ma but; *(eppure)* and yet; **dici?** what are you talking ~ *va!* nonsense!; ~ *no!* not ~ course not!

e•lude [ɪ'luːd] *v/t (escape from, ——‚* gire a; *(avoid)* sfuggire a; **the name** ~**s me** il nome mi sfugge

'**eve•ning class** corso *m* serale; '**eve•ning dress** *for woman* vestito *m* da sera; *for man* abito *m* scuro; **eve•ning** '**pa•per** giornale *m* della sera

◆**lay into** *v/t (attack)* aggredire
◆**lay on** *v/t (provide)* offrire

mim•ic ['mɪmɪk] **1** *n* imitatore *m*, -trice *f* **2** *v/t (pret & pp* -*ked)* imitare
critica *f (pl* -che*)* criticism

privato 1 *agg* private; *in* ~ in private **2** *m* private citizen

recitare <1l & b> **1** *v/t* recite; TEA play (the part of); *preghiera* say **2** *v/i* act

rospo *m* toad; *fig* F **ingoiare il** ~ lump it F
nerd [nɜːd] P fesso *m*, -a *f* P; *in style* tamarro *m* P

lampadina *f* light bulb; ~ *tascabile* torch, *Am* flashlight
sub•way ['sʌbweɪ] *Br (passageway)* sottopassaggio *m*; *Am* metropolitana *f*

Compounds
Termini composti

Phrasal verbs entered as headwords
Phrasal verbs lemmatizzati

Grammatical information
Informazioni grammaticali

Entries divided into grammatical categories
Articolazione dell'articolo in categorie grammaticali

Information on Italian conjugations
Rimando alle tabelle di coniugazione

Register labels
Marche di registro e linguaggio settoriale

American variants
Varianti americane

A
B
C
D
E
F
G
H
I
J
K
L
M
N
O
P
Q
R
S
T
U
V
W
X
Y
Z

Italian
Compact Dictionary

Italian – English
Inglese – Italiano

Berlitz Publishing
New York · Munich · Singapore

Original edition edited by the Langenscheidt editorial staff

Compiled by LEXUS Ltd.

Inset cover photo: © Punchstock/Medioimages

© 2006 Berlitz Publishing/APA Publications GmbH & Co. Verlag KG
Singapore Branch, Singapore

Berlitz Publishing
193 Morris Avenue
Springfield, NJ 07081
USA

Printed in Germany
ISBN 978-981-246-879-6 (vinyl edition)
ISBN 978-981-246-883-3 (UK paperback edition)

Preface

Here is a new dictionary of English and Italian, a tool with some 45,000 references for those who work with the English and Italian languages at beginner's or intermediate level.

Focusing on modern usage, the dictionary offers coverage of everyday language – and this means including vocabulary from areas such as computer use and business.

Having made the selection of vocabulary items to include, the editors of this book have set out to provide the means to enable you, the user of the dictionary, to get straight to the translation that fits a particular context of use. Is the *mouse* you need for your computer, for example, the same in Italian as the *mouse* you don't want in the house? Is *flimsy* referring to furniture the same in Italian as *flimsy* referring to an excuse? This dictionary is rich in sense distinctions like this – and in translation options tied to specific, identified senses.

Vocabulary needs grammar to back it up. So in this dictionary you'll find irregular verb forms, in both English and Italian, irregular English plural forms as well as detailed guidance on Italian plural and feminine endings.

And vocabulary items are often only clearly understood in a context. So a large number of idiomatic phrases are given to show how the two languages correspond in context.

All in all, this is a book full of information, which will, we hope, become a valuable part of your language toolkit.

Contents

How to use the dictionary

To get the most out of your dictionary you should understand how and where to find the information you need. Whether you are yourself writing text in a foreign language or wanting to understand text that has been written in a foreign language, the following pages should help.

1. How and where do I find a word?

1.1 The word list for each language is arranged in alphabetical order and also gives irregular forms of verbs and nouns in their correct alphabetical order.

Sometimes you might want to look up terms made up of two separate words, for example **falling star**, or hyphenated words, for example **absent-minded**. These words are treated as though they were a single word and their alphabetical ordering reflects this.

The only exception to this strict alphabetical ordering is made for English *phrasal verbs* – words like **go off**, **go out**, **go up**. These are positioned in an alphabetical block directly after their main verb (in this case **go**).

1.2 Italian feminine headwords of the form **-trice** are shown as follows:

> **albergatore** *m*, **-trice** *f* hotel keeper

Here **-trice** means **albergatrice**.

1.3 Pronunciation for English headwords is given in square brackets. You can look up the spelling of a word in your dictionary in the same way as you would in a spelling dictionary. American spelling variants are marked *Am*. If just a single letter is omitted in the American spelling, this is put between round brackets:

> **colo(u)r** — **hono(u)r** — **travel(l)er**

2. How do I split a word?

Italians find English hyphenation very difficult. All you have to do with this dictionary is look for the bold dots between syllables. These dots show you where you can split a word at the end of a line but you should avoid having just one letter before or after the hyphen as in **a•mend** or **thirst•y**. In such cases it is better to take the entire word over to the next line.

3. Swung dashes and long dashes

3.1 A swung dash (~) replaces the entire headword when the headword is repeated within an entry:

> **face** [feɪs] **1** *n* viso *m*, faccia *f*; **~ to ~** faccia a faccia

Here **~ to ~** means **face to face**.

> **incanto** *m* (*incantesimo*) spell; **come per ~** as if by magic

Here **come per ~** means **come per incanto**.

3.2 When a headword changes form in an entry, for example if it is put in the past tense or in the plural, then the past tense or plural ending is added to the swung dash – but only if the rest of the word doesn't change:

> **flame** [fleɪm] *n* fiamma *f*; *go up in ~s* incendiarsi
>
> **top** [tɒp] ... **3** *v/t* (*pret & pp* **-ped**): *~ped with cream* ricoperto di crema

But:

> ◆**make up 1** *v/i* ... *be made up of* essere composto da
>
> **sup•ply** [sə'plaɪ] ... **2** *v/t* ... *be supplied with* fitted with etc essere dotato di

3.3 Double headwords are replaced by a single swung dash:

> **'one-track mind** *hum*: *have a ~* essere fissato col sesso
>
> **sliced 'bread** [slaɪst] pane *m* a cassetta; *the greatest thing since ~* il non plus ultra

3.4 In the Italian-English part of the dictionary, when a headword is repeated in a phrase or compound with an altered form, a long dash is used:

> **impronta** *f* impression, mark; *-e pl* **digitali** fingerprints

Here **-e digitali** means **impronte digitali**.

4. What do the different typefaces mean?

4.1 All Italian and English headwords and the Arabic numerals differentiating between parts of speech appear in **bold**:

> **incisivo 1** *agg* incisive **2** *m* dente incisor
>
> **itch** [ɪtʃ] **1** *n* prurito *m* **2** *v/i* prudere

4.2 *Italics* are used for :

a) abbreviated grammatical labels: *adj, adv, v/i, v/t* etc

b) gender labels: *m, f, mpl* etc

c) all the indicating words which are the signposts pointing to the correct translation for your needs, eg:

> **mix•ture** ['mɪkstʃə(r)] miscuglio *m*; *medicine* sciroppo *m*
>
> **pro•fuse•ly** [prə'fjuːslɪ] *adv thank* con grande effusione; *bleed* copiosamente
>
> **rugoso** rough; *pelle* wrinkled; *albero* gnarled
>
> **terra** *f* earth; (*regione, proprietà, terreno agricolo*) land; (*superficie del suolo*) ground; (*pavimento*) floor

4.3 All phrases (examples and idioms) are given in **secondary bold italics**:

> **sym•pa•thet•ic** [sɪmpə'θetɪk] *adj* ... *be ~ towards an idea* simpatizzare per un'idea
>
> **premio** *m* (*pl* -mi) ... *~ Nobel per la pace* Nobel peace prize

4.4 The normal typeface is used for the translations. It is also used for Italian plural forms.

4.5 If a translation is given in italics, and not in the normal typeface, this means that the translation is more of an *explanation* in the other language and that an explanation has to be given because there just is no real equivalent:

>**'Mid•lands** *npl regione f nell'Inghilterra centrale*
>**ragioneria** *f* book-keeping; EDU *high school specializing in business studies*

5. Stress

To indicate where to put the **stress** in English words, the stress marker ' appears before the syllable on which the main stress falls:

>**on•ion** ['ʌnjən] cipolla *f*
>**rec•ord**[1] ['rekɔːd] *n* MUS disco *m* ...
>**record**[2] [rɪ'kɔːd] *v/t electronically* registrare ...

Stress is shown either in the pronunciation or, if there is no pronunciation given, in the actual headword or compound itself.

>**'rec•ord hold•er** primatista *m/f*

6. What do the various symbols and abbreviations tell you?

6.1 A solid blue diamond is used to indicate a phrasal verb:

>**♦auction off** *v/t* vendere all'asta

6.2 A white diamond is used to divide up longer entries into more easily digested chunks of related bits of text:

>**a** *prp* ◊ *stato in luogo:* **a Roma** in Rome; **a casa** at home
>◊ *moto a luogo:* **andare a Roma** go to Rome; **andare a casa** go home ◊ *tempo* ...

6.3 The abbreviation F tells you that the word or phrase is used colloquially rather than in formal contexts. The abbreviation V warns you that a word or phrase is vulgar or taboo. Be careful how you use these words. Words or phrases labelled P are slang.

These abbreviations, F, V and P are used both for headwords/phrases and for the translations of headwords/phrases. They come after the headword and before any phrase or indicated sense to be translated. They are given after the translation, but only if the translation has the same register as the headword/example. If there is no such label given, then the word or phrase is neutral.

6.4 A colon before an English or Italian phrase means that usage is restricted to this specific example (at least as far as this dictionary's translation is concerned):

>**tru•ant** ['truːənt]: **play** ~ marinare la scuola
>**tuck** [tʌk] ... 2 *v/t:* ~ **sth into sth** infilare qc in qc
>**'shoe•string** *n:* **do sth on a** ~ fare qc con pochi soldi

7. Does the dictionary deal with grammar too?

7.1 All English headwords are given a part of speech label:

> **tooth•less**['tu:θlɪs] *adj* sdentato
>
> **top•ple**['tɒpl] **1** *v/i* crollare **2** *v/t government* far cadere

But if a headword can only be used as a noun (in ordinary English) then no part of speech is given:

> **tooth•paste** dentifricio *m*

7.2 Italian headwords are not given parts of speech in cases where the grammar of the translation matches the grammar of the Italian:

> **esclusivo** exclusive
>
> **piuttosto** rather

But:

> **planetario**(*pl* -ri) **1** *agg* planetary **2** *m* planetarium

And Italian gender markers are given, as well as Italian plural forms:

> **pinacoteca** *f* (*pl* -che) art gallery
>
> **farmacista** *m/f* (*mpl* -i) chemist, *Am* pharmacist

7.3 If an English translation of an Italian adjective can only be used in front of a noun, and not after it, this is marked with *attr*:

> **fiabesco**(*pl* -chi) fairytale *attr*

7.4 If the Italian, unlike the English, doesn't change form if used in the plural, this is marked with *inv*:

> **fine settimana** *m inv* weekend

7.5 If the English, in spite of appearances, is not a plural form, this is marked with *nsg*:

> **mea•sles**['mi:zlz] *nsg* morbillo *m*

7.6 Irregular English plurals are identified:

> **the•sis**['θi:sɪs] (*pl* **theses** ['θi:si:z]) tesi *f inv*
>
> **thief**[θi:f] (*pl* **thieves** [θi:vz]) ladro *m*, -a *f*
>
> **trout**[traʊt] (*pl* **trout**) trota *f*

7.7 Words like **physics** or **media studies** have not been given a label to say if they are singular or plural for the simple reason that they can be either, depending on how they are used.

7.8 Irregular and semi-irregular verb forms are identified:

> **sim•pli•fy**['sɪmplɪfaɪ] *v/t* (*pret & pp* **-ied**) semplificare
>
> **sing**[sɪŋ] *v/t & v/i* (*pret* **sang**, *pp* **sung**) cantare

7.9 Cross-references are given to tables of Italian conjugations:

> **finire**<4d>   **fischiare**<1k>

7.10 Grammatical information is provided on the prepositions you'll need in order to create complete sentences:

> **ear•mark**['ɪəmɑːk] *v/t* riservare; ~ *sth for sth* riservare qc a qc
>
> **tremare**<1b> tremble, shake (*di, per* with)

Abbreviations

English	Abbr.	Italiano	English	Abbr.	Italiano
see	→	vedi	feminine plural	*fpl*	femminile plurale
registered trademark	®	marchio registrato	railway	FERR	ferrovia
abbreviation	*abbr*	abbreviazione	figurative	*fig*	figurato
adjective	*adj*	aggettivo	philosophy	FIL	filosofia
adverb	*adv*	avverbio	financial	FIN	finanze
adjective	*agg*	aggettivo	physics	FIS	fisica
agriculture	AGR	agricoltura	physiology	FISIOL	fisiologia
mountaineering	ALP	alpinismo	formal usage	*fml*	uso formale
American English	*Am*	inglese americano	photography	FOT	fotografia
anatomy	ANAT	anatomia	future	*fut*	futuro
architecture	ARCHI	architettura	cooking	GASTR	gastronomia
article	*art*	articolo	generally	*gen*	generalmente
astronomy	AST	astronomia	geography	GEOG	geografia
astrology	ASTR	astrologia	geology	GEOL	geology
attributive usage	*attr*	uso attributivo	gerund	*ger*	gerundio
motoring	AUTO	automobilismo	grammatical	GRAM	grammatica
civil aviation	AVIA	aviazione	humorous	*hum*	uso spiritoso
adverb	*avv*	avverbio	imperative	*imper*	imperativo
biology	BIO	biologia	imperfect	*imperf*	imperfetto
botany	BOT	botanica	indicative	*ind*	indicativo
British English	*Br*	inglese britannico	IT term	INFOR	informatica
chemistry	CHEM	chimica	interjection	*int*	interiezione
chemistry	CHIM	chimica	invariable	*inv*	invariabile
commerce, business	COM	commercio	ironic	*iron*	ironico
computers, IT term	COMPUT	informatica	law	LAW	diritto
conditional	*cond*	condizionale	masculine	*m*	maschile
conjunction	*cong*	congiunzione	masculine noun and adjective	*m/agg*	sostantivo maschile e aggettivo
subjunctive	*congiunt*	congiuntivo	masculine and feminine	*m/f*	maschile e femminile
conjunction	*conj*	congiunzione	masculine plural	*mpl*	maschile plurale
law	DIR	diritto	nautical	MAR	marineria, navigazione
et cetera	*ecc*	eccetera	mathematics	MAT	matematica
education	EDU	educazione	mathematics	MATH	matematica
for example	*eg*	per esempio	medicine	MED	medicina
electricity, electronics	EL	elettricità, elettronica	metallurgy	METAL	metallurgia
electricity, electronics	ELEC	elettricità, elettronica	meteorology	METEO	meteorologia
especially	*esp*	specialmente	military	MIL	militare
et cetera	*etc*	eccetera	mineralogy	MIN	mineralogia
euphemistic	*euph*	eufemismo	motoring	MOT	automobilismo
familiar, colloquial	F	familiare	music	MUS	musica
feminine	*f*	femminile	noun	*n*	sostantivo
feminine noun and adjective	*f/agg*	sostantivo femminile e aggettivo	nautical	NAUT	marineria, navigazione
			negative	*neg*	in senso negativo
			plural noun	*npl*	sostantivo plurale

singular noun	*nsg*	sostantivo singolare	something	qc	qualcosa
			someone	qu	qualcuno
optics	OPT	ottica	radio	RAD	radio
oneself	o.s.	sé, se stesso	railway	RAIL	ferrovia
optics	OTT	ottica	religion	REL	religione
popular, slang	P	popolare	skiing	SCI	sci
painting	PAINT	pittura	singular	sg	singolare
pejorative	*pej*	spregiativo	someone	s.o.	qualcuno
photography	PHOT	fotografia	sports	SP	sport
physics	PHYS	fisica	humorous	*spir*	uso spiritoso
painting	PITT	pittura	pejorative	*spreg*	spregiativo
plural	*pl*	plurale	something	sth	qualcosa
politics	POL	politica	theatre	TEA	teatro
past participle	*pp*	participio passato	technology	TEC	tecnica
			technology	TECH	tecnica
present participle	*p pr*	participio presente	telecommunications	TELEC	telecomunicazione
present	*pr*	presente	theatre	THEA	teatro
past historic	*p.r.*	passato remoto	typography, typesetting	TIP	tipografia
present subjunctive	*pr congiunt*	presente congiuntivo	television	TV	televisione
preposition	*prep*	preposizione	vulgar	V	volgare
preterite	*pret*	preterito	auxiliary verb	*v/aus*	verbo ausiliario
present indicative	*pr ind*	presente indicativo	auxiliary verb	*v/aux*	verbo ausiliario
pronoun	*pron*	pronome	intransitive verb	*v/i*	verbo intransitivo
preposition	*prp*	preposizione	reflexive verb	*v/r*	verbo riflessivo
psychology	PSI	psicologia	transitive verb	*v/t*	verbo transitivo
psychology	PSYCH	psicologia	zoology	ZO	zoologia

Italian Spelling and Pronunciation

1. The Italian Alphabet

The twenty-one letters of the Italian alphabet are listed below with their names and with their sounds given as approximate English equivalents.

LETTER	NAME	APPROXIMATE SOUND
a	a	Like *a* in English *father*, eg **facile**, **padre**.
b	bi	Like *b* in English *boat*, eg **bello**, **abate**.
c	ci	When followed by **e** or **i**, like *ch* in English *cherry*, eg **cento**, **cinque**; if the **i** is unstressed and followed by another vowel, its sound is not heard, eg **ciaria**, **cieco**. When followed by **a**, **o**, **u**, or a consonant like *c* in English *cook*, eg **casa**, **come**, **cura**, **credere**. **Ch**, which is used before **e** and **i**, has likewise the sound of *c* in English *cook*, eg **chiesa**, **perché**.
d	di	Like *d* in English *dance*, eg **dare**, **madre**.
e	e	Has two sounds. One like *a* in English *make*, eg **ferro**; and one like *e* in English *met*, eg **festa**.
f	effe	Like *f* in English *fool*, eg **farina**, **efelide**.
g	gi	When followed by **e** or **i**, like *g* in English *general*, eg **gelato**, **ginnasta**; if the **i** is unstressed and followed by another vowel, its sound is not heard, eg **giallo**, **giorno**. When followed by **a**, **o**, **u**, or a consonant, like *g* in English *go*, eg **gamba**, **goccia**, **gusto**, **grado**. **Gh**, which is used before **e** and **i**, has likewise the sound of *g* in English *go*, eg **ghisa**. When the combination **gli** (a) is a form of the definite article or the personal pronoun, (b) is final in a word, or (c) comes between two vowels, it has the sound of Castilian *ll*, which is somewhat like *lli* in English *million*, eg (a) **gli uomini**, **gli ho parlato ieri**, (b) **battagli**, (c) **figlio**, **migliore**. When it is (a) initial (except in the word **gli**, above), (b) preceded by a consonant, or (c) followed by a consonant, it is pronounced like *gli* in English *negligence*, eg (a) **glioma**, (b) **ganglio**, (c) **negligenza**. The combination **gl** followed by **a**, **e**, **o**, or **u** is pronounced like *gl* in English *globe*, eg **glabro**, **gleba**, **globo**, **gluteo**, **inglese**. **Gn** has the sound of Castilian *ñ*, which is somewhat like *ni* in English *onion*, eg **signore**, **gnocco**.
h	acca	Always silent, eg **ah**, **hanno**. See **ch** under **c** above and **gh** under **g** above.
i	i	Like *i* in English *machine*, eg **piccolo**, **sigla**.

		When unstressed and followed by another vowel, like *y* in English *yes*, eg **piatto**, **piede**, **fiore**, **fiume**. For **i** in **ci**, see **c** above, in **gi**, see **g** above, and in **sci**, see **s** below.
l	elle	Like *l* in English *lamb*, eg **labbro**, **lacrima**.
m	emme	Like *m* in English *money*, eg **mano**, **come**.
n	enne	Like *n* in English *net*, eg **nome**, **cane**.
o	o	Has two sounds. One like *o* in English *note*, eg **sole**; and one like *o* in English *hot*, eg **donna**.
p	pi	Like *p* in English *pot*, eg **passo**, **carpa**.
q	cu	This letter is always followed by the letter **u** and the combination has the sound of *qu* in English *quart*, eg **quanto**, **questo**.
r	erre	Like *r* in English *rubber*, with a slight trill, eg **roba**, **carta**.
s	esse	Has two sounds. When initial and followed by a vowel, when preceded by a consonant and followed by a vowel, and when followed by **c** [k] **f**, **p**, **q**, or **t**, like *s* in English *see*, eg **sale**, **falso**, **scappare**, **spazio**, **stoffa**. When standing between two vowels and when followed by **b**, **d**, **g** [g], **l**, **m**, **n**, **r** or **v**, like *z* in English *zero*, eg **paese**, **sbaglio**, **svenire**. However, **s** standing between two vowels in some words and initial *s* followed by **b**, **d**, **g** [g], **l**, **m**, **n**, **r**, or **v** in some foreign borrowings are pronounced like *s* in *see*, eg **casa**, **tesa**, **smoking**, **slam**. When initial s stands between two vowels in a compound, its pronunciation remains that of initial s, eg **autoservizio**. **Sc**, when followed by **e** or **i** has the sound of *sh* in English *shall*, eg **scelta**, **scimmia**; if the **i** is unstressed and followed by another vowel, its sound is not heard, eg **sciame**, **sciopero**. **Sch** has the sound of *sc* in English *scope*, eg **scherzo**, **schiavo**. An **s** coming between two vowels is generally pronounced like *z* in English *zero* in the north of Italy.
t	ti	Like *t* in English *table*, eg **terra**, **pasto**.
u	u	Like *u* in English *rule*, eg **luna**, **mulo**. When followed by a vowel, like *w* in English *was*, eg **quanto**, **guerra**, **nuovo**.
v	vu	Like *v* in *English vain*, eg **vita**, **uva**.
z	zeta	Has two sounds. One like *ts* in English *nuts*, eg **grazia**, **zuccero**; and one like *dz* in English *adze*, eg **zero**, **mezzo**.

The following five letters are found in borrowings from other languages.

LETTER	NAME	EXAMPLES
j	i lunga	**jazz**
k	cappa	**ko**
w	vu doppia	**whisky**
x	ics	**xenofobo**, *xilofono*
y	ìpsilon	**yacht**, **yoghurt**

Consonants written double are longer than consonants written single, that is, it takes a longer time to pronounce them, eg **camino** *chimney*, and **cammino** *road*, **capello** *hair* and **cappello** *hat*. Special attention is called to the following double consonants: **cc** followed by **e** or **i** has the sound of *ch ch* in English *beach chair*, that is a lengthened *ch*, eg **accento**; **cch** has the sound of *kk* in English *book-keeper*, eg **becchino**; **cq** has the sound of *kk* in English *book-keeper*, eg **acqua**; **gg** followed by **e** or **i** has the sound of *ge j* in English *carriage joiner*, eg **peggio**; **ggh** has the sound of *g g* in English *tag game*, eg **agghindare**.

2. Stress and Accent Marks

Whenever stress is shown as part of regular spelling, it is shown on **a, i**, and **u** by the grave accent mark, eg **libertà**, **giovedì**, **gioventù**, on close **e** and **o** by the acute accent mark, eg **perché**, and on open **e** and **o** by the grave accent mark, eg **caffè**, **parlò**.

Guidelines on Stress

(a) In words of two syllables, the stress falls on the syllable next to the last, eg **casa**, **muro**, **terra**. If the syllable next to the last contains a diphthong, that is, a combination of a strong vowel (**a**, **e**, or **o**) and a weak vowel (**i** or **u**), the strong vowel is stressed, regardless of which vowel comes first, eg **daino**, **eroico**, **neutro**, **fiato**, **duale**, **siepe**, **fiore**, **buono**.

(b) In words of more than two syllables, the stress may fall on the syllable next to the last, eg **andata**, **canzone**, **pastore** or on a preceding syllable, eg **missile**, **gondola**, **mandorla**. In these positions also the stressed syllable may contain a diphthong, eg **incauto**, **idraulico**, **fiocina**.

(c) If a weak vowel in juxtaposition with a strong vowel is stressed, the two vowels constitute two separate syllables, eg **abba•ino**, **ero•ina**, **pa•ura**, **miriade**, **via**.

(d) Two strong vowels in juxtaposition constitute two separate syllables, eg **pa•ese**, **aureola**, **idea**, **oceano**.

(e) Two weak vowels in juxtaposition generally constitute a diphthong in which the first vowel is stressed in some words, eg **fluido** and the second vowel in others, eg **piuma**.

(f) If a word ends in a diphthong, the diphthong is stressed, eg **marinai**, **parlai**, **eroi**.

English Pronunciation

Vowels

[ɑ:]	*father*	['fɑ:ðə(r)]
[æ]	*man*	[mæn]
[e]	*get*	[get]
[ə]	*about*	[ə'baʊt]
[ɜ:]	*absurd*	[əb'sɜ:d]
[ɪ]	*stick*	[stɪk]
[i:]	*need*	[ni:d]
[ɒ]	*hot*	[hɒt]
[ɔ:]	*law*	[lɔ:]
[ʌ]	*mother*	['mʌðə(r)]
[ʊ]	*book*	[bʊk]
[u:]	*fruit*	[fru:t]

Diphthongs

[aɪ]	*time*	[taɪm]
[aʊ]	*cloud*	[klaʊd]
[eɪ]	*name*	[neɪm]
[eə]	*hair*	[heə(r)]
[ɪə]	*here*	[hɪə(r)]
[ɔɪ]	*point*	[pɔɪnt]
[əʊ]	*oath*	[əʊθ]
[ʊə]	*tour*	[tʊə(r)]

Consonants

[b]	*bag*	[bæg]
[d]	*dear*	[dɪə(r)]
[f]	*fall*	[fɔ:l]
[g]	*give*	[gɪv]
[h]	*hole*	[həʊl]
[j]	*yes*	[jes]
[k]	*come*	[kʌm]
[l]	*land*	[lænd]
[m]	*mean*	[mi:n]
[n]	*night*	[naɪt]
[p]	*pot*	[pɒt]
[r]	*right*	[raɪt]
[(r)]	pronounced only at the end of a word followed by a word starting with a vowel: *where* [weə(r)]
[s]	*sun*	[sʌn]
[t]	*take*	[teɪk]
[v]	*vain*	[veɪn]
[w]	*wait*	[weɪt]
[z]	*rose*	[rəʊz]
[ŋ]	*bring*	[brɪŋ]
[ʃ]	*she*	[ʃi:]
[ʧ]	*chair*	[ʧeə(r)]
[dʒ]	*join*	[dʒɔɪn]
[ʒ]	*leisure*	['leʒə(r)]
[θ]	*think*	[θɪŋk]
[ð]	*the*	[ðə]
[']	means that the following syllable is stressed: *ability* [ə'bɪlətɪ]

A

A *abbr* (= **autostrada**) M (= motorway)

a *prp* ◊ *stato in luogo*: **a Roma** in Rome; **a casa** at home ◊ *moto a luogo*: **andare a Roma** go to Rome; **andare a casa** go home ◊ *tempo*: **alle quattro** at four o'clock; **a Natale** at Christmas; **a maggio** in May; **a vent'anni** at the age of twenty; **a giorni** any day now; **a domani!** see you tomorrow! ◊ *modo*: **a piedi** on foot; **alla moda** in fashion; **al burro** GASTR in butter ◊ *mezzo*: **ricamato a mano** embroidered by hand, hand-embroidered; **fatto a macchina** machine-made ◊ *con valore distributivo*: **a due a due** two at a time; **a poco a poco** little by little ◊ *prezzo, misura*: **a che prezzo** at what price; **al metro** by the metre; **100 km all'ora** 100 km an hour

AAS *abbr* (= **Azienda Autonoma di Soggiorno**) tourist board

ab. *abbr* (= **abitanti**) inhabitants

abate *m* abbot

abbacchiato downhearted

abbacchio *m* (*pl* -cchi) GASTR young lamb

abbagliante 1 *agg* dazzling **2** *m* gen *pl* -i AUTO full beam

abbagliare <1g> dazzle

abbaglio *m* (*pl* -gli): **prendere un ~** make a blunder

abbaiare <1i> bark

abbandonare <1a> abandon

abbandono *m* abandon; (*rinuncia*) abandonment; **stato di ~** state of disrepair

abbassamento *m* lowering

abbassare <1a> *prezzo* lower; *radio* turn down; **~ la voce** lower one's voice

abbassarsi (*chinarsi*) bend down; *prezzo* come down; *fig* **~ a** stoop to

abbasso *int*: **~ la scuola!** down with school!

abbastanza enough; (*alquanto*) quite; **ho mangiato ~** I've had enough to eat; **sono ~ soddisfatto** I'm quite satisfied

abbattere <3a> knock down; *casa* demolish; *albero* cut down; *aereo* shoot down; *fig* dishearten

abbattersi fall; *fig* become disheartened

abbattimento *m* knocking down; *casa* demolition; *albero* cutting down; *aereo* shooting down; *fig* despondency

abbattuto disheartened

abbazia *f* abbey

abbellire <4d> embellish

abbeverare <1m> water

abbì, abbia → **avere**

abbicì *m inv* abc; *fig* basics *pl*

abbigliamento *m* clothing; **~ sportivo** sportswear; **industria** *f* **dell'~** clothing industry

abbinare <1a> match; (*combinare*) combine

abboccare <1d> *di pesce* bite; TEC join; *fig* swallow the bait

abboccato *vino* medium sweet

abbonamento *m a giornale*, TEA subscription; *a treno*, bus season-ticket; **~ annuale** yearly subscription; yearly ticket; **~ mensile** monthly subscription; monthly ticket

abbonare <1c & o> take out a subscription for; (*condonare*) deduct

abbonarsi subscribe

abbonato *m* subscriber; TELEC **elenco** *m* **degli -i** telephone directory

abbondante abundant; *porzione* generous; *vestito* loose; *nevicata* heavy

abbondanza *f* abundance

abbordabile *persona* approachable;

prezzo reasonable

abbordare <1a> **1** *v/t persona* approach; F *persona dell'altro sesso* chat up F; *argomento* tackle **2** *v/t* MAR board

abbottonare <1a> button up

abbozzare <1c> sketch; **~ un sorriso** smile faintly

abbozzo *m* sketch

abbracciare <1f> embrace, hug; *fig* take up

abbracciarsi embrace, hug

abbraccio *m* (*pl* -cci) embrace, hug; **un ~ a fine lettera** love

abbreviare <1k & b> abbreviate

abbreviazione *f* abbreviation

abbronzante *m* sun-tan lotion; *lettino m* ~ sunbed

abbronzare <1a> *pelle* tan

abbronzarsi get a tan

abbronzato tanned

abbronzatura *f* tan

abbrustolire <4d> roast

abbuffarsi <1a> stuff o.s. (*di* with)

abbuono *m* FIN discount

abdicare <1l & d> abdicate

abdicazione *f* abdication

abete *m* fir

abile good (*in* at); fit (*a* for)

abilità *f inv* ability

abilitazione *f* qualification

abisso *m* abyss

abitabile habitable; *cucina f* ~ dining kitchen

abitacolo *m* AUTO passenger compartment

abitante *m/f* inhabitant

abitare <1l> **1** *v/t* live in **2** *v/i* live

abitato 1 *agg* inhabited **2** *m* built-up area

abitazione *f* house

abiti *mpl* clothes

abito *m* dress; *da uomo* suit; **~ da sera** evening dress

abituale usual

abituare <1l> accustom (*a* to)

abituarsi ~ a get used to

abitudinario (*pl* -ri) **1** *agg* of fixed habits **2** *m* creature of habit

abitudine *f* habit

abolire <4d> abolish

abolizione *f* abolition

abominevole abominable

aborigeno 1 *agg* aboriginal **2** *m* aboriginal

abortire <4d> MED miscarry; *volontariamente* have an abortion; *fig* fail

abortista *m/f* pro-choice campaigner

aborto *m* MED miscarriage; *provocato* abortion

abrogare <1e & c or 1l> repeal

abrogazione *f* repeal

abusare <1a>: ~ *di* abuse; (*approfittare*) take advantage of; ~ *nel bere* drink to excess

abusivo illegal

abuso *m* abuse; ~ *sessuale* sexual abuse

a.C. *abbr* (= *avanti Cristo*) BC (= before Christ)

acacia *f* (*pl* -cie) acacia

acca *f*: *non capire un'*~ not understand a thing

accademia *f* academy; ~ *di belle arti* art college

accademico (*pl* -ci) academic

accadere <2c> happen

accaduto *m*: *raccontami l'*~ tell me what happened

accaldarsi <1a> get overheated

accaldato overheated

accalorarsi <1a> *fig* get excited

accampamento *m* camp

accampare <1a> **1** *v/t*: ~ *scuse* come up with excuses **2** *v/i e* **accamparsi** camp

accanimento *m* (*tenacia*) tenacity; (*furia*) rage

accanirsi <4d> (*ostinarsi*) persist; ~ *contro qu* rage against s.o.

accanito *odio* fierce; *tifoso* dedicated; *fumatore* inveterate; *lavoratore m* ~ hard worker

accanto 1 *prp* - **a** next to **2** *avv* near, nearby; *abitare* next door

accantonare <1a> put aside

accappatoio *m* (*pl* -oi) bathrobe; *da mare* beachrobe

accarezzare <1a> caress; *speranza* cherish; *animale* stroke

accasciarsi <1f> flop down

accatastare <1a> pile up

accattonaggio *m* begging

accattone *m* beggar

accavallare <1a> cross

accavallarsi *fig* overlap

accecare <1b & d> **1** *v/t* blind **2** *v/i* be blinding

accedere <3a>: ~ *a* enter

accelerare <1b & m> speed up; AUTO accelerate

accelerato1 *agg* fast; *treno* slow **2** *m* slow train

acceleratore *m* AUTO accelerator

accelerazione *f* acceleration

accendere <3c> light; RAD, TV turn on

accendersi light up; *apparecchio* come on

accendino *m*, **accendisigari** *m inv* lighter

accennare <1a> indicate; *con parole* mention; ~ *a fare qc* show signs of doing sth

accenno *m* (*cenno*) gesture; (*indizio*) sign; (*allusione*) hint

accensione *f* ignition; AUTO ~ *elettronica* electronic ignition

accento *m* accent

accentuare <1b & m> accentuate

accertare <1b> check

accertarsi ~ *di qc* check sth

acceso *colore* bright; *motore* running; TV, *luce* on

accessibile accessible; *prezzo* reasonable

accesso *m* access; *fig e* MED fit; **divieto d'** ~ no entry

accessori *mpl* accessories

accessoriato AUTO complete with accessories

accessorio secondary

accetta *f* ax(e)

accettabile acceptable

accettare <1b> accept

accettazione *f* acceptance; (*di albergo*) reception; ~ *bagagli* check-in

accetta **bene** / **male** ~ welcome / not welcome

acchiappare <1a> catch

acciaio *m* (*pl* -ai) steel; ~ **inossi-dabile** stainless steel

accidentale accidental

accidentato *terreno* rough

accidenti *int* F damn! F; *di sorpresa* wow!

accigliato frowning

accingersi <3d>: ~ *a fare qc* be about to do sth

acciottolato *m* cobbles *pl*

acciuffare <1a> grab

acciuga *f* (*pl* -ghe) anchovy

acclamare <1a> applaud

acclimatarsi <1m> get acclimatized

accludere <3q> enclose

accluso enclosed; *qui* ~ enclosed

accogliente welcoming

accogliere <3ss> welcome; *richiesta* grant

accollare <1c> shoulder

accollarsi take on

accollato *abito* high-necked

accoltellare <1b> knife

accolto *pp* → **accogliere**

accomodamento *m* arrangement; (*accordo*) agreement

accomodante accommodating

accomodare <1c & m> (*riparare*) mend; *lite* resolve; (*sistemare*) arrange

accomodarsi make o.s. at home; *si accomodi!* come in!; (*sedersi*) have a seat!

accompagnamento *m* accompaniment; *lettera f di* ~ covering letter

accompagnare <1a> accompany

accompagnatore *m*, -trice *f* escort; MUS accompanist

acconciatura *f* hairdo

acconsentire <4b> consent (*a* to)

accontentare <1b> satisfy

accontentarsi be happy (*di* with)

acconto *m* deposit

accoppiare <1k & c> couple; *animali* mate

accoppiarsi pair off

accorciare <1f> shorten

accorciarsi get shorter

accordare <1c> grant; MUS tune; (*armonizzare*) harmonize

accordarsi agree; *di colori* match

accordo *m* agreement; (*armonia*)

harmony; MUS chord; *essere d'~* agree; *mettersi d'~* reach an agreement; *d'~!* OK!

accorgersi <3d>: ~ *di* notice

accorrere <3o> hurry; ~ *in aiuto di qu* rush to help s.o.

accortezza *f* forethought

accorto 1 *pp* → *accorgersi* **2** *agg* shrewd

accostare <1c> approach; *porta* leave ajar

accostarsi get close

accreditare <1b & m> confirm; FIN credit

accredito *m* credit

accrescere <3n> increase

accrescersi grow bigger

accudire <4d> **1** *v/t* look after **2** *v/i:* ~ *a qc* attend to sth

accumulare <1m> accumulate

accumulatore *m* battery

accumulazione *f* accumulation

accuratezza *f* care

accurato careful

accusa *f* accusation; DIR charge; *Pubblica Accusa* public prosecutor

accusare <1a> accuse; DIR charge; ~ *ricevuta* acknowledge receipt

accusato *m*, *-a f* accused

accusatore *m* prosecutor

acerbo unripe

acero *m* maple

aceto *m* vinegar; ~ *balsamico* balsamic vinegar; *mettere sott'~* pickle

acetone *m* nail varnish remover

ACI *abbr* (= *Automobile Club d'Italia*) Automobile Club of Italy

acidità *f* acidity; ~ *di stomaco* heartburn

acido 1 *agg* acid; *fig* sour; *piogge fpl acide* acid rain *sg* **2** *m* acid

ACLI *abbr* (= *Associazione Cristiana dei Lavoratori Italiani*) Italian trade union association

acne *f* acne

acqua *f* water; ~ *corrente* running water; ~ *minerale* mineral water; ~ *potabile* drinking water; ~ *di rubinetto* tap water; ~ *ossigenata* hydrogen peroxide; *una teoria che fa ~* a theory that doesn't hold water; ~ *in bocca!* keep it under your hat!; *ha l'~ alla gola* (*non ha tempo*) he's pushed for time; *-e pl* waters; *-e pl territoriali* territorial waters; *in cattive -e* in deep water

acquaforte *f* etching

acquaio *m* (*pl -ai*) sink

acquaragia *f* turpentine

acquario *m* (*pl -ri*) aquarium; ASTR *Acquario* Aquarius

acquatico (*pl -ci*) aquatic; *sci m ~* water skiing; *oggetto* waterski; *uccello m ~* waterfowl

acquavite *f* brandy

acquazzone *m* downpour

acquedotto *m* aqueduct

acqueo: *vapore m ~* water vapo(u)r

acquerello *m* water-colo(u)r

acquirente *m/f* purchaser

acquisizione *f* acquisition

acquistare <1a> **1** *v/t* buy; *fig* gain **2** *v/i* improve (*in* in)

acquisto *m* purchase; *potere m d'~* purchasing power; ~ *a rate* hire purchase, *Am* installment plan

acquolina *f*: *mi viene l'~ in bocca* my mouth's watering

acre sour; *voce* harsh

acrilico (*pl -ci*) acrylic

acrobata *m/f* acrobat

acustica *f* acoustics

acustico (*pl -ci*) acoustic

acuto 1 *agg* intense; *nota, dolore* sharp; *suono, voce* shrill; MED acute **2** *m* MUS high note

ad *prp* → *a* (*before vowels*)

adagiare <1f> *persona* lay down

adagiarsi lie down

adagio 1 *avv* slowly; *con cautela* cautiously **2** *m* (*pl -gi*) MUS adagio

adattamento *m* adaptation; (*rielaborazione*) reworking

adattare <1a> adapt

adattarsi (*adeguarsi*) adapt (*a* to); (*addirsi*) be suitable (*a* for); *questo colore non ti si adatta* the colour doesn't suit you

adattatore *m* adaptor

adatto right (*a* for)

addebitare <1m>: FIN ~ *qc a qu* debit s.o. with sth; *fig* ascribe sth to s.o.

addebito *m* FIN debit; *nota f di* ~ debit note

addensarsi <1b> thicken

addestramento *m* training

addestrare <1b> train

addetto 1 *agg* assigned (*a* to) 2 *m*, *-a f* person responsible; ~ *alle pubbliche relazioni* public relations officer; *fig* ~ *ai lavori* expert; ~ *culturale* cultural attaché; *vietato l'ingresso ai non -i* authorized personnel only

addio 1 *int* goodbye 2 *m* goodbye, farewell

addirittura (*assolutamente*) absolutely; (*perfino*) even

additivo *m* additive

addizionare <1a> add

addizione *f* addition

addobbare <1c> decorate

addobbo *m* decoration

addolcire <4d> sweeten; *fig* soften

addolorare <1a> grieve

addome *m* abdomen

addomesticare <1b, d & n> tame

addominale abdominal

addormentare <1b> get (off) to sleep

addormentarsi fall asleep

addormentato asleep; (*assonnato*) sleepy

addossare <1c> (*appoggiare*) lean (*a* on); *fig colpa* put, lay (*a* on)

addossarsi lean (*a* on); *fig* shoulder

addosso 1 *prp* on; *vicino* next to 2 *avv*: *avere* ~ *vestiti* have on; *avere* ~ *qu* have s.o. breathing down one's neck

addurre <3e> produce

adeguare <1a> adjust

adeguarsi conform; ~ *alle circostanze* adjust to circumstances

adeguato adequate

adempiere <4d & g>: ~ *a dovere* carry out, do

aderente 1 *agg vestito* tight 2 *m/f* follower

aderire <4d>: ~ *a* adhere to; *partito* support; *richiesta* agree to

adesione *f* adhesion; (*consenso*) agreement

adesivo 1 *agg* adhesive 2 *m* sticker

adesso now; *da* ~ *in poi* from now on; *fino* ~ up to now; *per* ~ for the moment

adiacente adjacent; ~ *a* next to, adjacent to

adibire <4d> use

adirarsi <1a> get angry

adirato angry

adolescente *m/f* adolescent, teenager

adolescenza *f* adolescence, teens *pl* F

adoperare <1m & c> use

adorare <1a> adore

adorazione *f* adoration

adornare <1a> adorn

adottare <1c> adopt

adottivo *genitori* adoptive; *figlio* adopted

adozione *f* adoption

adrenalina *f* adrenalin

adriatico (*pl* -ci) 1 *agg* Adriatic; *mare m* **Adriatico** Adriatic Sea 2 *m*: **Adriatico** Adriatic

adulare <1a> flatter

adulazione *f* flattery

adulterare <1m> adulterate

adulterio *m* (*pl* -ri) adultery

adulto 1 *agg* adult 2 *m*, *-a f* adult

adunare <1a> assemble

aerare <1l> air

aerazione *f* airing

aereo 1 *agg* air *attr*; *fotografia*, *radici* aerial; *base f* *-a* air base; *compagnia f* *-a* airline; *ponte m* ~ airlift; *posta f* *-a* airmail 2 *m* plane; ~ *di linea* airliner

aerobica *f* aerobics *sg*

aerobus *m inv* plane that makes short-haul flights

aerodinamico aerodynamic

aeronautica *f* aeronautics; ~ *militare* Air Force

aeroplano *m* plane, aeroplane, *Am* airplane

aeroporto *m* airport

aerosol *m inv* contenitore aerosol

aerospaziale aerospace *attr*
aerostato *m* aerostat, lighter-than-air aircraft
aerostazione *f* air terminal
afa *f* closeness, mugginess
affabile affable
affaccendarsi <1b> busy o.s. (*in* with)
affaccendato busy
affacciarsi <1f> appear
affamato starving
affannato breathless
affanno *m* breathlessness; *fig* anxiety
affare *m* matter, business; FIN transaction; *-i pl* business *sg*; **non sono -i tuoi** it's none of your business; **uomo *m* d'-i** businessman; **ministro *m* degli Affari Esteri** Foreign Secretary; **giro *m* d'-i** turnover
affarista *m/f* (*mpl* -i) wheeler-dealer
affascinante fascinating
affascinare <1m> fascinate
affaticare <1d> tire
affaticarsi tire o.s. out
affatto completely; **non è ~ vero!** there's not the slightest bit of truth in it!
affermare <1a> state
affermarsi become established
affermazione *f* assertion; (*successo*) achievement
afferrare <1b> seize, grab F; (*comprendere*) grasp
afferrarsi cling (*a* to), hold on (*a* to)
affettare¹ <1a> (*tagliare*) slice
affettare² <1b> *ammirazione ecc* affect
affettato¹ *m* sliced meat
affettato² *agg* affected
affettatrice *f* slicer
affetto *m* affection
affettuoso affectionate
affezionarsi <1a>: **~ a qu** become fond of s.o.
affezionato ~ a qu fond of s.o.
affiancare <1d> place side by side; *fig* support
affibbiare <1k>: **~ qc a qu** saddle s.o. with sth
affidabilità *f* dependability

affidamento *m* trust; **fare ~ su** rely on
affidare <1a> entrust
affidarsi ~ a rely on
affiggere <3mm> *avviso* put up
affilare <1a> sharpen; *fig* make thinner
affilato sharp; *naso* thin
affiliare <1g> *a una società* affiliate
affiliato 1 *m*, **-a** *f* member **2** *agg*: **società** *f* **-a** affiliate
affiliazione *f* affiliation
affinché so that
affine similar
affinità *f inv* affinity
affiorare <1a> *dall'acqua* emerge; *fig* (*mostrarsi*) appear
affissione *f* bill-posting
affisso 1 *pp* → **affiggere 2** *m* bill
affittacamere *m/f* landlord; *donna* landlady
affittare <1a> *locali, terre* let; (*prendere in affitto*) rent; **affittasi** to let
affitto *m* rent; **dare in ~** let; **prendere in ~** rent
affliggere <3cc> distress; *di malattia* trouble, plague
afflitto distressed
affluente *m* tributary
affluenza *f fig* influx
affluire <4d> flow; *di persone* pour in
afflusso *m* influx
affogare <1c & e> *v/t & v/i* drown
affollamento *m* crowd
affollare <1c>, **affollarsi** crowd
affollato crowded
affondare <1a> *v/t & v/i* sink
affrancare <1d> free; *posta* frank
affrancatura *f* franking; *tassa di spedizione* postage
affresco *m* (*pl* -chi) fresco
affrettare <1a> speed up
affrettarsi hurry
affrontare <1a> face, confront; *spese* meet
affronto *m* insult
affumicare <1d & m> *stanza* fill with smoke; *alimenti* smoke
affumicato smoked
affusolato tapering

afoso sultry

Africa *f* Africa

africano 1 *agg* African **2** *m*, **-a** *f* African

afrodisiaco *m/agg* aphrodisiac

agave *f* agave

agenda *f* diary

agente *m/f* agent; **~ di cambio** stockbroker; **~ immobiliare** estate agent, *Am* realtor; **~ inquinante** pollutant; **~ di pubblica sicurezza** police officer; **~ di vendita** sales representative; **~ di viaggio** travel agent

agenzia *f* agency; **~ di cambio** bureau de change; **~ immobiliare** estate agency, *Am* real estate office; **~ pubblicitaria** advertising agency; **~ di viaggi** travel agency

agevolare <1m> make easier

agevolato FIN on easy terms

agevolazione *f* FIN special term

agevole easy

agganciare <1f> hook; *cintura, collana* fasten

aggeggio *m* (*pl* -ggi) gadget

aggettivo *m* adjective

agghiacciante spine-chilling

aggiornamento *m* updating; (*rinvio*) postponement; **corso m d'~** refresher course

aggiornare <1a> (*mettere al corrente*) update; (*rinviare*) postpone

aggiornarsi keep up to date

aggirare <1a> surround; *fig ostacolo* get round

aggirarsi hang about; FIN be in the region of

aggiudicare <1d & m> award; *all'asta* knock down

aggiungere <3d> add

aggiunta *f* addition

aggiustare <1a> (*riparare*) repair; (*sistemare*) settle

agglomerato *m*: **~ urbano** built-up area

aggrapparsi <1a> cling, hold on (**a** to)

aggravante 1 *agg* aggravating **2** *f* aggravation

aggravare <1a> *punizione* increase; (*peggiorare*) make worse

aggravarsi worsen, deteriorate

aggravio *m* (*pl* -vi): **~ fiscale** tax increase

aggraziato graceful

aggredire <4d> attack

aggressione *f* aggression; (*attacco*) attack; POL **patto m di non ~** non-aggression pact

aggressività *f* aggressiveness

aggressivo aggressive

aggressore *m* attacker; POL aggressor

agguato *m* ambush; **tendere un ~ a qu** ambush s.o., set an ambush for s.o.

agguerrito hardened

agiatezza *f* comfort

agiato comfortable, well-off; (*comodo*) comfortable

agibile fit for human habitation

agile agile

agilità *f* agility; *fig* liveliness

agio *m* (*pl* -gi) ease; **vivere negli agi** live in comfort; **sentirsi a proprio ~** feel at ease

agire <4d> act; **comportarsi** behave, act; *di medicina* take effect; DIR take action (**contro** against)

agitare <1l> shake; *fazzoletto* wave; *fig* (*turbare*) upset, agitate; **~ prima dell'uso** shake before use

agitato agitated; *mare* rough

agitazione *f* agitation

agli *prp* **a** and *art* **gli**

aglio *m* (*pl* -gli) garlic

agnello *m* lamb

agnolotti *mpl* type of ravioli

ago *m* (*pl* -ghi) needle

agonia *f* agony

agonismo *m* competitiveness

agonistico (*pl* -ci) competitive

agopuntura *f* acupuncture

agorafobia *f* agoraphobia

agosto *m* August; **in ~** in August

agraria *f* agriculture

agrario (*pl* -ri) agricultural

agricolo agricultural

agricoltore *m* farmer

agricoltura *f* agriculture

agrifoglio *m* holly

agriturismo *m* farm holidays *pl*

agro sour

agrodolce bittersweet; GASTR sweet and sour

agronomo *m*, **-a** *f* agricultural economist

agrumi *mpl* citrus fruit *sg*

aguzzare <1a> sharpen; *~ la vista* keep one's eyes peeled

aguzzo pointed

ah! oh!

ahi! ouch!

ai *prp* **a** and *art* **i**

Aids *m* o *f* Aids

airbag *m inv* airbag

A.I.R.E. *abbr* (= *Anagrafe degli Italiani Residenti all'Estero*) register of Italian citizens resident overseas

airone *m* heron

aiuola *f* flower bed

aiutante *m/f* assistant

aiutare <1a> help

aiuto *m* help, assistance; *persona* assistant; *~ allo sviluppo* development aid *or* assistance; *chiedere ~ a qu* ask s.o. for help

aizzare <1a> incite

al *prp* **a** and *art* **il**

ala *f* (*pl* -i) wing

alabastro *m* alabaster

alano *m* Great Dane

alba *f* dawn; *all'~* at dawn

albanese *agg*, *m/f* Albanian

Albania *f* Albania

albeggiare <1f> dawn

alberato tree-lined

albergare <1b & e> put up

albergatore *m*, **-trice** *f* hotel keeper

alberghiero hotel *attr*

albergo *m* (*pl* -ghi) hotel; *guida f degli -ghi* hotel guide

albero *m* tree; MAR mast; AVIA, AUTO shaft; *~ genealogico* family tree; *~ motore* drive shaft; *~ di Natale* Christmas tree

albicocca *f* (*pl* -cche) apricot

albicocco *m* (*pl* -cchi) apricot (tree)

albo *m* notice board; (*registro*) register; *radiare dall'~* strike off

album *m inv* album

albume *m* albumen

alcalino alkaline

alcol *m* alcohol

alcolico (*pl* -ci) **1** *agg* alcoholic; *gradazione f -a* alcohol content **2** *m* alcoholic drink

alcolismo *m* alcoholism

alcolizzato *m*, **-a** *f* alcoholic

alcoltest *m inv* Breathalyzer®

alcuno **1** *agg* any; *non ~* no, not any **2** *pron* any; *-i pl* some, a few

aldilà *m*: *l'~* the next world

aletta *f* fin

alfabetico (*pl* -ci) alphabetical

alfabeto *m* alphabet

alfanumerico (*pl* -ci) INFOR alphanumeric

alfiere *m* scacchi bishop

alfine eventually

alga *f* (*pl* -ghe) seaweed

algebra *f* algebra

Algeria *f* Algeria

algerino **1** *agg* Algerian **2** *m*, **-a** *f* Algerian

aliante *m* glider

alice *f* anchovy

alienare <1b> DIR transfer; *persone* alienate

alienarsi become lienated

alienato **1** *agg* alienated **2** *m*, **-a** *f* madman; *donna* madwoman

alienazione *f* alienation; *~ mentale* madness

alimentare <1a> **1** *v/t* feed **2** *agg* food *attr*; *generi mpl -i* foodstuffs

alimentazione *f* feeding

alimento *m* food; *~ base* basic food(stuff); *-i pl* DIR alimony *sg*

aliquota *f* share; *~ d'imposta* rate of taxation

aliscafo *m* hydrofoil

all. *abbr* (= *allegato*) enc(l). (= enclosed)

all', **alla** *prp* **a** and *art* **l'**, **la**

allacciamento *m* TEC connection

allacciare <1f> fasten; TEC connect

allagamento *m* flooding

allagare <1e> flood

allargare <1e> widen; *vestito* let out; *braccia* open

allargarsi widen

allarmare <1a> alarm

allarmarsi become alarmed

allarme *m* alarm; *dare l'~* raise the alarm; *~ smog* smog alert

allattare <1a> *bambino* feed

alle *prp* **a** *and art* **le**

alleanza *f* alliance

allearsi <1b> ally o.s.

alleato 1 *agg* allied 2 *m*, **-a** *f* ally

allegare <1e> *documento* enclose

allegato *m* enclosure; INFOR attachment; *qui ~* enclosed

alleggerire <4d> lighten; *fig dolore* ease

allegria *f* cheerfulness

allegro 1 *agg* cheerful; *colore* bright 2 *m* MUS allegro

allenamento *m* training

allenare <1b>, **allenarsi** train (*per* for; *a* in)

allenatore *m*, **-trice** *f* trainer

allentare <1b> 1 *v/t* loosen; *fig disciplina* relax 2 *v/i e* **allentarsi** loosen

allergia *f* allergy

allergico (*pl* -ci) allergic (*a* to)

allestimento *m* preparation; MAR fitting out; TEA *~ scenico* sets *pl*, scenery

allestire <4d> prepare; MAR fit out; TEA stage

allevamento *m* BOT, ZO breeding

allevare <1b> BOT, ZO breed; *bambini* bring up, raise

allevatore *m*, **-trice** *f* breeder

alleviare <1b & k> alleviate

allievo *m*, **-a** *f* pupil, student

alligatore *m* alligator

allineamento *m* alignment

allineare <1m> line up; FIN adjust; TIP align

allinearsi line up; *fig* **~ con qu** align o.s. with s.o.

allo *prp* **a** *and art* **lo**

allodola *f* skylark

alloggiare <1f & c> 1 *v/t* put up; MIL billet 2 *v/i* stay, put up

alloggio *m* (*pl* -ggi) accommodation; *dare ~ a qu* put s.o. up; *vitto e ~* bed and board

allontanare <1a> take away; *fig pericolo, sospetto* avert

allontanarsi go away; *fig* grow apart

allora 1 *avv* then 2 *cong* then; *d'~ in poi* from then on; *fin d'~* since then

alloro *m* laurel; GASTR bay

alluce *m* big toe

allucinante F incredible, mind-blowing F

allucinazione *f* hallucination

alludere <3q> allude (*a* to)

alluminio *m* aluminium, *Am* aluminum

allungamento *m* lengthening

allungare <1e> lengthen; (*diluire*) dilute; *mano* stretch out, put out

allungarsi *di giorni* get longer; *di persona* stretch out, lie down

allusione *f* allusion

alluvione *f* flood

almeno at least

alogena *f* halogen

Alpi *fpl* Alps

alpinismo *m* mountaineering

alpinista *m/f* mountain climber

alpino Alpine

alquanto 1 *agg* some 2 *avv* a little, somewhat

alt *int* stop

altalena *f* swing

altare *m* altar

alterare <1l> alter

alterarsi (*guastarsi*) go bad *or* off; (*irritarsi*) get angry

alterazione *f* alteration

alterco *m* (*pl* -chi) altercation

alternare <1b>, **alternarsi** alternate

alternativa *f* alternative

alternativo alternative

alternato: *corrente f* **-a** alternating current

alterno: *a giorni pl* **-i** on alternate days

altezza *f* height; *titolo* Highness

alticcio (*pl* -cci) tipsy

altitudine *f* GEOG altitude

alto 1 *agg* high; *persona* tall; *a voce* **-a** in a loud voice; *leggere* aloud; *in ~* at the top; *moto* up; *a notte* **-a** in the middle of the night 2 *m* top

altoatesino 1 *agg* South Tyrolean 2 *m*, **-a** *f* person from South Tyrol

altoforno *m* blast furnace

altoparlante *m* loudspeaker

altopiano *m* (*pl* altipiani) plateau

altrettanto *agg*, *pron* as much; **-i** *pl* as many

altrimenti (*in modo diverso*) differently; (*in caso contrario*) otherwise

altro 1 *agg* other; **un ~** another; *l'altr'anno* last year; *l'~ giorno* the other day; *l'~ ieri* the day before yesterday **2** *pron* other; *l'un l'~* one another; *gli altri* other people; *tra l'~* what's more, moreover; *desidera ~?* anything else?; *tutt'~ che* anything but

altronde *d'~* on the other hand

altrove elsewhere

altruismo *m* altruism

altura *f* hill

alunno *m*, **-a** *f* pupil, student

alzacristallo *m inv* AUTO window winder

alzare <1a> raise, lift; *prezzi* increase, raise; (*costruire*) build, erect; *~ le spalle* shrug (one's shoulders)

alzarsi stand up, rise; *da letto* get up; *di sole* come up, rise

amabile lovable; (*gentile*) pleasant, kind; *vino* sweet

amabilità *f* pleasantness

amaca *f* (*pl* -che) hammock

amalgamare <1m> amalgamate

amante *m/f* lover

amare <1a> love; *amico* be fond of

amareggiare <1f> embitter

amareggiato embittered

amarena *f* sour black cherry

amarezza *f* bitterness

amaro 1 *agg* bitter **2** *m* liquore bitters *pl*

ambasciata *f* embassy

ambasciatore *m*, **-trice** *f* ambassador

ambedue both

ambientale environmental

ambientalista 1 *agg* environmental **2** *m/f* environmentalist

ambientarsi <1b> become acclimatized

ambiente *m* BIO environment; *~ di lavoro* work environment; *protezione f dell'~* environmental protection

ambiguità *f inv* ambiguity

ambiguo ambiguous

ambito *m* sphere

ambizione *f* ambition

ambizioso ambitious

ambo 1 *agg* both; *in -i casi* in both cases **2** *m* (*lotteria*) double

ambulante 1 *agg* travel(l)ing **2** *m/f* pedlar

ambulanza *f* ambulance

ambulatorio *m* MED (*pl* -ri) outpatients

America *f* America

americano 1 *agg* American **2** *m*, **-a** *f* American **3** *m* American English

ametista *f* amethyst

amianto *m* asbestos

amichevole friendly

amicizia *f* friendship

amico (*pl* -ci) **1** *agg* friendly **2** *m*, **-a** *f* (*pl* -che) friend; *~ intimo* close friend

amido *m* starch

ammaccare <1d> dent; *frutta* bruise

ammaccatura *f* dent; *su frutta* bruise

ammaestrare <1b> teach; *animali* train

ammalarsi <1a> fall ill

ammalato 1 *agg* ill **2** *m*, **-a** *f* ill person

ammanco *m* (*pl* -chi) deficit

ammanettare <1a> handcuff, put handcuffs on

ammarare <1a> *di aereo* put down in the water; *di navetta spaziale* splash down

ammassare <1a>, **ammassarsi** mass

ammasso *m* pile; GEOL mass

ammazzare <1a> kill; *animali* slaughter

ammazzarsi (*suicidarsi*) kill o.s.

ammenda *f* (*multa*) fine; *fare ~ di* make amends for

ammesso *pp* → **ammettere**

ammettere <3ee> admit; (*supporre*) suppose; (*riconoscere*) acknowledge; *ammesso che ...* supposing (that) ...

amministrare <1a> administer; *azienda* manage, run

amministrativo administrative

amministratore *m*, -**trice** *f* administrator; *di azienda* manager; ~ **delegato** managing director

amministrazione *f* administration; ~ **comunale** local council; **pubblica** ~ public administration; **spese** *fpl* **d'**~ administrative costs

ammiraglia *f* flagship

ammiraglio *m* (*pl* -gli) admiral

ammirare <1a> admire

ammiratore *m*, -**trice** *f* admirer

ammirazione *f* admiration

ammirevole admirable

ammissibile admissible

ammobiliare <1g> furnish

ammobiliato furnished

ammodo 1 *agg inv* respectable 2 *avv* properly

ammolla *in* ~ soaking

ammonimento *m* reprimand, admonishment; (*consiglio*) warning

ammonire <4d> reprimand, admonish; (*avvertire*) warn; DIR caution

ammonizione *f* reprimand, admonishment; SP warning; DIR caution

ammontare 1 *v/i* <1a>: ~ *a* amount to 2 *m* amount; **per un** ~ **di ...** in the amount of ...

ammorbidire <4d> soften

ammortamento *m* FIN amortization

ammortizzare <1a> FIN amortize

ammortizzatore *m* AUTO shock absorber

ammucchiare <1g> pile up

ammucchiarsi pile up, accumulate

ammuffire <4d> go mo(u)ldy; *fig* mo(u)lder away

ammutolire <4d> be struck dumb

amnesia *f* amnesia

amnistia *f* amnesty

amo *m* hook; *fig* bait

amore *m* love; **per l'**~ **di qu** for love of s.o.; **per l'amor di Dio** for goodness' sake, for the love of God; **fare l'**~ **con qu** make love to s.o.

amoreggiare <1f> flirt

amorevole loving

amoroso loving, affectionate; *sguardo* amorous; *lettera, poesia* love *attr*

amperaggio *m* (*pl* -gi) amperage

ampiezza *f di stanza* spaciousness; *di*
gonna fullness; *fig di cultura* breadth; *fig* ~ **di vedute** broad-mindedness

ampio (*pl* -pi) *stanza* spacious, large; *abito* roomy; *gonna* full

ampliamento *m* broadening, widening; *di edificio* extension

ampliare <1l> broaden, widen; *edificio* extend

amplificare <1m & d> TEC *suono* amplify

amplificatore *m* amplifier

ampolla *f* cruet

amputare <1l> amputate

amputazione *f* amputation

amuleto *m* amulet

anabbagliante dipped

anabolizzante *m* anabolic steroid

anacronistico (*pl* -ci) anachronistic

anagrafe *f ufficio* registry office

analcolico (*pl* -ci) 1 *agg* non-alcoholic 2 *m* non-alcoholic drink

anale anal

analfabeta *m/f* (*mpl* -i) illiterate person, person who cannot read or write

analfabetismo *m* illiteracy

analgesico (*pl* -ci) *m/agg* analgesic

analisi *f inv* analysis; ~ **del sangue** blood test

analista *m/f* (*mpl* -i) analyst; ~ **programmatore** systems analyst

analizzare <1a> analyse, *Am* analyze

analogia *f* analogy

analogo (*pl* -ghi) analogous

ananas *m inv* pineapple

anarchia *f* anarchy

anarchico (*pl* -ci) 1 *agg* anarchic 2 *m*, -**a** *f* anarchist

ANAS *abbr* (= **Azienda Nazionale Autonoma della Strada**) Italian Roads Department

anatomia *f* anatomy

anatomico (*pl* -ci) anatomical

anatra *f* duck

anca *f* (*pl* -che) hip

anche too, also, as well; (*perfino*) even; ~ **se** even if

ancora[1] *avv* still; *di nuovo* again; *di più* (some) more; **non** ~ not yet; ~

una volta once more, one more time; *dammene ~ un po'* give me a bit more

ancora² f anchor; *gettare l'~* drop anchor

ancoraggio m (pl -ggi) anchoring; *luogo* anchorage

ancorare <1l> anchor

ancorarsi anchor; *fig ~ a* cling to

andamento m *di vendite* performance

andare <1p> **1** v/i *e* go; *(funzionare)* work; *~ via (partire)* leave; *di macchia* come out; *~ bene* suit; *taglia* fit; *~ a cavallo* ride; *~ a passeggio* walk; *~ a male* go off; *~ a finire* turn out; *~ in bicicletta* cycle; *come va?* how are you?, how are things?; *non mi va di vestito* it doesn't fit me; *non mi va di venire* I don't feel like coming **2** m: *coll'~ del tempo* with the passage of time; *a lungo ~* in the long run

andarsene go away

andata f outward journey; *c'era più traffico all'~* there was more traffic on the way there; *biglietto m di ~* single (ticket), *Am* oneway ticket; *biglietto m di ~ e ritorno* return (ticket), *Am* roundtrip ticket

andatura f walk; SP pace

andirivieni m inv toing and froing

androne m hallway

aneddoto m anecdote

anello m ring; *~ di fidanzamento* engagement ring

anemia f an(a)emia

anemico (pl -ci) an(a)emic

anemone m anemone

anestesia f an(a)esthesia; *sostanza* an(a)esthetic

anestesista m/f (mpl -i) an(a)esthetist

anestetico m (pl -ci) an(a)esthetic

anfetamina f amphetamine

anfibio (pl -bi) **1** agg amphibious **2** m ZO amphibian; MIL amphibious vehicle

anfiteatro m amphitheatre, *Am* -theater

anfora f amphora

angelo m angel; *~ custode* guardian angel

anglicano 1 agg Anglican **2** m, **-a** f Anglican

anglista m/f student of English

anglosassone Anglo-Saxon

angolare angular

angolo m corner; MAT angle; *~ cottura* kitchenette; MAT *~ retto* right angle; SP *calcio m d'~* corner kick;

angoloso angular

angoscia f (pl -sce) anguish

angoscioso *pieno d'angoscia* anguished; *che da angoscia* distressing, heart-rending

anguilla f eel

anguria f water melon

angusto narrow

anice m GASTR aniseed

anidride f: *~ carbonica* carbon dioxide

anima f soul; *non c'è ~ viva* there isn't a soul to be seen; F *rompere l'~ a qu* get on s.o.'s nerves F

animale 1 agg animal attr **2** m animal; *~ domestico* pet

animare <1l> give life to; *conversazione* liven up; *(promuovere)* promote

animato *strada* busy; *conversazione, persona* animated

animatore m, **-trice** f *di gruppo* leader

animazione f animation; INFOR *~ al computer* computer animation

animo m nature; *(coraggio)* heart; *farsi ~* be brave; *perdersi d'~* lose heart

anisetta f aniseed-flavoured liqueur

anitra f duck

annacquare <1a> water down

annaffiare <1k> water

annaffiatoio m (pl -oi) watering can

annali mpl annals

annata f vintage; *(anno)* year; *importo* annual amount

annegare <1e> **1** v/t drown **2** v/i *e* **annegarsi** drown

annerire <4d> **1** v/t blacken **2** v/i *e* **annerirsi** turn black, blacken

annessione f POL annexation

annesso 1 pp → **annettere 2** agg annexed; (*allegato*) enclosed, attached **3** m edificio annex(e)

annettere <3m> POL annex; ARCHI add; (*allegare*) enclose, attach

annidarsi <1a> nest

anniversario m (pl -ri) anniversary

anno m year; **buon ~!** Happy New Year!; **~ finanziario** financial year; **~ scolastico** school year; **quanti -i hai?** how old are you?; **ho 33 -i** I'm 33 (years old)

annodare <1c> tie (together); *cravatta* tie, knot

annoiare <1i> bore; (*dare fastidio a*) annoy

annoiarsi get bored

annoiato bored

annotare <1c> make a note of; *testo* annotate

annotazione f note; *in testo* annotation

annuale annual, yearly; *di un anno* year-long

annuario m (pl -ri) yearbook

annuire <4d> (*assentire*) assent (**a** to)

annullamento m cancellation; *di matrimonio* annulment

annullare <1a> cancel; *matrimonio* annul; *gol* disallow; (*vanificare*) cancel out

annunciare <1f> announce

annunciatore m, **-trice** f RAD, TV announcer

Annunciazione f REL Annunciation

annuncio m (pl -ci) announcement; *in giornale* advertisement; **-i** pl **economici** classified ads, classifieds; **~ pubblicitario** ad(vert), advertisement

annunziare <1a> → **annunciare**

annuo annual, yearly

annusare <1a> sniff; *fig* smell

annuvolarsi <1a> cloud over

anomalo anomalous

anonimo anonymous; **società** f **-a** limited company

anoressia f anorexia

anoressico anorexic

anormale abnormal

ANSA abbr (= **Agenzia Nazionale Stampa Associata**) Italian Press Agency

ansa f handle; *di un fiume* bend

ansia f anxiety; **con ~** anxiously

ansimare <1l> wheeze

ansioso anxious

antagonismo m antagonism

antagonista m/f (mpl -i) antagonist

antartico (pl -ci) Antarctic attr

antecedente 1 agg preceding **2** m precedent

antefatto m prior event

anteguerra m pre-war years pl

antenato m, **-a** f ancestor

antenna f RAD, TV aerial; ZO antenna; **~ parabolica** satellite dish

anteporre <3ll> put before

anteposto pp → **anteporre**

anteprima f preview

anteriore front; *precedente* previous

anti ... anti ...

antiatomico (pl -ci) anti-nuclear; **rifugio** m **~** fallout shelter

antibiotico (pl -ci) m/agg antibiotic

anticamente in ancient times

anticamera f ante-room; **fare ~** be kept waiting

antichità f inv antiquity; **negozio** m **d'~** antique shop

anticiclone m anticyclone

anticipare <1m> anticipate; *denaro* pay in advance; *partenza, riunione ecc* bring forward

anticipo m advance; (*caparra*) deposit; **in ~** ahead of time, early

antico (pl -chi) **1** agg ancient; *mobile* antique **2 gli -chi** pl the ancients

anticoncezionale m/agg contraceptive

anticonformista m/f (mpl -i) nonconformist

anticongelante m anti-freeze

anticorpo m antibody

anticostituzionale unconstitutional

antidoto m antidote

antifurto 1 adj antitheft **2** m antitheft device

antigas inv gas attr

antincendio inv fire attr

antinebbia m inv foglamp
antioraria in senso ~ anticlockwise, Am counterclockwise
antipasto m starter
antipatia f antipathy
antipatico (pl -ci) disagreeable
antiquariato m antique business, antiques; **negozio** m **di** ~ antique shop
antiquario m (pl -ri), **-a** f antique dealer
antiquato antiquated
antiriflesso inv anti-glare
antiruggine m rust inhibitor
antirumore protezione f ~ soundproofing
antisemitismo m anti-Semitism
antisettico (pl -ci) m/agg antiseptic
antisismico (pl -ci) earthquakeproof
antitesi f FIL antithesis
antiurto shockproof
antologia f anthology
antracite f anthracite
antropologia f anthropology
anulare m ring finger
anzi in fact; (o meglio) (or) better still
anzianità f old age; ~ **di servizio** seniority
anziano 1 agg elderly; per servizio (most) senior 2 m, **-a** f old man; donna old woman; **gli -i** the elderly
anziché rather than
anzitutto first of all
aorta f aorta
apatia f apathy
apatico (pl -ci) apathetic
ape f bee
aperitivo m aperitif
aperto 1 pp → **aprire** 2 agg open; **di mentalità aperta** broad-minded; **all'** ~ piscina open-air; **mangiare all'**~ eat outside or in the open air
apertura f opening; PHOT aperture; ~ **di credito** loan agreement; ~ **alare** wingspan
apice m apex; fig height
apicoltore m, **-trice** f bee-keeper
apicoltura f bee-keeping
apnea f SP free diving
apolide 1 agg stateless 2 m stateless person

apolitico (pl -ci) apolitical
apoplessia f apoplexy
apostolico (pl -ci) apostolic
apostolo m apostle
apostrofare <1m & c> reprimand; GRAM add an apostrophe to
apostrofo m apostrophe
appagare <1e> satisfy
appaiare <1i> match
appallottolare <1c & n> roll up into a ball
appalto m (contratto) contract; **dare in** ~ contract out; **prendere in** ~ win the contract for; **gara** f **di** ~ call for tenders
appannare <1a> mist up
appannarsi di vetro mist up; di vista grow dim
apparato m TEC, fig apparatus; ~ **digerente** digestive system
apparecchiare <1g> tavola set, lay; (preparare) prepare
apparecchiatura f equipment
apparecchio m (pl -cchi) TEC device; AVIA F plane; per denti brace; ~ **fotografico** camera; F **portare l'**~ wear a hearing aid
apparente apparent
apparenza f appearance; **salvare le -e** save face
apparire <4e> appear
appariscente striking, eyecatching
apparizione f apparition
appartamento m flat, Am apartment
appartarsi <1a> withdraw
appartenere <2q> belong
appassionare <1a> excite; (commuovere) move
appassionarsi become excited (a by)
appassionato passionate
appassire <4d> wither
appellarsi <1b> appeal (a to; **contro** against)
appello m appeal; **fare** ~ **a qu** appeal to s.o.; DIR **ricorrere in** ~ lodge an appeal
appena 1 avv just 2 cong as soon as
appendere <3c> hang
appendiabiti m hatstand

appendice f appendix

appendicite f appendicitis

Appennini mpl Apennines

appesantire <4d> make heavier

appesi *appeso pp → appendere*

appetito m appetite; *buon ~!* enjoy your meal!

appetitoso appetizing

appianare <1a> level; *lite* smooth over

appiattire <4d> flatten

appiccicare <1m & d> stick

appiccicarsi stick

appiccicoso sticky; *fig* clingy

appigliarsi <1g> grab hold (*a* of)

appiglio m (*pl* -gli) *per mani* finger-hold; *per piedi* toehold; *fig* excuse

applaudire <4a *or* d> v/t & v/i applaud

applauso m applause

applicare <1l & d> *etichetta* attach; *regolamento* apply

applicarsi ~ *a qc* apply o.s. to sth

applicazione f application

appoggiare <1f & c> lean (*a* against); (*posare*) put; *fig* support, back

appoggiarsi ~ *a* lean on; *fig* rely on, lean on

appoggiatesta m inv headrest

appoggio m (*pl* -ggi) support

apporre <3ll> put; ~ *la firma su qc* put one's signature to sth

apportare <1c> bring; *fig* (*causare*) cause

apposito appropriate

apposta deliberately, on purpose; *specialmente* specifically

apprendere <3c> learn; *notizia* hear

apprendista m/f (*mpl* -i) apprentice

apprendistato m apprenticeship

apprensione f apprehension

apprensivo apprehensive

appreso pp → **apprendere**

appresso 1 prp close, near; (*dietro*) behind; ~ *a qu* near s.o., close to s.o. **2** avv near, close by; *portarsi qc ~* bring sth (with one)

apprezzare <1b> appreciate

approccio m (*pl* -cci) approach

approdare <1c> land; *di barca* moor,

tie up; *fig* **non ~ a nulla** come to nothing

approdo m landing; *luogo* landing stage

approfittare <1a>: ~ *di qc* take advantage of sth

approfondire <4d> deepen; *fig* study in depth

appropriarsi <1m & c>: ~ *di qc* appropriate sth

appropriato appropriate

approvare <1c> approve of; *legge* approve

approvazione f approval

approvvigionamento m supply

appuntamento m appointment

appuntare <1a> pin; *avviso* pin up

appuntito pointed; *matita* sharp

appunto 1 m note; *prendere -i* take notes **2** avv: (*per l'*)~ exactly

apribottiglie m inv bottle opener

aprile m April

aprire <4f> open; *rubinetto* turn on

aprirsi open; ~ *con qu* confide in s.o., open up to s.o.

apriscatole m inv can-opener, *Br* tin-opener

aquila f eagle

aquilone m kite

arabesco m (*pl* -chi) arabesque; *spir* scrawl, scribble

Arabia Saudita f Saudi (Arabia)

arabo 1 agg Arab **2** m, **-a** f Arab **3** m Arabic

arachide f peanut

aragosta f lobster

arancia f (*pl* -ce) orange

aranciata f orangeade

arancio 1 agg inv orange **2** m (*pl* -ci) *albero* orange tree; *colore* orange

arancione m/agg orange

arare <1a> plough, *Am* plow

aratro m plough, *Am* plow

arazzo m tapestry

arbitraggio m (*pl* -ggi) arbitration; *SP* refereeing

arbitrare <1l> arbitrate in; *SP* referee

arbitrario (*pl* -ri) arbitrary

arbitro m arbiter; *SP* referee

arbusto m shrub

arca f (*pl* -che) (*cassa*) chest; *REL l'~*

di Noè Noah's Ark

arcaico (*pl* -ci) archaic

arcangelo *m* archangel

arcata *f* ANAT, ARCHI arch

archeologia *f* arch(a)eology

archeologo *m* (*pl* -gi), **-a** *f* arch(a)eologist

archetto *m* MUS bow

architetto *m* architect

architettonico (*pl* -ci) architectural

archiviare <1k> file

archivio *m* (*pl* -vi) archives, records

arcipelago *m* (*pl* -ghi) archipelago

arcivescovo *m* archbishop

arco *m* (*pl* -chi) bow; ARCHI arch; ~ *di tempo* space of time; *orchestra f d'-chi* string orchestra

arcobaleno *m* rainbow

ardente *fig* ardent

ardere <3uu> *v/t & v/i* burn

area *f* surface; *zona* area; ~ *fabbricabile* site that may be built on; SP ~ *di rigore* penalty area; ~ *di servizio* service area

arena *f* arena

arenarsi <1a> run aground; *fig* come to a halt

areo ... → aereo ...

argano *m* winch

argentato silver-plated

argenteria *f* silver(ware)

Argentina *f* Argentina

argentino 1 *agg* Argentinian **2** *m*, **-a** *f* Argentinian

argento *m* silver; ~ *vivo* quicksilver; FERR *carta f d'~* travel pass for people over a certain age; *nozze fpl d'~* silver wedding *sg*

argilla *f* clay

argilloso clayey

arginare <1l> embank

argine *m* embankment

argomento *m* argument; (*contenuto*) subject; *cambiare ~* change the subject

arguto witty; (*perspicace*) shrewd

arguzia *f* wit; *espressione* witticism, witty remark; (*perspicacia*) shrewdness

arnese *m* tool

arnia *f* beehive

aroma *m* (*pl* -i) aroma

aromatico (*pl* -ci) aromatic

aromatizzare <1a> flavo(u)r

aria *f* **1** air; ~ *condizionata* air conditioning; *all'~ aperta* in the fresh air; *mandare all'~ qc* ruin sth **2** (*aspetto*) appearance; (*espressione*) air; *aver l'~ stanca* look tired; *ha l'~ di non capire* he looks as if he doesn't understand; *darsi delle -e* give o.s. airs **3** MUS tune; *di opera* aria

aridità *f* dryness

arido dry, arid

arieggiare <1f> *stanza* air

ariete *m* ZO ram; ASTR *Ariete* Aries

aringa *f* (*pl* -ghe) herring

arista *f* GASTR chine of pork

aristocratico (*pl* -ci) **1** *agg* aristocratic **2** *m*, **-a** *f* aristocrat

aristocrazia *f* aristocracy

aritmetica *f* arithmetic

arma *f* (*pl* -i) weapon; ~ *da fuoco* firearm; *-i pl convenzionali* conventional weapons; *-i pl nucleari* nuclear weapons; *-i pl atomiche, biologiche e chimiche* atomic, biological and chemical weapons; *chiamare alle -i* call up; *fig essere alle prime -i* be a beginner, be just starting out

armadio *m* (*pl* -di) cupboard; ~ *a muro* fitted cupboard

armamentario *m* (*pl* -ri) *gen spir* paraphernalia

armamento *m* armament; *industria f degli -i* armaments industry

armare <1a> arm; ARCHI reinforce

armarsi arm o.s. (*di* with)

armata *f* army; MAR fleet

armato armed

armatore *m* shipowner

armatura *f* armo(u)r; (*struttura*) framework

armistizio *m* (*pl* -zi) armistice

armonia *f* harmony

armonica *f* (*pl* -che) harmonica; ~ *a bocca* mouth organ

armonico (*pl* -ci) harmonic

armonioso harmonious

armonizzare <1a> *v/t & v/i* harmonize

aromaterapia f aromatherapy
arpa f harp
arpione m pesca harpoon
arrabattarsi <1a> do everything one can
arrabbiarsi <1k> get angry
arrabbiato angry; (idrofobo) rabid
arrampicarsi <1m & d> climb
arrampicata f climb
arrampicatore m, **-trice** f climber; ~ **sociale** social climber
arrangiamento m arrangement
arrangiare <1f> arrange
arrangiarsi (accordarsi) agree (**su** on); (destreggiarsi) manage
arrecare <1b & d> bring; fig cause
arredamento m décor; mobili furniture; arte interior design
arredare <1b> furnish
arredatore m, **-trice** f interior designer
arrendersi <3c> surrender; fig give up
arrendevole soft, yielding
arrestare <1b> stop, halt; DIR arrest
arrestarsi stop
arresto m coming to a stop; DIR arrest
arretrato 1 agg in arrears; paese underdeveloped; **numero** m ~ **di giornale** back number 2 **-i** mpl arrears
arricchire <4d> fig enrich
arricchirsi get rich
arricciare <1f> capelli curl; ~ **il naso** turn up one's nose
arringa f (pl -ghe) DIR closing speech for the defence
arrivare <1a> arrive; ~ **a** reach; ~ **primo** arrive first; ~ **puntuale** arrive on time; ~ **a fare qc** manage to do sth; F **non ci arriva** he doesn't get it F, he doesn't understand
arrivederci, **arrivederla** goodbye
arrivista m/f (mpl -i) social climber
arrivo m arrival; SP finishing line; **-i internazionali** international arrivals
arrogante arrogant
arroganza f arrogance
arrossire <4d> blush

arrostire <4d> carne roast; **ai ferri** grill
arrosto m roast; ~ **d'agnello** roast lamb
arrotolare <1m & c> roll up
arrotondare <1a> round off; stipendio supplement
arroventato red-hot
arruffare <1a> capelli ruffle
arruffato ruffled
arrugginire <4d> 1 v/t rust 2 v/i e **arrugginirsi** rust; fig become rusty
arruolamento m enlistment
arruolare <1o> enlist
arruolarsi enlist, join up
arsenale m arsenal; MAR dockyard
arso 1 pp → **ardere** 2 agg burnt; (secco) dried-up
arsura f blazing heat
arte f art; (abilità) gift; **le -i figurative** the figurative arts; **-i pl grafiche** graphic arts; **storia** f **dell'~** history of art; **un discorso fatto ad** ~ a masterly speech
artefatto voce disguised
artefice m/f fig author, architect
arteria f artery; ~ **stradale** arterial road
arterioso arterial
artico (pl -ci) Arctic attr
articolare 1 agg articular 2 v/t <1m> articulate; (suddividere) divide
articolazione f ANAT articulation
articolo m item, article; GRAM ~ **determinativo** definite article; GRAM ~ **indeterminativo** indefinite article; **-i pl di consumo** consumer goods; ~ **di fondo** leading article; ~ **di prima necessità** basic
artificiale artificial
artificio m (pl -ci) artifice; **fuochi** mpl **d'~** fireworks
artificioso maniere artificial
artigianale handmade, handcrafted
artigianato m craftsmanship
artigiano m, **-a** f craftsman; donna craftswoman
artiglieria f artillery
artiglio m (pl -gli) claw
artista m/f (mpl -i) artist
artistico (pl -ci) artistic

arto m limb
artrite f arthritis
artrosi f rheumatism
ascella f armpit
ascendente 1 agg ascending; *strada* sloping upwards; *movimento* upwards **2** m ASTR ascendant; *fig* influence
ascensione f di montagna ascent; REL Ascension
ascensore m lift, Am elevator
ascesa f ascent
ascesso m abscess
asceta m (pl -i) ascetic
ascia f (pl -sce) ax(e)
asciugacapelli m hairdryer
asciugamano m towel; **~ da bagno** bath towel
asciugare <1e> dry
asciugarsi dry o.s.; **~ i capelli** dry one's hair
asciugatrice f tumble dryer
asciutto 1 agg dry **2** m: fig *trovarsi all'~* be stony broke
ascoltare <1a> listen to
ascoltatore m, **-trice** f listener
ascolto m listening; **dare / prestare ~** listen (a to); **indice m di ~** ratings pl
asettico (pl -ci) aseptic
asfaltare <1a> asphalt
asfalto m asphalt
asfissia f asphyxia
asfissiare <1k> asphyxiate
Asia f Asia
asiatico (pl -ci) **1** agg Asian **2** m, **-a** f Asian
asilo m shelter; **richiesta f di ~ politico** request for political asylum; **~ infantile** nursery school; **~ nido** day nursery
asimmetrico (pl -ci) asymmetrical
asino m ass (anche fig)
asma f asthma
asmatico (pl -ci) asthmatic
asociale antisocial
asola f buttonhole
asparago m (pl -gi) spear of asparagus; **-gi** asparagus sg
aspettare <1b> wait for; **~ un bambino** be expecting a baby; **farsi**

~ keep people waiting
aspettarsi expect; **dovevo aspettarmelo** I should have expected it
aspettativa f expectation; **da lavoro** unpaid leave
aspetto¹ m look, appearance; *di problema* aspect; **sotto quest' ~** from that point of view
aspetto² m: **sala f d'~** waiting room
aspirante1 agg TEC suction attr **2** m/f applicant
aspirapolvere m vacuum cleaner
aspirare <1a> **1** v/t inhale; TEC suck up **2** v/i: **~ a qc** aspire to sth
aspirina f aspirin
asportare <1c> take away
aspro sour; (duro) harsh; *litigio* bitter
assaggiare <1f> taste, sample
assaggio m (pl -ggi) taste, sample
assai1 agg a lot of **2** avv con verbo a lot; con aggettivo very; (abbastanza) enough
assalire <4m> attack
assaltare <1a> → **assalire**
assalto m attack; fig **prendere d'~** storm
assassinare <1a> murder; POL assassinate
assassinio m murder; POL assassination
assassino1 agg murderous **2** m, **-a** f murderer; POL assassin
asse¹ f board; **~ da stiro** ironing board
asse² m TEC axle; MAT axis
assecondare <1a> support; (esaudire) satisfy
assediare <1k> besiege
assedio m (pl -di) siege
assegnare <1a> premio award; (destinare) assign
assegno m cheque, Am check; **~ in bianco** blank cheque (Am check); **~ sbarrato** crossed cheque (Am check); **~ turistico** traveller's cheque, Am traveler's check; **contro ~** cash on delivery; **-i familiari** child benefit; **emettere un ~** issue or write a cheque (Am check)
assemblea f meeting; **~ generale** annual general meeting

assennato sensible

assentarsi <1b> go away, leave

assente absent, away; *fig* absentminded

assenza *f* absence; **~ di qc** lack of sth

assessore *m* council(l)or; **~ comunale** local councillor

assetato thirsty

assetto *m* order; MAR trim

assicurare <1a> insure; (*legare*) secure; *lettera, pacco* register

assicurarsi make sure, ensure

assicurata *f* registered letter

assicurato 1 *agg* insured; *lettera, pacco* registered **2** *m*, **-a** *f* person with insurance

assicurazione *f* insurance; **~ dei bagagli** luggage insurance; **~ di responsabilità civile** liability insurance; **~ sulla vita** life insurance; **~ casco** comprehensive insurance

assideramento *m* exposure

assiduo (*diligente*) assiduous; (*regolare*) regular

assieme together

assillante nagging

assillare <1a> pester

assillo *m* *fig* *persona* pest, nuisance; (*preoccupazione*) nagging thought

assimilare <1m> assimilate

assimilazione *f* assimilation

assise *fpl*: **Corte f d'~** Crown Court

assistente *m/f* assistant; **~ sociale** social worker; **~ di volo** flight attendant

assistenza *f* assistance; **~ medica** medical care; **~ sociale** social work; **~ tecnica** after-sales service

assistere <3f> **1** *v/t* assist, help; (*curare*) nurse **2** *v/i* (*essere presente*) be present (**a** at), attend (**a** sth)

assom ace; *fig* **piantare in ~** leave in the lurch

associare <1f> take into partnership; *fig* **~ qu a qc** associate s.o. with sth

associarsi enter into partnership (**a** with); (*unirsi*) join forces; (*iscriversi*) subscribe (**a** to); (*prendere parte*) join (**a** sth)

associazione *f* association; **~ per la**

difesa dei consumatori consumer association

assoggettare <1b> subject

assolato sunny

assolo *m* *inv* MUS solo

assolto *pp* → **assolvere**

assolutamente absolutely

assoluto absolute

assoluzione *f* DIR acquittal; REL absolution

assolvere <3g> DIR acquit; *da un obbligo* release; *compito* carry out, perform; REL absolve, give absolution to

assomigliare <1g>: **~ a qu** be like, resemble s.o.

assomigliarsi be like *or* resemble each other

assonnato sleepy

assorbente 1 *agg* absorbent **2** *m*: **~ igienico** sanitary towel

assorbire <4c or 4d> absorb

assordante deafening

assordare <1a> **1** *v/t* deafen **2** *v/i* go deaf

assortimento *m* assortment

assortito assorted; **essere ben ~ con** go well with

assorto engrossed

assuefare <3aa> accustom (**a** to)

assuefarsi become accustomed (**a** to)

assuefatto *pp* → **assuefare**

assuefazione *f* resistance, tolerance; *agli alcolici, alla droga* addiction

assumere <3h> *impiegato* take on, hire; *incarico* take on

assunzione *f* *di impiegato* employment, hiring; REL **Assunzione** Assumption

assurdità *f* absurdity

assurdo absurd

asta *f* pole; FIN auction; **mettere all'~** sell at auction, put up for auction

astemio (*pl* -mi) **1** *agg* abstemious **2** *m*, **-a** *f* abstemious person

astenersi <2q>: **~ da** abstain from

astensione *f* abstention; **~ dal voto** abstention

asterisco *m* (*pl* -chi) asterisk

astigmatismo *m* astigmatism
astinenza *f* abstinence
astio *m* (*pl* -ti) ranco(u)r
astratto abstract
astringente *m/agg* MED astringent
astro *m* star
astrologia *f* astrology
astrologo *m* (*pl* -gi), **-a** *f* astrologer
astronauta *m/f* (*mpl* -i) astronaut
astronave *f* spaceship
astronomia *f* astronomy
astronomico (*pl* -ci) astronomical
astronomo *m*, **-a** *f* astronomer
astuccio *m* (*pl* -cci) case
astuto astute
ateismo *m* atheism
ateneo *m* university
ateo *m*, **-a** *f* atheist
atlante *m* atlas
atlantico (*pl* -ci) Atlantic; *Oceano m Atlantico* Atlantic Ocean
atleta *m/f* (*mpl* -i) athlete
atletica *f* athletics; *~ leggera* track and field (events)
atletico (*pl* -ci) athletic
atmosfera *f* atmosphere
atmosferico (*pl* -ci) atmospheric
atomico (*pl* -ci) atomic
atomo *m* atom
atrio *m* (*pl* -ri) foyer; *~ della stazione* station concourse
atroce appalling
atrocità *f* atrocity
attaccabrighe *m o f inv* F troublemaker
attaccamento *m* attachment
attaccante *m* SP forward
attaccapanni *m inv* clothes hook; *a stelo* clothes hanger
attaccare <1d> **1** *v/t* attach; (*incollare*) stick; (*appendere*) hang; (*assalire*) attack; (*iniziare*) begin, start **2** *v/i* stick; F *~ a fare qc* start doing sth
attaccarsi stick; (*aggrapparsi*) hold on (*a* to)
attacco *m* (*pl* -cchi) attack; (*punto di unione*) junction; EL socket; SCI binding; MED fit; (*inizio*) beginning
attardarsi <1a> linger
atteggiamento *m* attitude
atteggiarsi <1f>: *~ a* pose as

attendere <3c> **1** *v/t* wait for **2** *v/i*: *~ a* attend to
attendibile reliable
attenersi <2q> stick (*a* to)
attentare <1b>: *~ a* attack; *~ alla vita di qu* make an attempt on s.o.'s life
attentato *m* attempted assassination
attento 1 *agg* attentive; *stare ~ a* be careful of **2** *int* *~!* look out!, (be) careful!
attenuante *f* extenuating circumstance
attenuare <1m & b> reduce; *colpo* cushion
attenuarsi lessen, decrease
attenzione *f* attention; *~!* look out!, (be) careful!; *far ~ a qc* mind *or* watch sth
atterraggio *m* (*pl* -ggi) landing; *~ di fortuna* emergency landing
atterrare <1b> **1** *v/t* *avversario* knock down; *edificio* demolish, knock down **2** *v/i* land
attesa *f* waiting; (*tempo d'attesa*) wait; (*aspettativa*) expectation
atteso *pp* → **attendere**
attestare <1b> certify
attestato *m* certificate; *~ di frequenza* good attendance certificate
attico *m* (*pl* -ci) attic
attiguo adjacent (*a* to)
attimo *m* moment
attinente relevant (*a* to)
attirare <1a> attract
attitudine *f* attitude; *avere ~ per qc* have an aptitude for sth
attivare <1a> activate
attività *f* activity; *pl* FIN assets; *che ~ svolgi?* what do you do (for a living)?; *avere un'~ in proprio* have one's own business
attivo 1 *agg* active; FIN *bilancio ~* credit balance **2** *m* FIN assets *pl*; GRAM active voice
atto *m* act; (*gesto*) gesture; *documento* deed; *~ di fede* act of faith; *all'~ pratico* when it comes to the crunch; *mettere in ~* carry out; *prendere ~ di* note; DIR *mettere*

agli -*i* enter in the court records

attorcigliare <1g>, **attorcigliarsi** twist

attore *m*, -**trice** *f* actor; *donna* actress

attorno: ~ *a qc* round sth; *qui* ~ around here

attraccare <1d> MAR berth, dock

attracco *m* (*pl* -cchi) MAR berth

attraente attractive

attrarre <3xx> attract

attrattiva *f* attraction

attratto *pp* → **attrarre**

attraversare <1b> *strada, confine* cross; ~ *un momento difficile* be going through a bad time

attraverso across

attrazione *f* attraction

attrezzare <1a> equip

attrezzarsi get o.s. kitted out

attrezzato equipped

attrezzatura *f* equipment, gear F

attrezzo *m* piece of equipment; -*i pl da ginnastica* apparatus

attribuire <4d> attribute

attributo *m* attribute

attrice *f* → **attore**

attrito *m* friction

attuale current

attualità *f* news; *d'*~ topical

attualizzare <1a> update

attuare <1l> put into effect

attuazione *f* putting into effect

audace bold

audacia *f* boldness

audioleso 1 *agg* hearing-impaired 2 *m*, -**a** *f* person with hearing difficulties, person who is hearing-impaired

audiovisivo audiovisual

audizione *f* audition

augurare <1l> wish; ~ *a qu buon viaggio* wish s.o. a good trip

augurio *m* (*pl* -ri) wish; *fare gli* -*ri di Buon Natale a qu* wish s.o. a Merry Christmas; *tanti* -*ri!* all the best!

aula *f di scuola* class room; *di università* lecture theatre *or* room

aumentare <1a> 1 *v/t* increase; *prezzi* increase, raise, put up 2 *v/i* increase; *di prezzi* increase, rise, go up

aumento *m* increase, rise; ~ *salariale* pay rise; ~ *dei prezzi* increase *or* rise in prices

aureo golden

aureola *f* halo

auricolare *m* earphone

aurora *f* dawn; ~ *boreale* northern lights *pl*

ausiliare 1 *agg* auxiliary 2 *m* GRAM auxiliary

ausiliario (*pl* -ri) auxiliary

austerità *f* austerity

austero southern

Australia *f* Australia

australiano 1 *agg* Australian 2 *m*, -**a** *f* Australian

Austria *f* Austria

austriaco (*mpl* -ci) 1 *agg* Austrian 2 *m*, -**a** *f* Austrian

autenticare <1m, d & b> authenticate

autenticità *f* authenticity

autentico (*pl* -ci) authentic

autista *m/f* (*mpl* -i) driver

auto *f inv* → **automobile**

autoadesivo 1 *agg* self-adhesive 2 *m* sticker

autoambulanza *f* ambulance

autobiografia *f* autobiography

autobomba *f* car bomb

autobus *m* bus; ~ *di linea* city bus

autocaravan *f* camper van

autocarro *m* truck, *Br* lorry

autocisterna *f* tanker

autocontrollo *m* self-control

autocritica *f* self-criticism

autodidatta *m/f* (*mpl* -i) self-taught person

autodifesa *f* self-defence, *Am* -defense

autodromo *m* motor racing circuit

autofinanziamento *m* self-financing

autogol *m inv* own goal

autografo *m* autograph

autogrill *m inv* motorway café

autolavaggio *m* (*pl* -ggi) car-wash

automa *m* (*pl* -i) robot

automatico (*pl* -ci) 1 *agg* automatic 2 *m bottone* press stud fastener

automezzo *m* motor vehicle

automobile *f* car; ~ *da corsa* racing

car; ~ **da noleggio** hire car

automobilismo *m* driving; SP motor racing

automobilista *m/f* (*mpl* -i) driver

autonoleggio *m* (*pl* -ggi) car rental; (*azienda*) car-rental firm

autonomia *f* autonomy; TEC battery life

autonomo autonomous

autoradio *f inv* car radio

autore *m*, **-trice** *f* author; DIR perpetrator

autorevole authoritative

autorimessa *f* garage

autorità *f inv* authority; ~ **portuale** port authorities *pl*

autoritario (*pl* -ri) authoritarian

autorizzare <1a> authorize

autorizzazione *f* authorization

autoscatto *m* automatic shutter release

autoscuola *f* driving school

autosilo *m inv* multistorey car park, *Am* parking garage

autosoccorso *m* self-help

autostop *m*: **fare l'**~ hitchhike

autostoppista *m/f* (*mpl* -i) hitchhiker

autostrada *f* motorway, *Am* highway; ~ **informatica** information highway

autotreno *m* articulated lorry, *Am* semi

autovettura *f* motor vehicle

autrice *f* → **autore**

autunno *m* autumn, *Am* fall

avambraccio *m* (*pl* -cci) forearm

avanguardia *f* avant-garde; **all'**~ avant-garde *attr*; *azienda* leading-edge; **essere all'**~ **in** lead the way in

avanti 1 *avv* in front, ahead; **d'ora in** ~ from now on; **andare** ~ **di orologio** be fast; **mandare** ~ be the head of; **essere** ~ **nel programma** be ahead of schedule **2** *int* ~**!** come in! **3** *m* SP forward

avanzare <1a> **1** *v/i* advance; *fig* make progress; (*rimanere*) be left over **2** *v/t* put forward

avanzo *m* remainder; FIN surplus; **gli -i** *pl* the leftovers

avaria *f* failure

avariato damaged; *cibi* spoiled

avarizia *f* avarice

avaro 1 *agg* miserly **2** *m*, **-a** *f* miser

avena *f* oats *pl*

avere <2b> **1** *v/t* have; ~ **20 anni** be 20 (years old); ~ **fame / sonno** be hungry / sleepy; ~ **caldo / freddo** be hot / cold; ~ **qualcosa da fare** have something to do; **avercela con qu** have it in for s.o.; **che hai?** what's up with you? **2** *v/aus* have; **hai visto Tony?** have you seen Tony?; **hai visto Tony ieri?** did you see Tony yesterday? **3** *m* FIN credit; **dare e** ~ debits and credits; **-i** *mpl* wealth *sg*

avi *mpl* ancestors

aviatore *m* flyer

aviazione *f* aviation; MIL Air Force

avidità *f* avidness

avido avid

aviogetto *m* jet

AVIS *abbr* (= **Associazione Volontari Italiani del Sangue**) Italian blood donors' association

avocado *m* avocado

avorio *m* ivory

avvalersi <2r>: ~ **di qc** avail o.s. of sth

avvallamento *m* depression

avvantaggiare <1f> favo(u)r

avvantaggiarsi ~ **di qc** take advantage of sth

avvedersi <2s>: ~ **di qc** notice sth

avveduto astute

avvelenamento *m* poisoning

avvelenare <1a> poison

avvelenarsi poison o.s.

avvenimento *m* event

avvenire <4p> **1** *v/i* (*accadere*) happen **2** *m* future

Avvento *m* Advent

avventore *m* regular customer

avventura *f* adventure

avventurarsi <1a> venture

avventuriero *m*, **-a** *f* adventurer; *donna* adventuress

avventuroso adventurous

avvenuto *pp* → **avvenire**

avverarsi <1a> come true

avverbio m (pl -bi) adverb

avversario (pl -ri) **1** agg opposing **2** m, **-a** f opponent

avversione f aversion (**per** to)

avvertenza f (ammonimento) warning; (premessa) foreword; **avere l'~ di** be careful to; **-e** pl (istruzioni per l'uso) instructions

avvertimento m warning

avvertire <4b> warn; (percepire) catch

avviamento m introduction; TEC, AUTO start-up

avviare <1h> start

avviarsi set out, head off

avviato established

avvicendare <1b> alternate

avvicendarsi alternate

avvicinamento m approach

avvicinare <1a> approach; **~ qc a qc** move sth closer to sth

avvicinarsi approach, near (**a** sth)

avvilire <4d> depress; mortificare humiliate

avvilirsi demean o.s.; scoraggiarsi become depressed

avvilito scoraggiato depressed

avvio m: **dare l'~ a qc** get sth under way

avvisare <1a> (informare) inform, advise; (mettere in guardia) warn

avviso m notice; **a mio ~** in my opinion; **mettere qu sull'~** warn s.o.

avvitare <1a> screw in; fissare screw

avvocato m lawyer

avvolgere <3d> wrap

avvolgibile m roller blind

avvolto pp → **avvolgere**

avvoltoio m (pl -oi) vulture

azienda f business; **~ a conduzione familiare** family business; **~ autonoma di soggiorno** tourist information office

aziendale company attr

azionare <1a> activate; allarme set off

azionario share; **capitale** m **~** share capital

azione f action; (effetto) influence; FIN share; FIN **~ ordinaria** ordinary share; **emettere -i** issue shares

azionista m/f (mpl -i) shareholder; **maggiore ~** majority shareholder

azoto m nitrogen

azzannare <1a> bite into

azzardarsi <1a> dare

azzardato foolhardy

azzardo m hazard; **gioco** m **d'~** game of chance

azzerare <1b> TEC reset

azzuffarsi <1a> come to blows

azzurro 1 agg blue **2** m colore blue; SP **gli -i** pl the Italians, the Italian national team

B

babbo m F dad F, Am pop F; **Babbo Natale** Father Christmas, Santa (Claus)

babbuino m baboon

babordo m MAR port (side)

baby-sitter m/f inv baby-sitter

bacato wormeaten

bacca f (pl -cche) berry

baccalà m inv dried salt cod

baccano m din

bacchetta f rod; MUS del direttore d'orchestra baton; per suonare il tamburo (drum) stick; **~ magica** magic wand

bacheca f (pl -che) notice board; di museo showcase

baciare <1f> kiss

baciarsi kiss (each other)

bacillo m bacillus

bacinella f basin; FOT tray

bacino m basin; ANAT pelvis; MAR port

bacio m (pl -ci) kiss

baco m (pl -chi) worm; **~ da seta** silkworm

bada f: **tenere a ~ qu** keep s.o. at bay

badare <1a>: **~ a** look after; (fare attenzione a) look out for, mind; **~ ai fatti propri** mind one's own business; **non ~ a spese** spare no expense

baffo m: **-i** pl m(o)ustache; di animali whiskers

bagagliaio m (pl -ai) FERR luggage van, Am baggage car; AUTO boot, Am trunk

bagaglio m (pl -gli) luggage, Am baggage; **deposito** m **-i** left luggage (office), Am baggage checkroom; **fare i -i** pack; **spedire come ~ appresso** send as accompanied luggage

bagliore m glare; di speranza glimmer

bagnante m/f bather

bagnare <1a> wet; (immergere) dip; (inzuppare) soak; (annaffiare) water; di fiume flow through

bagnarsi get wet; in mare ecc swim, bathe

bagnato wet; **~ di sudore** dripping with sweat; **~ fradicio** soaked, wet through

bagnino m, **-a** f lifeguard

bagno m bath; stanza bathroom; gabinetto toilet; **~ di fango** mud bath; **fare il ~** have a bath; **mettere a ~** soak; nel mare ecc (have a) swim; **~ degli uomini** gents, Am men's room; **~ per donne** ladies' (room)

bagnomaria m inv double boiler, bain marie

baia f bay

baio m (pl bai): **cavallo** m **~** bay

baita f mountain chalet

balaustra f balustrade

balbettare <1a> stammer; bambino babble, prattle

balbettio m stammering; di bambino babble, prattle

balbuzie f stutter

balbuziente m/f stutterer

balcanico (pl -ci) Balkan; **paesi** mpl **-ci** Balkans

balconata f TEA dress circle, Am balcony

balcone m balcony

baldoria f revelry; **fare ~** have a riotous time

balena f whale

balenare <1a>: fig **gli è balenata un'idea** an idea flashed through his mind

baleno m lightning; **in un ~** in a flash

balestra f AUTO leaf spring

balia[1] f: **in ~ di** at the mercy of

balia[2] f: **~ asciutta** nanny

balla f bale; fig F (frottola) fib F

ballare <1a> v/t & v/i dance

ballata f MUS ballad

ballerina f dancer; di balletto ballet dancer; di rivista chorus girl; (scarpa) ballet shoe; ZO wagtail

ballerino m dancer; di balletto ballet dancer

balletto m ballet

ballo m dance; (il ballare) dancing; (festa) ball; **corpo** m **di ~** corps de ballet; **essere in ~** persona be involved; essere in gioco be at stake; **abbiamo in ~ un lavoro importante** we've got a big job on at the moment; **tirare in ~ qc** bring sth up

balneare località, centro seaside attr; **stagione** f **~** swimming season; **stabilimento** m **~** lido; **stazione** f **~** seaside resort

balocco m (pl -chi) toy

balordo 1 agg ragionamento shaky; idea stupid; tempo, consiglio unreliable 2 m (teppista) lout

balsamico (pl -ci) aceto balsamic; aria balmy

balsamo m per i capelli hair conditioner; fig balm, solace

baltico (pl -ci) Baltic

balzare <1a> jump, leap; **~ in piedi** jump or leap to one's feet; fig **un errore che balza subito agli occhi** a mistake that suddenly jumps out at you

balzo m jump, leap; fig **cogliere la**

palla al ~ jump at the chance

bambagia *f* cotton wool, *Am* absorbent cotton

bambinaia *f* nanny

bambino *m*, *-a f* child; *in fasce* baby; *~ in provetta* test-tube baby

bambola *f* doll

bambolotto *m* baby boy doll

bambù *m* bamboo; *canna f di ~* bamboo cane

banale banal

banalità *f inv* banality

banana *f* banana

banano *m* banana tree

banca *f* (*pl* -che) bank; INFOR *~ dati* data bank; *~ degli organi* organ bank

bancarella *f* stall

bancario (*pl* -ri) **1** *agg istituto, segreto* banking *attr; deposito, estratto conto* bank *attr* **2** *m*, *-a f* bank employee

bancarotta *f* bankruptcy

banchetto *m* banquet

banchiere *m* banker

banchina *f* FERR platform; MAR quay; *di strada* verge; *di autostrada* hard shoulder; *~ spartitraffico* central reservation, *Am* median strip

banchisa *f* ice floe

banco *m* (*pl* -chi) FIN bank; *di magistrati, di lavoro* bench; *di scuola* desk; *di bar* bar; *di chiesa* pew; *di negozio* counter; *~ corallino* coral reef; *~ di sabbia* sandbank; *~ del lotto* place that sells State lottery tickets; *vendere qc sotto ~* sell sth under the counter

bancogiro *m* giro

bancone *m* (work)bench

bancomat® *m inv* (*distributore*) cash-point, *Am* ATM; (*carta*) cash card

banconota *f* banknote, *Am* bill

banda *f* band; *di delinquenti* gang; INFOR *~ perforata* punched tape

banderuola *f* weathercock (*anche fig*)

bandiera *f* flag

bandire <4d> proclaim; *concorso* announce; (*esiliare*) banish; *fig* (*abolire*) dispense with

bandito *m* bandit

banditore *m all'asta* auctioneer

bando *m* proclamation; (*esilio*) banishment

bar *m inv* bar

bara *f* coffin

baracca *f* (*pl* -cche) hut; *spreg* hovel; F *mandare avanti la ~* keep one's head above water

baraccopoli *f inv* shanty town

barare <1a> cheat

baratro *m* abyss

barattare <1a> barter

baratto *m* barter

barattolo *m* tin, *Am* can; *di vetro* jar

barba *f* beard; *farsi la ~* shave; *fig che ~!* what a nuisance!, what a pain! F

barbabietola *f* beetroot, *Am* red beet; *~ da zucchero* sugar beet

barbarico (*pl* -ci) barbaric

barbarie *f* barbarity

barbaro 1 *agg* barbarous **2** *m* barbarian

barbecue *m inv* barbecue

barbiere *m* barber

barboncino *m* (miniature) poodle

barbone¹ *m* (*cane*) poodle

barbone² *m*, *-a f* (*vagabondo*) tramp

barca *f* (*pl* -che) boat; *~ a remi* rowing boat, *Am* rowboat; *~ a vela* sailing boat, *Am* sailboat

barcaiolo *m* boatman

barcollare <1c> stagger

barcone *m* barge

barella *f* stretcher

baricentro *m* centre of gravity

barile *m* barrel

barista *m/f* (*mpl* -i) barman, *Am* bartender; *donna* barmaid; *proprietario* bar owner

baritono *m* baritone

baro *m* cardsharp

barocco (*pl* -cchi) *m/agg* Baroque

barometro *m* barometer

barone *m*, *-essa f baron; donna* baroness; *fig ~ dell'industria* tycoon

barra *f* bar; MAR tiller; *~ spaziatrice* space bar

barricare <1l & d> barricade

barricata *f* barricade

B

barriera f barrier (anche fig); **~ doganale** tariff barrier

baruffa f (litigio) squabble; (zuffa) brawl; **far ~** squabble; (venirse alle mani) brawl

barzelletta f joke

basare <1a> base

basarsi be based (**su** on)

basco (pl -chi) **1** agg Basque **2** m, **-a** f Basque **3** m (berretto) beret

base f base; fig basis; **in ~ a** on the basis of

basette fpl sideburns

basilare basic

basilica f (pl -che) basilica

basilico m basil

bassezza f lowness; fig (viltà, azione meschina) vileness

basso1 agg low; di statura short; MUS bass; fig despicable; **a capo ~** with bowed head; **a occhi -i** looking downwards, with lowered eyes; **fare man -a di qc** steal sth **2** avv: **in ~** stato down below; **più in ~** further down; **da ~** in una casa downstairs **3** m MUS bass

bassopiano m (pl bassipiani) GEOG lowland

bassorilievo m (pl bassorilievi) bas-relief

bassotto m dachshund

basta → **bastare**

bastardo m, **-a** f cane mongrel; fig bastard

bastare <1a> be enough; (durare) last; **basta!** that's enough!; **adesso basta!** enough is enough!; **basta che** (purché) as long as

bastimento m ship

bastonare <1a> beat

bastone m stick; di pane baguette, French stick; fig **il ~ e la carota** the carrot and stick (approach); **~ da passeggio** walking stick

battaglia f battle (anche fig)

battagliero combative

battello m boat

battente m di porta wing; di finestra shutter

battere <3a> **1** v/i (bussare, dare colpi) knock **2** v/t beat; record break;

senza ~ ciglio without batting an eyelid; **~ le mani** clap (one's hands); **~ i piedi** stamp one's feet; **batteva i denti dal freddo** his teeth were chattering with cold; **~ a macchina** type; **~ bandiera** fly a flag

battersela run off

battersi fight

batteria f battery; MUS drums pl

batteri mpl bacteria

batterista m/f (pl -i) drummer

battesimo m christening, baptism

battezzare <1a> christen, baptize

battibaleno m: **in un ~** in a flash

battibecco m (pl -cchi) argument

batticuore m palpitations pl; fig **con un gran ~** with great anxiety

battimano m applause

battipanni m inv carpet beater

battistero m baptistry

battistrada m inv AUTO tread

battito m del polso pulse; delle ali flap (of its wings); della pioggia beating; **~ cardiaco** heartbeat

battuta f beat; in dattilografia keystroke; MUS bar; TEA cue; nel tennis service; **fare una ~ di caccia** go hunting; **~ di spirito** wisecrack; **non perdere una ~** not miss a word

baule m trunk; AUTO boot, Am trunk

bavaglino m bib

bavaglio m (pl -gli) gag

bavero m collar

bazar m inv bazaar

bazzecola f trifle

bazzicare <1l & d> **1** v/t un posto haunt; persone associate with **2** v/i hang about

Bce abbr (= **Banca centrale europea**) Central European Bank

beatificare <1n & d> beatify

beatitudine f bliss

beato happy; REL blessed; **~ te!** lucky you!

beauty-case m inv toilet bag

bebè m inv baby

beccaccia f (pl -cce) woodcock

beccare <1d> peck; F fig (cogliere sul fatto) nab F; F fig malattia catch, pick up F

beccarsi fig bisticciare squabble; F

malattia catch, pick up F

beccheggiare<1f> MAR pitch

becchino *m* grave digger

becco *m* (*pl* -cchi) beak; *di teiera ecc* spout; CHIM ~ **Bunsen** Bunsen burner; F *chiudi il* ~! shut up! F, shut it! F; *non avere il* ~ *di un quattrino* be broke

befana *f* kind old witch who brings presents to children on Twelfth Night; REL Twelfth Night; *fig* old witch

beffa *f* hoax; *farsi* -*e di qu* make a fool of s.o.

beffardo scornful

beffare<1b> mock

beffarsi ~ *di* mock

bega *f* (*pl* -ghe) (*litigio*) fight, argument; (*problema*) can of worms

begli → *bello*

begonia *f* begonia

Bei *abbr* (= *Banca europea per gli investimenti*) EIB (= European Investment Bank)

bei → *bello*

belare<1b> bleat

belga (*mpl* -gi) *agg*, *m/f* Belgian

Belgio *m* Belgium

belladonna *f* BOT deadly nightshade

bellezza *f* beauty; *istituto m di* ~ beauty salon; *prodotti mpl di* ~ cosmetics

bellico (*pl* -ci) (*di guerra*) war *attr*; (*del tempo di guerra*) wartime *attr*

bellicoso bellicose

bello 1 *agg* beautiful; *uomo* handsome; *tempo* fine, nice, beautiful; *questa è -a!* that's a good one!; *a -a posta* on purpose; *hai un bel dire* in spite of what you say; *nel bel mezzo* right in the middle; *farsi* ~ get dressed up; *scamparla* ~ have a narrow escape **2** *m* beauty; *sul più* ~ at the worst possible moment

belva *f* wild beast

belvedere *m inv* viewpoint

bemolle *m inv* MUS flat

benché though, although

benda *f* bandage; *per occhi* blindfold

bendare<1b> MED bandage

bene 1 *avv* well; ~! good!; *per* ~ properly; *stare* ~ *di salute* be well; *di*

vestito suit; *ben ti sta!* serves you right!; *va* ~! OK!; *andare* ~ *a qu di abito* fit s.o.; *di orario, appuntamento* suit s.o.; *di* ~ *in meglio* better and better; *sentirsi* ~ feel well **2** *m* good; *fare* ~ *alla salute* be good for you; *per il tuo* ~ for your own good; *voler* ~ *a qu* love s.o.; (*amare*) love s.o.; -*i pl* assets, property *sg*; -*i pl di consumo* consumer goods; -*i pl culturali* cultural heritage *sg*; -*i pl immobili* real estate *sg*; -*i pl pubblici* public property *sg*

benedetto 1 *pp* → **benedire 2** *agg* blessed; REL *acqua f* -*a* holy water

benedire<3t> bless

benedizione *f* blessing

beneducato well-mannered

benefattore *m*, -*trice* *f* benefactor

beneficenza *f* charity; *spettacolo m di* ~ benefit (performance)

beneficio *m* (*pl* -ci) benefit; *a* ~ *di* for the benefit of

benefico (*pl* -ci) beneficial; *organizzazione, istituto* charitable; *spettacolo* charity *attr*

benemerito worthy

benessere *m* well-being; (*agiatezza*) affluence

benestante 1 *agg* well-off **2** *m/f* person with money

benestare *m* consent

benevolenza *f* benevolence

benevolo benevolent

benigno MED benign

beninteso of course; ~ *che* provided that

benone splendid

benpensante *m/f* moderate; *spreg* conformist

benservito *m*: *dare il* ~ *a qu* thank s.o. for their services

bensì but rather

bentornato welcome back

benvenuto 1 *agg* welcome **2** *m* welcome; *dare il* ~ *a qu* welcome s.o.

benvisto well thought of

benvolere *farsi* ~ *da qu* win s.o. over

benvoluto well-liked

benzina *f* petrol, *Am* gas; *serbatoio*

m **della ~** petrol (*Am* gas) tank; **~ normale** 4-star, *Am* premium; **~ senza piombo** unleaded petrol (*Am* gas); **fare ~** get petrol (*Am* gas)

benzinaio *m* (*mpl* -ai), **-a** *f* petrol or *Am* gas station attendant

bere 1 *v/t* <3i> drink; *fig* swallow; *fig* **darla a ~ a qu** take s.o. in **2** *m* **bevanda** drink; *atto* drinking

berlina *f* AUTO saloon

berlinese 1 *agg* Berlin **2** *m/f* Berliner

Berlino *m* Berlin

bermuda *mpl* Bermuda shorts

bernoccolo *m* bump; *fig* flair; **aver il ~ di qc** have a flair for sth

berretto *m* cap

berrò → bere

bersaglio *m* (*pl* -gli) target; *fig* di *scherzi* butt

besciamella *f* béchamel

bestemmia *f* swear-word

bestemmiare <1k> **1** *v/i* swear (**contro** at) **2** *v/t* curse

bestia *f* animal; *persona brutale* beast; *persona sciocca* blockhead; *fig* **andare in ~** fly into a rage

bestiale bestial; F (*molto intenso*) terrible

bestiame *m* livestock

bettola *f* spreg dive

betulla *f* birch

bevanda *f* drink

beve → bere

bevibile drinkable

bevitore *m*, **-trice** *f* drinker

bevuta *f* drink; *azione* drinking

biada *f* fodder

biancheria *f* linen; **~ intima** underwear

bianco (*pl* -chi) **1** *agg* white; *foglio* blank; **dare carta -a a qu** give s.o. a free hand, give s.o. carte blanche; **notte f -a** sleepless night **2** *m* white; **~ d'uovo** egg white; **lasciare in ~** leave blank; **di punto in ~** point-blank; GASTR **riso m in ~** rice with butter and cheese; **mangiare in ~** avoid rich food; **in ~ e nero** *film* black and white; **in ~** *assegno* blank

biancospino *m* hawthorn

biasimare <1l> blame

biasimevole blameworthy

biasimo *m* blame

bibbia *f* bible

biberon *m inv* baby's bottle

bibita *f* soft drink

bibliografia *f* bibliography

bibliografico (*pl* -ci) bibliographical

biblioteca *f* (*pl* -che) library; *mobile* book-case

bibliotecario *m* (*pl* -ri), **-a** *f* librarian

bicamerale POL two-chamber

bicameralismo *m* two-chamber system

bicamere *m inv* two-room flat (*Am* apartment)

bicarbonato *m*: **~ (di sodio)** bicarbonate of soda

bicchiere *m* glass; **un ~ di birra** a glass of beer; **~ da birra** beer-glass; **~ di carta** paper cup

bicentenario *m* bicentenary

bici *f inv* F bike F

bicicletta *f* bike, bicycle; **andare in ~** cycle, ride a bicycle; **~ pieghevole** folding bike; **~ da corsa** racing bike; **gita f in ~** bike ride

bidè *m inv* bidet

bidone *m* drum; *della spazzatura* (dust)bin, *Am* garbage can; F (*imbroglio*) swindle F

biella *f* TEC connecting rod

biennale 1 *agg* che si fa ogni due anni biennial; *che dura due anni* two-year **2 Biennale** *f* (**di Venezia**) Venice Arts Festival

biennio *m* (*pl* -nni) period of two years

bietola *f* beet

bifase two-phase

bifora *f* ARCHI mullioned window

biforcarsi <1d> fork

biforcazione *f* fork

bigamia *f* bigamy

bigamo *m*, **-a** *f* bigamist

bigiotteria *f* costume jewellery, *Am* costume jewelry; (*negozio*) jewel(l)er's

bigliettaio *m* (*pl* -ai), **-a** *f* booking office clerk; *sul treno, tram* conductor

biglietteria f ticket office, booking office; *di cinema, teatro* box office

biglietto m ticket; ~ *aereo* airline or plane ticket; ~ *d'andata e ritorno* return ticket, *Am* roundtrip ticket; ~ *d'auguri* (greetings) card; ~ *da visita* business card; ~ *di banca* banknote, *Am* bill; ~ *della lotteria* lottery ticket; *un ~ da 10 dollari* a ten-dollar bill; *fare il ~* buy the ticket

bigodino m roller

bigotto 1 agg bigoted **2** m, -a f bigot

bikini m inv bikini

bilancia f (pl -ce) scales; FIN balance; ASTR *Bilancia* Libra; ~ *commerciale* balance of trade; ~ *dei pagamenti* balance of payments

bilanciare <1f> balance; (*pareggiare*) equal, be equal to; *fig* weigh up; FIN ~ *un conto* balance an account

bilanciarsi balance

bilancio m (pl -ci) balance; (*rendiconto*) balance sheet; ~ *annuale* annual accounts; ~ *consuntivo* closing balance; ~ *dello Stato* national budget; ~ *preventivo* budget; *fare il ~* draw up a balance sheet; *fig* take stock; *relazione f annuale di* ~ annual report

bilaterale bilateral

bile f bile; *fig* rage

biliardo m billiards sg

bilico m: *essere in* ~ be precariously balanced; *fig* be undecided

bilingue bilingual

bilione m (*mille miliardi*) million million, *Am* trillion; (*miliardo*) billion

bilocale m two-room flat (*Am* apartment)

bimbo m, -a f child

bimensile every two weeks, *Br* fortnightly

bimestrale ogni due mesi bimonthly; *che dura due mesi* two-month (long)

bimotore 1 agg twin-engine **2** m twin-engine plane

binario 1 agg binary **2** m (pl -ri) track; (*marciapiede*) platform

binocolo m binoculars pl

biochimica f biochemistry

biodegradabile biodegradable

biodinamica f biodynamics

biografia f biography

biografico (pl -ci) biographical

biografo m, -a f biographer

biologia f biology

biologico (pl -ci) biological; (*verde*) organic; *da culture -che* organic

biologo m (pl -gi), -a f biologist

biondo blonde

bioritmo m biorhythm

biossido m dioxide

biotopo m biotope

biplano m biplane

bipolare bipolar

biposto m/agg two-seater

birbante m rascal

birichino 1 agg naughty **2** m, -a f little devil

birillo m skittle

biro® f inv biro, ballpoint (pen)

birra f beer; ~ *chiara* lager; ~ *scura* brown ale; ~ *in lattina* canned beer; ~ *alla spina* draught (beer); *lievito m di* ~ brewer's yeast; *a tutta* ~ flat out

birreria f pub that sells only beer; *fabbrica* brewery

bis m inv, int encore

bisbetico (pl -ci) bad-tempered

bisbigliare <1g> whisper

bisbiglio m whisper

bisca f (pl -che) gambling den

biscia f (pl -sce) grass snake

biscotto m biscuit, *Am* cookie

bisessuale bisexual

bisestile: *anno* ~ leap year

bisettimanale every two weeks, *Br* fortnightly

bisnonno m, -a f great-grandfather; *donna* great-grandmother

bisognare <1a>: *bisogna farlo* it must be done, it needs to be done; *non bisogna farlo* it doesn't have to be done, there's no need to do it

bisogno m need; (*mancanza*) lack; (*fabbisogno*) requirements; *in caso di* ~ if necessary, if need be; *avere* ~ *di qc* need sth; *non ce n'è bisogno* there is no need

bisognoso needy

B

bisonte *m* zo bison

bistecca *f* (*pl* -cche) steak; ~ **ai ferri** grilled *or* Am broiled steak; ~ **alla fiorentina** charcoal grilled steak

bisticciare <1f> quarrel

bisticcio *m* (*pl* -cci) quarrel

bisturi *m* MED scalpel

bit *m inv* INFOR bit

bitter *m inv* aperitif

bivaccare <1d> bivouac

bivacco *m* (*pl* -cchi) bivouac

bivio *m* (*pl* -vi) junction; *fig* crossroads

bizantino Byzantine

bizzarro bizarre

bizzeffe *a* ~ galore

blando mild, gentle

blatta *f* cockroach

blindare <1a> armo(u)r-plate

blindato armo(u)red

blitz *m inv* blitz

bloccare <1c & d> block; MIL blockade; (*isolare*) cut off; *prezzi, conto* freeze

bloccarsi *di ascensore, persona* get stuck; *di freni, porta* jam

bloccaruota *m* AUTO wheel clamp, Am Denver boot; **mettere il** ~ **a** clamp

bloccasterzo *m* AUTO steering lock

blocchetto *m per appunti* notebook

blocco *m* (*pl* -cchi) block; *di carta* pad; MIL blockade; ~ **stradale** road block; ~ **dei fitti** rent control; **comprare in** ~ buy in bulk; ~ **dei prezzi** price-freeze; ~ **delle esportazioni** export ban, embargo

bloc-notes *m inv* writing pad

blu blue

blusa *f* blouse

boa[1] *m inv* zo boa constrictor

boa[2] *f* MAR buoy

boato *m* rumble

bob *m inv* SP bobsleigh, bobsled

bobbista *m/f* (*pl* -i) bobsledder

bobina *f* spool; *di film* reel; AUTO ~ **d'accensione** ignition coil

bocca *f* (*pl* -cche) mouth; (*apertura*) opening; **igiene** *f* **della** ~ oral hygiene; **in** ~ **al lupo!** good luck!; **vuoi essere sulla** ~ **di tutti?** do you want

to be the talk of the town?; **lasciare la** ~ **amara** leave a bad taste; **rimanere a** ~ **aperta** be dumbfounded; *fig* **rimanere a** ~ **asciutta** come away empty-handed

boccaccia *f* (*pl* -cce) (*smorfia*) grimace

boccaglio *m* (*pl* -gli) *di maschera per il nuoto* mouthpiece

boccale *m* jug; *da birra* tankard

boccetta *f* small bottle

boccheggiare <1f> gasp

bocchino *m per sigarette* cigarette holder; MUS, *di pipa* mouthpiece

boccia *f* (*pl* -cce) (*palla*) bowl; **gioco** *m* **delle -cce** bowls

bocciare <1c & f> (*respingere*) reject, vote down; EDU fail; *boccia* hit, strike

bocciatura *f* failure

bocciolo *m* bud

bocconcino *m* morsel

boccone *m* mouthful; ~ **amaro** bitter pill

bocconi face down

body *m inv* body

boia *m inv* executioner; F **fa un freddo** ~ it's bloody freezing F

boicottaggio *m* boycott

boicottare <1c> boycott

bolgia *f fig* bedlam

bolide *m* AST meteor; **come un** ~ like greased lightning

bolla[1] *f* bubble; MED blister

bolla[2] *f documento* note, docket; ~ **di consegna** delivery note

bollare <1a> stamp; *fig* brand

bollente boiling hot

bolletta *f* bill; ~ **della luce** electricity bill; ~ **di consegna** delivery note; F **essere in** ~ be hard up F

bollettino *m*: ~ **meteorologico** weather forecast

bollire <4c> *v/t & v/i* boil

bollito 1 *agg* boiled **2** *m* boiled meat

bollitore *m* kettle

bollo *m* stamp; ~ (**di circolazione**) road tax (disk); **marca** *f* **da** ~ revenue stamp

bomba *f* bomb; **a prova di** ~ bombproof; ~ **a mano** hand grenade; ~ **a**

orologeria time bomb; **~ atomica** atomic bomb

bombardamento m shelling, bombardment; (*attacco aereo*) air raid; *fig* bombardment

bombardare <1a> bomb; *fig* bombard

bombardiere m bomber

bombola f cylinder; **~ (di gas)** gas bottle, gas cylinder

bomboniera f wedding keep-sake

bonaccia f MAR calm

bonaccione m, **-a** f kind-hearted person

bonario (*pl* -ri) kind-hearted

bonifica f (*pl* -che) reclamation

bonificare <1m & d> FIN (*scontare*) allow, discount; (*accreditare*) credit; AGR reclaim; (*prosciugare*) drain

bonifico m FIN (*sconto*) allowance, rebate; (*trasferimento*) (money) transfer

bontà f inv goodness; (*gentilezza*) kindness

bonus-malus m inv assicurazione no-claims bonus system

bora f bora (*a cold north wind*)

borbottare <1a> mumble

bordello m brothel; *fig* F bedlam F; (*disordine*) mess

bordo m (*orlo*) edge; MAR, AVIA, AUTO **a ~** on board; **salire a ~** board, go on board

boreale northern; **aurora** f **~** northern lights *pl*

borgata f village; (*rione popolare*) suburb

borghese 1 agg middle-class; **in ~** in civilian clothes; **poliziotto** m **in ~** plainclothes policeman **2** m/f middle-class person; **piccolo ~** petty bourgeois, lower middle-class person

borghesia f middle classes *pl*

borgo m (*pl* -ghi) village

boria f conceit

borico (*pl* -ci): **acido** m **~** boric acid

borotalco m talcum powder, talc

borraccia f (*pl* -cce) flask

borsa f bag; (*borsetta*) handbag, Am purse; *per documenti* briefcase; FIN Stock Exchange; **~ della spesa** shopping bag; **~ termica** cool bag; **~ di studio** scholarship; **~ merci** Commodities Exchange; **~ nera** black market; **~ valori** Stock Exchange; **bollettino** m (o **listino** m) di **~** share index; **metter mano alla ~** put one's hand in one's pocket

borsaiolo m, **-a** f pickpocket

borseggio m (*pl* -ggi) pickpocketing

borsellino m purse, Am coin purse

borsetta f handbag, Am purse

borsista m/f (*mpl* -i) speculatore speculator; *studente* scholarship holder

boscaglia f brush, scrub

boscaiolo m woodcutter

bosco m (*pl* -schi) wood

boscoso wooded

bossolo m di proiettili (shell) case

BOT, bot abbr (= **Buono Ordinario del Tesoro**) treasury bond

botanica f botany

botanico (*pl* -ci) **1** agg botanical **2** m, **-a** f botanist

botola f trapdoor

botta f blow; (*rumore*) bang; **fare a -e** come to blows

botte f barrel; ARCHI **volta** f **a ~** barrel vault

bottega f (*pl* -ghe) shop; (*laboratorio*) workshop

bottegaio m (*pl* -ai), **-a** f shopkeeper

botteghino m box office; (*del lotto*) *sales outlet for lottery tickets*

bottiglia f bottle

bottiglieria f wine merchant's

bottino m loot

botto m (*rumore*) bang; **di ~** all of a sudden

bottone m button; **~ automatico** press-stud, Am snap fastener; **attaccare un ~ a qu** sew a button on for s.o.; *fig* buttonhole s.o.

bovino 1 agg bovine **2** m: **-i** pl cattle

box m inv *per auto* lock-up garage; *per bambini* playpen; *per cavalli* loose box

boxe f boxing

bozza f draft; TIP proof

bozzetto m sketch

B

bozzolo *m* cocoon

braccetto *m*: *a ~* arm in arm

bracciale *m* bracelet; (*fascia*) armband; *di orologio* watch strap

braccialetto *m* bracelet

bracciante *m/f* day labo(u)rer

bracciata *f nel nuoto* stroke

braccio *m* (*pl* le braccia *e* i bracci) arm; *~ di mare* sound; *a -a aperte* with open arms; *portare in ~ qu* carry s.o.; *fig* *essere il ~ destro di qu* be s.o.'s right-hand man; *incrociare le -a* fold one's arms; *fig* go on strike

bracciolo *m* arm(rest)

bracco *m* (*pl* -cchi) hound

bracconiere *m* poacher

brace *f* embers *pl*; *alla ~* char-grilled, *Am* -broiled

braciola *f* GASTR chop

branca *f* (*pl* -che) branch (*anche fig*)

branchia *f* gill

branco *m* (*pl* -chi) ZO *di cani, lupi* pack; *di pecore, uccelli* flock; *fig spreg* gang

brancolare <1l> grope

branda *f* camp-bed

brandello *m* shred, scrap; *a -i* in shreds *or* tatters

brano *m di testo, musica* passage

brasato *m* GASTR *di manzo* braised beef

Brasile *m* Brazil

brasiliano 1 *agg* Brazilian **2** *m*, -a *f* Brazilian

bravata *f* boasting; *azione* bravado

bravo good; (*abile*) clever, good; *~!* well done!

bravura *f* skill

break *m inv* break

breccia *f* (*pl* -cce) breach

bretella *f* (*raccordo*) slip road, *Am* ramp; *-e pl* braces, *Am* suspenders

breve short; *in ~* briefly, in short

brevettare <1a> patent

brevetto *m* patent; *di pilota* licence, *Am* license; *ufficio m dei -i* patent office

brevità *f* shortness

brezza *f* breeze

bricco *m* (*pl* -cchi) jug, *Am* pitcher

briciola *f* crumb

briciolo *m fig* grain, scrap

bricolage *m* do-it-yourself

briga *f* (*pl* -ghe): *darsi la ~ di fare qc* take the trouble to do sth; *attaccar ~ con qu* pick a quarrel with s.o.

brigadiere *m* MIL sergeant

brigante *m* bandit

brigata *f* party, group; MIL brigade

briglia *f* rein; *fig* *a ~ sciolta* at break-neck speed

brillante 1 *agg* sparkling; *colore* bright; *fig* brilliant **2** *m* diamond

brillare <1a> **1** *v/i* shine **2** *v/t mina* blow up

brillo tipsy

brina *f* hoar-frost

brindare <1a> drink a toast (*a* to), toast (*a* sth); *~ alla salute di qu* drink to *or* toast s.o.

brindisi *m inv* toast

brio *m* liveliness; MUS brio

brioche *f inv* brioche

brioso lively

britannico (*pl* -ci) **1** *agg* British **2** *m*, -a *f* Briton

brivido *m di freddo, spavento* shiver; *di emozione* thrill

brizzolato *capelli* greying, *Am* graying

brocca *f* (*pl* -cche) jug, *Am* pitcher

broccato *m* brocade

broccoli *mpl* broccoli *sg*

brodo *m* (clear) soup; *di pollo, di manzo, di verdura* stock; *minestra f in ~* soup; *~ ristretto* consommé

brodoso watery, thin

bronchiale bronchial

bronchite *f* bronchitis

broncio *m*: *avere* (*o tenere*) *il ~* sulk; *mi ha tenuto il ~ per tre giorni* he sulked for three days

broncopolmonite *f* bronchopneumonia

brontolare <1l> grumble; *di stomaco* rumble

brontolio *m* grumble; *di stomaco* rumble

brontolone 1 *agg* grumbling **2** *m*, -a *f* grumbler

bronzo *m* bronze

bruciapelo : *a ~* point-blank

bruciare <1f> **1** *v/t* burn; (*incendiare*) set fire to; *~ le tappe* forge ahead **2** *v/i* burn; *fig di occhi* sting

bruciarsi burn o.s.

bruciato burnt; *dal sole* scorched, parched

bruciatura *f* burn

bruciore *m* burning sensation; *~ di stomaco* heartburn

bruco *m* (*pl* -chi) grub; (*verme*) worm

brufolo *m* spot

brughiera *f* heath, moor

brulicare <1l & d> swarm

brulichio *m* swarming

brullo bare

bruno brown; *capelli* dark

brusco (*pl* -schi) sharp; *persona, modi* brusque, abrupt; (*improvviso*) sudden

brutale brutal

brutalità *f inv* brutality

bruto **1** *agg*: *forza f -a* brute force **2** *m* brute

brutta *f*: (*copia f*) *~* rough copy

bruttezza *f* ugliness

brutto ugly; (*cattivo*) bad; *tempo, tipo, situazione, affare* nasty

Bruxelles *f* Brussels

buca *f* (*pl* -che) hole; (*avvallamento*) hollow; *del biliardo* pocket; *~ delle lettere* letter-box, *Am* mailbox

bucaneve *m inv* snowdrop

bucare <1d> make a hole in; (*pungere*) prick; *biglietto* punch; *~ una gomma* have a puncture, *Am* have a flat (tire); *fig avere le mani bucate* be a spendthrift

bucarsi prick o.s.; *con droga* shoot up

bucato *m* washing, laundry; *fare il ~* do the washing

buccia *f* (*pl* -cce) peel

bucherellare <1b> make holes in; *bucherellato dai tarli* riddled with woodworm

buco *m* (*pl* -chi) hole; *~ dell' ozono* hole in the ozone layer; *~ nero* black hole

budello *m* (*pl le* budella) gut; (*vicolo*) alley

budget *m inv* budget

budino *m* pudding

bue *m* (*pl* buoi) ox, *pl* oxen; *carne* beef

bufalo *m* buffalo

bufera *f* storm; *~ di neve* snow-storm

buffet *m inv* buffet; *mobile* sideboard

buffo funny

buffone *m*, **-a** *f* buffoon, fool; *di corte* fool, jester

bugia¹ *f* candle holder

bugia² *f* (*menzogna*) lie; *dire -e* tell lies, lie

bugiardo **1** *agg* lying **2** *m*, **-a** *f* liar

bugigattolo *m* cubby-hole

buio **1** *agg* dark **2** *m* darkness; *al ~* in the dark; *~ pesto* pitch dark

bulbo *m* BOT bulb

Bulgaria *f* Bulgaria

bulgaro **1** *agg* Bulgarian **2** *m*, **-a** *f* Bulgarian

bulletta *f* tack

bullone *m* bolt

buoi → **bue**

buon → **buono**

buonafede *f*: *in ~* in good faith

buonanotte *int*, *f* good night; *dare la ~* say good night

buonasera *int*, *f* good evening; *dare la ~* say good evening

buongiorno *int*, *m* good morning, hello; *dare il ~* say good morning *or* hello

buongustaio *m* (*pl* -ai), **-a** *f* gour-met

buongusto *m* good taste; *di ~* in good taste

buono **1** *agg* good; (*valido*) good, valid; *momento, occasione* right; *alla -a* informal, casual; *di buon'ora* early; *di buon grado* willingly; *avere buon naso* have a good sense of smell; *~ a nulla* good-for-nothing **2** *m* good; FIN bond; (*tagliando*) coupon, voucher; *~ del tesoro* Treasury bond; *~ pasto o mensa* luncheon voucher; *~ regalo* gift voucher; *~ sconto* money-off coupon

buonsenso *m* common sense

B

buonuscita f (*liquidazione*) golden handshake

burattino m puppet

burbero gruff, surly

burla f practical joke, trick

burlarsi <1a>: ~ **di qu** make fun of s.o.

burlone m, **-a** f joker

burocrate m bureaucrat

burocratico (*pl* -ci) bureaucratic

burocrazia f bureaucracy

burrasca f (*pl* -sche) storm

burrascoso stormy

burro m butter; GASTR **al** ~ in butter; **tenero come il** ~ soft as butter

burrone m ravine

bussare <1a> knock; ~ **alla porta** knock at the door

bussola f compass; ~ **magnetica** magnetic compass; **perdere la** ~ lose one's bearings

busta f *per lettera* envelope; *per documenti* folder; (*astuccio*) case; ~ **paga** pay packet

bustarella f bribe

bustina f: ~ **di tè** tea bag

busto m ANAT torso; *scultura* bust; (*corsetto*) girdle

buttafuori m *inv* TEA call-boy; *di locale notturno* bouncer

buttare <1a> **1** *v/i* BOT shoot, sprout **2** *v/t* throw; ~ **via** throw away; *fig* waste; ~ **giù** knock down; *lettera* scribble down; *boccone* gulp down; F ~ **la pasta** put the pasta on

buttarsi throw o.s.; *fig* have a go (**in** at); ~ **giù** (*saltare*) jump; *fig* lose heart, get discouraged

by-pass m *inv* by-pass

byte m *inv* INFOR byte

C

ca. *abbr* (= **circa**) ca (= circa)

c.a. *abbr* (= **corrente alternata**) AC (= alternating current)

cabaret m *inv* cabaret

cabina f *di nave*, *aereo* cabin; *di ascensore*, *funivia* cage; ~ **balneare** beach hut; ~ **di guida** driver's cab; ~ **elettorale** polling booth; ~ **telefonica** phone box, *Am* pay phone

cabinato m cabin cruiser

cabriolè **cabriolet** m *inv* convertible

cacao m cocoa

caccia (*pl* -cce) **1** f hunting; **andare a** ~ go hunting (**di** sth); **dare la** ~ **a qu** chase after s.o. **2** m MIL *aereo* fighter; *nave* destroyer

cacciagione f GASTR game

cacciare <1f> hunt; (*scacciare*) drive out; (*ficcare*) shove; ~ (**via**) chase away

cacciarsi dove ti eri cacciato? where did you get to?

cacciatora f: GASTR **alla** ~ stewed

cacciatore m, **-trice** f hunter; ~ **di frodo** poacher

cacciavite m *inv* screwdriver

cachemire m *inv* cashmere

cachet m *inv* MED capsule

cacio m cheese

cactus m *inv* cactus

cadavere m corpse

cadente **stella** f ~ shooting star

cadere <2c> fall; *di edificio* fall down; *di capelli*, *denti* fall out; *di aereo* crash; ~ **dalle nuvole** be thunderstruck; **lasciar** ~ drop; **lasciarsi** ~ **su una poltrona** collapse into an armchair

caduta f fall; ~ **massi** falling rocks; ~ **di tensione** drop in voltage

caffè m *inv* coffee; *locale* café; ~ **corretto** espresso with a shot of alcohol; ~ **macchiato** espresso with a splash of milk

caffeina f caffeine; **senza ~** caffeine free

caffellatte m inv hot milk with a small amount of coffee

caffettiera f (bricco) coffee pot; (macchinetta) coffee maker

cafone m boor

cagionevole delicate, sickly

cagliare <1g> curdle

cagna f bitch

calabrese agg, m/f Calabrian

calabrone m hornet

calamari mpl squid

calamita f magnet

calamità f calamity; **~ naturale** natural disaster

calante luna f **~** waning moon

calare <1a> **1** v/t lower; prezzi reduce, lower **2** v/i di vento drop; di prezzi fall, come down; di sipario fall; di sole set, go down; **~ di peso** lose weight; **è calato del 20%** it's down 20%

calca f throng

calcagno m (pl i calcagni o le calcagna) heel

calcare[1] <1d> (pigiare) press down; con i piedi tread; parole emphasize; **~ la mano** exaggerate; **~ le scene** become an actor, take up acting

calcare[2] m limestone

calcareo chalky

calce[1] f lime

calce[2] m fig: **in ~** below

calcestruzzo m concrete

calciare <1f> kick

calciatore m footballer, soccer player

calcina f (malta) mortar

calcinaccio m (pl -cci) (intonaco) bit of plaster; di muro bit of rubble

calcio[1] m (pl -ci) kick; attività football, soccer; MIL butt; CHIM calcium; **giocare al ~** play football or soccer; **campionato** m **di ~** football or soccer championship; **~ di rigore** penalty kick

calcio[2] m (pl -chi) mo(u)ld

calcolare <1l> calculate; (valutare) weigh up

calcolatore m calculator; fig calculating person; elettronico computer

calcolatrice f calculator; **~ tascabile** pocket calculator; **~ da tavolo** desktop calculator

calcolo m calculation; MED stone; **~ preventivo** estimate

caldaia f boiler

caldarrosta f roast chestnut

caldo 1 agg warm; (molto caldo) hot; **non mi fa né ~ né freddo** it's all the same to me **2** m warmth; **molto caldo** heat; **ho ~** I'm warm; I'm hot

calendario m (pl -ri) calendar; **~ delle manifestazioni** calendar of events

calibrare <1l> calibrate

calibro m calibre, Am caliber; TEC callipers

calice m goblet; REL chalice

calle f a Venezia lane

calligrafia f calligraphy

callo m corn; **fare il ~ a qc** become hardened to sth

calma f calm; **prendersela con ~** take it easy

calmante m sedative

calmare <1a> calm; dolore soothe

calmarsi di dolore ease (off)

calmo calm

calo m di peso loss; dei prezzi drop, fall

calore m warmth; intenso heat

caloria f calorie

caloroso fig warm

calpestare <1a> walk on; fig trample over

calunnia f slander

calunniare <1k> slander

calura f heat

calvario m REL Calvary; fig ordeal

calvizie f baldness

calvo bald

calza f da donna stocking; da uomo sock; **~ elastica** support stocking; **fare la ~** knit

calzamaglia f tights pl, Am pantyhose; da ginnastica leotard

calzare 1 v/t scarpe put on; (indossare) wear **2** v/i fig fit

calzascarpe m shoehorn

calzatoio *m* (*pl* -oi) shoehorn

calzature *fpl* footwear *sg*

calzaturificio *m* (*pl* -ci) shoe factory

calzettone *m* knee sock

calzino *m* sock

calzolaio *m* (*pl* -ai) shoemaker

calzoleria *f* shoe shop

calzoncini *mpl* shorts; **~ da bagno** (swimming) trunks

calzone *m* GASTR *folded-over pizza*

calzoni *mpl* trousers, *Am* pants

camaleonte *m* chameleon

cambiale *f* bill (of exchange); **~ in bianco** blank bill; **girare una ~** endorse a bill; **pagare una ~** hono(u)r a bill; **~ a vista** sight bill; **~ a scadenza fissa** fixed-term bill

cambiamento *m* change; **~ climatico** climate change

cambiare <1k> *v/t* change; (*scambiare*) exchange; AUTO **~ la marcia** change gear; **~ casa** move (house); **~ idea** change one's mind **2** *v/i e* **cambiarsi** change

cambiavalute *m o f inv* currency dealer, money-broker

cambio *m* (*pl* -bi) change; FIN, (*scambio*) exchange; AUTO, TEC gear; **~ automatico** automatic gearshift; **~ dell'olio** oil change; **~ d'indirizzo** change of address; **in ~** in exchange (**di** for); **dare il ~ a qu** relieve s.o.; **fare ~ con qu** swap *or* exchange with s.o.

camelia *f* camellia

camera *f* room; **~ da letto** bedroom; **~ singola** single room; **~ matrimoniale** double room; **~ a due letti** twin room; **~ d'albergo** hotel room; **~ blindata** strong room; **Camera dei Deputati** House of Commons; FOT **~ oscura** darkroom; **~ d'aria** inner tube; **~ dell'industria e del commercio** chamber of commerce

cameraman *m inv* cameraman

camerata *f stanza* dormitory; *in ospedale* ward

cameriera *f* waitress; (*domestica*) maid

cameriere *m* waiter; (*domestico*) manservant

camerino *m* dressing room

camice *m di medico* white coat; *di chirurgo* gown

camicetta *f* blouse

camicia *f* (*pl* -cie) shirt; **~ sportiva** sports shirt; **~ da notte** nightdress

caminetto *m* fireplace

camino *m* chimney; (*focolare*) fireplace

camion *m inv* truck, *Br* lorry

camioncino *m* van

camionista *m* (*pl* -i) truck driver, *Br* lorry driver

cammello *m* camel; *stoffa* camel hair

camminare <1a> walk; (*funzionare*) work, go

camminata *f* walk

cammino *m*: **un'ora di ~** an hour's walk; **mettersi in ~** set out

camomilla *f* camomile; (*infuso*) camomile tea

camoscio *m* (*pl* -sci) chamois; **scarpe fpl di ~** suede shoes

campagna *f* country; *fig*, POL campaign; **vivere in ~** live in the country; **~ pubblicitaria** advertising campaign; **~ elettorale** election campaign

campana *f* bell

campanello *m* bell; *della porta* doorbell; **~ d'allarme** alarm bell

campanile *m* bell tower

campanula *f* campanula

campare <1a> live; **~ alla giornata** live for the moment

campeggiare <1f> camp

campeggiatore *m* camper

campeggio *m* camping; *posto* camp site

camper *m inv* camper van

campestre rural

camping *m* camp site

campionario *m* (*pl* -ri) samples

campionato *m* championship; **~ mondiale** world championship

campione *m* sample; (*esemplare*) specimen; *di stoffa* swatch; SP champion

campo *m* field; **~ giochi** playground; **~ di golf** golf course; **~ di calcio** football *or* soccer pitch; **~ di con-**

centramento concentration camp; **~ da tennis** tennis court; **~ di ricerche** area of research; **~ sportivo** sports ground; **~ profughi** refugee camp

camposanto *m* (*pl* camposanti) cemetery

camuffare <1a> disguise

Canada *m* Canada

canadese 1 *agg* Canadian **2** *m/f* Canadian **3** *f* half-litre (*Am* -liter) bottle of beer

canale *m* channel; *artificiale* canal

canalizzazione *f* channelling; (*conduttura*) pipe

canapa *f* hemp

canarino *m* canary

cancellare <1b> cross out; *con gomma* rub out, erase; INFOR delete; *debito* write off, cancel; *appuntamento* cancel

cancellata *f* railings *pl*

cancelleria *f*: *articoli mpl di ~* stationery

cancelliere *m* chancellor; DIR clerk of the court

cancello *m* gate

cancerogeno carcinogenic

cancrena *f* gangrene

cancro *m* MED cancer; ASTR, GEOG *Cancro* Cancer

candeggiante *m* stain remover

candeggina *f* bleach

candela *f* candle; **~ d'accensione** spark plug

candelabro *m* candelabra

candeliere *m* candlestick

candidarsi <1l> stand (for election)

candidato *m*, **-a** *f* candidate

candidatura *f* candidacy, candidature

candido pure white; (*sincero*) frank; (*innocente*) innocent, pure; (*ingenuo*) naive

canditi *mpl* candied fruit

cane *m* dog; *di arma da fuoco* hammer, cock; **~ da guardia** guard dog; *freddo ~* freezing cold; *non c'era un ~* there wasn't a soul about; F *fatto da -i* botched F

canestro *m* basket

canguro *m* kangaroo

canile *m* (*casotto*) kennel; *luogo* kennels

canino 1 *agg* dog *attr* **2** *m* (*dente*) canine (tooth)

canna *f* reed; (*bastone*) stick; P joint P; **~ fumaria** flue; **~ da pesca** fishing rod; **~ da zucchero** sugar cane

cannella *f* GASTR cinnamon

cannelloni *mpl* cannelloni *sg*

cannibale *m* cannibal

cannocchiale *m* telescope

cannonata *f* *fig*: *è una ~* it's terrific

cannone *m* MIL gun, cannon; (*asso*) ace

cannuccia *f* (*pl* -cce) straw

canoa *f* canoe

canone *m* FIN rental (fee); RAD, TV licence (fee); (*norma*) standard

canottaggio *m* a pagaie canoeing; *a remi* rowing; **circolo** *m* **di ~** rowing club

canottiera *f* vest

canotto *m* rowing boat, *Am* rowboat; **~ pneumatico** rubber dinghy; **~ di salvataggio** lifeboat

cantante *m/f* singer

cantare <1a> sing

cantautore *m*, **-trice** *f* singer-songwriter

cantiere *m* building *or* construction site; MAR shipyard

cantina *f* cellar; *locale* wineshop

canto¹ *m* (*canzone*) song; (*il cantare*) singing; **~ popolare** folk song; **~ del cigno** swan song

canto² *m*: *dal ~ mio* for my part; *d'altro ~* on the other hand

cantonata *f* (*grosso sbaglio*) blunder

cantone *m* POL canton; *Lago m dei Quattro Cantoni* Lake Lucerne

canzonare <1a> tease

canzone *f* song; *la solita ~* the same old story

canzoniere *m* songbook

caos *m* chaos

caotico (*pl* -ci) chaotic

C.A.P. *abbr* (= *Codice di Avviamento Postale*) postcode, *Am* zip code

capace (*abile*) capable; (*ampio*) large, capacious; **~ di fare qc**

capable of doing sth

capacità *f inv* ability; (*capienza*) capacity; FIN **~ di acquisto** purchasing power; INFOR **~ di memoria** memory

capanna *f* hut

capannone *m* shed; AVIA hangar

caparra *f* FIN deposit

capello *m* hair; **-i** *pl* hair *sg*; GASTR **-i d'angelo** very thin noodles; **ne ho fin sopra i -i!** I've had it up to here!; **per un ~** by the skin of one's teeth

capezzolo *m* nipple

capiente large, capacious

capienza *f* capacity

capigliatura *f* hair

capillare MED capillary

capire <4d> understand; **capisco** I see; **si capisce!** naturally!, of course!; **far ~ qc a qu** make s.o. understand sth, get s.o. to see sth; **farsi ~** make o.s. understood

capitale 1 *agg* capital; *fig* major **2** *f città* capital **3** *m* FIN capital; **~ d'esercizio** working capital; **~ disponibile** available capital; **~ fisso** fixed capital; **~ iniziale** start-up capital; **fuga f di -i** flight of capital; **~ proprio** equity capital; **~ sociale** share capital

capitalismo *m* capitalism

capitalista *agg, m/f* (*mpl* -i) capitalist

capitaneria *f*: **~ di porto** port authorities *pl*

capitano *m* captain

capitare <1l> *di avvenimento* happen; *di persona* find o.s.; **se mi capita l'occasione di venire** if I get a chance to come; **~ in cattive mani** fall into the wrong hands; **mangio dove capita** I don't always eat in the same place; **~ a proposito** come along at the right time; **sono cose che capitano** these things happen

capitello *m* ARCHI capital

capitolo *m* chapter; **avere voce in ~** have a say in the matter

capitombolo *m* tumble, fall

capo *m* ANAT head; *persona* head, chief, boss F; GEOG cape; **~ del governo** head of government; **~ dello**

Stato head of state; **~ di vestiario** item of clothing; **da ~** from the beginning; **ti seguirò in ~ al mondo** I'll follow you to the ends of the earth; **per sommi -i** briefly; **andare a ~** start a new paragraph; **non venire a ~ di nulla** be unable to come to any kind of conclusion; **questa storia non ha né ~ né coda** this story just doesn't make sense

capobanda *m/f di delinquenti* ringleader

capodanno *m* New Year's Day

capofamiglia *m/f* head of the family

capofitta *a* **~** headlong

capogiro *m* dizzy spell

capogruppo *m/f* group leader; POL leader

capolavoro *m* masterpiece

capolinea *m* terminus

capolista *f* SP leaders *pl*

capoluogo *m* (*pl* capoluoghi) principal town

capomastro (*pl* capomastri) master builder

caporeparto *m/f* (*mpl* capireparto, *fpl* caporeparto) *di fabbrica* foreman; *donna* forewoman; *di ufficio* superintendent

caposala *m/f* (*mpl* capisala, *fpl* caposala) *in ospedale* ward sister; *uomo* charge nurse

caposaldo *m* (*pl* capisaldi) stronghold

caposezione *m/f* (*mpl* capisezione, *fpl* caposezione) section chief

capostazione *m/f* (*mpl* capistazione, *fpl* capostazione) station master

capostipite *m/f* founder

capotavola *a* **~** at the head of the table

capote *f inv* AUTO hood, (soft) top

capotreno *m/f* (*mpl* capitreno, *fpl* capotreno) guard

capoufficio *m/f* (*mpl* capiufficio, *fpl* capoufficio) supervisor

capoverso *m* (*pl* capoversi) paragraph; TIP indent(ation)

capovolgere <3d> turn upside down; *piani* upset; *situazione* reverse

capovolgersi turn upside down; *di barca* capsize

capovolgimento *m* complete change

capovolto *pp* → *capovolgere*

cappa *f* (*mantello*) cloak; *di cucina* hood; *~ del camino* cowl

cappella *f* chapel

cappellano *m* chaplain

cappelletti *mpl* pasta, shaped like little hats, with meat, cheese and egg filling

cappello *m*; *~ di paglia* straw hat; *senza ~* hatless; *mettersi il ~* put one's hat on

cappero *m* caper

cappio *m* noose

cappone *m* capon; *far venire la pelle di ~ a qu* give s.o. the creeps

cappotto *m* coat

cappuccino *m bevanda* cappuccino

cappuccio *m* (*pl* -cci) hood; *di penna* top, cap

capra *f* (nanny)goat; (*cavalletto*) trestle

capretto *m* kid

capriccio *m* (*pl* -cci) whim; *di bambini* tantrum; *fare i -i* have tantrums

capriccioso capricious; *bambino* naughty; *tempo* changeable

Capricorno ASTR, GEOG Capricorn

capriola *f* somersault

capriolo *m* roe deer; GASTR venison

capro *m* billy goat; *~ espiatorio* scapegoat

capsula *f* capsule; *di dente* crown; *~ spaziale* space capsule

captare <1a> RAD pick up

carabina *f* carbine

carabiniere *m* police officer

caraffa *f* carafe

caramella *f* sweet

caramello *m* caramel

carato *m* carat

carattere *m* character; (*caratteristica*) characteristic; (*lettera*) character, letter; *-i pl* TIP typeface; INFOR font

caratteristica *f* characteristic

caratteristico (*pl* -ci) characteristic

caratterizzare <1a> characterize

caravan *m inv* caravan

caravanning *m inv* caravanning

carboidrato *m* carbohydrate

carbone *m* coal

carbonella *f* charcoal

carburante *m* fuel

carburatore *m* carburet(t)or

carcassa *f di animale* carcass; TEC (*intelaiatura*) frame; MAR, F wreck

carcerato *m*, **-a** *f* prisoner

carcerazione *f* imprisonment; *~ preventiva* preventive detention

carcere *m* (*pl* le -ri) jail, prison

carceriere *m*, **-a** *f* jailer, gaoler

carciofo *m* artichoke

cardellino *m* goldfinch

cardiaco (*pl* -ci) cardiac, heart

cardinale 1 *agg* cardinal; *punto m ~* cardinal point **2** *m* REL cardinal

cardine *m* hinge

cardiologia *f* cardiology

cardiologo *m* (*pl* -gi), **-a** *f* (*pl* -ghe) heart specialist, cardiologist

cardo *m* thistle

carena *f* MAR keel

carenza *f* lack (*di* of)

carestia *f* shortage

carezza *f* caress

carezzare <1a> caress

cargo *m aereo* air freighter; *nave* cargo ship

cariato *dente m ~* decayed tooth

carica *f* (*pl* -che) (*incarico*) office; *fig* (*slancio, energia*) drive; TEC load; MIL (*attacco*) charge; SP tackle; *in ~* in office; *durata f della ~* term of office; *tornare alla ~* insist

caricare <1d & l> load; MIL charge; *orologio* wind up

caricarsi overload o.s. (*di* with); PSI psych o.s. up; *~ di debiti* get heavily into debt

caricatura *f* caricature

caricaturista *m/f* (*mpl* -i) caricaturist

carico (*pl* -chi) **1** *agg* loaded; EL charged; *caffè* strong; *colore* deep; *orologio* wound up **2** *m* load; FIN charge, expense; MAR cargo; DIR *a ~ di* (*contro*) against; *essere a ~ di qu*

C

be dependent on s.o.; ~ *utile* payload; *lettera f (o polizza f) di ~* bill of lading; ~ *di lavoro* workload

carie *f inv* tooth decay

carino (*grazioso*) pretty; (*gentile*) nice

carisma *m* charisma

carità *f* charity; *per ~!* for goodness sake!, for pity's sake!

carnagione *f* complexion

carnale carnal; *fratello m ~* blood brother

carne *f* flesh; GASTR meat; ~ *di maiale/manzo* pork/beef; ~ *tritata* mince

carneficina *f* slaughter

carnevale *m* carnival

carnivoro *m* carnivore

carnoso fleshy

caro 1 *agg* dear; (*costoso*) dear, expensive; *mi è molto ~* I am very fond of him/it; *a ~ prezzo* dearly **2** *avv* a lot; *costare ~* be very expensive; *fig* have a high price **3** *m* dear; *~-i pl* loved ones, family

carogna *f* carrion; F swine

carosello *m* merry-go-round

carota *f* carrot

carotide *f* carotid artery

carovana *f* caravan

carovita *m* high cost of living; *indennità f di ~* cost of living allowance

carpa *f* carp

carpentiere *m* carpenter

carpire <4d>: ~ *qc a qu* get sth out of s.o.

carponi on all fours

carrabile → *carraio*

carraio: *passo m ~* driveway

carreggiata *f* roadway; *rimettersi in ~ fig* catch up

carrello *m* trolley; AVIA undercarriage; ~ *elevatore* fork-lift truck; ~ *portabagagli* baggage trolley, *Am* baggage cart

carretto *m* cart

carriera *f* career; *fare ~* come a long way; *di gran ~* at top speed

carriola *f* wheelbarrow

carro *m* cart; AST Bear; FERR *~ bestiame* cattle truck; FERR *~ merci*

goods wagon, *Am* freight car; ~ *armato* tank; ~ *attrezzi* breakdown van, tow truck, *Am* wrecker; ~ *funebre* hearse

carrozza *f* FERR carriage; ~ *con cuccette* sleeper; ~ *ristorante* restaurant car

carrozzella *f* per bambini pram; *per invalidi* wheelchair

carrozzeria *f* bodywork, coachwork

carrozziere *m* AUTO (*progettista*) (car) esigner; (*costruttore*) coachbuilder; *chi fa riparazioni* panel beater

carrozzina *f* pram

carta *f* paper; GASTR (*menù*) menu; GEOG ~ *geografica* map; ~ *assegni* cheque (guarantee) card; ~ *da bollo* official stamped paper; ~ *da gioco* (playing) card; ~ *da lettere* note paper; ~ *da macero* waste paper (for pulping); ~ *da parati* wallpaper; ~ *d'argento* card that entitles people over a certain age to reduced fares; ~ *di credito* credit card; ~ *d'identità* identity card; AVIA ~ *d'imbarco* boarding pass; ~ *igienica* toilet paper; ~ *stagnola* silver paper; GASTR tinfoil; ~ *stradale* road map; ~ *telefonica* phone card; ~ *velina* tissue paper; AUTO ~ *verde* green card; ~ *vetrata* sandpaper

cartacarbone *f* carbon paper

cartamodello *m* (*pl* cartamodelli) pattern

cartamoneta *f inv* paper money

cartapecora *f* parchment, vellum

cartapesta *f* papier-mâché

cartastraccia *f* waste paper

carteggio *m* (*pl* -ggi) correspondence

cartella *f* (*borsa*) briefcase; *di alunno* schoolbag, satchel; *copertina per documenti* folder, file; *foglio dattiloscritto* page; ~ *clinica* medical record

cartellino *m* (*etichetta*) label; *con prezzo* price tag; (*scheda*) card; SP ~ *giallo/rosso* yellow/red card; ~ *orario* clocking-in card

cartello *m* sign; *nelle dimostrazioni*

placard; FIN cartel; **~ stradale** road sign

cartellone *m pubblicitario* hoarding, *Am* billboard; TEA bill

cartiera *f* paper mill

cartilagine *f* cartilage

cartina *f* GEOG map; *(bustina)* packet; *per sigarette* cigarette paper

cartoccio *m (pl -cci)* paper bag; *a cono* paper cone; GASTR *al ~* baked in tinfoil, en papillote

cartografia *f* cartography

cartoleria *f* stationer's

cartolina *f* postcard; **~ illustrata** picture postcard; **~ postale** postcard

cartoncino *m (thin)* cardboard; *(biglietto)* card

cartone *m* cardboard; **-i pl animati** cartoons

cartuccia *f (pl -cce)* cartridge

casa *f edificio* house; *(abitazione)* home; FIN company; **~ di cura** nursing home; **~ editrice** publishing house; **~ dello studente** hall of residence; **~ a schiera** terraced house; **~ unifamiliare** single-family dwelling; **~ per le vacanze** holiday home; **case popolari** council houses; **seconda ~** second home; **essere di ~** be like one of the family; **dove stai di ~?** where do you live?; **cambiar ~** move (house); **fatto in ~** home-made; **andare a ~** go home; **essere a ~** be at home; SP **giocare in / fuori ~** play at home / away

casalinga *f (pl -ghe)* housewife

casalingo *(pl -ghi)* domestic; *(fatto in casa)* home-made; *persona* home-loving; **cucina *f* -a** home cooking; **-ghi** *mpl* household goods

cascare <1d> fall (down); *fig* **cascarci** fall for it

cascata *f* waterfall

cascina *f (casa colonica)* farmhouse; *(caseificio)* dairy farm

casco *m (pl -chi)* helmet; *dal parrucchiere* hair dryer; **-chi** *pl* **blu** UN forces, blue berets F

caseggiato *m (edificio)* block of flats, *Am* apartment block

caseificio *m (pl -ci)* dairy

casella *f di schedario* pigeon hole; *(quadratino)* square; **~ postale** post office box

casellario *m (pl -ri)* pigeon holes; **~ giudiziario** criminal records (office)

casello *m autostradale* toll booth

casereccio *(pl -cci)* homemade

caserma *f* barracks

casino P *m* brothel; *(rumore)* din, racket; *(disordine)* mess; **~ di caccia** hunting lodge

casinò *m inv* casino

caso *m* case; *(destino)* chance; *(occasione)* opportunity; **~ d'emergenza** emergency; **per ~** by chance; **a ~** at random; **(in) ~ che** in case; **in ~ contrario** should that not be the case; **in ogni ~** in any case, anyway; **in nessun ~** under no circumstances; **nel peggiore dei -i** if the worst comes to the worst

casolare *m* farmhouse

caspita! goodness (gracious)!, good heavens!

cassa *f* case; *di legno* crate; *di negozio* till; *sportello* cash desk, cashpoint; *(banca)* bank; **~ acustica** speaker; **~ comune** kitty; **~ continua** night safe; **~ da morto** coffin; **~ di risparmio** savings bank; **~ integrazione** form of income support; **~ malattia** department administering health insurance scheme; **~ toracica** ribcage; **orario *m* di ~** opening hours

cassaforte *f (pl casseforti)* safe

cassapanca *f (pl cassapanche)* chest

casseruola *f (sauce)* pan

cassetta *f* box; *per frutta, verdura* crate; *(musicassetta)* cassette; **~ delle lettere *(buca)*** post box, *Am* mailbox; *(casella)* letterbox, *Am* mailbox; **~ del pronto soccorso** first-aid kit; **~ di sicurezza** strong box; **successo *m* di ~** box office hit; **pane *m* a ~** sliced loaf

cassetto *m* drawer; AUTO **~ portaoggetti** glove compartment

cassettone *m* chest of drawers; **soffitto *m* a -i** panelled ceiling

cassiere m, **-a** f cashier; _di banca_ teller; _di supermercato_ checkout assistant

cassonetto m dustbin

casta f caste

castagna f chestnut

castagno m chestnut (tree)

castano _capelli_ chestnut; _occhi_ brown

castello m castle; TEC (_impalcatura_) scaffolding; **letti** mpl **a ~** bunk beds

castigare <1e> punish

castigo m (pl -ghi) punishment

castità f chastity

castoro m beaver

castrare <1a> castrate; _gatto_ neuter; _femmina di animale_ spay

casual 1 agg casual **2** m casual clothes, casual wear

casuale chance, casual

casualità f chance nature

cataclisma m (pl -i) disaster

catacomba f catacomb

catalizzatore m catalyst; AUTO catalytic converter; **~ a tre vie** three-way catalytic converter

catalogare <1m & e> catalog(ue)

catalogo m (pl -ghi) catalog(ue); **~ di vendita per corrispondenza** mail order catalog(ue)

catapecchia f shack

catapultare <1a> catapult

catarifrangente m reflector; _lungo la strada_ reflector, Br cat's eye

catarro m catarrh

catasta f pile, heap

catasto m land register

catastrofe f catastrophe

catastrofico (pl -ci) catastrophic

categoria f category; _di albergo_ class; **~ a rischio** at risk category

categorico (pl -ci) categoric(al)

catena f chain; **-e** pl **da neve** snow chains; **reazione** f **a ~** chain reaction; **~ di montaggio** assembly line; **~ montuosa** mountain range, chain of mountains

catenaccio m (pl -cci) bolt; SP defensive tactics

cateratta f (_chiusa_) sluice(gate); (_cascata_) falls; MED cataract

catino m basin

catrame m tar

cattedra f _scrivania_ desk; _incarico di insegnamento_ teaching post; **~ universitaria** university chair

cattedrale f cathedral

cattiveria f wickedness; _di bambini_ naughtiness; _azione_ nasty thing to do; _parole crudeli_ nasty thing to say

cattività f captivity

cattivo bad; _bambino_ naughty, bad; **con le buone o con le -e** by hook or by crook

cattolicesimo m (Roman) Catholicism

cattolico (pl -ci) **1** agg (Roman) Catholic **2** m, **-a** f (Roman) Catholic

cattura f capture; (_arresto_) arrest

catturare <1a> capture; (_arrestare_) arrest

caucciù m rubber

causa f cause; (_motivo_) reason; DIR lawsuit; **fare ~** sue (**a qu** s.o.); **a ~ di** because of; **per ~ tua** because of you

causale f cause, reason

causare <1a> cause

cautela f caution; (_precauzione_) precaution

cauto cautious

cauzione f (_deposito_) security; _per la libertà provvisoria_ bail

Cav. abbr (= **Cavaliere**) _Italian title awarded for services to the country_

cava f quarry

cavalcare <1d> ride

cavalcata f ride

cavalcavia m inv flyover

cavalcioni a ~ astride

cavaliere m rider; _accompagnatore_ escort; _al ballo_ partner

cavalla f mare

cavallerizzo m, **-a** f horseman; _donna_ horsewoman

cavalletta f grasshopper

cavalletto m trestle; FOT tripod; _da pittore_ easel

cavallo m horse; _scacchi_ knight; _dei pantaloni_ crotch; **~ da corsa** race horse; AUTO **~ vapore** horsepower;

C

andare a ~ go riding; **vivere a ~ di due secoli** straddle two centuries
cavallone *m* breaker
cavalluccio *m* (*pl* -cci): **~ marino** sea horse
cavare <1a> take out; *dente* take out, extract; **cavarsela** manage, get by
cavarsi ~ da un impiccio get out of trouble
cavatappi *m inv* corkscrew
caverna *f* cave
cavernoso *una voce* **-a** a deep voice
cavia *f* guinea pig (*anche fig*)
caviale *m* caviar
caviglia *f* (*pl* -glie) ANAT ankle
cavillo *m* quibble
cavità *f inv* cavity
cavo1 *agg* hollow **2** *m* cable; **~ d'accensione** plug lead; **~ di avviamento** jump leads; **~ di ormeggio** mooring rope; **~ da rimorchio** tow rope; **~ in fibra ottica** optic fibre cable; **televisione f via ~** cable TV
cavolfiore *m* cauliflower
cavolo *m* cabbage; **~ di Bruxelles** Brussels sprout; **~ rapa** kohlrabi; **~ verzotto** Savoy cabbage
cazzo *m* V prick V; **~!** fuck! V
CC *abbr* (= **Carabinieri**) Italian police force
cc *abbr* (= **centimetri cubici**) cc (= cubic centimetres)
c.c. *abbr* (= **corrente continua**) DC (= direct current)
c/c *abbr* (= **conto corrente**) current account, *Am* checking account
CD *m inv* CD; **lettore** *m* **~** CD player; **CD-Rom** *m inv* CD-Rom; **drive** *m* **per ~** CD-Rom drive
ce → **ci** (*before lo, la, li, le, ne*)
c'è there is
cecchino *m* sniper
cece *m* chickpea
cecità *f* blindness
ceco1 *agg* Czech **2** *m*, **-a** *f* Czech
cecoslovacco (*pl* -cchi) **1** *agg* Czechoslovakian **2** *m*, **-a** *f* Czechoslovakian
cedere <3a> **1** *v/t* (*dare*) hand over, give up; (*vendere*) sell, dispose of; **~**

il posto give up one's seat **2** *v/i* give in, surrender (*a* to); *muro, terreno* collapse, give way; **non ~!** don't give in!
cedevole soft
cedibile transferable, assignable
cedola *f* coupon; **~ di consegna** delivery note
cedro *m del Libano* cedar
CEE, **Cee** *abbr* (= **Comunità Economica Europea**) EEC (= European Economic Community)
cefalo *m* ZO mullet
ceffone *m* slap
celebrare <1l & b> celebrate
celebrazione *f* celebration
celebre famous
celebrità *f inv* fame; (*persona*) celebrity
celere fast, speedy, swift; **posta** *f* **~** swiftair®, *Am* Fedex®
celeste sky blue; (*divino*) heavenly (*anche fig*)
celibato *m* celibacy
celibe 1 *agg* single, unmarried **2** *m* bachelor
cella *f* cell
cellula *f* cell; **~ fotoelettrica** photoelectric cell; **~ solare** solar cell
cellulare1 *agg* cell *attr*; **telefono** *m* **~** mobile phone, *Am* cell(ular) phone **2** *m* prison van; (*telefono*) mobile
cellulite *f* cellulite
cellulosa *f* cellulose
celtico (*pl* -ci) Celtic
cemento *m* cement; **~ armato** reinforced concrete
cena *f* supper, evening meal; *importante, con ospiti* dinner; **~ in piedi** buffet
cenacolo *m* PITT Last Supper
cenare <1a> have supper; *formalmente* dine
cencio *m* (*pl* -ci) rag, piece of cloth; (*per spolverare*) duster; **bianco come un ~** white as a sheet
cenere *f* ash; **le Ceneri** *fpl* Ash Wednesday
cenno *m* sign; *della mano* wave; *del capo* nod; *con gli occhi* wink; (*breve notizia*) mention; (*allusione*) hint;

far ~ a qu *con la mano* wave to s.o.; *con il capo* nod to s.o.; *con gli occhi* wink at s.o.; **far ~ di voler andare** signal that one wants to leave; **far ~ di sì** nod (one's head); **far ~ di no** shake one's head

cenone *m* feast, banquet; **~ di San Silvestro** special celebratory meal on New Year's Eve

censimento *m* census

censura *f* censorship

censurare <1a> censor

centenario (*pl* -ri) **1** *agg* hundred-year-old **2** *m* (*persona*) centenarian; (*anniversario*) centenary

centesimo 1 *agg* hundredth **2** *m*: **~ di dollaro** cent; **badare al ~** count every penny

centigrado *m* centigrade

centimetro *m* centimetre, *Am* -meter; **~ cubo** cubic centimetre (*Am* -meter); **~ quadrato** square centimetre (*Am* -meter)

centinaio *m* (*pl* le centinaia) hundred; **un ~ di** about a hundred, a hundred or so

cento hundred; **per ~** per cent; **~ per ~** one hundred per cent; **~ di questi giorni** many happy returns

centrale 1 *agg* central **2** *f* station, plant; **~ atomica o nucleare** nuclear power station

centralinista *m/f* switchboard operator

centralino *m* switchboard

centralizzare <1a> centralize

centrare <1b> TEC centre, *Am* center; **~ il bersaglio** hit a bull's eye

centrifuga 1 *agg* centrifugal **2** *f* spin-dryer; TEC centrifuge

centrifugare <1e & m> spin-dry; TEC centrifuge

centro *m* centre, *Am* center; *di bersaglio* bull's eye; **~ commerciale** shopping centre; **~ della città** town or city centre, *Am* downtown; **~ residenziale** residential area; **~ storico** old (part of) town; **fare ~** hit the bull's eye; *fig* hit the nail on the head

ceppo *m*: **~ bloccaruota** wheel

clamp; **mettere il ~ a** clamp

cera[1] *f* wax; *per lucidare* polish; **~ da scarpe** shoe polish

cera[2] *f* look; **avere una brutta ~** look awful

ceralacca *f* sealing wax

ceramica *f* (*pl* -che) *arte* ceramics *sg*; *oggetto* piece of pottery

cerata *f* oilskins *pl*

cerca *f*: **in ~ di ...** in search of ...

cercare <1d> **1** *v/t* look for **2** *v/i*: **~ di fare** try to do

cerchia *f* circle

cerchio *m* (*pl* -chi) circle

cerchione *m* TEC rim

cereale 1 *agg* grain *attr* **2** -i *mpl* grain, cereals

cerealicoltura *f* grain farming

cerebrale: **commozione** *f* **~** concussion

cerimonia *f* ceremony; REL service; **-e** *pl* (*convenevoli*) pleasantries; **fare ~** stand on ceremony; **senza tante ~** (*bruscamente*) unceremoniously

cerimoniale *m/agg* ceremonial

cerimonioso ceremonious

cerino *m* (wax) match

cernia *f* grouper

cerniera *f* hinge; **~ lampo** zip (fastener), *Am* zipper

cernita *f* selection, choice

cero *m* (large) candle

cerotto *m* (sticking) plaster

certezza *f* certainty

certificare <1m & d> certify

certificato *m* certificate; **~ medico** medical certificate; **~ di garanzia** guarantee; **~ di nascita** birth certificate; **~ di sana e robusta costituzione** certificate of good health

certo 1 *agg* (*sicuro*) certain, sure (**di** of; **che** that); **un ~ signor Federici** a (certain) Mr Federici; **ci vuole un ~ coraggio** it takes (some) courage; **di una ~ età** of a certain age; **-i** some; **-e cose non si dicono** there are some things you just don't say; **un ~ non so che** a certain something, a certain je ne sais quoi **2** *avv* *(certamente)* certainly; *(naturalmente)* of course; **~ che ...** surely ... **3** *pron*: **-i, -e** some, some people

certosa *f* Carthusian monastery

cervello *m* (*pl* i cervelli, le cervella) brain; GASTR brains; **farsi saltare le -a** blow one's brains out; **lambiccarsi il ~** rack one's brains

cervo *m* deer; *carne* venison; **~ volante** stag beetle

cesareo: **taglio** *m* **~** C(a)esarean (section), C section

cesellare <1b> chisel

cesello *m* chisel

cesoie *fpl* shears

cespuglio *m* (*pl* -gli) bush, shrub

cessare <1b> stop, cease

cessate il fuoco *m* ceasefire

cessazione *f di contratto* termination; **~ di esercizio** closure, going out of business

cessione *f* transfer, handover

cesso *m* P bog P

cesta *f* basket

cestinare <1a> throw away, bin F

cestino *m* little basket; *per la carta* wastepaper basket

cesto *m* basket

cetaceo *m* cetacean

ceto *m* (social) class; **~ medio** middle class

cetra *f* zither

cetriolino *m* gherkin

cetriolo *m* cucumber

cf., cfr. *abbr* (= *confronta*) cf (= compare)

cg *abbr* (= *centigrammo*) cg (= centigram)

CGIL *abbr* (= **Confederazione Generale Italiana del Lavoro**) Italian trade union organization

chalet *m inv* chalet

charter *m inv* charter

che 1 *agg* what; **a ~ cosa serve?** what is that for?; **~ brutta giornata!** what a filthy day! **2** *pron persona*: *soggetto* who; *persona*: *oggetto* who, that, *fml* whom; *cosa* that, which; **~?** what?; **ciò ~** what; **non c'e di ~** don't mention it, you're welcome **3** *cong dopo il comparativo* than;

sono tre anni ~ non la vedo I haven't seen her for three years

check-in *m inv* AVIA check-in; **fare il ~** check in

chemioterapia *f* chemotherapy, chemo F

chetichella: **alla ~** stealthily

chi who; **di ~ è il libro?** whose book is this? **a ~ ha venduto la casa?** who did he sell the house to?; **c'è ~ dice che** some people say that; **~ ... ~** some ... others

chiacchiera *f* chat; *(maldicenza)* gossip; *(notizia infondata)* rumo(u)r; **far due -e con qu** have a chat with s.o.

chiacchierare <1l> chat, chatter; *spreg* gossip

chiacchierata *f* chat

chiacchierone 1 *agg* talkative, chatty; *(pettegolo)* gossipy **2** *m*, **-a** *f* chatterbox; *(pettegolo)* gossip

chiamare <1a> call; TELEC (tele)phone, ring; **andare a ~ qu** go and get s.o., fetch s.o.; **mandare a ~ qu** send for s.o.; *(convocare)* call in; TELEC **~ in teleselezione** call direct, dial direct

chiamarsi be called; **come ti chiami?** what's your name?; **mi chiamo ...** my name is ...

chiamata *f* call; TELEC (tele)phone call; **~ a carico del destinatario** reverse charge call, *Am* collect call; **~ interurbana** long-distance call

chiara *f* egg white

chiarezza *f* clarity

chiarimento *m* clarification

chiarire <4d> clarify

chiarirsi become clear

chiaro 1 *agg* clear; *colore* light, pale; *(luminoso)* bright; **~ e tondo** definite **2** *m* light; **~ di luna** moonlight; **mettere in ~** *(appurare)* throw light on; *(spiegare)* clarify **3** *avv* plainly; *(con franchezza)* frankly

chiaroscuro *m* PITT chiaroscuro

chiaroveggente *m/f* clairvoyant

chiasso *m* din, racket; **fare ~** make a din *or* racket; *fig* cause a sensation chiassoso noisy

chiatta *f* barge; **ponte** *m* **di -e** pontoon bridge

chiave **1** *agg inv* key **2** *f* key; MUS clef; ~ **d'accensione** ignition key; ~ **della macchina** car key; ~ **inglese** spanner, *Am* monkey wrench; **sotto** ~ under lock and key

chiavistello *m* bolt

chiazza *f* (*macchia*) stain; *sulla pelle, di colore* patch

chic *inv* chic, stylish, elegant

chicco *m* (*pl* -chi) grain; (*di caffè*) bean; ~ **d'uva** grape

chiedere <3k> *per sapere* ask (**di** about); *per avere* ask for; (*esigere*) demand, require; ~ **qc a qu** ask s.o. sth; ~ **di qu** (*chiedere notizie di*) ask about s.o.; *per parlargli* ask for s.o.; ~ **un piacere a qu** ask s.o. a favo(u)r, ask a favo(u)r of s.o.; ~ **scusa a qu** apologize to s.o.

chiedersi wonder (**se** whether)

chiesa *f* church

chiesto *pp* → **chiedere**

chiglia *f* MAR keel

chilo *m* kilo; **mezzo** ~ half a kilo

chilogrammo *m* kilogram

chilometraggio *m* AUTO mileage

chilometrico *indennità* per kilometre

chilometro *m* kilometre, *Am* -meter; **-i** *pl* **all'ora** kilometres (*Am* -meters) per hour

chilowatt *m inv* kilowatt

chimica *f* chemistry

chimico (*pl* -ci) **1** *agg* chemical; **sostanze** *fpl* **-che** chemicals **2** *m*, **-a** *f* chemist

chinare <1a> *testa* bend; *occhi* lower

chinarsi stoop, bend down

chincaglierie *fpl* knick-knacks, ornaments

chinino *m* quinine

chioccia *f fig* mother hen

chiocciola *f* snail; **scala** *f* **a** ~ spiral staircase

chiodata SP **scarpe** *fpl* **-e** spikes

chiodo *m* nail; ~ **di garofano** clove; *fig* ~ **fisso** obsession, idée fixe; **roba da -i!** it's unbelievable!

chioma *f* mane; *di cometa* tail

chiosco *m* (*pl* -chi) kiosk

chiostro *m* cloister

chip *m inv* chip

chiromante *m/f* palmist

chiropratico *m*, **-a** *f* chiropractor

chirurgia *f* surgery

chirurgico (*pl* -ci) surgical

chirurgo *m* (*pl* -ghi) surgeon

chissà who knows; (*forse*) maybe

chitarra *f* guitar

chitarrista *m/f* (*mpl* -i) guitarist

chiudere <3b> close, shut; *a chiave* lock; *strada* close off; *gas, luce* turn off; *fabbrica, negozio per sempre* close down, shut down; *fig* ~ **un occhio** turn a blind eye; FIN ~ **in pareggio** break even; ~ **in perdita / in attivo** show a loss / a profit

chiudersi *di porta, ombrello* close, shut; *di ferita* heal up; ~ **in se stesso** withdraw into o.s.

chiunque anyone; *relativo* whoever

chiusa *f di fiume* lock; *di discorso* conclusion

chiuso **1** *pp* → **chiudere 2** *agg* closed, shut; *a chiave* locked; (*nuvoloso*) cloudy, overcast; *persona* reserved

chiusura *f* closing, shutting; AUTO ~ **centralizzata** central locking; ~ **lampo** zip (fastener), *Am* zipper; **ora** *f* **di** ~ closing time

choc *m inv* shock

ci **1** *pron* us; **non** ~ **ha parlato** he didn't speak to us; ~ **siamo divertiti molto** we had a great time; ~ **vogliamo bene** we love each other; ~ **penso** I'm thinking about it **2** *avv* here; (*lì*) there; ~ **sei?** are you there?; **c'è ...** there is ...; ~ **sono ...** there are ...; ~ **vuole tempo** it takes time

C.ia *abbr* (= **compagnia**) Co. (= company)

ciabatta *f* slipper

cialda *f* wafer

ciambella *f* GASTR type of cake, *baked in a ring-shaped mo(u)ld*; (*salvagente*) lifebelt

cianfrusaglia *f* knick-knack

ciao! *nell'incontrarsi* hi!; *nel congedarsi* 'bye!, cheerio!

ciarlatano *m* charlatan

ciarpame *m* junk

ciascuno 1 *agg* each; (*ogni*) every **2** *pron* everyone

cibarsi <1a> feed on, eat (*di* sth)

cibernetica *f* cybernetics

cibo *m* food; **-i** *pl* foodstuffs, foods; **~ pronto** fast food

cicala *f* (*insetto*) cicada

cicalino *m* buzzer, bleeper

cicatrice *f* scar

cicatrizzare <1a>, **cicatrizzarsi** heal

cicca *f* (*pl* -che) (*mozzicone*) stub, butt; (*gomma da masticare*) (chewing) gum

ciccia *f* (*grasso*) flab

ciccione *m*, **-a** *f* fatty

cicciottello chubby

cicerone *m* guide

ciclamino *m* cyclamen

ciclico cyclical

ciclismo *m* cycling, bike riding

ciclista *m/f* (*mpl* -i) cyclist

ciclistico bike *attr*, cycle *attr*

ciclo *m* cycle

ciclomotore *m* moped

ciclone *m* cyclone

cicloturismo *m* cycling holidays

cicogna *f* stork

cicoria *f* chicory

cieco (*pl* -chi) **1** *agg* blind; **vicolo** *m* **~** dead end, blind alley **2** *m*, **-a** *f* blind man; **donna** blind woman

cielo *m* sky; REL heaven; **grazie al ~** thank heaven(s)

cifra *f* figure; (*monogramma*) monogram; (*somma*) amount, sum; (*codice*) cipher, code; **~ d'affari** turnover; **numero** *m* **di sei -e** six digit number

cifrato (*messaggio*) in cipher, in code

ciglio *m* (*pl* le ciglia) ANAT eyelash; (*pl* i cigli) (*bordo*) edge

cigno *m* swan

cigolare <1l> squeak

cigolio *m* squeak

Cile *m* Chile

cilecca **far ~** *di arma da fuoco* misfire

cileno 1 *agg* Chilean **2** *m*, **-a** *f* Chilean

ciliegia *f* (*pl* -ge) cherry

ciliegio *m* (*pl* -gi) cherry (tree)

cilindrata *f* TEC cubic capacity; **automobile** *f* **di media ~** middle of the range car

cilindrico (*pl* -ci) cylindrical

cilindro *m* cylinder; *cappello* top hat

cima *f* top; **in ~ all'armadio** on top of the wardrobe; **da ~ a fondo** from top to bottom; *fig* from beginning to end; **non è una ~** he's no Einstein

cimentarsi <1b>: **~ in** embark on

cimice *f* bug; *dei letti* bed bug; (*puntina da disegno*) drawing-pin

ciminiera *f* smokestack

cimitero *m* cemetery

Cina *f* China

cinciallegra *f* great tit

cincilla, **cincillà** *f* chinchilla

cin cin! F cheers!

cineamatore *m* video enthusiast

cineforum *m* *inv* film followed by a discussion; *club* film club

cinema *m* *inv* cinema, *Am luogo* movie theater; **~ d'essai** experimental cinema; *luogo* art cinema, art house

cinematografia *f* cinematography; *industria* film *or* movie industry

cinematografico (*pl* -ci) film *attr*, movie *attr*

cinepresa *f* cine camera

cinese *agg*, *m/f* Chinese

cineteca *f* film library

cinetico (*pl* -ci) kinetic

cingere <3d> (*circondare*) surround

cinghia *f* strap; (*cintura*) belt; **tirare la ~** tighten one's belt

cinghiale *m* wild boar; **pelle** *f* **di ~** pigskin

cinguettare <1a> twitter

cinguettio *m* twittering

cinico (*pl* -ci) **1** *agg* cynical **2** *m* **-a** *f* cynic

cinismo *m* cynicism

cinquanta fifty

cinquantenario *m* fiftieth anniversary

cinquantenne *m/f* 50-year-old

cinquantesimo *m/agg* fiftieth

cinquantina *f*: *una ~ di* about 50

cinque five

cinquecento 1 *agg* five hundred **2** *m*: *il Cinquecento* the sixteenth century

cinquemila five thousand

cintare <1a> enclose

cinto *pp* <- **cingere**

cintura *f* belt; (*vita*) waist; *~ di salvataggio* lifebelt; *~ di sicurezza* seat-belt

cinturino *m* strap

ciò (*questo*) this; (*quello*) that; *~ che* what; *con tutto ~* even so, in spite of all that; *~ nonostante* nevertheless

ciocca *f* (*pl* -cche) *di capelli* lock

cioccolata *f* chocolate

cioccolatino *m* chocolate

cioccolato *m* chocolate

cioè that is, i.e.

ciondolare <1l> dangle; *fig* hang about

ciondolo *m* pendant

ciotola *f* bowl

ciottolo *m* pebble

cipolla *f* onion; *di pianta* bulb

cipollina *f* small onion; *erba f ~* chives *pl*

cipresso *m* cypress (tree)

cipria *f* (face) powder

circa 1 *avv* (round) about **2** *prp* about

circo *m* (*pl* -chi) circus

circolare 1 *v/i* <1l> circulate; *di persone* move along; *le auto non possono ~* it's impossible to drive **2** *agg* circular **3** *f lettera* circular

circolazione *f* traffic; MED circulation; DIR *libera ~* freedom of movement; *~ del sangue* circulation of the blood; *mettere in ~ voci* spread; *ritirare dalla ~* withdraw from circulation

circolo *m* circle; (*club*) club; *~ vizioso* vicious circle

circondare <1a> surround

circonferenza *f* circumference

circonvallazione *f* ring road

circoscrivere <3tt> circumscribe

circoscrizione *f* area, district; *~ elettorale* constituency

circostante surrounding

circostanza *f* circumstance; (*occasione*) occasion

circuito *m* SP (*percorso*) track; EL circuit; EL *corto ~* short circuit

CISL *abbr* (= *Confederazione Italiana Sindacati Lavoratori*) Italian trade union organization

cisterna *f* cistern; (*serbatoio*) tank; *nave f ~* tanker

cisti *f* ANAT cyst

cistifellea *f* gall bladder

cistite *f* cystitis

CIT *abbr* (= *Compagnia Italiana del Turismo*) Italian Tourist Board

citare <1a> quote; *come esempio* cite, quote; DIR *testimone* summons; *in giudizio* sue

citazione *f* quotation, quote; DIR summons

citofono *m* entry phone; *in uffici* intercom

città *f* town; *grande* city; *~ dormitorio* dormitory town; *~ giardino* garden city; *~ universitaria* university town (*in the provinces*); *la ~ vecchia* old (part of) town; *Città del Vaticano* Vatican City; *la ~ eterna* the Eternal City

cittadina *f* (small) town

cittadinanza *f* citizenship; (*popolazione*) citizens; *~ onoraria* freedom of the city

cittadino 1 *agg* town *attr*, city *attr* **2** *m*, *-a f* citizen; (*abitante di città*) city dweller

ciuccio *m* F (*succhiotto*) dummy, *Am* pacifier

ciuffo *m* tuft

civetta *f* ZO (little) owl; *fig far la ~* flirt

civico *m* (*pl* -ci) (*della città*) municipal, town *attr*; *delle persone* civic; *numero m ~* (street) number

civile 1 *agg* civil; *civilizzato* civilized; (*non militare*) civilian; *guerra f ~* civil war; *matrimonio m ~* civil marriage; *stato m ~* marital status **2** *m* civilian

civiltà *f inv* civilization; (*cortesia*) civility

clacson *m inv* horn

clamoroso *fig* sensational

clandestino 1 *agg* clandestine; (*illegale*) illegal **2** *m*, **-a** *f* stowaway

clarinetto *m* clarinet

classe *f* class; (*aula*) classroom; **~ operaia** working class; **~ turistica** tourist class; **di ~** classy

classicismo *m* classicism

classico (*pl* -ci) **1** *agg* classical; (*tipico*) classic **2** *m* classic

classifica *f* classification; (*elenco*) list; **sportiva** league standings, league table; *musicale* charts

classificare <1m & d> classify

classificatore *m* (*cartella*) folder; *mobile* filing cabinet, *Am* file cabinet

classismo *m* class consciousness

clausola *f* clause; (*riserva*) proviso

claustrofobia *f* claustrophobia

clavicola *f* collar-bone, clavicle

clemente merciful; *tempo* mild

clemenza *f* clemency; *di tempo* mildness

cleptomane *m/f* kleptomaniac

clericale clerical

clero *m* clergy

clessidra *f* hourglass

clic *m inv* click; **mediante ~** by clicking

cliccare <1d> INFOR click (**su** on)

cliché *m inv fig* cliché

cliente *m/f* customer; *di professionista* client; *di albergo* guest; MED patient; **~ abituale** regular

clientela *f* customers *pl*, clientele; *di professionista* clients *pl*; *di medico* patients *pl*; **~ abituale** patrons *pl*, regular customers *pl*

clima *m* (*pl* -i) climate

climatico (*pl* -ci) climate *attr*, climatic; **stazione** *f* **climatica** health resort

clinica *f* (*pl* -che) (*ospedale*) clinic; (*casa di cura*) nursing home; **~ medica** clinical medicine

clinico (*pl* -ci) **1** *agg* clinical **2** *m* clinician

clip *m inv* clip

clonare <1a> BIO clone

cloro *m* chlorine

clorofilla *f* chlorophyl(l)

cloroformio *m* chloroform

club *m inv* club

cm *abbr* (= **centimetro**) cm (= centimetre)

c.m. *abbr* (= **corrente mese**) of this month, inst.

CNR *abbr* (= **Consiglio Nazionale delle Ricerche**) Italian National Research Council

coabitare <1m> share a flat (*Am* an apartment), be flatmates (*Am* roommates)

coagularsi <1m> *di sangue* coagulate, clot; *di latte* curdle

coalizione *f* coalition; **governo** *m* **di ~** coalition government

coalizzarsi <1a> join forces; POL form a coalition

cobra *m inv* cobra

cocaina *f* cocaine

cocainomane 1 *agg* addicted to cocaine **2** *m/f* cocaine addict

coccinella *f* ladybird, *Am* ladybug

coccio *m* (*pl* -cci) earthenware; *frammento* fragment (of pottery), shard

cocciuto stubborn, obstinate

cocco *m* (*pl* -cchi) (*albero*) coconut palm or tree; **noce** *f* **di ~** coconut **2** *m*, **-a** *f* (*persona prediletta*) darling

coccodrillo *m* crocodile

coccolare <1l & c> F cuddle; (*viziare*) spoil

cocente scorching; *fig* scathing

cocktail *m inv bevanda* cocktail; *festa* cocktail party

cocomero *m* water melon

coda *f* tail; (*fila*) queue, *Am* line; *di veicolo, treno* rear; MUS coda; **~ di paglia** guilty conscience; **~ dell'occhio** corner of the eye; **piano** *m* **a ~** grand piano; **fare la ~** queue (up), *Am* stand in line

codardo 1 *agg* cowardly **2** *m*, **-a** *f* coward

codazzo *m* swarm

codesto 1 *agg* that **2** *pron* that one

codice *m* code; **~ a barre** bar code; **~ civile** civil code; **~ di avviamento postale** post code, *Am* zip code; **~ fiscale** tax code; **~ stradale** Highway Code

codificare <1m & d> *dati* encode; DIR codify

codino *m* pigtail, plait

coefficiente *m* coefficient

coerente coherent; *fig* consistent

coerenza *f* coherence; *fig* consistency

coesione *f* cohesion

coesistenza *f* coexistence

coetaneo 1 *agg* the same age (**di** as) **2** *m*, **-a** *f* contemporary, person of the same age

cofanetto *m* casket

cofano *m* AUTO bonnet, *Am* hood

cogestione *f* joint management; **~ aziendale** worker participation

cogliere <3ss> pick; (*raccogliere*) gather; (*afferrare*) seize; *occasione* take, seize, jump at; (*capire*) grasp; **~ di sorpresa** catch unawares, take by surprise; **~ sul fatto** catch in the act, catch red-handed

cognac *m inv* cognac

cognato *m*, **-a** *f* brother-in-law; *donna* sister-in-law

cognizione *f* knowledge; FIL cognition; **parla con ~ di causa** he knows what he's talking about

cognome *m* surname; **nome** *m* **e ~** full name

coi *prp* con *and art* i

coincidenza *f* coincidence; FERR connection; **perdere la ~** miss one's connection

coincidere <3q> coincide

coinquilino *m*, **-a** *f in condominio* fellow tenant; *in appartamento* flatmate, *Am* roommate

coinvolgere <3d> involve (**in** in)

coinvolto *pp* → **coinvolgere**

col *prp* con *and art* il

colabrodo *m inv* strainer

colapasta *m inv* colander

colare <1a> **1** *v/t* strain; *pasta* drain **2** *v/i* drip; (*perdere*) leak; *di naso*

run; *di cera* melt; **~ a fondo** *o* **a pico** sink, go down

colata *f di metallo* casting; *di lava* flow

colazione *f* **prima** breakfast; *di mezzogiorno* lunch; **~ al sacco** picnic; **far ~** have breakfast, breakfast

colei *pron f* the one; **~ che** the one that

colera *m* cholera

colesterolo *m* cholesterol

colica *f* (*pl* -che) colic

colino *m* strainer

colla *f* glue; *di farina* paste

collaborare <1m> co-operate, collaborate; *con giornale* contribute

collaboratore *m*, **-trice** *f* collaborator; *di giornale* contributor; **~atore** *m* **esterno** freelance(r); **-trice** *f* **domestica** home help

collaborazione *f* co-operation, collaboration

collana *f* necklace; *di libri* series

collant *m inv* tights *pl*, *Am* pantyhose

collare *m* collar

collasso *m* collapse; **~ cardiaco** heart failure

collaudare <1a> test; *fig* put to the test

collaudo *m* test

colle *m* hill; (*valico*) pass

collegamento *m* connection; MIL liaison; RAD, TV link; **~ aereo / ferroviario** connecting flight / train

collegare <1a> connect, link

collegarsi RAD, TV link up

collegiale 1 *agg* collective **2** *m/f* boarder

collegio *m* (*pl* -gi) boarding school; **~ elettorale** constituency

collera *f* anger; **andare in ~** get angry; **essere in ~ con qu** be angry with s.o.

collerico (*pl* -ci) irascible

colletta *f* collection

collettività *f* community

collettivo *m/agg* collective

colletto *m* collar

collezionare <1a> collect

collezione f collection; **fare ~ di qc**
collect sth, make a collection of sth
collezionista m/f collector; **~ di
francobolli** stamp collector
collina f hill
collinoso hilly
collirio m eyewash
collisione f collision; **entrare in ~**
collide
collo m neck; (*bagaglio*) piece *or*
item of luggage; (*pacco*) package; **~
del piede** instep
collocamento m placing; (*impiego*)
employment; **agenzia** f **di ~** employment agency; **ufficio** m **di ~**
Jobcentre
collocare <1l & d> place, put; **~ a
riposo** retire
collocazione f place, job
colloquiale colloquial
colloquio m (*pl* -qui) talk, conversation; *ufficiale* interview; (*esame*) oral
(exam)
colluttazione f scuffle
colmare <1a> fill (**di** with); *fig di
gentilezze* overwhelm (**di** with); **~ un
vuoto** bridge a gap
colmo 1 *agg* full (**di** of) **2** m summit,
top; *fig* (*culmine*) height; **è il ~!** that's
the last straw!
colomba f ZO, *fig* dove
colombo m pigeon
colon m colon
Colonia f: **acqua** f **di ~** eau de Co-
logne
colonia f colony; *per bambini* holiday
camp; **~ marina** seaside holiday
camp
coloniale colonial
colonico (*pl* -ci): **casa** f **-a** farmhouse
colonizzare <1a> colonize
colonna f column; *di veicoli* line; *fig*
mainstay; **~ sonora** sound track; **~
vertebrale** spinal column
colonnato m colonnade
colonnello m colonel
colonnina f **della benzina** petrol (*Am*
gas) pump
colorante m dye; **senza -i** with no
artificial colo(u)rings

colorare <1a> colo(u)r; *disegno*
colo(u)r in
colorato colo(u)red
colorazione f colo(u)ring
colore m colo(u)r; *carte* suit; *poker*
flush; **gente** f **di ~** colo(u)red
people; **scatola** f **dei -i** paint box; **~
a olio** oil (paint); **a -i** *film, televisione*
colo(u)r; *attr;* **farne di tutti i -i** get up
to all sorts of mischief
colorito 1 *agg volto* rosy-cheeked; *fig*
(*vivace*) colo(u)rful **2** m complexion
coloro *pron pl* the ones; **~ che** those
who
colossale colossal
colosso m colossus
colpa f fault; REL sin; **dare a qu la ~
di qc** blame s.o. for sth; **non è ~ sua**
it's not her fault; **per ~ tua** because
of you; **senso** m **di ~** sense of guilt;
sentirsi in ~ feel guilty
colpevole 1 *agg* guilty **2** m/f culprit,
guilty party
colpire <4d> hit, strike; *fig* impress,
leave an impression on; **~ nel
segno** hit the nail on the head
colpo m blow; (*fig*) blow, shock; *di
pistola* shot; MED stroke; **~ -
apoplettico** apoplectic fit; **~ di calore** heat stroke; **~ di sole**
sunstroke; **~ di stato** coup d'état; **~
di telefono** phone call; **~ di testa**
whim; **fare ~** make an impact; **sul ~,
di ~** suddenly
coltellata f *ferita* stab wound
coltello m knife
coltivare <1a> AGR, *fig* cultivate
coltivatore m farmer
coltivazione f cultivation; *di prodotti
agricoli e piante* growing; *campi colti-
vati* crops
colto¹ *agg* cultured, learned
colto² *pp* → **cogliere**
coltura f growing; *piante* crop
colui *pron* m the one; **~ che** the one
that
coma m coma
comandamento m commandment
comandante m commander; AVIA,
MAR captain

comandare <1a> **1** v/t (*ordinare*) order, command; *esercito* command; *nave* captain, be captain of; FIN *merci* order; TEC control; **~ a distanza** operate by remote control **2** v/i be in charge

comando m order, command; TEC control; **~ a distanza** remote control

combaciare <1f> fit together; *fig* correspond

combattente m soldier, serviceman

combattere <3a> v/t & v/i fight

combattimento m fight; SP match, fight

combinare <1a> combine; (*organizzare*) arrange; **~ un guaio** make a mess; **oggi ho combinato poco** I got very little done today

combinarsi go well together

combinazione f combination; (*coincidenza*) coincidence; **per ~** by chance

combustibile 1 agg combustible **2** m fuel

combustione f combustion

come 1 avv as; (*in modo simile o uguale*) like; *interrogativo, esclamativo* how; (*prego?*) pardon?; **fa' ~ ti ho detto** do as I told you; **lavora ~ insegnante** he works as a teacher; **~ me** like me; **un cappello ~ il mio** a hat like mine; **~ sta?** how are you?, how are things?; **com'è bello!** how nice it is!; **~ mai?** how come?, why?; **oggi ~ oggi** nowadays; **~ se** as if **2** cong (*come se*) as if, as though; (*appena, quando*) as (soon as); **~ se niente fosse** as if nothing had happened

cometa f comet

comfort m inv comfort; **dotato di tutti i ~ moderni** with all mod cons

comicità f funniness

comico (*pl* -ci) **1** agg funny, comical; *genere comico* **2** m, **-a** f comedian; *donna* comedienne

comignolo m chimney pot

cominciare <1f> start, begin (**a** to); **a ~ da oggi** (starting) from today; **tanto per ~** to begin or start with

comitato m committee; **~ direttivo** steering committee

comitiva f group, party

comizio m meeting

Comm. abbr (= **Commendatore**) *Italian title awarded for services to the country*

commando m commando

commedia f comedy; *fig* play-acting

commediografo m, **-a** f playwright

commemorare <1m & b> commemorate

commemorazione f commemoration

commentare <1a> comment on

commentatore m, **-trice** f commentator

commento m comment

commerciale commercial; *relazioni, trattative* trade attr; *lettera* business attr

commercialista m/f accountant

commercializzare <1a> market

commerciante m/f merchant; (*negoziante*) shopkeeper

commerciare <1b & f> deal (**in** in)

commercio m (*pl* -ci) trade, business; *internazionale* trade; *di droga* traffic; **~ all'ingrosso** wholesale trade; **~ al minuto** retail trade; **camera f di ~** chamber of commerce; **essere in ~** be available; **mettere in ~ qc** put sth on the market

commessa f (*ordinazione*) order

commesso m, **-a** f shop assistant, *Am* sales clerk; (*impiegato*) clerk; **~ viaggiatore** travel(l)ing salesman

commestibile 1 agg edible **2** -i mpl foodstuffs

commettere <3ee> commit; *errore* make

commiserare <1m> feel sorry for

commissariato m: **~** (*di pubblica sicurezza*) police station

commissario m (*pl* -ri) *di polizia* (police) superintendent; *membro di commissione* commissioner

commissionare <1a> FIN commission

commissione f commission; (*incarico*) errand; ***Commissione europea*** European Commission; *-i pl* shopping *sg*; ***fatto su ~*** made to order

commosso 1 *pp* → ***commuovere*** 2 *agg fig* moved, touched

commovente moving, touching

commozione f emotion; *~ **cerebrale*** concussion

commuovere <3ff> move, touch

commuoversi be moved *or* touched

comò *m inv* chest of drawers

comodino *m* bedside table

comodità *f inv* comfort; (*vantaggio*) convenience

comodo 1 *agg* comfortable; *vestito* loose, comfortable; (*facilmente raggiungibile*) easy to get to; (*utile*) useful, handy; F *persona* laid back F; ***stia ~!*** don't get up! 2 *m* comfort; ***con ~*** at one's convenience; ***far ~ di denaro*** come in useful, be handy; ***le fa ~ così*** she finds it easier that way; ***fare il propio ~*** do as one pleases

compagnia f company; (*gruppo*) group; REL order; *~ **aerea*** airline; *~ **di assicurazioni*** insurance company; ***far ~ a qu*** keep s.o. company

compagno *m*, -a f companion; (*convivente*), FIN partner; POL comrade; *~ **di scuola*** schoolfriend, schoolmate; *~ **di squadra*** team mate; *~ **di viaggio*** travelling companion

comparativo *m/agg* comparative

comparire <4e> appear; (*essere pubblicato*) come out, appear; (*far figura*) stand out

comparizione f: DIR ***mandato m di ~*** summons

comparsa f appearance; TEA person with a walk-on part; *in film* extra

comparso *pp* → ***comparire***

compartimento *m* compartment

compassione f compassion, pity; ***provare ~ per qu*** feel sorry for s.o.

compasso *m* (pair of) compasses

compatibile compatible

compatire <4d>: *~ **qu*** feel sorry for s.o.

compatriota *m/f* (*mpl* -i) compatriot

compatto compact; *folla* dense; *fig* united

compensare <1b> (*controbilanciare*) compensate for, make up for; (*ricompensare*) reward; (*risarcire*) pay compensation to

compenso *m* (*ricompensa, risarcimento*) compensation; (*retribuzione*) fee; ***in ~*** (*d'altra parte*) on the other hand; ***dietro ~*** for a fee

compera f purchase; ***fare le -e*** go shopping

competente competent; (*responsabile*) appropriate

competenza f (*esperienza*) competence; ***essere di ~ di qu*** be s.o.'s responsibility

competere <3a> (*gareggiare*) compete

competitività f competitiveness

competitivo competitive

competizione f competition

compiacere too eager to please

compiacenza f overeagerness to please

compiacere <2k> please

compiacersi (*provare piacere*) be pleased (*di* with); ***mi compiaccio con te*** congratulations

compiaciuto *pp* → ***compiacere***

compiangere <3d> pity; *per lutto* mourn

compianto *pp* → ***compiangere***

compiere <4g> (*finire*) complete, finish; (*eseguire*) carry out; *~ **gli anni*** have one's birthday

compiersi (*avverarsi*) happen

compilare <1a> compile; *modulo* complete, fill in

compilatore *m* INFOR compiler

compilazione f compilation

compimento *m* completion

compito[1] *agg* polite

compito[2] *m* task; EDU *i -i pl* homework *sg*

compiuto *lavoro, opera* completed, finished; ***ha 10 anni -i*** he's 10

compleanno *m* birthday; ***buon ~!*** happy birthday!

complementare complementary

complemento *m* complement;

GRAM object

complessato full of complexes

complessivo all-in

complesso **1** *agg* complex, complicated **2** *m* complex; MUS group; *di circostanze* set, combination; **in** o **nel ~** on the whole

completamento *m* completion

completare <1b> complete

completo **1** *agg* complete; (*pieno*) full; TEA sold out **2** *m* set; (*vestito*) suit; **al ~** (*pieno*) full (up); TEA sold out

complicare <1l & d> complicate

complicarsi get complicated

complicato complicated, complex

complicazione *f* complication

complice *m/f* DIR accomplice

complimentarsi: **~ con qu** congratulate s.o. (**per** on)

complimento *m* compliment; **fare un ~ a qu** pay s.o. a compliment; **-i!** congratulations!; **non fare -i!** help yourself!

componente **1** *m* component **2** *m/f* (*persona*) member

componibile modular; *cucina* fitted

componimento *m* composition; DIR settlement

comporre <3ll> (*mettere in ordine*) arrange; MUS compose; TELEC **~ un numero** dial a number

comporsi: **~ di** consist of, be made up of

comportamento *m* behavio(u)r

comportare <1c> involve

comportarsi behave

compositore *m*, **-trice** *f* composer

composizione *f* composition; *di fiori* arrangement; DIR settlement

composta *f* stewed fruit; (*terricciato*) compost

composto **1** *pp* → **comporre 2** *agg* compound; *abiti, capelli* tidy, neat; **~ da** made up of; **stai ~** keep still; *seduto* sit properly **3** *m* compound

comprare <1a> buy, purchase; (*corrompere*) bribe, buy off

compratore *m*, **-trice** *f* buyer, purchaser

compravendita *f* buying and selling

comprendere <3c> (*includere*) comprise, include; (*capire*) understand

comprensibile understandable

comprensione *f* understanding

comprensivo (*tollerante*) understanding; **~ di** inclusive of

compreso **1** *pp* → **comprendere 2** *agg* inclusive; (*capito*) understood; **tutto ~** all in; **~ te** including you

compressa *f* (*pastiglia*) tablet; *di garza* compress

compresso *pp* → **comprimere**

comprimere <3r> press; (*reprimere*) repress; FIS compress

compromesso **1** *pp* → **compromettere 2** *m* compromise; DIR **~ di vendita** agreement to sell

compromettere <3ee> compromise

compromettersi compromise o.s.

computer *m inv* computer; **assistito dal ~** computer-assisted; **~ portatile** portable (computer), laptop

computerizzare <1a> computerize

computisteria *f* book-keeping, accountancy

comunale *del comune* municipal; town *attr*; **consiglio** *m* **~** town council; **palazzo** *m* **~** town hall

comune **1** *agg* common; *amico* mutual; (*ordinario*) ordinary, common; **in ~** in common; **non ~** unusual, uncommon; **fuori del ~** out of the ordinary **2** *m* municipality; **palazzo** *m* **del ~** town hall

comunemente commonly

comunicare <1m & d> **1** *v/t notizia* pass on, communicate; *contagio* pass on; REL give Communion to **2** *v/i* (*esprimersi*) communicate; *di persone* keep in touch, communicate

comunicato *m* announcement, communiqué; **~ stampa** press release

comunicazione *f* communication; (*annuncio*) announcement; TELEC (*collegamento*) connection; **dare ~ di qc a qu** tell s.o. about sth; TELEC **la ~ si è interrotta** I've been cut off; TELEC **~ internazionale** international call

comunione *f* REL communion; *di idee* sharing

comunismo *m* Communism

comunista *m/f* (*mpl* -i) Communist

comunità *f* community; **Comunità europea** European Community

comunitario community *attr*; *dell'UE* Community *attr*

comunque 1 *cong* however, no matter how; **~ vadano le cose** whatever happens **2** *avv* (*in ogni modo*) in any case, anyhow; (*in qualche modo*) somehow; (*tuttavia*) however

con with; (*mezzo*) by; **~ questo tempo** in this weather; **~ tutto ciò** for all that; **avere ~ sé** have with *or* on one

conato *m*: **~ di vomito** retching

concedere <3l> grant; *premio* award; **ti concedo che** I admit that

concedersi: **~ qc** treat o.s. to sth

concentramento *m* concentration

concentrare <1b>, **concentrarsi** concentrate

concentrazione *f* concentration

concentrico (*pl* -ci) concentric

concepibile conceivable

concepimento *m* conception

concepire <4d> conceive; (*ideare*) devise, conceive

concernere <3a> concern; **per quanto mi concerne** as far as I'm concerned

concerto *m* concert; *composizione* concerto

concessionario *m* (*pl* -ri) agent; **~ esclusivo** sole agent

concessione *f* concession

concesso *pp* → **concedere**

concetto *m* concept; (*giudizio*) opinion

concezione *f* conception; *fig* idea (**di** for)

conchiglia *f* shell

conciare <1f> *pelle* tan; (*sistemare*) arrange; **come ti sei conciato!** what a state *or* mess you're in!; **~ qu per le feste** tan s.o.'s hide, give s.o. a good hiding

conciliare <1k> reconcile; *multa* pay, settle; **~ il sonno** be conducive to sleep

conciliazione *f* reconciliation; DIR settlement

concimare <1a> *pianta* feed

concime *m* manure; **~ chimico** chemical fertilizer

conciso concise

concitato excited

concittadino *m*, **-a** *f* fellow citizen

concludere <3q> conclude; (*portare a termine*) achieve, carry off; **~ un affare** clinch a deal; **non ho concluso nulla** I got nowhere

concludersi end, close

conclusione *f* conclusion; **in ~** in short

conclusivo conclusive

concluso *pp* → **concludere**

concordanza *f* agreement

concordare <1c> **1** *v/t* agree (on); GRAM make agree **2** *v/i* (*essere d'accordo*) agree; (*coincidere*) tally

concordato 1 *agg* agreed on **2** *m* agreement; REL concordat; DIR settlement

concorde *agg* in agreement; (*unanime*) unanimous; (*simultaneo*) simultaneous

concordia *f* harmony

concorrente 1 *agg* (*rivale*) competing, rival **2** *m/f in una gara, gioco* competitor, contestant; FIN competitor

concorrenza *f* competition

concorrenziale competitive

concorrere <3o> (*contribuire*) concur; (*competere*) compete (**a** for); *di strade* converge; **~ per un posto** compete for a position

concorso 1 *pp* → **concorrere 2** *m* (*competizione*) competition, contest; **bandire un ~** announce a competition

concreto concrete; (*pratico*) practical

condanna *f* DIR sentence

condannare <1a> condemn (**a** to); DIR sentence (**a** to)

condensare <1b>, **condensarsi** condense

condensazione *f* condensation

condimento *m* seasoning; *di*

insalata dressing

condire <4d> season; *insalata* dress; *fig* spice up

condito seasoned

condividere <3q> share

condiviso *pp* → **condividere**

condizionale 1 *m/agg* conditional **2** *f* suspended sentence

condizionamento *m* PSI conditioning; **~ dell'aria** air conditioning

condizionare <1a> PSI condition

condizionato: con aria -a with air conditioning, air-conditioned

condizionatore *m* air conditioner

condizione *f* condition; **-i** *pl* **di lavoro** working conditions; **a ~ che** on condition that

condoglianze *fpl* condolences; **fare le ~ a qu** express one's condolences to s.o.

condominio *m* (*comproprietà*) joint ownership; *edificio* block of flats, *Am* condo

condomino *m* owner-occupier, *Am* condo owner

condonare <1a> remit

condono *m* remission; **~ fiscale** conditional amnesty for tax evaders

condotta *f* (*comportamento*) behavio(u)r; (*canale*) piping

condotto 1 *pp* → **condurre 2** *m* pipe; ANAT duct

conducente *m/f* driver; **~ di autobus** bus driver

condurre <3e> lead; (*accompagnare*) take; *veicolo* drive; *azienda* run; *acque, gas* carry, take

conduttore *m*, **-trice** *f* RAD, TV presenter; FERR (*controllore*) conductor

conduttura *f* (*condotto*) pipe

confederazione *f* confederation

conferenza *f* conference; **~ al vertice** summit (conference); **~ stampa** press conference

conferimento *m* conferring

conferire <4d> **1** *v/t* (*dare*) confer; *premio* award **2** *v/i*: **~ con qu** confer with s.o.

conferma *f* confirmation

confermare <1a> confirm

confessare <1b>, **confessarsi** confess

confessione *f* confession

confessore *m* confessor

confetto *m* GASTR sugared almond; MED pill

confettura *f* jam

confezionare <1a> *merce* wrap, package; *abiti* make

confezione *f* wrapping, packaging; *di abiti* making; **~ regalo** gift wrap; **-i** *pl* (*abiti*) garments

conficcare <1d> hammer, drive

confidare <1a> **1** *v/t* confide **2** *v/i*: **~ in** trust in, rely on

confidarsi: **~ con** confide in

confidenza *f* (*familiarità*) familiarity; (*fiducia*) confidence, trust; **avere ~ con qu** be familiar with s.o.; **prendere ~ con qc** familiarize o.s. with sth

confidenziale (*riservato*) confidential; **strettamente ~** strictly confidential

configurare <1a> configure

configurazione *f* configuration

confinante neighbo(u)ring

confinare <1a> border (**con** sth); *fig* confine

confine *m* border; *fra terreni, fig* boundary

confisca *f* (*pl* -che) seizure

confiscare <1d> confiscate

conflitto *m* conflict

confluire <4d> merge

confondere <3bb> confuse, mix up; (*imbarazzare*) embarrass

confondersi get mixed up

conformare <1a> (*rendere adatto*) adapt

conformarsi: **~ a** conform to; (*adattarsi*) adapt to

conforme (*simile*) similar; **~ a** in accordance with; **copia** *f* **~** (certified) true copy

conformismo *m* conformity

conformista *m/f* (*mpl* -i) conformist

conformità *f* conformity; **in ~ a** in accordance with

confortare <1c> comfort

confortevole comfortable

conforto *m* comfort

confrontare <1a> compare

confronto *m* confrontation; *(comparazione)* comparison; *a ~ di, in ~ a* compared with; *maleducato nei -i di qu* rude to s.o.

confusione *f* confusion; *(disordine)* muddle, mess; *(baccano)* noise, racket; *(imbarazzo)* embarrassment

confuso 1 *pp* → **confondere 2** *agg (non chiaro)* confused, muddled; *(imbarazzato)* embarrassed

congedare <1b> dismiss; MIL discharge

congedarsi take leave (*da* of)

congedo *m (permesso)* leave; MIL *assoluto* discharge

congelare <1b> **1** *v/t* freeze **2** *v/i e* **congelarsi** freeze

congelato frozen

congelatore *m* freezer

congenito congenital

congestionare <1a> congest

congestionato congested; *volto* flushed

congestione *f* congestion

congettura *f* conjecture

congiungere <3d> join

congiungersi join (up)

congiuntivite *f* conjunctivitis

congiuntivo *m* GRAM subjunctive

congiunto 1 *pp* → **congiungere 2** *m, -a f* relative, relation

congiuntura *f* ANAT joint; *~ economica* economic situation

congiunzione *f* GRAM conjunction

congiura *f* conspiracy, plot

congratularsi <1m>: *~ con qu* congratulate s.o. (*per* on)

congratulazioni *fpl*: *fare le propie ~ a qu* congratulate s.o.; *-i!* congratulations!

congressista *m/f (mpl* -i) convention participant

congresso *m* convention

conguaglio *m (pl* -gli) balance

CONI *abbr* (= *Comitato Olimpico Nazionale Italiano*) Italian Olympic Committee

coniare <1k & c> mint; *fig* coin

conifere *fpl* conifers

coniglio *m (pl* -gli) rabbit

coniugare <1l, c & e> conjugate

coniugato married

coniugazione *f* conjugation

coniuge *m/f* spouse; *-i pl* husband and wife; *i -i Rossi* Mr and Mrs Rossi

connazionale *m/f* compatriot

connessione *f* connection

connotati *mpl* features

cono *m* cone; *~ gelato* ice-cream cone

conoscente *m/f* acquaintance

conoscenza *f* knowledge; *persona* acquaintance; *(sensi)* consciousness; *per ~ cc*; *fare la ~ di qu* make s.o.'s acquaintance, meet s.o.; *perdere ~* lose consciousness, faint

conoscere <3n> know; *(fare la conoscenza di)* meet; *~ qu di vista* know s.o. by sight

conoscitore *m*, **-trice** *f* connoisseur

conosciuto well-known, famous

conquista *f* conquest

conquistare <1a> conquer; *fig* win

consacrare <1a> consecrate; *sacerdote* ordain; *(dedicare)* dedicate

consacrarsi devote o.s. (*a* to)

consacrazione *f* consecration; *di sacerdote* ordination

consanguineo *m*, **-a f** blood relative

consapevole: *~ di* conscious of, aware of

consapevolezza *f* consciousness, awareness

conscio conscious, aware

consecutivo *(di seguito)* consecutive; *tre giorni -i* three consecutive days, three days in a row

consegna *f di lavoro, documento* handing in; *di prigioniero, ostaggio* handover; *~ a domicilio* home delivery; *~ bagagli* left luggage, *Am* baggage checkroom

consegnare <1a> *lavoro, documento* hand in; *prigioniero, ostaggio* hand over; *merci, posta* deliver

conseguente consequent

conseguenza *f* consequence; *di ~* consequently; *in ~ qc* as a result of sth conseguire <4a> **1** v/t achieve; *laurea* obtain **2** v/i follow

consenso m (*permesso*) consent, permission

consentire <4b> **1** v/i (*accondiscendere*) consent **2** v/t allow

conserva f preserve; ~ **di pomodoro** tomato purée; ~ **di frutta** jam

conservante m preservative

conservare <1b> keep; GASTR preserve

conservarsi keep; *in salute* keep well

conservatore m, -**trice** f conservative

conservatorio m (*pl* -ri) music school, conservatoire

conservazione f preservation

considerare <1m> consider

considerazione f consideration; (*osservazione*) remark, comment; **prendere in** ~ take into consideration

considerevole considerable

consigliare <1g> advise; (*raccomandare*) recommend

consigliarsi ask for advice

consigliere m adviser; ~ **municipale** town council(l)or

consiglio m (*pl* -gli) piece of advice; (*organo amministrativo*) council; ~ **d'amministrazione** board (of directors); **Consiglio d'Europa** Council of Europe; ~ **dei ministri** Cabinet

consistente substantial; (*denso*) thick

consistenza f (*densità*) consistency, thickness; *di materiale* texture; *di argomento* basis

consistere <3f> consist (**in, di** of)

consocio m (*pl* -ci), -**a** f associate

consolare[1] <1c> console, comfort

consolare[2] agg consular

consolarsi console o.s.

consolato m consulate; ~ **generale** consulate general

consolazione f consolation

console[1] m *diplomatico* consul; ~ **generale** consul general

console[2] f *mobile* console

consolidare <1m & c> consolidate

consolidarsi stabilize

consonante f consonant

consorte m/f spouse; **principe** m ~ prince consort

consorzio m (*pl* -zi) *di imprese* consortium

constatare <1l> ascertain, determine; (*notare*) note

constatazione f statement

consueto usual

consuetudine f habit, custom; (*usanza*) custom, tradition

consulente m/f consultant; ~ **legale** legal adviser; ~ **tributario** tax consultant

consulenza f consultancy; ~ **aziendale** management consultancy

consultare <1a> consult

consultarsi: ~ **con qu** consult s.o.

consultazione f consultation; **opera** f di ~ reference book

consultorio m family planning clinic

consumare <1a> *acqua, gas* use, consume; (*logorare*) wear out; (*mangiare*) eat, consume; (*bere*) drink

consumarsi wear out

consumatore m, -**trice** f consumer

consumazione f food; (*bevanda*) drink

consumismo m consumerism

consumo m consumption; (*usura*) wear; **beni** mpl **di** ~ consumer goods

consuntivo m FIN closing balance

contabile m/f book keeper

contabilità f FIN *disciplina* accounting; *ufficio* accounts department; **tenere la** ~ keep the books

contachilometri m inv mileometer, clock F

contadino **1** agg rural, country attr **2** m, -**a** f peasant

contagiare <1f> infect

contagio m (*pl* -gi) infection; *per contatto diretto* contagion; (*epidemia*) outbreak

contagioso infectious

contagiri m inv rev(olution) counter

contagocce m inv dropper

container m inv container

contaminare <1m> contaminate, pollute

contaminazione *f* contamination, pollution

contante *m* cash; *in -i* cash

contare <1a> **1** *v/t* count **2** *v/i* count; *~ di fare qc* plan on doing sth

contascatti *m inv* time meter on phone

contatore *m* meter

contatto *m* contact

conte *m* count

contegno *m* behavio(u)r; *(atteggiamento)* restraint

contemplare <1b> contemplate; DIR provide for

contemplazione *f* contemplation

contemporaneamente at the same time

contemporaneo 1 *agg* contemporary *(di* with); *movimenti* simultaneous **2** *m*, *-a f* contemporary

contendere <3c> **1** *v/t: ~ qc a qu* compete with s.o. for sth **2** *v/i (competere)* contend

contendersi contend for, compete for

contenere <2q> contain, hold; *(reprimere)* repress; *(limitare)* limit

contenersi contain o.s.

contenitore *m* container

contentare <1b> please

contentarsi be content *(di* with)

contentezza *f* happiness

contento pleased *(di* with); *(lieto)* glad, happy

contenuto *m* contents *pl*

contesa *f* dispute

conteso *pp* → **contendere**

contessa *f* countess

contestare <1b> protest; DIR serve

contestatore *m*, *-trice f* protester

contestazione *f* protest

contesto *m* context

contiene → **contenere**

contiguo adjacent *(a* to)

continentale continental

continente *m* continent

continuare <1m> **1** *v/t* continue, carry on *(a fare* doing) **2** *v/i* continue

continuazione *f* continuation; *di film* sequel; *in ~* over and over again; *(ininterrottamente)* non stop

continuità *f* continuity

continuo *(ininterrotto)* continuous; *(molto frequente)* continual; *di ~ (ininterrottamente)* continuously; *(molto spesso)* continually; EL *corrente f -a* direct current

conto *m (calcolo)* calculation; FIN account; *in ristorante* bill, *Am* check; *~ corrente* current account, *Am* checking account; *~ corrente postale* Post Office account; *~ profitti e perdite* profit and loss account; *~ vincolato* term deposit; *rendere ~ di qc* account for sth; *rendersi ~ di qc* realize sth; *fare ~ su qu* count on s.o.; *tenere ~ di qc* take sth into account; *~ alla rovescia* countdown; *per ~ mio (secondo me)* in my opinion; *(da solo)* on my own; *sapere qc sul ~ di qu* know sth about s.o.; *in fin dei -i* when all's said and done, after all

contorcere <3d> twist

contorcersi: *~ dal dolore / dalle risate* roll about in pain / laughing

contorno *m* outline, contour; GASTR accompaniment

contorto twisted

contrabbandare <1a> smuggle

contrabbandiere *m* smuggler

contrabbando *m* contraband

contrabbasso *m* MUS double bass

contraccambiare <1k> return

contraccambio *m (pl* -bi) return

contraccettivo *m* contraceptive

contraccezione *f* contraception

contraccolpo *m* rebound; *di arma da fuoco* recoil

contraddire <3t> contradict

contraddizione *f* contradiction

contraffare <3aa> *(falsificare)* forge; *(imitare)* imitate

contraffatto forged; *voce* imitated

contraffazione *f (imitazione)* imitation; *(falsificazione)* forgery

contralto *m* MUS (contr)alto

contrappeso *m* counterbalance

contrapporre <3ll> set against

contrapporsi *(contrastare)* clash; *~ a* oppose

contrapposizione *f* opposition;

mettere in ~ contrast

contrapposto *pp* → **contrapporre**

contrariamente: ~ *a* contrary to

contrariare <1k> *piani* thwart, oppose; *persona* irritate, annoy

contrariato irritated, annoyed

contrarietà *fpl inv* difficulties, problems

contrario (*pl* -ri) **1** *agg* contrary; *direzione* opposite; *vento* adverse; *essere* ~ be against (*a* sth) **2** *m* contrary, opposite; *al* ~ on the contrary

contrarre <3xx> contract

contrarsi contract

contrassegnare <1a> mark

contrassegno *m* mark; FIN (*in*) ~ cash on delivery

contrastante contrasting

contrastare <1a> **1** *v/t* contrast; (*ostacolare*) hinder **2** *v/i* contrast (*con* with)

contrasto *m* contrast; (*litigio, discordia*) disagreement, dispute

contrattacco *m* (*pl* -cchi) counter-attack

contrattare <1a> negotiate; *persona* hire

contrattempo *m* hitch

contratto[1] *pp* → **contrarre**

contratto[2] *m* contract; ~ *d'affitto* lease

contrattuale contractual

contravvenire <4p> contravene

contravvenzione *f* contravention; (*multa*) fine

contrazione *f* contraction; (*riduzione*) reduction

contribuente *m/f* taxpayer

contribuire <4d> contribute

contributo *m* contribution; -*i pl sociali* social security (*Am* welfare) contributions

contro against

controbattere <3a> (*replicare*) answer back; (*confutare*) rebut

controcorrente 1 *agg* non-conformist **2** *avv* against the current; *in fiume* upstream

controffensiva counter-offensive

controfigura *f in film* stand in

controfirmare <1a> countersign

controindicazione *f* MED contraindication

controllare <1c> control; (*verificare*) check

controllo *m* control; (*verifica*) check; MED check-up; ~ *alla frontiera* customs inspection; ~ *dei biglietti* ticket inspection; ~ (*dei*) *passaporti* passport control; ~ *della qualità* quality control

controllore *m* controller; *di bus, treno* ticket inspector; ~ *di volo* air-traffic controller

controluce *f*: *in* ~ against the light

contromano: *andare a* ~ be going the wrong way

contromarca *f* (*pl* -che) token

contromisura *f* countermeasure

controproducente counterproductive

controproposta *f* counter-proposal

contrordine *m* counterorder

controsenso *m* contradiction in terms; (*assurdità*) nonsense

controversia *f* controversy, dispute; DIR litigation

controverso controversial

controvoglia unwillingly

contusione *f* bruise

contuso bruised

convalescente 1 *agg* convalescent **2** *m/f* person who is convalescent

convalescenza *f* convalescence; *essere in* ~ be convalescing

convalidare <1m> validate

convegno *m* convention; *luogo* meeting place

convenevoli *mpl* pleasantries

conveniente (*vantaggioso*) good; (*opportuno*) appropriate

convenienza *f di prezzo, offerta* good value; *di gesto* appropriateness; *fare qc per* ~ do sth out of self-interest

convenire <4p> **1** *v/i* gather, meet; (*concordare*) agree; (*essere opportuno*) be advisable, be better **2** *v/t* (*stabilire*) stipulate

convento *m di monache* convent; *di monaci* monastery

convenuto *pp* → **convenire**

convenzionale conventional

convenzione f convention; (*accordo*) agreement, convention

convergere <3uu> converge

conversare <1b> talk, make conversation

conversazione f conversation

conversione f conversion; AUTO U-turn

convertibile convertible

convertibilità f convertibility

convertire <4b or d> convert

convertirsi be converted

convincere <3d> convince

convinto pp → **convincere**

convinzione f conviction

convivente m/f common-law husband; *donna* common-law wife

convivenza f living together, cohabitation

convivere <3zz> live together

convocare <1l, c & d> call, convene

convocazione f calling, convening

convoglio m (pl -gli) MIL, MAR convoy; FERR train

cooperare <1m & c> co-operate (*a* in); (*contribuire*) contribute (*a* to)

cooperativa f: (*società* f) ~ co-operative; ~ **di consumo** cooperative (store)

cooperativo cooperative

cooperazione f cooperation

coordinamento m co-ordination

coordinare <1m> co-ordinate

coordinata f MAT co-ordinate

coordinatore m, **-trice** f co-ordinator

coordinazione f co-ordination

coperchio m (pl -chi) lid, top

coperta f blanket; MAR deck; ~ **imbottita** quilt

copertina f cover

coperto 1 pp → **coprire 2** agg covered (*di* with); *cielo* overcast, cloudy **3** m cover, shelter; *piatti e posate* place; *prezzo* cover charge; **essere al** ~ be under cover, be sheltered

copertone m AUTO tyre, Am tire

copertura f cover; ~ **delle spese** covering one's costs

copia f copy; FOT print, copy; **in**

duplice ~ in duplicate

copiare <1k & c> copy

copione m per attore script

copioso copious, abundant

copisteria f copy centre (Am center)

coppa f cup; (*calice*) glass; ~ (*di*) **gelato** dish of ice-cream; AUTO ~ **dell'olio** oil sump

coppetta f di gelato tub

coppia f couple, pair; **gara** f **a -e** doubles

copricapo m inv head covering

copricostume m inv beachrobe

coprifuoco m curfew

copriletto m inv bedspread, coverlet

coprire <4f & c> cover; *errore, suono* cover up

coprirsi (*vestirsi*) put something on; (*rannuvolarsi*) become overcast

coproduzione f co-production, joint production

coraggio m courage; (*sfacciataggine*) nerve; **farsi** ~ be brave

coraggioso brave, courageous

corallo m coral

Corano m Koran

corazza f MIL armo(u)r; ZO shell

corazzata f battleship

corazzato MIL armo(u)red; fig hardened (**contro** to)

corda f cord; (*fune*) rope; (*cordicella*) string; MUS string; ~ **vocale** vocal cord; **essere giù di** ~ feel down or depressed; **tenere qu sulla** ~ keep s.o. in suspense or on tenterhooks; **tagliare la** ~ cut and run

cordame m MAR rigging

cordata f ALP rope, roped party

cordiale 1 agg cordial; **-i saluti** mpl kind regards **2** m cordial

cordialità f cordiality

cordoglio m (*dolore*) grief, sorrow; (*condoglianze*) condolences pl

cordone m cord; di marciapiedi kerb, Am curb; (*sbarramento*) cordon; ~ **ombelicale** umbilical cord

coreografia f choreography

coreografo m, **-a** f choreographer

coriandolo m BOT coriander; **-i** mpl confetti

coricare <1l, c & d> (*adagiare*) lay

down; (*mettere a letto*) put to bed

coricarsi lie down

cornacchia f crow

cornamusa f bagpipes pl

cornea f cornea

cornetta f MUS cornet

cornetto m (*brioche*) croissant; (*gelato*) cone, cornet

cornice f frame

cornicione m ARCHI cornice

corno m (*pl gen* le corna) horn; *ramificate* antlers; **~ da scarpe** shoehorn; *fig* **fare le -a a qu** cheat on s.o. F; **facciamo le -a!** touch wood!; F **non m'importa un ~** I don't give a damn F

cornuto F cheated, betrayed

coro m chorus; *cantori* choir; **in ~** (*insieme*) all together

corona f crown; (*rosario*) rosary; **~ di fiori** wreath

coronaria f ANAT coronary artery

coronario: *vasi mpl* **-i** coronary arteries

corpetto m *da donna* bodice

corpo m body; MIL corps; **~ celeste** heavenly body; **~ diplomatico** diplomatic corps; **~ di ballo** dancers pl; **(a) ~ a ~** hand-to-hand

corporatura f build

corporazione f corporation

corpulento stout, corpulent

Corpus Domini m Corpus Christi

corredo m equipment; *da sposa* trousseau; *da neonato* layette

correggere <3cc> correct

correggersi correct o.s.

correlazione f correlation

corrente 1 agg current; *acqua* running; *lingua* fluent; **di uso** ~ in common use **2** m: **essere al** ~ know (*di* sth); **tenersi qu al** ~ keep s.o. up to date, keep s.o. informed **3** f current; *fig di opinione* trend; *fazione* faction; **~ continua** direct current; **~ d'aria** draught

correre <3o> **1** v/t run; **~ il pericolo** run the risk **2** v/i run; (*affrettarsi*) hurry; *di veicolo* speed; *di tempo* fly; **~ in aiuto di qu** rush to help s.o.; **~ dietro a qu** run after s.o.; **lascia ~!**

let it go!, leave it!; **corre voce** it is rumo(u)red

correttezza f correctness; (*onestà*) honesty

corretto 1 pp → **correggere 2** agg correct

correzione f TIP correction

corrida f bullfight

corridoio m (*pl* -oi) corridor; *in aereo, teatro* aisle

corridore m *in auto* racing driver; *a piedi* runner

corriera f coach, bus

corriere m courier; **~ della droga** drugs courier, mule P

corrispondente 1 agg corresponding **2** m/f correspondent; **~ estero** foreign correspondent

corrispondenza f correspondence; (*posta*) post; **vendita f per ~** mail order (shopping)

corrispondere <3hh> **1** v/t (*pagare*) pay; (*ricambiare*) reciprocate **2** v/i correspond; (*coincidere*) coincide; (*equivalere*) be equivalent

corrisposto 1 pp → **corrispondere 2** agg reciprocated

corrodere <3b>, **corrodersi** corrode, rust

corrompere <3rr> corrupt; *con denaro* bribe

corrosione f corrosion

corrosivo corrosive

corroso pp → **corrodere**

corrotto 1 pp → **corrompere 2** agg corrupt

corrugare <1e> wrinkle; **~ la fronte** frown

corruzione f corruption; *con denaro* bribery

corsa f run; *attività* running; *di autobus* trip, journey; (*gara*) race; **~ agli armamenti** arms race; **~ a ostacoli** *ippica* steeplechase; *atletica* hurdles; **di ~** at a run; *in fretta* in a rush; **vettura f da ~** racing car; **fare una ~** rush, dash; **-e** *pl* races

corsia f aisle; *di ospedale* ward; AUTO lane; **~ di emergenza** emergency lane; **~ di sorpasso** overtaking lane; **a tre -e** three-lane

Corsica *f* Corsica

corsivo *m* italics *pl*

corso[1] **1** *agg* Corsican **2** *m*, **-a** *f* Corsican

corso[2] **1** *pp* → **correre 2** *m* course; (*strada*) main street; FIN *di moneta* circulation; *di titoli* rate; **~ d'acqua** watercourse; **~ di lingue** language course; **~ dei cambi** exchange rate, rate of exchange; **~ di chiusura** closing rate; FIN **fuori ~** out of circulation; TIP **in ~ di stampa** being printed; **lavori** *mpl* **in ~** work in progress; **si sposeranno nel ~ dell'anno** they'll get married this year

corte *f* court; **Corte di giustizia europea** European Court of Justice

corteccia *f* (*pl* -cce) bark

corteggiare <1f> court

corteo *m* procession

cortese polite, courteous

cortesia *f* politeness, courtesy; **per ~!** please!

cortile *m* courtyard

cortina *f* curtain

corto short; **tagliar ~** cut it short; **essere a ~ di quattrini** be short of money

cortocircuito *m* short (circuit)

cortometraggio *m* short

corvo *m* rook; **~ imperiale** raven

cosa *f* thing; (*che*) **~** what; **qualche ~** something; **dimmi una ~** tell me something; **una ~ da nulla** a trifle; **un'altra ~** another thing; **-e** *pl* **da vedere** sights; **fra le altre -e** among other things; **tante belle -e!** all the best!

coscia *f* (*pl* -sce) thigh; GASTR leg

cosciente conscious

coscienza *f* conscience; (*consapevolezza*) consciousness; **agire secondo ~** listen to one's conscience; **senza coscienza** unscrupulous

coscienzioso conscientious

così so; (*in questo modo*) like this; **~ ~** so-so; **e ~ via** and so on; **per ~ dire** so to speak; **proprio ~!** exactly!; **basta ~!** that's enough!

cosicché and so

cosiddetto so called

cosiffatto such

cosmesi *f* cosmetics *pl*

cosmetico (*pl* -ci) **1** *agg* cosmetic **2** *m* cosmetic

cosmico (*pl* -ci) cosmic

cosmo *m* cosmos

cosmonauta *m/f* (*pl* -ti) cosmonaut

cosmopolita cosmopolitan

coso *m* F what-d'you-call-it F

cospargere <3uu> sprinkle; (*coprire*) cover (**di** with)

cosparso *pp* → **cospargere**

cospirare <1a> conspire

cospiratore *m*, **-trice** *f* conspirator

cospirazione *f* conspiracy

costa *f* coast, coastline; (*pendio*) hillside; ANAT rib; *di libro* spine

costante **1** *agg* constant, steady; MAT constant **2** *f* MAT constant

costanza *f* perseverance

costare <1c> cost; **~ caro** be expensive, cost a lot; *fig* cost dearly; **quanto costa?** how much is it?

costata *f* rib steak; **~ di agnello** lamb chop

costeggiare <1f> skirt, hug

costellazione f constellation

costiero coastal

costituire <4d> constitute; *società* form, create

costituirsi give o.s. up

costituzionale constitutional

costituzione *f* constitution

costo *m* cost; **~ della vita** cost of living; **prezzo** *m* **di ~** cost price; **-i** *pl* **di produzione** production costs; **a ~ di perdere** even if it means losing; **ad ogni ~** at all costs

costola *f* rib; *di libro* spine

costoletta *f* GASTR cutlet

costoro *pron pl* they; *complemento* them

costoso expensive, costly

costretto *pp* → **costringere**

costringere <3d> force, compel

costrizione *f* constraint

costruire <4d> build, construct

costruttivo *fig* constructive

costruttore *m*, **-trice** *f* builder; (*fab-*

bricante) manufacturer

costruzione *f* building, construction; GRAM construction

costui *pron m* he; *complemento* him

costume *m* (*usanza*) custom; (*condotta*) morals *pl*; (*indumento*) costume; **~ da bagno** swimming costume, swimsuit; *da uomo* (swimming) trunks; **~ nazionale** national costume

cotechino *m* kind of pork sausage

cotenna *f* pigskin; *della pancetta* rind

cotoletta *f* cutlet; **~ alla milanese** *breaded cutlet fried in butter*

cotone *m* cotton; MED **~ idrofilo** cotton wool, *Am* absorbent cotton

cotta *f* F crush

cottimo *m*: *lavorare a* **~** do piecework

cotto 1 *pp* → **cuocere 2** *agg* done, cooked; F *fig* head over heels in love (**di** with)

cottura *f* cooking

coupon *m inv* coupon

covare <1a> **1** *v/t* sit on, hatch; *fig malattia* sicken for, come down with; *rancore* harbo(u)r **2** *v/i* sit on eggs

covo *m* den; (*nido*) nest; *fig* hideout

covone *m* sheaf

cozza *f* mussel

cozzare <1c>: **~ contro** crash into; *fig* clash with

C.P. *abbr* (= **Casella Postale**) PO Box (= Post Office Box)

crac *m inv fig* crash

crampo *m* cramp

cranio *m* (*pl* -ni) skull

crash *m* INFOR: *andare in* **~** crash

cratere *m* crater

cravatta *f* tie; **~ a farfalla** bow-tie

crawl *m* SP crawl, freestyle

creare <1b> create; *fig* (*causare*) cause

creatività *f* creativity

creativo 1 *agg* creative **2** *m* copywriter

creato 1 *pp* → **creare 2** *m* creation

creatore 1 *agg* creative **2** *m* Creator **3** *m*, **-trice** *f* creator

creatura *f* creature

creazione *f* creation

credente *m/f* believer

credenza[1] *f* belief

credenza[2] *f* mobile dresser

credenziali *fpl* credentials

credere <3a> **1** *v/t* believe; (*pensare*) believe, think; *lo credo bene!* I should think so too!; **credersi** believe *or* think o.s. to be **2** *v/i* believe; **~ a qu** believe s.o.; **~ in qu** believe in s.o.; *credo in Dio* I believe in God; *non ci credo* I don't believe it; *non credevo ai miei occhi* I couldn't believe my eyes

credibile credible

credibilità *f* credibility

credito *m* credit; *fig* trust; (*attendibilità*) reliability; *comprare a* **~** buy on credit; *dare* **~ a qc** believe sth; *fare* **~ a qu** give s.o. credit

creditore *m*, **-trice** *f* creditor

credo *m inv* credo

crema *f* cream; *di latte e uova* custard; **~ da barba** shaving foam; **~ idratante** moisturizer, moisturizing cream; **~ solare** suntan lotion

cremare <1b> cremate

cremazione *f* cremation

cren *m* horseradish

crepa *f* crack

crepaccio *m* (*pl* -cci) cleft; *di ghiacciaio* crevasse

crepare <1b> (*spaccarsi*) crack; F (*morire*) kick the bucket F; **~ dalle risa** split one's sides laughing

crêpe *f inv* pancake

crepitare <1l & b> crackle

crepuscolo *m* twilight

crescendo *m* MUS crescendo

crescente growing; *luna* waxing

crescere <3n> **1** *v/t* bring up, raise **2** *v/i* grow; (*aumentare*) grow, increase

crescione *m* watercress

crescita *f* growth; (*aumento*) growth, increase; **~ economica** economic growth

cresima *f* confirmation

cresimare <1l & b> confirm

crespo *capelli* frizzy

cresta *f* crest; *di montagna* peak

creta *f* clay

cretino F **1** *agg* stupid, idiotic **2** *m*, **-a** *f* idiot

CRI *abbr* (= *Croce Rossa Italiana*) Italian Red Cross

cric *m inv* AUTO jack

criminale 1 *agg* criminal **2** *m/f* criminal; ~ **di guerra** war criminal

criminalità *f* crime

criminalizzare <1a> criminalize

crimine *m* crime

criniera *f* mane

cripta *f* crypt

crisantemo *m* chrysanthemum

crisi *f* crisis; MED fit; ~ **energetica** energy crisis; ~ **degli alloggi** housing shortage

cristallizzare, **cristallizzarsi** <1a> crystallize

cristallo *m* crystal; **bicchiere** *m* **di** ~ crystal glass

cristianesimo *m* Christianity

cristianità *f* (*i cristiani*) Christendom

cristiano 1 *agg* Christian **2** *m*, **-a** *f* Christian

Cristo *m* Christ

criterio *m* (*pl* -ri) criterion; (*buon senso*) common sense

critica *f* (*pl* -che) criticism

criticare <1l & d> criticize

critico (*pl* -ci) **1** *agg* critical **2** *m*, **-a** *f* critic

croato 1 *agg* Croatian **2** *m*, **-a** *f* Croat, Croatian

Croazia *f* Croatia

croccante 1 *agg* crisp, crunchy **2** *m* GASTR nut brittle

crocchetta *f* GASTR potato croquette

croce *f* cross; **Croce Rossa** Red Cross; **farsi il segno della** ~ cross o.s.; **a occhio e** ~ at a rough guess

crocevia *m* crossroads *inv*

crociata *f* crusade

crociera *f* cruise; ARCHI crossing; **velocità** *f* **di** ~ cruising speed

crocifiggere <3mm> crucify

crocifissione *f* crucifixion

crocifisso 1 *pp* → **crocifiggere 2** *m* crucifix

croco *m* BOT crocus

crollare <1c> collapse

crollo *m* collapse

cromare <1c> chromium-plate

cromatico (*pl* -ci) MUS chromatic

cromo *m* chrome

cronaca *f* (*pl* -che) chronicle; *di partita* commentary; **fatto di** ~ news item; ~ **nera** crime news; **essere al centro della** ~ be front-page news

cronico (*pl* -ci) chronic

cronista *m/f* (*mpl* -i) reporter; *di partita* commentator

cronologia *f* chronology

cronologico (*pl* -ci) chronological

cronometrare <1a> time

cronometro *m* chronometer; SP stopwatch

crosta *f* crust; MED scab; *di formaggio* rind

crostacei *mpl* shellfish

crostata *f* GASTR tart

crostino *m* GASTR crouton

cruciale crucial

cruciverba *m inv* crossword (puzzle)

crudele cruel

crudeltà *f* cruelty

crudo raw

crumiro *m*, **-a** *f* scab

crusca *f* bran

cruscotto *m* dashboard; *scomparto* glove compartment

c.s. *abbr* (= *come sopra*) as above

CSI *abbr* (= *Comunità di Stati Indipendenti*) CIS (= Commonwealth of Independent States)

c.to *abbr* (= *conto*) acct (= account)

Cuba *f* Cuba

cubano 1 *agg* Cuban **2** *m*, **-a** *f* Cuban

cubetto *m* (small) cube; ~ **di ghiaccio** ice cube

cubico (*pl* -ci) cubic

cubo 1 *agg* cubic **2** *m* cube

cuccagna *f*: (*paese m della*) ~ land of plenty

cuccetta *f* FERR couchette; MAR berth

cucchiaiata *f* spoonful

cucchiaino *m* teaspoon

cucchiaio *m* (*pl* -ai) spoon; ~ **da**

tavola tablespoon

cuccia *f* (*pl* -cce) dog's basket; *esterna* kennel

cucciolo *m* cub; *di cane* puppy

cucina *f* kitchen; *cibi* food; ~ *casalinga* home cooking; ~ *a gas* gas cooker *or* stove; *libro di* ~ cook book

cucinare <1a> cook

cucinino *m* kitchenette

cucire <4a> sew; *macchina f da* ~ sewing-machine

cucito 1 *agg* sewn **2** *m* sewing

cucitura *f* seam

cuculo *m* cuckoo

cuffia *f da piscina* swimming cap; RAD, TV headphones *pl*; ~ *da bagno* shower cap

cugino *m*, *-a f* cousin

cui *persona* who, whom *fml*; *cose* which; *la casa in* ~ *abitano* the house they live in, the house in which they live, the house where they live; *il* ~ *nome* whose name; *per* ~ so

culinario cookery *attr*, culinary; *arte f -a* culinary art, cookery

culla *f* cradle

cullare <1a> rock

culminante: *punto m* ~ climax

culminare <1l> culminate

culmine *m* peak

culo ∨ *m* arse ∨, *Am* ass ∨

culto *m* cult; *religione* religion

cultura *f* culture; ~ *di massa* mass culture; ~ *generale* general knowledge

culturale cultural

culturismo *m* body-building

cumulativo cumulative; *biglietto m* ~ group ticket

cumulo *m* heap, pile

cuneo *m* wedge

cunetta *f fondo stradale* bump

cuocere <3p> cook; *pane* bake

cuoco *m* (*pl* -chi), *-a f* cook

cuoio *m* leather; ~ *capelluto* scalp; F

tirare le -a kick the bucket F

cuore *m* heart; *carte -i* ∨ *pl* hearts; *di* ~ wholeheartedly; *senza* ~ heartless; *fig nel* ~ *di* in the heart of; *nel* ~ *della notte* in the middle of the night; *stare a* ~ *a qu* be very important to s.o.

cupo gloomy; *suono* deep

cupola *f* dome

cura *f* care; MED treatment; ~ *dimagrante* diet; *avere* ~ *di qc* take care of sth; *casa f di* ~ nursing home

curabile curable

curare <1a> take care of; MED treat

curarsi look after o.s.; *non curarti di loro* don't care about them

curato *m* parish priest

curatore *m*, *-trice f fiduciario* trustee; *di testo* editor; ~ *fallimentare* official receiver

curia *f* curia

curiosare <1a> have a look around; *spreg* pry (*in* into)

curiosità *f inv* curiosity

curioso curious

cursore *m* INFOR cursor

curva *f* curve

curvare <1a> curve; *schiena* bend

curvarsi bend

curvatura *f* curve

curvo curved; *persona* bent

cuscinetto *m* TEC bearing; ~ *a sfere* ball bearing; POL *stato m* ~ buffer state

cuscino *m* cushion; (*guanciale*) pillow

custode *m/f* caretaker; *angelo m* ~ guardian angel

custodia *f* care; DIR custody; (*astuccio*) case

custodire <4d> (*conservare*) keep

cute *f* skin

CV *abbr* (= *Cavallo Vapore*) HP (= horsepower); (= *curriculum vitae*) CV (= curriculum vitae)

cyclette *f* exercise bike

da *prp stato in luogo* at; *moto da luogo* from; *moto a luogo* to; *tempo* since; *con verbo passivo* by; *viene ~ Roma* he comes from Rome; *sono ~ mio fratello* I'm at my brother's (place); *ero ~ loro* I was at their place; *passo ~ Firenze* I'm going via Florence; *vado dal medico* I'm going to the doctor's; *~ ieri* since yesterday; *~ oggi in poi* from now on, starting from today; *~ bambino* as a child; *l'ho fatto ~ me* I did it myself; *qualcosa ~ mangiare* something to eat; *francobollo ~ 1000 lire* 1000 lire stamp; *la donna ~i capelli grigi* the woman with grey hair

dà → **dare**

daccapo → **capo**

dado *m* dice; GASTR stock cube; TEC nut

dagli *prp* **da** *and art* **gli**

dai[1] *prp* **da** *and art* **i**

dai[2] → **dare**

daino *m* deer; (*pelle*) buckskin

dal *prp* **da** *and art* **il**

dalia *f* dahlia

dall', **dalla**, **dalle**, **dallo** *prp* **da** *and art* **l'**, **la**, **le**, **lo**

daltonico *agg* (*pl* -ci) colo(u)r-blind

dama *f* lady; *gioco* draughts, *Am* checkers

damasco *m* (*pl* -chi) damask

damigiana *f* demijohn

danaro *m* → **denaro**

danese 1 *m/agg* Danish **2** *m/f* Dane

Danimarca *f* Denmark

danneggiare <1f> (*rovinare*) damage; (*nuocere*) harm

danno *m* damage; (*a persona*) harm; *risarcire i ~i a qu* compensate s.o. for the damage; *~i pl all'ambiente* environmental damage, damage to the environment

dannoso harmful

danza *f* dance; *~ classica* ballet

danzare <1a> *v/t & v/i* dance

dappertutto everywhere

dappoco *agg inv* (*inetto*) worthless; (*irrilevante*) minor, unimportant

dapprima at first

dare <1r> **1** *v/t* give; *~ qc a qu* give s.o. sth, give sth to s.o.; *~ uno sguardo a qc* have a look at sth; *dammi del tu* call me 'tu'; *mi dia del lei* address me as 'lei'; SP *il via* give the off; *fig ~ il via a qc* get sth under way **2** *v/i di finestra* overlook (*su* sth); *di porta* lead into (*su* sth); *fig ~ nell'occhio* attract attention, be noticed **3** *m* FIN debit; *~ e avere* debit and credit

darsi *v/r* give each other; (*dedicarsi*) devote o.s. (*a* to); *~ al commercio* go into business; *darsela a gambe* take to one's heels; *può ~* perhaps

darsena *f* dock

data *f* date; *~ di nascita* date of birth; *~ di scadenza* expiry date; *senza indicazione di ~* undated

datare <1a> **1** *v/t* date; *lettera* date, put the date on **2** *v/i*: *a ~ da oggi* from today

dato 1 *pp* → **dare 2** *agg* (*certo*) given, particular; (*dedito*) addicted (*a* to); *in -i casi* in certain cases; *~ che* given that **3** *m* piece of data; *-i pl* data; INFOR *elaborazione f dei dati* data processing; *supporto m ~* data medium

datore *m*, **-trice** *f*: *~ di lavoro* employer

dattero *m* date; (*albero*) date palm

dattilografare <1n> type

dattilografia *f* typing

dattilografo *m*, **-a** *f* typist

davanti 1 *prp*: *~ a* in front of **2** *avv* in front; (*dirimpetto*) opposite; *se mi stai ~* if you stand in front of me

3 *agg inv* front **4** *m* front

davanzale *m* window sill

davanzo more than enough

davvero really

dazio *m* (*pl* -zi) duty; (*posto*) customs; **~ d'importazione** import duty; **~ d'esportazione** export duty; **esente da ~** duty-free

d.C. *abbr* (**= dopo Cristo**) AD (= anno domini)

dea *f* goddess

debito 1 *agg* due, proper **2** *m* debt; (*dovere*) duty; FIN **~ pubblico** national debt; **avere un ~ con qu** be in debt to s.o.; *fig* **sentirsi in ~ verso qu** feel indebted to s.o.

debitore *m*, **-trice** *f* debtor; **essere ~ di qc a qu** owe s.o. sth, owe sth to s.o.

debole 1 *agg* weak; (*voce*) weak, faint; (*luce*) dim **2** *m* weakness; **avere un ~ per qu** have a soft spot for s.o.

debolezza *f* weakness

debuttante *m/f* beginner; *artista* performer at the start of his / her career

debuttare <1a> make one's début

debutto *m* début

decadente decadent

decadenza *f* decadence

decaffeinato decaffeinated, decaff F

decalcomania *f* transfer, *Am* decal

decano *m* dean

decappottabile *f/agg* AUTO convertible

decathlon *m* decathlon

decedere <3l> **è deceduto ieri** he died yesterday

decelerare <1b & m> *v/t & v/i* slow down

decennio *m* (*pl* -ni) decade

decente *agg* decent

decentramento *m* decentralization

decentrare <1b> decentralize

decesso *m* death

decidere <3q> **1** *v/t questione* settle; *data* decide on, settle on; **~ di fare qc** decide to do sth **2** *v/i* decide

decidersi decide (**a** to), make up one's mind (**a** to)

decifrare <1a> decipher

decimale *m/agg* decimal

decimetro *m* decimetre, *Am* -meter

decimo *m/agg* tenth

decina *f* MATH ten; **una ~** about ten

decisione *f* decision; (*risolutezza*) decisiveness; **prendere una ~** make a decision; **~ della maggioranza** majority decision

decisivo decisive

deciso 1 *pp* → **decidere 2** *agg* (*definito*) definite; (*risoluto*) determined; (*netto*) clear; (*spiccato*) marked

declassare <1a> *oggetto* downgrade; *persona* demote

declinare <1a> **1** *v/t* decline; **~ ogni responsabilità** disclaim all responsibility **2** *v/i* (*tramontare*) set; (*diminuire*) decline

declinazione *f* GRAM declension

declino *m* fig decline

decodificatore *m* decoder

decollare <1c> take off

decollo *m* take-off

decomporre <3ll> **1** *v/i* (*putrefarsi*) decompose **2** *v/t* CHIM break down

decomposizione *f* decomposition; CHIM breaking down

decompressione *f* decompression

decongestionare <1a> *strada*, MED relieve congestion in; **~ il traffico** relieve traffic congestion

decorare <1b> decorate

decoratore *m*, **-trice** *f* decorator

decorazione *f* decoration

decoro *m* decorum

decoroso decorous

decorrenza *f*: **con immediata ~** with immediate effect

decorrere <3o> *v/i* pass; **a ~ da oggi** with effect from today

decorso 1 *pp* → **decorrere 2** *m di malattia* course

decrepito decrepit

decrescere <3n> decrease, fall

decreto *m* decree; **~-legge** *m* decree passed in exceptional circumstances that has the force of law

dedica *f* (*pl* -che) dedication

dedicare <1b & d> dedicate

dedicarsi dedicate o.s.

dedito dedicated (**a** to); *a un vizio* addicted (**a** to)

dedizione *f* dedication

dedurre <3e> deduce; FIN deduct; (*derivare*) derive

deduttivo deductive

deduzione *f* deduction

defalcare <1d> deduct

defalco *m* (*pl* -chi) deduction

defezione *f* defection

deficiente **1** *agg* (*mancante*) deficient, lacking (**di** in) **2** *m/f* backward person; *insulto* idiot, moron

deficienza *f* (*scarsezza*) deficiency, lack (**di** of)

deficit *m inv* deficit; **~ del bilancio pubblico** budget deficit, public spending deficit

definire <4d> define; (*risolvere*) settle

definitivo definitive

definizione *f* definition; DIR settlement

deflettore *m* AUTO quarterlight

deflusso *m* ebb

deformare <1a> deform; *legno* warp; *metallo* buckle; *fig* distort

deformarsi *di legno* warp; *di metallo* buckle; *di scarpe* lose their shape

deformazione *f* deformation; *di legno* warping; *di metallo* buckling; *fisica* deformity; *fig*, OTT distortion

deforme deformed

defunto 1 *agg* dead; *fig* defunct **2** *m*, **-a** *f* DIR: **il ~** the deceased

degenerare <1m & b> degenerate (**in** into)

degente *m/f* patient

degenza *f* stay (in bed / hospital)

degli *prp* **di** and *art* **gli**

degnare <1a> **1** *v/t*: **~ qu di una parola** deign to speak to s.o. **2** *v/i* e **degnarsi**: **~ di** deign to, condescend to

degno worthy; **~ di nota** noteworthy; **~ di un re** fit for a king

degradante degrading, demeaning

degradare <1a> degrade; *da un rango* demote

degradarsi demean o.s., lower o.s.; CHIM degrade; *di ambiente, edifici* deteriorate

degradazione *f* degradation

degrado *m* deterioration; **~ ambientale** damage to the environment

degustazione *f* tasting; **~ del vino** wine tasting

dei[1] *prp* **di** and *art* **i**

dei[2] (*pl di* **dio**): **gli ~** *mpl* the Gods

del *prp* **di** and *art* **il**

delatore *m*, **-trice** *f* informer

delega *f* (*pl* -ghe) delegation; (*procura*) proxy

delegare <ll & b & e> delegate

delegato 1 *agg*: **amministratore** *m* **~** managing director **2** *m*, **-a** *f* delegate; **~ sindacale** (trade) union delegate

delegazione *f* delegation

delfino *m* dolphin

deliberare <1m> **1** *v/t* decide **2** *v/i* DIR deliberate (**su** on)

delicatezza *f* delicacy; (*discrezione*) tact, delicacy; (*debolezza*) frailty, delicacy

delicato delicate; (*persona*) frail, delicate; (*colore*) soft

delimitare <1m> define

delineare <1m> outline

delinquente *m/f* criminal; *fig* scoundrel; **~ minorile** juvenile delinquent

delinquenza *f* crime; **~ minorile** juvenile delinquency; **~ organizzata** organized crime

delirare <1a> be in raptures, rave; MED be delirious

delirio *m* (*pl* -ri) delirium; *fig* frenzy

delitto *m* crime; **corpo** *m* **del ~** corpus delicti

delizia *f* delight

delizioso delightful; *cibo* delicious

dell', **della**, **delle**, **dello** *prp* **di** and *art* **l'**, **la**, **le**, **lo**

delta *m* delta

deltaplanista *m/f* (*mpl* -ti) hang-glider

deltaplano *m* hang-glider; *attività* hang-gliding

deludere <3q> disappoint

delusione *f* disappointment

deluso disappointed

demagogo *m* (*pl* -ghi) demagog(ue)

demanio *m* State property

demente *m/f* MED person with dementia; F lunatic F

demenza *f* MED dementia; F lunacy F, madness F

democratico ⟨*pl* -ci⟩ **1** *agg* democratic **2** *m*, **-a** *f* democrat

democrazia *f* democracy

democristiano *m/agg* Christian Democrat

demografia *f* demography

demografico demographic

demolire ⟨4d⟩ demolish (*anche fig*); *macchine* crush

demolizione *f* demolition; *di macchine* crushing

demone *m* spirit

demonio *m* ⟨*pl* -ni⟩ devil

demoralizzarsi ⟨1a⟩ become demoralized, lose heart

demotivato demotivated

denaro *m* money; ~ **contante** cash

denatalità *f* decline in the birth rate

denaturato CHIM: **alcol** *m* ~ methlyated spirits *pl*

denominare ⟨1m & c⟩ name, call

denominazione *f* name; ~ **di origine controllata** term signifying that a wine is of a certain origin and quality

denotare ⟨11 & b or c⟩ denote, be indicative of

densità *f* density; *della nebbia* thickness, density; ~ **della popolazione** population density

denso dense; *fumo, nebbia* thick, dense

dentario ⟨*pl* -ri⟩ dental

dentata *f* bite; *segno* toothmark

dente *m* tooth; ~ **del giudizio** wisdom tooth; ~ **di leone** dandelion; **mal** *m* **di** *-i* toothache; *fig* **stringere i** *-i* grit one's teeth; *parlare fra i -i* mumble; GASTR **al** ~ al dente, *still slightly firm*

dentice *m* fish native to the Mediterranean

dentiera *f* dentures

dentifricio *m* ⟨*pl* -ci⟩ toothpaste

dentista *m/f* ⟨*mpl* -ti⟩ dentist

dentro 1 *prp* in, inside; (*entro*) within;

~ **di sé** inwardly **2** *avv* in, inside; (*nell'intimo*) inwardly; **qui/lì** ~ in here/there; F **metter** ~ put inside *or* away F

denuclearizzato nuclear-free, denuclearized

denuncia *f* ⟨*pl* -ce⟩ denunciation; *alla polizia, alla società di assicurazione* complaint, report; *di nascita, morte* registration; ~ **dei redditi** income tax return

denunciare ⟨1f⟩ denounce; *alla polizia, alla società di assicurazione* report; *nascita* register

denunzia → **denuncia**

denutrito undernourished

deodorante *m* deodorant

depilare ⟨1a⟩ *con pinzette* pluck; *con rasoio* shave; *con ceretta* wax

depilatorio ⟨*pl* -ri⟩ **1** *agg* depilatory **2** *m* hair-remover, depilatory

dépliant *m inv* leaflet; (*opuscolo*) brochure

deplorare ⟨1c⟩ deplore

deplorevole deplorable

deporre ⟨3ll⟩ **1** *v/t* put down; *uova* lay; *re, presidente* depose; ~ **il falso** commit perjury **2** *v/i* DIR testify, give evidence (**a favore di** for, **a carico di** against)

deportare ⟨1c⟩ deport

depositare ⟨1m & c⟩ deposit; (*posare*) put down, deposit; (*registrare*) register

depositato: marchio *m* ~ registered trademark

deposito *m* deposit; (*magazzino*) warehouse; MIL, *rimessa* depot; FERR ~ **bagagli** left-luggage office, *Am* baggage checkroom; ~ **di munizioni** ammunition dump; FIN ~ **vincolato** term deposit

deposizione *f* deposition; *da un'alta carica* removal; *di regnante*; overthrow

deposto *pp* → **deporre**

depravato *m*, **-a** *f* depraved person

depressione *f* depression; ~ **atmosferica** atmospheric depression; **zona** *f* **di** ~ **atmosferica** area of low pressure, low

depresso 1 *pp* → **deprimere 2** *agg* depressed

deprezzamento *m* depreciation

deprezzare <1b> lower the value of

deprezzare depreciate

deprimente depressing

deprimere <3r> depress

deprimersi get depressed

depurare <1a> purify

depuratore *m* purifier

depurazione *f* purification; *impianto m di ~* purification plant

deputato *m*, *-a f Member of Parliament*, *Am Representative*

deragliare <1g> FERR go off *or* leave the rails; *far ~* derail

deridere <3g> deride

derisione *f* derision

deriso *pp* → **deridere**

deriva *f* MAR drift; *andare alla ~* drift

derivare <1a> **1** *v/t* derive **2** *v/i*: *~ da* come from, derive from

derivazione *f* derivation; (*discendenza*) origin; EL shunt; TELEC extension

dermatologia *f* dermatology

dermatologo *m* (*pl -gi*), *-a f* dermatologist

derrate *fpl* food

derubare <1a> rob

descritto *pp* → **descrivere**

descrivere <3tt> describe

descrizione *f* description

deserto 1 *agg* deserted; *isola f -a* desert island **2** *m* desert

desiderare <1m> (*volere*) want, wish; *intensamente* long for, crave; *sessualmente* desire; *desidera?* can I help you?; *farsi ~* play hard to get; (*tardare*) keep people waiting; *lascia a ~* it leaves a lot to be desired

desiderio *m* (*pl -ri*) wish (*di* for); *intenso* longing (*di* for); *sessuale* desire (*di* for)

design *m inv* design

designare <1a> (*nominare*) appoint, name; (*fissare*) fix, set

designer *m/f inv* designer

desistere <3f>: *~ da* desist from

desolante distressing

desolato desolate; *sono ~!* I am so sorry

desolazione *f* desolation; (*dolore*) distress

dessert *m inv* dessert

destare <1a> *fig* (a)rouse, awaken

destarsi *fig* be aroused, be awakened

destinare <1a> destine; (*assegnare*) assign; *con il pensiero* mean, intend; *data* fix, set; (*indirizzare*) address (*a* to)

destinatario *m* (*pl -ri*), *-a f di lettera* addressee

destinazione *f*: (*luogo m di*) *~* destination

destino *m* destiny

destra *f* right; (*mano*) right hand; *a ~ stato* on the right, to the right; *moto* to the right

destreggiarsi <1f> manœuvre, *Am* maneuver

destrezza *f* skill, dexterity

destro right; (*abile*) skil(l)ful, dexterous

destrorso 1 *agg persona* right-handed; TEC clockwise **2** *m*, *-a f* right-hander, right-handed person

detenere <2q> hold; *in prigione* detain, hold

detenuto *m*, *-a f* prisoner

detenzione *f imprigionamento* detention; *~ abusiva di armi* possession of illegal weapons

detergente *m* detergent; *per cosmesi* cleanser

deteriorabile perishable

deteriorarsi <1a> deteriorate

determinare <1m & b> determine, establish; (*causare*) cause, lead to

determinato certain; (*specifico*) particular, specific; (*risoluto*) determined

determinazione *f* determination

detersivo *m* detergent; *per piatti* washing-up liquid, *Am* dishwashing liquid; *per biancheria* detergent, *Br* washing powder

detestare <1b> hate, detest

detonare <1c> detonate

detrarre <3xx> deduct (*da* from)

detratto

86

detratto pp → **detrarre**

detrazione f deduction

detrito m debris; GEOL detritus

detta f: **a ~ di** according to

dettaglio m (pl -gli) detail; FIN **commercio m al ~** retail trade

dettare <1a> dictate; **~ legge** lay down the law

dettato m dictation

dettatura f dictation; **scrivere sotto ~** take dictation

detto 1 pp → **dire**; **~ fatto** no sooner said than done; **come non ~** let's forget it **2** agg said; (soprannominato) known as **3** m saying

devastare <1a> devastate

devastazione f devastation

deve, **devi** → **dovere**

deviare <1h> **1** v/t traffico, sospetti divert **2** v/i deviate

deviazione f deviation; di traffico diversion

devo → **dovere**

devolvere <3g> POL devolve

devoluto pp → **devolvere**

devoluzione f POL devolution

devoto 1 agg devoted; REL devout **2** m, **-a** f devotee; REL **i ~i** the devout

devozione f devotion; REL devoutness

di 1 prp of; con il comparativo than; **~ ferro** (made of) iron; **io sono ~ Roma** I'm from Rome; **l'auto ~ mio padre** my father's car; **una tazza ~ caffè** a cup of coffee; **~ giorno** by day; **parlare ~ politica** talk about politics; **d'estate** in the summer; **~ questo passo** at this rate; **~ chi è questo libro?** whose is this book?, who does this book belong to?; **più bello ~** prettier than **2** art some; interrogativo any, some; neg any; **del vino** some wine

di' → **dire**

dia → **dare**

diabete m diabetes

diabetico (pl -ci) **1** agg diabetic **2** m, **-a** f diabetic

diadema m diadem

diaframma m (pl -i) diaphragm

diagnosi f inv diagnosis

diagnosticare <1n, c & d> diagnose

diagonale 1 agg diagonal **2** f diagonal (line)

diagramma m (pl -i) diagram

dialetto m dialect

dialisi f inv dialysis

dialogo m (pl -ghi) dialog(ue)

diamante m diamond

diametro m diameter

diapason m inv tuning fork

diapositiva f FOT slide

diario m (pl -ri) diary

diarrea f diarrh(o)ea

diavolo m devil; **un buon ~** a good fellow; **mandare qu al ~** tell s.o. to get lost

dibattere <3a> debate, discuss

dibattersi struggle; fig struggle (**in** with)

dibattito m debate

dicembre m December

diceria f rumo(u)r

dichiarare <1a> state; ufficialmente declare; nei giochi di carte bid; **ha qualcosa da ~?** anything to declare?

dichiararsi declare o.s.

dichiarazione f declaration; **~ dei redditi** income tax statement; **~ doganale** customs declaration

diciannove nineteen

diciannovesimo m/agg nineteenth

diciassette seventeen

diciassettesimo m/agg seventeenth

diciottenne m/f eighteen-year-old

diciotto eighteen

diciottesimo m/agg eighteenth

didattica f didactics

didattico (pl -ci) didactic

dieci ten; **alle/verso le ~** at/about ten (o'clock)

diesel m diesel

dieta f diet; **essere a ~** be on a diet

dietetica f dietetics

dietetico (pl -ci) diet attr

dietista m/f dietitian, dietician

dietro 1 prp behind; **~ l'angolo** round the corner; **~ di me** behind me; **uno ~ l'altro** nello spazio one behind the other; nel tempo one after the other; **~ ricevuta** on receipt

2 *avv* behind; *in auto* in the back; *di ~ stanza, porta* back; *zampe* hind; AUTO rear **3** *m inv* back

difatti *cong* in fact

difendere <3c> defend; (*proteggere*) protect

difensiva *f* defensive; *stare sulla ~* be on the defensive

difensivo defensive

difensore *m* defender; *~ d'ufficio* legal aid lawyer, *Am* public defender

difesa *f* defence, *Am* defense; *~ dei consumatori* consumer protection; *legittima ~* self-defence (*Am* -defense)

difeso *pp → difendere*

difetto *m* (*imperfezione*) defect; *morale* fault, flaw; (*mancanza*) lack; *far ~* be lacking

difettoso defective

diffamare <1a> slander; *scrivendo* libel

diffamazione *f* defamation of character

differente different (*da* from, *Am* than)

differenza *f* difference; *~ di prezzo* difference in price; *a ~ di* unlike

differenziare <1f> differentiate

differenziarsi differ (*da* from)

differire <4d> postpone

difficile difficult; (*improbabile*) unlikely

difficoltà *f inv* difficulty; *senza ~* easily, without any difficulty

diffida *f* DIR injunction

diffidare <1a> **1** *v/t* DIR issue an injunction against; *~ qu dal fare qc* warn s.o. not to do sth **2** *v/i*: *~ di qu* distrust s.o., mistrust s.o.

diffidente distrustful, mistrustful

diffidenza *f* distrust, mistrust

diffondere <3bb> diffuse; *fig* spread

diffondersi *fig* spread; (*dilungarsi*) enlarge

diffusione *f di luce, calore* diffusion; *di giornale* circulation

diffuso 1 *pp → diffondere* **2** *agg* widespread; (*luce*) diffuse

difterite *f* diphtheria

diga *f* (*pl* -ghe) *fluviale* dam; *litoranea*

dyke; *portuale* breakwater

digerire <4d> digest; F (*tollerare*) stomach F

digestione *f* digestion

digestivo 1 *agg* digestive **2** *m* after-dinner drink, digestif

digitale digital; *impronta ~* fingerprint

digitare <1l> INFOR key

digiunare <1a> fast

digiuno 1 *agg* fasting; *fig privo* lacking (*di* in); *essere ~ di notizie* have no news, not have any news **2** *m* fast; *a ~* on an empty stomach

dignità *f* dignity

dignitoso dignified

digrignare <1a> gnash

dilagare <1e> flood; *fig* spread rapidly

dilaniare <1k> tear apart

dilapidare <1m> squander

dilatare <1a> FIS expand; *occhi* open wide

dilatarsi *di materiali, metalli* expand; *di pupilla* dilate

dilatazione *f* expansion; *di pupilla* dilation

dilazionare <1a> defer, delay

dilazione *f* extension

dileguarsi <1a> vanish, disappear

dilemma *m* (*pl* -i) dilemma

dilettante *m/f* amateur; *spreg* dilettante

dilettare <1b> delight

dilettarsi: *~ di qc* dabble in sth, do sth as a hobby; *~ a fare qc* take delight in doing sth

diletto¹ 1 *agg* beloved **2** *m*, *-a f* beloved

**diletto² ** *m* (*piacere*) delight; *fare qc per ~* do sth for pleasure

diligente diligent; (*accurato*) accurate

diligenza *f* diligence

diluire <4d> dilute

dilungarsi <1e> *fig* dwell (*su* on)

diluviare <1k> pour down

diluvio *m* downpour; *fig* deluge; *~ universale* Flood

dimagrante: *cura f ~* diet

dimagrire <4d> lose weight

dimenare <1a> wave; *coda* wag

dimenarsi throw o.s. about

dimensione *f* dimension; *(grandezza)* size; *(misure)* dimensions

dimenticanza *f* forgetfulness, absent-mindedness; *(svista)* oversight

dimenticare <1m & d> forget

dimenticarsi forget (*di* sth; *di fare qc* to do sth)

dimestichezza *f* familiarity

dimettere <3ee> dismiss (*da* from); *da ospedali* discharge, release (*da* from); *da carceri* release (*da* from)

dimettersi resign (*da* from)

dimezzare <1b> halve; *(dividere)* halve, divide in two

diminuire <4d> **1** *v/t* reduce, diminish; *prezzi* reduce, lower **2** *v/i* decrease, diminish; *di prezzi, valore* fall, go down; *di vento, rumore* die down

diminuzione *f* decrease; *di prezzi, valore* fall, drop (*di* in)

dimissioni *fpl* resignation *sg*; *dare le ~* resign, hand in one's resignation

dimora *f* residence; *senza fissa ~* of no fixed abode

dimostrare <1a> demonstrate; *(interesse)* show; *(provare)* prove, show

dimostrarsi prove to be

dimostrazione *f* demonstration; *(prova)* proof

dinamica *f* dynamics

dinamico *(pl* -ci) dynamic

dinamismo *m* dynamism

dinamite *f* dynamite

dinamo *f inv* dynamo

dinanzi *prp*: *~ a* al cospetto di before

dinastia *f* dynasty

dingo *m inv* dingo

dinosauro *m* dinosaur

dintorno **1** *avv* around **2** *m*: *-i pl* neighbo(u)rhood

dio *m* (*pl* gli dei) *idolo* god; *Dio* God; *grazie a Dio!* thank God!, thank goodness!; *per l'amor di Dio* for God's *or* goodness sake

diocesi *f inv* diocese

diossina *f* dioxin

dipartimento *m* department

dipendente **1** *agg* dependent **2** *m/f* employee

dipendenza *f* dependence; *(edificio)* annex(e); *essere alle ~ di* work for

dipendere <3c>: *~ da (essere subordinato a)* depend on; *(essere mantenuto da)* be dependent on; *(essere causato da)* derive from, be due to; *dipende* it depends; *questo dipende da te* it's up to you

dipeso *pp* → **dipendere**

dipingere <3d> paint; *fig* describe, depict

dipinto **1** *pp* → **dipingere** **2** *m* painting, picture

diploma *m* (*pl* -i) diploma, certificate; *~ di laurea* degree (certificate)

diplomarsi <1c> obtain a diploma

diplomatico (*pl* -ci) **1** *agg* diplomatic **2** *m* diplomat

diplomato **1** *agg* qualified **2** *m*, *-a f* holder of a diploma

diplomazia *f* diplomacy

diporto *m*: *imbarcazione f da ~* pleasure boat

diradare <1a> thin out

diradarsi thin out; *di nebbia* clear, lift

dire <3t> **1** *v/t* say; *(raccontare)* tell; *~ qc a qu* tell s.o. sth; *vale a ~* that is, in other words; *a ~ il vero* to tell the truth; *come si dice ... in inglese?* what's the English for ... ?; *voler ~* mean **2** *v/i ~ bene di qu* speak highly of s.o.; *dico sul serio* I'm serious **3** *m*: *per sentito ~* by hearsay; *hai un bel ~* say what you like

direttissima *f* ALP shortest *or* most direct route; DIR *processo m per ~* summary proceedings *pl*

direttiva *f* directive

direttivo **1** *agg di direzione di società* managerial; *comitato, consiglio,* POL executive *attr* **2** *m di società* board (of directors); POL leadership

diretto **1** *pp* → **dirigere** **2** *agg (immediato)* direct; *~ a* aimed at; *lettera* addressed to; *essere ~ a casa* be heading for home; RAD, TV *in (ripresa) -a* live **3** *m* direct train; SP straight

direttore m, **-trice** f manager; *più in alto nella gerarchia* director; MUS conductor; EDU headmaster, headmistress f, Am principal; *di giornale, rivista* editor (in chief); **~ generale** chief executive officer; **~ delle vendite** sales manager; **~ d'orchestra** conductor; **~ tecnico** technical manager; SP coach and team manager

direzione f direction; *di società* management; *di partito* leadership; *ufficio* office; *sede generale* head office; **in ~ di Roma** in the direction of Rome

dirigente 1 agg *classe, partito* ruling; *personale* managerial **2** m/f executive; POL leader

dirigere <3u> direct; *azienda* run, manage; *orchestra* conduct

dirigersi head (**a, verso** for, towards)

dirigibile m airship, dirigible

dirimpetto opposite, across the way; **~ a** facing, in front of

diritto 1 agg straight **2** avv straight **3** m right; DIR law; **-i** pl *(il compenso)* fees; **-i d'autore** copyright; **~ commerciale** commercial law; **~ costituzionale** constitutional law; **~ internazionale** international law; **~ di precedenza** right of way; **~ di voto** right to vote; **-i** pl **umani** human rights; **parità f di -i** equal rights; **aver ~ a** be entitled to; **di ~** by rights

dirittura f straight line; SP straight; fig rectitude; **in ~ d'arrivo** in the home straight

diroccato ramshackle

dirottamento m hijack(ing)

dirottare <1c> *traffico* divert; *aereo* reroute; *con intenzioni criminali* hijack

dirottatore m, **-trice** f hijacker

dirotto: piove a ~ it's pouring

dirupo m precipice

disabile 1 agg disabled **2** m/f disabled person

disabitato uninhabited

disabituare <1n>: **~ qu a qc** get s.o. out of the habit of sth

disaccordo m disagreement

disadattato 1 agg maladjusted **2** m/f (social) misfit

disadatto unsuitable (**a** for); *persona* unsuited (**a un lavoro** to a job)

disadorno bare, unadorned

disagiato uncomfortable; *vita* hard

disagio m (pl -gi) (difficoltà) hardship; (scomodità) discomfort; (imbarazzo) embarrassment; **essere a ~** be ill at ease

disambientato out of place

disapprovare <1c> disapprove of

disapprovazione f disapproval

disappunto m disappointment

disarmare <1a> disarm

disarmato unarmed; fig defenceless

disarmo m POL disarmament

disastro m disaster

disastroso disastrous

disattento inattentive

disattenzione f inattention, lack of attention; *errore* careless mistake

disavanzo m deficit; **~ della bilancia commerciale** trade deficit; **~ commerciale con l'estero** foreign trade deficit

disavventura f misadventure

disboscamento m deforestation

disboscare <1d> deforest

disbrigo m (pl -ghi) dispatch

discapito m: **a ~ di qu** to the detriment or disadvantage of s.o.

discarica f (pl -che) dumping; (luogo) dump

discendente 1 agg inv descending **2** m/f descendant

discendenza f descent; (discendenti) descendants

discendere <3c> descend; (trarre origine) be a descendant (**da** of), be descended (**da** from); *da veicoli, da cavallo* alight (**da** from)

discepolo m disciple

discesa f descent; (pendio) slope; *di bus* exit; SCI **~ libera** downhill (race); **strada f in ~** street that slopes downwards

dischetto m INFOR diskette, floppy F

disciogliere <3ss> dissolve; *neve* melt

disciolto *pp* → **disciogliere**

disciplina *f* discipline

disciplinare 1 *agg* disciplinary **2** *v/t* <1a> discipline

disciplinato disciplined

disco *m* (*pl* -chi) disc, *Am* disk; SP discus; MUS record; INFOR disk; INFOR **~ rigido** hard disk; AUTO **~ orario** parking disc; **~ volante** flying saucer

discobolo *m* discus thrower

discografia *f* elenco recordings, discography; *attività* record industry

discolo 1 *agg* wild, unruly **2** *m* troublemaker

discolpare <1a> clear

discontinuo intermittent; (*disuguale*) erratic

discorde not in agreement, clashing

discordia *f* discord; (*differenza di opinioni*) disagreement; (*litigio*) argument

discorrere <3o> talk (*di* about)

discorso 1 *pp* → **discorrere 2** *m* *pubblico, ufficiale* speech; (*conversazione*) conversation, talk; **che –i!** what rubbish!

discoteca *f* (*pl* -che) *locale* disco; *raccolta* record library

discrepanza *f* discrepancy

discreto (*riservato*) discreet; (*abbastanza buono*) fairly good; (*moderato*) moderate, fair

discrezione *f* discretion; **a ~ di** at the discretion of

discriminare <1m> **1** *v/i* discriminate **2** *v/t* stranieri, donne discriminate against

discriminazione *f* discrimination

discussione *f* discussion; (*litigio*) argument

discusso *pp* → **discutere**

discutere <3v> **1** *v/t* proposta, caso discuss, talk about; questione debate; (*mettere in dubbio*) question; (*contestare*) dispute **2** *v/i* talk; (*litigare*) argue; (*negoziare*) negotiate

discutibile debatable

disdegnare <1a> disdain

disdetta *f* DIR notice; *fig* bad luck

disdetto *pp* → **disdire**

disdire <3t> *impegno* cancel; *contratto* terminate

disegnare <1a> draw; (*progettare*) design

disegnatore *m*, **-trice** *f* draughtsman, *Am* draftsman; *donna* draughtswoman, *Am* draftswoman; (*progettista*) designer

disegno *m* drawing; (*progetto*) design; **~ di legge** bill

diserbante *m* weed-killer, herbicide

diserbare <1a> weed

diseredare <1b> disinherit

diseredato underprivileged, disadvantaged

disertare <1b> **1** *v/t* desert; **~ una riunione** not attend a meeting **2** *v/i* desert

disertore *m* deserter

diserzione *f* desertion

disfare <3aa> undo; (*distruggere*) destroy; **~ la valigia** unpack

disfarsi *di neve, ghiaccio* melt; **~ di** get rid of

disfatta *f* defeat

disfatto *pp* → **disfare**

disfunzione *f* MED disorder

disgelo *m* thaw

disgrazia *f* misfortune; (*incidente*) accident; (*sfavore*) disgrace; **per ~** unfortunately

disgraziato 1 *agg* (*sfortunato*) unlucky, unfortunate **2** *m*, **-a** *f* poor soul; F (*farabutto*) bastard F

disgregare <1b> break up

disgregarsi break up, disintegrate

disguido *m* hiccup, hitch

disgustare <1a> disgust

disgustarsi be disgusted (*di* by)

disgusto *m* disgust

disgustoso disgusting

disidratato dehydrated

disilludere <3b> disillusion

disillusione *f* disillusionment

disilluso disillusioned

disimparare <1a> forget

disinfettante *m* disinfectant

disinfettare <1b> disinfect

disinfezione *f* disinfection

disingannare <1a> disillusion
disinibito uninhibited
disinnescare <1d> *bomba* defuse
disinnestare <1a> AUTO *marcia* disengage
disinquinare <1a> clean up
disinserire <4d> disconnect
disinteressarsi take no interest (*di* in)
disinteressato disinterested
disinteresse *m* lack of interest; (*generosità*) unselfishness
disintossicare <1m, c & d> detoxify
disintossicazione *f* treatment for drug/alcohol addiction, *Am* detox F
disinvolto confident
disinvoltura *f* confidence
dislessia *f* dyslexia
dislessico dyslexic
dislivello *m* difference in height; *fig* difference
disobbedire → **disubbidire**
disoccupato 1 *agg* unemployed, jobless **2** *m*, -**a** *f* person who is unemployed, person without a job; **i -i** the unemployed, the jobless
disoccupazione *f* unemployment; ~ **giovanile** unemployment among the young, youth unemployment
disonestà *f* dishonesty
disonesto dishonest
disonorare <1a> bring dishono(u)r on
disonore *m* dishono(u)r
disopra 1 *avv* above; **al ~ di** above **2** *agg* upper **3** *m* top
disordinato untidy, messy
disordine *m* untidiness, mess; **in ~** untidy, in a mess; -**i** *pl* riots, public disorder *sg*
disorganizzazione *f* disorganization, lack of organization
disorientare <1b> disorient(ate)
disorientamento *m* disorientation
disorientato disorient(at)ed
disotto 1 *avv* below; **al ~ di** beneath **2** *agg* lower **3** *m* underside
dispari odd
disparità *f* disparity
disparte: in ~ aside, to one side
dispendio *m* waste

dispendioso expensive
dispensa *f stanza* larder; *mobile* cupboard; *pubblicazione* instal(l)ment; DIR exemption; ~ **universitaria** duplicated lecture notes
dispensare <1b> dispense; (*esonerare*) exonerate
disperare <1b> despair (*di* of); **far ~ qu** drive s.o. to despair
disperarsi despair
disperato desperate
disperazione *f* despair, desperation
disperdere <3uu> disperse; *energie, sostanze* squander; **non ~ nell'ambiente** please dispose of carefully
disperdersi disperse
dispersione *f* dispersal; CHIM, FIS dispersion; *fig di energie* waste
disperso 1 *pp* → **disperdere 2** *agg* scattered; (*sperduto*) lost, missing
dispetto *m* spite; **per ~** out of spite; **a ~ di qc** in spite of sth; **fare -i a qu** annoy *or* tease s.o.
dispettoso mischievous
dispiacere 1 *v/i* <2k> (*causare dolore*) upset (*a* s.o.); (*non piacere*) displease (*a* s.o.); **mi dispiace** I'm sorry; **le dispiace se apro la finestra?** do you mind if I open the window? **2** *m* (*rammarico*) regret, sorrow; (*dolore*) grief, sadness; (*delusione*) disappointment; -**i** (*preoccupazioni*) worries, troubles
display *m* display
disponibile available; (*cortese*) helpful, obliging
disponibilità *f* availability; (*cortesia*) helpfulness
disporre <3ll> **1** *v/t* arrange; (*stabilire*) order **2** *v/i* (*decidere*) make arrangements; **abbiamo già disposto diversamente** we've made other arrangements; ~ **di qc** have sth (at one's disposal)
dispositivo *m* TEC device
disposizione *f* arrangement; (*norma*) provision; (*attitudine*) aptitude (*a* for); **stare/mettere a ~ di qu** be/put at s.o.'s disposal
disposto 1 *pp* → **disporre 2** *agg*: ~ **a** ready to, willing to; **essere ben ~**

verso qu be well disposed to s.o.

dispotico (*pl* -ci) despotic

disprezzare <1b> despise

disprezzo *m* contempt

disputa *f* dispute, argument

disputare <1l> **1** *v/i* argue **2** *v/t* SP take part in; **disputarsi qc** compete for sth

dissanguare <1a> *fig* bleed dry, bleed white

disseminare <1m> scatter, disseminate; *fig* spread

dissenso *m* dissent; (*dissapore*) argument, disagreement

dissenteria *f* dysentery

dissentire <4b> disagree (**da** with)

disseppellire <4d> exhume

dissertazione *f* dissertation

disservizio *m* (*pl* -zi) poor service; (*inefficienza*) inefficiency; (*cattiva gestione*) mismanagement

dissestare <1b> FIN destabilize

dissestato *strada* uneven; *finanze* precarious

dissesto *m* ruin, failure; **~ ecologico** environmental meltdown

dissetante thirst-quenching

dissetare <1a>: **~ qu** quench s.o.'s thirst

dissetarsi quench one's thirst

dissidente *m/f* dissident

dissimulare <1m> conceal, hide

dissimulazione *f* concealment

dissipare <1l> dissolve; (*sperperare*) squander

dissociare <1f> dissociate

dissociarsi dissociate o.s. (**da** from)

dissodare <1c> till

dissoluto dissolute

dissolvere <3g> dissolve; *dubbi*, *nebbia* dispel

dissolversi dissolve; (*svanire*) vanish

dissonante dissonant; *fig* discordant

dissonanza *f* MUS dissonance; *fig* clash

dissuadere <2i>: **~ qu da fare qc** dissuade s.o. from doing sth

dissuaso *pp* → **dissuadere**

distaccare <1d> detach; SP leave behind

distaccarsi *da persone* detach o.s.

(**da** from)

distacco *m* (*pl* -cchi) detachment (*anche fig*); (*separazione*) separation; SP lead

distante distant, remote, far-off; **~ da** far from

distanza *f* distance (*anche fig*); **comando** *m* **a ~** remote control

distanziare <1g> **1** *v/t* space out; SP leave behind; (*superare*) overtake

distare <1a>: **l'albergo dista 100 metri dalla stazione** the hotel is 100 metres from the station; **quanto dista da qui?** how far is it from here?

distendere <3c> (*adagiare*) lay; *gambe*, *braccia* stretch out; *muscoli* relax; *bucato* hang out; *nervi* calm

distendersi lie down; (*rilassarsi*) relax

distensione *f* relaxation; POL détente

distensivo relaxing

distesa *f* expanse

disteso **1** *pp* → **distendere** **2** *agg* stretched out; (*rilassato*) relaxed

distillare <1a> distil, *Am* distill

distilleria *f* distillery

distinguere <3d> distinguish

distintivo **1** *agg* distinctive **2** *m* badge

distinto **1** *pp* → **distinguere** **2** *agg* (*diverso*) different, distinct; (*chiaro*) distinct; *fig* distinguished; **~i saluti** yours faithfully

distinzione *f* distinction

distorsione *f* distortion; MED sprain

distrarre <3xx> distract; (*divertire*) entertain

distrarsi (*non essere attento*) get distracted; (*svagarsi*) take one's mind off things

distratto **1** *pp* → **distrarre** **2** *agg* absent-minded

distrazione *f* absent-mindedness; (*errore*) inattention; (*svago*) amusement; **che distrae da un'attività** distraction

distretto *m* district

distribuire <4d> distribute; *premi* award, present

distributore *m* distributor; **~ (di benzina)** (petrol, *Am* gas) pump; **~ automatico** vending machine; **~ automatico di biglietti** ticket machine

distribuzione *f* distribution; **posta** delivery

distruggere <3cc> destroy

distruttivo destructive

distrutto *pp* → **distruggere**

distruzione *f* destruction

disturbare <1a> disturb; (*dare fastidio a*) bother; (*sconvolgere*) upset

disturbarsi: non si disturbi please don't bother

disturbi *mpl* RAD interference *sg*

disturbo *m* trouble, bother; MED **-i pl di circolazione** circulation problems

disubbidiente disobedient

disubbidienza *f* disobedience

disubbidire <4d>: **~ a** disobey

disuguaglianza *f* disparity, difference

disuguale different; *terreno* uneven; *fig* inconsistent, erratic

disumano inhuman

disuso *m*: **in ~** in disuse, disused

ditale *m* thimble

dito *m* (*pl* le dita) finger; **del piede** toe; **un ~ di vino** a drop of wine

ditta *f* company, firm; **~ fornitrice** supplier; **~ di vendite per corrispondenza** mail-order company

dittafono® *m* dictaphone®

dittatore *m* dictator

dittatura *f* dictatorship

diurno daytime *attr*; **albergo *m* ~** place where travellers can have a shower / shave

diva *f* diva

divagare <1e> digress

divampare <1a> *di rivolta, incendio* break out; *di passione* blaze

divano *m* sofa; **~ letto** sofa bed

divaricare <1m & d> open (wide)

divario *m* (*pl* -ri) difference

divenire <4p> become

diventare <1b> become; *rosso, bianco* turn, go; **~ grande** grow up

diverbio *m* (*pl* -bi) argument

divergente diverging, divergent

divergenza *f* divergence; **di opinioni** difference

divergere <3uu & 3a> diverge

diversamente differently; (*altrimenti*) otherwise

diversificare <1n & d> **1** *v/t* diversify **2** *v/i e* **diversificarsi** differ

diversità *f* difference; (*varietà*) diversity

diversivo *m* diversion, distraction

diverso 1 *agg* (*differente*) different (**da** from, *Am* than); **-i pl** several; **da -i giorni** for the past few days **2** *mpl* **-i** several people

divertente amusing

divertimento *m* amusement; **buon ~!** have a good time!, enjoy yourself / yourselves!

divertire <4b> amuse

divertirsi enjoy o.s., have a good time

dividendo *m* dividend

dividere <3q> divide; (*condividere*) share

dividersi *di coppia* separate; (*scindersi*) be split, be divided (**in** into)

divieto *m* ban; **~ d'importazione** import ban; AUTO **~ di segnalazioni acustiche** please do not use your horn; **~ di sosta** no parking

divincolarsi <1m> twist, wriggle

divinità *f inv* divinity

divino divine

divisa *f* uniform; FIN currency

divisione *f* division; **~ del lavoro** division of labo(u)r

divisorio (*pl* -ri) **1** *agg* dividing; **parete *f* -a** partition wall, stud wall **2** *m* partition

divo *m* star

divorare <1c> devour

divorziare <1c & g> get a divorce

divorziato divorced

divorzio *m* (*pl* -zi) divorce

divulgare <1e> divulge, reveal; (*rendere accessibile*) popularize

divulgazione *f* divulging; *scientifica* popularization

dizionario *m* (*pl* -ri) dictionary

DNA *abbr* (= **acido deossiribonucleico**) DNA (= deoxyribonucleic acid)

do¹ → **dare**

do² *m inv* MUS C; *nel solfeggio della scala* doh

dobbiamo → **dovere**

D.O.C., doc *abbr* (= **Denominazione d'Origine Controllata**) term signifying that a wine is of a certain origin and quality

doccia *f* (*pl* -cce) shower; **fare la ~** take a shower

docente 1 *agg* teaching; **personale** *m* **~** teaching staff **2** *m/f* teacher

docile docile

documentare <1a> document

documentarsi collect information

documentario *m* documentary

documentazione *f* documentation

documento *m* document; **-i** *pl* papers; **-i dell'autoveicolo** car documents

dodici twelve

dogana *f* customs; (*dazio*) (customs) duty

doganale customs *attr*; **controllo** *m* **~** customs check; **dichiarazione** *f* **~** customs declaration; **formalità** *fpl* **-i** customs formalities

doganiere *m* customs officer

doglie *fpl*: **avere le ~** be in labo(u)r

dogma *m* (*pl* -i) dogma

dolce 1 *agg* sweet; *carattere, voce, pendio* gentle; *acqua* fresh; *clima* mild; *ricordo* pleasant; *suono* soft **2** *m* (*portata*) dessert, sweet; *di sapore* sweetness; (*torta*) cake; **-i** *pl* sweet things

dolcezza *f* sweetness; *di carattere, voce* gentleness; *di clima* mildness; *di ricordo* pleasantness; *di suono* softness

dolciastro sweetish; *fig* syrupy, sugary

dolcificante *m* sweetener

dolciumi *mpl* sweets, *Am* candy *sg*

dolente painful, sore

dolere <2e> hurt, be painful; **mi duole la schiena** my back hurts, I have a sore back

dolersi be sorry (**di** for); (*lagnarsi*) complain (**di** about)

dollaro *m* dollar

dolo *m* malice

Dolomiti *fpl* Dolomites

dolorante sore, painful

dolore *m* pain

doloroso painful

doloso malicious

domanda *f* question; (*richiesta*) request; FIN demand; **fare una ~ a qu** ask s.o. a question; **~ e offerta** supply and demand

domandare <1a> **1** *v/t per sapere: nome, ora, opinione ecc* ask; *per ottenere: informazioni, aiuto ecc* ask for; **~ un favore a qu** ask s.o. a favour; **~ scusa** apologize **2** *v/i*: **~ a qu** ask s.o.; **~ di qu** *per sapere come sta* ask after s.o.; *per parlargli* ask for s.o.

domandarsi wonder, ask o.s.

domani 1 *avv* tomorrow; **~ mattina** tomorrow morning; **~ sera** tomorrow evening; **a ~!** see you tomorrow! **2** *m* tomorrow

domare <1a> tame; *fig* control

domattina tomorrow morning

domenica *f* (*pl* -che) Sunday; **la ~, di ~** on Sundays

domestico (*pl* -ci) **1** *agg* domestic; **animale** *m* **~** pet **2** *m*, **-a** *f* servant; *donna* maid

domiciliato: **~ a** domiciled at

domicilio *m* domicile; (*casa*) home

dominante dominant; *idee* prevailing; *classe* ruling

dominare <1l & c> **1** *v/t* dominate; *materia* master; *passioni* master, overcome **2** *v/i* rule (**su** over), be master (**su** of); *fig di confusione* reign

dominazione *f* domination

dominio *m* (*pl* -ni) (*controllo*) control, power; *fig* (*campo*) domain, field

domino *m* mask, domino

donare <1a> donate, give; *sangue* give

donatore *m*, **-trice** *f* donor; **~ di sangue** blood donor

donazione f donation

dondolare <1l> **1** v/t culla rock; testa nod **2** v/i sway; (oscillare) swing

dondolarsi su altalena swing; su sedia rock; fig hang around

dondolio m (gentle) rocking

dondolo m: **cavallo** m **a ~** rocking horse; **sedia** f **a ~** rocking chair

donna f woman; carte da gioco queen; **~ di servizio** home help; **scarpe** fpl **da ~** women's or ladies' shoes

donnola f weasel

dono m gift

dopo 1 prp after; **~ di te** after you; **~ mangiato** after eating, after meals; **subito ~ il bar** just past the bar **2** avv (in seguito) afterward(s), after; (poi) then; (più tardi) later; **il giorno ~** the day after, the next day **3** conj: **~ che** after

dopobarba m inv aftershave

dopodomani the day after tomorrow

dopoguerra m inv post-war period

dopopranzo m afternoon

doposci m inv après-ski; **~ pl stivali** après-ski boots

dopotutto after all

doppiaggio m di film dubbing

doppiare <1k> film dub; SP lap; MAR round

doppiatore m, **-trice** f dubber

doppio (pl -pi) **1** agg double **2** m double; SP doubles

doppine f duplicate

doppipetto m double-breasted jacket

dorare <1c> gild; GASTR brown

dorato 1 pp → **dorare 2** agg gilded; sabbia, riflessi golden; GASTR browned

dorico (pl -ci) ARCHI Doric

dormicchiare <1k> doze

dormiglione m, **-a** f late riser

dormire <4c> sleep

dormita f (good) night's sleep

dormitorio m (pl -ri) dormitory

dormiveglia m: **essere nel ~** be only half awake

dorso m back; (di libro) spine; SP backstroke

dosaggio m (pl -gi) proportion; di medicina dosage

dosare <1c> measure out; fig be sparing with; parole weigh

dose f quantity, amount; MED dose; **una buona ~ di coraggio** a lot of courage

dosso m di strada hump; **togliersi gli abiti di ~** get undressed, take one's clothes off

dotare <1c> provide, supply (di with); fig provide, endow (di with)

dotato gifted; **~ di** equipped with

dotazione f equipment; finanziaria endowment; **dato in ~ a qu** issued to s.o.

dote f dowry; fig gift

dott. abbr (= **dottore**) Dr (= doctor)

dotto 1 agg learned **2** m scholar

dottorato m doctorate; **~ di ricerca** doctorate in scientific research

dottore m doctor (in of)

dottoressa f (woman) doctor

dottrina f doctrine

dott.ssa abbr (= **dottoressa**) Dr (= doctor)

dove where; **~ sei?** where are you?; **di ~ sei?** where are you from?; **fin ~?** how far?; **per ~ si passa?** which way do you go?; **mettilo ~ vuoi** put it wherever you like

dovere <2f> **1** v/i have to, must; **devo averlo** I must have it, I have to have it; **non devo dimenticare** I mustn't forget; **deve arrivare oggi** she is supposed to arrive today; **come si deve** (bene) properly; persona very decent; **doveva succedere** it was bound to happen; **dovresti avvertirlo** you ought to or should let him know **2** v/t owe **3** m duty; **per ~** out of duty

dovunque 1 avv (dappertutto) everywhere; (in qualsiasi luogo) anywhere **2** conj wherever

dovuto 1 pp → **dovere 2** agg due; **~ a** because of, due to

dozzina f dozen; **una ~ di uova** a dozen eggs; **se ne vendono a ~** they are sold by the dozen

dragare <1e> dredge

drago m (pl -ghi) dragon

dragoncello m tarragon

dramma m (pl -i) drama

drammatico (pl -ci) dramatic

drammatizzare <1a> dramatize

drammaturgia f theatre, Am theater

drammaturgo m (pl -ghi) playwright

drastico (pl -ci) drastic

drenaggio m drainage

drenare <1a> drain

dribblare <1a> SP dribble

dritto 1 agg straight 2 avv straight (ahead) 3 m di indumento, tessuto right side 4 m, **-a** f F crafty devil F

drive m inv INFOR drive

drizzare <1a> (raddrizzare) straighten; (erigere) put up, erect; **~ le orecchie** prick up one's ears

drizzarsi: **~ in piedi** rise to one's feet

droga f (pl -ghe) drug; **-ghe** pl **pesanti/leggere** hard/soft drugs

drogare <1c & e> drug

drogarsi SP take drugs

drogato m, **-a** f drug addict

drogheria f grocer's

dubbio (pl -bbi) 1 agg doubtful; (equivoco) dubious 2 m doubt; **essere in ~ fra** hesitate between; **mettere qc in ~** doubt sth; **senza ~** undoubtedly, without a doubt

dubbioso doubtful

dubitare <1l> doubt (**di** sth); **dubito che venga** I doubt whether he'll come

duca m (pl -chi) duke

ducato m (territorio) duchy

duchessa f duchess

due two; **a ~ a ~** in twos, two by two; **tutt'e ~** both of them; **vorrei dire ~ parole** I'd like to say a word or two

duecento 1 agg two hundred 2 m: **il Duecento** the thirteenth century

duello m duel

duemila two thousand

duepezzi m inv bikini; (vestito) two-piece (suit)

duetto m duet; (persone) duo, couple

duna f (sand) dune

dunque 1 conj so; (allora) well (then) 2 m: **venire al ~** come to the crunch

duomo m cathedral

duplex m inv party line

duplicato m duplicate

duplice double; **in ~ copia** in duplicate

durante prp during; **vita natural ~** for ever and ever

durare <1a> last; (conservarsi) keep, last

durata f duration, length; di prodotto life; **per tutta la ~ di** throughout; **~ di volo** flight time

duraturo lasting

durevole lasting

durezza f hardness; di carne toughness; (asprezza) harshness

duro 1 agg hard; carne, persona tough; inverno, voce harsh; congegno, meccanismo stiff; pane stale; (ostinato) stubborn; F (stupido) thick F; **~ d'orecchi** hard of hearing; **tieni ~!** don't give up!, hang in there! 2 m tough guy

durone m callus

duttile ductile; fig malleable

E

E *abbr* (= *est*) E (= east)

e and

è → **essere**

ebanista *m/f* (*mpl* -i) cabinet maker

ebano *m* ebony

ebbe, ebbi → **avere**

ebbene well

ebbrezza *f* drunkenness; *fig* thrill

ebraico (*pl* -ci) **1** *agg* Hebrew; *religione* Jewish **2** *m* Hebrew

ebreo **1** *m*, **-a** *f* Jew; **gli -i** the Jews **2** *agg* Jewish

ecc. *abbr* (= **eccetera**) etc (= et cetera)

eccedente excess

eccedenza *f* excess; (*il di più*) surplus; **peso** *m* **in** ~ excess weight

eccedere <3a> **1** *v/t* exceed, go beyond **2** *v/i* go too far; ~ **nel bere** drink too much

eccellente excellent

eccentrico (*pl* -ci) eccentric

eccessivo excessive

eccesso *m* excess; ~ **di personale** overmanning; ~ **di velocità** speeding

eccetera et cetera

eccetto except

eccettuare <1m & b> except

eccezionale exceptional; **in via** ~ as an exception

eccezionalmente exceptionally

eccezione *f* exception

ecchimosi *f inv* bruise

eccitante **1** *agg* exciting **2** *m* stimulant

eccitare <1l & b> excite

eccitarsi get excited

eccitazione *f* excitement

ecclesiastico (*pl* -ci) **1** *agg* ecclesiastical **2** *m* priest

ecco (*qui*) here; (*là*) there; ~ **come** this is how; ~ **fatto** that's that; ~ **tutto** that's all; ~**mi** here I am; ~**li**

here they are; ~**ti il libro** here is your book

eclissare <1a> eclipse

eclissarsi *fig* slip away

eclisse *f*, **eclissi** *f inv* eclipse; ~ **solare** solar eclipse; ~ **lunare** lunar eclipse

eco *m/f* (*pl* gli echi) echo

ecografia *f* scan

ecologia *f* ecology

ecologico (*pl* -ci) ecological

ecologista **1** *m/f* ecologist **2** *agg* ecological

ecologo *m* (*pl* -gi), **-a** *f* ecologist

economia *f* economy; *scienza* economics *sg*; **fare** ~ economize (**di** on); ~ **di mercato** market economy; **università Economia e Commercio** business school; **-e** *pl* savings

economico (*pl* -ci) economic; (*poco costoso*) economical; **classe** *f* ~ economy class

economista *m/f* (*mpl* -i) economist

economizzare <1a> **1** *v/t* save **2** *v/i* economize (**su** on)

economo **1** *agg* thrifty **2** *m*, **-a** *f* bursar

ecosistema *m* ecosystem

eczema *m* (*pl* -i) eczema

ed and

edera *f* ivy

edicola *f* newspaper kiosk

edificare <1m & d> build; *fig* edify

edificio *m* (*pl* -ci) building; *fig* structure

edile construction *attr*, building *attr*

edilizia *f* construction, building; (*urbanistica*) town planning

editare <1a> INFOR edit

editore **1** *agg* publishing **2** *m*, **-trice** *f* publisher; (*curatore*) editor

editoria *f* publishing

editoriale **1** *agg* publishing **2** *m* editorial

edizione f edition; **~ straordinaria di telegiornale** special news bulletin; **di giornale** extra (edition); **la quarta ~ del congresso XY** the fourth XY conference

educare <11, b & d> educate; (*allevare*) bring up; *gusto, orecchio, mente* train

educativo education attr; (*istruttivo*) educational

educato: (*ben*) ~ well brought-up, polite

educazione f education; *dei figli* upbringing; (*buone maniere*) (good) manners; **~ fisica** physical education

effervescente *bibita* fizzy, effervescent; *aspirina* soluble; *personalità* bubbly, effervescent

effettivamente (*in effetti*) in fact; *per rafforzare un'affermazione* really, actually

effettivo 1 agg (*reale*) real, actual; (*efficace*) effective; *personale* permanent; MIL regular **2** m FIN sum total

effetto m (*conseguenza*) effect; (*impressione*) impression; FIN (*cambiale*) bill (of exchange); **~ serra** greenhouse effect; **fare ~** (*funzionare*) work; (*impressionare*) make an impression; **fare l'~ di essere ...** give the impression of being ...; **-i pl collaterali** side effects; **-i pl personali** personal effects *or* belongings; **a tutti gli -i** to all intents and purposes; **in -i** in fact

effettuare <1m & b> carry out; *pagamento* make

effettuarsi take place; **il servizio non si effettua la domenica** there is no Sunday service

efficace effective

efficacia f effectiveness

efficiente efficient; (*funzionante*) in working order

efficienza f efficiency

Egitto m Egypt

egiziano 1 agg Egyptian **2** m, **-a** f Egyptian

egizio ancient Egyptian

egli pron m he

egocentrico egocentric

egoismo m selfishness, egoism

egoista 1 agg selfish **2** m/f (mpl -i) selfish person, egoist

egr. abbr (= **egregio**) form of address used in correspondence

egregio (pl -gi) distinguished; *nelle lettere* **~ signore** Dear Sir

eguale → **uguale**

eh? eh?, what?

ehi! oi!

E.I. abbr (= **Esercito Italiano**) Italian army

elaborare <1m> elaborate; *dati* process; *piano* draw up, work out

elaborato elaborate

elaboratore m: **~ elettronico** computer

elaborazione f elaboration; **~ elettronica dei dati** electronic data processing; **~ dei testi** word processing

elasticità f elasticity; (*agilità*) agility, suppleness; *fig* flexibility; *della mente* quickness

elastico (pl -ci) **1** agg elastic; *norme, orari* flexible **2** m rubber band

elefante m elephant

elegante elegant

eleganza f elegance

eleggere <3cc> elect

elementare elementary; **scuola** f ~ primary school, Am elementary school

elemento m element; (*componente*) component; **-i pl** (*rudimenti*) rudiments; (*fatti*) data

elemosina f charity; **chiedere l'~** beg

elemosinare <1n & c> v/t & v/i beg

elencare <1b & d> list

elenco m (pl -chi) list; **~ telefonico** phone book F, telephone directory

eletto 1 pp → **eleggere 2** agg chosen

elettorale electoral

elettorato m electorate

elettore m, **-trice** f voter

elettrauto m inv auto electrics garage; *persona* car electrician

elettricista m/f (pl -i) electrician

elettricità f electricity

elettrico (pl -ci) electric; **centrale** f **-a** power station

elettrocardiogramma m (pl -i) electrocardiogram

elettrodo m electrode

elettrodomestico m (pl -ci) household appliance

elettrolisi f electrolysis

elettromagnetico electromagnetic

elettromotore m electric motor

elettromotrice f FERR electric locomotive

elettrone m electron

elettronica f electronics

elettronico electronic

elettroshock electroshock

elettrotecnica f electrical engineering

elettrotecnico (pl -ci) **1** agg electrical **2** m electrical engineer

elevare <1b> raise; costruzioni erect; (promuovere) promote; fig migliorare better

elevato high; fig elevated, lofty

elevazione f elevation

elezione f election

eliambulanza f air ambulance

elica f (pl -che) MAR propeller, screw; AVIA propeller

elicottero m helicopter

eliminare <1m> eliminate

eliminatoria f SP heat

eliminazione f elimination

elio m helium

eliporto m heliport

élite f elite, élite

ella pron f she

ellenico (pl -ci) Hellenic

ellenismo m Hellenism

ellepì m inv LP

elmetto m helmet

elmo m helmet

elogiare <1f & c> praise

elogio m (pl -gi) praise

eloquente eloquent

eloquenza f eloquence

eludere <3q> elude; sorveglianza, domanda evade

elusivo elusive

elvetico (pl -ci) Swiss

emanare <1a> **1** v/t give off; legge pass **2** v/i emanate, come (**da** from)

emanazione f di calore, raggi emanation; di legge passing

emancipare <1m> emancipate

emanciparsi become emancipated

emancipazione f emancipation

emarginare <1m> marginalize

emarginato m, **-a** f person on the fringes of society

ematoma m (pl -i) h(a)ematoma

embargo m (pl -ghi) embargo

emblema m (pl -i) emblem

embolia f embolism

embrione m embryo

emergenza f emergency; **freno** m **d'~** emergency brake; **in caso di ~** in an emergency

emergere <3uu> emerge; (distinguersi) stand out

emersione f emersion

emerso pp → **emergere**

emesso pp → **emettere**

emettere <3ee> luce give out, emit; grido, verdetto give; calore give off; FIN issue; TEC emit

emicrania f migraine

emigrante m/f emigrant

emigrare <1a> emigrate

emigrato m, **-a** f person who has emigrated

emigrazione f emigration

emisfero m hemisphere

emissario m (pl -ri) GEOG outlet; (agente segreto) emissary

emissione f emission; di denaro, francobolli issue; RAD broadcast; **banca** f **di ~** bank of issue, issuing bank; **data** f **di ~** date of issue; **-i inquinanti** toxic emissions

emittente 1 agg issuing; (trasmittente) broadcasting **2** f RAD transmitter; TV channel; **~ privata** commercial channel

emoglobina f h(a)emoglobin

emorragia f h(a)emorrhage

emorroidi fpl h(a)emorroids

emostatico m h(a)emostat

emotivo emotional; (sensibile) sensitive

emozionante exciting, thrilling

emozionato excited; (*agitato*) nervous; (*commosso*) moved; (*turbato*) upset

emozionare <1a> (*appassionare*) excite; (*commuovere*) move; (*turbare*) upset

emozionarsi get excited; (*commuoversi*) be moved

emozione *f* emotion; (*agitazione*) excitement

empirico (*pl* -ci) empirical

emporio *m* (*pl* -ri) *negozio* department store

emulsione *f* emulsion

enciclopedia *f* encyclop(a)edia

enciclopedico (*pl* -ci) encyclop(a)edic

endovenoso intravenous

ENEL *abbr* (= **Ente Nazionale per l'Energia Elettrica**) Italian electricity board

energetico *fabbisogno, consumo ecc* energy *attr*; *alimento* energy-giving

energia *f* energy; **~ eolica** wind power; **~ nucleare** nuclear energy; **~ solare** solar power

energico (*pl* -ci) strong, energetic

enfasi *f* emphasis

enfatizzare <1a> emphasize

ENI *abbr* (= **Ente Nazionale Idrocarburi**) state-owned oil company

enigma *m* (*pl* -i) enigma

enigmatico (*pl* -ci) enigmatic

ENIT *abbr* (= **Ente Nazionale Italiano per il Turismo**) Italian tourist board

ennesimo MAT nth; F **per l'-a volta** for the hundredth time F

enorme enormous

enoteca *f* (*pl* -che) (*negozio*) wine merchant's (*specializing in fine wines*)

ente *m* organization; FIL being; **~ per il turismo** tourist board; **gli enti locali** the local authorities

entrambi both

entrare <1a> (*andare dentro*) go in, enter; (*venire dentro*) come in, enter; **la chiave non entra** the key won't go in, the key doesn't fit; *fig* **questo non c'entra** that has nothing to do with it; **~ in una stanza** enter a room, go into/come into a room; **~ in carica** take up one's duties; **non entro più nei pantaloni** I can't get into my trousers any more

entrata *f* entrance; *in parcheggio* entrance, way in; *in un paese* entry; INFOR input; FIN **-e** *pl* (*reddito*) income; (*guadagno*) earnings; **~ libera** admission free

entro within

entroterra *m inv* hinterland

entusiasmare <1a> arouse enthusiasm in

entusiasmo *m* enthusiasm

entusiasta enthusiastic

entusiastico (*pl* -ci) enthusiastic

enumerare <1m> enumerate

enumerazione *f* enumeration

enzima *m* (*pl* -i) enzyme

epatite *f* hepatitis; **~ virale** viral hepatitis

epica *f* epic

epicentro *m* epicentre, Am -center; *fig* centre

epidemia *f* epidemic; **~ di influenza** flu epidemic

epidermide *f* skin; MED epidermis

Epifania *f* Epiphany

epilessia *f* epilepsy

epilettico (*pl* -ci) **1** *agg* epileptic **2** *m*, **-a** *f* epileptic

episodio *m* (*pl* -di) episode

epistolare: **stile** *m* **~** style of letter-writing

epoca *f* (*pl* -che) age; (*periodo*) period, time; **auto** *f* **d'~** vintage car; **mobili** *mpl* **d'~** period furniture

epurare <1a> *fig* purge

eppure (and) yet

E.P.T. *abbr* (= **Ente Provinciale per il Turismo**) provincial tourist board

equatore *m* equator

equatoriale equatorial

equazione *f* equation

equilatero equilateral

equilibrare <1a> balance

equilibrato balanced; *fig* well-balanced

equilibrio *m* (*pl* -ri) balance; *fig* common sense

equino horse *attr*; *carne f -a* horse-meat

equinozio *m* (*pl* -zi) equinox

equipaggiamento *m* equipment

equipaggiare <1f> equip; MAR, AVIA *con personale* man, crew

equipaggio *m* (*pl* -ggi) crew

equiparare <1m> make equal

equiparazione *f* equalization; *~ di diritti* equal rights

équipe *f inv* team; *lavoro m di ~* team work

equitazione *f* horse riding

equivalente *m/agg* equivalent

equivalenza *f* equivalence

equivoco (*pl* -ci) **1** *agg* ambiguous; (*sospetto*) suspicious; F (*losco*) shady F **2** *m* misunderstanding

era *f* (*epoca*) age, era; GEOL era; *~ atomica* atomic age; *~ glaciale* Ice Age

era, erano → **essere**

erba *f* grass; GASTR *-e pl* herbs; *-e aromatiche* herbs; *alle -e* with herbs; *fig in ~* budding

erbaccia *f* (*pl* -cce) weed

erborista *m/f* (*pl* -i) herbalist

erboristeria *f* herbalist's

erboso grassy

erede *m/f* heir; *donna* heiress

eredità *f* inheritance; BIO heredity

ereditare <1m & b> inherit

ereditarietà *f* heredity

ereditario (*pl* -ri) hereditary

ereditiera *f* heiress

eremita *m* (*pl* -i) hermit

eresia *f* heresy

eretico 1 *agg* heretical **2** *m* (*pl* -ci), *-a f* heretic

eretto 1 *pp* → **erigere 2** *agg* erect

erezione *f* building; FISIOL erection

ergastolano *m*, *-a f* person serving a life sentence, lifer F

ergastolo *m* life sentence

ergonomico (*pl* -ci) ergonomic

erica *f* heather

erigere <3u> erect; *fig* (*fondare*) establish, found

erigersi *fig* set o.s. up (*a* as)

eritema *m* (*pl* -i) *cutaneo* rash; *~ solare* sunburn

ermafrodito *m* hermaphrodite

ermellino *m* ermine

ermetico (*pl* -ci) (*a tenuta d'aria*) airtight; *fig* obscure

ernia *f* MED hernia; *~ del disco* slipped disc

ero → **essere**

eroe *m* hero

erogare <1l, b & e> *denaro* allocate; *gas, acqua* supply

erogazione *f di denaro* allocation; *di gas ecc* supply

eroico (*pl* -ci) heroic

eroina *f droga* heroin; *donna eroica* heroine

eroinomane *m/f* heroin addict

erosione *f* GEOL erosion

erotico (*pl* -ci) erotic

erotismo *m* eroticism

errare <1b> wander, roam; (*sbagliare*) be mistaken

errata corrige *m inv* correction

erroneamente mistakenly

errore *m* mistake, error; *~ di battitura* typographical error, typo F; *~ di calcolo* mistake in the addition; *~ di ortografia* spelling mistake; *~ di stampa* misprint; *~ giudiziario* miscarriage of justice; *per ~* by mistake

erta *f*: *stare all'~* be on the alert

erudito 1 *agg* erudite, learned **2** *m*, *-a f* erudite person

erudizione *f* erudition, learning

eruttare <1a> *di vulcano* erupt

eruzione *f* eruption; MED rash

es. *abbr* (= *esempio*) eg (= for example)

esagerare <1m> **1** *v/t* exaggerate **2** *v/i* exaggerate; (*eccedere*) go too far (*in* in)

esagerato 1 *agg* exaggerated; *zelo* excessive; *prezzo* exorbitant **2** *m*, *-a f*: *sei il solito ~!* you're exaggerating as usual!

esagerazione *f* exaggeration

esagonale hexagonal, six-sided

esagono *m* hexagon

esalare <1a> **1** *v/t odori* give off; *~ il respiro* exhale **2** *v/i* come, emanate (*da* from)

esaltare <1a> exalt; (*entusiasmare*) elate

esaltarsi become elated

esaltato 1 *agg* elated; (*fanatico*) fanatical **2** *m* fanatic

esaltazione *f* exaltation; (*eccitazione*) elation

esame *m* exam(ination); MED (*test*) test; (*visita*) examination; ~ **d'idoneità** aptitude test; ~ **di guida** driving test; **prendere in** ~ examine

esaminare <1m> examine (*anche* MED)

esaminatore *m*, **-trice** *f* examiner

esasperante exasperating

esasperare <1m> (*inasprire*) exacerbate; (*irritare*) exasperate

esasperarsi become exasperated

esasperato exasperated

esasperazione *f* exasperation

esattezza *f* accuracy; **con** ~ exactly; **per l'** ~ to be precise

esatto 1 *pp* → **esigere 2** *agg* exact; *risposta* correct, right; **in punto** exactly; ~! that's right!

esattoria *f* tax office

esaudire <4d> grant; *speranze* fulfil

esauriente exhaustive

esaurimento *m* exhaustion; FIN **svendita** *f* **fino a** ~ **della merce** clearance sale; MED ~ **nervoso** nervous breakdown

esaurire <4d> exhaust; *merci* run out of

esaurito (*esausto*) exhausted; FIN sold out; *pubblicazioni* out of print; TEA **fa il tutto** ~ it is playing to a full house

esausto exhausted

esca *f* (*pl* -che) bait (*anche fig*)

esce → **uscire**

eschimese *agg*, *m/f* Inuit, Eskimo

esclamare <1a> exclaim

esclamazione *f* exclamation

escludere <3q> exclude; *possibilità, ipotesi* rule out

esclusione *f* exclusion

esclusiva *f* exclusive right, sole right; FIN ~ **di vendita** sole agency

esclusivo exclusive

escluso 1 *pp* → **escludere 2** *agg* excluded; (*impossibile*) out of the question, impossible **3** *m*, **-a** *f* person on the fringes of society

esco → **uscire**

escogitare <1m & c> contrive

escoriazione *f* graze

escrementi *mpl* excrement *sg*

escursione *f* trip, excursion; *a piedi* hike; ~ **di un giorno** day trip

escursionismo *m* touring; *a piedi* hiking, walking

escursionista *m/f* tourist; *a piedi* hiker, walker

esecutivo *m/agg* executive

esecutore *m*, **-trice** *f* DIR executor; MUS performer; ~ **testamentario** executor

esecuzione *f* (*realizzazione*) carrying out; MUS performance; DIR execution; ~ **capitale** execution

eseguire <4b or 4d> carry out; MUS perform

esempio *m* (*pl* -pi) example; **per** ~, **ad** ~ for example; **prendere** ~ **da qu** follow s.o.'s example

esemplare 1 *agg* exemplary **2** *m* specimen; (*copia*) copy

esentare <1b> exempt (**da** from)

esente exempt; ~ **da tasse** tax free

esequie *fpl* funeral (service) *sg*

esercente *m/f* shopkeeper

esercitare <1m & b> exercise; (*addestrare*) train; *professione* practise

esercitarsi practise

esercitazione *f* exercise

esercito *m* army

esercizio *m* (*pl* -zi) exercise; (*pratica*) practice; *di impianti* operation, use; (*anno finanziario*) financial year, *Am* fiscal year; FIN *azienda* business; *negozio* shop; ~ **pubblico** commercial premises

esibire <4d> *documenti* produce; *mettere in mostra* display

esibirsi *in uno spettacolo* perform; *fig* show off

esibizione *f* exhibition; (*ostentazione*) showing off; (*spettacolo*) performance

esibizionista *m/f* show-off; PSI exhibitionist

esigente exacting, demanding

esigenza *f* demand; (*bisogno*) need

esigere <3w> demand; (*riscuotere*) exact

esile slender; (*voce*) faint

esiliare <1k> exile

esilio *m* (*pl* -li) exile

esistente existing

esistenza *f* existence

esistere <3f> exist

esitare <1l & b> hesitate

esitazione *f* hesitation

esito *m* result, outcome; FIN sales, turnover

eskimo *m inv* giacca parka

esodo *m* exodus; *di capitali* flight

esofago *m* (*pl* -ghi) œsophagus, *Am* esophagus

esonerare <1m & c> exempt (*da* from)

esonero *m* exemption

esorbitante exorbitant

esordiente *m/f* beginner

esordio *m* (*pl* -di) introduction, preamble; (*inizio*) beginning; TEA début

esordire <4d> begin; TEA make one's début

esortare <1c> (*incitare*) urge; (*pregare*) beg

esortazione *f* urging

esoterico (*pl* -ci) esoteric

esoterismo *m* esotericism

esotico (*pl* -ci) exotic

espandere <3uu> expand

espandersi expand; (*diffondersi*) spread

espansione *f* expansion

espansività *f fig* warmth, friendliness

espansivo FIS, TEC expansive; *fig* warm, friendly

espatriare <1m & k> leave one's country

espatrio *m* (*pl* -i) expatriation

espediente *m* expedient; *vivere di -i* live by one's wits

espellere <3y> expel

esperienza *f* experience; *per ~* from experience

esperimento *m* experiment

esperto *m/agg* expert

espiare <1h> atone for

espirare <1a> breathe out, exhale

espirazione *f* exhalation

esplicito explicit

esplodere <3q> **1** *v/t colpo* fire **2** *v/i* explode

esplorare <1c> explore

esploratore *m*, -trice *f* explorer; *giovane m ~* boy scout

esplorazione *f* exploration

esplosione *f* explosion; *fig ~ demografica* population explosion

esplosivo *m/agg* explosive

esploso *pp* → **esplodere**

esponente *m/f* exponent

esporre <3ll> expose (*anche* PHOT); *avviso* put up; *in una mostra* exhibit, show; (*riferire*) present; *ragioni, caso* state; *teoria* explain

esporsi expose o.s. (*a* to); (*compromettersi*) compromise o.s.

esportare <1c> export

esportatore **1** *agg* exporting; *paese m ~* exporting country, exporter **2** *m*, -trice *f* exporter

esportazione *f* export

esposimetro *m* FOT exposure meter

espositore *m*, -trice *f* exhibitor

esposizione *f* (*mostra*) exhibition; (*narrazione*) presentation; FOT exposure

esposto **1** *pp* → **esporre 2** *agg in mostra* on show; *~ a* exposed to; *critiche* open to; *~ a sud* south facing **3** *m* statement; (*petizione*) petition

espressione *f* expression

espressivo expressive

espresso **1** *pp* → **esprimere 2** *agg* express **3** *m posta* express letter; FERR express; (*caffè m*) *~* espresso; *macchina f ~* espresso machine; *per ~* express

esprimere <3r> express

esprimersi express o.s.

espropriare <1m & c> expropriate

espropriazione *f* expropriation

esproprio *m* expropriation

espulsione *f* expulsion

espulso pp → **espellere**

essa pron f persona she; cosa, animale it

essenza f essence

essenziale **1** agg essential **2** m: l'~ è the main thing is

essere <3z> **1** v/i be; ~ **di** (provenire di) be or come from; ~ **di qu** (appartenere a) belong to s.o.; **lei è di Roma** she is or comes from Rome; **è di mio padre** it is my father's, it belongs to my father; **c'è** there is; **ci sono** there are; **sono io** it's me; **cosa c'è?** what's the matter?, what's wrong?; **non c'è di che!** don't mention it!; **chi è?** who is it?; **ci siamo!** here we are!; **sono le tre** it's three o'clock; **siamo in quattro** there are four of us; **se fossi in te** if I were you; **sarà!** if you say so! **2** v/aus: **siamo arrivati alle due** we arrived at two o'clock; **non siamo ancora arrivati** we haven't arrived yet; **è stato investito** he has been run over **3** m being; ~ **umano** human being

esso pron m persona he; cosa, animale it

est m east; **a ~ di** east of

estasi f ecstasy

estate f summer; ~ **di San Martino** Indian summer; **in ~, d'~** in (the) summer

estendere <3c> extend

estendersi di territorio extend; (allungarsi) stretch; fig (diffondersi) spread

estensione f extension; (vastità) expanse; MUS range

estenuante exhausting

esteriore m/agg exterior, outside

esteriorità f appearance

esterno **1** agg external; **per uso** ~ for external use only **2** m outside; in film location shot; **all'~** on the outside

estero **1** agg foreign; **ministro m degli Affari -i** Foreign Secretary, Am Secretary of State **2** m foreign countries; **all'~** abroad

esteso **1** pp → **estendere 2** agg extensive; (diffuso) widespread; **per ~** in full

estetica f (a)esthetics

estetista f beautician

estinguere <3d> extinguish, put out; (diffuso) pay off; sete quench

estinguersi die out

estinto **1** pp → **estinguere 2** agg extinct; debito paid off **3** m, -a f deceased

estintore m fire extinguisher

estinzione f extinction; FIN redemption, paying off

estirpare <1a> uproot; dente extract; fig eradicate

estivo summer attr

estorcere <3d> denaro extort

estorsione f extortion

estorto pp → **estorcere**

estradare <1a> extradite

estradizione f extradition

estraneo **1** adj outside (a sth); **corpo m** ~ foreign body **2** m, -a f stranger; persona non autorizzata unauthorized person

estrarre <3xx> extract; pistola draw out; ~ **a sorte** draw

estratto **1** pp → **estrarre 2** m extract; documento abstract; FIN ~ **conto** statement (of account)

estrazione f extraction

estremista m/f (pl -i) extremist

estremità f inv extremity; di corda end; (punta) tip; (punto superiore) top

estremo **1** agg extreme; (più lontano) farthest; (ultimo nel tempo) last, final; **l'-a sinistra** the far or extreme left; **l'Estremo Oriente** the Far East **2** m (estremità) extreme; **gli -i di un documento** the main points

estro m (ispirazione artistica) inspiration

estromettere <3ee> expel, Am expell

estroverso extrovert(ed)

estuario m (pl -ri) estuary

esuberante (vivace) exuberant

esuberanza f exuberance

esule m/f exile

esultare <1a> rejoice

età *f inv* age; *all'~ di* at the age of; ~ *della pietra* Stone Age; *raggiungere la maggiore ~* come of age; *limiti mpl d'~* age limit; *avere la stessa ~* be the same age; *di mezz' ~* middle-aged

etere *m* ether

eternità *f* eternity

eterno eternal; (*interminabile*) endless, never-ending; *questione, problema* age-old; *in ~* for ever and ever

eterogeneo heterogen(e)ous

eterosessuale heterosexual

etica *f* ethics

etichetta *f* label; *cerimoniale* etiquette

etico ethical

etimologia *f* etymology

etiope *agg*, *m/f* Ethiopian

Etiopia *f* Ethiopia

etiopico *m/agg* Ethiopian

etnico (*pl* -ci) ethnic

etrusco (*pl* -chi) **1** *agg* Etruscan **2** *m*, -a *f* Etruscan

ettaro *m* hectare

etto *m* hundred grams

ettogrammo *m* (*pl* -i) hundred grams *pl*, hectogram

ettolitro *m* hectolitre, *Am* -liter

eucalipto *m* eucalyptus

eucaristia *f* REL Eucharist

euforia *f* euphoria

euforico (*pl* -ci) euphoric

euro *m inv* euro

eurocheque *m inv* Eurocheque

eurodeputato *m*, -a *f* Euro MP

eurodollaro *m* Eurodollar

euromercato *m* euromarket

Europa *f* Europe

europeo **1** *agg* European **2** *m*, -a *f* European

eurovisione *f* Eurovision

evacuare <1m> evacuate

evacuazione *f* evacuation

evadere <3q> **1** *v/t* evade; (*sbrigare*) deal with; ~ *le tasse* evade taxes **2** *v/i* escape (*da* from)

evaporare <1m> evaporate

evaporazione *f* evaporation

evasione *f* escape; *fig* escapism; ~ *fiscale f* tax evasion

evasivo evasive

evaso **1** *pp* → **evadere 2** *m*, -a *f* fugitive

evasore *m*: ~ *fiscale* tax evader

evenienza *f* eventuality

evento *m* event

eventuale possible

eventualità *f inv* eventuality; *nell'~ che* in the event that; *per ogni ~* for every eventuality

eventualmente if necessary

evidente evident

evidenza *f* evidence; *mettere in ~* emphasize, highlight

evidenziatore *m* highlighter

evitare <1l & b> avoid; ~ *il fastidio a qu* spare s.o. the trouble

evoluto **1** *pp* → **evolvere 2** *agg* developed; (*progredito*) progressive, advanced; *senza pregiudizi* open minded, broad-minded

evoluzione *f* evolution

evolvere <3s> **1** *v/t* develop **2** *v/i* e evolversi evolve, develop

evviva hurray

ex ... (*nelle parole composte*) ex-, former

expertise *f inv* expertise

extra **1** *agg inv* extra; *di qualità ~* top quality **2** *m inv* extra

extracomunitario **1** *agg* non-EC, non-EU **2** *m*, -a *f* non-EC *or* non-EU citizen

extraconiugale extramarital

extraeuropeo non-European

extraterrestre *agg*, *m/f* extraterrestrial

F

fa 1 → **fare 2** *avv*: **5 anni ~** 5 years ago **3** *m* MUS F; *nel solfeggio della scala* fa(h)

fabbisogno *m* needs *pl*, requirements *pl*

fabbrica *f* (*pl* -che) factory, *Am* plant

fabbricante *m/f* manufacturer

fabbricare <1l & d> manufacture; ARCHI build; *fig* fabricate

fabbricato *m* building

fabbricazione *f* manufacturing; ARCHI building

fabbro *m*: **~** (*ferraio*) blacksmith

faccenda *f* matter

faccende *fpl* housework *sg*

facchino *m* porter

faccia *f* (*pl* -cce) face; (*risvolto, aspetto*) facet; (*lato*) side; **~ tosta** cheek; **~ a ~** face to face; *di* **~ a** opposite, in front of; *in* **~** in the face; *gliel'ha detto in* **~** he told him to his face

facciata *f* ARCHI front, façade; *di foglio* side; *fig* (*esteriorità*) appearance

faccio → **fare**

facile easy; *di carattere* easy-going; (*incline*) prone (**a** to); **è ~ a dirsi!** easier said than done!; **è ~ che venga** he is likely to come; *non è mica una cosa ~* it isn't that easy

facilità *f* ease; (*attitudine*) aptitude, facility; **con ~** easily; INFOR **~ d'uso** user-friendliness

facilitare <1m> facilitate

facilitazione *f* facility; **-i** *pl* **di prezzo** easy terms

facilmente easily

facoltà *f inv* faculty; (*potere*) power; **avere la ~ di scelta** have a choice, be able to choose

facoltativo optional

facoltoso wealthy

facsimile *m* facsimile

faggio *m* (*pl* -ggi) beech (tree)

fagiano *m* pheasant

fagiolini *mpl* green beans

fagiolo *m* bean

fagotto *m* bundle; MUS bassoon; *fig* **far ~** pack up and leave

fai → **fare**

fai da te *m inv* do-it-yourself, DIY

falce *f* scythe

falciare <1f> cut (with a scythe); *fig* mow down

falciatrice *f* lawn-mower

falco *m* (*pl* -chi) hawk

falda *f* layer; GEOL stratum; *di cappello* brim; (*pendio*) slope; (*piede di monte*) foot; **~ acquifera** water table

falegname *m* carpenter

falegnameria *f* carpentry

falena *f* moth

falla *f* MAR leak; **tappare una ~** stop or plug a leak (*anche fig*)

fallimento *m* failure; FIN bankruptcy

fallire <4d> **1** *v/t* miss **2** *v/i* fail; FIN go bankrupt

fallito 1 *agg* unsuccessful, failed; FIN bankrupt **2** *m* failure; FIN bankruptcy

fallo *m* fault; (*errore*) error, mistake; SP foul; **mettere il piede in ~** lose one's footing; **cogliere in ~** *qu* catch s.o. out; (*in flagrante*) catch s.o red-handed

falò *m inv* bonfire

falsare <1a> *verità, fatti* distort

falsario *m* (*pl* -ri) forger

falsificare <1m & d> forge

falsificazione *f* forgery

falsità *f* falsity, falseness; (*menzogna*) lie; (*ipocrisia*) insincerity

falso 1 *agg* false; (*sbagliato*) incorrect, wrong; *oro, gioielli* imitation, fake F; (*falsificato*) forged, fake F **2** *m* (*falsità*) falsehood; *oggetto falsificato* forgery, fake F; DIR forgery

fama *f* fame; (*reputazione*) reputa-

fastidio

tion; **di ~ mondiale** world-famous

fame f hunger; **aver ~** be hungry

famiglia f family; **~ numerosa** large family

familiare 1 agg family attr; (conosciuto) familiar; (semplice) informal **2** m/f relative, relation

familiarità f familiarity

familiarizzare <1a> familiarize

familiarizzarsi familiarize o.s.

famoso famous

fanale m AUTO, MAR, AVIA, FERR light; (lampione) street lamp

fanalino m AUTO: **~ di coda** tail-light; fig **essere il ~ di coda** bring up the rear

fanatico (pl -ci) **1** agg fanatical **2** m, **-a** f fanatic

fanciullo m, **-a** f lit (young) boy; ragazza (young) girl

fandonia f lie

fango m (pl -ghi) mud; MED **-ghi** pl mud-baths

fangoso muddy

fannullone m, **-a** f lazy good-for-nothing

fantascienza f science fiction

fantasia f fantasy; (immaginazione) imagination; (capriccio) fancy; MUS fantasia

fantasma m (pl -i) ghost

fantasticare <1m & d> day-dream (di about)

fantastico (pl -ci) fantastic

fante m carte da gioco jack

fanteria f MIL infantry

fantoccio m (pl -cci) puppet (anche fig)

farabutto m nasty piece of work

faraona f: (gallina f) ~ guinea fowl

farcire <4d> GASTR stuff; torta fill

farcito stuffed; dolce filled

fard m inv blusher

fardello m bundle; fig burden

fare <3aa> **1** v/t do; vestito, dolce, errore make; biglietto, benzina buy, get; **~ (dello) sport** play sport; **~ il pieno** fill up; **~ un bagno** have a bath; **~ il conto** al ristorante prepare the bill; **~ il medico / l'insegnante** be a doctor / teacher; **non fa niente** it

doesn't matter; **~ vedere qc a qu** show sth to s.o.; **~ fare qc** get sth done; **2 più 2 fa 4** 2 and 2 make(s) 4; **quanto fa?** how much is it?; **far ~ qc a qu** get s.o. to do sth **2** v/i: **questo non fa per me** this isn't for me; **faccia pure!** go ahead!, carry on!; **qui fa bello / brutto** the weather here is nice / awful; **fa freddo / caldo** it's cold / warm

farsi (diventare) grow; F (drogarsi) shoot up F; **~ grande** grow tall; **si sta facendo tardi** it's getting late; **~ avanti** step forward; **~ la barba** shave; **~ male** hurt o.s.

farfalla f butterfly

farina f flour

farinaceo 1 agg starchy **2 -cei** mpl starchy foodstuffs

faringe f pharynx

faringite f inflammation of the pharynx

farmaceutico (pl -ci) pharmaceutical

farmacia f pharmacy; negozio chemist's, Am drugstore

farmacista m/f (mpl -i) chemist, Am pharmacist

farmaco m (pl -ci) drug

faro m MAR lighthouse; AVIA beacon; AUTO headlight; **-i** pl **fendinebbia** fog lamps or lights

farsa f farce

fascia f (pl -sce) band; MED bandage; **~ elastica** crepe bandage; **~ oraria** (time) slot

fasciare <1f> MED bandage

fasciatura f (fascia) bandage; azione bandaging

fascicolo m (opuscolo) booklet, brochure; (incartamento) file, dossier

fascino m fascination, charm

fascio m (pl -sci) bundle; di fiori bunch; di luce beam

fascismo m Fascism

fascista agg, m/f (mpl -i) Fascist

fase f phase; AUTO stroke; fig **essere fuori ~** be out of sorts; **~ di lavorazione** production stage

fastidio m (pl -di) bother, trouble;

dare ~ **a qu** bother s.o.; **le dà** ~ **se ... ?** do you mind if ... ?; **un sacco di** ~ **-i** a lot of bother

fastidioso (*irritante*) irritating, annoying; (*irritabile*) irritable

fasto *m* pomp

fastoso sumptuous

fata *f* fairy

fatale fatal; **era** ~ **che non si sarebbero mai più rivisti** they were fated never to meet again

fatalità *f inv* (*il fato*) fate; (*disavventura*) misfortune

fatato magic, enchanted

fatica *f* (*pl* -**che**) (*sforzo*) effort; (*stanchezza*) fatigue; **a** ~ **with** a great deal of effort; **faccio** ~ **a crederci** I find it hard to believe

faticare <1d> toil; ~ **a** find it difficult to

faticoso tiring; (*difficile*) laborious

fatt. *abbr* (= **fattura**) *inv* (= invoice)

fattibile feasible

fatto 1 *pp* → **fare 2** *agg* done; AGR ripe; ~ **a mano** hand-made; ~ **di legno** made of wood; ~ **in casa** home-made; ~ **per qu/qc** (tailor-)made for s.o./sth **3** *m* fact; (*avvenimento*) event; (*faccenda*) affair, business; **il** ~ **è che ...** the fact is that ...; **cogliere sul** ~ catch red-handed; **di** ~ *agg* real; *avv* in fact, actually; **passare a vie di** ~ come to blows; **in** ~ **di** as regards

fattore *m* (*elemento*) factor; AGR farm manager; ~ **di protezione antisolare** sun protection factor

fattoria *f* farm; (*casa*) farmhouse

fattorino *m* messenger; *per consegne* delivery man; *posta* postman, *Am* mailman

fattura *f* (*lavorazione*) workmanship; *di abiti* cut; FIN invoice; **rilasciare una** ~ **a qu** invoice s.o.

fatturare <1a> FIN invoice

fatturato *m* FIN (*giro d'affari*) turnover

fauna *f* fauna

fava *f* broad bean

favola *f* (*fiaba*) fairy tale; (*storia*) story; *morale* fable; (*meraviglia*)

dream; **una vacanza da** ~ a dream holiday

favoloso fabulous

favore *m* favo(u)r; **prezzo** *m* **di** ~ special deal; **a** ~ **di qu** in favo(u)r of s.o.; **per** ~ **!** please!; **fare un** ~ **a qu** do s.o. a favo(u)r

favorevole favo(u)rable

favorire <4d> **1** *v/t* favo(u)r; (*promuovere*) promote **2** *v/i*: **vuol** ~? would you care to join me/us?; **favorisca i documenti!** your papers, please!; **favorisca nello studio** would you go into the study please

favorito *m/agg* favo(u)rite

fax *m inv* fax; **mandare un** ~ **a qc** send s.o. a fax, fax s.o.

faxare <1a> fax

fazione *f* faction

fazzolettino *m*: ~ **di carta** tissue

fazzoletto *m* handkerchief; **per la testa** headscarf

f.co *abbr* (= **franco**) free

febbraio *m* February

febbre *f* fever; **ha la** ~ he has a *or* is running a temperature; ~ **da fieno** hay fever

febbrifugo *m* (*pl* -**ghi**) MED *drug that reduces the temperature*

febbrile feverish

fecondare <1a> fertilize

fecondazione *f* fertilization; ~ **artificiale** artificial insemination

fecondità *f* fertility

fecondo fertile

fede *f* faith; (*fedeltà*) loyalty; *anello* wedding ring; **aver** ~ **in qc** have faith in s.o.; **tener** ~ **a una promessa** keep a promise

fedele 1 *agg* faithful; (*esatto, conforme all'originale*) true **2** *m* REL believer; **i** -**i** *pl* the faithful

fedeltà *f* faithfulness; MUS **alta** ~ hi-fi, high fidelity

federa *f* pillowcase

federale federal

federazione *f* federation

fegato *m* liver; *fig* courage, guts *pl* F

felce *f* fern

felice happy; (*fortunato*) lucky

felicità *f* happiness

felicitarsi <1m>: ~ *con qu per qc* congratulate s.o. on sth

felicitazioni *fpl* congratulations

felino feline

felpa *f* sweatshirt

feltro *m* felt

femmina *f* (*figlia*) girl, daughter; ZO, TEC female

femminile 1 *agg* feminine; (*da donna*) women's **2** *m* GRAM feminine

femminilità *f* feminity

femminismo *m* feminism

femminista *m/f* (*mpl* -i) feminist

femore *m* femur

fendinebbia *m inv* fog lamp *or* light

fenicottero *m* flamingo

fenomeno *m* phenomenon

feriale: *giorno m* ~ weekday

ferie *fpl* holiday *sg, Am* vacation *sg;* ***andare in*** ~ go on holiday (*Am* vacation)

ferimento *m* wounding

ferire <4d> wound; *in incidente* injure; *fig* hurt

ferirsi injure o.s.

ferita *f* wound; *in incidente* injury

ferito 1 *agg* wounded; *in incidente* injured; *fig sentimenti* hurt; *orgoglio* injured **2** *m* casualty

fermacarte *m inv* paperweight

fermacravatta *m* tiepin

fermaglio *m* (*pl* -gli) clasp; *per capelli* hair slide; (*gioiello*) brooch

fermare <1a> stop; DIR detain

fermarsi stop; (*restare*) stay, remain

fermata *f* stop; ~ *dell' autobus* bus stop; ~ *facoltativa o ~ a richiesta* request stop

fermentare <1a> ferment

fermentazione *f* fermentation

fermento *m* yeast; *fig* ferment

fermezza *f* firmness

fermo 1 *agg* still, motionless; *veicolo* stationary; (*saldo*) firm; *mano* steady; *star* ~ (*non muoversi*) keep still; *l'orologio è* ~ the watch has stopped **2** *int* ~*!* (*alt!*) stop!; (*immobile!*) keep still! **3** *m* DIR detention

fermoposta *m* poste restante

feroce fierce, ferocious; *animale* wild; (*insopportabile*) dreadful

ferocia *f* ferocity

ferragosto *m* August 15 public holiday; *periodo* August holidays

ferramenta *f* hardware; *negozio* hardware store, ironmonger's *Br*

ferrato FERR: *strada f -a* railway line, *Am* railroad; *fig essere* ~ *in qc* be well up in sth

ferro *m* iron; (*arnese*) tool; *fig di* ~ *memoria, salute* excellent; *stomaco* cast-iron; ~ *da calza* knitting needle; ~ *da stiro a vapore* steam iron; ~ *di cavallo* horseshoe; ~ *battuto* wrought iron; GASTR *ai -i* grilled, *Am* broiled

ferrovia *f* railway, *Am* railroad; ~ *metropolitana o sotterranea* underground, *Am* subway

ferrovecchio *m* (*pl* -cchi) scrap merchant

ferroviario (*pl* -ri) rail(way) *attr, Am* railroad *attr*

ferroviere *m* rail (*Am* railroad) worker

fertile fertile

fertilità *f* fertility

fertilizzante *m* fertilizer

fesso *m* F idiot F; *far* ~ *qu* con s.o F

fessura *f* (*spaccatura*) crack; (*fenditura*) slit, slot

festa *f* feast; *di santo* feast day; (*ricevimento*) party; (*compleanno*) birthday; (*onomastico*) name day; ~ *della mamma / del papà* Mother's / Father's Day; ~ *nazionale* national holiday; *buone* -*e! a Natale* Merry Christmas and a happy New Year!

festeggiamenti *mpl* celebrations

festeggiare <1f> celebrate; *persona* have a celebration for

festival *m inv* festival

festività *f inv* festival; ~ *pl* celebrations, festivities

festivo festive; *giorno m* ~ holiday

festoso happy, cheerful

feto *m* f(o)etus

fetta *f* slice; *a* -*e* sliced

feudale feudal

fiaba *f* fairy tale

fiabesco (*pl* -chi) fairytale *attr*

fiacca *f* weariness; (*svogliatezza*)

laziness; **battere la ~** slack, be a shirker

fiacco (*pl* -cchi) (*debole*) weak; (*svogliato*) lazy; FIN *mercato* sluggish

fiaccola *f* torch

fiala *f* phial

fiamma *f* flame; MAR pennant; GASTR **alla ~** flambé

fiammante: rosso ~ *m* fiery red; **nuovo ~** brand new

fiammifero *m* match

fiancheggiare <1f> border; *fig* support

fianco *m* (*pl* -chi) side; ANAT hip; **a ~ ~** side by side; **di ~ a qu** beside s.o.; **al tuo ~** by your side

fiasco *m* (*pl* -chi) flask; *fig* fiasco

fiato *m* breath; **senza ~** breathless; MUS **strumento** *m* **a ~** wind instrument; **tutto d'un ~** in one go; **riprendere ~** catch one's breath

fibbia *f* buckle

fibra *f* fibre, *Am* fiber; **di forte ~** robust, sturdy; **~ morale** moral fibre (*Am* fiber); **~ sintetica** synthetic; **~ di vetro** fibreglass, *Am* fiberglass

fibroso fibrous

ficcanaso *m/f* F nosy parker F

ficcare <1d> thrust; F (*mettere*) shove F

ficcarsi get; **~ nei guai** get into hot water; **~ qc in testa** get sth into one's head; **dove s'è ficcato?** where can it / he have got to?

fico *m* (*pl* -chi) *frutto* fig; *albero* fig (tree); **~ d'India** prickly pear

fidanzamento *m* engagement

fidanzarsi <1a> get engaged

fidanzata *f* fiancée

fidanzato *m* fiancé; **i -i** *pl* the engaged couple

fidarsi: ~ di qu / qc trust s.o. / sth, rely on s.o. / sth; **non mi fido di chiederlo a mio padre** I don't dare ask my father

fidato trustworthy

fideiussione *f* DIR guarantee

fido 1 *agg* trusted, trusty **2** *m* FIN credit

fiducia *f* confidence; **avere ~ in qu** have faith in s.o.; **di ~ persona** reliable, trustworthy; *incarico* responsible

fiduciaria *f* **~** FIN trust company

fiduciario (*pl* -ri) **1** *agg* DIR *atto*, *società* trust *attr* **2** *m* trustee

fiducioso trusting

fienile *m* barn

fieno *m* hay

fiera[1] *f animale* wild beast

fiera[2] *f mostra* fair

fierezza *f* pride

fiero proud

fifa F *f* nerves, jitters F; **aver ~** have the jitters, be jittery

figlia *f* daughter

figliastra *f* stepdaughter

figliastro *m* stepson

figlio *m* (*pl* -gli) son; **avere -gli** *pl* have children; **essere ~ unico** be an only child

figlioccia *f* (*pl* -cce) goddaughter

figlioccio *m* (*pl* -cci) godson

figura *f* figure; (*illustrazione*) illustration; (*apparenza*) appearance; **far brutta ~** make a bad impression

figurare <1a> **1** *v/t fig* imagine; **figurati!** just imagine!, just think!; **si figuri!** not at all!, of course not! **2** *v/i* (*apparire*) appear; (*far figura*) make a good impression

figurato (*illustrato*) illustrated; *linguaggio, espressione* figurative

figurina *f da raccolta* collector card, trading card

figurino *m* fashion sketch

fila *f* line, row; (*coda*) queue, *Am* line; **di ~** in succession; **tre giorni di ~** three days running, three days in succession; **in ~ indiana** in single file; **fare la ~** queue, *Am* wait in line

filamento *m* filament

filare <1a> **1** *v/t* spin **2** *v/i di ragno* spin; *di ragionamento* make sense; *di formaggio* go stringy; *di veicolo* travel; F (*andarsene*) take off F; **fila!** go away!, shoo!; **~ diritto** (*comportarsi bene*) behave (o.s.) **3** *m di alberi* row

filarmonico (*pl* -ci) philharmonic

filastrocca *f* (*pl* -cche) *m* nursery rhyme

F

filatelia *f* philately

filato 1 *agg* (*logico*) logical; **andare di ~ a casa** go straight home; **per 10 ore filate** for ten hours straight **2** *m* yarn; **per cucire** thread

file *m inv* INFOR file

filetto *m* GASTR fillet; TEC thread

filiale *f* branch; (*società affiliata*) affiliate

filigrana *f su carta* watermark; *in oreficeria* filigree

film *m inv* film, movie; **~ giallo** thriller; **~ in bianco e nero** black and white film

filmare <1a> film

filmato *m* short (film)

filo *m* (*pl anche* le -a) thread; *metallico* wire; *di lama* edge; *d'erba* blade; **fig un ~ di vergogna / rispetto** an ounce of shame / respect; *fig* **~ conduttore** lead; **~ interdentale** (dental) floss; **~ spinato** barbed wire; **~ di voce** whisper; **per ~ e per segno** in detail; **dare del ~ da torcere a qu** make things difficult for s.o.

filobus *m inv* trolley(bus)

filodrammatica *f* amateur dramatic society

filologia *f* philology

filologo *m* (*pl* -gi) philologist

filone *m* MIN vein; *pane* French stick; *fig* tradition

filosofia *f* philosophy

filosofico (*pl* -ci) philosophic(al)

filosofo *m* philosopher

filovia *f* trolley(bus)

filtrare <1a> **1** *v/t* strain, filter **2** *v/i fig* filter out

filtro *m* filter; **~ dell'olio** oil filter; **~ di carta** filter paper

fin → **fine, fino**

finale 1 *agg* final **2** *m* end **3** *f* SP final

finalista *m/f* finalist

finalmente (*alla fine*) at last; (*per ultimo*) finally

finanza *f* finance; **-e** *pl* finances; **ministro** *m* **delle -e** Minister of Finance

finanziamento *m* funding

finanziare <1g> fund, finance

finanziario (*pl* -ri) financial

finanziere *m* financier; (*guardia di finanza*) Customs and Excise officer; *lungo le coste* coastguard

finché until; (*per tutto il tempo che*) as long as

fine 1 *agg* fine; (*sottile*) thin; *udito, vista* sharp, keen; (*raffinato*) refined **2** *m* aim; **al ~ di ...** in order to ...; **secondo ~** ulterior motive **3** *f* end; **alla ~** in the end; **alla fin ~, in fin dei conti** after all, when all's said and done; **senza ~** endless

fine settimana *m inv* weekend

finestra *f* window

finestrino *m* window; AUTO **~ posteriore** rear window

finezza *f* fineness; (*sottigliezza*) thinness; (*raffinatezza*) refinement

fingere <3d> **1** *v/t:* **~ sorpresa / dolore** pretend to be surprised / to be in pain **2** *v/i:* **~ di** pretend to

fingersi pretend to be

finire <4d> **1** *v/t* finish, end; **finiscila!** stop it! **2** *v/i* end, finish (**in** in); **andrà a ~ male cosa** this will all end in tears; *persona* he / she will come to no good

finito finished; (*venduto*) sold out; **è finita** it's over; **farla finita con qc** put an end to sth

finlandese 1 *m/agg* Finnish **2** *m/f* Finn

Finlandia *f* Finland

fino¹ *agg* fine; (*acuto*) sharp; *oro* pure

fino² *prp tempo* till, until; *luogo* as far as; **~ a domani** until tomorrow; **~ a che** (*per tutto il tempo che*) as long as; (*fino al momento in cui*) until; **fin da ieri** since yesterday

fino³ *avv* even; **fin troppo** more than enough

finocchio *m* (*pl* -cchi) fennel

finora so far

finta *f* pretence, *Am* pretense, sham; SP feint; **far ~ di** pretend to

fintantoché until

finto 1 *pp* → **fingere 2** *agg* false; (*artificiale*) artificial; (*simulato*) feigned

finzione *f* pretence, *Am* pretense, sham

fiocco 112

fiocco *m* (*pl* -cchi) bow; ~ *di neve* snowflake; **-cchi** *pl d'avena* oat flakes, rolled oats; *fig* **coi -cchi** first-rate

fioco (*pl* -chi) weak; *luce* dim

fionda *f* catapult

fioraio *m* (*pl* -ai), **-a** *f* florist

fiordaliso *m* cornflower

fiordo *m* fiord

fiore *m* flower; *fig il* (*fior*) ~ the cream; *nelle carte* **-i** *pl* clubs; *disegno* **a** ~ *a* floral design; *a fior d'acqua* on the surface of the water; *essere in* ~ be in flower

fiorente flourishing

fiorentino 1 *agg* Florentine **2** *m*, **-a** *f* Florentine; GASTR *alla* **-a** with spinach; *bistecca* charcoal grilled **3** *f* GASTR T-bone steak

fioretto *m* SP foil

fiorire <4d> flower; *fig* flourish

fioritura *f* flowering (*anche fig*)

Firenze *f* Florence

firma *f* signature; (*il firmare*) signing; FIN *avere la* ~ be an authorized signatory

firmamento *m* firmament

firmare <1a> sign

firmatario *m* (*pl* -ri) signatory

firmato *abito*, *borsa* designer *attr*

fisarmonica *f* (*pl* -che) accordion

fiscale tax, fiscal; *fig spreg* rigid, unbending

fiscalità *f* taxation; (*pignoleria*) rigidity, lack of flexibility

fischiare <1k> 1 *v/t* whistle; ~ *qu* boo s.o. **2** *v/i di vento* whistle

fischio *m* (*pl* -chi) whistle; SP ~ *finale* final whistle

fisco *m* tax authorities *pl*, Inland Revenue, *Am* Internal Revenue; *il* ~ the taxman

fisica *f* physics; ~ *nucleare* nuclear physics

fisico (*pl* -ci) **1** *agg* physical **2** *m* physicist; ANAT physique

fisiologia *f* physiology

fisionomia *f* face; *fig di popolo*, *città* appearance; (*carattere*) character

fisioterapia *f* physiotherapy

fisioterapista *m/f* (*mpl* -i) physiotherapist

fissare <1a> (*fermare*) fix; (*guardare intensamente*) stare at; (*stabilire*) arrange; (*prenotare*) book

fissarsi (*stabilirsi*) settle; (*ostinarsi*) set one's mind (*di* on); (*avere un'idea fissa*) become obsessed (*di* with); ~ *in mente* memorize

fissatore *m* (*per capelli*) hair-spray; FOT fixer

fissazione *f* (*mania*) fixation (*di* about)

fisso 1 *agg* fixed; *stipendio*, *cliente* regular; *lavoro* permanent **2** *avv* fixedly

fitta *f* sharp pain

fitto¹ 1 *agg* (*denso*) thick; ~ *di* full of **2** *avv nevicare*, *piovere* hard

fitto² *m* rent

fiume *m* river; *fig* flood, torrent; *letto m del* ~ river bed

fiutare <1a> smell; *cocaina* snort; ~ *un imbroglio* smell a rat

fiuto *m* sense of smell; *fig* nose

flacone *m* bottle

flagrante flagrant; *cogliere qu in* ~ catch s.o. red-handed

flanella *f* flannel

flash *m inv* FOT flash; *stampa* newsflash

flatulenza *f* flatulence

flauto *m* flute

flemma *f* calm

flemmatico (*pl* -ci) phlegmatic

flessibile flexible

flessione *f* bending; GRAM inflection; (*diminuzione*) dip, (*slight*) drop

flipper *m inv* pinball machine; *giocare a* ~ play pinball

flirt *m inv* flirtation

flirtare <1a> flirt

F.lli *abbr* (= *fratelli*) Bros (= brothers)

floppy disk *m inv* floppy (disk)

flora *f* flora

floreale floral

floricultura *f* flower-growing industry

florido flourishing

floscio (*pl* -sci) limp; *muscoli* flabby
flotta *f* fleet
fluido *m/agg* fluid
fluorescente fluorescent
fluoro *m* fluorine
flusso *m* flow; **~ e riflusso** ebb and flow
fluttuare <1l> FIN, *fig* fluctuate
fluttuazione *f* fluctuation; **~ dei prezzi** price fluctuation
fluviale river *attr*
f.m. *abbr* (= **fine mese**) end of the month
FMI *abbr* (= **Fondo Monetario Internazionale**) IMF (= International Monetary Fund)
foca *f* (*pl* -che) seal
focaccia *f* (*pl* -cce) focaccia; *dolce* sweet type of bread; **rendere pan per ~** give tit for tat
focalizzare <1a> focus on
foce *f* mouth
focolaio *m* (*pl* -ai) *fig* hotbed
focolare *m* hearth; TEC furnace
focoso fiery
fodera *f interna* lining; *esterna* cover
foderare <1l & c> *all'interno* line; *all'esterno* cover
fodero *m* sheath
foggia *f* (*pl* -gge) *f di abito, acconciatura* style
foglia *f* leaf
fogliame *m* foliage
foglio *m* (*pl* -gli) sheet; INFOR **~ elettronico** spreadsheet; **~ rosa** provisional driving licence; **~ di via obbligatorio** expulsion order
fogna *f* sewer
fognatura *f* sewers *pl*, sewage pipes *pl*
folata *f* gust
folclore *m* folklore
folcloristico (*pl* -ci) folk *attr*
folgorare <1l> *di fulmine, idea* strike; *di corrente elettrica* electrocute; **~ qu con lo sguardo** glare at s.o.
folgorato struck
folklore *m* → **folclore**
folla *f* crowd; *fig* host
folle[1] *agg* mad

folle[2] AUTO: **in ~** in neutral
follia *f* madness
folto thick
fondale *m* MAR sea bed; TEA backcloth, backdrop
fondamentale fundamental
fondamento *m* foundation; **le -a** *fpl* the foundations; **senza ~** unfounded
fondare <1a> found
fondarsi be based (**su** on)
fondato founded
fondatore *m*, **-trice** *f* founder
fondazione *f* foundation
fondere <3bb> **1** *v/t* (*liquefare*) melt; METAL smelt; *colori* blend **2** *v/i* melt
fondersi melt; FIN merge
fonderia *f* foundry
fondiario (*pl* -ri) land *attr*
fondo 1 *agg* deep **2** *m* bottom; (*sfondo*) background; *terreno* property; FIN fund; SP long-distance; SCI cross-country, langlauf; **-i** *pl denaro* funds; **a ~** (*profondamente*) in depth; *fig* **in ~** basically; **in ~ alla strada/al corridoio** at the end or bottom of the road/of the corridor; **essere in ~ al treno** be at the rear of the train; FIN **~ d'ammortamento** depreciation fund; **andare a ~** (*affondare*) sink; (*approfondire*) get to the bottom (**di** of); **-i** *pl di magazzino* old or unsold stock *sg*
fondotinta *m inv* foundation
fonduta *f cheese fondue*
fonetica *f* phonetics
fontana *f* fountain
fonte *m/f* spring; *fig* source; **~ energetica** source of energy; **da ~ attendibile** from a reliable source
footing *m* jogging
foraggio *m* (*pl* -ggi) forage
forare <1a> *di proiettile* pierce; *con il trapano* drill; *biglietto* punch; *pneumatico* puncture
foratura *f di pneumatico* puncture
forbici *fpl* scissors; **un paio di ~** a pair of scissors
forca *f* (*forcone*) pitchfork
forcella *f* TEC fork
forchetta *f* fork; **essere una buona**

~ have a big appetite

forcina f hairpin

forcipe f forceps pl

forcone m pitchfork

foresta f forest

forestale forest attr

foresteria f guest accommodation

forestiero 1 agg foreign **2** m, -a f foreigner

forfait m inv lump sum; SP withdrawal; **a** ~ on a lump-sum basis

forfettario flat-rate, all in; **prezzo** m ~ lump sum

forfora f dandruff

forma f form; (sagoma) shape; TEC (stampo) mo(u)ld; **essere in** ~ be in good form

formaggiera f dish for grated cheese

formaggino m processed cheese

formaggio m (pl -ggi) cheese

formale formal

formalità f inv formality

formare <1a> shape; TELEC ~ **il numero** dial the number

formarsi form; (svilupparsi) develop; di un'idea take shape

formato m size; di libro format

formattare <1a> INFOR format

formazione f formation; fig addestramento training; SP line-up; ~ **professionale** vocational training

formica[1] f (pl -che) ZO ant

formica[2]® Formica®

formicaio m (pl -ai) anthill

formicolare <1m> di mano, gamba tingle; fig ~ **di** teem with

formicolio m sensazione pins and needles pl

formidabile (straordinario) incredible; (poderoso) powerful

formula f formula

formulare <1l> teoria, ipotesi formulate; (esprimere) express

fornaio m (pl -ai) baker; negozio bakery

fornello m stove

fornire <4d> supply (**qc a qu** s.o. with sth)

fornirsi get (**di** sth), get hold (**di** of)

fornitore m supplier

fornitura f supply

forno m oven; (panetteria) bakery; ~ **a microonde** microwave (oven); GASTR **al** ~ carne, patate roast; mele, pasta baked

foro[1] m (buco) hole

foro[2] m romano forum; DIR (tribunale) (law) court

forse perhaps, maybe; **mettere in** ~ cast doubt on

forte 1 agg strong; suono loud; pioggia heavy; taglia large; somma considerable, substantial; dolore severe **2** avv (con forza) hard; (ad alta voce) loudly; (velocemente) fast **3** m (fortezza) fort; **questo è il suo** ~ it's his strong point

fortezza f MIL fortress; ~ **d'animo** strength of character

fortificare <1m & d> rendere più forte strengthen; MIL fortify

fortino m MIL blockhouse

fortuito chance

fortuna f fortune; **avere** ~ be successful; (essere fortunato) be lucky; **buona ~!** good luck!; **fare** ~ make a fortune; **per** ~ luckily; **di** ~ makeshift; **atterraggio** m **di** ~ emergency landing

fortunatamente fortunately

fortunato lucky, fortunate

foruncolo m pimple

forza f strength; (potenza) power; muscolare force; ~ **di gravità** force of gravity; **per cause di** ~ **maggiore** because of circumstances beyond my/our control; **a viva** ~ by force; **a** ~ **di ...** by dint of ...; **per** ~ against my/our will; **per** ~! (naturalmente) of course!; ~! come on!; **-e** pl (armate) MIL armed forces

forzare <1c> force

foschia f haze

fosco (pl -schi) dark

fosfato m phosphate

fosforescente phosphorescent

fosforo m phosphorus

fossa f pit, hole; (tomba) grave; ~ **comune** mass grave

fossato m ditch; di fortezza moat

fossetta f dimple

fossile 1 agg fossil attr **2** m fossil

fosso *m* ditch

foto *f inv* photo, snap

fotocellula *f* photocell

fotocopia *f* photocopy

fotocopiare <1k & c> photocopy

fotocopiatrice *f* photocopier

fotogenico (*pl* -ci) photogenic

fotografare <1m & c> photograph

fotografia *f arte* photography; (*foto*) photograph; ~ *formato tessera* passport-size photograph; ~ *aerea* aerial photograph; ~ *a colori* colo(u)r photograph

fotografico (*pl* -ci) photographic; **macchina** *f* -*a* camera; **articoli** *mpl* -*ci* photographic equipment

fotografo *m* photographer

fotomontaggio *m* (*pl* -gi) photomontage

fotoreporter *m/f inv* photo journalist

fotoromanzo *m* story told in pictures

fra *prp* ◊ between; ~ *Roma e Londra* between Rome and London ◊ among; ~ *questi ragazzi* out of all these boys; ~ *di noi* between you and me; ~ *l'altro* what's more ◊ in; ~ *breve* in a very short time, soon; ~ *tre giorni* in three days ◊ ~ *sé e sé* to himself/herself

frac *m inv* tails

fracassare <1a> smash

fracasso *m di persone* din; *di oggetti che cadono* crash

fradicio (*pl* -ci) rotten; (*bagnato*) soaked, soaking wet; **ubriaco** ~ blind drunk F, blotto F

fragile fragile; *persona* frail, delicate

fragola *f* strawberry

fragore *m* roar; *di tuono* rumble

fraintendere <3c> misunderstand

frammentario (*pl* -ri) fragmentary

frammento *m* fragment

frana *f* landslide

franare <1a> collapse

francamente frankly

francese **1** *m/agg* French **2** *m/f* Frenchman; *donna* Frenchwoman; *i* -*i pl* the French

franchezza *f* frankness

franchigia *f* FIN exemption; *posta* freepost; ~ *doganale* exemption from customs duties

Francia *f* France

franco **1** *agg* frank; FIN free; *farla* -*a* get away with it; ~ *domicilio* free delivery, carriage paid **2** *m* FIN franc

francobollo *m* stamp; *due* -*i da …* *lire* two … lire stamps

frangente *m* (*onda*) breaker; (*situazione*) (difficult) situation

frangia *f* (*pl* -ge) fringe

frantumare <1a> shatter

frantumi *mpl* splinters; *in* ~ in smithereens; *mandare in* ~ smash to smithereens

frappé *m inv* milkshake

frase *f* phrase; ~ *fatta* cliché

frassino *m* ash (tree)

frastagliato: **costa** *f* -*a* jagged coastline

frastuono *m* racket

frate *m* REL friar, monk

fratellastro *m* step-brother; *con legami di consanguineità* half-brother

fratello *m* brother; -*i pl* fratello e sorella brother and sister

fraterno brotherly, fraternal

frattaglie *fpl* GASTR offal *sg*; *di pollo* giblets

frattanto meanwhile, in the meantime

frattempo *m*: *nel* ~ meanwhile, in the meantime

frattura *f* fracture

fratturare <1a> fracture

fratturarsi: ~ *una gamba* break one's leg

frazionare <1a> (*dividere in parti*) break up, split up

frazionarsi split (*in* into)

frazione *f* fraction; POL small group; (*borgata*) hamlet; ~ *decimale* decimal fraction; *una* ~ *di secondo* a split second

freccia *f* (*pl* -cce) arrow; AUTO ~ (*di direzione*) indicator

freddezza *f* coldness

freddo **1** *agg* cold; *fig* **a sangue** ~ in cold blood **2** *m* cold; *ho* ~ I'm cold;

fa ~ it's cold

freddoloso: *essere* ~ feel the cold

freddura *f* pun, play on words

freezer *m inv* freezer

fregare <1e> rub; F (*imbrogliare*) swindle F; F (*battere*) beat, wipe the floor with F; F *a un esame* fail; F (*rubare*) pinch F, lift F; P *me ne frego di quello che pensano* I don't give a damn what they think F

fregata *f* MAR frigate

fregatura *f* F (*imbroglio*) rip-off F; (*ostacolo, contrarietà*) pain F

fregio *m* ARCHI frieze

fremere <3a> (*tremare*) tremble, quiver

frenare <1a> AUTO brake; *folla, lacrime, risate* hold back; *entusiasmo, impulso* restrain

frenarsi (*dominarsi*) restrain o.s.

frenata *f* braking; *fare una* ~ brake; *segni* mpl di ~ tyre marks

freno *m* AUTO brake; *del cavallo* bit; ~ *d'allarme* emergency brake; ~ *a mano* handbrake, Am parking brake; ~ *a pedale* foot-brake; *porre* ~ *a qc* curb sth; *fig senza* ~ without restraint; *tenere a* ~ *la lingua* curb one's tongue

frequentare <1b> *luoghi* frequent; *scuola, corso* attend; *persona* associate with

frequentato popular; *strada* busy

frequente frequent; *di* ~ frequently

frequenza *f* frequency; *scolastica* attendance; *un'alta* ~ *di spettatori* a large audience; *con* ~ frequently

freschezza *f* freshness; *di temperatura* coolness

fresco (*pl* -chi) **1** *agg* fresh; *temperatura* cool; *fig* F *stai* ~ *!* you're for it! F, you've had it! F **2** *m* coolness; *prendere il* ~ take the air; *fa* ~ it's cool; *mettere in* ~ put in a cool place; *fig* F *al* ~ inside F

frescura *f* cool(ness)

fretta *f* hurry; *aver* ~ be in a hurry; *non c'è* ~ there's no hurry, there's no rush; *in tutta* ~, *in* ~ *e furia* in great haste

frettoloso *saluto, sorriso* hurried;

lavoro rushed; *persona* in a hurry

fricassea *f* GASTR fricassee

friggere <3cc> **1** *v/t* fry **2** *v/i* sizzle

friggitoria *f shop that sells deep fried fish etc*

friggitrice *f* deep fryer

frigido MED frigid

frigo *m* fridge

frigorifero 1 *agg* cold *attr*; *camion, nave, vagone* refrigerated **2** *m* refrigerator

fringuello *m* chaffinch

frittata *f* GASTR omelette, Am omelet; *fig ormai la* ~ *è fatta* the damage is done

frittella *f* fritter; *fig* (*macchia*) grease stain

fritto 1 *pp* → **friggere 2** *agg* fried **3** *m* fried food; ~ *misto* assortment of deep-fried food

frittura *f metodo* frying; ~ *di pesce* fried fish

frivolo frivolous

frizionare <1a> rub

frizione *f* friction; AUTO clutch

frizzante *bevanda* fizzy, sparkling; *aria* crisp; *fig parola, motto* biting, sharp

frodare <1c> defraud (*di* of); ~ *il fisco* evade *or* dodge F tax

frode *f* fraud

frontale frontal; *scontro m* ~ head-on collision

fronte 1 *f* forehead; *di* ~ *a* (*dirimpetto*) opposite, facing; *in presenza di* before; *a confronto di* compared to *or* with; *la casa, vista dal di* ~ the house, seen from the front **2** *m* front; ~ *caldo* warm front; *far* ~ *agli impegni* face up to one's responsibilities; *far* ~ *alle spese* make ends meet

fronteggiare <1f> (*stare di fronte a*) face; (*far fronte a*) face, confront

frontespizio *m* (*pl* -zi) title page; ARCHI frontispiece

frontiera *f* border, frontier; *guardia f di* ~ border guard; *valico m di* ~ border crossing

frontone *m* ARCHI pediment

fronzolo *m* frill

fuori

frottola f F fib F

frugale frugal

frugare <1e> **1** v/i (*rovistare*) rummage **2** v/t (*cercare con cura*) search, rummage through

fruire <4d>: ~ **di qc** benefit from sth

frullare <1a> GASTR blend, liquidize; *uova* whisk

frullato m milk-shake

frullatore m liquidizer, blender

frullino m whisk

frumento m wheat

frusciare <1f> rustle

fruscio m rustle

frusta f whip; GASTR whisk

frustare <1a> whip

frustino m riding crop

frustrare <1a> frustrate

frustrazione f frustration

frutta f fruit; ~ **candita** candied fruit; ~ **fresca** fresh fruit; ~ **secca** nuts

fruttare <1a> **1** v/t yield **2** v/i fruit

frutteto m orchard

fruttifero fruitful; FIN interest-bearing

fruttivendolo m, **-a** f greengrocer

frutto m fruit; **-i** pl **di mare** seafood sg

fruttuoso profitable

FS abbr (= **Ferrovie dello Stato**) Italian State railways

fu → **essere**

fucilare <1a> shoot

fucilata f shot

fucile m rifle

fucina f forge

fuga f (pl -ghe) escape; MUS fugue; ~ **di gas** gas leak; FIN ~ **di capitali** flight of capital

fuggevole fleeting

fuggiasco m (pl -schi) fugitive

fuggifuggi m inv stampede

fuggire <4a> flee

fuggitivo m fugitive

fulcro m fulcrum

fuliggine f soot

fuligginoso sooty

fulminante sguardo withering; malattia which strikes suddenly

fulminare <1l> di sguardo look daggers at, glare at; **rimanere fulminato** da fulmine be struck by light-

ning; da elettricità be electrocuted; fig be thunderstruck

fulminarsi di lampadina blow

fulmine m lightning

fulmineo fast, rapid

fumaiolo m MAR funnel; FERR chimney; di casa chimney pot

fumare <1a> smoke

fumatore m, **-trice** f smoker; FERR **scompartimento** m **per -i** / **non -i** smoking / non-smoking compartment

fumetto m comic strip; **-i** pl per ragazzi comics

fumo m smoke; (vapore) steam; fig **andare in** ~ (fallire) go up in smoke; (svanire) come to nothing; **mandare in** ~ shatter

fumoso smoky; fig (oscuro) muddled

fune f rope; (cavo) cable; **tiro** m **alla** ~ tug-of-war

funebre funeral attr; fig gloomy, funereal; **carro** m ~ hearse

funerale m funeral

fungere <3d> act (da as)

fungo m (pl -ghi) mushroom; MED fungus; ~ **velenoso** poisonous mushroom; ~ **prataiolo** field mushroom

funicolare f funicular railway

funivia f cableway

funzionamento m operation, functioning

funzionare <1a> operate, function; **non** ~ be out of order; di orologio have stopped

funzionario m (pl -ri) official, civil servant

funzione f function; (carica) office; REL service, ceremony; **mettere in** ~ put into operation; **in** ~ **di ...** depending on; **variare in** ~ **di ...** vary with ...

fuoco m (pl -chi) fire; FIS, FOT focus; **dar** ~ **a qc** set fire to sth; **-chi d'artificio** fireworks; MIL **far** ~ (open) fire; FOT **mettere a** ~ focus

fuorché except

fuori 1 prp stato outside, out of; moto out of, away from; ~ **di casa** outside the house; ~ **città** out of town; ~

luogo out of place; **~ mano** out of the way; **~ di sé** beside o.s.; **~ uso** out of use **2** *avv* outside; *all'aperto* out of doors; SP out; **di ~** outside; **~!** out!

fuoribordo *m inv* motorboat; *motore* outboard motor

fuoriclasse *agg*, *m/f inv* champion

fuorigioco *m inv* offside; **essere nel ~** be offside

fuoriserie 1 *agg* made to order, custom made **2** *f inv* AUTO custom-built model

fuoristrada *m inv* off-road vehicle

fuoriuscita *f* di gas leakage, escape

fuoriuscito *m* exile

fuorviare <1h> **1** *v/i* go astray **2** *v/t* lead astray

furbizia *f* cunning

furbo cunning, crafty

furfante *m* rascal, rogue

furgoncino *m* (small) van

furgone *m* van

furia *f* fury, rage; **a ~ di ...** by dint of ...

furibondo furious, livid

furioso furious; *vento, lotta* violent

furore *m* fury, rage; **far ~** be all the rage

furtivo furtive

furto *m* theft; **~ con scasso** burglary

fusa *fpl*: **fare le ~** purr

fuscello *m* twig

fuseaux *mpl* leggings

fusibile *m* EL fuse

fusione *f* fusion; FIN merger; **~ nucleare** nuclear fusion

fuso¹ *pp → fondere*; METAL molten; *burro* melted

fuso² *m* spindle; **~ orario** time zone

fusto *m* (*tronco*) trunk; (*stelo*) stem, stalk; *di metallo* drum; *di legno* barrel

futile futile

futilità *f* futility

futuristico futuristic

futuro *m/agg* future; **in ~** in future; **in un lontano / prossimo ~** in the distant / near future

G

g *abbr* (= **grammo**) g (= gram)

gabbia *f* cage; **~ di mattia** *fig* madhouse; **~ toracica** rib cage

gabbiano *m* (sea)gull

gabinetto *m* toilet; POL cabinet; **~ medico / dentistico** doctor's / dentist's surgery; POL **~ ombra** shadow cabinet

gaffe *f* blunder, gaffe

gaelico *m* Gaelic

gala *f* (*ricevimento*) gala; **serata f di ~** gala evening

galante gallant

galanteria *f* gallantry

galantuomo (*pl* -uomini) *m* gentleman

galassia *f* galaxy

galateo *m* *libro* book of etiquette; *comportamento* etiquette, (good) manners

galera *f* (*prigione*) jail, prison

galla *f* BOT gall; **a ~** afloat; **venire a ~** (come to the) surface; *fig* come to light; **tenersi a ~** stay *or* keep afloat

galleggiante 1 *agg* floating **2** *m* (*boa*) buoy

galleggiare <1f> float

galleria *f* gallery; *passaggio con negozi* (shopping) arcade; FERR, MIN tunnel; TEA circle

Galles *m* Wales

gallese 1 *m/agg* Welsh **2** *m/f* Welshman; *donna* Welshwoman

gallina *f* hen

gallo *m* cock; SP **peso m ~** bantam weight

gallone *m* MIL stripe; *unità di misura* gallon

galoppare <1c> gallop

galoppo *m* gallop; *al* ~ at a gallop

gamba *f* leg; *fig in* ~ (*capace*) smart, bright; (*in buona salute*) healthy, (*fighting*) fit; *persona anziana* spry, sprightly; *darsela a -e* take to one's heels

gamberetto *m* shrimp

gambero *m* prawn

gambo *m di fiore, bicchiere* stem; *di pianta, fungo* stalk

gamma *f* range; MUS scale

gancio *m* (*pl* -ci) hook; ~ *di traino* tow-hook

gara *f* competition; *di velocità* race; ~ *automobilistica* car race; ~ *eliminatoria* heat; *fare a* ~ compete

garage *m inv* garage; ~ *sotterraneo* underground car park (*Am* parking garage)

garagista *m* (*pl* -i) (*custode*) garage attendant; (*meccanico*) mechanic

garante *m* guarantor

garantire <4d> 1 *v/t* guarantee; (*assicurare*) ensure 2 *v/i* (*farsi garante*) stand guarantor (*per* for)

garantito guaranteed

garanzia *f* guarantee; *essere in* ~ be under guarantee

garbato courteous, polite

garbo *m* courtesy, politeness; (*modi gentili*) good manners *pl*; (*tatto*) tact

gardenia *f* gardenia

gareggiare <1f> compete

gargarismo *m* gargle; (*collutorio*) mouthwash; *fare i -i* gargle

garofano *m* carnation; GASTR *chiodi mpl di* ~ cloves

garza *f* gauze

garzone *m* boy

gas *m inv* gas; *a* ~ gas *attr*; AUTO *dare* ~ accelerate; ~ *asfissiante* poison gas; ~ *lacrimogeno* tear gas; ~ *naturale* natural gas; ~ *di scarico* exhaust (*fumes*)

gasato 1 *agg bibita* fizzy; (*eccitato*) excited 2 *m*, -**a** *f* bighead

gasolio *m per riscaldamento* oil; AUTO diesel fuel

gastrico (*pl* -ci) gastric; *succhi mpl -ci* digestive juices

gastrite *f* gastritis

gastronomia *f* gastronomy

gastronomico (*pl* -ci) gastronomic

gatta *f* (*female*) cat

gattino *m* kitten

gatto *m* cat; *maschio* (tom) cat; *c'erano quattro -i* there was hardly anybody there

gavetta *f* MIL mess tin; *fare la* ~ come up through the ranks

gay *m/agg* gay

gazza *f* magpie

gazzella *f* gazelle

gazzetta *f* gazette; ~ *ufficiale* official journal, gazette

gazzosa *f* fizzy drink

GB *abbr* (= *Gran Bretagna*) GB (= Great Britain)

G.d.F. *abbr* (= *Guardia di Finanza*) Customs and Excise

gel *m inv* gel

gelare <1b> 1 *v/t* freeze 2 *v/i e* **gelarsi** freeze; *mi si è gelato il sangue* my blood ran cold

gelata *f* frost

gelateria *f* ice-cream parlo(u)r

gelatina *f* gelatine; ~ *di frutta* fruit jelly

gelato 1 *agg* frozen 2 *m* ice cream; ~ *alla vaniglia* vanilla ice cream; ~ *di fragola* strawberry ice cream

gelido freezing

gelo *m* (*brina*) frost; *fig* chill

gelosia *f* jealousy

geloso jealous (*di* of)

gelso *m* mulberry (tree)

gelsomino *m* jasmine

gemellaggio *m* twinning

gemello 1 *agg* twin 2 *m di camicia* cuff link 3 *m*, -**a** *f* twin; ASTR *Gemelli pl* Gemini

gemere <3a> groan

gemito *m* groan

gemma *f* (*pietra preziosa*) gem, jewel; BOT bud; *fig* gem

gene *m* BIO gene

genealogia *f* genealogy

genealogico (*pl* -ci) genealogical; *albero m* ~ family tree

generale 1 *agg* general; *in ~* in general **2** *m* MIL general

generalità *f inv* general nature; *le ~ pl* personal details

generalizzare <1a> generalize

generalmente generally

generare <1l & b> *(dar vita a)* give birth to; *(causare)* generate, create; *sospetti* arouse; *elettricità, calore* generate

generatore *m* EL generator

generazione *f* generation

genere *m* *(tipo, specie)* kind; BIO genus; GRAM gender; *in ~* generally; *unico nel suo ~* unique; *-i pl alimentari* foodstuffs; *-i di consumo* consumer goods; *~ umano* mankind, humanity

generico *(pl -ci)* generic

genero *m* son-in-law

generosità *f* generosity

generoso generous (*con* to)

genesi *f* genesis

genetico *(pl -ci)* genetic; *ingegneria f -a* genetic engineering

gengiva *f* gum

geniale ingenious; *idea* brilliant

genialità *f* genius; *(ingegnosità)* ingeniousness

genio *m* *(pl -ni)* genius; *(inclinazione)* talent; *andare a ~* be to one's liking; *lampo m di ~* brainwave

genitali *mpl* genitals

genitori *mpl* parents

gennaio *m* January

genocidio *m* genocide

Genova Genoa

genovese *m/agg* Genoese

gentaglia *f* scum

gente *f* people *pl*; *quanta ~ !* what a crowd!; *iron ~ bene* upper-crust

gentile kind; *nelle lettere ~ signora* Dear Madam

gentilezza *f* kindness

gentiluomo *(pl -uomini)* *m* gentleman

genuino genuine; *prodotto alimentare* traditionally made; *risata* spontaneous

genziana *f* gentian

geografia *f* geography; *~ economica* economic geography

geografico *(pl -ci)* geographic

geologia *f* geology

geologico *(pl -ci)* geological

geologo *m* *(pl -gi)*, *-a f* geologist

geometra *m/f* surveyor

geometria *f* geometry

geometrico *(pl -ci)* geometric(al)

geranio *m* *(pl -ni)* geranium

gerarchia *f* hierarchy

gerarchico *(pl -ci)* hierarchical; *per via -a* through the proper channels

gerente *m/f* manager

gergo *m* *(pl -ghi)* slang; *di una professione* jargon

geriatrico *(pl -ci)* geriatric; *istituto m ~* old people's home

Germania *f* Germany

germe *m* germ; *fig* *(principio)* seeds *pl*; *in ~* in embryo

germinare <1l & b> germinate

germogliare <1g & c> sprout

germoglio *m* *(pl -gli)* shoot

geroglifico *m* *(pl -ci)* hieroglyph

gerundio *m* *(pl -di)* gerund

gesso *m* MIN gypsum; MED, *scultura* plaster cast; *per scrivere* chalk

gesticolare <1m> gesticulate

gestione *f* management

gestire <4d> manage

gesto *m* *con il braccio, la mano* gesture; *con la testa* nod

gestore *m* manager

Gesù *m* Jesus; *~ bambino* baby Jesus

gettare <1b> throw; *fondamenta* lay; *grido* give, let out; *~ fuori* throw out; *~ via* throw away

gettarsi throw o.s.; *di fiume* flow, empty (*in* into)

getto *m* jet; *di ~* in one go; *a ~ continuo* continuously

gettone *m* token; *per giochi* counter; *per giochi d'azzardo* chip; *~ (telefonico)* (telephone) token; *~ di presenza* *(indennità)* attendance fee; *telefono m a ~* phone taking tokens

ghetto *m* ghetto

ghiacciaio *m* *(pl -ai)* glacier

ghiacciare <1f> *v/t & v/i* freeze

ghiacciato *lago, stagno* frozen; *bibita*

ice-cold; *tè* m ~ iced tea

ghiaccio m (*pl* -cci) ice; *sulla strada* black ice

ghiacciolo m icicle; (*gelato*) ice lolly

ghiaia f gravel

ghianda f acorn

ghiandola f gland

ghigliottina f guillotine

ghignare <1a> sneer

ghigno m sneer

ghiotto *persona* greedy; *fig: di notizie ecc* avid (*di* for); (*appetitoso*) appetizing

ghiottoneria f *difetto* gluttony; *cibo* delicacy

ghirigoro m doodle

ghirlanda f garland

ghiro m dormouse; *dormire come un* ~ sleep like a log

ghisa f cast iron

già already; (*ex*) formerly; *~!* of course!

giacca f (*pl* -cche) jacket; *di abito maschile* jacket; *~ a vento* windproof jacket, windcheater; *~ di pelle* leather jacket

giacché since

giacenza f (*pl* -ze) (*merce per la vendita*) stock; (*merce invenduta*) unsold goods *pl*; *periodo* stock time; *~ di cassa* cash in *or* on hand; *-e pl di magazzino* stock in hand

giacere <2k> lie

giacimento m MIN deposit

giacinto m hyacinth

giada f jade

giaggiolo m iris

giaguaro m jaguar

giallo 1 *agg* yellow; *libro* m *~, film* m *~* thriller **2** m yellow; (*libro, film*) thriller

Giappone m Japan

giapponese *agg, m/f* Japanese

giardinaggio m gardening

giardiniera f *donna* gardener; *mobile* plant stand; GASTR (mixed) pickles

giardiniere m gardener

giardino m garden; *~ botanico* botanical gardens *pl*; *~ d'infanzia* kindergarten; *~ pubblico* park

giarrettiera f garter

giavellotto m javelin

gigante 1 *agg* gigantic, giant *attr* **2** m giant

gigantesco (*pl* -chi) gigantic

giglio m (*pl* -gli) lily

gilè m *inv* waistcoat, *Am* vest

gin m *inv* gin

ginecologo m (*pl* -gi), **-a** f gyn(a)e-cologist

ginepro m juniper

ginestra f broom

gingillarsi <1a> fiddle; (*perder tempo*) fool around

gingillo m plaything; (*ninnolo*) knick-knack

ginnastica f exercises *pl*; *disciplina sportiva* gymnastics; *in palestra* P.E., physical education; *~ presciistica* warm-up exercises (for skiers); *una ~ mentale* a mental exercise

ginocchio m (*pl* -chi e le -chia) knee; *stare in ~* be on one's knees, be kneeling

giocare <1o> **1** *v/i* play; *d'azzardo, in Borsa* gamble; (*scommettere*) bet; *~ a tennis, flipper* play; *~ d'astuzia* use cunning **2** *v/t* play; (*ingannare*) trick

giocarsi (*perdere al gioco*) gamble away; (*beffarsi*) make fun; *carriera* destroy, throw away

giocatore m, **-trice** f player; *d'azzardo* gambler

giocattolo m toy

gioco m (*pl* -chi) game; *il ~* gambling; *~ d'azzardo* game of chance; *~ da bambini* child's play; *~ di prestigio* conjuring trick; *~ elettronico* computer game; *Giochi Olimpici* Olympic Games; *l'ho detto per ~!* I was joking!

giocoliere m juggler

gioia f joy; (*gioiello*) jewel; *fig darsi alla pazza ~* go wild (with excitement)

gioielleria f jeweller's (shop), *Am* jewelry store

gioielliere m, **-a** f jeweller, *Am* jeweler

gioiello m jewel

gioire <4d> rejoice (*di* in)

giornalaio m (*pl* -ai), **-a** f newsagent

giornale m (news)paper; (*rivista*) magazine; (*registro*) journal; **~ radio** news (bulletin); **~ scandalistico** *testata* tabloid; *stampa in genere* gutter press

giornaliero 1 *agg* daily; **abbonamento** m ~ day pass; **spese** *fpl* **-e** day-to-day expenses **2** m day labo(u)rer

giornalino m *per ragazzi* comic; **~ aziendale** inhouse newspaper, staff magazine

giornalismo m journalism

giornalista m/f (mpl -sti) journalist, reporter

giornalistico (pl -ci) *attività, esperienza* journalistic; *agenzia, servizio* news *attr*

giornalmente daily

giornata f day; ~ (*lavorativa*) **di 8 ore** 8-hour day; **lo finiremo in ~** we'll finish it today *or* by the end of the day; **vivere alla ~** live from day to day

giorno m day; **~ di arrivo / partenza** arrival / departure date; **~ di paga** payday; **~ feriale** weekday, working day; **~ festivo** (public) holiday; **illuminato a ~** floodlit; **l'altro ~** the other day; **ogni ~** every day; **a -i** (*fra pochi giorni*) in a few days (time); **al ~** a day; **al ~ d'oggi** nowadays; **in pieno ~** in broad daylight; **di ~** by day

giostra f merry-go-round, *Am* carousel

giovane 1 *agg* young; (*giovanile*) youthful **2** m/f young man, youth; *ragazza* young woman, girl; **i -i** pl young people

giovanile youthful

giovanotto m young man, youth

giovare <1a> (*essere utile*) be useful (**a** to); (*far bene*) be good (**a** for)

giovarsi: **~ di** make use of; *consigli* take

Giove m Jupiter

giovedì m *inv* Thursday; **di ~** on Thursdays

gioventù f youth; (*i giovani*) young people pl

gioviale jovial, jolly

giovinezza f youth

giradischi m record player

giraffa f giraffe

giramondo m/f rolling stone, wanderer

girandola f (*fuoco d'artificio*) Catherine wheel; (*giocattolo*) windmill; (*banderuola*) weather vane

girare <1a> **1** v/t turn; *ostacolo* get round; *posto, città, negozi* go round; *mondo, paese* travel round; *film* shoot; (*mescolare*) mix; FIN endorse **2** v/i turn; *rapidamente* spin; (*andare in giro*) wander *or* roam around; *con un veicolo* drive around; **mi gira la testa** I feel dizzy, my head is spinning

girarrosto m GASTR spit

girasole m sunflower

girata f turn; (*passeggiata a piedi*) walk, stroll; *in macchina* drive; FIN endorsement; **~ in bianco** blank endorsement

giravolta f turn; AUTO spin; *fig* U-turn

girevole revolving

girino m tadpole

giro m turn; (*circolo*) circle; (*percorso abituale*) round; (*deviazione*) detour; (*passeggiata a piedi*) walk, stroll; *in macchina* drive; *in bicicletta* ride; *di pista* lap; *di motore* rev(olution); (*viaggio*) tour; **~ d'affari** turnover; **~ di capitali** circulation of capital; **~ turistico della città** city sightseeing tour; **fare il ~ dei negozi** go round the shops; **nel ~ di una settimana** within a week; **senza tanti -i di parole** without beating about the bush so much; **~ di prova** test drive; **essere in ~** (*a qualche parte*) be around (somewhere); (*fuori*) be out; **mettere in ~** spread; *fig* **prendere in ~ qu** pull s.o.'s leg; **a ~ di posta** by return of post

girocollo m *inv*: **maglione** m **a ~** crewneck (sweater)

gironzolare <1m> hang around; **~ per negozi** wander about the shops

girovagare <1m, c & e> wander about

girovago (*pl* -ghi) **1** *agg* gente nomadic **2** *m* wanderer; (*ambulante*) itinerant

gita *f* trip, excursion; **andare in ~** go on a trip *or* excursion; **~ domenicale** Sunday outing; **~ in bicicletta** bike ride

gitano *m*, **-a** *f* gypsy

gitante *m/f* (day) tripper

giù down; (*sotto*) below; (*da basso*) downstairs; **andar ~** go down; *fig* **non mi va** ~ it sticks in my throat; *fig* **essere** ~ be down *or* depressed; *di salute* be run down; **male qu** swallow (*anche fig*); **un po' più in** ~ a bit lower down; **su e** ~ up and down; **da Roma in** ~ south of Rome

giubbotto *m* sports jacket; **~ di salvataggio** life jacket

giudicare <1l & d> **1** *v/t* judge; (*considerare*) consider, judge; **~ male qu** misjudge s.o.; **lo hanno giudicato colpevole** he has been found guilty. **2** *v/i* judge

giudice *m* judge; **~ istruttore** examining magistrate; **~ di gara** referee

giudiziario (*pl* -ri) judicial; **vendita f -a** a sale by order of the court

giudizio *m* (*pl* -zi) judg(e)ment; (*senno*) wisdom; DIR (*causa*) trial; (*sentenza*) verdict; **a mio** ~ in my opinion; **~ civile** civil action, lawsuit; **mettere** ~ turn over a new leaf

giudizioso sensible

giugno *m* June

giunco *m* (*pl* -chi) reed

giungere <3d> **1** *v/t*: **~ le mani** clasp one's hands **2** *v/i* arrive (**a** in, at), reach (**a** sth); **~ a Roma / alla stazione** arrive in Rome / at the station, reach Rome / the station; *fig* **~ in porto** reach one's goal; **questa mi giunge nuova** it's news to me

giungla *f* jungle

giunta *f* addition; POL junta; **~ comunale** town council; **per** ~ in addition, moreover

giunto *pp* → **giungere**

giuntura *f* ANAT joint

giuramento *m* oath; **falso** ~ perjury; **fare un** ~ swear an oath; **prestare** ~ take the oath

giurare <1a> swear

giurato 1 *agg* sworn **2** *m* member of the jury

giuria *f* jury

giuridico (*pl* -ci) legal

giurisdizione *f* jurisdiction

giurisprudenza *f* jurisprudence

giurista *m/f* (*mpl* -sti) jurist

giustezza *f* accuracy; *di argomentazione* soundness; TIP justification

giustificare <1m & d> justify

giustificazione *f* justification

giustizia *f* justice; **fare** ~ **sommaria** administer summary justice

giusto 1 *agg* just, fair; (*adatto*) right, appropriate; (*esatto*) correct, right, exact **2** *avv* correctly; *mirare* accurately; (*proprio, per l'appunto*) just; **~!** that's right! **3** *m* (*uomo giusto*) just man; **pretendo solo il** ~ I just want what is rightfully mine

glaciale glacial, icy

gladiolo *m* gladiolus

glassa *f* GASTR icing

gli 1 *art mpl* the; **avere gli occhi azzurri** have blue eyes **2** *pron* (*a lui*) (to) him; (*a esso*) (to) it; (*a loro*) (to) them; **dagli i libri** give him / them the books, give the books to him / them

glicemia *f* glyc(a)emia

glicerina *f* glycerine

glicine *m* wisteria

glie-: **~-la, ~-lo, ~-li, ~-le, ~-ne** = *pron* **gli** *or* **le** with *pron* **la, lo, li, le, ne**

globale global

globo *m* globe; **~ oculare** eyeball; **~ terrestre** globe

globulo *m* globule; MED corpuscle; **~ rosso / bianco** red / white blood cell

gloria *f* glory

glorificare <1m & d> glorify

glorioso glorious

glossa *f* gloss

glossario *m* (*pl* -ri) glossary

glucosio *m* glucose

gnocchi *mpl* (*di patate*) gnocchi (*small potato dumplings*)

G

gnorri m F: **fare lo ~** act dumb F

goal m inv SP goal

gobba f hump

gobbo 1 agg hunchbacked **2** m hunchback

goccia f (pl -cce) drop; **a ~ a ~** little by little

gocciolare <1l> drip

gocciolio m (pl -ii) drip

godere <2a> **1** v/t enjoy; **godersela** enjoy o.s. **2** v/i (rallegrarsi) be delighted (**di** at)

godimento m enjoyment

goffo awkward, clumsy

gol m inv SP goal

gola f throat; (ingordigia) greed-(iness), gluttony; GEOG gorge; **mal m di ~** sore throat; **far ~ a** tempt

golf m inv golf; (cardigan) cardigan; (maglione) sweater; **giocatore m di ~** golf player, golfer

golfista m/f golfer

golfo m gulf

golosità f (ghiottoneria) greed-(iness), gluttony; (leccornia) delicacy

goloso greedy; **essere ~ di dolci** have a sweet tooth

golpe m inv coup

gomito m elbow; **curva f a ~** sharp bend; fig **alzare il ~** hit the bottle

gomitolo m ball (of wool)

gomma f rubber; per cancellare eraser; (pneumatico) tyre, Am tire; **~ da masticare** (chewing) gum; AUTO **~ di scorta** spare tyre (Am tire); **avere una ~ a terra** have a flat tyre (Am tire)

gommapiuma f foam rubber

gommato carta gummed; tessuto rubberized

gommista m (pl -i) tyre (Am tire) specialist

gommone m rubber dinghy

gondola f gondola

gondoliere m gondolier

gonfiare <1k> **1** v/t con aria inflate; le guance puff out; fig (esagerare) exaggerate, magnify **2** v/i e **gonfiarsi** swell up; fig puff up

gonfio (pl -fi) swollen; pneumatico inflated; stomaco bloated; fig puffed up (**di** with); fig **a -e vele** splendidly

gonfiore m swelling

gonna f skirt; **~ a pieghe** pleated skirt; **~ pantalone** culottes pl

gorgo m (pl -ghi) whirlpool

gorgogliare <1g> di stomaco rumble; dell'acqua gurgle

gorilla m inv gorilla; F (guardia del corpo) bodyguard, gorilla F

gotico (pl -ci) m/agg Gothic

gotta f MED gout

governante 1 f housekeeper **2** m ruler

governare <1b> POL govern, rule; MAR steer

governativo government attr; scuola state attr

governatore m governor

governo m government; MAR steering; **~ di coalizione** coalition government; **~ di minoranza** minority government

gozzo m MED goitre, Am goiter

gozzovigliare <1g> make merry

gracchiare <1k> di corvo caw; di rane croak; di persona squawk

gracidare <1l> croak

gracile (debole) delicate

gradasso m boaster

gradazione f gradation; (sfumatura) shade; **~ alcolica** alcohol(ic) content

gradevole pleasant, agreeable

gradimento m liking

gradinata f flight of steps; stadio stand; a teatro gallery, balcony

gradino m step

gradire <4d> like; (desiderare) wish; **gradirei sapere** I would like to know; **gradisce un po' di vino?** would you like some wine?

gradito pleasant; (bene accetto) welcome

grado[1] m degree; in una gerarchia, MIL rank; **30 -i all'ombra** 30 degrees in the shade; **in ~ di lavorare** capable of working, fit for work; **essere in ~ di** be in a position to; **per -i** by degrees

grado[2] m: **di buon ~** willingly

graduale gradual

graduare <1l> graduate

graduatoria f list

graduazione f graduation

graffa f TIP brace

graffiare <1k> scratch

graffio m (pl -ffi) scratch

graffiti mpl graffiti

grafia f (hand)writing

grafica f graphics pl

grafico (pl -ci) **1** agg graphic **2** m (diagramma) graph; (disegnatore) graphic artist

grafite f graphite

grafologia f handwriting analysis

grammatica f grammar

grammaticale grammatical

grammo m gram(me)

gran → **grande**

grana 1 f grain; F (seccatura) trouble; F soldi dough F, cash; F **piantare una ~** stir up trouble; F **pieni di ~** rolling in money F **2** m inv cheese similar to Parmesan

granaio m (pl -ai) barn

granata f MIL grenade; BOT pomegranate

Gran Bretagna f Great Britain

granchio m (pl -chi) crab; fig blunder; fig **prendere un ~** make a blunder

grandangolare m FOT wide-angle lens

grande big, large; (alto) big, tall; (largo) wide; fig (intenso, notevole) great; (adulto) grown-up, big; (vecchio) old; FERR **~ velocità** high speed; **non è un gran che** it's nothing special

grandezza f (dimensione) size; (larghezza) width; (ampiezza) breadth; (altezza) height; fig (eccellenza) greatness; (grandiosità) grandeur

grandinare <1l> hail

grandinata f hailstorm

grandine f hail

grandioso grand

granduca m (pl -chi) grand duke

granducato m grand duchy

granduchessa f grand duchess

granello m grain; **~ di pepe** pepper-

corn; **~ di polvere** speck of dust; **~ di sabbia** grain of sand

granita f type of ice made of frozen crystals of coffee or fruit syrup

granito m granite

grano m (chicco) grain; (frumento) wheat; fig grain, ounce

granturco m maize, corn

grappa f grappa, brandy made from the remains of the grapes used in wine-making

grappolo m bunch

grassetto m TIP bold (type)

grasso 1 agg fat; (unto) greasy; cibo fatty **2** m fat; di bue, pecora suet; **macchia f di ~** grease stain; **~ lubrificante** grease; **privo di -i** fat-free

grassoccio (pl -cci) plump

grata f grating

gratella f, **graticola** f GASTR grill

gratifica f bonus

gratin m: **al ~** au gratin

gratinato → **al gratin**

gratis free (of charge)

gratitudine f gratitude

grato grateful; (gradito) welcome; **vi sarei grato se …** I would be grateful if …, I would appreciate it if …

grattacapo m problem, headache F

grattacielo m skyscraper

grattare <1a> scratch; (raschiare) scrape; (grattugiare) grate; F swipe F, pinch F

grattugia f (pl -ge) grater

grattugiare <1f> grate; **pane m grattugiato** breadcrumbs pl

gratuito free (of charge); (infondato) gratuitous

gravare <1a> **1** v/t burden **2** v/i weigh (su on)

grave (pesante) heavy; (serio) serious; (difficile) hard

gravidanza f pregnancy

gravità f seriousness, gravity; FIS (forza f di) ~ (force of) gravity

gravoso onerous

grazia f grace; (gentilezza) favo(u)r; REL grace; DIR pardon; **in ~ di** thanks to; **con ~** gracefully; **colpo m di ~** coup de grâce

graziare <1g> pardon

grazie *int* thank you, thanks; *tante ~* thank you so much; *~ a* thanks to; *~ a Dio!* thank goodness!

grazioso charming; *(carino)* pretty

Grecia *f* Greece

greco *(pl -ci)* **1** *agg* Greek **2** *m*, *-a f* Greek

gregge *m (pl le -ggi)* flock

greggio *(pl -ggi)* **1** *agg (non lavorato)* raw, crude **2** *m* crude *(petroleum)*

grembiule *m* apron

grembo *m* lap; *(materno)* womb; *fig* bosom

gremito crowded

gretto *(avaro)* mean; *(di mente ristretta)* narrow-minded

gridare <1a> **1** *v/t* shout, yell; *~ aiuto* shout for help **2** *v/i* shout, yell; *(strillare)* scream

grido *m (pl gen le -da)* shout, cry

grigio *(pl -gi)* grey, *Am* gray; *fig (triste)* sad; *(scialbo)* dull, dreary

grigiore *m* greyness, *Am* grayness; *fig (monotonia)* dullness, dreariness

griglia *f (grata)* grating; GASTR grill; *alla ~* grilled

grilletto *m* trigger

grillo *m* cricket; *fig (capriccio)* fancy, whim

grimaldello *m* device for picking locks

grinfie *fpl* clutches

grinta *f* grit; *fig* determination

grinza *f di stoffa* crease

grinzoso *viso* wrinkled; *(spiegazzato)* creased

grissino *m* bread stick

grondaia *f* gutter

grondare <1a> **1** *v/i (colare)* pour; *(gocciolare)* drip; *~ di sudore* be dripping with sweat **2** *v/t* drip with

groppa *f* back

groppo *m*: *avere un ~ alla gola* have a lump in one's throat

grossezza *f (dimensione)* size; *(spessore)* thickness; *(l'essere grosso)* largeness

grossista *m/f (mpl -i)* wholesaler

grosso 1 *agg* big, large; *(spesso)* thick; *mare* rough; *sale, ghiaia* coarse;

F *pezzo m* ~ big shot F; *questa è -a!* this is too much!; *sbagliarsi di ~* make a big mistake; *farla -a* make a fine mess **2** *m* bulk

grossolano coarse; *errore* serious

grossomodo roughly

grotta *f* cave; *artificiale* grotto

grottesco *(pl -chi)* grotesque

groviglio *m (pl -gli)* tangle; *fig* muddle

gru *f inv* crane

gruccia *f (pl -cce)* crutch; *per vestiti* hanger

grumo *m* clot; *di farina* lump

gruppo *m* group; *~ sanguigno* blood group; *~ di lavoro* working group; *a -i* in groups

guadagnare <1a> earn; *(ottenere)* gain

guadagno *m* gain; *(profitto)* profit; *(entrate)* earnings *pl*; *margine m di ~* profit margin

guaina *f sheath; (busto)* corset, girdle

guaio *m (pl -ai)* trouble; *(danno)* damage; *-ai a te se lo fai!* woe betide you if you do!; *essere nei -ai* be in trouble

guancia *f (pl -ce)* cheek

guanciale *m* pillow

guanto *m* glove

guantone *m*: *~ da boxe* boxing glove

guardaboschi *m inv* forest ranger

guardacaccia *m inv* gamekeeper

guardacoste *m inv* MAR coastguard

guardalinee *m inv* SP assistant referee, linesman

guardamacchine *m* car park (*Am* parking lot) attendant

guardare <1a> **1** *v/t* look at; *(osservare, stare a vedere)* watch; *(custodire)* watch, look after; *(esaminare)* check **2** *v/i* look; *(controllare)* check; *di finestra* overlook (*su* sth); *di porta* lead (*su* to); *~ a sud* face south

guardarsi look at o.s.; *~ da* beware of; *(astenersi)* refrain from

guardaroba *m inv* cloakroom, *Am* checkroom; *armadio* wardrobe

guardarobiere *m*, *-a f* cloakroom attendant

guardia *f* guard; ~ **forestale** forest ranger; ~ **di finanza** Customs and Excise officer; ~ **di pubblica sicurezza** policeman; ~ **del corpo** bodyguard; ~ **medica, medico** *m* **di** ~ doctor on duty; **fare la** ~ keep guard; **stare in** ~ be on one's guard

guardiano *m* **-a** *f* (*custode*) warden; (*portiere*) caretaker; (*guardia*) guard; *di parco* keeper; ~ **notturno** night watchman

guardone *m* voyeur

guardrail *m inv* guardrail

guarigione *f* recovery; **in via di** ~ on the mend

guarire <4d> **1** *v/t* cure **2** *v/i* recover; *di ferita* heal

guarnire <4d> decorate; *abiti* trim; GASTR garnish

guarnizione *f* (*abbellimento*) trimming; GASTR garnish; *di rubinetto* washer; AUTO ~ **del freno** brake lining

guastafeste *m/f inv* spoilsport

guastare <1a> spoil, ruin; *meccanismo* break

guastarsi break down; *di tempo* change for the worse; *di cibi* go bad, spoil

guasto **1** *agg* broken; *telefono, ascensore* out of order; AUTO broken down; *cibi* bad, off F; *dente* rotten, decayed **2** *m* fault, failure; AUTO breakdown

guerra *f* war; ~ **civile** civil war; ~ **lampo** blitz; ~ **fredda** Cold War

guerrafondaio *m* (*pl* -ai) warmonger

guerriglia *f* guerrilla warfare

guerrigliero *m*, **-a** *f* guerrilla

gufo *m* owl

guida *f* guidance; (*persona, libro*) guide; AUTO driving; ~ **alpina** mountain guide; ~ **telefonica** phone book; ~ **turistica** tourist guide; AUTO ~ **a destra/a sinistra** right-hand/left-hand drive

guidare <1a> guide; AUTO drive

guidatore *m*, **-trice** *f* driver

guinzaglio *m* (*pl* -gli) lead, leash

guizzare <1a> dart

guscio *m* (*pl* -sci) shell

gustare <1a> taste; *fig* enjoy

gusto *m* taste; (*sapore*) flavo(u)r; *fig* (*piacere*) pleasure; **buon/cattivo** ~ good/bad taste; **senza** ~ tasteless

gustoso tasty; *fig* delightful

H

h *abbr* (= **ora**) h (= hour)

ha *abbr* (= **ettaro**) ha (= hectare)

ha, hai, hanno → **avere**

habitat *m inv* BIO habitat

habitué *m/f inv* regular customer

hacker *m/f* INFOR *inv* hacker

hall *f inv* foyer

hamburger *m inv* hamburger

handicap *m inv* handicap

handicappato **1** *agg* disabled, handicapped **2** *m*, **-a** *f* disabled *or* handicapped person

hard disk *m inv* INFOR hard disk

hardware *m inv* INFOR hardware

harem *m inv* harem

hashish *m inv* hashish

henné *m inv* henna

herpes *m inv* herpes

hg *abbr* (= **ettogrammo**) hg (= hectogram)

hinterland *m inv* hinterland

hit parade *f inv* hit parade

hl *abbr* (= **ettolitro**) hl (= hectolitre)

hm *abbr* (= **ettometro**) hm (= hectometre)

ho → **avere**

hobby *m inv* hobby
hockey *m inv* hockey; **~ su ghiaccio** ice hockey
holding *f inv* holding

hostess *f inv* hostess; **~ di terra** (*guida*) member of ground staff
hotel *m inv* hotel
hot dog *m inv* hot dog

I

i *art mpl* the

iberico (*pl* -ci) Iberian
iceberg *m inv* iceberg
icona *f* icon
iconografia *f* iconography
Iddio *m* God
idea *f* idea; (*opinione*) opinion; **~ fissa** obsession, idée fixe; **cambiare ~** change one's mind; **non avere la minima ~ di qc** not have the slightest idea about sth; **scambio *m* di -e** exchange of views; **neanche per ~!** of course not!
ideale *m/agg* ideal
idealizzare <1a> idealize
ideare <1b> *scherzo, scusa* think up; *metodo, oggetto nuovo* invent; *piano, progetto* devise
ideatore *m*, **-trice** *f* originator; *di metodo, oggetto nuovo* inventor
idem ditto
identico (*pl* -ci) identical
identificare <1n & d> identify
identificazione *f* identification
identikit® *m inv* Identikit
identità *f inv* identity
ideologia *f* ideology
ideologico (*pl* -ci) ideological
idioma *m* (*pl* -i) idiom
idiomatico (*pl* -ci) idiomatic
idiota **1** *agg* idiotic, stupid **2** *m/f* (*mpl* -i) idiot, fool
idiozia *f* stupidity, idiocy; (*assurdità*) nonsense; **un'~** a stupid *or* idiotic thing to do / say
idolo *m* idol
idoneità *f* suitability; *qualifica* qualification

idoneo suitable (**a** for)
idrante *m* hydrant
idratante *della pelle* moisturizing
idratare <1a> *la pelle* moisturize
idraulico **1** *agg* hydraulic; **impianto *m* ~** plumbing **2** *m* (*pl* -ci) plumber
idrico water *attr*
idromassaggio *m* Jacuzzi®, whirlpool bath
idroelettrico hydroelectric
idrofilo: **cotone ~** cotton wool, *Am* absorbent cotton
idrofobo ZO rabid; (*furioso*) foaming at the mouth
idrogeno *m* hydrogen
idroplano *m* hydroplane
iena *f* hyena
ieri yesterday; **~ l'altro, l'altro ~** the day before yesterday; **~ mattina** yesterday morning
igiene *f* hygiene; **~ del corpo** personal hygiene; **ufficio *m* d'~** public health office
igienico (*pl* -ci) hygienic; **carta *f* -a** toilet paper
ignaro unaware (**di** of)
ignorante (*non informato*) ignorant; (*incolto*) uneducated; (*maleducato*) rude
ignoranza *f* ignorance
ignorare <1a> (*non considerare*) ignore; (*non sapere*) not know; **lo ignoro** I don't know
ignoto unknown
il *art m sg* the; **~ signor Conte** Mr Conte; **~ martedì** on Tuesdays; **3000 lire ~ chilo** 3000 lire a kilo; **mi piace il caffè** I like coffee

illecito illicit

illegale illegal

illegalità f illegality

illeggibile illegible

illegittimo illegitimate

illeso unhurt

illimitato unlimited

ill.mo *abbr* (= *illustrissimo*) formal style of address in correspondence

illogico (*pl* -ci) illogical

illudere <3q> deceive

illudersi delude o.s.

illuminare <1m> light up; *fig* enlighten

illuminazione f lighting; *fig* flash of inspiration; **~ stradale** street lighting

illusione f illusion

illuso 1 *pp* → **illudere** 2 *m/f* (*sognatore*) dreamer

illusorio (*pl* -ri) illusory

illustrare <1a> illustrate

illustratore *m*, **-trice** f illustrator

illustrazione f illustration

illustre illustrious

imballaggio *m* (*pl* -ggi) *operazione* packing; (*involucro*) package

imballare <1a> pack; AUTO **~ il motore** race the engine

imballo *m* → **imballaggio**

imbalsamare <1a> embalm; *animale* stuff

imbambolato *occhi, sguardo* blank; *dal sonno* bleary-eyed; **non star lì fermo ~!** don't stand there gawping!

imbarazzante embarrassing

imbarazzare <1a> embarrass

imbarazzato embarrassed

imbarazzo *m* embarrassment; (*disturbo*) trouble; **non avere che l'~ della scelta** be spoilt for choice; **~ di stomaco** upset stomach; **mettere in ~ qu** embarrass s.o.

imbarcadero *m* landing stage

imbarcare <1d> embark; *carico* load

imbarcarsi go on board, embark; **~ in un'impresa** embark on an undertaking

imbarcazione f boat; **~ da diporto** pleasure boat

imbarco *m* (*pl* -chi) *di passeggeri* boarding, embarkation; *di carico* loading; (*banchina*) landing stage

imbattersi <3a>: **~ in qu** bump into s.o.

imbattibile unbeatable

imbecille 1 *agg* idiotic, stupid 2 *m/f* imbecile, fool

imbiancare <1d> 1 *v/t* whiten; *con pitture* paint; *tessuti* bleach 2 *v/i e* **imbiancarsi** go white

imbianchino *m* (house) painter

imboccare <1d> *persona* feed; *fig* prompt; **~ una strada** turn into a road

imboccatura f (*apertura*) opening; (*ingresso*) entrance; MUS mouthpiece

imbocco *m* entrance

imboscata f ambush

imbottigliamento *m* bottling; AUTO traffic jam

imbottigliare <1g> bottle; *di veicoli* hold up; **sono rimasto imbottigliato nel traffico** I was stuck in a traffic jam

imbottire <4d> stuff; *giacca* pad; *fig* (*riempire*) cram, stuff

imbottito stuffed; *panino* filled

imbottitura f stuffing; *di giacca* padding

imbranato clumsy

imbrattare <1a> soil; (*macchiare*) stain

imbrattatele *m/f inv* dauber

imbrogliare <1g & c> 1 *v/t* (*raggirare*) take in; (*truffare*) cheat, swindle; *fig* confuse 2 *v/i* cheat

imbroglio *m* (*pl* -gli) (*truffa*) trick; *fig* (*pasticcio*) mess

imbroglione *m*, **-a** f cheat, swindler

imbronciato sulky

imbrunire <4d> get dark

imbruttire <4d> 1 *v/t* make ugly 2 *v/i* become ugly

imbucare <1d> *posta* post, *Am* mail

imburrare <1a> butter

imbuto *m* funnel

imitare <1a *or* 1l> imitate

imitazione f imitation

immagazzinare <1a> store

immaginare <1m> imagine; (*supporre*) suppose; **s'immagini!** not at all!

immaginario (*pl* -ri) imaginary

immaginazione *f* imagination

immagine *f* image

immancabile *cortesia, sorriso* unfailing; *persona* ever present; *macchina fotografica* inevitable

immangiabile inedible

immatricolare <1n> register

immatricolarsi enrol, *Am* enroll; *all'università* matriculate, enrol

immatricolazione *f* registration; *all'università* matriculation, enrol(l)ment

immaturità *f* immaturity

immaturo *persona* immature; (*precoce*) premature; *frutto* unripe

immedesimarsi <1n> identify (*in* with)

immediatamente immediately

immediato immediate; (*pronto*) prompt

immenso immense

immergere <3uu> immerse, dip; (*lasciare immerso*) soak

immergersi plunge; *di subacqueo, sottomarino* dive; *fig* immerse o.s. (*in* in)

immeritato undeserved

immersione *f* immersion; *di subacqueo, sottomarino* dive

immerso 1 *pp* → **immergere 2** *agg* immersed

immettere <3ee> introduce (*in* into); INFOR *dati* enter; (*portare*) lead (*in* into)

immettersi: ~ *in* get into

immigrante *m/f* immigrant

immigrare <1a> immigrate

immigrato *m*, **-a** *f* immigrant

immigrazione *f* immigration; (*immigrati*) immigrants *pl*; FIN inflow

imminente imminent; *pericolo* impending; *pubblicazione* forthcoming

imminenza *f* imminence

immischiare <1k> involve

immischiarsi meddle (*in* with), interfere (*in* in)

immissione *f* introduction; *di manodopera* intake; INFOR *di dati* entry

immobile 1 *agg* motionless, still **2** *mpl*: **-i** real estate *sg*

immobiliare: **agente** *m/f* ~ estate agent, *Am* realtor; **società** *f* ~ *di compravendita* property company; *di costruzione* construction company

immobilismo *m* inactivity; POL opposition to progress

immobilità *f* immobility; POL, FIN inactivity

immobilizzare <1a> immobilize; FIN *capitali* tie up

immondizia *f* (*gen pl*) rubbish, refuse, *Am* trash

immorale immoral

immoralità *f* immorality

immortale immortal

immortalità *f* immortality

immune MED immune (*a* to); (*esente*) free (*da* from)

immunità *f* immunity

immunitario: **sistema** *m* ~ immune system

immunizzare <1a> immunize

immunodeficienza *f* immunodeficiency

immutabile *decisione, legge* unchangeable; *principi, tradizioni* unchanging

immutato unchanged

impacchettare <1a> (*confezionare*) wrap (up); (*mettere in pacchetti*) package

impacciare <1f> *movimenti* hamper; *persona* hinder

impacciato (*imbarazzato*) embarrassed; (*goffo*) awkward, clumsy

impaccio *m* (*pl* -cci) (*ostacolo*) hindrance; (*situazione difficile*) awkward situation; (*imbarazzo*) awkwardness

impacco *m* (*pl* -cchi) MED compress

impadronirsi <4d>: ~ *di qc* take possession of sth, seize sth; *fig* master sth

impagabile priceless

impaginare <1m> TIP paginate

impaginazione *f* pagination

impalcatura *f temporanea* scaffolding; *fig* framework, structure

impallidire <4d> *di persona* turn pale

impanare <1a> GASTR coat with breadcrumbs

impanato in breadcrumbs, breaded

impantanarsi <1a> get bogged down

impaperarsi <1m> falter

imparare <1a> learn (*a* to)

imparentarsi <1b>: **~ con qu** become related to s.o.

impari unequal; MAT odd

impartire <4d> give

imparziale impartial

imparzialità *f* impartiality

impassibile impassive

impastare <1a> mix; *pane* knead

impasto *m* GASTR dough; (*mescolanza*) mixture

impatto *m* impact

impaurire <4d> frighten

impaurirsi become frightened

impaziente impatient

impazienza *f* impatience

impazzata: **all'~** *correre* at breakneck speed; *colpire* wildly

impazzire <4d> go mad *or* crazy; **far ~ qu** drive s.o. mad *or* crazy

impeccabile impeccable

impedimento *m* hindrance; (*ostacolo*) obstacle; DIR impediment; **essere d'~** be a hindrance

impedire <4d> prevent; (*ostruire*) block, obstruct; (*impacciare*) hinder; **~ a qu di fare qc** prevent s.o. *or* keep s.o. from doing sth

impegnare <1a> (*dare come pegno*) pawn; (*riservare*) reserve, book; *spazio*, *corsia* occupy, take up; SP *avversario* keep under pressure; (*costringere*) oblige; **~ qu** di lavoro keep s.o. busy *or* occupied; **~ qu per contratto** bind s.o. by contract

impegnarsi (*prendersi l'impegno*) commit o.s., undertake (*a* to); (*concentrarsi*) apply o.s. (*in* to); **mi sono impegnata a farlo** I've committed myself to doing it, I've undertaken to do it

impegnativo (*che richiede impegno*) demanding; *pranzo*, *serata*, *abito* formal; (*vincolante*) binding

impegnato (*occupato*) busy; *fig* (*politically*) committed; **sono già ~** I've made other arrangements, I'm doing something else

impegno *m* commitment; (*appuntamento*) engagement; (*zelo*) zeal, care; COM **senza ~** with no commitment

impensabile unthinkable

impensato unexpected

imperante (*dominante*) prevailing

imperare <1b> rule (**su** over)

imperativo *m*/*agg* imperative

imperatore *m*, **-trice** *f* emperor; *donna* empress

impercettibile imperceptible

imperdonabile unforgivable

imperfetto *m*/*agg* imperfect

imperfezione *f* imperfection

impermeabile 1 *agg* waterproof **2** *m* raincoat

impermeabilità *f* impermeability

impermeabilizzare <1a> waterproof

impero *m* empire; (*potere*) rule

impersonale impersonal

impersonare <1a> personify; (*interpretare*) play (the part of)

impertinente impertinent

impertinenza *f* impertinence

imperturbabile imperturbable

imperturbabilità *f* imperturbability

imperversare <1b> rage; *fig di moda* be all the rage

impeto *m* impetus, force; (*accesso*) outburst; (*slancio*) passion, heat; **parlare con ~** speak forcefully

impetuoso impetuous

impiantare <1a> *azienda*, *ufficio* set up; (*apparecchiatura*, *apparecchiatura* install; MED implant

impianto *m operazione* installation; (*apparecchiature*) plant; (*sistema*) system; MED implant; **~ elettrico** wiring; **~ di risalita** ski lift; **~ di riscaldamento** heating system; **~ stereo** stereo (system); **-i** *pl* **sanitari** bathroom fixtures and fittings

impiastro *m* poultice; *fig* pain in the neck

impiccare <1d> hang

impiccarsi hang o.s.

impicciare <1f> be in the way

impicciarsi: **~ di** *o* **in qc** interfere *or* meddle in sth

impiccio *m* (*pl* -cci) (*ostacolo*) hindrance; (*seccatura*) bother; **essere d'~** be in the way; **essere in un ~** be in trouble

impiegare <1b & e> (*usare*) use; *tempo, soldi* spend; (*metterci*) take; (*assumere*) employ; **ho impiegato un'ora** it took me an hour

impiegato *m*, **-a** *f* employee; **~ di banca** bank clerk; **~ di ruolo** permanent employee

impiego *m* (*pl* -ghi) (*uso*) use; (*occupazione*) employment; (*posto*) job; FIN investment; **domanda** *f* **d'~** job application; **offerta** *f* **d'~** job offer

impietosire <4d> move to pity

impietosirsi be moved to pity

impigliare <1g> entangle

impigliarsi get entangled

impigrire <4d> **1** *v/t* make lazy **2** *v/i e* **impigrirsi** get lazy

implacabile implacable

implicare <1l & d> (*coinvolgere*) implicate; (*comportare*) imply

implicito implicit

implorare <1c> implore

impolverato dusty, covered with *or* in dust

imponente imposing, impressive

imponibile 1 *agg* taxable **2** *m* taxable income

impopolare unpopular

impopolarità *f* unpopularity

imporre <3ll> impose; *prezzo* fix

imporsi (*farsi valere*) assert o.s.; (*avere successo*) be successful, become established; (*essere necessario*) be necessary

importante important

importanza *f* importance; **darsi ~** give o.s. airs; **senza ~** not important, unimportant

importare <1c> **1** *v/t* FIN, INFOR import **2** *v/i* matter, be important;

(*essere necessario*) be necessary; **e a te che te ne importa?** what's it to you?; **non importa** it doesn't matter; **non gliene importa niente** he couldn't care less

importatore *m*, **-trice** *f* importer

importazione *f* import; **~ clandestina** smuggling; **permesso** *m* **d'~** import permit

importo *m* amount

importunare <1a> (*assillare*) pester; (*disturbare*) bother

importuno troublesome; *domanda, osservazione* ill-timed

imposizione *f* imposition; (*tassazione*) taxation; (*tassa*) tax

impossessarsi <1b>: **~ di** seize

impossibile impossible

impossibilità *f* impossibility

imposta[1] *f* tax; **~ di consumo** excise duty; **~ diretta** / **indiretta** direct / indirect tax; **~ sul reddito** income tax; **~ sul valore aggiunto** value added tax; **~ sul fatturato** sales tax; **ufficio** *m* **delle -e** tax office

imposta[2] *f di finestra* shutter

impostare <1c> *lavoro* plan; *problema* set out; *lettera* post, *Am* mail

imposto *pp* → **imporre**

impostore *m* impostor

impotente powerless; (*inefficace*) ineffectual; MED impotent

impotenza *f* powerlessness; MED impotence

impraticabile *strada* impassable

impratichirsi <4d> get practice (**in** in)

imprecare <1d & b> curse, swear (**contro** at)

imprecazione *f* curse

imprecisato *numero, quantità* indeterminate; *motivi, circostanze* not clear

imprecisione *f* inaccuracy

impreciso inaccurate

impregnare <1a> impregnate; (*imbevere*) soak

impregnarsi become impregnated (**di** with)

imprenditore *m*, **-trice** *f* entrepreneur

imprenditoriale entrepreneurial

impreparato unprepared

impresa f (*iniziativa*) enterprise, undertaking; (*azienda*) business, firm; *~ familiare* family business; *piccola ~* small business; *~ di servizi pubblici* utility company

impresario m (*pl* -ri) contractor; TEA impresario

impressionabile impressionable; FOT sensitive

impressionante impressive; (*spaventoso*) frightening; (*sconvolgente*) upsetting, shocking

impressionare <1a> (*turbare*) upset, shock; (*spaventare*) frighten; (*colpire*) impress; FOT expose

impressionato FOT exposed; *~ favorevolmente* (favourably) impressed

impressione f impression; (*turbamento*) shock; (*paura*) fright; TIP printing

impresso pp → **imprimere**

imprevedibile unforeseeable; *persona* unpredictable

imprevisto **1** *agg* unexpected **2** *m* unforeseen event; *salvo imprevisti* all being well

imprigionare <1a> imprison

imprimere <3r> impress; *fig nella mente* fix firmly, imprint; *movimento* impart; TIP print

improbabile unlikely, improbable

improbabilità f unlikelihood, improbability

improduttivo unproductive

impronta f impression, mark; (*orma*) footprint; (*traccia*) track; *fig* mark; *-e pl digitali* fingerprints

improprio (*pl* -ri) improper

improvvisamente suddenly

improvvisare <1a> improvize

improvvisarsi take on the role of

improvvisata f surprise

improvvisato improvized, impromptu

improvviso sudden; (*inaspettato*) unexpected; *all'~* suddenly; (*inaspettatamente*) unexpectedly

imprudente careless; (*non saggio*) imprudent, rash

imprudenza f carelessness; (*mancanza di saggezza*) imprudence, rashness

impugnare <1a> grasp; DIR contest

impugnatura f grip; (*manico*) handle

impulsivo impulsive

impulso m impulse

impunità f impunity

impunito unpunished

impuntarsi (*ostinarsi*) dig one's heels in

imputato m, **-a** f accused

imputazione f charge

imputridire rot

in *prp* in; *moto a luogo* to; *~ casa* at home; *è ~ Scozia* he is in Scotland; *va ~ Inghilterra* he is going to England; *~ italiano* in Italian; *~ campagna* in the country; *essere ~ viaggio* be travelling; *viaggiare ~ macchina* travel by car; *nel 1999* in 1999; *una giacca ~ pelle* a leather jacket; *~ vacanza* on holiday; *se fossi ~ te* if I were you, if I were in your place

inabile unfit (*a* for); (*disabile*) disabled

inabitabile uninhabitable

inabitato uninhabited

inaccessibile inaccessible, out of reach; *fig persona* unapproachable; *prezzi* exorbitant

inaccettabile unacceptable

inacidire <4d>, **inacidirsi** turn sour

inadatto unsuitable (*a* for), unsuited (*a* to)

inadeguato inadequate

inafferrabile elusive; (*incomprensibile*) incomprehensible

inalare <1a> inhale

inalatore m inhaler, puffer F

inalazione f inhalation

inalterabile *sentimento* unchangeable; *colore* fast; *metallo* non-tarnish

inalterato unchanged

inamidare <1m> starch

inammissibile inadmissible

inanimato inanimate; (*senza vita*) lifeless

inappellabile final, irrevocable

inappetenza f lack of appetite

inarcare <1d> *schiena* arch; *sopracciglia* raise

inaridire <4d> **1** v/t parch **2** v/i dry up

inaspettato unexpected

inasprimento m (*intensificazione*) worsening; *di carattere* embitterment

inasprire <4d> exacerbate, make worse; *carattere* embitter

inasprirsi get worse; *di persona* become embittered

inattaccabile unassailable

inattendibile unreliable

inatteso unexpected

inattività f inactivity

inattivo *persona, capitale* idle; *vulcano* dormant

inattuabile (*non fattibile*) impracticable; (*non realistico*) unrealistic

inaugurare <1m> *mostra* (officially) open, inaugurate; *lapide, monumento* unveil; F *oggetto nuovo* christen F

inaugurazione f *di mostra* (official) opening, inauguration; *di lapide* unveiling; F *di oggetto nuovo* christening F

inavvertenza f inadvertence

inavvertito unnoticed

incagliarsi <1g> MAR run aground

incalcolabile incalculable

incalzante *pericolo* imminent; *richieste* pressing

incalzare <1a> pursue; *fig con richieste* ply

incamminarsi <1m> set out

incandescente incandescent; *fig* heated

incantare <1a> enchant

incantarsi (*restare affascinato*) be spellbound; (*sognare a occhi aperti*) be in a daze; TEC jam

incantato *per effetto di magia* enchanted; (*trasognato*) in a daze; (*affascinato*) spellbound

incantesimo m spell

incantevole delightful, charming

incanto[1] m (*incantesimo*) spell; **come per ~** as if by magic

incanto[2] m COM auction; **mettere**

all'~ sell at auction, put up for auction

incapace 1 agg incapable (**di** of); (*incompetente*) incompetent **2** m/f incompetent person

incapacità f (*inabilità*) inability; (*incompetenza*) incompetence

incappare <1a>: **~ in** nebbia, difficoltà run into

incapricciarsi <1f>: **~ di qu** take a liking to s.o.

incarcerare <1m> imprison

incaricare <1d> (*dare istruzioni a*) instruct; **~ qu di fare qc** tell or instruct s.o. to do sth

incaricarsi: **~ di qc** (*occuparsi di*) see to sth, deal with sth

incaricato m, **-a** f (*responsabile*) person in charge; (*funzionario*) official, representative

incarico m (pl -chi) (*compito*) task, assignment; (*nomina*) appointment; **per ~ di** on behalf of

incarnare <1a> embody

incarnazione f incarnation

incartamento m file, dossier

incartare <1a> wrap (up) (in paper)

incarto m wrapping; (*incartamento*) file, dossier

incassare <1a> COM (*riscuotere*) cash; *fig colpi, insulti ecc* take

incasso m (*riscossione*) collection; (*somma incassata*) takings pl

incastonare <1a> set

incastonatura f setting

incastrare <1a> fit in; F *fig* (*far apparire colpevole*) frame F; (*mettere in una posizione difficile*) corner F

incastro m joint

incatenare <1a> chain

incavato *occhi* deep-set

incendiare <1b & k> set fire to

incendiario m (pl m -ri), **-a** f arsonist, firebug F

incendio m (pl -di) fire; **~ doloso** arson

incenerimento m incineration

incenerire <4d> reduce to ashes

inceneritore m incinerator

incenso m incense

incensurato irreproachable; DIR **es-**

sere ~ have a clean record

incentivare <1a> (*incrementare*) boost

incentivo *m* incentive

incerata *f* oilcloth

incertezza *f* uncertainty

incerto 1 *agg* uncertain **2** *m* uncertainty

incessante incessant

incetta *f:* **fare ~ di qc** stockpile sth

inchiesta *f* investigation; FIN ~ *di mercato* market survey; **commissione** *f* **d'~** committee *or* board of inquiry

inchinare <1a> bow

inchinarsi bow

inchino *m* bow; *di donna* curtsy

inchiodare <1c> **1** *v/t* nail; *coperchio* nail down; *fig* **essere inchiodato in un luogo** be stuck in a place **2** *v/i* AUTO jam on the brakes

inchiostro *m* ink; ~ *di china* Indian ink

inciampare <1a> trip (*in* over); ~ *in qu* run into s.o.

incidentale (*casuale*) accidental; (*secondario*) incidental

incidente *m* (*episodio*) incident; ~ *aereo* plane crash; ~ *stradale* road accident

incidere[1] <3q> *v/i* affect (*su* sth)

incidere[2] <3q> *v/t* engrave; (*tagliare*) cut; (*registrare*) record

incidersi *fig* (*restare impresso*) be engraved (*in* on)

incinta pregnant

incirca *all'~* more or less

incisione *f* engraving; (*acquaforte*) etching; (*taglio*) cut; MED incision; (*registrazione*) recording

incisivo 1 *agg* incisive **2** *m* (*dente*) incisor

incitare <1l> incite

incivile uncivilized; (*villano*) rude, impolite

inclinare <1a> **1** *v/t* tilt **2** *v/i:* ~ *a* (*tendere a*) be inclined to

inclinato tilted

inclinazione *f* inclination

incline inclined (*a* to)

includere <3q> include; (*allegare*)

enclose, inclose; **incluso il servizio** service included

inclusivo inclusive

incluso 1 *pp* → **includere 2** *agg* included; (*compreso*) inclusive; (*allegato*) enclosed

incoerente (*incongruente*) inconsistent

incoerenza *f* inconsistency

incognita *f* unknown quantity

incognito *m:* **in** ~ incognito

incollare <1c> stick; *con colla liquida* glue

incollarsi stick (**a** to)

incolonnare <1a> *numeri ecc* put in a column; *persone* line up

incolore colo(u)rless

incolpare <1a> blame

incolparsi: ~ **a vicenda** blame each other

incolto uneducated; (*trascurato*) unkempt; AGR uncultivated

incolume unharmed

incolumità *f* safety

incombente *pericolo* impending

incombenza *f* task

incominciare <1f> start, begin (**a** to)

incomodare <1m & c> inconvenience

incomodarsi put o.s. out; **non si incomodi!** don't put yourself out!, please don't go to any trouble!

incomodo 1 *agg* (*inopportuno*) inconvenient; (*scomodo*) uncomfortable **2** *m* inconvenience

incompatibile incompatible; (*intollerabile*) unacceptable

incompatibilità *f* incompatibility

incompetente incompetent; **sono ~ in materia** I'm no expert

incompetenza *f* incompetence

incompiuto unfinished

incompleto incomplete

incomprensibile incomprehensible, impossible to understand

incomprensione *f* lack of understanding; (*malinteso*) misunderstanding

incompreso misunderstood

inconcepibile inconceivable

inconciliabile irreconcilable
inconcludente inconclusive; *persona* ineffectual
incondizionato unconditional
inconfondibile unmistakable
inconfutabile indisputable
inconsapevole (*ignaro*) unaware
inconsapevolezza *f* lack of awareness
inconscio *m/agg* unconscious
inconsistente insubstantial; *fig* (*infondato*) unfounded; (*vago*) vague
inconsistenza *f* flimsiness
inconsolabile inconsolable
inconsueto unusual
incontentabile hard to please, very demanding; (*perfezionista*) perfectionist
incontestato undisputed
incontrare <1a> 1 *v/t* meet; *difficoltà* come up against, encounter 2 *v/i e* incontrarsi meet (con s.o.)
incontrario: all'~ the other way round; (*nel modo sbagliato*) the wrong way round
incontrastato undisputed
incontro 1 *m* meeting; ~ di calcio football match; POL ~ al vertice summit (meeting) 2 *prp*: ~ a towards; andare ~ a qu go and meet s.o.; *fig* meet s.o. halfway
inconveniente *m* (*svantaggio*) drawback; (*ostacolo*) hitch
incoraggiamento *m* encouragement
incoraggiante encouraging
incoraggiare <1f> encourage
incorniciare <1f> frame
incoronare <1a> crown
incoronazione *f* coronation
incorporare <1m & c> incorporate
incorreggibile incorrigible
incorrere <3o>: ~ in sanzioni incur; *errore* make
incorruttibile incorruptible
incosciente unconscious; (*irresponsabile*) reckless
incoscienza *f* unconsciousness; (*insensatezza*) recklessness
incostante changeable; *negli affetti* fickle

incostanza *f* changeableness; *negli affetti* fickleness
incostituzionale unconstitutional
incostituzionalità *f* unconstitutionality
incredibile incredible
incredulo incredulous, disbelieving
incrementare <1a> increase
incremento *m* increase, growth; ~ demografico population growth
increspare <1a> *acque* ripple; *capelli* frizz; *tessuto* gather
incriminare <1m> indict
incrociare <1f> 1 *v/t* cross 2 *v/i* MAR, AVIA cruise
incrocio *m* (*pl* -ci) (*intersezione*) crossing; (*crocevia*) crossroads; *di razze animali* cross(-breed)
incrollabile indestructible; *fig* unshakeable
incubatrice *f* incubator
incubazione *f* incubation
incubo *m* nightmare
incudine *f* anvil
incurabile incurable
incurante heedless (di of)
incuria *f* negligence
incuriosire <4d>: ~ qu make s.o. curious, arouse s.o.'s curiosity
incuriosirsi become curious
incursione *f* raid; ~ aerea air raid
incurvare <1a> bend
incustodito unattended, unguarded; *passaggio a livello* unmanned
indaco *m/agg* indigo
indaffarato busy
indagare <1e> 1 *v/t* cause, *fenomeni* investigate 2 *v/i* investigate (su, intorno a sth)
indagine *f* (*ricerca, studio*) research; *della polizia* investigation; ~ di mercato market survey; ~ demoscopica (*public*) opinion poll
indebitare <1m>, indebitarsi get into debt
indebitato in debt
indebolimento *m* weakening
indebolire <4d> *v/t & v/i* weaken
indecente indecent
indecenza *f* (*vergogna*) disgrace,

outrage; (*mancanza di pudore*) indecency

indecisione *f* indecision; *abituale* indecisiveness

indeciso undecided; *abitualmente* indecisive

indefinito indefinite

indegno unworthy

indelebile indelible; *colore* fast

indenne *persona* uninjured; *cosa* undamaged

indennità *f inv* (*gratifica*) allowance, benefit; (*risarcimento*) compensation; **~ di trasferta** travel allowance; **~ parlamentare** MP's allowance

indennizzare <1a> compensate (**per** for)

indennizzo *m* (*compenso*) compensation

indescrivibile indescribable

indesiderato unwanted

indeterminato *tempo* unspecified, indefinite; *quantità* indeterminate

India *f* India

indiano 1 *agg* Indian; *in fila* **-a** in single file **2** *m*, **-a** *f* Indian

indicare <1l & d> show, indicate; *col dito* point at *or* to; (*consigliare*) suggest, recommend; (*significare*) mean

indicativo *m* GRAM indicative

indicato (*consigliabile*) advisable; (*adatto*) suitable

indicatore 1 *agg* indicative; **cartello** *m* **~** road sign **2** *m* indicator; (*strumento*) gauge, indicator; **~ del livello di carburante** fuel gauge; AUTO **~ di direzione** indicator

indicazione *f* indication; (*direttiva*) direction; (*informazione*) piece of information; MED **-i** *pl* directions (for use); **-i** *pl* **stradali** road signs

indice *m* index; ANAT index finger, forefinger; TV **~ di ascolto** ratings *pl*

indicibile indescribable

indietreggiare <1f> draw back; *camminando all'indietro* step back; MIL retreat

indietro behind; *tornare, girarsi* back; **essere ~ con il lavoro** be behind; *mentalmente* be backward; *nei*

pagamenti be in arrears; *di orologio* be slow; **dare ~** (*restituire*) give back; **tirarsi ~** draw back; *fig* back out; **all'~** backwards; AUTO **fare marcia ~** reverse; *fig* back-pedal

indifeso undefended; (*inerme*) defenceless, helpless

indifferente indifferent; **lasciare qu ~** leave s.o. cold, cut no ice with s.o.; **non ~** appreciable, considerable; **per me è ~** it's all the same to me

indifferenza *f* indifference

indigeno 1 *agg* native, indigenous **2** *m*, **-a** *f* native

indigestione *f* indigestion

indigesto indigestible

indignare <1a>: **~ qu** make s.o. indignant, arouse s.o.'s indignation

indignarsi get indignant (**per** about)

indignazione *f* indignation

indimenticabile unforgettable

indipendente independent (**da** of); **~ dalla mia volontà** outside my control

indipendentemente independently; **~ dall'età** regardless of age, whatever the age

indipendenza *f* independence

indire <3t> *conferenza, elezioni, sciopero* call; *concorso* announce

indiretto indirect

indirizzare <1a> direct; *lettera* address; (*spedire*) send

indirizzario *m* address book; *per spedizione* mailing list

indirizzo *m* address; (*direzione*) direction

indisciplina *f* lack of discipline, indiscipline

indisciplinato undisciplined

indiscreto indiscreet

indiscrezione *f* indiscretion

indiscriminato indiscriminate

indiscusso unquestioned

indiscutibile unquestionable

indispensabile 1 *agg* indispensable, essential **2** *m* essentials *pl*

indispettire <4d> irritate

indispettirsi get irritated

indispettito irritated

indisporre <3ll> irritate

indisposizione f indisposition

indisposto (*ammalato*) indisposed

indistinto indistinct, faint

indistruttibile indestructible

indivia f endive

individuale individual

individualismo m individualism

individualista m/f (mpl -i) individualist

individualità f individuality

individuo m individual

indivisibile indivisible

indiviso undivided

indizio m (pl -zi) clue; (*segno*) sign; (*sintomo*) symptom; DIR **-i** pl circumstantial evidence sg

indole f nature

indolente indolent

indolenza f indolence

indolore painless

indomani m: **l'~** the next day

indossare <1c> (*mettersi*) put on; (*portare*) wear

indossatore m, **-trice** f model

indotto pp → **indurre**

indovinare <1a> guess; *futuro* predict

indovinato (*ben riuscito*) successful; (*ben scelto*) well chosen

indovinello m riddle

indovino m, **-a** f fortune-teller

indubbiamente undoubtedly

indugiare <1f> **1** v/t *partenza* delay **2** v/i (*tardare*) delay; (*esitare*) hesitate; (*attardarsi*) linger

indugiarsi linger

indugio m (pl -gi) delay; **senza ~** without delay

indulgente indulgent; *giudice, sentenza* lenient

indulgenza f indulgence; *di giudice, sentenza* leniency

indumento m garment, item of clothing; **gli -i** pl clothes

indurire <4d> **1** v/t harden; *fig cuore* harden; *corpo* toughen (up) **2** v/i e **indurirsi** go hard, harden

indurito hardened

indurre <3e> induce

industria f industry; (*operosità*) industriousness; **~ automobilistica** car industry; **~ dei servizi** service industry, services; **~ pesante** heavy industry

industriale 1 agg industrial **2** m industrialist

industrializzare <1a> industrialize

industrializzazione f industrialization

ineccepibile irreproachable; *ragionamento* faultless

inedito unpublished; *fig* novel

inefficace ineffective

inefficacia f ineffectiveness

inefficiente inefficient

inefficienza f inefficiency

ineguagliabile (*senza rivali*) unrivalled; (*senza confronto*) incomparable, beyond compare

ineguaglianza f inequality

ineguale (*non uguale*) unequal; (*discontinuo*) uneven

inequivocabile unequivocal

inerte (*inoperoso*) idle; (*immobile*) inert, motionless; (*senza vita*) lifeless; FIS inert

inerzia f inertia; (*inattività*) inactivity; **forza** f **d'~** force of inertia

inesattezza f inaccuracy

inesatto inaccurate

inesauribile inexhaustible

inesorabile inexorable

inesperienza f inexperience, lack of experience

inesperto inexperienced

inesplicabile inexplicable

inesplorato unexplored

inesploso unexploded

inesprimibile (*indicibile*) indescribable

inestimabile inestimable; *bene* invaluable

inetto inept

inevaso pending

inevitabile inevitable

inezia f trifle

infallibile infallible

infame 1 agg (*turpe*) infamous, foul; *spir* horrible, terrible **2** m/f P (*delatore*) grass P

infantile *letteratura, giochi* children's;

malattie childhood; (*immaturo*) childish, infantile

infanzia *f* childhood; (*primi mesi*) infancy (*anche fig*); (*bambini*) children

infarinare <1a> (dust with) flour

infarinatura *f fig* smattering

infarto *m cardiaco* heart attack

infastidire <4d> annoy, irritate

infaticabile tireless

infatti in fact

infatuarsi <1m>: *~ di qu* become infatuated with s.o.

infedele 1 *agg* unfaithful; *traduzione* inaccurate **2** *m/f* REL infidel

infedeltà *f inv* unfaithfulness

infelice unhappy; (*inopportuno*) unfortunate; (*malriuscito*) bad

infelicità *f* unhappiness

inferiore 1 *agg* lower; *fig* inferior (*a* to); *di qualità* ~ of inferior quality; *essere ~ a qu* be inferior to s.o., be s.o.'s inferior; *~ alla media* below average **2** *m/f* inferior; (*subalterno*) subordinate

inferiorità *f* inferiority; *complesso m d'~* inferiority complex

infermeria *f* infirmary

infermiere *m*, **-a** *f* nurse

infermità *f inv* illness

infermo 1 *agg* (*ammalato*) ill; (*invalido*) invalid **2** *m*, **-a** *f* invalid

infernale infernal

inferno *m* hell

inferriata *f* grating; (*cancellata*) railings *pl*

infertilità *f* infertility

infestare <1b> infest

infettare <1b> infect

infettarsi become infected

infettivo infectious

infetto infected

infezione *f* infection

infiammabile flammable

infiammare <1a> *fig*, MED inflame

infiammarsi become inflamed

infiammazione *f* inflammation; *~ alla gola* inflammation of the throat

infierire <4d> *di maltempo, malattia* rage; *~ su* o *contro* savagely attack

infilare <1a> *fili, corde, ago* thread;

(*inserire*) insert, put in; (*indossare*) put on; *strada* take; *~ le mani in tasca* put one's hands in one's pockets; *~ la porta uscendo / entrando* slip out / in

infilarsi *indumento* slip on; (*conficcarsi*) stick; (*introdursi*) slip (*in* into); (*stiparsi*) squeeze (*in* into)

infiltrare <1a> infiltrate

infiltrarsi seep; *fig* infiltrate

infiltrazione *f* infiltration; *di liquidi* seepage

infilzare <1a> pierce; *perle* thread; *fig* string together

infimo lowest

infine (*alla fine*) finally, eventually; (*insomma*) in short

infinità *f* infinity; *ho un'~ di cose da fare* I've got no end of things to do

infinito 1 *agg* infinite **2** *m* infinity; GRAM infinitive; *ripetere all'~* say over and over again

infischiarsi <1k> F: *~ di* not give a hoot about F; *me ne infischio* I couldn't care less F

infittire *v/t & v/i* <4d> thicken

inflazione *f* inflation; *tasso m d'~* (rate of) inflation

inflessibile inflexible

inflessibilità *f* inflexibility

inflessione *f* inflection

infliggere <3cc> inflict

inflitto *pp → infliggere*

influente influential

influenza *f* influence; MED flu, influenza

influenzabile easily influenced, impressionable

influenzare <1b> influence

influire <4d>: *~ su* influence, have an effect on

influsso *m* influence

infondato unfounded, without foundation

infondere <3bb> *fig* instil

inforcare <1d> *occhiali* put on; *bicicletta* get on, mount

informale informal

informare <1a> inform (*di* of)

informarsi find out (*di, su* about)

informatica *f scienza* information

technology, computer science

informatico (*pl* -ci) **1** *agg* computer *attr* **2** *m*, **-a** *f* computer scientist

informato informed

informatore *m*, **-trice** *f* informant; *della polizia* informer

informazione *f* piece of information; **ufficio** *m* **-i** information office

informe shapeless

informicolirsi <4d> have pins and needles

infortunio *m* (*pl* -ni) accident; **~ sul lavoro** accident at work, industrial accident; **assicurazione** *f* **contro gli -i** accident insurance

infossato *occhi* deep-set, sunken

infrangere <3d> break

infrangibile unbreakable; **vetro** *m* **~** shatterproof glass

infranto *pp* → **infrangere**

infrarosso infrared

infrasettimanale midweek

infrastruttura *f* infrastructure

infrazione *f* offence, *Am* offense; **~ al codice stradale** traffic offence (*Am* offense)

infreddatura *f* cold

infruttuoso fruitless

infuocare *fig* inflame

infuocato (*caldissimo*) scorching, blistering; *discorso, tramonto* fiery

infuori: **all'~** outwards; **all'~ di** except

infuriare <1k> **1** *v/t* infuriate, enrage **2** *v/i* rage

infuriarsi fly into a rage

infuriato furious

infusione *f*, **infuso** *m* infusion; (*tisana*) herbal tea

ingaggiare <1f> (*reclutare*) recruit; *attore, cantante lirico* engage; SP sign (up); (*iniziare*) start, begin

ingaggio *m* (*pl* -ggi) (*reclutamento*) recruitment; SP signing; (*somma*) fee

ingannare <1a> deceive; **~ il tempo** kill time

ingannarsi deceive o.s.

inganno *m* deception, deceit

ingarbugliare <1g> tangle; *fig* confuse, muddle

ingarbugliarsi get entangled; *fig* get confused

ingegnarsi <1a> do one's utmost (**a, per** to)

ingegnere *m* engineer

ingegneria *f* engineering; **~ genetica** genetic engineering; **~ meccanica** mechanical engineering

ingegno *m* (*mente*) mind; (*intelligenza*) brains *pl*; (*genio*) genius; (*inventiva*) ingenuity

ingegnoso ingenious

ingelosire <4d> **1** *v/t* make jealous **2** *v/i* be jealous

ingente enormous

ingenuità *f* ingenuousness

ingenuo ingenuous

ingerenza *f* interference

ingerire <4d> swallow

ingerirsi interfere

ingessare <1b> put in plaster

ingessatura *f* plaster

Inghilterra *f* England

inghiottire <4d> swallow

ingiallire <4d> *v/t* & *v/i* yellow, turn yellow

ingiallito yellowed

inginocchiarsi <1k> kneel (down)

ingiù: **all'~** down(wards)

ingiungere <3d>: **~ a qu di fare qc** order s.o. to do sth

ingiunzione *f* injunction; **~ di pagamento** final demand

ingiuria *f* insult

ingiuriare <1k> insult

ingiustificato unjustified

ingiustizia *f* injustice

ingiusto unjust, unfair

inglese 1 *m/agg* English **2** *m/f* Englishman; *donna* Englishwoman *f*

ingoiare <1i> swallow

ingolfare <1a>, **ingolfarsi** flood

ingombrante cumbersome, bulky

ingombrare <1a> *passaggio* block (up); *stanza, mente* clutter (up)

ingombro 1 *agg passaggio* blocked; *stanza, mente* cluttered (up) **2** *m* hindrance, obstacle; **essere d'~** be in the way

ingordo greedy

ingorgare <1e> block

ingorgarsi get blocked

ingorgo *m* (*pl* -ghi) blockage; ~ **stradale** traffic jam

ingovernabile ungovernable

ingozzare <1a> *cibo* devour, gobble up; *persona* stuff (**di** with)

ingozzarsi stuff o.s (**di** with)

ingranaggio *m* (*pl* -ggi) gear; *fig* machine)

ingranare <1a> engage; *fig* F **le cose cominciano a ~** things are beginning to work out

ingrandimento *m* enlargement; *di azienda, città* expansion, growth

ingrandire <4d> enlarge; *azienda, città* expand, develop; (*esagerare*) exaggerate

ingrandirsi grow

ingrassare <1a> 1 *v/t animali* fatten (up); (*lubrificare*) grease 2 *v/i* get fat, put on weight; *di birra, burro ecc* be fattening

ingratitudine *f* ingratitude

ingrato ungrateful; *lavoro, compito* thankless

ingrediente *m* ingredient

ingresso *m* entrance; (*atrio*) hall; (*accesso*) admittance; INFOR input; ~ **libero** admission free; *vietato l'*~ no entry, no admittance

ingrossare <1c> 1 *v/t* make bigger; (*gonfiare, accrescere*) swell 2 *v/i e* **ingrossarsi** get bigger; (*gonfiarsi*) swell

ingrossato swollen

ingrosso: *all'*~ (*all'incirca*) roughly, about; COM wholesale; *commercio m all'*~ wholesale (trade)

ingualcibile crease-resistant

inguaribile incurable

inguinale groin *attr*; **ernia** *f* ~ hernia

inguine *m* ANAT groin

ingurgitare <1m> gulp down

inibire <4d> prohibit, forbid; PSI inhibit

inibito inhibited

inibizione *f* PSI inhibition

iniettare <1b> inject; ~ *qc a qu* inject s.o. with sth; *occhi mpl* **iniettati di sangue** bloodshot eyes

iniettarsi: ~ *qc* inject o.s. with sth

iniezione *f* injection; **motore** *m* **a ~** fuel-injection engine

inimicarsi <1d> fall out (**con** with)

inimicizia *f* enmity

inimitabile inimitable

inimmaginabile unimaginable

ininterrotto continuous

iniziale 1 *agg* initial; **stipendio** *m* ~ starting salary 2 *f* initial

inizializzare <1a> INFOR initialize

iniziare <1g> 1 *v/t* begin, start; *ostilità, dibattito* open; *fig* initiate 2 *v/i* begin, start; *di ostilità, dibattito* open; ~ *a fare qc* begin *or* start doing sth, begin *or* start to do sth

iniziativa *f* initiative; ~ **privata** private enterprise; *di mia* ~ on my own initiative; **spirito** *m* **d'**~ initiative

inizio *m* (*pl* -zi) start, beginning; **avere** ~ start, begin; **dare** *a qc* start sth

in loco on the premises

innaffiare <1k> water

innaffiatoio *m* (*pl* -oi) watering can

innalzare <1a> raise; (*erigere*) erect

innalzarsi rise

innamorarsi <1a> fall in love (**di** with)

innamorato 1 *agg* in love (**di** with) 2 *m*, -a *f* boyfriend; *donna* girlfriend

innanzi 1 *prp* before; ~ *a* in front of; ~ *tutto* first of all; (*soprattutto*) above all 2 *avv stato in luogo* in front; (*avanti*) forward; (*prima*) before; *d'ora* ~ from now on

innato innate, inborn

innaturale unnatural

innervosire <4d>: ~ *qu* make s.o. nervous; (*irritare*) get on s.o.'s nerves

innervosirsi get nervous; (*irritarsi*) get irritated

innestare <1b> BOT, MED graft; EL *spina* insert; AUTO *marcia* engage

innesto *m* BOT, MED graft; AUTO clutch; EL connection

inno *m* hymn; ~ **nazionale** national anthem

innocente innocent

innocenza *f* innocence

innocuo innocuous, harmless

innovativo innovative
innovazione f innovation
innumerevole innumerable
inodore odo(u)rless
inoffensivo harmless, inoffensive
inoltrare <1a> forward
inoltrarsi advance, penetrate (**in** into)
inoltrato late
inoltre besides
inondare <1a> flood
inondazione f flood
inoperoso idle
inopportuno (*inadatto*) inappropriate; (*intempestivo*) untimely; *persona* tactless
inorridire <4d> **1** v/t horrify **2** v/i be horrified
inorridito horrified
inospitale inhospitable, unwelcoming
inosservato unobserved, unnoticed; (*non rispettato*) disregarded; *passare* ~ go unnoticed
inossidabile stainless
inquadrare <1a> *dipinto, fotografia* frame; *fig* put into context
inquadrarsi be part of
inquadratura f frame
inqualificabile *fig* unspeakable
inquietante *che preoccupa* worrying; *che turba* disturbing
inquietare <1b> (*preoccupare*) worry; (*turbare*) disturb; *fare* ~ *qu* make s.o. cross
inquietarsi (*preoccuparsi*) get worried; (*impazientirsi*) get cross
inquieto restless; (*preoccupato*) worried, anxious; (*adirato*) angry
inquietudine f anxiety
inquilino m, **-a** f tenant
inquinamento m pollution; *da sostanze radioattive* contamination; ~ *acustico* noise pollution; ~ *atmosferico* air pollution; ~ *dell'ambiente* pollution
inquinante **1** *agg* polluting; *non* ~ environmentally friendly; *sostanza* f ~ pollutant **2** m pollutant
inquinare <1a> pollute; *fig* (*corrom-*

pere) corrupt; DIR *prove* tamper with
insabbiamento m *di porto* silting up; *fig* shelving
insabbiare <1k> *fig* shelve
insabbiarsi *di porto* get silted up; *fig* grind to a halt
insaccare <1d> put in bags
insaccati mpl sausages
insalata f salad; ~ *mista* mixed salad; ~ *verde* green salad
insalatiera f salad bowl
insanabile (*incurabile*) incurable; *fig* (*irrimediabile*) irreparable
insanguinato bloodstained
insaponare <1a> soap
insapore tasteless
insaporire <4d> flavo(u)r
insaputa: *all'~ di qu* unknown to s.o.
insaziabile insatiable
inscatolare <1m> tin, can
inscenare <1a> stage
inscindibile inseparable
insegna f sign; (*bandiera*) flag; (*stemma*) symbol; (*decorazione*) decoration
insegnamento m teaching
insegnante **1** *agg* teaching; *corpo* ~ staff **2** m/f teacher
insegnare <1a> teach; ~ *qc a qu* teach s.o. sth
inseguimento m chase, pursuit
inseguire <4b> chase, pursue
inseminazione f insemination; ~ *artificiale* artificial insemination
insenatura f inlet
insensato **1** *agg* senseless, idiotic **2** m, **-a** f fool, idiot
insensibile insensitive (**a** to); *parte del corpo* numb
insensibilità f insensitivity; *di parte del corpo* numbness
inseparabile inseparable
inserire <4d> insert; (*collegare: in elettrotecnica*) connect; *annuncio* put in, place
inserirsi fit in; *in una conversazione* join in
inserto m (*pubblicazione*) supplement; (*insieme di documenti*) file
inservibile unusable

inserviente *m/f* attendant

inserzione *f* insertion; *sul giornale* ad(vert), advertisement

insetticida *m* (*pl* -i) insecticide

insettifugo *m* (*pl* -ghi) insect repellent

insetto *m* insect

insicurezza *f* insecurity, lack of security

insicuro insecure

insidia *f* (*tranello*) snare; (*inganno*) trick

insidioso insidious

insieme 1 *avv* together; (*contemporaneamente*) at the same time **2** *prp*: **~ a, ~ con** together with **3** *m* whole; *di abiti* outfit; **nell'~** on the whole

insignificante insignificant

insinuare <1m> insert; *fig dubbio, sospetto* sow the seeds of; **~ che** insinuate that

insinuarsi penetrate; *fig* **~ in** creep into

insinuazione *f* insinuation

insipido insipid

insistente insistent

insistenza *f* insistence

insistere <3f> insist; (*perseverare*) persevere; **~ a fare qc** insist on doing sth

insoddisfacente unsatisfactory

insoddisfatto unsatisfied; (*scontento*) dissatisfied

insoddisfazione *f* dissatisfaction

insofferente intolerant

insofferenza *f* intolerance

insolazione *f* sunstroke

insolente insolent

insolenza *f* insolence; *espressione* insolent remark

insolito unusual

insolubile insoluble

insoluto unsolved; *debito* unpaid, outstanding

insolvente insolvent

insolvenza *f* insolvency

insolvibile insolvent

insomma (*in breve*) briefly, in short; **~!** well, really!

insonne sleepless

insonnia *f* insomnia

insonnolito sleepy

insonorizzazione *f* soundproofing

insopportabile unbearable, intolerable

insorgere <3d> rise (up) (**contro** against); *di difficoltà* come up, crop up

insormontabile insurmountable

insorto 1 *pp* → **insorgere 2** *m* rebel

insospettabile above suspicion; (*impensato*) unsuspected

insospettato unsuspected

insospettire <4d> **1** *v/t*: **~ qu** make s.o. suspicious, arouse s.o.'s suspicion **2** *v/i e* **insospettirsi** become suspicious

insostenibile untenable; (*insopportabile*) unbearable

insostituibile irreplaceable

insperato unhoped for; (*inatteso*) unexpected

inspiegabile inexplicable

inspirare <1a> breathe in, inhale

instabile unstable; *tempo* changeable

instabilità *f* instability; *del tempo* changeability

installare <1a> install

installazione *f* installation

instancabile tireless, untiring

insù: **all'~** upwards

insubordinato insubordinate

insubordinazione *f* insubordination

insuccesso *m* failure

insufficiente insufficient; (*inadeguato*) inadequate

insufficienza *f* (*scarsità*) insufficiency; (*inadeguatezza*) inadequacy; **~ cardiaca** cardiac insufficiency

insulare *popolazione, flora ecc* island *attr*

insulina *f* insulin

insulso *fig* (*privo di vivacità*) dull; (*vacuo*) inane; (*sciocco*) silly

insultare <1a> insult

insulto *m* insult

insuperabile insuperable; (*ineguagliabile*) incomparable

insuperato unsurpassed

insurrezione *f* insurrection

intaccare <1d> (*corrodere*) corrode;

fig (*danneggiare*) damage; *scorte, capitale* make inroads into

intagliare <1g> carve

intaglio *m* carving

intanto (*nel frattempo*) meanwhile; (*per ora*) for the time being; (*invece*) yet; **~ che** while

intarsio *m* (*pl* -si) inlay

intasamento *m* blockage; **~ del traffico** traffic jam

intasare <1a> block

intasarsi get blocked

intasato blocked

intascare <1d> pocket

intatto intact

integrale 1 *agg* whole; MAT integral; *edizione* unabridged; **pane** *m* **~** wholemeal bread **2** *m* MAT integral

integrare <1l> integrate; (*aumentare*) supplement

integrarsi integrate

integrazione *f* integration; **cassa** *f* **~** form of income support

integrità *f* integrity

intelaiatura *f* framework

intelletto *m* intellect

intellettuale *agg, m/f* intellectual

intelligente intelligent

intelligenza *f* intelligence; **~ artificiale** artifical intelligence, AI

intendere <3c> (*comprendere*) understand; (*udire*) hear; (*voler dire*) mean; (*avere intenzione*) intend; (*pretendere*) want; **s'intende!** naturally!, of course!

intendersi (*capirsi*) understand each other; (*accordarsi*) agree; **~ di qc** know a lot about sth; **intendersela** have an affair (**con** with)

intenditore *m*, **-trice** *f* connoisseur, expert

intensificare <1n & d> intensify

intensificarsi intensify

intensità *f* intensity; EL strength

intensivo intensive

intenso intense

intento 1 *agg* engrossed (**a** in), intent (**a** on) **2** *m* aim, purpose

intenzionale intentional, deliberate

intenzione *f* intention; **avere l'~ di fare qc** intend to do sth; **con ~** in-

tentionally; **senza ~** uninentionally

interamente entirely, wholly

interagire <4d> interact

interattivo interactive

interazione *f* interaction

intercalare 1 *v/t* insert **2** *m* stock phrase

intercambiabile interchangeable

intercapedine *f* cavity

intercedere <3a> intercede (**presso** with; **per** on behalf of)

intercettare <1b> intercept

intercettazione *f* interception; **-i** *pl* **telefoniche** phone tapping *sg*

intercontinentale intercontinental

intercorrere <3o> *di tempo* elapse; (*esserci*) exist, be

interdentale: filo *m* **~** (dental) floss

interdetto 1 *pp* → **interdire 2** *agg* (*sbalordito*) astonished; (*sconcertato*) puzzled **3** *m*, **-a** *f* F idiot F

interdire <3t> forbid; **~ a qu di fare qc** forbid s.o. to do sth; DIR **~ qu** deprive s.o. of his/her civil rights

interdizione *f* ban

interessamento *m* interest; (*intervento*) intervention

interessante interesting; **in stato ~** pregnant

interessare <1b> **1** *v/t* interest; (*riguardare*) concern **2** *v/i* matter

interessarsi be interested, take an interest (**a, di** in); (*occuparsi*) take care (**di** of)

interessato 1 *agg* interested (**a** in); (*implicato*) involved (**a** in); *spreg parere, opinione* biased; *persona* self-interested **2** *m*, **-a** *f* person concerned

interesse *m* interest; (*tornaconto*) benefit; **tasso** *m* **d'~** interest rate; **~ composto** compound interest; **per ~** out of self-interest; **senza ~** of no interest; FIN **senza -i** interest-free

interfaccia *f* (*pl* -cce) INFOR interface

interferenza *f* interference

interferire <4d> interfere

interfono *m* intercom

interiezione *f* interjection

interiora *fpl* entrails

interiore *m/agg* interior

interlocutore *m*, **-trice** *f*: **la sua -trice** the woman he was in conversation with

interludio *m* interlude

intermediario *m* (*pl* -ri), **-a** *f* intermediary

intermedio (*pl* -di) intermediate; *bilancio*, *relazione* interim

intermezzo *m* intermezzo

interminabile interminable

intermittente intermittent

internamento *m* internment; *in manicomio* committal

internare <1b> intern; *in manicomio* commit

internazionale international

internet *m* Internet; **navigare nell'~** surf the Net

internista *m/f* (*pl* -i) internist

interno 1 *agg* internal, inside *attr*; GEOG inland; POL, FIN domestic; *fig* inner; *alunno m* ~ boarder **2** *m* (*parte interna*) inside, interior; GEOG interior; TELEC extension; *via Dante n. 6* ~ *9* 6 via Dante, Flat 9; *ministero m dell'Interno o degli Interni* Home Office, *Am* Department of the Interior; *all'~* inside; SP ~ *destro / sinistro* inside right / left

intero whole, entire; (*completo*) complete; *latte m* ~ whole milk; MAT *numero m* ~ integer; *l'-a somma* the full amount

interpellare <1b> consult

interporre <3ll> *autorità*, *influenza* bring to bear

interporsi intervene

interpretare <1m & b> interpret; *personnagio* play; MUS play, perform

interpretazione *f* interpretation; TEA, MUS, *film* performance

interprete *m/f* interpreter; *attore*, *musicista* performer; ~ *simultaneo* (*-a*) interpreter; *fare da* ~ interpret, act as interpreter

interpunzione *f* punctuation

interrogare <1m, b & e> question; EDU test

interrogativo 1 *agg* GRAM interrogative; *occhiata* questioning; *pun-*

to *m* ~ question mark **2** *m* (*domanda*) question; (*dubbio*) doubt

interrogatorio *m* (*pl* -ri) questioning

interrogazione *f* questioning; *domanda* question; EDU oral test

interrompere <3rr> interrupt; (*sospendere*) break off, stop; *comunicazioni, forniture* cut off

interrotto *pp* → **interrompere**

interruttore *m* EL switch

interruzione *f* interruption

intersecare <1m, b & d> intersect

intersezione *f* intersection

interurbana *f* long-distance (phone) call

interurbano intercity; *comunicazione f* **-a** long-distance (phone) call

intervallo *m* interval; *di scuola, lavoro* break

intervenire <4p> intervene; (*partecipare*) take part, participate (**a** in); MED operate

intervento *m* intervention; (*partecipazione*) participation; MED operation; *pronto* ~ emergency services

intervista *f* interview

intervistare <1a> interview

intervistatore *m*, **-trice** *f* interviewer

intesa *f* (*accordo*) understanding; (*patto*) agreement; SP team work

inteso 1 *pp* → **intendere 2** *agg* (*capito*) understood; (*destinato*) intended, meant (**a** to); *siamo -i?* agreed?; *ben* ~ needless to say, of course

intestare <1b> *assegno* make out (**a** to); *proprietà* register (**a** in the name of); *carta f intestata* letterhead, letterheaded notepaper

intestatario *m* (*pl* -ri), **-a** *f di assegno* payee; *di proprietà* registered owner

intestazione *f* heading; *su carta da lettere* letterhead

intestinale intestinal

intestino *m* intestine, gut

intimare <1l or 1a> order

intimazione *f* order

intimidazione *f* intimidation

intimidire <4d> intimidate

intimità f privacy; *di un rapporto* intimacy

intimo 1 *agg* intimate; (*segreto*) private; (*accogliente*) cosy, *Am* cozy; *amico* close, intimate **2** *m persona* close friend, intimate; (*abbigliamento*) underwear

intimorire <4d> frighten

intingere <3d> dip

intingolo *m* sauce

intitolare <1m> (*dare il titolo a*) call, entitle; (*dedicare*) dedicate (**a** to)

intitolarsi be called

intollerabile intolerable

intollerante intolerant

intolleranza f intolerance

intonacare <1m, c & d> plaster

intonaco *m* (*pl* -chi) plaster

intonare <1c> *strumento* tune; *colori* co-ordinate

intonarsi (*armonizzare*) go well (**a, con** with)

intonato MUS in tune; **colori** *pl* **-i** colours that go well together

intontire <4d> daze

intontito dazed

intoppo *m* (*ostacolo*) hindrance; (*contrattempo*) snag

intorno 1 *prp*: ~ around; (*circa*) (round) about, around; (*riguardo a*) about **2** *avv* around; **tutt'~** all around; **guardarsi** ~ look around

intossicare <1m, c & d> poison

intossicazione f poisoning; ~ **alimentare** food poisoning

intralciare <1f> hinder, hamper

intralcio *m* (*pl* -ci) hindrance

intramuscolare MED intramuscular

intransigente intransigent

intransitivo intransitive

intraprendente enterprising

intraprendenza f enterprise

intraprendere <3c> undertake

intrattabile intractable; *prezzo* fixed, non-negotiable

intrattenere <2q> entertain; ~ **buoni rapporti con qu** be on good terms with s.o.

intrattenersi dwell (**su** on)

intravedere <2s> glimpse, catch a glimpse of; *fig* (*presagire*) anticipate, see

intravisto *pp* → **intravedere**

intrecciare <1f> plait, braid; (*intessere*) weave

intrecciarsi intertwine

intreccio *m* (*pl* -cci) *fig* (*trama*) plot

intricato tangled; *disegno* intricate; *fig* complicated

intrigante scheming; (*affascinante*) intriguing

intrigo *m* (*pl* -ghi) plot

intrinseco (*pl* -ci) intrinsic

introdurre <3e> introduce; (*inserire*) insert

introdursi get in

introduzione f introduction

introito *m* income; (*incasso*) takings *pl*

intromettersi <3ee> interfere; (*interporsi*) intervene

intromissione f interference; (*intervento*) intervention

introvabile impossible to find

introverso 1 *agg* introverted **2** *m*, **-a** f introvert

intrufolarsi <1m> sneak in

intruglio *m* (*pl* -gli) concoction

intrusione f intrusion

intruso *m*, **-a** f intruder

intuire <4d> know instinctively

intuito *m* intuition

intuizione f intuition

inumano inhuman

inumidire <4d> dampen, moisten

inumidirsi get damp

inutile useless; (*superfluo*) unnecessary, pointless

inutilità f uselessness

inutilizzabile unusable

inutilizzato unused

inutilmente pointlessly, needlessly

invadente 1 *agg* nosy **2** *m/f* busybody

invadenza f nosiness

invadere <3q> invade; (*occupare*) occupy; (*inondare*) flood

invaghirsi <4d>: ~ **di** take a fancy to

invalidare <1m> invalidate

invalidità f disability

invalido 1 *agg* disabled; DIR invalid

2 *m*, **-a** *f* disabled person

invano in vain

invariabile invariable

invariabilità *f* unchanging nature

invariato unchanged

invasione *f* invasion (*di* of)

invasore *m* invader

invecchiare <1k> **1** *v/t* age **2** *v/i* age, get older; *di vini, cibi* mature; *fig* (*cadere in disuso*) date

invece instead; (*ma*) but; **~ di fare** instead of doing

inveire <4d>: **~ contro** inveigh against

invenduto unsold

inventare <1b> invent

inventario *m* (*pl* -ri) inventory

inventore *m*, **-trice** *f* inventor

invenzione *f* invention

invernale winter *attr*; *sport mpl* **-i** winter sports

inverno *m* winter; **d'~** in winter

inverosimile improbable, unlikely

inversione *f* (*scambio*) reversal; AUTO **~ di marcia** U-turn

inverso 1 *agg* reverse **2** *m* opposite

invertire <4b or 4d> reverse; (*capovolgere*) turn upside down; CHIM, EL invert; **~ la marcia** turn round; **~ le parti** exchange roles

investigare <1m, b & e> investigate

investigatore *m*, **-trice** *f* investigator

investigazione *f* investigation

investimento *m* investment; *di veicolo* crash; *di pedone* running over; **~ di capitali** capital investment

investire <4d or 4b> *pedone* run over; *veicolo* smash into, collide with; FIN, *fig* invest

inviare <1h> send

inviato *m*, **-a** *f* envoy; *di giornale* correspondent

invidia *f* envy

invidiare <1k> envy

invidioso *m* envious

invincibile invincible

invio *m* (*pl* -vii) dispatch; INFO **tasto** *m* **d'~** enter key

inviolabile inviolable

invisibile invisible

invitante *profumo* enticing; *offerta* tempting

invitare <1a> invite

invitato *m*, **-a** *f* guest

invito *m* invitation; **~ a presentarsi** summons *sg*

invocare <1c & d> invoke; (*implorare*) plead for, beg for

invocazione *f* invocation; (*richiesta*) plea

invogliare <1g & c> induce

involontario (*pl* -ri) involuntary

involtini *mpl* GASTR rolled stuffed slices of meat

involto *m* bundle; (*pacco*) parcel

involucro *m* wrapping

inzaccherare <1m> spatter with mud

inzuppare <1a> soak; (*intingere*) dip

inzuppato soaked

io 1 *pron* I; **~ stesso** myself; **sono ~!** it's me! **2** *m inv* ego

iodio *m* iodine

ionico (*pl* -ci) ARCHI Ionic

iosa: **a ~** in abundance, aplenty

iperalimentazione *f* overfeeding

iperattivo hyperactive

iperbole *f figura retorica* hyperbole; MAT hyperbola

ipermercato *m* hypermarket

ipersensibile hypersensitive

ipertensione *f* high blood pressure

ipnosi *f* hypnosis

ipnotizzare <1a> hypnotize

ipocalorico (*pl* -ci) low in calories

ipocrisia *f* hypocrisy

ipocrita 1 *agg* hypocritical **2** *m/f* (*mpl* -i) hypocrite

ipoteca *f* (*pl* -che) mortgage; **accendere un'~** take out a mortgage

ipotecare <1b & d> mortgage

ipotesi *f* hypothesis

ipotetico (*pl* -ci) hypothetical

ipotizzare <1a> hypothesize

ippica *f* (horse) riding

ippocastano *m* horse chestnut

ippodromo *m* race-course

ippopotamo *m* hippo(potamus)

ira *f* anger; **avere uno scatto d'~** fly into a rage

iracheno 1 *agg* Iraqi **2** *m*, **-a** *f* Iraqi

Iran *m* Iran

iraniano 1 *agg* Iranian 2 *m*, **-a** *f* Iranian

Iraq *m* Iraq

irascibile irritable, irascible

iride *f* (*arcobaleno*) rainbow; ANAT, BOT iris

Irlanda *f* Ireland

irlandese 1 *agg* Irish 2 *m* Irish Gaelic 3 *m/f* Irishman; *donna* Irishwoman

ironia *f* irony

ironico (*pl* -ci) ironic(al)

ironizzare <1a> be ironic

IRPEF *abbr* (= *Imposta sul Reddito delle Persone Fisiche*) income tax

irradiare <1k> *v/t & v/i* radiate

irradiazione *f* radiation

irraggiungibile unattainable

irragionevole unreasonable

irrazionale irrational

irreale unreal

irrealizzabile unattainable

irrefrenabile uncontrollable

irregolare irregular

irregolarità *f inv* irregularity

irreparabile irreparable

irreperibile impossible to find

irreprensibile irreproachable

irreprimibile irrepressible

irrequietezza *f* restlessness

irrequieto restless

irresistibile irresistible

irresponsabile irresponsible

irresponsabilità *f* irresponsibility

irrestringibile non-shrink; *parzialmente* shrink-resistant

irrevocabile irrevocable

irriconoscibile unrecognizable

irrigare <1e> irrigate

irrigazione *f* irrigation

irrigidire <4d> stiffen; *fig disciplina* tighten

irrigidirsi stiffen

irrigidito stiff

irrilevante irrelevant

irrimediabile irremediable

irrinunciabile *diritto* inalienable

irripetibile unrepeatable

irrisorio (*pl* -ri) derisive; *quantità, somma di denaro* derisory; *prezzo*

ridiculously low

irritabile irritable

irritabilità *f* irritability

irritante irritating

irritare <1l or 1a> irritate

irritarsi become irritated

irrobustire <4d> strengthen, build up

irrompere <3rr> burst (*in* into)

irruzione *f*: *fare ~ in* burst into; *di polizia* raid

iscritto 1 *pp* → *iscrivere* 2 *m*, **-a** *f* member; *a gare, concorsi* entrant; EDU pupil, student 3 *m*: *per ~ in* writing

iscrivere <3tt> register; *a gare, concorsi* enter (*a* for, in); EDU enrol(l) (*a* at)

iscriversi *in un elenco* register; *~ a partito, associazione* join; *gara* enter; EDU enrol(l) at

iscrizione *f* inscription

islamico (*pl* -ci) Islamic

Islanda *f* Iceland

islandese 1 *m/agg* Icelandic 2 *m/f* Icelander

isola *f* island; *~ pedonale* pedestrian precinct; *~ spartitraffico* traffic island

isolamento *m* isolation; TEC insulation; *~ acustico* soundproofing

isolano *m*, **-a** *f* islander

isolante 1 *agg* insulating 2 *m* insulator

isolare <1l> isolate; TECH insulate

isolarsi isolate o.s., cut o.s. off

isolato 1 *agg* isolated; TECH insulated 2 *m* outsider; *di case* block

ispettore *m*, **-trice** *f* inspector

ispezionare <1a> inspect

ispezione *f* inspection

ispirare <1a> inspire

ispirarsi *di artista* get inspiration (*a* from)

ispirazione *f* inspiration; (*impulso*) impulse; (*idea*) idea

Israele *m* Israel

israeliano *m*, **-a** *f* Israeli

issare <1a> hoist

istallare <1a> → *installare*

istantanea *f* snap

istantaneo instantaneous
istante m instant; **all'~** instantly
istanza f (esigenza) need; (domanda) application; DIR petition
ISTAT abbr (= **Istituto Centrale di Statistica**) central statistics office
isterico (pl -ci) hysterical
istigare <11 & e> instigate
istintivo instinctive
istinto m instinct
istituire <4d> establish
istituto m institute; assistenziale institution, home; **~ di bellezza** beauty salon; **~ di credito** bank
istituzione f institution
istmo m isthmus
istruire <4d> educate, teach; (dare istruzioni a, addestrare) instruct
istruirsi educate o.s.
istruito educated
istruttivo instructive
istruttore m, **-trice** f instructor
istruzione f education; (direttiva) instruction; **-i** pl **per l'uso** instructions (for use)
Italia f Italy
italiano 1 m/agg Italian; **parla ~?** do you speak Italian? **2** m, **-a** f Italian
itinerario m (pl -ri) route, itinerary
ittico (pl -ci) fish
iugoslavo → **yugoslavo**
iuta f jute
IVA abbr (= **Imposta sul Valore Aggiunto**) VAT (= value-added tax)

J

jazz m jazz
jazzista m/f (mpl -i) jazz musician
jeans mpl jeans
jeep f inv jeep
jet m inv jet
jet-lag m inv jet lag
jet-set m inv jet set
jockey m inv jockey
jogging m jogging; **fare ~** jog, go for a jog
joint-venture f inv joint venture
jolly m inv joker
joule m inv joule
joy-stick m inv joystick
judo m judo
juke-box m inv jukebox
jumbo m jumbo
junior m/agg (pl juniores) junior

K

karatè m karate
kg abbr (= **chilogrammo**) kg (= kilogram)
killer m inv killer
kit m inv kit
kitsch agg inv, m kitsch
kiwi m inv BOT kiwi (fruit)
km abbr (= **chilometro**) km (= kilometre)
km/h abbr (= **chilometri all'ora**) km/h (= kilometres per hour)
kmq abbr (= **chilometri quadrati**) km² (= square kilometres)
knock-out knock-out

k.o.: *mettere qu* ~ knock s.o. out; *fig* trounce s.o.

kolossal *m inv* epic

krapfen *m inv* GASTR doughnut

kümmel *m* kümmel

kV *abbr* (= *chilovolt*) kV (= kilovolt)

kW *abbr* (= *chilowatt*) kW (= kilowatt)

kWh *abbr* (= *chilowattora*) kWh (= kilowatt hour)

L

L *abbr* (= *lira*) L (= lire)

l *abbr* (= *litro*) l (= litre)

l' = *lo, la*

la¹ *art fsg* the; ~ *signora Rossi* Mrs Rossi; ~ *domenica* on Sundays; *mi piace la birra* I like beer

la² *pron* **1** *sg* (*persona*) her; (*cosa, animale*) it; ~ *prenderò* I'll take it **2** *anche* **La** *sg* you

la³ *m* MUS A; *nel solfeggio della scala* la(h)

là there; *di* ~that way; (*in quel luogo*) in there; *di* ~ *di* on the other side of; *più in* ~ further on; *nel tempo* later on

labbro *m* (*pl* le -a) lip

labile (*passeggero*) fleeting, short-lived

labirinto *m* labyrinth

laboratorio *m* (*pl* -ri) lab, laboratory; (*officina*) workshop

laboriosità *f* laboriousness; *di persona* industriousness

laborioso laborious; *persona* hard-working, industrious

laburista **1** *agg* Labo(u)r **2** *m/f* Labo(u)r Party member; *elettore* Labo(u)r supporter

lacca *f* (*pl* -cche) lacquer; *per capelli* hair spray, lacquer

laccare <1d> lacquer

laccio *m* (*pl* -cci) tie, (draw)string; *-cci pl* **delle scarpe** shoe laces

lacerante *dolore, grido* piercing

lacero tattered, in tatters

lacrima *f* tear

lacrimare <1l> water

lacrimevole heart-rending; *film m* ~ tear-jerker

lacrimogeno: *gas m* ~ tear gas

lacuna *f* gap

lacunoso incomplete

ladino 1 *agg* South Tyrolean **2** *m*, -a *f* South Tyrolean

ladro *m*, -a *f* thief

laggiù down there; *distante* over there

laghetto *m* pond

lagna *f* (*lamentela*) whining; *persona* whiner; (*cosa noiosa*) bore

lagnanza *f* complaint

lagnarsi <1a> complain (*di* about)

lago *m* (*pl* -ghi) lake; ~ *artificiale* reservoir; ~ *di Garda* Lake Garda

laguna *f* lagoon

laico (*pl* -ci) **1** *agg scuola, stato* secular **2** *m*, -a *f* member of the laity

lama *f* blade; ~ *di coltello* knife blade

lamentare <1a> lament, deplore

lamentarsi complain (*di* about)

lamentela *f* complaint

lamento *m* whimper

lamentoso whining

lametta *f*: ~ (*da barba*) razor blade

lamiera *f* metal sheet; ~ *ondulata* corrugated iron

lamina *f* foil; ~ *d'oro* gold leaf

lampada *f* lamp; ~ *alogena* halogen lamp; ~ *a stelo* floor lamp, *Br* standard lamp; ~ *al neon* neon light

lampadario *m* (*pl* -ri) chandelier

lampadina *f* light bulb; ~ *tascabile*

torch, *Am* flashlight

lampante blindingly obvious

lampeggiare <1f> flash

lampeggiatore *m* AUTO indicator; FOT flashlight

lampione *m* streetlight

lampo *m* lightning; *in un* ~ in a flash

lampone *m* raspberry

lana *f* wool; *pura ~ vergine* pure new wool

lancetta *f* needle, indicator; *di orologio* hand

lancia *f* (*pl* -ce) spear; MAR launch; *~ di salvataggio* lifeboat

lanciare <1f> throw; *prodotto* launch; *~ un'occhiata* glance, take a quick look; *~ un urlo* give a shout, shout

lanciarsi rush; *~ contro* throw o.s at, attack; F *~ in un' impresa* embark on a venture; F *mi lancio* I'll go for it F, I'll take the plunge F

lancinante *dolore* piercing

lancio *m* (*pl* -ci) throwing; *di prodotto* launch; *~ del disco* discus; *~ del giavellotto* javelin; *~ del peso* putting the shot

languire <4a or 4d> languish

languore *m* lang(u)or; *ho un ~ allo stomaco* I'm feeling peckish

lanificio *m* (*pl* -ci) wool mill

lanterna *f* lantern; (*faro*) lighthouse

lapide *f* gravestone; *su monumento* plaque

lapis *m inv* pencil

lardo *m* lard

larghezza *f* width, breadth; *~ di vedute* broad-mindedness

largo (*pl* -ghi) **1** *agg* wide, broad; *indumento* loose, big; (*abbondante*) large, generous; *~ di manica* generous **2** *m* width; (*piazza*) square; *andare al* ~ head for the open sea; *al ~ di* off the coast of; *farsi ~* elbow one's way through; *stare alla -a da* steer clear of, keep away from

larice *m* larch

laringe *f* larynx

laringite *f* laryngitis

larva *f* ZO larva

lasagne *fpl* lasagne *sg*

lasciapassare *m inv* pass

lasciare <1f> leave; (*abbandonare*) give up; (*concedere*) let; (*smettere di tenere*) let go; *lascia andare!, lascia perdere!* forget it!

lasciarsi separate, leave each other; *~ andare* let o.s go

lascito *m* legacy

lascivo lascivious

laser *m inv, agg inv* laser

lassativo *m/agg* laxative

lasso *m*: *~ di tempo* period of time

lassù up there

lastra *f di pietra* slab; *di metallo, ghiaccio, vetro* sheet; MED x-ray

lastrico *m* (*pl* -chi *o* -ci): *fig ridursi sul* ~ lose everything

latente latent

laterale lateral

laterizio *m* (*mpl* -zi) bricks and tiles *pl*

latino 1 *agg* Latin; *~-americano* Latin-American **2** *m* Latin; *~-americano, -a f* Latin-American

latitante *m/f* fugitive

latitudine *f* latitude

lato *m* side; *a ~ di, di ~ a* beside; *d'altro* ~ on the other hand

latrare <1a> bark

latrato *m* barking

latrina *f* latrine

latta *f* can, tin; *~ di benzina* petrol can, *Am* gas can

lattaio *m* (*pl* -ai), *-a f* milkman; *donna* milkwoman

lattante *m* infant, small baby

latte *m* milk; *~ a lunga conservazione* long-life milk; *~ intero* whole milk; *~ materno* mother's milk; *~ scremato* skim(med) milk

latteo milk *attr*; *Via f Lattea* Milky Way

latteria *f* dairy

lattice *m* latex

latticinio *m* (*pl* -ni) dairy product

lattina *f* can, tin

lattuga *f* (*pl* -ghe) lettuce

laurea *f* degree

laurearsi <1l> graduate

laureato *m*, *-a f* graduate

lava *f* lava

lavabile washable; **~ in lavatrice** machine-washable
lavabo m basin
lavacristallo m AUTO windscreen (Am windshield) washer
lavaggio m (pl -ggi) washing; **~ a secco** dry-cleaning; **~ del cervello** brainwashing
lavagna f blackboard; GEOL slate; **~ luminosa** overhead projector
lavanda f BOT lavender
lavanderia f laundry; **~ a gettone** laundrette
lavandino m basin; *nella cucina* sink
lavapiatti m/f inv dishwasher
lavare <1a> wash; **~ i panni** do the washing
lavarsi wash; **~ le mani** wash one's hands; **~ i denti** brush *or* clean one's teeth
lavastoviglie f inv dishwasher
lavatoio m (pl -oi) laundry; *di casa* laundry (room), utility room
lavatrice f washing machine
lavello m basin; *nella cucina* sink
lavina f avalanche
lavorare <1a> **1** v/i work **2** v/t *materia prima* process; *legno* carve; *terra* work
lavorativo: giorno m **~** working day
lavorato *legno* carved
lavoratore m, **-trice** f worker; **~ autonomo** self-employed person; **~ dipendente** employee
lavorazione f *di materia prima* processing; *di legno* carving
lavoro m work; *(impiego)* job; **~ di gruppo** teamwork; **~ malfatto** botched job; **~ nero** moonlighting; **-i** pl **occasionali** o **saltuari** odd jobs; **per ~** on business; **condizioni** fpl **di ~** working conditions; **permesso** m **di ~** work permit; **posto** m **di ~** place of work, workplace; **-i in corso** roadworks, work in progress; **senza ~** unemployed
le¹ art fpl the
le² pron fsg to her; fpl them; *anche* **Le** you
leader m/f inv leader
leale loyal

lealtà f loyalty
lebbra f leprosy
lebbroso m, **-a** f leper
lecca-lecca m inv lollipop
leccare <1d> lick; F **~ qu** suck up to s.o. F, lick s.o.'s boots F
leccio m (pl -cci) holm oak
leccornia f appetizing dish, delicacy
lecito legal, permissible; **se mi è ~** if I may
lega f (pl -ghe) league; METAL alloy
legale 1 agg legal **2** m/f lawyer
legalità f legality
legalizzare <1a> legalize
legame m tie, relationship; *(nesso)* link, connection
legamento m ANAT ligament
legare <1e> tie; *persona* tie up; *(collegare)* link; *fig di lavoro* tie down
legarsi fig tie o.s. down
legazione f legation
legge f law; **studiare ~** study *or* read law; **a norma di ~** up to standard; **a norma di ~ ...** complies with ...; **fuori ~** illegal, unlawful
leggenda f legend; *di carta geografica ecc* key
leggendario (pl -ri) legendary
leggere <3cc> read; **~ le labbra** lipread; **~ nel pensiero a qu** read s.o.'s mind
leggerezza f lightness; fig casualness; **con ~** thoughtlessly, unthinkingly
leggero light; *(lieve, di poca importanza)* slight; *(superficiale)* thoughtless; *caffè* weak; **alla -a** lightly, lightheartedly
leggibile legible
leggio m (pl -ii) lectern; MUS music stand
legislativo legislative
legislatore m legislator
legislatura f *periodo* term of parliament
legislazione f legislation
legittimare <1m> approve
legittimazione f approval
legittimo legitimate

legna *f* (fire)wood; **far ~** collect firewood

legname *m* timber; **~ da costruzione** lumber

legno *m* (*pl* i -i) wood; **di ~** wooden

legumi *mpl* peas and beans; *secchi* pulses

lei *pron fsg soggetto* she; *oggetto, con preposizione* her; **~ stessa** herself; *anche* **Lei** you; **dare del ~ a qu** address s.o. as 'lei'

lembo *m di gonna* hem, bottom; *di terra* stip

lente *f* lens; **-i** *pl* glasses, spectacles, specs F; **-i** *pl* (**a contatto**) contact lenses, contacts F; **~ d'ingrandimento** magnifying glass

lentezza *f* slowness

lenticchia *f* lentil

lentiggine *f* freckle

lento slow; (*allentato*) slack; *abito* loose

lenza *f* fishing rod

lenzuolo *m* (*pl* i -i e le -a) sheet

leone *m* lion; ASTR **Leone** Leo

leonessa *f* lioness

leopardo *m* leopard

lepre *f* hare

lercio filthy

lesbica *f* lesbian

lesionare damage

lesione *f* MED injury

lessare <1a> boil

lessico *m* (*pl* -ci) vocabulary; (*dizionario*) glossary

lesso 1 *agg* boiled **2** *m* boiled beef

letale lethal

letame *m* manure, dung

letargo *m* (*pl* -ghi) lethargy

lettera *f* letter; **alla ~** to the letter; **~ assicurata** registered letter; **~ commerciale** business letter; **~ di accompagnamento** covering letter; FIN **~ di cambio** bill of exchange; **~ espresso** (letter sent) express delivery; **~ raccomandata** recorded delivery letter

letterale literal

letterario (*pl* -ri) literary

letterato *m*, **-a** *f* man/woman of letters

letteratura *f* literature

lettino *m* cot; *dal medico* bed; *dallo psicologo* couch; **~ solare** sunbed

letto[1] *m* bed; **~ a una piazza** single bed; **~ matrimoniale** double bed; **andare a ~** go to bed; **essere a ~** be in bed

letto[2] *pp* → **leggere**

lettore *m*, **-trice** *f* reader; *all'università* lecturer in a foreign language; INFOR disk drive; **~ compact disc** CD player; **~ ottico** optical character reader

lettura *f* reading

leucemia *f* leuk(a)emia

leva *f* lever; MIL call-up, *Am* draft; AUTO **~ del cambio** gear lever

levante *m* east

levare <1b> (*alzare*) raise, lift; (*togliere*) take, (re)move; (*rimuovere*) take out, remove; *macchia* remove, get out; *dente* take out, extract; **~ l'ancora** weigh anchor

levarsi get up, rise; *di sole* rise, come up; *indumento* take off; **~ il vizio di fare qc** get out of the habit of doing sth; **levatelo dalla testa!** you can get that idea out of your head!

levata *f di posta* collection

levatrice *f* midwife

levigare <1l, b & e> smooth down

levigato smooth

lezione *f* lesson; *all'università* lecture; *fig* **dare una ~ a qu** teach s.o. a lesson

li *pron mpl* them

lì there; **~ per ~** there and then; **giù di ~** thereabouts; **di ~ a pochi giorni** a few days later

libanese *agg*, *m/f* Lebanese

Libano *m* (the) Lebanon

libbra *f* pound

libellula *f* dragon-fly

liberale 1 *agg* generous; POL liberal **2** *m/f* liberal

liberalità *f* generosity

liberalizzare <1a> liberalize

liberalizzazione *f* liberalization

liberamente freely

liberare <1l> release, free;

(*sgombrare*) empty; *stanza* vacate
liberarsi: ~ *di* get rid of
liberazione *f* release; *di nazione* liberation
libero free; *camera d'albergo* vacant, free
libertà *f inv* freedom, liberty; **mettersi in** ~ change into more comfortable clothes; ~ *di stampa* freedom of the press; **prendersi la ~ di fare qc** take the liberty of doing sth; ~ **provvisoria** bail
Libia *f* Libya
libico (*pl* -ci) **1** *agg* Libyan **2** *m*, -**a** *f* Libyan
libraio *m* (*pl* -ai) bookseller
librario (*pl* -ri) book *attr*
libreria *f* bookstore, *Br* -shop; (*biblioteca*) book collection, library; *mobile* bookcase
libretto *m* booklet; MUS libretto; ~ *di assegni* cheque book, *Am* check book; AUTO ~ *di circolazione* registration document; ~ *di risparmio* bank book
libro *m* book; ~ *di testo* textbook; ~ *illustrato* picture book
licenza *f* FIN licence, *Am* license, permit; MIL leave; EDU school leaving certificate; ~ *di costruzione* building *or* construction permit; ~ *di esercizio* trading licence (*Am* license)
licenziamento *m* dismissal; *per motivi economici* dismissal, *Br* redundancy
licenziare <1g> dismiss; *per motivi economici* dismiss, lay off, *Br* make redundant; ~ *alle stampe* pass for press
licenziarsi resign
liceo *m* high school; ~ *classico* (**scientifico**) high school that *specializes in arts* (*science*) *subjects*
lido *m* beach
lieto happy; ~ *di conoscerla* nice *or* pleased to meet you
lieve light; (*di poca gravità*) slight, minor; *sorriso, rumore* faint
lievitare <1l & b> rise; *fig* rise, be on the increase

lievito *m* yeast; ~ *in polvere* baking powder
lilla *m/agg* lilac
lillà *m* lilac (tree)
lima *f* file
limare <1a> file
limetta *f* emery board; *di metallo* nail file
limitare <1l> limit, restrict (**a** to); (*contenere*) limit, contain
limitato limited; FIN **società** *f* **a responsabilità -a** limited company; **è** ~ *di persona* he's got his limitations
limitazione *f* limitation; ~ *delle nascite* birth control; **senza -i** without restriction
limite *m* limit; (*confine*) boundary; ~ *di età* age limit; ~ *di velocità* speed limit; **al** ~ at most, at the outside; **nei -i del possibile** to the best of one's ability
limitrofo bordering, neighbo(u)ring
limonata *f* lemonade
limone *m* lemon; (*albero*) lemon tree
limpidezza *f* cleanness
limpido clear; *acqua* crystal-clear, limpid
lince *f* lynx
linciare <1f> lynch
linea *f* line; ~ *dell'autobus* bus route; **mantenere la** ~ keep one's figure; TELEC **restare in** ~ stay on the line, not hang up
lineamenti *mpl* (*fisionomia*) features
lineare linear
lineetta *f* dash
linfonodo *m* lymph node
lingotto *m* ingot
lingua *f* tongue; (*linguaggio*) language; ~ *madre* mother tongue; ~ *parlata* colloquial language; ~ *straniera* foreign language; ~ *nazionale* official language
linguaggio *m* (*pl* -ggi) language; ~ *tecnico* technical language, jargon; INFOR ~ *di programmazione* programming language
linguistica *f* linguistics
lino *m* BOT flax; *tessuto* linen
liofilizzato freeze-dried

liquidare <1l> (*pagare*) pay; *merci* clear; *azienda* liquidate; *fig questione* settle; *problema* dispose of; *persona* F liquidate F, dispose of F

liquidazione f liquidation; **~ totale** clearance sale

liquidità f liquid assets pl, liquidity

liquido m/agg liquid

liquirizia f liquorice

liquore m liqueur

lira f lira

lirica f (pl -che) lyric poem; MUS **la ~** opera

lirico (pl -ci) lyric; *cantante* opera attr; *teatro* m ~ opera house

lisca f (pl -che) fishbone

lisciare <1f> smooth (down); (*accarezzare*) stroke; *capelli* straighten

liscio (pl -sci) smooth; *bevanda* straight, neat; *fig* **passarla -a** get away with it

liso worn

lista f (*elenco*) list; (*striscia*) strip; **~ d'attesa** waiting list; **in ~ d'attesa** on the waiting list, wait-listed; AVIA on standby; **~ dei vini** wine list

listino m: **~ di borsa** share index; **~ prezzi** price list

Lit. abbr (= **lire italiane**) L (= lire)

lite f quarrel, argument; JUR lawsuit; **~ coniugale** marital dispute

litigare <1l & e> quarrel, argue

litigio m (pl -gi) quarrel, argument

litigioso argumentative, quarrelsome

litografia f lithography

litografo m lithograph

litorale 1 agg coastal **2** m coast

litoranea f coast road

litoraneo coast attr, coastal

litro m litre, Am liter

Lituania f Lithuania

lituano 1 agg Lithuanian **2** m, **-a** f Lithuanian

liturgia f liturgy

liturgico (pl -ci) liturgical

liutaio m (pl -ai) lute maker

liuto m lute

livella f level

livellamento m levelling

livellare <1b> level

livello m level; AUTO **~ dell'olio** oil level; *fig* **ad altissimo ~** first-class, first-rate; **sopra il ~ del mare** above sea level; **~ di vita** standard of living

livido 1 agg livid; *braccio, viso* black and blue; *occhio* black; *per il freddo* blue **2** m bruise

lo 1 art m/sg the **2** pron m/sg him; *cosa, animale* it; **non ~ so** I don't know

lobo m lobe

locale 1 agg local; MED **anestesia** f **~** local an(a)esthetic **2** m room; *luogo pubblico* place; FERR local train

località f inv town; **~ balneare** seaside resort; **~ turistica** tourist resort

localizzare <1a> locate; (*delimitare*) localize

locandina f TEA bill

locatario m (pl -ri), **-a** f tenant

locatore m, **-trice** f landlord; *donna* landlady

locazione f rental

locomotiva f locomotive

locomozione f locomotion; **mezzo** m **di ~** means of transport

locuzione f fixed expression

lodare <1c> praise

lode f praise

lodevole praiseworthy, laudable

loggia f (pl -gge) loggia

loggione m TEA gallery

logica f logic

logico (pl -ci) logical

logorare <1l> wear out

logorio m wear and tear

logoro *indumento* worn (out), threadbare

lombaggine f lumbago

Lombardia f Lombardy

lombardo 1 agg of Lombardy **2** m, **-a** f native of Lombardy

lombata f loin

lombo m loin

lombrico m (pl -chi) earthworm

Londra f London

longevo longlived

longitudine f GEOG longitude

lontananza f distance; *tra persone* separation

lontano 1 agg far; *nel tempo* far-off;

L

passato, futuro, parente distant; **alla -a** *conoscere* vaguely, slightly; **siamo cugini alla -a** we're distant cousins **2** *avv* far (away); **da ~** from a distance; **abita molto ~?** do you live very far away?

lontra *f* otter

loquace talkative

lordo dirty; *peso, reddito ecc* gross

loro 1 *pron soggetto* they; *oggetto* them; *forma di cortesia, anche* **Loro** you **2** *possessivo* their; *forma di cortesia, anche* **Loro** your; *il ~ amico* their / your friend; *i ~ genitori* their / your parents **3** *pron: il ~* theirs; *forma di cortesia, anche* **Loro** yours

lotta *f* struggle; SP wrestling; *fig* fight

lottare <1c> wrestle, struggle (**con** with); *fig* fight (**contro** against; **per** for)

lottatore *m* wrestler

lotteria *f* lottery; **biglietto** *m* **della ~** lottery ticket

lotto *m* lottery; *di terreno* plot

lozione *f* lotion; **~ dopobarba** aftershave

L.st. *abbr* (= **lira sterlina**) £ (= pound)

lubrificante *m* lubricant; AUTO lubricating oil

lubrificare <1m & qc> lubricate

lucchetto *m* padlock

luccicare <1l & d> sparkle

luccio *m* (*pl* -cci) pike

lucciola *f* glowworm

luce *f* light; **~ al neon** neon light; **dare alla ~ un figlio** give birth to a son; *fig* **far ~ su qc** shed light on sth; AUTO **-i** *pl* **di posizione** side lights; **-i** *pl* **posteriori** rear lights

lucente shining, gleaming

lucentezza *f* shininess

lucertola *f* lizard

lucidare <1l> polish; *disegno* trace

lucidatrice *f* floor polisher

lucido 1 *agg superficie, scarpe* shiny; FOT glossy; *persona* lucid **2** *m* polish; *disegno* transparency; **~ da scarpe** shoe polish

lucrativo lucrative

lucro *m*: **a scopo di ~** profit-making;

senza fini di ~ non-profit-making

luglio *m* July

lugubre sombre, *Am* somber, lugubrious

lui *pron msg soggetto* he; *oggetto* him; **a ~** to him; **~ stesso** himself

lumaca *f* (*pl* -che) slug

lume *m* (*lampada*) lamp; *luce* light; *fig* **perdere il ~ della ragione** lose one's mind

luminosità *f* luminosity; FOT speed

luminoso luminous; *stanza* bright, full of light; **sorgente** *f* **-a** light source

luna *f* moon; *fig* **avere la ~ storta** be in a mood; **~ crescente / calante** crescent / waning moon; **~ piena** full moon; **~ di miele** honeymoon

luna-park *m inv* amusement park, *Br* funfair

lunario *m*: **sbarcare il ~** make ends meet

lunatico (*pl* -ci) moody

lunedì *m inv* Monday; **il o di ~** on Mondays

lunetta *f* ARCHI lunette

lunghezza *f* length

lungo (*pl* -ghi) **1** *agg* long; *caffè* weak; **non essere ~!** don't be long!, don't take forever!; **a ~** at length, for a long time; *fig* **alla -a** in the long run; **andare per le -ghe** drag on; **di gran -a** by far **2** *prp* along; (*durante*) throughout

lungolago *m* (*pl* -ghi) lakeside, lakeshore

lungomare *m inv* sea front

lunotto *m* AUTO rear window

luogo *m* (*pl* -ghi) place; **~ di nascita** birthplace, place of birth; **avere ~** take place, be held; **fuori ~** out of place; **in primo ~** in the first place; **in qualche ~** somewhere, someplace; **in nessun ~** nowhere

lupo *m* wolf

lurido filthy

lusinga *f* (*pl* -ghe) flattery

lusingare <1e> flatter

lusinghiero flattering

lussazione *f* dislocation

lusso *m* luxury; **albergo** *m* **di ~**

luxury hotel
lussuoso luxurious
lustrare <1a> polish

lustro *m* shine, lustre, *Am* luster; *fig* prestige; (*periodo*) five-year period
lutto *m* mourning

M

m *abbr* (= **metro**) m (= metre)
ma but; (*eppure*) and yet; ~ **cosa dici?** what are you talking about?; ~ **va!** nonsense!; ~ **no!** not at all!, of course not!
maccheroni *mpl* macaroni *sg*
macchia *f* spot; *di sporco* stain; (*bosco*) scrub; **allargarsi a ~ d'olio** spread like wildfire
macchiare <1k> stain, mark
macchiato stained; **caffè m ~** espresso with a splash of milk
macchina *f* machine; (*auto*) car; *fig* machinery; ~ **fotografica** camera; ~ **da cucire** sewing machine; ~ **da presa** cine camera; ~ **da scrivere** typewriter; ~ **sportiva** sports car; ~ **a noleggio** hire car, rental car; **fatto a ~** machine made
macchinario *m* (*pl* -ri) machinery
macchinista *m* (*pl* -i) FERR train driver
macedonia *f*: ~ (**di frutta**) fruit salad
macellaio *m* (*pl* -ai), -**a** *f* butcher
macellare <1b> butcher
macelleria *f* butcher's
macerie *fpl* rubble *sg*
macigno *m* boulder
macinacaffè *m inv* coffee mill, coffee grinder
macinapepe *m inv* pepper mill, pepper grinder
macinare <1l> grind
macinino *m* mill; *spir* old banger
macrobiotica *f* health food; **negozio m di ~** health food shop
macrobiotico (*mpl* -ci) macrobiotic
macroscopico (*pl* -ci) *fig* huge, enormous; **errore** monumental, colossal
Madonna *f* Madonna, Our Lady; PITT ~ **con bambino** Madonna and Child
madonnaro *m* pavement artist specializing in sacred images
madre *f* mother
madrelingua 1 *f* mother tongue **2** *m/f* native speaker
madrepatria *f* native land, mother country
madreperla *f* mother-of-pearl
madrevite *f* nut
madrina *f* godmother
maestà *f* majesty
maestoso majestic
maestrale *m* north-west wind
maestranze *fpl* workers
maestria *f* mastery
maestro 1 *agg* (*principale*) main; MAR **albero m ~** main mast; **muro m ~** loadbearing wall **2** *m* master; MUS, PITT maestro, master; **colpo m da ~** masterstroke **3** *m*, -**a** *f* teacher; ~ **di nuoto** swimming teacher *or* instructor; ~ **di sci** ski instructor
mafia *f* Mafia
maga *f* witch
magari 1 *avv* maybe, perhaps **2** *int* ~**!** if only! **3** *cong* ~ **venisse** if only he would come
magazzinaggio *m* storage
magazzino *m* warehouse; *di negozio* stock room; (*emporio*) factory shop; **grandi -i** *pl* department stores
maggio *m* May
maggiolino *m* June bug, May beetle
maggiorana *f* marjoram

maggioranza *f* majority; **~ azionaria** majority shareholding

maggiorare <1a> increase

maggiore 1 *agg* bigger; (*più vecchio*) older; MUS major; **il ~** the biggest; *figlio* the oldest; *artista* the greatest; *azionista* the major, the largest; **la maggior parte del tempo / di noi** most of the time / of us, the majority of the time / of us; **andare per la ~** be a crowd pleaser **2** *m* MIL major

maggiorenne adult *attr*

maggioritario (*pl* -ri) majority; **sistema** *m* **~** first-past-the-post system

magia *f* magic

magico (*pl* -ci) magic(al)

magistrale (*eccellente*) masterful; **istituto** *m* **~** teacher training college

magistrato DIR *m* magistrate

maglia *f* top; (*maglione*) sweater; SP shirt, jersey; *ai ferri* stitch; **lavorare a ~** knit; SP **~ gialla** yellow jersey

maglieria *f* knitwear

maglietta *f* tee-shirt

maglione *m* sweater

magnanimo magnanimous

magnesia *f* magnesia

magnesio *m* magnesium

magnete *m* magnet

magnetico (*pl* -ci) magnetic

magnifico (*pl* -ci) magnificent

magnolia *f* magnolia

mago *m* **1** (*pl* -ghi) wizard **2** (*pl* -gi) *i re* -gi the Three Wise Men, the Magi

magro thin; *cibo* low in fat; *fig consolazione* small; *guadagno* meagre, *Am* meager

mai never; (*qualche volta*) ever; **~ più** never again; **più che ~** more than ever; **non accetterò ~ e poi ~** I will never agree, never; **chi ha ~ detto che ...** who said that ...; **come ~?** how come?; **se ~** if ever; **meglio tardi che ~** better late than never; **dove / perché ~?** where / why on earth?

maiale *m* pig; (*carne f di*) **~** pork

maiolica *f* (*pl* -che) majolica

maionese *f* mayonnaise

mais *m* maize

maiuscola *f* capital (letter)

maiuscolo capital

mal → **male**

malandato *vestito, divano, macchina* dilapidated; *persona* poorly, not very well

malanno *m* misfortune; (*malattia*) illness

malapena: a ~ hardly, barely

malaria *f* malaria

malaticcio (*pl* -ci) sickly

malato 1 *agg* ill; **essere ~ di cuore** have heart problems; **~ di mente** mentally ill **2** *m*, **-a** *f* ill person

malattia *f* illness; **essere / mettersi in ~** be / go on sick leave; **~ infettiva** infectious disease; **-e** *pl* **della pelle** skin diseases; **-e** *pl* **veneree** sexually transmitted diseases

malavita *f* underworld

malavoglia *f* unwillingness, reluctance; **di ~** unwillingly, grudgingly, reluctantly

malconcio (*pl* -ci) *vestito, divano, macchina* dilapidated, the worse for wear; *persona* poorly, not very well

malcontento 1 *agg* discontented, dissatisfied **2** *m* discontent

malcostume *m* immorality

maldestro awkward, clumsy

male 1 *m* evil; **che c'è di ~?** where's the harm in it?; **andare a ~** go off, go bad; **aversela o prendersela a ~** take it the wrong way; MED **mal di gola** sore throat; **mal di testa / di denti** headache / toothache; **mal di mare** seasickness; **far ~ a qu** hurt s.o.; **mi fa ~ il braccio** my arm hurts; **il cioccolato mi fa ~** chocolate doesn't agree with me; **fare ~ alla salute** be bad for you; **farsi ~** hurt o.s. **2** *avv* badly; **capire ~** misunderstand; **di ~ in peggio** from bad to worse; **meno ~!** thank goodness!; **stare ~** (*essere malato*) be ill; (*essere giù*) be depressed; **il giallo mi sta ~** yellow doesn't suit me, I don't suit yellow; **il divano sta ~ qui** the couch doesn't look right here; **sta ~ ...** it's not done to ...; **mi ha**

risposto ~ he gave me a rude answer

maledetto 1 *pp* → **maledire 2** *agg* dratted, damn(ed)

maledire <3t> curse

maledizione *f* curse; **~!** damn!

maleducato bad-mannered, uncouth

malessere *m* indisposition; *fig* malaise

malfamato disreputable

malfatto *cosa* badly made

malfattore *m* criminal

malformazione *f* MED, BIO malformation

malgoverno *m* POL misgovernment

malgrado 1 *prp* in spite of, despite **2** *avv* **mio/tuo** ~ against my/your will **3** *cong* although

maligno malicious, spiteful; MED malignant

malinconia *f* melancholy

malinconico (*pl* -ci) melancholic

malincuore: a ~ reluctantly, unwilling

malintenzionato 1 *agg* shady, suspicious **2** *m*, **-a** *f* shady character

malinteso *m* misunderstanding

malizia *f* (*cattiveria*) malice, spite; (*astuzia*) trick; **con** ~ maliciously, spitefully

malizioso malicious, spiteful; *sorriso* mischievous

malloppo *m* (*refurtiva*) loot

malmenare <1a> mistreat

malmesso *vestito, divano, macchina* the worse for wear; **sono un po'** ~ I'm a bit hard up

malnutrito under-nourished

malnutrizione *f* malnutrition

malore *m*: **è stato colto da un** ~ he was suddenly taken ill

malsano unhealthy

malsicuro unsafe

malta *f* mortar

maltempo *m* bad weather

malto *m* malt

maltrattare <1a> mistreat, ill-treat

malumore *m* bad mood; **essere di** ~ be in a bad mood

malvagio (*pl* -gi) evil, wicked

malvisto unpopular

malvivente *m* lout

malvolentieri unwillingly, reluctantly

mamma *f* mother, mum; **~ mia!** goodness!

mammella *f* breast

mammifero *m* mammal

mammografia *f* mammography

manager *m/f* manager

manageriale managerial, management *attr*

mancanza *f* lack (**di** of); (*errore*) oversight; **~ di abitazioni** housing shortage; **~ di corrente** power failure; **~ di personale** lack of staff, staff shortage; **per ~ di tempo** for lack of time

mancare <1d> **1** *v/i* be missing; (*venire meno*) fail; (*morire*) pass away; **a qu manca qc** s.o. lacks sth; **mi mancano le forze** I don't have the strength; **mi manca la casa** I miss home; **mi mancano 5000 lire** I'm 5000 lire short; **manca la benzina nella macchina** the car needs filling up; **mancano tre mesi a Natale** it's three months to Christmas; **sentirsi** ~ feel faint; **non mancherò** I'll do that, I'll be sure to do it; **c'è mancato poco che cadesse** he almost fell; **ci mancherebbe altro!** no way!, you must be joking!; **~ di qc** (*non avere*) lack sth, be lacking in sth; **~ di fare qc** fail *or* omit to do sth; **~ di parola** break one's promise **2** *v/t* miss

mancato *occasione* missed, lost; *tentativo* unsuccessful; **è un poeta** ~ he should have been a poet; **~ pagamento** non-payment

manchevole faulty, defective

mancia *f* (*pl* -ce) tip

manciata *f* handful

mancino 1 *agg* left-handed; *fig* **colpo** *m* ~ blow beneath the belt, dirty trick **2** *m*, **-a** *f* left-hander

mandante *m/f* DIR client; *F* person who hires a contract killer

mandare <1a> send; **~ qu a prendere qc** send s.o. for sth; **~ a monte**

M

ruin, send up in smoke F; *fig* **~ giù** digest, take in

mandarino *m* BOT mandarin (orange)

mandato *m* POL mandate; DIR warrant; **~ bancario** banker's order; **~ di pagamento** payment order; **~ d'arresto** arrest warrant

mandibola *f* jaw

mandolino *m* mandolin

mandorla *f* almond

mandorlo *m* almond tree

mandria *f* herd

maneggevole easy to handle, manageable

maneggiare <1f> handle (*anche fig*)

maneggio *m* (*pl* -ggi) handling; *per cavalli* riding school

manesco (*pl* -chi) a bit too ready with one's fists

manette *fpl* handcuffs

manganello *m* truncheon

mangereccio (*pl* -ci) edible

mangiabile edible

mangiacassette *m inv*, **mangianastri** *m inv* cassette player

mangiare **1** *v/t* <1f> eat; *fig* squander; **mangiarsi le parole** mumble; **mangiarsi un'occasione** throw away *or* waste an opportunity **2** *m* food

mangime *m* fodder

mangiucchiare <1g> snack, eat between meals

mango *m* (*pl* -ghi) mango

mania *f* mania

Manica *f*: **la ~** the (English) Channel

manica *f* (*pl* -che) sleeve; **senza -che** sleeveless; **è un altro paio di -che!** that's another kettle of fish

manicaretto *m* delicacy

manichino *m* dummy

manico *m* (*pl* -chi *o* -ci) handle; *di violino* neck

manicomio *m* (*pl* -mi) mental home

manicotto *m* TEC sleeve

manicure *f inv* manicure; (*persona*) manicurist

maniera *f* (*modo*) way, manner; (*stile*) manner; **-e** *pl* manners

manifattura *f* manufacture; (*stabili-*

mento) factory

manifestante *m/f* demonstrator

manifestare <1b> **1** *v/t* (*esprimere*) express; (*mostrare*) show, demonstrate **2** *v/i* demonstrate

manifestarsi appear, show up; *di malattia* manifest itself

manifestazione *f* expression; *il mostrare* show, demonstration; **~ di protesta** demonstration, demo F; **~ sportiva** sporting event

manifesto **1** *agg* obvious **2** *m* poster

maniglia *f* handle; *di autobus, metro* strap

manipolare <1m> manipulate; *vino* adulterate

manipolazione *f* manipulation; *di vino* adulteration

mano *f* (*pl* -i) hand; **fuori ~** out of the way, not easy to get at; *fig* **alla ~** approachable; **di seconda ~** second-hand; **dare una ~ a qu** give s.o. a hand; **mettere ~ a qc** start sth; **lavo le pentole che sporco a ~ a ~** I wash the dirty pots as I go along; **tenersi per ~** hold hands; **man ~ che** as (and when); **-i in alto!** hands up!

manodopera *f* labo(u)r

manomettere <3ee> tamper with

manopola *f* knob

manoscritto *m* manuscript

manovale *m* hod carrier

manovella *f* starting handle; TEC crank

manovra *f* manoeuvre, *Am* maneuver

manovrare <1c> **1** *v/t* TEC operate; FERR shunt; *fig* manipulate **2** *v/i* manoeuvre, *Am* maneuver

mansarda *f* (*locale*) attic

mansueto docile

mantello *m* (*cappa*) cloak; *di animale* coat; (*strato*) covering, layer

mantenere <2q> keep; *famiglia* keep, maintain; *in buono stato* maintain; **mantenersi in forma** keep in shape

mantenimento *m* maintenance; *di famiglia* keep

manto *m* cloak; *di animale* coat; *fig* **~**

di neve mantle of snow

Mantova *f* Mantua

mantovano 1 *agg* Mantuan **2** *m*, **-a** *f* native of Mantua

manuale 1 *agg* manual **2** *m* manual, handbook

manubrio *m* (*pl* -ri) handlebars *pl*

manutenzione *f* maintenance

manzo *m* steer, bullock; *carne* beef

mappa *f* map

mappamondo *m* globe

maratona *f* marathon

maratoneta *m/f* (*mpl* -i) marathon runner

marca *f* (*pl* -che) brand, make; (*etichetta*) label; **~ da bollo** revenue stamp

marcare <1d> mark; *goal* score

marcato *accento, lineamenti* strong

marchiare <1k> brand (*anche fig*)

marchio *m* (*pl* -chi) FIN brand; **~ depositato** registered trademark

marcia *f* (*pl* -ce) march; SP walk; TEC AUTO gear; **~ indietro** reverse; **mettersi in ~** set off

marciapiede *m* pavement, *Am* sidewalk; FERR platform

marciare <1f> march

marcio (*pl* -ci) bad, rotten; (*corrotto*) corrupt, rotten to the core; **avere torto ~** be totally wrong

marcire <4d> go bad, rot; *fig* rot

marco *m* (*pl* -chi) mark

mare *m* sea; **in alto ~** on the high seas

marea *f* tide; *fig* **una ~ di** loads of; **alta ~** high tide; **bassa ~** low tide; **~ nera** oil slick

mareggiata *f* storm

maremoto *m* tidal wave

margarina *f* margarine

margherita *f* marguerite

margheritina *f* daisy

margine *m* margin; (*orlo*) edge, brink; **vivere ai -i della società** live on the fringes of society

marina *f* coast(line); MAR navy; PITT seascape

marinaio *m* (*pl* -ai) sailor

marinare <1a> GASTR marinate; F **~ la scuola** play truant, *Br* bunk off school F

marinato GASTR marinated

marino sea, marine

marionetta *f* puppet, marionette

marito *m* husband

marittimo maritime

marmellata *f* jam; **~ di arance** marmalade

marmitta *f* AUTO silencer, *Am* muffler; **~ catalitica** catalytic converter

marmo *m* marble

marmotta *f* marmot; **dormire come una ~** sleep like a log

marocchino 1 *agg* Moroccan **2** *m*, **-a** *f* Moroccan

Marocco *m* Morocco

marrone 1 *agg* (chestnut) brown **2** *m colore* (chestnut) brown; (*castagno*) chestnut

marsala *m* Marsala, *dessert wine*

marsina *f* tails

Marte *m* Mars

martedì *m inv* Tuesday; **~ grasso** Shrove Tuesday, *Br* Pancake Day F

martello *m* hammer; **~ pneumatico** pneumatic drill

martire *m/f* martyr

martirio *m* (*pl* -ri) martyrdom

martora *f* marten

marxismo *m* Marxism

marxista *m/f* (*mpl* -i) Marxist

marzapane *m* marzipan

marziano *m* Martian

marzo *m* March

mascalzone *m* rogue, rascal

mascara *m inv* mascara

mascarpone *m* mascarpone

mascella *f* jaw

maschera *f* mask; *in cinema, teatro* usher; *donna* usherette; **~ antigas** gas mask; **~ subacquea** face mask; **ballo in ~** masked ball

mascherare <1l> mask; *fig* camouflage, conceal

mascherarsi put on a mask; (*travestirsi*) dress up (**da** as)

maschile *spogliatoio, abito* men's; *caratteristica* male; GRAM masculine

maschilista (*pl* -i) **1** *m* male chauvinist, sexist **2** *agg* chauvinistic, sexist

maschio (*pl* -chi) **1** *agg* male; **hanno**

tre figli **-i** they have three sons or boys **2** *m* (*ragazzo*) boy; (*uomo*) man; ZO male

mascolino masculine

mascotte *f inv* mascot

massa *f* mass; EL earth; F *una ~ di cosa da fare* masses of things to do F

massacrare <1a> massacre

massacro *m* massacre

massaggiare <1f> massage

massaggiatore *m*, **-trice** *f* masseur; *donna* masseuse

massaggio *m* (*pl* -ggi) massage

massaia *f* housewife

massiccio (*pl* -cci) **1** *agg* massive; *oro, noce ecc* solid **2** *m* massif

massima *f* saying, maxim; (*temperatura*) maximum; *di ~ progetto* preliminary; *in linea di ~* generally speaking, on the whole

massimale *m* maximum

massimo **1** *agg* greatest, maximum **2** *m* maximum; *al ~* at most

mass media *mpl* mass media

masso *m* rock

masterizzare <1a> INFOR burn

masterizzatore *m* INFOR writer

masticare <1l & d> chew

mastice *m* mastic; (*stucco*) putty

mastino *m* mastiff

mastodontico (*pl* -ci) gigantic, enormous

masturbare <1a>, *gen* **masturbarsi** masturbate

masturbazione *f* masturbation

matassa *f* skein

matematica *f* mathematics, maths F, *Am* math F

matematico (*pl* -ci) **1** *agg* mathematical **2** *m*, **-a** *f* mathematician

materassino *m* airbed, lilo®

materasso *m* mattress

materia *f* matter; (*materiale*) material; (*disciplina*) subject; *~ facoltativa* optional subject; *~ obbligatoria* compulsory subject; *~ prima* raw material; *~ sintetica* synthetic (material)

materiale **1** *agg* material; (*rozzo*) coarse, rough **2** *m* material; TEC equipment

materialista (*mpl* -i) **1** *agg* materialistic **2** *m/f* materialist

maternità *f inv* motherhood; *in ospedale* maternity

materno maternal; *scuola f* **-a** nursery school

matita *f* pencil; *~ colorata* colo(u)red pencil; *~ per gli occhi* eye pencil; *~ per sopracciglia* eyebrow pencil

matrice *f* matrix

matricola *f* register; *all'università* first-year student

matrigna *f* stepmother

matrimoniale *agg* matrimonial

matrimonio *m* (*pl* -ni) marriage; *rito* wedding

mattina *f* morning; *di ~* in the morning; *questa ~* this morning; *domani ~* tomorrow morning

mattinata *f* morning; TEA matinee

mattiniero: essere ~ be an early bird

mattino *m* morning; *di buon ~* early in the morning

matto **1** *agg* mad, crazy, insane (*per* about); *avere una voglia* **-a** *di qc* be dying for sth; *essere ~ da legare* be insane, be mad as a hatter **2** *m*, **-a** *f* madman, lunatic; *donna* madwoman, lunatic; *mi piace da* **-i** *andare al cinema* I'm mad about the cinema

mattone *m* brick; *fig che ~!* what a turgid piece of writing!

mattonella *f* tile

mattutino morning *attr*

maturare <1a> *interessi* accrue; *~ una decisione* reach a decision

maturità *f* maturity; (*diploma*) A level

maturo *frutto* ripe; *persona* mature; *i tempi sono* **-i** the time is ripe

mausoleo *m* mausoleum

mazza *f* club; (*martello*) sledgehammer; *da baseball* bat; *~ da golf* golf club

mazzo *m* bunch, bundle; *~ di fiori* bunch of flowers, bouquet; *~ di chiavi* bunch of keys; *~ di carte* pack or deck of cards

mc *abbr* (= *metro cubo*) m³ (= cubic metre)

me (= *mi* before *lo, la, li, le, ne*) me; *dammelo* give me it, give it to me; *come* ~ like me; *fai come* ~ do what I do; *per* ~ for me; *secondo* ~ in my opinion

meccanica *f* mechanics; *di orologio* mechanism; *la* ~ *di un incidente* how an accident happened; ~ *di precisione* precision engineering

meccanicamente mechanically

meccanico (*pl* -ci) **1** *agg* mechanical **2** *m* mechanic

meccanismo *m* mechanism

mecenate *m/f* sponsor

mèche *f inv* streak

medaglia *f* medal

medesimo (very) same; *il* ~ the (very) same; *la* -*a* the (very) same

media *f* average; *in* ~ on average; *superiore* (*inferiore*) *alla* ~ above (below) average; ~ *oraria* average speed

mediano 1 *agg* central, middle **2** *m* SP half-back

mediante by (means of)

mediatore *m*, -*trice* *f* mediator

mediazione *f* mediation

medicamento *m* medicine

medicare <1l, b & d> *persona* treat; *ferita* clean, disinfect

medicazione *f* treatment; (*bende*) dressing

medicina *f* medicine; ~ *interna* internal medicine; ~ *legale* forensic medicine; ~ *sportiva* sports medicine

medicinale 1 *agg* medicinal **2** *m* medicine

medico (*pl* -ci) **1** *agg* medical; *visita f* -*a* medical examination, physical F **2** *m* doctor; ~ *generico* general practitioner, *Br* GP; ~ *di famiglia* family doctor; ~ *di guardia* duty doctor

medievale medi(a)eval

medio (*pl* -di) **1** *agg età, classe ecc* middle *attr, guadagno, statura, rendimento* average **2** *m* middle finger

mediocre mediocre

mediocrità *f* mediocrity

medioevo *m* Middle Ages

meditare <1l & b> **1** *v/t* think about; (*progettare*) plan **2** *v/i* meditate; (*riflettere*) think; ~ *su qc* think about sth

meditazione *f* meditation; (*riflessione*) consideration, reflection

mediterraneo 1 *agg* Mediterranean **2** *m Mediterraneo* Mediterranean (Sea)

medium *m/f inv* medium

medusa *f* ZO jellyfish

megalomania *m* megalomania

meglio 1 *avv* better; ~*!, tanto* ~*!* so much the better!, good!; *alla* ~ to the best of one's ability; *di bene in* ~ better and better **2** *agg* better; *superlativo* best **3** *m* best; *fare del proprio* ~ do one's best **4** *f avere la* ~ *su* get the better of

mela *f* apple

melagrana *f* pomegranate

melanzana *f* aubergine, *Am* eggplant

melma *f* mud

melo *m* apple (tree)

melodia *f* melody

melodico (*pl* -ci) melodic

melodramma *m* (*pl* -i) melodrama

melodrammatico melodramatic

melograno *m* pomegranate tree

melone *m* melon

membrana *f* membrane; ~ *del timpano* eardrum

membro *m* (*pl* le membra) ANAT limb; *persona* (*pl* i -i) member

memorabile memorable

memorandum *m inv* memo(randum); (*promemoria*) memo

memoria *f* memory; INFOR storage capacity; *a* ~ by heart; *in* ~ *di* in memory of; ~ *centrale* main memory; *questo nome non ti richiama alla* ~ *niente* doesn't that name remind you of anything?; -*e pl* memoirs

memorizzare <1a> memorize; INFOR save

menare <1a> lead; F (*picchiare*) hit

mendicante *m/f* beggar

M

mendicare <1l, d or 1d> **1** v/t beg (for); *aiuto*, *lavoro ecc* beg for, plead for **2** v/i beg

menefreghismo m couldn't-careless attitude

meninge f: F **spremersi le -i** rack one's brains F

meningite f meningitis

meno 1 avv less; *superlativo* least; MATH minus; *il ~ possibile* as little as possible; *di ~* at least; *a ~ che* unless; *per lo ~* at least; *sono le sei ~ un quarto* it's a quarter to six; *sempre ~* less and less; *fare a ~ di qc* do without sth; *venir ~ a qcno forze* desert s.o.; *venir ~ alla parola data* not keep one's word **2** prp except

menomato damaged; *(handicappato)* disabled

menomazioni fpl damage sg

mensa f di fabbrica canteen; MIL mess; *~ universitaria* refectory

mensile 1 agg monthly; *tessera f ~ per treno, autobus* monthly season ticket **2** m *(periodico)* monthly

mensilità f inv salary

mensola f bracket

menta f mint; *~ piperita* peppermint

mentale mental

mentalità f inv mentality

mentalmente mentally

mente f mind; *malato di ~* mentally ill; *avere in ~ di fare qc* be planning to do sth, be thinking about doing sth; *tenere a ~ qc* bear sth in mind; *non mi viene in ~ il nome di ...* I can't remember the name of ...; *mi è uscito di ~* it slipped my mind

mentire <4d or b> lie

mento m chin

mentre while

menù m inv menu anche INFOR

menzionare <1a> mention

menzogna f lie

meraviglia f wonder; *a ~* marvel(l)ously, wonderfully

meravigliare <1g> astonish

meravigliarsi: *~ di* be astonished by;

mi meraviglio di te you astonish me

meravigliato astonished

meraviglioso marvel(l)ous, wonderful

mercante m merchant

mercanteggiare <1f> bargain, haggle

mercantile 1 agg nave cargo attr; porto commercial **2** m cargo ship

mercanzia f merchandise

mercato m market; *~ coperto* covered market, indoor market; *~ estero* foreign market; *~ mondiale* world market; *~ interno* domestic market; *~ unico europeo* single European market; *~ nero* black market; *~ delle pulci* flea market; *a buon ~* cheap, inexpensive

merce f goods; *~ di contrabbando* contraband

merceria f (pl -ie) haberdashery

mercoledì m inv Wednesday; *~ delle Ceneri* Ash Wednesday

mercurio m mercury; AST **Mercurio** Mercury

merda P shit P

merenda f snack

meridiana f sundial

meridiano 1 agg midday attr **2** m meridian

meridionale 1 agg southern; *Italia f ~* southern Italy **2** m/f southerner

meridione m south; *il Meridione* southern Italy

meringa f (pl -ghe) meringue

meritare <1l & b> **1** v/t deserve; *non merita un prezzo così alto* it's not worth that much **2** v/i: *un libro che merita* a worthwhile book; *non ti arrabbiare, non merita* don't get angry, it's/he's not worth it

meritevole worthy (*di* of)

merito m merit; *in ~ a* as regards; *per ~ suo* thanks to him

merletto m lace

merlo m ZO blackbird; ARCHI *-i* pl battlements

merluzzo m cod

meschino mean, petty; *(infelice)* wretched

mescolanza f mixture

mescolare <1l> mix; *insalata* toss; *caffè* stir

mescolarsi mix, blend

mese m month; *una volta al ~* once a month; *ai primi del ~* on the first of every month

messa[1]: *~ in piega* set; *~ in scena* production; AUTO *~ in marcia* starting; *~ in moto* start-up; FOT *~ a fuoco* focussing; *~ a punto di meccanismo* adjustment; *di motore* (fine-)tuning; *di testo* finalization

messa[2] f REL mass; *~ solenne* high mass

messaggero m messenger

messaggio m (*pl* -ggi) message

messale m missal

messicano 1 *agg* Mexican **2** m, -a f Mexican

Messico m Mexico

messinscena f production; *fig* act

messo pp → **mettere**

mestiere m trade; (*professione*) profession; *essere del ~* be a professional *or* an expert

mestolo m ladle

mestruazione f menstruation

meta f destination; SP try; *fig* goal, aim

metà f inv half; *punto centrale* middle, centre; *siamo a ~ del viaggio* we're half-way there; *a ~ prezzo* half price; *a ~ strada* halfway; *fare a ~* go halves (*di* on)

metabolico metabolic

metabolismo m metabolism

metadone m methadone

metafora f metaphor

metaforico (*pl* -ci) metaphorical

metallico (*pl* -ci) metallic

metallizzato metallic

metallo m metal; *~ prezioso* precious metal

metallurgia f metallurgy

metamorfosi f inv metamorphosis

metano m methane

metanodotto m gas pipeline

meteora f meteor

meteorite m *o* f meteorite

meteorologico (*pl* -ci) meteorological, weather *attr*; *bollettino* m ~ weather forecast; *servizio* m ~ weather service

meticoloso meticulous

metodico (*pl* -ci) methodical

metodo m method

metrica f metrics

metrico (*pl* -ci) metric

metro[1] m metre, *Am* meter; *~ quadrato* square metre (*Am* meter); *~ cubo* cubic metre (*Am* meter)

metrò[2] m inv (*metropolitana*) underground, *Am* subway

metronotte m inv night watchman

metropoli f inv metropolis

metropolitana f underground, *Am* subway

mettere <3ee> put; *vestito* put on; *~ a punto meccanismo* adjust; *motore* (fine-)tune; *~ in moto* start (up); *~ in ordine* tidy up; *~ al sicuro* put away safely; *~ su casa* set up house; *mettiamo che* let's assume that

mettersi *abito, cappello ecc* put on; *~ a letto* go to bed, take to one's bed; *~ a sedere* sit down; AVIA, AUTO *~ la cintura* fasten one's seat belt; *~ a fare qc* start to do sth; *~ in cammino* set out, get going

mezzaluna f (*pl* mezzelune) half moon, crescent; GASTR two-handled chopper

mezzanino m mezzanine

mezzanotte f midnight

mezzo 1 *agg* half; *uno e ~* one and a half; *mezz'ora* half-hour; *le sei e ~* half past six; *~ chilo* a half kilo; *a ~ strada* halfway; *di -a età* middle-aged **2** *avv* half **3** m (*parte centrale*) middle; (*metà*) half; (*strumento*) means sg; (*veicolo*) means sg of transport; *prendere un ~ pubblico* use public transport; *-i pl di comunicazione di massa* mass media; *-i pl di pagamento* means of payment; *per ~ di* by means of; *a ~ posta* by post,; *in ~ a due persone, due libri* between; *in ~ a quei documenti* in the middle of *or* among those papers; *in ~ alla stanza* in the middle of the room;

M

nel ~ di in the middle of; **giusto ~** happy medium

mezzobusto m (pl mezzobusti) half-length photograph / portrait

mezzofondo m middle distance

mezzogiorno m midday; GEOG **Mezzogiorno** south (of Italy), southern Italy

mezzoservizio m: **lavorare a ~** work part-time

mg abbr (= **milligrammo**) mg (= milligram)

mi¹ m MUS E; nel solfeggio della scala me, mi

mi² pron me; riflessivo myself; **eccomi** here I am

miagolare <1l> miaow, mew

miagolio m miaowing, mewing

mica: **non ho ~ finito** I'm nowhere near finished; **non è ~ vero** there's not the slightest bit of truth in it; **~ male** not bad at all

miccia f fuse

micidiale veleno, clima deadly; fatica, sforza exhausting, killing

micio F m (pl -ci) (pussy) cat

micosi f inv mycosis

microbiologia f microbiology

microbo m microbe

microcamera f miniature camera

microchirurgia f microsurgery

microclima m microclimate

microcomputer m inv microcomputer

microcosmo m microcosm

microfilm m inv microfilm

microfono m microphone, mike F

microonda f microwave; **forno m a -e** microwave (oven)

microprocessore m microprocessor

microrganismo m microorganism

microscopico (pl -ci) microscopic

microscopio m (pl -pi) microscope

midollo m marrow; **~ osseo** bone marrow; **~ spinale** spinal cord

miei mpl di **mio** my

miele m honey

mietere <3a> harvest

migliaio m (pl -aia f) thousand; **un ~** a or one thousand; fig **un ~ di per-sone** thousands of people; **a migliaia** in their thousands

miglio¹ m (pl -glia f) misura mile; **~ marino** nautical mile

miglio² m grano millet

miglioramento m improvement

migliorare <1a> **1** v/t improve **2** v/i e **migliorarsi** improve, get better

migliore better; **il ~** the best

mignolo m (o **dito ~**) little finger; del piede little toe

migrare <1a> migrate

migrazione f migration

-mila thousand; **due~** two thousand

milanese 1 agg of Milan **2** m/f in-habitant of Milan

Milano f Milan

miliardario m (pl -ri), **-a** f billionaire, multimillionaire

miliardo m billion

milionario m (pl -ri), **-a** f millionaire; donna millionairess

milione m million

militare <1l> fight, militate (**contro** against; **per** for); **~ in un partito** be a member of a party **2** agg military **3** m soldier; **fare il ~** do one's military service

militarismo m militarism

militarista m/f (mpl -i) militarist

militarizzare <1a> hand over to the military; partito structure like the army

milite m soldier; **il ~ ignoto** the Unknown Soldier

militesente exempt from military service

milizia f militia

mille (pl mila) a thousand

millefoglie m inv vanilla slice

millennio m (pl -nni) millennium

millepiedi m inv millipede

millesimo m/agg thousandth

milligrammo m milligram(me)

millimetro m millimetre, Am -meter

milza f spleen

mimetizzare <1a> MIL camouflage

mimetizzarsi camouflage o.s.; fig **~ tra la folla** get lost in the crowd

mimica f mime

mimo m mime

mimosa *f* mimosa

mina *f* mine; *di matita* lead

minaccia *f* (*pl* -cce) threat

minacciare <1f> threaten

minaccioso threatening

minare <1a> mine; *fig* undermine

minato: *campo m ~* minefield

minareto *m* minaret

minatore *m* miner

minatorio (*pl* -ri) threatening

minerale *m*/*agg* mineral

minestra *f* soup; *~ di fagioli* bean soup; *~ di verdura* vegetable soup

minestrina *f* clear soup, broth

minestrone *m* minestrone

miniatura *f* miniature

miniera *f* mine (*anche fig*)

minigolf *m inv* miniature golf

minigonna *f* mini(skirt)

minimizzare <1a> minimize

minimo 1 *agg* least, slightest; *prezzo, offerta* lowest; *salario, temperatura* minimum **2** *m* minimum; *come ~, dovresti …* you should at least …

ministero *m* ministry; (*gabinetto*) government, ministry; *pubblico ~* state prosecutor

ministro *m* minister; *~ degli Esteri* Foreign Secretary, *Am* Secretary of State; *~ degli Interni* Home Secretary, *Am* Secretary of the Interior; *primo ~* Prime Minister; *consiglio m dei -i* Cabinet

minoranza *f* minority

minorato 1 *agg* severely handicapped **2** *m*, **-a** *f* severely handicapped person

minore 1 *agg* minor; *di età* younger; *distanza* shorter; *più piccolo* smaller; **2** *m*/*f*: *vietato ai -i di 18 anni* no admittance to those under 18 years of age; *film* X-rated

minorenne 1 *agg* under-age **2** *m*/*f* minor

minuscola *f* small letter, lower case letter

minuscolo tiny, miniscule

minuto 1 *agg persona* tiny; *oggetto* minute; *descrizione, indagine* detailed; *commercio m al ~* retail trade **2** *m* minute; *60 pulsazioni al ~* 60 beats a minute; *ho i -i contati* I don't have a minute to spare

minuzioso *descrizione* detailed; *ricerca* meticulous

mio (*pl* miei) **1** *agg* my; *un ~ amico* a friend of mine, one of my friends; *i miei amici* my friends **2** *pron*: *il ~* mine; *questo libro è ~* this book is mine, this is my book; *i miei* my parents

miope short-sighted

miopia *f* short-sightedness, myopia

mira *f* aim; (*obiettivo*) target; *prendere la ~* take aim; *prendere di ~* aim at; *fig prendere di ~ qu* have it in for s.o.

miracolo *m* miracle; *per ~* by a miracle, miraculously

miraggio *m* (*pl* -ggi) mirage

mirare <1a> aim (*a* at)

mirino *m* MIL sight; FOT viewfinder

mirtillo *m* bilberry

mirto *m* myrtle

miscela *f* mixture; *di caffè, tabacco* blend

miscelatore *m* GASTR mixer; *rubinetto* mixer tap

mischia *f* (*rissa*) scuffle; SP, (*folla*) scrum

mischiare <1k> mix; *carte* shuffle

mischiarsi mix

miscuglio *m* (*pl* -gli) mixture

miserabile wretched, miserable

miserevole pitiful

miseria *f* (*povertà*) poverty; (*infelicità*) misery; *costare una ~* cost next to nothing; F *porca ~!* damn and blast! F

misericordia *f* mercy; *avere ~ di qu* have pity on s.o.

misero wretched

misfatto *m* misdeed

missaggio *m* (*pl* -ggi) → *mixaggio*

missare → *mixare*

missile *m* missile; *~ a lunga gittata* long-range missile

missionario *m* (*pl* -ri), **-a** *f* missionary

missione *f* mission

misterioso mysterious

mistero *m* mystery

M

mistico (*pl* -ci) mystic(al)

misto 1 *agg* mixed **2** *m* mixture; **~ lana** wool mix

misura *f* measurement; (*taglia*) size; (*provvedimento*), *fig* measure; MUS bar; **-e** *pl* **preventive** preventive measures; **unità f di ~** unit of measurement; **con ~** in moderation; **su ~** made to measure

misurabile measurable, which can be measured

misurare <1a> measure; *vestito* try on; **~ le spese** limit one's spending

misurarsi *in una gara* compete; **~ con** compete with

misurato restrained

misurino *m* measuring spoon

mite *persona, inverno* mild; *condanna* light

mitigare <1l & e> lessen; *dolore* ease, lessen

mito *m* myth

mitologia *f* mythology

mitologico (*pl* -ci) mythological

mitra *m inv*, **mitragliatrice** *f* machine gun

mitt. *abbr* (= **mittente**) from

mittente *m/f* sender

mixaggio *m* mixing

mixare <1k> mix

ml *abbr* (= **millilitro**) ml (= millilitre)

M.M. *abbr* (= **Marina Militare**) Italian navy

mm *abbr* (= **millimetro**) mm (= millimetre)

mobile 1 *agg* mobile; *ripiano, pannello* removeable; **squadra f ~** flying squad **2** *m* piece of furniture; **-i** *pl* furniture

mobilia *f* furnishings

mobilificio *m* furniture-making factory

mobilio *m → mobilia*

mobilità *f* mobility

mobilitare <1m> mobilize

moca *m* mocha

mocassino *m* moccasin

moda *f* fashion; **alla ~** fashionable, in fashion; *vestirsi* fashionably; **di ~** fashionable, in fashion; **fuori ~** out of fashion, unfashionable

modalità *f inv* method

modella *f* model

modellare <1b> model

modello 1 *agg* model **2** *m* model; (*indossatore*) male model; *di vestito* style; (*formulario*) form

modem *m inv* INFOR modem

moderare <1l & c> moderate

moderato moderate

moderatore *m*, **-trice** *f* moderator

moderazione *f* moderation

modernizzare <1a> modernize

moderno modern

modestia *f* modesty

modesto modest; *prezzo* very reasonable

modico (*pl* -ci) reasonable

modifica *f* (*pl* -che) modification

modificare <1m & d> modify

modo *m* (*maniera*) way, manner; (*mezzo*) way; MUS mode; GRAM mood; **~ di dire** expression; **~ di vedere** way of looking at things; **per ~ di dire** so to speak; **se hai ~ di passare da me** if you could drop by; **a ~ mio** in my own way; **ad ogni ~** anyway, anyhow; **di ~ che** so that; **in che ~?** how?; **in special ~** especially

modulo *m* form; (*elemento*) module; **~ di domanda** application form; **~ d'iscrizione** registration form; **~ di versamento** *banca* pay-in slip

mogano *m* mahogany

moglie *f* (*pl* -gli) wife

mola *f* grindstone; *di mulino* millstone

molare 1 *v/t* <1c> grind **2** *m* molar

mole *f* (*grandezza*) size

molecola *f* molecule

molestare <1b> bother, trouble; *sessualmente* sexually harass

molestia *f* bother, nuisance; **~ sessuale** sexual harassment

molesto annoying

molla *f* spring; *fig* spur; **-e** *pl* tongs

mollare <1c> *corda* release, let go; F *schiaffo, ceffone* give; F *fidanzato* dump; **~ la presa** let go

molle soft; (*bagnato*) wet

molleggiare <1f> be springy

molleggio *m* springs

molletta *f* hairgrip; *da bucato* clothes peg *or* pin

mollica *f* (*pl* -che) crumb

mollusco *m* (*pl* -chi) mollusc, *Am* mollusk

molo *m* pier

molotov *f inv* Molotov cocktail

molteplice multifaceted

moltiplicare <1m & d> **1** *v/t* multiply (**per** by) **2** *v/i e* **moltiplicarsi** multiply

moltitudine *f* multitude, host

molto 1 *agg* a lot of; *con nomi plurali* a lot of, many **2** *avv* a lot; *con aggettivi* very; **~ meglio** much better, a lot better; **da ~** for a long time; **fra non ~** before long

momentaneo momentary, temporary

momento *m* moment; **dal ~ che** from the moment that; *causale* since; **a -i** sometimes, at moments; **per il ~** for the moment; **del ~** short-lived; **sul ~** at the time

monaca *f* (*pl* -che) nun

monaco *m* (*pl* -ci) monk

monarca *m* (*pl* -chi) monarch

monarchia *f* monarchy

monarchico (*pl* -ci) **1** *agg* monarchical **2** *m*, **-a** *f* monarchist

monastero *m* monastery; *di monache* convent

mondano society; (*terreno*) worldly; **fare vita -a** go out

mondare <1a> *frutta* peel

mondiale 1 *agg* world *attr*, *economia* world *attr*, global; *fenomeno, scala* worldwide; **di fama ~** world-famous **2** *m*: **i -i** *di calcio* the World Cup

mondo *m* world; **giro** *m* **del ~** world tour, tour round the world; **l'altro ~** the next world; **il più bello del ~** the most beautiful in the world; **divertirsi un ~** enjoy o.s. enormously *or* a lot

monello *m*, **-a** *f imp*, little devil

moneta *f* coin; (*valuta*) currency; (*denaro*) money; (*spiccioli*) change; **~ d'oro** gold coin

monetario (*pl* -ri) monetary; **Fondo**

m **~ internazionale** International Monetary Fund

mongolfiera *m* hot-air balloon

monito *m* reprimand

monografia *f* monograph

monogramma *m* (*pl* -i) monogram

monolocale *m* bedsit

monologo *m* (*pl* -ghi) monolog(ue)

monopattino *m* child's scooter

monopolio *m* (*pl* -li) monopoly

monopolizzare <1a> monopolize

monoposto *m* single-seater

monotonia *f* monotony

monotono monotonous

monouso disposable, throwaway

montacarichi *m inv* hoist

montaggio *m* (*pl* -ggi) TECH assembly; *di film* editing

montagna *f* mountain; *fig* **-e** *pl* **russe** rollercoaster *sg*

montagnoso mountainous

montanaro *m*, **-a** *f* person who lives in the mountains

montare <1a> **1** *v/t* go up, climb; *cavallo* get onto, mount; TEC assemble; *film* edit; GASTR whip; **~ la guardia** mount guard **2** *v/i* go up; *venire* come up; **~ in macchina** get into; **~ su** *scala* climb; *pullman* get on

montarsi: **~ la testa** get a swollen head, get bigheaded

montatura *f di occhiali* frame; *di gioiello* mount; *fig* set-up F, frame-up F

monte *m* mountain; *fig* mountain, pile; **a ~** upstream; *fig* **mandare a ~** ruin, mess up F

montone *m* ram; *pelle, giacca* sheepskin

montuoso mountainous

monumento *m* monument

moquette *f inv* fitted carpet

mora *f* BOT *del gelso* mulberry; *del rovo* blackberry

morale 1 *agg* moral **2** *f* morals *pl*; *di favola ecc* moral **3** *m* morale; **essere giù di ~** be feeling a bit down; **tirare su il ~ a qu** cheer s.o. up, lift s.o.'s spirits

moralista *m/f* (*mpl* -i) moralist

M

morbidezza f softness
morbido soft
morbillo m measles sg
morbo m disease
morboso fig unhealthy, unnatural; *curiosità* morbid
mordace fig biting, mordant
mordere <3uu> bite
morena f moraine
morfina f morphine
moribondo dying
morire <4k> die; fig ~ *di paura* be scared to death; F *muoio dalla voglia di una birra* I could murder a pint F, I'm dying for a beer F
mormorare <1l> murmur; (*bisbigliare, lamentarsi*) mutter
mormorio m murmuring; (*brontolio*) muttering
morsetto m TEC clamp; EL terminal
morsicare <1l, c & d> bite
morso 1 pp → **mordere** 2 m bite; *di cibo* bit, mouthful; *per cavallo* bit; *i -i pl della fame* the pangs of hunger
mortale *ferita, malattia* fatal; *offesa, nemico* deadly; *uomo* mortal
mortalità f mortality
morte f death
mortificare <1m & d> mortify
mortificazione f mortification
morto 1 pp → **morire** 2 agg dead; *stanco ~* dead tired 3 m, -a f dead man; *donna* dead woman; *i -i pl* the dead
mortorio m: F *essere un ~* be deadly dull or boring
mortuario (*pl* -ri) death; *camera f -a* chapel
mosaico m (*pl* -ci) mosaic
mosca f (*pl* -che) fly; *peso m ~* flyweight; *~ cieca* blindman's buff; *restare con un pugno di -e* come away empty-handed
moscatello m muscatel
moscato 1 agg muscat; *noce f -a* nutmeg 2 m muscatel
moscerino m gnat, midge
moschea f mosque
moscio (*pl* -sci) thin, flimsy; fig limp, washed out
moscone m ZO bluebottle; (*imbar-*

cazione) pedalo
mossa f movement; fig e di judo, karate move
mosso 1 pp → **muovere** 2 agg mare rough
mostarda f mustard
mosto m must, *unfermented grape juice*
mostra f show; (*esposizione*) exhibition; fig *mettere in ~* show off
mostrare <1a> show; (*indicare*) point out
mostrarsi appear
mostro m monster
mostruoso monstrous
motel m inv motel
motivare <1a> cause; *personale* motivate; (*spiegare*) explain, give reasons for
motivazione f (*spiegazione*) explanation; (*stimolo*) motivation
motivo m reason; MUS theme, motif; *su tessuto* pattern; *per quale ~?* for what reason?, why?
moto[1] m movement; *fare ~* get some exercise; *mettere in ~* motore start (up); fig set in motion
moto[2] f (motor)bike
motocicletta f motorcycle
motociclista m/f (*mpl* -i) motorcyclist
motociclo m motorcycling
motore m engine; *~ Diesel* diesel engine; *~ a due tempi* two-stroke engine; *~ a quattro tempi* four-stroke engine; *~ a combustione* internal combustion engine; INFOR *~ di ricerca* search engine; *~ fuoribordo* outboard (motor or engine); *veicolo m a ~* motor vehicle; *accendere il ~* start (up) the engine, turn the key in the ignition; *fermare il ~* turn off the engine
motorino m moped; *~ d'avviamento* starter
motorizzato motorized; F *sei ~* have you got wheels? F
motoscafo m motorboat
motoscooter m inv (motor) scooter
motrice f FERR railcar
motteggio m (*pl* -ggi) joke

motto *m* motto

mouse *m inv* INFOR mouse

movente *m* motive

movimento *m* movement; (*vita*) life, bustle

mozione *f* motion; **~ di fiducia** vote of confidence

mozzarella *f* mozzarella, *buffalo-milk cheese*

mozzicone *m* cigarette end, (cigarette) stub

mozzo *m* TEC hub

mq *abbr* (= **metro quadrato**) sq m (= square metre)

mucca *f* (*pl* -cche) cow

mucchio *m* (*pl* -cchi) pile, heap

muco *m* (*pl* -chi) mucus

mucosa *f* mucous membrane

muffa *f* mo(u)ld; **sapere di ~** taste mo(u)ldy; **fare la ~** go mo(u)ldy

mughetto *m* lily-of-the-valley

mugolare <1l> *di cane* whine; (*gemere*) moan, whine

mugolio *m* whining

mugugnare <1a> grumble

mulattiera *f* mule track

mulatto *m*, **-a** *f* mulatto

mulinello *m su canna da pesca* reel; *vortice d'acqua* eddy

mulino *m* mill; **~ a vento** windmill

mulo *m* mule

multa *f* fine

multare <1a> fine

multicolore multicolo(u)red

multiculturale multicultural

multimediale multimedia

multinazionale *f/agg* multinational

multiplo multiple

multiuso multipurpose

mungere <3d> milk

municipale municipal; **consiglio** *m* **~** town council

municipio *m* (*pl* -pi) town council, municipality; *edificio* town hall

munire <4d>: **~ di** supply with, provide with

munizioni *fpl* ammunition

muovere <3ff> **1** *v/t* move **2** *v/i partire* move off (**da** from); **~ incontro a qu** move towards s.o.

muoversi move; F (*sbrigarsi*) get a

move on F

muraglia *f* wall

murale 1 *agg* wall *attr* **2** *m* PITT mural

murare <1a> (*chiudere*) wall up

muratore *m* bricklayer

muratura *f* brickwork

murena *f* moray (eel)

muro *m* (*pl anche le mura*) wall; **~ del suono** sound barrier; *fig* **mi ha messo con le spalle al ~** he'd got my back against the wall; **le -a** *fpl* (city) walls

muschio *m* (*pl* -chi) BOT moss

muscolare muscular; **strappo** *m* **~** strained muscle

muscolatura *f* muscles *pl*

muscolo *m* muscle

muscoloso muscular

museo *m* museum; **~ etnologico** folk museum; **~ d'arte** museum

museruola *f* muzzle

musica *f* music; **~ da camera** chamber music; **~ leggera** light music, easy-listening music

musicale musical; **strumento** *m* **~** musical instrument

musicassetta *f* (music) tape

musicista *m/f* (*mpl* -i) musician

muso *m di animale* muzzle; **tenere il ~ a qu** be in a huff with s.o.

musone *m* sulker

musulmano 1 *agg* Muslim, Moslem **2** *m*, **-a** *f* Muslim, Moslem

muta *f di cani* pack; SP wetsuit

mutabile changeable

mutamento *m* change

mutande *fpl di donna* knickers; *di uomo* (under)pants

mutandine *fpl* knickers;**~ (da bagno)** (swimming) trunks

mutare <1a> *v/t & v/i* change

mutevole → **mutabile**

mutilare <1l> mutilate

mutilato *m* disabled ex-serviceman

mutilazione *f* mutilation

muto 1 *agg* dumb; (*silenzioso*) silent, dumb; **essere ~ dallo stupore** be struck dumb with astonishment; **film** *m* **~** silent movie **2** *m*, **-a** *f* mute

mutua *f* fund that pays out sickness benefit; **medico** *m* **della ~a** doctor

recognized by the mutua
mutuato *m*, **-a** *f* person entitled to

sickness benefit
mutuo 1 *agg* mutual **2** *m* mortgage

N

N *abbr* (= **nord**) N (= north)

n. *abbr* (= **numero**) No. (= number)

nacchere *fpl* castanets

nafta *f* naphtha

nano 1 *agg* dwarf **2** *m*, **-a** *f* dwarf

napoletano 1 *agg* Neapolitan **2** *m*, **-a** *f* Neapolitan

Napoli *f* Naples

nappa *f* tassel; (*pelle*) nappa (*type of soft leather*)

narciso *m* BOT narcissus

narcosi *f inv* narcosis

narcotico *m* (*pl* -ci) narcotic

narcotizzare <1a> drug

narice *f* nostril

narrare <1a> tell, narrate

narratore, **-trice** *f* narrator

nascere <3gg> be born; BOT come up; *fig* develop, grow up; *di sole* rise, come up; **sono nato a Roma** I was born in Rome; **le è nata una figlia** she's had a little girl

nascita *f* birth; **fin dalla ~** from birth

nascondere <3hh> hide, conceal

nascondersi hide

nascondiglio *m* (*pl* -gli) hiding place

nascosto 1 *pp* → **nascondere**
2 *avv*: **di ~** in secret; **di ~ a qu** unbeknownst to s.o.

nasello *m* (*pesce*) hake

naso *m* nose

nastro *m* tape; *per capelli, di decorazione* ribbon; **~ adesivo** adhesive tape, Sellotape®, *Am* Scotch tape®; **~ isolante** insulating tape, *Am* friction tape; **~ magnetico** magnetic tape

Natale *m* Christmas; **vigilia** *f* **di ~**

Christmas Eve; **buon ~!** Merry Christmas!

natale *agg* of one's birth

natalità *f* birth rate, number of births

natalizio (*pl* -zi) Christmas

natante 1 *agg* floating **2** *m* boat

nativo 1 *agg* native **2** *m*, **-a** *f* native

NATO *abbr* (= **Organizzazione del Trattato nord-atlantico**) NATO (= North Atlantic Treaty Organization

nato → **nascere**

natura *f* nature; PITT **~ morta** still life; **contro ~** unnatural; **essere paziente per ~** be patient by nature, be naturally patient; **secondo ~** in harmony with nature

naturale natural; **scienze** *fpl* **-i** natural sciences

naturalezza *f* naturalness; **con ~** naturally

naturalizzare <1a>: **è naturalizzato americano** he's a naturalized American

naturalmente naturally, of course; *comportarsi* naturally

naufragare <1l & e> *di nave* be wrecked; *di persona* be shipwrecked; *fig* be ruined, come to grief

naufragio *m* (*pl* -gi) shipwreck; *fig* ruin; **fare ~** *di nave* be wrecked; *di persona* be shipwrecked

naufrago *m* (*pl* -ghi), **-a** *f* survivor of a shipwreck

nausea *f* nausea; **avere la ~** feel sick, *Am* feel nauseous; **dare la ~ a qu** make s.o. feel sick, nauseate s.o. (*anche fig*)

nauseare <1l> nauseate (*anche fig*)

nautica *f* seamanship

nautico (*pl* -ci) nautical

navale naval; *cantiere m* ~ shipyard

navata *f* ARCHI: ~ *centrale* nave; ~ *laterale* aisle

nave *f* ship; ~ *da carico* cargo ship *or* vessel; ~ *passeggeri* passenger ship; ~ *traghetto* ferry

navetta 1 *agg inv*: *bus m* ~ shuttle bus **2** *f* shuttle; ~ *spaziale* space shuttle

navicella *f di astronave* nose cone

navigabile navigable

navigare <11 & e> sail; INFOR navigate

navigatore *m* navigator

navigazione *f* navigation

nazionale 1 *agg* national **2** *f* national team; *la ~ italiana* the Italian team

nazionalismo *m* nationalism

nazionalista *m/f* (*mpl* -i) nationalist

nazionalistico (*pl* -ci) nationalistic

nazionalità *f inv* nationality

nazionalizzare <1a> nationalize

nazione *f* nation

N.B. *abbr* (= *nota bene*) NB (= nota bene)

N.d.A. *abbr* (= *nota dell'autore*) author's note

N.d.E. *abbr* (= *nota dell'editore*) publisher's note

N.d.T. *abbr* (= *nota del traduttore*) translator's note

NE *abbr* (= *nord-est*) NE (= northeast)

ne ~ *pron* (*di lui*) about him; (*di lei*) about her; (*di loro*) about them; (*di ciò*) about it; ~ *sono contento* I'm happy about it; ~ *ho abbastanza* I have enough **2** *avv* from there; ~ *vengo adesso* I've just come back from there

né: ~ *...* ~ neither ... nor; *non l'ho trovato* ~ *a casa* ~ *in ufficio* I couldn't find him either at home or in the office

neanche neither; *io non vado* ~ *neanch'io* I'm not going – neither am I *or* me neither F; *non l'ho visto* I didn't even see him; ~ *per sogno!* in your dreams!

nebbia *f* fog

nebbioso foggy

nebulosa *f* AST nebula

nebuloso *fig* vague, hazy

necessaire *m inv*: ~ (*da viaggio*) beauty case

necessario (*pl* -ri) **1** *agg* necessary **2** *m*: *il* ~ *per vivere* the basic necessities *pl*

necessità *f inv* need; *ho* ~ *di parlarti* I need to talk to you; *articolo m di prima* ~ essential; *in caso di* ~ if necessary, if need be; *fare qc senza* ~ do sth needlessly; *per* ~ out of necessity

nefrite *f* MED nephritis

negare <1e> deny; (*rifiutare*) refuse

negativa *f* negative

negativo *m/agg* negative

negato: *essere* ~ *per qc* be hopeless at sth

negazione *f* denial; GRAM negative

negli *prp* *in* and *art* gli

negligente careless, negligent

negligenza *f* carelessness, negligence

negoziante *m/f* shopkeeper

negoziare <1g & c> **1** *v/t* negotiate **2** *v/i* negotiate, bargain; FIN ~ *in* trade in, deal in

negoziato *m* negotiation; *-i pl di pace* peace negotiations

negoziazione *f* negotiation

negozio *m* (*pl* -zi) shop; (*affare*) deal; ~ *di generi alimentari* food shop; ~ *specializzato* specialist shop

negro 1 *agg* black **2** *m*, *-a f* black (man/woman)

nei, nel, nell', nella, nelle, nello *prp* *in* and *art* i, il, l', la, le, lo

nemico (*pl* -ci) **1** *agg* enemy *attr* **2** *m*, *-a f* enemy

nemmeno neither; ~ *io* me neither; ~ *per idea!* don't even think about it!

neo *m* mole; *fig* flaw

neonato *m*, *-a f* infant, newborn baby

neppure not even; *non ci vado* – – ~ *io* I'm not going – neither am I *or* me neither F

nero 1 agg black; fig giornata, periodo black; umore awful, filthy F **2** m black; di seppia ink **3** m, **-a** f black (man/woman)

nerofumo m lampblack

nervo m nerve; dare sui (o ai) **-i a qu** get on s.o.'s nerves

nervosismo m nervousness

nervoso 1 agg nervous; (irritabile) edgy; (asciutto) sinewy; **esaurimento** m ~ nervous breakdown **2** m F: **il ~** irritation; **mi viene il ~** I'm beginning to get really irritated, this is getting on my nerves

nespola f medlar

nespolo m medlar (tree)

nessuno 1 agg no; **non chiamare in nessun caso** don't call in any circumstances; **c'è ~ a notizia?** is there any news? **2** pron nobody, no one; **hai visto ~?** did you see anyone or anybody?

nettezza f cleanliness; **~ urbana** cleansing department

netto clean; (chiaro) clear; reddito, peso net; **interrompere qu di ~** break in on s.o.

netturbino m, **-a** f dustman

neurologia f neurology

neurologico neurological

neurologo m (pl -gi), **-a** f neurologist

neutrale neutral

neutralità f neutrality

neutralizzare <1a> neutralize

neutro neutral; GRAM neuter

neve f snow

nevicare <11 & d> snow

nevicata f snowfall

nevoso snowy

nevralgia f neuralgia

nevralgico (pl -ci) neuralgic; **punto** m ~ specially painful point; fig weak point

nevrosi f neurosis

nevrotico (pl -ci) **1** agg neurotic; F short-tempered, quick to fly off the handle **2** m, **-a** f neurotic

nicchia f niche

nichel m nickel

nicotina f nicotine

nido m nest

niente 1 pron m nothing **2** avv nothing; **non ho ~** I don't have anything, I have nothing; **lo fai tu? – ~ affatto!** are you going to do it? – no, I am not!; **tu hai detto che … – ~ affatto!** you said that … – no, I did not!; **non ho per ~ fame** I'm not at all hungry; **non ho capito per ~** I didn't understand a thing

niente(di)meno no less; **~!** that's incredible! you don't say!

ninfea f water-lily

nipote m/f di zio nephew; donna, ragazza niece f; di nonno grandson; donna, ragazza granddaughter f

nitidezza f clarity, clearness; FOT sharpness

nitido clear; FOT sharp

nitrire <4d> neigh

NO abbr (= nord-ovest) NW (= northwest)

no no; **~ e poi ~** absolutely not!, no and that's final!; **come ~!** of course!, naturally!; **se ~** otherwise; **dire di ~** say no; **credo di ~** I don't think so

nobile 1 agg noble **2** m/f aristocrat

nobiltà f nobility

nocca f (pl -cche) knuckle

nocciola f hazelnut; **color** m ~ hazel

nocciolina f: ~ (americana) peanut, ground-nut, monkey-nut

nocciolo[1] m (albero) hazel (tree)

nocciolo[2] m di frutto stone; di questione heart, kernel

noce 1 m walnut (tree); (legno) walnut **2** f walnut; **~ di cocco** coconut; **~ moscata** nutmeg

nocepesca f nectarine

nocivo harmful

nodo m knot; fig crux; FERR junction; **avere un ~ in gola** have a lump in one's throat

noi pron soggetto we; con prp us; **a ~** to us; **con ~** with us; **senza di ~** without us

noia f boredom; **-e** pl trouble sg; **dar ~ a qu** annoy s.o.; **venire a ~ a qu** start to bore s.o.

noioso boring; (molesto) annoying

noleggiare <1f> hire; MAR, AVIA charter

noleggio *m* hire; MAR, AVIA charter; *~* (*di*) *biciclette* bike hire

nolo *m* hire; **prendere a ~** hire; **dare a ~** hire out

nome *m* name; GRAM noun; *~ di battesimo* Christian name; *~ e cognome* full name; **conoscere qu di ~** know s.o. by name; *in ~ di* in the name of

nomignolo *m* nickname

nomina *f* appointment

nominare <1l & c> (*menzionare*) mention; *a un incarico* appoint (*a* to)

non not; *~ ho fratelli* I don't have any brothers, I have no brothers; *~ ancora* not yet; *~ che io non voglia* not that I don't want to; *~ cedibile* not transferable, non-transferable

nonché let alone; (*e anche*) as well as

noncurante nonchalant, casual; *~ di* mindless of, heedless of

noncuranza *f* nonchalance, casualness

nondimeno nevertheless

nonno *m*, **-a** *f* grandfather; *donna grandmother*; *-i pl* grandparents

nonnulla *m inv* trifle

nono *m*/*agg* ninth

nonostante despite; *ciò ~* however

nonsenso *m* nonsense

non stop *agg inv* nonstop

nontiscordardimé *m inv* forget-me-not

non vedente *m*/*f* blind person

nord *m* north; *mare m del ~* North Sea; *a(l) ~ di* (to the) north of

nordest *m* north-east

nordico (*pl -ci*) northern; *lingue* Nordic

nordovest *m* north-west

norma *f* (*precetto*) rule, precept; TEC standard; *-e per l'uso* instructions (for use); *a ~ di legge* up to standard; *a ~ di legge ...* complies with ...

normale normal

normalità *f* normality

normalizzare <1a> normalize;

(*uniformare*) standardize

norvegese *agg*, *m*/*f* Norwegian

Norvegia *f* Norway

nostalgia *f* nostalgia; *avere ~ di casa* feel homesick; *avere ~ di qu* miss s.o.

nostrale local, home *attr*

nostrano local, home *attr*

nostro **1** *agg* our; *i -i genitori pl* our parents; *un ~ amico* a friend of ours **2** *pron*: *il ~* ours

nota *f* note; FIN bill; *degno di ~* noteworthy; *~ spese* expense account; *prendere ~ di qc* make a note of sth; *situazione, comportamento* take note of sth

notaio *m* (*pl -ai*) notary (public)

notare <1c> (*osservare*) notice; (*annotare*) make a note of, note down; *con segni* mark; *è da ~ che* please note that; *ti faccio ~ che* I'll have you know that

notariato *m* notaryship

notarile notarial

notevole *degno di nota* notable, noteworthy; *grande* considerable, substantial

notificare <1m & d> serve (*a* on)

notizia *f* piece *or* bit *or* item of news; *avere -e di qu* have news of s.o., hear from s.o.; *-e pl sportive* sports news; *le ultime -e pl* the latest news

notiziario *m* (*pl -ri*) RAD, TV news

noto well-known; *rendere ~* announce

notorietà *f* fame; *spreg* notoriety

notorio (*pl -ri*) well-known; *spreg* notorious

nottambulo *m*, **-a** *f* night owl

nottata *f* night; *fare la ~* stay up all night

notte *f* night; *di ~* at night; *buona ~!* good night!; *nel cuore della ~* in the middle of the night

notturno night(-time) *attr*; *animale* nocturnal; *ore fpl -e* hours of darkness

novanta ninety

novantesimo *m*/*agg* ninetieth

nove nine

novecento 1 *agg* nine hundred **2** *m*:

N

*il **Novecento*** the twentieth century

novella *f* short story

novembre *m* November

novità *f inv* novelty; (*notizia*) piece *or* item of news; ***essere una ~ sul mercato*** be new on the market

novizio (*pl* -zi) **1** *agg* novice **2** *m*, -a *f* beginner, novice; REL novice

nozione *f* notion, idea; *-i pl di base* rudiments

nozionistico (*pl* -ci) superficial

nozze *fpl* wedding *sg*; ***~ d'argento*** silver wedding (anniversary); ***sposarsi in seconde ~*** get married for the second time, remarry

ns. *abbr* (= *nostro*) our(s), *used in correspondence*

NU *abbr* (= *Nazioni Unite*) UN (= United Nations); (= *nettezza urbana*) cleansing department

nube *f* cloud

nubifragio *m* (*pl* -gi) cloudburst

nubile *donna* single, unmarried

nuca *f* (*pl* -che) nape of the neck

nucleare nuclear

nucleo *m* FIS nucleus (*anche fig*); ***~ urbano*** urban centre

nudismo *m* naturism, nudism

nudista *m/f* (*mpl* -i) naturist, nudist

nudità *f* nudity, nakedness

nudo 1 *agg* nude, naked; (*spoglio*) bare; ***a occhio ~*** to the naked eye **2** *m* PITT nude

nulla 1 *avv* nothing; *è **solo una cosa da ~*** it's nothing; ***per ~*** for nothing; ***non per ~*** not for nothing **2** *m* nothing; ***non ti ho portato un bel ~*** I haven't brought you anything at all

nullaosta *m*: *fig* ***ottenere il ~*** get the green light *or* go-ahead

nullo invalid; *gol* disallowed; *voto* spoiled; ***dichiarare ~*** declare null and void

numerale *m* numeral

numerare <1l> number

numerato numbered

numerico (*pl* -ci) numerical

numero *m* number; *arabo, romano* numeral; *di scarpa* size; ***~ di casa*** home (tele)phone number; ***~ di targa*** registration number, Am license number; ***~ di telefono*** phone number; ***~ di volo*** flight number; TELEC ***sbagliare ~*** dial the wrong number; ***~ verde*** 0800 number, Am toll-free number; ***~ legale*** quorum; EDU ***~ chiuso*** restricted enrol(l)ment; ***sono venuti in gran*** lots of them came; F ***dare i -i*** talk nonsense

numeroso numerous; *famiglia, classe* large

nuocere <3ii>: *~ a* harm; *il fumo **nuoce alla salute*** smoking is bad for you

nuora *f* daughter-in-law

nuotare <1c> swim

nuotata *f* swim

nuotatore *m*, **-trice** *f* swimmer

nuoto *m* swimming; ***attraversare la Manica a ~*** swim across the Channel

nuovamente again

nuovo 1 *agg* new; *di ~* again; ***essere ~ in una città*** be new to a town; ***~ fiammante*** brand new **2** *m*: ***che c'è di ~?*** what's new?

nutriente nourishing

nutrimento *m* food

nutrire <4d or 4a> feed

nutrirsi: *~ di* live on

nutritivo nutritious

nutrizione *f* nutrition

nuvola *f* cloud; *fig **cadere dalle -e*** be taken aback

nuvoloso cloudy

nylon *m* nylon

O

O *abbr* (= *ovest*) W (= west)

o *cong* or; ~ ... ~ either ... or

oasi *f inv* oasis

obbedire → **ubbidire**

obbligare <1l, c & e>: ~ **qu a fare qc** oblige *or* compel s.o. to do sth

obbligarsi commit o.s. (*a fare* to doing), undertake (*a fare* to do)

obbligatorio (*pl* -ri) obligatory, compulsory

obbligazione *f* obligation; FIN bond

obbligo *m* (*pl* -ghi) obligation; *d'~* obligatory

obesità *f* obesity

obeso obese

obiettare <1b> object, say (*a* to)

obiettivo **1** *agg* objective **2** *m* aim, objective; FOT lens

obiettore *m*: ~ **di coscienza** conscientious objector

obiezione *f* objection; *fare ~ di coscienza* be a conscientious objector

obliquo oblique

obliterare <1m> *biglietto* punch

oblò *m inv* MAR porthole

oca *f* (*pl* -che) *f* goose; *fig* silly woman

occasionale casual; *i rapporti mpl -i* casual sex

occasionalmente occasionally

occasione *f* (*opportunità*) opportunity, chance; (*evento*) occasion; (*affare*) bargain; *automobile f d'~* second-hand *or* used car; *cogliere l'~* seize the opportunity, jump at the chance F; *all'~* if necessary; *in ~ di* on the occasion of

occhiaie *fpl* bags under the eyes

occhiali *mpl* glasses, specs *Br* F; ~ *da sole* sunglasses

occhiata *f* look, glance; *dare un'~ a* have a look at, glance at; (*sorvegliare*) keep an eye on

occhiello *m* buttonhole

occhio *m* (*pl* -cchi) eye; *a ~ nudo* to the naked eye; *a ~ e croce* roughly; *dare nell'~* attract attention, be noticed; *a quattr' ~i* in private

occidentale western; *Europa f ~* Western Europe

occidente *m* west; *a ~ di* (to the) west of

occorrente **1** *agg* necessary **2** *m* necessary materials *pl*

occorrenza *f*: *all'~* if necessary, if need be

occorrere <3o> be necessary; (*accadere*) occur; *mi occorre* I need; *Le occorre altro?* (do you need) anything else?; *occorre programmare le cose* we / you need to plan things; *non occorre!* there's no need!

occupare <1l & c> *spazio* take up, occupy; *tempo* occupy, fill; *posto* have, hold; *persona* keep busy; *di esercizio* occupy

occuparsi take care (*di* of), deal (*di* with); *occupati degli affari tuoi!* mind your own business!; ~ *di qu* look after s.o., take care of s.o.

occupato TELEC engaged, *Am* busy; *posto, appartamento* taken; *gabinetto* engaged; *persona* busy; *città, nazione* occupied

occupazione *f di città, paese* occupation; (*attività*) pastime; (*impiego*) job

oceano *m* ocean; *Oceano Atlantico* Atlantic Ocean; *Oceano Pacifico* Pacific Ocean

OCSE *abbr* (= *Organizzazione per la Cooperazione e lo Sviluppo Economico*) OECD (= Organization for Economic Co-operation and Development)

oculista *m/f* (*pl* -i) ophthalmologist

od = **o** (*before a vowel*)

odiare <1k> hate, detest

odierno modern-day *attr*, of today, today's

odio *m* hatred

odioso hateful, odious

odontotecnico *m*, **-a** *f* dental technician

odorare <1a> **1** *v/t* smell **2** *v/i* smell (*di* of)

odorato *m* sense of smell

odore *m* smell, odo(u)r; **-i** *pl* GASTR herbs

odoroso fragrant, sweet-smelling

offendere <3c> offend

offendersi take offence, *Am* offense

offensiva *f* offensive

offensivo offensive

offerente *m* bidder; **maggior ~** highest bidder

offerta *f* offer; FIN supply; REL offering; (*dono*) donation; *in asta* bid; **~ d'impiego** job offer; **~ pubblica di acquisto** takeover bid; **~ speciale** special offer

offesa *f* offence, *Am* offense

offeso *pp* → **offendere**

officina *f* workshop; *per macchine* garage

offrire <4f & c> offer; **ti offro da bere** I'll buy *or* stand F you a drink; **posso offrirti qualcosa?** can I get you anything?

oggettivo objective

oggetto *m* object; **-i** *pl* **di valore** valuables

oggi today; **d'~** of today, today's; **da ~ a domani** overnight; **da ~ in poi** from now on; **~ stesso** today, this very day; **~ come ~** at the moment; **~ pomeriggio** this afternoon

oggigiorno nowadays

ogni every; **~ tanto** every so often; **~ sei giorni** every six days

Ognissanti *m inv* All Saints Day

ognuno everyone, everybody

Olanda *f* Holland

olandese **1** *agg m* Dutch **2** *m/f* Dutchman; *donna* Dutchwoman

oleandro *m* oleander

oleoso oily

olfatto *m* sense of smell

oliare <1k> oil

oliera *f* type of cruet for oil and vinegar bottles

Olimpiadi *fpl* Olympic Games, Olympics; **~ invernali** Winter Olympics

olimpionico (*pl* -ci) **1** *agg* Olympic *attr* **2** *m*, **-a** *f* Olympic contestant

olio *m* (*pl* -li) oil; **~ dei freni** brake fluid; **~ lubrificante** lubricating oil, lube; **~ per il cambio** gearbox oil; **~ extra-vergine d'oliva** extra-virgin olive oil; **~ solare** suntan oil

oliva *f* olive

olivo *m* olive (tree)

olmo *m* elm (tree)

OLP *abbr* (= *Organizzazione per la Liberazione della Palestina*) PLO (= Palestine Liberation Organization)

oltraggiare <1f> offend, outrage

oltraggio *m* (*pl* -ggi) offence, *Am* offense, outrage

oltre **1** *prp in spazio, tempo* after, past; (*più di*) over; **vai ~ il semaforo** go past the traffic lights; **aspetto da ~ un'ora** I've been waiting for more than *or* over an hour; **~ a** apart from **2** *avv nello spazio* further; *nel tempo* longer

oltremare overseas

omaggio *m* (*pl* -ggi) homage; (*dono*) gift; **copia (in) ~** free *or* complimentary copy; **~ pubblicitario** (free) gift; **essere in ~ con** come free with

ombelico *m* (*pl* -chi) navel

ombra *f* shadow; *zona non illuminata* shade; *fig* **un'~ di tristezza** a touch of sadness; **all'~** in the shade

ombrello *m* umbrella

ombrellone *m* parasol; *sulla spiaggia* beach umbrella

ombretto *m* eye shadow

ombroso shady; *fig persona* touchy

omelette *f inv* omelette, *Am* omelet

omeopatia *f* homeopathy

omeopatico (*pl* -ci) **1** *agg* homeopathic **2** *m*, **-a** *f* homeopath

omero *m* humerus

omesso *pp* → **omettere**

omettere <3ee> omit, leave out

omicida *(mpl -di)* **1** *agg* murderous **2** *m/f* murderer

omicidio *m (pl -di)* murder; **~ colposo** manslaughter; **tentato ~** attempted murder

omogeneizzato homogenized

omogeneo homogenous

omologare <1m, c & e> approve

omonimo 1 *agg* of the same name **2** *m* homonym **3** *m, -a f* namesake

omosessuale *agg, m/f* homosexual

omosessualità *f* homosexuality

OMS *abbr* (= **Organizzazione Mondiale della Sanità**) WHO (= World Health Organization)

on. *abbr* (= **onorevole**) Hon (= honourable)

oncologia *f* oncology

oncologo *m, -a f* oncologist

onda *f* wave; **-e** *pl* **corte** short wave; **-e** *pl* **lunghe** long wave; **-e** *pl* **medie** medium wave; RAD **andare in ~** go on the air

ondata *f* wave; **~ di caldo** heat wave; **~ di freddo** cold spell

ondeggiare <1f> *di barca* rock; *di bandiera* flutter

ondulato *capelli* wavy; *superficie* uneven; *cartone, lamiera* corrugated

onestà *f* honesty

onesto honest; *prezzo, critica* fair

onice *m* onyx

onnipotente omnipotent

onnipotenza *f* omnipotence

onnipresente ubiquitous

onnisciente omniscient

onniscienza *f* omniscience

onnivoro 1 *agg* omnivorous **2** *m, -a f* omnivore

onomastico *m (pl -ci)* name day

onorare <1a> be a credit to; **~ qu di qc** hono(u)r s.o. with sth

onorario *(pl -ri)* **1** *agg* honorary **2** *m* fee

onorato respected, hono(u)red

onore *m* hono(u)r; **in ~ di** in hono(u)r of

onorevole **1** *agg* hono(u)rable **2** *Onorevole m/f* Member of Parliament

onorificenza *f* hono(u)r

ONU *abbr* (= **Organizzazione delle Nazioni Unite**) UN (= United Nations)

OPA *abbr* (= **Offerta Pubblica di Acquisto (di azioni di società)**) takeover bid

opacità *f di vetro* opaqueness; *di colore, foto* darkness

opaco *(pl -chi) vetro* opaque; *calze, rossetto* dark

opera *f* work; MUS opera; **~ d'arte** work of art; **~ buona** good deed; **mettersi all'~** set to work

operaio *(pl -ai)* **1** *agg* working **2** *m, -a f* worker; **~ specializzato** skilled worker

operare <1l & c> **1** *v/t cambiamento* make; *miracoli* work; MED operate on **2** *v/i* act

operativo operational; *ricerca* applied; *ordine* operative; **piano** *m* **~** plan of operations

operatore *m, -trice f* operator; *televisivo, cinematografico* cameraman; **~ di Borsa** market trader; **~ sociale** social worker; **~ turistico** tour operator

operazione *f* operation; **~ finanziaria** transaction

operetta *f* operetta

operoso hard-working, industrious

opinione *f* opinion; **secondo la tua ~** in your opinion

oppio *m* opium

opporre <3ll> put forward, offer; *scuse, resistenza* offer

opporsi be opposed

opportunista *m/f* opportunist

opportunità *f inv* opportunity; *di decisione* timeliness; **pari ~** *pl* equal opportunities

opportuno suitable, appropriate; **al momento ~** at a suitable time, at the opportune moment

opposizione *f* opposition; POL **all'~** in opposition

opposto 1 *pp* → **opporre 2** *agg* opposite **3** *m* POL opposition

oppressione *f* oppression

oppressore *m* oppressor

opprimente oppressive

opprimere <3r> oppress

oppure or (else)

optare <1c>: **~ per** choose, opt for

opuscolo *m* brochure

opzione *f* option

ora ¹ *f* time; *unità di misura* hour; *che è?, che -e sono?* what time is it?, what's the time?; **~ legale** daylight saving time; **~ locale** local time; **-e pl straordinarie** overtime *sg*; **~ di punta** rush hour; TELEC peak time; **di buon'~** early

ora ² ¹ *avv* now; *sono rientrato or ~* I've only just got back; *per ~* for the moment, for the time being; **~ come ~** at the moment; **d'~ in poi** from now on **2** *cong* now

orafo *m*, **-a** *f* goldsmith

orale **1** *agg* oral **2** *m* oral (exam)

orario (*pl* -ri) **1** *agg tariffa*, hourly; *velocità* per hour; RAD **segnale ~** time signal; **in senso ~** clockwise **2** *m di treno*, *bus*, *aeroplano* timetable, *Am* schedule; *di negozio* hours of business; *al lavoro* hours of work; **~ di apertura/chiusura** opening/closing time; **~ di sportello** banking hours; **~ flessibile** flexitime; **in ~** on time

orata *f* gilthead bream

oratore *m*, **-trice** *f* speaker

oratorio **1** *agg* (*pl* -ri) as an orator **2** *m* oratory

orbita *f*; AST orbit; ANAT eye-socket; **in ~** in orbit

orchestra *f* orchestra; (*luogo*) (orchestra) pit

orchestrale **1** *agg* orchestral **2** *m/f* member of an orchestra

orchestrare <1b> orchestrate (*anche fig*)

orchestrazione *f* orchestration

orchidea *f* orchid

ordigno *m* device; **~ esplosivo** explosive device

ordinale *m/agg* ordinal

ordinamento *m* rules and regulations; **~ sociale** rules governing society

ordinare <1l> order; *stanza* tidy up; MED prescribe; REL ordain

ordinario (*pl* -ri) ordinary; *mediocre* pretty average

ordinato tidy

ordinazione *f* order; REL ordination

ordine *m* order; **mettere in ~** tidy up; **~ alfabetico** alphabetical order; **~ di pagamento** payment order; **di prim'~** first-rate, first-class; **~ del giorno** agenda; **l'~ dei medici** the medical association; **~ permanente** FIN standing order

orecchino *m* earring

orecchio *m* (*pl* -cchi) ear; MUS **a ~ by ear**

orecchioni *mpl* mumps *sg*

orefice *m/f* goldsmith

oreficeria *f* goldsmithing; (*gioielleria*) jewel(l)er's

orfano **1** *agg* orphan **2** *m*, **-a** *f* orphan

orfanotrofio *m* orphanage

organico (*pl* -ci) organic

organismo *m* organism; *fig* body

organista *m/f* (*mpl* -i) organist

organizzare <1a> organize

organizzazione *f* organization

organo *m* organ

orgasmo *m* orgasm

orgoglio *m* pride

orgoglioso proud

orientabile adjustable, swivelling

orientale **1** *agg* eastern; (*dell'Oriente*) Oriental; **Europa** *f* **~** Eastern Europe **2** *m/f* Oriental

orientamento *m*: **senso** *m* **d'~** sense of direction; **~ professionale** professional advice

orientare <1b> *antenna*, *schermo* turn; **~ qu verso una carriera** guide *or* steer s.o. towards a career

orientarsi get one's bearings

oriente *m* east; **l'Oriente** the Orient; **Medio Oriente** Middle East; **Estremo Oriente** Far East; **ad ~ di** (to the) east of

origano *m* oregano

originale *m/agg* original

originalità *f* originality

originalmente originally

originario (*pl* -ri) original; **essere ~ di** come from, be a native of;

popolo originate in

origine *f* origin; **in ~** originally

origliare <1g> eavesdrop

orizzontale horizontal

orizzonte *m* horizon

orlare <1a> hem

orlo *m* edge; *di vestito* hem

orma *f* footprint; *fig* **seguire le -e di qu** follow in s.o.'s footsteps

ormai by now

ormonale hormonal

ormone *m* hormone

ornamentale ornamental

ornamento *m* ornament

ornare <1a> decorate

ornitologia *f* ornithology

ornitologico ornithological

ornitologo *m*, **-a** *f* ornithologist

oro *m* gold; **d'~** (made of) gold

orologeria *f* clock- and watch-making; *negozio* watchmaker's

orologiaio *m* (*pl* -ai) (clock- and) watch-maker

orologio *m* (*pl* -gi) clock; *portatile* watch; **~ a cucù** cuckoo clock; **~ da polso** wristwatch; **~ da tasca** pocket watch; **~ subacqueo** waterproof watch

oroscopo *m* horoscope

orrendo horrendous

orribile horrible

orrore *m* horror (**di** of); **avere qc in ~** hate sth

Orsa *f*: **~ maggiore / minore** Ursa Major / Minor, the Great / Little Bear

orsacchiotto *m* bear cub; (*giocattolo*) teddy (bear)

orso *m* bear; *fig* hermit; **~ bianco** polar bear

ortaggio *m* (*pl* -ggi) vegetable

ortica *f* (*pl* -che) nettle

orticaria *f* nettle rash

orticoltura *f* horticulture

orto *m* vegetable garden, kitchen garden; **~ botanico** botanical gardens

ortodossia *f* orthodoxy

ortodosso orthodox

ortografia *f* spelling

ortolano *m*, **-a** *f* market gardener

ortopedia *f* orthop(a)edics

ortopedico (*pl* -ci) **1** *agg* orthop(a)edic **2** *m*, **-a** *f* orthop(a)edist

orzaiolo *m* stye

orzata *f* drink made from crushed almonds, sugar and water

orzo *m* barley; **~ perlato** pearl barley

osare <1c> dare

oscenità *f inv* obscenity

osceno obscene

oscillare <1a> *di corda* sway, swing; *di barca* rock; FIS oscillate; *fig di persona* waver, hesitate; *di prezzi* fluctuate

oscillazione *f di barca* rocking; **~ dei prezzi** price fluctuations *pl*

oscurare <1a> obscure; *luce* block out

oscurità *f* darkness; *fig* obscurity; **nell'~** in the dark

oscuro 1 *agg* dark; (*sconosciuto*) obscure **2** *m* dark; **essere all'~ di qc** be in the dark about sth

ospedale *m* hospital

ospitale hospitable

ospitalità *f* hospitality

ospitare <1l & c> put up; SP be at home to

ospite *m/f* guest; *chi ospita* host; *donna* hostess

ospizio *m* (*pl* -zi) old folk's home

ossatura *f* bone structure; *fig*, ARCHI structure

osseo bone *attr*

osservare <1b> (*guardare*) look at, observe; (*notare*) see, notice, observe; (*far notare*) point out, remark; (*seguire*) abide by, obey; **~ una dieta** keep to a diet, follow a diet; **le faccio ~ che** I'll have you know that

osservatore *m*, **-trice** *f* observer, watcher

osservatorio *m* (*pl* -ri) AST observatory; **~ meteorologico** *f* weather station

osservazione *f* observation; (*affermazione*) remark, observation

ossessione *f* obsession (**di** with); **avere l'~ di** be obsessed with

ossessivo obsessive

ossia or rather

ossidabile liable to tarnish

ossidare <1l & c> tarnish

ossidazione f tarnish

ossigeno m oxygen; **tenda** f ~ oxygen tent

osso m (ANAT pl le ossa) bone; **di ~** bone attr, made of bone; **~ sacro** sacrum; **in carne e -a** in the flesh

ossobuco m (pl ossibuchi) marrowbone; GASTR ossobuco, stew made with knuckle of veal

ostacolare <1m> hinder

ostacolo m obstacle; nell'atletica hurdle; nell'equitazione fence, jump; fig stumbling block, obstacle

ostaggio m (pl -ggi) hostage; **prendere qu in ~** take s.o. hostage

ostello m: **~ della gioventù** youth hostel

osteoporosi f osteoporosis

osteria f inn

ostetrica f obstetrician; (levatrice) midwife

ostetricia f obstetrics

ostetrico (pl -ci) **1** agg obstetric(al) **2** m obstetrician

ostia f Host

ostile hostile

ostilità f inv hostility

ostinarsi <1a> dig one's heels in: **~ a fare qc** persist in doing sth

ostinato obstinate

ostinazione f obstinacy

ostrica f (pl -che) oyster

ostruire <4d> block, obstruct

ostruito blocked

ostruzione f (ostacolo) obstruction, blockage

otite f ear infection

otorinolaringoiatra m/f (pl -i) ear, nose and throat specialist, ENT specialist

ottagonale octagonal

ottagono octagon

ottano m octane; **numero m di -i** octane rating or number

ottanta eighty

ottantesimo m/agg eightieth

ottava f MUS octave

ottavo m/agg eighth

ottenere <2q> get, obtain

ottengo → **ottenere**

ottenibile obtainable

ottica f optics; fig viewpoint, point of view

ottico (pl -ci) **1** agg optical **2** m optician

ottimale optimum

ottimismo m optimism

ottimista m/f (mpl -i) optimist

ottimistico (pl -ci) optimistic

ottimizzare <1a> optimize

ottimo excellent, extremely good

otto 1 agg eight; **oggi a ~** a week today **2** m eight; **~ volante** big dipper

ottobre m October

ottocento 1 agg eight hundred **2** m: **il Ottocento** the nineteenth century

ottone m brass; MUS **-i** pl brass (instruments)

otturare <1a> block; dente fill

otturatore m FOT shutter

otturazione f blocking; di dente filling

ottuso obtuse

ovaia f ANAT ovary

ovale m/agg oval

ovazione f ovation

overdose f inv overdose

ovest m west

ovile m sheep pen; fig fold

ovini mpl sheep

ovunque everywhere

ovvero or rather; (cioè) that is

ovvio (pl -vvi) obvious

oziare <1g> laze around, be idle

ozio m (pl -zi) laziness, idleness

ozioso lazy, idle

ozono m ozone; **buco m nell'~** hole in the ozone layer; **strato m d' ~** ozone layer

P

p. *abbr* (= *pagina*) p (= page)

pacato calm, unhurried

pacchetto *m* package, small parcel; *di sigarette, biscotti* packet; ~ *azionario* block of shares; ~ *turistico* package holiday

pacchiano vulgar, in bad taste

pacco *m* (*pl* -cchi) parcel, package; ~ *bomba* parcel bomb; ~ *postale* parcel

pace *f* peace; *lasciare in* ~ *qu* leave s.o. alone *or* in peace

pacifico (*pl* -ci) **1** *agg* peaceful **2** *m*: *il Pacifico* the Pacific

pacifismo *m* pacifism

pacifista *m/f* (*mpl* -i) pacifist

padano *agg* of the Po; *pianura f* -**a** Po Valley

padella *f di cucina* frying pan

padiglione *m* pavilion; ~ *auricolare* auricle

Padova *f* Padua

padovano 1 *agg* Paduan **2** *m*, -**a** *f* native of Padua

padre *m* father

padrino *m* godfather

padronanza *f* (*controllo*) control; (*conoscenza*) mastery; ~ *di sé* self-control

padrone *m*, -**a** *f* boss; (*proprietario*) owner; *di cane* master; *donna* mistress; ~ *di casa* man / lady of the house; *per inquilino* landlord; *donna* landlady

paesaggio *m* (*pl* -ggi) scenery; PITT, GEOG landscape

paesaggista *m/f* PITT landscape painter *or* artist

paesano 1 *agg* country *attr* **2** *m*, -**a** *f* person from the country; *spreg* country bumpkin

paese *m* country; (*villaggio*) village; (*territorio*) region, area; *i Paesi Bassi pl* the Netherlands; ~ *d'origi-*

ne country of origin; -**i** *pl in via di sviluppo* developing countries; ~ *membro* member state

paga *f* (*pl* -ghe) pay

pagabile payable; ~ *a vista* payable at sight

pagamento *m* payment; ~ *anticipato* payment in advance; ~ *alla consegna* cash on delivery; ~ *in contanti* payment in cash, cash payment; ~ *a rate* payment in insta(l)lments; *altre sono a* ~ others you have to pay for

pagare <1e> **1** *v/t acquisto* pay for; *conto, fattura, debito* pay; *ti pago qualcosa da bere* I'll buy you *or* stand you a drink; *gliela faccio* ~ he'll pay for this **2** *v/i* pay; ~ *anticipatamente* pay in advance; ~ *in contanti* pay (in) cash; ~ *a rate* pay in instal(l)ments

pagella *f* report, *Am* report card

paghetta *f* pocket money

pagina *f* page; *a* ~ *10* on page 10; -**e** *gialle* Yellow Pages; ~ *elettronica* screen page; ~ *Web* Web site

paglia *f* straw

paio *m* (*pl le* **paia**): *un* ~ *di scarpe, guanti ecc* a pair of; *un* ~ *di volte* a couple of times

pala *f* shovel; *di elica, turbina, remo* blade; ~ *d'altare* altarpiece

palasport *m inv* indoor sports arena

palato *m* palate

palazzina *f* luxury home

palazzo *m* palace; (*edificio*) building; *con appartamenti* block of flats, *Am* apartment block; ~ *comunale* town hall; ~ *di giustizia* courthouse; ~ *dello sport* indoor sports arena

palco *m* (*pl* -chi) dais; TEA stage

palcoscenico *m* (*pl* -ci) stage

palese obvious

Palestina *f* Palestine

palestinese *agg, m/f* Palestinian

palestra *f* gym

paletta *f* shovel; *per la spiaggia* spade; FERR signal(l)ing paddle

paletto *m* tent peg

palla *f* ball; **~ di neve** snowball; *fig* **cogliere la ~ al balzo** jump at the chance

pallacanestro *f* basketball

pallanuoto *f* water polo

pallavolo *f* volley ball

palliativo *m* palliative

pallido pale

pallina *f* **di vetro** marble; **~ da golf** golf ball; **~ da tennis** tennis ball

pallino *m* nel biliardo cue ball; *nelle bocce* jack; *munizione* pellet; *fig* **avere il ~ della pesca** be mad about fishing, be fishing mad; **a -i** *pl* with spots, spotted

palloncino *m* balloon

pallone *m* ball; *calcio* football, soccer; AVIA balloon; **~ sonda** weather balloon

pallore *m* paleness, pallor

pallottola *f* pellet; *di pistola* bullet

palma *f* palm

palmo *m* hand's breadth; ANAT palm; **a ~ a ~** gradually, bit by bit, inch by inch

palo *m* pole; *nel calcio* (goal)post

palombaro *m* diver

palpabile *fig* palpable

palpare <1a> feel; MED palpate

palpebra *f* eyelid

palpitare <1l> *del cuore* pound

palpitazione *f* palpitation

palpito *m* del cuore beat

paltò *m inv* overcoat, heavy coat

palude *f* marsh

paludoso marshy

palustre marshy; *pianta* marsh

panacea *f* panacea

panca *f* (*pl* -che) bench; *in chiesa* pew

pancarré *m* sliced loaf

pancetta *f* pancetta, *cured belly of pork*

panchetto *m* footstool

panchina *f* bench

pancia *f* (*pl* -ce) *m* stomach, belly F; *di animale* belly; **mal m di ~** stomach-ache, belly-ache F; **mettere su ~** develop a paunch

panciotto *m* waistcoat, *Am* vest

panciuto big-bellied

pancreas *m inv* pancreas

pane *m* bread; **~ bianco** white bread; **~ nero** (o **di segala**) black *or* rye bread; **~ integrale** wholewheat bread

panetteria *f* bakery

panettiere *m/f* baker

panettone *m* panettone, *cake made with candied fruit*

panfilo *m* yacht; **~ a motore** motor yacht

pangrattato *m* breadcrumbs *pl*

panico (*pl* -ci) *m* panic

paniere *m* basket

panificio *m* (*pl* -ci) bakery

panino *m* roll; **~ imbottito** filled roll

paninoteca *f* sandwich shop

panna *f* cream; **~ montata** whipped cream

panne *f*: **essere in ~** have broken down, have had a breakdown

pannello *m* panel; **~ solare** solar panel

panno *m* pezzo di stoffa cloth; **-i** *pl* clothes; **se fossi nei tuoi -i** if I were in your shoes

pannocchia *f* cob

pannolino *m* nappy; *per donne* sanitary towel

panorama *m* (*pl* -i) panorama; *fig* overview

panoramica *f* FOT panorama, panoramic view; *fig* overview

pantaloncini *mpl* shorts

pantaloni *mpl* trousers, *Am* pants

pantera *f* ZO panther

pantofola *f* slipper

pantomima *f* pantomime

paonazzo purple

papà *m inv* daddy, dad

papa *m* Pope

papale papal

paparazzo *m*: **i -i** *pl* the paparazzi

papavero *m* poppy

papera *f* fig (*errore*) slip of the tongue

papero *m*, **-a** *f* gosling
papillon *m inv* bow tie
papiro *m* papyrus
pappa *f* food
pappagallo *m* parrot
paprica *f* paprika
par. *abbr* (= **paragrafo**) para (= paragraph)
parabrezza *m inv* windscreen, *Am* windshield
paracadutare <1a> parachute in
paracadute *m inv* parachute
paracadutista *m/f* (*mpl* -i) parachutist
paracarro *m* post
paradiso *m* heaven, paradise; **~ terrestre** heaven on earth, Eden
paradossale paradoxical
paradosso *m* paradox
parafango *m* (*pl* -ghi) mudguard, *Am* fender
parafulmine *m* lightning rod
paraggi *mpl* neighbo(u)rhood *sg*; **nei ~ di** (somewhere) near
paragonabile comparable
paragonare <1a> compare
paragone *m* comparison; **a ~ di** compared with, in *or* by comparison with; **senza ~** incomparable
paragrafo *m* paragraph
paralisi *f* paralysis
paralitico *m*, **-a** *f* (*mpl* -ci) paralyzed person
paralizzare <1a> paralyze
parallela *f* parallel line; **-e** *pl* parallel bars
parallelo *m/agg* parallel
paraluce *m inv* FOT lens hood
paralume *m* lampshade
parametro *m* parameter
paranoia *f* paranoia
paranoico (*pl* -ci) **1** *agg* paranoid **2** *m*, **-a** *f* person with paranoia
paranormale *m/agg* paranormal
paraocchi *mpl* blinkers (*anche fig*)
parapendio *m* SP paragliding
parapetto *m* parapet; MAR rail
paraplegico 1 *agg* paraplegic **2** *m*, **-a** *f* paraplegic
parare <1a> **1** *v/t ornare* decorate; *proteggere* shelter; *occhi* shield; *scan-*

sare parry **2** *v/i* save
parasole *m* parasol; FOT lens hood
parassita *m/f* (*mpl* -i) parasite
parata *f* parade
paraurti *m inv* bumper
parcheggiare <1f> *v/t & v/i* park
parcheggio *m* parking; *luogo* car park, *Am* parking lot; **~ sotterraneo** underground car park; **divieto di ~** no parking
parchimetro *m* parking meter
parco[1] (*pl* -chi) *agg*: **essere ~ nel mangiare** eat sparingly
parco[2] *m* (*pl* -chi) park; **~ dei divertimenti** amusement park; **~ naturale** nature reserve; **~ nazionale** national park; **~ macchine** fleet (of vehicles)
parecchio 1 *agg* a lot of **2** *pron* **parecchi** *mpl*, **parecchie** *fpl* quite a few **3** *avv* quite a lot
pareggiare <1f> **1** *v/t* even up; (*uguagliare*) match, equal; *conto* balance **2** *v/i* SP draw
pareggio *m* (*pl* -ggi) SP draw
parente *m/f* relative
parentela *f* relationship; *parenti* relatives, relations
parentesi *f* bracket; (*detto*) **fra ~** by the by; *fig* **aprire una ~** digress slightly
parere 1 *v/i* <2h> seem, appear; **pare che** it seems that, it would appear that; **che te ne pare?** what do you think (of it)?; **non ti pare?** don't you think?; **a quanto pare** by all accounts; **non mi pare vero!** I can't believe it! **2** *m* opinion; **a mio ~** in my opinion, to my way of thinking
parete *f* wall; **~ divisoria** partition wall
pari 1 *agg* equal; *numero* even; **essere di ~ altezza** be the same height; **al ~ di** like; **alla ~** the same; SP **finire alla ~** end in a draw; **senza ~** unrivalled, unequalled **2** *m* (social) equal, peer; **da ~ a ~** as an equal
Parigi Paris
parigino (of) Paris, Parisian
parità *f* equality, parity; **~ di diritti** equal rights; **a ~ di condizioni** all

P

things being equal

parka *m inv* parka

parlamentare 1 *agg* Parliamentary **2** *v/i* <1a> negotiate **3** *m/f* (*pl* -ri) Member of Parliament, MP

parlamento *m* Parliament; *Parlamento europeo* European Parliament

parlare <1a> talk, speak (*a qu* to s.o.; *di qc* about sth); ~ *del più e del meno* make small talk; *parla inglese?* do you speak English?

parmigiano *m* (*formaggio*) Parmesan

parodia *f* parody

parola *f* word; (*facoltà*) speech; ~ *d'ordine* password; -e *pl crociate* crossword (puzzle) *sg*; *essere di* ~ keep one's word; *chiedere la* ~ ask for the floor; ~ *per* ~ word for word

parolaccia *f* swear word

parquet *m* parquet floor

parrocchia *f* parish

parrochiale parish *attr*

parroco *m* (*pl* -ci) parish priest

parrucca *f* (*pl* -cche) wig

parrucchiere *m*, **-a** *f* hairdresser; ~ *per signora* ladies' hairdresser

parte *f* part; (*porzione*) portion; (*lato*) side; DIR party; ~ *civile* plaintiff; *far* ~ *di una società* belong to a society, be a member of a society; *prendere* ~ a take part in; *a* ~ separate; *scherzi a* ~ joking apart; *mettere da* ~ *qc* put sth aside; *dall'altra* ~ *della strada* on the other side of the street; *da nessuna* ~ nowhere; *da tutte le* -*i* everywhere; *da* ~ *mia* for my part, as far as I'm concerned; *regalo ecc* from me; *in* ~ in part, partly; *in gran* ~ largely

partecipante *m/f* participant

partecipare <1m> **1** *v/t* announce **2** *v/i*: ~ *a gara* take part in; *dolore, gioia* share

partecipazione *f* (*intervento*) participation; (*annunzio*) announcement; FIN holding; ~ *agli utili* profit-sharing

parteggiare <1f>: ~ *per* support

partenza *f* departure; SP start; INFOR ~ *a freddo* cold start; *essere di* ~ be just about to leave, be on the point of leaving; *fig punto m di* ~ starting point, point of departure

participio *m* (*pl* -pi) participle

particolare 1 *agg* particular; *segretario* private; *in* ~ in particular **2** *m* particular, detail

particolareggiato detailed

particolarità *f inv* special nature

partigiano *m*, **-a** *f* partisan

partire <4a> leave; AUTO, SP start; ~ *per* leave for; ~ *per l'estero* go abroad

partita *f* SP match; *di carte* game; *di merce* shipment; ~ *IVA* VAT registration number; ~ *amichevole* friendly (match); ~ *di calcio* football match

partito *m* POL party; ~ *d'opposizione* opposition (party); *prendere* ~ make up one's mind; *essere ridotto a mal* ~ be in a bad way

partitura *f* score

partner *m/f inv* partner

parto *m* birth; ~ *cesareo* C(a)esarean (section)

partorire <4d> give birth to

part time 1 *agg* part-time **2** *avv* part time

parziale partial; *fig* biased

pascolo *m* pasture

Pasqua *f* Easter

pasquale Easter *attr*

Pasquetta *f* Easter Monday

passaggio *m* (*pl* -ggi) passage; *in macchina* lift, *Am* ride; *atto* passing; SP pass; *essere di* ~ be passing through; ~ *pedonale* pedestrian crossing, *Br* zebra crossing; ~ *a livello* level crossing, *Am* grade crossing; *dare un* ~ *a qu* give s.o. a lift (*Am* ride)

passante *m/f* passer-by

passaporto *m* passport; *controllo m dei* -*i* passport control

passare <1a> **1** *v/i* (*trasferirsi*) go (*in* into); SP pass; *di legge* be passed, pass; *di tempo* go by *or* past, pass; ~ *attraverso delle difficoltà* have a difficult time; **~ da / per Milano** go through Milan; **~ dal panettiere** drop by the baker's; **mi è passato di mente** it slipped my mind; **~ di moda** go out of fashion; **~ inosservato** go unnoticed; **~ per imbecille** be taken for a fool **2** v/t *confine* cross; (*sorpassare*) overstep; (*porgere*) pass; (*trascorrere*) spend; TELEC **ti passo Claudio** here's Claudio

passata f quick wipe; GASTR **~ (di pomodoro)** passata, *sieved tomato pulp*

passatempo m pastime, hobby

passato 1 pp → **passare 2** agg past; *alimento* pureed; **l'anno ~** last year **3** m past; GASTR puree

passatoia f runner

passaverdura m inv food mill

passeggero 1 agg passing, short-lived **2** m, -a f passenger

passeggiare <1f> stroll, walk

passeggiata f stroll, walk; (*percorso*) walk

passeggino m pushchair

passeggio m (pl -ggi): **andare a ~** go for a walk

passe-partout m inv (*chiave*) master key

passerella f (*foot*)bridge; MAR gangway; AVIA ramp; *per sfilate* catwalk

passero m sparrow

passionale passionate; *delitto* of passion

passione f passion; REL Passion

passivo 1 agg passive; **fumo** m **~** second-hand smoke **2** m GRAM passive; FIN liabilities pl

passo m step; (*impronta*) footprint; *di libro* passage; GEOG pass; **a ~ di lumaca** at a snail's pace; **~ falso** false move; AUTO **avanzare a ~ d'uomo** crawl; **~ carrabile** driveway; **fare due -i** go for a walk or a stroll; fig **fare il primo ~** take the first step

pasta f paste; (*pastasciutta*) pasta; (*impasto*) dough; (*dolce*) pastry; **~ dentifricia** toothpaste; **~ frolla** shortcrust pastry; **~ sfoglia** puff pastry

pastasciutta f pasta

pastella f batter

pastello m pastel

pasticca f (pl -cche) pastille

pasticceria f pastries pl, cakes pl; *negozio* cake shop

pasticciere m, **-a** f confectioner

pasticcino m pastry

pasticcio m (pl -cci) GASTR pie; fig mess; **~ di fegato d'oca** pâté de foie gras; **essere nei -i** be in a mess

pastiglia f MED tablet, pill

pastina f *small pasta shapes for soup*

pasto m meal

pastorale 1 m bishop's staff, crozier **2** f REL pastoral letter

pastore 1 m, **-a** f shepherd **2** m REL: **~ (evangelico)** pastor

pastorizzato pasteurized

patata f potato; **-e** pl **fritte** (French) fries, Br chips; **-e** pl **lesse** boiled potatoes; **-e** pl **arrosto** roast potatoes

patatine fpl crisps, Am chips; (*fritte*) French fries, Br chips

patente f: **~ (di guida)** driving licence, Am driver's license

paternalismo m paternalism

paternità f paternity

paterno paternal, fatherly

patetico (pl -ci) pathetic

patire <4d> **1** v/i suffer (**di** from) **2** v/t suffer (from)

patito 1 agg of suffering **2** m, **-a** f fan; **~ del jazz** jazz fan

patologia f pathology

patologico pathological

patria f homeland

patrigno m stepfather

patrimonio m (pl -ni) estate; **~ artistico** artistic heritage; **~ ereditario** genetic inheritance; fig **un ~** a fortune

patriota m/f (mpl -i) patriot

patriottico patriotic

patriottismo m patriotism

patrocinio m support, patronage

patrono m, **-a** f REL patron saint

patteggiare <1f> negotiate

pattinaggio m (pl -ggi) skating; ~ **artistico** figure skating; ~ **su ghiaccio** ice skating; ~ **a rotelle** roller skating

pattinare <1l> skate; AUTO skid

pattinatore m, **-trice** f skater

pattino m SP skate; ~ **a rotelle** roller skate; ~ **in linea** roller blade

patto m pact; **a** ~ **che** on condition that; **venire a -i** come to terms

pattuglia f patrol

pattumiera f dustbin

paura f fear; **avere** ~ **di** be frightened of; **mettere** (o **fare**) ~ **a qu** frighten s.o.

pauroso fearful; **che fa paura** frightening

pausa f pause; **durante il lavoro** break

pavimento m floor

pavone m peacock

pazientare <1b> be patient

paziente agg, m/f patient

pazienza f patience

pazzesco (pl -chi) crazy

pazzia f madness

pazzo 1 agg mad, crazy; **è ~ da legare** he's off his head; **andare ~ per** be mad or crazy about **2** m, **-a** f madman; **donna** madwoman

p.c. abbr (= **per conoscenza**) cc (= carbon copy)

p.e. abbr (= **per esempio**) eg (= for example)

pecca f (pl -cche) fault

peccare <1b & d> sin; ~ **di** be guilty of

peccato m sin; (**che**) ~ **!** what a pity!

pecora f sheep

pecorino m/agg: (**formaggio** m) ~ pecorino (**ewe's milk cheese**)

peculiarità f inv special feature, peculiarity

pedaggio m (pl -ggi) toll

pedalare <1a> pedal

pedale m pedal; ~ **dell'acceleratore** accelerator

pedalò m inv pedalo

pedana f footrest; SP springboard

pedante pedantic

pedata f kick; (**impronta**) footprint

pediatra m/f (mpl -i) p(a)ediatrician

pediatria f p(a)ediatrics

pedicure 1 m/f chiropodist, Am podiatrist **2** m inv pedicure

pedina f draughtsman; fig cog in the wheel

pedinare <1a> shadow, follow

pedofilia f p(a)edophilia

pedofilo m, **-a** f p(a)edophile

pedonale pedestrian; **zona** f ~ pedestrian precinct; **strisce** fpl **-i** pedestrian crossing sg

pedone m pedestrian

peggio 1 avv worse **2** m: **il ~ è che** the worst of it is that; **avere la ~** get the worst of it; **di male in ~** from bad to worse

peggioramento m deterioration, worsening

peggiorare <1a> **1** v/t make worse, worsen **2** v/i get worse, worsen

peggiore worse; superlativo worst; **il ~** the worst; **nel ~ dei casi** if the worst comes to the worst

pegno m d'amore, respetto ecc token; **dare qc in ~** pawn sth

pelare <1a> peel; **pollo** pluck; fig F fleece F

pellame m skin, pelt

pelle f skin; ~ **scamosciata** suede; **avere la ~ d'oca** get gooseflesh; fig **essere ~ e ossa** be nothing but skin and bones

pellegrinaggio m (pl -ggi) pilgrimage

pellegrino m, **-a** f pilgrim

pelletteria f leatherwork; **-e** pl leather goods

pellicano m pelican

pelliccia f furrier's

pelliccia f (pl -cce) fur; **cappotto** fur coat

pellicola f film; ~ **a colori** colo(u)r film; ~ **trasparente** cling film

pelo m hair, coat; (**pelliccia**) coat; **a ~ dell'acqua** on the surface of the water; fig **per un ~** by the skin of one's teeth

peluria f down

pena f (**sofferenza**) pain, suffering; (**punizione**) punishment; ~ **di morte** death penalty; **stare in ~ per qu**

worry about s.o.; *vale la ~ soffrire tanto?* is it worth suffering so much?; *non ne vale la ~* it's not worth it; *mi fa ~* I feel sorry for him / her; *a mala ~* hardly

penale 1 *agg* criminal; *codice penal* 2 *f* penalty

penalista *m/f* (*mpl* -i) criminal lawyer

penalità *f inv* penalty

penalizzare <1a> penalize

pendenza *f* slope

pendere <3a> hang; (*essere inclinato*) slope; *fig ~ dalle labbra di qu* hang on s.o.'s every word

pendio *m* slope

pendolare *m/f* commuter

pendolo *m* pendulum

pene *m* penis

penetrante *dolore, freddo* piercing; *fig sguardo* piercing, penetrating; *analisi* penetrating

penetrare <1l & b> 1 *v/t* penetrate 2 *v/i*: *~ in* enter

penicillina *f* penicillin

peninsulare peninsular

penisola *f* peninsula; *~ iberica* Iberian peninsula

penitenza *f* REL penance; *in gioco* forfeit

penitenziario *m* (*pl* -ri) prison

penna *f* pen; *di uccello* feather; *~ biro®* ballpoint (pen), biro; *~ stilografica* fountain pen; *~ a feltro* felt-tip (pen)

pennarello *m* felt-tip (pen)

pennello *m* brush

penombra *f* half-light

penoso painful

pensare <1b> think; *~ a* think about *or* of; *~ a fare qc* (*ricordarsi di*) remember to do sth; *~ di fare qc* think of doing sth; *che ne pensa?* what do you think?; *cosa stai pensando?* what are you thinking about?; *ci penso io* I'll take care of it; *senza ~* without thinking

pensiero *m* thought; (*preoccupazione*) worry; *stare in ~* be worried *or* anxious (*per* about); *un piccolo ~* (*regalo*) a little something

pensieroso pensive

pensile hanging

pensilina *f* shelter

pensionamento *m* retirement

pensionato *m*, -a *f* pensioner, retired person; (*alloggio*) boarding house

pensione *f* pension; (*albergo*) boarding house; *~ completa* full board; *mezza ~* half board; *andare in ~* retire

pensoso pensive, thoughtful

pentagono *m* pentagon

Pentecoste *f* Whitsun

pentimento *m* remorse

pentirsi <4b *or* 4d> *di peccato* repent; *~ di aver fatto qc* be sorry for doing sth

pentola *f* pot, pan; *~ a pressione* pressure cooker

penultimo last but one, penultimate

penuria *f* shortage (*di* of); *~ di alloggi* housing shortage

penzolare <1l> dangle

penzoloni dangling

peonia *f* peony

pepare <1a> pepper

pepato peppered

pepe *m* pepper

peperone *m* pepper

per 1 *prp* for; *mezzo* by; *~ qualche giorno* for a few days; *~ questa ragione* for that reason; *~ tutta la notte* throughout the night; *~ iscritto* in writing; *~ esempio* for example; *dieci ~ cento* ten per cent; *uno ~ uno* one by one 2 *cong*: *~ fare qc* (in order) to do sth; *stare ~* be about to

pera *f* pear

peraltro however

perbene 1 *agg* respectable 2 *avv* properly

percento 1 *m* percentage 2 *avv* per cent

percentuale *f/agg* percentage

percepire <4d> perceive; (*riscuotere*) cash

percezione *f* perception

perché because; (*affinché*) so that; *~?* why?

P

perciò so, therefore

percorrere <3o> *distanza* cover; *strada, fiume* travel along

percorso 1 *pp* → **percorrere 2** *m* (*tragitto*) route

percossa *f* blow

percosso → **percuotere**

percuotere <3ff> strike

percussione *f* percussion; MUS *-i pl* percussion

perdere <3b & 3uu> **1** *v/t* lose; *treno, occasione* miss; **~ tempo** waste time; **~ di vista** lose sight of; *fig* lose touch with **2** *v/i* lose; *di rubinetto, tubo* leak; **a ~** disposable

perdersi get lost; **~ d'animo** lose heart

perdita *f* loss; *di gas, di acqua* leak; **essere in ~** be making a loss; **~ di tempo** waste of time; **si estendeva a ~ d'occhio** it stretched as far as the eye could see

perditempo 1 *m/f inv* idler **2** *m inv* waste of time

perdonare <1a> forgive

perdono *m* forgiveness; **ti chiedo ~** please forgive me

perenne eternal, never-ending; BOT perennial

perfettamente perfectly

perfetto 1 *agg* perfect **2** *m* GRAM perfect (tense)

perfezionamento *m* adjustment, further improvement; **corso m di ~** further training

perfezionare <1a> perfect, further improve

perfezione *f* perfection; **a ~** to perfection, perfectly

perfezionista *m/f* perfectionist

perfido treacherous

perfino even

perforare <1c> drill through

perforazione *f* perforation

pergola *f* pergola

pergolato *m* pergola

pericolante on the verge of collapse

pericolo *m* danger; (*rischio*) risk; **fuori ~** out of danger; **mettere in ~** endanger, put at risk

pericoloso dangerous

periferia *f* periphery; *di città* outskirts

periferico (*pl* -ci) peripheral; *quartiere* outlying; INFOR **unità f -a** peripheral

perifrasi *f inv* circumlocution

periodico (*pl* -ci) **1** *agg* periodic **2** *m* periodical; **~ mensile** monthly

periodo *m* period; **~ di transizione** transition period

peripezia *f* misadventure

perito 1 *agg* expert **2** *m*, **-a** *f* expert

peritonite *f* peritonitis

perizia *f* skill, expertise; *esame* examination (by an expert)

perla *f* pearl; **~ coltivata** cultured pearl; **collana f di -e** pearl necklace

perlina *f* bead

perlomeno at least

perlopiù usually

perlustrare <1a> patrol

permaloso easily offended, touchy

permanente 1 *agg* permanent **2** *f* perm

permanenza *f* permanence; **in un luogo** stay

permesso 1 *pp* → **permettere 2** *m* permission; (*breve licenza*) permit; MIL leave; **~ d'atterraggio** permission to land; **~ di lavoro** work permit; **~ di soggiorno** residence permit; **(è) ~?** may I?; **con ~** excuse me

permettere <3ee> allow, permit

permettersi afford

pernacchia *f* F raspberry F

pernice *f* partridge

perno *m* pivot

pernottamento *m* night, overnight stay

pernottare <1c> spend the night, stay overnight

pero *m* pear (tree)

però but

perpendicolare *f/agg* perpendicular

perpetuo perpetual

perplesso perplexed

perquisire <4d> search

perquisizione *f* search; **~ personale** body search; **mandato m di ~** search warrant

persecuzione *f* persecution; **mania**

f **di** ~ persecution complex

perseguitare <1m> persecute

perseguitato m: ~ **politico** person being persecuted for their political views

perseverante persevering

perseveranza f perseverance

perseverare <1m & b> persevere

persiana f shutter

persiano Persian

persino → **perfino**

persistente persistent

persistenza f persistence

persistere <3f> persist

perso pp → **perdere**

persona f person; **a** (**o per**) ~ a head, each; **in** ~, **di** ~ in person, personally

personaggio m (pl -ggi) character; (celebrità) personality

personale 1 agg personal **2** m staff, personnel; AVIA ~ **di terra** ground staff or crew; **riduzione** f **del** ~ cuts in staff, personnel cutbacks

personalità f inv personality

personalmente personally

personificare <1n & d> personify

perspicace shrewd

perspicacia f shrewdness

persuadere <2i> convince; ~ **qu a fare qc** persuade s.o. to do sth

persuasione f persuasion

persuasivo persuasive

persuaso pp → **persuadere**

pertanto and so, therefore

pertinente relevant, pertinent

pertinenza f relevance, pertinence

perturbazione f disturbance; ~ **atmosferica** atmospheric disturbance

peruviano 1 agg Peruvian **2** m, **-a** f Peruvian

pervenire <4p> arrive; **far** ~ send

perverso perverse

pervertito m, **-a** f pervert

p.es. abbr (= **per esempio**) eg (= for example)

pesante heavy; fig libro, film boring

pesantezza f heaviness; ~ **di stomaco** indigestion

pesapersone f inv scales; in negozio ecc weighing machine

pesare <1a> **1** v/t weigh; ingredienti weigh out **2** v/i weigh

pesca¹ f (pl -che) (frutto) peach

pesca² f fishing; ~ **con la lenza** angling

pescare <1d> fish for; (prendere) catch; fig dig up; ladro, svaligiatore ecc catch (red-handed)

pescatore m fisherman

pesce m fish; ~ **spada** swordfish; ~ **d'aprile** April Fool; ASTR **Pesci** pl Pisces

pescecane m (pl pescicani) shark

peschereccio m (pl -cci) fishing boat

pescheria f fishmonger's

pescivendolo m, **-a** f fishmonger

pesco m (pl -chi) peach (tree)

pescoso with abundant supplies of fish

peso m weight; ~ **netto** net weight; **di nessun** ~ of no importance, unimportant; **a** ~ by weight; fig **non voglio essere un** ~ **per te** I don't want to be a burden to you

pessimismo m pessimism

pessimista 1 agg pessimistic **2** m/f (mpl -i) pessimist

pessimistico (pl -ci) pessimistic

pessimo very bad, terrible

pestaggio m (pl -ggi) F going-over F

pestare <1a> carne, prezzemolo pound; con piede step on; (picchiare) beat up

peste f plague; persona pest

pesticida m (pl -ci) pesticide

pesto m pesto, paste of basil, olive oil and pine nuts

petalo m petal

petardo m banger

petizione f petition

peto m F fart F

petroliera f (oil) tanker

petrolifero oil attr

petrolio m oil, petroleum, ~ **greggio** crude

pettegolare <1m> gossip

pettegolezzo m piece or item of gossip

pettegolo 1 agg gossipy **2** m, **-a** f gossip

P

pettinare <ll & b> comb

pettinarsi comb one's hair

pettinatura *f* hairstyle, hairdo

pettine *m* comb

pettirosso *m* robin

petto *m* chest; (*seno*) breast; **~ di pollo** chicken breast; **a doppio ~** double-breasted

pezza *f* cloth; (*toppa*) patch

pezzo *m* piece; *di motore* part; **da / per un ~** for a long time; **due -i** bikini; **~ di ricambio** spare (part); *fig* **~ grosso** big shot; **andare in -i** break into pieces; **in -i da cento mila lire** in denominations of one hundred thousand lira

ph *m* pH

piacente attractive

piacere 1 *v/i* <2k>: **le piace il vino?** do you like wine?; **non mi piace il cioccolato** I don't like chocolate; **non mi piacciono i tuoi amici** I don't like your friends; **mi piacerebbe saperlo** I'd really like to know; **faccio come mi pare e piace** I do as I please **2** *m* pleasure; (*favore*) favo(u)r; **~!** pleased to meet you!; **viaggio** *m* **di ~** pleasure trip; **aver ~ di** be delighted to; **mi fa ~** I'm happy to; **con ~** with pleasure; **per ~** please; **serviti a ~** take as much as you like

piacevole pleasant

piacimento *m*: **a ~** as much as you like

piaga *f* (*pl* -ghe) (*ferita*) wound; *fig* scourge; **agitare il coltello nella ~** rub salt into the wound

pialla *f* plane

piallare <1a> plane

piana *f* plain

pianerottolo *m* landing

pianeta *m* planet

piangere <3d> **1** *v/i* cry, weep **2** *v/t* mourn

pianificare <1m & d> plan

pianificazione *f* planning

pianista *m/f* (*mpl* -i) pianist

piano 1 *agg* flat **2** *avv* (*adagio*) slowly; (*a voce bassa*) quietly, in a low voice **3** *m* plan; (*pianura*) plane;

di edificio floor; MUS piano; **~ rialzato** mezzanine (floor); **primo ~** foreground; PHOT close-up

pianoforte *m* piano; **~ a coda** grand piano

pianta *f* plant; *di città* map; *del piede* sole; **~ di appartamento** house plant; **~ medicinale** medicinal plant; **di sana ~** from start to finish

piantare <1a> plant; *chiodo* hammer in; F **piantala!** cut that out! F; F **~ qu** dump s.o. F; **~ grane** make difficulties

piantarsi F: **si sono piantati** they've split up F

pianterreno *m* ground floor, *Am* first floor

pianto 1 *pp* → **piangere 2** *m* crying, weeping; (*lacrime*) tears

pianura *f* plain

piastra *f* plate

piastrella *f* tile

piattaforma *f* platform; **~ di lancio** launch pad

piattino *m* saucer

piatto 1 *agg* flat **2** *m* plate; GASTR dish; MUS **-i** *pl* cymbals; **~ forte** main course; **~ fondo** soup plate; **~ nazionale** national dish; **~ piano** flat plate; **primo ~** first course; **~ del giorno** day's special

piazza *f* square; COM market(place); *fig* **fare ~ pulita** make a clean sweep

piazzale *m* large square; *in autostrada* toll-booth area

piazzare <1a> place, put; (*vendere*) sell

piazzista *m/f* salesman; *donna* saleswoman

piazzola *f* small square; **~ di sosta** layby

piccante spicy, hot

picchiare <1a> beat

picchiata *f* AVIA nosedive

picchio *m* (*pl* -cchi); ZO woodpecker

piccionaia *f* TEA gods

piccione *m* pigeon; **~ viaggiatore** carrier pigeon; **prendere due -i con una fava** kill two birds with one stone

picco *m* (*pl* -cchi) peak; MAR **colare**

a ~ sink

piccolezza *f* smallness; (*inezia*) trifle; *fig* pettiness, small-mindedness

piccolo 1 *agg* small, little; *di statura* short; *meschino* petty **2** *m*, *-a f* child; **la gatta con i suoi** *-i* the cat and her young; *da* ~ as a child; *fin da* ~ since I/he was a child

piccozza *f* ice ax(e)

picnic *m inv* picnic; *fare un* ~ have a picnic, picnic

pidocchio *m* (*pl* -cchi) louse

piede *m* foot; *-i pi piatti* flat feet; P cops P, flatfoots P; *a* -i on foot; *su due -i* suddenly; *stare in* -i stand; *a* ~ *libero* at large; *a -i nudi* barefoot, with bare feet

piedistallo *m* pedestal

piega *f* (*pl* -ghe) wrinkle; *di pantaloni* crease; *di gonna* pleat; *a* -*ghe gonna* pleated

piegare <1b & e> **1** *v/t* bend; (*ripiegare*) fold **2** *v/i* bend

piegarsi bend; *fig* ~ *a* comply with

pieghevole *sedia* folding

Piemonte *m* Piedmont

piemontese *agg, m/f* Piedmontese

piena *f* flood; *a teatro* full house

pienezza *f* fullness

pieno 1 *agg* full (*di* of); (*non cavo*) solid; *in* ~ *giorno* in broad daylight; *in -a notte* in the middle of the night **2** *m: nel* ~ *dell'inverno* in the depths of winter; *AUTO fare il* ~ fill up

pietà *f* pity (*di* for); *PITT* pietà; *avere* ~ *di qu* take pity on s.o.; *senza* ~ pitiless, merciless

pietanza *f* dish

pietoso pitiful; (*compassionevole*) merciful

pietra *f* stone; ~ *focaia* flint; ~ *preziosa* precious stone; ~ *miliare* milestone (*anche fig*)

pietrina *f* flint

pietroso stony

pigiama *m* pyjamas *pl*, PJs F

pigiare <1f> crush

pigione *f* rent

pigliare <1g> catch; ~ *fiato* catch

one's breath

pigmeo *m*, *-a f* pygmy

pigna *f* pinecone

pignolo pedantic, nit-picking F

pignoramento *m* distraint

pignorare <1a> distrain

pigrizia *f* laziness

pigro lazy

PIL *abbr* (= *prodotto interno lordo*) GDP (= gross domestic product)

pila *f* EL battery; (*catasta*) pile, heap

pilastro *m* pillar

pillola *f* pill; ~ (*anticoncezionale*) pill; *prendere la* ~ be on the pill

pilone *m* pier; EL pylon

pilota (*pl* -*i*) **1** *m/f* AVIA, MAR pilot; ~ *automatico* automatic pilot **2** *agg* pilot *attr*

pilotare <1c> pilot; AUTO drive

pinacoteca *f* (*pl* -che) art gallery

pineta *f* pine forest

ping-pong *m* table tennis, ping-pong

pinna *f di pesce* fin; SP flipper

pino *m* pine

pinolo *m* pine nut

pinza *f* pliers *pl*; MED forceps *pl*

pinzare <1a> staple

pinzatrice *f* stapler

pinzette *fpl* tweezers

pio pious

pioggerella *f* drizzle

pioggia *f* (*pl* -gge) rain; ~ *acida* acid rain

piombare <1a> **1** *v/t dente* fill **2** *v/i* fall; *precipitarsi* rush (*su* at); *mi è piombato in casa* he dropped in unexpectedly

piombatura *f di dente* filling

piombino *m* sinker

piombo *m* lead; *a* ~ plumb; *con* / *senza* ~ *benzina* leaded / unleaded; *fig andare con i piedi di* ~ tread carefully

pioniere *m*, *-a f* pioneer

pioppo *m* poplar

piovere <3kk> rain; *piove a dirotto* it's raining cats and dogs

piovigginare <1m> drizzle

piovigginoso drizzly

piovoso rainy

piovra *f* octopus

P

pipa f pipe; **fumare la** ~ smoke a pipe

pipì f F pee F; F **fare la** ~ go for a pee F

pipistrello m bat

piramide f pyramid

pirata m (pl -i) pirate; ~ **dell'aria** hijacker; ~ **della strada** hit-and-run driver; (guidatore spericolato) roadhog

pirofila f oven-proof dish

piroscafo m steamer, steamship

pirotecnica f fireworks pl

pirotecnico (pl -ci) fireworks attr

pisciare <1f> P piss P

piscina f (swimming) pool; ~ **coperta** indoor pool

pisello m pea

pisolino m nap

pista f di atletica track; di circo ring; (traccia) trail; di autostrada toll-lane; ~ **d'atterraggio** runway; ~ **da ballo** dance floor; ~ **da sci** ski slope; ~ **da sci da fondo** cross country ski trail; ~ **ciclabile** bike path

pistacchio m (pl -cchi) pistachio

pistola f pistol; ~ **ad acqua** water pistol; ~ **automatica** automatic (pistol); ~ **a spruzzo** spray gun

pistone m piston

pittore m, **-trice** f painter

pittoresco (pl -chi) picturesque

pittura f painting

pitturare <1a> paint

più 1 avv more (**di, che** than); superlativo most; MAT plus; ~ **grande** bigger; **il ~ grande** the biggest; **di ~** more; **non** ~ no more; tempo no longer; ~ **o meno** more or less; **per di** ~ what's more; **mai** ~ never again; **al ~ presto** as soon as possible; **al ~ tardi** at the latest **2** agg more; superlativo most; ~ **volte** several times **3** m most; MAT plus sign; **per lo** ~ mainly; **i ~, le** ~ the majority

piuma f feather

piumaggio m plumage

piumino m down; giacca down jacket

piumone m Continental quilt, duvet

piuttosto rather

pizza f pizza

pizzaiolo m pizza maker

pizzeria f pizzeria, pizza parlo(u)r

pizzicare <1l & d> **1** v/t braccio, persona pinch; F ladro catch (redhanded), nick F **2** v/i pinch

pizzico m (pl -chi) pinch

pizzicotto m pinch

pizzo m (merletto) lace

placare <1d> placate; dolore ease

placca f (pl -cche) plate; (targhetta) plaque; ~ **dentaria** plaque

placcare <1d> plate; nel rugby tackle; **placcato d'oro** gold-plated

placido placid

planare <1a> glide

planata f: **fare una** ~ glide

plancia f bridge; (passerella) gangway, gangplank

planetario (pl -ri) **1** agg planetary **2** m planetarium

plasma m plasma; ~ **sanguigno** blood plasma

plasmabile malleable

plasmare <1a> mo(u)ld

plastica f plastic; MED plastic surgery; **posate** fpl **di** ~ plastic cutlery

plastico (pl -ci) **1** agg plastic **2** m ARCHI scale model; **esplosivo** m **al** ~ plastic bomb

plastilina® f Plasticine®

platano m plane (tree)

platea f TEA stalls

platino m platinum

plausibile plausible

plenilunio m (pl -ni) full moon

pletora f fig plethora

plettro m plectrum

pleurite f pleurisy

plico m (pl -chi) envelope; **in ~ separato** under separate cover

plurale m/agg plural

pluripartitico (pl -ci) multiparty

plusvalore m capital gains; **tassa** f **sul** ~ capital gains tax

plutonio m plutonium

pneumatico (pl -ci) **1** agg pneumatic **2** m tyre, Am tire; **-i da neve** pl snow tyres (Am tires)

PNL abbr (= **prodotto nazionale lordo**) GNP (= gross national product)

po¹: *un* ~ a little (*di* sth), a little bit (*di* of); *un bel* ~ quite a lot

poco (*pl* -chi) **1** *agg* little; *con nomi plurali* few **2** *avv* not much; *con aggettivi* not very, not greatly; *senti un po'!* just listen!; *a* ~ *a* ~ little by little, gradually; ~ *fa* a little while ago; *fra* ~ in a little while, soon; ~ *dopo* a little while later, soon after; *per* ~ cheap; (*quasi*) almost, nearly

podere *m* farm

podio *m* (*pl* -di) podium, dais; MUS podium

podismo *m* walking

poesia *f* poetry; *componimento* poem

poeta *m* (*pl* -i), **-essa** *f* poet

poetico (*pl* -ci) poetic

poggiare <1f & c> lean; (*posare*) put, place

poggiarsi ~ *a* lean on

poggiatesta *m inv* head rest

poggio *m* (*pl* -ggi) mound

poi *avv* then; *d'ora in* ~ from now on; *questa* ~! well I'm blowed!; *dalle 6 in* ~ from 6 o'clock on(wards); *prima o* ~ sooner or later

poiché since

poker *m* poker

polacco (*pl* -cchi) **1** *m/agg* Polish **2** *m*, **-a** *f* Pole

polare Polar; *circolo* *m* ~ *artico* / *antartico* Arctic / Antarctic circle

polarizzare <1a> polarize

polemica *f* (*pl* -che) argument; *fare* **-che** argue

polemico (*pl* -ci) argumentative

polemizzare <1a> argue

polenta *f* polenta, *kind of porridge made from cornmeal*

policlinico *m* (*pl* -ci) general hospital

poliglotta **1** *agg* multilingual **2** *m/f* polyglot

poligono *m* MAT polygon; MIL ~ *di tiro* firing range

polio *f* F polio F

poliomielite *f* poliomyelitis

polipo *m* polyp

politica *f* politics; (*strategia*) policy; ~ *estera* foreign policy; ~ *interna* domestic policy; ~ *sanitaria* health policy

politico (*pl* -ci) **1** *agg* political **2** *m*, **-a** *f* politician

polizia *f* police; ~ *ferroviaria* transport police; ~ *stradale* (o *della strada*) traffic police, *Am* highway patrol; *agente* *m di* ~ police officer

poliziesco (*pl* -chi) police *attr*; *romanzo* *m* ~ detective story

poliziotto **1** *m* policeman **2** *agg*: *donna* *f* -a policewoman; *cane* *m* ~ police dog

polizza *f* policy; ~ *di assicurazione* insurance policy

pollame *m* poultry

pollice *m* thumb; *unità di misura* inch

polline *m* pollen

pollo *m* chicken; ~ *arrosto* roast chicken

polmonare pulmonary

polmone *m* lung

polmonite *f* pneumonia

polo¹ *m* GEOG pole; ~ *nord* North Pole; ~ *sud* South Pole

polo² **1** *m* SP polo **2** *f inv* polo shirt

Polonia *f* Poland

polpa *f* flesh; *di manzo, vitello* meat

polpaccio *m* (*pl* -cci) calf

polpastrello *m* fingertip

polpetta *f di carne* meatball

polpettone *m* meat loaf

polpo *m* octopus

polposo fleshy

polsino *m* cuff

polso *m* ANAT wrist; *di camicia* cuff; *pulsazione* pulse; *tastare il* ~ *a qu* take s.o.'s pulse

poltiglia *f* mush

poltrire <4d> laze around

poltrona *f* armchair; TEA stall (seat)

poltrone *m*, **-a** *f* lazybones

polvere *f* dust; (*sostanza polverizzata*) powder; *caffè* *m in* ~ instant coffee; *latte* *m in* ~ powdered milk

polverina *f* powder

polverizzare <1a> crush, pulverize; *fig* pulverize

polveroso dusty

pomata *f* cream

pomello *m* cheek; *di porta* knob

P

pomeridiano afternoon *attr*; **alle tre -e** at three in the afternoon, at three pm

pomeriggio *m* (*pl* -ggi) afternoon; **di ~, nel ~** in the afternoon; **domani ~** tomorrow afternoon

pomice *f* agg: (**pietra** *f*) ~ pumice (stone)

pomo *m* knob; ~ **d'Adamo** Adam's apple

pomodoro *m* tomato

pompa[1] *f* pomp; **impresa** *f* **di -e funebri** undertaker's, *Am* mortician

pompa[2] *f* TEC pump

pompelmo *m* grapefruit

pompiere *m* firefighter, *Br* fireman; **-i** *pl* firefighters, *Br* fire brigade

pomposo pompous

ponderare <1l & c> ponder

ponderato *decisione, scelta* carefully considered; *persona* reflective

pone → **porre**

ponente *m* west

pongo → **porre**

ponte *m* bridge; ARCHI scaffolding; MAR deck; ~ **girevole** swing bridge; ~ **sospeso** suspension bridge; ~ **radio** radio link; ~ **aereo** airlift; **fare il ~** have a four-day weekend

pontefice *m* pontiff

ponteggio *m* scaffolding

ponticello *m* MUS bridge

pontificio (*pl* -ci) papal; **Stato** *m* ~ Papal States *pl*

pontile *m* jetty

pop: **musica** *f* ~ pop (music)

popolamento *m di città, Stato* population

popolare 1 *agg* popular; *quartiere* working-class; **ballo** *m* ~ folk dance **2** *v/t* <1l>populate

popolarità *f* popularity

popolato populated; (*abitato*) inhabited; (*pieno*) crowded

popolazione *f* population

popolo *m* people

poppa *f* MAR stern

porcellana *f* porcelain, china

porcellino *m* piglet; ~ **d'India** guinea-pig

porcheria *f* disgusting thing; *fig* **una**

~ filth; **mangiare -e** eat junk food

porchetta *f* suckling pig roasted whole in the oven

porcile *m* pigsty, *Am* pigpen

porcino *m* cep

porco *m* (*pl* -chi) pig

porcospino *m* porcupine

porgere <3d> *mano, oggetto* hold out; *aiuto, saluto ecc* proffer

porno F **1** *agg* porn(o) F **2** *m* porn F

pornografia *f* pornography

pornografico (*pl* -ci) pornographic

poro *m* pore

poroso porous

porre <3ll> place, put; ~ **una domanda** ask a question; **poniàmo che ...** let's suppose (that) ...

porro *m* leek; MED wart

porta *f* door; ~ **scorrevole** sliding door; **a -e chiuse** behind closed doors

portabagagli *m inv* luggage rack; AUTO roof rack

portacenere *m inv* ashtray

portachiavi *m inv* keyring

portacipria *m inv* powder compact

portafinestra *f* (*pl* portefinestre) French window

portafoglio *m* (*pl* -gli) wallet

portafortuna *m inv* good luck charm, talisman

portale *m* door

portalettere *m/f inv* → **postino**

portamento *m* bearing

portamonete *m inv* purse

portaombrelli *m inv* umbrella stand

portapacchi *m inv di macchina* roof rack; *di bicicletta* carrier

portapenne *m inv* pencil case

portare <1c> (*trasportare*) carry; (*accompagnare*) take; (*avere adosso*) wear; (*condurre*) lead; ~ **via** take away; **mi ha portato un regalo** he brought me a present; **portale un regalo** take her a present; ~ **in tavola** serve; **essere portato per qc/per fare qc** have a gift for sth/ for doing sth; ~ **fortuna** be lucky; **porta bene i propri anni** he doesn't look his age

portasci *m inv* AUTO ski rack

portasigarette *m inv* cigarette case

portata *f* GASTR course; *di danni* extent; TEC *di camion* load capacity; *di cannocchiale* range; *alla ~ di* film, *libro ecc* suitable for; *a ~ di mano* within reach

portatile portable; *computer m ~* portable (computer); *radio f ~* portable (radio); *telefono m ~* mobile (phone), *Am* cell(ular) phone; *farmacia f ~* first-aid kit

portatore *m*, **-trice** *f* bearer; *di malattia* carrier

portauovo *m inv* eggcup

portavoce *m/f inv* spokesperson

portico *m (pl -ci)* porch; *-i pl* arcades

portiera *f* door

portiere *m* doorman; *(portinaio)* caretaker; SP goalkeeper, goalie F

portinaio *m (pl -ai)*, **-a** *f* caretaker

portineria *f* caretaker's flat (*Am* apartment)

porto¹ *pp →* **porgere**

porto² *m* posta postage; *~ d'armi* gun licence (*Am* license)

porto³ *m* MAR port; *~ d'imbarco* port of embarkation

Portogallo *m* Portugal

portoghese *agg*, *m/f* Portuguese

portone *m* main entrance

porzione *f* share; GASTR portion

posa *f* di cavi, tubi laying; FOT exposure; FOT *mettersi in ~* pose

posacenere *m inv* ashtray

posare <1c> **1** *v/t* put, place **2** *v/i* (*stare in posa*) pose; *~ su* rest on; *fig ~ da intellettuale* pose as an intellectual

posarsi alight

posate *fpl* cutlery *sg*

posato composed

positivo positive

posizione *f* position; *~ chiave* key position

possedere <2o> own, possess

possedimento *m* possession

possessivo possessive

possesso *m* possession

possessore *m* owner, possessor

possiamo → **potere**

possibile **1** *agg* possible; *il più*

presto ~ as soon as possible **2** *m*: *fare il ~* do everything one can, do one's best

possibilità *f inv* possibility; (*occasione*) opportunity, chance; *~ di guadagno* earning potential

possibilmente if possible, if I/you *etc* can

posso → **potere**

posta *f* mail, *Br* post; (*ufficio postale*) post office; *~ aerea* airmail; *per ~* by post; *a giro di ~* by return of post; INFOR *~ elettronica* e-mail; *fermo ~* poste restante

postale postal; *servizio m ~* postal service; *cartolina f ~* postcard

postdatare <1a> postdate

posteggiare <1f> park

posteggio *m (pl -ggi)* carpark; *~ dei taxi* taxi rank

posteriore back *attr*, rear *attr*; (*successivo*) later; *sedile m ~* back seat

posticipare <1m> postpone

posticipato: *pagamento m ~* payment in arrears

postino *m*, **-a** *f* postman, *Am* mailman; *donna* postwoman, *Am* mailwoman

posto¹ *pp →* **porre**; *~ che* supposing that

posto² *m* place; (*lavoro*) job, position; *mettere a ~ stanza* tidy (up); *la tua camera è a ~?* is your room tidy?; *~ macchina* parking space; *~ finestrino / corridoio* window / aisle seat; *ho trovato solo un ~ in piedi* I had to stand; *~ a sedere* seat; *~ di guardia* guard post; INFOR *~ di lavoro* workstation; *~ di polizia* police station; *~ di pronto soccorso* first aid post; *~ di villeggiatura* holiday resort; *vado io al ~ tuo* I'll go in your place, I'll go instead of you; *fuori ~* out of place

postoperatorio *(pl -ri)* postoperative

postumo posthumous

potabile fit to drink; *acqua f ~* drinking water

potare <1a> prune

potassio *m* potassium

P

potente powerful; (*efficace*) potent

potenza *f* power; ~ **mondiale** world power; ~ **del motore** engine power

potenziare <1a> strengthen

potere 1 *v/i* <2l> can, be able to; **non posso andare** I can't go; **non ho potuto farlo** I couldn't do it, I was unable to do it; **posso fumare?** do you mind if I smoke?; *formale* may I smoke?; **può essere** perhaps, maybe; ~**può darsi** perhaps, maybe **2** *m* power; ~ **d'acquisto** purchasing power; **essere al** ~ be in power

poveraccio *m* (*pl* -cci), **-a** *f* poor thing, poor creature

poveretto *m*, **poverino** *m* poor man

povero 1 *agg* poor **2** *m*, **-a** *f* poor man; *donna* poor woman; **i -i** *pl* the poor

povertà *f* poverty

pozzanghera *f* puddle

pozzo *m* well; ~ **petrolifero** oil well

pp. *abbr* (= **pagine**) pp (= pages)

p.p. *abbr* (= **per procura**) pp (= for, on behalf of); (= **pacco postale**) small parcel

PP.TT. *abbr* (= **Poste e Telecomunicazioni**) Italian Post Office

pranzare <1a> *a mezzogiorno* have lunch; *la sera* have dinner

pranzo *m a mezzogiorno* lunch; *la sera* dinner

prassi *f inv* standard procedure

prataiolo *m* field mushroom

pratica *f* (*pl* -che) practice; (*esperienza*) experience; (*atto*) file; **mettere in** ~ put into practice; **fare** ~ gain experience, become more experienced; **-che** *pl* papers, documents; **fare le -che necessarie per qc** take the necessary steps for sth; **fare le -che per** *passaporto* gather together the necessary documentation for; **in** ~ in practice; **avere** ~ **di qc** have experience of sth

praticabile *sport* which can be practised; *strada* passable

praticantato *m* apprenticeship

praticare <1l & d> *virtù, pazienza* show; *professione, sport* practise;

locale frequent; ~ **molto sport** do a lot of sport

pratico (*pl* -ci) practical; **essere** ~ **di conoscere bene** know a lot about

prato *m* meadow

preavviso *m* notice

precario (*pl* -ri) precarious

precauzione *f* caution; **-i** *pl* precautions

precedente 1 *agg* preceding **2** *m* precedent; **avere dei -i penali** have a record

precedenza *f* precedence; AUTO **diritto** *m* **di** ~ right of way; **avere la** ~ have precedence; AUTO **have right of way**; **dare la** ~ give priority; AUTO give way

precedere <3a> precede

precipitare <1m> **1** *v/t* throw; *fig* rush **2** *v/i* fall, plunge

precipitarsi (*affrettarsi*) rush

precipitazione *f* (*fretta*) haste, hurry; **-i** *pl* **atmosferiche** atmospheric precipitation *sg*

precipitoso hasty

precipizio *m* (*pl* -zi) precipice

precisamente precisely

precisare <1a> specify

precisione *f* precision, accuracy; **con** ~ precisely

preciso accurate; *persona* precise; **alle tre -e** at three o'clock exactly *o* precisely, at three o'clock sharp

precoce precocious; *pianta* early

precotto *m* ready-made, pre-cooked

preda *f* prey; **in** ~ **alla disperazione** in despair

predecessore *m*, **-a** *f* predecessor

predestinare <1a> predestine

predica *f* (*pl* -che) sermon

predicare <1l, b & d> preach

prediletto 1 *pp* → **prediligere 2** *agg* favo(u)rite

predilezione *f* predilection

prediligere <3u> prefer

predire <3t> predict

predisporre <3ll> draw up in advance; ~ **a** encourage, promote

predisposto *pp* → **predisporre**

predominare <1m & c> predominate

predominio *m* (*pl* -ni) predominance

prefabbricato 1 *agg* prefabricated **2** *m* prefabricated building

prefazione *f* preface

preferenza *f* preference

preferenziale preferential

preferire <4d> prefer

preferito favo(u)rite

prefetto *m* prefect

prefettura *f* prefecture

prefiggersi <3mm> set o.s.

prefisso 1 *pp* → **prefiggersi 2** *m* TELEC code

pregare <1b & e> beg (*di fare* to do); *divinità* pray to; *ti prego di ascoltarmi* please listen to me; *farsi ~* be coaxed; *prego* please; *prego?* I'm sorry (what did you say)?; *grazie! – prego!* thank you! – you're welcome! *or* not at all!

preghiera *f* request; REL prayer

pregiato *metallo, pietra* precious

pregio *m* (*qualità*) good point

pregiudicato *m*, **-a** *f* previous offender

pregiudizio *m* (*pl* -zi) prejudice

preg.mo *abbr* (= **pregiatissimo**) formal style of address used in correspondence

pregustare <1a> look forward to

preistoria *f* prehistory

preistorico (*pl* -ci) prehistoric

prelato *m* REL prelate

prelavaggio *m* pre-wash

prelevamento *m di sangue, campione* taking; FIN withdrawal; **~ in contanti** cash withdrawal

prelevare <1b> *sangue, campione* take; *denaro* withdraw

prelibato exquisite

prelievo *m* (*prelevamento*) taking; FIN withdrawal; **~ del sangue** blood sample

pre-maman 1 *agg* maternity *attr* **2** *m inv* maternity dress

prematrimoniale premarital

prematuro premature

premeditato premeditated

premere <3a> **1** *v/t* press **2** *v/i* press (*su* on); *mi preme che* it is

important to me that

premessa *f* introduction

premesso *pp* → **premettere**

premettere <3ee> say first

premiare <1k & b> give an award *or* prize to; *onestà, coraggio* reward

premiato prize-winning, award-winning

premiazione *f* award ceremony

premio *m* (*pl* -mi) prize, award; FIN premium; **~ Nobel per la pace** Nobel peace prize; **assegnare un ~** award a prize

premura *f* (*fretta*) hurry, rush; *essere pieno di -e nei confronti di qu* be very attentive to s.o.; *mettere ~ a qu* hurry s.o. along; *non c'è ~* there's no hurry *o* rush

premuroso attentive

prenatale prenatal

prendere <3c> **1** *v/t* take; *malattia, treno* catch; *cosa prendi?* what will you have?; **~ qu per un italiano** take *or* mistake s.o. for an Italian; *andare / venire a ~ qu* fetch s.o.; **~ fuoco** catch fire; **~ il sole** sunbathe; **~ paura** take fright, get frightened; AVIA **~ quota** gain height; **~ in giro qu** pull s.o.'s leg; *prendersela* get upset (*per* about; *con* with); *che ti prende?* what's got into you? **2** *v/i* **~ a destra** turn right

prendisole *m inv* sundress

prenotare <1c> book, reserve

prenotato booked, reserved

prenotazione *f* booking, reservation

preoccupare <1m & c> worry, preoccupy

preoccuparsi worry

preoccupato worried, preoccupied

preoccupazione *f* worry

preparare <1a> prepare

prepararsi get ready (*a* to), prepare (*a* to)

preparativi *mpl* preparations

preparato 1 *agg* ready, prepared **2** *m* preparation

preparazione *f* preparation

preposizione *f* preposition

prepotente domineering; *bisogno* pressing

prepotenza f di persona domineering nature; di bisogno pressing nature

presa f grip, hold; **abbandonare la ~** let go; **fare una ~ presso corriere** call a courier; EL **~ di corrente** socket; fig **~ di possesso** conquest, capture; **essere alle -e con qc** be grappling with sth

presagio m (pl -gi) omen, sign

presalario m scholarship

presbite far-sighted, long-sighted

prescindere <3v>: **~ da** have nothing to do with, not be connected with

prescritto pp → **prescrivere**

prescrivere <3tt> prescribe

prescrizione f prescription

presentare <1b> documenti, biglietto show, present; domanda submit; scuse make; TEA present; (contenere) contain; (far conoscere) introduce (a to)

presentarsi look; (esporre) show itself; occasione present itself, occur

presentatore m, **-trice** f presenter

presentazione f presentation; di richiesta submission; **fare le -i** make the introductions

presente 1 agg present; **hai ~ il negozio … ?** do you know the shop … ? **2** m present; GRAM present (tense); **i -i** pl those present, those in attendance

presentimento m premonition

presenza f presence; **alla** (o **in**) **~ di** in the presence of; **di bella ~** fine-looking

presepe m

presepio m (pl -pi) crèche

preservare <1b> protect, keep (da from)

preservativo m condom

presidente m/f chairman; POL **Presidente dello Stato** President; **~ del Consiglio** (**dei ministri**) Prime Minister

presidenza f chairmanship; POL presidency

preso pp → **prendere**

pressappoco more or less

pressare <1b> crush; TEC press

pressione f pressure; **~ atmosferica** atmospheric pressure; **~ delle gomme** tyre pressure; **~ sanguigna** blood pressure; fig **far ~ su** put pressure on, pressure

presso 1 prp (vicino a) near; **nella sede di** on the premises of; posta care of; **vive ~ i genitori** he lives with his parents; **lavoro ~ la FIAT** I work for Fiat **2** m: **nei -i di** in the vicinity of, in the neighbo(u)rhood of

pressoché almost

prestare <1b> lend; **~ ascolto** / **aiuto a qu** listen to / help s.o.; **~ un servizio** provide a service

prestarsi offer one's services; (essere adatto) lend itself (a to)

prestatore m di servizio provider

prestazione f service

prestigio m prestige

prestito m loan; **in ~** on loan; **dare in ~** lend; **prendere in ~** borrow

presto (fra poco) soon; (in fretta) quickly; (di buon'ora) early; **a ~!** see you soon!; **far ~** be quick

presumere <3h> presume

presuntuoso presumptuous

presunzione f presumption

prete m priest

pretendente m/f claimant

pretendere <3c> claim

pretensioso pretentious

pretesa f pretension; **avanzare -e** put forward claims; **senza -e** unpretentious

pretesto m pretext

pretore m magistrate

pretura f magistrates' court

prevalenza f prevalence; **in ~** prevalently

prevalere <2r> prevail

prevedere <2s> foresee, predict; tempo forecast; di legge provide for

prevedibile predictable

prevendita f advance sale

prevenire <4p> domanda, desiderio anticipate; (evitare) prevent

preventivo 1 agg preventive **2** m estimate

prevenzione f prevention

previdente foresighted

previdenza f foresight; **~ sociale** social security, Am welfare

previsione f forecast; **-i** pl **del tempo** weather forecast sg

previsto pp → **prevedere**

prezioso precious

prezzemolo m parsley

prezzo m price; **~ di listino** recommended retail price; **~ promozionale** special introductory price; **aumento** m **del ~** price increase; **a buon ~** cheap; fig **a caro ~** dearly; **a metà ~** half-price; **a qualunque ~** at any cost; **~ netto** net price

prigione f prison

prigionia f imprisonment

prigioniero m, **-a** f prisoner; **fare ~** take prisoner

prima¹ avv before; (in primo luogo) first; **~ di** before; **~ di fare qc** before doing sth; **o poi** sooner or later; **~ che** before; **quanto ~** as soon as possible

prima² f FERR first class; AUTO first gear; TEA first night

primario (pl -ri) prime

primavera f spring

primaverile spring attr

primitivo primitive; (iniziale) original

primizia f early crop

primo 1 agg first; **~ piano** m first floor; **in -a visione** film just out **2** m, **-a** f first; **ai -i del mese** at the beginning of the month; **sulle -e** in the beginning, at first **3** m GASTR first course, starter

primogenito 1 agg first-born **2** m, **-a** f first-born

principale 1 agg main **2** m boss

principato m principality

principe m prince

principessa f princess

principiante m/f beginner

principio m (pl -pi) (inizio) start, beginning; (norma) principle; **al ~** at the start, in the beginning; **da ~** from the start or beginning or outset; **per ~** as a matter of principle; **in**

linea di ~ in theory

privare <1a> deprive (**di** of)

privarsi deprive o.s. (**di** of)

privatizzare <1a> privatize

privato 1 agg private; **in ~** in private **2** m private citizen

privazione f deprivation; (sacrificio) privation

privilegiare <1f> favo(u)r, prefer

privilegiato privileged

privilegio m (pl -gi) privilege

privo: ~ di lacking in, devoid of; **~ di sensi** unconscious

pro 1 m inv **i ~ e i contro** the pros and cons; **a che ~?** what's the point or use? **2** prp for; **~ capite** per capita, each

probabile probable

probabilità f inv probability

problema m (pl -i) problem

problematico (pl -ci) problematic

proboscide f trunk

procedere <3a> carry on; fig (agire) proceed; DIR **~ contro qu** take legal proceedings against s.o.

procedimento m process

procedura f procedure; DIR proceedings pl

processare <1b> try

processione f procession

processo m process; DIR trial; **~ civile** civil proceedings; **~ di fabbricazione** manufacturing process; **~ verbale** minutes pl; **essere sotto ~** be on trial

processuale DIR trial attr

procinto m: **essere in ~ di** be about to, be on the point of

proclamare <1a> proclaim

proclamazione f proclamation

procura f power of attorney; **Procura di Stato** public prosecutor's office; **per ~** by proxy

procurare <1a> (causare) cause; **~ qc a qu** cause s.o. sth

procurarsi get hold of, obtain

procuratore m, **-trice** f person with power of attorney; DIR lawyer for the prosecution; **~ generale** Attorney General

prodigio m (pl -gi) prodigy

prodigioso 202

prodigioso tremendous, prodigious
prodotto 1 pp → **produrre** 2 m
product; *-i pl alimentari* foodstuffs;
-i pl farmaceutici pharmaceuticals;
~ finito finished product; *~ interno /
nazionale lordo* gross domestic /
national product; *-i pl di bellezza*
cosmetics
produco → **produrre**
produrre <3e> produce; *danni* cause
produttività f productivity
produttivo productive
produttore m, -trice f producer
produzione f production; *~ giorna-
liera* daily production or output; *~
in serie* mass production
prof. *abbr* (= **professore**) Prof. (=
Professor)
profanare <1a> desecrate
profano 1 agg profane 2 m fig: *sono
un ~ di* I know nothing about
professionale *esperienza, impegno*
professional; *scuola, corso* vocational
professione f profession; *~ di fede*
profession of faith; *calciatore m di
~* professional footballer
professionista m/f (mpl -i) professional, pro F; *libero ~* self-employed
person
professore m, -essa f teacher; *d'università* professor
profeta m (pl -i) prophet
profezia f prophecy
proficuo profitable
profilassi f inv prophylaxis
profilattico (pl -ci) prophylactic
profilo m profile
profitto m (*vantaggio*) advantage;
FIN *conto -i e perdite* profit and
loss account
profondità f inv depth; FOT *~ di campo* depth of field
profondo deep
prof. ssa *abbr* (= **professoressa**)
Prof. (= Professor)
profugo m (pl -ghi), -a f refugee
profumare <1a> perfume, scent
profumatamente: *pagare ~* pay
through the nose, pay a fortune
profumeria f perfume shop

profumo m perfume
progettare <1b> plan
progettazione f design
progetto m design; *di costruzione*
project; *~ pilota* pilot project; *~ di
legge* bill
prognosi f inv prognosis
programma m (pl -i) programme,
Am program; INFOR program; *~
applicativo* application; *~ di scrittura* word processor; *~ televisivo*
TV program(me); *fuori ~* unsched-
uled; *avere in ~ qualcosa* have
something planned
programmare <1a> plan; INFOR
program
programmatore m, -trice f pro-
grammer
programmazione f programming;
FIN *~ economica* economic planning; INFOR *linguaggio m di ~* programming language
progredire <4d> progress
progredito advanced
progressione f progression
progressivo progressive
progresso m progress; *fare -i* make
progress
proibire <4d> ban, prohibit; *~ a qu di
fare qc* forbid s.o. to do sth
proibizione f ban
proiettare <1b> throw; *film* screen,
show; *fig* project
proiettile m projectile
proiettore m projector; *~ per dia-
positive* slide projector
proiezione f projection; *di film*
screening, showing
prole f children, offspring
proletariato (pl -ri) 1 agg proletariat
2 m proletarian
pro loco f inv local tourist board
prologo m (pl -ghi) prolog(ue)
prolunga f EL extension cord
prolungamento m extension
prolungare <1e> *nel spazio* extend;
nel tempo prolong, extend
prolungarsi *di strada* extend; *di riunione* go on, continue
promemoria m inv memo
promessa f promise

promesso *pp* → **promettere**

promettente promising

promettere <3ee> promise; ~ *bene* look promising

promontorio *m* (*pl* -ri) promontory, headland

promosso *pp* → **promuovere**

promozione *f* promotion; EDU year; ~ *delle vendite* sales promotion

promuovere <3ff> promote; EDU move up

pronipote *m/f di nonni* great-grandson; *donna, ragazza* great-granddaughter; *di zii* great-nephew; *donna, ragazza* great-niece

pronome *m* pronoun

prontezza *f* readiness, promptness; (*rapidità*) speediness, promptness; ~ *di spirito* quick thinking

pronto (*preparato*) ready (*a fare qc* to do sth; *per qc* for sth); (*rapido*) speedy, prompt; TELEC ~*!* hello!; *pagamento m* -*a cassa* payment in cash, cash payment; ~ *soccorso* first aid; *in ospedale* accident and emergency, A&E; ~ *per l'uso* ready to use

pronuncia *f* pronunciation

pronunciare <1f> pronounce; *non ha pronunciato una parola* he didn't say a word

pronunciarsi give an opinion (*su* on)

pronunciato *fig* definite, pronounced

propaganda *f* propaganda; POL ~ *elettorale* electioneering

propagare <1e> propagate; *fig* spread

propagarsi spread (*anche fig*)

propano *m* propane

propenso inclined (*a fare qc* to do sth)

propizio (*pl* -zi) suitable

propongo → **proporre**

proponimento *m* resolution; *fare* ~ *di fare qc* decide *or* make up one's mind to do sth

proporre <3ll> propose

proporsi stand (*come* as); ~ *di fare qc* intend to do sth

proporzionale proportional

proporzionato in proportion (*a* to)

proporzione *f* proportion; *in* ~ in proportion (*a, con* to)

proposito *m* intention; *a che* ~*?* what about?; *a* ~ by the way; *a* ~ *di* about, with reference to; *di* ~ deliberately, on purpose; *capitare a* ~ turn up at just the right moment

proposizione *f* GRAM sentence

proposta *f* proposal

proposto *pp* → **proporre**

propriamente really

proprietà *f inv* property; *diritto* ownership; ~ *privata* private property; *essere di* ~ *di qu* belong to s.o., be s.o.'s property

proprietario *m* (*pl* -ri), -*a f* owner

proprio (*pl* -ri) **1** *agg* own; (*caratteristico*) typical; (*adatto*) proper; *nome m* ~ proper noun; *amor m* ~ pride; *a* -*e spese* at one's own expense **2** *avv* (*davvero*) really; *è* ~ *lui che me l'ha chiesto* he's the one who asked me!; *è* ~ *impossibile* that is quite impossible **3** *m* (*beni*) personal property; *lavorare in* ~ be self-employed

propulsione *f* propulsion

propulsore *m* propeller

prora *f* prow

proroga *f* (*pl* -ghe) postponement; (*prolungamento*) extension

prorogare <1l, e & c> (*rinviare*) postpone; (*prolungare*) extend

prosa *f* prose

prosciogliere <3ss> release; DIR acquit

prosciugare <1e> drain; *di sole* dry up

prosciutto *m* ham, prosciutto; ~ *cotto* cooked ham; ~ *crudo* salted air-dried ham

proseguimento *m* continuation

proseguire <4a> **1** *v/t* continue **2** *v/i* continue, carry on, go on

prosperare <1l & c> prosper

prosperità *f* prosperity

prospero prosperous

prospettiva *f* perspective; (*panorama*) view; *fig* point of view;

P

senza -e without prospects

prospetto *m disegno* elevation; (*facciata*) facade; (*tabella*) table; ~ **pubblicitario** brochure

prossimamente shortly, soon

prossimità *f inv* proximity; **in ~ di** near, close to

prossimo 1 *agg* close; **la -a volta** the next time; **il lavoro è ~ alla fine** the work is nearly finished **2** *m* fellow human being, neighbo(u)r

prostituta *f* prostitute

prostituzione *f* prostitution

protagonista *m/f* (*mpl* -i) protagonist

proteggere <3cc> protect (**da** from)

proteico protein *attr*

proteina *f* protein

protesi *f inv* prosthesis; ~ **dentaria** false teeth, dentures

protesta *f* protest

protestante *agg*, *m/f* Protestant

protestare <1b> *v/t e v/i* protest

protettivo protective

protetto *pp* → **proteggere**

protezione *f* protection; ~ **degli animali** prevention of cruelty to animals; ~ **dell'ambiente** environmental protection, protection of the environment; ~ **del paesaggio** nature conservation; ~ **delle acque** prevention of water pollution; INFOR ~ **dati** data protection

protocollare 1 *agg* official **2** *v/t* <1c> register

protocollo *m* protocol; (*registro*) register; TEC standard; **foglio** *m* ~ foolscap; **mettere a** ~ register

prototipo *m* prototype

prova *f* (*esame*) test; (*tentativo*) attempt; (*testimonianza*) proof; *di abito* fitting; SP heat; TEA **-e** *pl* rehearsal *sg*; TEA **-e** *pl* **generali** dress rehearsal *sg*; ~ **di laboratorio** lab test; **banco** *m* **di** ~ test bench; **a** ~ **di bomba** bombproof; **salvo** ~ **contraria** unless otherwise stated; **per insufficienza di -e** for lack of evidence; **mettere alla** ~ put to the test

provare <1c> test, try out; *vestito* try (on); (*dimostrare*) prove; TEA re-

hearse; ~ **a fare qc** try to do sth

provato proven; *fig* marked (**da** by)

provengo → **provenire**

provenienza *f* origin

provenire <4p> come (**da** from)

proventi *mpl* income *sg*

proverbio *m* (*pl* -i) proverb

provetta *f* test-tube; **bambino** *m* **in ~** test-tube baby

provincia *f* (*pl* -ce) province

provinciale 1 *agg* provincial; **strada** *f* ~ B road **2** *m/f* provincial **3** *f* B road

provino *m* screen-test; (*campione*) sample

provocante provocative

provocare <1l, c & d> (*causare*) cause; (*sfidare*) provoke; *invidia* arouse

provvedere <2s> **1** *v/t* provide (**di** with) **2** *v/i*: ~ **a** take care of

provvedimento *m* measure; ~ **d'urgenza** emergency measure

provvidenza *f* providence

provvigione *f* commission

provvisorio (*pl* -ri) provisional

provvista *f*: **fare -e** go (food) shopping; **far ~ di qc** stock up on sth

provvisto 1 *pp* → **provvedere 2** *agg*: **essere ~ di** be provided with, have; **essere ben ~ di** have lots of sth

prozio *m*, **-a** *f* great-uncle; *donna* great-aunt

prua *f* prow

prudente careful, cautious

prudenza *f* care, caution

prudere <3a>: **mi prude la mano** my hand itches

prugna *f* plum; ~ **secca** prune

prurito *m* itch

P.S. *abbr* (= **Pubblica Sicurezza**) police; (= **post scriptum**) PS (= post scriptum)

pseudo ... pseudo ...

pseudonimo *m* pseudonym

psicanalisi *f* psychoanalysis

psicanalista *m/f* (*mpl* -i) psychoanalyst

psiche *f* psyche

psichiatra *m/f* (*mpl* -i) psychiatrist

psichiatria *f* psychiatry

psichiatrico (*pl* -ci) psychiatric

psicologia *f* psychology
psicologico (*pl* -ci) psychological
psicologo *m* (*pl* -gi), **-a** *f* psychologist
psicosi *f inv* psychosis
psicoterapia *f* psychotherapy
P.T.P. *abbr* (= *Posto Telefonico Pubblico*) public telephone
pubblicare <1l & d> publish
pubblicazione *f* publication; **-i** *pl* **matrimoniali** banns
pubblicità *f inv* publicity, advertising; *annuncio* ad(vert); **~ televisiva** TV ad, *Br* commercial; *fare* **~** *a evento* publicize; *prodotto* advertise
pubblicitario 1 *agg* advertising **2** *m*, **-a** *f* publicist
pubblico (*pl* -ci) **1** *agg* public; **Pubblico Ministero** public prosecutor **2** *m* public; (*spettatori*) audience; *in* **~** in public
pube *m* pubis
pubertà *f* puberty
pudore *m* modesty; *senza* **~** shameless, immodest
pugilato *m* boxing; *incontro m di* **~** boxing match
pugile *m* boxer
pugnalare <1a> stab
pugnale *m* dagger
pugno *m* fist; (*colpo*) punch; *quantità* handful; *di proprio* **~** in one's own handwriting; *avere in* **~** *qc* have sth in one's grasp; *ti ho in* **~** I've got you now; *rimanere con un* **~** *di mosche* come away empty-handed; *fare a* **-i** fight, come to blows
pulce *f* flea
pulcino *m* chick
puledro *m*, **-a** *f* colt; (*femmina*) filly
pulire <4d> clean
pulito clean; *fig* cleaned-out
pulitura *f* cleaning; **~** *a secco* dry cleaning
pulizia *f* cleanliness; *fig* **~** *etnica* ethnic cleansing; *donna f delle* **-e** cleaner; *fare le* **-e** do the cleaning, clean
pullman *m inv* coach, bus
pullover *m inv* pullover
pullulare <1l>: **~** *di* be teeming or swarming with
pulpito *m* pulpit
pulsante *m* button
pulsare <1a> pulsate
pulsazione *f* pulsation
pulviscolo *m* dust
pungente *foglia* prickly; *freddo, parola* sharp, biting; *desiderio* sharp
pungere <3d> prick; *di ape, vespa* sting; **~** *qu sul vivo* cut s.o. to the quick
pungiglione *m* sting
punibile punishable (*con* by)
punire <4d> punish
punizione *f* punishment; SP *calcio m di* **~** free kick
punta *f di spillo, coltello* point; *di dita, lingua* tip; GEOG peak; *fig* touch, trace; *ora f di* **~** peak hour; *ce l'ho sulla* **~** *della lingua* it's on the tip of my tongue; *fig prendere qc di* **~** face sth head-on
puntare <1a> **1** *v/t* pin (*su* to); (*dirigere*) point (*verso* at); (*scommettere*) bet (*su* on); *fig* **-i** *piedi* dig one's heels in **2** *v/i* (*dirigersi*) head (*verso* for); **~** *a successo, matrimonio* aspire to, set one's sights on; **~** *su contare su* rely on
puntata *f* instal(l)ment; (*scommessa*) bet
punteggiatura *f* punctuation
punteggio *m* score
puntiglio *m* obstinacy
puntiglioso punctilious
puntina *f*; *di giradischi* stylus; **~** (*da disegno*) drawing pin, *Am* thumbtack
puntino *m* dot; *a* **~** perfectly, to perfection
punto 1 *pp* → **pungere 2** *m* point; MED, (*maglia*) stitch; **~** *di vista* point of view, viewpoint; **~** *cardinale* point of the compass; **~** *culminante* height; **~** *di partenza* starting point; **~** *di fusione* melting point; *fino a che* **~** *sei arrivato?* how far have you got?; *alle dieci in* **~** at ten o'clock exactly *or* on the dot; **~** *fermo* full stop, *Am* period; *due* **-i** colon; **~** *e virgola* semi-colon;

P

~ *esclamativo* exclamation mark; ~ *interrogativo* question mark; *di ~ in bianco* suddenly, without warning; *essere sul ~ di fare qc* be on the point of doing sth, be about to do sth

puntuale punctual

puntualità *f* punctuality

puntualizzare <1a> make clear

puntura *f di ape, vespa* sting; *di ago* prick; MED injection; ~ *d'insetto* insect bite

punzecchiare <1k> prick; *fig (provocare)* tease

può, puoi → *potere*

pupazzo *m* puppet; ~ *di neve* snowman

pupilla *f* pupil

purché provided, on condition that

pure 1 *cong* even if; *(tuttavia)* (and) yet 2 *avv* too, as well; *pur di* in order to; *venga ~ avanti !* do come in!

purè *m* puree

purezza *f* purity

purga *f* (*pl* -ghe) purge

purgante *m* laxative

puro pure

purtroppo unfortunately

pus *m* pus

pustola *f* pimple

putrefare <3aa> rot, putrefy

puttana *f* P whore P

puzza *f* stink

puzzare <1a> stink (*di* of)

puzzo *m* stink

puzzola *f* ZO polecat

puzzolente stinking, evil-smelling

p.v. *abbr* (= *prossimo venturo*) next

Q

q *abbr* (= *quintale*) 100 kilograms

qua here; *passa di ~* come this way; *al di ~ di* on this side of

quaderno *m* exercise book

quadrangolare four-sided

quadrangolo *m* quadrangle

quadrante *m* quadrant; *di orologio* dial

quadrare <1a> 1 *v/t* MAT square; *conti* balance 2 *v/i di conti* balance, square F; *fig i conti non quadrano* there's something fishy going on

quadrato 1 *agg* square; *fig persona* rational 2 *m* square; *tabella ecc* list

quadrifoglio *m* (*pl* -gli) four-leaf clover

quadro 1 *agg* square 2 *m* painting, picture; MAT square; *fig nel ~ di* as part of; ~ *(sinottico)* table; *-i pl direttivi* senior executives, senior management *sg*; ~ *di comando* control panel; ~ *a olio* oil painting; *a -i* check *attr*

quadruplo *m/agg* quadruple

quaggiù down here

quaglia *f* quail

qualche a few; *(un certo)* some; *interrogativo* any; *rimango ~ giorno* I'm staying for a few days; ~ *giorno usciamo insieme* we'll go out some day; ~ *cosa* something; ~ *volta* sometime; *alcune volte* a few times; *a volte* sometimes; *in ~ luogo* somewhere; ~ *mese fa* a few months ago; *in ~ modo* somehow

qualcheduno someone, somebody

qualcosa something; *interrogativo* anything, something; *qualcos'altro* something else; ~ *da mangiare* something to eat; ~ *di bello* something beautiful

qualcuno someone, somebody; *in interrogazioni anche* anyone, anybody; *qualcun'altro* someone *or* somebody else; *c'è ~?* (is) anybody *or* anyone home?

quale 1 *agg* what; *~ libro vuoi?* which book do you want?; *città ~ Roma* cities like Rome **2** *pron*: *prendi un libro – ~?* take a book – which one?; *il/la ~ persona* who, that; *cosa* which, that; *la persona della ~ stai parlando* the person you're talking about **3** *avv* as

qualifica *f* (*pl* -che) qualification; *professionale* profession

qualificare <1m & d> qualify; (*definire*) describe

qualificarsi give one's name (*come* as); *a esame, gara* qualify

qualificato qualified

qualificazione *f* qualification

qualità *f inv* quality; *merce f di prima ~* top quality goods; *~ della vita* quality of life

qualora in the event that

qualsiasi any; *non importa quale* whatever; *~ persona* anyone; *~ cosa faccia* whatever I do

qualunque any; *uno ~* any one; *~ cosa* anything; *~ cosa faccia* whatever I do; *in ~ stagione* whatever the season; *l'uomo ~* the man in the street

qualvolta: *ogni ~* every time that

quando when; *per ~?* when?; *da ~?* how long?; *~ vengo* when I come; *ogni volta che* whenever I come; *di ~ in ~* now and then, from time to time

quantità *f inv* quantity, amount

quantitativo *m* quantity, amount

quanto **1** *agg* how much; *con nomi plurali* how many; *tutto ~ il libro* the whole book; *tutti -i* *pl* every single one *sg*; *-i ne abbiamo oggi?* what is the date today?, what is today's date? **2** *avv*: *~ dura ancora?* how long will it go on for?; *~ a me* as for me; *~ costa?* how much is it?; *~ prima* as soon as possible; *in ~* since, because; *per ~ ne sappia* as far as I know **3** *m*: *teoria f dei ~i* quantum theory

quaranta forty

quarantena *f* quarantine

quarantenne 1 *agg* forty or so **2** *m/f*

person in his/her forties

quarantesimo *m/agg* fortieth

quaresima *f* Lent

quarta *f* AUTO fourth (gear)

quartiere *m* district; MIL quarters *pl*; *~ generale* headquarters

quarto 1 *agg* fourth **2** *m* fourth; (*quarta parte*) quarter; *~ d'ora* quarter of an hour; *sono le due e un ~* it's (a) quarter past two; *un ~ di rosso* a quarter-litre (*Am* liter) of red; *-i di finale* quarter-finals

quarzo *m* quartz; *orologio m al ~* quartz watch

quasi almost; *~ mai* hardly ever

quassù up here

quattordicesimo *m/agg* fourteenth

quattordici fourteen

quattrini *mpl* money *sg*, cash *sg*

quattro four; *al ~ per cento* at four per cent; *fare ~ passi* go for a stroll; *farsi in ~ per fare qc* go to a lot of trouble to do sth

quattrocchi *m inv*: *a ~* in private

quattrocento 1 *agg* four hundred **2** *m*: *il Quattrocento* the fifteenth century

quattromila four thousand

quegli, quei → *quello*

quello 1 *agg* that, *pl* those **2** *pron* that (one), *pl* those (ones); *~ che* the one that; *tutto ~ che* all (that), everything (that)

quercia *f* (*pl* -ce) oak

querela *f* legal action; *sporgere ~ contro qc* take legal action against s.o., sue s.o.; *~ per diffamazione* action for slander

quesito *m* question

questi → *questo*

questionario *m* (*pl* -ri) questionnaire

questione *f* question; *~ di fiducia* question *or* matter of trust; *qui non è ~ di* it is not a question *or* matter of; *è ~ di fortuna* it's a matter of luck; *è fuori ~* it is out of the question; *mettere qc in ~* cast doubt on sth

questo 1 *agg* this, *pl* these; *quest'oggi* today **2** *pron* this (one), *pl* these (ones); **~ qui** this one here; **con ~** with that; **per ~** for that reason; **quest'oggi** today; **-a poi!** well I'm blowed!; **ci mancherebbe anche -a!** that's all we'd need!; **-a non me l'aspettavo** I wasn't expecting this

questore *m* chief of police

questura *f* offices of the chief of police

qui here; **~ vicino** near here; **fin ~** up to here; **passa di ~!** come this way!; **voglio uscire di ~** I want to get out of here; **di ~ a un mese** a month from now, in a month's time

quietanza *f* receipt

quiete *f* peace and quiet

quieto quiet

quindecismo *m/agg* fifteenth

quindi 1 *avv* then **2** *cong* therefore

quindici fifteen; **tra ~ giorni** in two weeks (time), *Br* in a fortnight('s time)

quindicina *f*: **una ~** about fifteen;

una ~ di giorni about two weeks, *Br* about a fortnight

quinta *f* AUTO fifth (gear); TEA **le -e** the wings; *fig* **dietro le -e** behind the scenes

quintale *m* hundred kilos; **mezzo ~** fifty kilos

quinto *m/agg* fifth

quota *f* (*parte*) share, quota; (*altitudine*) **perdere ~** lose altitude; **prendere ~** gain altitude

quotare <1c> (*valutare*) value; FIN **azioni** *pl* **quotate in borsa** shares listed *or* quoted on the Stock Exchange

quotato respected

quotazione *f di azioni* value, price; **~ d'acquisto** bid price; **~ di vendita** offer price

quotidianamente daily

quotidiano 1 *agg* daily **2** *m* daily (newspaper)

quoziente *m*: **~ d'intelligenza** IQ

R

R. *abbr* (= **raccomandata**) recorded delivery, *Am* certified mail

rabarbaro *m* rhubarb

rabbia *f rage*; (*stizza*) anger; MED rabies; **accesso m di ~** fit of rage; **fare ~ a qu** make s.o. cross

rabbino *m* rabbi

rabbioso *gesto, sguardo* of rage; *cane* rabid

rabbrividire <4d> shudder; *per paura* shiver

rabbuiarsi <1i> get dark, darken; *fig* darken

racc. *abbr* (= **raccomandata**) recorded delivery, *Am* certified mail

raccapricciante appalling, sickening

raccattare <1a> (*tirar su*) pick up

racchetta *f* racquet; **~ da sci** ski pole

racchiudere <3b> contain

raccogliere <3ss> (*tirar su*) pick up; (*radunare*) gather, collect; AGR harvest; **~ i frutti di qc** reap the benefits of sth

raccoglitore *m* ring binder; **~ del vetro** bottle bank

raccolgo → **raccogliere**

raccolta *f* collection; AGR harvest; **fare ~ di francobolli** collect stamps

raccolto 1 *pp* → **raccogliere 2** *m* harvest

raccomandabile: **un tipo poco ~** a shady character

raccomandare <1a> **1** *v/t* recommend **2** *v/i*: **~ a qu di fare qc** tell s.o. to do sth

raccomandata *f* recorded delivery (letter), *Am* certified mail raccomandazione *f* recommendation

raccontare <1a> tell; **~ per filo e per segno** tell in great detail

racconto *m* story

raccordo *m* TEC connection; *strada* slip road; **~ anulare** ring road; **~ autostradale** junction

rada *f* roads *pl*, roadstead

radar *m inv* radar; **impianto** *m* **~** radar installation; **uomini** *pl* **~** air traffic controllers

raddolcire <4d> sweeten; *fig* soften

raddolcirsi *di aria* grow milder; *di carattere* mellow

raddoppiare <1k> double; *sforzi* redouble

raddrizzare <1a> straighten

raddrizzarsi straighten up

radere <3b> shave; *sfiorare* skim; **~ al suolo** raze (to the ground)

radersi shave

radiare <1k> strike off

radiatore *m* radiator

radiazione *f* radiation

radicale radical

radice *f* root; **~ quadrata** square root; **mettere -i** put down roots

radio *f inv* radio; (*stazione*) radio station; **giornale** *m* **~** (radio) news; **via ~** by radio; **ascoltare la ~** listen to the radio

radioascoltatore *m*, **-trice** *f* (radio) listener

radioattività *f* radioactivity

radioattivo radioactive

radiocronaca *f* (radio) commentary

radiocronista *m/f* (*pl* -i) (radio) commentator

radiodramma *m* (*pl* -i) (radio) play

radiofonico radio *attr*

radiografia *f* x-ray

radiografico (*pl* -ci): **esame** *m* **~** x-ray

radioregistratore *m* radio cassette recorder

radioso radiant

radiosveglia *f* clock radio

radiotaxi *m inv* taxi, cab

radiotelefono *m* radio

radioterapia *f* radiation treatment

radiotrasmittente *f apparecchio* radio transmitter; *stazione* radio station

rado *pettine* wide-toothed; *alberi, capelli* sparse; **di ~** seldom

radunare <1a> collect, gather

radunarsi collect, gather

raduno *m* rally

rafano *m* horseradish

raffermo *pane* stale

raffica *f* (*pl* -che) gust; *di mitragliatrice* burst

raffigurare <1a> represent

raffinare <1a> refine

raffinatezza *f* refinement; **gli piacciono le -e** he likes the finer things in life

raffinato *fig* refined

raffineria *f* refinery

rafforzare <1c> strengthen

raffreddamento *m* cooling; **~ ad acqua** water cooling

raffreddare <1a> cool

raffreddarsi cool down; MED catch cold

raffreddato *fig*: **essere molto ~** have a very bad cold

raffreddore *m* cold; **~ da fieno** hay fever

rag. *abbr* (= **ragioniere**) accountant

ragazza *f* girl; **la mia ~** my girlfriend; **~ alla pari** au pair; **nome** *m* **da ~** maiden name

ragazzo *m* boy; **il mio ~** my boyfriend

raggio *m* (*pl* -ggi) ray; MAT radius; **~ d'azione** range; *fig* duties, responsibilities; **~ di sole** ray of sunshine; **-i** *pl* **X** x-rays; **-i** *pl* **infrarossi** / **ultravioletti** infrared / ultraviolet rays

raggirare <1a> fool, take in

raggiro *m* trick

raggiungere <3d> *luogo* reach, get to; *persona* join; *scopo* achieve

raggomitolare <1n> wind *or* roll into a ball

raggomitolarsi curl up

raggrinzito wrinkled

ragionamento *m* reasoning

ragionare <1a> reason; **~ di** talk about, discuss

R

ragione f reason; (diritto) right; ~ **sociale** company name; **per -i di salute** for health reasons; **aver** ~ be right; **dare** ~ **a qu** admit that s.o. is right; **a** ~, **con** ~ rightly; **senza** ~ for no reason

ragioneria f book-keeping; EDU high school specializing in business studies

ragionevole reasonable

ragioniere m, **-a** f accountant

ragnatela f spider's web

ragno m spider

ragù m inv meat sauce for pasta

RAI-TV abbr (= **Radio Televisione Italiana**) Italian state radio and television

rallegramenti mpl congratulations

rallegrare <1a> cheer up, brighten up

rallegrarsi cheer up, brighten up; ~ **con qu di qc** congratulate s.o. on sth

rallentare <1b> slow down; fig ~ **il lavoro** ease off in one's work

rallentatore m: **al** ~ in slow motion

ramanzina f lecture

rame m copper

ramificarsi <1m & d> di fiume branch

ramificazione f ramification

ramino m (gioco) rummy

rammaricare <1m & d> disappoint

rammaricarsi be disappointed (di at)

rammarico m (pl -chi) regret

rammendare <1a> darn

rammendo m darn

rammollire <4d> v/t & v/i soften

ramo m branch

ramoscello m twig

rampa f flight; ~ **di carico** loading ramp; ~ **d'accesso** slip road; ~ **di lancio** launch(ing) pad

rampicante 1 agg climbing; **pianta** f ~ climber 2 m climber

rampone m crampon

rana f frog; **uomo** m ~ frogman

rancido rancid

rancore m ranco(u)r

randagio (pl -gi) stray

randello m club

rango m (pl -ghi) rank

rannicchiarsi <1k> huddle up

rannuvolamento m clouding over

rannuvolarsi <1m> cloud over

ranocchio m (pl -cchi) frog

rapa f turnip

rapace 1 m bird of prey 2 agg fig predatory; **uccello** m ~ bird of prey

rapida f rapids pl

rapidità f speed, rapidity

rapido 1 agg quick, fast; crescita, aumento rapid 2 m (**treno** m)~ intercity train

rapimento m abduction, kidnap-(p)ing

rapina f robbery

rapinare <1a> rob

rapinatore m, **-trice** f robber

rapire <4d> abduct, kidnap

rapitore m, **-trice** f abductor, kidnap(p)er

rappacificare <1n & d> reconcile

rappacificazione f reconciliation

rappezzare <1b> patch; fig discorso, articolo cobble together

rappezzo m patch

rapporto m resoconto report; relazione relationship; nesso connection, link; **-i pl interpersonali** personal relationships; **avere -i pl di lavoro con qu** be a colleague of s.o., work with s.o.; **in** ~ **a** in connection with; **le due cose sono in** ~ the two things are related or connected

rappresentante m/f representative

rappresentanza f agency; ~ **esclusiva** sole agency

rappresentare <1b> represent; TEA perform

rappresentazione f representation; TEA performance

rarità f inv rarity

raro rare

rasare <1a> shave

rasatura f shaving

raschiare <1k> scrape; ruggine, sporco scrape off

raschiarsi: ~ **la gola** clear one's throat

rasentare <1b> (sfiorare) scrape; fig (avvicinarsi) verge on; ~ **il muro** hug the wall

rasente: ~ *a* very close to

rasoio *m* (*pl* -oi) razor; ~ *di sicurezza* safety razor; ~ *elettrico* electric razor

raspo *m* cluster

rassegna *f* festival; *di pittura ecc* exhibition; *passare in* ~ review

rassegnarsi <1a> resign o.s (*a* to)

rassegnato resigned

rassegnazione *f* resignation

rasserenare <1a> calm down

rasserenarsi *di cielo, tempo* clear up

rassicurare <1a> reassure

rassicurarsi feel reassured

rassomigliante similar

rassomiglianza *f* resemblance

rassomigliare <1g>: ~ *a* look like, resemble

rassomigliarsi look like *or* resemble each other

rastrellare <1b> rake; *fig* comb

rastrelliera *f* rack; ~ *per biciclette* bike rack

rastrello *m* rake

rata *f* instal(l)ment; *a* -*e* in instalments; ~ *qc a rate* buy sth on hire purchase *or Am* the installment plan

rateale: *pagamento m* ~ payment in insta(l)lments; *vendita f* ~ hire purchase, *Am* installment plan

ratificare <1m & d> ratify

ratto *m* ZO rat

rattoppare <1c> patch

rattoppo *m* patch

rattrappirsi <4d>, **rattrappirsi** go stiff

rattrappito stiff

rattristare <1a> sadden, make sad

rattristarsi become sad

raucedine *f* hoarseness

rauco (*pl* -chi) hoarse

ravanello *m* radish

ravioli *mpl* ravioli *sg*

ravvicinamento *m* approach; *fig* reconciliation

ravvicinare <1a> move closer; *fig* (*confrontare*) compare; (*riappacificare*) reconcile

ravvivare <1a> revive

razionale rational

razionalizzare <1a> rationalize

razionare <1a> ration

razione *f* ration

razza *f* race; *fig* sort, kind; ZO breed

razzia *f* raid

razziale racial

razzismo *m* racism

razzista *agg, m/f* (*mpl* -i) racist

razzo *m* rocket; *come un* ~ like greased lightning, like a bat out of hell

re *m inv* king; MUS D

reagire <4d> react (*a* to)

reale *vero* real; *regale* royal

realismo *m* realism

realista *m/f* (*mpl* -i) realist

realistico (*pl* -ci) realistic

realizzabile feasible

realizzare <1a> realize; *piano, progetto* carry out

realizzarsi *di sogno* come true; *di persona* find o.s., find fulfilment

realizzazione *f* fulfilment; (*cosa realizzata*) achievement

realmente really

realtà *f* reality; *in* ~ in fact, actually; ~ *virtuale* virtual reality

reato *m* (criminal) offence (*Am* offense); -*i pl minori* minor offences

reattore *m* AVIA jet engine; *aereo* jet; ~ *nucleare* nuclear reactor

reazionario (*pl* -ri) **1** *agg* reactionary **2** *m*, -**a** *f* reactionary

reazione *f* reaction

recapitare <1m> deliver

recapito *m* delivery; (*indirizzo*) address; ~ *telefonico* phone number

recare <1d> *portare* bring; *arrecare* cause

recarsi go

recensione *f* review

recensire <4d> review

recensore *m* reviewer, critic

recente recent

recentemente recently

recintare <1a> enclose

recinto *m* enclosure; *per animali* pen, enclosure; *steccato* fence

recipiente *m* container, recipient

reciproco (*pl* -ci) mutual, reciprocal

R

recita *f* performance

recitare <ll & b> **1** *v/t* recite; TEA play (the part of); *preghiera* say **2** *v/i* act

reclamare <1a> **1** *v/i* complain **2** *v/t* claim

réclame *f inv* advert

reclamizzare <1a> advertise

reclamo *m* complaint

reclusione *f* seclusion

recluso *m* prisoner

recluta *f* recruit

record *m inv* record; **stabilire il ~** set the record; **a tempo di ~** in record time

recuperare → **ricuperare**

recupero → **ricupero**

redatto *pp* → **redigere**

redattore *m*, **-trice** *f* editor; *di articolo* writer; **~ capo** editor-in-chief

redazione *f* editorial staff; *di articolo* writing

redditizio (*pl* -zi) profitable

reddito *m* income; **~ annuo** annual income

Redentore *m* REL Redeemer

redigere <3oo> *testo, articolo* write; *lista* draw up

redini *fpl* reins

reduce *m/f* ex-serviceman

referendum *m inv* referendum

referenza *f* reference

referto *m* (official) report

refettorio *m* (*pl* -ri) refectory

refill *m inv* refill

refrigerante cooling

refrigerare <1m> refrigerate

refrigerio *m* (*pl* -ri) coolness

refurtiva *f* stolen property

regalare <1a> give; **regalarsi qc** treat o.s. to sth

regale regal

regalino *m* gift, present, little something F

regalo *m* gift, present; **articolo m da ~** gift

regata *f* (boat) race

reggere <3cc> **1** *v/t* (*sostenere*) support; (*tenere in mano*) hold; (*sopportare*) bear; GRAM take **2** *v/i di tempo* last; *di ragionamento* stand up; *fig*

non reggo più I can't take any more

reggersi stand

reggia *f* (*pl* -gge) palace

reggicalze *m inv* suspender belt

reggipetto *m*, **reggiseno** *m* bra, *Am* brassiere

regia *f* production; *di film* direction

regime *m* régime; MED diet; MED **essere a ~** be on a diet

regina *f* queen

regionale regional

regione *f* region

regista *m/f* director; TEA producer

registrare <1a> *in un registro* enter, record, register; *rilevare* show, register; *canzone, messaggio* record

registratore *m*: **~ (a cassetta)** cassette recorder; **~ a nastro** tape recorder; **~ di cassa** cash register

registrazione *f* recording

registro *m* register

regnare <1a> reign

regno *m* kingdom; *periodo* reign

regola *f* rule; **in ~** in order; **di ~** as a rule

regolabile adjustable

regolamento *m* regulation; **~ dei conti** settling of accounts

regolare **1** *v/t* <ll & b> regulate; *spese, consumo* cut down on; TEC adjust; *questione* sort out, settle; *conto, debito* settle **2** *agg* regular

regolarità *f* regularity

regolarizzare <1a> *situazione* sort out, put in order

regredire <4d> regress

regressione *f* regression

regressivo regressive

regresso *m* regression

reimpiego *m* (*pl* -ghi) *di capitali* reinvestment; *di personale* re-employment

relatività *f* relativity; **teoria f della ~** theory of relativity

relativo relative (**a** to); (*corrispondente*) relevant

relatore *m*, **-trice** *f* speaker

relazione *f legame* relationship; *esposizione* report; **avere una ~ con qu** have an affair *or* a relationship with s.o.; **in ~ a** with reference to; **-i pubbliche** public relations, PR

religione *f* religion

religiosa *f* nun

religiosità *f* religion

religioso **1** *agg* religious **2** *m* monk

relitto *m* wreck

remare <1b> row

rematore *m* rower

remo *m* oar

remoto remote

remunerare <1m> pay

remunerativo remunerative, well-paid; **non ~** unpaid

remunerazione *f* payment, remuneration

rendere <3c> *restituire* give back, return; *fruttare* yield; *senso, idea* render; **~ un servizio a qu** do s.o. a favo(u)r; **~ conto a qu di qc** account to s.o. for sth; **~ felice** make happy

rendimento *m di macchina, impiegato* performance; **~ giornaliero** daily output *or* production

rendita *f* income; **~ vitalizia** annuity; **vivere di ~** have private means

rene *m* kidney

reparto *m* department

repentaglio *m*: **mettere a ~** risk, endanger

reperibile available; **difficilmente ~** difficult to find

reperire <4d> find

reperto *m* find; DIR exhibit

repertorio *m* (*pl* -ri) TEA, MUS repertory

replica *f* (*pl* -che) (*copia*) replica; TV repeat; TEA repeat performance; (*risposta*) answer, response; **il suo tono non ammette -e** his tone of voice leaves no room for discussion

replicare <1l, b & d> *ripetere* repeat; *ribattere* reply, answer

reportage *m inv* report

reporter *m/f inv* reporter, journalist

repressione *f* repression

repressivo repressive

represso *pp* → **reprimere**

reprimere <3r> repress

repubblica *f* (*pl* -che) republic

repubblicano republican

repulsione *f* repulsion

reputare <1l & b> consider, deem

reputarsi consider o.s.

reputazione *f* reputation

requisire <4d> requisition

requisito *m* requirement

resa *f* surrender; *restituzione* return; **~ dei conti** settling of accounts

residence *m inv* block of service flats (*Am* apartments)

residente resident

residenza *f* (official) address; *sede* seat; *soggiorno* stay

residenziale residential; **zona *f* ~** residential area

residuo *m* remainder

resina *f* resin

resistente sturdy, strong; **~ al fuoco** fire-resistant

resistenza *f* resistance; *instancabilità* stamina

resistere <3f> *al freddo ecc* stand up to; *opporsi* resist; **non resisto più** I can't take any more

reso *pp* → **rendere**

resoconto *m* report

respingere <3d> *richiesta, pretendente* reject, turn down; *nemico, attacco* repel

respinto *pp* → **respingere**

respirare <1a> **1** *v/t* breathe (in) **2** *v/i* breathe; *fig* draw breath

respiratore *m* respirator; *per apnea* snorkel

respirazione *f* breathing; **~ artificiale** artificial respiration

respiro *m* breathing; **trattenere il ~** hold one's breath; *fig* **un attimo di ~** a moment's rest

responsabile responsible (**di** for); DIR liable (**di** for)

responsabilità *f inv* responsibility; DIR liability; **~ civile** civil liability; **~ limitata** limited liability

ressa *f* crowd

restare <1b> stay, remain; *avanzare* be left; **~ indietro** stay behind; **~ perplesso/vedovo** be puzzled/widowed; **restarci male** be hurt

restaurare <1a> restore

R

restauratore *m*, **-trice** *f* restorer
restauro *m* restoration; *chiuso per -i* closed for restoration
restituire <4d> return; *salute* restore
restituzione *f* return
resto *m* rest, remainder; (*soldi*) change; *-i pl* remains; *del ~* anyway, besides
restringere <3d> narrow; *vestito, giacca* take in
restringersi *di strada* narrow; *di stoffa* shrink
restrizione *f* restriction
rete *f per pescare ecc* net; SP goal; INFOR, TELEC, FERR network; *~ autostradale* road network
retina *f* ANAT retina
retribuire <4d> pay
retribuzione *f* payment
retroattivo retroactive
retrobottega *m inv* back shop
retrocedere <3l> retreat; *fig* lose ground
retrodatare <1a> backdate
retrogrado reactionary
retromarcia *f* (*pl* -ce) AUTO reverse (gear)
retroscena *mpl fig* background *sg*
retrospettivo *mostra* retrospective
retroterra *m inv* hinterland
retrovisivo: specchietto *m ~* rearview mirror
retta¹ *f somma* fee
retta² *f* MAT straight line
retta³ *f*: *dare ~ a qu* listen to s.o.
rettangolare rectangular
rettangolo *m* rectangle
rettifica *f* (*pl* -che) correction
rettificare <1m & d> correct
rettile *m* reptile
rettilineo straight
rettorato *m* rectorship
rettore *m* rector
reumatico (*pl* -ci) rheumatic
reumatismo *m* rheumatism
revisionare <1a> *conti* audit; AUTO MOT, put through the MOT test; *testo* revise
revisione *f di conti* audit; AUTO MOT; *di testo* revision
revoca *f* (*pl* -che) repeal

revocare <1l, b & d> repeal, revoke
R.I. *abbr* (= **Repubblica Italiana**) Italian Republic
ri- *prefisso* re-.
riabilitare <1n> rehabilitate
riabilitazione *f* rehabilitation
riacquistare <1a> get back, regain; *casa* buy back
riagganciare <1f> TELEC hang up
riallacciare <1f> refasten; TELEC reconnect
rialzare <1a> *alzare di nuovo* pick up; *aumentare* raise, increase
rialzo *m* rise, increase
rianimare <1m> *speranze, entusiasmo* revive; (*rallegrare*) cheer up; MED resuscitate
rianimarsi revive
rianimazione *f* resuscitation; *centro m di ~* intensive care unit, ICU
riapertura *f* reopening
riaprire <4f> reopen
riarmare <1a> rearm
riarmo *m* rearmament
riassettare <1b> tidy up
riassetto *m* tidy-up
riassumere <3h> re-employ; (*riepilogare*) summarize
riassunto 1 *pp* → **riassumere 2** *m* summary
riavere <2b> get back, regain; *ho riavuto il raffreddore* I've got another cold
riaversi recover (*da* from), get over (*da* sth)
riavviare <1h> INFOR reboot
ribaltabile folding
ribaltare <1a> **1** *v/t* overturn **2** *v/i di macchina, barca* turn over
ribassare <1a> **1** *v/t* lower **2** *v/i* fall, drop
ribasso *m* fall, drop; *sconto* discount; *essere in ~* be falling *or* dropping
ribattere <3a> **1** *v/t argomento* refute **2** *v/i* (*replicare*) answer back; (*insistere*) insist; *~ a un'accusa* deny an accusation
ribellarsi <1b> rebel (*a* against)
ribelle 1 *agg* rebellious **2** *m/f* rebel
ribellione *f* rebellion
ribes *m inv* currant; *~ nero*

blackcurrant; **~ rosso** redcurrant

ribrezzo *m* horror; **fare ~ a** disgust

ricadere <2c> fall; *cadere di nuovo* fall back; *fig* relapse

ricaduta *f* relapse

ricamare <1a> embroider

ricambiare <1k> change; *contraccambiare* return, reciprocate

ricambio *m* change; *(sostituzione)* replacement; *pezzo* (spare) part; **pezzo di ~** spare part

ricamo *m* embroidery

ricapitolare <1n> sum up, recapitulate

ricaricare <1m & d> *batteria* recharge

ricattare <1a> blackmail

ricattatore *m*, **-trice** *f* blackmailer

ricatto *m* blackmail

ricavare <1a> derive; *denaro* get

ricavato *m* **di vendita** proceeds

ricchezza *f* wealth

riccio¹ *m* (*pl* -cci) ZO hedgehog; BOT *spiny outer casing of the chestnut*; **~ di mare** sea urchin

riccio² (*pl* -cci) **1** *agg* curly **2** *m* curl

ricciolo *m* curl

ricco (*pl* -cchi) **1** *agg* rich, wealthy; **~ di** rich in **2** *m*, **-a** *f* rich or wealthy man / woman; **i -i** *pl* the rich

ricerca *f* (*pl* -che) research; *di persona scomparsa, informazione ecc* search (*di* for); EDU project; **alla ~ di** in search of

ricercare <1d> *(cercare di nuovo)* look again for; *(cercare con cura)* search or look for

ricercato 1 *agg oggetto, artista* sought-after **2** *m* man wanted by the police

ricercatore *m*, **-trice** *f* researcher

ricetta *f* prescription; GASTR recipe

ricevere <3a> receive; *di medico* see patients; **~ gente** have guests

ricevimento *m* receipt; *festa* reception

ricevitore *m* receiver

ricevuta *f* receipt; **accusare ~** acknowledge receipt

richiamare <1a> *(chiamare di nuovo)* call again; *(chiamare indietro)* call back; *attirare* draw; *fig rimproverare* rebuke, reprimand; **~ l'attenzione di qu** draw s.o.'s attention (**su** to); **~ qu all'ordine** call s.o. to order

richiamarsi: ~ a refer to

richiedente *m/f* applicant

richiedere <3k> ask for again; *(necessitare di)* take, require; *documento* apply for

richiesta *f* request (**di qc** for sth); FIN demand; **a** (*o su*) **~ di** at the request of; **più informazioni saranno disponibili su ~** further information on request

richiesto 1 *pp → richiedere* **2** *agg*: **molto ~** much in demand, much sought after

riciclaggio *m* (*pl* -ggi) recycling

riciclare <1a> recycle

ricompensa *f* reward

ricompensare <1b> reward (**qu di qc** s.o. for sth)

riconciliare <1g> reconcile

riconciliazione *f* reconciliation

ricondurre <3e> *(riportare)* take back (**a** to); *(imputare)* attribute (**a** to)

riconoscente grateful; **mostrarsi ~** show one's gratitude

riconoscenza *f* gratitude; **per ~** out of gratitude

riconoscere <3n> recognise; *ammettere* acknowledge; **riconosco che** I admit that; **non si riconosce più** he's unrecognisable

riconoscibile recognizable

riconoscimento *m* recognition

riconquistare <1a> reconquer

ricordare <1c> remember; *(menzionare)* mention; **~ qc a qu** remind s.o. of sth

ricordarsi remember (**di qc** sth; **di fare qc** to do sth)

ricordo *m* memory; *oggetto* memento; **~ di viaggio** souvenir

ricorrente recurrent, recurring

ricorrenza *f* recurrence; *di evento* anniversary

ricorrere <3o> *di date, di festa* take place, happen; **~ a qu** turn to s.o.; **~ a qc** have recourse to sth; **oggi**

R

ricorre l'aniversario del nostro matrimonio today is our wedding anniversary

ricorso 1 *pp* → **ricorrere 2** *m* DIR appeal; *avere ~ a avvocato, medico* see; *avere ~ all'aiuto di qu* ask for s.o.'s help; *presentare ~* appeal

ricostruire <4d> rebuild; *fig* reconstruct

ricostruzione *f* rebuilding; *fig* reconstruction

ricotta *f* ricotta, *soft cheese made from ewe's milk*

ricoverare <1m & c> admit

ricoverato 1 *agg* admitted **2** *m*, -**a** *f* *in ospedale* patient

ricovero *m in ospedale* admission; *(refugio)* shelter

ricreazione *f* recreation; *nelle scuole* break, recreation, *Am* recess

ricredersi <3a> change one's mind

ricuperare <1m> **1** *v/t* get back, recover; *libertà, fiducia* regain; *spazio* gain; *tempo* make up; *~ il tempo perso* make up for lost time **2** *v/i* catch up

ricupero *m* recovery; *~ del centro storico* development of the old part of town; *~ di debiti* debt collection; EDU *corso m di ~* remedial course; *materiale m di ~* scrap; SP *partita f di ~* rescheduled match

ricurvo bent, crooked

ridare <1r> *restituire* give back, return; *fiducia, forze* restore

ridere <3b> laugh *(di* at); *far ~ di sé* make a fool of o.s.; *se la ride del parere degli altri* he couldn't care less what people think

ridicolizzare <1a> ridicule

ridicolo 1 *agg* ridiculous **2** *m* ridicule; *mettere qu in ~, gettare il ~ su qu* ridicule s.o.

ridimensionare <1a> downsize; *fig* get into perspective

ridotto 1 *pp* → **ridurre 2** *agg*: *a prezzi -i* at reduced prices

riduco → **ridurre**

ridurre <3e> reduce *(a* to); *prezzi, sprechi* reduce, cut; *personale*

reduce, cut back; *~ al silenzio* reduce to silence

ridursi decrease, diminish; *~ a fare qc* be reduced to doing sth; *~ male* be in a bad way; *~ in miseria* ruin o.s.

riduzione *f* reduction, cut; *~ del personale* staff cutbacks

riempire <4g> fill (up); *formulario* fill in

rientrare <1a> come back; *a casa* come home; *questo non rientrava nei miei piani* that was not part of the plan

rientro *m* return; *al tuo ~* when you get back

rifare <3aa> do again; *(rinnovare)* do up; *stanza* tidy (up); *letto* make

rifarsi *vita* rebuild; *casa* renovate; *guardaroba* replace; *~ di qc* make up for sth

riferimento *m* reference; *punto m di ~* point of reference; *con ~ a* with reference to

riferire <4d> report

riferirsi: *~ a* refer to

rifiutare <1a> e **rifiutarsi** refuse

rifiuto *m* refusal; *-i pl* waste *sg*, refuse *sg*; *(spazzatura)* rubbish *sg*; *-i tossici* toxic waste

riflessione *f* thought, reflection; FIS reflection

riflessivo thoughtful; GRAM reflexive

riflesso 1 *pp* → **riflettere 2** *m* reflection; *(gesto istintivo)* reflex *(movement)*; *ho agito di ~* it was a reflex action, I did it automatically

riflettere <3qq> **1** *v/t* reflect **2** *v/i* think; *~ su qc* think about sth, reflect on sth

riflettersi be reflected

riflettore *m* floodlight

riflusso *m* ebb

riforma *f* reform; REL Reformation; *~ monetaria* monetary reform

riformare <1a> *(rifare)* re-shape, reform; *(cambiare)* reform; MIL declare unfit

riformato REL Reformed; MIL declared unfit

rifornimento *m* AVIA refuelling; *-i pl* supplies, provisions; *fare ~ di cibo* stock up on food; *fare ~ di benzina* fill up

rifornire <4d> *macchina* fill (up); *frigo* restock, fill (*di* with); *~ il magazzino* restock

rifornirsi stock up (*di* on)

rifugiarsi <1f> take refuge

rifugiato *m*, *-a f* refugee; *~ politico* political refugee

rifugio *m* (*pl* -gi) shelter; *~ alpino* mountain hut; *~ antiaereo* air-raid shelter

riga *f* (*pl* -ghe) *f* line; (*fila*) row; (*regolo*) rule; *in stoffa* stripe; *nei capelli* parting, *Am* part; *stoffa f a -ghe* striped fabric

rigatoni *mpl* rigatoni *sg*

rigenerare <1m & b> regenerate

rigenerazione *f* regeneration

rigetto *m* MED rejection; *fig* mental block

rigido (*duro*) rigid; *muscolo, articolazione* stiff; *clima* harsh; *fig*: *severo* strict

rigirare <1a> **1** *v/i* walk around **2** *v/t* turn over and over; *denaro* launder; *~ il discorso* change the subject

rigirarsi turn round; *nel letto* toss and turn

rigo *m* (*pl* -ghi) line; *~ musicale* staff, stave

rigoglioso lush, luxuriant

rigore *m di clima* harshness; (*severità*) strictness; SP (*anche calcio m di ~*) penalty (kick); *area f di ~* penalty area; *di ~* compulsory

rigoroso rigorous

riguardante about, regarding

riguardare <1a> look at again; (*rivedere*) review, look at; (*riferirsi*) be about, concern; *per quanto riguarda ...* as far as ... is concerned; *non ti riguarda* it's none of your business, it doesn't concern you

riguardarsi take care of o.s.

riguardo *m* (*attenzione*) care; (*rispetto*) respect; *mancanza f di ~* lack of respect; *di ~* important; *~ a*

as regards, about; *senza ~* carelessly

rilasciare <1f> release; *documento* issue

rilascio *m* release; *di passaporto* issue

rilassamento *m* relaxation

rilassare <1a> *e* **rilassarsi** relax

rilassato relaxed

rilegare <1e> *libro* bind

rilegatore *m* bookbinder

rilegatura *f* binding

rilevare <1b> (*ricavare*) find; (*osservare*) note, notice; *ditta* acquire, buy up; *da quanto è successo si rileva che ...* from what has happened, we can gather that ...

rilievo *m* relief; *fig dare ~ a qc, mettere qc in ~* emphasize or highlight sth; *di ~* important; *di nessun ~* of no importance

rima *f* rhyme; *far ~* rhyme

rimandare <1a> send again; (*restituire*) send back, return; *palla* return; (*rinviare*) postpone

rimanente **1** *agg* remaining **2** *m* rest, balance

rimanenza *f* remainder

rimanere <2m> stay, remain; (*avanzare*) be left (over); *rimanerci male* be hurt; *come siete rimasti per stasera?* what arrangements did you make for this evening?

rimango → **rimanere**

rimarginare <1m> *e* **rimarginarsi** heal

rimasto *pp* → **rimanere**

rimbalzare <1a> bounce

rimbalzo *m* bounce

rimboccare <1d> *coperte* tuck in; *rimboccarsi le maniche* roll up one's sleeves

rimborsare <1a> reimburse, refund, pay back

rimborso *m* reimbursement, repayment; *~ spese* reimbursement of expenses; *contro ~* COD, cash on delivery

rimboschimento *m* reforestation

rimboschire <4d> reforest

rimediare <1k & b> **1** *v/i* **~ a** make

up for, remedy; **come posso ~?**
how can I put things right? **2** v/t
find, scrape together

rimedio m (pl -di) remedy; MED
medicine; **senza ~** hopeless

rimescolare <1m> mix again; più
volte mix thoroughly; caffè stir again

rimessa f di auto garage; degli
autobus depot; FIN remittance; SP **~
laterale** throw-in

rimettere <3ee> put back, return; ~
(affidare) refer; vomitare bring up; ~
a posto put back; **~ in ordine** tidy
up; **ci ho rimesso molti soldi** I lost a
lot of money

rimettersi di tempo improve; **~ da qc**
get over sth; **~ a qu** put o.s. in s.o.'s
hands

rimmel® m inv mascara

rimodernare <1b> modernize

rimorchiare <1k & c> AUTO tow
(away)

rimorchiatore m tug

rimorchio m AUTO tow; veicolo
trailer

rimorso m remorse

rimozione f removal

rimpatriare <1k & m> **1** v/t repatri-
ate **2** v/i return or go home

rimpatrio m (pl -ri) repatriation

rimpiangere <3d> regret (**di avere
fatto qc** doing sth); tempi passati,
giovinezza miss

rimpianto 1 pp → **rimpiangere 2** m
regret

rimpiazzare <1a> replace

rimpicciolire <4d> **1** v/t make
smaller **2** v/i become smaller, shrink

rimproverare <1m & c> scold;
impiegato reprimand; **~ qc a qu** re-
proach s.o. for sth

rimprovero m scolding; dal capo reprimand; **-i** pl reproaches

rimuovere <3ff> remove; muovere di
nuovo move again

rinascere <3gg> be born again; di
passione, speranza be revived; fig
sentirsi ~ feel rejuvenated

Rinascimento m Renaissance

rincarare <1a> **1** v/t increase, put up;
~ la dose make matters worse **2** v/i

increase in price

rincaro m increase in price

rincasare <1a> venire come home;
andare go home

rinchiudere <3b> shut up

rinchiudersi shut o.s. up

rincorrere <3o> run or chase after

rincorsa f run-up

rincorso pp → **rincorrere**

rincrescere <3n>: **mi rincresce** I'm
sorry; **se non ti rincresce** if you
don't mind

rincrescimento m regret

rinfacciare <1f>: **~ qc a qu** cast sth
up to s.o.

rinforzare <1c> strengthen

rinforzarsi get stronger

rinforzo m reinforcement; MIL **-i** pl
reinforcements

rinfrescare <1d> **1** v/t cool down,
make cooler; (ristorare) refresh;
(rinnovare) freshen up; **~ la memoria a qu** refresh s.o.'s memory **2** v/i
cool down

rinfrescarsi freshen up

rinfresco m (pl -chi) buffet (party)

rinfusa: alla ~ any which way, all
higgledy-piggledy

ringhiare <1k> growl

ringhiera f railing

ringiovanire <4d> **1** v/t make feel
younger; di aspetto make look
younger **2** v/i feel younger; di aspetto look younger

ringraziamento: un ~ a word of
thanks; **lettera f di ~** thank you letter, letter of thanks; **i miei -i** pl my
thanks

ringraziare <1g> thank (**di** for)

rinnovamento m change; di contratto, tessera renewal

rinnovare <1c> renovate; guardaroba replace; abbonamento renew; (ripetere) renew, repeat

rinnovarsi renew itself; (ripetersi) be
repeated, happen again

rinnovo m renovation; di guardaroba
replacement; di abbonamento renewal; di richiesta repetition

rinsavire <4d> **1** v/t: **~ qu** bring s.o.
back to his / her senses **2** v/i come to

one's senses

rintanarsi <1a> hide, go to earth

rintracciare <1f> track down

rinuncia f (pl -ce) renunciation (**a** of)

rinunciare <1f> give up (**a** sth)

rinunzia → **rinuncia**

rinvenimento m recovery; di resti discovery

rinvenire <4p> **1** v/t recover; resti discover **2** v/i regain consciousness, come round

rinviare <1h> (mandare indietro) return; (posticipare) postpone, put off; a letteratura refer

rinvio m (pl -vii) return; di riunione postponement; in un testo cross-reference

rione m district

riordinare <1m> tidy up; **~ le idee** set one's ideas in order

riorganizzare <1a> reorganize

riorganizzazione f reorganization

riparare <1a> **1** v/t (proteggere) protect (**da** from); (aggiustare) repair; un torto make up for **2** v/i escape

ripararsi dalla pioggia shelter, take shelter (**da** from)

riparato sheltered

riparazione f repair; fig di torta, ingiustizia putting right, reparation; officina f **-i** garage

riparo m shelter; **mettersi al ~** take shelter

ripartire¹ v/i <4a> leave again

ripartire² v/t <4d> divide (up)

ripartizione f division

ripassare <1a> **1** v/i → **passare 2** v/t col ferro iron; lezione revise, Am review

ripensamento m: **avere un ~** have second thoughts

ripensare <1b> riflettere think; **~ a qc** think about sth again; **ci ho ripensato** I've changed my mind

ripetere <3a> repeat; **ti ho ripetuto mille volte la stessa cosa** I've told you the same thing a thousand times

ripetizione f repetition; **dare -i a qu** tutor s.o.

ripetuto repeated

ripido steep

ripiegare <1b & e> **1** v/t fold (up) again **2** v/i fall back

ripiego m (pl -ghi) makeshift (solution)

ripieno 1 agg full; GASTR stuffed **2** m stuffing

riporre <3ll> put away; speranze place

riportare <1c> take back; (riferire) report; vittoria, successo achieve; MAT carry over; tasche sew on; danni, ferite sustain

riporto m amount carried over

riposare <1c> v/t & v/i rest

riposarsi rest

riposato: a mente -a once I've/you've had some rest

riposo m rest; **giorno** m **di ~** day off; **collocare a ~** retire; **senza ~** nonstop

ripostiglio m (pl -gli) boxroom, storeroom

riprendere <3c> take again; (prendere indietro) take back; lavoro go back to; FOT record; **~ coscienza** regain consciousness; **~ a fare qc** start doing sth again

riprendersi: ~ da qc get over sth

ripresa f resumption; di vestito alteration; film shot; AUTO acceleration; RAD, TV **in ~ diretta** (broadcast) live; **a più -e** several times, on several occasions

riprodurre → **riprodurre**

riprodurre <3e> reproduce

riprodursi di animali breed, reproduce; di situazione happen again

riproduzione f reproduction; **~ vietata** copyright

riprovare <1c> **1** v/t feel again; vestito try on again **2** v/i try again

ripugnante disgusting, repugnant

ripugnanza f disgust, repugnance

ripugnare <1a>: **~ a qu** disgust s.o.

ripulire <4d> clean again; (rimettere in ordine) tidy (up); spir empty, clean out

risa fpl laughter sg

risaia f rice field

risalire <4m> **1** v/t scale go back up **2** v/i (rincarare) go up again; **~ alle origini** go back to source

risalita f ascent; **impianti** mpl **di ~** ski lifts

risaltare <1a> stand out

risalto m: **fare ~** stand out; **mettere in ~, dare ~ a** highlight

risanamento m redevelopment; FIN improvement; **~ del deficit pubblico** reduction in the public deficit

risanare <1a> redevelop; FIN improve

risarcimento m compensation

risarcire <4d> persona compensate (**di** for); danno compensate for

risata f laugh

riscaldamento m heating; **~ centrale** central heating system (for a block of flats)

riscaldare <1a> heat or warm up

riscaldarsi warm o.s.

rischiararsi <1a> clear (up); cielo clear (up); **~ in volto** cheer up

rischiare <1k> **1** v/t risk **2** v/i: **~ di sbagliare** risk making a mistake

rischio m (pl -chi) risk; **a ~ della propria vita** risking one's own life; **mettere a ~** put at risk

rischioso risky

riscontrare <1a> (confrontare) compare; (controllare) check; (incontrare) come up against; errori come across

riscontro m comparison; check; **in ~ alla Vostra** in response to yours

riscuotere <3ff> FIN soldi draw; assegno cash; fig earn

risentimento m resentment

risentire <4b> **1** v/t hear again **2** v/i feel the effects (**di** of)

risentirsi TELEC talk again; (offendersi) take offence (Am offense)

riserbo m reserve; **senza ~** openly

riserva f reserve; (scorta) stock, reserve; fig reservation; AUTO **essere in ~** be running out of fuel; **fondo m di ~** reserve stock; **avere delle -e pl su qc** have reservations about sth; **senza -e** without reservation, wholeheartedly; **~ naturale** nature

reserve; **fare ~ di** stock up on

riservare <1b> keep; (prenotare) book, reserve

riservarsi reserve; **mi riservo di non accettare** I reserve the right not to accept

riservatezza f reserve

riservato reserved; (confidenziale) confidential

risiedere <3a> be resident, reside

riso[1] **1** pp → **ridere 2** m laughing

riso[2] m rice

risolto pp → **risolvere**

risolutezza f determination, resolution; **con ~** with determination

risoluto determined

risoluzione f resolution; (soluzione) solution; **~ d'un contratto** cancellation of a contract; **prendere una ~** make a decision

risolvere <3g> solve; (decidere) resolve

risolversi be solved; (decidersi) decide, resolve; **~ in nulla** come to nothing

risonanza f MUS resonance; fig: di scandalo reverberations pl

risorgere <3d> rise; fig: di industria ecc experience a rebirth

Risorgimento m Risorgimento, the reunification of Italy

risorsa f resource

risotto m risotto

risparmiare <1k> save; fig spare

risparmiarsi conserve one's energy

risparmiatore m saver

risparmio m (pl -mi) saving; **-i** pl savings; **cassa f di ~** savings bank

rispecchiare <1k> reflect

rispettare <1b> respect; legge, contratto abide by

rispettivo respective

rispetto 1 m respect **2** prp: **~ a** (confronto a) compared with; (in relazione a) as regards

risplendere <3a> shine, glitter

rispondere <3hh> answer (a sth), reply (a to); (reagire) respond; saluto acknowledge; **~ alle speranze** come up to expectations; **~ di qc** be accountable for sth (a to); **~ male**

answer back; TELEC **non risponde** there's no answer

risposta f answer, reply; *(reazione)* response; **~ pagata** reply paid

rissa f brawl

ristabilimento m *di ordine* restoration; *di regolamento* re-introduction; *(guarigione)* recovery

ristabilire <4d> *ordine* restore; *regolamento* re-introduce; **~ la verità** set the record straight

ristabilirsi recover

ristampa f reprint

ristampare <1a> reprint

ristorante m restaurant

ristrettezza f *di idee* narrowness; **vivere nelle -e** live in straitened circumstances

ristretto: **caffè** m inv **~** very strong coffee

ristrutturare <1a> *azienda* restructure

ristrutturazione f restructuring

risultare <1a> *(derivare)* result; *(rivelarsi)* turn out; **mi risulta che ...** as far as I know ...

risultato m result; **senza ~** unsuccessfully

risurrezione f REL Resurrection

risvegliare <1g>, risvegliarsi *fig* reawaken

risveglio m *(pl -gli)* awakening; *fig* reawakening; **al mio ~** when I woke

ritardare <1a> **1** *v/t* delay **2** *v/i* be late; *orologio* be slow

ritardatario m *(pl -ri)*, **-a** f latecomer

ritardo m delay; **senza ~** without delay; **essere in ~** be late

ritenere <2q> *(credere)* believe

ritenersi: **si ritiene molto intelligente** he thinks he is very intelligent

ritenuta f deduction *(su* from); **~ alla fonte** deduction at source

ritirare <1a> withdraw, pull back; *(tirare di nuovo)* throw again; *proposta* withdraw; *(prelevare)* collect, pick up

ritirarsi *(restringersi)* shrink; **~ a vita privata** retire into private life; **~ da**

gara, esame ecc withdraw from

ritiro m withdrawal

ritmo m rhythm

rito m ceremony; **essere di ~** be customary

ritoccare <1d> touch up

ritornare <1a> **1** *v/i venire* get back, come back, return; *andare* go back, return; *su argomento* go back **(su** over); **~ verde** turn green again; **~ in sé** come to one's senses **2** *v/t* return

ritornello m refrain

ritorno m return; **far ~** come back, return; **essere di ~** be back; **viaggio** m **di ~** return trip

ritrarre <3xx> pull away; PITT paint; *(rappresentare)* depict

ritrattare <1a> retract

ritrattazione f retraction

ritratto m portrait; *fig* **il ~ di qu** the spitting image of s.o.

ritrovare <1c> find; *(riacquistare)* regain

ritrovarsi meet again; *(capitare)* find o.s.; *(orientarsi)* get one's bearings

ritrovo m meeting; *luogo* meeting place; **~ notturno** nightclub

ritto straight

riunificazione f reunification

riunione f meeting; *di amici, famiglia* reunion

riunire <4d> gather

riunirsi meet

riuscire <4o> succeed; *(essere capace)* manage; **non riesco a capire** I can't understand; **~ bene / male** be a success / a failure; *di foto* come out well / badly; **~ in qc** be successful in sth

riuscita f success

riuscito successful

riutilizzare <1a> re-use

riutilizzazione f re-use

riva f shore

rivale **1** *agg* rival *attr* **2** *m/f* rival

rivaleggiare <1f> compete

rivalità f rivalry

rivalutare <1a> revalue; *persona* change one's mind about

rivalutazione f revaluation

rivedere <2s> see again; (*ripassare*) review, look at again; (*verificare*) check

rivelare <1a> reveal

rivelazione *f* revelation

rivendere <3a> resell

rivendicare <1m & d> demand

rivendicazione *f* demand; *-i pl salariali* wage demands

rivendita *f negozio* retail outlet

rivenditore *m*, **-trice** *f* retailer; ~ *specializzato* dealer

rivestimento *m* covering

rivestire <4b> (*foderare*) cover; *ruolo* play; *carica* fill

rivestirsi get dressed again

rivincita *f* return match; *prendersi la* ~ get one's revenge

rivista *f* magazine; TEA revue; MIL review; ~ *di moda* fashion magazine

rivolgere <3d> turn; *domanda* address (*a qu* to s.o.); *non mi rivolge mai il saluto* he never acknowledges me; ~ *la parola a qu* speak to s.o., address s.o.; ~ *l'attenzione a qc* turn one's attention to sth

rivolgersi: ~ *a qu* apply to s.o. (*per* for)

rivolgimento *m fig* upheaval

rivolta *f* revolt

rivoltare <1c> turn; (*mettere sottosopra*) turn upside down; (*disgustare*) revolt

rivoltella *f* revolver

rivoluzionario (*pl* -ri) revolutionary

rivoluzione *f* revolution

rizzare <1a> put up; *bandiera* raise; *orecchie* prick up

rizzarsi straighten up; *mi si sono rizzati i capelli in testa* my hair stood on end

roba *f* things *pl*, stuff; ~ *da mangiare* food, things *or* stuff to eat; ~ *da matti!* would you believe it!

robot *m inv* robot; *da cucina* food processor

robustezza *f* sturdiness

robusto sturdy

rocca *f* (*pl* -cche) fortress

roccia *f* (*pl* -cce) rock

rocciatore *m* rock climber

roccioso rocky

rock *m inv* MUS rock; *concerto* *m* ~ rock concert

rockettaro *m*, **-a** *f* rocker

roco (*pl* -chi) hoarse

rodaggio *m* running in; *fig* *sono ancora in* ~ I'm still finding my feet; *in* ~ running in

rodere <3b> gnaw at

rodersi: ~ *dalla gelosia* be eaten up with jealousy

roditore *m* rodent

rogna *f* F *di cane* mange; *problema* hassle

rognone *m di animale* kidney

Roma *f* Rome

romanico (*pl* -ci) Romanesque

romano 1 *agg* Roman; *fare alla -a* go Dutch **2** *m*, **-a** *f* Roman

romanticismo *m* Romanticism

romantico (*pl* -ci) **1** *agg* romantic **2** *m*, **-a** *f* romantic

romanziere *m* novelist

romanzo 1 *agg* Romance **2** *m* novel; ~ *giallo* thriller

rombare <1a> rumble

rombo[1] *m* rumble

rombo[2] *m* ZO turbot

rombo[3] *m* MAT rhombus

romeno 1 *agg* Romanian **2** *m*, **-a** *f* Romanian

rompere <3rr> **1** *v/t* break; F ~ *le scatole a qu* get on s.o.'s nerves F **2** *v/i* F be a pain F; *fig* ~ *con qu* break it off with s.o.

rompersi break; ~ *un braccio* break one's arm

rompicapo *m inv* puzzle; (*problema*) headache

rompighiaccio *m inv* ice-breaker; ALP ice-pick

rondine *f* swallow

ronzare <1a> buzz

ronzio *m* buzzing

rosa 1 *f* rose; ~ *dei venti* wind rose **2** *m/agg inv* pink

rosaio *m* (*pl* -ai) *pianta* rosebush

rosario *m* (*pl* -ri) REL rosary

rosato *m* rosé

rosbif *m inv* roast beef

roseo pink; *avvenire* rosy

roseto *m* rose garden

rosmarino *m* rosemary

rosolare <1l & c> brown

rosolia *f* German measles *sg*

rosone *m* ARCHI rose window

rospo *m* toad; *fig* F *ingoiare il ~* lump it F

rossastro reddish

rossetto *m* lipstick

rossiccio (*pl* -cci) reddish

rosso 1 *agg* red 2 *m* red; ~ *d'uovo* egg yolk; *fermarsi al ~* stop at a red light; *passare col ~* go through a red light

rossore *m* red patch

rosticceria *f* rotisserie (*shop selling roast meat*)

rotaia *f* rail

rotare <1o> rotate

rotatoria *f* roundabout, *Am* traffic circle

rotazione *f* rotation

rotella *f* castor

rotocalco *m* (*pl* -chi) magazine

rotolare <1l & c> *v/t & v/i* roll

rotolarsi roll (around)

rotolino *m* FOTO film

rotolo *m* roll; FOTO film; *andare a -i* go to rack and ruin; *mandare a -i* ruin

rotondo round

rotta *f* MAR, AVIA course; *fig (giusta direzione)* straight and narrow; *cambiare ~* change course; *a ~ di collo* at breakneck speed

rottame *m* wreck

rotto 1 *pp* → *rompere* 2 *agg* broken

rottura *f* breaking; F *tra innamorati* break-up; F *che ~!* what a pain! F

rotula *f* kneecap

roulotte *f inv* caravan

routine *f* routine

rovesciare <1f & b> *liquidi* spill; *oggetto* knock over; *(capovolgere)* overturn, upset; *fig* turn upside down

rovesciarsi overturn, capsize

rovesciata *f calcio* bicycle kick

rovescio (*pl* -sci) reverse; *in tennis* backhand; *fig* ~ *d'acqua* downpour, cloudburst; ~ *di fortuna* reversal of

fortune; *il ~ della medaglia* the other side of the coin; *mettersi una maglia al ~* put a sweater on inside out

rovina *f* ruin; *andare in -e* go to rack and ruin; *mandare in -e* ruin; *-e pl* ruins

rovinare <1a> ruin

rovinarsi ruin o.s.

rovo *m* bramble

rozzo rough and ready

RSM *abbr* (= **Repubblica di San Marino**) Republic of San Marino

R.U. *abbr* (= **Regno Unito**) UK (= United Kingdom)

ruba *f*: *andare a ~* sell like hot cakes, walk out the door

rubare <1a> steal

rubinetto *m* tap; ~ *dell'acqua calda* hot water tap

rubino *m* ruby

rubrica *f* (*pl* -che) *di libro* table of contents; *quaderno* address book; *di giornale* column; TV report

rude rough and ready

rudere *m* ruin; *-i pl* ruins

rudimentale rudimentary, basic

rudimenti *mpl* basics, rudiments

ruga *f* (*pl* -ghe) wrinkle, line

ruggine *f* rust

ruggire <4d> roar

ruggito *m* roar

rugiada *f* dew

rugoso rough; *pelle* wrinkled; *albero* gnarled

rullare <1a> MAR roll; AVIA taxi

rullino *m* FOTO film

rullio *m* roll

rullo *m* roll; ~ *compressore* steam roller

rum *m* rum

ruminare <1a> chew the cud; *fig* ruminate

rumore *m* noise; *far ~* make a noise, be noisy

rumoreggiare <1f> be noisy; *di tuono* growl, rumble; *di folla* mutter

rumoroso noisy

ruolo *m* role; *personale m di ~* (permanent) members of staff

ruota *f* wheel; ~ *anteriore* front

wheel; ~ **dentata** cog; ~ **posteriore** back wheel; ~ **motrice** drive wheel; ~ **di scorta** spare wheel; *fig* **mettere i bastoni tra le -e a qu** put a spoke in s.o.'s wheel

rupe *f* cliff

rupestre *inv* rock *attr;* **arte** *f* ~ wall painting

ruscello *m* stream

russare <1a> snore

Russia *f* Russia

russo 1 *agg* Russian **2** *m,* **-a** *f* Russian

rustico (*pl* -ci) rural, rustic; *fig* unsophisticated

ruttare <1a> belch; *di bambino* burp

ruttino *m* burp

rutto *m* belch

ruvidezza *f* roughness

ruvido rough

ruzzolare <1l> fall

ruzzolone *m* fall; **fare un** ~ fall

S

S *abbr* (= **sud**) S (= south)

S. *abbr* (= **santo**) St (= Saint)

s *abbr* (= **secondo**) s, sec (= second)

S.A. *abbr* (= **Società Anonima**) Ltd (= Limited)

sa → **sapere**

sabato *m* Saturday; **di** ~ on Saturdays; **è meglio uscire di** ~ it's better to go out on a Saturday

sabbia *f* sand

sabbioso sandy

sabotaggio *m* sabotage

sabotare <1a> sabotage

sabotatore *m,* **-trice** *f* saboteur

sacca *f* (*pl* -cche) bag; ANAT, BIO sac

saccarina *f* saccharin

saccheggiare <1f> sack; *spir* raid

saccheggio *m* (*pl* -ggi) sack, sacking

sacchetto *m* bag

sacco *m* (*pl* -cchi) sack; *fig* F **un** ~ **di** piles of F; **costa un** ~ it costs a fortune; ~ **a pelo** sleeping bag; ~ **da montagna** backpack, rucksack; *fig* **vuotare il** ~ spill the beans; *confidarsi* pour one's heart out

saccopelista *m/f* backpacker, hiker

sacerdote *m* priest

sacramento *m* sacrament

sacrificare <1m & d> sacrifice

sacrificarsi sacrifice o.s.

sacrificio *m* (*pl* -ci) sacrifice

sacrilegio *m* sacrilege

sacro sacred; **osso** *m* ~ sacrum

sadico (*pl* -ci) **1** *agg* sadistic **2** *m,* **-a** *f* sadist

sadismo *m* sadism

safari *m inv* safari; ~ **fotografico** photo safari

saggezza *f* wisdom

saggiare <1f> test

saggio[1] (*pl* -ggi) **1** *agg* wise **2** *m* wise man, sage

saggio[2] *m* (*pl* -ggi) test; (*campione*) sample; *scritto* essay; *di danza, musica* end of term show; ~ **d'interesse** interest rate, rate of interest; ~ **di sconto** discount rate

saggista *m/f* essayist

saggistica *f* essay-writing

Sagittario *m* ASTR Sagittarius

sahariana *f* safari jacket

sala *f* room; (*soggiorno*) living room; ~ **da pranzo** dining room; ~ **di lettura** reading room; ~ **giochi** amusement arcade; ~ **operatoria** (operating) theatre, *Am* operating room

salamandra *f* salamander

salame *m* salami

salamoia *f:* **in** ~ in brine

salare <1a> salt

salariale pay *attr*

salariato *m* employee

salario *m* (*pl* -ri) salary, wages; ~ **base** basic salary *or* wage

salatino *m* savo(u)ry

salato savo(u)ry; *acqua* salt; *cibo* salted; F (*caro*) steep F; **troppo ~** salty

saldare <1a> weld; *ossa* set; *fattura* pay (off)

saldatura *f* welding; **una ~** a weld

saldo 1 *agg* steady, secure; *fig* **essere ~ nelle proprie convizioni** be unshakeable in one's beliefs; **tenersi ~** hold on tight **2** *m* payment; *in svendita* sale item; (*resto*) balance; **-i** *pl* **di fine stagione** end-of-season sales; **articolo in ~** sale item; **~ attivo** net assets; **~ passivo** net liabilities

sale *m* salt; **ha poco ~ in zucca** he's not very bright

salgo → **salire**

salice *m* willow; **~ piangente** weeping willow

saliera *f* salt cellar

salina *f* salt works

salire <4m> **1** *v/i* climb; *di livello, prezzi, temperatura,* rise; **~ in macchina** get in; **~ su scala** climb; *treno, autobus* get on **2** *v/t:* **~ le scale** andare go up, climb; *venire* come up, climb

saliscendi *m inv:* **finestra** *f* **a ~** sash window

salita *f* climb; *strada* slope; **strada** *f* **in ~** steep street

saliva *f* saliva

salma *f* corpse, body

salmastro 1 *agg* briny **2** *m* salt

salmone *m* salmon; **~ affumicato** smoked salmon

salmonella *f* salmonella (poisoning)

salone *m* living room; (*esposizione*) show; **~ dell'automobile** motor show; **~ di bellezza** beauty salon

salotto *m* lounge

salpare <1a> sail

salsa *f* sauce; **~ di pomodoro** tomato sauce

salsiccia *f* (*pl* -cce) sausage

saltare <1a> **1** *v/t* jump; (*omettere*) skip; **~ (in padella)** sauté **2** *v/i* jump; *di bottone* come off; *di fusibile* blow;

F di impegno be cancelled; **~ (giù) dal letto** jump out of bed; **~ dalla gioia** jump for joy; **è saltata la corrente** there's been a power cut; **~/ far ~ in aria** blow up; **~ fuori** turn up

saltellare <1b> hop

saltimbocca *m inv* fried veal topped with prosciutto and a sage leaf

salto *m* jump; (*dislivello*) change in level; **~ mortale** somersault; **~ in alto** high jump; **~ in lungo** long jump; *fig* **~ nel buio** leap in the dark; **faccio un ~ da te** I'll drop by *or* in

saltuariamente occasionally

saltuario (*pl* -ri) occasional; **lavoro** *m* **~** casual work

salubre healthy

salumeria *f* shop that sells salumi

salumi *mpl* cold meat *sg*

salutare 1 *agg* healthy; *fig discussione* helpful **2** *v/t* <1a> say hello to, greet; **salutami la tua famiglia** say hello to the family for me

salute *f* health; **~!** cheers!; **alla tua ~!** cheers!, here's to you!

salutista *m/f* (*mpl* -i) health fanatic

saluto *m* wave; **tanti -i** greetings

salvagente *m inv* lifebelt; *giubbotto* life jacket; *per bambini* ring; (*isola spartitraffico*) traffic island

salvaguardare <1a> protect, safeguard

salvaguardia *f* protection

salvare <1a> save, rescue

salvataggio *m* (*pl* -ggi) salvage; **barca** *f* **di ~** lifeboat

salve! hello!

salvezza *f* salvation

salvia *f* sage

salvietta *f* napkin, *Br* serviette

salvo 1 *agg* safe **2** *prp* except; **~ che** unless; **~ imprevisti** barring accidents, all being well **3** *m:* **mettersi in ~** take shelter

sambuco *m* (*pl* -chi) elder

San = Santo

sanare <1a> heal; FIN, ARCHI restore

sanatorio *m* (*pl* -ri) sanatorium, *Am* sanitarium

sandalo *m* sandal; BOT sandalwood

sangue *m* blood; **a ~ freddo** in cold

blood; ***donare il ~*** give blood; GASTR ***al ~*** rare

sanguigno: ***gruppo*** *m* ~ blood group; ***vaso*** *m* ~ blood vessel

sanguinare <1l> bleed; ***mi sanguina il naso*** my nose is bleeding

sanguinoso bloody

sanguisuga *f* (*pl* -ghe) leech

sanità *f* health; ***amministrazione*** ~ health care

sanitario (*pl* -ri) health *attr*; ***assistenza*** *f* -*a* health care

sanno → ***sapere***

sano healthy; ~ ***e salvo*** safe and sound

santo 1 *agg* holy; ***acqua*** *f* -*a* holy water; ***tutto il ~ giorno*** the whole blessed day **2** *m*, -*a* *f* saint; *davanti al nome* St

santuario *m* (*pl* -ri) sanctuary

sanzione *f* sanction

sapere <2n> **1** *v/t* know; (*essere capace di*) be able to; (*venire a*) ~ hear; ***sai nuotare?*** can you swim?; ***lo so*** I know **2** *v/i*: ***far ~ qc a qu*** let s.o. know sth; ***saperla lunga*** know all about it; ***non si sa mai*** you never know; ***per quel che ne so*** as far as I know; ~ *di* (*avere sapore di*) taste of; ***non sa di nulla*** it doesn't taste of anything **3** *m* knowledge

sapiente 1 *agg* wise **2** *m/f* (*scienziato*) scientist

sapienza *f* wisdom

sapone *m* soap

saponetta *f* toilet soap

sapore *m* taste (*di* of); -*i pl* aromatic herbs; ***avere ~ di qc*** taste of sth; ***senza ~*** tasteless

saporito tasty

saracinesca *f* (*pl* -sche) roller shutter

sarcasmo *m* sarcasm; ***non fare ~!*** don't be sarcastic!

sarcastico (*pl* -ci) sarcastic

sarcofago *m* (*pl* -gi *e* -ghi) sarcophagus

Sardegna *f* Sardinia

sardina *f* sardine

sardo 1 *agg* Sardinian **2** *m*, -*a* *f* Sardinian

sarò → ***essere***

sarto *m*, -*a* *f* tailor; *per donne* dressmaker

sartoria *f* tailor's; *per donne* dressmaker's

sasso *m* stone; ***restare di ~*** be thunderstruck

sassofonista *m/f* (*mpl* -i) saxophone player, saxophonist

sassofono *m* saxophone

satellite 1 *m* satellite **2** *agg* satellite *attr*; ***città*** *f* ~ satellite town

satira *f* satire

satirico (*pl* -ci) satirical

saturare <1l> saturate (*di* with)

saturazione *f* saturation

saturo saturated

sauna *f* sauna

saziare <1g> satiate

saziarsi eat one's fill; ***non ~ mai di fare qc*** never get tired of doing sth

sazietà *f*: ***mangiare a ~*** eat one's fill

sazio (*pl* -zi) full (up)

sbadato absent-minded

sbadigliare <1g> yawn

sbadiglio *m* (*pl* -gli) yawn

sbagliare <1g> **1** *v/i e* **sbagliarsi** make a mistake; ***hai sbagliato a dirle la verità*** you were wrong to tell her the truth **2** *v/t* make a mistake in; ~ ***persona*** have the wrong person; ~ ***strada*** go the wrong way

sbagliato wrong

sbaglio *m* (*pl* -gli) mistake; ***per ~*** by mistake; ***senza -i*** flawless

sbalordimento *m* amazement, stupefaction

sbalordire <4d> stun, amaze

sbalorditivo amazing, incredible

sbalzare <1a> throw; *temperatura* change

sbalzo *m* jump; ~ ***di temperatura*** change in temperature

sbandare <1a> AUTO skid; FERR, *fig* go off the rails

sbandata *f* AUTO skid; F ***prendersi una ~ per qu*** develop a crush on s.o.

sbarazzare <1a> clear

sbarazzarsi: ~ *di* get rid of

sbarcare <1d> **1** *v/t merci* unload; *persone* disembark; *fig* ~ ***il lunario***

make ends meet **2** *v/i* disembark

sbarco *m* (*pl* -chi) *di merce* unloading; *di persone* disembarkation

sbarra *f* bar; **essere alla ~** be on trial

sbarramento *m* fence; (*ostacolo*) barrier

sbarrare <1a> bar; *assegno* cross; *occhi* open wide

sbarrato *assegno* crossed; *occhi* wide open

sbattere <3a> **1** *v/t porta* slam, bang; (*urtare*) bang; GASTR beat; **~ la porta in faccia a qu** close the door in s.o.'s face **2** *v/i* bang

sbattitore *m* hand mixer

sbendare <1b> take the bandage(s) off

sberla *f* F slap

sbiadire <4d> fade

sbiadito faded; *stile* colo(u)rless

sbiancare <1d> **1** *v/t* bleach **2** *v/i* turn pale

sbilanciare <1f> unbalance, throw off balance

sbilanciarsi lose one's balance; *fig* commit o.s.

sbizzarrirsi <4d> indulge o.s.

sbloccare <1c & d> clear; *macchina* unblock; *prezzi* deregulate

sblocco *m* (*pl* -chi) *f* clearing; *di macchina* unblocking; *di prezzi* deregulation

sboccare <1d>: **~ in** *di fiume* flow into; *di strada* lead to

sbocciare <1f & c> open (out)

sbocco *m* (*pl* -chi) FIN outlet; *di situazione* way out; **strada** *f* **senza ~** dead end, cul-de-sac

sbornia *f* F hangover; **prendersi una ~** get drunk

sborsare <1a> F cough up F

sbottonare <1a> unbutton

sbottonarsi *fig* open up (**con** to); **la giacca** unbutton one's jacket

sbozzare <1c> draft, rough out

sbraitare <1c> shout, yell

sbranare <1a> tear apart

sbriciolare <1l> spread crumbs

sbrigare <1e> attend to

sbrigarsi hurry up

sbrigativo (*rapido*) hurried, rushed; (*brusco*) brusque

sbrinare <1a> *frigorifero* defrost

sbrinatore *m* defrost control

sbrogliare <1g & c> untangle, disentangle; **sbrogliarsela** sort things out

sbronza *f* F hangover

sbronzarsi <1a> F get drunk

sbronzo F tight F, sloshed F

sbucare <1d> emerge; **da dove sei sbucato?** where did you spring from?

sbucciare <1f> *frutta*, *patate* peel; **sbucciarsi le ginocchia** skin one's knees

sbucciato peeled; *ginocchio* skinned

sbucciatura *f* graze

s.c. *abbr* (= **sopra citato**) above-mentioned

scabroso rough, uneven; *fig* offensive

scacchiera *f* chessboard

scacciare <1f> chase away

scacco *m* (*pl* -chi) (chess) piece; *fig* setback; **~ matto** checkmate; **-cchi** *pl* chess *sg*; **giocare a -cchi** play chess; **a -cchi** checked

scadente **1** → **scadere 2** *agg* second-rate

scadenza *f* deadline; *su alimento* best before date; **~ del termine** deadline, last date; **a breve ~** short-term; **a lunga ~** long-term

scadere <2c> *di passaporto* expire; *di cambiale* fall due; (*perdere valore*) decline (in quality)

scaduto expired; *alimento* past its sell-by date

scaffale *m* shelves *pl*

scaglia *f* flake; *di legno* chip; *di pesce* scale

scagliare <1g> hurl

scagliarsi: **~ contro** attack

scala *f* staircase; GEOG scale; **~ (a pioli)** ladder; **~ mobile** escalator; FIN sliding scale; **~ musicale** (musical) scale; **disegno** *m* **in ~** scale drawing; **su larga ~** on a large scale; **su ~ nazionale** country-wide; **fare le -e** climb the stairs

scalare <1a> climb

scalata f climb; **~ al successo** rise to fame

scalatore m, **-trice** f climber

scaldabagno m water heater

scaldare <1a> heat (up); fig **~ la testa a qu** get s.o. worked up

scaldarsi warm up; fig get worked up, get excited

scaldavivande m inv food warmer

scalinata f steps pl

scalino m step

scalo m AVIA stop; MAR port of call; **volo** m **senza ~** nonstop flight; **fare ~ a** call at

scalogna f bad luck; **portare ~** be unlucky

scalognato unlucky

scaloppina f escalope

scalpello m chisel

scaltro shrewd

scalzo barefoot

scambiare <1k> (confondere) mistake (**per** for); (barattare) exchange, swap F (**con** for)

scambio m (pl -bi) exchange; di persona mistake; FERR points pl; **-i commerciali** trade sg; **~ di lettere** exchange of letters; **~ d'opinioni** exchange of views; **-i culturali** cultural exchange sg; **libero ~** free trade

scampagnata f day out in the country

scampanellare <1b> ring

scampanellata f ring

scampi mpl ZO scampi

scampo m escape, way out

scampolo m remnant

scandagliare <1g> sound; fig sound out

scandalistico (pl -ci) scandal-mongering

scandalizzare <1a> scandalize, shock

scandalizzarsi be scandalized or shocked (**di** by)

scandalizzato scandalized

scandalo m scandal

scandaloso scandalous

scandinavo 1 agg Scandinavian 2 m, **-a** f Scandinavian

scanner m inv INFOR scanner

scannerizzare <1a> INFOR scan

scansafatiche m/f inv lazybones

scansare <1a> (allontanare) move; (evitare) avoid

scansarsi move out of the way

scansia f bookcase

scantinato m cellar

scapito m: **a ~ di** to the detriment of

scapola f shoulder blade, ANAT scapula

scapolo 1 agg single, unmarried 2 m bachelor

scappamento m TEC exhaust

scappare <1a> (fuggire) run away; (affrettarsi) rush, run; **lasciarsi ~ l'occasione** let the opportunity slip; **mi è scappata la pazienza** I lost patience

scappatella f di bambino escapade; **fare delle -lle** get into mischief

scappatoia f way out

scarabocchiare <1k & c> scribble

scarabocchio m (pl -chi) scribble

scarafaggio m (pl -ggi) cockroach

scaraventare <1b> throw, hurl

scaraventarsi throw or hurl o.s. (**contro** at)

scarcerare <1l> release

scarcerazione f release

scardinare <1l> take off the hinges

scarica f (pl -che) discharge

scaricare <1l & d> unload; batteria run down; rifiuti, sostanze nocive dump; responsabilità offload, get rid of; **-arsi la coscienza** ease one's conscience; F **~ qu** get rid of s.o.; INFOR **~ dalla rete** download; INFOR **~ su dischetto** download to disk

scaricarsi relax, unwind F; di batteria run down

scarico (pl -chi) 1 agg camion empty; batteria run-down 2 m di merce unloading; luogo dump; di responsabilità offloading; **gas** m **di ~** exhaust (fumes); **tubo** m **di ~** exhaust (pipe); **divieto di ~** no dumping; **-chi** pl **industriali** industrial waste sg

scarlattina f scarlet fever

scarpa f shoe; **-e** pl **da uomo/da**

donna men's/women's shoes

scarpata f (*burrone*) escarpment

scarpetta f shoe; **-e** pl **da ginnastica** trainers

scarpinare <1a> trek

scarpinata f trek

scarpone m (heavy) boot; **~ da sci** ski boot

scarseggiare <1f> become scarce; **~ di qc** not have much of sth, be short of sth

scarsezza f, **scarsità** f shortage, scarcity; **~ di viveri** food shortage

scarso scarce, in short supply; **esse-re ~ di qc** be lacking in sth; **quattro chilometri -si** barely four kilometres

scartare <1a> (*svolgere*) unwrap; (*eliminare*) reject

scarto m rejection; (*cosa scartata*) reject; **merce** f **di ~** imperfect goods

scassare <1a> F ruin, wreck

scassarsi F give up the ghost F

scassato F done for F

scassinare <1a> force open

scassinatore m, **-trice** f burglar

scasso m forced entry; **furto** m **con ~** breaking and entering, burglary

scatenare <1a> fig unleash

scatenarsi fig: di tempesta break; di collera break out; di persona let one's hair down

scatenato unrestrained

scatola f box; di tonno, piselli tin, can; **in ~** cibo tinned, canned; AVIA **~ nera** black box

scattare <1a> **1** v/t FOT take **2** v/i go off; di serratura catch; (*arrabbiarsi*) lose one's temper; SP spurt; di atleta put on a spurt; **~ in piedi** jump up; **far ~** activate

scatto m click; SP spurt; FOTO exposure; di foto taking; TELEC unit; FOTO **~ automatico** automatic timer; **uno ~ di rabbia** an angry gesture; **~ di stipendio** automatic raise

scavalcare <1d> muro climb (over)

scavare <1a> con pala dig; con trivella excavate

scavi mpl archeologici dig sg

scegliere <3ss> choose, pick, select

scelgo → **scegliere**

scelta f choice, selection; **di prima ~** first-rate; **prendine uno a ~** take your pick

scelto 1 pp → **scegliere 2** agg hand-picked; merce, pubblico (specially) selected

scemo 1 agg stupid, idiotic **2** m, **-a** f idiot

scena theatre, Am theater; (*scenata*) scene; fig **colpo** m **di ~** coup de théâtre; **mettere in ~** produce; fig **fare ~ muta** be struck dumb

scenario m (pl -ri) screenplay; fig scenery

scenata f scene; **fare una ~ (a qu)** make a scene

scendere <3c> **1** v/i andare go down, descend; venire come down, descend; da cavallo get down, dismount; dal treno, dall' autobus get off; dalla macchina get out; di temperatura, prezzi go down, drop; **~ a terra** come (back) down to earth **2** v/t: **~ le scale** andare go down the stairs; venire come down the stairs

scendiletto m bedside rug

sceneggiatura f screenplay

scenografia f sets pl

scenografo m, **-a** f set designer

scetticismo m scepticism, Am skepticism

scettico 1 agg sceptical, Am skeptical **2** m, **-a** f sceptic, Am skeptic

scheda f card; (*formulario*) form; **~ elettorale** ballot (paper); INFOR **~ grafica** graphics card; **~ telefonica** phonecard

schedario m (pl -ri) file

schedina f pools coupon

scheggia f (pl -gge) sliver

scheletro m skeleton

schema m (pl -i) diagram; (*abbozzo*) outline

schematico (pl -ci) general; disegno schematic

schematizzare <1a> outline

scherma f fencing; **tirare di ~** fence

schermo m screen; (*riparo*) shield

scherzare <1a> play; (*burlare*) joke

scherzo m joke; MUS scherzo;

essere uno ~ (*facile*) be child's play; **-i a parte** joking aside; **per ~ fare, dire qc** as a joke

scherzoso playful

schiaccianoci *m inv* pair of nutcrackers, nutcrackers *pl*

schiacciare <1f> **1** *v/t* crush; *noce* crack; **~ un piede a qu** step on s.o.'s toes; F **~ un sonnellino** have a snooze F, have forty winks F **2** *v/i* SP smash

schiacciato crushed, squashed

schiaffeggiare <1f> slap

schiaffo *m* slap

schiamazzare <1a> make a din

schiamazzo *m* yell, scream

schiantare <1a> **1** *v/t* crash, smash **2** *v/i* e **schiantarsi** crash

schianto *m* crash

schiarire <4d> lighten

schiarirsi brighten up

schiarita *f* bright spell

schiavitù *f* slavery

schiavo 1 *agg:* **essere ~ di** be a slave to **2** *m,* **-a** *f* slave

schiena *f* back; **mal m di ~** back ache

schienale *m* di sedile back

schiera *f* group; **a ~** in ranks

schierare <1b> line up

schierarsi: ~ in favore di qu come out in favo(u)r of s.o.

schietto pure; *fig* frank

schifezza *f:* **che ~!** how disgusting!

schifo *m* disgust; **fare ~ a qu** disgust s.o.

schifoso disgusting; (*pessimo*) dreadful

schioppo *m* shotgun

schiuma *f* foam; **~ da bagno** bubble bath; **~ da barba** shaving foam

schiumoso foamy

schivare <1a> avoid, dodge F

schivo shy

schizzare <1a> **1** *v/t* (*spruzzare*) squirt; (*abbozzare*) sketch **2** *v/i* squirt; (*saltare*) jump

schizzinoso fussy

schizzo *m* squirt; (*abbozzo*) (lightning) sketch

sci *m inv* ski; *attività* skiing; **~ acquatico** water ski/skiing; **~ di**

fondo cross-country ski/skiing

sciacquare <1a> rinse

sciacquatura *f* rinse

sciagura *f* disaster

sciagurato *giorno, evento* unfortunate

scialle *m* shawl

scialuppa *f* dinghy; **~ di salvataggio** lifeboat

sciame *m* swarm

sciare <1h> ski

sciarpa *f* scarf

sciatica *f* sciatica

sciatore *m,* **-trice** *f* skier

sciatteria *f* untidiness, sloppiness F

sciatto untidy, sloppy F

scientifico (*pl* -ci) scientific

scienza *f* science; **-e** *pl* **naturali** natural science

scienziato *m,* **-a** *f* scientist

scimmia *f* monkey

scimmiottare <1c> ape

scimpanzè *m inv* chimpanzee, chimp F

scintilla *f* spark

scintillante sparkling

scintillare <1a> sparkle

scintillio *m* sparkle

sciocchezza *f* (*idiozia*) stupidity; **è solo una ~** it's nothing

sciocco (*pl* -chi) **1** *agg* silly **2** *m,* **-a** *f* silly thing

sciogliere <3ss> untie; *capelli* undo, let down; *matrimonio* dissolve; *neve* melt; *dubbio, problema* clear up

sciogliersi *di corda, nodo* come undone; *di burro, neve* melt; *di questione, problema* resolve itself

scioglilingua *m inv* tongue-twister

scioltezza *f* nimbleness; *fisica* agility

sciolto 1 *pp → sciogliere* **2** *agg neve, ghiaccio* melted; *matrimonio* dissolved; **a briglia -a** at breakneck speed

scioperante *m/f* striker

scioperare <1l & c> strike

sciopero *m* strike; **fare ~** go on strike; **~ bianco** work-to-rule; **~ generale** general strike; **~ della fame** hunger strike

sciovia *f* ski-lift

sciovinismo *m* chauvinism

sciovinista *m/f* (*mpl* -i) chauvinist

scipito bland

scippatore *m*, **-trice** *f* bag-snatcher

scippo *m* bag-snatching

scirocco *m* sirocco

sciroppo *m* syrup

scissione *f* splitting

scisto *m* GEOL schist

sciupare <1a> (*logorare*) wear out; *salute* ruin; *tempo, denaro* waste, fritter away

sciupato *persona* drawn; *cosa* worn out

scivolare <1l> slide; (*cadere*) slip

scivolo *m* slide; (*caduta*) slip; *gioco* chute; **~ d'emergenza** escape chute

scivoloso slippery

sclerosi *f inv* MED sclerosis; **~ multipla** multiple sclerosis, MS

scocciare F <1f> bother, annoy, hassle F

scocciatore F *m*, **-trice** *f* pest F, nuisance F

scocciatura F *f* nuisance F

scodella *f* bowl

scogliera *f* cliff

scoglio *m* (*pl* -gli) rock; *fig* stumbling block

scoiattolo *m* squirrel

scolapasta *m inv* colander

scolare <1a> drain

scolaro *m*, **-a** *f* schoolboy; *ragazza* schoolgirl

scolastico (*pl* -ci) school *attr*

scoliosi *f inv* curvature of the spine

scollato low-necked; *donna* wearing a low neck

scollatura *f* neck(line)

scollo *m* neck

scolo *m* drainage

scolorire <4d> **1** *v/t* fade **2** *v/i e* **scolorirsi** fade

scolorito faded

scolpire <4d> *marmo, statua* sculpt; *legno* carve; *fig* engrave

scommessa *f* bet

scommesso *pp* → **scommettere**

scommettere <3ee> bet

scomodare <1l & c> disturb

scomodarsi put o.s. out; **non si sco-**

modi please don't go to any bother

scomodo uncomfortable; (*non pratico*) inconvenient

scomparire <4e> disappear

scomparsa *f* disappearance

scomparso *pp* → **scomparire**

scompartimento *m* compartment; FERR **~ per (non) fumatori** (non-)smoking compartment

scompenso *m* imbalance; **~ cardiaco** cardiac insufficiency

scompigliare <1g> *persona* ruffle the hair of; *capelli* ruffle

scompiglio *m* (*pl* -gli) confusion

scomponibile flat pack *attr*, modular

scomporre <3ll> break down

scomporsi: **senza ~** without showing any emotion

sconcertante disconcerting

sconcio (*pl* -ci) indecent; *parola* disgusting, filthy

sconclusionato incoherent

sconfiggere <3cc> defeat

sconfinare <1a> trespass; MIL cross the border

sconfinato vast, boundless

sconfitta *f* defeat

sconfitto *pp* → **sconfiggere**

sconfortante discouraging, disheartening

sconfortare <1c> discourage, dishearten

sconforto *m* discouragement

scongelare <1b> thaw

scongiurare <1a> beg; *pericolo* avert

sconosciuto 1 *agg* unknown **2** *m*, **-a** *f* stranger

sconsigliare <1g> advise against; **~ qc a qu** advise s.o. against sth

sconsolato disconsolate

scontare <1a> FIN deduct, discount; *pena* serve

scontato discounted; (*previsto*) expected; **~ del 30%** 30% discount *or* deduction

scontento 1 *agg* unhappy, not satisfied (*di* with) **2** *m* unhappiness, dissatisfaction

sconto *m* discount; **praticare uno ~**

give a discount

scontrarsi <1a> collide (**con** with); *fig* clash (**con** with)

scontrino *m* receipt; **fare lo ~ alla cassa** please pay at the cash desk before ordering

scontro *m* AUTO collision; *fig* clash

scontroso unpleasant, disagreeable

sconveniente inappropriate, unacceptable

sconvolgente upsetting, distressing; **di un'intelligenza ~** incredibly intelligent

sconvolgere <3d> upset

sconvolto 1 *pp* → **sconvolgere** 2 *agg paese* in upheaval

scopa *f* broom

scopare <1a> sweep; P shag P

scoperchiare <1k> *pentola* take the lid off

scoperta *f* discovery

scoperto 1 *pp* → **scoprire** 2 *agg pentola* uncovered; **a capo ~** bareheaded; **assegno** *m* **~** bad cheque, rubber cheque F 3 *m* FIN overdraft; **allo ~** in the open

scopo *m* aim, purpose; **allo ~ di fare qc** in order to do sth; **senza ~** aimlessly

scoppiare <1k & c> *di bomba, petardo* explode; *di palloncino, pneumatico* burst; **~ in lacrime** burst into tears; **~ a ridere** burst out laughing; **~ di caldo** be boiling hot

scoppio *m* (*pl* -ppi) explosion; *di palloncino* bursting; *fig* outbreak

scoprire <4f> *contenitore* take the lid off; (*denudare*) uncover; *piani, verità* discover, find out

scoraggiare <1f> discourage, dishearten

scoraggiarsi become discouraged, lose heart

scoraggiato discouraged, disheartened

scorciatoia *f* short cut

scordare <1c>, **scordarsi di** forget

scordato MUS out of tune

scoreggia *f* (*pl* -gge) F fart F

scoreggiare <1f> F fart F

scorgere <3d> see, make out; **non**

farsi ~ not let o.s. be seen

scoria *f* waste

scorpione *m* scorpion; ASTR **Scorpione** Scorpio

scorrere <3o> 1 *v/i* flow, run; *di tempo* go past, pass 2 *v/t giornale* skim

scorretto (*errato*) incorrect; (*non onesto*) unfair

scorrevole *porta* sliding; *stile* flowing

scorso 1 *pp* → **scorrere** 2 *agg*: **l'anno ~** last year

scorta *f* escort; (*provvista*) supply, stock

scortare <1c> escort

scortese rude, discourteous

scortesia *f* rudeness, lack of courtesy

scorto *pp* → **scorgere**

scorza *f* peel; *fig* exterior

scossa *f* shake; **~ di terremoto** (earth) tremor; **~ elettrica** electric shock

scosso *pp* → **scuotere**

scostare <1c> move away (**da** from)

scostarsi move (aside); *fig* **~ della retta via** leave the straight and narrow

scottante delicate

scottare <1c> 1 *v/t* burn; GASTR *verdure* blanch; **mi sono scottato le dita** I burned my fingers 2 *v/i* burn; **scotta!** it's hot!

scottato *verdure* blanched

scottatura *f* burn; **ho già avuto troppe -e** I've had my fingers burned once too often

Scozia *f* Scotland

scozzese 1 *agg* Scottish 2 *m/f* Scot

screditare <1l> discredit

scremato skimmed; **parzialmente ~** semi-skimmed

screpolare <1l & b> e **screpolarsi** crack

screpolatura *f* crack

scricchiolare <1l> creak

scricchiolio *m* (*pl* -ii) creak

scricciolo *m* ZO wren

scritta *f* inscription

scritto 1 *pp* → **scrivere** 2 *m* writing; **per ~** in writing

scrittore *m*, **-trice** *f* writer

scrittura *f* writing; REL scripture

scritturare <1a> engage, sign F

scrivania *f* desk

scrivere <3tt> write; (*annotare*) write down; *come si scrive ... ?* how do you spell ... ?

scroccare <1c & d> F scrounge F

scrollare <1c> shake; *~ le spalle* shrug (one's shoulders)

scrosciare <1f & c> *di pioggia* fall in torrents

scrupolo *m* scruple; *senza -i* unscrupulous

scrupolosità *f* scrupulousness

scrupoloso scrupulous

scrutare <1a> look at intently; *orizzonte* scan

scrutatore *m*, **-trice** *f* POL person counting votes

scrutinio *m* (*pl* -ni) POL counting; EDU *teachers' meeting to discuss pupils' performance*

scucire <4a> unpick; F *scuci i soldi!* cough up! F

scucirsi come apart at the seams

scuderia *f* stable

scudetto *m* SP championship

scudo *m* shield

sculacciare <1f> spank

scultore *m*, **-trice** *f* sculptor

scultura *f* sculpture

scuola *f* school; *~ di lingue* language school; *~ elementare* primary school; *~ media* secondary school; *~ parificata* private school officially recognized by the state; *~ serale* evening classes *pl*; *~ superiore* high school; *~ guida* driving school; *andare a ~* go to school

scuotere <3ff> shake

scuotersi shake off

scure *f* ax(e)

scurire <4d> *v/t* & *v/i* darken

scuro 1 *agg* dark **2** *m* darkness; *essere allo ~ di qc* be in the dark about sth

scusa *f* excuse; *chiedere ~* apologize

scusare <1a> forgive; (*giustificare*) excuse; *mi scusi* I'm sorry; *scusi, scusa* excuse me

scusarsi apologize

S.C.V. *abbr* (= **Stato della Città del Vaticano**) Vatican City

s.d. *abbr* (= **senza data**) undated

sdebitarsi <1l> pay one's debts

sdegnare <1a> (*disprezzare*) despise; (*fare arrabbiare*) incense

sdegnarsi get angry (*con* with)

sdegno *m* moral indignation

sdentato toothless

sdoganamento *m* customs clearance

sdoganare <1a> clear through customs

sdolcinato sloppy

sdraiare <1i> lay

sdraiarsi lie down

sdraiato lying down

sdraio *m*: (*sedia f a*) *~* deck chair

se¹ *cong* if; *~ mai* if need be; *~ mai arrivasse ...* should he arrive ...; *come ~* as if; *~ no* if not

se² *pron* = *si* in front of *lo, la, li, le, ne*

sé oneself; *lui* himself; *lei* herself; *loro* themselves; *esso, essa* itself; *da ~* (by) himself / herself / themselves

sebbene even though, although; *~ abbia detto la verità* even though he told the truth

secca *f* (*pl* -cche) shallows

seccante *fig* annoying

seccare <1d> **1** *v/t* dry; *fig* annoy **2** *v/i* e **seccarsi** dry; *fig* get annoyed

seccatore *m*, **-trice** *f* nuisance, pest

seccatura *f* nuisance

secchio *m* (*pl* -cchi) bucket, pail

secco (*pl* -cchi) **1** *agg* dry; *fiori, pomodori* dried; *risposta, tono* curt; *frutta f -a* dried fruit; (*noci*) nuts *pl* **2** *m*: *rimanere a ~* run out of petrol; *fig* run out of money; *pulire a ~* dryclean

secolare *albero, tradizione* hundred-year old

secolo *m* century; *ti ho aspettato un ~!* I waited hours for you!

seconda *f* AUTO second (gear); FERR second class; EDU second year

secondario (*pl* -ri) secondary

secondo 1 *agg* second; *di -a mano* second-hand; *~ fine* ulterior motive,

S

hidden agenda **2** *prp* according to; *~ me* in my opinion; *~ le istruzioni* as per instructions **3** *m* second; GASTR main course

secrétaire *m inv mobile* writing desk

sedano *m* celery

sedare <1b> calm (down)

sedativo *m* sedative

sede *f* headquarters; *la Santa Sede* the Holy See

sedentario (*pl* -ri) sedentary

sedere 1 *m* F rear end **F 2** *v/i* <2o> e *sedersi* sit down

sedia *f* chair; *~ a sdraio* deck chair; *~ a dondolo* rocking chair; *~ a rotelle* wheelchair

sedicesimo *m/agg* sixteenth

sedicente so-called, self-styled

sedici sixteen

sedile *m* seat; AUTO *~ posteriore* back seat

seducente attractive

sedurre <3e> seduce; (*attrarre*) attract

seduta *f* session; (*posa*) sitting; *~ plenaria* plenary session

seduto seated

seduttore *m*, **-trice** *f* seducer; *donna* seductress

seduzione *f* seduction

S.E. e O. *abbr* (= *salvo errori e omissioni*) E & OE (= errors and omissions excepted)

seg. *abbr* (= *seguente*) foll. (= following)

sega *f* (*pl* -ghe) saw

segale *f* rye; *pane m di ~* rye bread

segare <1e> saw

segatura *f* sawdust

seggio *m* (*pl* -ggi) seat; *~ (elettorale*) polling station

seggiola *f* chair

seggiolino *m di macchina, bicicletta* child's seat

seggiolone *m* high chair

seggiovia *f* chair lift

seggo → *sedere*

segnalare <1a> signal; (*annunciare*) report

segnale *m* signal; (*segno*) sign; *~ d'allarme* alarm; *~ orario* (*alla ra-*

dio) time signal; *~ stradale* road sign

segnaletica *f* signs *pl*; *~ stradale* road signs *pl*

segnalibro *m* bookmark

segnare <1a> (*marcare*) mark; (*annotare*) note down; SP score; *~ a dito qu* point s.o. out, point to s.o.; *sentirsi segnato a dita* feel the finger pointed at you; *ha segnato due gol* he scored two goals

segno *m* sign; (*traccia*) mark, trace; (*cenno*) gesture, sign; *-i pl caratteristici* distinguishing marks; *fig non dar -i di vita* not get in touch; *cogliere nel ~* hit the nail on the head; *~ zodiacale* sign of the zodiac; *farsi il ~ della croce* cross o.s.; *lasciare il ~* leave a mark

segretaria *f* secretary; *~ di direzione* executive secretary

segretariato *m* secretariat

segretario *m* (*pl* -ri) secretary; POL *~ di partito* party leader

segreteria *f carica* secretaryship; *ufficio* administrative office; *attività* secretarial duties *pl*; *~ telefonica* answering machine, answerphone

segreto 1 *agg* secret **2** *m* secret; *~ professionale* confidentiality

seguace *m/f* disciple, follower

seguente next, following

seguire <4a> **1** *v/t* follow; *corso* take **2** *v/i* follow (*a qc* sth); *come segue* as follows

seguitare <1l>: *~ a fare qc* carry on doing sth

seguito *m persone* retinue; (*sostenitori*) followers; *di film* sequel; *di ~* one after the other, in succession; *in ~* after that; *in ~ a* following, in the wake of

sei[1] → *essere*

sei[2] six

seicento 1 *agg* six hundred **2** *m*: *il Seicento* the seventeenth century

selciato *m* paving

selezione *f* selection

self-service *m inv* self-service

sella *f* saddle

sellino *m* saddle

seltz *m*: **acqua** *f di ~* soda (water)
selva *f* forest
selvaggina *f* game
selvaggio (*pl* -ggi) **1** *agg animale, fiori* wild; *tribù, omicidio* savage **2** *m*, **-a** *f* savage
selvatico (*pl* -ci) wild
semaforo *m* traffic lights
sembrare <1a> seem; (*assomigliare a*) resemble, look like
seme *m* seed
semestre *m* six months; EDU term
semicerchio *m* (*pl* -chi) semi-circle, half-moon
semicircolare semi-circular
semiconduttore *m* EL semi-conductor
semifinale *f* semi-final
semifreddo *m* soft ice cream
semilavorato *m* semi-finished
semina *f* sowing
seminare <1l> sow
seminario *m* (*pl* -ri) seminar
seminudo half-naked
seminuovo practically new
semisfera *f* hemisphere
semolino *m* semolina
semplice simple; (*non doppio*) single; (*spontaneo*) natural
semplicità *f* simplicity
semplificare <1m & d> simplify
semplificazione *f* simplification
sempre always; *ci conosciamo da ~* we've known each other practically for ever; *è quello di ~* he's the same as always; *per ~* for ever; *~ più* more and more; *~ più vecchio* older and older; *piove ~ di più* the rain's getting heavier and heavier; *~ che* as long as, on condition that
sen. *abbr* (= **senatore**) Sen (= senator)
senape *f* mustard
senato *m* senate
senatore *m*, **-trice** *f* senator
senile senile
senno *m* common sense; *uscire di ~* lose one's mind; (*arrabbiarsi*) lose control
seno *m* breast; GEOG inlet; MAT sine; *in ~ a* in

sensato sensible
sensazionale sensational
sensazione *f* sensation, feeling; (*impressione*) feeling; *fare ~* cause a sensation; *ho la ~ che* I have a feeling that
sensibile sensitive; (*evidente*) significant, substantial
sensibilità *f* sensitivity
sensibilizzare <1a> make more aware (*a* of)
senso *m* sense; (*significato*) meaning; (*direzione*) direction; *buon ~* common sense; *~ unico* one way; *~ vietato* no entry; *in ~ orario* clockwise; *privo di -i* unconscious; *perdere i -i* faint
sensore *m* TEC sensor
sensuale sensual
sensualità *f* sensuality
sentenza *f* DIR verdict; *~ di morte* death sentence
sentenziare <1g> *fig* pass judgment
sentiero *m* path
sentimentale sentimental
sentimento *m* feeling, sentiment
sentinella *f* sentry
sentire <4b> feel; (*udire*) hear; (*ascoltare*) listen to; *odore* smell; *cibo* taste
sentirsi feel; *sentirsela di fare qc* feel up to doing sth
senza without; *senz'altro* definitely; *~ dubbio* more than likely, probably; *~ impegno* (with) no obligation *or* commitment; *~ di me* without me
senzatetto *m/f inv* homeless person; *i -i pl* the homeless
separare <1a or 1l & b> separate
separarsi separate, split up F
separazione *f* separation; *~ dei beni* division of property
sepolto *pp* → **seppellire**
sepoltura *f* burial
seppellire <4d> bury
seppia *f* cuttle fish
seppure even if
sequestrare <1b> confiscate; DIR impound, seize; (*rapire*) kidnap
sequestro *m* kidnap(ping); DIR

sera f evening; *di* ~ in the evenings; *questa* ~ this evening; *verso* ~ towards evening

serale evening *attr*

serata f evening; (*festa*) party; ~ *danzante* dance; ~ *di gala* gala (evening)

serbatoio m (*pl* -oi) tank; ~ *di riserva* reserve tank

serbo¹ 1 *agg* Serbian **2** m, -a f Serb

serbo² m: *tenere qc* ~ keep; *avere qc in* ~ have sth in store

serenata f serenade

serenità f serenity

sereno serene; *fig* relaxed, calm

serial m *inv* serial

seriale INFOR serial; *porta* f ~ serial port

sericoltura f silk-worm farming

serie f *inv* series; *articolo* m *di* ~ mass produced item; *produzione* f *in* ~ mass production

serietà f seriousness

serigrafia f silk-screen printing

serio (*pl* -ri) **1** *agg* serious; (*affidabile*) reliable **2** m: *sul* ~ seriously

sermone m sermon

serpe f grass snake

serpeggiare <1f> wind

serpente m snake

serpentina f *linea* wavy line; *strada* winding street

serra f greenhouse

serramanico m: *coltello* m *a* ~ flick knife

serranda f shutter

serrare <1b> close; *denti, pugni* clench; ~ *il ritmo* step up the pace

serrata f lock-out

serratura f lock; ~ *a combinazione* combination lock

servire <4b> **1** v/i be useful; *non mi serve* I don't need it; *a che serve questo?* what's this for?; ~ *da bere a qu* pour s.o. a drink **2** v/t serve; *mi serve aiuto* I need help

servirsi (*usare*) use (*di* sth); *prego, si serva!* a tavola please help yourself!

servitù f slavery, servitude; (*persona-le*) servants *pl*

servizio m (*pl* -zi) service; (*favore*) favo(u)r; (*dipartimento*) department; *in giornale* feature (story); *lavorare a mezzo* ~ work part-time; ~ *assistenza tecnica* after-sales service; ~ *civile* community service in lieu of military service; ~ *militare* military service; ~ *d'emergenza* emergency service; ~ *da tavola* dinner service; *di* ~ on duty; *fuori* ~ out of order; *in* ~ on duty; *-zi* *pl* services

servofreno m servo brake

servosterzo m power steering

sesamo m sesame

sessanta sixty

sessantenne sixty-year-old

sessantesimo m/agg sixtieth

sessantina f: *una* ~ about sixty (*di* sth); *sulla* ~ about sixty

sesso m sex

sessuale sexual

sessualità f sexuality

sesto m/agg sixth

seta f silk; ~ *artificiale* artificial silk

sete f thirst; *aver* ~ be thirsty

setola f bristle

setta f sect

settanta seventy

settantenne seventy-year-old

settantesimo m/agg seventieth

settantina f: *una* ~ about seventy (*di* sth); *sulla* ~ about seventy

settare <1a> *macchina, computer* set up

sette seven

settecento 1 *agg* seven hundred **2** m: *il Settecento* the eighteenth century

settembre m September

settentrionale 1 *agg* northern **2** m/f northerner

settentrione m north

setticemia f septic(a)emia

settimana f week; ~ *corta* five-day week; ~ *santa* Easter week

settimanale m/agg weekly

settimo m/agg seventh

settore m sector

severità f severity

severo severe

sezione f section

sfaccendato idle

sfacchinata f backbreaking job

sfacciato cheeky

sfacelo m ruin

sfamare <1a> feed

sfarfallio m flicker

sfarzo m splendo(u)r

sfarzoso magnificent

sfasciare <1f> smash; MED unbandage

sfasciarsi smash

sfaticato m, **-a** f idler

sfavillare <1a> di occhi sparkle; di fuoco flicker

sfavillio m di occhi sparkle

sfavore m disadvantage

sfavorevole unfavourable

sfera f sphere; **- d'azione** responsibilities, duties; **~ di competenza** area of expertise

sferico (pl -ci) spherical

sfida f challenge

sfidare <1a> challenge

sfiducia f distrust, mistrust; **voto m di ~** vote of no confidence

sfiduciato discouraged, disheartened

sfigurare <1a> **1** v/t disfigure **2** v/i look out of place

sfigurato disfigured

sfilare <1a> **1** v/t unthread; (togliere) take off **2** v/i parade

sfilata f: **~ di moda** fashion show

sfinimento m exhaustion

sfinito exhausted

sfiorare <1a> brush; argomento touch on

sfiorire <4d> fade, wither

sfitto empty, not let

sfocato foto blurred

sfociare <1f> flow

sfogare <1e> rabbia, frustrazione vent, get rid of (**con, su** on)

sfogarsi vent one's feelings; **non ti sfogare su di me** don't take it out on me; **~ con qu** confide in s.o., pour one's heart out to s.o.

sfoglia: **pasta** f **~** puff pastry

sfogliare <1g & c> libro leaf through

sfogo m (pl -ghi) outlet; MED rash

sfoltire <4d> thin

sfondare <1a> break; porta break down; muro knock down; pavimento break through

sfondo m background

sformare <1a> stretch out of shape

sformato m GASTR soufflé

sfornito: **essere ~ di qc** be out of sth

sfortuna f bad luck, misfortune

sfortunatamente unfortunately

sfortunato unlucky, unfortunate

sforzare <1c> strain

sforzarsi try very hard, make every effort

sforzo m effort; fisico strain; **fare uno ~** make an effort; fisicamente strain o.s.; **senza ~** effortlessly

sfracellarsi <1b> break into pieces, shatter

sfrattare <1a> evict

sfratto m eviction; avviso notice to quit

sfregare <1e> rub

sfrenato unrestrained

sfrontato insolent

sfruttamento m exploitation

sfruttare <1a> exploit

sfuggevole fleeting

sfuggire <4a> (scampare) escape (**a** from); **mi è sfuggito di mente** it slipped my mind

sfuggita f: **di ~** in passing

sfumatura f nuance; di colore shade

sfuriata f (angry) tirade

sfuso loose; burro melted; vino in bulk

sgabello m stool

sgabuzzino m cupboard

sgambetto m: **fare lo ~ a qu** trip s.o. up

sganciare <1f> unhook; FERR uncouple; F soldi fork out F

sganciarsi become unhooked; di persona release o.s.; fig free o.s.

sgarbato rude

sgarbo m discourtesy

sgelare <1b> thaw

sgelo m thaw

sghembo crooked; **di ~** crookedly, not in a straight line

sgobbare <1c> slave

sgobbone *m*, **-a** *f* F swot F

sgocciolare <1l> *v/t & v/i* drip

sgomberare <1l> → **sgombrare**

sgombero *m di strada* clearing; *(trasloco)* removal

sgombrare <1a> *strada, stanza* clear; *ostacolo* remove; *appartamento* clear out, empty

sgombro[1] *agg strada, stanza* empty

sgombro[2] *m* mackerel

sgomentare <1a> frighten

sgomentarsi be frightened

sgomento *m* fear

sgonfiare <1k> **1** *v/t* let the air out of **2** *v/i e* **sgonfiarsi** become deflated; *il braccio si è sgonfiato* the swelling in the arm has gone down

sgonfio (*pl* -fi) flat; MED not swollen

sgradevole unpleasant

sgradito unwelcome

sgranchire <4d>, **sgranchirsi**: **~ le gambe** stretch one's legs

sgraziato awkward

sgridare <1a> scold, tell off F

sgridata *f* scolding, telling off F

sguaiato raucous

sgualdrina *f* tart

sguardo *m* look; *(occhiata)* glance; *al primo ~* at first glance

sguazzare <1a> splash about; *fig* F **~ nei soldi** be rolling in (it) F

sgusciare <1f> **1** *v/t* shell **2** *v/i* slip away; *mi è sgusciato di mano* it slipped out of my hand

shampoo *m inv* shampoo

shock *m inv* shock; **~ culturale** culture shock

si[1] *pron* oneself; *lui* himself; *lei* herself; *esso, essa* itself; *loro* themselves; *reciproco* each other; **spazzolarsi i capelli** brush one's hair; **~ è spazzolato i capelli** he brushed his hair; **~ dice** they say; **cosa ~ può dire?** what can one say?, what can I say?; **~ capisce da sé** it's self-evident

si[2] *m* MUS B

sì *avv* yes; **dire di ~** say yes; **~ e no** yes and no; **penso di ~** I think so

sia: **~ ... ~ ...** both ... and ...; *(o l'uno*

o l'altro) either ... or ...; **~ che ... ~ che ...** whether ... or whether ...

siamo → **essere**

sibilare <1l> hiss; *di vento* whistle

sibilo *m* hiss; *di vento* whistle

sicario *m* hired killer, hit man F

sicché (and) so

siccità *f* drought

siccome since

Sicilia *f* Sicily

siciliano 1 *agg* Sicilian **2** *m*, **-a** *f* Sicilian

sicura *f* safety catch

sicurezza *f* security; *(protezione)* safety; *(certezza)* certainty; **pubblica** ~ police; **cintura di** ~ safety belt; **misure fpl di** ~ safety measures

sicuro 1 *agg luogo* safe; *investimento* sound, safe; *(certo)* sure; **~ di sé** self-confident, sure of o.s.; **di** ~ definitely **2** *m*: **essere al** ~ **da qc** be safe from sth; **mettere al** ~ put in a safe place

siderurgia *f* iron and steel industry

sidro *m* cider

siedo → **sedere**

siepe *f* hedge

siero *m* MED serum

sieropositivo HIV positive

siesta *f* siesta

siete → **essere**

sifilide *f* MED syphilis

sig. *abbr* (= **signore**) Mr (= mister)

sigaretta *f* cigarette; **~ col filtro** filter tip

sigaro *m* cigar

sigg. *abbr* (= **signori**) Messrs

sigillare <1a> seal

sigillo *m* seal

sigla *f* initials *pl*; *musicale* theme (tune)

sig.na *abbr* (= **signorina**) Miss, Ms

significare <1m & d> mean

significativo significant

significato *m* meaning

signora *f* lady; **mi scusi, ~!** excuse me!; **la ~ Rossi** Mrs Rossi; **-e e signori** ladies and gentlemen

signore *m* gentleman; **mi scusi, ~!** excuse me!; **il signor Rossi** Mr Rossi; **i -i Rossi** Mr and Mrs Rossi signorile *appartamento* luxury; *modi* gentlemanly

signorina *f* young lady; **è ancora ~** she's not married; **la ~ Rossi** Miss Rossi

sig.ra *abbr* (= **signora**) Mrs

silenziatore *m* silencer, *Am* muffler

silenzio *m* silence; **fare ~** be quiet; **~!** silence!, quiet!

silenzioso silent

sillaba *f* syllable

sillabare <1l> split into syllables

silo *m* silo

siluro *m* MAR torpedo

simboleggiare <1f> symbolize

simbolico (*pl* -ci) symbolic

simbolismo *m* symbolism

simbolo *m* symbol

simile similar

simmetria *f* symmetry

simmetrico (*pl* -ci) symmetric(al)

simpatia *f* liking; (*affinità*) sympathy; **avere ~ per qu** like s.o.

simpatico (*pl* -ci) likeable

simpatizzare <1a> become friends

simposio *m* (*pl* -si) symposium

simulare <1l> feign; TEC simulate

simulazione *f* pretence, *Am* pretense; TECH simulation; **~ elettronica** electronic simulation

sinagoga *f* (*pl* -ghe) synagogue

sinceramente sincerely; (*in verità*) honestly

sincerarsi <1b> make sure

sincerità *f* sincerity

sincero sincere

sincronizzare <1a> synchronize

sindacalista *m/f* (*mpl* -i) trade unionist

sindacato *m* trade union

sindaco *m* (*pl* -ci) mayor

sinfonia *f* symphony

sinfonico (*pl* -ci) symphonic

singhiozzare <1a> sob

singhiozzo *m:* **avere il ~** have hiccups; **-zi** *pl* sobs

single *m/f inv* single

singolare **1** *agg* singular; (*insolito*) unusual; (*strano*) strange **2** *m* singular; SP singles

singolo **1** *agg* individual; *camera,* *letto* single **2** *m* individual; SP singles

sinistra *f* left; **a ~** on the left; *andare* to the left

sinistro **1** *agg* left, left-hand; *fig* sinister **2** *m* accident

sino → *fino*

sinonimo **1** *agg* synonymous **2** *m* synonym

sintesi *f inv* synthesis; (*riassunto*) summary

sintetico (*pl* -ci) synthetic; (*riassunto*) brief; **materiale *m* ~** synthetic (material)

sintetizzare <1a> synthesize; (*riassumere*) summarize, sum up

sintomo *m* symptom

sintonia *f* RAD tuning; *fig* **essere in ~** be on the same wavelength (**con** with)

sintonizzare <1a> RAD tune

sintonizzarsi tune in (**su** to)

sinusite *f* sinusitis

sipario *m* (*pl* -ri) curtain

sirena *f* siren; *mitologica* mermaid; **~ d'allarme** alarm

siringa *f* (*pl* -ghe) MED syringe; **~ monouso** disposable syringe

sismico (*pl* -ci) seismic

sistema *m* (*pl* -i) system; **~ antibloccaggio** anti-lock braking system; **~ elettorale proporzionale** proportional representation; **~ immunitario** immune system; **~ monetario** monetary system; INFOR **~ operativo** operating system

sistemare <1b> put; (*mettere in ordine*) arrange; *casa* do up

sistemarsi tidy o.s. up; (*trovare casa, sposarsi*) settle down

sistematico (*pl* -ci) systematic

sistemazione *f* place; (*lavoro*) job; *in albergo* accommodation

sito site; *in* **~** on the premises

situare <1l> locate, find

situato: **essere ~** be situated

situazione *f* situation

slacciare <1f> undo

slalom *m* slalom

slanciato slender

slancio *m* (*pl* -ci) impulse

slavo **1** *agg* Slav, Slavonic **2** *m*, **-a** *f* Slav

sleale disloyal

slealtà f disloyalty

slegare <1e> untie

slegarsi free o.s.

slegato fig incoherent, disjointed

slip m inv underpants; **da donna** knickers; **~ da bagno** bathing trunks

slitta f sledge

slittino m sled; SP bobsleigh

s.l.m. abbr (= **sul livello del mare**) above sea level

slogan m inv slogan

slogare <1e> dislocate

slogarsi: **~ una caviglia** sprain one's ankle

slogatura f sprain

sloggiare <1f> move out

smacchiare <1k> take the stains out of

smacchiatore m stain remover

smagliatura f ladder, Am run; MED stretch mark

smaltare <1a> enamel

smaltimento m FIN disposal of stock; di rifiuti tossici disposal

smaltire <4d> dispose of

smalto m enamel; per ceramiche glaze; **~ per unghie** nail varnish or polish

smantellamento m dismantling

smantellare <1b> dismantle

smarrimento m loss

smarrire <4d> lose

smarrirsi get lost

smarrito 1 pp → **smarrire 2** agg lost

smascherare <1l> unmask

Sme abbr (= **Sistema monetario europeo**) EMS (= European Monetary System)

smemorato forgetful

smentire <4d> prove to be wrong; **non si smentisce mai!** he doesn't change!

smentita f denial

smeraldo 1 m emerald **2** agg emerald (green)

smercio m (pl -ci) sale

smesso pp → **smettere**

smettere <3ee> **1** v/t stop; abiti stop

wearing **2** v/i stop (**di fare qc** doing sth)

smilitarizzare <1a> demilitarize

smilitarizzazione f demilitarization

sminuire <4d> problema downplay; persona belittle

smistamento m FERR shunting

smistare <1a> FERR shunt

smisurato boundless

smodato excessive

smog m smog

smontabile which can be taken apart, Am knockdown

smontaggio m dismantling

smontare <1a> **1** v/i (da cavallo) dismount **2** v/t dismantle; persona deflate

smorfia f grimace

smorfioso affected, simpering

smorto persona deathly pale; colore dull

smorzare <1c> colore tone down; luce dim; entusiasmo dampen

smuovere <3ff> shift, move

snellezza f slenderness

snellire <4d> slim down; fig pare down

snello slim, slender

snervante irritating, wearing on the nerves

snob 1 agg snobbish **2** m/f inv snob

SO abbr (= **sud-ovest**) SW (= southwest)

so → **sapere**

sobborgo m (pl -ghi) suburb

sobrietà f sobriety

sobrio (pl -ri) sober

Soc. abbr (= **società**) Co (= company); soc. (= society)

socchiudere <3b> half-close

socchiuso 1 pp → **socchiudere 2** agg half-closed; porta ajar

soccombere <3a> succumb

soccorrere <3o> help

soccorritore m rescue worker

soccorso 1 pp → **soccorrere 2** m rescue; **venire in ~ a qu** come to s.o.'s rescue; **pronto ~** first aid; **~ stradale** breakdown service, Am wrecking service; **segnale m di ~** distress signal

sociale social
socialismo *m* socialism
socialista (*mpl* -i) *agg, m/f* socialist
socializzare <1a> socialize
società *f inv* company; (*associazione*) society; *~ a responsabilità limitata* limited liability company; *~ in nome collettivo* general partnership; *~ per azioni* joint stock company; *~ del benessere* welfare society; *~ dei consumi* consumer society
socievole sociable
socio *m* (*pl* -ci), **-a** *f* member; FIN partner
sociologia *f* sociology
sociologo *m* (*pl* -gi), **-a** *f* sociologist
soddisfacente satisfying
soddisfare <3aa> satisfy
soddisfatto 1 *pp* → **soddisfare 2** *agg* satisfied; *essere ~ di qu* be satisfied with s.o.
soddisfazione *f* satisfaction
sodio *m* sodium
sodo *uovo* hard-boiled; *fig venire al ~* get down to brass tacks
sofà *m inv* sofa
sofferente suffering
sofferenza *f* suffering
soffermare <1a> *attenzione* turn
soffermarsi dwell (*su* on)
sofferto *pp* → **soffrire**
soffiare <1k> blow; F swipe F; *~arsi il naso* blow one's nose
soffice soft
soffio *m* puff
soffitta *f* attic
soffitto *m* ceiling
soffocante suffocating
soffocare <1l, c & d> suffocate
soffriggere <3cc> fry gently
soffrire <4f> **1** *v/t* suffer; *persone* bear, stand F **2** *v/i* suffer (*di* from)
sofisticato sophisticated
software *m inv* software
softwarista *m/f* software engineer
soggettivo subjective
soggetto 1 *agg* subject; *~ a tassa* subject to tax; *andare ~ a qc* suffer from sth **2** *m* GRAM subject
soggezione *f* subjection

soggiornare <1a> stay
soggiorno *m* stay; *permesso m di ~* residence permit
soglia *f* threshold
sogliola *f* sole
sognare <1a> *e* **sognarsi** dream (*di* about, of)
sognatore *m*, **-trice** *f* dreamer
sogno *m* dream; *neppure per ~!* in your dreams!
soia *f* soya
sol *m inv* MUS G
solaio *m* (*pl* -ai) attic, loft
solamente only; *~ ieri* just yesterday
solare solar
solarium *m inv* solarium
solco *m* (*pl* -chi) furrow
soldato *m* soldier
soldi *mpl* money *sg*
sole *m* sun; *c'è il ~* it's sunny; *colpo m di ~* sunstroke; *prendere il ~* sunbathe
soleggiare <1f> dry in the sun
soleggiato sun-dried
solenne solemn
solennità *f* solemnity
solere <2p>: *~ fare* be in the habit of doing
soletta *f* insole
solforico (*pl* -ci) sulphur, *Am* sulfur *attr*; *acido m ~* sulphuric, *Am* sulfuric acid
solidale *fig* in agreement
solidarietà *f* solidarity
solidarizzare <1a> agree, be in agreement
solidità *f* solidity
solido solid; (*robusto*) sturdy
solista *m/f* (*mpl* -i) soloist
solitario (*pl* -ri) **1** *agg* solitary; *luogo* lonely; *navigatore solo* **2** *m* solitaire; *gioco* patience
solito usual, same; *al o di ~* usually; *come al ~* as usual; *più del ~* more than usual
solitudine *f* solitude, being alone
sollecitare <1m> (*stimolare*) urge; *risposta* ask (again) for
sollecito 1 *agg persona* diligent; *risposta, reazione* prompt; *lettera f di ~* reminder **2** *m* reminder

sollecitudine f di persona diligence; di risposta promptness

solleticare <1m & d> tickle; appetito whet

solletico m tickling; **fare il ~ a qu** tickle s.o.; **soffrire il ~** be ticklish

sollevamento m lifting; (insurrezione) rising; **~ pesi** weightlifting

sollevare <1b> lift; problema, obiezione bring up

sollevarsi di popolo rise up; AVIA climb, rise

sollievo m relief

solo 1 agg lonely; (non accompagnato) alone; (unico) only; MUS solo; **da ~** by myself/yourself etc, on my/your etc own **2** avv only **3** m MUS solo

solstizio m (pl -zi) solstice

soltanto only; **~ ieri** only yesterday

solubile soluble

soluzione f solution; **~ provvisoria** stopgap

solvente 1 agg FIN solvent **2** m CHIM solvent

somigliante similar

somiglianza f resemblance

somigliare <1g>: **~ a qu** resemble s.o.

somma f (addizione) addition; risultato sum; (importo) amount (of money), sum; **fare la ~ di** add (up); fig **tirare le -e** sum up

sommare <1a> add; **~ a** total, come to

sommario (pl -ri) **1** agg summary **2** m summary; di libro table of contents

sommato: tutto ~ all things considered, on the whole

sommergere <3uu> submerge; fig overwhelm (**di** with)

sommergersi submerge, dive

sommergibile m submarine

sommerso città submerged; strade inches deep in water

sommesso voce quiet

somministrare <1a> MED administer

sommo 1 agg supreme **2** m summit; fig height

sommossa f uprising

sondaggio m (pl -ggi): **~ (d'opinione)** (opinion) poll

sondare <1a> sound; fig test

sonnambulo m, **-a** f sleepwalker

sonnecchiare <1k> doze

sonnifero m sleeping tablet

sonno m sleep; **aver ~** be sleepy; **prendere ~** fall asleep

sonnolento drowsy

sonnolenza f drowsiness

sono → essere

sonorità f inv sonority

sonoro sound attr; risa, applausi loud; **colonna f -a** sound-track

sontuosità f magnificence

sontuoso sumptuous, magnificent

soppesare <1a> weigh; fig weigh up

sopportabile bearable, tolerable

sopportare <1c> peso bear; fig bear, stand F

soppressione f deletion; di regola abolition

soppresso pp → sopprimere

sopprimere <3r> delete; regola abolish

sopra 1 prp on; (più in alto di) above; (riguardo a) about, on; **~ il tavolo** on the table; **l'uno ~ l'altro** one on top of the other; **i bambini ~ cinque anni** children over five; **5 gradi ~ zero** 5 degrees above zero; **al di ~ di qc** over sth **2** avv on top; (al piano superiore) upstairs; **dormirci ~** sleep on it; **vedi ~** see above; **la parte di ~** the top or upper part

soprabito m (over)coat

sopracciglio m (fpl -a) eyebrow

sopraccoperta f di letto bedspread; di libro dustjacket

sopraffare <3aa> overwhelm

sopraggiungere <3d> di persona turn up, arrive on the scene; di difficoltà arise, come up F

sopralluogo m (pl -ghi) inspection (of the site)

soprammobile m ornament

soprannaturale supernatural

soprannome m nickname

soprannumero m: **in ~** overcrowded

soprano m soprano; **mezzo ~**

mezzo(-soprano)

soprappensiero → **sovrappensiero**

soprassalto: *di* ~ with a start

soprattassa *f* surcharge

soprattutto particularly, (e)specially, above all

sopravvalutare <1a> overvalue; *fig* overestimate

sopravvenire <4p> turn up, appear

sopravvento *m*: *avere o prendere il* ~ have the upper hand

sopravvissuto 1 *agg* surviving **2** *m*, **-a** *f* survivor

sopravvivenza *f* survival

sopravvivere <3zz> survive, outlive (*a qu* s.o.)

soprintendente *m/f* supervisor

sopruso *m* abuse of power

soqquadro *m*: *mettere a* ~ turn upside down

sorbetto *m* sorbet

sorbire <4d> sip

sorbirsi put up with

sorcio *m* (*pl* -ci) mouse

sordina *f* mute; *in* ~ in secret, on the quiet F

sordità *f* deafness

sordo deaf

sordomuto deaf and dumb

sorella *f* sister

sorellastra *f* stepsister

sorgente *f* spring; *fig* source

sorgere <3d> *di sole* rise, come up; *fig* arise, come up

sormontare <1a> *difficoltà* overcome, surmount

sorpassare <1a> go past; AUTO pass, overtake; *fig* exceed

sorpassato out of date

sorpasso *m*: *divieto di* ~ no passing, no overtaking; *fare un* ~ pass, overtake

sorprendente surprising

sorprendere <3c> surprise; (*cogliere sul fatto*) catch

sorpresa *f* surprise

sorpreso *pp* → **sorprendere**

sorridere <3b> smile

sorriso 1 *pp* → **sorridere 2** *m* smile

sorseggiare <1f> sip

sorso *m* mouthful

sorta *f* sort, kind

sorte *f* fate; *tirare a* ~ draw lots

sorteggiare <1f> draw

sorteggio *m* (*pl* -ggi) draw

sorto *pp* → **sorgere**

sorveglianza *f* supervision; *di edificio* security

sorvegliare <1g> supervise; *edificio* provide security for; *bagagli ecc* look after, take care of

sorvolare <1a> **1** *v/t* AVIA fly over **2** *v/i fig*: ~ *su* skim over, skip

sosia *m inv* double

sospendere <3c> suspend; (*appendere*) hang

sospensione *f* suspension

sospeso 1 *pp* → **sospendere 2** *agg* hanging; *fig questione* pending; *tenere in* ~ *persona* keep in suspense

sospettare <1b> suspect; ~ *qu o di qu* suspect s.o.

sospetto 1 *agg* suspicious **2** *m*, **-a** *f* suspect

sospettoso suspicious

sospirare <1a> **1** *v/i* sigh **2** *v/t* long for

sospiro *m* sigh

sosta *f* stop; (*pausa*) break, pause; *senza* ~ nonstop; *divieto di* ~ no parking

sostantivo *m* noun

sostanza *f* substance; *in* ~ in short, to sum up

sostare <1c> stop

sostegno *m* support; *a* ~ *di* in support of

sostenere <2q> support; (*affermare*) maintain

sostengo → **sostenere**

sostenitore *m*, **-trice** *f* supporter

sostentamento *m* support

sostenuto *stile* formal; *velocità* high

sostituibile which can be replaced, replaceable

sostituire <4d>: ~ *X con Y* replace X with Y, substitute Y for X

sostituto *m*, **-a** *f* substitute, replacement

sostituzione *f* substitution, replacement

S

sottaceti *mpl* pickles

sottana *f* slip, underskirt; (*gonna*) skirt; REL cassock

sotterranea *f* underground

sotterraneo 1 *agg* underground *attr* **2** *m* cellar

sotterrare <1b> bury

sottile fine; *fig* subtle; *udito* keen

sottintendere <3c> imply

sottinteso 1 *pp* → **sottintendere 2** *m* allusion

sotto 1 *prp* under; *i bambini ~ cin-que anni* children under five; *5 gra-di ~ zero* 5 degrees below (zero); *~ la pioggia* in the rain; *al di ~ di qc* under sth **2** *avv* below; (*più in bas-so*) lower down; (*al di sotto*) underneath; (*al piano di ~*) downstairs

sottobanco under the counter

sottobraccio: camminare ~ walk arm-in-arm; **prendere qu ~** take s.o.'s arm

sottocchio: tenere ~ qc keep an eye on sth

sottochiave under lock and key

sottocosto at less than cost price

sottoesposto FOT underexposed

sottofondo *m* background

sottolineare <1n> *anche fig* underline

sottomarino 1 *agg* underwater *attr* **2** *m* submarine

sottomesso 1 *pp* → **sottomettere 2** *agg* submissive; *popolo* subject *attr*

sottomettere <3ee> submit; *popolo* subdue

sottomissione *f* submission

sottopassaggio *m* (*pl* -ggi) underpass

sottoporre <3ll> submit

sottoporsi: ~ a undergo

sottoscritto 1 *pp* → **sottoscrivere 2** *m* undersigned

sottoscrivere <3tt> *documento* sign; *teoria* subscribe to; *abbonamento* take out

sottoscrizione *f* signing; (*abbona-mento*) subscription

sottosopra *fig* upside-down

sottosuolo *m* subsoil; *ricchezze fpl*

del ~ mineral wealth; **nel ~** underground

sottosviluppato underdeveloped

sottovalutare <1a> undervalue; *per-sona* underestimate

sottoveste *f* slip, underskirt

sottovoce quietly, sotto voce

sottrarre <3xx> MAT subtract; *dena-ro* embezzle

sottrarsi: ~ a qc avoid sth

sottratto *pp* → **sottrarre**

sottrazione *f* MAT subtraction; *di de-naro* embezzlement

sottufficiale *m* non-commissioned officer, NCO

souvenir *m inv* souvenir

sovietico (*pl* -ci) Soviet

sovrabbondante overabundant

sovrabbondanza *f* overabundance

sovrabbondare <1a> be overabundant; *~ di* have an overabundance of

sovraccarico 1 *agg* overloaded (*di* with) **2** *m* overload

sovrano 1 *agg* sovereign **2** *m*, **-a** *f* sovereign

sovrappensiero: essere ~ be lost in thought

sovrappeso 1 *agg* overweight **2** *m* excess weight

sovrappopolato overpopulated

sovrapporre <3ll> overlap

sovrapposizione *f* overlapping

sovrapproduzione *f* overproduction

sovrastare <1a> overlook, dominate

sovrintendente *m/f* → **soprinten-dente**

sovrumano superhuman

sovvenzionare <1a> give a grant to

sovvenzione *f* grant

sovversivo subversive

S.P. *abbr* (= **Strada Provinciale**) B road

S.p.A. *abbr* (= **Società per Azioni**) joint stock company

spaccare <1d> break in two; *legna* split, chop

spaccarsi break in two

spaccatura *f* crevice

spacciare <1f> *droga* deal in, push F; *siamo spacciati!* we've had it!

spacciarsi: ~ *per* pass o.s. off as

spacciatore *m,* **-trice** *f di droga* dealer

spaccio *m (pl* -cci) *di droga* dealing; *negozio* general store

spacco *m (pl* -cchi) *m in gonna* slit; *in giacca* vent

spaccone *m,* **-a** *f* braggart

spada *f* sword

spadroneggiare <1f> throw one's weight around

spaesato disorient(at)ed, confused

spaghetti *mpl* spaghetti *sg*

Spagna *f* Spain

spagnolo 1 *m/agg* Spanish **2** *m,* **-a** *f* Spaniard

spago *m (pl* -ghi) string

spalancare <1d> open wide

spalla *f* shoulder; *girare le* -*e a qu* turn one's back on s.o.; *era di* -*e* he had his back to me; *stringersi nelle* -*e* shrug; *vivere alle* -*e di qu* live off s.o.

spalleggiare <1f> support, back up

spalliera *f* wallbars

spallina *f* shoulder pad

spalmare <1a> spread

spalti *mpl* terraces

spandere <3a> spread

spandersi spread

spanto *pp* → **spandere**

sparare <1a> **1** *v/i* shoot (*a* at) **2** *v/t:* ~ *un colpo* fire a shot

sparatoria *f* gunfire, series of shots

sparecchiare <1k> clear

spareggio *m* SP play-off

spargere <3uu> spread; *lagrime, sangue* shed

sparire <4d or 4e> disappear

sparizione *f* disappearance

sparo *m* (gun)shot

sparpagliare <1g> scatter

sparso 1 *pp* → **spargere 2** *agg* scattered

spartiacque *m inv* watershed

spartire <4d> divide (up), split F

spartito *m* score

spartitraffico *m (pl* -ci) traffic island

spartizione *f* division

spasimante *m/f* admirer

spasimo *m* agony

spasmo *m* MED spasm

spasso *m* fun; *andare a* ~ go for a walk; *fig essere a* ~ be out of work, be unemployed; *è uno* ~ he/it's a good laugh; *per* ~ as a joke, for fun

spassoso very funny

spastico (*pl* -ci) spastic

spaurito frightened

spavaldo cocky, over-confident

spaventapasseri *m inv* scarecrow

spaventare <1b> frighten, scare

spaventarsi be frightened, be scared

spavento *m* fright; *mi sono preso uno* ~ I got a fright

spaventoso frightening

spaziale space *attr*

spazientirsi <4d> get impatient, lose one's patience

spazio *m (pl* -zi) space; ~ *aereo* airspace

spazioso spacious

spazzacamino *m* chimney sweep

spazzaneve *m inv* snowplough, *Am* -plow

spazzare <1a> sweep

spazzatura *f* rubbish, garbage

spazzino *m,* **-a** *f* street sweeper

spazzola *f* brush

spazzolare <1l> brush

spazzolino *m* brush; ~ *da denti* toothbrush

specchiarsi <1k> look at o.s.; *(riflettersi)* be mirrored, be reflected

specchietto *m* mirror; *(prospetto)* table; AUTO ~ *retrovisore* rear-view mirror

specchio *m (pl* -cchi) mirror

speciale special

specialista *m/f (mpl* -i) specialist

specialità *f inv* special(i)ty

specializzarsi <1a> specialize

specialmente especially

specie *f inv* species; *una* ~ *di* a sort or kind of **2** *avv* especially

specificare <1m & d> specify

specifico (*pl* -ci) specific

speculare <1l & b> speculate (*in* in, *su* on)

speculativo speculative

speculatore *m*, **-trice** *f* speculator

speculazione *f* speculation

spedire <4d> send

spedito fast

spedizione *f* dispatch, sending; *di merce* shipping; (*viaggio*) expedition; *agenzia f di* ~ shipping agency; **spese** *pl* **di** ~ shipping costs

spedizioniere *m* courier

spegnere <3vv> put out; *luce, motore, radio* turn off, switch off

spegnersi *di fuoco* go out; *di motore* stop, die F

spellare <1a> skin

spellarsi peel

spelonca *f* (*pl* -che) cave

spendere <3c> spend; *fig* invest

spennare <1a> *pollo* pluck

spensierato carefree

spento *pp* → **spegnere**

speranza *f* hope; *senza* ~ hopeless

sperare <1b> **1** *v/t* hope for **2** *v/i* trust (**in** in)

sperduto lost; *luogo* remote, isolated

spergiuro **1** *m* perjury **2** *m*, **-a** *f* perjurer

sperimentale experimental

sperimentare <1a> try; *in laboratorio* test; *fig: fatica, dolore* feel; *droga* experiment with

sperma *m* sperm

sperperare <1l & b> fritter away, squander

sperpero *m* frittering away, squandering

spesa *f* expense; *fare la* ~ do the shopping; *fare* -*e* go shopping; -*e pl di produzione* production costs; -*e pl di pubblicità* advertising costs; -*e pl vive* incidental expenses; *a proprie* -*e* at one's own expense

spesso **1** *agg* thick; -*e volte* many times, often **2** *avv* often, frequently

spessore *m* thickness

spett. *abbr* (= **spettabile**) Messrs; *in lettera* **Spett. Ditta** Dear Sirs

spettacolare spectacular

spettacolo *m* show; (*panorama*) spectacle, sight; ~ **teatrale** show

spettare <1b>: *questo spetta a te*

this is yours; *non spetta a te giudicare* it's not up to you to judge

spettatore *m*, **-trice** *f* spectator; TEA member of the audience

spettinare <1l & b>: ~ *qu* ruffle s.o.'s hair

spettro *m* ghost; FIS spectrum

spezie *fpl* spices

spezzare <1b> break in two

spezzarsi break

spezzatino *m* stew

spezzato **1** *agg* broken (in two) **2** *m* co-ordinated two-piece suit

spezzettare <1a> break up

spia *f* spy; TEC pilot light; *fare la* ~ tell, sneak

spiacente: *essere* ~ be sorry; *sono molto* ~ I am very sorry

spiacere <2k>: *mi spiace* I am sorry

spiacevole unpleasant

spiaggia *f* (*pl* -gge) beach

spianare <1a> roll

spiare <1h> spy on

spiazzo *m* empty space; *in bosco* clearing

spiccato strong

spicchio *m* (*pl* -cchi) *di frutto* section; ~ *d'aglio* clove of garlic

spicciarsi <1f> hurry up

spiccioli *mpl* (small) change *sg*

spiedo *m* spit; *allo* ~ spit-roasted

spiegabile possible to explain

spiegare <1b & e> (*stendere*) spread; (*chiarire*) explain

spiegarsi explain what one means; *mi spiego?* have I made myself clear?; *non so se mi spiego* I don't know if I make myself clear

spiegazione *f* explanation

spiegazzare <1a> crease

spietato merciless, pitiless

spiga *f* (*pl* -ghe) *di grano* ear

spigato herring-bone *attr*

spigliato confident

spigola *f* sea bass

spigolo *m* corner

spilla *f* *gioiello* brooch; ~ *da balia* safety pin

spillo *m* pin; ~ *di sicurezza* safety pin

spina *f* BOT thorn; ZO spine; *di pesce*

bone; EL plug; ANAT **~ dorsale** spine; **parcheggio m a ~ di pesce** angle parking; **birra f alla ~** draught beer, beer on tap; *fig* **stare sulle -e** be on tenterhooks

spinaci *mpl* spinach *sg*

spinale spinal

spinello F *m* joint F

spingere <3d> push; *fig* drive

spino *m* thorn

spinoso thorny

spinta *f* push

spinterogeno *m* AUTO distributor

spinto *pp* → **spingere**

spionaggio *m* (*pl* -ggi) espionage

spiraglio *m* (*pl* -gli) crack; *di luce, speranza* gleam, glimmer

spirale *f* spiral; *contraccettivo* coil

spirare <1a> blow; *fig* die

spirito *m* spirit; (*disposizione*) mind; (*umorismo*) wit; **avere ~ d'osservazione** be observant; **fare dello ~** be witty

spiritoso witty

spirituale spiritual

splendere <3a> shine

splendente bright

splendido wonderful, splendid

splendore *m* splendo(u)r

spogliare <1g> undress; (*rubare*) rob

spogliarsi undress, strip; **~ di qc** give sth up

spogliarello *m* striptease

spogliatoio *m* (*pl* -oi) dressing room, locker room

spoglio (*pl* -gli) bare

spola *f*: **fare la ~ da un posto all'altro** shuttle backwards and forwards between two places

spolverare <1l> dust

spolverizzare <1a> dust (**di** with)

sponda *f di letto* edge, side; *di fiume* bank; *nel biliardo* cushion

sponsor *m inv* sponsor

sponsorizzare <1a> sponsor

spontaneità *f* spontaneity

spontaneo spontaneous

sporadico (*pl* -ci) sporadic

sporcare <1c & d> dirty

sporcarsi get dirty

sporcizia *f* dirt

sporco (*pl* -chi) **1** *agg* dirty **2** *m* dirt

sporgere <3d> **1** *v/t* hold out; *denuncia* make **2** *v/i* jut out

sporgersi lean out

sport *m inv* sport; **~pl invernali** winter sports; **fare dello ~** do sport; **per ~** for fun

sporta *f* shopping bag; *di vimini* shopping basket

sportello *m* door; **~ automatico** automatic teller machine, cash dispenser

sportivo 1 *agg* sports *attr; persona* sporty; **campo m ~** playing field **2** *m*, **-a** *f* sportsman; **donna** sportswoman

sporto *pp* → **sporgere**

sposa *f* bride; **abito m da ~** wedding dress

sposare <1c> marry

sposarsi get married

sposato married

sposo *m* bridegroom; **-i** *pl* newlyweds

spostare <1a> (*trasferire*) move, shift; (*rimandare*) postpone

spostarsi move

S.P.Q.R. *abbr* (= **Senatus Populusque Romanus**) the Senate and People of Rome

spranga *f* (*pl* -ghe) bar

sprangare <1e> bar

sprecare <1b & d> waste, squander

spreco *m* (*pl* -chi) waste

spregevole contemptible, despicable

spregiudicato unprejudiced, unbiased; *spreg* unscrupulous

spremere <3a> squeeze

spremilimoni *m inv* lemon squeezer

spremuta *f* juice; **~ di limone** lemon juice; **~ d'arancia** orange juice

sprizzare <1a> spurt; *fig* exude

sprofondare <1a> sink; *fig* **~ dalla vergogna** be overcome with embarrassment

spronare <1a> spur on

sprone *m* spur

sproporzionato disproportionate (**a** to), out of proportion (**a** to)

sproposito *m* blunder; **fare uno ~**

do something silly; **costare uno ~** cost a fortune; **a ~** out of turn

sprovveduto inexperienced

sprovvisto: **~ di** lacking; **sono ~ di ...** I don't have any ...; **alla -a** unexpectedly

spruzzare <1a> spray

spruzzatore m spray

spruzzo m spray; **fango** splatter

spudorato shameless

spugna f sponge

spuma f foam

spumante: **(vino** m**) ~** sparkling wine

spumeggiante frothy; **persona** bubbly

spuntare <1a> stick out; BOT come up; **di sole** appear; **di giorno** break; **gli è spuntato un dente** he has cut a tooth

spuntino m snack

spunto m suggestion; **prendere ~ da** be inspired by

sputare <1a> **1** v/i spit **2** v/t spit out

sputo m spittle

squadra f **strumento** set square; **(gruppo)** squad; SP team; **~ volante** flying squad

squalifica f (pl -che) disqualification

squalificare <1m & d> disqualify

squallido squalid

squallore m squalor

squalo m shark

squama f flake; **di pesce** scale

squarcio m (pl -ci) in **stoffa** rip, tear; in **nuvole** break

squilibrato 1 agg insane **2** m, **-a** f lunatic

squilibrio m (pl -ri) imbalance

squillare <1a> ring

squillo m ring; **ragazza** f **~** callgirl

squisito cibo delicious

sradicare <1l & d> uproot; fig **(eliminare)** eradicate, uproot

S.r.l. abbr **(= Società a responsabilità limitata)** Ltd (= limited)

SS. abbr **(= santi)** Saints

S.S. abbr **(= Sua Santità)** His Holiness (the Pope); **(= Strada Statale)** A road

stabile 1 agg steady; **(duraturo)** stable; **tempo** settled **2** m building

stabilimento m **(fabbrica)** plant, Br factory; **~ balneare** lido

stabilire <4d> **data, obiettivi, record** set; **(decidere)** decide, settle

stabilirsi settle

stabilità f steadiness; **di relazione, moneta** stability

stabilizzare <1a> stabilize

staccare <1d> remove, detach; EL unplug; TELEC **il ricevitore** lift the receiver

stadio m (pl -di) stage; SP stadium

staffa f stirrup; **perdere le -e** blow one's top

staffetta f SP relay; **corsa** f **a ~** relay race

stage m inv training period

stagionale seasonal

stagionare <1a> age, mature; **legno** season

stagionato aged, mature; **legno** seasoned

stagione f season; **alta ~** high season; **bassa ~** low season; **~ morta** off-season; **frutta** f **di ~** fruit in season, seasonal fruit

stagnare <1a> **dell'acqua** grow stagnant; FIN stagnate

stagnante stagnant

stagno 1 m pond; TEC tin **2** agg watertight

stalla f **per bovini** cowshed; **per cavalli** stable

stamani, stamattina this morning

stambecco m (pl -cchi) ibex

stampa f press; **tecnica** printing; FOT print; **posta -e** pl printed matter; **libro** m **in corso di ~** book that has gone to press; **~ locale** local press; **~ scandalistica** tabloids, gutter press; **libertà** f **di ~** freedom of the press

stampante f INFOR printer; **~ a getto di inchiostro** ink-jet printer; **~ laser** laser printer

stampare <1a> print

stampatello m block letters pl

stampato m INFOR printout, hard copy

stampella f crutch

stampo m mo(u)ld

stancare <1d> tire (out)

stancarsi get tired, tire

stanchezza f tiredness, fatigue

stanco (pl -chi) tired; ~ **morto** dead beat

stand m inv stand

standard m/agg inv standard

standardizzare <1a> standardize

standardizzazione f standardization

stanga f (pl -ghe) bar

stanghetta f leg

stanotte tonight; (la notte scorsa) last night

stantuffo m piston

stanza f room

stanziare <1g> somma di denaro allocate, earmark

stanzino m boxroom

stappare <1a> take the top off

star f inv star

stare <1q> be; (restare) stay; (abitare) live; ~ **in piedi** stand; ~ **bene** be well; di vestiti suit; ~ **per fare qc** be about to do sth; **stammi a sentire** listen to me; **lascialo** ~ leave him alone, let him be; ~ **telefonando** be on the phone, be making a phonecall; **come sta?** how are you?, how are things?; **ben ti sta!** serves you right!; **ci sto!** here I am!; **sta bene** all right, ok

starnutire <4d> sneeze

starnuto m sneeze

start m inv start

starter m inv SP starter; AUTO choke

stasera this evening, tonight

statale 1 agg state attr **2** m/f (gen pl -i) civil servant **3** f main road

statistica f (pl -che) statistics

Stati Uniti d'America mpl United States of America, USA

statizzare <1a> nationalize

stato 1 pp → **essere** e **stare 2** m anche POL state; ~ **assistenziale** Welfare State; ~ **civile** marital status; ~ **maggiore** general staff; ~ **di salute** state of health, condition; **essere in ~ di fare** be in a position

to do; **essere in ~ interessante** be pregnant

statua f statue

statunitense 1 agg US attr, American **2** m/f US citizen, citizen of the United States

statura f height; fig stature

statuto m statute

stavolta this time

stazionamento m parking

stazionare <1a> be parked

stazionario (pl -ri) stationary

stazione f station; ~ **di servizio** service station; ~ **balneare** seaside resort; ~ **centrale** main station; ~ **climatica** health resort; ~ **termale** spa; ~ **trasmittente** radio station

stecca f (pl -cche) di biliardo cue; di sigarette carton; MED splint; MUS wrong note

stecchino m toothpick

stella f star; ~ **alpina** edelweiss; ~ **polare** North Star, Pole Star; ~ **cadente** shooting star; ~ **di mare** starfish; fig **vedere le -e** see stars

stelo m stem, stalk

stemma m (pl -i) coat of arms

stendere <3c> spread; braccio stretch out; biancheria hang out, hang up; verbale draw up

stendersi stretch out

stendibiancheria m inv clothes dryer

stenodattilografa f shorthand typist

stenodattilografia f shorthand typing

stenografare <1m & c> take down in shorthand

stenografia f shorthand

stentare <1b>: ~ **a fare qc** find it hard to do sth, have difficulty doing sth

stento m: **a** ~ with difficulty; **-i** pl hardship

stereo m inv stereo

stereotipo 1 agg stereotypical **2** m stereotype

sterile sterile

sterilità f sterility

sterilizzare <1a> sterilize

S

sterilizzazione *f* sterilization

sterlina *f* sterling

sterminare <1l & b> exterminate

sterminato vast

sterminio *m* (*pl* -ni) extermination

sterno *m* breastbone, ANAT sternum

sterzare <1b> steer; **~ *a sinistra*** turn left

sterzata *f* swerve

sterzo *m* AUTO steering

steso *pp* → **stendere**

stesso same; ***lo ~, la stessa*** the same one; ***è lo ~*** it's all the same; ***oggi ~*** this very day; ***io ~*** myself; ***se ~*** himself; ***l'ho visto coi miei stessi occhi*** I saw it with my very own eyes

stile *m* style; SP **~ *libero*** freestyle

stilografica *f* fountain pen

stima *f* (*ammirazione*) esteem; (*valutazione*) estimate

stimare <1a> *persona* esteem; *oggetto* value, estimate (the value of); (*ritenere*) think, consider

stimarsi think *or* consider o.s.

stimato respected

stimolante 1 *agg* stimulating **2** *m* stimulant

stimolare <1l> stimulate

stimolo *m* stimulus

stinco *m* (*pl* -chi) shin

stingere <3d> **1** *v/t* fade **2** *v/i e* **stingersi** fade

stinto *pp* → **stingere**

stipare <1a> cram

stipato crammed (*di* with)

stipendiato *m*, **-a** *f* person on a salary

stipendio *m* (*pl* -di) salary

stipulare <1l> stipulate

stipulazione *f* stipulation

stiramento *m* MED pulled muscle

stirare <1a> iron; ***non si stira*** it's non-iron

stirarsi pull

stiratura *f* ironing

stiro *m*: ***ferro m da ~*** iron; ***non ~*** non-iron

stirpe *f* (*origine*) birth

stitichezza *f* constipation

stivale *m* boots; **-i** *pl di gomma* rubber boots, Br wellingtons

sto → **stare**

stoccafisso *m* stockfish (*air-dried cod*)

stoccaggio *m* (*pl* -ggi) stocking

stoffa *f* material; *fig* ***avere ~*** be talented

stomaco *m* (*pl* -chi) stomach; ***dolori mpl di ~*** stomach pains; ***mi sono tolto un peso dallo ~*** I got it off my chest

stonare <1c> *di cantante* sing out of tune; *fig* be out of place; *di colori* clash

stonato *persona* tone deaf; *nota* false; *strumento* out of tune

stop *m inv* AUTO brake light; *cartello* stop sign

stoppare <1c> stop

storcere <3d> twist; **~ *il naso*** make a face

storcersi bend; **~ *un piede*** twist one's ankle

stordimento *m* dizziness

stordire <4d> stun

stordito stunned

storia *f* history; (*narrazione*) story; **~ *dell'arte*** history of art; ***non far -e!*** don't make a fuss *or* scene!

storico (*pl* -ci) **1** *agg* historical; (*memorabile*) historic **2** *m*, **-a** *f* historian

storiografia *f* historiography

storiografo *m*, **-a** *f* historiographer

storione *m* sturgeon

stormo *m di uccelli* flock

stornare <1a> *pericolo* avert

storno *m uccello* starling

storpio (*pl* -pi) **1** *agg* crippled **2** *m* **-a** *f* cripple

storta *f*: ***prendere una ~ al piede*** twist one's ankle

storto crooked

stoviglie *fpl* dishes

strabico (*pl* -ci) cross-eyed

strabismo *m* strabismus

stracarico (*pl* -chi) overloaded

stracaro exceedingly expensive

stracciare <1f> tear up

stracciatella *f* type of soup; *gelato* chocolate chip

stracciato in shreds

straccio (*pl* -cci) **1** *m per pulire* cloth; *per spolverare* duster **2** *agg*: **carta** *f* **~ -a** waste paper

strada *f* road; **per ~** down the road; **sono (già) per ~** I'm coming, I'm on my way; **provinciale** B road; **~ a senso unico** one-way street; **~ statale** A road; **farsi ~** push one's way through; *nella vita* get on in life; **a mezza ~** half-way

stradale road *attr*; **incidente** *m* **~** road accident; **polizia** *f* **~** traffic police; **regolamento** *m* **~** rule of the road; **rete** *f* **~** road network

stradario *m* street-finder, street map

strafare <3aa> exaggerate

strage *f* slaughter; **fare ~ di cuori** be a heartbreaker

stragrande: **la ~ maggioranza** the vast majority

stranezza *f* strangeness

strangolare <1l> strangle

straniero 1 *agg* foreign **2** *m*, **-a** *f* foreigner

strano strange

straordinario (*pl* -ri) **1** *agg* special; *eccezionale* extraordinary **2** *m* overtime

strapazzare <1a> treat badly; **uova** *fpl* **strapazzate** scrambled eggs

strapazzarsi overdo it

strapazzo *m* strain; **essere uno ~** be exhausting; **da ~** third-rate

strapieno crowded

strapiombo *m*: **a ~** overhanging

strappare <1a> tear, rip; (*staccare*) tear down; (*togliere*) grab, snatch (**a qu** out of s.o.'s hands)

strappo *m* tear, rip; MED torn ligament; *fig* **uno ~ alla regola** an exception to the rule

straricco (*pl* -cchi) extremely rich

straripare <1a> flood, overflow its banks

strascico *m* (*pl* -chi) train; *fig* after-effects

stratagemma *m* (*pl* -i) stratagem

strategia *f* strategy

strategico (*pl* -ci) strategic

strato *m* layer; **~ d'ozono** ozone layer; **~ protettivo** protective coating; **~ sociale** social stratum

stravagante extravagant

stravaganza *f* extravagance

stravecchio (*pl* -cchi) ancient

stravedere <2s>: **~ per qu** worship s.o.

stravincere <3d> win by a mile

stravolgere <3d> change radically; (*travisare*) twist; (*stancare*) exhaust

stravolto 1 *pp* → **stravolgere 2** *agg* (*stanco*) exhausted

strazio *m* (*pl* -zi): **era uno ~** it was painful

strega *f* (*pl* -ghe) witch

stregare <1e> bewitch

stregone *m* wizard

stremare <1b> exhaust

stremato exhausted

stress *m inv* stress

stressante stressful

stressare <1b> stress

stretta *f* hold; **~ di mano** handshake; **mettere qu alle -e** put s.o. in a tight corner

strettamente closely; **tenere qc ~ (in mano)** clutch sth (in one's hand)

strettezza *f* narrowness

stretto 1 *pp* → **stringere 2** *agg* narrow; *vestito*, *scarpe* too tight; **lo ~ necessario** the bare minimum **3** *m* GEOG strait

strettoia *f* bottleneck

stridere <3a> *di porta* squeak; *di colori* clash

stridulo shrill

strillare <1a> scream

strillo *m* scream

striminzito skimpy

strimpellare <1b> strum

stringa *f* (*pl* -ghe) lace

stringere <3d> **1** *v/t* make narrower; *abito* take in; *vite* tighten; **~ amicizia** become friends **2** *v/i* di tempo press

stringersi *intorno a tavolo* squeeze up

striscia *f* (*pl* -sce) strip; *dipinta* stripe; **-sce** *pl* **pedonali** pedestrian crossing *sg*, *Br* zebra crossing *sg*; **a -sce** striped

strisciare <1f> **1** *v/t piedi* scrape; (*sfiorare*) brush, smear (**contro**

against) **2** v/i crawl
striscio m MED smear
striscione m banner
strizzare <1a> wring; **~ l'occhio a qu** wink at s.o.
strofa f verse
strofinaccio m (pl -cci) dish towel
strofinare <1a> rub
stroncare <1d> albero knock down; vita snuff out; F idea shoot down
stropicciare <1f> crush, wrinkle
strozzare <1c> strangle
strozzatura f narrowing
strozzino m, **-a** f loan shark F
struggente all-consuming
struggere <3cc> consume
strumentalizzare make use of
strumento m instrument; **~ musicale** musical instrument; **~ ad arco / a fiato** string / wind instrument
strutto m lard
struttura f structure
strutturale structural
strutturare <1a> structure
struzzo m ZO ostrich
stuccare <1d> plaster
stucco m (pl -cchi) plaster; **rimanere di ~** be thunderstruck, Br be gobsmacked F
studente m, **-essa** f student; **casa f dello ~** hall of residence
studiare <1k> study
studio m (pl -di) study; di artista, RAD, TV studio; di professionista office; di medico surgery; **borsa f di ~** bursary
studioso 1 agg studious **2** m, **-a** f scholar
stufa f stove; **~ elettrica / a gas** electric / gas fire
stufare <1a> GASTR stew; fig bore
stufarsi get bored (**di** with)
stufato m stew
stufo: **essere ~ di qc** be bored with sth
stuolo m host
stupefacente 1 agg amazing, stupefying **2** m narcotic
stupefatto amazed, stupefied
stupendo stupendous
stupidaggine f stupidity; **è una ~**

(cosa senza importanza) it's nothing
stupidità f stupidity
stupido 1 agg stupid **2** m, **-a** f idiot
stupire <4d> **1** v/t amaze **2** v/i e **stupirsi** be amazed
stupore m amazement
stuprare <1a> rape
stupratore m rapist
stupro m rape
sturare <1a> clear, unblock
stuzzicadenti m inv toothpick
stuzzicare <1l & d> tease; **~ l'appetito** whet the appetite
su 1 prp on; argomento about; (circa) (round) about; **sul tavolo** on the table; **sul mare** by the sea; **sulle tremila lire** round about three thousand lire; **~ misura** made to measure; **nove volte ~ dieci** nine times out of ten **2** avv up; (al piano di sopra) upstairs; **~!** come on!; **avere ~ vestito** have on; **guardare in ~** look up
sub m/f inv skin diver
subacqueo 1 agg underwater **2** m, **-a** f skin diver
subaffittare <1a> sublet
subaffitto m sublet
subdolo underhand
subentrare <1a>: **~ a qu** replace s.o., take s.o.'s place
subire <4d> danni, perdita suffer
subito immediately
subordinare <1m> subordinate
suburbano suburban
succedere <3a o 3l> (accadere) happen; **~ a in carica** succeed; **che succede?** what's going on?
successione f succession
successivo successive
successo 1 pp → **succedere 2** m success; **di ~** successful
successore m successor
succhiare <1k> suck
succo m (pl -cchi) juice; **~ d'arancia** orange juice
succoso juicy
succursale f branch
sud m south; **~ ovest** south-west; **~ est** south-east; **al ~ di** (to the) south of

sudare <1a> perspire, sweat
sudata *f* perspiration, sweat
sudato sweaty
suddividere <3q> subdivide
suddivisione *f* subdivision
sudicio (*pl* -ci) **1** *agg* dirty **2** *m* dirt
sudiciume *m* dirt
sudore *m* perspiration, sweat
sufficiente sufficient
sufficienza *f* sufficiency; *a* ~ enough
suffragio *m* (*pl* -gi) suffrage; ~ *universale* universal suffrage
suggerimento *m* suggestion
suggerire <4d> suggest; TEA prompt
suggeritore *m* TEA prompter
suggestionare <1a> influence
suggestione *f* influence
suggestivo picturesque
sughero *m* cork
sugli *prp* **su** *and art* **gli**
sugo *m* (*pl* -ghi) sauce; *di arrosto* juice; *al* ~ with sauce
sui *prp* **su** *and art* **i**
suicida *m/f* suicide (victim)
suicidarsi <1a> commit suicide, kill o.s.
suicidio *m* (*pl* -di) suicide
suino pork *attr*
sul *prp* **su** *and art* **il**
sull', **sulla**, **sulle**, **sullo** *prp* **su** *and art* **l'**, **la**, **le**, **lo**
suo 1 *agg* his; *di cosa* its; *-a f* her; *di cosa* its; *il* ~ *maestro* his teacher; *i suoi amici* his friends; *questo libro è* ~ this is his book; *Suo* your **2** *pron*: *il* ~ his; *di cosa* its; *la -a f* hers; *di cosa* its
suocera *f* mother-in-law
suocero *m* father-in-law; *-i pl* mother- and father-in-law, in-laws F
suola *f* sole
suolo *m* ground; (*terreno*) soil
suonare <1o> **1** *v/t* play; *campanello* ring **2** *v/i* play; *alla porta* ring
suono *m* sound
suora *f* REL nun
super *f inv* F 4-star
superare <1l> go past; *fig* overcome; *esame* pass
superato out of date
superbia *f* haughtiness

superbo haughty
superficiale superficial
superficie *f* surface; *in* ~ on the surface
superfluo superfluous
superiora *f* Mother Superior
superiore 1 *agg* top; *qualità* superior; ~ *alla media* better than average **2** *m* superior
superiorità *f* superiority
superlativo *m/agg* superlative
supermarket *m inv*, **supermercato** *m* supermarket
superstite 1 *agg* surviving **2** *m/f* survivor
superstizione *f* superstition
superstizioso superstitious
superstrada *f* motorway, *Am* highway (*with no tolls*)
superuomo *m* (*pl* -uomini) superman
suppergiù about
supplementare additional, supplementary
supplemento *m* supplement; ~ *intercity* intercity supplement; FERR *fare il* ~ pay a supplement
supplente *m/f* replacement; EDU supply teacher
supplenza *f* supply teaching
supplicare <1l & d> beg
supplizio *m* (*pl* -zi) torture
suppongo → **supporre**
supporre <3ll> suppose
supporto *m* TEC support; INFOR ~ *dati* data support
supposizione *f* supposition
supposta *f* MED suppository
supposto *pp* → **supporre**
suppurare <1a> MED suppurate
suppurazione *f* suppuration
supremazia *f* supremacy
supremo supreme
surf *m inv* surfboard; *fare* ~ surf, go surfing
surfista *m/f* (*mpl* -i) surfer
surgelare <1b> freeze
surgelato 1 *agg* frozen **2** *m*: *-i pl* frozen food *sg*
surriscaldare <1a> overheat
surrogato *m* substitute

suscettibile touchy; **è ~ di migliora-mento** it's likely to improve
suscettibilità *f* touchiness
suscitare <1l> arouse
susina *f* plum
susino *m* plum (tree)
sussidio *m* (*pl* -di) grant, allowance; **~ di disoccupazione** unemployment benefit
sussultare <1a> start, jump
sussulto *m* start, jump
sussurrare <1a> *v/t & v/i* whisper
sussurro *m* whisper
sutura *f* MED stitches *pl*
svagarsi <1e> take one's mind off things
svago *m* (*pl* -ghi) distraction; **per ~** to take one's mind off things
svaligiare <1f> burgle, *Am* burglarize
svalutare <1a> devalue
svalutazione *f* devaluation
svanire <4d> vanish
svantaggio *m* (*pl* -ggi) disadvantage
svantaggioso disadvantageous
svariato varied
svedese **1** *m/agg* Swedish **2** *m/f* Swede
sveglia *f* alarm clock
svegliare <1g> waken (up)
svegliarsi waken up
sveglio awake; *fig* alert
svelare <1a> *segreto* reveal
svelto quick; **alla -a** quickly
svendere <3a> sell at a reduced price
svendita *f* clearance

svenimento *m* fainting fit
svenire <4p> faint
sventolare <1l & b> *v/t & v/i* wave
sventura *f* misfortune
sventurato unfortunate
svenuto *pp* → **svenire**
svergognato shameless
svernare <1b> spend the winter in
svestire <4b> undress
svestirsi get undressed, undress
Svezia *f* Sweden
sviare <1h> deflect; *fig* divert
svignarsela <1a> slip away
sviluppare <1a> develop
svilupparsi develop
sviluppato developed
sviluppo *m* development
svincolo *m* di strada junction
svista *f* oversight; **per ~** by some oversight
svitare <1a> unscrew
svitato unscrewed; *fig* **essere ~** have a screw loose
Svizzera *f* Switzerland
svizzero **1** *agg* Swiss **2** *m*, **-a** *f* Swiss
svogliatezza *f* laziness
svogliato lazy
svolazzare <1a> flutter
svolgere <3d> *rotolo* unwrap; *tema* develop; *attività* carry out
svolgersi happen; *di film* be set
svolgimento *m* course; *di tema* development
svolta *f* turning; *fig* turning point
svoltare <1c>: **~ a destra** turn right
svolto *pp* → **svolgere**
svuotare <1c> empty

S

T

t *abbr* (= **tonnellata**) t (= tonne)
tabaccaio *m* (*pl* -ai), **-a** *f* tobacconist
tabaccheria *f* tobacconist's
tabacco *m* (*pl* -cchi) tobacco

tabagismo *m* smoking
tabella *f* table; **~ dei prezzi** price list; *fig* **~ di marcia** schedule
tabellina *f* multiplication table

tabellone m board; per avvisi notice board; **~ pubblicitario** billboard

tabernacolo m tabernacle

tabù m/agg inv taboo

tabulato m printout

TAC abbr (= **Tomografia Assiale Computerizzata**) CAT (= computerized axial tomography)

taccagno mean, stingy F

taccheggio m shoplifting

tacchino m turkey

tacco m (pl -cchi) heel

taccuino m notebook

tacere <2k> **1** v/t keep quiet about, say nothing about **2** v/i not say anything, be silent

tachicardia f tachycardia

tachimetro m speedometer

tacitare <1l> scandalo hush up

tacito tacit

taciturno taciturn

tafano m ZO horsefly

tafferuglio m (pl -gli) scuffle

taglia f (misura) size; **di ~ media** medium; **~ forte** outsize; **~ unica** one size

tagliacarte m inv paper-knife

tagliando m coupon; AUTO service; **fare il ~** have the vehicle serviced

tagliare <1g> cut; albero cut down; legna chop; **~ i capelli** have one's hair cut; fig **~ la strada a qu** cut in front of s.o.

tagliarsi cut o.s.; **mi sono tagliata un dito** I've cut my finger

tagliatelle fpl tagliatelle sg

tagliente sharp

tagliere m chopping board

taglierini mpl type of noodles

taglio m (pl -gli) cut; **~ cesareo** C(a)esarean (section)

tailleur m inv suit

talco m (pl -chi) talc, talcum powder

tale such a; **-i pl** such; **~ e quale** just like; **un ~** someone; **il signor tal dei -i** Mr So-and-so

talento m talent

tallonare <1a> persona follow close behind; nel rugby heel

talloncino m coupon

tallone m heel

talmente so

talora sometimes

talpa f mole

talvolta sometimes

tamburo m drum

tamponamento m AUTO collision; **~ a catena** multi-vehicle pile-up

tamponare <1a> falla plug; AUTO collide with, crash into

tampone m MED swab; per donne tampon; per timbri (ink) pad; INFOR buffer

tana f den

tandem m inv tandem

tangente f MAT tangent; F (percentuale illecita) kickback F; F (bustarella) bribe; F (pizzo) protection money

tangenziale f ring road

tanica f container; MAR per fuoribordo tank

tanto 1 agg so much; **-i pl** so many; **-i saluti** best wishes; **-e grazie** thank you so much, many thanks **2** pron much; **-i pl** many **3** avv (così) so; con verbi so much; **di ~ in ~** from time to time; **~ quanto** as much as; **è da ~ (tempo) che non lo vedo** I haven't seen him for a long time; **~ per cambiare** for a change

tappa f stop; di viaggio stage

tappare <1a> plug; bottiglia put the cork in

tapparella f rolling shutter

tappeto m carpet

tappezzare <1a> (wall)paper

tappezzeria f di pareti wallpaper; di sedili upholstery

tappo m cap, top; di sughero cork; di lavandini, vasche plug

tarare <1a> TEC calibrate

tarchiato stocky

tardare <1a> **1** v/t delay **2** v/i be late

tardi late; **più ~** later (on); **al più ~** at the latest; **a più ~!** see you later!; **far ~** (arrivare in ritardo) be late; (stare alzato) stay up late; in ufficio work late

tardivo late; fig retarded, slow

tardo late

targa f (pl -ghe) nameplate; AUTO numberplate

targhetta f tag; *su porta* nameplate

tariffa f rate; *nei trasporti* fare; *doganale* tariff

tarlato worm-eaten

tarlo m woodworm

tarma f (clothes) moth

tartaro m tartar

tartaruga f (pl -ghe) *terrestre* tortoise; *aquatica* turtle

tartina f canapé

tartufo m truffle

tasca f (pl -che) pocket; **ne ho piene le -che** I'm fed up with this

tascabile 1 agg pocket attr **2** m paperback

tassa f tax; **~ di circolazione** road tax; **~ di soggiorno** visitor tax; **esente da ~** tax free; **soggetto a ~** subject to tax

tassametro m meter, clock F

tassare <1a> tax

tassello m *nel muro* plug

tassista m/f (mpl -i) taxi driver

tasso[1] m FIN rate; **~ d'inflazione** inflation rate, rate of inflation; **~ d'interesse** interest rate; **~ di sconto** discount rate

tasso[2] m ZO badger

tasso[3] m BOT yew

tastare <1a> feel; *fig* **~ il terreno** test the water, see how the land lies

tastiera f keyboard

tastierista m/f (mpl -i) keyboarder

tasto m key; INFOR **~ operativo** function key

tattica f (pl -che) tactics pl

tattico (pl -ci) tactical

tatto m *(senso)* touch; *fig* tact; **mancanza f di ~** tactlessness, lack of tact

tatuaggio m (pl -ggi) tattoo

tatuare <1l> tattoo

taverna f country-style restaurant

tavola f table; *(asse)* plank, board; *in libro* plate; **~ calda** snackbar; **~ rotonda** round table; SP **~ a vela** sailboard; **mettersi a ~** sit down to eat; **a ~!** lunch/dinner is ready!, come and get it! F

tavoletta f: **~ di cioccolata** bar of chocolate

tavolo m table

taxi m inv taxi

tazza f cup

tazzina f espresso cup

tbc, TBC abbr (= *tubercolosi*) TB (= tuberculosis)

TCI abbr (= *Touring Club Italiano*) Italian motoring organization

te you; **~ l'ho venduto** I sold it to you

tè m tea; **~ freddo** iced tea; **sala f da ~** tearoom; **tazza f da ~** teacup

teatrale theatre, Am theater; *fig* theatrical; **rappresentazione f ~** play

teatro m theatre, Am theater; *fig (luogo)* scene; **~ all'aperto** open air theatre (Am theater); **~ lirico** opera (house)

tecnica f (pl -che) technique; *(tecnologia)* technology

tecnico (pl -ci) **1** agg technical **2** m technician

tecnologia f technology; **alta ~** high technology, high tech F

tecnologico (pl -ci) technological

tedesco (pl -chi) **1** m/agg German **2** m, **-a** f German

tegame m (sauce)pan

teglia f baking tin

tegola f tile

teiera f teapot

tel. abbr (= *telefono*) tel (= telephone)

tela f cloth; PITT canvas; **~ cerata** oilcloth

telaio m (pl -ai) loom; *di automobile* chassis; *di bicicletta, finestra* frame

telecamera f television camera

telecomando m remote control

telecomunicazioni fpl telecommunications, telecomms

telefax m inv fax

teleferica f (pl -che) cableway

telefilm m inv film made for television

telefonare <1m & b> (tele)phone, ring (*a qu* s.o.)

telefonata f (tele)phone call; **~ interurbana** long-distance (phone) call; **~ urbana** local call; **fare una ~ a qu** ring or phone s.o.

telefonico (pl -ci) (tele)phone attr

telefonista m/f (mpl -i) (switch-

257 tentare

board) operator

telefonino *m* mobile (phone), *Am* cell(ular) phone

telefono *m* (tele)phone; **~ a gettoni** *telephone that takes tokens*; **~ a scheda (magnetica)** cardphone; **~ a tastiera** push-button (tele)phone; **~ cellulare** cellphone, cellular (tele)phone; **dare un colpo di ~ a qu** give s.o. a ring

telegiornale *m* news *sg*

telegrafare <1m & b> telegraph

telegrafico (*pl* -ci) *stile* telegraphic; *risposta* very brief

telegrafo *m* telegraph

telegramma *m* (*pl* -i) telegram

teleguidato remote controlled

telelavoro *m* teleworking

teleobiettivo *m* telephoto lens

telepatia *f* telepathy

teleschermo *m* TV screen

telescopio *m* (*pl* -pi) telescope

teleselezione *f* STD

telespettatore *m*, **-trice** *f* TV viewer

televisione *f* television, TV; **~ via cavo** cable television *or* TV; **~ via satellite** satellite television *or* TV

televisivo television *attr*, TV *attr*

televisore *m* television (set), TV (set); **~ a colori** colo(u)r TV

telex *m inv* telex

telone *m* tarpaulin; TEA curtain

tema *m* theme, subject

temerario (*pl* -ri) reckless

temere <2a> be afraid *or* frightened of

temperamatite *m inv* pencil sharpener

temperamento *m* temperament

temperare <1l & b> *acciaio* temper; *matita* sharpen

temperato *acciaio* tempered; *matita* sharp; *clima* temperate

temperatura *f* temperature; **~ ambiente** room temperature

tempesta *f* storm

tempestoso stormy

tempia *f* temple

tempio *m* (*pl* -pli) temple

tempo *m* time; METEO weather; **~ libero** free time; **a ~ parziale** part-

time; **a ~ perso** in one's spare time; **a ~ pieno** full-time; SP **-i pl supplementari** extra time *sg*, *Am* overtime *sg*; **a ~, in ~** in time; **col ~** in time, eventually; **un ~** once, long ago; **per ~ (presto)** in good time; **(di buon'ora)** early; **non ho ~** I don't have (the) time; **lavora da molto ~** he has been working for a long time; **fa bel / brutto ~** the weather is lovely / nasty

temporale *m* thunderstorm

temporaneo temporary

tenace *materiali, sostanze* strong; *fig* tenacious

tenacia *f fig* tenacity

tenaglie *fpl* pincers *pl*

tenda *f* curtain; **da campeggio** tent

tendenza *f* tendency

tendere <3c> **1** *v/t molla, elastico, muscoli* stretch; *corde del violino* tighten; *mano* hold out, stretch out; *fig trappola* lay; **~ un braccio per fare qc** reach out to do sth; **~ le braccia a qu** hold one's arms out to s.o. **2** *v/i:* **~ a** (*aspirare a*) aim at; (*essere portati a*) tend to; (*avvicinarsi a*) verge on

tendina *f* net curtain

tendine *m* tendon

tenebre *fpl* darkness *sg*

tenente *m* lieutenant

tenere <2q> **1** *v/t* hold; (*conservare, mantenere*) keep; (*gestire*) run; *spazio* take up; *conferenza* give; **~ d'occhio** keep an eye on, watch **2** *v/i* hold (on); **~ a** (*dare importanza a*) care about; SP support

tenerezza *f* tenderness

tenero tender; *pietra, legno* soft

tenersi (*reggersi*) hold on (**a** to); (*mantenersi*) keep o.s.; **~ in piedi** stand (up)

tengo → **tenere**

tennis *m* tennis; **~ da tavolo** table tennis

tennista *m/f* (*mpl* -i) tennis player

tenore *m* MUS tenor; **~ di vita** standard of living

tensione *f* voltage; *fig* tension

tentare <1b> try, attempt; (*allettare*)

tempt; **~ tutto il possibile** do everything possible

tentativo m attempt

tentazione f temptation

tenue *colore* pale; *luce, speranza* faint

tenuta f (*capacità*) capacity; (*resistenza*) stamina; (*divisa*) uniform; (*abbigliamento*) outfit; AGR estate; **a ~ d'aria** airtight; AUTO **~ di strada** roadholding ability

teologia f theology

teologico (*pl* -ci) theological

teologo m (*pl* -gi), **-a** f theologian

teorema m (*pl* -i) theorem

teoria f theory

teorico (*pl* -ci) theoretical

tepore m warmth

teppista m/f (*pl* -i) hooligan

terapia f therapy

tergicristallo m AUTO windscreen (*Am* windshield) wiper

termale thermal; **stazione f ~** spa; **stabilimento m ~** baths *pl*

terme *fpl* baths

terminal m *inv* AVIA air terminal, terminal building

terminale 1 *agg* terminal; **stazione f ~** terminus **2** m INFOR, EL terminal

terminare <11 & b> v/t & v/i end, finish, terminate

termine m end; (*confine*) limit; FIN (*scadenza*) deadline; (*parola*) term; **-i di consegna** terms of delivery; **~ tecnico** technical term; **a breve / lungo ~** in the short / long term; **in altri -i** in other words; **volgere al ~** come to an end

termocoperta f electric blanket

termometro m thermometer

termos m *inv* thermos®

termosifone m radiator

termostato m thermostat

terra f earth; (*regione, proprietà, terreno agricolo*) land; (*superficie del suolo*) ground; (*pavimento*) floor; **a ~** on the ground; AVIA, MAR **scendere a ~** get off; TEC **mettere a ~** earth; **cadere a o per ~** fall (down)

terracotta f (*pl* terrecotte) terracotta

terraferma f dry land, terra firma

terrapieno m embankment

terrazza f, **terrazzo** m balcony, terrace

terremoto m earthquake

terreno 1 *agg* earthly; *piano* ground, *Am* first **2** m (*superficie*) ground; (*suolo, materiale*) soil; (*appezzamento*) plot of land; *fig* (*settore, tema*) field, area; **perdere / guadagnare ~** lose / gain ground; **~ fabbricabile** land that may be built on

terrestre land *attr*, terrestrial; *della Terra* of the Earth; **globo m ~** globe

terribile terrible

terrina f bowl

territoriale territorial

territorio m (*pl* -ri) territory

terrore m terror

terrorismo m terrorism

terrorista m/f (*mpl* -i) terrorist

terrorizzare <1a> terrorize

terza f AUTO third (gear)

terziario m (*pl* -ri) tertiary sector, services *pl*

terzino m SP back

terzo 1 *agg* third; **il ~ mondo** the Third World; **-a pagina** arts page **2** m third

teschio m (*pl* -chi) skull

tesi f *inv*: **~ (di laurea)** thesis

teso 1 *pp* → **tendere 2** *agg* taut; *fig* tense

tesoro m treasure; (*tesoreria*) treasury

tessera f card; **~ d'abbonamento** season ticket

tessile 1 *agg* textile **2** **-i** *mpl* textiles

tessuto m fabric, material; **~ di lana** wool; **-i** *pl* fabrics, material *sg*

test m *inv* test

testa f head; **a ~** each, a head; **alla ~ di** at the head of; **essere in ~** lead

testamento m will

testardaggine f stubbornness

testardo stubborn

testata f (*giornale*) newspaper; *di letto* headboard; AUTO cylinder head; **~ nucleare** nuclear warhead

teste m/f witness

testicolo m testicle

testimone m/f witness; **~ oculare**

eyewitness: **Testimoni** pl **di Geova** Jehovah's Witnesses

testimonianza f testimony; (prova) proof

testimoniare <1k & c> **1** v/i testify, give evidence **2** v/t fig testify to; DIR ~ **il falso** commit perjury

testo m text

tetano m tetanus

tetro gloomy

tetto m roof

tettoia f roof

Tevere m Tiber

TG abbr (= **Telegiornale**) TV news

thermos → **termos**

ti you; riflessivo yourself

tibia f shinbone, tibia

tic m inv di orologio tick; MED tic

ticchettio m di orologio ticking; di pioggia patter

ticket m inv MED charge

tiene → **tenere**

tiepido lukewarm, tepid; fig half-hearted, lukewarm

tifo m MED typhus; fig **fare il ~ per una squadra** be a fan or supporter of a team

tifoso m, **-a** f fan, supporter

tiglio m (pl -gli) lime tree

tigre f tiger

timbrare <1a> stamp

timbro m stamp; MUS timbre; ~ **postale** postage stamp

timidezza f shyness, timidity

timido shy, timid

timo m BOT thyme

timone m MAR, AVIA rudder; fig helm

timoniere m helmsman

timore m fear

timoroso timorous

timpano m MUS kettledrum; ANAT eardrum

tingere <3d> dye

tinta f (colorante) dye; (colore) colo(u)r

tintarella f (sun)tan

tinto pp → **tingere**

tintoria f dry-cleaner's

tintura f dyeing; (colorante) dye; ~ **di iodio** iodine

tipico (pl -ci) typical

tipo m sort, kind, type; F fig guy

tipografia f printing; stabilimento printer's

tipografo m printer

tipografico typographical

tir m heavy goods vehicle, HGV

tiranneggiare <1f> tyrannize

tirannia f tyranny

tiranno 1 agg tyrannical **2** m tyrant

tirare <1a> **1** v/t pull; (tendere) stretch; (lanciare) throw; (sparare) fire; (tracciare) draw; ~ **fuori** take out; ~ **su** da terra pick up; bambino bring up; ~ **giù** take down **2** v/i pull; di abito be too tight; di vento blow; (sparare) shoot; ~ **avanti** (arrangiarsi) get by, manage; (continuare) keep going; ~ **dritto** go straight on; ~ **a sorte** draw lots

tirarsi ~ **indietro** back off; fig back out

tiratore m, **-trice** f shot

tiratura f di libro print run; di giornale circulation

tirchio (pl -chi) **1** agg mean, stingy F **2** m, **-a** f miser, skinflint F

tiro m (lancio) throw; (sparo) shot; ~ **con l'arco** archery; fig **un brutto ~** a nasty trick; **essere a ~** be within range

tirocinante m/f trainee

tirocinio m (pl -ni) training

tiroide f thyroid

tirolese agg, m/f Tyrolean, Tyrolese

Tirolo m Tyrol

tisana f herbal tea, tisane

titolare m/f owner

titolo m title; dei giornali headline; FIN security; ~ **a reddito fisso** fixed income security; **a ~ di** as; ~ **di studio** qualification

titubare <1l> hesitate

tizio m, **-a** f: **un ~** somebody, some man; **una -a** somebody, some woman

toccare <1d> **1** v/t touch; (riguardare) concern, be about **2** v/i happen (a to); **gli tocca metà dell'eredità** half the estate is going to him; **tocca a me** it's my turn; **mi tocca partire** I must go, I have to go

tocco m (pl -cchi) touch

togliere <3ss> take (away), remove; (eliminare) take off; (tirare fuori) take out, remove; (revocare) lift, raise; dente take out, extract; **~ di mezzo** get rid of; **ciò non toglie che** the fact remains that

togliersi giacca take off, remove; (spostarsi) take o.s. off; **~ dai piedi** get out of the way

tolgo → **togliere**

tollerante tolerant

tolleranza f tolerance

tollerare <1l & c> tolerate

tolto pp → **togliere**

tomba f grave

tombola f bingo

tomografia f MED tomography; **~ assiale computerizzata** computerized axial tomography

tonaca f (pl -che) habit

tonalità f inv tonality

tondeggiante roundish

tondo round; (grassoccio) plump; **chiaro e ~** quite clearly

tonfo m in acqua splash

tonico m (pl -ci) tonic

tonificare <1m & d> tone up

tonnellata f tonne

tonno m tuna

tono m tone; **rispondere a ~** (a proposito) answer to the point; **per le rime** answer back

tonsille fpl ANAT tonsils

tonsillite f tonsillitis

topazio m (pl -zi) topaz

topo m mouse

topografia f topography

Topolino m Mickey Mouse

toppa f (serratura) keyhole; (rattoppo) patch

torace m chest

torbido liquid cloudy

torcere <3d> twist; biancheria wring

torchio m (pl -chi) press

torcia f (pl -ce) f torch

torcicollo m stiff neck

tordo m thrush

torinese of Turin

Torino f Turin

tormenta f snowstorm

tormentare <1a> torment

tormentarsi torment o.s.

tormento m torment

tornaconto m benefit

tornante m hairpin bend

tornare <1a> venire come back, return; andare go back, return; (quadrare) balance; **~ utile** prove useful; **~ a fare / dire qc** do / say sth again; **ben tornato!** welcome back!; **~ in sé** come to one's senses

torneo m tournament; **Torneo delle Sei Nazioni** Six Nations Cup

tornio m (pl -ni) lathe

toro m bull; ASTR **Toro** Taurus

torpedine m ZO electric ray

torpore m torpor

torre f tower

torrefare <3aa> roast

torrefazione f roasting

torreggiare <1f> tower (su over)

torrente m stream

torrido torrid

torrone m nougat

torsione f twisting; TEC torsion

torso m torso

torsolo m core

torta f cake

tortellini mpl tortellini sg

torto m wrong; **aver ~** be wrong; **a ~** wrongly

tortora f turtledove

tortuoso (sinuoso) winding; (ambiguo) devious

tortura f torture

torturare <1a> torture

torvo sguardo dark, black

tosaerba f e m lawnmower

tosare <1a> pecore shear

Toscana f Tuscany

toscano Tuscan

tosse f cough; **~ canina** whooping cough; **aver la ~** have a cough

tossico (pl -ci) **1** agg toxic **2** m, **-a** f F druggie F

tossicodipendente m/f drug addict

tossicodipendenza f drug addiction

tossicomane m/f drug addict

tossire <4a & d> cough

tostapane m toaster

tostare <1c> *pane* toast; *caffè* roast

tot 1 *agg* so many **2** *pron* so much

totale *m/agg* total

totalità *f* (*interezza*) entirety, totality; **nella ~ dei casi** in all cases

totip *m* competition similar to football pools, based on horse racing

totocalcio *m* competition similar to football pools

tovaglia *f* tablecloth

tovagliolo *m* napkin, serviette

tozzo 1 *agg* stocky **2** *m di pane* crust

tra → *fra*

traballare <1a> stagger; *mobile* wobble

traboccare <1d> overflow (*anche fig*)

traccia *f* (*pl* -cce) (*orma*) footprint; *di veicolo* track; (*indizio*) clue; (*segno*) trace; (*abbozzo*) sketch

tracciare <1f> *linea* draw; (*delineare*) outline; (*abbozzare*) sketch

trachea *f* windpipe

tracolla *f* (shoulder) strap; **a ~** slung over one's shoulder; **borsa f a ~** shoulder bag

tracollo *m* collapse

tradimento *m* betrayal; POL treason; **a ~** treacherously

tradire <4d> betray; *coniuge* be unfaithful to

tradirsi give o.s. away

traditore 1 *agg* (*infedele*) unfaithful **2** *m*, **-trice** *f* traitor

tradizionale traditional

tradizione *f* tradition

tradotto *pp* → *tradurre*

tradurre <3e> translate; **~ in inglese** translate into English

traduttore *m*, **-trice** *f* translator

traduzione *f* translation

trafficante *m/f spreg* dealer; **~ di droga** drug dealer

trafficare <1l & d> deal, trade (**in** in); *spreg* traffic (**in** in); (*armeggiare*) tinker; (*affaccendarsi*) bustle about

traffico *m* (*pl* -chi e -ci) traffic; **~ aereo** air traffic; **~ stradale** road traffic; **densità f del ~** volume of traffic

traforo *m* tunnel

tragedia *f* tragedy

traghettare <1a> ferry

traghetto *m* ferry

tragico (*pl* -ci) tragic

tragitto *m* journey

traguardo *m* finishing line

traiettoria *f* trajectory

trainare <1l> (*rimorchiare*) tow; *di animali* pull, draw

traino *m* towing; *veicolo* vehicle on tow; **a ~** on tow

tralasciare <1f> (*omettere*) omit, leave out; (*interrompere*) interrupt

traliccio *m* (*pl* -cci) EL pylon; TEC trellis

tram *m inv* tram

trama *f fig* plot

tramandare <1a> hand down

tramare <1a> *fig* plot

trambusto *m* (*confusione*) bustle; (*tumulto*) uproar, commotion

tramezzino *m* sandwich

tramezzo *m* partition

tramite 1 *m* (*collegamento*) link; (*intermediario*) go-between **2** *prep* through

tramontana *f* north wind

tramontare <1a> set

tramonto *m* sunset; *fig* decline

trampolino *m* diving board; SCI ski jump

tranello *m* trap

tranne except

tranquillante *m* tranquil(l)izer

tranquillità *f* peacefulness, tranquillity

tranquillizzare <1a>: **~ qu** set s.o.'s mind at rest

tranquillo calm, peaceful

transatlantico (*pl* -ci) **1** *agg* transatlantic **2** *m* liner

transazione *f* DIR settlement; FIN transaction

transenna *f* barrier

transistor *m inv* transistor

transitabile *strada* passable

transitare <1l> pass

transitivo GRAM transitive

transito *m* transit; **divieto di ~** no thoroughfare

transitorio (*pl* -ri) transitory

transizione f transition

transoceanico (pl -ci) ocean attr

trantran m F routine

tranviere m (manovratore) tram driver; (controllore) tram conductor

trapanare <1b> drill

trapano m drill; **~ a percussione** percussion drill

trapezio m (pl -zi) trapeze; MAT trapezium

trapezista m/f (mpl -i) trapeze artist

trapiantare <1a> transplant

trapianto m transplant

trappola f trap

trapunta f quilt

trarre <3xx> conclusioni draw; vantaggio derive; **tratto da un libro di** taken from a book by

trasalire <4m> jump

trasandato scruffy; lavoro slipshod

trasbordare <1a> transfer

trasbordo m transfer

trascinare <1a> drag; (travolgere) sweep away; fig (entusiasmare) carry away

trascorrere <3o> 1 v/t spend 2 v/i pass, go by

trascorso pp → **trascorrere**

trascrivere <3tt> transcribe

trascrizione f transcription

trascurabile unimportant

trascurare <1a> neglect; (tralasciare) ignore; **~ di fare qc** fail to do sth

trascuratezza f negligence

trascurato careless, negligent; (trasandato) slovenly; (ignorato) neglected

trasferibile transferable

trasferimento m transfer

trasferire <4d> transfer

trasferirsi move

trasferta f transfer; SP away game

trasformare <1a> transform; TEC process; nel rugby convert

trasformarsi change, turn (**in** into)

trasformatore m transformer

trasformazione f transformation

trasfusione f transfusion

trasgredire <4d> disobey

trasgressione f disobedience

trasgressore m transgressor

traslocare <1c & d> v/t & v/i move

trasloco m (pl -chi) move

trasmettere <3ee> pass on; RAD, TV broadcast, transmit; DIR diritti transfer

trasmissibile transmissible

trasmissione f transmission; RAD, TV broadcast, transmission; (programma) programme, Am program; RAD, TV **~ in diretta** live broadcast; INFOR **~ dati** data transmission

trasognato dreamy

trasparente 1 agg transparent **2** m transparency

trasparenza f transparency

trasportare <1c> transport

trasporto m transport; **~ combinato rotaia-strada** piggyback transport; **-i** pl **pubblici** public transport sg

trasversale 1 agg transverse **2** f MAT transversal

tratta f trade; FIN draft

trattamento m treatment

trattare <1a> **1** v/t treat; TEC treat, process; FIN deal in; (negoziare) negotiate **2** v/i deal; **~ di** be about; FIN **~ in** deal in

trattarsi di che si tratta? what's it about?

trattative fpl negotiations, talks

trattato m treatise; DIR, POL treaty; **~ di pace** peace treaty

trattenere <2q> (far restare) keep, hold; (far perder tempo) hold up; (frenare) restrain; fiato, respiro hold; lacrime hold back; somma withhold

trattenersi (rimanere) stay; (frenarsi) restrain o.s.; **~ dal fare qc** refrain from doing sth

trattenuta f deduction

trattino m dash; in parole composte hyphen

tratto 1 pp → **trarre 2** m di spazio, tempo stretch; di penna stroke; (linea) line; **a un ~** all of a sudden; **-i** pl (lineamenti) features; **a -i** at intervals

trattore m tractor

trattoria f restaurant

trauma m (pl -i) trauma

traumatico (*pl* -ci) traumatic

travaglio *m*: MED **~ di parto** labo(u)r

travasare <1a> decant

trave *f* beam

traversa *f* crossbeam

traversare <1b> cross

traversata *f* crossing

traverso *flauto m* **~** flute; **andare di ~ di cibi** go down the wrong way; **per vie -e** by devious means

travestimento *m* disguise

travestire <4b> disguise

travestirsi disguise o.s., dress up (**da** as)

travestito *m* transvestite

travolgere <3d> carry away (*anche fig*); **con un veicolo** run over

travolto *pp* → **travolgere**

trazione *f* TEC traction; AUTO **~ anteriore / posteriore** front- / rear-wheel drive

tre three

trebbiare <1k> AGR thresh

treccia *f* (*pl* -cce) plait

trecento 1 *agg* three hundred **2** *m*: **il Trecento** the fourteenth century

tredicesimo *m*/*agg* thirteenth

tredici thirteen

tregua *f* truce; *fig* break, let-up

trekking *m* hiking

tremante trembling, shaking

tremare <1b> tremble, shake (**di, per** with)

tremendo terrible, tremendous

tremila three thousand

treno *m* train; **~ intercity** intercity train; **~ merci** goods train; **in ~** by train

trenta thirty

trentenne *agg, m*/*f* thirty-year-old

trentesimo *m*/*agg* thirtieth

trentina una ~ about thirty; **essere sulla ~** be about thirty, be in one's thirties

treppiedi *m inv* tripod

treruote *m inv* three-wheeler

triangolare triangular

triangolo *m* triangle; AUTO warning triangle

tribù *f inv* tribe

tribuna *f* platform

tribunale *m* court; **~ per i minorenni** juvenile court

tributario (*pl* -ri) tax

tributo *m* tax; *fig* tribute

tricheco *m* (*pl* -chi) walrus

triciclo *m* tricycle

tricolore 1 *agg* tricolo(u)r(ed) **2** *m* tricolo(u)r

triennale *contratto, progetto* three-year; *mostra, festival* three-yearly

triennio *m* (*pl* -nni) three-year period

triestino of Trieste

trifoglio *m* (*pl* -gli) clover

triglia *f* red mullet

trilaterale trilateral

trillare <1a> trill

trillo *m* trill

trim. *abbr* (= **trimestre**) term

trimestrale quarterly

trimestre *m* quarter; EDU term

trincea *f* trench

trincerare <1b> entrench

trincerarsi entrench o.s.

trinchetto *m* foremast

trinciare <1f> cut up, chop

Trinità *f* Trinity

trio *m* trio

trionfare <1a> triumph (**su** over)

trionfo *m* triumph

triplicare <1l & d> triple

triplice triple

triplo 1 *agg* triple **2** *m*: **il ~** three times as much (**di** as)

trippa *f* tripe

triste sad

tristezza *f* sadness

tritacarne *m inv* mincer

tritare <1a> mince

tritatutto *m inv* mincer

trito minced; *fig* **~ e ritrito** rehashed

trittico *m* (*pl* -ci) triptych

triturare <1a> grind

trivellare <1b> drill

trivella *f* drill

triviale trivial

trofeo *m* trophy

tromba *f* MUS trumpet; AUTO horn; **~ d'aria** whirlwind; **~ delle scale** stairwell

trombone *m* trombone

trombosi *f* thrombosis

troncare <1d> cut off; *fig* break off

tronchese *m* wire cutters *pl*

tronco *m* (*pl* -chi) ANAT, BOT trunk; FERR section; **licenziare in ~** fire on the spot *or* there and then

trono *m* throne

tropicale tropical

tropici *mpl* tropics

troppo 1 *agg* too much; **-i** *pl* too many **2** *avv* too much; **non ~** not too much; **è ~ tardi** it's too late

trota *f* trout

trottare <1c> trot

trotto *m* trot

trottola *f* (spinning) top

trovare <1c> find; (*inventare*) find, come up with; **andare a ~ qu** (go and) see s.o.

trovarsi be; **~ bene** be happy

trovata *f* good idea

truccare <1d> make up; *motore* soup up; *partita, elezioni* fix

truccarsi put on one's make-up

truccatore *m*, **-trice** *f* make-up artist

trucco *m* (*pl* -cchi) make-up; (*inganno, astuzia*) trick

truce fierce; (*crudele*) cruel

truffa *f* fraud

truffare <1a> defraud (*di* of)

truffatore *m*, **-trice** *f* trickster, con artist F

truppa *f* troops *pl*; *fig* horde

tu you; **dammi del tu** call me 'tu'; **sei ~?** is that you?

tuba *f* tuba

tubatura *f*, **tubazione** *f* pipes *pl*, piping

tubercolosi *f* tuberculosis

tubero *m* tuber

tubetto *m* tube

tubo *m* pipe; *flessibile* hose; AUTO **~ di scappamento** exhaust (pipe); **~ fluorescente** fluorescent light

tuffare <1a> dip

tuffarsi (*immergersi*) dive; (*buttarsi dentro*) throw o.s. (*anche fig*)

tuffo *m* dip; SP dive

tugurio *m* (*pl* -ri) hovel

tulipano *m* tulip

tumore *m* tumo(u)r

tumulto *m* riot

tumultuoso tumultuous

tunica *f* (*pl* -che) tunic

Tunisia *f* Tunisia

tunisino 1 *agg* Tunisian **2** *m*, **-a** *f* Tunisian

tunnel *m inv* tunnel; **~ dell'orrore** ghost train

tuo (*pl* tuoi) **1** *agg* your; **il ~ amico** your friend; **un ~ amico** a friend of yours **2** *pron*: **il ~** yours

tuonare <1c> thunder

tuono *m* thunder

tuorlo *m* yolk

turare <1a> stop; *bottiglia* put the top on

turbamento *m* perturbation

turbante *m* turban

turbare <1a> upset, disturb

turbina *f* turbine

turbine *m* whirlwind

turbolenza *f* turbulence

turboreattore *m* turbojet

turchese *m/agg* turquoise

Turchia *f* Turkey

turco (*pl* -chi) **1** *m/agg* Turkish **2** *m*, **-a** *f* Turk

turismo *m* tourism; **~ di massa** mass tourism

turista *m/f* (*mpl* -i) tourist

turistico (*pl* -ci) tourist; **assegno** *m* **~** traveller's cheque, *Am* traveler's check

turno *m* turn; *di lavoro* shift; **a ~** in turn; **di ~** on duty; **è il mio ~** it's my turn; **~ di riposo** rest day; **darsi il ~** take turns

tuta *f* da lavoro boiler suit, overalls; **~ da ginnastica** track suit; **~ da sci** salopettes

tutela *f* protection; DIR guardianship

tutelare <1b> protect

tutore *m*, **-trice** *f* guardian

tuttavia still

tutto 1 *agg* whole; **-i, -e** *pl* all; **~ il libro** the whole book; **-i i giorni** every day; **-i e tre** all three; **noi -i** all of us **2** *avv* all; **era ~ solo** he was all alone; **del ~** quite; **in ~** altogether, in all **3** *pron* all; *gente* everybody, everyone; *cose* everything; **lo ha**

mangiato ~ he ate it all
tuttora still

TV *abbr* (= *televisione*) TV (= television)

U

ubbidiente obedient
ubbidienza *f* obedience
ubbidire <4d> obey; ~ *ai genitori* obey one's parents
ubriacare <1d>: ~ **qu** get s.o. drunk
ubriacarsi get drunk
ubriachezza *f* drunkenness
ubriaco (*pl* -chi) **1** *agg* drunk **2** *m*, -**a** *f* drunk
uccello *m* bird; ~ *rapace* bird of prey
uccidere <3q> kill
uccidersi kill o.s.
ucciso *pp* → *uccidere*
uccisione *f* killing
udienza *f* (audience) audience; DIR hearing
udire <4n> hear
udito *m* hearing
uditorio *m* (*pl* -ri) audience
Ue *abbr* (= *Unione europea*) EU (= European Union)
Uem *abbr* (= *Unione economica e monetaria europea*) EMU (= Economic and Monetary Union)
ufficiale 1 *agg* official; *non* ~ unofficial **2** *m* official; MIL officer
ufficio *m* (*pl* -ci) office; ~ *cambi* bureau de change; ~ *oggetti smarriti* lost property; ~ *postale* post office; ~ *stampa* press office; ~ *di collocamento* Jobcentre; ~ *turistico* tourist information office
ufficioso unofficial
ufo[1] *m*: *a* ~ at other people's expense, free (of charge)
ufo[2] *m* UFO
uguaglianza *f* equality
uguagliare <1g> make equal; (*livellare*) level; (*essere pari a*) equal
uguale equal; *lo stesso* the same;

terreno level
UIL *abbr* (= *Unione Italiana del Lavoro*) Italian trade union organization
ulcera *f* ulcer; ~ *gastrica* gastric ulcer
ulteriore further
ultimamente recently
ultimare <1l> complete
ultimatum *m inv* ultimatum
ultimo 1 *agg* last; *più recente* latest; ~ *piano* top floor **2** *m*, -**a** *f* last; *fino all'*~ till the end
ultracorto: *onde fpl* -e ultrashort waves
ultrasuono *m* ultrasound
ultravioletto ultraviolet
ululare <1l> howl
ululato *m* howl
umanità *f* humanity
umanitario (*pl* -ri) humanitarian
umano human; *trattamento ecc* humane
Ume *abbr* (= *unione monetaria (europea)*) EMU (= European Monetary Union)
umidificatore *m* humidifier
umidità *f* dampness
umido 1 *agg* damp **2** *m* dampness; GASTR *in* ~ stewed
umile (*modesto*) humble; *mestiere* menial
umiliante humiliating
umiliare <1g> humiliate
umiliazione *f* humiliation
umiltà *f* humility
umore *m* mood; *di buon* ~ in a good mood; *di cattivo* ~ in a bad mood
umorismo *m* humo(u)r
umorista *m/f* (*mpl* -i) humorist

U

un, una → **uno**

unanime unanimous

unanimità f unanimity; **all'~** unanimously

uncinetto m crochet hook; **lavorare all'~** crochet

uncino m hook

undicesimo m/agg eleventh

undici eleven

ungere <3d> grease

ungherese agg, m/f Hungarian

Ungheria f Hungary

unghia f nail

unguento m ointment, cream

unico (pl -ci) only; (senza uguali) unique; **moneta f -a** single currency

unifamiliare: casa f ~ detached house

unificare <1m & d> unify

unificazione f unification

uniformare <1a> standardize

uniformarsi: ~ a conform to; **regole, direttive** comply with

uniforme f/agg uniform

uniformità f uniformity

unione f union; fig unity; **Unione economica e monetaria** Economic and Monetary Union; **Unione europea** European Union; **Unione monetaria (europea)** (European) Monetary Union

unire <4d> unite; congiungere join

unirsi unite; **~ in matrimonio** marry

unità f inv unit; **~ monetaria** monetary unit; **~ di misura** unit of measurement; INFOR **~ a dischi flessibili** disk drive; **~ pl periferiche** peripherals

unito united

universale universal

università f inv university

universitario (pl -ri) **1** agg university attr **2** m, **-a** f university student; (professore) university lecturer

universo m universe

uno 1 art a; before a vowel or silent h an; **un' uovo** an egg **2** agg a, one **3** m one; **~ e mezzo** one and a half **4** pron one; **a ~ a ~** one by one; **l'~ dopo l'altro** one after the other; **l'un l'altro** each other, one another

unto 1 pp → **ungere 2** agg greasy **3** m grease

unzione f: **estrema ~** last rites

uomo m (pl uomini) man; **~ d'affari** businessman; **~ di fiducia** right-hand man; **~ qualunque** man in the street; **da ~** abbigliamento ecc for men, men's

uovo m (pl le -a) egg; **~ alla coque** soft-boiled egg; **~ di Pasqua** Easter egg; **~ al tegame** fried egg; **-a pl strapazzate** scrambled eggs

uragano m hurricane

uranio m uranium

urbanistica f town planning

urbano urban; fig urbane

uretra f urethra

urgente urgent

urgenza f urgency; **in caso d'~** in an emergency

urina f urine

urlare <1a> scream

urlo m (pl anche le -a) scream

urna f urn; **elettorale** ballot box

urologo m (pl -gi), **-a** f urologist

urrà! hooray!

urtare <1a> bump into, collide with; **con un veicolo** hit; fig offend; **~ i nervi a qu** get on s.o.'s nerves

urto m bump; (scontro) collision

u.s. abbr (= **ultimo scorso**) last, ult.

USA abbr (= **Stati uniti d'America**) USA (= United States of America)

usa- e getta disposable

usanza f custom, tradition

usare <1a> **1** v/t use **2** v/i use; (essere di moda) be in fashion

usato used; (di seconda mano) second-hand

uscire <4o> come out; (andare fuori) go out

uscita f exit, way out; INFOR output; **~ di sicurezza** emergency exit; **via d'~** way out

usignolo m nightingale

uso m use; (abitudine) custom; **pronto per l'~** ready to use; **fuori ~** out of use; **~ indebito** misuse; **per ~ interno** for internal use; **per ~ esterno** not to be taken internally

US(S)L, **Us(s)l** abbr (= **Unità**

(Socio-)sanitaria Locale) local health authority

ustionarsi <1a> burn o.s.

ustione *f* burn

usuale usual

usufruire <4d>: **~ di qc** have the use of sth

usura *f di denaro* illegal money lending; *(logorio)* wear and tear

usuraio *m (pl -i)* loan shark

utensile 1 *agg*: **macchina** *f* **~** machine tool **2** *m* utensil

utente *m/f* user; **~ della strada** road user

utero *m* womb

utile 1 *agg* useful; **in tempo ~** within the time limit **2** *m* FIN profit; **unire l'~ al dilettevole** combine business with pleasure; **~ netto** net profit; **~ d'esercizio** operating profit

utilità *f* usefulness

utilitaria *f* economy car

utilizzare <1a> use

utilizzazione *f* use

utopia *f* utopia

utopista *m/f (mpl -i)* dreamer

uva *f* grapes *pl*; **~ passa** raisins *pl*; **~ spina** gooseberry

V

V *abbr* (= **volt**) V (= volt)

V. *abbr* (= **via**) St (= street)

v. *abbr* (= **vedi**) see

va → andare

vacante vacant

vacanza *f* holiday; **-e** *pl* **estive** summer holiday(s); **andare in ~** go on holiday

vacca *f (pl -cche)* cow

vaccinare <1a> vaccinate

vaccinazione *f* vaccination; **~ antitetanica** tetanus injection *or* shot

vaccino *m* vaccine

vado → andare

vagabondare <1a> wander

vagabondo 1 *agg (girovago)* wandering; *(fannullone)* idle **2** *m*, **-a** *f* *(giramondo)* wanderer; *(fannullone)* idler, layabout F; *(barbone)* tramp

vagare <1e> wander (aimlessly)

vagina *f* ANAT vagina

vaglia *m inv*: **~ (postale)** postal order; **~ bancario** bill of exchange, draft

vago *(pl -ghi)* vague

vagone *m* carriage; **~ letto** sleeper; **~ merci** goods wagon; **~ ristorante** dining car

vai → andare

vaiolo *m* smallpox

valanga *f (pl -ghe)* avalanche

valere <2r> be worth; *(essere valido)* be valid; **non vale nulla** it's worthless, it isn't worth anything; **far ~ diritti, autorità** assert; **non vale!** that's not fair!

valersi: **~ di qc** avail o.s. of sth

valeriana *f* valerian

valevole valid

valgo → valere

valico *m (pl -chi)* pass

validità *f* validity

valido valid; *persona* fit; **non ~** invalid

valigia *f (pl -gie)* suitcase; **fare le -e** pack

valle *f* valley

valore *m* value; *(coraggio)* bravery, valo(u)r; **~ aggiunto** added value; **~ commerciale** market value; **~ corrente** current value; **~ energetico** energy value; **-i** *pl* securities; **di ~** valuable; **senza ~** worthless

valorizzare <1a> increase the value of; *(far risaltare)* show off

valoroso courageous

valuta f currency; *stabilità f della ~* monetary stability

valutare <1a> value

valutario monetary

valutazione f valuation

valvola f valve; EL fuse; *~ dell'aria* air valve

valzer m inv waltz

vandalismo m vandalism

vandalo m vandal

vanga f (pl -ghe) spade

vangelo m gospel

vaniglia f vanilla

vanità f vanity

vanitoso vain

vanno → **andare**

vano 1 agg minacce, promesse empty; (inutile) vain 2 m (spazio vuoto) hollow; (stanza) room; AUTO *~ porta-oggetti* glove compartment

vantaggio m (pl -ggi) advantage; *in gara* lead

vantaggioso advantageous

vantare <1a> speak highly of; *possedere* boast

vantarsi boast (*di* of)

vanto m boast

vapore m vapo(u)r; MAR steamer; *~ (d'acqua)* steam

vaporetto m water bus

vaporizzare <1a> (*nebulizzare*) spray

vaporoso floaty; (*vago*) woolly

variabile 1 agg changeable 2 f MAT variable

variare <1k> v/t & v/i vary

variazione f variation

varice f varicose vein

varicella f chickenpox

varietà 1 f inv variety 2 m inv variety, Am vaudeville; (*spettacolo m di*) *~* variety, Am vaudeville) show

vario (pl -ri) varied; *-ri pl* various

variopinto multicolo(u)red

vasca f (pl -che) (*serbatoio, cisterna*) tank; (*lunghezza di piscina*) length; *di fontana* basin; *~ (da bagno)* bath, (bath)tub

vaselina f vaseline

vasellame m dishes

vaso m pot; ANAT vessel

vassoio m (pl -oi) tray

vasto vast

V.d.F. abbr (= *vigili del fuoco*) fire brigade, Am fire department

ve = **vi** (*before* **lo, la, li, le, ne**)

vecchiaia f old age

vecchio (pl -cchi) 1 agg old 2 m, -a f old man; *donna vecchia* old woman

vece f: *in ~ di* instead of; *fare le -i di qu* take s.o.'s place

vedere <2s> see; *far ~* show; *stare a ~* watch

vedovo 1 agg widowed 2 m, -a f widower; *donna* widow

veduta f view (*su* of); *~ aerea* aerial view; fig *larghezza f di -e* broadmindedness

vegetale 1 agg vegetable attr; *regno, vita* plant attr 2 m plant

vegetare <1l & b> vegetate

vegetariano 1 agg vegetarian attr 2 m, -a f vegetarian

vegetazione f vegetation

vegeto vecchio spry; *vivo e ~* hale and hearty

veggente m/f (*chiaroveggente*) clairvoyant

veglia f (*l'essere svegli*) wakefulness; (*il vegliare*) vigil; *essere tra la ~ e il sonno* be half asleep

vegliare <1g> 1 v/i keep watch 2 v/t: *~ qu* watch over s.o.

veicolo m vehicle; *~ spaziale* spaceship

vela f sail; *attività* sailing; *fare ~* set sail; *tutto è andato a gonfie -e* everything went swimmingly

veleggiare <1f> sail

veleno m poison; *di animali* venom (*anche fig*)

velenoso poisonous; fig venomous

veliero m sailing ship

velina f: *carta f ~ per imballaggio* tissue paper

velismo m sailing

velista m/f sailor

velivolo m aircraft

velluto m velvet; *~ a coste* corduroy

velo m veil

veloce fast, quick

velocemente quickly

velocità f inv speed; **limite** m **di** ~ speed limit; **eccesso** m **di** ~ speeding; ~ **della luce** speed of light; ~ **di crociera** cruising speed

velodromo m velodrome

vena f vein; **essere in** ~ be in the mood

vendemmia f (grape) harvest

vendemmiare <1k> v/t v/i harvest

vendere <3a> sell; ~ **all'ingrosso** sell wholesale; ~ **al minuto** retail

vendetta f revenge

vendicare <1f & d> avenge

vendicarsi get one's own revenge (**di qu** on s.o.; **di qc** for sth)

vendita f sale; ~ **di fine stagione** end-of-season sale; ~ **diretta** direct selling

venditore m, **-trice** f salesman; **donna** saleswoman

venerare <1l & b> revere

venerazione f veneration

venerdì m inv Friday; **Venerdì Santo** Good Friday

Venere f Venus

Venezia f Venice

veneziano 1 agg of Venice, Venetian **2** m, **-a** f Venetian

vengo → **venire**

venire <4p> come; (riuscire) turn out; come ausiliare be; **i suoi disegni vengono ammirati da tutti** his drawings are admired by all; ~ **a costare** total, work out at; ~ **a sapere qc** learn sth, find sth out; ~ **al dunque** get to the point; **mi sta venendo fame** I'm getting hungry

ventaglio m (pl -gli) fan

ventenne agg, m/f twenty-year-old

ventesimo m/agg twentieth

venti twenty

ventilatore m fan

ventilazione f ventilation

ventina f: **una** ~ about twenty

ventiquattrore f inv (valigetta) overnight bag

vento m wind; **c'è** ~ it's windy

ventoso windy

ventre m stomach; **basso** ~ lower abdomen

venturo next

venuta f arrival

venuto 1 pp → **venire 2** m, **-a** f: **il primo** ~ just anyone; **non è certo il primo** ~ he's not just anyone

veramente really

veranda f veranda

verbale 1 agg verbal **2** m record; **di riunione** minutes pl

verbalizzare <1a> record (in writing), take down; riunione take the minutes of; (esprimere a parole) verbalize

verbalmente verbally

verbo m GRAM verb

verde 1 agg green; benzina unleaded; **numero** ~ freephone number; **essere al** ~ be broke **2** m green; POL **i -i** pl the Greens

verdetto m verdict

verdura f vegetables pl

vergine 1 agg virgin attr **2** f virgin; ASTR **Vergine** Virgo

verginità f virginity

vergogna f shame; (timidezza) shyness

vergognarsi <1a> be ashamed; (essere timido) be shy

vergognoso ashamed; (timido) shy; azione shameful

verifica f (pl -che) check

verificare <1m & d> check

verificarsi (accadere) occur, take place; (avverarsi) come true

verità f truth

verme m worm; ~ **solitario** tapeworm

vermut m vermouth

vernice f paint; trasparente varnish; pelle patent leather; fig veneer; ~ **antiruggine** rust-proofing paint; ~ **fresca** wet paint; ~ **protettiva** protective coating

verniciare <1f> paint; con vernice trasparente varnish; **verniciato di fresco** wet paint

verniciatura f painting; con vernice trasparente varnishing; fig veneer

vero 1 agg (rispondente a verità) true; (autentico) real; **sei contento, ~?** you're happy, aren't you?; **ti piace il**

gelato, ~? you like icecream, don't you?; **fosse ~!** if only (it were true)! **2** *m* truth; PITT **dal ~** from life

veronese 1 *agg* of Verona **2** *m/f* inhabitant of Verona

verosimile likely

verruca *f* (*pl* -che) wart

versamento *m* payment; **ricevuta** *f* **di ~** receipt for payment

versante *m* slope

versare <1b> **1** *v/t vino* pour; *denaro* pay; (*rovesciare*) spill **2** *v/i* (*trovarsi*, *essere*) be

versione *f* version; (*traduzione*) translation; **in ~ originale** original language version

verso 1 *prp* towards; **andare ~ casa** head for home; **~ le otto** about eight o'clock **2** *m di poesie* verse; (*modo*) manner; **non c'è ~** there is no way

vertebra *f* vertebra

vertebrale: colonna *f* **~** spinal column

verticale 1 *agg* vertical **2** *f* vertical (line); *in ginnastica* handstand

vertice *m* summit; **incontro** *m* **al ~** summit (meeting)

vertigine *f* vertigo, dizziness; **ho le -i** I feel dizzy

vertiginoso *altezza* dizzy; *prezzi* staggering, sky-high; *velocità* breakneck

verza *f* savoy (cabbage)

vescica *f* (*pl* -che) ANAT bladder

vescovo *m* bishop

vespa *f* ZO wasp

vespaio *m* (*pl* -ai) wasps' nest; *fig* hornets' nest

vestaglia *f* dressing gown, *Am* robe

veste *f* fig (*capacità*, *funzione*) capacity; **in ~ ufficiale** in an offical capacity

vestiario *m* wardrobe

vestire <4b> dress; (*portare*) wear

vestirsi get dressed; *in un certo modo* dress; **~irsi da** (*travestirsi*) dress up as

vestito *m* **da uomo** suit; *da donna* dress; (*capo di vestiario*) item of clothing, garment; **-i** *pl* clothes; **-i da uomo** men's wear

veterinario *m* (*pl* -ri), **-a** *f* veterinary surgeon, vet F

veto *m* veto; **porre il ~ a** veto

vetraio *m* (*pl* -i), (*installatore*) glazier

vetrata *f finestra* large window; *porta* glass door; *di chiesa* stained-glass window

vetreria *f* (*fabbrica*) glass works; (*negozio*) glazier's

vetrina *f* (shop) window; *mobile* display cabinet; *di museo*, *fig* showcase

vetrinista *m/f* (*mpl* -i) window dresser

vetro *m* glass; *di finestra*, *porta* pane; **di ~** glass *attr*; **~ armato** reinforced glass; **~ smerigliato** frosted glass

vetta *f* top; *di montagna* peak

vettura *f* AUTO car; FERR carriage; **~ da corsa** racing car; **in ~!** all aboard!

vi 1 *pron* you; *riflessivo* yourselves; *reciproco* each other **2** *avv* → **ci**

via 1 *f* street, road; (*in*); **Marconi** Marconi St; **lettera** *f* (*per*) **~ aerea** airmail letter; **Via lattea** Milky Way; **ricorrere alle -e legali** take legal action; **in ~ eccezionale** as an exception; **per ~ di** by; (*a causa di*) because of **2** *m* off, starting signal; SP **dare il ~** give the off; *fig* **dare il ~ a qc** get sth under way **3** *avv* away; **andar ~** go away, leave; **~ ~** (*gradualmente*) little by little, gradually; (*man mano*) as (and when); **e così ~** and so on; **~! per scacciare** go away!, scram! F; (*suvvia*) come on! **4** *prp* via, by way of

viabilità *f* road conditions *pl*; (*rete stradale*) road network; (*traffico stradale*) road traffic

viadotto *m* viaduct

viaggiare <1f> travel; **~ per affari** travel on business

viaggiatore *m*, **-trice** *f* travel(l)er

viaggio *m* (*pl* -ggi) journey; **~ aereo** flight; **~ per mare** voyage; **~ di nozze** honeymoon; **~ in comitiva** group travel; **~ in treno** train journey; **~ d'affari** business trip; **~ di studio** study trip; **cestino** *m* **da ~** packed meal; **mettersi in ~** set out;

essere in ~ be away, be travelling
viale *m* avenue
viavai *m inv* coming and going
vibrare <1a> vibrate
vibrazione *f* vibration
vice- *prefisso* vice-
vice *m/f inv* deputy
vicedirettore *m* assistant manager
vicenda *f* (*episodio*) event; (*storia*) story; ***alterne* -e** changing fortunes; ***a* ~** (*a turno*) in turn; (*scambievolmente*) each other, one another
viceversa vice versa
vicinanza *f* nearness, proximity; **-e** *pl* neighbo(u)rhood *sg*, vicinity *sg*
vicinato *m* neighbo(u)rhood; (*persone*) neighbo(u)rs *pl*
vicino 1 *agg* near, close; ~ *a* near, close to; (*accanto a*) next to; *da* ~ *esaminare* closely; *visto* close up **2** *avv* nearby, close by **3** *m*, **-a** *f* neighbo(u)r
vicolo *m* lane; ~ *cieco* dead end
videata *f* INFOR display
video *m* video; F (*schermo*) screen
videocamera *f* videocamera
videocassetta *f* video (cassette)
videocontrollo *m* video surveillance
videogioco *m* video game
videoregistratore *m* video (recorder)
videoteca *f* video library; (*negozio*) video shop
videotel *m inv Italian Videotex*®
videotelefono *m* videophone, viewphone
vietare <1b> forbid; ~ *a qu di fare qc* forbid s.o. to do sth
vietato: ~ *fumare* no smoking
vigente in force
vigilante *m* security guard
vigilanza *f* vigilance; *sotto* ~ under surveillance
vigilare <1l> *persone* watch (over); (*pattugliare*) patrol
vigile 1 *agg* watchful **2** *m/f:* ~ (*urbano*) local police officer; ~ *del fuoco* firefighter
vigilia *f* night before, eve; ~ *di Natale* Christmas Eve
vigliacco (*pl* -cchi) **1** *agg* cowardly **2** *m*, **-a** *f* coward
vigna *f* (small) vineyard
vigneto *m* vineyard
vignetta *f* cartoon
vigore *m* vigo(u)r
vigoroso vigorous
vile 1 *agg* vile; (*codardo*) cowardly **2** *m* coward
villa *f* villa
villaggio *m* (*pl* -ggi) village; ~ *turistico* holiday village
villeggiatura *f* holiday
villino *m* house
vincere <3d> **1** *v/t* win; *avversario, nemico* defeat, beat; *difficoltà* overcome **2** *v/i* win
vincersi (*dominarsi*) control o.s.
vincita *f* win
vincitore *m*, **-trice** *f* winner
vincolare <1l> bind; *capitale* tie up
vincolo *m* bond
vino *m* wine; ~ *bianco* white wine; ~ *rosso* red wine; ~ *da pasto* table wine
vinto *pp* → **vincere**
viola *f* MUS viola; BOT violet; ~ *del pensiero* pansy
violare <1l> violate; *legge* break
violazione *f* violation; *di leggi, patti, accordi* breach; ~ *di domicilio* unlawful entry
violentare <1b> rape
violentatore *m* rapist
violento violent
violenza *f* violence
violinista *m/f* (*mpl* -i) violinist
violino *m* violin
violoncello *m* cello
vipera *f* viper
virgola *f* comma; MAT decimal point
virile manly, virile
virtù *f inv* virtue
virtuoso 1 *agg* virtuous **2** *m* virtuoso
virus *m inv* virus
viscere *fpl* insides; *fig: della terra* bowels
vischio *m* (*pl* -chi) mistletoe
viscido slimy
viscosa *f* viscose
viscoso viscous
visibile visible

visibilità f visibility

visiera f di berretto peak; di casco visor

visione f sight, vision; **prendere ~ di qc** have a look at sth; **in ~** for examination

visita f visit; **~ medica** medical (examination); **far ~ a qu** visit s.o.

visitare <1l> visit; MED examine

visitatore m, **-trice** f visitor

visivo visual

viso m face

visone m mink

vissuto pp → **vivere**

vista f (senso) sight; (capacità visiva) eyesight; (veduta) view; **a prima ~** at first sight; MUS at sight; **in ~ di** in sight of; fig in view of; **conoscere qu di ~** know s.o. by sight; fig **perdere qu di ~** lose touch with s.o.

visto 1 pp → **vedere**; **~ che** seeing that **2** m visa; **~ d'entrata** entry visa; **~ di transito** transit visa; **~ d'uscita** exit visa

vistoso eye-catching

visuale 1 agg visual **2** f (veduta) view

vita f life; (durata della vita) lifetime; ANAT waist; **a ~** for life; **costo m della ~** cost of living; **senza ~** lifeless

vitale vital; persona lively, full of life

vitalità f inv vitality

vitamina f vitamin

vite[1] f TEC screw

vite[2] f AGR vine

vitello m calf; GASTR veal

viticoltore m vinegrower

viticoltura f vinegrowing

vitreo fig: sguardo, occhio glazed, glassy

vittima f victim

vitto m diet food; **~ e alloggio** bed and board

vittoria f victory

vittorioso victorious

vivace lively; colore bright

vivacità f liveliness; di colori brightness

vivaio m di pesci tank; di piante nursery; fig breeding ground

vivanda f food

viva voce m inv speakerphone

vivente living

vivere <3zz> **1** v/i live (di on) **2** v/t (passare, provare) experience; **~ una vita tranquilla** live quietly, lead a quiet life

viveri mpl food (supplies)

vivisezione f vivisection

vivo 1 agg (in vita) alive; (vivente) living; colore bright; **farsi ~** get in touch; (arrivare) turn up; **~ e vegeto** hale and hearty **2** m: **dal ~** trasmissione, concerto live; **entrare nel ~ della questione** get to the heart of the matter; **i -i** pl the living

viziare <1g> persona spoil

viziato persona spoiled; **aria** f **-a** stale air

vizio m (pl -zi) vice; (cattiva abitudine) (bad) habit; (dipendenza) addiction; **~ cardiaco** heart defect

vizioso persona dissolute; **circolo** m **~** vicious circle

v.le abbr (= **viale**) St (= street)

vocabolario m (pl -ri) (lessico) vocabulary; (dizionario) dictionary

vocabolo m word

vocale 1 agg vocal **2** f vowel

vocazione f vocation

voce f voice; fig rumo(u)r; in dizionario, elenco entry; **ad alta ~** in a loud voice, loudly; **a bassa ~** in a low voice, quietly; **spargere la ~** spread rumo(u)rs

voglia f (desiderio) wish, desire; (volontà) will; sulla pelle birthmark; **avere ~ di fare qc** feel like doing sth; **morire dalla ~ di fare qc** be dying to do sth; **contro ~, di mala ~** unwillingly, reluctantly

voglio → **volere**

voi you; riflessivo yourselves; reciproco each other; **a ~** to you; **senza di ~** without you

vol. abbr (= **volume**) vol (= volume)

volano m shuttlecock

volante 1 agg flying **2** m AUTO (steering) wheel **3** f flying squad

volantino m leaflet

volare <1a> fly

volata f SP final sprint; **di ~** in a rush

volenteroso willing

volentieri willingly; **~!** with pleasure!

volere 1 <2t> *v/t & v/i* want; **vorrei ...** I would *or* I'd like ...; **vorrei partire** I'd like to leave; **~ dire** mean; **~ bene a qu** (*amare*) love s.o.; **ci vogliono dieci mesi** it takes ten months; **senza ~** without meaning to **2** *m* will

volgare vulgar

volgarità *f* vulgarity

volgere <3d> **1** *v/t:* **~ le spalle** turn one's back **2** *v/i:* **~ al termine** draw to a close; **il tempo volge al brutto** the weather is getting worse; **~ al peggio** take a turn for the worse

volo *m* flight; (*caduta*) fall; **prendere il ~** *di uccello* fly away; *di persona* run away; **~ a vela** gliding; **~ diretto** direct flight; **~ di linea** scheduled flight; **~ internazionale** international flight; **~ nazionale** domestic flight; **~ senza scalo** nonstop flight; *fig* **afferrare qc al ~** be quick to grasp sth

volontà *f* will; **a ~** as much as you like; **buona ~** goodwill

volontariato *m* voluntary work

volontario (*pl* -ri) **1** *agg* voluntary **2** *m*, **-a** *f* volunteer

volpe *f* fox; *femmina* vixen

volt *m inv* volt

volta *f* time; (*turno*) turn; ARCHI vault; **una ~** once; **due -e** twice; **qualche ~** sometimes; **questa ~** this time; **ogni ~** every time; **una ~ per sempre** once and for all; **poco per ~** little by little; **un'altra ~** ancora una volta one more time; **lo faremo un'altra** we'll do it some other time; **molte -e** many times, often

voltaggio *m* (*pl* -ggi) voltage

voltare <1c> **1** *v/t* turn; *pagina* turn (over); **~ le spalle a qu** *azione* turn one's back on s.o.; *posizione* have one's back to s.o. **2** *v/i* turn; **~ a destra** turn right

voltarsi turn (round)

volto¹ *m* face

volto² *pp* → **volgere**

volume *m* volume

voluminoso bulky

voluttà *f* voluptuousness

vomitare <1l & c> vomit, throw up F; *fig* **mi fa ~** it makes me sick

vomito *m* vomit

vongola *f* ZO, GASTR clam

voragine *f* chasm, abyss

vortice *m* whirl; *in acqua* whirlpool; *di vento* whirlwind

vostro 1 *agg* your; **i -i amici** your friends **2** *pron: il ~* yours; **questi libri sono -i** these books are yours

votare <1a> vote

votazione *f* vote

voto *m* POL vote; EDU mark; REL, *fig* vow; **mettere qc ai -i** put sth to the vote, take a vote on sth

v.r. *abbr* (= **vedi retro**) see over

Vs. *abbr* (= **vostro**) your

v.s. *abbr* (= **vedi sopra**) see above

V.U. *abbr* (= **Vigili Urbani**) police

vulcanico (*pl* -ci) volcanic

vulcano *m* volcano

vulnerabile vulnerable

vuole → **volere**

vuotare <1c> empty

vuotarsi empty

vuoto 1 *agg* empty; (*non occupato*) vacant; (*privo*) devoid (*di* of) **2** *m* (*spazio*) empty space; (*recipiente*) empty; FIS vacuum; *fig* void; **~ d'aria** air pocket; **~ a perdere** non-returnable container; **~ a rendere** returnable container; **andare a ~** fall through; (*confezionato*) **sotto ~** vacuum-packed

W

W *abbr* (= *watt*) W (= watt); (= *viva*) long live
walkman *m inv* Walkman®
watt *m inv* watt
WC *abbr* (= *gabinetto*) WC (= water closet)
week-end *m inv* weekend

western *m inv* Western; **~ all'italiana** spaghetti Western
whisky *m inv* whisky
windsurf *m inv* (*tavola*) sailboard; *attività* windsurfing; **fare ~** go windsurfing
W.L. *abbr* (= *vagone letto*) sleeper

XY

X, x *f* x; **raggi** *mpl* **~** X-rays
xenofobia *f* xenophobia
xenofobo 1 *agg* xenophobic **2** *m*, **-a** *f* xenophobe
xilofono *m* xylophone

yacht *m inv* yacht
yoga *m* yoga
yogurt *m inv* yoghurt
yugoslavo 1 *agg* Yugoslav(ian) **2** *m*, **-a** *f* Yugoslav(ian)

Z

zabaione *m* zabaglione
zafferano *m* saffron
zaffiro *m* sapphire
zagara *f* orange blossom
zaino *m* rucksack
zampa *f* ZO (*piede*) paw; *di uccello* claw; (*zoccolo*) hoof; (*arto*) leg; GASTR *di maiale* trotter; *fig* **giù le -e!** hands off!; **a ~ di elefante** flared
zampillare <1a> gush
zampillo *m* spurt
zampone *m* GASTR stuffed pig's trotter
zanzara *f* mosquito

zanzariera *f* mosquito net; *su finestre* insect screen
zappa *f* hoe
zappare <1a> hoe
zapping *m inv*: **fare lo ~** zap
zattera *f* raft
zavorra *f* ballast
zebra *f* zebra
zecca¹ *f* (*pl* -cche) ZO tick
zecca² *f* (*pl* -cche) Mint; **nuovo di ~** brand-new
zelante zealous
zelo *m* zeal
zenit *m* zenith

zenzero *m* ginger

zeppo: pieno ~ crammed (*di* with)

zerbino *m* doormat

zero *m* zero; *nel tennis* love; *nel calcio* nil; *fig* **partire da ~** start from scratch; **2 gradi sotto ~** 2 degrees below zero

zigomo *m* cheekbone

zigzag *m inv* zigzag

zimbello *m* decoy; *fig* laughing stock

zinco *m* zinc

zingaro m, **-a** *f* gipsy

zio m, **-a** *f* uncle; *donna* aunt

zitto quiet; **sta ~!** be quiet!; *in tono minaccioso* keep your mouth shut! F

zoccolo *m* clog; ZO hoof; ARCHI base

zodiacale: segni *mpl* **-i** signs of the Zodiac

zodiaco *m* Zodiac

zolfo *m* sulphur, *Am* sulfur

zona *f* zone, area; **~ di libero scambio** free trade area; **~ disco** short-stay parking area; **~ industriale** industrial area; **~ pedonale** pedestrian precinct; **~ residenziale** residential area; **~ verde** green belt

zonzo: andare a ~ wander around

zoo *m inv* zoo

zoppicare <1l, c & d> limp; *di mobile* wobble

zoppo lame; (*zoppicante*) limping; *mobile* wobbly

zucca *f* (*pl* -cche) marrow; *fig* F (*testa*) bonce F, nut F

zuccherare <1l> sugar

zuccheriera *f* sugar bowl

zucchero *m* sugar; **~ greggio** brown sugar; **~ vanigliato** vanilla sugar; **~ in zollette** sugar cubes

zucchini *mpl* courgettes, *Am* zucchini(s)

zuffa *f* scuffle

zuppa *f* soup; **~ di verdura** vegetable soup; **~ di pesce** fish soup; **~ inglese** trifle

zuppiera *f* tureen

zuppo soaked, wet through

Z

A

a [ə] *stressed* [eɪ] *art* un *m*, una *f*; *masculine before s + consonant, gn, ps, z* uno; *feminine before vowel* un'; **~ cat** un gatto; **~ joke** uno scherzo; **~ girl** una ragazza; **an island** un'isola; **£5 ~ ride** una corsa 5 sterline; **£2 ~ litre** 2 sterline al litro; **five flights ~ day** cinque voli al giorno

a·back [ə'bæk] *adv*: **taken ~** preso alla sprovvista

a·ban·don [ə'bændən] *v/t* abbandonare; *hope, scheme* rinunciare a

a·bashed [ə'bæʃt] *adj* imbarazzato

a·bate [ə'beɪt] *v/i of storm, flood waters* calmarsi

ab·at·toir ['æbətwɑː(r)] mattatoio *m*

ab·bey ['æbɪ] abbazia *f*

ab·bre·vi·ate [ə'briːvɪeɪt] *v/t* abbreviare

ab·bre·vi·a·tion [əbriːvɪ'eɪʃn] abbreviazione *f*

ab·di·cate ['æbdɪkeɪt] *v/i* abdicare

ab·di·ca·tion [æbdɪ'keɪʃn] abdicazione *f*

ab·do·men ['æbdəmən] addome *m*

ab·dom·i·nal [æb'dɒmɪnl] *adj* addominale

ab·duct [əb'dʌkt] *v/t* sequestrare, rapire

ab·duc·tion [əb'dʌkʃn] sequestro *m*, rapimento *m*

ab·hor·rence [əb'hɒrəns] *fml* orrore *m*

ab·hor·rent [əb'hɒrənt] *adj fml* ripugnante

♦ **abide by** [ə'baɪd] *v/t* attenersi a

a·bil·i·ty [ə'bɪlətɪ] abilità *f inv*

a·blaze [ə'bleɪz] *adj* in fiamme

a·ble ['eɪbl] *adj* (*skilful*) capace; **be ~ to** essere capace a; **I wasn't ~ to see/hear** non ero in grado di vedere/sentire

a·ble-bod·ied [eɪbl'bɒdɪːd] *adj* robusto; MIL abile

ab·nor·mal [æb'nɔːml] *adj* anormale

ab·nor·mal·ly [æb'nɔːməlɪ] *adv* in modo anomalo

a·board [ə'bɔːd] **1** *prep* a bordo di **2** *adv*: **be ~** essere a bordo; **go ~** salire a bordo

a·bol·ish [ə'bɒlɪʃ] *v/t* abolire

ab·o·li·tion [æbə'lɪʃn] abolizione *f*

a·bort [ə'bɔːt] *v/t mission, rocket launch* annullare; COMPUT: *program* interrompere

a·bor·tion [ə'bɔːʃn] aborto *m*; **have an ~** abortire

a·bor·tive [ə'bɔːtɪv] *adj* fallito; **the plan proved ~** il piano si è rivelato un fallimento

a·bout [ə'baʊt] **1** *prep* (*concerning*) su; **I'll tell you all ~ it** ti dirò tutto al riguardo; **talk ~ sth** parlare di qc; **be angry ~ sth** essere arrabbiato per qc; **there's nothing you can do ~ it** non ci puoi fare niente; **what's it ~?** *of book, film* di cosa parla?; *of complaint, problem* di cosa si tratta? **2** *adv* (*roughly*) quasi; (*nearly*) quasi; **it's ~ ready** è quasi pronto; **be ~ to ...** (*be going to*) essere sul punto di ...; **be ~** (*somewhere near*) essere nei paraggi; **there are a lot of people ~** c'è un sacco di gente qui

a·bove [ə'bʌv] **1** *prep* (*higher than*) sopra; (*more than*) sopra, oltre; **~ all** soprattutto **2** *adv* sopra; **on the floor ~** al piano di sopra

a·bove-men·tioned [əbʌv'menʃnd] *adj* suddetto

ab·ra·sion [ə'breɪʒn] abrasione *f*

ab·ra·sive [ə'breɪsɪv] *adj personality* ruvido

a·breast [ə'brest] *adv* fianco a fianco; **keep ~ of** tenere al corrente di

a·bridge [ə'brɪdʒ] *v/t* ridurre

a·broad [ə'brɔːd] *adv* all'estero

a·brupt [ə'brʌpt] *adj departure* improvviso; *manner* brusco

a·brupt·ly [ə'brʌptlɪ] *adv leave* improvvisamente; *say* bruscamente

ab·scess ['æbsɪs] ascesso *m*

ab·sence ['æbsəns] assenza *f*

ab·sent ['æbsənt] *adj* assente

ab·sen·tee [æbsən'tiː] *n* assente *m/f*

ab·sen·tee·ism [æbsən'tiːɪzm] assenteismo *m*

ab·sent-mind·ed [æbsənt'maɪndɪd] *adj* distratto

ab·sent-mind·ed·ly [æbsənt'maɪndɪdlɪ] *adv* distrattamente

ab·so·lute ['æbsəluːt] *adj power* assoluto; *idiot* totale

ab·so·lute·ly ['æbsəluːtlɪ] *adv (completely)* assolutamente; **~ not!** assolutamente no!; **do you agree? ~** sei d'accordo? – assolutamente sì

ab·so·lu·tion [æbsə'luːʃn] REL assoluzione *f*

ab·solve [əb'zɒlv] *v/t* assolvere

ab·sorb [əb'sɔːb] *v/t* assorbire; **~ed in ...** assorto in ...

ab·sorb·en·cy [əb'sɔːbənsɪ] assorbenza *f*

ab·sorb·ent [əb'sɔːbənt] *adj* assorbente

ab·sorb·ing [əb'sɔːbɪŋ] *adj* avvincente

ab·stain [əb'steɪn] *v/i from voting* astenersi

ab·sten·tion [əb'stenʃn] *in voting* astensione *f*

ab·sti·nence ['æbstɪnəns] astinenza *f*

ab·stract ['æbstrækt] *adj* astratto

ab·struse [əb'struːs] *adj* astruso

ab·surd [əb'sɜːd] *adj* assurdo

ab·surd·i·ty [əb'sɜːdətɪ] assurdità *f*

ab·surd·ly [əb'sɜːdlɪ] *adv* in modo assurdo

a·bun·dance [ə'bʌndəns] abbondanza *f*

a·bun·dant [ə'bʌndənt] *adj* abbondante

a·buse¹ [ə'bjuːs] *n* abuso *m*; *(ill treatment)* maltrattamento *m*; *(insults)* insulti *mpl*

a·buse² [ə'bjuːz] *v/t* abusare di; *(treat badly)* maltrattare; *(insult)* insultare

a·bu·sive [ə'bjuːsɪv] *adj language* offensivo; **become ~** diventare aggressivo

a·bys·mal [ə'bɪzml] *adj* F *(very bad)* pessimo

a·byss [ə'bɪs] abisso *m*

AC ['eɪsiː] *abbr* (= **alternating current**) c.a. (corrente *f* alternata)

ac·a·dem·ic [ækə'demɪk] **1** *n* docente *m/f* universitario, -a **2** *adj* accademico; *person* portato per lo studio

a·cad·e·my [ə'kædəmɪ] accademia *f*

ac·cede [ək'siːd] *v/i*: **~ to** *throne* salire a

ac·cel·e·rate [ək'seləreɪt] *v/t & v/i* accelerare

ac·cel·e·ra·tion [əkselə'reɪʃn] *of car* accelerazione *f*

ac·cel·e·ra·tor [ək'seləreɪtə(r)] *of car* acceleratore *m*

ac·cent ['æksənt] accento *m*

ac·cen·tu·ate [ək'sentjueɪt] *v/t* accentuare

ac·cept [ək'sept] *v/t* accettare

ac·cep·ta·ble [ək'septəbl] *adj* accettabile

ac·cept·ance [ək'septəns] accettazione *f*

ac·cess ['ækses] **1** *n* accesso *m*; **have ~ to** *computer* avere accesso a; *child* avere il permesso di vedere **2** *v/t* accedere a

'ac·cess code COMPUT codice *m* di accesso

ac·ces·si·ble [ək'sesəbl] *adj* accessibile

ac·ces·sion [ək'seʃn] ascesa *f*

ac·ces·so·ry [ək'sesərɪ] *for wearing* accessorio *m*; LAW complice *m/f*

'ac·cess road svincolo *m*

'ac·cess time COMPUT tempo *m* di accesso

ac·ci·dent ['æksɪdənt] incidente *m*; **by ~** per caso

ac·ci·den·tal [æksɪ'dentl] *adj* accidentale

ac·ci·den·tal·ly [æksɪ'dentlɪ] *adv* accidentalmente

ac·claim [ə'kleɪm] **1** *n* consenso *m* **2** *v/t* acclamare

acid test

ac·cla·ma·tion [ækləˈmeɪʃn] acclamazioni *fpl*

ac·cli·mate, ac·cli·ma·tize [əˈklaɪmət, əˈklaɪmətaɪz] **1** *v/t* acclimatare **2** *v/i* acclimatarsi

ac·com·mo·date [əˈkɒmədeɪt] *v/t* ospitare; *special requirements* tenere conto di

ac·com·mo·da·tion [əkɒməˈdeɪʃn] sistemazione *f*

ac·com·pa·ni·ment [əˈkʌmpənɪmənt] MUS accompagnamento *m*

ac·com·pa·nist [əˈkʌmpənɪst] MUS: **with Gerald Moore as his ~** con l'accompagnamento di Gerald Moore

ac·com·pa·ny [əˈkʌmpənɪ] *v/t* (*pret & pp -ied*) accompagnare

ac·com·plice [əˈkʌmplɪs] complice *m/f*

ac·com·plish [əˈkʌmplɪʃ] *v/t* *task* compiere; *goal* conseguire

ac·com·plished [əˈkʌmplɪʃt] *adj* dotato

ac·com·plish·ment [əˈkʌmplɪʃmənt] *of a task* realizzazione *f*; (*talent*) talento *m*; (*achievement*) risultato *m*

ac·cord [əˈkɔːd] accordo *m*; **of his / my own ~** di sua / mia spontanea volontà

ac·cord·ance [əˈkɔːdəns]: **in ~ with** conformemente a

ac·cord·ing [əˈkɔːdɪŋ] *adv*: **~ to** secondo

ac·cord·ing·ly [əˈkɔːdɪŋlɪ] *adv* di conseguenza

ac·cor·di·on [əˈkɔːdɪən] fisarmonica *f*

ac·cor·di·on·ist [əˈkɔːdɪənɪst] fisarmonicista *m/f*

ac·count [əˈkaʊnt] *financial* conto *m*; (*report, description*) resoconto *m*; **give an ~ of** fare un resoconto di; **on no ~** per nessuna ragione; **on ~ of** a causa di; **take ... into ~, take ~ of ...** tenere conto di ...

♦ **account for** *v/t* (*explain*) giustificare; (*make up, constitute*) ammontare a

ac·count·abil·i·ty [əkaʊntəˈbɪlətɪ]

responsabilità *f*

ac·coun·ta·ble [əˈkaʊntəbl] *adj* responsabile; **be held ~** essere considerato responsabile

ac·coun·tant [əˈkaʊntənt] contabile *m/f*; *running own business* commercialista *m/f*

ac'count hol·der titolare *m/f* di conto; *of current account* correntista *m/f*

ac'count num·ber numero *m* di conto

ac·counts [əˈkaʊnts] *npl* contabilità *f*

ac·cu·mu·late [əˈkjuːmjʊleɪt] **1** *v/t* accumulare **2** *v/i* accumularsi

ac·cu·mu·la·tion [əkjuːmjʊˈleɪʃn] accumulazione *f*

ac·cu·ra·cy [ˈækjʊrəsɪ] precisione *f*

ac·cu·rate [ˈækjʊrət] *adj* preciso

ac·cu·rate·ly [ˈækjʊrətlɪ] *adv* con precisione

ac·cu·sa·tion [ækjuːˈzeɪʃn] accusa *f*

ac·cuse [əˈkjuːz] *v/t* accusare; **he ~d me of lying** mi ha accusato di mentire; **be ~d of ...** LAW essere accusato di ...

ac·cused [əˈkjuːzd] *n* LAW accusato *m*, -a *f*

ac·cus·ing [əˈkjuːzɪŋ] *adj* accusatorio

ac·cus·ing·ly [əˈkjuːzɪŋlɪ] *adv* look, point con aria accusatoria; *say* con tono accusatorio

ac·cus·tom [əˈkʌstəm] *v/t*: **get ~ed to** abituarsi a; **be ~ed to** essere abituato a

ace [eɪs] *in cards* asso *m*; (*in tennis: shot*) ace *m inv*

ache [eɪk] **1** *n* dolore *m* **2** *v/i* fare male; **my head ~s** mi fa male la testa

a·chieve [əˈtʃiːv] *v/t* realizzare; *success, fame* ottenere

a·chieve·ment [əˈtʃiːvmənt] *of ambition* realizzazione *f*; (*thing achieved*) successo *m*

ac·id [ˈæsɪd] *n* acido *m*

a·cid·i·ty [əˈsɪdətɪ] *also fig* acidità *f*

ac·id 'rain pioggia *f* acida

'ac·id test *fig* prova *f* della verità

ac·knowl·edge [ək'nɒlɪdʒ] v/t riconoscere; *by smile, nod* far capire di aver notato; *he ~d the applause with a smile* ha risposto all'applauso con un sorriso; ~ *(receipt of a) letter* accusare ricezione di una lettera

ac·knowl·edg(e)·ment [ək'nɒlɪdʒmənt] riconoscimento m; *(smile, nod)* cenno m; *(letter)* lettera f di accusata ricezione; *in ~ of thanking* come pegno di riconoscenza di; *~s (in book)* ringraziamenti mpl

ac·ne ['æknɪ] MED acne m

a·corn ['eɪkɔːn] BOT ghianda f

a·cous·tics [ə'kuːstɪks] acustica f

ac·quaint [ə'kweɪnt] v/t: *be ~ed with* fml conoscere

ac·quaint·ance [ə'kweɪntəns] *person* conoscenza f

ac·qui·esce [ækwɪ'es] v/i fml acconsentire

ac·qui·es·cence [ækwɪ'esns] fml consentimento m

ac·quire [ə'kwaɪə(r)] v/t acquisire

ac·qui·si·tion [ækwɪ'zɪʃn] acquisizione f

ac·quis·i·tive [ə'kwɪzətɪv] adj avido

ac·quit [ə'kwɪt] v/t LAW assolvere

ac·quit·tal [ə'kwɪtl] LAW assoluzione f

a·cre ['eɪkə(r)] acro m

a·cre·age ['eɪkrɪdʒ] estensione f in acri

ac·rid ['ækrɪd] adj *smell* acre

ac·ri·mo·ni·ous [ækrɪ'məʊnɪəs] adj aspro

ac·ro·bat ['ækrəbæt] acrobata m/f

ac·ro·bat·ic [ækrə'bætɪk] adj acrobatico

ac·ro·bat·ics [ækrə'bætɪks] npl acrobazie fpl

ac·ro·nym ['ækrənɪm] acronimo m

a·cross [ə'krɒs] **1** prep *on other side of* dall'altro lato di; *sail ~ the Atlantic* attraversare l'Atlantico in barca a vela; *walk ~ the street* attraversare la strada; *a bridge ~ the river* un ponte sul fiume; *~ Europe* all over in tutta Europa **2** adv *to other side* dall'altro lato; *10 m ~* largo 10 m; *they*

came to the river and swam ~ sono arrivati al fiume e l'hanno attraversato a nuoto

a·cryl·ic [ə'krɪlɪk] adj acrilico

act [ækt] **1** v/i agire; THEA recitare; *(pretend)* fare finta; *~ as* fare le funzioni di **2** n *(deed)* atto m; *of play* atto m; *in variety show* numero m; *(pretence)* finta f; *(law)* atto m; *~ of God* causa f di forza maggiore

act·ing ['æktɪŋ] **1** n recitazione f; *she went into ~* si è data alla recitazione **2** adj *(temporary)* facente funzione; *the ~ president* il facente funzione di presidente

ac·tion ['ækʃn] azione f; *out of ~ (not functioning)* fuori uso; *take ~* agire; *bring an ~ against* LAW fare causa a

ac·tion 're·play TV replay m inv

ac·tive ['æktɪv] adj attivo; GRAM attivo

ac·tiv·ist ['æktɪvɪst] POL attivista m/f

ac·tiv·i·ty [æk'tɪvətɪ] attività f

ac·tor ['æktə(r)] attore m

ac·tress ['æktrɪs] attrice f

ac·tu·al ['æktʃʊəl] adj reale; *cost* effettivo; *the ~ ceremony starts at 10* la cerimonia vera e propria comincia alle 10

ac·tu·al·ly ['æktʃʊəlɪ] adv *(in fact, to tell the truth)* in realtà; *expressing surprise* veramente; ~ *I do know him* stressing the converse a dire il vero, lo conosco

ac·u·punc·ture ['ækjʊpʌŋktʃə(r)] agopuntura f

a·cute [ə'kjuːt] adj *pain, sense* acuto; *shortage* estremo

a·cute·ly [ə'kjuːtlɪ] adv *(extremely)* estremamente

AD [eɪ'diː] abbr (= *anno domini*) d.C. (= dopo Cristo)

ad [æd] → *advertisement*

ad·a·mant ['ædəmənt] adj categorico

ad·a·mant·ly ['ædəməntlɪ] adv categoricamente

Ad·am's ap·ple [ædəmz'æpəl] pomo m di Adamo

a·dapt [ə'dæpt] **1** v/t adattare **2** v/i of

person adattarsi

a·dapt·a·bil·i·ty [ədæptə'bɪlətɪ] adattabilità *f*

a·dap·ta·ble [ə'dæptəbl] *adj* adattabile

a·dap·ta·tion [ædæp'teɪʃn] *of play etc* adattamento *m*

a·dapt·or [ə'dæptə(r)] *electrical* adattatore *m*

add [æd] **1** *v/t* aggiungere; MATH addizionare **2** *v/i of person* fare le somme

♦ **add on** *v/t* 15% *etc* aggiungere

♦ **add up 1** *v/t* sommare **2** *v/i fig* quadrare

ad·der ['ædə(r)] vipera *f* rossa

ad·dict ['ædɪkt] *to football, chess* maniaco *m*, -a *f*; **drug ~** tossicomane *m/f*, tossicodipendente *m/f*; **heroin ~** eroinomane *m/f*; **TV ~** teledipendente *m/f*

ad·dic·ted [ə'dɪktɪd] *adj* dipendente; **be ~ to** *drugs, alcohol* essere dedito a; *football, computer games etc* essere un maniaco di

ad·dic·tion [ə'dɪkʃn] *to drugs* dipendenza *f*, assuefazione *f*; *to TV, chocolate etc* dipendenza *f*

ad·dic·tive [ə'dɪktɪv] *adj*: **be ~ of** *drugs* provocare dipendenza o assuefazione; *of TV, chocolate etc* provocare dipendenza

ad·di·tion [ə'dɪʃn] MATH addizione *f*; *to list, company etc* aggiunta *f*; **in ~ to** in aggiunta a

ad·di·tion·al [ə'dɪʃnl] *adj* aggiuntivo

ad·di·tive ['ædɪtɪv] additivo *m*

add-on ['ædɒn] complemento *m*

ad·dress [ə'dres] **1** *n* indirizzo *m*; **form of ~** appellativo *m* **2** *v/t letter* indirizzare; *audience* tenere un discorso a; *person* rivolgersi a

ad'dress book indirizzario *m*

ad·dress·ee [ædre'siː] destinatario *m*, -a *f*

ad·ept [ə'dept] *adj* esperto; **be ~ at** essere esperto in

ad·e·quate ['ædɪkwət] *adj* adeguato

ad·e·quate·ly ['ædɪkwətlɪ] *adv* adeguatamente

ad·here [əd'hɪə(r)] *v/i* aderire

♦ **adhere to** *v/t surface* aderire a; *rules* attenersi a

ad·he·sive [əd'hiːsɪv] *n* adesivo *m*

ad·he·sive 'plas·ter cerotto *m*

ad·he·sive 'tape nastro *m* adesivo

ad·ja·cent [ə'dʒeɪsnt] *adj* adiacente

ad·jec·tive ['ædʒɪktɪv] aggettivo *m*

ad·join [ə'dʒɔɪn] *v/t* essere adiacente a

ad·join·ing [ə'dʒɔɪnɪŋ] *adj* adiacente

ad·journ [ə'dʒɜːn] *v/i* aggiornare

ad·journ·ment [ə'dʒɜːnmənt] aggiornamento *m*

ad·just [ə'dʒʌst] *v/t* regolare; **~ o.s. to** adattarsi a

ad·just·a·ble [ə'dʒʌstəbl] *adj* regolabile

ad·just·ment [ə'dʒʌstmənt] regolazione *f*; *psychological* adattamento *m*

ad lib [æd'lɪb] **1** *adj & adv* a braccio F **2** *v/i* (*pret & pp* **-bed**) improvvisare

ad·min·is·ter [əd'mɪnɪstə(r)] *v/t medicine* somministrare; *company* amministrare; *country* governare

ad·min·is·tra·tion [ədmɪnɪ'streɪʃn] amministrazione *f*; (*government*) governo *m*

ad·min·is·tra·tive [ədmɪnɪ'strətɪv] *adj* amministrativo

ad·min·is·tra·tor [əd'mɪnɪstreɪtə(r)] amministratore *m*, -trice *f*

ad·mi·ra·ble ['ædmərəbl] *adj* ammirevole

ad·mi·ra·bly ['ædmərəblɪ] *adv* ammirevolmente

ad·mi·ral ['ædmərəl] ammiraglio *m*

ad·mi·ra·tion [ædmə'reɪʃn] ammirazione *f*

ad·mire [əd'maɪə(r)] *v/t* ammirare

ad·mir·er [əd'maɪərə(r)] ammiratore *m*, -trice *f*

ad·mir·ing [əd'maɪərɪŋ] *adj* ammirativo

ad·mir·ing·ly [əd'maɪərɪŋlɪ] *adv* con ammirazione

ad·mis·si·ble [əd'mɪsəbl] *adj* ammissibile

ad·mis·sion [əd'mɪʃn] (*confession*) ammissione *f*; **~ free** entrata *f* libera

ad·mit [əd'mɪt] *v/t* (*pret & pp* **-ted**)

ammettere; *to a place* lasciare entrare; *to school, club etc* ammettere; *to hospital* ricoverare

ad·mit·tance [əd'mɪtəns]: *no* ~ vietato l'accesso

ad·mit·ted·ly [əd'mɪtedlɪ] *adv* effettivamente

ad·mon·ish [əd'mɒnɪʃ] *v/t fml* ammonire

a·do [ə'duː]: *without further* ~ senza ulteriori indugi

ad·o·les·cence [ædə'lesns] adolescenza *f*

ad·o·les·cent [ædə'lesnt] **1** *n* adolescente *m/f* **2** *adj* adolescenziale

a·dopt [ə'dɒpt] *v/t* adottare

a·dop·tion [ə'dɒpʃn] adozione *f*

adop·tive par·ents [ədɒptɪv 'peərənts] *npl* genitori *mpl* adottivi

a·dor·a·ble [ə'dɔːrəbl] *adj* adorabile

ad·o·ra·tion [ædə'reɪʃn] adorazione *f*

a·dore [ə'dɔː(r)] *v/t* adorare

a·dor·ing [ə'dɔːrɪŋ] *adj* in adorazione

ad·ren·al·in [ə'drenəlɪn] adrenalina *f*

a·drift [ə'drɪft] *adj* alla deriva; *fig* sbandato

ad·u·la·tion [ædjʊ'leɪʃn] adulazione *f*

ad·ult ['ædʌlt] **1** *n* adulto *m*, -a *f* **2** *adj* adulto

ad·ult ed·u·ca·tion corsi *mpl* per adulti

a·dul·ter·ous [ə'dʌltərəs] *adj* relationship extraconiugale

a·dul·ter·y [ə'dʌltərɪ] adulterio *m*

'adult film *euph* film *m inv* per adulti

ad·vance [əd'vɑːns] **1** *n* (*money*) anticipo *m*; *in science etc* progresso *m*; MIL avanzata *f*; *in* ~ in anticipo; *make* ~*s* (*progress*) fare progressi; *sexually* fare delle avances **2** *v/i* MIL avanzare; (*make progress*) fare progressi **3** *v/t theory* avanzare; *sum of money* anticipare; *human knowledge, a cause* fare progredire

ad·vance 'book·ing prenotazione *f*

ad·vanced [əd'vɑːnst] *adj country, level* avanzato; *learner* di livello avanzato

ad·vance 'no·tice preavviso *m*

ad·vance 'pay·ment pagamento *m* anticipato

ad·van·tage [əd'vɑːntɪdʒ] vantaggio *m*; *it's to your* ~ è a tuo vantaggio; *take* ~ *of opportunity* approfittare di

ad·van·ta·geous [ædvən'teɪdʒəs] *adj* vantaggioso

ad·vent ['ædvent] *fig* avvento *m*

'ad·vent cal·en·dar *calendario m dell'Avvento con finestrelle numerate che i bambini aprono giorno per giorno*

ad·ven·ture [əd'ventʃə(r)] avventura *f*

ad·ven·tur·ous [əd'ventʃərəs] *adj* avventuroso

ad·verb ['ædvɜːb] avverbio *m*

ad·ver·sa·ry ['ædvəsərɪ] avversario *m*, -a *f*

ad·verse ['ædvɜːs] *adj* avverso

ad·vert ['ædvɜːt] → *advertisement*

ad·ver·tise ['ædvətaɪz] **1** *v/t job* mettere un annuncio per; *product* reclamizzare **2** *v/i for job* mettere un annuncio; *for product* fare pubblicità

ad·ver·tise·ment [əd'vɜːtɪsmənt] annuncio *m*, inserzione *f*; *for product* pubblicità *f inv*

ad·ver·tis·er ['ædvətaɪzə(r)] acquirente *m/f* di uno spazio pubblicitario; *in magazine, newspaper* inserzionista *m/f*

ad·ver·tis·ing ['ædvətaɪzɪŋ] pubblicità *f inv*

'ad·ver·tis·ing a·gen·cy agenzia *f* pubblicitaria; **'ad·ver·tis·ing budg·et** budget *m inv* per la pubblicità; **'ad·ver·tis·ing cam·paign** campagna *f* pubblicitaria; **'ad·ver·tis·ing rev·e·nue** proventi *mpl* della pubblicità

ad·vice [əd'vaɪs] consigli *mpl*; *legal, financial* consulenza *f*; *a bit of* ~ un consiglio; *take s.o.'s* ~ seguire il consiglio di qu

ad·vis·a·ble [əd'vaɪzəbl] *adj* consigliabile

ad·vise [əd'vaɪz] *v/t person* consiglia-

re a; *caution etc* consigliare; **~ s.o.
to ...** consigliare a qu di ...

ad·vis·er [əd'vaɪzə(r)] consulente
m/f

ad·vo·cate ['ædvəkeɪt] *v/t* propugnare

aer·i·al ['eərɪəl] *n* antenna *f*

aer·i·al 'pho·to·graph fotografia *f*
aerea

aer·o·bics [eə'rəʊbɪks] *nsg* aerobica
f

aer·o·dy·nam·ic [eərəʊdaɪ'næmɪk]
adj aerodinamico

aer·o·nau·ti·cal [eərəʊ'nɔːtɪkl] *adj*
aeronautico

aer·o·plane ['eərəpleɪn] aeroplano
m

aer·o·sol ['eərəsɒl] spray *m inv*

aer·o·space in·dus·try ['eərəspeɪs
ɪndʌstrɪ] industria *f* aerospaziale

aes·thet·ic [iːs'θetɪk] *adj* estetico

af·fa·ble ['æfəbl] *adj* affabile

af·fair [ə'feə(r)] (*matter*) affare *m*;
(*event*) caso *m*; (*business*) affare *m*;
(*love*) relazione *f*; **foreign ~s** affari
mpl esteri; **have an ~ with** avere
una relazione con

affect [ə'fekt] *v/t* MED colpire; (*influence*) influire su; (*concern*) riguardare; (*cause feelings to*) colpire

af·fec·tion [ə'fekʃn] affetto *m*

af·fec·tion·ate [ə'fekʃnət] *adj* affettuoso

af·fec·tion·ate·ly [ə'fekʃnətlɪ] *adv*
affettuosamente

af·fin·i·ty [ə'fɪnətɪ] affinità *f inv*

af·fir·ma·tive [ə'fɜːmətɪv] *adj* affermativo; **answer in the ~** rispondere
affermativamente

af·flict [ə'flɪkt] *v/t* tormentare; **be
~ed with** soffrire di

af·flu·ence ['æfluəns] benessere *m*

af·flu·ent ['æfluənt] *adj* benestante;
~ society società *f inv* del benessere

af·ford [ə'fɔːd] *v/t*: **be able to ~ sth**
financially potersi permettere qc; **I
can't ~ the time** non ne ho il tempo; **it's a risk we can't ~ to take** è
un rischio che non possiamo permetterci di correre

af·ford·a·ble [ə'fɔːdəbl] *adj* abbordabile

af·front [ə'frʌnt] *n* affronto *m*

a·float [ə'fləʊt] *adj* boat a galla; **keep
the company ~** tenere a galla
l'azienda

a·fraid [ə'freɪd] *adj*: **be ~** avere paura; **be ~ of** avere paura di; **I'm ~**
expressing regret sono spiacente; **I'm
~ so** temo che sia così; **I'm ~ not**
purtroppo no

a·fresh [ə'freʃ] *adv* da capo

Af·ri·ca ['æfrɪkə] Africa *f*

Af·ri·can ['æfrɪkən] **1** *n* africano *m*,
-a f **2** *adj* africano

af·ter ['ɑːftə(r)] **1** *prep* dopo; **~ her/
me/you** dopo di lei/me/te; **~ all**
dopo tutto; **~ that** dopo ciò; **the day ~
tomorrow** dopodomani **2** *adv*
dopo; **the day ~** il giorno dopo

af·ter·math ['ɑːftəmɑːθ]: **the ~ of
war** il dopoguerra; **in the ~ of** nel
periodo immediatamente successivo a

afternoon [ɑːftə'nuːn] pomeriggio
m; **in the ~** nel pomeriggio; **this ~**
oggi pomeriggio; **good ~** buon giorno

'af·ter sales serv·ice servizio *m* dopovendita; **'af·ter·shave** dopobarba *m inv*; **'af·ter·taste** retrogusto
m

af·ter·wards ['ɑːftəwədz] *adv* dopo

a·gain [ə'geɪn] *adv* di nuovo; **I never
saw him ~** non l'ho mai più visto

a·gainst [ə'geɪnst] *prep* lean contro;
America ~ Brazil SP America contro Brasile; **I'm ~ the idea** sono contrario all'idea; **what do you have ~
her?** cos'hai contro di lei?; **~ the
law** contro la legge

age [eɪdʒ] **1** *n* (*also era*) età *f inv*; **at
the ~ of** all'età di; **under ~** minorenne; **she's five years of ~** ha cinque
anni; **I've been waiting for ~s** ho
aspettato un secolo F **2** *v/i* invecchiare

aged¹ [eɪdʒd] *adj*: **a boy ~ 16** un ragazzo di 16 anni; **he was ~ 16** aveva
16 anni

aged² ['eɪdʒɪd] **1** *adj*: **her ~ parents** i

suoi anziani genitori **2** *n*: **the ~** gli anziani

'**age group** fascia *f* d'età

'**age lim·it** limite *m* d'età

a·gen·cy ['eɪdʒənsɪ] agenzia *f*

a·gen·da [ə'dʒendə] ordine *m* del giorno; **on the ~** all'ordine del giorno

a·gent ['eɪdʒənt] agente *m/f*

ag·gra·vate ['ægrəveɪt] *v/t* aggravare; (*annoy*) seccare

ag·gre·gate ['ægrɪgət] *n* insieme *m*; **in (the) ~** nel complesso; **win on ~** SP vincere ai punti

ag·gres·sion [ə'greʃn] aggressione *f*

ag·gres·sive [ə'gresɪv] *adj* (*also dynamic*) aggressivo

ag·gres·sive·ly [ə'gresɪvlɪ] *adv* con aggressività

ag·gro ['ægrəʊ] ℙ grane *fpl*

a·ghast [ə'gɑːst] *adj* inorridito

ag·ile ['ædʒaɪl] *adj* agile

a·gil·i·ty [ə'dʒɪlətɪ] agilità *f*

ag·i·tate ['ædʒɪteɪt] *v/i*: ~ **for** / **against** mobilitarsi per / contro

ag·i·tat·ed ['ædʒɪteɪtɪd] *adj* agitato

ag·i·ta·tion [ædʒɪ'teɪʃn] agitazione *f*

ag·i·ta·tor [ædʒɪ'teɪtə(r)] agitatore *m*, -trice *f*

AGM [eɪdʒiː'em] *abbr* (= **annual general meeting**) assemblea *f* annuale

a·go [ə'gəʊ] *adv*: **2 days ~** due giorni fa; **long ~** molto tempo fa; **how long ~?** quanto tempo fa?

ag·o·nize ['ægənaɪz] *v/i* angosciarsi; ~ **over** angosciarsi per

ag·o·niz·ing ['ægənaɪzɪŋ] *adj* angosciante

ag·o·ny ['ægənɪ] agonia *f*; *mental* angoscia *f*

a·gree [ə'griː] **1** *v/i* essere d'accordo; *of figures, accounts* quadrare; (*reach agreement*) mettersi d'accordo; **I ~** sono d'accordo; **it doesn't ~ with me** *of food* mi fa male **2** *v/t price* concordare; ~ **that sth should be done** concordare che si dovrebbe fare qc

a·gree·a·ble [ə'griːəbl] *adj* (*pleasant*) piacevole; **be ~** (*in agreement*) essere d'accordo

a·gree·ment [ə'griːmənt] (*consent*, *contract*) accordo *m*; **reach ~ on** trovare un accordo su

ag·ri·cul·tur·al [ægrɪ'kʌltʃərəl] *adj* agricolo

ag·ri·cul·ture ['ægrɪkʌltʃə(r)] agricoltura *f*

a·head [ə'hed] *adv* davanti; (*in advance*) avanti; **200 m ~** 200 m più avanti; **be ~ of** essere davanti a; **plan** / **think ~** programmare per tempo; **arrive ~ of the others** arrivare prima degli altri

aid [eɪd] **1** *n* aiuto *m* **2** *v/t* aiutare

aide [eɪd] assistente *m/f*

Aids [eɪdz] Aids *m*

ail·ing ['eɪlɪŋ] *adj economy* malato

ail·ment ['eɪlmənt] disturbo *m*

aim [eɪm] **1** *n in shooting* mira *f*; (*objective*) obiettivo *m*; **take ~** prendere la mira; **2** *v/i in shooting* mirare; ~ **at doing sth,** ~ **to do sth** aspirare a fare qc **3** *v/t*: **be ~ed at** *of remark etc* essere rivolto a; *of guns* essere puntato contro

aim·less ['eɪmlɪs] *adj* senza obiettivi; *wandering* senza meta

air [eə(r)] **1** *n* aria *f*; **by ~** *travel* in aereo; *send mail* per via aerea; **in the open** all'aperto; **on the ~** RAD, TV in onda **2** *v/t room* arieggiare; *fig*: *views* rendere noto

'**air·bag** airbag *m inv*; '**air·base** base *f* aerea; '**air-con·di·tioned** *adj* con aria condizionata; '**air-con·di·tion·ing** aria condizionata; '**air·craft** aereo *m*; '**air·craft car·ri·er** portaerei *f inv*; '**air fare** tariffa *f* aerea; '**air·field** campo *m* d'aviazione; '**air force** aeronautica *f* militare; '**air host·ess** hostess *f inv*; '**air let·ter** aerogramma *m*; '**air·lift 1** *n* ponte *m* aereo **2** *v/t* trasportare per via aerea; '**air·line** compagnia *f* aerea; '**air·lin·er** aereo *m* di linea; '**air·mail**: **by ~** per via aerea; '**air·plane** aeroplano *m*; '**air·pock·et** vuoto *m* d'aria; '**air pol·lu·tion** inquinamento *m* atmosferico; '**air·port** aeroporto *m*; '**air·sick**: **get** ~ soffrire il mal d'aereo *o* l'aereo; '**air·space** spazio *m* aereo; '**air ter·mi·nal** terminale *m*; '**air·tight** *adj* container ermetico; '**air traf·fic** traffico *m* aereo; **air-traf·fic con·trol** controllo *m* del traffico aereo; **air-traf·fic con'trol·ler** controllore *m* di volo

air·y ['eərɪ] *adj* room arieggiato; *attitude* noncurante

aisle [aɪl] corridoio *m*; *in supermarket* corsia *f*; *in church* navata *f* laterale

'**aisle seat** posto *m* corridoio

a·jar [ə'dʒɑː(r)] *adj*: **be** ~ essere socchiuso

a·lac·ri·ty [ə'lækrɪtɪ] alacrità *f*

a·larm [ə'lɑːm] **1** *n* allarme *m*; **raise the** ~ dare l'allarme **2** *v/t* allarmare

a'larm clock sveglia *f*

a·larm·ing [ə'lɑːmɪŋ] *adj* allarmante

a·larm·ing·ly [ə'lɑːmɪŋlɪ] *adv* in modo allarmante

al·bum ['ælbəm] *for photographs*, *(record)* album *m* *inv*

al·co·hol ['ælkəhɒl] alcol *m*; **~-free** analcolico

al·co·hol·ic [ælkə'hɒlɪk] **1** *n* alcolizzato *m*, -a *f* **2** *adj* alcolico

a·lert [ə'lɜːt] **1** *n* (*signal*) allarme *m*; **be on the** ~ stare all'erta; *of troops*, *police* essere in stato di allerta **2** *v/t* mettere in guardia **3** *adj* all'erta *inv*

A-lev·el ['eɪlevl] diploma *f* di scuola media superiore in Gran Bretagna che permette di accedere all'università

al·ge·bra ['ældʒɪbrə] algebra *f*

al·i·bi ['ælɪbaɪ] alibi *m* *inv*

a·li·en ['eɪlɪən] **1** *n* (*foreigner*) straniero *m*, -a *f*; *from space* alieno *m*, -a *f* **2** *adj* estraneo; **be** ~ **to s.o.** essere estraneo a qu

a·li·en·ate ['eɪlɪəneɪt] *v/t* alienarsi

a·light [ə'laɪt] *adj*: **be** ~ essere in fiamme; **set sth** ~ dare fuoco a qc

a·lign [ə'laɪn] *v/t* allineare

a·like [ə'laɪk] **1** *adj* simile; **be** ~ assomigliarsi **2** *adv*: **it appeals to old and young** ~ attira vecchi e giovani allo stesso tempo

al·i·mo·ny ['ælɪmənɪ] alimenti *mpl*

a·live [ə'laɪv] *adj*: **be** ~ essere vivo; **~ and kicking** vivo e vegeto

all [ɔːl] **1** *adj* tutto; (*any whatever*) qualsiasi; ~ **day** / **month** tutto il giorno / mese; **beyond** ~ **doubt** al di là di qualsiasi dubbio **2** *pron* tutto; ~ **of us** / **them** tutti noi / loro; **he ate** ~ **of it** lo ha mangiato tutto; **that's** ~, **thanks** è tutto, grazie; **for** ~ **I care** per quello che me ne importa; **for** ~ **I know** per quel che ne so; **at once** tutto in una volta; (*suddenly*) tutt'a un tratto; ~ **but** (*nearly*) quasi; ~ **but John agreed** (*except*) erano tutti d'accordo tranne John; ~ **the better** molto meglio; ~ **the time** tutto il tempo; **they're not at** ~ **alike** non si assomigliano affatto; **not at** ~! niente affatto!; **two** ~ SP due pari; ~ **right** → **alright**

al·lay [ə'leɪ] *v/t* attenuare

al·le·ga·tion [ælɪ'geɪʃn] accusa *f*

al·lege [ə'ledʒ] *v/t* dichiarare

al·leged [ə'ledʒd] *adj* presunto

al·leg·ed·ly [ə'ledʒɪdlɪ] *adv* a quanto si suppone

al·le·giance [ə'liːdʒəns] fedeltà *f*

al·ler·gic [ə'lɜːdʒɪk] *adj* allergico; **be** ~ **to** essere allergico a

al·ler·gy ['ælədʒɪ] allergia *f*

al·le·vi·ate [ə'liːvɪeɪt] *v/t* alleviare

al·ley ['ælɪ] vicolo *m*

al·li·ance [ə'laɪəns] alleanza *f*

al·lied ['ælaɪd] MIL alleato

al·lo·cate ['æləkeɪt] *v/t* assegnare

al·lo·ca·tion [ælə'keɪʃn] assegnazione *f*; (*amount*) parte *f*

al·lot [ə'lɒt] *v/t* (*pret & pp* **-ted**) assegnare

al·lot·ment [ə'lɒtmənt] *Br* lotto *m* da coltivare

al·low [ə'laʊ] *v/t* (*permit*) permettere; (*calculate for*) calcolare; **be ~ed** essere autorizzato; **it's not ~ed** è vietato; **passengers are not ~ed to smoke** è vietato ai passeggeri fumare; **dogs not ~ed** vietato l'ingresso ai cani; ~ **s.o. to ...** permettere a qu di ...

♦ **allow for** *v/t* tenere conto di

al·low·ance [ə'lauəns] (*money*) sussidio *m*; (*pocket money*) paghetta *f*; **make ~s for sth** tenere conto di qc; **make ~s for s.o.** essere indulgente con qu

al·loy ['ælɔɪ] lega *m*

'all-pur·pose *adj* multiuso *inv*; **'all-round** *adj improvement* generale; *person* eclettico; **'all-time: be at an ~ low** *of inflation, unemployment* aver raggiunto il minimo storico

♦ **allude to** [ə'lu:d] *v/t* alludere a

al·lur·ing [ə'lu:rɪŋ] *adj* attraente

al·lu·sion [ə'lu:ʒn] allusione *f*

al·ly ['ælaɪ] *n* alleato *m*, -a *f*

Al·might·y [ɔ:l'maɪtɪ]: **the ~** l'Onnipotente

al·mond ['ɑ:mənd] mandorla *f*

al·most ['ɔ:lməʊst] *adv* quasi

a·lone [ə'ləʊn] *adj* solo

a·long [ə'lɒŋ] **1** *prep* lungo; **walk ~ the street** camminare lungo la strada **2** *adv*: **~ with** insieme con; **all ~** (*all the time*) per tutto il tempo; **we're going, would you like to come ~?** noi andiamo, vuoi venire con noi?

a·long·side [əlɒŋ'saɪd] *prep* di fianco a; *person* vicino a; **draw up ~** accostare; **draw up ~ s.o.** accostare vicino a qu; **~ him** al suo fianco

a·loof [ə'lu:f] *adj* in disparte

a·loud [ə'laʊd] *adv* ad alta voce; *laugh, call* forte

al·pha·bet ['ælfəbet] alfabeto *m*

al·pha·bet·i·cal [ælfə'betɪkl] *adj* alfabetico

al·pine ['ælpaɪn] *adj* alpino

Alps [ælps] *npl* Alpi *fpl*

al·read·y [ɔ:l'redɪ] *adv* già

al·right [ɔ:l'raɪt] *adj*: **it's ~** va bene; **are you ~?** (*not hurt*) stai bene?; **I'm ~** (*not hurt*) sto bene; (*have got enough*) va bene così; **is the monitor ~?** (*in working order*) funziona il monitor?; **is it ~ with you if I ...?** va bene se ...?; **~, you can have one!** va bene, puoi averne uno!; **~, I heard you!** sì, ti ho sentito!; **everything is ~ now between them** adesso va tutto bene tra di loro;

that's ~ (*don't mention it*) non c'è di che; (*I don't mind*) non fa niente; **~, that's enough!** basta così!

Al·sa·tian [æl'seɪʃn] *Br* pastore *m* tedesco

al·so ['ɔ:lsəʊ] *adv* anche

al·tar ['ɒltə(r)] REL altare *m*

al·ter ['ɒltə(r)] *v/t* modificare; *clothes* aggiustare

al·ter·a·tion [ɒltə'reɪʃn] modifica *f*

al·ter·nate ['ɒltəneɪt] **1** *v/i* alternare **2** *adj* ['ɒltənət] alternato; **on ~ days** a giorni alterni; **on ~ Mondays** un lunedì su due

al·ter·nat·ing 'cur·rent ['ɒltəneɪtɪŋ] corrente *f* alternata

al·ter·na·tive [ɒl'tɜ:nətɪv] **1** *n* alternativa *f* **2** *adj* alternativo

al·ter·na·tive·ly [ɒl'tɜ:nətɪvlɪ] *adv* alternativamente

al·though [ɔ:l'ðəʊ] *conj* benché, sebbene

al·ti·tude ['æltɪtju:d] altitudine *f*

al·to·geth·er [ɔ:ltə'geðə(r)] *adv* (*completely*) completamente; (*in all*) complessivamente

al·tru·ism ['æltru:ɪzm] altruismo *m*

al·tru·is·tic [æltru:'ɪstɪk] *adj* altruistico

a·lu·min·i·um [ælju'mɪniəm], *Am* **a·lu·mi·num** [ə'lu:mɪnəm] alluminio *m*

al·ways ['ɔ:lweɪz] *adv* sempre

a.m. [eɪ'em] *abbr* (= *ante meridiem*) di mattina

a·mal·gam·ate [ə'mælgəmeɪt] *v/i* di *companies* fondersi

a·mass [ə'mæs] *v/t* accumulare

am·a·teur ['æmətə(r)] *n* (*unskilled*) dilettante *m/f*; SP non professionista *m/f*

am·a·teur·ish ['æmətərɪʃ] *adj pej* dilettantesco

a·maze [ə'meɪz] *v/t* stupire

a·mazed [ə'meɪzd] *adj* stupito

a·maze·ment [ə'meɪzmənt] stupore *m*

a·maz·ing [ə'meɪzɪŋ] *adj* (*surprising*) sorprendente; F (*good*) incredibile

a·maz·ing·ly [ə'meɪzɪŋlɪ] *adv* incredibilmente

am·bas·sa·dor [æm'bæsədə(r)] ambasciatore *m*, -trice *f*

am·ber ['æmbə(r)] *n* ambra *f*; **at ~** giallo

am·bi·dex·trous [æmbɪ'dekstrəs] *adj* ambidestro

am·bi·ence ['æmbɪəns] atmosfera *f*

am·bi·gu·i·ty [æmbɪ'gjuːətɪ] ambiguità *f*

am·big·u·ous [æm'bɪgjʊəs] *adj* ambiguo

am·bi·tion [æm'bɪʃn] ambizione *f*

am·bi·tious [æm'bɪʃəs] *adj* ambizioso

am·biv·a·lent [æm'bɪvələnt] *adj* ambiguo

am·ble ['æmbl] *v/i* camminare con calma; **we were ambling along the riverbank** stavamo passeggiando lungo il fiume

am·bu·lance ['æmbjʊləns] ambulanza *f*

am·bush ['æmbʊʃ] **1** *n* agguato *m* **2** *v/t* tendere un agguato a; **be ~ed by** subire un agguato da parte di

a·mend [ə'mend] *v/t* emendare

a·mend·ment [ə'mendmənt] emendamento *m*

a·mends [ə'mendz]: **make ~** fare ammenda

a·men·i·ties [ə'miːnətɪz] *npl* comodità *fpl*

A·mer·i·ca [ə'merɪkə] America *f*

A·mer·i·can [ə'merɪkən] **1** *n* americano *m*, -a *f* **2** *adj* americano

a·mi·a·ble ['eɪmɪəbl] *adj* amichevole

a·mi·ca·ble ['æmɪkəbl] *adj* amichevole

a·mi·ca·bly ['æmɪkəblɪ] *adv* amichevolmente

am·mu·ni·tion [æmjʊ'nɪʃn] munizioni *fpl*; *fig* arma *f*

am·ne·sia [æm'niːzɪə] amnesia *f*

am·nes·ty ['æmnəstɪ] amnistia *f*

a·mong(st) [ə'mʌŋ(st)] *prep* tra

a·mor·al [eɪ'mɒrəl] *adj* amorale

a·mount [ə'maʊnt] quantità *f inv*; (*sum of money*) importo *m*

♦ **amount to** *v/t* of income, sum ammontare a; (*be equal to*) equivalere a

am·phib·i·an [æm'fɪbɪən] anfibio *m*

am·phib·i·ous [æm'fɪbɪəs] *adj animal* anfibio; *vehicle* anfibio

am·phi·the·a·ter *Am*, **am·phi·the·a·tre** ['æmfɪθɪətə(r)] anfiteatro *m*

am·ple ['æmpl] *adj* abbondante; (*more than enough*) in abbondanza

am·pli·fi·er ['æmplɪfaɪə(r)] amplificatore *m*

am·pli·fy ['æmplɪfaɪ] *v/t* (*pret & pp -ied*) *sound* amplificare

am·pu·tate ['æmpjuːteɪt] *v/t* amputare

am·pu·ta·tion [æmpjʊ'teɪʃn] amputazione *f*

a·muse [ə'mjuːz] *v/t* (*make laugh etc*) divertire; (*entertain*) intrattenere

a·muse·ment [ə'mjuːzmənt] (*merriment*) divertimento *m*; (*entertainment*) intrattenimento *m*; **~s** (*games*) divertimenti *mpl*; **to our great ~** con nostro grande divertimento

a·muse·ment ar·cade sala *f* giochi

a·muse·ment park parco *m* giochi

a·mus·ing [ə'mjuːzɪŋ] *adj* divertente

an [æn] → **a**

an·a·bol·ic 'ste·roid [ænə'bɒlɪk] anabolizzante *m*

an·ae·mi·a [ə'niːmɪə] anemia *f*

an·aem·ic [ə'niːmɪk] *adj* anemico

an·aes·thet·ic [ænəs'θetɪk] *n* anestetico *m*

an·aes·the·tist [ə'niːsθətɪst] anestesista *m/f*

an·a·log ['ænəlɒg] *adj* COMPUT analogico

a·nal·o·gy [ə'nælədʒɪ] analogia *f*

an·a·lyse ['ænəlaɪz] *v/t* analizzare; (*psychoanalyse*) psicanalizzare

a·nal·y·sis [ə'næləsɪs] (*pl* **analyses** [ə'næləsiːz]) analisi *f inv*

an·a·lyst ['ænəlɪst] *also* PSYCH analista *m/f*

an·a·lyt·i·cal [ænə'lɪtɪkl] *adj* analitico

an·a·lyze *Am* → **analyse**

an·arch·y ['ænəkɪ] anarchia *f*

a·nat·o·my [ə'nætəmɪ] anatomia *f*

an·ces·tor ['ænsestə(r)] antenato *m*, -a *f*

an·chor ['æŋkə(r)] **1** n NAUT ancora f **2** v/i NAUT gettare l'ancora

'an·chor·man TV presentatore m, anchorman m inv

an·cient ['eɪnʃənt] adj antico

an·cil·lar·y [æn'sɪləri] adj staff ausiliario

and [ənd] stressed [ænd] conj e; **5 ~ 5 makes 10** 5 più 5 fa 10; **three hundred ~ sixty** trecentosessanta; **worse ~ worse** sempre peggio; **I'll come ~ pick you up** vengo a prenderti

an·ec·dote ['ænɪkdəʊt] aneddoto m

a·ne·mi·a etc Am → anaemia etc

an·es·thet·ic etc Am → anaesthetic etc

an·gel ['eɪndʒl] REL, fig angelo m

an·ger ['æŋgə(r)] **1** n rabbia f **2** v/t fare arrabbiare

an·gi·na [æn'dʒaɪnə] angina f (pectoris)

an·gle ['æŋgl] n angolo m; (position, fig) angolazione f

an·gler ['æŋglə(r)] pescatore m, -trice f (con amo e lenza)

An·gli·can ['æŋglɪkən] REL **1** adj anglicano **2** n anglicano m, -a f

An·glo-Sax·on [æŋgləʊ'sæksn] **1** adj anglosassone **2** n person anglosassone m/f

an·gry ['æŋgrɪ] adj arrabbiato; **be ~ with s.o.** essere arrabbiato con qu

an·guish ['æŋgwɪʃ] angoscia f

an·gu·lar ['æŋgjʊlə(r)] adj face, shape spigoloso

an·i·mal ['ænɪml] animale m

an·i·mat·ed ['ænɪmeɪtɪd] adj animato

an·i·mat·ed car'toon cartone m animato

an·i·ma·tion [ænɪ'meɪʃn] animazione f

an·i·mos·i·ty [ænɪ'mɒsətɪ] animosità f

an·kle ['æŋkl] caviglia f

an·nex [ə'neks] v/t state annettere

an·nexe ['æneks] n (building) edificio m annesso; to document annesso m

an·ni·hi·late [ə'naɪəleɪt] v/t annientare

an·ni·hi·la·tion [ənaɪə'leɪʃn] annientamento m

an·ni·ver·sa·ry [ænɪ'vɜːsərɪ] (wedding ~) anniversario m

an·no·tate ['ænəteɪt] v/t report annotare

an·nounce [ə'naʊns] v/t annunciare

an·nounce·ment [ə'naʊnsmənt] annuncio m

an·nounc·er [ə'naʊnsə(r)] TV, Radio annunciatore m, -trice f

an·noy [ə'nɔɪ] v/t infastidire; **be ~ed** essere infastidito

an·noy·ance [ə'nɔɪəns] (anger) irritazione f; (nuisance) fastidio m

an·noy·ing [ə'nɔɪɪŋ] adj irritante

an·nu·al ['ænjʊəl] adj annuale

an·nu·al gen·er·al 'meet·ing assemblea f annuale

an·nu·i·ty [ə'njuːətɪ] rendita f annuale

an·nul [ə'nʌl] v/t (pret & pp **-led**) marriage annullare

an·nul·ment [ə'nʌlmənt] annullamento m

a·non·y·mous [ə'nɒnɪməs] adj anonimo

an·o·rak ['ænəræk] Br giacca f a vento

an·o·rex·i·a [ænə'reksɪə] anoressia f

an·o·rex·ic [ænə'reksɪk] adj anoressico

an·oth·er [ə'nʌðə(r)] **1** adj un altro m, un'altra f **2** pron un altro m, un'altra f; **one ~** l'un l'altro; **do they know one ~?** si conoscono?

ans·wer ['ɑːnsə(r)] **1** n to letter, person, problem risposta f **2** v/t letter, person rispondere a; **~ the door** aprire la porta; **~ the telephone** rispondere al telefono

♦ **answer back 1** v/t person ribattere a **2** v/i ribattere

♦ **answer for** v/t rispondere di

an·swer·ing ma·chine ['ɑːnsərɪŋ] TELEC segreteria f telefonica

ans·wer·phone ['ɑːnsəfəʊn] segreteria f telefonica

ant [ænt] formica f

an·tag·o·nis·m [æn'tægənɪzm] antagonismo m

an·tag·o·nis·tic [æntægə'nɪstɪk] *adj* ostile

an·tag·o·nize [æn'tægənaɪz] *v/t* contrariare

Ant·arc·tic [ænt'ɑ:ktɪk] *n* Antartico *m*

an·te·lope ['æntɪləʊp] antilope *f*

an·te·na·tal [æntɪ'neɪtl] *adj* durante la gravidanza; **~ classes** corso *m* di preparazione al parto; **~ clinic** clinica *f* per gestanti

an·ten·na [æn'tenə] antenna *f*

an·thol·o·gy [æn'θɒlədʒɪ] antologia *f*

an·thro·pol·o·gy [ænθrə'pɒlədʒɪ] antropologia *f*

an·ti·bi·ot·ic [æntɪbaɪ'ɒtɪk] *n* antibiotico *m*

an·ti·bod·y ['æntɪbɒdɪ] anticorpo *m*

an·tic·i·pate [æn'tɪsɪpeɪt] *v/t* prevedere

an·tic·i·pa·tion [æntɪsɪ'peɪʃn] previsione *f*

an·ti·clock·wise ['æntɪklɒkwaɪz] *Br* **1** *adj* antiorario **2** *adv* in senso antiorario

an·tics ['æntɪks] *npl* buffonate *fpl*

an·ti·dote ['æntɪdəʊt] antidoto *m*

an·ti·freeze ['æntɪfri:z] antigelo *m inv*

an·tip·a·thy [æn'tɪpəθɪ] antipatia *f*

an·ti·quat·ed ['æntɪkweɪtɪd] *adj* antiquato

an·tique [æn'ti:k] *n* pezzo *m* d'antiquariato

an·tique dealer antiquario *m*, -a *f*

an·tiq·ui·ty [æn'tɪkwɪtɪ] antichità *f inv*

an·ti·sep·tic [æntɪ'septɪk] **1** *adj* antisettico **2** *n* antisettico *m*

an·ti·so·cial [æntɪ'səʊʃl] *adj* asociale

an·ti·vi·rus pro·gram [æntɪ'vaɪrəs] COMPUT programma *m* antivirus

anx·i·e·ty [æn'zaɪətɪ] ansia *f*

anx·ious ['æŋkʃəs] *adj* ansioso; **be ~ for ...** *for news etc* essere ansioso di avere ...

an·y ['enɪ] **1** *adj* qualche; **are there ~ diskettes/glasses?** ci sono dei diskettes/bicchieri?; **is there ~ bread?** c'è del pane?; **is there ~**

improvement? c'è qualche miglioramento?; **there aren't ~ diskettes/glasses** non ci sono diskettes/bicchieri; **there isn't ~ bread** non c'è pane; **there isn't ~ improvement** non c'è nessun miglioramento; **have you ~ idea at all?** hai qualche idea?; **take ~ one you like** prendi quello che vuoi **2** *pron*: **do you have ~?** ne hai?; **there aren't ~ left** non ce ne sono più; **there isn't ~ left** non ce n'è più; **~ of them could be guilty** chiunque di loro potrebbe essere colpevole **3** *adv* un po'; **is that ~ better/easier?** è un po' meglio/più facile?; **I don't like it ~ more** non mi piace più

an·y·bod·y ['enɪbɒdɪ] *pron* qualcuno; *with negative* nessuno; *(whoever)* chiunque; **is there ~ there?** c'è qualcuno?; **there wasn't ~ there** non c'era nessuno; **~ could do it** lo potrebbe fare chiunque

an·y·how ['enɪhaʊ] comunque; **if I can help you ~, let me know** se ti posso aiutare in qualsiasi modo, fammi sapere

an·y·one ['enɪwʌn] → **anybody**

an·y·thing ['enɪθɪŋ] *pron* qualcosa; *with negatives* niente, nulla; **I didn't hear ~** non ho sentito niente *o* nulla; **~ but** per niente; **she was ~ but helpful** non è stata per niente d'aiuto; **~ else?** qualcos'altro?

an·y·way ['enɪweɪ] → **anyhow**

an·y·where ['enɪweə(r)] *adv* da qualche parte; *with negative* da nessuna parte; *(wherever)* dovunque; **I can't find it ~** non riesco a trovarlo da nessuna parte

a·part [ə'pɑ:t] *adv in distance* distante; **the two cities are 250 miles ~** le due città distano 250 miglia l'una dall'altra; **live ~** *of people* vivere separati; **~ from** *(excepting)* a parte, tranne; *(in addition to)* oltre a

a·part·ment [ə'pɑ:tmənt] appartamento *m*

a·part·ment block *Am* palazzo *m* (d'appartamenti)

ap·a·thet·ic [æpə'θetɪk] *adj* apatico

ap·a·thy ['æpəθɪ] apatia *f*

ape [eɪp] scimmia *f*

a·pe·ri·tif [ə'perɪtiːf] aperitivo *m*

ap·er·ture ['æpətʃə(r)] PHOT apertura *f*

a·piece [ə'piːs] *adv* l'uno *m*, l'una *f*; **you can have one ~** potete averne uno a testa

a·pol·o·get·ic [əpɒlə'dʒetɪk] *adj letter, smile* di scuse; **he was very ~ for being late** si è scusato molto di essere in ritardo

a·pol·o·gize [ə'pɒlədʒaɪz] *v/i* scusarsi; **~ to s.o.** scusarsi con qu

a·pol·o·gy [ə'pɒlədʒɪ] scusa *f*; **make an ~ to s.o.** fare le proprie scuse a qu

a·pos·tle [ə'pɒsl] REL apostolo *m*

a·pos·tro·phe [ə'pɒstrəfɪ] GRAM apostrofo *m*

ap·pal [ə'pɔːl] *v/t* sconvolgere

ap·pal·ling [ə'pɔːlɪŋ] *adj* sconvolgente; *language* scioccante

ap·pa·ra·tus [æpə'reɪtəs] apparecchio *m*

ap·par·ent [ə'pærənt] *adj* evidente; (*seeming real*) apparente; **become ~ that …** diventare evidente che …

ap·par·ent·ly [ə'pærəntlɪ] *adv* apparentemente

ap·pa·ri·tion [æpə'rɪʃn] (*ghost*) apparizione *f*

ap·peal [ə'piːl] **1** *n* (*charm*) attrattiva *f*; *for funds etc*, LAW appello *m* **2** *v/i* LAW fare appello

♦ **appeal to** (*be attractive to*) attirare

♦ **appeal for** *v/t blood, help* fare un appello per ottenere; **the President appealed for calm** il Presidente ha fatto appello alla calma

ap·peal·ing [ə'piːlɪŋ] *adj idea, offer* allettante; *glance* supplichevole

ap·pear [ə'pɪə(r)] *v/i* apparire, comparire; *in film etc* apparire; *of new product* comparire; *in court* comparire; (*look, seem*) apparire; **it ~s that …** sembra che …

ap·pear·ance [ə'pɪərəns)] (*arrival*) apparizione *f*, comparsa *f*; *in film etc* apparizione *f*; *in court* comparizione *f*; (*look*) aspetto *m*; **put in an ~** fare un salto; **judge by ~s** giudicare dalle apparenze

ap·pease [ə'piːz] *v/t gods, anger* placare; *tyrant* compiacere

ap·pen·di·ci·tis [əpendɪ'saɪtɪs] appendicite *f*

ap·pen·dix [ə'pendɪks] MED, *of book etc* appendice *f*

ap·pe·tite ['æpɪtaɪt] appetito *m*; **~ for sth** *fig* sete *f* di qc

ap·pe·tiz·er ['æpɪtaɪzə(r)] *food* stuzzichino *m*; *drink* aperitivo *m*

ap·pe·tiz·ing ['æpɪtaɪzɪŋ] *adj* appetitoso

ap·plaud [ə'plɔːd] **1** *v/i* applaudire **2** *v/t also fig* applaudire

ap·plause [ə'plɔːz] applauso *m*; (*praise*) approvazione *f*

ap·ple ['æpl] mela *f*

ap·ple 'pie torta *f* di mele

ap·ple 'sauce composta *f* di mele

ap·pli·ance [ə'plaɪəns] apparecchio *m*; *household* elettrodomestico *m*

ap·plic·a·ble [ə'plɪkəbl] *adj* applicabile

ap·pli·cant ['æplɪkənt] candidato *m*, -a *f*

ap·pli·ca·tion [æplɪ'keɪʃn] *for job etc* candidatura *f*; *for passport, visa* domanda *f*, richiesta *f*; *for university* domanda *f* di iscrizione

ap·pli'ca·tion form modulo *m* di richiesta; *for passport, visa* modulo *m* di richiesta; *for university* modulo *f* di richiesta di iscrizione

ap·ply [ə'plaɪ] (*pret & pp -ied*) **1** *v/t* applicare **2** *v/i of rule, law* applicarsi

♦ **apply for** *v/t job, passport* fare domanda per; *university* fare domanda di iscrizione a

♦ **apply to** *v/t* (*contact*) rivolgersi a; (*affect*) applicarsi a

ap·point [ə'pɔɪnt] *v/t to position* nominare

ap·point·ment [ə'pɔɪntmənt] *to position* nomina *f*; (*meeting*) appuntamento *m*

ap'point·ments di·a·ry agenda *f* degli appuntamenti

ap·prais·al [ə'preɪz(ə)l] valutazione f

ap·pre·cia·ble [ə'priːʃəbl] adj notevole

ap·pre·ci·ate [ə'priːʃɪeɪt] 1 v/t apprezzare; (acknowledge) rendersi conto di; *thanks, I ~ it* grazie, te ne sono grato; *I ~ that ...* mi rendo conto che ... 2 v/i FIN rivalutarsi

ap·pre·ci·a·tion [əpriːʃɪ'eɪʃn] of kindness etc riconoscenza f; of music etc apprezzamento m

ap·pre·ci·a·tive [ə'priːʃətɪv] adj (showing gratitude) riconoscente; (showing pleasure) soddisfatto

ap·pre·hen·sion [æprɪ'henʃn] apprensione f

ap·pre·hen·sive [æprɪ'hensɪv] adj apprensivo

ap·pren·tice [ə'prentɪs] apprendista m/f

ap·pren·tice·ship [ə'prentɪsʃɪp] apprendistato m

ap·proach [ə'prəʊtʃ] 1 n avvicinamento m; (proposal) contatto m; *to problem* approccio m 2 v/t (get near to) avvicinarsi a; (contact) contattare; *problem* abbordare

ap·proach·a·ble [ə'prəʊtʃəbl] adj person abbordabile

ap·pro·pri·ate¹ [ə'prəʊprɪət] adj appropriato

ap·pro·pri·ate² [ə'prəʊprɪeɪt] v/t also euph appropriarsi di

ap·prov·al [ə'pruːvl] approvazione f

ap·prove [ə'pruːv] v/t & v/i approvare

♦ **approve of** v/t approvare

ap·prox·i·mate [ə'prɒksɪmət] adj approssimativo

ap·prox·i·mate·ly [ə'prɒksɪmətlɪ] adv approssimativamente

ap·prox·i·ma·tion [əprɒksɪ'meɪʃn] approssimazione f

APR [eɪpiː'ɑː] abbr (= **annual percentage rate**) tasso m di interesse annuale

a·pri·cot ['eɪprɪkɒt] albicocca f

A·pril ['eɪprəl] aprile m

a·pron ['eɪprən] grembiule m

apt [æpt] adj pupil portato; remark

appropriato; *be ~ to ...* avere tendenza a ...

ap·ti·tude ['æptɪtjuːd] attitudine f

'ap·ti·tude test test m inv attitudinale

aq·ua·lung ['ækwəlʌŋ] autorespiratore m

a·quar·i·um [ə'kweərɪəm] acquario m

A·quar·i·us [ə'kweərɪəs] ASTR Acquario m

a·quat·ic [ə'kwætɪk] adj acquatico

Ar·ab ['ærəb] 1 n arabo m, -a f 2 adj arabo

Ar·a·bic ['ærəbɪk] 1 n arabo m 2 adj arabo

ar·a·ble ['ærəbl] adj coltivabile

ar·bi·tra·ry ['ɑːbɪtrərɪ] adj arbitrario

ar·bi·trate ['ɑːbɪtreɪt] v/i arbitrare

ar·bi·tra·tion [ɑːbɪ'treɪʃn] arbitrato m

ar·bi·tra·tor ['ɑːbɪtreɪtə(r)] arbitro m

ar·cade [ɑː'keɪd] (games ~) sala f giochi

arch [ɑːtʃ] n arco m

ar·chae·o·log·i·cal [ɑːkɪə'lɒdʒɪkl] adj archeologico

ar·chae·ol·o·gist [ɑːkɪ'ɒlədʒɪst] archeologo m, -a f

ar·chae·ol·o·gy [ɑːkɪ'ɒlədʒɪ] archeologia f

ar·cha·ic [ɑː'keɪɪk] adj arcaico

arch·bish·op [ɑːtʃ'bɪʃəp] arcivescovo m

ar·che·ol·o·gy etc Am → **archaeology** etc

arch·er ['ɑːtʃə(r)] arciere m, -a f

ar·chi·tect ['ɑːkɪtekt] architetto m

ar·chi·tec·tur·al [ɑːkɪ'tektʃərəl] adj architettonico

ar·chi·tec·ture [ɑːkɪtektʃə(r)] architettura f

ar·chives ['ɑːkaɪvz] npl archivi mpl

arch·way ['ɑːtʃweɪ] arco m

Arc·tic ['ɑːktɪk] n Artico m

ar·dent ['ɑːdənt] adj ardente

ar·du·ous [ɑː'djuːəs] adj arduo

ar·e·a ['eərɪə] area f; (region) zona f

'ar·e·a code Am TELEC prefisso m

telefonico; *official name* indicativo *m* distrettuale

Ar·gen·ti·na [ɑːdʒən'tiːnə] Argentina *f*

Ar·gen·tin·i·an [ɑːdʒən'tɪnɪən] **1** *adj* argentino **2** *n* argentino *m*, -a *f*

ar·gu·a·bly ['ɑːɡjuəblɪ] *adv* probabilmente; **he's ~ the best** si può dire che è il migliore

ar·gue ['ɑːɡjuː] **1** *v/i* (*quarrel*) litigare; (*reason*) sostenere **2** *v/t*: **~ that ...** sostenere che ...

ar·gu·ment ['ɑːɡjʊmənt] (*quarrel*) litigio *m*; (*reasoning*) argomento *m*

ar·gu·ment·a·tive [ɑːɡjʊ'mentətɪv] *adj* polemico

a·ri·a ['ɑːrɪə] MUS aria *f*

ar·id ['ærɪd] *adj land* arido

Ar·i·es ['eərɪːz] ASTR Ariete *m*

a·rise [ə'raɪz] *v/i* (*pret* **arose**, *pp* **arisen**) *of situation, problem* emergere

a·ris·en [ə'rɪzn] *pp* → **arise**

ar·is·toc·ra·cy [ærɪ'stɒkrəsɪ] aristocrazia *f*

ar·is·to·crat ['ærɪstəkræt] aristocratico *m*, -a *f*

ar·is·to·crat·ic [ærɪstə'krætɪk] *adj* aristocratico

a·rith·me·tic [ə'rɪθmətɪk] aritmetica *f*

arm[1] [ɑːm] *n of person* braccio *m*; *of chair* bracciolo *m*

arm[2] [ɑːm] *v/t* armare; **~ s.o. / sth with sth** armare qu / qc di qc

ar·ma·ments ['ɑːməmənts] *npl* armamenti *mpl*

arm·chair ['ɑːmtʃeə(r)] poltrona *f*

armed [ɑːmd] *adj* armato

armed 'forc·es *npl* forze *fpl* armate

armed 'rob·ber·y rapina *f* a mano armata

ar·mor *Am*, **ar·mour** ['ɑːmə(r)] armatura *f*; (*metal plates*) blindatura *f*

ar·mored ve·hi·cle *Am*, **ar·moured ve·hi·cle** [ɑːməd'viːɪkl] veicolo *m* blindato

arm·pit ['ɑːmpɪt] ascella *f*

arms [ɑːmz] *npl* (*weapons*) armi *fpl*

ar·my ['ɑːmɪ] esercito *m*

a·ro·ma [ə'rəumə] aroma *m*

a·rose [ə'rəuz] *pret* → **arise**

a·round [ə'raund] **1** *prep* (*in circle, roughly*) intorno a; *room, world* attraverso; **it's ~ the corner** è dietro l'angolo **2** *adv* (*in the area*) qui intorno; (*encircling*) intorno; **he lives ~ here** abita da queste parti; **walk ~** andare in giro; **she has been ~** (*has travelled, is experienced*) ha girato; **he's still ~** F (*alive*) è ancora in circolazione

a·rouse [ə'rauz] *v/t* suscitare; (*sexually*) eccitare

ar·range [ə'reɪndʒ] *v/t* (*put in order*) sistemare; *music* arrangiare; *meeting, party etc* organizzare; *time and place* combinare; **I've ~d to meet her** ho combinato di incontrarla

♦ **arrange for** *v/t* provvedere a; **I've arranged for him to meet us** ho provveduto affinché ci incontrasse

ar·range·ment [ə'reɪndʒmənt] (*agreement*) accordo *m*; *of party, meeting* organizzazione *f*; (*layout: of furniture etc*) disposizione *f*; *of music* arrangiamento *m*; **~s for party, meeting** preparativi *mpl*; **make ~s** prendere disposizioni

ar·rears [ə'rɪəz] *npl* arretrati *mpl*; **be in ~** *of person* essere in arretrato; **be paid in ~** *for job* essere pagato a lavoro effettuato

ar·rest [ə'rest] **1** *n* arresto *m*; **be under ~** essere in arresto **2** *v/t* arrestare

ar·riv·al [ə'raɪvl] arrivo *m*; **~s** *at airport* arrivi *mpl*

ar·rive [ə'raɪv] *v/i* arrivare

♦ **arrive at** *v/t place, decision* arrivare a

ar·ro·gance ['ærəɡəns] arroganza *f*

ar·ro·gant ['ærəɡənt] *adj* arrogante

ar·ro·gant·ly ['ærəɡəntlɪ] *adv* con arroganza

ar·row ['ærəu] freccia *f*

arse [ɑːs] V culo *m* V

ar·se·nic ['ɑːsənɪk] arsenico *m*

ar·son ['ɑːsn] incendio *m* doloso

ar·son·ist ['ɑːsənɪst] piromane *m/f*

art [ɑːt] arte f; **the ~s** l'arte

ar·te·ry ['ɑːtəri] MED arteria f

'art gal·ler·y galleria f d'arte

ar·thri·tis [ɑː'θraɪtɪs] artrite f

ar·ti·choke ['ɑːtɪtʃəʊk] carciofo m

ar·ti·cle ['ɑːtɪkl] articolo m

ar·tic·u·late [ɑː'tɪkjʊlət] adj speech chiaro; **be ~ of** person esprimersi bene

ar·tic·u·lat·ed 'lor·ry [ɑːtɪkjʊleɪtɪd] Br autoarticolato m

ar·ti·fi·cial [ɑːtɪ'fɪʃl] adj artificiale; (not sincere) finto

ar·ti·fi·cial in·tel·li·gence intelligenza f artificiale

ar·til·le·ry [ɑː'tɪləri] artiglieria f

ar·ti·san ['ɑːtɪzæn] artigiano m, -a f

ar·tist ['ɑːtɪst] artista m/f

ar·tis·tic [ɑː'tɪstɪk] adj artistico

'arts de·gree laurea f in discipline umanistiche

as [æz] **1** conj (while, when) mentre; (because) dato che; (like) come; **~ he grew older, ...** diventando più vecchio, ...; **~ if** come se; **~ usual** come al solito; **~ necessary** in base alla necessità; **2** adv: **~ high / pretty ~ ...** alto / carino come ...; **~ much ~ that?** così tanto?; **run ~ fast ~ you can** corri più veloce che puoi **3** prep come; **~ a child** da bambino; **~ a schoolgirl** quando andava a scuola; **I'm talking to you ~ a friend** ti parlo come amico; **dressed ~ a policeman** vestito da poliziotto; **work ~ a teacher / translator** essere insegnante / traduttore; **~ for** quanto a; **~ Hamlet** nel ruolo di Amleto

asap ['eɪzæp] abbr (= **as soon as possible**) quanto prima

as·bes·tos [æz'bestɒs] amianto m

As·cen·sion [ə'senʃn] REL Ascensione f

as·cent [ə'sent] path salita f; of mountain ascensione f; fig ascesa f

ash [æʃ] cenere f; **-es** ceneri fpl

a·shamed [ə'ʃeɪmd] adj: **be ~ of** vergognarsi di; **you should be ~ of yourself** dovresti vergognarti

a·shore [ə'ʃɔː(r)] adv a terra; **go ~** sbarcare

ash·tray ['æʃtreɪ] posacenere m, portacenere m

Ash 'Wednes·day mercoledì m inv delle Ceneri

A·sia ['eɪʃə] Asia f

A·sian ['eɪʃn] **1** n asiatico m, -a f; (Indian, Pakistani) indiano m, -a f **2** adj asiatico; (Indian, Pakistani) indiano

a·side [ə'saɪd] adv da parte; **take s.o. ~** prendere a parte qu; **joking ~** scherzi a parte; **~ from** a parte

ask [ɑːsk] **1** v/t person chiedere a; (invite) invitare; question fare; favour chiedere; **can I ~ you something?** posso chiederti una cosa?; **~ s.o. about sth** chiedere a qu di qc; **~ s.o. for ...** chiedere a qu ...; **~ s.o. to ...** chiedere a qu di ... **2** v/i chiedere

♦ **ask after** v/t person chiedere di

♦ **ask for** v/t chiedere; person chiedere di

♦ **ask out** v/t for a drink, night out chiedere di uscire a

ask·ing price ['ɑːskɪnpraɪs] prezzo m di domanda

a·sleep [ə'sliːp] adj: **he's (fast) ~** sta dormendo (profondamente); **fall ~** addormentarsi

as·par·a·gus [ə'spærəgəs] asparagi mpl

as·pect ['æspekt] aspetto m

as·phalt ['æsfælt] n asfalto m

as·phyx·i·ate [æ'sfɪksɪeɪt] v/t asfissiare

as·phyx·i·a·tion [əsfɪksɪ'eɪʃn] asfissia f

as·pi·ra·tion [æspə'reɪʃn] aspirazione f

as·pi·rin ['æsprɪn] aspirina f

ass [æs] F (idiot) cretino m, -a; Am P (backside) culo m P

as·sai·lant [ə'seɪlənt] assalitore m, -trice f

as·sas·sin [ə'sæsɪn] assassino m, -a f

as·sas·si·nate [ə'sæsɪneɪt] v/t assassinare

as·sas·si·na·tion [əsæsɪ'neɪʃn] assassinio m

as·sault [ə'sɒlt] **1** n assalto m; LAW aggressione f **2** v/t aggredire

as·sem·ble [ə'sembl] **1** v/t parts assemblare, montare **2** v/i of people radunarsi

as·sem·bly [ə'semblɪ] assemblea f; of parts assemblaggio m

as'sem·bly line catena f di montaggio

as'sem·bly plant officina f di montaggio

as·sent [ə'sent] v/i acconsentire

as·sert [ə'sɜːt]: v/t: **~ o.s.** farsi valere

as·ser·tive [ə'sɜːtɪv] adj person sicuro di sé

as·sess [ə'ses] v/t valutare

as·sess·ment [ə'sesmənt] valutazione f

as·set ['æset] FIN attivo m; fig: thing vantaggio m; person elemento m prezioso

as·sign [ə'saɪn] v/t: person destinare; thing assegnare

as·sign·ment [ə'saɪnmənt] (task, study) compito m

as·sim·i·late [ə'sɪmɪleɪt] v/t information assimilare; person into group integrare

as·sist [ə'sɪst] v/t assistere

as·sist·ance [ə'sɪstəns] assistenza f

as·sist·ant [ə'sɪstənt] assistente m/f; in shop commesso m, -a f

as·sist·ant di'rec·tor vice-direttore m; of film assistente m/f

as·sist·ant 'man·ag·er of business vice-responsabile m/f; of hotel, restaurant vice-direttore m

as·so·ci·ate [ə'səʊʃɪeɪt] **1** v/t associare **2** v/i: **~ with** frequentare **3** n [ə'səʊʃɪət] socio m, -a f

as·so·ci·ate pro'fes·sor professore m associato, professoressa f associata

as·so·ci·a·tion [əsəʊsɪ'eɪʃn] associazione f; **in ~ with** in associazione con

as·sort·ed [ə'sɔːtɪd] adj assortito

as·sort·ment [ə'sɔːtmənt] assortimento m; **there was a whole ~ of people** c'era gente di tutti i tipi

as·sume [ə'sjuːm] v/t (suppose) supporre

as·sump·tion [ə'sʌmpʃn] supposi-

zione f; **The Assumption** REL l'Assunzione f

as·sur·ance [ə'ʃʊərəns] assicurazione f, garanzia f; (confidence) sicurezza f; **he gave me his personal ~ that ...** mi ha assicurato personalmente che ...

as·sure [ə'ʃʊə(r)] v/t (reassure): **~ s.o. of sth** assicurare qc a qu

as·sured [ə'ʃʊəd] adj (confident) sicuro

as·ter·isk ['æstərɪsk] asterisco m

asth·ma ['æsmə] asma f

asth·mat·ic [æs'mætɪk] adj asmatico

as·ton·ish [ə'stɒnɪʃ] v/t sbalordire; **be ~ed** essere sbalordito

as·ton·ish·ing [ə'stɒnɪʃɪŋ] adj sbalorditivo

as·ton·ish·ing·ly [ə'stɒnɪʃɪŋlɪ] adv in modo sbalorditivo

as·ton·ish·ment [ə'stɒnɪʃmənt] stupore m

as·tound [ə'staʊnd] v/t stupefare

as·tound·ing [ə'staʊndɪŋ] adj stupefacente

a·stray [ə'streɪ] adv: **go ~** smarrirsi; morally uscire dalla retta via

a·stride [ə'straɪd] **1** adv a cavalcioni **2** prep a cavalcioni di

as·trol·o·ger [ə'strɒlədʒə(r)] astrologo m, -a f

as·trol·o·gy [ə'strɒlədʒɪ] astrologia f

as·tro·naut ['æstrənɔːt] astronauta m/f

as·tron·o·mer [ə'strɒnəmə(r)] astronomo m, -a f

as·tro·nom·i·cal [æstrə'nɒmɪkl] adj price etc astronomico

as·tron·o·my [ə'strɒnəmɪ] astronomia f

as·tute [ə'stjuːt] adj astuto

a·sy·lum [ə'saɪləm] mental manicomio m; political asilo m

at [ət] stressed [æt] prep (with places) a; **he works ~ the hospital** lavora in ospedale; **~ the baker's** dal panettiere o in panetteria; **~ Joe's** da Joe; **~ the door** alla porta; **~ 10 pounds** a 10 sterline; **~ the age of 18** all'età di 18 anni; **~ 5 o'clock** alle cinque; **~ war** in guerra; **~ night** di notte; **~**

the moment you called nel momento in cui hai chiamato; **~ 150 km/h** a 150 km/h; **be good/bad ~ sth** essere/non essere bravo in qc

ate [eɪt] *pret of* **eat**

a·the·is·m ['eɪθɪɪzm] ateismo *m*

a·the·ist ['eɪθɪɪst] ateo *m*, -a *f*

ath·lete ['æθliːt] atleta *m/f*

ath·let·ic [æθ'letɪk] *adj* atletico

ath·let·ics [æθ'letɪks] *nsg* atletica *f*

At·lan·tic [ət'læntɪk] *n* Atlantico *m*

at·las ['ætləs] atlante *m*

at·mos·phere ['ætməsfɪə(r)] *of earth, mood* atmosfera *f*

at·mos·pher·ic pol·lu·tion [ætməs'ferɪk] inquinamento *m* atmosferico

at·om ['ætəm] atomo *m*

'at·om bomb bomba *f* atomica

a·tom·ic [ə'tɒmɪk] *adj* atomico

a·tom·ic 'en·er·gy energia *f* nucleare

a·tom·ic 'waste scorie *fpl* nucleari

a·tom·iz·er ['ætəmaɪzə(r)] vaporizzatore *m*

a·tone [ə'təun] *v/i:* **~ for** scontare

a·tro·cious [ə'trəuʃəs] *adj* atroce

a·troc·i·ty [ə'trɒsətɪ] atrocità *f inv*

at·tach [ə'tætʃ] *v/t* attaccare; *importance* attribuire; *document, file* allegare; **be ~ed to** (*fond of*) essere attaccato a

at·tach·ment [ə'tætʃmənt] (*fondness*) attaccamento *m*; *to email* allegato *m*

at·tack [ə'tæk] **1** *n* aggressione *f*; MIL attacco *m* **2** *v/t* aggredire; MIL attaccare

at·tempt [ə'tempt] **1** *n* tentativo *m* **2** *v/t* tentare

at·tend [ə'tend] *v/t wedding, funeral* partecipare a; *school, classes* frequentare

♦ **attend to** *v/t* (*deal with*) sbrigare; *customer* servire; *patient* assistere

at·tend·ance [ə'tendəns] partecipazione *f*; *at school* frequenza *f*

at·tend·ant [ə'tendənt] *in museum etc* sorvegliante *m/f*

at·ten·tion [ə'tenʃn] attenzione *f*; **bring sth to s.o.'s ~** informare qu di qc; **your ~ please** attenzione; **pay ~**

fare attenzione; **for the ~ of** in *faxes etc* alla cortese attenzione di

at·ten·tive [ə'tentɪv] *adj listener* attento

at·tic ['ætɪk] soffitta *f*

at·ti·tude ['ætɪtjuːd] atteggiamento *m*

attn *abbr* (= **attention**) c.a. (= alla cortese attenzione di)

at·tor·ney [ə'tɜːnɪ] avvocato *m*; **power of ~** delega *f*

at·tract [ə'trækt] *v/t* attirare; **be ~ed to s.o.** essere attirato da qu

at·trac·tion [ə'trækʃn] attrazione *f*

at·trac·tive [ə'træktɪv] *adj* attrattivo; *person* attraente

at·trib·ute[1] [ə'trɪbjuːt] *v/t* attribuire; **~ sth to ...** attribuire qc a ...

at·trib·ute[2] ['ætrɪbjuːt] *n* attributo *m*

au·ber·gine ['əubəʒiːn] melanzana *f*

auc·tion ['ɔːkʃn] **1** *n* asta *f* **2** *v/t* mettere all'asta

♦ **auction off** *v/t* vendere all'asta

auc·tio·neer [ɔːkʃə'nɪə(r)] banditore *m*, -trice *f*

au·da·cious [ɔː'deɪʃəs] *adj* audace

au·dac·i·ty [ɔː'dæsətɪ] audacia *f*

au·di·ble ['ɔːdəbl] *adj* udibile

au·di·ence ['ɔːdɪəns] pubblico *m*; TV telespettatori *mpl*; *with the Pope etc* udienza *f*

au·di·o ['ɔːdɪəu] *adj* audio *inv*

au·di·o·vi·su·al [ɔːdɪəu'vɪʒuəl] *adj* audiovisivo

au·dit ['ɔːdɪt] **1** *n of accounts* revisione *f o* verifica *f* contabile; **software ~** inventario *m* dei software **2** *v/t* verificare

au·di·tion [ɔː'dɪʃn] **1** *n* audizione *f* **2** *v/i* fare un'audizione

au·di·tor ['ɔːdɪtə(r)] revisore *m* contabile

au·di·to·ri·um [ɔːdɪ'tɔːrɪəm] *of theatre etc* sala *f*

Au·gust ['ɔːgəst] agosto *m*

aunt [ɑːnt] zia *f*

au pair (girl) [əu'peə(r)] ragazza *f* alla pari

au·ra ['ɔːrə]: **she has an ~ of confidence** emana sicurezza

aus·pic·es ['ɔːspɪsɪz]: **under the ~**

of sotto l'egida di
aus·pi·cious [ɔːˈspɪʃəs] *adj* propizio
aus·tere [ɔːˈstɪə(r)] *adj* austero
aus·ter·i·ty [ɒsˈterətɪ] *economic* austerità *f*
Aus·tra·li·a [ɒˈstreɪlɪə] Australia *f*
Aus·tra·li·an [ɒˈstreɪlɪən] **1** *adj* australiano **2** *n* australiano *m*, -a *f*
Aus·tri·a [ˈɒstrɪə] Austria *f*
Aus·tri·an [ˈɒstrɪən] **1** *adj* austriaco **2** *n* austriaco *m*, -a *f*
au·then·tic [ɔːˈθentɪk] *adj* autentico
au·then·tic·i·ty [ɔːθenˈtɪsətɪ] autenticità *f*
au·thor [ˈɔːθə(r)] autore *m*, autrice *f*
au·thor·i·tar·i·an [ɔːθɒrɪˈteərɪən] *adj* autoritario
au·thor·i·ta·tive [ɔːˈθɒrɪtətɪv] *adj* autoritario; *information* autorevole
au·thor·i·ty [ɔːˈθɒrətɪ] autorità *f inv*; (*permission*) autorizzazione *f*; **be in ~** avere l'autorità; **be an ~ on** essere un'autorità in materia di; **the authorities** le autorità
au·thor·i·za·tion [ɔːθəraɪˈzeɪʃn] autorizzazione *f*
au·thor·ize [ˈɔːθəraɪz] *v/t* autorizzare; **be ~d to ...** essere autorizzato a ...
au·tis·tic [ɔːˈtɪstɪk] *adj* autistico
au·to·bi·og·ra·phy [ɔːtəbaɪˈɒgrəfɪ] autobiografia *f*
au·to·crat·ic [ɔːtəˈkrætɪk] *adj* autocratico
au·to·graph [ˈɔːtəgrɑːf] autografo *m*
au·to·mate [ˈɔːtəmeɪt] *v/t* automatizzare
au·to·mat·ic [ɔːtəˈmætɪk] **1** *adj* automatico **2** *n* car macchina *f* con il cambio automatico; *gun* pistola *f* automatica; *washing machine* lavatrice *f* automatica
au·to·mat·i·cal·ly [ɔːtəˈmætɪklɪ] *adv* automaticamente
au·to·ma·tion [ɔːtəˈmeɪʃn] automazione *f*
au·to·mo·bile [ˈɔːtəməbiːl] automobile *f*
au·ton·o·mous [ɔːˈtɒnəməs] *adj* autonomo

au·ton·o·my [ɔːˈtɒnəmɪ] autonomia *f*
au·to·pi·lot [ˈɔːtəʊpaɪlət] pilota *m* automatico
au·top·sy [ˈɔːtɒpsɪ] autopsia *f*
au·tumn [ˈɔːtəm] autunno *m*
aux·il·ia·ry [ɔːgˈzɪlɪərɪ] *adj* ausiliario
a·vail [əˈveɪl] **1** *n*: **to no ~** invano **2** *v/t*: **~ o.s. of** avvalersi di
a·vai·la·ble [əˈveɪləbl] *adj* disponibile
av·a·lanche [ˈævəlɑːnʃ] valanga *f*
av·a·rice [ˈævərɪs] avarizia *f*
a·venge [əˈvendʒ] *v/t* vendicare
av·e·nue [ˈævənjuː] corso *m*; *fig* strada *f*
av·e·rage [ˈævərɪdʒ] **1** *adj* medio; (*of mediocre quality*) mediocre **2** *n* media *f*; **above/below** ~ sopra/sotto la media; **on** ~ in media, mediamente **3** *v/t* raggiungere in media
♦ **average out** *v/t* fare la media di
♦ **average out at** *v/t* risultare in media a
a·verse [əˈvɜːs] *adj*: **not be ~ to** non avere niente contro
a·ver·sion [əˈvɜːʃn] avversione *f*; **have an ~ to** avere un'avversione per
a·vert [əˈvɜːt] *v/t* one's eyes distogliere; *crisis* evitare
a·vi·a·ry [ˈeɪvɪərɪ] voliera *f*
a·vi·a·tion [eɪvɪˈeɪʃn] aviazione *f*; ~ **industry** industria *f* aeronautica
av·id [ˈævɪd] *adj* avido
av·o·ca·do [ævəˈkɑːdəʊ] avocado *m inv*
a·void [əˈvɔɪd] *v/t* evitare
a·void·a·ble [əˈvɔɪdəbl] *adj* evitabile
a·wait [əˈweɪt] *v/t* attendere
a·wake [əˈweɪk] *adj* sveglio; **it's keeping me ~** mi impedisce di dormire
a·ward [əˈwɔːd] **1** *n* (*prize*) premio *m* **2** *v/t* assegnare; *damages* riconoscere; **she was ~ed the Nobel Prize for ...** le hanno assegnato il premio Nobel per ...
a·ware [əˈweə(r)] *adj* conscio, consapevole; **be ~ of sth** essere conscio *o* consapevole di qc; **become ~ of sth**

rendersi conto di qc

a·ware·ness [ə'weənɪs] consapevolezza f

a·way [ə'weɪ] adv via; SP fuori casa; **be** ~ *travelling, sick etc* essere via; **go**/**run** ~ andare/correre via; **look** ~ guardare da un'altra parte; **it's 2 miles** ~ dista 2 miglia; **Christmas is still six weeks** ~ mancano ancora sei settimane a Natale; **take sth ~ from s.o.** togliere qc a qu; **put sth** ~ mettere via qc

a'way match SP partita f fuori casa

awe [ɔː] soggezione f

awe·some ['ɔːsm] adj F (terrific) fantastico

aw·ful ['ɔːfl] adj tremendo, terribile; **I feel** ~ F sto da cani F

aw·ful·ly ['ɔːflɪ] adv F (very) da matti F

awk·ward ['ɔːkwəd] adj (clumsy) goffo; (difficult) difficile; (embarrassing) scomodo; **feel** ~ sentirsi a disagio

awn·ing ['ɔːnɪŋ] tenda f

ax Am, **axe** [æks] **1** n scure f, accetta f **2** v/t project, job sopprimere

ax·le ['æksl] asse f

BA [biː'eɪ] abbr (= **Bachelor of Arts**) (degree) laurea f in lettere; (person) laureato m, -a f in lettere

ba·by ['beɪbɪ] n bambino m, -a f

'baby boom baby boom m inv

ba·by·ish ['beɪbɪɪʃ] adj infantile

'ba·by·sit v/i (pret & pp **-sat**) fare il/la baby-sitter

'bab·y·sit·ter baby-sitter m/f inv

bach·e·lor ['bætʃələ(r)] scapolo m

back [bæk] **1** n of person schiena f; of animal, hand dorso m; of car, bus parte f posteriore; of book, house retro m; of clothes rovescio m; of drawer fondo m; of chair schienale m; SP terzino m; **in the ~ (of the car)** (nei sedili) di dietro; **at the ~ of the bus** in fondo all'autobus; ~ **to front** al contrario; **at the ~ of beyond** in capo al mondo **2** adj door, steps di dietro; wheels, legs posteriore; garden, room sul retro; payment, issue arretrato; ~ **road** strada secondaria **3** adv: **please move**/**stand** ~ indietro, per favore; **2 metres ~ from the edge** a 2 metri dal bordo; ~ **in 1935** nel 1935; **give sth ~ to s.o.** restituire qc a qu; **she'll be** ~

tomorrow sarà di ritorno domani; **when are you coming ~?** quando torni?; **take sth ~ to the store** because unsatisfactory riportare qc indietro al negozio; **they wrote**/**phoned** ~ hanno risposto alla lettera/telefonata; **he hit me** ~ mi ha restituito il colpo **4** v/t (support) appoggiare; car guidare in retromarcia; horse puntare su; ~ **the car into the garage** mettere la macchina in garage in retromarcia **5** v/i of driver fare retromarcia

♦**back away** v/i indietreggiare

♦**back down** v/i fig fare marcia indietro

♦**back off** v/i spostarsi indietro; from danger tirarsi indietro

♦**back onto** v/i dare su

♦**back out** v/i fig tirarsi indietro

♦**back up 1** v/t (support) confermare; claim, argument supportare; file fare un backup di; **back s.o. up** spalleggiare qu; **be backed up** of traffic essere congestionato **2** v/i in car fare retromarcia

'back·ache mal m inv di schiena; **back·bench·er** [bæk'bentʃə(r)]

B

parlamentare *m/f* ordinario, -a;
'**back·bit·ing** maldicenze *fpl*;
'**back·bone** *also fig* spina *f* dorsale;
'**back-break·ing** *adj* massacrante;
back 'burn·er: put sth on the ~
accantonare qc; '**back·date** *v/t* retrodatare; '**back·door** porta *f* di
dietro

back·er ['bækə(r)] FIN finanziatore
m, -trice *f*

back'fire *v/i fig* avere effetto contrario; **~ on s.o.** ritorcersi contro qu;
'**back·ground** *n* sfondo *m*; *fig: of
person* background *m inv*; *of story,
event* retroscena *mpl*; '**back·hand** *n*
in tennis rovescio *m*; **back·hand·er**
['bækhændə(r)] F bustarella *f* F

'**back·ing** ['bækɪŋ] *n moral* appoggio
m; *financial* finanziamento *m*; MUS
accompagnamento *m*
'**back·ing group** MUS gruppo *m*
d'accompagnamento

'**back·lash** reazione *f* violenta;
'**back·log: ~ of work** lavoro *m* arretrato; **~ of unanswered letters** corrispondenza *f* arretrata; '**back·pack**
n zaino *m*; '**back·pack·er** saccopelista *m/f*; '**back·pack·ing** *il
viaggiare con zaino e sacco a pelo*;
'**back·ped·al** *v/i fig* fare marcia indietro; '**back seat** *of car* sedile *m*
posteriore; **back-seat 'driv·er:
you're a terrible ~!** smettila di dire
come si deve guidare!; '**back·side** F
sedere *m*; '**back·space (key)** (tasto di) ritorno *m*; '**back·stairs** *npl*
scala *f* di servizio; '**back streets** *npl*
vicoli *mpl*; '**back·stroke** SP dorso
m; '**back·track** *v/i* tornare indietro;
'**back·up** (*support*) rinforzi *mpl*;
COMPUT backup *m inv*; '**back·up
disk** COMPUT disco *m* di backup

back·ward ['bækwəd] *adj child* tardivo; *society* arretrato; *glance* all'indietro

backwards ['bækwədz] *adv* indietro
back'yard cortile *m*; **not in my ~** *fig*
non in casa mia

ba·con ['beɪkn] pancetta *f*

bac·te·ri·a [bæk'tɪərɪə] *npl* batteri
mpl

bad [bæd] *adj news, manners* cattivo;
weather, cold, headache brutto; *mistake, accident* grave; *egg, food* guasto;
smoking is ~ for you il fumo fa
male; **it's not ~** non è male; **that's
too ~** *shame* peccato!; **feel ~ about
sth** (*guilty*) sentirsi in colpa per
qc; **be ~ at** essere negato per;
Friday's ~, how about Thursday?
venerdì non posso, che ne dici di
giovedì?

bad 'debt debito *m* insoluto
badge [bædʒ] distintivo *m*
bad·ger ['bædʒə(r)] *v/t* tasso *m*
bad 'lan·guage parolacce *fpl*
bad·ly ['bædlɪ] *adv* male; *injured,
damaged* gravemente; **he ~ needs a
haircut / rest** ha urgente bisogno di
tagliarsi i capelli / riposare; **he is ~
off** (*poor*) è povero
bad-man·nered [bæd'mænəd] *adj*
maleducato
bad·min·ton ['bædmɪntən] badmin-
ton *m inv*
bad-tem·pered [bæd'tempəd] *adj*
irascibile
baf·fle ['bæfl] *v/t:* **be ~d** essere perplesso
baf·fling ['bæflɪŋ] *adj* sconcertante
bag [bæg] borsa *f*; *plastic, paper* busta
f
bag·gage ['bægɪdʒ] bagagli *mpl*
bag·gage re·claim ['riːkleɪm] ritiro
m bagagli
'**bag·gage trol·ley** carrello *m*
bag·gy ['bægɪ] *adj* senza forma
'**bag·pipes** *npl* cornamusa *fsg*
bail [beɪl] *n* LAW cauzione *f*; **on ~** su
cauzione
◆**bail out 1** *v/t* LAW scarcerare su
cauzione; *fig* tirare fuori dai guai
2 *v/i of aeroplane* lanciarsi col paracadute
bai·liff ['beɪlɪf] *ufficiale m giudiziario*
bait [beɪt] *n* esca *f*
bake [beɪk] *v/t* cuocere al forno
baked 'beans [beɪkt] *npl* fagioli *mpl*
in salsa rossa
baked po'ta·toes *npl* patate *fpl* cotte
al forno con la buccia
bak·er ['beɪkə(r)] fornaio *m*, -a *f*

bak·er's ['beɪkəz] panetteria *f*
bak·er·y ['beɪkərɪ] panetteria *f*
bak·ing pow·der ['beɪkɪŋ] lievito *m*
bal·ance ['bæləns] **1** *n* equilibrio *m*; (*remainder*) resto *m*; *of bank account* saldo *m* **2** *v/t* tenere in equilibrio; **~ the books** fare il bilancio **3** *v/i* stare in equilibrio; *of accounts* quadrare
bal·anced ['bælənst] *adj* (*fair*) obiettivo; *diet, personality* equilibrato
bal·ance of 'pay·ments bilancia *f* dei pagamenti
bal·ance of 'trade bilancia *f* commerciale
'bal·ance sheet bilancio *m* (di esercizio)
bal·co·ny ['bælkənɪ] *of house* balcone *m*; *in theatre* prima galleria *f*
bald [bɔːld] *adj man* calvo; **he's going ~** sta perdendo i capelli
bald·ing ['bɔːldɪŋ] *adj* stempiato
Bal·kan ['bɔːlkən] *adj* balcanico
Bal·kans ['bɔːlkənz] *npl*: **the ~** i Balcani *mpl*
ball¹ [bɔːl] palla *f*; *football* pallone *m*; **be on the ~** essere sveglio; **play ~** *fig* collaborare; **the ~'s in his court** la prossima mossa è sua
ball² [bɔːl] (*dance*) ballo *m*
bal·lad ['bæləd] ballata *f*
ball 'bear·ing cuscinetto *m* a sfere
bal·le·ri·na [bælə'riːnə] ballerina *f*
bal·let ['bæleɪ] *art* danza *f* classica; *dance* balletto *m*
'bal·let danc·er ballerino *m* classico, ballerina *f* classica
'ball game F: **that's a different ~** è un altro paio di maniche
bal·lis·tic mis·sile [bə'lɪstɪk] missile *m* balistico
bal·loon [bə'luːn] *child's* palloncino *m*; *for flight* mongolfiera *f*
bal·loon·ist [bə'luːnɪst] aeronauta *m/f*
bal·lot ['bælət] **1** *n* votazione *f* **2** *v/t members* consultare tramite votazione
'bal·lot box urna *f* elettorale
'bal·lot pa·per scheda *f* elettorale
'ball·park F: **be in the right ~** essere nell'ordine corretto di cifre; **'ball-**

park fig·ure F cifra *f* approssimativa
'ball·point (pen) penna *f* a sfera
balls [bɔːlz] *npl* V (*also courage*) palle *fpl* V
bam·boo [bæm'buː] *n* bambù *m inv*
ban [bæn] **1** *n* divieto *m* (**on** di) **2** *v/t* (*pret & pp* **-ned**) proibire
ba·nal [bə'nɑːl] *adj* banale
ba·na·na [bə'nɑːnə] banana *f*
band [bænd] banda *f*; *pop* gruppo *m*; *of material* nastro *m*
ban·dage ['bændɪdʒ] **1** *n* benda *f* **2** *v/t* bendare
B&B [biːn'biː] *abbr* (= **bed and breakfast**) pensione *f* familiare, bed and breakfast *m inv*
ban·dit ['bændɪt] brigante *m*
'band·wag·on *n*: **jump on the ~** seguire la corrente
ban·dy ['bændɪ] *adj legs* storto
bang [bæŋ] **1** *n* colpo *m* **2** *v/t door* chiudere violentemente; (*hit*) sbattere; **I ~ed my knee on the table** ho battuto il ginocchio contro il tavolo **3** *v/i* sbattere; **the door ~ed shut** la porta si è chiusa con un colpo
bang·er ['bæŋə(r)] F (*sausage*) salamino *m*; **an old ~** (*car*) una vecchia carretta
ban·gle ['bæŋgl] braccialetto *m*
ban·is·ters ['bænɪstəz] *npl* ringhiera *fsg*
ban·jo ['bændʒəʊ] banjo *m inv*
bank¹ [bæŋk] *of river* riva *f*
bank² [bæŋk] **1** *n* FIN banca *f* **2** *v/i*: **~ with** avere un conto presso **3** *v/t money* mettere in banca
♦ **bank on** *v/t* contare su; **don't bank on it** non ci contare; **bank on s.o. doing sth** dare per scontato che qu faccia qc
'bank ac·count conto *m* bancario
'bank bal·ance saldo *m*
bank·er ['bæŋkə(r)] banchiere *m*
'bank·er's card carta *f* assegni
bank·er's 'or·der ordine *m* di pagamento
bank 'hol·i·day giorno *m* festivo
bank·ing ['bæŋkɪŋ] professione *f* bancaria

B

'bank loan prestito *m* bancario; 'bank man·ag·er direttore *m* di banca; 'bank note banconota *f*; 'bank rate tasso *m* ufficiale di sconto; 'bank·roll *v/t* finanziare

bank·rupt ['bæŋkrʌpt] **1** *adj* fallito; go ~ fallire **2** *v/t* portare al fallimento

bank·rupt·cy ['bæŋkrʌpsɪ] bancarotta *f*

'bank state·ment estratto *m* conto

ban·ner ['bænə(r)] *n* striscione *m*

banns [bænz] *npl* pubblicazioni *mpl* (matrimoniali)

ban·quet ['bæŋkwɪt] *n* banchetto *m*

ban·ter ['bæntə(r)] *n* scambio *m* di battute

bap·tis·m ['bæptɪzm] battesimo *m*

bap·tize [bæp'taɪz] *v/t* battezzare

bar¹ [bɑː(r)] *n of iron* spranga *f*; *of chocolate* tavoletta *f*; *for drinks* bar *m inv*; (*counter*) bancone *m*; a ~ of soap una saponetta; be behind ~s (*in prison*) essere dietro le sbarre

bar² [bɑː(r)] *v/t* (*pret & pp -red*) vietare l'ingresso a; he's been ~red from the club gli hanno vietato l'ingresso al club

bar³ [bɑː(r)] *prep* (*except*) tranne

bar·bar·i·an [bɑː'beərɪən] barbaro *m*, -a *f*

bar·bar·ic [bɑː'bærɪk] *adj* barbaro

bar·be·cue ['bɑːbɪkjuː] **1** *n* barbecue *m inv* **2** *v/t* cuocere al barbecue

barbed 'wire [bɑːbd] filo *m* spinato

bar·ber ['bɑːbə(r)] barbiere *m*

bar·bi·tu·rate [bɑː'bɪtjʊrət] barbiturico *m*

'bar code codice *m* a barre

bare [beə(r)] *adj* (*naked*) nudo; (*empty: room*) spoglio; *mountainside* brullo

'bare·foot *adj*: be ~ essere scalzo

bare·head·ed [beə'hedɪd] *adj* senza cappello

bare·ly ['beəlɪ] *adv* appena

bar·gain ['bɑːgɪn] **1** *n* (*deal*) patto *m*; (*good buy*) affare *m*; it's a ~! (*deal*) è un affare!; *into the* ~ per giunta **2** *v/i* tirare sul prezzo

♦ bargain for *v/t* (*expect*) aspettarsi;

he got more than he bargained for non se l'aspettava

barge [bɑːdʒ] *n* NAUT chiatta *f*

♦ barge into *v/t* piombare su

bar·i·tone ['bærɪtəʊn] *n* baritono *m*

bark¹ [bɑːk] **1** *n of dog* abbaiare *m* **2** *v/i* abbaiare

bark² [bɑːk] *of tree* corteccia *f*

bar·ley ['bɑːlɪ] orzo *m*

'bar·maid barista *f*

'bar·man barista *m*

barm·y ['bɑːmɪ] *adj* F pazzoide F

barn [bɑːn] granaio *m*

ba·rom·e·ter [bə'rɒmɪtə(r)] *also fig* barometro *m*

Ba·roque [bə'rɒk] *adj* barocco

bar·racks ['bærəks] *npl* MIL caserma *fsg*

bar·rage ['bærɑːʒ] MIL sbarramento *m*; *fig* raffica *f*

bar·rel ['bærəl] (*container*) barile *m*

bar·ren ['bærən] *adj* land arido

bar·ri·cade [bærɪ'keɪd] *n* barricata *f*

bar·ri·er ['bærɪə(r)] barriera *f*; *language* ~ l'ostacolo *m* della lingua

bar·ring ['bɑːrɪŋ] *prep*: ~ accidents salvo imprevisti

bar·ris·ter ['bærɪstə(r)] avvocato *m*

bar·row ['bærəʊ] carriola *f*

'bar ten·der barista *m/f*

bar·ter ['bɑːtə(r)] **1** *n* baratto *m* **2** *v/i* barattare

base [beɪs] **1** *n* base *f* **2** *v/t* basare; ~ sth on sth basare qc su qc; be ~d in *in city, country* essere di base a; be ~d on essere basato su

'base·ball baseball *m inv*

'base·ball bat mazza *f* da baseball

'base·ball cap berretto *m* da baseball

base·less ['beɪslɪs] *adj* infondato

base·ment ['beɪsmənt] seminterrato *m*

'base rate FIN tasso *m* base

bash [bæʃ] **1** *n* F colpo *m* **2** *v/t* F sbattere

ba·sic ['beɪsɪk] *adj knowledge, equipment* rudimentale; *salary* di base; *beliefs* fondamentale

ba·sic·al·ly ['beɪsɪklɪ] *adv* essenzialmente

be

ba·sics ['beɪsɪks] *npl*: **the ~** i rudimenti *mpl*; **get down to ~** venire al sodo

bas·il ['bæzɪl] basilico *m*

ba·sil·i·ca [bə'zɪlɪkə] basilica *f*

ba·sin ['beɪsn] *for washing* lavandino *m*

ba·sis ['beɪsɪs] (*pl* **bases** ['beɪsiːz]) base *f*

bask [baːsk] *v/i* crogiolarsi

bas·ket ['baːskɪt] cestino *m*; *in basketball* cesto *m*

'bas·ket·ball basket *m inv*, pallacanestro *f*

bass [beɪs] **1** *n* (*part*) voce *f* di basso; (*singer*) basso *m*; (*double bass*) contrabbasso *m*; (*guitar*) basso *m* **2** *adj* di basso

bas·tard ['baːstəd] F bastardo *m*, -a *f*

bat¹ [bæt] **1** *n* mazza *f*; *for table tennis* racchetta *f* **2** *v/i* (*pret & pp* **-ted**) SP battere

bat² [bæt] *v/t* (*pret & pp* **-ted**): **he didn't ~ an eyelid** non ha battuto ciglio

bat³ [bæt] (*animal*) pipistrello *m*

batch [bætʃ] *n of students* gruppo *m*; *of goods* lotto *m*; *of bread* infornata *f*

ba·ted ['beɪtɪd] *adj*: **with ~ breath** col fiato sospeso

bath [baːθ] bagno *m*; **have a ~**, **take a ~** fare il bagno

bathe [beɪð] *v/i* (*swim, have bath*) fare il bagno

'bath·ing cost·ume, **'bath·ing suit** costume *m* da bagno

'bath mat tappetino *m* da bagno; **'bath·robe** accappatoio *m*; **'bath·room** (stanza *f* da) bagno *m*

baths [baːðz] *npl Br* bagni *mpl* pubblici

'bath tow·el asciugamano *m* da bagno

'bath·tub vasca *f* da bagno

bat·on ['bætən] *of conductor* bacchetta *f*

bat·tal·i·on [bə'tæljən] MIL battaglione *m*

bat·ter ['bætə(r)] *n* pastella *f*

bat·tered ['bætəd] *adj* maltrattato;

old hat, suitcase etc malridotto

bat·ter·y ['bætrɪ] pila *f*; MOT batteria *f*

'bat·ter·y charg·er caricabatterie *m inv*

bat·ter·y-op·e·rat·ed [bætrɪ'ɒpəreɪtɪd] *adj* a pile

bat·tle ['bætl] **1** *n also fig* battaglia *f* **2** *v/i against illness etc* lottare

'bat·tle·field, **'bat·tle·ground** campo *m* di battaglia

'bat·tle·ship corazzata *f*

bawd·y ['bɔːdɪ] *adj* spinto

bawl [bɔːl] *v/i* (*shout*) urlare; (*weep*) strillare

♦**bawl out** *v/t* F fare una lavata di capo a

bay [beɪ] (*inlet*) baia *f*

bay·o·net ['beɪənət] *n* baionetta *f*

bay 'win·dow bovindo *m*

BBC [biːbiː'siː] *abbr* (= **British Broadcasting Corporation**) BBC *f inv*

BC [biː'siː] *abbr* (= **before Christ**) a. C. (= avanti Cristo)

be [biː] *v/i* (*pret* **was** / **were**, *pp* **been**) essere; *it's me* sono io; *was she there?* era lì?; *how much is* / *are ...?* quant'è / quanto sono ...?; *there is, there are* c'è, ci sono; ~ *careful* sta' attento; *don't ~ sad* non essere triste; *how are you?* come stai?; *he's very well* sta bene; *I'm hot* / *cold* ho freddo / caldo; *it's hot* / *cold* fa freddo / caldo; *he's seven* ha sette anni ◊ *has the postman been?* è passato il postino?; *I've never been to Japan* non sono mai stato in Giappone; *I've been here for hours* sono qui da tanto ◊ *tags: that's right, isn't it?* giusto, no?; *she's American, isn't she?* è americana, vero? ◊ *v aux*: *I am thinking* sto pensando; *he was running* stava correndo; *you're ~ing silly* stai facendo lo sciocco; *he's working in London* lavora a Londra; *I'll be waiting for an answer* aspetterò una risposta ◊ *obligation*: *you are to do what I tell you* devi fare quello che ti dico; *I* was to tell you this dovevo dirtelo; **you were not to tell anyone** non dovevi dirlo a nessuno ◊ passive essere, venire (not with past tenses); **he was killed** è stato ucciso; **they have been sold** sono stati venduti; **it will ~ sold for £100** sarà o verrà venduto a 100 sterline

♦ **be in for** v/t doversi aspettare; **you're in for a disappointment** resterai deluso

beach [bi:tʃ] n spiaggia f

'**beach ball** pallone m da spiaggia

'**beach·wear** abbigliamento m da spiaggia

beads [bi:dz] npl perline fpl

beak [bi:k] becco m

bea·ker ['bi:kə(r)] bicchiere m

'**be-all: the ~ and end-all** la cosa più importante

beam [bi:m] **1** n in ceiling etc trave f **2** v/i (smile) fare un sorriso radioso **3** v/t (transmit) trasmettere

bean [bi:n] (vegetable) fagiolo m; of coffee chicco m; **be full of ~s** F essere particolarmente vivace

'**bean·bag** seat poltrona f sacco

bear[1] [beə(r)] animal orso m

bear[2] [beə(r)] (pret **bore**, pp **borne**) **1** v/t weight portare; costs sostenere; (tolerate) sopportare; child dare alla luce **2** v/i: **bring pressure to ~ on** fare pressione su

♦ **bear out** v/t (confirm) confermare; **bear s.o. out** appoggiare qu

bear·a·ble ['beərəbl] adj sopportabile

beard [bɪəd] barba f

beard·ed ['bɪədɪd] adj con la barba

bear·ing ['beərɪŋ] in machine cuscinetto m; **that has no ~ on the case** ciò non ha alcuna attinenza col caso

'**bear mar·ket** FIN mercato m cedente

beast [bi:st] bestia f

beat [bi:t] **1** n of heart battito m; of music ritmo m **2** v/i (pret **beat**, pp **beaten**) of heart battere; of rain picchiettare; **~ about the bush** menar il can per l'aia **3** v/t (pret **beat**, pp **beaten**) in competition battere; (hit)

picchiare; drum suonare; ~ **it!** F fila!; **it ~s me** non capisco

♦ **beat up** v/t picchiare

beat·en ['bi:tən] **1** adj: **off the ~ track** fuori mano **2** pp → **beat**

beat·ing ['bi:tɪŋ] (physical) botte fpl

beat-up adj F malconcio

beau·ti·cian [bju:'tɪʃn] estetista m/f

beau·ti·ful ['bju:tɪfʊl] adj bello; **thanks, that's just ~!** grazie, così va bene

beau·ti·ful·ly ['bju:tɪflɪ] adv stupendamente

beau·ty ['bju:tɪ] of woman, sunset bellezza f

'**beau·ty sal·on** istituto m di bellezza

♦ **beaver away** v/i F sgobbare F

be·came [bɪ'keɪm] pret → **become**

be·cause [bɪ'kɒz] conj perché; ~ **of** a causa di

beck·on ['bekn] v/i fare cenno

be·come [bɪ'kʌm] (pret **became**, pp **become**) diventare; **what's ~ of her?** che ne è stato di lei?

be·com·ing [bɪ'kʌmɪŋ] adj grazioso

bed [bed] n letto m; ~ **of flowers** aiuola f; **go to ~** andare a letto; **he's still in ~** è ancora a letto; **go to ~ with** andare a letto con

bed and 'break·fast pensione f familiare, bed and breakfast m inv

'**bed·clothes** npl coperte e lenzuola fpl

bed·ding ['bedɪŋ] materasso m e lenzuola fpl

bed·lam ['bedləm] F manicomio m

bed·rid·den ['bedrɪdən] adj costretto a letto; '**bed·room** camera f da letto; '**bed·side: be at the ~ of** essere al capezzale di; **bed·side 'lamp** lampada f da comodino; **bed·side 'ta·ble** comodino m; '**bed·sit**, **bed-'sit·ter** monolocale m; '**bed·spread** copriletto m; '**bed·time** ora f di andare a letto

bee [bi:] ape f

beech [bi:tʃ] faggio m

beef [bi:f] **1** n manzo m; F (complaint) problema m **2** v/i F (complain) lagnarsi

♦ **beef up** v/t rinforzare

'beef·bur·ger hamburger *m inv*

'bee·hive alveare *m*

'bee·line: *make a ~ for* andare diritto a

been [biːn] *pp* → *be*

beep [biːp] **1** *n* bip *m inv* **2** *v/i* suonare **3** *v/t* (*call on pager*) chiamare sul cercapersone

beep·er ['biːpə(r)] (*pager*) cercapersone *m inv*

beer [bɪə(r)] birra *f*

bee·tle ['biːtl] coleottero *m*

beet·root ['biːtruːt] barbabietola *f*; *as red as a ~* rosso come un peperone

be·fore [bɪ'fɔː(r)] **1** *prep* prima di; *~ eight o'clock* prima delle otto **2** *adv* prima; *have you been to England ~?* sei già stato in Inghilterra?; *I've seen this film ~* questo film l'ho già visto **3** *conj* prima che; *I saw him ~ he left* l'ho visto prima che partisse; *I saw him ~ I left* l'ho visto prima di partire

be·fore·hand *adv* prima

be·friend [bɪ'frend] *v/t* fare amicizia con

beg [beg] (*pret & pp -ged*) **1** *v/i* mendicare **2** *v/t*: *~ s.o. to ...* pregare qu di ...

be·gan [bɪ'gæn] *pret* → *begin*

beg·gar ['begə(r)] *n* mendicante *m/f*

be·gin [bɪ'gɪn] *v/t & v/i* (*pret began, pp begun*) cominciare; *to ~ with* per cominciare

be·gin·ner [bɪ'gɪnə(r)] principiante *m/f*

be·gin·ning [bɪ'gɪnɪŋ] inizio *m*; (*origin*) origine *f*

be·grudge [bɪ'grʌdʒ] *v/t* (*envy*) invidiare; (*give reluctantly*) dare malvolentieri

be·gun [bɪ'gʌn] *pp* → *begin*

be·half: *on ~ of* a nome di; *on my / his ~* a nome mio / suo

be·have [bɪ'heɪv] *v/i* comportarsi; *~ (o.s.)* comportarsi bene; *~ (yourself)!* comportati bene!

be·hav·iour [bɪ'heɪvjə(r)] comportamento *m*

be·hind [bɪ'haɪnd] **1** *prep in position* dietro; *in progress* indietro rispetto a; *in order* dietro a; *be ~* (*responsible for*) essere dietro a; (*support*) appoggiare **2** *adv* (*at the back*) dietro; *she had to stay* ~ è dovuta rimanere; *be ~ in match* essere in svantaggio; *be ~ with sth* essere indietro con qc

beige [beɪʒ] *adj* beige *inv*

be·ing ['biːɪŋ] (*existence*) esistenza *f*; (*creature*) essere *m*

be·lat·ed [bɪ'leɪtɪd] *adj* in ritardo

belch [beltʃ] **1** *n* rutto *m* **2** *v/i* ruttare

Bel·gian ['beldʒən] **1** *adj* belga **2** *n* belga *m/f*

Bel·gium ['beldʒəm] Belgio *m*

be·lief [bɪ'liːf] convinzione *f*; *in God* fede *f*; *your ~ in me* il fatto che tu creda in me

be·lieve [bɪ'liːv] *v/t* credere

♦ believe in *v/t God, person* credere in; *ghost, person* credere a

be·liev·er [bɪ'liːvə(r)] REL credente *m/f*; *I'm a great ~ in ...* credo fermamente in ...

be·lit·tle [bɪ'lɪtl] *v/t* sminuire

bell [bel] *in church, school* campana *f*; *on door* campanello *m*

bel·lig·er·ent [bɪ'lɪdʒərənt] *adj* bellicoso

bel·low ['beləʊ] **1** *n* urlo *m*; *of bull* muggito *m* **2** *v/i* urlare; *of bull* muggire

bel·ly ['belɪ] pancia *f*

'bel·ly·ache *v/i* F brontolare F

be·long [bɪ'lɒŋ] *v/i*: *where does this ~?* dove va questo?; *I don't ~ here* mi sento un estraneo; *at last he found a place where he ~ed* finalmente ha trovato un posto adatto a lui

♦ belong to *v/t* appartenere a

be·long·ings [bɪ'lɒŋɪŋz] *npl* cose *fpl*

be·lov·ed [bɪ'lʌvɪd] *adj* adorato

be·low [bɪ'ləʊ] **1** *prep* sotto **2** *adv* di sotto; *in text* sotto; *see* ~ vedi sotto; *10 degrees ~* 10 gradi sotto zero

belt [belt] *n* cintura *f*; *tighten one's ~ fig* stringere la cinghia

♦ belt up *v/i* (*fasten seat belt*) allacciare la cintura (di sicurezza); **belt up!** F sta' zitto!

be·moan [bɪˈməʊn] *v/t* lamentarsi di

bench [bentʃ] (*seat*) panchina *f*; (*work~*) banco *m*

'bench·mark punto *m* di riferimento

bend [bend] **1** *n* curva *f* **2** *v/t* (*pret & pp* **bent**) piegare **3** *v/i* (*pret & pp* **bent**) curvarsi; *of person* inchinarsi
♦ **bend down** *v/i* chinarsi

bend·er [ˈbendə(r)] F sbronza *f* F

be·neath [bɪˈniːθ] **1** *prep* sotto **2** *adv* di sotto; **they think he's ~ her** lo considerano inferiore a lei

ben·e·dic·tion [benɪˈdɪkʃn] benedizione *f*

ben·e·fac·tor [ˈbenɪfæktə(r)] benefattore *m*, -trice *f*

ben·e·fi·cial [benɪˈfɪʃl] *adj* vantaggioso

ben·e·fit [ˈbenɪfɪt] **1** *n* (*advantage*) vantaggio *m*; *payment* indennità *f inv* **2** *v/t* andare a vantaggio di **3** *v/i* trarre vantaggio (*from* da)

be·nev·o·lence [bɪˈnevələns] benevolenza *f*

be·nev·o·lent [bɪˈnevələnt] *adj* benevolo

be·nign [bɪˈnaɪn] *adj* benevolo; MED benigno

bent [bent] **1** *adj* F corrotto **2** *pret & pp* → **bend**

be·queath [bɪˈkwiːð] *v/t also fig* lasciare in eredità

be·quest [bɪˈkwest] lascito *m*

be·reaved [bɪˈriːvd] **1** *adj* addolorato **2** *n*: **the ~** i familiari *mpl* del defunto

be·ret [ˈbereɪ] berretto *m*

ber·ry [ˈberɪ] bacca *f*

ber·serk [bəˈzɜːk] *adv*: **go ~** dare in escandescenze

berth [bɜːθ] *on ship, train* cuccetta *f*; **give s.o. a wide ~** stare alla larga da qu

be·seech [bɪˈsiːtʃ] *v/t*: **~ s.o. to do sth** implorare qu di fare qc

be·side [bɪˈsaɪd] *prep* accanto a; **be ~ o.s.** essere fuori di sé; **that's ~ the point** questo non c'entra

be·sides [bɪˈsaɪdz] **1** *adv* inoltre **2** *prep* (*apart from*) oltre a

be·siege [bɪˈsiːdʒ] *v/t also fig* assediare

best [best] **1** *adj* migliore **2** *adv* meglio; **it would be ~ if ...** sarebbe meglio se ...; **I like her ~** lei è quella che mi piace di più **3** *n*: **do one's ~** fare del proprio meglio; **the ~** il meglio; (*outstanding thing or person*) il/la migliore; **they've done the ~ they can** hanno fatto tutto il possibile; **make the ~ of** cogliere il lato buono di; **all the ~!** tanti auguri!

best be'fore date scadenza *f*; **best 'man** *at wedding* testimone *m* dello sposo; **'best-sell·er** bestseller *m inv*

bet [bet] **1** *n* scommessa *f* **2** *v/i* scommettere; **you ~!** ci puoi scommettere!

be·tray [bɪˈtreɪ] *v/t* tradire

be·tray·al [bɪˈtreɪəl] tradimento *m*

bet·ter [ˈbetə(r)] **1** *adj* migliore; **get ~** migliorare **2** *adv* meglio; **you'd ~ ask permission** faresti meglio a chiedere il permesso; **I'd really ~ not** sarebbe meglio di no; **the ~ for us** tanto meglio per noi; **I like her ~** lei mi piace di più

bet·ter 'off *adj*: **be ~** stare meglio finanziariamente; **the ~** la classe abbiente

be·tween [bɪˈtwiːn] *prep* tra; **~ you and me** tra me e te

bev·er·age [ˈbevərɪdʒ] *fml* bevanda *f*

be·ware [bɪˈweə(r)] *v/t*: **~ of ...!** (stai) attento a ...!

be·wil·der [bɪˈwɪldə(r)] *v/t* sconcertare

be·wil·der·ment [bɪˈwɪldəmənt] perplessità *f inv*

be·yond [bɪˈjɒnd] **1** *prep* oltre, al di là di; **it's ~ me** (*don't understand*) non capisco; (*can't do it*) va oltre le mie capacità **2** *adv* più in là

bi·as [ˈbaɪəs] *n against* pregiudizio *m*; *in favour of* preferenza *f*

bi·as(s)ed [ˈbaɪəst] *adj* parziale

bib [bɪb] *for baby* bavaglino *m*

Bible ['baɪbl] bibbia *f*
bib·li·cal ['bɪblɪkl] *adj* biblico
bib·li·og·ra·phy [bɪblɪ'ɒgrəfɪ] bibliografia *f*
bi·car·bon·ate of so·da [baɪ'kɑːbənət] bicarbonato *m* di sodio
bi·cen·te·na·ry [baɪsen'tiːnərɪ] bicentenario *m*
bi·ceps ['baɪseps] *npl* bicipiti *mpl*
bick·er ['bɪkə(r)] *v/i* bisticciare
bi·cy·cle ['baɪsɪkl] *n* bicicletta *f*
bid [bɪd] **1** *n at auction* offerta *f*; (*attempt*) tentativo *m* **2** *v/t & v/i* (*pret & pp* **bid**) *at auction* offrire
bid·der ['bɪdə(r)] offerente *m/f*
bi·fo·cals [baɪ'fəʊkəlz] *npl* occhiali *mpl* bifocali
big [bɪg] **1** *adj* grande; *my* ~ *brother / sister* mio fratello / mia sorella maggiore; ~ *name* nome importante **2** *adv*: *talk* ~ sparlare grosse
big·a·mist ['bɪgəmɪst] bigamo *m*, -a *f*
big·a·mous ['bɪgəməs] *adj* bigamo
big·a·my ['bɪgəmɪ] bigamia *f*
'big·head F pallone *m* gonfiato F
big·head·ed [bɪg'hedɪd] *adj* F presuntuoso
big·ot ['bɪgət] fanatico *m*, -a *f*
bike [baɪk] **1** *n* F bici *f inv* F **2** *v/i* andare in bici; *I ~d here* sono venuto in bici
bik·er ['baɪkə(r)] motociclista *m/f*; (*courier*) corriere *m*
bi·ki·ni [bɪ'kiːnɪ] bikini *m inv*
bi·lat·er·al [baɪ'lætərəl] *adj* bilaterale
bi·lin·gual [baɪ'lɪŋgwəl] *adj* bilingue
bill [bɪl] **1** *n in hotel, restaurant* conto *m*; (*gas / electricity* ~) bolletta *f*; (*invoice*) fattura *f*; *Am: money* banconota *f*; POL disegno *m* di legge; (*poster*) avviso *m* **2** *v/t* (*invoice*) mandare la fattura a
'bill·fold *Am* portafoglio *m*
bil·liards ['bɪljədz] *nsg* biliardo *m*
bil·li·on ['bɪljən] (*1,000,000,000*) miliardo *m*
bill of ex'change FIN cambiale *f*
bill of 'sale atto *m* di vendita
bin [bɪn] *n* bidone *m*

bi·na·ry ['baɪnərɪ] *adj* binario
bind [baɪnd] *v/t* (*pret & pp* **bound**) *also fig* legare; (LAW: *oblige*) obbligare
bind·ing ['baɪndɪŋ] **1** *adj agreement, promise* vincolante **2** *n of book* rilegatura *f*; *of ski* attacco *m*
bin·go ['bɪŋgəʊ] tombola *f*
bi·noc·u·lars [bɪ'nɒkjʊləz] *npl* binocolo *msg*
bi·o·chem·ist [baɪəʊ'kemɪst] biochimico *m*, -a *f*
bi·o·chem·is·try [baɪəʊ'kemɪstrɪ] biochimica *f*
bi·o·de·grad·a·bil·i·ty [baɪəʊdɪgreɪdə'bɪlətɪ] biodegradabilità *f inv*
bi·o·de·gra·da·ble [baɪəʊdɪ'greɪdəbl] *adj* biodegradabile
bi·og·ra·pher [baɪ'ɒgrəfə(r)] biografo *m*, -a *f*
bi·og·ra·phy [baɪ'ɒgrəfɪ] biografia *f*
bi·o·log·i·cal [baɪə'lɒdʒɪkl] *adj* biologico
bi·ol·o·gist [baɪ'ɒlədʒɪst] biologo *m*, -a *f*
bi·ol·o·gy [baɪ'ɒlədʒɪ] biologia *f*
bi·o·tech·nol·o·gy [baɪəʊtek'nɒlədʒɪ] biotecnologia *f*
bird [bɜːd] uccello *m*
'bird·cage gabbia *f* per uccelli; **bird of 'prey** (uccello *m*) rapace *m*; **'bird sanc·tu·a·ry** rifugio *m* per uccelli; **bird's eye 'view** vista *f* a volo d'uccello
bi·ro® ['baɪrəʊ] biro *f*
birth [bɜːθ] *also fig* nascita *f*; (*labour*) parto *m*; *give* ~ *to child* partorire; *date of* ~ data di nascita
'birth cer·tif·i·cate certificato *m* di nascita; **'birth con·trol** controllo *m* delle nascite; **'birth·day** compleanno *m*; *happy* ~! buon compleanno!; **'birth·mark** voglia *f*; **'birth·place** luogo *m* di nascita; **'birth·rate** tasso *m* di nascita
bis·cuit ['bɪskɪt] biscotto *m*
bi·sex·u·al ['baɪseksjʊəl] **1** *adj* bisessuale **2** *n* bisessuale *m/f*
bish·op ['bɪʃəp] vescovo *m*
bit¹ [bɪt] *n* (*piece*) pezzo *m*; (*part*) parte *f*; COMPUT bit *m inv*; *a* ~ (*a*

B

little) un po'; *a ~ of* (*a little*) un po' di; *a ~ of news / advice* una notizia / un consiglio; *~ by ~* poco a poco; *I'll be there in a ~* (*in a little while*) sarò lì tra poco

bit²[bɪt] *for a horse* morso *m*

bit³[bɪt] *pret* → **bite**

bitch[bɪtʃ] **1** *n dog* cagna *f*; F *woman* bastarda *f*, stronza *f* V **2** *v/i* F (*complain*) lamentarsi

bitch·y ['bɪtʃɪ] *adj* F *person, remark* velenoso

bite[baɪt] **1** *n* morso *m*; *let's have a ~* (*to eat*) mangiamo un boccone; *he didn't get a ~ of angler* non ha abboccato neanche un pesce **2** *v/t* (*pret bit, pp bitten*) mordere; *one's nails* mangiarsi **3** *v/i* (*pret bit, pp bitten*) mordere; *of fish* abboccare

bit·ten ['bɪtn] *pp* → **bite**

bit·ter ['bɪtə(r)] **1** *adj taste* amaro; *person* amareggiato; *weather* gelido; *argument* aspro **2** *n beer* birra *f* amara

bit·ter·ly ['bɪtəlɪ] *adv resent* profondamente; *~ cold* gelido

bi·zarre [bɪ'zɑː(r)] *adj* bizzarro

blab [blæb] *v/i* (*pret & pp -bed*) F spifferare F

blab·ber·mouth ['blæbəmaʊθ] F spione *m*, -a *f*

black [blæk] **1** *adj also fig* nero; *person* negro, nero; *tea* senza latte **2** *n* (*colour*) nero *m*; (*person*) nero *m*, -a *f*; *in the ~* FIN in attivo; *in ~ and white fig* nero su bianco

♦ **black out** *v/i* svenire

'**black·ber·ry** mora *f* di rovo; '**black·bird** merlo *m*; '**black·board** lavagna *f*; **black 'box** scatola *f* nera; **black e'con·o·my** economia *f* sommersa

black·en ['blækn] *v/t fig: person's name* infangare

black 'eye occhio *m* nero; '**black·head** punto *m* nero, comedone *m*; **black 'ice** ghiaccio *m* (sulla strada); '**black·list 1** *n* lista *f* nera **2** *v/t* mettere sulla lista nera; '**black·mail 1** *n also fig* ricatto *m* **2** *v/t* ricattare; '**black·mail·er** ricattatore *m*, -trice

f; **black 'mar·ket** mercato *m* nero

black·ness ['blæknɪs] *of night* oscurità *f inv*

'**black·out** ELEC black-out *m inv*; MED svenimento *m*

black 'pud·ding *sanguinaccio m*

'**black·smith** fabbro *m* ferraio

blad·der ['blædə(r)] vescica *f*

blade [bleɪd] *of knife, sword* lama *f*; *of helicopter* pala *f*; *of grass* filo *m*

blame [bleɪm] **1** *n* colpa *f*; (*responsibility*) responsabilità *f inv* **2** *v/t* biasimare; *~ s.o. for sth* ritenere qu responsabile di qc

bland [blænd] *adj smile, answer* insulso; *food* insipido

blank [blæŋk] **1** *adj* (*not written on*) bianco; *tape* vergine; *look* vuoto **2** *n* (*empty space*) spazio *m*; *my mind's a ~* ho la testa vuota

blank 'check *Am*, **blank 'cheque** assegno *m* in bianco

blan·ket ['blæŋkɪt] *n also fig* coperta *f*

blare [bleə(r)] *v/i* suonare a tutto volume

♦ **blare out 1** *v/i* strepitare **2** *v/t* rimbombare

blas·pheme [blæs'fiːm] *v/i* bestemmiare

blas·phe·my ['blæsfəmɪ] bestemmia *f*

blast [blɑːst] **1** *n* (*explosion*) esplosione *f*; (*gust*) raffica *f* **2** *v/t* far esplodere; *~!* accidenti!

♦ **blast off** *v/i of rocket* essere lanciato

blast fur·nace altoforno *m*

'**blast-off** lancio *m*

bla·tant ['bleɪtənt] *adj* palese

blaze [bleɪz] **1** *n* (*fire*) incendio *m*; *a ~ of colour* un'esplosione di colore **2** *v/i of fire* ardere

♦ **blaze away** *v/i with gun* sparare a raffica

blaz·er ['bleɪzə(r)] blazer *m inv*

bleach [bliːtʃ] **1** *n for clothes* varechina *f*; *for hair* acqua *f* ossigenata **2** *v/t hair* ossigenarsi

bleak [bliːk] *adj countryside* desolato; *weather* cupo; *future* deprimente

B

blear·y-eyed ['blɪəraɪd] *adj*: **be ~** avere lo sguardo appannato

bleat [bli:t] *v/i of sheep* belare

bled [bled] *pret & pp* → **bleed**

bleed [bli:d] (*pret & pp* **bled**) **1** *v/i* sanguinare **2** *v/t fig* dissanguare

bleed·ing ['bli:dɪŋ] *n* emorragia *f*

bleep [bli:p] **1** *n* blip *m inv* **2** *v/i* suonare **3** *v/t* (*call on pager*) chiamare sul cercapersone

bleep·er ['bli:pə(r)] (*pager*) cercapersone *m inv*

blem·ish ['blemɪʃ] **1** *n on skin* imperfezione *f*; *on fruit* ammaccatura *f* **2** *v/t reputation* infangare

blend [blend] **1** *n* miscela *f* **2** *v/t* miscelare

◆ **blend in 1** *v/i* inserirsi; (*look good*) armonizzare **2** *v/t in cooking* incorporare

blend·er ['blendə(r)] *machine* frullatore *m*

bless [bles] *v/t* benedire; (*God*) **~ you!** Dio ti benedica!; **~ you!** (*in response to sneeze*) salute!; **~ me!, ~ my soul!** santo cielo!; **be ~ed with** godere di

bless·ing ['blesɪŋ] *also fig* benedizione *f*

blew [blu:] *pret* → **blow**

blind [blaɪnd] **1** *adj* cieco; **be ~ to** *fig* non vedere **2** *n*: **the ~** i ciechi **3** *v/t* accecare

blind 'al·ley vicolo *m* cieco; **blind 'date** appuntamento *m* al buio; **'blind·fold 1** *n* benda *f* **2** *v/t* bendare (gli occhi a) **3** *adv* con gli occhi bendati

blind·ing ['blaɪndɪŋ] *adj* atroce; *light* accecante, abbagliante

blind·ly ['blaɪndlɪ] *adv feel, grope* a tastoni; *fig* ciecamente

'blind spot *in road* punto *m* cieco; (*ability that is lacking*) punto *m* debole

blink [blɪŋk] *v/i of person* sbattere le palpebre; *of light* tremolare

blink·ered ['blɪŋkəd] *adj fig* ottuso

blip [blɪp] *on radar screen* segnale *m*; *fig* battuta *f* d'arresto

bliss [blɪs] felicità *f inv*

blis·ter ['blɪstə(r)] **1** *n* vescichetta *f* **2** *v/i* formare una vescichetta; *of paint* formare delle bolle

blis·ter pack blister *m inv*

bliz·zard ['blɪzəd] bufera *f* di neve

bloat·ed ['bləʊtɪd] *adj* gonfio

blob [blɒb] *of liquid* goccia *f*

bloc [blɒk] POL blocco *m*

block [blɒk] **1** *n* blocco *m*; *in town* isolato *m*; *of shares* pacchetto *m*; (*blockage*) blocco *m*; **~ of flats** palazzo *m* (d'appartamenti) **2** *v/t* bloccare

◆ **block in** *v/t with vehicle* bloccare la macchina di; **somebody's car was blocking me** in qualcuno ha bloccato la mia macchina parcheggiando la sua

◆ **block out** *v/t light* impedire

◆ **block up** *v/t sink etc* otturare

block·ade [blɒˈkeɪd] **1** *n* blocco *m* **2** *v/t* bloccare

block·age ['blɒkɪdʒ] ingorgo *m*

block·bust·er ['blɒkbʌstə(r)] successone *m*

block 'let·ters *npl* maiuscole *fpl*

bloke [bləʊk] F tipo *m* F

blond [blɒnd] *adj* biondo

blonde [blɒnd] *n* (*woman*) bionda *f*

blood [blʌd] sangue *m*; **in cold ~** a sangue freddo

'blood al·co·hol lev·el concentrazione *f* di alcol etilico nel sangue; **'blood bank** banca *f* del sangue; **'blood bath** bagno *m* di sangue; **'blood do·nor** donatore *m*, -trice *f* di sangue; **'blood group** gruppo *m* sanguigno

blood·less ['blʌdlɪs] *adj coup* senza spargimento di sangue

'blood poi·son·ing setticemia *f*; **'blood pres·sure** pressione *f* del sangue; **'blood re·la·tion, 'blood rel·a·tive** consanguineo *m*, -a *f*; **'blood sam·ple** prelievo *m* di sangue; **'blood·shed** spargimento *m* di sangue; **'blood·shot** *adj* iniettato di sangue; **'blood·stain** macchia *f* di sangue; **'blood·stain·ed** *adj* macchiato di sangue; **'blood·stream** circolazione *f* (del sangue); **'blood**

B

test analisi *f inv* del sangue; '**blood·thirst·y** *adj* assetato di sangue; '**blood trans·fu·sion** trasfusione *f* di sangue; '**blood ves·sel** vaso *m* sanguigno

blood·y ['blʌdɪ] **1** *adj hands etc* insanguinato; *battle* sanguinoso; F maledetto; ~ *hell!* porca miseria! F; *it's a* ~ *nuisance* è una gran rottura F; *you're a* ~ *genius!* sei un geniaccio! F **2** *adv: that's* ~ *difficult / easy!* è facile / difficile da morire!; *I'm* ~ *tired* sono stanco morto; *you'll* ~ *well do it!* eccome se lo farai!

blood·y-mind·ed [blʌdɪ'maɪndɪd] *adj* F ostinato

bloom [bluːm] **1** *n* fiore *m*; *in full* ~ in piena fioritura **2** *v/i also fig* fiorire

blos·som ['blɒsəm] **1** *n* fiori *mpl* **2** *v/i also fig* fiorire

blot [blɒt] **1** *n* macchia *f* **2** *v/t* (*pret & pp -ted*) (*dry*) asciugare
♦ **blot out** *v/t memory* cancellare; *view* nascondere

blotch [blɒtʃ] chiazza *f*

blotch·y ['blɒtʃɪ] *adj* coperto di chiazze

blouse [blaʊz] camicetta *f*

blow [bləʊ] **1** *n* colpo *m* **2** *v/t* (*pret* ***blew***, *pp* ***blown***) *of wind* spingere; *smoke* soffiare; F (*spend*) sperperare; F *opportunity* mandare all'aria; ~ *a whistle* fischiare; ~ *one's nose* soffiarsi il naso **3** *v/i* (*pret* ***blew***, *pp* ***blown***) *of wind*, *person* soffiare; *of fuse* saltare; *of tyre* scoppiare; *the whistle blew for half-time* è stato fischiato l'intervallo
♦ **blow off 1** *v/t* portar via **2** *v/i* volar via
♦ **blow out 1** *v/t candle* spegnere **2** *v/i of candle* spegnersi
♦ **blow over 1** *v/t* abbattere **2** *v/i of storm, upset* calmarsi
♦ **blow up 1** *v/t with explosives* far saltare; *balloon* gonfiare; *photograph* ingrandire **2** *v/i also fig* esplodere
'**blow-dry** *v/t* (*pret & pp -ied*) asciugare col phon
'**blow job** ∨ pompino *m* ∨
blown [bləʊn] *pp* → **blow**

'**blow-out** *of tyre* scoppio *m*; F (*big meal*) abbuffata *f*
'**blow-up** *of photo* ingrandimento *m*
blue [bluː] **1** *adj* blu; F *film* porno **2** *n* blu *m inv*
blue 'chip *adj* sicuro; *company* di alto livello; **blue-'col·lar work·er** operaio *m*, -a *f*; '**blue·print** cianografia *f*; (*fig: plan*) programma *m*
blues [bluːz] *npl* MUS blues *m inv*; *have the* ~ essere giù
'**blues sing·er** cantante *m/f* blues
bluff [blʌf] **1** *n* (*deception*) bluff *m inv* **2** *v/i* bluffare
blun·der ['blʌndə(r)] **1** *n* errore *m* **2** *v/i* fare un errore
blunt [blʌnt] *adj* spuntato; *person* diretto
blunt·ly ['blʌntlɪ] *adv speak* senza mezzi termini
blur [blɜː(r)] **1** *n* massa *f* indistinta **2** *v/t* (*pret & pp -red*) offuscare
blurb [blɜːb] *on book* note *fpl* di copertina
♦ **blurt out** *v/t* spiattellare
blush [blʌʃ] **1** *n* rossore *m* **2** *v/i* arrossire
blush·er ['blʌʃə(r)] *cosmetic* fard *m inv*
blus·ter ['blʌstə(r)] *v/i* protestare
blus·ter·y ['blʌstərɪ] *adj* ventoso
BO [biː'əʊ] *abbr* (= *body odour*) odori *mpl* corporei
board [bɔːd] **1** *n* asse *f*; *for game* scacchiera *f*; *for notices* tabellone *m*; ~ (*of directors*) consiglio *m* (d'amministrazione); *on* ~ (*plane, train, boat*) a bordo; *take on* ~ *comments etc* prendere in esame; (*fully realize truth of*) accettare; *across the* ~ a tutti i livelli **2** *v/t aeroplane etc* salire a bordo di **3** *v/i of passengers* salire a bordo
♦ **board up** *v/t* chiudere con assi
♦ **board with** *v/t* essere a pensione da
board and 'lodg·ing vitto e alloggio *m*
board·er ['bɔːdə(r)] pensionante *m/f*; EDU convittore *m*, -trice *f*
'**board game** gioco *m* da tavolo
'**board·ing card** carta *f* d'imbarco;

'board·ing house pensione f;
'board·ing pass carta f d'imbarco;
'board·ing school collegio m
'board meet·ing riunione f di consiglio
'board room sala f del consiglio
boast [bəʊst] 1 n vanteria f 2 v/i vantarsi
boat [bəʊt] (small, for leisure) barca f; (ship) nave f; go by ~ andare in nave
bob¹ [bɒb] (haircut) caschetto m
bob² [bɒb] v/i (pret & pp -bed) of boat etc andare su e giù
♦ bob up v/i spuntare
'bob·sleigh, 'bob·sled bob m inv
bod·ice ['bɒdɪs] corpetto m
bod·i·ly ['bɒdɪlɪ] 1 adj corporale 2 adv eject di peso
bod·y ['bɒdɪ] corpo m; dead cadavere m; ~ of water massa f d'acqua; ~ (suit) (undergarment) body m inv
'bod·y ar·mour giubbotto m antiproiettile; 'body·guard guardia f del corpo; 'body lan·guage linguaggio m del corpo; 'bod·y o·dour odori mpl corporei; 'bod·y pierc·ing piercing m inv; 'body shop MOT carrozzeria f; 'bod·y stock·ing body m inv; 'body·work MOT carrozzeria f
bog palude f
bog·gle ['bɒgl] v/i: the mind ~s! è incredibile!
bo·gus ['bəʊgəs] adj fasullo
boil¹ [bɔɪl] n (swelling) foruncolo m
boil² [bɔɪl] 1 v/t far bollire 2 v/i bollire
♦ boil down to v/t ridursi a
♦ boil over v/i of milk etc traboccare bollendo
boil·er ['bɔɪlə(r)] caldaia f
boil·ing point ['bɔɪlɪŋ] of liquid punto m d'ebollizione; reach ~ fig perdere le staffe
bois·ter·ous ['bɔɪstərəs] adj turbolento
bold [bəʊld] 1 adj (brave) audace 2 n print neretto m; in ~ in neretto
bol·ster ['bəʊlstə(r)] v/t confidence rafforzare

bolt [bəʊlt] 1 n on door catenaccio m; (metal pin) bullone m; of lightning fulmine m; like a ~ from the blue come un fulmine a ciel sereno 2 adv: ~ upright diritto come un fuso 3 v/t (fix with bolts) fissare con bulloni; (close) chiudere col catenaccio 4 v/i (run off) scappare via
bomb [bɒm] 1 n bomba f 2 v/t bombardare; (blow up) fare esplodere una bomba in, far saltare
bom·bard [bɒm'bɑːd] v/t (attack) bombardare; ~ with questions bombardare di domande
'bomb attack attacco m dinamitardo
bomb·er ['bɒmə(r)] (aeroplane) bombardiere m; (terrorist) dinamitardo m, -a f
'bomb·er jack·et bomber m inv
'bomb·proof adj a prova di bomba; 'bomb scare allarme-bomba m; 'bomb·shell fig: news bomba f
bond [bɒnd] 1 n (tie) legame m; FIN obbligazione f; government ~s titoli mpl di Stato 2 v/i aderire
bone [bəʊn] 1 n osso m 2 v/t meat disossare; fish togliere la lisca a
bon·fire ['bɒnfaɪə(r)] falò m inv
bonk [bɒŋk] v/t & v/i P scopare P
bon·net ['bɒnɪt] of car cofano m
bo·nus ['bəʊnəs] (money) gratifica f; (something extra) vantaggio m in più
boo [buː] 1 n fischio m 2 v/t & v/i actor, speaker fischiare
boob¹ [buːb] 1 n F (mistake) errore m 2 v/i F (make a mistake) fare un errore
boob² [buːb] n F (breast) tetta f P
boo·boo ['buːbuː] n F → boob¹
book [bʊk] 1 n libro m; ~ of matches bustina f di fiammiferi 2 v/t (reserve) prenotare; of policeman multare; SP ammonire 3 v/i (reserve) prenotare
♦ book in 1 v/i prenotare una camera; (check in) registrarsi 2 v/t prenotare una camera per
'book·case scaffale m
booked up [bʊkt'ʌp] adj tutto esaurito; person occupatissimo
book·ie ['bʊkɪ] F allibratore m

B

book·ing ['bʊkɪŋ] (*reservation*) prenotazione *f*

'**book·ing clerk** impiegato *m* della biglietteria

'**book·ing of·fice** biglietteria *f*

'**book·keep·er** contabile *m/f*

'**book·keep·ing** contabilità *f inv*

book·let ['bʊklɪt] libretto *m*

'**book·mak·er** allibratore *m*

books [bʊks] *npl* (*accounts*) libri *mpl* contabili; **do the ~** tenere la contabilità; **cook the ~s** falsificare i libri contabili

'**book·sell·er** libraio *m*, -a *f*; '**book-shelf** mensola *f*; '**book·shop** libreria *f*; '**book·stall** edicola *f*; '**book to·ken** buono *m* libro

boom[1] [buːm] **1** *n* boom *m inv* **2** *v/i of business* andare a gonfie vele

boom[2] [buːm] **1** *n* (*bang*) rimbombo *m* **2** *v/i* rimbombare

boor [bʊr] zotico *m*

boor·ish ['bʊrɪʃ] *adj* da zotico

boost [buːst] **1** *n* spinta *f* **2** *v/t production, sales* incrementare; *confidence* aumentare

boot[1] [buːt] *n* stivale *m*; (*climbing ~*) scarpone *m*; *for football* scarpetta *m*

boot[2] [buːt] *of car* bagagliaio *m*

♦ **boot out** *v/t* F sbattere fuori F

♦ **boot up** *v/t & v/i* COMPUT inizializzare

booth [buːθ] *at market, fair* bancarella *f*; (*telephone ~*) cabina *f*

booze [buːz] *n* F alcolici *mpl*

booz·er ['buːzə] F (*pub*) pub *m inv*; (*person*) beone *m*, -a *f* F

'**booze-up** F bevuta *f*

bor·der ['bɔːdə(r)] **1** *n between countries* confine *m*; (*edge*) bordo *m* **2** *v/t country* confinare con

♦ **border on** *country* confinare con; (*be almost*) rasentare

'**bor·der·line** *adj* al limite; **a ~ case** un caso limite

bore[1] [bɔː(r)] *v/t hole* praticare

bore[2] [bɔː(r)] **1** *n* (*person*) persona *f* noiosa; *it's such a ~* è una seccatura **2** *v/t* annoiare

bore[3] [bɔː(r)] *pret* → **bear**[2]

bored [bɔːd] *adj* annoiato; *I'm ~* mi sto annoiando

bore·dom ['bɔːdəm] noia *f*

bor·ing ['bɔːrɪŋ] *adj* noioso

born [bɔːn] *adj*: **be ~** essere nato; **where were you ~?** dove sei nato?; **be a ~ ...** essere un ... nato

borne [bɔːn] *pp* → **bear**[2]

bor·row ['bɒrəʊ] *v/t* prendere in prestito

bos·om ['bʊzm] *of woman* seno *m*

boss [bɒs] boss *m inv*

♦ **boss about** *v/t* dare ordini a

boss·y ['bɒsɪ] *adj* prepotente

bo·tan·i·cal [bə'tænɪkl] *adj* botanico

bo·tan·ic(·al) gar·dens *npl* orto *m* botanico

bot·a·nist ['bɒtənɪst] botanico *m*, -a *f*

bot·a·ny ['bɒtənɪ] botanica *f*

botch [bɒtʃ] *v/t* fare un pasticcio con

both [bəʊθ] **1** *adj pron* entrambi, tutti *mpl* e due, tutte *fpl* e due, tutt'e due; *I know ~* (*of the*) *brothers* conosco tutt'e due i fratelli; *~ (of the) brothers were there* tutt'e due i fratelli erano lì; *~ of them* entrambi **2** *adv*: *~ my mother and I* sia mia madre che io; *is it business or pleasure?* – *~* per piacere o per affari? – tutt'e due

both·er ['bɒðə(r)] **1** *n* disturbo *m*; *it's no ~* non c'è problema **2** *v/t* (*disturb*) disturbare; (*worry*) preoccupare **3** *v/i*: *don't ~* (*you needn't do it*) non preoccuparti; *you needn't have ~ed!* non dovevi!

bot·tle ['bɒtl] **1** *n* bottiglia *f*; *for baby* biberon *m* **2** *v/t* imbottigliare

♦ **bot·tle out** *v/i* P tirarsi indietro

♦ **bottle up** *v/t feelings* reprimere

'**bot·tle bank** contenitore *m* per la raccolta del vetro

bot·tled wa·ter ['bɒtld] acqua *f* in bottiglia

'**bot·tle·neck** *n* ingorgo *m*

'**bot·tle-o·pen·er** apribottiglie *m inv*

bot·tom ['bɒtəm] **1** *adj* più basso **2** *n* fondo *m*; (*buttocks*) sedere *m*; *at the ~ of the screen* in basso sullo schermo; *at the ~ of the page / street* in fondo alla pagina / strada; *she* *started at the ~ and she's a manager now* ha cominciato dal basso e ora è dirigente

♦ **bottom out** *v/i* toccare il fondo

bot·tom 'line (*fig: financial outcome*) risultato *m* finanziario; *the ~* (*the real issue*) l'essenziale *m*

bought [bɔːt] *pret & pp* → **buy**

boul·der ['bəʊldə(r)] macigno *m*

bounce [baʊns] **1** *v/t ball* far rimbalzare **2** *v/i of ball* rimbalzare; *on sofa etc* saltare; *of cheque* essere protestato

bounc·er ['baʊnsə(r)] buttafuori *m inv*

bouncy ['baʊnsɪ] *adj ball* che rimbalza bene; *chair* molleggiato

bound¹ [baʊnd] *adj*: *be ~ to do sth* (*sure to*) dover fare per forza qc; (*obliged to*) essere obbligato a fare qc; *the train is ~ to be late* il treno sarà senz'altro in ritardo

bound² [baʊnd] *adj*: *be ~ for of ship* essere diretto a

bound³ [baʊnd] **1** *n* (*jump*) balzo *m* **2** *v/i* saltellare

bound⁴ [baʊnd] *pret & pp* → **bind**

bound·a·ry ['baʊndərɪ] confine *m*

bound·less ['baʊndlɪs] *adj* illimitato

bou·quet [buˈkeɪ] bouquet *m inv*

bour·bon ['bɜːbən] bourbon *m*

bout [baʊt] MED attacco *m*; *in boxing* incontro *m*

bou·tique [buːˈtiːk] boutique *f inv*

bo·vine spon·gi·form en·ceph·a·lo·pa·thy [bəʊvaɪnspʌdʒɪfɔːmensefəˈlɒpəθɪ] encefalite *f* spongiforme bovina

bow¹ [baʊ] **1** *n as greeting* inchino *m* **2** *v/i* inchinarsi **3** *v/t head* chinare

bow² [bəʊ] (*knot*) fiocco *m*; MUS archetto *m*

bow³ [baʊ] *of ship* prua *f*

bow·els ['baʊəlz] *npl* intestino *msg*

bowl¹ [bəʊl] (*container*) bacinella *f*; *for soup, cereal* ciotola *f*; *for cooking, salad* terrina *f*; *plastic* contenitore *m* di plastica

bowl² [bəʊl] **1** *n ball* boccia *f* **2** *v/i in bowling* lanciare

♦ **bowl over** *v/t* (*fig: astonish*) strabiliare

bowl·er ['bəʊlə(r)] (*hat*) bombetta *f*; *in cricket* lanciatore *m*

bowl·ing ['bəʊlɪŋ] bowling *m inv*

'bowl·ing al·ley pista *f* da bowling

bowls [bəʊlz] *nsg* (*game*) bocce *fpl*

bow 'tie (*cravatta f a*) farfalla *f*

box¹ [bɒks] *n container* scatola *f*; *on form* casella *f*

box² [bɒks] *v/i do boxing* fare pugilato; *he ~ed well* ha combattuto bene

box·er ['bɒksə(r)] pugile *m*

'box·er shorts *npl* boxer *mpl*

box·ing ['bɒksɪŋ] pugilato *m*, boxe *f inv*

'Box·ing Day *Br* Santo Stefano; **'box·ing glove** guantone *m* da pugile; **'box·ing match** incontro *m* di pugilato; **'box·ing ring** quadrato *m*, ring *m inv*

'box num·ber *at post office* casella *f*

'box of·fice botteghino *m*

boy [bɔɪ] *child* bambino *m*; *youth* ragazzo *m*; *son* figlio *m*

boy·cott ['bɔɪkɒt] **1** *n* boicottaggio *m* **2** *v/t* boicottare

'boy·friend ragazzo *m*

boy·ish ['bɔɪɪʃ] *adj* da ragazzo

boy'scout boy-scout *m inv*

bra [brɑː] reggiseno *m*

brace [breɪs] *on teeth* apparecchio *m* (ai denti)

brace·let ['breɪslɪt] braccialetto *m*

brac·es ['breɪsɪz] *npl* bretelle *fpl*

brack·et ['brækɪt] *for shelf* staffa *f*; *in text* parentesi *f inv*

brag [bræg] *v/i* (*pret & pp* -**ged**) vantarsi

braid [breɪd] (*trimming*) passamaneria *f*

braille [breɪl] braille *m*

brain [breɪn] cervello *m*; *use your ~* usa il cervello

'brain dead *adj* MED cerebralmente morto

brain·less ['breɪnlɪs] *adj* F deficiente

brains [breɪnz] *npl* (*intelligence*) cervello *msg*

'brain·storm *Br* attacco *m* di follia; **brain·storm·ing** ['breɪnstɔːmɪŋ]

B

brain-storming *m inv*; **'brain sur·geon** neurochirurgo *m*; **'brain surger·y** neurochirurgia *f*; **'brain tumour** tumore *m* al cervello; **'brainwash** *v/t* fare il lavaggio del cervello a; **we've been ~ed into believing that ...** ci hanno fatto il lavaggio del cervello per convincerci che ...; **'brain·wave** (*brilliant idea*) lampo *m* di genio

brain·y ['breini] *adj* F geniale

brake [breik] **1** *n* freno *m* **2** *v/i* frenare

'brake flu·id MOT liquido *m* dei freni; **'brake light** MOT fanalino *m* d'arresto; **'brake ped·al** MOT pedale *m* del freno

branch [brɑːntʃ] *n of tree* ramo *m*; *of bank, company* filiale *f*

♦ **branch off** *v/i of road* diramarsi

♦ **branch out** *v/i* diversificarsi

brand [brænd] **1** *n* marca *f*; **2** *v/t:* **be ~ed a traitor** essere tacciato di tradimento

brand 'im·age brand image *f inv*

bran·dish ['brændɪʃ] *v/t* brandire

brand 'lead·er marca *f* leader di mercato; **brand 'loy·al·ty** fedeltà *f inv* alla marca; **'brand name** marca *f*

brand-'new *adj* nuovo di zecca

bran·dy ['brændi] brandy *m inv*

brass [brɑːs] (*alloy*) ottone *m*; **the ~** MUS gli ottoni

brass 'band fanfara *f*

bras·sière [brə'zɪə(r)] *Am* reggiseno *m*

brat [bræt] *pej* marmocchio *m*

bra·va·do [brə'vɑːdəʊ] spavalderia *f*

brave [breiv] *adj* coraggioso

brave·ly ['breivli] *adv* coraggiosamente

brav·er·y ['breivəri] coraggio *m*

brawl [brɔːl] **1** *n* rissa *f* **2** *v/i* azzuffarsi

brawn·y ['brɔːni] *adj* muscoloso

Bra·zil [brə'zɪl] Brasile *m*

Bra·zil·ian [brə'zɪliən] **1** *adj* brasiliano **2** *n* brasiliano *m*, -a *f*

breach [briːtʃ] *n* (*violation*) violazione *f*; *in party* rottura *f*

breach of 'con·tract LAW inadempienza *f* di contratto

bread [bred] *n* pane *m*

'bread·crumbs *npl for cooking* pane *msg* grattato; *for bird* briciole *fpl*

'bread knife coltello *m* per il pane

breadth [bredθ] larghezza *f*

'bread·win·ner: **be the ~** mantenere la famiglia

break [breik] **1** *n also fig* rottura *f*; (*rest*) pausa *f*; **give s.o. a ~** F (*opportunity*) dare un'opportunità a qu; **take a ~** fare una pausa; **without a ~** *work, travel* senza sosta; **lucky ~** colpo di fortuna **2** *v/t* (*pret* **broke**, *pp* **broken**) *china, egg, bone* rompere; *rules, law* violare; *promise* non mantenere; *news* comunicare; *record* battere **3** *v/i* (*pret* **broke**, *pp* **broken**) *of china, egg, toy* rompersi; *of news* diffondersi; *of storm* scoppiare; *of boy's voice* cambiare

♦ **break away** *v/i* scappare; *from organization, tradition* staccarsi

♦ **break down 1** *v/i of vehicle, machine* avere un guasto; *of talks* arenarsi; *in tears* scoppiare in lacrime; (*mentally*) avere un esaurimento **2** *v/t door* buttare giù; *figures* analizzare

♦ **break even** *v/i* COM coprire le spese

♦ **break in** *v/i* (*interrupt*) interrompere; *of burglar* entrare con la forza

♦ **break off 1** *v/t* staccare; *engagement* rompere; **they've broken it off** si sono lasciati **2** *v/i* (*stop talking*) interrompersi

♦ **break out** *v/i* (*start up*) scoppiare; *of prisoners* evadere; **he broke out in a rash** gli è venuta l'orticaria

♦ **break up 1** *v/t* (*into component parts*) scomporre; *fight* far cessare **2** *v/i of ice* spaccarsi; *of couple* separarsi; *of band, meeting* sciogliersi

break·a·ble ['breikəbl] *adj* fragile

break·age ['breikɪdʒ] danni *mpl*

'break·down *of vehicle, machine* guasto *m*; *of talks* rottura *f*; (*nervous ~*) esaurimento *m* (nervoso); *of figures* analisi *f inv*

'break·down ser·vice servizio *m* di soccorso stradale

'break·down truck carro *m* attrezzi

break·'e·ven point punto *m* di rottura di pareggio

break·fast ['brekfəst] *n* colazione *f*; **have ~** fare colazione

'break·fast tel·e·vi·sion programmi *mpl* televisivi del mattino

'break-in furto *m* (con scasso); **'break·through** *in plan, negotiations* passo *m* avanti; *of science, technology* scoperta *f*; **'break-up** *of marriage, partnership* rottura *f*

breast [brest] *of woman* seno *m*

'breast·feed *v/t* (*pret* & *pp* **breastfed**) allattare

'breast·stroke nuoto *m* a rana

breath [breθ] *n* respiro *m*; **there wasn't a ~ of air** non c'era un filo d'aria; **be out of ~** essere senza fiato; **take a deep ~** fai un respiro profondo

breath·a·lyse ['breθəlaɪz] *v/t* sottoporre ad alcoltest

breath·a·lys·er® ['breθəlaɪzə(r)] alcoltest *m inv*

breathe [briːð] *v/t* & *v/i* respirare

◆ **breathe in 1** *v/i* inspirare **2** *v/t* respirare

◆ **breathe out** *v/i* espirare

breath·ing ['briːðɪŋ] *n* respiro *m*

breath·less ['breθlɪs] *adj* senza fiato

breath·less·ness ['breθlɪsnɪs] fiato *m* corto

breath·tak·ing ['breθteɪkɪŋ] *adj* mozzafiato

bred [bred] *pret* & *pp* → **breed**

breed [briːd] **1** *n* razza *f* **2** *v/t* (*pret* & *pp* **bred**) allevare; *fig* generare **3** *v/i* (*pret* & *pp* **bred**) *of animals* riprodursi

breed·er ['briːdə(r)] allevatore *m*, -trice *f*

breed·ing ['briːdɪŋ] allevamento *m*; *of person* educazione *f*

'breed·ing ground *fig* terreno *m* fertile

breeze [briːz] brezza *f*

breez·i·ly ['briːzɪlɪ] *adv fig* con disinvoltura

breez·y ['briːzɪ] *adj* ventoso; *fig* brioso

brew [bruː] **1** *v/t beer* produrre; *tea* fare **2** *v/i of storm* prepararsi; **there's trouble ~ing** ci sono guai in vista

brew·er ['bruːə(r)] produttore *m* di birra

brew·er·y ['bruːərɪ] fabbrica *f* di birra

bribe [braɪb] **1** *n* bustarella *f* **2** *v/t* corrompere

brib·er·y ['braɪbərɪ] corruzione *f*

brick [brɪk] mattone *m*

'brick·lay·er muratore *m*

brid·al suite ['braɪdl] suite *f inv* nuziale

bride [braɪd] sposa *f*

'bride·groom sposo *m*

'brides·maid damigella *f* d'onore

bridge¹ [brɪdʒ] **1** *n* ponte *m*; *of ship* ponte *m* di comando; **~ of the nose** setto *m* nasale; **2** *v/t gap* colmare

bridge² [brɪdʒ] (*card game*) bridge *m inv*

bri·dle ['braɪdl] briglia *f*

brief¹ [briːf] *adj* breve

brief² [briːf] **1** *n* (*mission*) missione *f*; (P: *lawyer*) avvocato *m* **2** *v/t*: **~ s.o. on sth** *instruct* dare istruzioni a qu su qc; *inform* mettere qu al corrente di qc

'brief·case valigetta *f*

brief·ing ['briːfɪŋ] briefing *m inv*

brief·ly ['briːflɪ] *adv* (*for a short period of time*) brevemente; (*in a few words, to sum up*) in breve

briefs [briːfs] *npl* slip *m inv*

bright [braɪt] *adj colour* vivace; *smile, future* radioso; (*sunny*) luminoso; (*intelligent*) intelligente; **~ red** rosso vivo

◆ **brighten up** ['braɪtn] **1** *v/t* ravvivare; **2** *v/i of weather* schiarirsi; *of face, person* rallegrarsi

bright·ly ['braɪtlɪ] *adv smile* in modo radioso; *shine, lit* intensamente; *coloured* in modo sgargiante

bright·ness ['braɪtnɪs] luminosità *f inv*

bril·liance ['brɪljəns] *of person*

B

genialità f inv; of colour vivacità f inv

bril·liant ['brɪljənt] adj sunshine etc sfolgorante; (very good) eccezionale; (very intelligent) brillante

brim [brɪm] of container orlo m; of hat falda f

brim·ful ['brɪmful] adj colmo

bring [brɪŋ] v/t (pret & pp brought) portare; ~ it here, will you portalo qui, per favore; can I ~ a friend? posso portare un amico?

♦ bring about v/t causare

♦ bring around v/t from a faint far rinvenire; (persuade) convincere

♦ bring back v/t (return) restituire; (re-introduce) reintrodurre; memories risvegliare

♦ bring down v/t tree, government, aeroplane abbattere; rates, inflation, price far scendere

♦ bring in v/t interest, income rendere; legislation introdurre; verdict emettere; (involve) coinvolgere

♦ bring on v/t illness provocare

♦ bring out v/t (produce) book pubblicare; new product lanciare

♦ bring to v/t from a faint far rinvenire

♦ bring up v/t child allevare; subject sollevare; (vomit) vomitare

brink [brɪŋk] also fig orlo m

brisk [brɪsk] adj person, tone spiccio; walk svelto; trade vivace

brist·les ['brɪslz] npl peli mpl

brist·ling ['brɪslɪŋ] adj: be ~ with brulicare di

Brit [brɪt] F britannico m, -a f

Brit·ain ['brɪtn] Gran Bretagna f

Brit·ish ['brɪtɪʃ] 1 adj britannico 2 n: the ~ i britannici

Brit·on ['brɪtn] britannico m, -a f

brit·tle ['brɪtl] adj fragile

broach [brəʊtʃ] v/t subject affrontare

broad [brɔːd] adj largo; (general) generale; in ~ daylight in pieno giorno

'broad·cast 1 n trasmissione f 2 v/t trasmettere

'broad·cast·er giornalista m/f radiotelevisivo, -a

'broad·cast·ing diffusione f radiotelevisiva

broad·en ['brɔːdn] 1 v/i allargarsi 2 v/t allargare

broad·ly ['brɔːdlɪ] adv: ~ speaking parlando in senso lato

broad-mind·ed [brɔːd'maɪndɪd] adj di larghe vedute

broad-mind·ed·ness [brɔːd'maɪnd-ɪdnɪs] larghezza f di vedute

broc·co·li ['brɒkəlɪ] broccoli mpl

bro·chure ['brəʊʃə(r)] dépliant m inv, opuscolo m

broke [brəʊk] 1 adj al verde; go ~ (go bankrupt) andare sul lastrico 2 pret → break

bro·ken ['brəʊkn] 1 adj rotto; English stentato; marriage fallito; she's from a ~ home i suoi sono separati 2 pp → break

bro·ken-heart·ed [brəʊkn'hɑːtɪd] adj col cuore spezzato

bro·ker ['brəʊkə(r)] mediatore m, -trice f

brol·ly ['brɒlɪ] F ombrello m

bron·chi·tis [brɒŋ'kaɪtɪs] bronchite f

bronze [brɒnz] n bronzo m

brooch [brəʊtʃ] spilla f

brood [bruːd] v/i of person rimuginare

broom [bruːm] scopa f

broth [brɒθ] (soup) minestra f; (stock) brodo m

broth·el ['brɒθl] bordello m

broth·er ['brʌðə(r)] fratello m; they're ~s sono fratelli; ~s and sisters fratelli e sorelle

'broth·er-in-law (pl brothers-in-law) cognato m

broth·er·ly ['brʌðəlɪ] adj fraterno

brought [brɔːt] pret & pp → bring

brow [braʊ] (forehead) fronte f; of hill cima f

brown [braʊn] 1 n marrone m; eyes, hair castano 2 adj marrone; (tanned) abbronzato 3 v/t in cooking rosolare 4 v/i in cooking rosolarsi

Brown·ie ['braʊnɪ] giovane esploratrice f

brown 'pa·per carta f da pacchi;

brown pa·per 'bag sacchetto *m* di carta; **'brown sug·ar** zucchero *m* non raffinato

browse [brauz] *v/i in shop* curiosare; **~ through a book** sfogliare un libro

brows·er ['brauzə(r)] COMPUT browser *m inv*

bruise [bru:z] **1** *n* livido *m*; *on fruit* ammaccatura *f* **2** *v/t person* fare un livido a; *fruit* ammaccare **3** *v/i of person* coprirsi di lividi; *of fruit* ammaccarsi

bruis·ing ['bru:zɪŋ] *adj fig* doloroso

brunch [brʌntʃ] brunch *m inv*

bru·nette [bru:'net] *n* brunetta *f*

brunt [brʌnt] *n*: **bear the ~ of ...** subire il peggio di ...

brush [brʌʃ] **1** *n* spazzola *f*; *(paint~)* pennello *m*; *(tooth~)* spazzolino *m* da denti; *(conflict)* scontro *m* **2** *v/t* spazzolare; *(touch lightly)* sfiorare; *(move away)* spostare; **~ your teeth** lavati i denti

♦**brush against** *v/t* sfiorare

♦**brush aside** *v/t* ignorare

♦**brush off** *v/t* spazzolare via; *criticism* ignorare

♦**brush up** *v/t* ripassare

'brush-off give s.o. the ~ F rispondere picche a qu F

'brush·work PAINT pennellata *f*

brusque [brusk] *adj* brusco

Brus·sels ['brʌslz] Bruxelles *f inv*

Brus·sels 'sprout cavolino *m* di Bruxelles

bru·tal ['bru:tl] *adj* brutale

bru·tal·i·ty [bru:'tælətɪ] brutalità *f inv*

bru·tal·ly ['bru:təlɪ] *adv* brutalmente

brute [bru:t] bruto *m*

brute force forza *f* bruta

BSE [bi:es'i:] *abbr* (= **bovine spongiform encephalopathy**)

bub·ble ['bʌbl] *n* bolla *f*

'bub·ble bath bagnoschiuma *m inv*; **'bub·ble gum** gomma *f* da masticare; **'bub·ble wrap** *n* involucro *m* a bolle

bub·bly ['bʌblɪ] *n* F *(champagne)* champagne *m inv*

buck[1] [bʌk] *n Am* F *(dollar)* dollaro *m*

buck[2] [bʌk] *v/i of horse* sgroppare

buck[3] [bʌk] *n*: **pass the ~** scaricare la responsabilità

buck·et ['bʌkɪt] *n* secchio *m*

'buck·et shop agenzia *f* di viaggi che pratica forti sconti

buck·le[1] ['bʌkl] **1** *n* fibbia *f* **2** *v/t belt* allacciare

buck·le[2] ['bʌkl] *v/i of wood, metal* piegarsi

♦**buck·le down** *v/i* mettersi a lavorare

bud [bʌd] *n* BOT bocciolo *m*

bud·dy ['bʌdɪ] F amico *m*, -a *f*

budge [bʌdʒ] **1** *v/t* smuovere; *(make reconsider)* far cambiare idea a **2** *v/i* muoversi; *(change one's mind)* cambiare idea

bud·ger·i·gar ['bʌdʒərɪgɑ:(r)] pappagallino *m*

bud·get ['bʌdʒɪt] **1** *n* budget *m inv*; *of company* bilancio *m* preventivo; *of state* bilancio *m* dello Stato; **I'm on a ~** devo stare attento ai soldi **2** *v/i* prevedere le spese

♦**budget for** *v/t* preventivare

bud·gie ['bʌdʒɪ] F pappagallino *m*

buff[1] [bʌf] *adj (colour)* beige *inv*

buff[2] [bʌf] *n* appassionato *m*, -a *f*

buf·fa·lo ['bʌfələʊ] bufalo *m*

buff·er ['bʌfə(r)] RAIL respingente *m*; COMPUT buffer *m inv*; *fig* cuscinetto *m*

buf·fet[1] ['bufeɪ] *n (meal)* buffet *m inv*

buf·fet[2] ['bʌfɪt] *v/t of wind* sballottare

bug [bʌg] **1** *n (insect)* insetto *m*; *(virus)* virus *m inv*; *(spying device)* microspia *f*; COMPUT bug *m inv* **2** *v/t (pret & pp -ged) room* installare microspie in; *telephone* mettere sotto controllo; F *(annoy)* seccare

bug·gy ['bʌgɪ] *for baby* passeggino *m*

build [bɪld] **1** *n of person* corporatura *f* **2** *v/t (pret & pp built)* costruire

♦**build up 1** *v/t relationship* consolidare; *collection* mettere insieme **2** *v/i of tension, traffic* aumentare; **build up one's strength** rimettersi in forze

'build·er ['bɪldə(r)] *person* muratore

B

m; *company* impresario *m* edile
'build·ing ['bɪldɪŋ] edificio *m*, palazzo *m*; (*activity*) costruzione *f*
'build·ing blocks *npl for child*
mattoncini *mpl*; **'build·ing site** cantiere *m* edile; **'build·ing so·ci·e·ty**
Br istituto *m* di credito immobiliare;
'build·ing trade edilizia *f*
'build·up *of traffic, pressure* aumento
m; *of arms, forces* ammassamento *m*;
(*publicity*) pubblicità *f inv*
built [bɪlt] *pret & pp* → **build**
built-in ['bɪltɪn] *adj wardrobe* a muro;
flash incorporato
built-up 'ar·e·a abitato *m*
bulb [bʌlb] BOT bulbo *m*; (*light* ~)
lampadina *f*
bulge [bʌldʒ] **1** *n* rigonfiamento *m*
2 *v/i* sporgere
bu·lim·i·a [buˈlɪmɪə] bulimia *f*
bulk [bʌlk] grosso *m*; **in ~** in grande
quantità; *wholesale* all'ingrosso
bulk·y ['bʌlkɪ] *adj* voluminoso
bull [bʊl] toro *m*
bull·doze ['bʊldəʊz] *v/t* (*demolish*)
abbattere con il bulldozer; ~ **s.o.
into sth** *fig* costringere qu a fare qc
bull·doz·er ['bʊldəʊzə(r)] bulldozer
m inv
bul·let ['bʊlɪt] proiettile *m*, pallottola
f
bul·le·tin ['bʊlɪtɪn] bollettino *m*
'bul·le·tin board COMPUT bulletin
board *m inv*; *Am: on wall* bacheca *f*
'bul·let-proof *adj* a prova di proiettile
'bull mar·ket FIN mercato *m* in ascesa
'bull's-eye centro *m* del bersaglio;
hit the ~ fare centro
'bull·shit 1 *n* V stronzate *fpl* V **2** *v/i*
(*pret & pp* **-ted**) V dire stronzate V
bul·ly ['bʊlɪ] **1** *n* prepotente *m/f* **2** *v/t*
(*pret & pp* **-ied**) tiranneggiare
bul·ly·ing ['bʊlɪɪŋ] *n* prepotenze *fpl*
bum [bʌm] **1** *n* F *worthless person*
mezza calzetta *f* F; (*Br: bottom*) sedere *m*; (*Am: tramp*) barbone *m*
2 *adj* F (*useless*) del piffero **3** *v/t*
(*pret & pp* **-med**) F *cigarette etc*
scroccare

♦**bum around, bum about** *v/i* F
(*travel*) vagabondare; (*be lazy*)
oziare
'bum·bag F marsupio *m*
bum·ble·bee ['bʌmblbiː] bombo *m*
bump [bʌmp] **1** *n* (*swelling*) gonfiore
m; (*lump*) bernoccolo *m*; *on road*
cunetta *f*; **get a ~ on the head** prendere un colpo in testa **2** *v/t* battere
♦**bump into** *v/t table* battere contro;
(*meet*) incontrare
♦**bump off** *v/t* F (*murder*) far fuori
♦**bump up** *v/t* F (*prices*) aumentare
bump·er ['bʌmpə(r)] **1** *n* MOT paraurti *m inv*; **the traffic was ~ to ~**
c'era una coda di macchine **2** *adj*
(*extremely good*) eccezionale
bumph [bʌmf] *Br* F scartoffie *fpl*
'bump-start *v/t car* mettere in moto
a spinte; (*fig: economy*) dare una
spinta a
bump·y ['bʌmpɪ] *adj road* accidentato; *flight* movimentato
bun [bʌn] *hairstyle* chignon *m inv*; *for
eating* panino *m* dolce
bunch [bʌntʃ] *of people* gruppo *m*; *of
keys, flowers* mazzo *m*; **a ~ of grapes**
un grappolo d'uva
bun·dle ['bʌndl] *of clothes* fagotto *m*;
of wood fascina *f*
♦**bundle up** *v/t* fare un fagotto di;
(*dress warmly*) coprire bene
bung [bʌŋ] *v/t* F buttare
bun·ga·low ['bʌŋgələʊ] bungalow *m
inv*
bun·gee jump·ing ['bʌndʒɪdʒʌmp-
ɪŋ] salto *m* con l'elastico
bun·gle ['bʌŋgl] *v/t* pasticciare
bunk [bʌŋk] cuccetta *f*
'bunk beds *npl* letti *mpl* a castello
buoy [bɔɪ] *n* NAUT boa *f*
buoy·ant ['bɔɪənt] *adj* (*cheerful*) allegro; *fig: economy* sostenuto
bur·den ['bɜːdn] **1** *n also fig* peso *m*
2 *v/t*: ~ **s.o. with sth** *fig* opprimere
qu con qc
bur·eau ['bjʊərəʊ] (*office*) ufficio *m*
bu·reauc·ra·cy [bjʊəˈrɒkrəsɪ] burocrazia *f*
bu·reau·crat ['bjʊərəkræt] burocrate *m/f*

bu·reau·crat·ic [bjʊərə'krætɪk] adj burocratico

burg·er ['bɜːɡə(r)] hamburger m inv

bur·glar ['bɜːɡlə(r)] ladro m

'bur·glar a·larm antifurto m

bur·glar·ize ['bɜːɡləraɪz] v/t Am svaligiare

bur·glar·y ['bɜːɡlərɪ] furto m (con scasso)

bur·gle ['bɜːɡl] v/t svaligiare

bur·i·al ['berɪəl] sepoltura f

bur·ly ['bɜːlɪ] adj robusto

burn [bɜːn] **1** n bruciatura f; superficial scottatura f; very serious ustione f **2** v/t (pret & pp **burnt**) bruciare; of sun scottare **3** v/i (pret & pp **burnt**) ardere; of house bruciare; of toast bruciarsi; (get sunburnt) scottarsi, bruciarsi; **~ to death** morire carbonizzato

♦ **burn down 1** v/t dare alle fiamme **2** v/i essere distrutto dal fuoco

♦ **burn out** v/t: **burn o.s. out** esaurirsi; **a burned-out car** un'auto bruciata

burnt [bɜːnt] pret & pp → **burn**

burp [bɜːp] **1** n rutto m **2** v/i ruttare **3** v/t baby far fare il ruttino a

burst [bɜːst] **1** n in water pipe rottura f; of gunfire raffica f; **a ~ of energy** un'esplosione d'energia **2** adj tyre bucato **3** v/t (pret & pp **burst**) balloon far scoppiare **4** v/i (pret & pp **burst**) of balloon, tyre scoppiare; **~ into a room** irrompere in una stanza; **~ into tears** scoppiare in lacrime; **~ out laughing** scoppiare a ridere

bur·y ['berɪ] v/t (pret & pp **-ied**) seppellire; hide nascondere; **~ o.s. in work** immergersi nel lavoro

bus [bʌs] **1** n autobus m inv; (long distance) pullman m inv **2** v/t (pret & pp **-sed**) trasportare in autobus

'bus driv·er autista m/f di autobus

bush [bʊʃ] (plant) cespuglio m; (land) boscaglia f

bushed [bʊʃt] adj F (tired) distrutto

bush·y ['bʊʃɪ] adj eyebrows irsuto

busi·ness ['bɪznɪs] (trade) affari mpl; (company) impresa f; (work) lavoro

m; (affair, matter) faccenda f; (as subject of study) economia f aziendale; **in the insurance ~ (sector)** nel campo delle assicurazioni; **on ~** per affari; **that's none of your ~!, mind your own ~!** fatti gli affari tuoi!

'busi·ness card biglietto m da visita (della ditta); **'busi·ness class** business class f inv; **'busi·ness hours** npl orario msg di apertura; **busi·ness·like** ['bɪznɪslaɪk] adj efficiente; **'busi·ness lunch** pranzo m d'affari; **'busi·ness·man** uomo m d'affari; **'busi·ness meet·ing** riunione f d'affari; **'busi·ness school** istituto m commerciale; **'busi·ness stud·ies** nsg (course) economia f aziendale; **'busi·ness trip** viaggio m d'affari; **'busi·ness·wom·an** donna f d'affari

busk·er ['bʌskə(r)] musicista m/f ambulante

'bus lane corsia f riservata (ai mezzi pubblici); **'bus shel·ter** pensilina f (dell'autobus); **'bus sta·tion** autostazione f; **'bus stop** fermata f dell'autobus

bust¹ [bʌst] n of woman petto m

bust² [bʌst] **1** adj F (broken) scassato; **go ~** fallire v/t scassare

'bus tick·et biglietto m dell'autobus

♦ **bus·tle about** ['bʌsl] v/i affaccendarsi

'bust-up F rottura f

bust·y ['bʌstɪ] adj prosperoso

bus·y ['bɪzɪ] **1** adj occupato; day intenso; street animato; shop, restaurant affollato; TELEC occupato; **be ~ doing sth** essere occupato a fare qc; **I'm ~ talking to Gran** sto parlando con la nonna **2** v/t (pret & pp **-ied**): **~ o.s. with** tenersi occupato con

'bus·y·bod·y impiccione m, -a f

but [bʌt] unstressed [bət] **1** conj ma; **~ then (again)** d'altra parte **2** prep: **all ~ him** tutti tranne lui; **the last ~ one** il penultimo; **the next ~ one** il secondo; **~ for you** se non fosse per te; **nothing ~ the best** solo il meglio

butch·er ['bʊtʃə(r)] macellaio m, -a f

butch·er's ['bʊtʃəz] macelleria f

B

butt [bʌt] **1** n of cigarette mozzicone m; of joke bersaglio m; Am P (backside) culo m P **2** v/t dare una testata a; of goat, bull dare una cornata a
♦ **butt in** v/i interrompere
but·ter ['bʌtə(r)] **1** n burro m **2** v/t imburrare
♦ **butter up** v/t F arruffianarsi F
'**but·ter·cup** ranuncolo m
'**but·ter·fly** also swimming farfalla f
but·tocks ['bʌtəks] npl natiche fpl
but·ton ['bʌtn] **1** n bottone m; on machine pulsante m **2** v/t abbottonare
♦ **button up** → **button**
'**but·ton·hole 1** n in suit occhiello m **2** v/t attaccare un bottone a
but·tress ['bʌtrəs] contrafforte m
bux·om ['bʌksəm] adj formoso
buy [baɪ] **1** n acquisto m **2** v/t (pret & pp **bought**) comprare; **can I ~ you a drink?** posso offrirti da bere?; **£5 doesn't ~ much** con 5 sterline non si compra granché
♦ **buy off** v/t (bribe) comprare
♦ **buy out** v/t COM rilevare
♦ **buy up** v/t accaparrarsi
buy·er ['baɪə(r)] acquirente m/f; for department store, supermarket buyer m inv
buzz [bʌz] **1** n ronzio m; F (thrill) emozione f **2** v/i of insect ronzare; with buzzer suonare **3** v/t with

buzzer chiamare
♦ **buzz off** v/i F levarsi di torno F
buzz·er ['bʌzə(r)] cicalino m
by [baɪ] **1** prep agency da; (near, next to) vicino a, accanto a; (no later than) entro, per; (past) davanti a; (mode of transport) in; **side ~ side** fianco a fianco; **~ day / night** di giorno / notte; **~ bus / train** in autobus / treno; **~ the hour / ton** a ore / tonnellate; **~ my watch** secondo il mio orologio; **a book ~ …** un libro di …; **murdered ~ her husband** assassinata dal marito; **~ o.s.** da solo; **pay ~ cheque** pagare con un assegno; **~ a couple of minutes** per pochi minuti; **2 ~ 4** (measurement) 2 per 4; **this time tomorrow** domani a quest'ora **2** adv: **~ and ~** (soon) tra breve
bye(-bye) [baɪ] ciao
'**by-e·lec·tion** elezione f straordinaria di un parlamentare; **by·gone** ['baɪgɒn] **1** n: **let ~s be ~s** metterci una pietra sopra **2** adj: **in ~ days** nei giorni andati; '**by·pass 1** n (road) circonvallazione f; MED by-pass m inv **2** v/t aggirare; '**by-prod·uct** sottoprodotto m; **by·stand·er** ['baɪstændə(r)] astante m/f
byte [baɪt] byte m inv
'**by·word** n: **be a ~ for** essere sinonimo di

C

cab [kæb] (taxi) taxi m inv; of truck cabina f; **~ driver** tassista m/f
cab·a·ret ['kæbəreɪ] spettacolo m di cabaret
cab·bage ['kæbɪdʒ] cavolo m
cab·in ['kæbɪn] of plane, ship cabina f
'**cab·in at·tend·ant** assistente m/f di volo
'**cab·in crew** equipaggio m di volo
cab·i·net ['kæbɪnɪt] armadietto m; POL Consiglio m dei ministri; **display ~** vetrina f; **drinks ~** mobile m bar
'**cab·i·net mak·er** ebanista m/f;
'**cab·i·net meet·ing** riunione f del Consiglio dei ministri; '**cab·i·net min·is·ter** membro m del Consiglio dei ministri; '**cab·i·net re·shuf·fle**

rimpasto *m* del governo

ca·ble ['keɪbl] ELEC, *for securing* cavo *m*; ~ (*TV*) tv *f* via cavo

'**ca·ble car** cabina *f* (di funivia)

'**ca·ble tel·e·vi·sion** televisione *f* via cavo

cac·tus ['kæktəs] cactus *m inv*

CAD-CAM ['kædkæm] *abbr* (= *computer assisted design-computer assisted manufacture*) CAD-CAM *m*

cad·die ['kædɪ] **1** *n in golf* portamazze *m inv* **2** *v/i* portare le mazze

ca·det [kə'det] cadetto *m*

cadge [kædʒ] *v/t:* ~ **sth from s.o.** scroccare qc a qu

Cae·sar·e·an [sɪ'zeərɪən] *n* parto *m* cesareo

caf·é ['kæfeɪ] caffè *m inv*, bar *m*

caf·e·te·ri·a [kæfə'tɪərɪə] tavola *f* calda

caf·feine ['kæfiːn] caffeina *f*

cage [keɪdʒ] gabbia *f*

ca·gey ['keɪdʒɪ] *adj* evasivo

ca·hoots [kə'huːts] F: *be in* ~ *with* essere in combutta con

ca·jole [kə'dʒəʊl] *v/t* convincere con le lusinghe

cake [keɪk] **1** *n* dolce *m*, torta *f*; *be a piece of* ~ F essere un gioco da ragazzi **2** *v/i of mud, blood* indurirsi

ca·lam·i·ty [kə'læmətɪ] calamità *f inv*

cal·ci·um ['kælsɪəm] calcio *m*

cal·cu·late ['kælkjuleɪt] *v/t* calcolare

cal·cu·lat·ing ['kælkjuleɪtɪŋ] *adj* calcolatore

cal·cu·la·tion [kælkju'leɪʃn] calcolo *m*

cal·cu·la·tor ['kælkjuleɪtə(r)] calcolatrice *f*

cal·en·dar ['kælɪndə(r)] calendario *m*

calf[1] [kɑːf] (*pl calves* [kɑːvz]) *young cow* vitello *m*

calf[2] [kɑːf] (*pl calves* [kɑːvz]) *of leg* polpaccio *m*

'**calf·skin** *n* vitello *m*

cal·i·ber *Am*, **cal·i·bre** ['kælɪbə(r)] *of gun* calibro *m*; *a man of his* ~ un uomo del suo calibro

call [kɔːl] **1** *n* (*phone* ~) telefonata *f*; (*shout*) grido *m*; (*demand*) richiesta *f*; (*visit*) visita *f*; *be on* ~ *of doctor* essere di guardia; *pay s.o. a* ~ far visita a qu **2** *v/t on phone* chiamare; (*summon*) chiamare; (*shout*) gridare; (*describe as*) definire; *meeting, election* indire, convocare; *what have they* ~*ed the baby?* come hanno chiamato il bambino?; ~ *s.o. as a witness* citare qu a testimoniare; ~ *a flight* annunciare un volo; ~ *s.o. names* dare dei titoli a qu **3** *v/i on phone* chiamare; (*shout*) gridare; (*visit*) passare

♦ **call at** (*stop at*) passare da

♦ **call back 1** *v/t also* TELEC richiamare **2** *v/i on phone* richiamare; (*make another visit*) ripassare

♦ **call for** *v/t* (*collect*) passare a prendere; (*demand*) reclamare; (*require*) richiedere

♦ **call in 1** *v/t* (*summon*) far venire **2** *v/i on phone* chiamare; *call in sick* chiamare per dire di essere ammalato

♦ **call off** *v/t strike* revocare; *wedding, appointment* disdire

♦ **call on** *v/t* (*urge*) sollecitare; (*visit*) visitare

♦ **call out** *v/t* (*shout*) chiamare ad alta voce; (*summon*) chiamare

♦ **call up** *v/t on phone* chiamare; COMPUT aprire

'**call box** cabina *f* telefonica

'**call cen·tre** centro *m* chiamate

call·er ['kɔːlə(r)] *on phone* persona *f* che ha chiamato; (*visitor*) visitatore *m*, -trice *f*

'**call girl** squillo *f inv*

cal·lous ['kæləs] *adj* freddo, insensibile

cal·lous·ly ['kæləslɪ] *adv* freddamente, insensibilmente

cal·lous·ness ['kæləsnɪs] freddezza *f*, insensibilità *f*

calm [kɑːm] **1** *adj* calmo **2** *n* calma *f*

♦ **calm down 1** *v/t* calmare **2** *v/i* calmarsi

calm·ly ['kɑːmlɪ] *adv* con calma

cal·o·rie ['kælərɪ] caloria *f*

cam·cor·der ['kæmkɔːdə(r)] video-camera *f*

came [keɪm] *pret* → **come**

cam·e·ra ['kæmərə] macchina *f* fotografica; (*video* ~) videocamera *f*; (*television* ~) telecamera *f*

'cam·e·ra·man cameraman *m inv*

cam·ou·flage ['kæməflɑːʒ] **1** *n* mimetizzazione *f*; *of soldiers* tuta *f* mimetica **2** *v/t* mimetizzare; *fig* mascherare

camp [kæmp] **1** *n* campo *m*; **make** ~ accamparsi **2** *v/i* accamparsi

cam·paign [kæm'peɪn] **1** *n* campagna *f* **2** *v/i* militare

cam·paign·er [kæm'peɪnə(r)] militante *m/f*

camp·er ['kæmpə(r)] *person* campeggiatore *m*, -trice *f*; *vehicle* camper *m inv*

camp·ing ['kæmpɪŋ] campeggio *m*; **go** ~ andare in campeggio

'camp·site camping *m inv*, campeggio *m*

cam·pus ['kæmpəs] campus *m inv*

can¹ [kæn] *unstressed* [kən] *v/aux* (*pret* **could**) ◊ (*ability*) potere; ~ **you hear me?** mi senti?; **I can't see** non vedo; ~ **you speak French?** sai parlare il francese?; ~ **he call me back?** mi può richiamare?; **as fast as you** ~ più veloce che puoi; **as well as you** ~ meglio che puoi ◊ (*permission*) potere; ~ **I help you?** posso aiutarla?; ~ **you help me?** mi può aiutare?; ~ **I have a beer / coffee?** posso avere una birra / un caffè?; **that can't be right** non può essere giusto

can² [kæn] **1** *n for drinks* lattina *f*; *for food* scatola *f* **2** *v/t* (*pret & pp* **-ned**) inscatolare

Can·a·da ['kænədə] Canada *m*

Ca·na·di·an [kə'neɪdɪən] **1** *adj* canadese **2** *n* canadese *m/f*

ca·nal [kə'næl] (*waterway*) canale *m*

ca·nar·y [kə'neərɪ] canarino *m*

can·cel ['kænsl] *v/t* annullare

can·cel·la·tion [kænsə'leɪʃn] annullamento *m*

can·cel·la·tion fee penalità *f* (per annullamento)

can·cer ['kænsə(r)] cancro *m*

Can·cer ['kænsə(r)] ASTR Cancro *m*

can·cer·ous ['kænsərəs] *adj* canceroso

c&f *abbr* (= **cost and freight**) c&f

can·did ['kændɪd] *adj* franco

can·di·da·cy ['kændɪdəsɪ] candidatura *f*

can·di·date ['kændɪdət] candidato *m*, -a *f*

can·did·ly ['kændɪdlɪ] *adv* francamente

can·died ['kændiːd] *adj* candito

can·dle ['kændl] candela *f*

'can·dle·stick portacandele *m inv*

can·dor *Am*, **can·dour** ['kændə(r)] franchezza *f*

can·dy ['kændɪ] *Am* (*sweet*) caramella *f*; (*sweets*) dolciumi *mpl*

can·dy·floss ['kændɪflɒs] zucchero *m* filato

cane [keɪn] canna *f*; *for walking* bastone *m*

can·is·ter ['kænɪstə(r)] barattolo *m*; *spray* bombola *f*

can·na·bis ['kænəbɪs] hashish *m*

canned [kænd] *adj fruit, tomatoes* in scatola; (*recorded*) registrato

can·ni·bal·ize ['kænɪbəlaɪz] *v/t* riciclare parti di

can·not ['kænɒt] → **can¹**

can·ny ['kænɪ] *adj* (*astute*) arguto

ca·noe [kə'nuː] canoa *f*

'can o·pen·er apriscatole *m inv*

can't [kɑːnt] → **can¹**

can·tan·ker·ous [kæn'tæŋkərəs] *adj* irascibile

can·teen [kæn'tiːn] *in factory* mensa *f*

can·vas ['kænvəs] tela *f*

can·vass ['kænvəs] **1** *v/t* (*seek opinion of*) fare un sondaggio tra **2** *v/i* POL fare propaganda elettorale

can·yon ['kænjən] canyon *m inv*

cap [kæp] (*hat*) berretto *m*; *of bottle, jar* tappo *m*; *of pen* cappuccio *m*; *for lens* coperchio *m*

ca·pa·bil·i·ty [keɪpə'bɪlətɪ] *of person* capacità *f inv*; MIL potenziale *m*

care for

ca·pa·ble ['keɪpəbl] *adj* (*efficient*) capace; *be ~ of* essere capace di

ca·pac·i·ty [kə'pæsɪtɪ] capacità *f inv*; *of car engine* potenza *f*; *of factory* capacità *f inv* produttiva; *in my ~ as ...* in qualità di ...

cap·i·tal ['kæpɪtl] *n of country* capitale *f*; (*capital letter*) maiuscola *f*; *money* capitale *m*

cap·i·tal ex'pend·i·ture spese *fpl* in conto capitale

cap·i·tal 'gains tax imposta *f* sui redditi di capitale

cap·i·tal 'growth aumento *m* del capitale

cap·i·tal·is·m ['kæpɪtəlɪzm] capitalismo *m*

cap·i·tal·ist ['kæpɪtəlɪst] **1** *adj* capitalista **2** *n* capitalista *m/f*

♦**cap·i·tal·ize on** ['kæpɪtəlaɪz] *v/t* trarre vantaggio da

cap·i·tal 'let·ter lettera *f* maiuscola

cap·i·tal 'pun·ish·ment pena *f* capitale

ca·pit·u·late [kə'pɪtjʊleɪt] *v/i* capitolare

ca·pit·u·la·tion [kæpɪtjʊ'leɪʃn] capitolazione *f*

Cap·ri·corn ['kæprɪkɔːn] ASTR Capricorno *m*

cap·size [kæp'saɪz] **1** *v/i* ribaltarsi **2** *v/t* far ribaltare

cap·sule ['kæpsjul] *of medicine* cachet *m inv*; (*space ~*) capsula *f*

cap·tain ['kæptɪn] *n* capitano *m*

cap·tion ['kæpʃn] *n* didascalia *f*

cap·ti·vate ['kæptɪveɪt] *v/t* affascinare

cap·tive ['kæptɪv] *adj* prigioniero

cap·tiv·i·ty [kæp'tɪvətɪ] cattività *f*

cap·ture ['kæptʃə(r)] **1** *n of building, city* occupazione *f*, *of city* presa *f*; *of criminal, animal* cattura *f* **2** *v/t person, animal* catturare; *city, building* occupare; *city* prendere; *market share* conquistare; (*portray*) cogliere

car [kɑː(r)] macchina *f*, auto *f inv*; *of train* vagone *m*; *by ~* in macchina

ca·rafe [kə'ræf] caraffa *f*

car·a·mel ['kærəmel] *sweet* caramel-

la *f* morbida

car·at ['kærət] carato *m*

car·a·van ['kærəvæn] roulotte *f inv*

'car·a·van site campeggio *m* per roulotte

car·bo·hy·drate [kɑːbə'haɪdreɪt] carboidrato *m*

'car bomb autobomba *f*

car·bon mon·ox·ide [kɑːbənmɒn'ɒksaɪd] monossido *m* di carbonio

car·bu·ret·or [kɑːbjʊ'retə(r)] carburatore *m*

car·cass ['kɑːkəs] carcassa *f*

car·cin·o·gen ['kɑːsɪnədʒen] cancerogeno *m*

car·cin·o·gen·ic [kɑːsɪnə'dʒenɪk] *adj* cancerogeno

card [kɑːd] *to mark special occasion* biglietto *m*; (*post~*) cartolina *f*; (*business ~*) biglietto *m* (da visita); (*playing ~*) carta *f*; COMPUT scheda *f*; *material* cartoncino *m*

'card·board cartone *m*

card·board 'box scatola *f* di cartone

car·di·ac ['kɑːdɪæk] *adj* cardiaco

car·di·ac ar'rest arresto *m* cardiaco

car·di·gan ['kɑːdɪgən] cardigan *m inv*

car·di·nal ['kɑːdɪnl] *n* REL cardinale *m*

'card in·dex schedario *m*; **'card key** tessera *f* magnetica; **'card phone** telefono *m* a scheda

care [keə(r)] **1** *n of baby, pet* cure *fpl*; *of the elderly* assistenza *f*; *of the sick* cura *f*; (*worry*) preoccupazione *f*; *take ~* (*be cautious*) fare attenzione; *take ~* (*of yourself*)! (*goodbye*) stammi bene; *take ~ of* (*look after*: *baby, dog*) prendersi cura di; *tool, house, garden* tenere bene; (*deal with*) occuparsi di; (*handle*) *with ~!* *on label* maneggiare con cura **2** *v/i* interessarsi; *I don't ~!* non m'importa; *I couldn't ~ less* non potrebbe importarmene di meno

care for ♦ *c/o*

♦ **care about** *v/t* interessarsi a

♦ **care for** *v/t* (*look after*) prendersi cura di; *I don't care for your tone* non mi piace il tuo tono; *would you* *care for a tea?* *fml* gradirebbe un tè?

ca·reer [kə'rɪə(r)] (*profession*) carriera *f*; (*path through life*) vita *f*

ca·reers of·fi·cer consulente *m/f* professionale

'care·free *adj* spensierato

care·ful ['keəful] *adj* (*cautious*) attento; (*thorough*) attento; (**be**) **~!** (stai) attento

care·ful·ly ['keəfulɪ] *adv* con cautela

care·less ['keəlɪs] *adj* incurante; *driver, worker* sbadato; *work* fatto senza attenzione; *error* di disattenzione; **you are so ~!** sei così sbadato!

care·less·ly ['keəlɪslɪ] *adv* senza cura

carer ['keərə(r)] accompagnatore *m*, -trice *f*

ca·ress [kə'res] **1** *n* carezza *f* **2** *v/t* accarezzare

care·tak·er ['keəteɪkə(r)] custode *m/f*

'care·worn *adj* provato

'car fer·ry traghetto *m* (per le macchine)

car·go ['kɑːgəʊ] carico *m*

'car hire autonoleggio *m*

'car hire com·pa·ny compagnia *f* di autonoleggio

car·i·ca·ture ['kærɪkətjʊə(r)] *n* caricatura *f*

car·ing ['keərɪŋ] *adj* premuroso

'car me·chan·ic meccanico *m* per auto

car·nage ['kɑːnɪdʒ] carneficina *f*

car·na·tion [kɑː'neɪʃn] garofano *m*

car·ni·val ['kɑːnɪvl] carnevale *m*

car·ol ['kærəl] *n* canzone *f* di Natale

car·ou·sel [kærə'sel] *at airport* nastro *m* trasportatore; *for slide projector* carrello *m*

'car park parcheggio *m*

'car park at·tend·ant parcheggiatore *m*, -trice *f*

car·pen·ter ['kɑːpɪntə(r)] falegname *m*

car·pet ['kɑːpɪt] tappeto *m*; (*fitted ~*) moquette *f inv*

'car phone telefono *m* da automobi-

le; **'car·pool** *n* uso *m* condiviso della macchina dell'uno o dell'altro tra un gruppo di persone; **'car port** posto *m* auto coperto; **car 'ra·di·o** autoradio *f inv*

car·riage ['kærɪdʒ] carrozza *f*; COM trasporto *m*

car·ri·er ['kærɪə(r)] (*company*) compagnia *f* di trasporto; *of disease* portatore *m* sano, portatrice *f* sana

'car·ri·er bag sacchetto *m*

car·rot ['kærət] carota *f*

car·ry ['kærɪ] (*pret & pp -ied*) **1** *v/t* portare; *of pregnant woman* portare in grembo; *of ship, plane, bus etc* trasportare; *proposal* approvare; **get carried away** farsi prendere dall'entusiasmo **2** *v/i* of sound sentirsi

♦ **carry on 1** *v/i* (*continue*) andare avanti, continuare; (*make a fuss*) fare storie; (*have an affair*) avere una storia **2** *v/t* (*conduct*) portare avanti

♦ **carry out** *v/t survey etc* effettuare; *orders etc* eseguire

'car·ry·cot porte-enfant *m inv*

'car seat *for child* seggiolino *m* per auto

cart [kɑːt] carretto *m*

car·tel [kɑː'tel] cartello *m*

car·ton ['kɑːtn] *for storage, transport* cartone *m*; *of cigarettes* stecca *f*

car·toon [kɑː'tuːn] *in newspaper, magazine* fumetto *m*; *on TV, film* cartone *m* animato

car·toon·ist [kɑː'tuːnɪst] *for newspaper etc* vignettista *m/f*

car·tridge ['kɑːtrɪdʒ] *for gun, printer* cartuccia *f*

carve [kɑːv] *v/t meat* tagliare; *wood* intagliare

carv·ing ['kɑːvɪŋ] *figure* scultura *f*

'car wash lavaggio *m* per auto

case¹ [keɪs] *for glasses, pen* astuccio *m*; *of whisky, wine* cassa *f*; (*suitcase*) valigia *f*; **glass ~** teca *f*

case² [keɪs] *n* (*instance, for police*), MED caso *m*; (*argument*) argomentazione *f*; LAW causa *f*; **in ~ ...** in caso ...; **take an umbrella in ~ it rains** prendi un ombrello in caso

piovesse; *in any* ~ in ogni caso; *in that* ~ in questo caso
'case his·to·ry MED cartella *f* clinica
'case·load numero *m* di assistiti; *my doctor's* ~ il numero dei pazienti del mio dottore
cash [kæʃ] **1** *n* contanti *mpl*; F *(money)* soldi *mpl*; ~ *down* in contanti; *pay (in)* ~ pagare in contanti; ~ *in advance* pagamento *m* anticipato; ~ *on delivery* → COD **2** *v/t cheque* incassare
♦ cash in on *v/t* guadagnare su
'cash card carta *f* per prelievi; 'cash cow vacca *f* da mungere; 'cash desk cassa *f*; cash 'dis·count sconto *m* su pagamento in contanti; 'cash di·spens·er (sportello *m*) Bancomat® *m*; 'cash flow flusso *m* di cassa
cash·ier [kæˈʃɪə(r)] *n in shop etc* cassiere *m*, -a *f*
'cash ma·chine (sportello *m*) Bancomat® *m*
cash·mere ['kæʃmɪər] *adj* cashmere *m inv*
'cash·point (sportello *m*) Bancomat® *m*
'cash re·gis·ter cassa *f*
ca·si·no [kəˈsiːnəʊ] casinò *m inv*
cas·ket ['kæskɪt] *Am (coffin)* bara *f*
cas·se·role ['kæsərəʊl] *n meal* stufato *m*; *container* casseruola *f*
cas·sette [kəˈset] cassetta *f*
cas'sette play·er mangiacassette *m inv*
cas'sette re·cord·er registratore *m* (a cassette)
cast [kɑːst] **1** *n of play* cast *m inv*; *(mould)* stampo *m* **2** *v/t (pret & pp* **cast**) *doubt, suspicion* far sorgere *(on* su); *shadow* proiettare; *metal* colare (in uno stampo); *play* assegnare le parti per; ~ *s.o. as ... for play* far fare a qu il ruolo di ...; *he was* ~ *as Romeo* gli è stata assegnata la parte di Romeo; ~ *a glance at s.o. / sth* gettare uno sguardo su qu/qc
♦ cast off *v/i/t of ship* sciogliere gli ormeggi

caste [kɑːst] casta *f*
cast·er ['kɑːstə(r)] *on chair etc* rotella *f*
'cast·er sug·ar zucchero *m* raffinato
cast 'iron ghisa *f*
cast-'iron *adj* di ghisa
cas·tle ['kɑːsl] castello *m*
'cast·or ['kɑːstə(r)] → *caster*
cas·trate [kæˈstreɪt] *v/t* castrare
cas·tra·tion [kæˈstreɪʃn] castrazione *f*
cas·u·al ['kæʒʊəl] *adj (chance)* casuale; *(offhand)* disinvolto; *(irresponsible)* noncurante; *remark* poco importante; *clothes* casual *inv*; *(not permanent)* occasionale; ~ *sex* rapporti *mpl* occasionali
cas·u·al·ly ['kæʒʊəlɪ] *adv dressed* (in modo) casual; *say* con disinvoltura
cas·u·al·ty ['kæʒʊəltɪ] *dead person* vittima *f*; *injured* ferito *m*
'cas·u·al wear abbigliamento *m* casual
cat [kæt] gatto *m*; *wild* felino *m*
cat·a·log *Am*, cat·a·logue ['kætəlɒg] *n* catalogo *m*
cat·a·lyst ['kætəlɪst] catalizzatore *m*
cat·a·lyt·ic con·vert·er [kætəˈlɪtɪk] marmitta *f* catalitica
cat·a·pult ['kætəpʌlt] **1** *v/t fig: to fame, stardom* catapultare **2** *n* catapulta *f*; *toy* fionda *f*
cat·a·ract ['kætərækt] MED cataratta *f*
ca·tas·tro·phe [kəˈtæstrəfɪ] catastrofe *f*
cat·a·stroph·ic [kætəˈstrɒfɪk] *adj* catastrofico
catch [kætʃ] **1** *n* presa *f*; *of fish* pesca *f*; *on handbag, box* chiusura *f*; *on door, window* fermo *m*; *on brooch* fermaglio *m*; *(problem)* inghippo *m* **2** *v/t (pret & pp* **caught**) *ball, escaped prisoner* prendere; *bus, train* prendere; *fish* prendere; *(in order to speak to)* trovare; *(hear)* afferrare; *illness* prendere; ~ *(a) cold* prendere un raffreddore; ~ *s.o.'s eye of person, object* attirare l'attenzione di qu; ~ *sight of,* ~ *a glimpse of* intravedere; ~ *s.o. doing sth* sorpren-

dere qu a fare qc

♦ **catch on** v/i (*become popular*) fare presa; (*understand*) afferrare

♦ **catch up** v/i recuperare; **catch up with s.o.** raggiungere qu; **catch up with sth** work, studies mettersi in pari con qc

♦ **catch up on** v/t recuperare

catch-22 [kætʃtwentɪˈtuː]: **it's a ~ situation** è una situazione senza via d'uscita

catch·ing [ˈkætʃɪŋ] adj also fig contagioso

catch·y [ˈkætʃɪ] adj tune orecchiabile

cat·e·go·ric [kætəˈɡɒrɪk] adj categorico

cat·e·gor·i·cal·ly [kætəˈɡɒrɪklɪ] adv categoricamente

cat·e·go·ry [ˈkætɪɡərɪ] categoria f

♦ **cater for** [ˈkeɪtə(r)] v/t (*meet the needs of*) rispondere alle esigenze di; (*provide food for*) organizzare rinfreschi per

ca·ter·er [ˈkeɪtərə(r)] ristoratore m, -trice f

ca·ter·pil·lar [ˈkætəpɪlə(r)] bruco m

ca·the·dral [kəˈθiːdrəl] cattedrale f, duomo m

Cath·o·lic [ˈkæθəlɪk] **1** adj cattolico **2** n cattolico m, -a f

Ca·thol·i·cism [kəˈθɒlɪsɪzm] cattolicesimo m

'**cat·nap 1** n pisolino m **2** v/i (pret & pp -**ped**) schiacciare un pisolino

'**cat's eye** on road catarifrangente m

cat·tle [ˈkætl] npl bestiame m

cat·ty [ˈkætɪ] adj maligno

'**cat·walk** passerella f

caught [kɔːt] pret & pp → **catch**

cau·li·flow·er [ˈkɒlɪflaʊə(r)] cavolfiore m

cause [kɔːz] **1** n causa f; (*grounds*) motivo m; (*objective*) causa f **2** v/t causare; **what ~d you to leave so early?** perché sei andato via così presto?

caus·tic [ˈkɔːstɪk] adj fig caustico

cau·tion [ˈkɔːʃn] **1** n (*carefulness*) cautela f, prudenza f; **~ is advised** si raccomanda la prudenza **2** v/t (*warn*) mettere in guardia

cau·tious [ˈkɔːʃəs] adj cauto, prudente

cau·tious·ly [ˈkɔːʃəslɪ] adv con cautela

cave [keɪv] caverna f, grotta f

♦ **cave in** v/i of roof crollare

cav·i·ar [ˈkævɪɑː(r)] caviale m

cav·i·ty [ˈkævətɪ] cavità f inv; in tooth carie f inv

cc [siːˈsiː] **1** abbr (= **carbon copy**) cc (= copia f carbone); (= **cubic centimetres**) cc m inv (= centimetri cubici); MOT cilindrata f **2** v/t memo fare una copia di; person mandare una copia per conoscenza a

CD [siːˈdiː] abbr (= **compact disc**) CD m inv

CD play·er lettore m CD; **CD-ROM** [siːdiːˈrɒm] CD-ROM m inv; **CD-ROM drive** drive m inv per CD-ROM

cease [siːs] v/t & v/i cessare

'**cease-fire** cessate il fuoco m inv

cei·ling [ˈsiːlɪŋ] of room soffitto m; (*limit*) tetto m, plafond m inv

cel·e·brate [ˈselɪbreɪt] **1** v/i festeggiare **2** v/t celebrare, festeggiare; (*observe*) festeggiare

cel·e·brat·ed [ˈselɪbreɪtɪd] adj acclamato; **be ~ for** essere famoso per

cel·e·bra·tion [selɪˈbreɪʃn] celebrazione f, festeggiamento m

ce·leb·ri·ty [sɪˈlebrətɪ] celebrità f inv

cel·e·ry [ˈselərɪ] sedano m

cel·i·ba·cy [ˈselɪbəsɪ] celibato m

cel·i·bate [ˈselɪbət] adj man celibe; woman nubile

cell [sel] for prisoner cella f; BIO cellula f; in spreadsheet casella f, cella f

cel·lar [ˈselə(r)] of house cantina f; of wine collezione f di vini

cel·list [ˈtʃelɪst] violoncellista m/f

cel·lo [ˈtʃeləʊ] violoncello m

cel·lo·phane [ˈseləfeɪn] cellofan m inv

cel·lu·lar phone [seljuːlərˈfəʊn] telefono m cellulare, cellulare m

cel·lu·lite [ˈseljuːlaɪt] cellulite f

ce·ment [sɪˈment] **1** n cemento m; (*adhesive*) mastice m **2** v/t cementare; friendship consolidare

cem·e·tery ['semətrɪ] cimitero *m*
cen·sor ['sensə(r)] *v/t* censurare
cen·sor·ship ['sensəʃɪp] censura *f*
cen·sus ['sensəs] censimento *m*
cent [sent] centesimo *m*
cen·te·na·ry [sen'tiːnərɪ] centenario *m*
cen·ter *Am* → **centre**
cen·ti·grade ['sentɪgreɪd] *adj* centigrado; **10 degrees ~** 10 gradi centigradi
cen·ti·me·ter *Am*, **cen·ti·me·tre** ['sentɪmiːtə(r)] centimetro *m*
cen·tral ['sentrəl] *adj location, flat* centrale; (*main*) principale, centrale; **~ London / France** il centro di Londra / della Francia; **be ~ to sth** essere fondamentale per qc
cen·tral 'heat·ing riscaldamento *m* autonomo
cen·tral·ize ['sentrəlaɪz] *v/t decision making* accentrare
cen·tral 'lock·ing MOT chiusura *f* centralizzata
cen·tral 'pro·ces·sing u·nit unità *f inv* centrale
cen·tral res·er·va·tion MOT banchina *f* spartitraffico
cen·tre ['sentə(r)] **1** *n* centro *m*; **in the ~ of** al centro di **2** *v/t* centrare
♦ **centre on** *v/t* essere incentrato su
cen·tre of 'grav·i·ty centro *m* di gravità
cen·tu·ry ['sentʃərɪ] secolo *m*
CEO [siːiːˈəʊ] *abbr* (= *Chief Executive Officer*) direttore *m* generale
ce·ram·ic [sɪˈræmɪk] *adj* ceramico
ce·ram·ics [sɪˈræmɪks] (*pl: objects*) ceramiche *fpl*; (*sg: art*) ceramica *f*
ce·re·al ['sɪərɪəl] (*grain*) cereale *m*; (*breakfast ~*) cereali *mpl*
cer·e·mo·ni·al [serɪˈməʊnɪəl] **1** *adj* da cerimonia **2** *n* cerimoniale *m*
cer·e·mo·ny ['serɪmənɪ] (*event*) cerimonia *f*; (*ritual*) cerimonie *fpl*
cer·tain ['sɜːtn] *adj* (*sure, particular*) certo; **it's ~ that ...** è certo che ...; **a ~ Mr S.** un certo Sig S.; **make ~** accertarsi; **know / say for ~** sapere / dire con certezza

cer·tain·ly ['sɜːtnlɪ] *adv* certamente; **~ not!** certo che no!
cer·tain·ty ['sɜːtntɪ]) certezza *f*; **it's a ~** è una cosa certa; **he's a ~ to win** vincerà di certo
cer·tif·i·cate [səˈtɪfɪkət] *qualification* certificazione *f*; *official paper* certificato *m*
cer·ti·fy ['sɜːtɪfaɪ] *v/t* (*pret & pp -ied*) dichiarare ufficialmente
Ce·sar·e·an *Am* → **Caesarean**
ces·sa·tion [seˈseɪʃn] cessazione *f*
c/f *abbr* (= *cost and freight*) c/f
CFC [siːefˈsiː] *abbr* (= *chlorofluorocarbon*) CFC *m inv* (= clorofluorocarburi *mpl*)
chain [tʃeɪn] **1** *n* catena *f* **2** *v/t*: **~ sth / s.o. to sth** incatenare qc / qu a qc
chain re'ac·tion reazione *f* a catena; **'chain smoke** *v/i* fumare una sigaretta dopo l'altra; **'chain smok·er** fumatore *m*, -trice *f* incallito; **'chain store** *store* negozio *m* di una catena; *company* catena *f* di negozi
chair [tʃeə(r)] **1** *n* sedia *f*; (*arm ~*) poltrona *f*; *at university* cattedra *f*; **the ~** (*electric ~*) la sedia elettrica; *at meeting* presidente *m/f*; **take the ~** presiedere **2** *v/t meeting* presiedere
'chair lift seggiovia *f*
'chair·man presidente *m*
chair·man·ship ['tʃeəmənʃɪp] presidenza *f*
'chair·per·son presidente *m/f*
'chair·wom·an presidente *m/f*
cha·let ['ʃæleɪ] chalet *m inv*
chal·ice ['tʃælɪs] REL calice *m*
chalk [tʃɔːk] gesso *m*
chal·lenge ['tʃælɪndʒ] **1** *n* sfida *f* **2** *v/t* sfidare; (*call into question*) mettere alla prova
chal·len·ger ['tʃælɪndʒə(r)] sfidante *m/f*
chal·len·ging ['tʃælɪndʒɪŋ] *adj job, undertaking* stimolante
'cham·ber·maid ['tʃeɪmbəmeɪd] cameriera *f*; **'cham·ber mu·sic** musica *f* da camera; **Cham·ber of 'Com·merce** Camera *f* di Commercio

cham·ois (leather) [ˈʃæmɪ] camoscio *m*

cham·pagne [ʃæmˈpeɪn] champagne *m inv*

cham·pi·on [ˈtʃæmpɪən] **1** *n* SP campione *m*, -essa *f*; *of cause* difensore *m*, -a *f* **2** *v/t (cause)* difendere

cham·pi·on·ship [ˈtʃæmpɪənʃɪp] *event* campionato *m*; *title* titolo *m* di campione; *of cause* difesa *f*

chance [tʃɑːns] *(possibility)* probabilità *f inv*; *(opportunity)* opportunità *f inv*, occasione *f*; *(risk)* rischio *m*; *(luck)* caso *m*; **by ~** per caso; **take a ~** correre un rischio; **I'm not taking any ~s** non voglio correre nessun rischio; **you don't stand a ~** non hai nessuna possibilità

Chan·cel·lor [ˈtʃɑːnsələ(r)] *in Germany* cancelliere *m*; **~ (of the Exchequer)** *in Britain* ministro *m* del tesoro

chan·de·lier [ʃændəˈlɪə(r)] lampadario *m*

change [tʃeɪndʒ] **1** *n* cambiamento *m*; *small coins* moneta *f*; *from purchase* resto *m*; **for a ~** per cambiare; **a ~ of clothes** un ricambio di vestiti **2** *v/t (alter)* cambiare; *one's clothes* cambiarsi **3** *v/i* cambiare; *(put on different clothes)* cambiarsi; **you ~ at Crewe** devi cambiare a Crewe

change·a·ble [ˈtʃeɪndʒəbl] *adj* incostante; *weather* variabile

ˈchange·o·ver passaggio *m*; *period* fase *f* di transizione; *in relay race* passaggio *m* del testimone

chang·ing room SP spogliatoio *m*; *in shop* camerino *m*

chan·nel [ˈtʃænl] *on TV, in water* canale *m*

Chan·nel ˈTun·nel tunnel *m* della Manica

chant [tʃɑːnt] **1** *n* slogan *m inv*; REL canto *m* **2** *v/i* gridare; *of demonstrators* gridare slogan; REL cantare

cha·os [ˈkeɪɒs] caos *m inv*

cha·ot·ic [keɪˈɒtɪk] *adj* caotico

chap [tʃæp] *n* F tipo *m* F

chap·el [ˈtʃæpl] cappella *f*

chapped [tʃæpt] *adj* screpolato

chap·ter [ˈtʃæptə(r)] *of book* capitolo *m*; *of organization* filiale *f*

char·ac·ter [ˈkærɪktə(r)] *(nature)* carattere *m*; *(person)* tipo *m*; *in book, play* personaggio *m*; *in writing* carattere *m*; **he's a real ~** è un tipo speciale

char·ac·ter·is·tic [kærɪktəˈrɪstɪk] **1** *n* caratteristica *f* **2** *adj* caratteristico

char·ac·ter·is·ti·cal·ly [kærɪktəˈrɪstɪklɪ] *adv* in modo caratteristico; **he was ~ rude** era maleducato, come al solito

char·ac·ter·ize [ˈkærɪktəraɪz] *v/t* caratterizzare

cha·rade [ʃəˈrɑːd] *fig* farsa *f*

char·coal [ˈtʃɑːkəʊl] *for barbecue* carbonella *f*; *for drawing* carboncino *m*

charge [tʃɑːdʒ] **1** *n (fee)* costo *m*; LAW accusa *f*; **free of ~** gratis; **be in ~** essere responsabile; **take ~** assumersi l'incombenza; **take ~ of sth** farsi carico di qc **2** *v/t sum of money* far pagare; *person* far pagare a; *(put on account)* addebitare; LAW accusare; *battery* caricare; **how much do you ~ for ...?** quanto prende per ...? **3** *v/i (attack)* attaccare

ˈcharge ac·count conto *m* (spese)

ˈcharge card carta *f* di addebito

cha·ris·ma [kəˈrɪzmə] carisma *m*

char·is·mat·ic [kærɪzˈmætɪk] *adj* carismatico

char·i·ta·ble [ˈtʃærɪtəbl] *adj* *institution* di beneficenza; *donation* in beneficenza; *person* caritatevole

char·i·ty [ˈtʃærɪtɪ] *assistance* carità *f*; *organization* associazione *f* di beneficenza

char·la·tan [ˈʃɑːlətən] ciarlatano *m*, -a *f*

charm [tʃɑːm] **1** *n appealing quality* fascino *m*; *on bracelet etc* ciondolo *m* **2** *v/t (delight)* conquistare

charm·ing [ˈtʃɑːmɪŋ] *adj* affascinante; *house, village* incantevole

charred [tʃɑːd] *adj* carbonizzato

chart [tʃɑːt] *diagram* diagramma *m*; *for ship* carta *f* nautica; *for aeroplane*

cheeseburger

carta *f* aeronautica; *the ~s* MUS l'hit parade *f inv*

char·ter ['tʃɑːtə(r)] *v/t plane, boat* noleggiare

'char·ter flight volo *m* charter *inv*

chase [tʃeɪs] **1** *n* inseguimento *m* **2** *v/t* inseguire

♦ **chase away** *v/t* cacciare (via)

chas·er ['tʃeɪsə(r)] alcolico bevuto dopo un altro di diverso tipo

chas·sis ['ʃæsɪ] *of car* telaio *m*

chat [tʃæt] **1** *n* chiacchierata *f*; *useless talk* chiacchiere *fpl* **2** *v/i* (*pret & pp* **-ted**) chiacchierare

♦ **chat up** *v/t* F abbordare F

'chat room stanza *f* di chat; **'chat show** talk show *m inv*; **'chat show host** conduttore *m*, -trice *f* di un talk show

chat·ter ['tʃætə(r)] **1** *n* parlantina *f* **2** *v/i talk* fare chiacchiere; *of teeth* battere

'chat·ter·box chiacchierone *m*, -a *f*

chat·ty ['tʃætɪ] *adj person* chiacchierone; *letter* familiare

chauf·feur ['ʃəʊfə(r)] *n* autista *m/f*

'chauf·feur-driv·en *adj* con autista

chau·vin·ist ['ʃəʊvɪnɪst] *n* sciovinista *m/f*; (*male ~*) maschilista *m*

chau·vin·ist·ic [ʃəʊvɪˈnɪstɪk] *adj* sciovinista

cheap [tʃiːp] *adj* (*inexpensive*) economico; (*nasty*) cattivo; (*mean*) tirchio

cheat [tʃiːt] **1** *n person* imbroglione *m*, -a *f* in *cards* baro *m*; (*deception*) truffa *f* **2** *v/t* imbrogliare; *~ s.o. out of sth* estorcere qc a qu con l'inganno **3** *v/i* imbrogliare; in *cards* barare; *~ on one's wife* tradire la propria moglie

check¹ [tʃek] **1** *adj shirt* a quadri **2** *n* quadro *m*

check² [tʃek] **1** *n to verify sth* verifica *f*; *keep in ~, hold in ~* tenere sotto controllo; *keep a ~ on* tenere sotto controllo **2** *v/t* (*verify*) verificare; (*restrain*) controllare; (*stop*) bloccare; *with a tick* marcare **3** *v/i* verificare; *did you ~ check for signs of forced entry?* hai guardato se c'erano segni di infrazione?

♦ **check in** *v/i* registrarsi

♦ **check off** *v/t* segnare

♦ **check on** *v/t* controllare

♦ **check out 1** *v/i of hotel* saldare il conto **2** *v/t* (*look into*) verificare; *club, restaurant etc* provare

♦ **check up on** *v/t* fare dei controlli su

♦ **check with** *v/i of person* verificare con; (*tally*) combaciare con

check³ [tʃek] *Am* → **cheque**

checked [tʃekt] *adj material* a quadri

checkers ['tʃekəz] *nsg Am: game* dama *f*

'check-in (coun·ter) banco *m* dell'accettazione

'check·ing ac·count *Am* conto *m* corrente

'check-in time check in *m inv*; **'check-list** lista *f* di verifica; **'check·mark** *Am* segno *m*; **'check·mate** *n* scacco *m* matto; **'check·out** cassa *f*; **'check-out time** *from hotel* ora *f* di check-out; **'check·point** *military, police* posto *m* di blocco; **'check·room** *Am for coats* guardaroba *m inv*; **'check-up** *medical* check up *m inv*; *dental* visita *f* di controllo

cheek [tʃiːk] guancia *f*; (*impudence*) sfacciataggine *f*

'cheek·bone zigomo *m*

cheek·i·ly ['tʃiːkɪlɪ] *adv* sfacciatamente

cheek·y ['tʃiːkɪ] *adj* sfacciato

cheer [tʃɪə(r)] **1** *n* acclamazione *f*; *three ~s for ...* hip, hip, hurrà per ...; *~s!* (*toast*) salute!; *~s!* F (*thanks*) grazie! **2** *v/t* acclamare **3** *v/i* fare acclamazioni

♦ **cheer on** *v/t* incitare

♦ **cheer up 1** *v/i* consolarsi; *cheer up!* su con la vita! **2** *v/t* tirare su

cheer·ful ['tʃɪəfʊl] *adj* allegro

cheer·ing ['tʃɪərɪŋ] *n* acclamazioni *fpl*

cheer·i·o [tʃɪərɪˈəʊ] F ciao F

cheer·y ['tʃɪərɪ] *adj* → **cheerful**

cheese [tʃiːz] formaggio *m*

'cheese·burg·er cheeseburger *m inv*

'cheese·cake dolce *m* al formaggio

chef [ʃef] chef *m/f inv*

chem·i·cal ['kemɪkl] **1** *adj* chimico **2** *n* sostanza *f* chimica

chem·i·cal 'war·fare guerra *f* chimica

chemist ['kemɪst] *in laboratory* chimico *m*, -a *f*; *who dispenses medicine* farmacista *m/f*

chem·is·try ['kemɪstrɪ] chimica *f*; *fig* alchimia *f*

'chem·ist's (shop) farmacia *f*

chem·o·ther·a·py [ki:məʊˈθerəpɪ] chemioterapia *f*

cheque [ʃek] assegno *m*

'cheque·book libretto *m* degli assegni

cheque (guar·an·tee) card carta *f* assegni

cher·ish ['ʃerɪʃ] *v/t* avere a cuore

cher·ry ['ʃerɪ] *fruit* ciliegia *f*; *tree* ciliegio *m*

cher·ub ['ʃerəb] cherubino *m*

chess [ʃes] scacchi *mpl*

'chess·board scacchiera *f*

'chess·man, chess·piece pezzo *m* degli scacchi

chest [ʃest] *of person* petto *m*; *(box)* cassa *f*; **I'm glad I've got that off my ~** sono contento di essermi tolto questo peso dallo stomaco

chest·nut ['ʃesnʌt] castagna *f*; *tree* castagno *m*

chest of 'drawers comò *m inv*, cassettone *m*

chew [ʃu:] *v/t* masticare; *of dog, rats* rosicchiare

chew·ing gum ['ʃu:ɪŋ] gomma *f* da masticare

chic [ʃi:k] *adj* chic *inv*

chick [ʃɪk] pulcino *m*; F *(girl)* ragazza *f*

chick·en ['ʃɪkɪn] **1** *n* pollo *m*; F fifone *m*, -a *f* F **2** *adj* F *(cowardly)* fifone

♦ **chicken out** *v/i* F tirarsi indietro per la fifa F

'chick·en·feed F una bazzecola

'chick·en·pox varicella *f*

chief [ʃi:f] **1** *n (head)* principale *m/f*; *of tribe* capo *m* **2** *adj* principale

chief·ly ['ʃi:flɪ] *adv* principalmente

chil·blain ['ʃɪlbleɪn] gelone *m*

child [ʃaɪld] *(pl* **children** ['ʃɪldrən]) *also pej* bambino *m*, -a *f*; **they have two children** hanno due figli

'child a·buse violenza *f* sui minori; **'child·birth** parto *m*; **child·hood** ['ʃaɪldhʊd] infanzia *f*

child·ish ['ʃaɪldɪʃ] *adj pej* infantile, puerile

child·ish·ly ['ʃaɪldɪʃlɪ] *adv pej* puerilmente

child·ish·ness ['ʃaɪldɪʃnɪs] *pej* puerilità *f inv*

child·less ['ʃaɪldlɪs] *adj* senza figli

child·like ['ʃaɪldlaɪk] *adj* innocente

'child·mind·er baby-sitter *m/f inv*

'child·ren ['ʃɪldrən] *pl* → **child**

Chil·e ['ʃɪlɪ] Cile *m*

Chil·e·an ['ʃɪlɪən] **1** *adj* cileno **2** *n* cileno *m*, -a *f*

chill [ʃɪl] **1** *n in air* freddo *m*; *illness* colpo *m* di freddo; **there's a ~ in the air** l'aria è fredda **2** *v/t wine* mettere in fresco

♦ **chill out** *v/i* P rilassarsi

chilli (pepper) ['ʃɪlɪ] peperoncino *m*

chill·y ['ʃɪlɪ] *adj weather, welcome* freddo; **I'm feeling a bit ~** ho un po' freddo; **it's a bit ~ this morning** sta freddino stamattina

chime [ʃaɪm] *v/i* suonare

chim·ney ['ʃɪmnɪ] camino *m*

chim·pan·zee [ʃɪmpænˈzi:] scimpanzé *m inv*

chin [ʃɪn] mento *m*

Chi·na ['ʃaɪnə] Cina *f*

chi·na ['ʃaɪnə] porcellana *f*

Chi·nese [ʃaɪˈni:z] **1** *adj* cinese **2** *n language* cinese *m*; *person* cinese *m/f*

chink [ʃɪŋk] *gap* fessura *f*; *sound* tintinnio *m*

chip [ʃɪp] **1** *n fragment* scheggia *f*; *damage* scheggiatura *f*; *in gambling* fiche *f inv*; COMPUT chip *m inv*; **~s** patate *fpl* fritte; *Am* patatine *fpl* **2** *v/t (pret & pp* **-ped**) *damage* scheggiare

♦ **chip in** *v/i (interrupt)* intervenire; *with money* contribuire

chi·rop·o·dist [kɪ'rɒpədɪst] pedicure *m/f inv*

chi·ro·prac·tor ['kaɪrəʊpræktə(r)] chiroterapeuta *m/f*

chirp [tʃɜːp] *v/i* cinguettare

chis·el ['tʃɪzl] *n* scalpello *m*

chit-chat ['tʃɪtʃæt] chiacchiere *fpl*

chiv·al·rous ['ʃɪvlrəs] *adj* cavalleresco

chive [tʃaɪv] erba *f* cipollina

chlo·rine ['klɔːriːn] cloro *m*

chlor·o·form ['klɒrəfɔːm] *n* cloroformio *m*

choc·a·hol·ic [tʃɒkə'hɒlɪk] *n* F fanatico *m*, -a *f* del cioccolato

chock-a-block [tʃɒkə'blɒk] *adj* F pieno zeppo

chock-full [tʃɒk'fʊl] *adj* F strapieno

choc·o·late ['tʃɒkələt] cioccolato *m*; *in box* cioccolatino *m*; *hot* ~ cioccolata *f* calda

'**choc·o·late cake** dolce *m* al cioccolato

choice [tʃɔɪs] **1** *n* scelta *f*; *I had no* ~ non avevo scelta **2** *adj* (*top quality*) di prima scelta

choir ['kwaɪə(r)] coro *m*

'**choir·boy** corista *m*

choke [tʃəʊk] **1** *n* MOT starter *m inv* **2** *v/i* soffocare; *he ~d on a bone* si è strozzato con un osso **3** *v/t* soffocare

cho·les·te·rol [kə'lestərɒl] colesterolo *m*

choose [tʃuːz] *v/t & v/i* (*pret chose*, *pp chosen*) scegliere

choos·ey ['tʃuːzɪ] *adj* F selettivo

chop [tʃɒp] **1** *n action* colpo *m*; *meat* braciola *f* **2** *v/t* (*pret & pp -ped*) *wood* spaccare; *meat*, *vegetables* tagliare a pezzi

♦ **chop down** *v/t tree* abbattere

chop·per ['tʃɒpə(r)] *tool* accetta *f*; F (*helicopter*) elicottero *m*

'**chop·ping board** ['tʃɒpɪŋ] tagliere *m*

'**chop·sticks** *npl* bastoncini *mpl* (cinesi)

cho·ral ['kɔːrəl] *adj* corale

chord [kɔːd] MUS accordo *m*

chore [tʃɔː(r)] *household* faccenda *f* domestica

chor·e·o·graph ['kɒrɪəgrɑːf] *v/t* coreografare

chor·e·og·ra·pher [kɒrɪ'ɒgrəfə(r)] coreografo *m*, -a *f*

chor·e·og·ra·phy [kɒrɪ'ɒgrəfɪ] coreografia *f*

cho·rus ['kɔːrəs] *singers, of song* coro *m*

chose [tʃəʊz] *pret* → **choose**

cho·sen ['tʃəʊzn] *pp* → **choose**

Christ [kraɪst] Cristo *m*; ~! Cristo!

chris·ten ['krɪsn] *v/t* battezzare

chris·ten·ing ['krɪsnɪŋ] battesimo *m*

Chris·tian ['krɪstʃən] **1** *n* cristiano *m*, -a *f* **2** *adj* cristiano; *attitude* da cristiano

Chris·ti·an·i·ty [krɪstɪ'ænɪtɪ] cristianesimo *m*

'**Chris·tian name** nome *m* di battesimo

Christ·mas ['krɪsməs] Natale *m*; *at* ~ a Natale; *Merry* ~! Buon Natale!

'**Christ·mas card** biglietto *m* di auguri natalizi; **Christ·mas 'Day** giorno *m* di Natale; **Christ·mas 'Eve** vigilia *f* di Natale; '**Christ·mas present** regalo *m* di Natale; '**Christ·mas tree** albero *m* di Natale

chrome, chro·mi·um [krəʊm, 'krəʊmɪəm] cromo *m*

chro·mo·some ['krəʊməsəʊm] cromosomo *m*

chron·ic ['krɒnɪk] *adj* cronico

chron·o·log·i·cal [krɒnə'lɒdʒɪkl] *adj* cronologico; *in* ~ *order* in ordine cronologico

chrys·an·the·mum [krɪ'sænθəməm] crisantemo *m*

chub·by ['tʃʌbɪ] *adj* paffuto

chuck [tʃʌk] *v/t* F buttare

♦ **chuck out** *v/t* F *object* buttare via; *person* buttare fuori

chuck·ing-out time ['tʃʌkɪŋ'aʊt] F ora *f* di chiusura

chuck·le ['tʃʌkl] **1** *n* risatina *f* **2** *v/i* ridacchiare

chum [tʃʌm] amico *m*, -a *f*

chum·my ['tʃʌmɪ] *adj* F pappa e ciccia F; *be* ~ *with* essere pappa e ciccia con

chunk [tʃʌŋk] pezzo m

chunk·y ['tʃʌŋkɪ] adj sweater spesso; tumbler tozzo; person, build tarchiato

church [tʃɜːtʃ] chiesa f

church 'hall sala f parrocchiale; **church 'serv·ice** funzione f religiosa; **'church·yard** cimitero m (di una chiesa)

churl·ish ['tʃɜːlɪʃ] adj sgarbato

chute [ʃuːt] scivolo m; for waste disposal canale m di scarico

CIA [siːaɪ'eɪ] abbr (= **Central Intelligence Agency**) CIA f

ci·der ['saɪdə(r)] sidro m

CIF [siːaɪ'ef] abbr (= **cost insurance freight**) CIF

ci·gar [sɪ'gɑː(r)] sigaro m

cig·a·rette [sɪgə'ret] sigaretta f

cig·a'rette end mozzicone m di sigaretta; **cig·a'rette light·er** accendino m; **cig·a'rette pa·per** carta f per sigarette

cin·e·ma ['sɪnɪmə] cinema m

cin·na·mon ['sɪnəmən] canella f

cir·cle ['sɜːkl] **1** n cerchio m; (group) cerchia f **2** v/t (draw circle around) cerchiare **3** v/i of plane girare in tondo; of bird volteggiare

cir·cuit ['sɜːkɪt] ELEC circuito m; (lap) giro m

'cir·cuit board COMPUT circuito m stampato; **'cir·cuit break·er** ELEC interruttore m automatico; **'cir·cuit train·ing** SP percorso m ginnico

cir·cu·lar ['sɜːkjʊlə(r)] **1** n giving information circolare f **2** adj circolare

cir·cu·late ['sɜːkjʊleɪt] **1** v/i circolare **2** v/t memo far circolare

cir·cu·la·tion [sɜːkjʊ'leɪʃn] BIO circolazione f; of newspaper, magazine tiratura f

cir·cum·fer·ence [sə'kʌmfərəns] circonferenza f

cir·cum·stances ['sɜːkəmstənsɪs] npl circostanze fpl; (financial) situazione fsg (economica); **under no ~** in nessuna circostanza; **under the ~** date le circostanze

cir·cus ['sɜːkəs] circo m

cir·rho·sis (of the liv·er) [sɪ'rəʊsɪs] cirrosi f (epatica)

cis·tern ['sɪstən] cisterna f; of WC serbatoio m

cite [saɪt] v/t citare

cit·i·zen ['sɪtɪzn] cittadino m, -a f

cit·i·zen·ship ['sɪtɪznʃɪp] cittadinanza f

citr·us fruit ['sɪtrəs] agrume m

cit·y ['sɪtɪ] città f inv

city 'centre centro m (della città)

city 'hall sala f municipale

civ·ic ['sɪvɪk] adj civico

civ·il ['sɪvl] adj civile

civ·il en·gi'neer ingegnere m civile

ci·vil·i·an [sɪ'vɪljən] **1** n civile m/f **2** adj clothes civile

ci·vil·i·ty [sɪ'vɪlɪtɪ] civiltà f

civ·i·li·za·tion [sɪvəlaɪ'zeɪʃn] civilizzazione f

civ·i·lize ['sɪvəlaɪz] v/t person civilizzare

civ·il 'rights npl diritti mpl civili; **civ·il 'ser·vant** impiegato m, -a f statale; **civ·il 'ser·vice** pubblica amministrazione f; **civ·il 'war** guerra f civile

claim [kleɪm] **1** n (request) richiesta f; (right) diritto m; (assertion) affermazione f **2** v/t (ask for as a right) rivendicare; damages richiedere; (assert) affermare; lost property reclamare; **they have ~ed responsibility for the attack** hanno rivendicato l'attentato

claim·ant ['kleɪmənt] richiedente m/f

clair·voy·ant [kleə'vɔɪənt] n chiaroveggente m/f

clam [klæm] vongola f

♦ **clam up** v/i (pret & pp **-med**) F chiudersi come un riccio

clam·ber ['klæmbə(r)] v/i arrampicarsi

clam·my ['klæmɪ] adj hands appiccicaticcio; weather afoso

clam·or Am, **clam·our** ['klæmə(r)] noise clamore m; (outcry) protesta f

♦ **clamour** for v/t chiedere a gran voce

clamp [klæmp] **1** n fastener morsa f;

for wheel ceppo *m* (bloccaruote) **2** *v/t fasten* bloccare (con una morsa); *fig: hand etc* stringere; *car* mettere i ceppi a

♦ **clamp down** *v/i* usare il pugno di ferro

♦ **clamp down on** *v/t* mettere un freno a

clan [klæn] clan *m inv*

clan·des·tine [klæn'destɪn] *adj* clandestino

clang [klæŋ] **1** *n* suono *m* metallico **2** *v/i*: ~ **shut** chiudersi con un suono metallico

clang·er ['klæŋə(r)] F gaffe *f inv*; **drop a ~** fare una gaffe

clap [klæp] *v/t & v/i* (*pret & pp* **-ped**) (*applaud*) applaudire

clar·et ['klærɪt] *wine* claret *m inv*

clar·i·fi·ca·tion [klærɪfɪ'keɪʃn] chiarimento *m*

clar·i·fy ['klærɪfaɪ] *v/t* (*pret & pp* **-ied**) chiarire

clar·i·net [klærɪ'net] clarinetto *m*

clar·i·ty ['klærətɪ] chiarezza *f*

clash [klæʃ] **1** *n* scontro *m* **2** *v/i* scontrarsi; *of opinions* essere in contrasto; *of colours* stonare; *of events* coincidere

clasp [klɑːsp] **1** *n fastener* chiusura *f* **2** *v/t in hand* stringere

class [klɑːs] **1** *n* (*lesson*) lezione *f*; (*group of people, category*) classe *f*; **social ~** classe *f* sociale **2** *v/t* classificare

clas·sic ['klæsɪk] **1** *adj* (*typical*) classico; (*definitive*) eccellente; **she wrote the ~ biography of ...** la sua biografia di ... è un classico **2** *n* classico *m*

clas·si·cal ['klæsɪkl] *adj* classico

clas·si·fi·ca·tion [klæsɪfɪ'keɪʃn] classificazione *f*

clas·si·fied ['klæsɪfaɪd] *adj information* riservato

'**clas·si·fied ad**(·**ver·tise·ment**) inserzione *f*, annuncio *m*

clas·si·fy ['klæsɪfaɪ] *v/t* (*pret & pp* **-ied**) (*categorize*) classificare

'**class·mate** compagno *m*, -a *f* di classe; '**class·room** aula *f*; '**class**

war·fare lotta *f* di classe

classy ['klɑːsɪ] *adj* F d'alta classe

clat·ter ['klætə(r)] **1** *n* frastuono *m* **2** *v/i* fare baccano; ~ **down the stairs** scendere rumorosamente le scale

clause [klɔːz] *in agreement* articolo *m*; GRAM proposizione *f*

claus·tro·pho·bi·a [klɒːstrə'fəʊbɪə] claustrofobia *f*

claw [klɔː] **1** *n* artiglio *m*; *of lobster* chela *m* **2** *v/t* (*scratch*) graffiare

clay [kleɪ] argilla *f*

clean [kliːn] **1** *adj* pulito **2** *adv* F (*completely*) completamente **3** *v/t* pulire; *teeth* lavarsi; *car, hands, face* lavare; *clothes* lavare *o* pulire a secco

♦ **clean out** *v/t room, cupboard* pulire a fondo; *fig* ripulire

♦ **clean up 1** *v/t also fig* ripulire **2** *v/i* pulire; (*wash*) ripulirsi; *on stock market etc* fare fortuna

clean·er ['kliːnə(r)] *male* uomo *m* delle pulizie; *female* donna *f* delle pulizie; (*dry ~*) lavanderia *f*, tintoria *f*

'**clean·ing wom·an** donna *f* delle pulizie

cleanse [klenz] *v/t skin* detergere

cleans·er ['klenzə(r)] *for skin* detergente *m*

'**cleans·ing cream** ['klenzɪŋ] latte *f* detergente

clear [klɪə(r)] **1** *adj* chiaro; *weather, sky* sereno; *water, eyes* limpido; *skin* uniforme; *conscience* pulito; **I'm not ~ about it** non l'ho capito bene; **I didn't make myself ~** non mi sono spiegato bene; **I made it ~ to him** gliel'ho fatto capire **2** *adv: loud and ~* forte e chiaro; **stand ~ of** stare lontano da; **steer ~ of** stare alla larga da **3** *v/t roads etc* sgomb(e)rare; (*acquit*) scagionare; (*authorize*) autorizzare; (*earn*) guadagnare al netto; *fence* saltare; ~ **one's throat** schiarirsi la gola; ~ **the table** sparecchiare (la tavola) **4** *v/i of sky* schiarirsi; *of mist* diradarsi

♦ **clear away** v/t mettere via

♦ **clear off** v/i F filarsela F

♦ **clear out 1** v/t cupboard sgomb(e)rare **2** v/i sparire

♦ **clear up 1** v/i (tidy up) mettere in ordine; of weather schiarirsi; of illness, rash sparire **2** v/t (tidy) mettere in ordine; mystery, problem risolvere

clear·ance ['klɪərəns] space spazio m libero; (authorization) autorizzazione f

clear·ance sale liquidazione f

clear·ing ['klɪərɪŋ] in woods radura f

clear·ly ['klɪəlɪ] adv chiaramente

cleav·age ['kliːvɪdʒ] décolleté m inv

cleav·er ['kliːvə(r)] mannaia f

clem·en·cy ['klemənsɪ] clemenza f

clench [klentʃ] v/t serrare

cler·gy ['klɜːdʒɪ] clero m

cler·gy·man ['klɜːdʒɪmæn] ecclesiastico m

clerk [klɑːk, Am klɜːrk] impiegato m, -a f; Am: in shop commesso m, -a f

clev·er ['klevə(r)] adj intelligente; gadget, device ingegnoso; **don't get ~ with me** non fare il furbo con me

clev·er·ly ['klevəlɪ] adv intelligentemente

cli·ché ['kliːʃeɪ] frase f stereotipata

cli·chéd ['kliːʃeɪd] adj stereotipato

click [klɪk] **1** n COMPUT click m inv **2** v/i of camera etc scattare

♦ **click on** v/t COMPUT cliccare su

cli·ent ['klaɪənt] cliente m/f

cli·en·tele [kliːən'tel] clientela f

cliff [klɪf] scogliera f

cli·mate ['klaɪmət] clima m

cli·mate change mutazione f climatica

cli·mat·ic [klaɪ'mætɪk] adj climatico

cli·max ['klaɪmæks] n punto m culminante

climb [klaɪm] **1** n up mountain scalata f, arrampicata f **2** v/t salire su; clamber up arrampicarsi su; mountaineering scalare **3** v/i of plane, road, inflation salire; clamber arrampicarsi

♦ **climb down** v/i scendere; fig fare marcia indietro

climb·er ['klaɪmə(r)] person alpinista m/f

climb·ing ['klaɪmɪŋ] alpinismo m

climb·ing wall parete f artificiale per esercitarsi nella scalata

clinch [klɪntʃ] v/t deal concludere; **that ~es it** questo risolve la questione

cling [klɪŋ] v/i (pret & pp **clung**) of clothes essere attillato

♦ **cling to** v/t of child avvinghiarsi a; ideas, tradition aggrapparsi a

cling·film pellicola f trasparente

cling·y ['klɪŋɪ] adj child, boyfriend appiccicoso

clin·ic ['klɪnɪk] clinica f

clin·i·cal ['klɪnɪkl] adj clinico

clink [klɪŋk] **1** n noise tintinnio m **2** v/i tintinnare

clip[1] [klɪp] **1** n fastener fermaglio m; for hair molletta f; for paper graffetta f **2** v/t (pret & pp **-ped**): **~ sth to sth** attaccare qc a qc

clip[2] [klɪp] **1** n from film spezzone f **2** v/t (pret & pp **-ped**) hair, hedge, grass tagliare

clip·board fermablocco m inv

clip·pers ['klɪpəz] npl for hair rasoio m; for nails tronchesina f; for gardening tosasiepi fpl

clip·ping ['klɪpɪŋ] from newspaper ritaglio m

clique [kliːk] combriccola f

cloak n cappa f

cloak·room guardaroba m inv; (euph: toilet) servizi mpl

clock [klɒk] orologio m; F (speedometer) contachilometri m inv

clock ra·di·o radiosveglia f; **clock·wise** adv in senso orario; **clock·work** meccanismo m di orologio; **it went like ~** è andato liscio come l'olio

♦ **clog up** [klɒg] (pret & pp **-ged**) **1** v/i intasarsi **2** v/t intasare

clone [kləun] **1** n clone m **2** v/t clonare

close[1] [kləus] **1** adj family, friend intimo; resemblance stretto; **we are very ~** siamo molto uniti; **be ~ to s.o.** emotionally essere vicino a qu

2 *adv* vicino; ~ **at hand** a portata di mano; ~ **by** nelle vicinanze

close² [kləuz] **1** *v/t* chiudere **2** *v/i of door, eyes* chiudersi; *of shop* chiudere
♦ **close down** *v/t & v/i* chiudere
♦ **close in** *v/i* circondare; *of fog, night* calare
♦ **close up 1** *v/t building* chiudere **2** *v/i (move closer)* avvicinarsi

closed [kləuzd] *adj* chiuso
closed-cir·cuit 'tel·e·vi·sion televisione *f* a circuito chiuso
'close-knit *adj* affiatato
close·ly ['kləuslɪ] *adv listen, watch* attentamente; *cooperate* fianco a fianco
clos·et ['klɒzɪt] *Am* armadio *m*
close-up ['kləusʌp] primo piano *m*
clos·ing date ['kləuzɪŋ] termine *m*
clos·ing time ['kləuzɪŋ] ora *f* di chiusura
clo·sure ['kləuʒə(r)] chiusura *f*
clot [klɒt] **1** *n of blood* grumo *m* **2** *v/i (pret & pp -ted) of blood* coagularsi
cloth [klɒθ] *(fabric)* tessuto *m*; *for cleaning* straccio *m*
clothes [kləuðz] *npl* vestiti *mpl*
'clothes brush spazzola *f* per vestiti; **'clothes hang·er** attaccapanni *m inv*; **'clothes·horse** stendibiancheria *m inv*; **'clothes·line** filo *m* stendibiancheria *inv*; **'clothes peg** molletta *f* per i panni
cloth·ing ['kləuðɪŋ] abbigliamento *m*
cloud [klaud] *n* nuvola *f*; **a ~ of smoke / dust** una nuvola di fumo / polvere
♦ **cloud over** *v/i of sky* rannuvolarsi
'cloud·burst temporale *m*
cloud·less ['klaudlɪs] *adj sky* sereno
cloud·y ['klaudɪ] *adj* nuvoloso
clout [klaut] *F (blow)* botta *f*; *(fig: influence)* impatto *m*
clove of 'gar·lic [kləuv] spicchio *m* d'aglio
clown [klaun] *in circus* pagliaccio *m*; *(joker, also pej)* pagliaccio *m*
club [klʌb] *n weapon* clava *f*; *in golf* mazza *f*; *organization* club *m inv*

clue [klu:] indizio *m*; **I haven't a ~** F non ne ho la minima idea; **he hasn't a ~** *(is useless)* non ci capisce niente
clued-up [klu:d'ʌp] *adj* F beninformato
clump [klʌmp] *n of earth* zolla *f*; *group* gruppo *m*
clum·si·ness ['klʌmzɪnɪs] goffaggine *f*
clum·sy ['klʌmzɪ] *adj person* goffo, maldestro
clung [klʌŋ] *pret & pp* → **cling**
clus·ter ['klʌstə(r)] **1** *n* gruppo *m* **2** *v/i of people* raggrupparsi; *of houses* essere raggruppato
clutch [klʌtʃ] **1** *n* MOT frizione *f* **2** *v/t* stringere
♦ **clutch at** *v/t* cercare di afferrare
clut·ter ['klʌtə(r)] **1** *n* oggetti *mpl* alla rinfusa **2** *v/t (also: ~ up)* ingombrare
Co. *abbr (= Company)* C.ia *(= compagnia)*
c/o *abbr (= care of)* presso
coach [kəutʃ] **1** *n (trainer)* allenatore *m*, -trice *f*; *of singer etc* maestro *m*, -a *f*; *on train* vagone *m*; *(Br: bus)* pullman *m inv* **2** *v/t* allenare; *singer, actor* dare lezioni a
coach·ing ['kəutʃɪŋ] allenamento *m*; *of singer, actor* lezioni *fpl*
'coach par·ty gruppo *m* di turisti; **'coach sta·tion** stazione *f* dei pullman; **'coach tour** viaggio *m* turistico in pullman
co·ag·u·late [kəu'ægjuleɪt] *v/i of blood* coagularsi
coal [kəul] carbone *m*
co·a·li·tion [kəuə'lɪʃn] coalizione *f*
'coal·mine miniera *f* di carbone
coarse [kɔ:s] *adj skin, fabric* ruvido; *hair* spesso; *(vulgar)* grossolano
coarse·ly ['kɔ:slɪ] *adv (vulgarly)* grossolanamente; *ground* a grani grossi
coast [kəust] *n* costa *f*; **at the ~** sulla costa
coast·al ['kəustl] *adj* costiero
coast·er ['kəustə(r)] *for glass* sottobicchiere *m*; *for bottle* sottobottiglia *m*

'coast·guard *organization, person* guardia *f* costiera

'coast·line costa *f*, litorale *m*

coat [kəʊt] **1** *n (over~)* cappotto *m*; *of animal* pelliccia *f*; *of paint etc* mano *f* **2** *v/t (cover)* ricoprire

'coat·hang·er attaccapanni *m inv*, gruccia *f*

coat·ing ['kəʊtɪŋ] strato *m*

co·au·thor ['kəʊːθə(r)] **1** *n* co-autore *m*, -trice *f* **2** *v/t* scrivere insieme

coax [kəʊks] *v/t* convincere con le moine; **~ sth out of s.o.** ottenere qc da qu con le moine

cob·bled ['kɒbld] *adj* lastricato (a ciottoli)

cob·ble·stone ['kɒblstəʊn] ciottolo *m*

cob·web ['kɒbweb] ragnatela *f*

co·caine [kə'keɪn] cocaina *f*

cock [kɒk] *n chicken* gallo *m*; *any male bird* maschio *m* (di uccelli); V *(penis)* cazzo *m* V

cock-eyed [kɒk'aɪd] *adj* F *idea etc* strampalato

'cock·pit *of plane* cabina *f* (di pilotaggio)

cock·roach ['kɒkrəʊʧ] scarafaggio *m*

'cock·tail cocktail *m inv*

'cock·tail par·ty cocktail party *m inv*

'cock·tail shak·er shaker *m inv*

cock·y ['kɒkɪ] *adj* F arrogante

co·coa ['kəʊkəʊ] *drink* cioccolata *f* calda

co·co·nut ['kəʊkənʌt] cocco *m*

co·co·nut palm palma *f* di cocco

COD [siːəʊ'diː] *abbr* (= **cash on delivery**) pagamento *m* contrassegno

cod·dle ['kɒdl] *v/t sick person* coccolare; *pej: child* viziare

code [kəʊd] *n* codice *m*

co·ed·u·ca·tion·al [kəʊedjʊ'keɪʃnl] *adj* misto

co·erce [kəʊ'ɜːs] *v/t* costringere

co·ex·ist [kəʊɪg'zɪst] *v/i* coesistere

co·ex·ist·ence [kəʊɪg'zɪstəns] coesistenza *f*

cof·fee ['kɒfɪ] caffè *m inv*

'cof·fee bar caffè *m inv*; **'cof·fee bean** chicco *m* di caffè; **'cof·fee**

break pausa *f* per il caffè; **'cof·fee cup** tazza *f* da caffè; **'cof·fee grind·er** ['graɪndə(r)] macinacaffè *m inv*; **'cof·fee mak·er** caffettiera *f*; **'cof·fee pot** caffettiera *f*; **'cof·fee shop** caffetteria *f*; **'cof·fee ta·ble** tavolino *m*

cof·fin ['kɒfɪn] bara *f*

cog [kɒg] dente *m*

cog·nac ['kɒnjæk] cognac *m inv*

'cog·wheel ruota *f* dentata

co·hab·it [kəʊ'hæbɪt] *v/i* convivere

co·her·ent [kəʊ'hɪərənt] *adj* coerente

coil [kɔɪl] **1** *n of rope* rotolo *m* **2** *v/t*: **~ (up)** avvolgere

coin [kɔɪn] *n* moneta *f*

co·in·cide [kəʊɪn'saɪd] *v/i* coincidere

co·in·ci·dence [kəʊ'ɪnsɪdəns] coincidenza *f*

coke [kəʊk] P *(cocaine)* coca P *f*

Coke® [kəʊk] Coca® *f*

cold [kəʊld] **1** *adj* freddo; *I'm (feeling)* **~** ho freddo; *it's* **~** *of weather* fa freddo; *in* **~** *blood* a sangue freddo; *get* **~** *feet* F farsi prendere dalla fifa **2** *n* freddo *m*; MED raffreddore *m*; *I have a* **~** ho il raffreddore

cold-blood·ed [kəʊld'blʌdɪd] *adj also murder* a sangue freddo; *person* spietato

cold 'call·ing porta-a-porta *m*; *by phone* televendite *fpl*

'cold cuts *npl* affettati *mpl*

cold·ly ['kəʊldlɪ] *adv* freddamente

'cold meat affettati *mpl*

cold·ness ['kəʊldnɪs] *fig* freddezza *f*

'cold sore febbre *f* del labbro

cole·slaw ['kəʊlslɔː] insalata *f* di cavolo, carote, cipolle tritati e maionese

col·ic ['kɒlɪk] colica *f*

col·lab·o·rate [kə'læbəreɪt] *v/i* collaborare

col·lab·o·ra·tion [kəlæbə'reɪʃn] collaborazione *f*; *with enemy* collaborazionismo *m*

col·lab·o·ra·tor [kə'læbəreɪtə(r)] collaboratore *m*, -trice *f*; *with enemy* collaborazionista *m/f*

col·lapse [kə'læps] *v/i* crollare; *of*

person accacciarsi

col·lap·si·ble [kə'læpsəbl] *adj* pieghevole

col·lar ['kɒlə(r)] collo *m*, colletto *m*; *of dog, cat* collare *m*

'col·lar·bone clavicola *f*

col·league ['kɒliːg] collega *m/f*

col·lect [kə'lekt] **1** *v/t person*: go andare a prendere; *person*: come venire a prendere; *tickets, cleaning etc* ritirare; *as hobby* collezionare; *(gather)* raccogliere **2** *v/i (gather together)* radunarsi **3** *adv Am*: **call ~** telefonare a carico del destinatario

col·lect·ed [kə'lektɪd] *adj person* controllato; **the ~ works of ...** l'opera critica di ...

col·lec·tion [kə'lekʃn] collezione *f*; *in church* colletta *f*; *of poems, stories* raccolta *f*

col·lec·tive [kə'lektɪv] *adj* collettivo

col·lec·tive 'bar·gain·ing trattative *fpl* sindacali

col·lec·tor [kə'lektə(r)] collezionista *m/f*

col·lege ['kɒlɪdʒ] istituto *m* parauniversitario; *at Oxford and Cambridge* college *m inv*

col·lide [kə'laɪd] *v/i* scontrarsi

col·li·sion [kə'lɪʒn] collisione *f*, scontro *m*

col·lo·qui·al [kə'ləʊkwɪəl] *adj* colloquiale

co·lon ['kəʊlən] *punctuation* due punti *mpl*; ANAT colon *m inv*

colo·nel ['kɜːnl] colonnello *m*

co·lo·ni·al [kə'ləʊnɪəl] *adj* coloniale

co·lo·nize ['kɒlənaɪz] *v/t country* colonizzare

co·lo·ny ['kɒlənɪ] colonia *f*

col·or ['kʌlə(r)] *Am* → **colour** *etc*

co·los·sal [kə'lɒsl] *adj* colossale

col·our ['kʌlə(r)] **1** *n* colore *m*; *in cheeks* colorito *m*; **in ~** *film etc* a colori; **~s** MIL bandiera *f* **2** *v/t* colorare; *one's hair* tingere **3** *v/i (blush)* diventare rosso

'col·our-blind *adj* daltonico

col·oured ['kʌləd] *adj person* di colore

'col·our fast *adj* con colori resistenti

col·our·ful ['kʌləfʊl] *adj* pieno di colori; *account* pittoresco

col·our·ing ['kʌlərɪŋ] colorito *m*

'col·our pho·to·graph fotografia *f* a colori

'col·our scheme abbinamento *m* dei colori

'col·our TV tv *f inv* a colori

colt [kəʊlt] puledro *m*

col·umn ['kɒləm] colonna *f*; *(newspaper feature)* rubrica *f*

col·umn·ist ['kɒləm(n)ɪst] giornalista *m/f* che cura una rubrica

co·ma ['kəʊmə] coma *m inv*

comb [kəʊm] **1** *n* pettine *m* **2** *v/t* pettinare; *area* rastrellare

com·bat ['kɒmbæt] **1** *n* combattimento *m* **2** *v/t* combattere

com·bi·na·tion [kɒmbɪ'neɪʃn] combinazione *f*

com·bine [kəm'baɪn] **1** *v/t* unire; *ingredients* mescolare **2** *v/i of chemical elements* combinarsi

com·bine har·vest·er [kɒmbaɪn-'hɑːvɪstə(r)] mietitrebbia *f*

com·bus·ti·ble [kəm'bʌstɪbl] *adj* combustibile

com·bus·tion [kəm'bʌstʃn] combustione *f*

come [kʌm] *v/i (pret* **came**, *pp* **come**) venire; *of train, bus* arrivare; **you'll ~ to like it** finirà per piacerti; **how ~?** F come mai? F

◆ **come about** *v/i (happen)* succedere

◆ **come across 1** *v/t (find)* trovare **2** *v/i of idea, humour* essere capito; **she comes across as ...** dà l'impressione di essere ...

◆ **come along** *v/i (come too)* venire; *(turn up)* presentarsi; *(progress)* fare progressi; **how is it coming along?** come sta andando?; **your Italian has come along a lot** il tuo italiano è migliorato molto

◆ **come apart** *v/i* smontarsi; *(break)* andare in pezzi

◆ **come away** *v/i of person, button* venire via

◆ **come back** *v/i* ritornare; **it came back to me** mi è tornato in mente

♦ **come by 1** *v/i* passare **2** *v/t* (*acquire*) ottenere

♦ **come down** *v/i* venire giù; *in price, amount etc* scendere; *of rain, snow* cadere; **he came down the stairs** è sceso dalle scale

♦ **come for** *v/t* (*attack*) assalire; (*collect*) venire a prendere

♦ **come forward** *v/i* (*present o.s.*) farsi avanti

♦ **come from** *v/t* venire da; **where do you come from?** di dove sei?

♦ **come in** *v/i* entrare; *of train, in race* arrivare; *of tide* salire; **come in!** entra!

♦ **come in for** *v/t* attirare; **come in for criticism** attirare delle critiche

♦ **come in on** *v/t* partecipare a; **come in on a deal** stare a un accordo

♦ **come off** *v/i of handle etc* staccarsi

♦ **come on** *v/i* (*progress*) fare progressi; **how's the work coming on?** come sta venendo il lavoro?; **come on!** dai!; *in disbelief* ma dai!

♦ **come out** *v/i of person, book, sun* uscire; *of results, product* venir fuori; *of stain* venire via; *of gay* rendere nota la propria omosessualità

♦ **come round** *v/i to s.o.'s home* passare; (*regain consciousness*) rinvenire

♦ **come to 1** *v/t place, position* arrivare a; **that comes to £70** fanno 70 sterline **2** *v/i* (*regain consciousness*) rinvenire

♦ **come up** *v/i* salire; *of sun* sorgere; **something has come up** si è presentato qualcosa

♦ **come up with** *v/t new idea etc* venir fuori con

'**come·back** ritorno *m*; **make a ~** tornare alla ribalta

co·me·di·an [kə'miːdɪən] comico *m*, -a *f; pej* buffone *m*

'**come·down** passo *m* indietro

com·e·dy ['kɒmədɪ] commedia *f*

com·et ['kɒmɪt] cometa *f*

come·up·pance [kʌm'ʌpəns] *n* F: **he'll get his ~** avrà quello che si merita

com·fort ['kʌmfət] **1** *n* comodità *f inv*; (*consolation*) conforto *m* **2** *v/t* confortare

'**com·for·ta·ble** ['kʌmfətəbl] *adj chair, room* comodo; **be ~** *in chair* stare comodo; *in situation* essere a proprio agio; (*financially*) essere agiato

com·fy ['kʌmfɪ] *adj* F → **comfortable**

com·ic ['kɒmɪk] **1** *n to read* fumetto *m*; (*comedian*) comico *m*, -a *f* **2** *adj* comico

com·i·cal ['kɒmɪkl] *adj* comico

comic book fumetto *m*

comic strip striscia *f* (di fumetti)

com·ma ['kɒmə] virgola *f*

com·mand [kə'mɑːnd] **1** *n* comando *m* **2** *v/t person* comandare a

com·man·deer [kɒmən'dɪə(r)] *v/t* appropriarsi di

com·mand·er [kə'mɑːndə(r)] comandante *m*

com·mand·er-in-'chief comandante *m* in capo

com·mand·ing of·fi·cer [kə'mɑːndɪŋ] ufficiale *m* comandante

com·mand·ment [kə'mɑːndmənt]: **the Ten Commandments** REL i Dieci Comandamenti

com·mem·o·rate [kə'meməreɪt] *v/t* commemorare

com·mem·o·ra·tion [kəmemə'reɪʃn]: **in ~ of** in commemorazione di

com·mence [kə'mens] *v/t & v/i* cominciare

com·mend [kə'mend] *v/t* (*praise*) lodare; (*recommend*) raccomandare

com·mend·a·ble [kə'mendəbl] *adj* lodevole

com·men·da·tion [kɒmen'deɪʃn] *for bravery* riconoscimento *m*

com·men·su·rate [kə'menʃərət] *adj*: **~ with** commisurato a

com·ment ['kɒment] **1** *n* commento *m*; **no ~!** no comment! **2** *v/i* fare commenti

com·men·ta·ry ['kɒməntrɪ] cronaca *f*

com·men·tate ['kɒmənteɪt] *v/i* commentare

com·men·ta·tor ['kɒmənteɪtə(r)] *on TV* telecronista *m/f*; *on radio* radiocronista *m/f*

com·merce ['kɒmɜːs] commercio *m*

com·mer·cial [kəˈmɜːʃl] **1** *adj* commerciale **2** *n (advert)* pubblicità *f inv*

com·mer·cial 'break interruzione *f* pubblicitaria

com·mer·cial·ize [kəˈmɜːʃlaɪz] *v/t Christmas etc* commercializzare

com·mer·cial 'tel·e·vi·sion televisione *f* privata

com·mer·cial 'trav·el·ler rappresentante *m/f*

com·mis·e·rate [kəˈmɪzəreɪt] *v/i* esprimere rincrescimento (**with** *a*)

com·mis·sion [kəˈmɪʃn] **1** *n (payment, committee)* commissione *f*; *(job)* incarico *m* **2** *v/t for a job* incaricare

com·mis·sion·aire [kəmɪʃəˈneə(r)] portiere *m*

Com·mis·sion·er [kəˈmɪʃənə(r)] *in European Union* Commissario *m*, -a *f*

com·mit [kəˈmɪt] *v/t (pret & pp -ted) crime* commettere; *money* assegnare; **~ o.s.** impegnarsi

com·mit·ment [kəˈmɪtmənt] impegno *m*

com·mit·tee [kəˈmɪtɪ] comitato *m*

com·mod·i·ty [kəˈmɒdətɪ] prodotto *m*

com·mon ['kɒmən] *adj* comune; **in ~** in comune; **have sth in ~ with s.o.** avere qc in comune con qu

com·mon·er ['kɒmənə(r)] persona *f* non nobile

com·mon 'law husband / wife *convivente al quale spettano legalmente i diritti di una moglie / un marito*

com·mon·ly ['kɒmənlɪ] *adv* comunemente

Com·mon 'Mar·ket Mercato *m* Comune

'com·mon·place *adj* luogo *m* comune

Com·mons ['kɒmənz] *npl*: **the ~** la Camera dei Comuni

com·mon 'sense buon senso *m*

com·mo·tion [kəˈməʊʃn] confusione *f*

com·mu·nal ['kɒmjunl] *adj* comune

com·mu·nal·ly ['kɒmjunəlɪ] *adv* in comune

com·mu·ni·cate [kəˈmjuːnɪkeɪt] *v/t & v/i* comunicare

com·mu·ni·ca·tion [kəmjuːnɪˈkeɪʃn] comunicazione *f*

com·mu·ni·ca·tions *npl* comunicazioni *fpl*

com·mu·ni·ca·tions sat·el·lite satellite *m* per telecomunicazioni

com·mu·ni·ca·tive [kəˈmjuːnɪkətɪv] *adj person* comunicativo

Com·mun·ion [kəˈmjuːnɪən] REL comunione *f*

com·mu·ni·qué [kəˈmjuːnɪkeɪ] comunicato *m* ufficiale

Com·mu·nism ['kɒmjunɪzm] comunismo *m*

Com·mu·nist ['kɒmjunɪst] **1** *adj* comunista **2** *n* comunista *m/f*

com·mu·ni·ty [kəˈmjuːnətɪ] comunità *f inv*

com·mu·ni·ty cen·tre centro *m* comunitario

com·mu·ni·ty serv·ice servizio *m* civile (come pena per reati minori)

com·mute [kəˈmjuːt] **1** *v/i* fare il / la pendolare **2** *v/t* LAW commutare

com·mut·er [kəˈmjuːtə(r)] pendolare *m/f*

com·mut·er traf·fic traffico *m* dei pendolari

com·mut·er train treno *m* dei pendolari

com·pact [kəmˈpækt] **1** *adj* compatto **2** *n* ['kɒmpækt] *for powder* portacipria *m inv*

com·pact 'disc → *CD*

com·pan·ion [kəmˈpænjən] compagno *m*, -a *f*

com·pan·ion·ship [kəmˈpænjənʃɪp] compagnia *f*

com·pa·ny ['kʌmpənɪ] COM società *f inv*; *(ballet ~, theatre ~)* compagnia *f*; *(companionship, guests)* compagnia *f*

com·pa·ny: **keep s.o. ~** fare compagnia a qu

com·pa·ny 'car auto *f inv* della ditta

com·pa·ny 'law diritto *m* societario

com·pa·ra·ble ['kɒmpərəbl] *adj* paragonabile; (*similar*) simile

com·par·a·tive [kəm'pærətɪv] **1** *adj* (*relative*) relativo; *study, method* comparato; GRAM comparativo **2** *n* GRAM comparativo *m*

com·par·a·tive·ly [kəm'pærətɪvlɪ] *adv* relativamente

com·pare [kəm'peə(r)] **1** *v/t* paragonare; **~ sth with sth / s.o. with s.o.** paragonare qc a qc/qu a qu; **~d with ...** rispetto a ... **2** *v/i* reggere il confronto; **how did he ~?** com'era rispetto agli altri?

com·pa·ri·son [kəm'pærɪsn] paragone *m*, confronto *m*; **in ~ with** in confronto a; **there's no ~** non c'è paragone

com·part·ment [kəm'pɑːtmənt] scomparto *m*; RAIL scompartimento *m*

com·pass ['kʌmpəs] bussola *f*; (*pair of*) **~es** *for geometry* compasso *m*

com·pas·sion [kəm'pæʃn] compassione *f*

com·pas·sion·ate [kəm'pæʃənət] *adj* compassionevole

com·pas·sion·ate leave congedo *m* per motivi familiari

com·pat·i·bil·i·ty [kəmpætə'bɪlɪtɪ] compatibilità *f inv*

com·pat·i·ble [kəm'pætəbl] *adj also* COMPUT compatibile; **we're not ~** siamo incompatibili

com·pel [kəm'pel] *v/t* (*pret & pp* **-led**) costringere

com·pel·ling [kəm'pelɪŋ] *adj argument* convincente; *film, book* avvincente

com·pen·sate ['kɒmpənseɪt] **1** *v/t with money* risarcire **2** *v/i*: **~ for** compensare

com·pen·sa·tion [kɒmpən'seɪʃn] *money* risarcimento *m*; *reward* vantaggio *m*; *comfort* consolazione *f*

com·père ['kɒmpeə(r)] presentatore *m*, -trice *f*

com·pete [kəm'piːt] *v/i* competere; (*take part*) gareggiare; **~ for** contendersi

com·pe·tence ['kɒmpɪtəns] competenza *f*

com·pe·tent ['kɒmpɪtənt] *adj* competente

com·pe·tent·ly ['kɒmpɪtəntlɪ] *adv* con competenza

com·pe·ti·tion [kɒmpə'tɪʃn] (*contest*) concorso *m*; SP gara *f*; (*competing, competitors*) concorrenza *f*

com·pet·i·tive [kəm'petətɪv] *adj* competitivo; *sport* agonistico; *price, offer* concorrenziale

com·pet·i·tive·ly [kəm'petətɪvlɪ] *adv*: **~ priced** a prezzi concorrenziali

com·pet·i·tive·ness competitività *f inv*

com·pet·i·tor [kəm'petɪtə(r)] *in contest* concorrente *m/f*; **our ~s** COM la concorrenza

com·pile [kəm'paɪl] *v/t* compilare

com·pla·cen·cy [kəm'pleɪsənsɪ] autocompiacimento *m*

com·pla·cent [kəm'pleɪsənt] *adj* compiaciuto; **be ~ about sth** compiacersi di qc

com·plain [kəm'pleɪn] *v/i* lamentarsi; *to shop, manager* reclamare; **~ of** MED accusare

com·plaint [kəm'pleɪnt] lamentela *f*; *to shop* reclamo *m*; MED disturbo *m*

com·ple·ment ['kɒmplɪmənt] *v/t* completare; **they ~ each other** si completano bene

com·ple·men·ta·ry [kɒmplɪ'mentərɪ] *adj* complementare

com·plete [kəm'pliːt] **1** *adj* (*total*) completo; (*finished*) terminato; **I made a ~ fool of myself** mi sono comportato da perfetto idiota **2** *v/t task, building etc* completare; *form* compilare

com·plete·ly [kəm'pliːtlɪ] *adv* completamente

com·ple·tion [kəm'pliːʃn] completamento *m*; **payment on ~** pagamento a conclusione lavori

com·plex ['kɒmpleks] **1** *adj* complesso **2** *n also* PSYCH complesso *m*

com·plex·ion [kəmˈplekʃn] *facial* carnagione *f*

com·plex·i·ty [kəmˈpleksɪtɪ] complessità *f inv*

com·pli·ance [kəmˈplaɪəns] conformità *f inv*

com·pli·cate [ˈkɒmplɪkeɪt] *v/t* complicare

com·pli·cat·ed [ˈkɒmplɪkeɪtɪd] *adj* complicato

com·pli·ca·tion [kɒmplɪˈkeɪʃn] complicazione *f*; **~s** MED complicazioni

com·pli·ment [ˈkɒmplɪmənt] **1** *n* complimento *m* **2** *v/t* fare i complimenti a

com·pli·men·ta·ry [kɒmplɪˈmentərɪ] *adj* lusinghiero; (*free*) in omaggio

'com·pli·ments slip [ˈkɒmplɪmənts] biglietto *m* intestato della ditta

com·ply [kəmˈplaɪ] *v/i* (*pret & pp* **-ied**) ubbidire; **~ with** osservare; *of products, equipment* essere conforme a

com·po·nent [kəmˈpəʊnənt] componente *m*

com·pose [kəmˈpəʊz] *v/t also* MUS comporre; **be ~d of** essere composto da; **~ o.s.** ricomporsi

com·posed [kəmˈpəʊzd] *adj* (*calm*) calmo

com·pos·er [kəmˈpəʊzə(r)] MUS compositore *m*, -trice *f*

com·po·si·tion [kɒmpəˈzɪʃn] *also* MUS composizione *f*; (*essay*) tema *m*

com·po·sure [kəmˈpəʊʒə(r)] calma *f*

com·pound [ˈkɒmpaʊnd] *n* CHEM composto *m*

com·pound 'in·ter·est interesse *m* composto

com·pre·hend [kɒmprɪˈhend] *v/t* (*understand*) capire

com·pre·hen·sion [kɒmprɪˈhenʃn] comprensione *f*

com·pre·hen·sive [kɒmprɪˈhensɪv] *adj* esauriente

com·pre·hen·sive in'sur·ance polizza *f* casco

com·pre·hen·sive·ly [kɒmprɪˈhensɪvlɪ] *adv* in modo esauriente

com·pre·hen·sive school scuola *f* secondaria

com·press [ˈkɒmpres] **1** *n* MED impacco *m* **2** *v/t* [kəmˈpres] *air, gas* comprimere; *information* condensare

com·prise [kəmˈpraɪz] *v/t* comprendere; (*make-up*) costituire; **be ~d of** essere composto da

com·pro·mise [ˈkɒmprəmaɪz] **1** *n* compromesso *m* **2** *v/i* arrivare a un compromesso **3** *v/t* (*jeopardize*) compromettere; **~ o.s.** compromettersi

com·pul·sion [kəmˈpʌlʃn] PSYCH coazione *f*

com·pul·sive [kəmˈpʌlsɪv] *adj* *behaviour* patologico; *reading, viewing* avvincente

com·pul·so·ry [kəmˈpʌlsərɪ] *adj* obbligatorio; **~ education** scuola *f* dell'obbligo

com·put·er [kəmˈpjuːtə(r)] computer *m inv*; **have sth on ~** avere qc sul computer

com·put·er-aid·ed de'sign progettazione *f* assistita dall'elaboratore; **com·put·er-aid·ed man·u'fac·ture** produzione *f* computerizzata; **com·put·er-con'trolled** *adj* controllato dal computer; **com'puter game** computer game *m inv*

com·put·er·ize [kəmˈpjuːtəraɪz] *v/t* computerizzare

com·put·er 'lit·er·ate *adj* che ha la dimestichezza con il computer; **com·put·er 'sci·ence** informatica *f*; **com·put·er 'sci·en·tist** informatico *m*, -a *f*

com·put·ing [kəmˈpjuːtɪŋ] *n* informatica *f*

com·rade [ˈkɒmreɪd] *also* POL compagno *m*, -a *f*

com·rade·ship [ˈkɒmreɪdʃɪp] cameratismo *m*

con [kɒn] **1** *n* F truffa *f* **2** *v/t* (*pret & pp* **-ned**) F truffare; **~ s.o. into doing sth** far fare qc a qu con l'inganno

con·ceal [kənˈsiːl] *v/t* nascondere

con·ceal·ment [kənˈsiːlmənt] occultazione *f*

con·cede [kənˈsiːd] *v/t* (*admit*) ammettere; *goal* concedere

con·ceit [kənˈsiːt] presunzione *f*

con·ceit·ed [kənˈsiːtɪd] *adj* presuntuoso

con·cei·va·ble [kənˈsiːvəbl] *adj* concepibile

con·ceive [kənˈsiːv] *v/i of woman* concepire; ~ **of** (*imagine*) immaginare

con·cen·trate [ˈkɒnsəntreɪt] **1** *v/i* concentrarsi **2** *v/t one's attention, energies* concentrare

con·cen·trat·ed [ˈkɒnsəntreɪtɪd] *adj juice etc* concentrato

con·cen·tra·tion [kɒnsənˈtreɪʃn] concentrazione *f*

con·cept [ˈkɒnsept] concetto *m*

con·cep·tion [kənˈsepʃn] *of child* concepimento *m*

con·cern [kənˈsɜːn] **1** *n* (*anxiety*) preoccupazione *f*; (*care*) interesse *m*; (*business*) affare *m*; (*company*) impresa *f*; **there's no cause for ~** non c'è motivo di preoccuparsi; **it's none of your ~** non sono affari tuoi **2** *v/t* (*involve*) riguardare; (*worry*) preoccupare; ~ **o.s. with** preoccuparsi di

con·cerned [kənˈsɜːnd] *adj* (*anxious*) preoccupato; (*caring*) interessato; (*involved*) in questione; **as far as I'm** ~ per quanto mi riguarda

con·cern·ing [kənˈsɜːnɪŋ] *prep* riguardo a

con·cert [ˈkɒnsət] concerto *m*

con·cert·ed [kənˈsɜːtɪd] *adj* (*joint*) congiunto

con·cer·to [kənˈtʃeətəʊ] concerto *m*

con·ces·sion [kənˈseʃn] (*compromise*) concessione *f*

con·cil·i·a·to·ry [kənsɪlɪˈeɪtərɪ] *adj* conciliatorio

con·cise [kənˈsaɪs] *adj* conciso

con·clude [kənˈkluːd] **1** *v/t* concludere; ~ **sth from sth** concludere qc da qc **2** *v/i* concludere

con·clu·sion [kənˈkluːʒn] conclusione *f*; **in** ~ in conclusione

con·clu·sive [kənˈkluːsɪv] *adj* conclusivo

con·coct [kənˈkɒkt] *v/t meal, drink* mettere insieme; *excuse, story* inventare

con·coc·tion [kənˈkɒkʃn] *food, drink* intruglio *m*

con·crete[1] [ˈkɒŋkriːt] *adj* concreto

con·crete[2] [ˈkɒŋkriːt] *n* calcestruzzo *m*; ~ **jungle** giungla *f* di cemento

con·cur [kənˈkɜː(r)] *v/i* (*pret & pp* **-red**) essere d'accordo

con·cus·sion [kənˈkʌʃn] commozione *f* cerebrale

con·demn [kənˈdem] *v/t action* condannare; *building* dichiarare inagibile; (*doom*) condannare

con·dem·na·tion [kɒndəmˈneɪʃn] *of action* condanna *f*

con·den·sa·tion [kɒndenˈseɪʃn] *on walls, windows* condensa *f*

con·dense [kənˈdens] **1** *v/t* (*make shorter*) condensare **2** *v/i of steam* condensarsi

con·densed 'milk [kənˈdensd] latte *m* condensato

con·de·scend [kɒndɪˈsend] *v/i:* **he ~ed to speak to me** si è degnato di rivolgermi la parola

con·de·scend·ing [kɒndɪˈsendɪŋ] *adj* (*patronizing*) borioso

con·di·tion [kənˈdɪʃn] **1** *n* condizione *f*; MED malattia *f*; ~ **s** (*circumstances*) condizioni; **on** ~ **that** a condizione che; **in/out of** ~ in/ fuori forma **2** *v/t* PSYCH condizionare

con·di·tion·al [kənˈdɪʃnl] **1** *adj* acceptance condizionale **2** *n* GRAM condizionale *m*

con·di·tion·er [kənˈdɪʃnə(r)] *for hair* balsamo *m*; *for fabric* ammorbidente *m*

con·di·tion·ing [kənˈdɪʃnɪŋ] PSYCH condizionamento *m*

con·do·lences [kənˈdəʊlənsɪz] *npl* condoglianze *fpl*

con·dom [ˈkɒndəm] preservativo *m*

con·done [kənˈdəʊn] *v/t actions* scusare

con·du·cive [kənˈdjuːsɪv] *adj:* **be** ~ **to** favorire

con·duct [ˈkɒndʌkt] **1** *n* (*behaviour*)

con·dot·ta *f* **2** *v/t* [kən'dʌkt] (*carry out*) condurre; ELEC condurre; MUS dirigere; **~ o.s.** comportarsi

con·duct·ed tour [kən'dʌktɪd] visita *f* guidata

con·duc·tor [kən'dʌktə(r)] MUS direttore *m* d'orchestra; *on bus* bigliettaio *m*; PHYS conduttore *m*

con·duc·tress [kən'dʌktrɪs] bigliettaia *f*

cone [kəʊn] cono *m*; *of pine tree* pigna *f*; *on motorway* birillo *m*

♦ **cone off** *v/t* chiudere al traffico

con·fec·tion·er [kən'fekʃənə(r)] pasticciere *m*, -a *f*

con·fec·tion·e·ry [kən'fekʃənərɪ] dolciumi *mpl*

con·fed·e·ra·tion [kənfedə'reɪʃn] confederazione *f*

con·fer [kən'fɜː(r)] (*pret & pp* **-red**) **1** *v/t* (*bestow*) conferire **2** *v/i* (*discuss*) confabulare

con·fe·rence ['kɒnfərəns] congresso *m*; *family* ~ consiglio *m* di famiglia

'con·fe·rence cen·tre centro *m* congressi

'con·fe·rence room sala *f* riunioni

con·fess [kən'fes] **1** *v/t* *sin*, *crime* confessare **2** *v/i* confessare; REL confessarsi; ~ **to sth** confessare qc; ~ **to a weakness for sth** confessare di avere un debole per qc

con·fes·sion [kən'feʃn] confessione *f*

con·fes·sion·al [kən'feʃnl] REL confessionale *m*

con·fes·sor [kən'fesə(r)] REL confessore *m*

con·fide [kən'faɪd] **1** *v/t* confidare **2** *v/i*: ~ **in s.o.** confidarsi con qu

con·fi·dence ['kɒnfɪdəns] (*assurance*) sicurezza *f* (di sé); (*trust*) fiducia *f*; **in** ~ in confidenza

con·fi·dent ['kɒnfɪdənt] *adj* sicuro; *person* sicuro di sé

con·fi·den·tial [kɒnfɪ'denʃl] *adj* riservato, confidenziale; *adviser* di fiducia

con·fi·den·tial·ly [kɒnfɪ'denʃlɪ] *adv* in confidenza

con·fi·dent·ly ['kɒnfɪdəntlɪ] *adv* con sicurezza

con·fine [kən'faɪn] *v/t* (*imprison*) richiudere; (*restrict*) limitare; **be ~d to one's bed** essere costretto a letto

con·fined [kən'faɪnd] *adj* space ristretto

con·fine·ment [kən'faɪnmənt] (*imprisonment*) reclusione *f*; MED parto *m*

con·firm [kən'fɜːm] *v/t* confermare

con·fir·ma·tion [kɒnfə'meɪʃn] conferma *f*

con·firmed [kən'fɜːmd] *adj* bachelor incallito

con·fis·cate ['kɒnfɪskeɪt] *v/t* sequestrare

con·flict ['kɒnflɪkt] **1** *n* conflitto *m* **2** *v/i* [kən'flɪkt] *of statements*, *accounts* essere in conflitto; *of dates* coincidere

con·form [kən'fɔːm] *v/i* conformarsi; ~ **to** *of products*, *acts etc* essere conforme a

con·form·ist [kən'fɔːmɪst] *n* conformista *m/f*

con·front [kən'frʌnt] *v/t* (*face*) affrontare; ~ **s.o. with sth** mettere qu di fronte a qc; *the problems ~ing us* i problemi che dobbiamo affrontare

con·fron·ta·tion [kɒnfrən'teɪʃn] scontro *m*

con·fuse [kən'fjuːz] *v/t*) confondere; ~ **s.o. with s.o.** confondere qu con qu

con·fused [kən'fjuːzd] *adj* confuso

con·fus·ing [kən'fjuːzɪŋ] *adj* che confonde

con·fu·sion [kən'fjuːʒn] confusione *f*

con·geal [kən'dʒiːl] *v/i of blood, fat* rapprendersi

con·gen·ial [kən'dʒiːnɪəl] *adj* (*pleasant*) simpatico

con·gen·i·tal [kən'dʒenɪtl] *adj* MED congenito

con·gest·ed [kən'dʒestɪd] *adj* congestionato

con·ges·tion [kən'dʒestʃn] congestione f; **traffic ~** la congestione del traffico

con·grat·u·late [kənˈgrætjʊleɪt] v/t congratularsi con

con·grat·u·la·tions [kəngrætjʊˈleɪʃnz] npl congratulazioni fpl; **~ on ...** congratulazioni per ...

con·grat·u·la·to·ry [kəngrætjʊˈleɪtəri] adj di congratulazioni

con·gre·gate [ˈkɒŋgrɪgeɪt] v/i (gather) riunirsi

con·gre·ga·tion [kɒŋgrɪˈgeɪʃn] REL fedeli mpl

con·gress [ˈkɒŋgres] (conference) congresso m; **Congress in US** il Congresso

Con·gres·sion·al [kənˈgreʃnl] adj del Congresso

Con·gress·man [ˈkɒŋgresmən] membro m del Congresso

co·ni·fer [ˈkɒnɪfə(r)] conifera f

con·jec·ture [kənˈdʒektʃə(r)] n (speculation) congettura f

con·ju·gate [ˈkɒndʒʊgeɪt] v/t GRAM coniugare

con·junc·tion [kənˈdʒʌŋkʃn] GRAM congiunzione f; **in ~ with** insieme a

con·junc·ti·vi·tis [kəndʒʌŋktɪˈvaɪtɪs] congiuntivite f

♦ **con·jure up** [ˈkʌndʒə(r)] v/t (produce) far apparire (come) per magia; (evoke) evocare

con·jur·er, con·jur·or [ˈkʌndʒərə(r)] (magician) prestigiatore m, -trice f

'**con·jur·ing tricks** [ˈkʌndʒərɪŋ] npl giochi mpl di prestigio

con man [ˈkɒnmæn] F truffatore m

con·nect [kəˈnekt] v/t (join, link) collegare; (to power supply) allacciare; **~ s.o. with s.o.** TELEC mettere in comunicazione qu con qu

con·nect·ed [kəˈnektɪd] adj: **be well-~** avere conoscenze influenti; **be ~ with ...** essere collegato con; **by marriage** essere imparentato con

con·nect·ing flight [kəˈnektɪŋ] coincidenza f (volo)

con·nec·tion [kəˈnekʃn] (link) collegamento m; when travelling coinci-

denza f; (personal contact) conoscenza f; **in ~ with** a proposito di

con·nois·seur [kɒnəˈsɜː(r)] intenditore m, -trice f

con·quer [ˈkɒŋkə(r)] v/t conquistare; fig: fear etc vincere

con·quer·or [ˈkɒŋkərə(r)] conquistatore m, -trice f

con·quest [ˈkɒŋkwest] conquista f

con·science [ˈkɒnʃəns] coscienza f; **have a guilty / clear ~** avere la coscienza sporca / a posto; **on one's ~** sulla coscienza

con·sci·en·tious [kɒnʃɪˈenʃəs] adj coscienzioso

con·sci·en·tious·ness [kɒnʃɪˈenʃəsnəs] coscienziosità f inv

con·sci·en·tious ob·ject·or obiettore m di coscienza

con·scious [ˈkɒnʃəs] adj (aware) consapevole; (deliberate) conscio; MED cosciente; **be / become ~ of** rendersi conto di

con·scious·ly [ˈkɒnʃəslɪ] adv consapevolmente

con·scious·ness [ˈkɒnʃəsnɪs] (awareness) consapevolezza f; MED conoscenza f; **lose / regain ~** perdere / riprendere conoscenza

con·sec·u·tive [kənˈsekjʊtɪv] adj consecutivo

con·sen·sus [kənˈsensəs] consenso m

con·sent [kənˈsent] **1** n consenso m **2** v/i acconsentire

con·se·quence [ˈkɒnsɪkwəns] (result) conseguenza f

con·se·quent·ly [ˈkɒnsɪkwəntlɪ] adv (therefore) di conseguenza

con·ser·va·tion [kɒnsəˈveɪʃn] (preservation) tutela f

con·ser·va·tion area area f soggetta a vincoli urbanistici e ambientali

con·ser·va·tion·ist [kɒnsəˈveɪʃnɪst] ambientalista m/f

con·ser·va·tive [kənˈsɜːvətɪv] **1** adj (conventional) conservatore; clothes tradizionale; estimate cauto; **Conservative** Br POL conservatore **2** n Br POL **Conservative** conservatore m, -trice f

con·ser·va·to·ry [kən'sɜːvətrɪ] veranda *f*; MUS conservatorio *m*

con·serve [kən'sɜːv] **1** *n* (*jam*) marmellata *f* **2** *v/t* [kən'sɜːv] *energy, strength* risparmiare

con·sid·er [kən'sɪdə(r)] *v/t* (*regard*) considerare; (*show regard for*) tener conto di; (*think about*) pensare a; *~ doing sth* prendere in considerazione la possibilità di fare qc; *it is ~ed to be his best work* è considerata la sua opera migliore

con·sid·e·ra·ble [kən'sɪdrəbl] *adj* considerevole

con·sid·e·ra·bly [kən'sɪdrəblɪ] *adv* considerevolmente

con·sid·er·ate [kən'sɪdərət] *adj person, attitude* premuroso; *be ~ of* avere riguardo per

con·sid·er·ate·ly [kən'sɪdərətlɪ] *adv* premurosamente

con·sid·e·ra·tion [kənsɪdə'reɪʃn] (*thought*) considerazione *f*; (*thoughtfulness, concern*) riguardo *m*; (*factor*) fattore *m*; *take sth into ~* prendere in considerazione qc; *under ~* in esame

con·sign·ment [kən'saɪnmənt] COM consegna *f*

♦ **con·sist of** [kən'sɪst] *v/t* consistere in

con·sis·ten·cy [kən'sɪstənsɪ] (*texture*) consistenza *f*; (*unchangingness*) coerenza *f*

con·sis·tent [kən'sɪstənt] *adj* (*unchanging*) coerente

con·sis·tent·ly [kən'sɪstəntlɪ] *adv* in modo coerente; *always* costantemente

con·so·la·tion [kɒnsə'leɪʃn] consolazione *f*

con·sole [kən'səʊl] *v/t* consolare

con·sol·i·date [kən'sɒlɪdeɪt] *v/t* consolidare

con·so·nant ['kɒnsənənt] *n* GRAM consonante *f*

con·sor·ti·um [kən'sɔːtɪəm] consorzio *m*

con·spic·u·ous [kən'spɪkjʊəs] *adj*: *be / look ~* spiccare; *feel ~* sentirsi fuori posto

con·spi·ra·cy [kən'spɪrəsɪ] cospirazione *f*

con·spi·ra·tor [kən'spɪrətə(r)] cospiratore *m*, -trice *f*

con·spire [kən'spaɪə(r)] *v/i* cospirare

con·stant ['kɒnstənt] *adj* (*continuous*) costante

con·stant·ly ['kɒnstəntlɪ] *adv* costantemente

con·ster·na·tion [kɒnstə'neɪʃn] costernazione *f*

con·sti·pat·ed ['kɒnstɪpeɪtɪd] *adj* stitico

con·sti·pa·tion [kɒnstɪ'peɪʃn] stitichezza *f*

con·sti·tu·en·cy [kən'stɪtjʊənsɪ] Br POL circoscrizione *f* elettorale

con·sti·tu·ent [kən'stɪtjʊənt] *n* (*component*) componente *m*; Br POL elettore *m*, -trice *f*

con·sti·tute ['kɒnstɪtjuːt] *v/t* costituire

con·sti·tu·tion [kɒnstɪ'tjuːʃn] *also* POL costituzione *f*

con·sti·tu·tion·al [kɒnstɪ'tjuːʃənl] *adj* POL costituzionale

con·straint [kən'streɪnt] (*restriction*) restrizione *f*

con·struct [kən'strʌkt] *v/t building etc* costruire

con·struc·tion [kən'strʌkʃn] costruzione *f*; *under ~* in costruzione; **con'struc·tion in·dus·try** edilizia *f*; **con'struc·tion site** cantiere *m* edile; **con'struc·tion work·er** operaio *m* edile

con·struc·tive [kən'strʌktɪv] *adj* costruttivo

con·sul ['kɒnsl] console *m*

con·su·late ['kɒnsjʊlət] consolato *m*

con·sult [kən'sʌlt] *v/t* (*seek the advice of*) consultare

con·sul·tan·cy [kən'sʌltənsɪ] (*company*) società *f* inv di consulenza; (*advice*) consulenza *f*

con·sul·tant [kən'sʌltənt] *n* (*adviser*) consulente *m/f*

consultation [kɒnsəl'teɪʃn] consultazione *f*

con·sult·ing hours orario *m* di visita

con·sult·ing room ambulatorio *m*

con·sume [kən'sju:m] *v/t* consumare

con·sum·er [kən'sju:mə(r)] (*purchaser*) consumatore *m*, -trice *f*; **con'sum·er con·fi·dence** fiducia *f* dei consumatori; **con'sum·er goods** *npl* beni *mpl* di consumo; **con'sum·er so·ci·e·ty** società *f inv* dei consumi

con·sump·tion [kən'sʌmpʃn] consumo *m*

con·tact ['kɒntækt] **1** *n* contatto *m*; (*person*) conoscenza *f*; **keep in ∼ with s.o.** mantenere i contatti con qu **2** *v/t* mettersi in contatto con

'con·tact lens lente *f* a contatto

'con·tact num·ber *numero m presso cui si è reperibili*

con·ta·gious [kən'teɪdʒəs] *adj also fig* contagioso

con·tain [kən'teɪn] *v/t* (*hold*) contenere; *flood, disease, revolt* contenere; **∼ o.s.** contenersi

con·tain·er [kən'teɪnə(r)] (*recipient*) contenitore *m*; COM container *m inv*

con'tain·er ship nave *f* portacontainer

con·tam·i·nate [kən'tæmɪneɪt] *v/t* contaminare

con·tam·i·na·tion [kəntæmɪ'neɪʃn] contaminazione *f*

con·tem·plate ['kɒntəmpleɪt] *v/t* (*look at*) contemplare; (*think about*) considerare; **∼ doing sth** considerare la possibilità di fare qc

con·tem·po·ra·ry [kən'tempərəri] **1** *adj* contemporaneo **2** *n* coetaneo *m*, -a *f*

con·tempt [kən'tempt] disprezzo *m*; **be beneath ∼** essere spregevole

con·temp·ti·ble [kən'temptəbl] *adj* spregevole

con·temp·tu·ous [kən'temptjuəs] *adj* sprezzante

con·tend [kən'tend] *v/i*: **∼ for sth** contendersi qc; **∼ with s.o. / sth** confrontarsi con qc / qu

con·tend·er [kən'tendə(r)] *in sport, competition* concorrente *m/f*; *against*

champion sfidante *m/f*; POL candidato *m*, -a *f*

con·tent¹ ['kɒntent] *n* contenuto *m*

con·tent² [kən'tent] **1** *adj* contento **2** *v/t*: **∼ o.s. with** accontentarsi di

con·tent·ed [kən'tentɪd] *adj* contento

con·ten·tion [kən'tenʃn] (*assertion*) opinione *f*; **be in ∼ for** essere in lizza per

con·ten·tious [kən'tenʃəs] *adj* polemico

con·tent·ment [kən'tentmənt] soddisfazione *f*

con·tents ['kɒntents] *npl of house, letter, bag etc* contenuto *m*

con·test¹ ['kɒntest] *n* (*competition*) concorso *m*; (*struggle, for power*) lotta *f*

con·test² [kən'test] *v/t leadership etc* essere in lizza per; *will* impugnare

con·tes·tant [kən'testənt] concorrente *m/f*

con·text ['kɒntekst] contesto *m*; **look at sth in ∼ / out of ∼** considerare qc in / fuori contesto

con·ti·nent ['kɒntɪnənt] *n* continente *m*; **the ∼** l'Europa continentale

con·ti·nen·tal [kɒntɪ'nentl] *adj* continentale

con·ti·nen·tal 'break·fast *colazione f a base di caffè, pane, burro e marmellata*

con·tin·gen·cy [kən'tɪndʒənsɪ] eventualità *f inv*

con·tin·u·al [kən'tɪnjuəl] *adj* continuo

con·tin·u·al·ly [kən'tɪnjuəlɪ] *adv* continuamente

con·tin·u·a·tion [kəntɪnju'eɪʃn] seguito *m*

con·tin·ue [kən'tɪnju:] **1** *v/t* continuare; **∼ doing sth** continuare a fare qc; **to be ∼d** continua … **2** *v/i* continuare

con·ti·nu·i·ty [kɒntɪ'nju:ətɪ] continuità *f inv*; *in films* ordine *m* della sceneggiatura

con·tin·u·ous [kən'tɪnjuəs] *adj* ininterrotto

con·tin·u·ous·ly [kənˈtɪnjʊəslɪ] *adv* ininterrottamente

con·tort [kənˈtɔːt] *v/t* contorcere

con·tour [ˈkɒntʊə(r)] profilo *m*; *on map* curva *f* di livello

con·tra·cep·tion [kɒntrəˈsepʃn] contraccezione *f*

con·tra·cep·tive [kɒntrəˈseptɪv] *n* anticoncezionale *m*, contraccettivo *m*

con·tract¹ [ˈkɒntrækt] *n* contratto *m*

con·tract² [kənˈtrækt] **1** *v/i* (*shrink*) contrarsi **2** *v/t illness* contrarre

con·trac·tor [kənˈtræktə(r)] appaltatore *m*, -trice *f*; *building* ~ ditta *f* di appalti (edili)

con·trac·tu·al [kənˈtræktjʊəl] *adj* contrattuale

con·tra·dict [kɒntrəˈdɪkt] *v/t* contraddire

con·tra·dic·tion [kɒntrəˈdɪkʃn] contraddizione *f*

con·tra·dic·to·ry [kɒntrəˈdɪktrɪ] *adj account* contraddittorio

con·trap·tion [kənˈtræpʃn] F aggeggio *m*

con·trar·y¹ [ˈkɒntrərɪ] **1** *adj* contrario; ~ *to* contrariamente a **2** *n*: *on the* ~ al contrario

con·tra·ry² [kənˈtreərɪ] *adj*: *be* ~ (*perverse*) essere un bastian contrario

con·trast [ˈkɒntrɑːst] **1** *n* contrasto *m*; *by* ~ invece **2** *v/t* [kənˈtrɑːst] confrontare **3** *v/i* contrastare

con·trast·ing [kənˈtrɑːstɪŋ] *adj* contrastante

con·tra·vene [kɒntrəˈviːn] *v/t* contravvenire a

con·trib·ute [kənˈtrɪbjuːt] **1** *v/i with money, material, time* contribuire; *to magazine, paper* collaborare (*to* con); *to discussion* intervenire (*to* in); (*help to cause*) contribuire a creare **2** *v/t money* contribuire con

con·tri·bu·tion [kɒntrɪˈbjuːʃn] *money* offerta *f*; *to political party, church* donazione *f*; *of time, effort* contributo *m*; *to debate* intervento *m*; *to magazine* collaborazione *f*

con·trib·u·tor [kənˈtrɪbjʊtə(r)] *of money* finanziatore *m*, -trice *f*; *to magazine* collaboratore *m*, -trice *f*

con·trol [kənˈtrəʊl] **1** *n* controllo *m*; *take* ~ *of* assumere il controllo di; *lose* ~ *of* perdere il controllo di; *lose* ~ *of o.s.* perdere il controllo; *circumstances beyond our* ~ cause indipendenti dalla nostra volontà; *be in* ~ *of sth* tenere qc sotto controllo; *get out of* ~ diventare incontrollabile; *the situation is under* ~ la situazione è sotto controllo; *bring a blaze under* ~ circoscrivere un incendio; ~*s of aircraft, vehicle* comandi; ~*s* (*restrictions*) restrizioni **2** *v/t* (*pret & pp* -**led**) (*govern*) controllare; *traffic* dirigere; (*restrict*) contenere; (*regulate*) regolare; ~ *o.s.* controllarsi

con·trol cen·ter *Am,* **con·trol cen·tre** centro *m* di controllo

con·trol freak F persona *f* che vuole avere tutto e tutti sotto controllo

con·trolled ˈsub·stance [kənˈtrəʊld] sostanza *f* stupefacente

con·trol·ling ˈin·ter·est [kənˈtrəʊlɪŋ] FIN maggioranza *f* delle azioni

con·trol pan·el quadro *m* dei comandi

con·trol tow·er torre *f* di controllo

con·tro·ver·sial [kɒntrəˈvɜːʃl] *adj* controverso

con·tro·ver·sy [ˈkɒntrəvɜːsɪ] polemica *f*

con·va·lesce [kɒnvəˈles] *v/i* rimettersi (in salute)

con·va·les·cence [kɒnvəˈlesns] convalescenza *f*

con·vene [kənˈviːn] *v/t* indire

con·ve·ni·ence [kənˈviːnɪəns] *of having sth, location* comodità *f inv*; *at my*/*your* ~ a mio/tuo comodo; *all* (*modern*) ~*s* tutti i comfort

con·ve·ni·ence food scatolame *m*, cibi precotti ecc

con·ve·ni·ence store negozio *m* alimentari

con·ve·ni·ent [kənˈviːnɪənt] *adj location, device* comodo; *whenever*

C

it's ~ quando ti va bene

con•ve•ni•ent•ly [kən'viːnɪəntlɪ] *adv* comodamente

con•vent ['kɒnvənt] convento *m*

con•ven•tion [kən'venʃn] (*tradition*) convenzione *f*; (*conference*) congresso *m*

con•ven•tion•al [kən'venʃnl] *adj person, ideas* convenzionale; *method* tradizionale

♦ con•verge on [kən'vɜːdʒ] *v/t* convergere su

con•ver•sant [kən'vɜːsənt] *adj*: *be ~ with* essere pratico di

con•ver•sa•tion [kɒnvə'seɪʃn] conversazione *f*

con•ver•sa•tion•al [kɒnvə'seɪʃnl] *adj* colloquiale

con•verse ['kɒnvɜːs] *n* (*opposite*) contrario *m*

con•verse•ly [kən'vɜːslɪ] *adv* per contro

con•ver•sion [kən'vɜːʃn] conversione *f*; *of house* trasformazione *f*

con•ver•sion ta•ble tabella *f* di conversione

con•vert ['kɒnvɜːt] **1** *n* convertito *m*, -a *f* **2** *v/t* [kən'vɜːt] convertire **3** *v/i* trasformarsi (*into* in); *house, room* trasformare

con•ver•ti•ble [kən'vɜːtəbl] *n car* cabriolet *f inv*, decappottabile *f*

con•vey [kən'veɪ] *v/t* (*transmit*) comunicare; (*carry*) trasportare

con•vey•or belt [kən'veɪə(r)] nastro *m* trasportatore

con•vict ['kɒnvɪkt] **1** *n* carcerato *m*, -a *f* **2** *v/t* [kən'vɪkt] LAW condannare; *~ s.o. of sth* condannare qu per qc

con•vic•tion [kən'vɪkʃn] LAW condanna *f*; (*belief*) convinzione *f*

con•vince [kən'vɪns] *v/t* convincere

con•vinc•ing [kən'vɪnsɪŋ] *adj* convincente

con•viv•i•al [kən'vɪvɪəl] *adj* (*friendly*) gioviale

con•voy ['kɒnvɔɪ] convoglio *m*

con•vul•sion [kən'vʌlʃn] MED convulsione *f*

cook [kʊk] **1** *n* cuoco *m*, -a *f*; *I'm a*

good ~ cucino bene **2** *v/t vegetables, meat* cucinare; *meal, dinner* preparare; *a ~ed meal* un pasto caldo; *~ the books* F falsificare i registri **3** *v/i of person* cucinare; *of vegetables, meat* cuocere

'cook•book ricettario *m*

cook•er ['kʊkə(r)] cucina *f*

cook•e•ry ['kʊkərɪ] cucina *f*

'cook•e•ry book ricettario *m*

cook•ie ['kʊkɪ] *Am* biscotto *m*

cook•ing ['kʊkɪŋ] *food* cucina *f*; *he does all the* ~ è lui che cucina

cool [kuːl] **1** *n* F: *keep / lose one's* ~ conservare / perdere la calma **2** *adj weather, breeze, drink* fresco; (*calm*) calmo; (*unfriendly*) freddo **3** *v/i of food* raffreddarsi; *of tempers* calmarsi; *of interest* raffreddarsi **4** *v/t* F: *~ it!* calma!

♦ cool down **1** *v/i* raffreddarsi; *of weather* rinfrescare; *fig: of tempers* calmarsi **2** *v/t food* raffreddare; *fig* calmare

cool•ing-'off pe•ri•od periodo *m* di riflessione

co•op•e•rate [kəʊ'ɒpəreɪt] *v/i* cooperare

co•op•e•ra•tion [kəʊɒpə'reɪʃn] cooperazione *f*

co•op•e•ra•tive [kəʊ'ɒpərətɪv] **1** *n* COM cooperativa *f* **2** *adj* COM cooperativo; (*helpful*) disponibile (a collaborare)

co•or•di•nate [kəʊ'ɔːdɪneɪt] *v/t* coordinare

co•or•di•na•tion [kəʊɔː di'neɪʃn] *of activities* coordinamento *m*; *of body* coordinazione *f*

cop [kɒp] *n* F poliziotto *m*

cope [kəʊp] *v/i* farcela; *~ with* farcela con

cop•i•er ['kɒpɪə(r)] *machine* fotocopiatrice *f*

co•pi•lot ['kəʊpaɪlət] secondo pilota *m*

co•pi•ous ['kəʊpɪəs] *adj* abbondante

cop•per ['kɒpə(r)] *n metal* rame *m*

cop•y ['kɒpɪ] **1** *n* copia *f*; *written material* materiale *m*; *fair* ~ bella copia *f*; *rough* ~ brutta copia *f*;

make a ~ of a file fare una copia di un file **2** v/t (*pret & pp -ied*) copiare

'cop·y·cat F copione *m*, -a *f* F; **copy·cat 'crime** *reato m a imitazione di un altro*; **'cop·y·right** *n diritti mpl d'autore, copyright m inv*; **'cop·y·writ·er** *in advertising* copywriter *m*

cor·al ['kɔːrəl] corallo *m*

cord [kɔːd] (*string*) corda *f*; (*cable*) filo *m*

cor·di·al ['kɔːdɪəl] *adj* cordiale

cord·less 'phone ['kɔːdlɪs] cordless *m inv*

cor·don ['kɔːdn] cordone *m*

◆**cor·don off** v/t transennare; *put cordon around* recintare

cords [kɔːdz] *npl trousers* pantaloni *mpl* di velluto a coste

cor·du·roy ['kɔːdərɔɪ] velluto *m* a coste

core [kɔː(r)] **1** *n of fruit* torsolo *m*; *of problem* nocciolo *m*; *of organization, party* cuore *m* **2** v/t *fruit* togliere il torsolo a **3** *adj issue, meaning* essenziale

cork [kɔːk] *in bottle* tappo *m* di sughero; (*material*) sughero *m*

'cork·screw *n* cavatappi *m inv*

corn [kɔːn] *grain* frumento *m*; *Am* (*maize*) granturco *m*

cor·ner ['kɔːnə(r)] **1** *n of page, room, street* angolo *m*; (*equivalent*) spigolo *m*; *in football* calcio *m* d'angolo, corner *m inv*; **in the ~** nell'angolo; **on the ~** *of street* all'angolo; **around the ~** dietro l'angolo **2** v/t *person* bloccare; **~ a market** prendersi il monopolio di un mercato **3** v/i *of driver, car* affrontare una curva

'cor·ner kick *in football* calcio *m* d'angolo

'cor·ner shop piccola drogheria *f*

'corn·flakes *npl* fiocchi *mpl* di granturco, cornflakes *mpl*

'corn·flour farina *f* di granturco

corn·y ['kɔːnɪ] *adj* F scontato; *sentimental* sdolcinato

cor·o·na·ry ['kɔrənərɪ] **1** *adj* coronario **2** *n* infarto *m*

cor·o·ner ['kɒrənə(r)] *ufficiale m*

pubblico che indaga sui casi di morte sospetta

cor·po·ral ['kɔːpərəl] *n* caporale *m* maggiore

cor·po·ral 'pun·ish·ment punizione *f* corporale

cor·po·rate ['kɔːpərət] *adj* COM aziendale; **~ image** corporate image *f inv*; **sense of ~ loyalty** corporativismo *m*

cor·po·ra·tion [kɔːpə'reɪʃn] (*business*) corporation *f inv*

corps [kɔː(r)] *nsg* corpo *m*

corpse [kɔːps] cadavere *m*

cor·pu·lent ['kɔːpjulənt] *adj* corpulento

cor·pus·cle ['kɔːpʌsl] globulo *m*

cor·rect [kə'rekt] **1** *adj* giusto; *behaviour* corretto; **she's ~** ha ragione **2** v/t correggere

cor·rec·tion [kə'rekʃn] correzione *f*

cor·rect·ly [kə'rektlɪ] *adv* giustamente; *behave* correttamente

cor·re·spond [kɒrɪ'spɒnd] v/i (*match, write*) corrispondere; **~ to** corrispondere a; **~ with** corrispondere con

cor·re·spon·dence [kɒrɪ'spɒndəns] (*agreement, letters*) corrispondenza *f*

cor·re·spon·dent [kɒrɪ'spɒndənt] corrispondente *m/f*

cor·re·spon·ding [kɒrɪ'spɒndɪŋ] *adj* (*equivalent*) corrispondente

cor·ri·dor ['kɒrɪdɔː(r)] *in building* corridoio *m*

cor·rob·o·rate [kə'rɒbəreɪt] v/t corroborare

cor·rode [kə'rəud] v/t & v/i corrodere

cor·ro·sion [kə'rəuʒn] corrosione *f*

cor·ru·gat·ed 'card·board ['kɒrəgeɪtɪd] cartone *m* ondulato

cor·ru·gat·ed 'i·ron lamiera *f* (di ferro) ondulata

cor·rupt [kə'rʌpt] **1** *adj also* COMPUT corrotto **2** v/t *morals, youth* traviare; (*bribe*) corrompere

cor·rup·tion [kə'rʌpʃn] corruzione *f*

Cor·si·ca ['kɔːsɪkə] Corsica *f*

Cor·si·can ['kɔːsɪkən] **1** *adj* corso **2** *n* corso *m*, -a *f*

cos·met·ic [kɒzˈmetɪk] adj cosmetico; surgery estetico; fig di facciata

cos·met·ics [kɒzˈmetɪks] npl cosmetici mpl

cos·met·ic 'sur·geon chirurgo m estetico

cos·met·ic 'sur·ger·y chirurgia f estetica

cos·mo·naut [ˈkɒzmənɔːt] cosmonauta m/f

cos·mo·pol·i·tan [kɒzməˈpɒlɪtən] adj city cosmopolitano

cost¹ [kɒst] **1** n also fig costo m; at all ~s a ogni costo; I've learnt to my ~s l'ho imparato a mie spese; ~s LAW spese **2** v/t (pret & pp cost) costare; FIN: proposal, project fare il preventivo di; how much does it ~? quanto costa?; it ~ me my health ci ho rimesso la salute

cost² [kɒst] v/t (pret & pp costed) FIN: proposal, project fare il preventivo di

cost and 'freight COM costo e nolo; **'cost-con·scious** adj: be ~ fare attenzione ai consumi; **'cost-ef·fec·tive** adj conveniente; **'cost, insurance and freight** COM costo, assicurazione e nolo

cost·ly [ˈkɒstlɪ] adj mistake costoso; it would be a ~ mistake potresti pagarla cara

cost of 'liv·ing costo m della vita

cost 'price prezzo m di costo

cos·tume [ˈkɒstjuːm] for actor costume m

cos·tume 'jew·el·lery, Am **cos·tume 'jew·el·ry** bigiotteria f

co·sy adj (comfortable) gradevole; (intimate and friendly) intimo; be nice and ~ in bed starsene al calduccio a letto; a nice ~ little job un lavoretto tranquillo

cot [kɒt] for child lettino m

cot·tage [ˈkɒtɪdʒ] cottage m inv

cot·tage 'cheese fiocchi mpl di latte

cot·ton [ˈkɒtn] **1** n cotone m **2** adj di cotone
♦ **cotton on** v/i F afferrare F
♦ **cotton on to** v/t F afferrare F

cot·ton 'wool ovatta f

couch [kaʊtʃ] n divano m

'couch po·ta·to F teledipendente m/f

cou·chette [kuːˈʃet] cuccetta f

cough [kɒf] **1** n tosse f; to get attention colpetto m di tosse **2** v/i tossire; to get attention tossicchiare
♦ **cough up 1** v/t blood etc sputare; F money cacciar fuori F **2** v/i F (pay) cacciare i soldi F

'cough medicine, 'cough syrup sciroppo m per la tosse

could¹ [kʊd] v/aux: ~ I have my key? mi dà la chiave?; ~ you help me? mi puoi dare una mano?; this ~ be our bus questo potrebbe essere il nostro autobus; you ~ be right magari hai ragione; I ~n't say for sure non potrei giurarci; he ~ have got lost può darsi che si sia smarrito; you ~ have warned me! in indignation avresti potuto avvisarmi!

could² [kʊd] pret → can

coun·cil [ˈkaʊnsl] n (assembly) consiglio m; (city ~) comune m

'coun·cil house casa f popolare

coun·cil·lor [ˈkaʊnsələ(r)] consigliere m, -a f (comunale)

'coun·cil tax imposta f comunale sugli immobili

coun·sel [ˈkaʊnsl] **1** n (advice) consiglio m; (lawyer) avvocato m **2** v/t course of action consigliare; person offrire consulenza a

coun·sel·ing Am, **coun·sel·ling** [ˈkaʊnslɪŋ] terapia f

coun·sel·or, Am **coun·sel·or** [ˈkaʊnslə(r)] (adviser) consulente m/f

count¹ [kaʊnt] aristocrat conte m

count² [kaʊnt] **1** n conteggio m; keep / lose ~ of tenere / perdere il conto di; what's your ~? quanti ne hai contati? **2** v/i contare; that doesn't ~ questo non conta **3** v/t contare; ~ yourself lucky considerati fortunato
♦ **count on** v/t contare su

'count·down conto m alla rovescia

coun·te·nance [ˈkaʊntənəns] v/t approvare

coun·ter¹ ['kaʊntə(r)] *in shop, café* banco *m; in game* segnalino *m*

coun·ter² ['kaʊntə(r)] **1** *v/t* neutralizzare **2** *v/i* (*retaliate*) rispondere

coun·ter 3 ['kaʊntə(r)] *adv*: **run ~ to** andare contro

'coun·ter·act *v/t* neutralizzare

coun·ter-at·tack 1 *n* contrattacco *m* **2** *v/i* contrattaccare

'coun·terbal·ance 1 *n* contrappeso *m* **2** *v/t* fare da contrappeso a

coun·ter·es·pi·o·nage controspionaggio *m*

coun·ter·feit ['kaʊntəfɪt] **1** *v/t* falsificare **2** *adj* falso

coun·ter·foil ['kaʊntəfɔɪl] matrice *f*

'coun·ter·part *person* omologo *m*, -a *f*

coun·ter·pro'duc·tive *adj* controproducente

'coun·ter·sign *v/t* controfirmare

coun·tess ['kaʊntes] contessa *f*

count·less ['kaʊntlɪs] *adj* innumerevole

coun·try ['kʌntrɪ] **1** *n* (*nation*) paese *m; as opposed to town* campagna *f; in the ~* in campagna **2** *adj roads, life* di campagna

coun·try and 'west·ern MUS country and western *m inv*; **'coun·try·man** (*fellow ~*) connazionale *m*; **'coun·try·side** campagna *f*

coun·ty ['kaʊntɪ] contea *f*

coup [kuː] POL colpo *m* di stato, golpe *m inv; fig* colpo *m*

cou·ple ['kʌpl] *n* coppia *f; just a ~* solo un paio; **a ~ of** un paio di

cou·pon ['kuːpɒn] buono *m*

cour·age ['kʌrɪdʒ] coraggio *m*

cou·ra·geous [kə'reɪdʒəs] *adj* coraggioso

cou·ri·er ['kʊrɪə(r)] (*messenger*) corriere *m; with tourist party* accompagnatore *m* turistico, accompagnatrice *f* turistica

course [kɔːs] *n series of lessons* corso *m; part of meal* portata *f; of ship, plane* rotta *f; for golf* campo *m; for race, skiing* pista *f; of ~* (*certainly*) certo; (*naturally*) ovviamente; **of ~ not** certo che no; **first ~** primo *m;*

second ~ secondo *m; ~ of action** linea *f* di condotta; **~ of treatment** cura *f; in the ~ of** nel corso di

court [kɔːt] *n* LAW corte *f;* (*courthouse*) tribunale *m;* SP campo *m;* **take s.o. to ~** fare causa a qu; **out of ~** in via amichevole

'court case caso *m* (giudiziario)

cour·te·ous ['kɜːtɪəs] *adj* cortese

cour·te·sy ['kɜːtəsɪ] cortesia *f*

'court·house tribunale *m*, palazzo *m* di giustizia; **court 'mar·tial 1** *n* corte *f* marziale **2** *v/t* processare in corte marziale; **'court or·der** ingiunzione *f* del tribunale; **'court·room** aula *f* del tribunale; **'court·yard** cortile *m*

cous·in ['kʌzn] cugino *m*, -a *f*

cove [kəʊv] *small bay* cala *f*

cov·er ['kʌvə(r)] **1** *n protective* fodera *f; of book, magazine* copertina *f;* (*shelter*) riparo *m; insurance* copertura *f; ~s for bed* coperte fpl; **take ~** ripararsi **2** *v/t* coprire; *distance* percorrere; *of journalist* fare un servizio su; **we're not ~ed for theft** non siamo coperti contro i furti

♦ **cover up 1** *v/t* coprire; *fig* insabbiare **2** *v/i*: **cover up for s.o.** *fig* coprire qu

cov·er·age ['kʌvərɪdʒ] *by media* copertura *f; the trial got a lot of ~* il processo ha avuto molta risonanza

cov·er·ing let·ter ['kʌvrɪŋ] lettera *f* d'accompagnamento

cov·ert [kəʊ'vɜːt] *adj* segreto

'cov·er-up insabbiamento *m; it looks like a ~** sembra che qualcuno stia cercando di insabbiare le prove

cow [kaʊ] mucca *f*

cow·ard ['kaʊəd] vigliacco *m*, -a *f*

cow·ard·ice ['kaʊədɪs] vigliaccheria *f*

cow·ard·ly ['kaʊədlɪ] *adj* vile

'cow·boy cow-boy *m inv*

cow·er ['kaʊə(r)] *v/i* rannicchiarsi

coy [kɔɪ] *adj* (*evasive*) evasivo; (*flirtatious*) civettuolo

'coz·y *Am* → **cosy**

CPU [siːpiː'juː] *abbr* (= **central**

processing unit) unità f centrale di elaborazione

crab [kræb] n granchio m

crack [kræk] **1** n crepa f; (*joke*) battuta f **2** v/t cup, glass incrinare; nut schiacciare; code decifrare; F (*solve*) risolvere; ~ **a joke** fare una battuta **3** v/i incrinarsi; **get ~ing** F darsi una mossa

♦ **crack down on** v/t prendere serie misure contro

♦ **crack up** v/i (*have breakdown*) avere un esaurimento; F (*laugh*) scoppiare a ridere

'**crack·brained** adj F pazzoide f

'**crack·down** intensificazione f dei controlli (**on** su)

cracked [krækt] adj cup, glass incrinato; F (*crazy*) tocco F

crack·er ['krækə(r)] to eat cracker m inv

crack·le ['krækl] v/i of fire schioppettare

cra·dle ['kreidl] n for baby culla f

craft[1] [krɑːft] NAUT imbarcazione f

craft[2] [krɑːft] (*skill*) attività f inv artigiana; (*trade*) mestiere m

crafts·man ['krɑːftsmən] artigiano m

craft·y ['krɑːfti] adj astuto

crag [kræg] rock rupe f

cram [kræm] v/t papers, food infilare; people stipare

cramp [kræmp] n crampo m

cramped [kræmpt] adj room, flat esiguo

cran·ber·ry ['krænbəri] mirtillo m

crane [krein] **1** n machine gru f inv **2** v/t: ~ **one's neck** allungare il collo

crank [kræŋk] n strange person tipo m strambo

'**crank·shaft** albero m a gomiti

crash [kræʃ] **1** n noise fragore m; accident incidente m; COM crollo m; COMPUT crash m inv **2** v/i fall noisily fracassarsi; of thunder rombare; of car schiantarsi; of two cars scontrarsi, schiantarsi; of plane precipitare; COM: of market crollare; COMPUT fare un crash; F (*sleep*) dormire **3** v/t car avere un incidente con

♦ **crash out** v/i F (*fall asleep*) addormentarsi; without meaning to crollare F

'**crash bar·ri·er** barriera f protettiva; '**crash course** corso m intensivo; '**crash di·et** dieta f lampo; '**crash hel·met** casco m (di protezione); '**crash-land** v/i fare un atterraggio di fortuna; '**crash land·ing** atterraggio m di fortuna

crate [kreit] (*packing case*) cassetta f

cra·ter ['kreitə(r)] of volcano cratere m

crave [kreiv] v/t smaniare dalla voglia di

crav·ing ['kreiviŋ] voglia f; pej smania f

crawl [krɔːl] **1** n in swimming crawl m, stile m libero; **at a ~** (*very slowly*) a passo d'uomo **2** v/i on floor andare (a) carponi; (*move slowly*) avanzare lentamente

♦ **crawl with** v/t brulicare di

cray·on ['kreiɒn] n matita f colorata; wax pastello m a cera

craze [kreiz] moda f

cra·zy ['kreizi] adj pazzo; **be ~ about s.o.** essere pazzo di qu; **be ~ about sth** andare matto per qc

creak [kriːk] **1** n scricchiolio m **2** v/i scricchiolare

creak·y ['kriːki] adj che scricchiola

cream [kriːm] **1** n for skin crema f; for coffee, cake panna f; colour color m panna **2** adj color panna

cream 'cheese formaggio m fresco da spalmare

cream·er ['kriːmə(r)] for coffee panna f liofilizzata

cream·y ['kriːmi] adj (with lots of cream) cremoso

crease [kriːs] **1** n accidental grinza f; deliberate piega f **2** v/t accidentally sgualcire

cre·ate [kriː'eit] v/t creare

cre·a·tion [kriː'eiʃn] creazione f

cre·a·tive [kriː'eitiv] adj creativo

cre·a·tor [kriː'eitə(r)] creatore m, -trice f; **the Creator** REL il Creatore

crea·ture ['kriːtʃə(r)] creatura f

crop up

crèche [kreʃ] *for children* asilo *m* nido; REL presepe *m*

cred·i·bil·i·ty [kredə'bɪlətɪ] credibilità *f inv*

cred·i·ble ['kredəbl] *adj* credibile

cred·it ['kredɪt] **1** *n* FIN credito *m*; *(honour)* merito *m*; **be in ~** avere un saldo attivo; **get the ~ for sth** prendersi il merito di qc **2** *v/t (believe)* credere; **~ an amount to an account** accreditare una cifra su un conto

cred·i·ta·ble ['kredɪtəbl] *adj* lodevole

'cred·it card carta *f* di credito

'cred·it lim·it limite *m* di credito

cred·i·tor ['kredɪtə(r)] creditore *m*, -trice *f*

'cred·it·wor·thy *adj* solvibile

cred·u·lous ['kredjʊləs] *adj* credulo

creed [kriːd] credo *m inv*

creep [kriːp] **1** *n pej* tipo *m* odioso **2** *v/i (pret & pp crept)* quietly avanzare quatto quatto; *slowly* avanzare lentamente

creep·er ['kriːpə(r)] BOT rampicante *m*

creeps [kriːps] *npl* F: **the house / he gives me the ~** la casa / lui mi fa venire la pelle d'oca

creep·y ['kriːpɪ] *adj* F che dà i brividi; **be ~** far paura

cre·mate [krɪ'meɪt] *v/t* cremare

cre·ma·tion [krɪ'meɪʃn] cremazione *f*

cre·ma·to·ri·um [kremə'tɔːrɪəm] crematorio *m*

crept [krept] *pret & pp* → **creep**

cres·cent ['kresənt] *n shape* mezzaluna *f*

crest [krest] *of hill, bird* cresta *f*

crest·fal·len *adj* abbattuto

cre·vasse [krə'væs] voragine *f*

crev·ice ['krevɪs] crepa *f*

crew [kruː] *n of ship, plane* equipaggio *m*; *of workers etc* squadra *f*; *(film ~)* troupe *f inv*; *(crowd, group)* ghenga *f*

'crew cut taglio *m* a spazzola

'crew neck girocollo *m*

crick [krɪk] *n*: **~ in the neck** torcicollo *m*

crick·et ['krɪkɪt] *insect* grillo *m*; *game* cricket *m inv*

crime [kraɪm] *(offence)* reato *m*; *(criminality)* criminalità *f inv*; *(shameful act)* crimine *m*

crim·i·nal ['krɪmɪnl] **1** *n* delinquente *m/f* **2** *adj* LAW penale; *(shameful)* vergognoso; **a ~ offence** un reato

crim·son ['krɪmzn] *adj* cremisi *inv*

cringe [krɪndʒ] *v/i* morire di vergogna

crip·ple ['krɪpl] **1** *n (disabled person)* invalido *m*, -a *f* **2** *v/t person* rendere invalido; *fig* paralizzare

cri·sis ['kraɪsɪs] *(pl crises ['kraɪsiːz])* crisi *f inv*

crisp [krɪsp] *adj weather, air, lettuce, new shirt* fresco; *bacon, toast* croccante; *bank notes* nuovo di zecca

crisps [krɪsps] *npl Br* patatine *fpl*

cri·te·ri·on [kraɪ'tɪərɪən] criterio *m*

crit·ic ['krɪtɪk] critico *m*, -a *f*

crit·i·cal ['krɪtɪkl] *adj* critico

crit·i·cal·ly ['krɪtɪklɪ] *adv speak etc* criticamente; **~ ill** gravemente malato

crit·i·cis·m ['krɪtɪsɪzm] critica *f*

crit·i·cize ['krɪtɪsaɪz] *v/t* criticare

croak [krəʊk] **1** *n of frog* gracidio *m*; *of person* rantolo *m* **2** *v/i of frog* gracidare; *of person* parlare con voce rauca

cro·chet ['krəʊʃeɪ] **1** *n* lavoro *m* all'uncinetto **2** *v/t* lavorare all'uncinetto

crock·e·ry ['krɒkərɪ] stoviglie *fpl*

croc·o·dile ['krɒkədaɪl] coccodrillo *m*

cro·cus ['krəʊkəs] croco *m*

cro·ny ['krəʊnɪ] F amico *m*, -a *f*

crook [krʊk] *n* truffatore *m*, -trice *f*

crook·ed ['krʊkɪd] *adj streets* tortuoso; *picture* storto; *(dishonest)* disonesto

crop [krɒp] **1** *n* raccolto *m*; *type of grain etc* coltura *f*; *fig* scaglione *m* **2** *v/t (pret & pp -ped) hair, photo* tagliare

♦ **crop up** *v/i* venir fuori

C

cross [krɒs] **1** adj (angry) arrabbiato **2** n croce f **3** v/t (go across) attraversare; ~ **one's legs** accavallare le gambe; **keep one's fingers ~ed** fare gli scongiuri; **it never ~ed my mind** non mi è passato per la testa **4** v/i (go across) attraversare; of lines intersecarsi

♦ **cross off, cross out** v/t depennare

'**cross·bar** of goal traversa f; of bicycle canna f; in high jump asticella f

'**cross-check 1** n controllo m incrociato **2** v/t fare un controllo incrociato su

cross-'coun·try corsa f campestre

cross-coun·try ('skiing) sci m inv di fondo

crossed 'check Am, crossed 'cheque [krɒst] assegno m sbarrato

cross-ex·am·i'na·tion LAW interrogatorio m in contraddittorio

cross-ex'am·ine v/t LAW interrogare in contraddittorio

cross-eyed ['krɒsaɪd] adj strabico

cross·ing ['krɒsɪŋ] NAUT traversata f; for pedestrians attraversamento m pedonale

'**cross·roads** nsg incrocio m; fig bivio m; '**cross-sec·tion** of people campione m rappresentativo; '**cross-walk** Am passaggio m pedonale; '**cross·word** (**puz·zle**) cruciverba m inv

crotch [krɒtʃ] of person inguine m; of trousers cavallo m

crouch [krautʃ] v/i accovacciarsi

crow [krəʊ] n bird corvo m; **as the ~ flies** in linea d'aria

'**crow·bar** piede m di porco

crowd [kraud] n folla f

crowd·ed ['kraudɪd] adj affollato

crown [kraun] **1** n corona f; on tooth capsula f **2** v/t king incoronare; tooth incapsulare

cru·cial ['kruːʃl] adj essenziale

cru·ci·fix ['kruːsɪfɪks] crocifisso m

cru·ci·fix·ion [kruːsɪ'fɪkʃn] crocifissione f

cru·ci·fy ['kruːsɪfaɪ] v/t (pret & pp -ied) REL crocifiggere; fig fare a pezzi

crude [kruːd] **1** adj (vulgar) volgare; (unsophisticated) rudimentale **2** n: ~ (oil) (petrolio m) greggio m

crude·ly ['kruːdlɪ] adv speak volgarmente; made rozzamente

cru·el ['kruːəl] adj crudele

cru·el·ty ['kruːəltɪ] crudeltà f inv

cruise [kruːz] **1** n crociera f **2** v/i of people fare una crociera; of car, plane viaggiare a velocità di crociera

'**cruise lin·er** nave f da crociera

cruis·ing speed ['kruːzɪŋ] also fig velocità f inv di crociera

crumb [krʌm] briciola f

crum·ble ['krʌmbl] **1** v/t sbriciolare **2** v/i of bread sbriciolarsi; of stonework sgretolarsi; fig: of opposition etc crollare

crum·bly ['krʌmblɪ] adj friabile

crum·ple ['krʌmpl] **1** v/t (crease) sgualcire **2** v/i (collapse) accasciarsi

crunch [krʌntʃ] **1** n F: **when it comes to the ~** al momento cruciale **2** v/i of snow, gravel scricchiolare

cru·sade [kruː'seɪd] n also fig crociata f

crush [krʌʃ] **1** n crowd ressa f; **have a ~ on** avere una cotta per **2** v/t schiacciare; (crease) sgualcire; **they were ~ed to death** sono morti schiacciati **3** v/i (crease) sgualcire

crust [krʌst] on bread crosta f

crust·y ['krʌstɪ] adj bread croccante

crutch [krʌtʃ] for injured person stampella f

cry [kraɪ] **1** n (call) grido m; **have a ~** piangere **2** v/t (pret & pp -ied) (call) gridare **3** v/i (pret & pp -ied) (weep) piangere

♦ **cry out** v/t & v/i gridare

♦ **cry out for** v/t (need) aver fortemente bisogno di

cryp·tic ['krɪptɪk] adj sibillino

crys·tal ['krɪstl] **1** n mineral cristallo m; glass cristalli mpl **2** adj di cristallo

crys·tal·lize ['krɪstlaɪz] **1** v/t concretizzare **2** v/i *of thoughts etc* concretizzarsi

cub [kʌb] cucciolo *m*

Cu·ba ['kjuːbə] Cuba *f*

Cu·ban ['kjuːbən] **1** *adj* cubano **2** *n* cubano *m*, -a *f*

cube [kjuːb] *shape* cubo *m*

cu·bic ['kjuːbɪk] *adj* cubico

cu·bic ca'pac·i·ty TECH cilindrata *f*

cu·bi·cle ['kjuːbɪkl] (*changing room*) cabina *f*

cu·cum·ber ['kjuːkʌmbə(r)] cetriolo *m*

cud·dle ['kʌdl] **1** *n* coccole *fpl* **2** v/t coccolare

cud·dly ['kʌdlɪ] *adj kitten etc* tenero; *liking cuddles* coccolone

cue [kjuː] *n for actor etc* imbeccata *f*; *for billiards* stecca *f*

cuff [kʌf] **1** *n of shirt* polsino *m*; (*blow*) schiaffo *m*; *Am* (*of trousers*) risvolto *m*; **off the ~** improvvisando **2** v/t *hit* dare uno schiaffo a

'cuff link gemello *m*

'cul-de-sac ['kʌldəsæk] vicolo *m* cieco

cu·li·nar·y ['kʌlɪnərɪ] *adj* culinario

cul·mi·nate ['kʌlmɪneɪt] v/i culminare; **~ in** culminare in

cul·mi·na·tion [kʌlmɪ'neɪʃn] culmine *m*

cu·lottes ['kjuːlɒt] *npl* gonna *f* pantalone

cul·prit ['kʌlprɪt] colpevole *m/f*

cult [kʌlt] culto *m*

cul·ti·vate ['kʌltɪveɪt] v/t *land* coltivare; *person* coltivarsi

cul·ti·vat·ed ['kʌltɪveɪtɪd] *adj person* colto

cul·ti·va·tion [kʌltɪ'veɪʃn] *of land* coltivazione *f*

cul·tu·ral ['kʌltʃərəl] *adj* culturale

cul·ture ['kʌltʃə(r)] *n* cultura *f*

cul·tured ['kʌltʃəd] *adj* (*cultivated*) colto

'cul·ture shock shock *m inv* culturale

cum·ber·some ['kʌmbəsəm] *adj* ingombrante; *procedure* macchinoso

cu·mu·la·tive ['kjuːmjʊlətɪv] *adj* cumulativo

cun·ning ['kʌnɪŋ] **1** *n* astuzia *f* **2** *adj* astuto

cup [kʌp] *n* tazza *f*; (*trophy*) coppa *f*; **a ~ of tea** una tazza di tè

'cup·board ['kʌbəd] armadio *m*

'cup fi·nal finale *f* di coppa

cu·po·la ['kjuːpələ] cupola *f*

'cup tie partita *f* di coppa

cu·ra·ble ['kjʊərəbl] *adj* curabile

cu·ra·tor [kjʊə'reɪtə(r)] direttore *m*, -trice *f* di museo

curb [kɜːb] **1** *n on powers etc* freno *m* **2** v/t tenere a freno

cur·dle ['kɜːdl] v/i *of milk* cagliare

cure [kjʊə(r)] **1** *n* MED cura *f* **2** v/t MED guarire; *by drying* essiccare; *by salting* salare; *by smoking* affumicare

cur·few ['kɜːfjuː] coprifuoco *m*

cu·ri·os·i·ty [kjʊərɪ'ɒsɪtɪ] curiosità *f inv*

cu·ri·ous ['kjʊərɪəs] *adj* (*inquisitive*) curioso; (*strange*) strano

cu·ri·ous·ly ['kjʊərɪəslɪ] *adv* (*inquisitively*) con curiosità; (*strangely*) stranamente; **~ enough ...** sembrerà strano ma ...

curl [kɜːl] **1** *n in hair* ricciolo *m*; *of smoke* spirale *f* **2** v/t arricciare **3** v/i *of hair* arricciarsi; *of leaf, paper etc* accartocciarsi

♦ **curl up** v/i acciambellarsi

curl·y ['kɜːlɪ] *adj hair* riccio; *tail* a ricciolo

cur·rant ['kʌrənt] (*dried fruit*) uva *f* passa

cur·ren·cy ['kʌrənsɪ] *money* valuta *f*; **foreign ~** valuta estera

cur·rent ['kʌrənt] **1** *n* corrente *f* **2** *adj* (*present*) attuale

'cur·rent ac·count conto *m* corrente

cur·rent af'fairs, cur·rent e'vents *npl* attualità *f inv*

cur·rent af'fairs pro·gramme programma *m* di attualità

cur·rent·ly ['kʌrəntlɪ] *adv* attualmente

cur·ric·u·lum [kə'rɪkjʊləm] programma *m* (scolastico)

cur·ric·u·lum vi·tae ['viːtaɪ]

curriculum *m inv* vitae

cur·ry ['kʌrɪ] *dish* piatto *m* al curry; *spice* curry *m inv*

curse [kɜːs] **1** *n spell* maledizione *f*; (*swearword*) imprecazione *f* **2** *v/t* maledire; (*swear at*) imprecare contro **3** *v/i* (*swear*) imprecare

cur·sor ['kɜːsə(r)] COMPUT cursore *m*

cur·so·ry ['kɜːsərɪ] *adj* di sfuggita

curt [kɜːt] *adj* brusco

cur·tail [kɜː'teɪl] *v/t trip etc* accorciare

cur·tain ['kɜːtn] tenda *f*; THEA sipario *m*

curve [kɜːv] **1** *n* curva *f* **2** *v/i* (*bend*) fare una curva

cush·ion ['kʊʃn] **1** *n for couch etc* cuscino *m* **2** *v/t blow, fall* attutire

cus·tard ['kʌstəd] crema *f* (pasticcera)

cus·to·dy ['kʌstədɪ] *of children* custodia *f*; **in ~** LAW in detenzione preventiva

cus·tom ['kʌstəm] (*tradition*) usanza *f*; COM clientela *f*; **as was his ~** com'era suo solito

cus·tom·a·ry ['kʌstəmərɪ] *adj* consueto; **it is ~ to ...** è consuetudine ...

cus·tom·er ['kʌstəmə(r)] cliente *m/f*

cus·tom·er re'la·tions *npl* relazione *f* clienti

cus·tom·er 'serv·ice servizio *m* assistenza al cliente

cus·toms ['kʌstəmz] *npl* dogana *f*

Cus·toms and 'Ex·cise Ufficio *m* Dazi e Dogana; **'cus·toms clear·ance** sdoganamento *m*; **'cus·toms in·spec·tion** controllo *m* doganale; **'cus·toms of·fi·cer** doganiere *m*, -a *f*

cut [kʌt] **1** *n with knife, of hair, clothes* taglio *m*; (*reduction*) riduzione *f*; *in public spending* taglio *m*; **my hair needs a ~** devo tagliarmi i capelli **2** *v/t* (*pret & pp* **cut**) tagliare; (*reduce*) ridurre; **get one's hair ~** tagliarsi i capelli; **I ~ my finger** mi sono tagliato un dito

♦ **cut back 1** *v/i in costs* limitare le spese **2** *v/t employees* ridurre

♦ **cut down 1** *v/t tree* abbattere **2** *v/i in smoking etc* limitarsi

♦ **cut down on** *v/t cigarettes, chocolate* ridurre la quantità di; **cut down on smoking** fumare di meno

♦ **cut off** *v/t with knife, scissors etc* tagliare; (*isolate*) isolare; **I've been cut off** TELEC è caduta la linea

♦ **cut out** *v/t with scissors* ritagliare; (*eliminate*) eliminare; **cut that out!** F smettila!; **be cut out for sth** essere tagliato per qc

♦ **cut up** *v/t meat etc* sminuzzare

cut·back *in production* riduzione *f*; *in public spending* taglio *m*

cute [kjuːt] *adj* (*pretty*) carino; (*smart, clever*) furbo

cu·ti·cle ['kjuːtɪkl] pellicina *f*

cut·le·ry ['kʌtlərɪ] posate *fpl*

'cut-off date scadenza *f*

cut-'price *adj goods* a prezzo ridotto; *store* di articoli scontati

'cut-throat *adj competition* spietato

cut·ting ['kʌtɪŋ] **1** *n from newspaper etc* ritaglio *m* **2** *adj remark* tagliente

CV [siː'viː] *abbr* (= **curriculum vitae**) CV *m inv* (= curriculum *m inv* vitae)

'cy·ber·space ['saɪbəspeɪs] ciberspazio *m*

cy·cle ['saɪkl] **1** *n* (*bicycle*) bicicletta *f*; *of events* ciclo *m* **2** *v/i to work* andare in bicicletta

'cy·cle path pista *f* ciclabile

cy·cling ['saɪklɪŋ] ciclismo *m*; **he's taken up ~** ha cominciato ad andare in bicicletta

cy·clist ['saɪklɪst] ciclista *m/f*

cyl·in·der ['sɪlɪndə(r)] cilindro *m*

cy·lin·dri·cal [sɪ'lɪndrɪkl] *adj* cilindrico

cyn·ic ['sɪnɪk] cinico *m*, -a *f*

cyn·i·cal ['sɪnɪkl] *adj* cinico

cyn·i·cal·ly ['sɪnɪklɪ] *adv* cinicamente

cyn·i·cism ['sɪnɪsɪzm] cinismo *m*

cy·press ['saɪprəs] cipresso *m*

cyst [sɪst] cisti *f inv*

Czech [tʃek] **1** *adj* ceco; **the ~ Republic** la Repubblica Ceca **2** *n person* ceco *m*, -a *f*; *language* ceco *m*

D

dab [dæb] **1** n (small amount) tocco m, pochino m **2** v/t (remove) (pret & pp **-bed**) tamponare; (apply) applicare; **~ a cut with ointment** applicare una pomata sul taglio
♦ **dabble in** v/t dilettarsi di

dad [dæd] papà m inv

dad·dy ['dædɪ] papà m inv

dad·dy long·legs zanzarone m

daf·fo·dil ['dæfədɪl] trombone m

daft [dɑːft] adj stupido

dag·ge r ['dægə(r)] pugnale m

dai·ly ['deɪlɪ] **1** n (paper) quotidiano m; (cleaning woman) domestica f **2** adj quotidiano

dain·ty ['deɪntɪ] adj aggraziato

dair·y cat·tle ['deərɪ] vacche fpl da latte; **'dair·y farm·ing** produzione f di latticini; **'dair·y prod·ucts** npl latticini mpl

dais ['deɪɪs] palco m

dai·sy ['deɪzɪ] margherita f

dam [dæm] **1** n for water diga f **2** v/t (pret & pp **-med**) river costruire una diga su

dam·age ['dæmɪdʒ] **1** n also fig danno m **2** v/t danneggiare; fig: reputation etc compromettere

dam·ages ['dæmɪdʒɪz] npl LAW risarcimento msg

dam·ag·ing ['dæmɪdʒɪŋ] adj nocivo

dame [deɪm] Am F (woman) tizia f F; **she's quite a ~!** che donna!

damn [dæm] **1** int F accidenti **2** n: F **I don't give a ~!** non me ne frega niente! F **3** adj F maledetto **4** adv F incredibilmente **5** v/t (condemn) maledire; **~ it!** F accidenti!; **I'm ~ed if I will** F non me lo sogno nemmeno

damned [dæmd] → **damn** adj & adv

damn·ing ['dæmɪŋ] adj evidence schiacciante; report incriminante

damp [dæmp] adj umido

damp·en ['dæmpən] v/t inumidire

dance [dɑːns] **1** n ballo m **2** v/i ballare; of ballerina danzare; **would you like to ~?** ti va di ballare?; fml posso invitarla a ballare?

danc·er ['dɑːnsə(r)] (performer) ballerino m, -a f; **be a good ~** ballare bene

danc·ing ['dɑːnsɪŋ] ballo m, danza f

dan·de·lion ['dændɪlaɪən] dente m di leone

dan·druff ['dændrʌf] forfora f

dan·druff sham·poo shampoo m inv antiforfora inv

Dane [deɪn] danese m/f

dan·ger ['deɪndʒə(r)] pericolo m; **be in ~** essere in pericolo; **out of ~** of patient fuori pericolo

dan·ger·ous ['deɪndʒərəs] adj pericoloso

dan·ger·ous 'driv·ing guida f pericolosa

dan·ger·ous·ly ['deɪndʒərəslɪ] adv drive spericolatamente; **~ ill** gravemente malato

dan·gle ['dæŋgl] **1** v/t dondolare **2** v/i pendere

Da·nish ['deɪnɪʃ] **1** adj danese **2** n (language) danese m

Da·nish ('pastry) dolcetto m ripieno

dare [deə(r)] **1** v/i osare; **~ to do sth** osare fare qc; **how ~ you!** come osi! **2** v/t: **~ s.o. to do sth** sfidare qu a fare qc

dare·dev·il ['deədevɪl] scavezzacollo m

dar·ing ['deərɪŋ] adj audace

dark [dɑːk] **1** n buio m, oscurità f; **after ~** dopo il calare della notte; **keep s.o. in the ~** fig tenere qu all'oscuro **2** adj room, night buio; hair, eyes, colour scuro; **~ green/blue** verde/blu scuro

dark·en ['dɑːkn] v/i of sky oscurarsi

dark 'glass·es npl occhiali mpl scuri

dark·ness ['dɑːknɪs] oscurità *f*

'dark·room PHOT camera *f* oscura

dar·ling ['dɑːlɪŋ] **1** *n* tesoro *m*; **be a ~ and ...** sii carino e ... **2** *adj* caro

darn [dɑːn] **1** *n* (*mend*) rammendo *m* **2** *v/t* (*mend*) rammendare

dart [dɑːt] **1** *n for throwing* freccetta *f* **2** *v/i* scagliarsi

darts [dɑːts] *nsg* (*game*) freccette *fpl*

'dart(s)·board tabellone *m* delle freccette

dash [dæʃ] **1** *n in punctuation* trattino *m*, lineetta *f*; *of whisky, milk* goccio *m*; *of salt* pizzico *m*; (MOT: *dashboard*) cruscotto *m*; **make a ~ for** precipitarsi su **2** *v/i* precipitarsi; **I must ~** devo scappare **3** *v/t hopes* stroncare

♦ **dash off 1** *v/i* scappare **2** *v/t* (*write quickly*) buttare giù

'dash·board cruscotto *m*

data ['deɪtə] dati *mpl*

'data·base base *f* dati; **da·ta 'cap·ture** inserimento *f* dati; **da·ta 'pro·cess·ing** elaborazione *f* dati; **da·ta pro'tec·tion** protezione *f* dati; **da·ta 'stor·age** memorizzazione *f* dati, archiviazione *f* dati

date¹ [deɪt] (*fruit*) dattero *m*

date² [deɪt] **1** *n* data *f*; (*meeting*) appuntamento *m*; **your ~ is here** è arrivato il tuo ragazzo, è arrivata la tua ragazza; **what's the ~ today?** quanti ne abbiamo oggi?; **out of ~** *clothes* fuori moda; *passport* scaduto; **up to ~** aggiornato; (*fashionable*) attuale **2** *v/t letter, cheque* datare; (*go out with*) uscire con; **that ~s you** (*shows your age*) quanto sei vecchio

dat·ed ['deɪtɪd] *adj* superato

daub [dɔːb] *v/t*: **~ paint on a wall** imbrattare il muro di vernice

daugh·ter ['dɔːtə(r)] figlia *f*

'daugh·ter-in-law (*pl* **daughters-in-law**) nuora *f*

daunt [dɔːnt] *v/t* scoraggiare

daw·dle ['dɔːdl] *v/i* ciondolare

dawn [dɔːn] **1** *n* alba *f*; *fig: of new age* albori *mpl* **2** *v/i*: **it ~ed on me that ...** mi sono reso conto che ...

day [deɪ] giorno *m*; **what ~ is it today?** che giorno è oggi?; **~ off** giorno *m* di ferie; **by ~** di giorno; **~ by ~** giorno per giorno; **the ~ after** il giorno dopo; **the ~ after tomorrow** dopodomani; **the ~ before** il giorno prima; **the ~ before yesterday** l'altro ieri; **~ in ~ out** senza tregua; **in those ~s** a quei tempi; **one ~** un giorno; **the other ~** (*recently*) l'altro giorno; **let's call it a ~!** lasciamo perdere!

'day boy alunno *m* esterno; **'day·break: at ~** allo spuntare del giorno; **'day care** asilo *m*; **'day·dream 1** *n* sogno *m* ad occhi aperti **2** *v/i* essere sovrappensiero; **'day dream·er** sognatore *m*, -trice *f*; **'day girl** alunna *f* esterna; **day re'turn** biglietto *m* di andata e ritorno in giornata; **'day·time: in the ~** durante il giorno; **day·light 'sav·ing time** ora *f* legale; **'day-trip** gita *f* di un giorno

daze [deɪz] *n*: **in a ~** sbalordito

dazed [deɪzd] *adj by good / bad news* sbalordito; *by a blow* stordito

daz·zle ['dæzl] *v/t of light, fig* abbagliare

DC [diː'siː] *abbr* (= *direct current*) c.c.; (=corrente *f* continua); **District of Columbia**) DC

dead [ded] **1** *adj person, plant* morto; *battery* scarica; *phone* muto; *light bulb* bruciato; **be ~** F *of place* essere un mortorio F **2** *adv* F (*very*) da matti F; **~ beat, ~ tired** stanco morto; **that's ~ right** è assolutamente vero; **it's ~ interesting** è interessante da matti **3** *n*: **the ~** (*dead people*) i morti; **in the ~ of night** nel cuore della notte

dead·en ['dedn] *v/t pain* attenuare; *sound* attutire

dead 'end (*street*) vicolo *m* cieco; **dead-'end job** lavoro *m* senza prospettive; **dead 'heat** pareggio *m*; **'dead·line** scadenza *f*; *for newspaper, magazine* termine *m* per l'invio in stampa; **'dead·lock** *n in talks* punto *m* morto

dead·ly ['dedlɪ] *adj* (*fatal*) mortale; F

(*boring*) di una noia mortale F

deaf [def] *adj* sordo

deaf-and-'dumb *adj* sordomuto

deaf-en ['defn] *v/t* assordare

deaf-en-ing ['defnɪŋ] *adj* assordante

deaf-ness ['defnɪs] sordità *f inv*

deal [di:l] **1** *n* accordo *m*; *it's a ~!* affare fatto!; *a good ~* (*bargain*) un affare; (*a lot*) molto; *a great ~ of* (*lots*) un bel po' di; *it's your ~ in games* tocca a te **2** *v/t* (*pret & pp dealt*) *cards* distribuire; *~ a blow to* inferire un duro colpo a

♦ **deal in** *v/t* (*trade in*) trattare; *drugs* trafficare

♦ **deal out** *v/t cards* distribuire

♦ **deal with** *v/t* (*handle*) occuparsi di; *situation* gestire; (*do business with*) trattare con

deal-er ['di:lə(r)] (*merchant*) commerciante *m/f*; (*drug ~*) spacciatore *m*, -trice *f*

deal-ing ['di:lɪŋ] (*drug ~*) spaccio *m*

deal-ings ['di:lɪŋz] *npl* (*business*) rapporti *mpl*

dealt [delt] *pret & pp* → **deal**

dean [di:n] *of college* preside *m*

dear [dɪə(r)] *adj* caro; *Dear Sir* Egregio Signore; *Dear Richard / Dear Margaret* caro Richard / cara Margareth; (*oh*) *~!*, *~ me!* povero / a me!

dear-ly ['dɪəlɪ] *adv love* teneramente

death [deθ] morte *f*

'death cer-tif-i-cate certificato *m* di decesso; **'death pen-al-ty** pena *f* di morte; **'death toll** numero *m* delle vittime

de-ba-ta-ble [dɪ'beɪtəbl] *adj* discutibile

de-bate [dɪ'beɪt] **1** *n* dibattimento *m*; POL dibattito *m*; *after much ~* dopo molto dibattere **2** *v/i* dibattere; *~ with o.s. whether ...* considerare se ... **3** *v/t* dibattere su

de-bauch-er-y [dɪ'bɔ:ʃərɪ] depravazione *f*

deb-it ['debɪt] **1** *n* addebito *m* **2** *v/t*: *~ £150 to s.o.'s account* addebitare £150 a qu; *~ an account with £150*

addebitare £150 su un conto

'deb-it card carta *f* di debito

deb-ris ['debri:] *of plane* rottami *mpl*; *of building* macerie *fpl*

debt [det] debito *m*; *be in ~* (*financially*) avere dei debiti

debt-or ['detə(r)] debitore *m*, -trice *f*

de-bug [di:'bʌg] *v/t* (*pret & pp -ged*) *room* togliere le microspie da; COMPUT togliere gli errori da

dé-but ['deɪbju:] *n* debutto *m*

dec-ade ['dekeɪd] decennio *m*, decade *f*

dec-a-dence ['dekədəns] decadenza *f*

dec-a-dent ['dekədənt] *adj* decadente

de-caf-fein-at-ed [dɪ'kæfɪneɪtɪd] *adj* decaffeinato

de-cant-er [dɪ'kæntə(r)] caraffa *f*

de-cap-i-tate [dɪ'kæpɪteɪt] *v/t* decapitare

de-cay [dɪ'keɪ] **1** *n of organic matter* decomposizione *f*; *of civilization* declino *m*; (*decayed matter*) marciume *m*; *in teeth* carie *f inv* **2** *v/i of organic matter* decomporsi; *of civilization* declinare; *of teeth* cariarsi

de-ceased [dɪ'si:st]: *the ~* il defunto *m*, la defunta *f*

de-ceit [dɪ'si:t] falsità *f*, disonestà *f*

de-ceit-ful [dɪ'si:tful] *adj* falso, disonesto

de-ceive [dɪ'si:v] *v/t* ingannare

De-cem-ber [dɪ'sembə(r)] dicembre *m*

de-cen-cy ['di:sənsɪ] decenza *f*; *he had the ~ to ...* ha avuto la decenza di ...

de-cent ['di:sənt] *adj price, proposition* corretto; *meal, sleep* decente; (*adequately dressed*) presentabile; *a ~ guy* un uomo per bene; *that's very ~ of you* è molto gentile da parte tua

de-cen-tral-ize [di:'sentrəlaɪz] *v/t* decentralizzare

de-cep-tion [dɪ'sepʃn] inganno *m*

de-cep-tive [dɪ'septɪv] *adj* ingannevole

de-cep-tive-ly [dɪ'septɪvlɪ] *adv*: *it*

looks ~ simple sembra semplice solo all'apparenza

dec·i·bel ['desɪbel] decibel m inv

de·cide [dɪ'saɪd] **1** v/t (make up one's mind) decidere; (conclude, settle) risolvere **2** v/i decidere; **you ~** decidi tu

de·cid·ed [dɪ'saɪdɪd] adj (definite) deciso

de·cid·er [dɪ'saɪdə(r)]: **be the ~ of** match etc essere decisivo

dec·i·du·ous [dɪ'sɪdjʊəs] adj che perde le foglie in inverno

dec·i·mal ['desɪml] n decimale

dec·i·mal 'point punto m che separa i decimali; in Italy virgola f

dec·i·mate ['desɪmeɪt] v/t decimare

de·ci·pher [dɪ'saɪfə(r)] v/t decifrare

de·ci·sion [dɪ'sɪʒn] decisione f; (conclusion) risoluzione f; **come to a ~** prendere una decisione

de'ci·sion-mak·er responsabile m/f; **be a ~** (be able to make decisions) saper prendere delle decisioni

de·ci·sive [dɪ'saɪsɪv] adj risoluto; (crucial) decisivo

deck [dek] of ship ponte m; of bus piano m; of cards mazzo m

'deck·chair sedia f a sdraio, sdraio f inv

dec·la·ra·tion [deklə'reɪʃn] dichiarazione f

de·clare [dɪ'kleə(r)] v/t dichiarare

de·cline [dɪ'klaɪn] **1** n in number, standards calo m; in health peggioramento m **2** v/t invitation declinare; **~ to comment / accept** esimersi dal commentare / accettare **3** v/i (refuse) declinare; (decrease) diminuire; of health peggiorare

de·clutch [diː'klʌtʃ] v/i lasciare andare la frizione

de·code [diː'kəʊd] v/t decodificare

de·com·pose [diːkəm'pəʊz] v/i decomporsi

dé·cor ['deɪkɔː(r)] arredamento m

dec·o·rate ['dekəreɪt] v/t with paint imbiancare; with paper tappezzare; (adorn), MIL decorare

dec·o·ra·tion [dekə'reɪʃn] paint vernice f; paper tappezzeria f;

(ornament) addobbi mpl; MIL decorazione f

dec·o·ra·tive ['dekərətɪv] adj decorativo

dec·o·ra·tor ['dekəreɪtə(r)] (interior ~) imbianchino m

de·co·rum [dɪ'kɔːrəm] decoro m

de·coy ['diːkɔɪ] n esca f

de·crease ['diːkriːs] **1** n diminuzione f **2** v/t ridurre **3** v/i ridursi

de·crep·it [dɪ'krepɪt] adj decrepito

ded·i·cate ['dedɪkeɪt] v/t book etc dedicare; **~ o.s. to ...** consacrarsi a ...

ded·i·ca·ted ['dedɪkeɪtɪd] adj dedito

ded·i·ca·tion [dedɪ'keɪʃn] in book dedica f; to cause, work dedizione f

de·duce [dɪ'djuːs] v/t dedurre

de·duct [dɪ'dʌkt] v/t detrarre; **~ sth from sth** detrarre qc da qc

de·duc·tion [dɪ'dʌkʃn] from salary trattenuta f; (conclusion) deduzione f; **~ at source** ritenuta f alla fonte

dee·jay ['diːdʒeɪ] F dj m/f inv

deed [diːd] n (act) azione f; LAW atto m

deem [diːm] v/t ritenere

deep [diːp] adj hole, water, voice, thinker profondo; colour intenso; **you're in ~ trouble** sei davvero nei guai

deep·en ['diːpn] **1** v/t rendere più profondo **2** v/i diventare più profondo; of crisis aggravarsi; of mystery infittirsi

'deep freeze n congelatore m; **'deep-froz·en food** surgelati mpl; **'deep-fry** v/t (pret & pp -ied) friggere (immergendo nell'olio); **deep 'fry·er** padella f (per friggere); **electric** friggitrice f

deer [dɪə(r)] (pl deer) cervo m

de·face [dɪ'feɪs] v/t vandalizzare

def·a·ma·tion [defə'meɪʃn] diffamazione f

de·fam·a·to·ry [dɪ'fæmətərɪ] adj diffamatorio

de·fault ['dɪfɒlt] adj COMPUT di default

de·feat [dɪ'fiːt] **1** n sconfitta f **2** v/t sconfiggere; **this problem ~s me**

D

questo problema è troppo grande per me

de·feat·ist [dɪ'fiːtɪst] *adj attitude* disfattista

de·fect ['diːfekt] *n* difetto *m*

de·fec·tive [dɪ'fektɪv] *adj* difettoso

de·fend [dɪ'fend] *v/t* difendere

de·fend·ant [dɪ'fendənt] accusato *m*, -a *f*; *in criminal case* imputato *m*, -a *f*

de·fence [dɪ'fens] difesa *f*; **come to s.o.'s ~** venire in aiuto a qu

de'fence budg·et POL budget *m inv* della difesa

de'fence law·yer avvocato *m* difensore

de'fence·less [dɪ'fenslɪs] *adj* indifeso

de'fence play·er SP difensore *m*

de'fence wit·ness LAW testimone *m/f* della difesa

de'fense *etc Am* → **defence** *etc*

de·fen·sive [dɪ'fensɪv] **1** *n*: **on the ~** sulla difensiva; **go on the ~** mettersi sulla difensiva **2** *adj weaponry* difensivo; *person* sulla difensiva

de·fen·sive·ly [dɪ'fensɪvlɪ] *adv* sulla difensiva; **play ~** SP ritirarsi in difesa

de·fer [dɪ'fɜː(r)] *v/t* (*pret & pp* **-red**) (*postpone*) rinviare

def·er·ence ['defərəns] deferenza *f*

def·er·en·tial [defə'renʃl] *adj* deferente

de·fi·ance [dɪ'faɪəns] sfida *f*; **in ~ of** a dispetto di

de·fi·ant [dɪ'faɪənt] *adj* provocatorio

de·fi·cien·cy [dɪ'fɪʃənsɪ] (*lack*) carenza *f*

de·fi·cient [dɪ'fɪʃənt] *adj* carente; **be ~ in ...** essere carente di ...

de·fi·cit ['defɪsɪt] deficit *m inv*

de·fine [dɪ'faɪn] *v/t* definire

def·i·nite ['defɪnɪt] *adj date, time, answer* preciso; *improvement* netto; (*certain*) certo; **are you ~ about that?** ne sei sicuro?; **nothing ~ has been arranged** non è stato previsto niente di preciso

def·i·nite 'ar·ti·cle GRAM articolo *m* determinativo

def·i·nite·ly ['defɪnɪtlɪ] *adv* senza dubbio; *smell, hear* distintamente

def·i·ni·tion [defɪ'nɪʃn] definizione *f*

de·fi·ni·tive [dɪ'fɪnətɪv] *adj biography* più completo; *performance* migliore

de·flect [dɪ'flekt] *v/t ball, blow* deviare; sviare; **be ~ed from** essere sviato da

de·for·est·a·tion [dɪforɪs'teɪʃn] disboscamento *m*

de·form [dɪ'fɔːm] *v/t* deformare

de·for·mi·ty [dɪ'fɔːmɪtɪ] deformità *f inv*

de·fraud [dɪ'frɔːd] *v/t* defraudare; *Inland Revenue* frodare

de·frost [diː'frɒst] *v/t food* scongelare; *fridge* sbrinare

deft [deft] *adj* agile

de·fuse [diː'fjuːz] *v/t bomb* disinnescare; *situation* placare

de·fy [dɪ'faɪ] *v/t* (*pret & pp* **-ied**) (*disobey*) disobbedire a

de·gen·e·rate [dɪ'dʒenəreɪt] *v/i* degenerare; **~ into** degenerare in

de·grade [dɪ'greɪd] *v/t* degradare

de·grad·ing [dɪ'greɪdɪŋ] *adj position, work* degradante

de·gree [dɪ'griː] *from university* laurea *f*; *of temperature, angle, latitude* grado *m*; **a ~ of** (*amount*) un po' di; **by ~s** per gradi; **to a certain ~** fino a un certo punto; **there is a ~ of truth in that** c'è del vero in questo; **get one's ~** prendere la laurea

de·hy·drat·ed [diːhaɪ'dreɪtɪd] *adj* disidratato

de-ice [diː'aɪs] *v/t* togliere il ghiaccio da

de-ic·er [diː'aɪsə(r)] (*spray*) antigelo *m inv*

deign [deɪn] *v/i*: **~ to ...** degnarsi di ...

de·i·ty ['diːɪtɪ] divinità *f inv*

de·jec·ted [dɪ'dʒektɪd] *adj* sconfortato

de·lay [dɪ'leɪ] **1** *n* ritardo **2** *v/t* ritardare; **be ~ed** (*be late*) essere in ritardo; **~ doing sth** tardare a fare qc; **sorry, I've been ~ed** scusa, sono stato trattenuto **3** *v/i* tardare

del·e·gate ['delɪgət] **1** *n* delegato *m*,

-a *f* **2** *v/t* ['delɪgeɪt] *task, person* delegare

del·e·ga·tion [delɪ'geɪʃn] *of task* delega *f*; (*people*) delegazione *f*

de·lete [dɪ'liːt] *v/t* cancellare

de'lete key COMPUT tasto *m* 'cancella'

de·le·tion [dɪ'liːʃn] *act* cancellazione *f*; *that deleted* cancellatura *f*

del·i ['delɪ] → **delicatessen**

de·lib·e·rate [dɪ'lɪbərət] **1** *adj* deliberato **2** *v/i* [dɪ'lɪbəreɪt] riflettere

de·lib·e·rate·ly [dɪ'lɪbərətlɪ] *adv* deliberatamente

del·i·ca·cy ['delɪkəsɪ] delicatezza *f*; (*food*) prelibatezza *f*

del·i·cate ['delɪkət] *adj* delicato

del·i·ca·tes·sen [delɪkə'tesn] gastronomia *f*

del·i·cious [dɪ'lɪʃəs] *adj* delizioso, ottimo

de·light [dɪ'laɪt] *n* gioia *f*; **to my great ~** con mio grande piacere

de·light·ed [dɪ'laɪtɪd] *adj* lieto

de·light·ful [dɪ'laɪtful] *adj* molto piacevole

de·lim·it [diː'lɪmɪt] *v/t* delimitare

de·lin·quen·cy [dɪ'lɪŋkwənsɪ] delinquenza *f* (minorile)

de·lin·quent [dɪ'lɪŋkwənt] *n* delinquente *m/f*

de·lir·i·ous [dɪ'lɪrɪəs] *adj* MED delirante; (*ecstatic*) in delirio

de·liv·er [dɪ'lɪvə(r)] *v/t* consegnare; *message* trasmettere; *baby* far nascere; **~ a speech** tenere un discorso

de·liv·er·y [dɪ'lɪvərɪ] *of goods, mail* consegna *f*; *of baby* parto *m*

de'liv·ery charge: there is no ~ la consegna è gratuita; **de'liv·er·y date** termine *m* di consegna; **de'liv·ery man** fattorino *m*; **de'liv·er·y note** bolla *f*, documento *m* di trasporto; **de'liv·ery serv·ice** consegna *f* a domicilio; **de'liv·er·y van** furgone *m* delle consegne

de·lude [dɪ'luːd] *v/t* ingannare; **~ s.o. into believing sth** far credere qc a qu; **you're deluding yourself** ti sbagli

de·luge ['deljuːdʒ] **1** *n* temporale *m*; *fig* valanga *f* **2** *v/t fig* sommergere

de·lu·sion [dɪ'luːʒn] illusione *f*; *of others* inganno *m*

de luxe [də'lʌks] *adj* di lusso

♦ **delve into** [delv] *v/t* addentrarsi in; *s.o.'s past* scavare in

de·mand [dɪ'mɑːnd] **1** *n* rivendicazione *f*; COM domanda *f*; **in ~** richiesto **2** *v/t* esigere; (*require*) richiedere

de·mand·ing [dɪ'mɑːndɪŋ] *adj job* impegnativo; *person* esigente

de·mean·ing [dɪ'miːnɪŋ] *adj* avvilente

de·ment·ed [dɪ'mentɪd] *adj* demente

de·mise [dɪ'maɪz] scomparsa *f*

dem·o ['deməʊ] (*protest*) manifestazione *f*; *of video etc* dimostrazione *f*

de·moc·ra·cy [dɪ'mɒkrəsɪ] democrazia *f*

dem·o·crat ['deməkræt] democratico *m*, -a *f*; **Democrat** POL democratico *m*, -a *f*

dem·o·crat·ic [demə'krætɪk] *adj* democratico

dem·o·crat·ic·al·ly [demə'krætɪklɪ] *adv* democraticamente

'**dem·o disk** disco *m* dimostrativo

de·mo·graph·ic [deməʊ'græfɪk] *adj* demografico

de·mol·ish [dɪ'mɒlɪʃ] *v/t* demolire

de·mo·li·tion [demə'lɪʃn] demolizione *f*

de·mon ['diːmən] demone *m*

dem·on·strate ['demənstreɪt] **1** *v/t* (*prove*) dimostrare; *machine* fare una dimostrazione di **2** *v/i politically* manifestare

dem·on·stra·tion [demən'streɪʃn] dimostrazione *f*; (*protest*) manifestazione *f*

de·mon·stra·tive [dɪ'mɒnstrətɪv] *adj* espansivo

de·mon·stra·tor ['demənstreɪtə(r)] (*protester*) manifestante *m/f*

de·mor·al·ized [dɪ'mɒrəlaɪzd] *adj* demoralizzato

de·mor·al·iz·ing [dɪ'mɒrəlaɪzɪŋ] *adj* demoralizzante

de·mote [diː'məʊt] *v/t* retrocedere;

MIL degradare

de·mure [dɪ'mjʊə(r)] *adj* contegnoso

den [den] (*study*) studio *m*

de·ni·al [dɪ'naɪəl] *of rumour, accusation* negazione *f*; *of request, right* negazione *f*, rifiuto *m*

den·im ['denɪm] denim *m inv*

den·ims ['denɪmz] *npl* (*jeans*) jeans *m inv*

Den·mark ['denmɑːk] Danimarca *f*

de·nom·i·na·tion [dɪnɒmɪ'neɪʃn] *of money* banconota *f*; REL confessione *f*; *money in small ~s* denaro *m* in banconote di piccolo taglio

de·nounce [dɪ'naʊns] *v/t* denunciare

dense [dens] *adj* fitto; (*stupid*) ottuso

dense·ly ['densli] *adv*: *~ populated* densamente popolato

den·si·ty ['densɪti] *of population* densità *f inv*

dent [dent] **1** *n* ammaccatura *f* **2** *v/t* ammaccare

den·tal ['dentl] *adj treatment* dentario, dentale; *hospital* dentistico

den·ted ['dentɪd] *adj* ammaccato

den·tist ['dentɪst] dentista *m/f*

den·tist·ry ['dentɪstrɪ] odontoiatria *f*

den·tures ['dentʃəz] *npl* dentiera *f*

de·ny [dɪ'naɪ] *v/t* (*pret & pp -ied*) negare; *rumour* smentire; *I was denied the right to …* mi è stato negato il diritto di …

de·o·do·rant [diː'əʊdərənt] deodorante *m*

de·part [dɪ'pɑːt] *v/i* partire; *~ from* (*deviate from*) allontanarsi da

de·part·ment [dɪ'pɑːtmənt] *of university* dipartimento *m*; *of government* ministero *m*; *of store, company* reparto *m*

de·part·ment store grande magazzino *m*

de·par·ture [dɪ'pɑːtʃə(r)] partenza *f*; (*deviation*) allontanamento *m*; *a new ~ for government, organization* una svolta

de·par·ture lounge sala *f* partenze

de·par·ture time ora *f* di partenza

de·pend [dɪ'pend] *v/i*: *that ~s* dipen-

de; *it ~s on the weather* dipende dal tempo; *I am ~ing on you* conto su di te

de·pen·da·ble [dɪ'pendəbl] *adj* affidabile

de·pen·dant [dɪ'pendənt] → **dependent**

de·pen·dence, de·pen·den·cy [dɪ'pendəns, dɪ'pendənsɪ] dipendenza *f*

de·pen·dent [dɪ'pendənt] **1** *n* persona *f* a carico; *a married man with ~s* un uomo sposato con famiglia a carico **2** *adj* dipendente; *~ children* figli *mpl* a carico

de·pict [dɪ'pɪkt] *v/t in painting, writing* raffigurare

de·plete [dɪ'pliːt] *v/t* intaccare

de·plor·a·ble [dɪ'plɔːrəbl] *adj* deplorevole

de·plore [dɪ'plɔː(r)] *v/t* deplorare, lamentarsi di

de·ploy [dɪ'plɔɪ] *v/t* (*use*) spiegare; (*position*) schierare

de·pop·u·la·tion [diːpɒpjʊ'leɪʃn] spopolamento *m*

de·port [dɪ'pɔːt] *v/t* deportare

de·por·ta·tion [diːpɔː'teɪʃn] deportazione *f*

de·por·ta·tion or·der ordine *m* di deportazione

de·pose [dɪ'pəʊz] *v/t* deporre

de·pos·it [dɪ'pɒzɪt] **1** *n in bank* versamento *m*, deposito *m*; *of mineral* deposito *m*; *on purchase* acconto *m*; (*against loss, damage*) cauzione *f* **2** *v/t money* versare, depositare; (*put down*) lasciare; *silt, mud* depositare

de·pos·it ac·count libretto *m* di risparmio

dep·ot ['depəʊ] (*train station*) stazione *f* ferroviaria; (*bus station*) rimessa *f* degli autobus; *for storage* magazzino *m*

de·praved [dɪ'preɪvd] *adj* depravato

de·pre·ci·ate [dɪ'priːʃɪeɪt] *v/i* FIN svalutarsi

de·pre·ci·a·tion [dɪpriːʃɪ'eɪʃn] FIN svalutazione *f*

de·press [dɪ'pres] v/t person deprimere

de·pressed [dɪ'prest] adj person depresso

de·press·ing [dɪ'presɪŋ] adj deprimente

de·pres·sion [dɪ'preʃn] depressione f

dep·ri·va·tion [deprɪ'veɪʃn] privazione f; (lack: of sleep, food) carenza f

de·prive [dɪ'praɪv] v/t: ~ s.o. of sth privare qu di qc

de·prived [dɪ'praɪvd] adj socialmente svantaggiato

depth [depθ] profondità f inv; in ~ (thoroughly) a fondo; in the ~s of winter in pieno inverno; be out of one's ~ in water non toccare (il fondo); when they talk about politics I'm out of my ~ la politica va al di là della mia comprensione

dep·u·ta·tion [depjʊ'teɪʃn] deputazione f

♦**deputize for** ['depjʊtaɪz] v/t fare le veci di

dep·u·ty ['depjʊtɪ] vice m/f inv

'dep·u·ty lead·er of party vice segretario m

de·rail [dɪ'reɪl] v/t: be ~ed of train essere deragliato

de·ranged [dɪ'reɪndʒd] adj squilibrato

de·reg·u·late [diː'regjʊleɪt] v/t deregolamentare

de·reg·u·la·tion [dɪregjʊ'leɪʃn] deregolamentazione f

der·e·lict ['derəlɪkt] adj desolato

de·ride [dɪ'raɪd] v/t deridere

de·ri·sion [dɪ'rɪʒn] derisione f

de·ri·sive [dɪ'raɪsɪv] adj remarks, laughter derisorio

de·ri·sive·ly [dɪ'raɪsɪvlɪ] adv con aria derisoria

de·ri·so·ry [dɪ'raɪsərɪ] adj amount, salary irrisorio

de·riv·a·tive [dɪ'rɪvətɪv] adj (not original) derivato

de·rive [dɪ'raɪv] v/t trarre; be ~d from of word derivare da

der·ma·tol·o·gist [dɜːmə'tɒlədʒɪst] dermatologo m, -a f

de·rog·a·to·ry [dɪ'rɒgətrɪ] adj peggiorativo

de·scend [dɪ'send] 1 v/t scendere; be ~ed from discendere da 2 v/i scendere; of mood, darkness calare

de·scen·dant [dɪ'sendənt] discendente m/f

de·scent [dɪ'sent] discesa f; (ancestry) discendenza f, of Chinese ~ di origini cinesi

de·scribe [dɪ'skraɪb] v/t descrivere; ~ sth as sth descrivere qc come qc

de·scrip·tion [dɪ'skrɪpʃn] descrizione f

des·e·crate ['desɪkreɪt] v/t profanare

des·e·cra·tion [desɪ'kreɪʃn] profanazione f

de·seg·re·gate [diː'segrəgeɪt] eliminare la segregazione in

des·ert¹ ['dezət] n also fig deserto m

des·ert² [dɪ'zɜːt] 1 v/t (abandon) abbandonare 2 v/i of soldier disertare

des·ert·ed [dɪ'zɜːtɪd] adj deserto

de·sert·er [dɪ'zɜːtə(r)] MIL disertore m

de·ser·ti·fi·ca·tion [dɪzɜːtɪfɪ'keɪʃn] desertificazione f

de·ser·tion [dɪ'zɜːʃn] (abandoning) abbandono m; MIL diserzione f

des·ert 'is·land isola f deserta

de·serve [dɪ'zɜːv] v/t meritare

de·sign [dɪ'zaɪn] 1 n design m; technical progettazione f; (drawing) progetto m, disegno m; (pattern) motivo m; the machine's unique ~ la concezione unica della macchina 2 v/t house, car progettare; clothes disegnare; this machine is not ~ed for ... questa macchina non è stata concepita per ...

des·ig·nate ['dezɪgneɪt] v/t person designare; it has been ~d a non smoking area quest'area è riservata ai non fumatori

de·sign·er [dɪ'zaɪnə(r)] designer m/f inv; of building, car, ship progettista m/f; costume ~ costumista m/f; fashion ~ stilista m/f; interior ~ arredatore m, -trice f de'sign·er clothes *npl* abiti *mpl* firmati

de'sign fault difetto *m* di concezione

de'sign school scuola *f* di design

de·sir·a·ble [dɪˈzaɪrəbl] *adj* desiderabile; (*advisable*) preferibile

de·sire [dɪˈzaɪə(r)] *n* desiderio *m*

desk [desk] scrivania *f*; *in hotel* reception *f inv*

'desk clerk *Am* receptionist *m/f inv*; 'desk di·a·ry agenda *f* da tavolo; 'desk·top scrivania *f*; (*computer*) computer *m inv* da tavolo; (*screen*) desktop *m inv*; desk·top 'pub·lish·ing editoria *f* elettronica

des·o·late [ˈdesələt] *adj* place desolato

de·spair [dɪˈspeə(r)] **1** *n* disperazione *f*; *in* ~ disperato **2** *v/i* disperare; ~ *of sth / s.o.* aver perso la fiducia in qc / qu; ~ *of doing sth* disperare di fare qualcosa

des·per·ate [ˈdespərət] *adj* disperato; *be ~ for a cigarette / drink* morire dalla voglia di una sigaretta / bere qualcosa

des·per·a·tion [despəˈreɪʃn] disperazione *f*

des·pic·a·ble [dɪsˈpɪkəbl] *adj* deplorevole

de·spise [dɪˈspaɪz] *v/t* disprezzare

de·spite [dɪˈspaɪt] *prep* malgrado, nonostante

de·spon·dent [dɪˈspɒndənt] *adj* abbattuto

des·pot [ˈdespɒt] despota *m*

des·sert [dɪˈzɜːt] dolce *m*, dessert *m inv*

des·ti·na·tion [destɪˈneɪʃn] destinazione *f*

des·tined [ˈdestɪnd] *adj*: *be ~ for fig* essere destinato a

des·ti·ny [ˈdestɪnɪ] destino *m*

des·ti·tute [ˈdestɪtjuːt] *adj* indigente

de·stroy [dɪˈstrɔɪ] *v/t* distruggere

de·stroy·er [dɪˈstrɔɪə(r)] NAUT cacciatorpediniere *m*

de·struc·tion [dɪˈstrʌkʃn] distruzione *f*

de·struc·tive [dɪˈstrʌktɪv] *adj* distruttivo; *child* scalmanato

de·tach [dɪˈtætʃ] *v/t* staccare

de·tach·a·ble [dɪˈtætʃəbl] *adj* staccabile

de·tached [dɪˈtætʃt] *adj* (*objective*) distaccato

de'tached house villetta *f*

de·tach·ment [dɪˈtætʃmənt] (*objectivity*) distacco *m*

de·tail [ˈdiːteɪl] *n* dettaglio *m*; *in* ~ dettagliatamente

de·tailed [ˈdiːteɪld] *adj* dettagliato

de·tain [dɪˈteɪn] *v/t* (*hold back*) trattenere; *as prisoner* trattenere

de·tain·ee [diːteɪnˈiː] detenuto *m*, -a *f*

de·tect [dɪˈtekt] *v/t* rilevare; *anxiety, irony* cogliere

de·tec·tion [dɪˈtekʃn] *of criminal, crime* investigazione *f*; *of smoke etc* rilevamento *m*

de·tec·tive [dɪˈtektɪv] (*policeman*) agente *m/f* investigativo

de'tec·tive nov·el romanzo *m* giallo, giallo *m*

de·tec·tor [dɪˈtektə(r)] rilevatore *m*

dé·tente [ˈdeɪtɒnt] POL distensione *f*

de·ten·tion [dɪˈtenʃn] (*imprisonment*) detenzione *f*

de·ter [dɪˈtɜː(r)] *v/t* (*pret & pp* **-red**) dissuadere; ~ *s.o. from doing sth* dissuadere qu dal fare qc

de·ter·gent [dɪˈtɜːdʒənt] detergente *m*

de·te·ri·o·rate [dɪˈtɪərɪəreɪt] *v/i* deteriorarsi

de·te·ri·o·ra·tion [dɪtɪərɪəˈreɪʃn] deterioramento *m*

de·ter·mi·na·tion [dɪtɜːmɪˈneɪʃn] (*resolution*) determinazione *f*

de·ter·mine [dɪˈtɜːmɪn] *v/t* (*establish*) determinare

de·ter·mined [dɪˈtɜːmɪnd] *adj* determinato, deciso

de·ter·rent [dɪˈterənt] *n* deterrente *m*

de·test [dɪˈtest] *v/t* detestare

de·test·a·ble [dɪˈtestəbl] *adj* detestabile

de·to·nate [ˈdetəneɪt] **1** *v/t* fare detonare **2** *v/i* detonare

de·to·na·tion [detə'neɪʃn] detonazione *f*

de·tour ['di:tʊə(r)] *n* deviazione *f*

♦ **de·tract from** [dɪ'trækt] *v/t* merit, value sminuire; enjoyment rovinare; room, décor rovinare l'effetto di

de·tri·ment [detrɪmənt]: **to the ~ of** a scapito di

de·tri·men·tal [detrɪ'mentl] *adj* nocivo

deuce [dju:s] *in tennis* 40 pari *m inv*

de·val·u·a·tion [di:vælju'eɪʃn] *of currency* svalutazione *f*

de·val·ue [di:'vælju:] *v/t* currency svalutare

dev·a·state ['devəsteɪt] *v/t also fig* devastare

dev·a·stat·ing ['devəsteɪtɪŋ] *adj* devastante

de·vel·op [dɪ'veləp] **1** *v/t* film, business sviluppare; land, site valorizzare; (originate) scoprire; illness, cold contrarre **2** *v/i* (grow) svilupparsi; **~ into** diventare

de·vel·op·er [dɪ'veləpə(r)] of property impresario *m*, a *f* edile

de·vel·op·ing coun·try paese *m* in via di sviluppo

de·vel·op·ment [dɪ'veləpmənt] sviluppo *m*; of land, site valorizzazione *f*; (origination) scoperta *f*

de·vice [dɪ'vaɪs] (tool) dispositivo *m*

dev·il ['devl] diavolo *m*

de·vi·ous ['di:vɪəs] (sly) subdolo

de·vise [dɪ'vaɪz] *v/t* escogitare

de·void [dɪ'vɔɪd] *adj*: **be ~ of** essere privo di

dev·o·lu·tion [di:və'lu:ʃn] POL decentramento *m*

de·vote [dɪ'vəʊt] *v/t* time, effort, money dedicare

de·vot·ed [dɪ'vəʊtɪd] *adj* son etc devoto; **be ~ to a person** essere molto attaccato a una persona

dev·o·tee [dɪvəʊ'ti:] appassionato *m*, -a *f*

de·vo·tion [dɪ'vəʊʃn] to a person attaccamento *m*; to one's job dedizione *f*

de·vour [dɪ'vaʊə(r)] *v/t* food, book divorare

de·vout [dɪ'vaʊt] *adj* devoto; **a ~ Catholic** un cattolico fervente

dew [dju:] rugiada *f*

dex·ter·i·ty [dek'sterətɪ] destrezza *f*

di·a·be·tes [daɪə'bi:ti:z] *nsg* diabete *m*

di·a·bet·ic [daɪə'betɪk] **1** *n* diabetico *m*, -a *f* **2** *adj* diabetico; foods per diabetici

di·a·bol·i·cal [daɪə'bɒlɪkl] *adj* P (very bad) penoso

di·ag·nose ['daɪəgnəʊz] *v/t* diagnosticare

di·ag·no·sis [daɪəg'nəʊsɪs] (pl diagnoses [daɪəg'nəʊsi:z]) diagnosi *f inv*

di·ag·o·nal [daɪ'ægənl] *adj* diagonale

di·ag·o·nal·ly [daɪ'ægənlɪ] *adv* diagonalmente

di·a·gram ['daɪəgræm] diagramma *m*

di·al ['daɪəl] **1** *n* of clock, meter quadrante *m*; TELEC disco *m* combinatore **2** *v/i* (pret & pp **-led**, Am **-ed**) TELEC comporre il numero **3** *v/t* (pret & pp **-led**, Am **-ed**) TELEC number comporre

di·a·lect ['daɪəlekt] dialetto *m*

di·al·ling code ['daɪlɪŋ] prefisso *m*

'di·al·ling tone, Am **'dial tone** segnale *m* di linea libera

di·a·log Am, **di·a·logue** ['daɪəlɒg] dialogo *m*

di·a·logue box COMPUT riquadro *m* di dialogo

di·am·e·ter [daɪ'æmɪtə(r)] diametro *m*

di·a·met·ri·cal·ly [daɪə'metrɪkəlɪ] *adv*: **~ opposed** diametralmente opposto

di·a·mond ['daɪəmənd] (jewel) diamante *m*; (shape) losanga *f*; **~s** in cards quadri *mpl*

di·a·per ['daɪəpər] Am pannolino *m*

di·a·phragm ['daɪəfræm] diaframma *m*

di·ar·rhe·a Am, **di·ar·rhoe·a** [daɪə'rɪə] diarrea *f*

di·a·ry ['daɪərɪ] for thoughts diario *m*; for appointments agenda *f*

dice [daɪs] **1** *n* dado *m* **2** *v/t* (*cut*) tagliare a dadini

di·chot·o·my [daɪ'kɒtəmɪ] dicotomia *f*

dic·ta·te [dɪk'teɪt] *v/t letter, novel* dettare; *course of action* imporre

dic·ta·tion [dɪk'teɪʃn] dettatura *f*

dic·ta·tor [dɪk'teɪtə(r)] POL dittatore *m*

dic·ta·tori·al [dɪktə'tɔːrɪəl] *adj* dittatoriale

dic·ta·tor·ship [dɪk'teɪtəʃɪp] dittatura *f*

dic·tion·a·ry ['dɪkʃənrɪ] dizionario *m*

did [dɪd] *pret* → **do**

die [daɪ] *v/i* morire; **~ of cancer / Aids** morire di cancro / AIDS; *I'm dying to know / leave* muoio dalla voglia di sapere / andare via

♦ **die away** *v/i of noise* estinguersi

♦ **die down** *v/i of noise, fire* estinguersi; *of storm, excitement* placarsi

♦ **die out** *v/i of custom* scomparire; *of species* estinguersi

die·sel ['diːzl] (*fuel*) diesel *m*

di·et ['daɪət] **1** *n* dieta *f* **2** *v/i to lose weight* essere a dieta

di·e·ti·tian [daɪə'tɪʃn] dietologo *m*, -a *f*

dif·fer ['dɪfə(r)] *v/i* (*be different*) differire, essere differente; (*disagree*) non essere d'accordo

dif·fe·rence ['dɪfrəns] differenza *f*; (*disagreement*) divergenza *f*; *it doesn't make any ~* non fa nessuna differenza

dif·fe·rent ['dɪfrənt] *adj* diverso, differente

dif·fe·ren·ti·ate [dɪfə'renʃɪeɪt]: *v/i* distinguere; **~ between** *things* distinguere tra; *people* fare distinzioni tra

dif·fe·rent·ly ['dɪfrəntlɪ] *adv* diversamente, differentemente

dif·fi·cult ['dɪfɪkəlt] *adj* difficile

dif·fi·cul·ty ['dɪfɪkəltɪ] difficoltà *f inv*; **with ~** a fatica

dif·fi·dence ['dɪfɪdəns] diffidenza *f*

dif·fi·dent ['dɪfɪdənt] *adj* diffidente

dig [dɪg] (*pret & pp dug*) **1** *v/t* scava-

re **2** *v/i*: *it was ~ging into me* mi si stava conficcando dentro

♦ **dig out** *v/t* tirar fuori

♦ **dig up** *v/t garden* scavare; *buried object* dissotterrare; *tree* sradicare; *information* scovare

di·gest [daɪ'dʒest] *v/t also fig* digerire

di·gest·i·ble [daɪ'dʒestəbl] *adj food* digeribile

di·ges·tion [daɪ'dʒestʃn] digestione *f*

di·ges·tive [daɪ'dʒestɪv] *adj* digestivo; **~ juices** succhi *mpl* gastrici; **~ system** apparato *m* digerente

dig·ger ['dɪgə(r)] (*machine*) scavatrice *f*

di·git ['dɪdʒɪt] (*number*) cifra *f*; *a 4 ~ number* un numero di 4 cifre

di·gi·tal ['dɪdʒɪtl] *adj* digitale

dig·ni·fied ['dɪgnɪfaɪd] *adj* dignitoso

dig·ni·ta·ry ['dɪgnɪtərɪ] dignitario *m*

dig·ni·ty ['dɪgnɪtɪ] dignità *f*

di·gress [daɪ'gres] *v/i* fare una digressione

di·gres·sion [daɪ'greʃn] digressione *f*

digs [dɪgz] *npl* camera *f* in affitto

dike [daɪk] *along a river* argine *m*; *across a river* diga *f*

di·lap·i·dat·ed [dɪ'læpɪdeɪtɪd] *adj* rovinato; *house* cadente

di·late [daɪ'leɪt] *v/i of pupils* dilatarsi

di·lem·ma [dɪ'lemə] dilemma *m*; *be in a ~* trovarsi in un dilemma

dil·et·tante [dɪle'tæntɪ] dilettante *m/f*

dil·i·gent ['dɪlɪdʒənt] *adj* diligente

di·lute [daɪ'luːt] *v/t* diluire

dim [dɪm] **1** *adj room* buio; *light* fioco; *outline* indistinto; (*stupid*) idiota; *prospects* vago **2** *v/t* (*pret & pp -med*): **~ the headlights** abbassare le luci **3** *v/i* (*pret & pp -med*) *of lights* abbassarsi

di·men·sion [daɪ'menʃn] (*measurement*) dimensione *f*

di·min·ish [dɪ'mɪnɪʃ] *v/t & v/i* diminuire

di·min·u·tive [dɪ'mɪnjʊtɪv] **1** *n* diminutivo *m* **2** *adj* minuscolo

dim·ple ['dɪmpl] fossetta *f*

din [dɪn] *n* baccano *m*

dine [daɪn] *v/i fml* cenare

din·er ['daɪnə(r)] *in a restaurant* cliente *m/f*; ***fellow* ~** commensale *m/f*

din·ghy ['dɪŋgɪ] *small yacht* dinghy *m*; *rubber boat* gommone *m*

din·gy ['dɪndʒɪ] *adj atmosphere* offuscato; (*dirty*) sporco

din·ing car ['daɪnɪŋ] RAIL vagone *m* ristorante; **'din·ing room** *in house* sala *f* da pranzo; *in hotel* sala *f* ristorante; **'din·ing ta·ble** tavolo *m* da pranzo

din·ner ['dɪnə(r)] *in the evening* cena *f*; *at midday* pranzo *m*; *formal gathering* ricevimento *m*

'din·ner guest invitato *m*, -a; **'dinner jack·et** smoking *m inv*; **'dinner par·ty** cena *f*; **'din·ner serv·ice** servizio *m* (di piatti)

di·no·saur ['daɪnəsɔː(r)] dinosauro *m*

dip [dɪp] **1** *n* (*swim*) tuffo *m*; *for food* salsa *f*; *in road* pendenza *f* **2** *v/t* (*pret & pp* **-ped**) immergere; **~ the headlights** abbassare le luci **3** *v/i* (*pret & pp* **-ped**) *of road* scendere

di·plo·ma [dɪ'pləʊmə] diploma *m*

di·plo·ma·cy [dɪ'pləʊməsɪ] diplomazia *f*

di·plo·mat ['dɪpləmæt] diplomatico *m*, -a *f*

di·plo·mat·ic [dɪplə'mætɪk] *adj* diplomatico

dip·lo·mat·i·cal·ly [dɪplə'mætɪklɪ] *adv* con diplomazia

dip·lo·mat·ic im'mu·ni·ty immunità *f* diplomatica

dire ['daɪə(r)] *adj* tremendo

di·rect [daɪ'rekt] **1** *adj* diretto **2** *v/t play* mettere in scena; *film* curare la regia di; *attention* dirigere; **could you please ~ me to ...?** mi può per favore indicare la strada per ...?

di·rect 'cur·rent ELEC corrente *f* continua

di·rect 'deb·it FIN ordine *m* di addebito automatico

di·rec·tion [dɪ'rekʃn] direzione *f*; *of film, play* regia *f*; **~s** (*instructions*), *to a place* indicazioni *fpl*; *for use* istruzioni *fpl*

di·rec·tion 'in·di·ca·tor MOT freccia *f*

di·rec·tive [dɪ'rektɪv] *of EU etc* direttiva *f*

di·rect·ly [dɪ'rektlɪ] **1** *adv* (*straight*) direttamente; (*soon, immediately*) immediatamente **2** *conj* (non) appena; **I'll do it ~ I've finished this** lo faccio (non) appena ho finito questo

di·rec·tor [dɪ'rektə(r)] *of company* direttore *m*, -trice *f*; *of play, film* regista *m/f*

di·rec·to·ry [dɪ'rektərɪ] elenco *m*; TELEC guida *f* telefonica

dirt [dɜːt] sporco *m*, sporcizia *f*

'dirt cheap *adj* F a un prezzo stracciato

dirt·y ['dɜːtɪ] **1** *adj* sporco; (*pornographic*) sconcio **2** *v/t* (*pret & pp* **-ied**) sporcare

dirt·y 'trick tiro *m* mancino

dis·a·bil·i·ty [dɪsə'bɪlətɪ] handicap *m inv*, invalidità *f inv*

dis·a·bled [dɪs'eɪbld] **1** *n* handicappato *m*, -a *f*; **the ~** i disabili **2** *adj* handicappato

dis·ad·van·tage [dɪsəd'vɑːntɪdʒ] (*drawback*) svantaggio *m*; **be at a ~** essere svantaggiato

dis·ad·van·taged [dɪsəd'vɑːntɪdʒd] *adj* penalizzato

dis·ad·van·ta·geous [dɪsədvɑn'teɪdʒəs] *adj* svantaggioso

dis·a·gree [dɪsə'griː] *v/i of person* non essere d'accordo

♦ **disagree with** *v/t of person* non essere d'accordo con; *of food* fare male a

dis·a·gree·a·ble [dɪsə'griːəbl] *adj* sgradevole

dis·a·gree·ment [dɪsə'griːmənt] disaccordo *m*; (*argument*) discussione *f*

dis·al·low [dɪsə'laʊ] *v/t goal* annullare

dis·ap·pear [dɪsə'pɪə(r)] *v/i* sparire, scomparire

dis·ap·pear·ance [dɪsə'pɪərəns] sparizione *f*, scomparsa *f*

dis·ap·point [dɪsə'pɔɪnt] v/t deludere

dis·ap·point·ed [dɪsə'pɔɪntɪd] adj deluso

dis·ap·point·ing [dɪsə'pɔɪntɪŋ] adj deludente

dis·ap·point·ment [dɪsə'pɔɪntmənt] delusione f

dis·ap·prov·al [dɪsə'pruːvl] disapprovazione f

dis·ap·prove [dɪsə'pruːv] v/i disapprovare; **~ of** disapprovare

dis·ap·prov·ing [dɪsə'pruːvɪŋ] adj look di disapprovazione

dis·ap·prov·ing·ly [dɪsə'pruːvɪŋlɪ] adv con disapprovazione

dis·arm [dɪs'ɑːm] **1** v/t disarmare **2** v/i disarmarsi

dis·ar·ma·ment [dɪs'ɑːməmənt] disarmo m

dis·arm·ing [dɪs'ɑːmɪŋ] adj disarmante

dis·as·ter [dɪ'zɑːstə(r)] disastro m

di'sas·ter ar·e·a area f disastrata; (fig: person) disastro m

di·sas·trous [dɪ'zɑːstrəs] adj disastroso

dis·band [dɪs'bænd] **1** v/t sciogliere **2** v/i sciogliersi

dis·be·lief [dɪsbə'liːf] incredulità f; **in ~** con incredulità

disc [dɪsk] disco m

dis·card [dɪ'skɑːd] v/t sbarazzarsi di

di·scern [dɪ'sɜːn] v/t improvement, intentions percepire; outline distinguere

di·scern·i·ble [dɪ'sɜːnəbl] adj improvement percepibile; outline distinguibile

di·scern·ing [dɪ'sɜːnɪŋ] adj person perspicace; **the car for the ~ driver** la macchina per i guidatori che sanno fare la differenza

dis·charge ['dɪstʃɑːdʒ] **1** n from hospital dimissione f; from army congedo m **2** v/t [dɪs'tʃɑːdʒ] from hospital dimettere; from army congedare; from job licenziare; LAW prosciogliere

di·sci·ple [dɪ'saɪpl] discepolo m, -a f

dis·ci·pli·nar·y [dɪsɪ'plɪnərɪ] adj disciplinare

dis·ci·pline ['dɪsɪplɪn] **1** n disciplina f **2** v/t child, dog imporre disciplina a; employee applicare provvedimenti disciplinari a

'disc jock·ey disc jockey m/f inv

dis·claim [dɪs'kleɪm] v/t negare; responsibility declinare

dis·close [dɪs'kləʊs] v/t svelare, rivelare

dis·clo·sure [dɪs'kləʊʒə(r)] rivelazione f

dis·co ['dɪskəʊ] discoteca f

dis·col·or Am, **dis·col·our** [dɪs'kʌlə(r)] v/i scolorire

dis·com·fort [dɪs'kʌmfət] n disagio m; (pain) fastidio m

dis·con·cert [dɪskən'sɜːt] v/t sconcertare

dis·con·cert·ed [dɪskən'sɜːtɪd] adj sconcertato

dis·con·nect [dɪskə'nekt] v/t (detach) sconnettere; supply, telephones staccare; **they'll ~ you if you don't pay your phone bill** ti staccheranno il telefono se non paghi la bolletta; **I was ~ed** TELEC è caduta la linea

dis·con·so·late [dɪs'kɒnsələt] adj sconsolato

dis·con·tent [dɪskən'tent] malcontento m

dis·con·tent·ed [dɪskən'tentɪd] adj scontento

dis·con·tin·ue [dɪskən'tɪnjuː] v/t interrompere; **be a ~d line** essere fuori produzione

dis·cord ['dɪskɔːd] MUS dissonanza f; in relations contrasto m

dis·co·theque ['dɪskətek] discoteca f

dis·count ['dɪskaʊnt] **1** n sconto m; **a 10% ~** uno sconto del 10% **2** v/t [dɪs'kaʊnt] goods scontare; theory trascurare

dis·cour·age [dɪs'kʌrɪdʒ] v/t (dissuade) scoraggiare

dis·cour·age·ment [dɪs'kʌrɪdʒmənt] being disheartened scoraggiamento m; **meet with ~** non avere incoraggiamento

dis·cov·er [dɪ'skʌvə(r)] v/t scoprire

dis·cov·er·er [dɪ'skʌvərə(r)] scopritore m, -trice f

dis·cov·e·ry [dɪ'skʌvərɪ] scoperta f

dis·cred·it [dɪs'kredɪt] v/t screditare

dis·creet [dɪ'skriːt] adj discreto

dis·creet·ly [dɪ'skriːtlɪ] adv discretamente

dis·crep·an·cy [dɪ'skrepənsɪ] incongruenza f

dis·cre·tion [dɪ'skreʃn] discrezione f; **at your ~** a tua discrezione

dis·crim·i·nate [dɪ'skrɪmɪneɪt] v/i: ~ **against** discriminare; ~ **between** (distinguish between) distinguere tra

dis·crim·i·nat·ing [dɪ'skrɪmɪneɪtɪŋ] adj esigente

dis·crim·i·na·tion [dɪ'skrɪmɪneɪʃn] sexual, racial etc discriminazione f

dis·cus ['dɪskəs] SP: object disco m; SP: event lancio m del disco

dis·cuss [dɪ'skʌs] v/t discutere; of article trattare di; **the article ~es whether ...** l'articolo esamina se ...

dis·cus·sion [dɪ'skʌʃn] discussione f

'dis·cus throw·er lanciatore m, -trice f di disco

dis·dain [dɪs'deɪn] n sdegno m

dis·ease [dɪ'ziːz] malattia f

dis·em·bark [dɪsəm'bɑːk] v/i sbarcare

dis·en·chant·ed [dɪsən'tʃɑːntɪd] adj disincantato; ~ **with** disilluso di

dis·en·gage [dɪsən'geɪdʒ] v/t svincolare

dis·en·tan·gle [dɪsən'tæŋgl] v/t districare

dis·fig·ure [dɪs'fɪgə(r)] v/t sfigurare; fig deturpare

dis·grace [dɪs'greɪs] 1 n vergogna f; **it's a ~** è una vergogna; **in ~** in disgrazia 2 v/t disonorare

dis·grace·ful [dɪs'greɪsful] adj behaviour, situation vergognoso

dis·grun·tled [dɪs'grʌntld] adj scontento

dis·guise [dɪs'gaɪz] 1 n travestimento m; **be in ~** essere travestito 2 v/t one's voice, handwriting camuffare; fear, anxiety dissimulare; ~ **o.s. as**

travestirsi da; **he was ~d as a woman** era travestito da donna

dis·gust [dɪs'gʌst] 1 n disgusto m; **in ~** disgustato 2 v/t disgustare

dis·gust·ing [dɪs'gʌstɪŋ] adj disgustoso

dish [dɪʃ] part of meal piatto m; for serving piatto m; for cooking recipiente m

'dish·cloth strofinaccio m

dis·heart·ened [dɪs'hɑːtnd] adj demoralizzato

dis·heart·en·ing [dɪs'hɑːtnɪŋ] adj demoralizzante

di·shev·eled [dɪ'ʃevld] adj person, appearance arruffato; after effort scompigliato

dis·hon·est [dɪs'ɒnɪst] adj disonesto

dis·hon·es·ty [dɪs'ɒnɪstɪ] disonestà f

dis·hon·or etc Am → **dishonour** etc

dis·hon·our [dɪs'ɒnə(r)] n disonore m; **bring ~ on** coprire di disonore

dis·hon·our·a·ble [dɪs'ɒnərəbl] adj disdicevole

'dish·wash·er machine lavastoviglie f inv; person lavapiatti m/f inv

'dish·wash·ing liq·uid Am detersivo m per i piatti

'dish·wa·ter acqua f dei piatti

dis·il·lu·sion [dɪsɪ'luːʒn] v/t disilludere

dis·il·lu·sion·ment [dɪsɪ'luːʒnmənt] disillusione f

dis·in·clined [dɪsɪn'klaɪnd] adj restio (**to** a)

dis·in·fect [dɪsɪn'fekt] v/t disinfettare

dis·in·fec·tant [dɪsɪn'fektənt] disinfettante m

dis·in·her·it [dɪsɪn'herɪt] v/t diseredare

dis·in·te·grate [dɪs'ɪntəgreɪt] v/i disintegrarsi; of marriage, building andare in pezzi

dis·in·ter·est·ed [dɪs'ɪntərestɪd] adj (unbiased) disinteressato

dis·joint·ed [dɪs'dʒɔɪntɪd] adj sconnesso

disk [dɪsk] disco m; (diskette) dischetto m; **on ~** su dischetto m 'disk drive COMPUT lettore *m o* drive *m inv* di dischetti

disk·ette [dɪs'ket] dischetto *m*

dis·like [dɪs'laɪk] **1** *n* antipatia *f*; **take a ~ to s.o.** prendere qu in antipatia **2** *v/t*: **I ~ cats** non mi piacciono i gatti; **I ~ watching TV** non mi piace guardare la TV

dis·lo·cate ['dɪsləkeɪt] *v/t shoulder* lussare

dis·lodge [dɪs'lɒdʒ] *v/t* rimuovere

dis·loy·al [dɪs'lɔɪəl] *adj* sleale

dis·loy·al·ty [dɪs'lɔɪəltɪ] slealtà *f*

dis·mal ['dɪzməl] *adj weather, news* deprimente; *person (sad), failure* triste; *person (negative)* ombroso

dis·man·tle [dɪs'mæntl] *v/t* smontare; *organization* demolire

dis·may [dɪs'meɪ] **1** *n* costernazione *f* **2** *v/t* costernare

dis·miss [dɪs'mɪs] *v/t employee* licenziare; *suggestion, possibility* scartare; *idea, thought* accantonare

dis·miss·al [dɪs'mɪsl] *of employee* licenziamento *m*

dis·mount [dɪs'maʊnt] *v/i* smontare

dis·o·be·di·ence [dɪsə'biːdɪəns] disobbidienza *f*

dis·o·be·di·ent [dɪsə'biːdɪənt] *adj* disobbidiente

dis·o·bey [dɪsə'beɪ] *v/t* disobbedire a

dis·or·der [dɪs'ɔːdə(r)] *(untidiness)* disordine *m*; *(unrest)* disordini *mpl*; MED disturbo *m*

dis·or·der·ly [dɪs'ɔːdəlɪ] *adj room, desk* in disordine; *mob* turbolento

dis·or·gan·ized [dɪs'ɔːgənaɪzd] *adj* disorganizzato

dis·o·ri·ent·ed [dɪs'ɔːrɪentɪd], dis·o·ri·en·tat·ed [dɪs'ɔːrɪənteɪtɪd] *adj* disorientato

dis·own [dɪs'əʊn] *v/t* disconoscere

di·spar·ag·ing [dɪ'spærɪdʒɪŋ] *adj* dispregiativo

dis·par·i·ty [dɪ'spærətɪ] disparità *f inv*

dis·pas·sion·ate [dɪs'pæʃənət] *adj (objective)* spassionato

dis·patch [dɪ'spætʃ] *v/t (send)* spedire

di·spen·sa·ry [dɪ'spensərɪ] *in phar-*

macy dispensario *m*

♦ di·spense with [dɪ'spens] *v/t* fare a meno di

di·sperse [dɪ'spɜːs] **1** *v/t* dissipare **2** *v/i of crowd* disperdersi; *of mist* dissiparsi

di·spir·it·ed [dɪs'pɪrɪtɪd] *adj* abbattuto

dis·place [dɪs'pleɪs] *v/t (supplant)* rimpiazzare

di·splay [dɪ'spleɪ] **1** *n* esposizione *f*, mostra *f*; *in shop window* articoli *mpl* in esposizione; COMPUT visualizzazione *f*; **be on ~** *at exhibition* essere in esposizione *o* mostra; *(be for sale)* essere esposto in vendita **2** *v/t emotion* manifestare; *at exhibition* esporre; *(for sale)* esporre in vendita; COMPUT visualizzare

di'splay cab·i·net *in museum* teca *f*; *in shop* vetrinetta *f*

dis·please [dɪs'pliːz] *v/t* contrariare; **they were ~d with her** erano contrariati con lei

dis·plea·sure [dɪs'pleʒə(r)] disappunto *m*

dis·po·sa·ble [dɪ'spəʊzəbl] *adj* usa e getta *inv*

dis·po·sa·ble 'in·come reddito *m* disponibile

dis·pos·al [dɪ'spəʊzl] *(getting rid of)* eliminazione *f*; *of pollutants, nuclear waste* smaltimento *m*; **I am at your ~** sono a tua disposizione; **put sth at s.o.'s ~** mettere qc a disposizione di qu

♦ dis·pose of [dɪ'spəʊz] *v/t (get rid of)* sbarazzarsi di

dis·posed [dɪ'spəʊzd] *adj*: **be ~ to do sth** *(willing)* essere disposto a fare qc; **be well ~ towards** essere ben disposto verso

dis·po·si·tion [dɪspə'zɪʃn] *(nature)* indole *f*

dis·pro·por·tion·ate [dɪsprə'pɔːʃənət] *adj* sproporzionato

dis·prove [dɪs'pruːv] *v/t* smentire

di·spute [dɪ'spjuːt] **1** *n* controversia *f*; *(industrial)* contestazione *f*; **be in ~** essere controverso **2** *v/t* contestare; *(fight over)* contendersi

dis·qual·i·fi·ca·tion [dɪskwɒlɪfɪ'keɪ-ʃn] squalifica f; *it's a ~* è penalizzante

dis·qual·i·fy [dɪs'kwɒlɪfaɪ] v/t (pret & pp *-ied*) squalificare

dis·re·gard [dɪsrə'ɡɑːd] **1** n mancanza f di considerazione **2** v/t ignorare

dis·re·pair [dɪsrə'peə(r)]: *in a state of* ~ in cattivo stato

dis·rep·u·ta·ble [dɪs'repjʊtəbl] adj depravato; *area* malfamato

dis·re·spect [dɪsrə'spekt] mancanza f di rispetto

dis·re·spect·ful [dɪsrə'spektfʊl] adj irriverente

dis·rupt [dɪs'rʌpt] v/t *train service* creare disagi a; *meeting, class* disturbare; (*intentionally*) creare scompiglio in

dis·rup·tion [dɪs'rʌpʃn] *of train service* disagio m; *of meeting, class* disturbo m; (*intentional*) scompiglio m

dis·rup·tive [dɪs'rʌptɪv] adj *influence* deleterio; *he's very ~ in class* è un elemento di disturbo nella classe

dis·sat·is·fac·tion [dɪssætɪs'fækʃn] insoddisfazione f

dis·sat·is·fied [dɪs'sætɪsfaɪd] adj insoddisfatto

dis·sen·sion [dɪ'senʃn] dissenso m

dis·sent [dɪ'sent] **1** n dissenso m **2** v/i ~ *from* dissentire da

dis·si·dent ['dɪsɪdənt] n dissidente m/f

dis·sim·i·lar [dɪs'sɪmɪlə(r)] adj dissimile

dis·so·ci·ate [dɪ'səʊʃɪeɪt] v/t: ~ *o.s. from* dissociarsi da

dis·so·lute ['dɪsəluːt] adj dissoluto

dis·so·lu·tion ['dɪsəluːʃn] POL scioglimento m

dis·solve [dɪ'zɒlv] **1** v/t *substance* sciogliere **2** v/i *of substance* sciogliersi

dis·suade [dɪ'sweɪd] v/t dissuadere; ~ *s.o. from doing sth* dissuadere qu dal fare qc

dis·tance ['dɪstəns] **1** n distanza f; *in the* ~ in lontananza **2** v/t: ~ *o.s. from* prendere le distanze da

dis·tant ['dɪstənt] adj lontano

dis·taste [dɪs'teɪst] avversione f

dis·taste·ful [dɪs'teɪstfʊl] adj spiacevole

dis·till·er·y [dɪs'tɪlərɪ] distilleria f

dis·tinct [dɪ'stɪŋkt] adj (*clear*) netto; (*different*) distinto; *as ~ from* contrariamente a

dis·tinc·tion [dɪ'stɪŋkʃn] (*differentiation*) distinzione f; *hotel / product of* ~ hotel / prodotto d'eccezione

dis·tinc·tive [dɪ'stɪŋktɪv] adj caratteristico

dis·tinct·ly [dɪ'stɪŋktlɪ] adv distintamente; (*decidedly*) decisamente

dis·tin·guish [dɪ'stɪŋɡwɪʃ] v/t (*see*) distinguere; ~ *between X and Y* distinguere tra X e Y

dis·tin·guished [dɪ'stɪŋɡwɪʃt] adj (*famous*) insigne; (*dignified*) distinto

dis·tort [dɪ'stɔːt] v/t distorcere

dis·tract [dɪ'strækt] v/t *person* distrarre; *attention* distogliere

dis·tract·ed [dɪ'stræktɪd] adj assente

dis·trac·tion [dɪ'strækʃn] *of attention* distrazione f; *drive s.o. to* ~ fare impazzire qu

dis·traught [dɪ'strɔːt] adj affranto

dis·tress [dɪ'stres] **1** n sofferenza f; *in* ~ *of ship, aircraft* in difficoltà **2** v/t (*upset*) angosciare

dis·tress·ing [dɪ'stresɪŋ] adj sconvolgente

dis·tress sig·nal segnale m di pericolo

dis·trib·ute [dɪ'strɪbjuːt] v/t distribuire

dis·tri·bu·tion [dɪstrɪ'bjuːʃn] distribuzione f

dis·trib·u·tor [dɪs'trɪbjuːtə(r)] COM distributore m

dis·trict ['dɪstrɪkt] quartiere m

dis·trust [dɪs'trʌst] **1** n diffidenza f **2** v/t non fidarsi di

dis·turb [dɪ'stɜːb] v/t disturbare; *do not* ~ non disturbare

dis·turb·ance [dɪ'stɜːbəns] (*interruption*) fastidio m; ~*s* (*civil unrest*) disordini mpl

dis·turbed [dɪ'stɜːbd] *adj* (*concerned, worried*) turbato; *psychologically* malato di mente

dis·turb·ing [dɪ'stɜːbɪŋ] *adj* inquietante

dis·used [dɪs'juːzd] *adj* inutilizzato

ditch [dɪtʃ] **1** *n* fosso *m* **2** *v/t* F *boyfriend* scaricare F; F *car* sbarazzarsi di

dith·er ['dɪθə(r)] *v/i* titubare

di·van [dɪ'væn] (*bed*) divano *m*

dive [daɪv] **1** *n* tuffo *m*; (*underwater*) immersione *f*; *of plane* picchiata *f*; F (*bar etc*) bettola *f* F; **take a ~** F *of sterling etc* crollare **2** *v/i* tuffarsi; (*underwater*) fare immersione; *of submarine* immergersi; *of plane* scendere in picchiata; **the goalie ~d for the ball** il portiere si è tuffato per prendere la palla

div·er ['daɪvə(r)] *off board* tuffatore *m*, -trice *f*; (*underwater*) sub *m/f inv*, sommozzatore *m*, -trice *f*

di·verge [daɪ'vɜːdʒ] *v/i* divergere

di·verse [daɪ'vɜːs] *adj* svariato

di·ver·si·fi·ca·tion [daɪvɜːsɪfɪ'keɪʃn] COM diversificazione *f*

di·ver·si·fy [daɪ'vɜːsɪfaɪ] *v/i* (*pret & pp* **-ied**) COM diversificare

di·ver·sion [daɪ'vɜːʃn] *for traffic* deviazione *f*; *to distract attention* diversivo *m*

di·ver·si·ty [daɪ'vɜːsətɪ] varietà *f inv*

di·vert [daɪ'vɜːt] *v/t traffic* deviare; *attention* sviare, distogliere

di·vest [daɪ'vest] *v/t*: **~ s.o. of sth** privare qu di qc

di·vide [dɪ'vaɪd] *v/t* dividere

div·i·dend ['dɪvɪdend] FIN dividendo *m*; **pay ~s** *fig* dare i suoi frutti

di·vine [dɪ'vaɪn] *adj* REL, F divino

div·ing ['daɪvɪŋ] *from board* tuffi *mpl*; (*scuba ~*) immersione *f*

'div·ing board trampolino *m*

di·vis·i·ble [dɪ'vɪzəbl] *adj* divisibile

di·vi·sion [dɪ'vɪʒn] divisione *f*; *of company* sezione *f*

di·vorce [dɪ'vɔːs] **1** *n* divorzio *m*; **get a ~** divorziare **2** *v/t* divorziare da; **get ~d** divorziare **3** *v/i* divorziare

di·vorced [dɪ'vɔːst] *adj* divorziato

di·vor·cee [dɪvɔː'siː] divorziato *m*, -a *f*

di·vulge [daɪ'vʌldʒ] *v/t* divulgare

DIY [diːaɪ'waɪ] *abbr* (= *do it yourself*) fai da te *m inv*, bricolage *m*

DI'Y store negozio *m* di bricolage; *smaller shop* ferramenta *f*

diz·zi·ness ['dɪzɪnɪs] giramento *m* di testa, vertigini *fpl*

diz·zy ['dɪzɪ] *adj* stordito; **I feel ~** mi gira la testa

DJ [diː'dʒeɪ] *abbr* (= *disc jockey*) dj *m/f inv*; (= *dinner jacket*) smoking *m inv*

DNA [diːen'eɪ] *abbr* (= *deoxyribonucleic acid*) DNA *m inv* (= acido *m* deossiribonucleico)

do [duː] (*pret* **did**, *pp* **done**) **1** *v/t* fare; *one's hair* farsi; *100mph etc* andare a; **~ the ironing/cooking** stirare/cucinare; **what are you ~ing tonight?** cosa fai stasera?; **I don't know what to ~** non so cosa fare; **no, I'll ~ it** no, lo faccio; *stress on I* no, lo faccio io; **~ it right now!** fallo subito!; **have you done this before?** lo hai già fatto?; **have you had your hair done** farsi fare i capelli **2** *v/i* (*be suitable, enough*) andare bene; **that will ~!** basta così!; **~ well** (*do a good job*) essere bravo; (*be in good health*) stare bene; **well done!** (*congratulations!*) bravo!; **how ~ you ~?** molto piacere **3** *v/aux*: **~ you know him?** lo conosci?; **I ~n't know** non (lo) so; **~ be quick** sii veloce; **~ you like London? – yes I ~** ti piace Londra? – sì (mi piace); **he works hard, doesn't he?** lavora sodo, no?; **~n't you believe me?** non mi credi?; **you ~ believe me, ~n't you?** mi credi, non è vero?; **you ~n't know the answer, ~ you? – no I ~n't** non sai la risposta, vero? – no, non la so

♦ **do away with** *v/t* (*abolish*) abolire

♦ **do in** *v/t* F (*exhaust*) stravolgere F; **I'm done in** sono stravolto

♦ **do out of** *v/t*: **do s.o. out of sth** F fregare qc a qu F

♦ **do up** *v/t* (*renovate*) restaurare;

D

(*fasten*) allacciare; ***do up your buttons*** abbottonati; ***do up your shoe-laces*** allacciati le scarpe

♦ **do with** *v/t:* ***I could do with ...*** mi ci vorrebbe ...; ***he won't have anything to do with it*** (*won't get involved*) non vuole averci niente a che fare

♦ **do without 1** *v/i* farne a meno **2** *v/t* fare a meno di

do·cile ['dəʊsaɪl] *adj* docile

dock¹ [dɒk] **1** *n* NAUT bacino *m* **2** *v/i of ship* entrare in porto; *of spaceship* agganciarsi

dock² [dɒk] LAW banco *m* degli imputati

dock·er ['dɒkə(r)] portuale *m*

'dock·yard cantiere *m* navale

doc·tor ['dɒktə(r)] *n* MED dottore *m*, -essa *f*

doc·tor·ate ['dɒktərət] dottorato *m*

doc·trine ['dɒktrɪn] dottrina *f*

doc·u·dra·ma ['dɒkjʊdrɑːmə] ricostruzione *f* filmata

doc·u·ment ['dɒkjʊmənt] *n* documento *m*

doc·u·men·ta·ry [dɒkjʊ'mentərɪ] *n programme* documentario *m*

doc·u·men·ta·tion [dɒkjʊmen'teɪʃn] documentazione *f*

dodge [dɒdʒ] *v/t blow* schivare; *person, issue* evitare; *question* aggirare

dodg·ems ['dɒdʒəms] *npl* autoscontro *m*

dog [dɒg] **1** *n* cane *m* **2** *v/t* (*pret & pp* **-ged**) *of bad luck* perseguitare

'dog catch·er accalappiacani *m inv*

dog-eared ['dɒgɪəd] *adj book* con le orecchie

dog·ged ['dɒgɪd] *adj* accanito

dog·gie ['dɒgɪ] *in children's language* cagnolino *m*

'dog·gy bag ['dɒgɪbæg] pacchetto *m* con gli avanzi di una cena al ristorante per l'asporto

'dog·house: be in the ~ F essere nei casini F

dog·ma ['dɒgmə] dogma *m*

dog·mat·ic [dɒg'mætɪk] *adj* dogmatico

do-good·er [duː'gʊdə(r)] *pej* impiccione *m*, -a *f*

dogs·bod·y ['dɒgzbɒdɪ] F bestia *m* da soma

'dog-tired *adj* F stravolto

do-it-your·self [duːɪtjə'self] fai da te *m inv*

dol·drums ['dɒldrəmz]: ***be in the ~*** *of economy* essere in stallo; *of person* essere giù di corda

dole [dəʊl] *Br* F assegno *m* di disoccupazione; ***be on the ~*** ricevere l'assegno di disoccupazione

'dole money *Br* F assegni *mpl* di disoccupazione

♦ **dole out** *v/t* distribuire

doll [dɒl] *toy*, F *woman* bambola *f*

♦ **doll up** *v/t:* ***get dolled up*** mettersi in ghingheri

dol·lar ['dɒlə(r)] dollaro *m*

dol·lop ['dɒləp] *n* F cucchiaiata *f*

dol·phin ['dɒlfɪn] delfino *m*

dome [dəʊm] *of building* cupola *f*

do·mes·tic [də'mestɪk] *adj* domestico; *news, policy* interno

do·mes·tic 'an·i·mal animale *m* domestico

do·mes·ti·cate [də'mestɪkeɪt] *v/t animal* addomesticare; ***be ~d*** *of person* essere incline a fare i lavori di casa

do'mes·tic flight volo *m* nazionale

dom·i·nant ['dɒmɪnənt] *adj* dominante; *member* principale

dom·i·nate ['dɒmɪneɪt] *v/t* dominare

dom·i·na·tion [dɒmɪ'neɪʃn] dominio *m*

dom·i·neer·ing [dɒmɪ'nɪərɪŋ] *adj* autoritario

dom·i·no ['dɒmɪnəʊ] domino *m*; ***play ~s*** giocare a domino

do·nate [dəʊ'neɪt] *v/t* donare

do·na·tion [dəʊ'neɪʃn] donazione *f*

done [dʌn] *pp* → **do**

don·key ['dɒŋkɪ] asino *m*

do·nor ['dəʊnə(r)] donatore *m*, -trice *f*

do·nut ['dəʊnʌt] *Am* → **doughnut**

doo·dle ['duːdl] *v/i* scarabocchiare

doom [duːm] *n* (*fate*) destino *f*; (*ruin*) rovina *f*

doomed [du:md] *adj project* condannato al fallimento; **we are ~** siamo condannati; **the ~ ship** la nave destinata ad affondare; **the ~ plane** l'aereo destinato a cadere

door [dɔː(r)] porta *f*; *of car* portiera *f*; **there's someone at the ~** stanno suonando alla porta

'**door·bell** campanello *m*; '**door·knob** pomello *m* della porta; '**door·man** usciere *m*; '**door·mat** zerbino *m*; '**door·step** gradino *m* della porta; '**door·way** vano *m* della porta

dope [dəʊp] **1** *n* (*drugs*) droga *f* leggera; *in sport* doping *m inv*; F (*idiot*) cretino *m*, -a *f*; F (*information*) soffiata *f* **2** *v/t* dopare

dor·mant ['dɔːmənt] *adj*: **~ volcano** vulcano *m* inattivo; **lie ~** *ofplant* rimanere latente

dor·mi·to·ry ['dɔːmɪtrɪ] dormitorio *m*

dos·age ['dəʊsɪdʒ] dosaggio *m*

dose [dəʊs] *n* dose *f*

dot [dɒt] *n* puntino *m*; *in email address* punto *m*; **on the ~** (*exactly*) in punto

◆ **dote on** [dəʊt] *v/t* stravedere per

dot·ing ['dəʊtɪŋ] *adj* adorante

dot·ted line ['dɒtɪd] linea *f* tratteggiata

dot·ty ['dɒtɪ] *adj* F svitato

dou·ble ['dʌbl] **1** *n* (*amount*) doppio; (*person*) sosia *m inv*; *of film star* controfigura *f*; (*room with two beds*) doppio; (*room with double bed*) matrimoniale **2** *adj* doppio; **in ~ figures** a due cifre **3** *adv*: **~ the amount** il doppio della quantità **4** *v/t* raddoppiare **5** *v/i* raddoppiare

◆ **double back** *v/i* (*go back*) fare dietrofront

◆ **double up** *v/i in pain* piegarsi in due; (*share a room*) dividere la stanza

dou·ble-'bass contrabbasso *m*; **dou·ble 'bed** letto *m* matrimoniale; **dou·ble-'breast·ed** *adj* a doppio petto; **dou·ble 'check** *v/t & v/i* ricontrollare; **dou·ble 'chin** doppio mento *m*; **dou·ble'cross** *v/t* fare il

doppio gioco con; **dou·ble deck·er 'bus** autobus *m inv* a due piani; **dou·ble 'glaz·ing** doppi vetri *mpl*; **dou·ble·park** *v/i* parcheggiare in doppia fila; '**dou·ble-quick** *adj*: **in ~ time** in un batter d'occhio; '**dou·ble room** *with two beds* camera *f* doppia; *with double bed* camera *f* matrimoniale

dou·bles ['dʌblz] *npl in tennis* doppio *msg*

doubt [daʊt] **1** *n* dubbio *m*; **be in ~** essere in dubbio; **no ~** (*probably*) senz'altro **2** *v/t*: **~ s.o. / sth** dubitare di qu / qc; **~ that ...** dubitare che ...

doubt·ful ['daʊtful] *adj remark, look* dubbio; **be ~** *of person* essere dubbioso; **it is ~ whether ...** è in dubbio se ...

doubt·ful·ly ['daʊtflɪ] *adv* con aria dubbiosa

doubt·less ['daʊtlɪs] *adj* senza dubbio

dough [dəʊ] impasto *m*; F (*money*) quattrini *mpl*

dough·nut ['dəʊnʌt] bombolone *m*, krapfen *m inv*

dove [dʌv] colomba *f*; *fig* pacifista *m/f*

dow·dy ['daʊdɪ] *adj* scialbo

down[1] [daʊn] *n* (*feathers*) piuma *f*, piumino *m*

down[2] [daʊn] **1** *adv* (*downwards*) giù; **~ there** laggiù; **fall ~** cadere giù; **die ~** calmarsi; **£200 ~** (*as deposit*) un acconto di £200; **~ south** a sud; **be ~** *of price, rate* essere diminuito; (*not working*) non funzionare; F (*depressed*) essere giù **2** *prep* giù da; (*along*) lungo; **I looked ~ the list** ho scorso la lista; **the third door ~ this corridor** la terza porta lungo questo corridoio; **walk ~ a street** percorrere una strada **3** *v/t* (*swallow*) buttare giù; (*destroy*) abbattere

'**down-and-out** *n* senza tetto *m/f inv*; '**down-cast** *adj* (*dejected*) abbattuto; '**down·fall** rovina *f*; *of politician, government* caduta *f*; '**down·grade** *v/t* ridimensionare; *employee* retrocedere di livello; **down·heart·ed** [daʊn'hɑːtɪd] *adj* abbattuto; **down·** 'hill *adv* in discesa; *go ~ fig* peggiorare; **'down·hill ski·ing** discesa *f* libera; **'down·load** *v/t* COMPUT scaricare; **'down·mark·et** *adj* di fascia medio-bassa; **'down·pay·ment** deposito *m*, acconto *m*; **'down·play** *v/t* minimizzare; **'down·pour** acquazzone *m*; **'down·right 1** *adj*: *it's a ~ lie* è una bugia bella e buona; *he's a ~ idiot* è un perfetto idiota **2** *adv dangerous, stupid etc* assolutamente; **'downside** (*disadvantage*) contropartita *f*; **'down·size 1** *v/t*: *company* ridimensionare; *the ~ed version of car* la versione ridotta **2** *v/i of company* ridimensionarsi; **'down·stairs** *adj & adv* al piano di sotto; **down-to-'earth** *adj approach* pratico; *she's very ~ about it* ha i piedi molto ben per terra al riguardo; **'down·town** *adj & adv* in centro; **'down·turn** *in economy* flessione *f* **'down·wards** *adj & adv* verso il basso

doze [dəʊz] **1** *n* sonnellino *m* **2** *v/i* fare un sonnellino

♦ **doze off** *v/i* assopirsi

doz·en ['dʌzn] dozzina *f*; *~s of ...* F un sacco di ... F

drab [dræb] *adj* scialbo

draft [drɑːft] *of document* bozza *f*; *Am* MIL leva *f*; *Am* → **draught 2** *v/t document* fare una bozza di; *Am* MIL arruolare

'draft dodg·er *Am* MIL renitente *m* alla leva

drag [dræg] **1** *n*: *it's a ~ having to ...* F è una rottura dover ... F; *he's a ~* F è una pizza F; P il corso principale; *in ~* vestito da donna; *a man in ~* un travestito **2** *v/t* (*pret & pp* **-ged**) (*pull*) trascinare; (*search*) dragare **3** *v/i* (*pret & pp* **-ged**) *of time* non passare mai; *of show, film* trascinarsi; *~ s.o. into sth* (*involve*) tirare in ballo qu in qc; *~ sth out of s.o.* (*get information from*) tirare fuori qc da qu

♦ **drag away**: *v/t*: *drag o.s. away*

from the TV staccarsi dalla TV

♦ **drag in** *v/t into conversation* tirare fuori

♦ **drag on** *v/i* (*last long time*) trascinarsi

♦ **drag out** *v/t* (*prolong*) tirare per le lunghe

♦ **drag up** *v/t* F (*mention*) rivangare

drag·on ['drægn] drago *m*; *fig* strega *f*

drain [dreɪn] **1** *n* (*pipe*) tubo *m* di scarico; *under street* tombino *m*; *a ~ on resources* un salasso per le risorse **2** *v/t water* fare colare; *oil fare* uscire; *vegetables* scolare; *land* drenare; *glass, tank* svuotare; (*exhaust: person*) svuotare **3** *v/i of dishes* scolare

♦ **drain away** *v/i of liquid* defluire

♦ **drain off** *v/t water* fare defluire

drain·age ['dreɪnɪdʒ] (*drains*) fognatura *f*; *of water from soil* drenaggio *m*

'drain·pipe tubo *m* di scarico

dra·ma ['drɑːmə] (*art form*) arte *f* drammatica; (*acting*) recitazione *f*; (*excitement*) dramma *m*; (*play: on* TV) sceneggiato *m*; *~ classes* corso *m* di recitazione

dra·mat·ic [drə'mætɪk] *adj* drammatico; (*exciting*) sorprendente; *gesture* teatrale

dra·mat·i·cal·ly [drə'mætɪklɪ] *adv say* drammaticamente; *decline, rise, change etc* drasticamente

dram·a·tist ['dræmətɪst] drammaturgo *m*, -a *f*

dram·a·ti·za·tion [dræmətaɪ'zeɪʃn] (*play*) adattamento *m* teatrale

dram·a·tize ['dræmətaɪz] *v/t story* adattare; *fig* drammatizzare

drank [dræŋk] *pret* → **drink**

drape [dreɪp] *v/t cloth, coat* appoggiare; *~d in* (*covered with*) avvolto in

drap·er·y ['dreɪpərɪ] drappeggio *m*

drapes [dreɪps] *npl Am* tende *fpl*

dras·tic ['dræstɪk] *adj* drastico

draught [drɑːft] **1** *n of air* corrente *f* (d'aria); *~* (*beer*), *beer on ~* birra *f* alla spina

draughts [drɑːfts] *nsg game* dama *f*

draughts·man ['drɑːftsmən] disegnatore *m* industriale; *of plan* disegnatore *m*, -trice *f*

draught·y [ˈdrɑːftɪ] *adj* pieno di correnti d'aria

draw [drɔː] **1** *n in match, competition* pareggio *m*; *in lottery* estrazione *f*, sorteggio *m*; (*attraction*) attrazione *f* **2** *v/t t* (*pret* **drew**, *pp* **drawn**) *picture, map* disegnare; *cart, curtain*, tirare; *in lottery, gun, knife* estrarre; (*attract*) attirare; (*lead*) tirare; *from bank account* ritirare **3** *v/i t* (*pret* **drew**, *pp* **drawn**) disegnare; *in match, competition* pareggiare; **~ near** avvicinarsi

♦ **draw back 1** *v/t* (*recoil*) tirarsi indietro **2** *v/t hand* ritirare; *curtains* aprire

♦ **draw on 1** *v/i* (*approach*) avvicinarsi **2** *v/t* (*make use of*) attingere a

♦ **draw out** *v/t wallet etc* estrarre; *money from bank* ritirare

♦ **draw up 1** *v/t document* redigere; *chair* accostare **2** *v/i of vehicle* fermarsi; **draw up alongside s.o.** accostarsi a qu

'draw·back inconveniente *m*

draw·er¹ [drɔː(r)] *of desk etc* cassetto *m*

draw·er² [drɔː(r)] (*person*) disegnatore *m*, -trice *f*; **she's a good ~** disegna bene

draw·ing [ˈdrɔːɪŋ] disegno *m*

'draw·ing board tecnigrafo *m*; **go back to the ~** *fig* ricominciare da capo

'draw·ing pin puntina *f*

drawl [drɔːl] *n* pronuncia *f* strascicata

drawn [drɔːn] *pp* → **draw**

dread [dred] *v/t* aver il terrore di; **I ~ him finding it out** ho il terrore che lo scopra

dread·ful [ˈdredfʊl] *adj* terribile

dread·ful·ly [ˈdredflɪ] *adv* F (*extremely*) terribilmente; *behave* malissimo

dream [driːm] **1** *n* sogno *m* **2** *adj* F *house etc* dei sogni **3** *v/t* sognare **4** *v/i* sognare; **I ~t about you** ti ho sognato

♦ **dream up** *v/t* sognare

dream·er [ˈdriːmə(r)] (*daydreamer*)

sognatore *m*, -trice *f*

dream·y [ˈdriːmɪ] *adj voice, look* sognante

drear·y [ˈdrɪərɪ] *adj* deprimente; (*boring*) noioso

dredge [dredʒ] *v/t harbour, canal* dragare

♦ **dredge up** *v/t fig* scovare

dregs [dregz] *npl of coffee* fondi *mpl*; **the ~ of society** la feccia della società

drench [drentʃ] *v/t* inzuppare; **get ~ed** inzupparsi; **I'm ~ed** sono fradicio

dress [dres] **1** *n for woman* vestito *m*; (*clothing*) abbigliamento *m* **2** *v/t person* vestire; *wound* medicare; *salad* condire; **get ~ed** vestirsi **3** *v/i* vestirsi; **~ in red** vestirsi di rosso

♦ **dress up** *v/i* vestirsi elegante; (*wear a disguise*) travestirsi; **dress up as a ghost** travestirsi da fantasma

'dress cir·cle prima galleria *f*

dress·er [ˈdresə(r)] *in kitchen* credenza *f*

dress·ing [ˈdresɪŋ] *for salad* condimento *m*; *for wound* medicazione *f*

'dress·ing 'down sgridata *f*; **'dress·ing gown** vestaglia *f*; **'dress·ing room** *in theatre* spogliatoio *m*; **'dress·ing ta·ble** toilette *f inv*

'dress·mak·er sarto *m*, -a *f*

'dress re·hears·al prova *f* generale

dress·y [ˈdresɪ] *adj* F sull'elegante F

drew [druː] *pret* → **draw**

drib·ble [ˈdrɪbl] *v/i of person* sbavare; *of water* gocciolare; *SP* dribblare

dried [draɪd] *adj fruit etc* essicato

dri·er [ˈdraɪə(r)] → **dryer**

drift [drɪft] **1** *n of snow* cumulo *m* **2** *v/i of snow* accumularsi; *of ship* andare alla deriva; (*go off course*) uscire dalla rotta; *of person* vagabondare

♦ **drift apart** *v/i of couple* allontanarsi (l'uno dall'altro)

drift·er [ˈdrɪftə(r)] vagabondo *m*, -a *f*

drill [drɪl] **1** *n* (*tool*) trapano *m*; (*exercise*), *MIL* esercitazione *f* **2** *v/t tunnel* scavare; **~ a hole** fare un foro col trapano **3** v/i *for oil* trivellare; MIL addestrarsi

dril·ling rig ['drɪlɪŋrɪg] (*platform*) sonda *f*

dri·ly ['draɪlɪ] *adv remark* ironicamente

drink [drɪŋk] **1** *n* bevanda *f*; *non-alcoholic ~* bibita *f* (*analcolica*); *a ~ of ...* un bicchiere di ...; *go for a ~* andare a bere qualcosa **2** v/t & v/i (*pret* **drank**, *pp* **drunk**) bere; *I don't ~* non bevo

♦ **drink up 1** v/i (*finish drink*) finire il bicchiere **2** v/t (*drink completely*) finire di bere

drink·a·ble ['drɪŋkəbl] *adj* potabile

drink 'driv·ing guida *f* in stato di ebbrezza

drink·er ['drɪŋkə(r)] bevitore *m*, -trice *f*

drink·ing ['drɪŋkɪŋ] *of alcohol* consumo *m* di alcolici; *he has a ~ problem* beve troppi alcolici

'drink·ing wa·ter acqua *f* potabile

'drinks ma·chine distributore *m* di bevande

drip [drɪp] **1** *n action* gocciolamento *m*; *amount* goccia *f*; MED flebo *f inv* **2** v/i (*pret* & *pp* **-ped**) gocciolare

'drip-dry *adj* non-stiro

drip·ping ['drɪpɪŋ] *adv:* **~ wet** fradicio

drive [draɪv] **1** *n* percorso *m* in macchina; (*outing*) giro *m* in macchina; (*driveway*) viale *m*; (*energy*) grinta *f*; COMPUT lettore *m*; (*campaign*) campagna *f*; *left-/right-hand ~* MOT guida *f* a sinistra/destra **2** v/t (*pret* **drove**, *pp* **driven**) *vehicle* guidare; (*take in car*) portare (in macchina); TECH azionare; *that noise/this man is driving me mad* questo rumore/quest'uomo mi fa diventare matto **3** v/i (*pret* **drove**, *pp* **driven**) guidare; *I ~ to work* vado al lavoro in macchina

♦ **drive at** v/t: *what are you driving at?* dove vuoi andare a parare?

♦ **drive away 1** v/t portare via (in macchina); (*chase off*) cacciare **2** v/i andare via (in macchina)

♦ **drive in** v/t *nail* piantare

♦ **drive off** → **drive away**

driv·el ['drɪvl] *n* sciocchezze *fpl*

driv·en ['drɪvn] *pp* → **drive**

driv·er ['draɪvə(r)] guidatore *m*, -trice *f*, conducente *m/f*; *of train* macchinista *m/f*; COMPUT driver *m inv*

'driv·er's li·cense *Am* patente *f* (di guida)

'drive·way viale *m*

driv·ing ['draɪvɪŋ] **1** *n* guida *f* **2** *adj rain* violento

'driv·ing force elemento *m* motore; **'driv·ing in·struct·or** istruttore *m*, -trice *f* di guida; **'driv·ing les·son** lezione *f* di guida; **'driv·ing li·cence** patente *f* (di guida); **'driv·ing school** scuola *f* guida; **'driv·ing test** esame *m* di guida

driz·zle ['drɪzl] **1** *n* pioggerella *f* **2** v/i piovvigginare

drone [drəʊn] *n* (*noise*) ronzio *m*

droop [druːp] v/i abbassarsi; *of plant* afflosciarsi

drop [drɒp] **1** *n of rain* goccia *f*; (*small amount*) goccio *m*; *in price, temperature* calo *m*; *in number* calo *m* **2** v/t (*pret* & *pp* **-ped**) far cadere; *from plane* sganciare; *person from car* lasciare; *person from team* scartare; (*stop seeing*) smettere di frequentare; *charges, demand etc* abbandonare; (*give up*) lasciare perdere; *~ a line to* scrivere due righe a **3** v/i (*pret* & *pp* **-ped**) cadere; (*decline*) calare

♦ **drop in** v/i (*visit*) passare

♦ **drop off 1** v/t *person, goods* lasciare **2** v/i (*fall asleep*) addormentarsi; (*decline*) calare

♦ **drop out** v/i *from competition, school* ritirarsi

'drop·out (*from school*) persona *f* che ha abbandonato gli studi; (*from society*) emarginato *m*, -a *f*

drops [drɒps] *npl for eyes* collirio *m*

drought [draʊt] siccità *f*

drove [drəʊv] *pret* → **drive**

drown [draʊn] **1** v/i annegare **2** v/t *person* annegare; *sound* coprire; *be ~ed* annegare

drow·sy ['draʊzɪ] *adj* sonnolento

drudg·e·ry ['drʌdʒərɪ] lavoro *m* ingrato

drug [drʌg] **1** *n* droga *f*; **be on ~s** drogarsi **2** *v/t* (*pret & pp* **-ged**) drogare

'**drug addict** tossicodipendente *m/f*

'**drug deal·er** spacciatore *m*, -trice *f* (di droga)

'**drug·store** *esp Am* negozio-bar *m* che vende articoli vari, inclusi medicinali

'**drug traf·fick·ing** traffico *m* di droga

drum [drʌm] *n* MUS tamburo *m*; (*container*) bidone *m*; **~s** *in pop music* batteria *f*
  ◆ **drum into** *v/t* (*pret & pp* **-med**): **drum sth into s.o.** inculcare qc in qu
  ◆ **drum up** *v/t*: **drum up support** cercare supporto

drum·mer [drʌmə(r)] batterista *m/f*; *in brass band* percussionista *m/f*

'**drum·stick** MUS bacchetta *f*; *of poultry* coscia *f*

drunk [drʌŋk] **1** *n* ubriacone *m*, -a *f* **2** *adj* ubriaco; **get ~** ubriacarsi **3** *pp* → **drink**

drunk·en [drʌŋkn] *voices, laughter* da ubriaco; **~ party** festa *f* in cui si beve molto

drunk 'driv·ing guida *f* in stato di ebbrezza

dry [draɪ] **1** *adj* secco; (*ironic*) ironico; *clothes* asciutto; (*where alcohol is banned*) dove la vendita e il consumo di alcolici sono illegali **2** *v/t & v/i* (*pret & pp* **-ied**) asciugare
  ◆ **dry out** *v/i* asciugare; *of alcoholic* disintossicarsi
  ◆ **dry up** *v/i of river* prosciugarsi; F (*be quiet*) stare zitto

'**dry-clean** *v/t* pulire *o* lavare a secco; '**dry clean·er** tintoria *f*; '**dry-clean·ing** (*clothes*) abiti *mpl* portati in tintoria

dry·er ['draɪə(r)] (*machine*) asciugatrice *f*

DTP [diːtiːˈpiː] *abbr* (= **desktop publishing**) desk-top publishing *m*, impaginazione *f* elettronica

du·al ['djuːəl] *adj* doppio

du·al 'car·riage·way *Br* carreggiata *f* a due corsie

dub [dʌb] *v/t* (*pret & pp* **-bed**) *film* doppiare

du·bi·ous ['djuːbɪəs] *adj* equivoco; (*having doubts*) dubbioso

duch·ess duchessa *f*

duck [dʌk] **1** *n* anatra *f* **2** *v/i* piegarsi **3** *v/t one's head* piegare; *question* aggirare

dud [dʌd] *n* F (*false note*) falso *m*

due [djuː] *adj* (*owed, proper*) dovuto; **be ~** *of train, baby etc* essere previsto; *I'm ~ to meet him* dovrei incontrarlo; **~ to** (*because of*) a causa di; **be ~ to** (*be caused by*) essere dovuto a; *in ~ course* a tempo debito

dues [djuːz] *npl* quota *fsg*

du·et [djuːˈet] MUS duetto *m*

dug [dʌg] *pret & pp* → **dig**

duke [djuːk] duca *m*

dull [dʌl] *adj weather* grigio; *sound, pain* sordo; (*boring*) noioso

du·ly ['djuːlɪ] *adv* (*as expected*) come previsto; (*properly*) debitamente

dumb [dʌm] *adj* (*mute*) muto; F (*stupid*) stupido

dumb·found·ed [dʌmˈfaʊndɪd] *adj* ammutolito

dum·my ['dʌmɪ] *for clothes* manichino *m*; *for baby* succhiotto *m*

dump [dʌmp] **1** *n for rubbish* discarica *f*; (*unpleasant place*) postaccio *m* **2** *v/t* (*deposit*) lasciare; (*dispose of*) scaricare; *toxic waste etc* sbarazzarsi di

dump·ling ['dʌmplɪŋ] *fagotto m di pasta ripieno, sia dolce che salato*

dune [djuːn] duna *f*

dung [dʌŋ] sterco *m*

dun·ga·rees [dʌŋgəˈriːz] *npl* salopette *f inv*

dunk [dʌŋk] *v/t in coffee etc* inzuppare

du·o ['djuːəʊ] MUS duo *m inv*

du·pli·cate ['djuːplɪkət] **1** *n* duplicato *m*; *in ~* in duplicato **2** *v/t* ['djuːplɪkeɪt] (*copy*) duplicare; (*repeat*) rifare

du·pli·cate 'key chiave *f* di scorta

du·ra·ble ['djuərəbl] *adj material* resistente; *relationship* durevole

du·ra·tion [djuə'reɪʃn] durata *f*

du·ress [djuə'res]: *under ~* sotto costrizione

dur·ing ['djuərɪŋ] *prep* durante

dusk [dʌsk] crepuscolo *m*

dust [dʌst] **1** *n* polvere *f* **2** *v/t* spolverare; *~ sth with sth* (*sprinkle*) spolverare qc con qc

'dust·bin bidone *m* della spazzatura

'dust cov·er *for book* sopracoperta *f*

duster ['dʌstə(r)] (*cloth*) straccio *m* (per spolverare)

'dust jack·et *of book* sopracoperta *f*; **'dust·man** spazzino *m*; **'dust·pan** paletta *f*

dust·y ['dʌsti] *adj table* impolverato; *road* polveroso

Dutch [dʌtʃ] **1** *adj* olandese; *go ~* F fare alla romana F **2** *n language* olandese *m*; *the ~* gli Olandesi

du·ty ['dju:tɪ] dovere *m*; *on goods* tassa *f* doganale, dazio *m*; *be on ~* essere di servizio; *be off ~* essere fuori servizio

du·ty 'free 1 *adj* duty free *inv* **2** *n* acquisto *m* fatto in un duty free

du·ty free al'low·ance limite *m* di acquisto in un duty free

du·ty'free shop duty free *m inv*

dwarf [dwɔ:f] **1** *n* nano *m*, -a *f* **2** *v/t* fare scomparire

♦ **dwell on** [dwel] *v/t* rimuginare

dwin·dle ['dwɪndl] *v/i* diminuire

dye [daɪ] **1** *n* tintura *f*; *for food* colorante *m* **2** *v/t* colorare, tingere

dy·ing ['daɪɪŋ] *adj person* morente; *industry*, *tradition* in via di disparizione; *his ~ day* il giorno della sua morte

dy·nam·ic [daɪ'næmɪk] *adj person* dinamico

dy·na·mism ['daɪnəmɪzm] dinamismo *m*

dy·na·mite ['daɪnəmaɪt] *n* dinamite *f*

dy·na·mo ['daɪnəməʊ] TECH dinamo *f inv*

dy·nas·ty ['dɪnəstɪ] dinastia *f*

dys·lex·i·a [dɪs'leksɪə] dislessia *f*

dys·lex·ic [dɪs'leksɪk] **1** *adj* dislessico **2** *n* dislessico *m*, -a *f*

E

each [i:tʃ] **1** *adj* ogni **2** *adv* ciascuno; *they're £1.50 ~* costano £1,50 ciascuno **3** *pron* ciascuno *m*, -a *f*, ognuno *m*, -a *f*; *~ other* l'un l'altro *m*, l'una l'altra *f*; *we know ~ other* ci conosciamo; *we drive ~ other's car* guidiamo l'uno la macchina dell'altro

ea·ger ['i:gə(r)] *adj* entusiasta; *be ~ to do sth* essere ansioso di fare qc; *be ~ for* essere desideroso di

ea·ger 'bea·ver F fanatico *m*, -a *f* F

ea·ger·ly ['i:gəlɪ] *adv* ansiosamente

ea·ger·ness ['i:gənɪs] smania *f*

ea·gle ['i:gl] aquila *f*

ea·gle-eyed [i:gl'aɪd] *adj*: *be ~ eyed* avere l'occhio di falco

ear¹ [ɪə(r)] *of person, animal* orecchio *m*

ear² [ɪə(r)] *of corn* spiga *f*

'ear·ache mal *m* d'orecchi

'ear·drum timpano *m*

earl [ɜ:l] conte *m*

'ear·lobe lobo *m* dell'orecchio

ear·ly ['ɜ:lɪ] **1** *adj* (*not late*) primo; *arrival* anticipato; (*farther back in time*) antico; *in the ~ hours* nelle prime ore; *in the ~ stages* nelle fasi iniziali; *in ~ spring* all'inizio della primavera; *~ October* inizio ottobre; *at an ~ age* in giovane età; *I'm an ~ riser* mi alzo sempre presto; *let's have an ~ supper* ceniamo troppo presto; *an ~ Picasso* un Picasso primo periodo; *the ~ Romans* gli antichi Romani; *~ music* musica *f* primitiva; *I look forward to an ~ reply* resto in attesa di una sollecita risposta **2** *adv* (*not late*) presto; (*ahead of time*) in anticipo; *it's too ~* è troppo presto; *you're a bit ~* sei un po' in anticipo

'**ear·ly bird** persona *f* mattiniera; *planning ahead* persona *f* previdente

ear·mark ['ɪəmɑːk] *v/t* riservare; *~ sth for sth* riservare qc a qc

earn [ɜːn] *v/t* guadagnare; *of interest* fruttare; *holiday, drink etc* guadagnarsi; *~ one's living* guadagnarsi da vivere; *his honesty ~ed him everybody's respect* la sua onestà gli è valsa il rispetto di tutti

ear·nest ['ɜːnɪst] serio; *in ~* sul serio

earn·ings ['ɜːnɪŋz] *npl* guadagno *m*

'**ear·phones** *npl* cuffie *fpl* (d'ascolto); '**ear·pierc·ing** *adj* perforante; '**ear·ring** orecchino *m*; '**ear·shot**: *within ~* a portata d'orecchio; *out of ~* fuori dalla portata d'orecchio

earth [ɜːθ] (*soil, planet*) terra *f*; *where on ~ have you been?* F dove cavolo sei stato? F

earth·en·ware ['ɜːθnweə(r)] *n* terracotta *f*

earth·ly ['ɜːθlɪ] *adj* terreno; *it's no ~ use ...* F è perfettamente inutile ...

earth·quake ['ɜːθkweɪk] terremoto *m*

earth-shat·ter·ing ['ɜːθʃætərɪŋ] *adj* sconvolgente

ease [iːz] **1** *n* facilità *f*; *be at* (*one's*) *~, feel at ~* essere *o* sentirsi a proprio agio; *be or feel ill at ~* essere *o* sentirsi a disagio **2** *v/t* (*relieve*) alleviare; *it will ~ my mind* mi darà sollievo **3** *v/i of pain* alleviarsi

♦ **ease off 1** *v/t* (*remove*) togliere con cautela **2** *v/i of pain, rain* diminuire

ea·sel ['iːzl] cavalletto *m*

eas·i·ly ['iːzəlɪ] *adv* (*with ease*) facilmente; (*by far*) di gran lunga

east [iːst] **1** *n* est *m* **2** *adj* orientale **3** *adv travel* a est

Eas·ter ['iːstə(r)] Pasqua *f*

Eas·ter 'Day il giorno *o* la domenica di Pasqua

'**Eas·ter egg** uovo *m* di Pasqua

eas·ter·ly ['iːstəlɪ] *adj*: *~ wind* vento *m* dell'est; *in an ~ direction* verso est

Eas·ter 'Mon·day lunedì *m inv* di Pasqua, Pasquetta *f*

east·ern ['iːstən] *adj* orientale

east·ward(s) ['iːstwəd(z)] *adv* verso est

eas·y ['iːzɪ] *adj* facile; (*relaxed*) tranquillo; *take things ~* (*slow down*) prendersela con calma; *take it ~!* (*calm down*) calma!; *I've had it ~* ho avuto una vita facile

'**eas·y chair** poltrona *f*

eas·y-go·ing ['iːzɪɡəʊɪŋ] *adj*: *he's very ~* gli va bene quasi tutto

eat [iːt] *v/t & v/i* (*pret ate, pp eaten*) mangiare

♦ **eat out** *v/i* mangiare fuori

♦ **eat up** *v/t finish food* finire di mangiare; *fig* mangiare; *with jealousy* consumare; *eat up your beans* eat them all mangia tutti i fagioli

eat·a·ble ['iːtəbl] *adj* commestibile; *lunch, dish* mangiabile

eat·en ['iːtn] *pp* → **eat**

eau de Co·logne [əʊdəkə'ləʊn] acqua *f* di Colonia

eaves [iːvz] *npl* cornicione *m*

eaves·drop ['iːvzdrɒp] *v/i* (*pret & pp -ped*) origliare; *~ on s.o. / sth* origliare qu / qc

ebb [eb] *v/i of tide* rifluire

♦ **ebb away** *v/i fig: of courage, strength* venire meno

ec·cen·tric [ɪk'sentrɪk] **1** *adj* eccentrico **2** *n* eccentrico *m*, -a *f*

ec·cen·tric·i·ty [ɪksen'trɪsɪtɪ] eccentricità *f inv*

ech·o ['ekəʊ] **1** *n* eco *f* **2** *v/i* risuonare **3** *v/t words* ripetere; *views* condividere

e·clipse [ɪ'klɪps] **1** *n* eclissi *f inv* **2** *v/t* *fig* eclissare

e·co·lo·gi·cal [iːkə'lɒdʒɪkl] *adj* ecologico; **~ balance** equilibrio *m* ecologico

e·co·lo·gi·cal·ly [iːkə'lɒdʒɪklɪ] *adv* ecologicamente

e·co·lo·gi·cal·ly 'friend·ly *adj* ecologico

e·col·o·gist [ɪ'kɒlədʒɪst] ecologista *m/f*

e·col·o·gy [ɪ'kɒlədʒɪ] ecologia *f*

ec·o·nom·ic [iːkə'nɒmɪk] *adj* economico

ec·o·nom·i·cal [iːkə'nɒmɪkl] *adj* (*cheap*) economico; (*thrifty*) parsimonioso

ec·o·nom·i·cal·ly [iːkə'nɒmɪklɪ] *adv* (*in terms of economics*) economicamente; (*thriftily*) con parsimonia

ec·o·nom·ics [iːkə'nɒmɪks] *science* economia *f*; *financial aspects* aspetti *mpl* economici

e·con·o·mist [ɪ'kɒnəmɪst] economista *m/f*

e·con·o·mize [ɪ'kɒnəmaɪz] *v/i* risparmiare, fare economia

♦ **economize on** *v/t* risparmiare su

e·con·o·my [ɪ'kɒnəmɪ] *of a country* economia *f*; (*saving*) risparmio *m*, economia *f*

e·con·o·my class classe *f* economica; **e·con·o·my drive** regime *m* di risparmio; **e·con·o·my size** confezione *f* famiglia

e·co·sys·tem ['iːkəʊsɪstm] ecosistema *m*

e·co·tour·ism ['iːkəʊtʊərɪzm] agriturismo *m*

ec·sta·sy ['ekstəsɪ] estasi *f*

ec·sta·tic [ɪk'stætɪk] *adj* in estasi

ec·ze·ma ['eksmə] eczema *m*

edge [edʒ] **1** *n of knife* filo *m*; *of table, seat, lawn* bordo *m*; *of road* ciglio *m*; *of cliff* orlo *m*; *in voice* sfumatura *f* tagliente; **there's an ~ of cynicism in his voice** c'è una punta di cinismo nella sua voce; **on ~** → **edgy 2** *v/t* profilare **3** *v/i* (*move slowly*) muoversi con cautela

edge·ways ['edʒweɪz] *adv*: **I couldn't get a word in ~** non sono

riuscito a piazzare una parola

edg·y ['edʒɪ] *adj* teso

ed·i·ble ['edɪbl] *adj* commestibile

ed·it ['edɪt] *v/t text* rivedere; *prepare for publication* curare; *newspaper* dirigere; *TV program, film* montare; COMPUT editare

e·di·tion [ɪ'dɪʃn] edizione *f*

ed·i·tor ['edɪtə(r)] *of text* revisore *m*; *of publication* curatore *m*, -trice *f*; *of newspaper* direttore *m*, -trice; *of TV program* responsabile *m/f* del montaggio; *of film* tecnico *m* del montaggio; **sports ~** redattore *m*, -trice sportivo, -a; *in charge* caporedattore *m*, -trice *f* sportivo, -a

ed·i·to·ri·al [edɪ'tɔːrɪəl] **1** *adj* editoriale; **the ~ staff** la redazione **2** *n* editoriale *m*, articolo *m* di fondo

EDP [iːdiː'piː] *abbr* (= **electronic data processing**) EDP (= elaborazione *f* elettronica dei dati)

ed·u·cate ['edjʊkeɪt] *v/t child* istruire; *consumers* educare; **he was ~d at Cambridge** ha studiato a Cambridge

ed·u·cat·ed ['edjʊkeɪtɪd] *adj person* istruito

ed·u·ca·tion [edjʊ'keɪʃn] istruzione *f*; **the ~ system** la pubblica istruzione

ed·u·ca·tion·al [edjʊ'keɪʃnl] *adj* didattico; (*informative*) istruttivo

eel [iːl] anguilla *f*

ee·rie ['ɪərɪ] *adj* inquietante

ef·fect [ɪ'fekt] effetto *m*; **take ~ of** *medicine, drug* fare effetto; **come into ~ of** *law* entrare in vigore

ef·fec·tive [ɪ'fektɪv] *adj* (*efficient*) efficace; (*striking*) d'effetto; **~ May 1** con decorrenza dal 1 maggio; **a very ~ combination** un abbinamento di grande effetto

ef·fem·i·nate [ɪ'femɪnət] *adj* effeminato

ef·fer·ves·cent [efə'vesnt] *adj also fig* effervescente

ef·fi·cien·cy [ɪ'fɪʃənsɪ] efficienza *f*; *of machine* rendimento *m*

ef·fi·cient [ɪ'fɪʃənt] *adj* efficiente; *machine* ad alto rendimento ef·fi·cient·ly [ɪ'fɪʃəntlɪ] adv con efficienza

ef·flu·ent ['efluənt] scarichi mpl

ef·fort ['efət] sforzo m; **make an ~ to do sth** fare uno sforzo per fare qc

ef·fort·less ['efətlɪs] adj facile

ef·fron·te·ry [ɪ'frʌntərɪ] sfrontatezza f, sfacciataggine f

ef·fu·sive [ɪ'fjuːsɪv] adj thanks, welcome caloroso

e.g. [iː'dʒiː] ad o per esempio

e·gal·i·tar·i·an [ɪgælɪ'teərɪən] adj egualitario

egg [eg] uovo m; of woman ovulo m

♦ egg on v/t istigare

'egg·cup portauovo m inv; 'egg·head F intellettualoide m/f; 'egg·plant Am melanzana f; 'egg·shell guscio m d'uovo; 'egg tim·er timer m per misurare il tempo di cottura delle uova

e·go ['iːgəʊ] ego m

e·go·cen·tric [iːgəʊ'sentrɪk] adj egocentrico

e·go·ism ['iːgəʊɪzm] egoismo m

e·go·ist ['iːgəʊɪst] egoista m/f

E·gypt ['iːdʒɪpt] Egitto m

E·gyp·tian [ɪ'dʒɪpʃn] 1 adj egiziano 2 n egiziano m, -a f

ei·der·down ['aɪdədaʊn] (quilt) piumino m

eight [eɪt] otto

eigh·teen [eɪ'tiːn] diciotto

eigh·teenth [eɪ'tiːnθ] n & adj diciottesimo, -a

eighth [eɪtθ] n & adj ottavo, -a

eigh·ti·eth ['eɪtɪɪθ] n & adj ottantesimo, -a

eigh·ty ['eɪtɪ] ottanta

ei·ther ['aɪðə(r)] 1 adj l'uno o l'altro; (both) entrambi pl; **at ~ side of the street** da entrambi i lati della strada 2 pron l'uno o l'altro m, l'una o l'altra f 3 adv nemmeno, neppure; **I won't go** ~ non vado nemmeno o neppure io 4 conj: ~ **my mother or my sister** mia madre o mia sorella; **he doesn't like** ~ **wine or beer** non gli piacciono né il vino, né la birra; ~ **you write or phone** o scrivi, o telefoni

e·ject [ɪ'dʒekt] 1 v/t espellere 2 v/i from plane eiettarsi

♦ eke out [iːk] v/t usare con parsimonia; grant etc arrotondare

e·lab·o·rate [ɪ'læbərət] 1 adj elaborato 2 v/i [ɪ'læbəreɪt] fornire particolari

e·lab·o·rate·ly [ɪ'læbərətlɪ] adv in modo elaborato

e·lapse [ɪ'læps] v/i trascorrere

e·las·tic [ɪ'læstɪk] 1 adj elastico 2 n elastico m

e·las·ti·cat·ed [ɪ'læstɪkeɪtɪd] adj elasticizzato

e·las·tic 'band elastico m

e·las·tic·i·ty [ɪlæs'tɪsətɪ] elasticità f

E·las·to·plast® [ɪ'læstəpluːst] cerotto m

e·lat·ed [ɪ'leɪtɪd] adj esultante

e·la·tion [ɪ'leɪʃn] esultanza f

el·bow ['elbəʊ] 1 n gomito m 2 v/t: ~ **out of the way** allontanare a spintoni

el·der ['eldə(r)] 1 adj maggiore 2 n maggiore m/f; **she's two years my** ~ è più vecchia di me di due anni

el·der·ly ['eldəlɪ] adj anziano

el·dest ['eldəst] 1 adj maggiore 2 n maggiore m/f; **the** ~ il/la maggiore

e·lect [ɪ'lekt] 1 v/t eleggere; ~ **to ...** decidere di ... 2 adj: **the president** ~ il futuro presidente

e·lec·tion [ɪ'lekʃn] elezione f

e·lec·tion cam·paign campagna f elettorale

e·lec·tion day giorno m delle elezioni

e·lec·tive [ɪ'lektɪv] adj facoltativo

e·lec·tor [ɪ'lektə(r)] elettore m, -trice f

e·lec·to·ral sys·tem [ɪ'lektərəlsɪstm] sistema m elettorale

e·lec·to·rate [ɪ'lektərət] elettorato m

e·lec·tric [ɪ'lektrɪk] adj also fig elettrico

e·lec·tri·cal [ɪ'lektrɪkl] adj elettrico

e·lec·tri·cal en·gi'neer ingegnere m elettrico

e·lec·tri·cal en·gi·neer·ing ingegneria f elettrica

e·lec·tric 'blan·ket coperta *f* elettrica

e·lec·tric 'chair sedia *f* elettrica

e·lec·tri·cian [ɪlek'trɪʃn] elettricista *m/f*

e·lec·tri·ci·ty [ɪlek'trɪsəti] elettricità *f*

e·lec·tric 'ra·zor rasoio *m* elettrico

e·lec·tri·fy [ɪ'lektrɪfaɪ] *v/t* (*pret & pp -ied*) elettrificare; *fig* elettrizzare

e·lec·tro·cute [ɪ'lektrəkju:t] *v/t* fulminare

e·lec·trode [ɪ'lektrəʊd] elettrodo *m*

e·lec·tron [ɪ'lektrɒn] elettrone *m*

e·lec·tron·ic [ɪlek'trɒnɪk] *adj* elettronico

e·lec·tron·ic da·ta 'pro·ces·sing elaborazione *f* elettronica dei dati

e·lec·tron·ic 'mail posta *f* elettronica

e·lec·tron·ics [ɪlek'trɒnɪks] elettronica *f*

el·e·gance ['elɪgəns] eleganza *f*

el·e·gant ['elɪgənt] *adj* elegante

el·e·gant·ly ['elɪgəntlɪ] *adv* elegantemente

el·e·ment ['elɪmənt] elemento *m*

el·e·men·ta·ry [elɪ'mentərɪ] *adj* (*rudimentary*) elementare

el·e·men·ta·ry school *Am* scuola *f* elementare

el·e·men·ta·ry teacher maestro *m*, -a *f* elementare

el·e·phant ['elɪfənt] elefante *m*

el·e·vate ['elɪveɪt] *v/t* elevare

el·e·va·tion [elɪ'veɪʃn] (*altitude*) altitudine *f*

el·e·va·tor ['elɪveɪtə(r)] *Am* ascensore *m*

el·e·ven [ɪ'levn] undici

el·e·venth [ɪ'levnθ] *n & adj* undicesimo, -a; *at the ~ hour* all'ultima ora, all'ultimo momento

el·i·gi·ble ['elɪdʒəbl] *adj*: *be ~ to do sth* avere il diritto di fare qc; *be ~ for sth* avere diritto a qc

el·i·gi·ble 'bach·e·lor buon partito *m*

e·lim·i·nate [ɪ'lɪmɪneɪt] *v/t* eliminare; *be ~d from competition* essere eliminato

e·lim·i·na·tion [ɪ'lɪmɪneɪʃn] eliminazione *f*

e·lite [eɪ'li:t] **1** *n* elite *f inv* **2** *adj* elitario

el·lipse [ɪ'lɪps] ellisse *f*

elm [elm] olmo *m*

e·lope [ɪ'ləʊp] *v/i* scappare (per sposarsi)

el·o·quence ['eləkwəns] eloquenza *f*

el·o·quent ['eləkwənt] *adj* eloquente

el·o·quent·ly ['eləkwəntlɪ] *adv* con eloquenza

else [els] *adv*: *anything ~* qualcos'altro; *anything ~? in shop* (desidera) altro?; *nothing ~* nient'altro; *if you've got nothing ~ to do* se non hai altro da fare; *nobody ~* nessun altro; *everyone ~ is going* tutti gli altri vanno; *who ~ was there?* chi altro c'era?; *someone ~* qualcun altro; *something ~* qualcos'altro; *let's go somewhere ~* andiamo da qualche altra parte; *or ~* altrimenti

else·where ['elsweə(r)] *adv* altrove

e·lude [ɪ'lu:d] *v/t* (*escape from*) sfuggire a; (*avoid*) sfuggire a; *the name ~s me* il nome mi sfugge

e·lu·sive [ɪ'lu:sɪv] *adj person* difficile da trovare; *quality* raro; *criminal* inafferrabile

e·ma·ci·ated [ɪ'meɪsɪeɪtɪd] *adj* emaciato

e-mail ['i:meɪl] **1** *n* e-mail *m inv* **2** *v/t person* mandare un e-mail a; *text* mandare per e-mail

'e-mail ad·dress indirizzo *m* e-mail

e·man·ci·pat·ed [ɪ'mænsɪpeɪtɪd] *adj woman* emancipato

e·man·ci·pa·tion [ɪmænsɪ'peɪʃn] emancipazione *f*

em·balm [ɪm'bɑ:m] *v/t* imbalsamare

em·bank·ment [ɪm'bæŋkmənt] *of river* argine *m*; RAIL massicciata *f*

em·bar·go [em'bɑ:gəʊ] embargo *m inv*

em·bark [ɪm'bɑ:k] *v/i* imbarcarsi

♦embark on *v/t* imbarcarsi in

em·bar·rass [ɪm'bærəs] *v/t* imbarazzare

em·bar·rassed [ɪm'bærəst] *adj* imbarazzato

em·bar·rass·ing [ɪm'bærəsɪŋ] *adj* imbarazzante

em·bar·rass·ment [ɪm'bærəsmənt] imbarazzo *m*

em·bas·sy ['embəsɪ] ambasciata *f*

em·bel·lish [ɪm'belɪʃ] *v/t* ornare; *story* ricamare su

em·bers ['embəz] *npl* brace *fsg*

em·bez·zle [ɪm'bezl] *v/t* appropriarsi indebitamente di

em·bez·zle·ment [ɪm'bezlmənt] appropriazione *f* indebita

em·bez·zler [ɪm'bezlə(r)] malversatore *m*, -trice *f*

em·bit·ter [ɪm'bɪtə(r)] *v/t* amareggiare

em·blem ['embləm] emblema *f*

em·bod·i·ment [ɪm'bɒdɪmənt] incarnazione *f*

em·bod·y [ɪm'bɒdɪ] *v/t* (*pret & pp -ied*) incarnare

em·bo·lis·m ['embəlɪzm] embolia *f*

em·boss [ɪm'bɒs] *v/t metal* lavorare a sbalzo; *paper, fabric* stampare in rilievo

em·brace [ɪm'breɪs] **1** *n* abbraccio *m* **2** *v/t* (*hug, include*) abbracciare **3** *v/i of two people* abbracciarsi

em·broi·der [ɪm'brɔɪdə(r)] *v/t* ricamare; *fig* ricamare su

em·broi·der·y [ɪm'brɔɪdərɪ] ricamo *m*

em·bry·o ['embrɪəʊ] embrione *m*

em·bry·on·ic [embrɪ'ɒnɪk] *adj fig* embrionale

em·e·rald ['emərəld] *precious stone* smeraldo *m; colour* verde *m* smeraldo

e·merge [ɪ'mɜːdʒ] *v/i* (*appear*) emergere; *it has ~d that ...* è emerso che ...

e·mer·gen·cy [ɪ'mɜːdʒənsɪ] emergenza *f; in an ~* in caso di emergenza; **emer·gen·cy 'ex·it** uscita *f* di sicurezza; **e'mer·gen·cy land·ing** atterraggio *m* di fortuna; **e'mer·gen·cy serv·ices** *npl* servizi *mpl* di soccorso

em·er·y board ['emərɪbɔːd] limetta *f* (da unghie)

em·i·grant ['emɪgrənt] emigrante *m/f*

em·i·grate ['emɪgreɪt] *v/i* emigrare

em·i·gra·tion [emɪ'greɪʃn] emigrazione *f*

Em·i·nence ['emɪnəns]: REL **His ~** Sua Eminenza

em·i·nent ['emɪnənt] *adj* eminente

em·i·nent·ly ['emɪnəntlɪ] *adv* decisamente

e·mis·sion [ɪ'mɪʃn] *of gases* emanazione *f*

e·mit [ɪ'mɪt] *v/t* (*pret & pp -ted*) *heat, gases* emanare; *light, smoke* emettere; *smell* esalare

e·mo·tion [ɪ'məʊʃn] emozione *f*

e·mo·tion·al [ɪ'məʊʃnl] *adj problems, development* emozionale; (*causing emotion*) commovente; (*showing emotion*) commosso

em·pa·thize ['empəθaɪz] *v/i* immedesimarsi; **~ with s.o.** immedesimarsi con qu; **~ with sth** capire qc

em·per·or ['empərə(r)] imperatore *m*

em·pha·sis ['emfəsɪs] enfasi *f; on word* rilievo *m*

em·pha·size ['emfəsaɪz] *v/t* enfatizzare; *word* dare rilievo a

em·phat·ic [ɪm'fætɪk] *adj* enfatico

em·pire ['empaɪə(r)] impero *m*

em·ploy [ɪm'plɔɪ] *v/t* dare lavoro a; (*take on*) assumere; (*use*) impiegare; **she's ~ed as a secretary** lavora come segretaria; **he hasn't been ~ed for six months** non lavora da sei mesi

em·ploy·ee [emplɔɪ'iː] dipendente *m/f*

em·ploy·er [em plɔɪ'ə(r)] datore *m*, -trice *f* di lavoro

em·ploy·ment [em plɔɪmənt] occupazione *f;* (*work*) impiego *m; be seeking ~* essere in cerca di occupazione

em'ploy·ment a·gen·cy agenzia *f* di collocamento

em·press ['emprɪs] imperatrice *f*

emp·ti·ness ['emptɪnɪs] vuoto *m*

emp·ty ['emptɪ] **1** *adj* vuoto **2** *v/t*

E

(*pret & pp* **-ied**) vuotare **3** *v/i* (*pret & pp* **-ied**) *of room, street* svuotarsi

em·u·late ['emjʊleɪt] *v/t* emulare

e·mul·sion [ɪ'mʌlʃn] *n paint* emulsione *f*

en·a·ble [ɪ'neɪbl] *v/t person* permettere a; *thing* permettere; **~ *s.o. to do sth*** permettere a qu di fare qc

en·act [ɪ'nækt] *v/t law* emanare; THEA rappresentare

e·nam·el [ɪ'næml] smalto *m*

enc *abbr* (= **enclosure(s)**) all. (= allegato *m*)

en·chant [ɪn'tʃɑːnt] *v/t* (*delight*) incantare

en·chant·ing [ɪn'tʃɑːntɪŋ] *adj smile, village, person* incantevole

en·cir·cle [ɪn'sɜːkl] *v/t* circondare

encl *abbr* (= **enclosure(s)**) all. (= allegato *m*)

en·close [ɪn'kləʊz] *v/t in letter* allegare; *please find* **~d ...** in allegato, ...; *area* recintare

en·clo·sure [ɪn'kləʊʒə(r)] *with letter* allegato *m*

en·core ['ɒŋkɔː(r)] bis *m inv*

en·coun·ter [ɪn'kaʊntə(r)] **1** *n* incontro *m* **2** *v/t* incontrare

en·cour·age [ɪn'kʌrɪdʒ] *v/t* incoraggiare

en·cour·age·ment [ɪn'kʌrɪdʒmənt] incoraggiamento *m*

en·cour·ag·ing [ɪn'kʌrɪdʒɪŋ] *adj* incoraggiante

♦ **encroach on** [ɪn'krəʊtʃ] *v/t land, time* invadere; *rights* violare

en·cy·clo·pe·di·a [ɪnsaɪklə'piːdɪə] enciclopedia *f*

end [end] **1** *n* (*extremity*) estremità *f inv*; (*conclusion*) fine *f*; (*purpose*) fine *m*; *in the* **~** alla fine; *for hours on* **~** senza sosta; *stand sth on* **~** mettere qc verticale; *at the* **~ *of July*** alla fine di luglio; *put an* **~ *to*** mettere fine a **2** *v/t* terminare **3** *v/i* finire

♦ **end up** *v/i* finire; *I'll end up doing it myself* finirò per farlo io stesso

en·dan·ger [ɪn'deɪndʒə(r)] *v/t* mettere in pericolo

en'dan·gered spe·cies specie *f* in via d'estinzione

en·dear·ing [ɪn'dɪərɪŋ] *adj* accattivante

en·deav·our [ɪn'devə(r)] **1** *n* tentativo *m* **2** *v/t* tentare

en·dem·ic [ɪn'demɪk] *adj* endemico

end·ing ['endɪŋ] finale *m*; GRAM desinenza *f*

end·less ['endlɪs] *adj* interminabile

en·dorse [en'dɔːs] *v/t cheque* girare; *candidacy* appoggiare; *product* fare pubblicità a

en·dorse·ment [en'dɔːsmənt] *of cheque* girata *f*; *of candidacy* appoggio *m*; *of product* pubblicità *f*

end 'prod·uct prodotto *m* finale

end re'sult risultato *m* finale

en·dur·ance [ɪn'djʊrəns] resistenza *f*

en·dure [ɪn'djʊə(r)] **1** *v/t* sopportare **2** *v/i* (*last*) resistere

en·dur·ing [ɪn'djʊərɪŋ] *adj* durevole

end-us·er [end'juːzə(r)] utente *m* finale

en·e·my ['enəmɪ] nemico *m*, -a *f*

en·er·get·ic [enə'dʒetɪk] *adj* energico

en·er·get·i·cal·ly [enə'dʒetɪklɪ] *adv* con energia

en·er·gy ['enədʒɪ] energia *f*

en·er·gy-sav·ing ['enədʒɪseɪvɪŋ] *adj device* per risparmiare energia

'en·er·gy sup·ply rifornimento *m* di energia elettrica

en·force [ɪn'fɔːs] *v/t* far rispettare

en·gage [ɪn'geɪdʒ] **1** *v/t* (*hire*) ingaggiare **2** *v/i* TECH ingranare

♦ **engage in** *v/t* occuparsi di; *conversation* coinvolgere in

en·gaged [ɪn'geɪdʒd] *adj to be married* fidanzato; *get* **~** fidanzarsi

en'gaged tone *Br* TELEC segnale *m* d'occupato

en·gage·ment [ɪn'geɪdʒmənt] (*appointment*) impegno *m*; *to be married* fidanzamento *m*; MIL scontro *m*

en'gage·ment ring anello *m* di fidanzamento

en·gag·ing [ɪn'geɪdʒɪŋ] *adj smile, person* accattivante

en·gine ['endʒɪn] motore *m*

en·gi·neer [endʒɪ'nɪə(r)] **1** *n* ingegnere *m*; *for sound, software* tecnico *m*; NAUT macchinista *m* **2** *v/t fig*: *meeting etc* macchinare, architettare

en·gi·neer·ing [endʒɪ'nɪərɪŋ] ingegneria *f*

En·gland ['ɪŋɡlənd] Inghilterra *f*

En·glish ['ɪŋɡlɪʃ] **1** *adj* inglese **2** *n* (*language*) inglese *m*; **the ~** gli inglesi

En·glish 'Chan·nel Manica *f*

'En·glish·man inglese *m*

'En·glish·wom·an inglese *f*

en·grave [ɪn'ɡreɪv] *v/t* incidere

en·grav·ing [ɪn'ɡreɪvɪŋ] (*drawing*) stampa *f*; (*design*) incisione *f*

en·grossed [ɪn'ɡrəʊst] *adj*: **~ in** assorto in

en·gulf [ɪn'ɡʌlf] *v/t* avvolgere

en·hance [ɪn'hɑːns] *v/t* accrescere; *performance, reputation* migliorare

e·nig·ma [ɪ'nɪɡmə] enigma *m*

e·nig·mat·ic [enɪɡ'mætɪk] *adj* enigmatico

en·joy [ɪn'dʒɔɪ] *v/t*: **did you ~ the film?** ti è piaciuto il film?; **I ~ reading** mi piace leggere; **~ your meal!** buon appetito!; **~ o.s.** divertirsi

en·joy·a·ble [ɪn'dʒɔɪəbl] *adj* piacevole

en·joy·ment [ɪn'dʒɔɪmənt] piacere *m*, divertimento *m*

en·large [ɪn'lɑːdʒ] *v/t* ingrandire

en·large·ment [ɪn'lɑːdʒmənt] ingrandimento *m*

en·light·en [ɪn'laɪtn] *v/t* illuminare

en·list [ɪn'lɪst] **1** *v/i* MIL arruolarsi **2** *v/t*: **~ the help of ...** ottenere l'appoggio di ...

en·liv·en [ɪn'laɪvn] *v/t* animare

en·mi·ty ['enmətɪ] inimicizia *f*

e·nor·mi·ty [ɪ'nɔːmətɪ] enormità *f inv*

e·nor·mous [ɪ'nɔːməs] *adj* enorme

e·nor·mous·ly [ɪ'nɔːməslɪ] *adv* enormemente

e·nough [ɪ'nʌf] **1** *adj* sufficiente, abbastanza *inv* **2** *pron* abbastanza; **will £50 be ~?** saranno sufficienti £50?;

I've had ~! ne ho abbastanza!; *thanks, I've had ~ food, drinks* grazie, basta così; *that's ~, calm down!* adesso basta, calmati! **3** *adv* abbastanza; *strangely ~* per quanto strano

en·quire [ɪn'kwaɪə(r)] *v/i* chiedere informazioni, informarsi; **~ about sth** chiedere informazioni su qc; **~ into sth** fare delle ricerche su qc

en·quir·ing [ɪn'kwaɪərɪŋ] *adj*: **have an ~ mind** avere una mente curiosa

en·quir·y [ɪn'kwaɪərɪ] richiesta *f* di informazioni; (*public ~*) indagine *f*

en·raged [ɪn'reɪdʒd] *adj* arrabbiato

en·rich [ɪn'rɪtʃ] *v/t* arricchire

en·roll [ɪn'rəʊl] *v/i* iscriversi

en·rol·ment [ɪn'rəʊlmənt] iscrizione *f*

en·sue [ɪn'sjuː] *v/i* seguire

en suite (bath·room) ['ɒnswiːt] bagno *m* in camera

en·sure [ɪn'ʃʊə(r)] *v/t* assicurare

en·tail [ɪn'teɪl] *v/t* comportare

en·tan·gle [ɪn'tæŋɡl] *v/t in rope* impigliare; **become ~d in** impigliarsi in; *in love affair* invischiarsi in

en·ter ['entə(r)] **1** *v/t room, house* entrare in; *competition* inscriversi a; *person, horse in race* iscrivere; (*write down*) registrare; COMPUT inserire **2** *v/i* entrare; THEA entrare in scena; *in competition* iscriversi **3** *n* COMPUT invio *m*

en·ter·prise ['entəpraɪz] (*initiative*) intraprendenza *f*; (*venture*) impresa *f*

en·ter·pris·ing ['entəpraɪzɪŋ] *adj* intraprendente

en·ter·tain [entə'teɪn] **1** *v/t* (*amuse*) intrattenere; (*consider: idea*) considerare **2** *v/i* (*have guests*) ricevere

en·ter·tain·er [entə'teɪnə(r)] artista *m/f*

en·ter·tain·ing [entə'teɪnɪŋ] *adj* divertente

en·ter·tain·ment [entə'teɪnmənt] *adj* divertimento *m*

en·thrall [ɪn'θrɔːl] *v/t* affascinare

en·thu·si·as·m [ɪn'θjuːzɪæzm] entusiasmo *m*

E

en·thu·si·ast [ɪnˈθjuːzɪˈæst] appassionato *m*, -a *f*

en·thu·si·as·tic [ɪnθjuːzɪˈæstɪk] *adj* entusiasta

en·thu·si·as·tic·al·ly [ɪnθjuːzɪˈæstɪklɪ] *adv* con entusiasmo

en·tice [ɪnˈtaɪs] *v/t* attirare

en·tire [ɪnˈtaɪə(r)] *adj* intero

en·tire·ly [ɪnˈtaɪəlɪ] *adv* interamente

en·ti·tle [ɪnˈtaɪtl] *v/t* dare il diritto a; **be ~d to do sth** avere il diritto di fare qc

en·ti·tled [ɪnˈtaɪtld] *adj book* intitolato

en·trance ['entrəns] entrata *f*, ingresso *m*; THEA entrata *f* in scena; (*admission*) ammissione *f*

en·tranced [ɪnˈtrɑːnst] *adj* incantato

'en·trance ex·am·i·na·tion esame *m* di ammissione

'en·trance fee quota *f* di ingresso

en·trant ['entrənt] concorrente *m/f*

en·treat [ɪnˈtriːt] *v/t* supplicare; **~ s.o. to do sth** supplicare qu di fare qc

en·trenched [ɪnˈtrentʃt] *adj attitudes* radicato

en·tre·pre·neur [ɒntrəprəˈnɜː] imprenditore *m*, -trice *f*

en·tre·pre·neur·i·al [ɒntrəprəˈnɜːrɪəl] *adj* imprenditoriale

en·trust [ɪnˈtrʌst] *v/t* affidare; **~ s.o. with sth, ~ sth to s.o.** affidare qc a qu

en·try ['entrɪ] (*way in*) entrata *f*; (*admission*) ingresso *m*; *in diary* annotazione *f*; *in accounts, dictionary* voce *f*

'en·try form modulo *m* d'iscrizione; '**en·try·phone** citofono *m*; '**en·try vi·sa** visto *m* d'ingresso

e·nu·me·rate [ɪˈnjuːməreɪt] *v/t* enumerare

en·vel·op [ɪnˈveləp] *v/t* avviluppare

en·ve·lope ['envələʊp] busta *f*

en·vi·a·ble ['envɪəbl] *adj* invidiabile

en·vi·ous ['envɪəs] *adj* invidioso; **be ~ of s.o.** essere invidioso di qu

en·vi·ron·ment [ɪnˈvaɪərənmənt] ambiente *m*

en·vi·ron·men·tal [ɪnvaɪərənˈmentl] *adj* ambientale

en·vi·ron·men·tal·ist [ɪnvaɪərənˈmentəlɪst] ambientalista *m/f*

en·vi·ron·men·tal·ly friend·ly [ɪnvaɪərənˈmentəlɪ] *adj* ecologico

en·vi·ron·men·tal pol·lu·tion inquinamento *m* ambientale

en·vi·ron·men·tal pro·tec·tion tutela *f* dell'ambiente

en·vi·rons [ɪnˈvaɪərənz] *npl* dintorni *mpl*

en·vis·age [ɪnˈvɪzɪdʒ] *v/t* prevedere

en·voy ['envɔɪ] inviato *m*, -a *f*

en·vy ['envɪ] **1** *n* invidia *f*; **be the ~ of** essere invidiato da **2** *v/t* (*pret & pp* **-ied**): **~ s.o. sth** invidiare qc a qu

e·phem·er·al *adj* effimero

ep·ic ['epɪk] **1** *n* epopea *f* **2** *adj journey* mitico; **a task of ~ proportions** un'impresa titanica

ep·i·cen·tre ['epɪsentr] epicentro *m*

ep·i·dem·ic [epɪˈdemɪk] epidemia *f*

ep·i·lep·sy ['epɪlepsɪ] epilessia *f*

ep·i·lep·tic [epɪˈleptɪk] epilettico *m*, -a *f*

ep·i·lep·tic 'fit attacco *m* epilettico

ep·i·log *Am*, **ep·i·logue** ['epɪlɒg] epilogo *m*

ep·i·sode ['epɪsəʊd] episodio *m*

ep·i·taph ['epɪtɑːf] epitaffio *m*

e·poch ['iːpɒk] epoca *f*

'e·poch-mak·ing ['iːpɒkmeɪkɪŋ] *adj* che fa epoca

e·qual ['iːkwl] **1** *adj* uguale, pari *inv*; **be ~ to** *task* essere all'altezza di **2** *n*: **be the ~ of** essere equivalente a; **treat s.o. as his ~** trattare qualcuno alla pari **3** *v/t* (*pret & pp* **-led**, *Am* **-ed**) (*be as good as*) uguagliare; **4 times 12 ~s 48** 4 per 12 fa 48

e·qual·i·ty [ɪˈkwɒlətɪ] uguaglianza *f*, parità *f*

e·qual·ize ['iːkwəlaɪz] **1** *v/t* uniformare **2** *v/i Br* SP pareggiare

e·qual·iz·er ['iːkwəlaɪzə(r)] *Br* SP gol *m inv* del pareggio

e·qual·ly ['iːkwəlɪ] *adv* ugualmente; **~, ...** allo stesso modo, ...

e·qual 'rights *npl* parità *f* di diritti

e·quate [ɪˈkweɪt] *v/t* equiparare; **~ sth with sth** equiparare qc e qc

e·qua·tion [ɪˈkweɪʒn] MATH equazione f

e·qua·tor [ɪˈkweɪtə(r)] equatore m

e·qui·lib·ri·um [iːkwɪˈlɪbrɪəm] equilibrio m

e·qui·nox [ˈiːkwɪnɒks] equinozio m

e·quip [ɪˈkwɪp] v/t (pret & pp **-ped**) equipaggiare; ~ **s.o. / sth with sth** equipaggiare qu / qc di qc; **he's not ~ped to handle it** fig non ha la capacità di gestirlo

e·quip·ment equipaggiamento m; electrical, electronic apparecchiature fpl

equi·ui·ty [ˈekwətɪ] FIN capitale m azionario

e·quiv·a·lent [ɪˈkwɪvələnt] **1** adj equivalente; **be ~ to** essere equivalente a **2** n equivalente m

e·ra [ˈɪərə] era f

e·rad·i·cate [ɪˈrædɪkeɪt] v/t sradicare

e·rase [ɪˈreɪz] v/t cancellare

e·ras·er [ɪˈreɪzə(r)] gomma f (da cancellare)

e·rect [ɪˈrekt] **1** adj eretto **2** v/t erigere

e·rec·tion [ɪˈrekʃn] erezione f

er·go·nom·ic [ɜːɡəʊˈnɒmɪk] adj furniture ergonomico

e·rode [ɪˈrəʊd] v/t erodere; of acid corrodere; fig: rights, power eliminare

e·ro·sion [ɪˈrəʊʒn] erosione f; of acid corrosione f; fig eliminazione f

e·rot·ic [ɪˈrɒtɪk] adj erotico

e·rot·i·cism [ɪˈrɒtɪsɪzm] erotismo m

er·rand [ˈerənd] commissione f; **run ~s** fare commissioni

er·rat·ic [ɪˈrætɪk] adj irregolare

er·ror [ˈerə(r)] errore m

'er·ror mes·sage COMPUT messaggio m di errore

e·rupt [ɪˈrʌpt] v/i of volcano eruttare; of violence esplodere; of person dare in escandescenze

e·rup·tion [ɪˈrʌpʃn] of volcano eruzione f; of violence esplosione f

es·ca·late [ˈeskəleɪt] v/i of costs aumentare; of war intensificarsi

es·ca·la·tion [eskəˈleɪʃn] escalation f inv

es·ca·la·tor [ˈeskəleɪtə(r)] scala f mobile

es·cape [ɪˈskeɪp] **1** n of prisoner, animal, gas fuga f; **have a narrow ~** scamparla per un pelo **2** v/i of prisoner, animal scappare, fuggire; of gas fuoriuscire **3** v/t: **the word ~s me** la parola mi sfugge

es'cape chute AVIA scivolo m

es·cort [ˈeskɔːt] **1** n accompagnatore m, -trice f; (guard) scorta f **2** v/t [ɪˈskɔːt] socially accompagnare; act as guard to scortare

es·pe·cial [ɪˈspeʃl] → **special**

es·pe·cial·ly [ɪˈspeʃlɪ] adv specialmente

es·pi·o·nage [ˈespɪənɑːʒ] spionaggio m

es·pres·so (cof·fee) [esˈpresəʊ] espresso m

es·say [ˈeseɪ] n saggio m; in school tema m

es·sen·tial [ɪˈsenʃl] adj essenziale

es·sen·tial·ly [ɪˈsenʃlɪ] adv essenzialmente

es·tab·lish [ɪˈstæblɪʃ] v/t company fondare; (create, determine) stabilire; **~ o.s. as** imporsi come

es·tab·lish·ment [ɪˈstæblɪʃmənt] firm azienda f; hotel, restaurant struttura f; **the Establishment** la classe dirigente

es·tate [ɪˈsteɪt] (area of land) tenuta f; (possessions of dead person) patrimonio m

es·tate a·gen·cy agenzia f immobiliare; **es·tate a·gent** agente m/f immobiliare; **es·tate car** giardiniera f

es·thet·ic etc Am → **aesthetic** etc

es·ti·mate [ˈestɪmət] **1** n stima f, valutazione f; COM preventivo m **2** v/t stimare

es·ti·ma·tion [estɪˈmeɪʃn] stima f; **he has gone up / down in my ~** è salito / sceso nella mia stima; **in my ~** (opinion) a mio giudizio

es·tranged [ɪsˈtreɪndʒd] adj wife, husband separato

es·tu·a·ry [ˈestjʊərɪ] estuario m

ETA [iːtiːˈeɪ] abbr (= **estimated time of arrival**) ora f d'arrivo prevista

etc [et'setrə] *abbr* (= *et cetera*) ecc. (= eccetera)

etch·ing ['etʃɪŋ] acquaforte *f*

e·ter·nal [ɪ'tɜ:nl] *adj* eterno

e·ter·ni·ty [ɪ'tɜ:nətɪ] eternità *f*

eth·i·cal ['eθɪkl] *adj* etico

eth·ics ['eθɪks] etica *f*

eth·nic ['eθnɪk] *adj* etnico

eth·nic 'group gruppo *m* etnico, etnia *f*

eth·nic mi'nor·i·ty minoranza *f* etnica

EU [i:'ju:] *abbr* (= *European Union*) UE *f* (= Unione *f* europea)

eu·phe·mism ['ju:fəmɪzm] eufemismo *m*

eu·pho·ri·a [ju:'fɔ:rɪə] euforia *f*

eu·ro ['jʊərəu] euro *m inv*; **'Eu·ro·cheque** Eurocheque *m inv*; **Eu·ro·crat** ['jʊərəukræt] funzionario *m*, -a *f* della Commissione europea; **'Eu·ro MP** eurodeputato *m*, -a *f*

Eu·rope ['jʊərəp] Europa *f*

Eu·ro·pe·an [jʊərə'pɪən] **1** *adj* europeo **2** *n* europeo *m*, -a *f*; **Eu·ro·pe·an Com'mis·sion** Commissione *f* europea; **Eu·ro·pe·an Com'mis·sion·er** Commissario *m* europeo; **Eu·ro·pe·an 'Par·lia·ment** Parlamento *m* europeo; **Eu·ro·pe·an 'Un·ion** Unione *f* europea

eu·tha·na·si·a [ju:θə'neɪzɪə] eutanasia *f*

e·vac·u·ate [ɪ'vækjueɪt] *v/t* evacuare

e·vade [ɪ'veɪd] *v/t* eludere; *taxes* evadere

e·val·u·ate [ɪ'væljueɪt] *v/t* valutare

e·val·u·a·tion [ɪvælju'eɪʃn] valutazione *f*

e·van·gel·ist [ɪ'vændʒəlɪst] evangelizzatore *m*, -trice *f*

e·vap·o·rate [ɪ'væpəreɪt] *v/i of water* evaporare; *of confidence* svanire

e·vap·o·ra·tion [ɪvæpə'reɪʃn] *of water* evaporazione *f*

e·va·sion [ɪ'veɪʒn] elusione *f*; *of taxes* evasione *f*

e·va·sive [ɪ'veɪsɪv] *adj* evasivo

eve [i:v] vigilia *f*

e·ven ['i:vn] **1** *adj* (*regular*) omoge-

neo; *breathing* regolare; *surface* piano; *hem* diritto; (*number*) pari *inv*; *players, game* alla pari; **get ~ with ...** farla pagare a ... **2** *adv* persino; **the car ~ has a CD player** la macchina ha persino un lettore CD; **~ bigger** ancora più grande; **~ better / worse** ancora meglio / peggio; **not ~** nemmeno, neppure; **~ so** nonostante questo; **~ if** anche se **3** *v/t*: **~ the score** pareggiare

eve·ning ['i:vnɪŋ] sera *f*; **in the ~** di sera; **this ~** stasera; **good ~** buona sera

'eve·ning class corso *m* serale; **'eve·ning dress** *for woman* vestito *m* da sera; *for man* abito *m* scuro; **eve·ning 'pa·per** giornale *m* della sera

e·ven·ly ['i:vnlɪ] *adv* (*regularly*) in modo omogeneo; *breathe* regolarmente

e·vent [ɪ'vent] evento *m*, avvenimento *m*; *social* manifestazione *f*; SP prova *f*; **at all ~s** ad ogni modo

e·vent·ful [ɪ'ventful] *adj* movimentato

e·ven·tu·al [ɪ'ventjuəl] *adj* finale

e·ven·tu·al·ly [ɪ'ventjuəlɪ] *adv* finalmente, alla fine

ev·er ['evə(r)] *adv* mai; **have you ~ been to ...?** sei mai stato in ...?; **for ~ per** sempre; **as ~** come sempre; **~ more** sempre di più; **~ since he left I have been worried** da quando è partito sono preoccupato; **~ since his sister's death** dalla morte di sua sorella; **he's been depressed ~ since** è depresso da allora

ev·er·green ['evəgri:n] *n* sempreverde *m*

ev·er·last·ing [evə'lɑ:stɪŋ] *adj* eterno

ev·ery ['evrɪ] *adj* ogni; **one in ~ ten houses** una casa su dieci; **~ other day** un giorno sì, uno no; **~ now and then** ogni tanto

ev·ery·bod·y ['evrɪbɒdɪ] → **everyone**

ev·ery·day ['evrɪdeɪ] *adj* di tutti i giorni

ev·ery·one ['evrɪwʌn] *pron* tutti *pl*

ev·ery·thing ['evrɪθɪŋ] *pron* tutto

ev·ery·where ['evrɪweə(r)] *adv* dovunque, dappertutto; (*wherever*) dovunque

e·vict [ɪ'vɪkt] *v/t* sfrattare

ev·i·dence ['evɪdəns] prova *f*; *give ~* testimoniare

ev·i·dent ['evɪdənt] *adj* evidente

ev·i·dent·ly ['evɪdəntlɪ] *adv* evidentemente

e·vil ['iːvl] **1** *adj* cattivo **2** *n* male *m*

e·voke [ɪ'vəʊk] *v/t image* evocare

ev·o·lu·tion [iːvə'luːʃn] evoluzione *f*

e·volve [ɪ'vɒlv] *v/i* evolvere

ewe [juː] pecora *f* femmina

ex- [eks] *pref* ex-

ex [eks] F (*former wife*) ex *f inv* F; (*former husband*) ex *m inv* F

ex·act [ɪg'zækt] *adj* esatto

ex·act·ing [ɪg'zæktɪŋ] *adj task* impegnativo; *employer* esigente; *standards* rigido

ex·act·ly [ɪg'zæktlɪ] *adv* esattamente; *~!* esatto!, esattamente!; *not ~* non esattamente

ex·ag·ge·rate [ɪg'zædʒəreɪt] *v/t & v/i* esagerare

ex·ag·ge·ra·tion [ɪgzædʒə'reɪʃn] esagerazione *f*

ex·am [ɪg'zæm] esame *m*; *sit an ~* dare o sostenere un esame; *pass an ~* passare o superare un esame; *fail an ~* essere bocciato a un esame

ex·am·i·na·tion [ɪgzæmɪ'neɪʃn] esame *m*; *of patient* visita *f*

ex·am·ine [ɪg'zæmɪn] *v/t* esaminare; *patient* visitare

ex·am·in·er [ɪg'zæmɪnə(r)] EDU esaminatore *m*, -trice *f*

ex·am·ple [ɪg'zɑːmpl] esempio *m*; *for ~* ad o per esempio; *set a good / bad ~* dare il buon / cattivo esempio

ex·as·pe·rat·ed [ɪg'zæspəreɪt] *adj* esasperato

ex·as·pe·rat·ing [ɪg'zæspəreɪtɪŋ] *adj* esasperante

ex·ca·vate ['ekskəveɪt] *v/t* (*dig*) scavare; *of archaeologist* riportare alla luce

ex·ca·va·tion [ekskə'veɪʃn] scavo *m*

ex·ca·va·tor ['ekskəveɪtə(r)] escavatrice *f*

ex·ceed [ɪk'siːd] *v/t* (*be more than*) eccedere, superare; (*go beyond*) oltrepassare, superare

ex·ceed·ing·ly [ɪk'siːdɪŋlɪ] *adj* estremamente

ex·cel [ɪk'sel] (*pret & pp* **-led**) **1** *v/i* eccellere; *~ at* eccellere in **2** *v/t*: *~ o.s.* superare se stesso

ex·cel·lence ['eksələns] eccellenza *f*

ex·cel·lent ['eksələnt] *adj* eccellente

ex·cept [ɪk'sept] *prep* eccetto; *~ for* fatta eccezione per; *~ that …* eccetto che …

ex·cep·tion [ɪk'sepʃn] eccezione *f*; *with the ~ of* con l'eccezione di; *take ~ to* avere da ridire su; (*be offended by*) risentirsi per

ex·cep·tion·al [ɪk'sepʃnl] *adj* eccezionale

ex·cep·tion·al·ly [ɪk'sepʃnlɪ] *adv* (*extremely*) eccezionalmente

ex·cerpt ['eksɜːpt] estratto *m*

ex·cess [ɪk'ses] **1** *n* eccesso *m*; *eat / drink to ~* mangiare / bere all'eccesso; *be in ~ of* eccedere **2** *adj* eccesso

ex·cess 'bag·gage eccedenza *f* di bagaglio

ex·cess 'fare supplemento *m* tariffa

ex·ces·sive [ɪk'sesɪv] *adj* eccessivo

ex·change [ɪks'tʃeɪndʒ] **1** *n of views, information* scambio *m*; *between schools* scambio *m* culturale; *in ~* (*for*) in cambio (di) **2** *v/t* cambiare; *~ sth for sth* cambiare qc con qc

ex'change rate FIN tasso *m* di cambio

ex·ci·ta·ble [ɪk'saɪtəbl] *adj* eccitabile

ex·cite [ɪk'saɪt] *v/t* (*make enthusiastic*) eccitare

ex·cit·ed [ɪk'saɪtɪd] *adj* eccitato; *get ~* eccitarsi; *get ~ about sth* eccitarsi per qc

ex·cite·ment [ɪk'saɪtmənt] eccitazione *f*

ex·cit·ing [ɪk'saɪtɪŋ] *adj* eccitante, emozionante

E

ex·claim [ɪk'skleɪm] v/t esclamare

ex·cla·ma·tion [eksklə'meɪʃn] esclamazione f

ex·cla·ma·tion mark punto m esclamativo

ex·clude [ɪk'sklu:d] v/t escludere

ex·clud·ing [ɪk'sklu:dɪŋ] prep ad esclusione di

ex·clu·sive [ɪk'sklu:sɪv] adj esclusivo

ex·com·mu·ni·cate [ekskə'mju:nɪkeɪt] v/t REL scomunicare

ex·cru·ci·at·ing [ɪk'skru:ʃɪeɪtɪŋ] adj pain lancinante

ex·cur·sion [ɪk'skɜ:ʃn] escursione f, gita f

ex·cuse [ɪk'skju:s] 1 n scusa f 2 v/t [ɪk'skju:z] scusare; ~ s.o. from sth dispensare qu da qc; ~ me to get attention, interrupting scusami, mi scusi fml; to get past permesso

ex·di·rec·to·ry Br be ~ non comparire sull'elenco telefonico

e·x·e·cute ['eksɪkju:t] v/t criminal giustiziare; plan attuare

ex·e·cu·tion [eksɪ'kju:ʃn] of criminal esecuzione f; of plan attuazione f

ex·e·cu·tion·er [eksɪ'kju:ʃnə(r)] carnefice m

ex·ec·u·tive [ɪg'zekjʊtɪv] dirigente m/f

ex·ec·u·tive 'brief·case ventiquattrore f inv

ex·ec·u·tive 'wash·room bagno m della direzione

ex·em·pla·ry [ɪg'zemplərɪ] adj esemplare

ex·empt [ɪg'zempt] adj: be ~ from essere esente da

ex·er·cise ['eksəsaɪz] 1 n (physical), EDU esercizio m; MIL esercitazione f; take ~ fare esercizio 2 v/t muscle fare esercizio con; dog far fare esercizio a; caution, restraint adoperare 3 v/i fare esercizio

'ex·er·cise bike cyclette f inv; **'ex·er·cise book** EDU quaderno m di esercizi; **'ex·er·cise class** esercitazione f

ex·ert [ɪg'zɜ:t] v/t authority esercitare; ~ o.s. sforzarsi

ex·er·tion [ɪg'zɜ:ʃn] sforzo m

ex·hale [eks'heɪl] v/t esalare

ex·haust [ɪg'zɔ:st] 1 n fumes gas mpl di scarico; pipe tubo m di scappamento 2 v/t (tire) estenuare; (use up) esaurire

ex·haust·ed [ɪg'zɔ:stɪd] adj (tired) esausto

ex·haust fumes npl gas mpl di scarico

ex·haust·ing [ɪg'zɔ:stɪŋ] adj estenuante

ex·haus·tion [ɪg'zɔ:stʃn] spossatezza f

ex·haus·tive [ɪg'zɔ:stɪv] adj esauriente

ex'haust pipe tubo m di scappamento

ex·hib·it [ɪg'zɪbɪt] 1 n in exhibition oggetto m esposto; LAW prova f 2 v/t of gallery, artist esporre; (give evidence of) manifestare

ex·hi·bi·tion [eksɪ'bɪʃn] esposizione f; of bad behaviour manifestazione f; of skill dimostrazione f

ex·hi·bi·tion·ist [eksɪ'bɪʃnɪst] esibizionista m/f

ex·hil·a·rat·ing [ɪg'zɪləreɪtɪŋ] adj emozionante

ex·ile ['eksaɪl] 1 n esilio m; person esiliato m, -a f 2 v/t esiliare

ex·ist [ɪg'zɪst] v/i esistere; ~ on vivere di

ex·ist·ence [ɪg'zɪstəns] esistenza f; in ~ esistente; **come into** ~ nascere

ex·ist·ing [ɪg'zɪstɪŋ] adj attuale

ex·it ['eksɪt] 1 n uscita f 2 v/i COMPUT uscire

ex·on·e·rate [ɪg'zɒnəreɪt] v/t scagionare

ex·or·bi·tant [ɪg'zɔ:bɪtənt] adj esorbitante

ex·ot·ic [ɪg'zɒtɪk] adj esotico

ex·pand [ɪk'spænd] 1 v/t espandere 2 v/i espandersi; of metal dilatarsi

♦ expand on v/t dilungarsi su

ex·panse [ɪk'spæns] distesa f

ex·pan·sion [ɪk'spænʃn] espansione f; of metal dilatazione f

ex·pat·ri·ate [eks'pætrɪət] 1 adj

residente all'estero **2** *n* residente *m/f* all'estero

ex·pect [ɪk'spekt] **1** *v/t* aspettare; (*suppose, demand*) aspettarsi **2** *v/i:* **be ~ing** aspettare un bambino; **I ~ so** immagino di sì

ex·pec·tant [ɪk'spektənt] *adj* pieno di aspettativa

ex·pec·tant 'moth·er donna *f* in stato interessante

ex·pec·ta·tion [ekspek'teɪʃn] aspettativa *f*; **~s** (*demands*) aspettative *fpl*

ex·pe·di·ent [ɪk'spiːdɪənt] *n* espediente *m*

ex·pe·di·tion [ekspɪ'dɪʃn] spedizione *f*; **go on a shopping/sightseeing ~** andare a fare spese/in giro a visitare

ex·pel [ɪk'spel] *v/t* (*pret & pp -led*) espellere

ex·pend [ɪk'spend] *v/t energy* spendere

ex·pend·a·ble [ɪk'spendəbl] *adj person* sacrificabile

ex·pen·di·ture [ɪk'spendɪtʃə(r)] spesa *f*

ex·pense [ɪk'spens] spesa *f*; **at the company's ~** a spese della società; **a joke at my ~** uno scherzo a mie spese; **at the ~ of his health** a spese della sua salute

ex'pense ac·count nota *f* spese

ex·pen·ses [ɪk'spensɪz] *npl* spese *fpl*

ex·pen·sive [ɪk'spensɪv] *adj* caro

ex·pe·ri·ence [ɪk'spɪərɪəns] **1** *n* esperienza *f* **2** *v/t pain, pleasure* provare; *problem, difficulty* incontrare

ex·pe·ri·enced [ɪk'spɪərɪənst] *adj* con esperienza; **he's ~ in teaching** ha esperienza nell'insegnamento

ex·per·i·ment [ɪk'sperɪmənt] **1** *n* esperimento *m* **2** *v/i* fare esperimenti; **~ on animals** sperimentare su; **~ with** (*try out*) sperimentare

ex·per·i·men·tal [ɪksperɪ'mentl] *adj* sperimentale

ex·pert [ɪk'spɜːt] **1** *adj* esperto **2** *n* esperto *m*, -a *f*

ex·pert ad'vice parere *m* di un esperto

ex·per·tise [ekspɜː'tiːz] competenza *f*

ex·pire [ɪk'spaɪə(r)] *v/i* scadere

ex·pi·ry [ɪk'spaɪərɪ] scadenza *f*

ex'pi·ry date data *f* di scadenza

ex·plain [ɪk'spleɪn] **1** *v/t* spiegare **2** *v/i* spiegarsi

ex·pla·na·tion [eksplə'neɪʃn] spiegazione *f*

ex·plic·it [ɪk'splɪsɪt] *adj instructions* esplicito

ex·plic·it·ly [ɪk'splɪsɪtlɪ] *adv state, forbid* esplicitamente

ex·plode [ɪk'spləʊd] **1** *v/i of bomb* esplodere **2** *v/t bomb* fare esplodere

ex·ploit¹ ['eksplɔɪt] *n* exploit *m inv*

ex·ploit² [ɪk'splɔɪt] *v/t person, resources* sfruttare

ex·ploi·ta·tion [eksplɔɪ'teɪʃn] sfruttamento *m*

ex·plo·ra·tion [eksplə'reɪʃn] esplorazione *f*

ex·plor·a·to·ry [ɪk'splɒrətərɪ] *adj surgery* esplorativo

ex·plore [ɪk'splɔː(r)] *v/t country, possibility etc* esplorare

ex·plo·rer [ɪk'splɔːrə(r)] esploratore *m*, -trice *f*

ex·plo·sion [ɪk'spləʊʒn] esplosione *f*; **a population ~** un'esplosione demografica

ex·plo·sive [ɪk'spləʊsɪv] *n* esplosivo *m*

ex·port ['ekspɔːt] **1** *n action* esportazione *f*; *item* prodotto *m* di esportazione **2** *v/t goods*, COMPUT esportare

'ex·port cam·paign campagna *f* per l'esportazione

ex·port·er [ɪk'spɔːtə(r)] esportatore *m*, -trice *f*

ex·pose [ɪk'spəʊz] *v/t* (*uncover*) scoprire; *scandal, person* denunciare; **~ sth to sth** esporre qc a qc

ex·po·sure [ɪk'spəʊʒə(r)] esposizione *f*; *to cold weather* esposizione *f* prolungata al freddo; *of dishonest behaviour* denuncia *f*; PHOT posa *f*

ex·press [ɪk'spres] **1** *adj* (*fast, explicit*) espresso **2** *n* (*train*) espresso *m*

expression

392

3 v/t (speak of, voice) esprimere; **~ o.s. well / clearly** esprimersi bene / chiaramente; **~ o.s.** (emotionally) esprimersi

ex·pres·sion [ɪk'spreʃn] espressione f; (expressiveness) espressività f

ex·pres·sive [ɪk'spresɪv] adj espressivo

ex·press·ly [ɪk'spreslɪ] adv espressamente

ex·press·way [ɪk'spresweɪ] autostrada f

ex·pul·sion [ɪk'spʌlʃn] espulsione f

ex·qui·site [ek'skwɪzɪt] adj (beautiful) squisito

ex·tend [ɪk'stend] **1** v/t estendere; house, repertoire ampliare; runway, path prolungare; contract, visa prorogare; thanks, congratulations porgere **2** v/i of garden etc estendersi

ex·ten·sion [ɪk'stenʃn] to house annesso m; of contract, visa proroga f; TELEC interno m

ex·ten·sion ca·ble prolunga f

ex·ten·sive [ɪk'stensɪv] adj ampio

ex·tent [ɪk'stent] ampiezza f, portata f; **to such an ~ that** a un punto tale che; **to a certain ~** fino a un certo punto

ex·ten·u·at·ing cir·cum·stances [ɪk'stenjueɪtɪŋ] npl circostanze fpl attenuanti

ex·te·ri·or [ɪk'stɪərɪə(r)] **1** adj esterno **2** n of building esterno m; of person aspetto m esteriore

ex·ter·mi·nate [ɪk'stɜːmɪneɪt] v/t sterminare

ex·ter·nal [ɪk'stɜːnl] adj (outside) esterno

ex·tinct [ɪk'stɪŋkt] adj species estinto

ex·tinc·tion [ɪk'stɪŋkʃn] of species estinzione f

ex·tin·guish [ɪk'stɪŋgwɪʃ] v/t spegnere

ex·tin·guish·er [ɪk'stɪŋgwɪʃə(r)] estintore m

ex·tort [ɪk'stɔːt] v/t estorcere; **~ money from ...** estorcere denaro da ...

ex·tor·tion [ɪk'stɔːʃn] estorsione f

ex·tor·tion·ate [ɪk'stɔːʃənət] adj prices esorbitante; **that's ~!** è un furto!

ex·tra ['ekstrə] **1** n extra m inv **2** adj in più; **be ~** (cost more) essere a parte **3** adv particolarmente; **an ~ special day** un giorno particolarmente speciale

ex·tra 'charge costo m aggiuntivo

ex·tract¹ ['ekstrækt] n estratto m

ex·tract² [ɪk'strækt] v/t estrarre; information estorcere

ex·trac·tion [ɪk'strækʃn] estrazione f

ex·tra·dite ['ekstrədaɪt] v/t estradare

ex·tra·di·tion [ekstrə'dɪʃn] estradizione f

ex·tra·di·tion trea·ty accordo m di estradizione

ex·tra·mar·i·tal [ekstrə'mærɪtl] adj extraconiugale

ex·tra·or·di·nar·i·ly [ekstrɔː'dɪn'eərɪlɪ] adv eccezionalmente

ex·tra·or·di·na·ry [ɪk'strɔːdɪnərɪ] adj straordinario

ex·tra 'time SP tempi mpl supplementari

ex·trav·a·gance [ɪk'strævəgəns] stravaganza f

ex·trav·a·gant [ɪk'strævəgənt] adj with money stravagante

ex·treme [ɪk'striːm] **1** n estremo m **2** adj estremo

ex·treme·ly [ɪk'striːmlɪ] adv estremamente

ex·trem·ist [ɪk'striːmɪst] estremista m/f

ex·tri·cate ['ekstrɪkeɪt] v/t districare

ex·tro·vert ['ekstrəvɜːt] n / adj estroverso m, -a f

ex·u·be·rant [ɪg'zjuːbərənt] adj esuberante

ex·ult [ɪg'zʌlt] v/i esultare

eye [aɪ] **1** n occhio m; of needle cruna f; **keep an ~ on** tenere d'occhio **2** v/t scrutare

'eye·ball bulbo m oculare; **'eye·brow** sopracciglio m; **'eye·catch·ing** adj appariscente; **'eye·lash** ciglio m; **'eye·lid** palpebra f; **'eye·lin·er** eyeliner m inv; **'eye·sha·dow** ombretto m; **'eye·sight**

vista *f*; **'eye·sore** pugno *m* in un occhio; **'eye strain** affaticamento *m* della vista; **'eye·wit·ness** testimone *m/f* oculare

F

F *abbr* (= **Fahrenheit**) F (= Fahrenheit)
fab·ric ['fæbrɪk] (*material*) tessuto *m*
fab·u·lous ['fæbjʊləs] *adj* fantastico
fab·u·lous·ly ['fæbjʊləslɪ] *adv* incredibilmente
fa·çade [fə'sɑːd] *of building, person* facciata *f*
face [feɪs] **1** *n* viso *m*, faccia *f*; **~ to ~** faccia a faccia; **lose ~** perdere la faccia **2** *v/t person, the sea etc* essere di fronte a; *facts, truth* affrontare
♦ **face up to** *v/t* affrontare
'face·cloth guanto *m* di spugna; **'face·lift** lifting *m inv* del viso; **'face pack** maschera *f* di bellezza; **face 'val·ue** valore *m* nominale; **take sth at ~** giudicare qc dalle apparenze
fa·cial ['feɪʃl] *n* pulizia *f* del viso
fa·cil·i·tate [fə'sɪlɪteɪt] *v/t* facilitare
fa·cil·i·ties [fə'sɪlətɪz] *npl* strutture *fpl*
fact [fækt] fatto *m*; **in ~, as a matter of ~** in realtà
faction ['fækʃn] fazione *f*
fac·tor ['fæktə(r)] fattore *m*
fac·to·ry ['fæktərɪ] fabbrica *f*
fac·ul·ty ['fækəltɪ] facoltà *f inv*
fad [fæd] mania *f* passeggera
fade [feɪd] *v/i of colours* sbiadire; *of light* smorzarsi; *of memories* svanire
fad·ed ['feɪdɪd] *adj colour, jeans* sbiadito
fag [fæg] F (*cigarette*) sigaretta *f*
'fag end F (*cigarette end*) mozzicone *m* di sigaretta
Fahr·en·heit ['færənhaɪt] *adj* Fahrenheit
fail [feɪl] **1** *v/i* fallire **2** *v/t test, exam* essere bocciato a; **he ~ed to arrive in time** non è riuscito ad arrivare in tempo; **he never ~s to write** non manca mai di scrivere **2** *n*: **without ~** con certezza
fail·ing ['feɪlɪŋ] *n* difetto *m*
fail·ure ['feɪljə(r)] fallimento *m*
faint [feɪnt] **1** *adj* vago **2** *v/i* svenire
faint·ly ['feɪntlɪ] *adv* vagamente
fair[1] [feə(r)] *n* (*fun ~*) luna park *m inv*; COM fiera *f*
fair[2] [feə(r)] *adj hair* biondo; *complexion* chiaro; (*just*) giusto; **it's not ~** non è giusto *adv*: **~ enough** e va bene
fair·ly ['feəlɪ] *adv treat* giustamente; (*quite*) piuttosto
fair·ness ['feənɪs] *of treatment* giustizia *f*
fai·ry ['feərɪ] fata *f*
'fai·ry tale fiaba *f*, favola *f*
faith [feɪθ] fede *f*
faith·ful ['feɪθfl] *adj* fedele; **be ~ to one's partner** essere fedele al proprio compagno
faith·ful·ly ['feɪθflɪ] *adv* fedelmente; **Yours ~** distinti saluti
fake [feɪk] **1** *n* falso *m* **2** *adj* falso **3** *v/t* (*forge*) falsificare; (*feign*) simulare
fall[1] [fɔːl] *n Am* autunno *m*
fall[2] [fɔːl] **1** *v/i* (*pret* **fell**, *pp* **fallen**) *of person, government, prices, temperature* calare; **it ~s on a Tuesday** cade di martedì; **~ ill** ammalarsi **2** *n of person, government* caduta *f*; *in price, temperature* calo *m*
♦ **fall back on** *v/t* ricorrere a
♦ **fall behind** *v/i with work, studies* rimanere indietro

F

◆ **fall down** v/i cadere

◆ **fall for** v/t (*fall in love with*) innamorarsi di; (*be deceived by*) abboccare a

◆ **fall out** v/i *of hair* cadere; (*argue*) litigare

◆ **fall over** v/i cadere

◆ **fall through** v/i *of plans* andare a monte

fal·len ['fɔːlən] pp → **fall**

fal·li·ble ['fæləbl] adj fallibile

'**fallout** precipitazione f

false [fɔːls] adj falso

false a'larm falso allarme m

false·ly ['fɔːlslɪ] adv: **be ~ accused of sth** essere ingiustamente accusato di qc

false 'start *in race* falsa partenza f

false 'teeth npl dentiera f

fal·si·fy ['fɔːlsɪfaɪ] v/t (*pret & pp -ied*) falsificare

fame [feɪm] fama f

fa·mil·i·ar [fə'mɪljə(r)] adj (*intimate*) intimo; *form of address*, (*well-known*) familiare; **be ~ with sth** conoscere bene qc; **that looks/ sounds ~** ha un'aria familiare

fa·mil·i·ar·i·ty [fəmɪlɪ'jærɪtɪ] *with subject etc* buona conoscenza f

fa·mil·i·ar·ize [fə'mɪljəraɪz] v/t familiarizzare; **~ o.s. with ...** familiarizzarsi con ...

fam·i·ly ['fæməlɪ] famiglia f

fam·i·ly 'doc·tor medico m di famiglia; **fam·i·ly 'name** cognome m; **fam·i·ly 'plan·ning** pianificazione f familiare; **fam·i·ly 'plan·ning clin·ic** consultorio m per la pianificazione familiare; **fam·i·ly 'tree** albero m genealogico

fam·ine ['fæmɪn] fame f

fam·ished ['fæmɪʃt] adj F affamato

fa·mous ['feɪməs] adj famoso; **be ~ for ...** essere noto per ...

fan¹ [fæn] n (*supporter*) fan m/f

fan² [fæn] **1** n *for cooling: electric* ventilatore m; *handheld* ventaglio m **2** v/t (*pret & pp -ned*): **~ o.s.** farsi aria

fa·nat·ic [fə'nætɪk] n fanatico m, -a f

fa·nat·i·cal [fə'nætɪkl] adj fanatico

fa·nat·i·cism [fə'nætɪsɪzm] fanatismo m

'**fan belt** MOT cinghia f della ventola

'**fan club** fan club m inv

fan·cy ['fænsɪ] **1** adj design stravagante **2** n: **as the ~ takes you** quanto ti va; **take a ~ to s.o.** prendere a benvolere qu **3** v/t (*pret & pp -ied*) F avere voglia di; **I'm sure he fancies you** sono sicuro che gli piaci

fan·cy 'dress costume m

fan·cy-'dress par·ty festa f in maschera

fang [fæŋ] dente m aguzzo

'**fan mail** lettere fpl dei fans

fan·ta·size ['fæntəsaɪz] v/i fantasticare

fan·tas·tic [fæn'tæstɪk] adj (*very good*) fantastico; (*very big*) enorme

fan·tas·tic·al·ly [fæn'tæstɪklɪ] adv (*extremely*) incredibilmente

fan·ta·sy ['fæntəsɪ] fantasia f

far [fɑː(r)] adv lontano; (*much*) molto; **~ away** lontano; **how ~ is it to ...?** quanto dista ...?; **as ~ as the corner/hotel** fino all'angolo/hotel; **as ~ as I can see** per quanto posso vedere; **as ~ as I know** per quanto ne so; **you've gone too ~** *in behaviour* sei andato troppo oltre; **so ~ so good** fin qui tutto bene

farce [fɑːs] farsa f

fare [feə] n *for travel* tariffa f

Far 'East Estremo Oriente m

fare·well [feə'wel] n addio m

fare·well par·ty festa f d'addio

far-fetched [fɑː'fetʃt] adj inverosimile

farm [fɑːm] n fattoria f

farm·er ['fɑːmə(r)] agricoltore m, -trice f

'**farm·house** cascina f

farm·ing ['fɑːmɪŋ] n agricoltura f

'**farm·work·er** bracciante m/f

'**farm·yard** cortile m di una cascina

far-'off adj lontano

far·sight·ed [fɑː'saɪtɪd] adj previdente; *Am* OPT presbite

fart [fɑːt] **1** n F scoreggia f F, peto m

2 v/i F scoreggiare F, petare

far·ther ['fɑːðə(r)] adv più lontano

far·thest ['fɑːðəst] adv travel etc più lontano

fas·ci·nate ['fæsɪneɪt] v/t affascinare; *I always was ~d by the idea of ...* mi ha sempre affascinato l'idea di ...

fas·ci·nat·ing ['fæsɪneɪtɪŋ] adj affascinante

fas·ci·na·tion [fæsɪ'neɪʃn] with subject fascino m

fas·cis·m ['fæʃɪzm] fascismo m

fas·cist ['fæʃɪst] **1** n fascista m/f **2** adj fascista

fash·ion ['fæʃn] n moda f; (manner) maniera f, modo m; *in* ~ alla moda; *out of* ~ fuori moda

fash·ion·a·ble ['fæʃnəbl] adj alla moda

fash·ion·a·bly ['fæʃnəblɪ] adv dressed alla moda

'**fash·ion-con·scious** adj fanatico della moda; '**fash·ion de·sign·er** stilista m/f; '**fash·ion mag·a·zine** rivista f di moda; '**fash·ion show** sfilata f di moda

fast[1] [fɑːst] **1** adj veloce, rapido; *be ~ of clock* essere avanti **2** adv velocemente; *stuck* ~ fissato saldamente; *~ asleep* profondamente addormentato

fast[2] [fɑːst] n not eating digiuno m

fas·ten ['fɑːsn] v/t chiudere; dress, seat-belt allacciare; *~ sth onto sth* attaccare qc a qc; brooch appuntare qc su qc **2** v/i of dress etc allacciarsi

fas·ten·er ['fɑːsnə(r)] chiusura f

fast '**food** fast food m; **fast-food** '**res·tau·rant** fast food m inv; **fast** '**for·ward 1** n on video etc riavvolgimento m rapido **2** v/i riavvolgere rapidamente; '**fast lane** on road corsia f di sorpasso; *in the* ~ fig: of life a cento all'ora; '**fast train** rapido m

fat [fæt] **1** adj grasso **2** n grasso m

fa·tal ['feɪtl] adj fatale

fa·tal·i·ty [fə'tælətɪ] fatalità f inv

fa·tal·ly ['feɪtəlɪ] adv: *~ injured* ferito a morte

fate [feɪt] fato m

fat·ed ['feɪtɪd] adj: *be ~ to do sth* essere destinato a fare qc

fa·ther ['fɑːðə(r)] n padre m; *Father Martin* REL padre Martin

Fa·ther 'Christ·mas Babbo m Natale

fa·ther·hood ['fɑːðəhʊd] paternità f

'**fa·ther-in-law** (pl *fathers-in-law*) suocero m

fa·ther·ly ['fɑːðəlɪ] adj paterno

fath·om ['fæðəm] n NAUT fathom m inv

♦ **fathom out** v/t fig spiegarsi; *I just can't fathom you out* proprio non ti capisco

fa·tigue [fə'tiːg] n stanchezza f

fat·so ['fætsəʊ] n F ciccione m, -a f F

fat·ten ['fætn] v/t animal ingrassare

fat·ty ['fætɪ] **1** adj grasso **2** n F person ciccione m, -a f F

fau·cet ['fɔːsɪt] Am rubinetto m

fault [fɔːlt] n (defect) difetto m; *it's your / my* ~ è colpa tua / mia; *find ~ with* criticare

fault·less ['fɔːltlɪs] adj person, performance impeccabile

fault·y ['fɔːltɪ] adj goods difettoso

fa·vor etc Am → **favour** etc

fa·vour ['feɪvə(r)] **1** n favore m; *do s.o. a* ~ fare un favore a qu; *do me a* ~! (don't be stupid) fammi il piacere!; *in* ~ of ... a favore di ...; *be in* ~ of ... essere a favore di ... **2** v/t (prefer) preferire, prediligere

fa·vou·ra·ble ['feɪvərəbl] adj reply etc favorevole

fa·vou·rite ['feɪvərɪt] **1** n prediletto m, -a f; (food) piatto m preferito; in race, competition favorito m, -a f **2** adj preferito

fa·vou·rit·ism ['feɪvrɪtɪzm] favoritismo m

fax [fæks] **1** n fax m inv; *send sth by* ~ inviare qc per fax **2** v/t inviare per fax; *~ sth to s.o.* inviare qc per fax a qc

FBI abbr (= *Federal Bureau of Investigation*) FBI f

fear [fɪə(r)] **1** n paura f **2** v/t avere paura di

F

fear·less ['fɪəlɪs] *adj* intrepido

fear·less·ly ['fɪəlɪslɪ] *adv* intrepidamente

fea·si·bil·i·ty stud·y [fiːzə'bɪlətɪ] studio *m* di fattibilità

fea·si·ble ['fiːzəbl] *adj* fattibile

feast [fiːst] *n* banchetto *m*

feat [fiːt] prodezza *f*

feath·er ['feðə(r)] piuma *f*

fea·ture ['fiːtʃə(r)] **1** *n on face* tratto *m*; *of city, building, plan, style* caratteristica *f*; *in paper* servizio *m*; (*film*) lungometraggio *m*; **make a ~ of ...** mettere l'accento su ... **2** *v/t of film* avere come protagonista

'fea·ture film lungometraggio *m*

Feb·ru·a·ry ['februərɪ] febbraio *m*

fed [fed] *pret & pp → feed*

fed·e·ral ['fedərəl] *adj* federale

fed·e·ra·tion [fedə'reɪʃn] federazione *f*

fed 'up *adj* F stufo F; **be ~ with ...** essere stufo di ...

fee [fiː] tariffa *f*; *of lawyer, doctor etc* onorario *m*

fee·ble ['fiːbl] *adj* debole

feed [fiːd] *v/t (pret & pp fed)* nutrire; *family* mantenere; *baby* dare da mangiare a

'feed·back *n* riscontro *m*, feedback *m inv*

feel [fiːl] (*pret & pp felt*) **1** *v/t (touch)* toccare; (*sense*) sentire; *pain, pleasure, sensation* sentire; (*think*) pensare **2** *v/i* sentirsi; *it ~s like silk / cotton* sembra seta / cotone al tatto; *your hand ~s hot / cold* la tua mano è calda / fredda; *I ~ hungry* ho fame; *I ~ tired* sono stanco; *how are you ~ing today?* come ti senti oggi?; *how does it ~ to be rich?* che sensazione fa essere ricchi?; *do you ~ like a drink / meal?* hai voglia di bere / mangiare qualcosa?; *I ~ like going / staying* ho voglia di andare / rimanere; *I don't ~ like it* non ne ho voglia

♦ feel up to *v/t* sentirsi in grado di

feel·er ['fiːlə(r)] *of insect* antenna *f*

'feel·good fac·tor fattore *m* tranquillizzante

feel·ing ['fiːlɪŋ] sentimento *m*; (*emotion*) sensazione *f*; (*sensation*) sensibilità *f*; *what are your ~s about it?* quali sono le tue impressioni in proposito?; *I have mixed ~s about him* ho sensazioni contrastanti nei suoi riguardi; *I have this ~ that ...* ho la sensazione che ...

feet [fiːt] *pl → foot*

fe·line ['fiːlaɪn] *adj* felino

fell [fel] *pret → fall*

fel·low ['feləʊ] *n (man)* tipo *m*

fel·low 'cit·i·zen concittadino *m*, -a *f*; **fel·low 'coun·try·man** compatriota *m/f*; **fel·low·man** prossimo *m*

fel·o·ny ['felənɪ] *Am* delitto *m*

felt[1] [felt] *n* feltro *m*

felt[2] [felt] *pret & pp → feel*

felt 'tip, felt-tip(·ped) 'pen pennarello *m*

fe·male ['fiːmeɪl] **1** *adj* femmina; *typical of women* femminile **2** *n* femmina *f*, F (*woman*) donna *f*

fem·i·nine ['femɪnɪn] **1** *adj* femminile **2** *n* GRAM femminile *m*

fem·i·nis·m ['femɪnɪzm] femminismo *m*

fem·i·nist ['femɪnɪst] **1** *n* femminista *f* **2** *adj* femminista

fence [fens] *n round garden etc* recinto *m*; F *criminal* ricettatore *m*, -trice *f*; **sit on the ~** non prendere partito

♦ fence in *v/t land* recintare

fenc·ing ['fensɪŋ] SP scherma *f*

fend [fend] *v/i*: **~ for o.s.** badare a se stesso

fer·ment[1] [fə'ment] *v/i of liquid* fermentare

fer·ment[2] ['fɜːment] *n (unrest)* fermento *m*

fer·men·ta·tion [fɜːmen'teɪʃn] fermentazione *f*

fern [fɜːn] felce *f*

fe·ro·cious [fə'rəʊʃəs] *adj* feroce

fer·ry ['ferɪ] *n* traghetto *m*

fer·tile ['fɜːtaɪl] *adj* fertile

fer·til·i·ty [fɜː'tɪlətɪ] fertilità *f*

fer·til·i·ty drug cura *f* per sviluppare la fertilità

fer·ti·lize ['fɜːtəlaɪz] *v/t ovum* fecondare

fer·ti·liz·er ['fɜːtəlaɪzə(r)] *for soil* fertilizzante *m*

fer·vent ['fɜːvənt] *adj admirer* fervente

fer·vent·ly ['fɜːvəntlɪ] *adv* ardentemente

fes·ter ['festə(r)] *v/i of wound* fare infezione

fes·ti·val ['festɪvl] festival *m inv*

fes·tive ['festɪv] *adj* festivo; *the ~ season* le festività

fes·tiv·i·ties [fe'stɪvətɪz] *npl* festeggiamenti *mpl*

fe·tal ['fiːtl] *adj* fetale

fetch [fetʃ] *v/t (go and ~)* andare a prendere; *(come and ~)* venire a prendere; *thing* prendere; *price* rendere

fe·tus ['fiːtəs] feto *m*

feud [fjuːd] **1** *n* faida *f* **2** *v/i* litigare

fe·ver ['fiːvə(r)] febbre *f*

fe·ver·ish ['fiːvərɪʃ] *adj also fig* febbrile; *I'm feeling ~* mi sento la febbre

few [fjuː] **1** *adj (not many)* pochi; *a ~ ...* alcuni ...; *a ~ people* alcune persone, qualche persona; *a ~ books* alcuni libri, qualche libro; *quite a ~, a good ~ (a lot)* parecchi **2** *pron (not many)* pochi; *a ~ (some)* alcuni; *quite a ~, a good ~ (a lot)* parecchi

fewer ['fjuːə(r)] *adj* meno; *~ than ...* meno di ...

fi·an·cé [fɪ'ɒnseɪ] fidanzato *m*

fi·an·cée [fɪ'ɒnseɪ] fidanzata *f*

fi·as·co [fɪ'æskəʊ] fiasco *m*

fib [fɪb] *n* frottola *f*

fi·ber *Am* → **fibre**

fi·bre ['faɪbə(r)] fibra *f*

'fi·bre·glass *n* fibra *f* di vetro; **fi·bre 'op·tic** *adj* fibra *f* ottica; **fi·bre 'op·tics** tecnologia *f* delle fibre ottiche

fick·le ['fɪkl] *adj* incostante

fic·tion ['fɪkʃn] *n (novels)* narrativa *f*; *(made-up story)* storia *f*

fic·tion·al ['fɪkʃnl] *adj* immaginario

fic·ti·tious [fɪk'tɪʃəs] *adj* fittizio

fid·dle ['fɪdl] **1** *n* F *(violin)* violino *m*; *it's a ~* F *(cheat)* è una fregatura F **2** *v/i*: *~ with ...* giocherellare con ...;

~ around with ... trafficare con ... **3** *v/t accounts, results* truccare

fi·del·i·ty [fɪ'delətɪ] fedeltà *f*

fid·get ['fɪdʒɪt] *v/i* agitarsi

fid·get·y ['fɪdʒɪtɪ] *adj* in agitazione; *get ~* mettersi in agitazione

field [fiːld] campo *m*; *(competitors in race)* formazione *f*; *that's not my ~* non è il mio campo

field·er ['fiːldə(r)] *in cricket* esterno *m*

'field e·vents *npl* atletica *f* leggera (escluse le specialità su pista)

fierce [fɪəs] *adj animal* feroce; *wind, storm* violento

fierce·ly ['fɪəslɪ] *adv* ferocemente; *say sth* ~ dire qc in tono aggressivo

fi·er·y ['faɪərɪ] *adj personality, temper* focoso

fif·teen [fɪf'tiːn] quindici

fif·teenth [fɪf'tiːnθ] *n & adj* quindicesimo, -a

fifth [fɪfθ] *n & adj* quinto, -a

fifth·ly ['fɪfθlɪ] *adv* al quinto posto

fif·ti·eth ['fɪftɪɪθ] *n & adj* cinquantesimo, -a

fif·ty ['fɪftɪ] cinquanta

fif·ty-'fif·ty *adv* metà e metà; *go ~ with s.o.* fare metà con qu

fig [fɪg] fico *m*

fight [faɪt] **1** *n* lotta *f*; *in war* combattimento *m*; *(argument)* litigio *m*; *in boxing* incontro *m* **2** *v/t (pret & pp fought) (brawl)* azzuffare; *in war* combattere; *in boxing* battersi contro; *disease, injustice* combattere **3** *v/i (pret & pp fought)* in war combattere; *of drunks, schoolkids* azzuffarsi; *(argue)* litigare

♦ **fight for** *v/t one's rights, a cause* lottare per

fight·er ['faɪtə(r)] combattente *m/f*; *aeroplane* caccia *m inv*; *(boxer)* pugile *m*; *she's a ~* è combattiva

fight·ing ['faɪtɪŋ] *n* risse *fpl*; *he's always in trouble for ~* è sempre nei guai perché scatena risse

fig·u·ra·tive ['fɪgjərətɪv] *adj use of word* figurato; *art* figurativo

fig·ure ['fɪgə(r)] *n (digit)* cifra *f*; *of person* linea *f*; *(form, shape)* figura *f*

♦ **figure out** *v/t* (*understand*) capire; *calculation* calcolare

'**fig·ure skat·er** pattinatore *m*, -trice *f* artistico, -a

'**fig·ure skat·ing** pattinaggio *m* artistico

file[1] [faɪl] **1** *n for papers* raccoglitore *m*; *contents* dossier *m inv*, pratica *f*; COMPUT file *m inv*; **on ~** in archivio **2** *v/t documents* schedare

♦ **file away** *v/t documents* archiviare

file[2] [faɪl] *n for wood, fingernails* lima *f*

'**file man·ag·er** COMPUT file manager *m inv*

fi·li·al ['fɪlɪəl] *adj* filiale

fil·ing cab·i·net ['faɪlɪŋkæbɪnət] schedario *m*

fill [fɪl] **1** *v/t* riempire; *tooth* otturare **2** *n*: **eat one's ~** mangiare a sazietà

♦ **fill in** *v/t form* compilare; *hole* riempire; **fill s.o. in** mettere al corrente qu

♦ **fill in for** *v/t* sostituire temporaneamente

♦ **fill out 1** *v/t form* compilare **2** *v/i* (*get fatter*) arrotondarsi

♦ **fill up 1** *v/t* riempire **2** *v/i of stadium, theatre* riempirsi

fil·let ['fɪlɪt] *n* filetto *m*

fil·let 'steak filetto *m*

fill·ing ['fɪlɪŋ] **1** *n in sandwich* ripieno *m*; *in tooth* otturazione *f* **2** *adj food* pesante

'**fill·ing sta·tion** stazione *f* di rifornimento

film [fɪlm] **1** *n for camera* pellicola *f*; *at cinema* film *m inv* **2** *v/t person, event* riprendere, filmare; *scene* girare

'**film-mak·er** regista *m/f*

'**film star** stella *f* del cinema

fil·ter ['fɪltə(r)] **1** *n* filtro *m* **2** *v/t coffee, liquid* filtrare

♦ **filter through** *v/i of news, reports* diffondersi

'**fil·ter pa·per** carta *f* filtrante

'**fil·ter tip** (*cigarette*) filtro *m*

filth [fɪlθ] *n* sporcizia *f*; (*obscenities*) sconcezze *fpl*

filth·y [fɪlθɪ] *adj* sporco; *language etc* volgare

fin [fɪn] *of fish* pinna *f*

fi·nal ['faɪnl] **1** *adj* finale **2** *n* SP finale *f*

fi·na·le [fɪ'nɑːlɪ] *n* finale *m*

fi·nal·ist ['faɪnəlɪst] finalista *m/f*

fi·nal·ize ['faɪnəlaɪz] *v/t plans, design* mettere a punto

fi·nal·ly ['faɪnəlɪ] *adv* infine; (*at last*) finalmente

fi·nals ['faɪnəlz] *npl* EDU esami *mpl* finali

fi·nance ['faɪnæns] **1** *n* finanza *f* **2** *v/t* finanziare

fi·nan·ces ['faɪnænsɪz] *npl* finanze *fpl*

fi·nan·cial [faɪ'nænʃl] *adj* finanziario

fi·nan·cial·ly [faɪ'nænʃəlɪ] *adv* finanziariamente

fi·nan·cial 'year esercizio *m* (finanziario)

fi·nan·cier [faɪ'nænsɪə(r)] *n* finanziatore *m*, -trice *f*

find [faɪnd] *v/t* (*pret & pp found*) trovare; **if you ~ it too hot / cold** se lo trovi troppo caldo / freddo; **~ a person innocent / guilty** LAW giudicare una persona innocente / colpevole

♦ **find out** *v/t & v/i* scoprire

find·ings ['faɪndɪŋz] *npl of report* conclusioni *fpl*

fine[1] [faɪn] *adj day, weather, city* bello; *wine, performance* buono; *distinction, line* sottile; **how's that? – that's ~** com'è? – va benissimo; **that's ~ by me** a me sta bene; **how are you? – ~** come stai? – bene

fine[2] [faɪn] **1** *n penalty* multa *f* **2** *v/t* multare

fine-'tooth comb: **go through it with a ~** passare qc al setaccio

fine-'tune *v/t also fig* mettere a punto

fin·ger ['fɪŋɡə(r)] **1** *n* dito *m* **2** *v/t* passare le dita su

'**fin·ger·nail** unghia *f*; '**fin·ger·print 1** *n* impronta *f* digitale **2** *v/t* prendere le impronte digitali di; '**fin·ger·tip** punta *f* del dito; **have sth at one's ~s** *knowledge* sapere qc a menadito

fin·i·cky ['fɪnɪkɪ] *adj person* pignolo; *design, pattern* complicato

fin·ish ['fɪnɪʃ] **1** *v/t* finire; ~ *doing sth* finire di fare qc **2** *v/i* finire **3** *n of product* finitura *f; finishing line* traguardo *m*

♦ **finish off** *v/t* finire

♦ **finish up** *v/t food* finire; *he finished up liking London* Londra ha finito per piacergli

♦ **finish with** *v/t boyfriend etc* lasciare

fin·ish·ing line ['fɪnɪʃɪŋ] traguardo *m*

Fin·land ['fɪnlənd] Finlandia *f*

Finn [fɪn] finlandese *m/f*

Finn·ish ['fɪnɪʃ] **1** *adj* finlandese, finnico **2** *n language* finlandese *m*

fir [fɜ:(r)] abete *m*

fire ['faɪə(r)] **1** *n* fuoco *m; (blaze)* incendio *m; (bonfire, campfire etc)* falò *m inv; be on* ~ essere in fiamme; *catch* ~ prendere fuoco; *set sth on* ~, *set* ~ *to sth* dare fuoco a qc **2** *v/i (shoot)* sparare **3** *v/t* F *(dismiss)* licenziare

'**fire a·larm** allarme *m* antincendio; '**fire·arm** arma *f* da fuoco; '**fire bri·gade** vigili *mpl* del fuoco; '**fire·crack·er** petardo *m*; '**fire door** porta *f* taglia-fuoco; '**fire drill** esercitazione *f* antincendio; '**fire en·gine** autopompa *f*; '**fire es·cape** scala *f* antincendio; **fire ex·tin·guish·er** ['faɪərɪkstɪŋgwɪʃə(r)] estintore *m*; '**fire fight·er** pompiere *m*; '**fire·guard** parafuoco *m inv*; '**fire·man** pompiere *m*; '**fire·place** camino *m*; '**fire sta·tion** caserma *f* dei pompieri; '**fire truck** *Am* autopompa *f*; '**fire·wood** legna *f* da ardere; '**fire·works** *npl* fuochi *mpl* d'artificio

firm¹ [fɜ:m] *adj grip, handshake* energico; *flesh, muscles* sodo; *voice, parents* deciso; *decision* risoluto; *date, offer* definitivo; *control* rigido; *foundations* solido; *believer* convinto; *a ~ deal* un accordo definito

firm² [fɜ:m] *n* COM azienda *f*

first [fɜ:st] **1** *adj* primo; *who's please?* chi è il primo, per favore? **2** *n* primo *m*, -a *f* **3** *adv arrive, finish* per primo; *(beforehand)* prima; ~ *of*

all (for one reason) innanzitutto; *at* ~ in un primo tempo, al principio

first 'aid pronto soccorso *m*; '**first-'aid box, first-'aid kit** cassetta *f* del pronto soccorso; '**first-born** *adj* primogenito; '**first class 1** *adj* di prima classe **2** *adv travel* in prima classe; **first 'floor** primo piano *m; Am* piano *m* terra; **first'hand** *adj* diretto; **First 'La·dy** *of US* First Lady *f inv*

first·ly ['fɜ:stlɪ] *adv* in primo luogo

first 'name nome *m* di battesimo; **first 'night** prima serata *f*; **first of'fend·er** delinquente *m/f* non pregiudicato, -a; **first-'rate** *adj* di prima qualità

fis·cal ['fɪskl] *adj* fiscale

fish [fɪʃ] **1** *n (pl fish)* pesce *m; drink like a* ~ F bere come una spugna F; *feel like a* ~ *out of water* sentirsi come un pesce fuor d'acqua **2** *v/i* pescare

fish and 'chips *npl* pesce e patate fritte

'**fish·bone** lisca *f*

fish·er·man ['fɪʃəmən] pescatore *m*

fish 'fin·ger bastoncino *m* di pesce

fish·ing ['fɪʃɪŋ] pesca *f*

'**fish·ing boat** peschereccio *m*; '**fishing line** lenza *f*; '**fish·ing rod** canna *f* da pesca

fish·mon·ger ['fɪʃmʌŋgə(r)] pescivendolo *m*

fish·y ['fɪʃɪ] *adj* F *(suspicious)* sospetto

fist [fɪst] pugno *m*

fit¹ [fɪt] *n* MED attacco *m; a* ~ *of rage / jealousy* un accesso di rabbia / gelosia

fit² [fɪt] *adj physically* in forma; *morally* adatto; *keep* ~ tenersi in forma

fit³ [fɪt] **1** *v/t (pret & pp -ted) of clothes* andare bene a; *(attach)* installare **2** *v/i (pret & pp -ted) of clothes* andare bene; *of piece of furniture etc* starci **3** *n: of piece of furniture etc* ci sta perfettamente; *of clothes* calza a pennello; *it's a tight* ~ *of piece of furniture etc* ci sta appena; *of clothes* va giusto giusto

♦ **fit in 1** *v/i of person in group* integrarsi; *it fits in with our plans* si concilia con i nostri programmi **2** *v/t*: *fit s.o. in into schedule* fissare un appuntamento a qu

fit·ful ['fɪtfʊl] *adj sleep* a tratti

fit·ness ['fɪtnɪs] *physical* forma *f*

'fit·ness cen·ter *Am*, **'fit·ness cen·tre** palestra *f*

fit·ted 'car·pet ['fɪtɪd] moquette *f inv*; **fit·ted 'kitch·en** cucina *f* componibile; **fit·ted 'sheet** lenzuolo *m* con gli angoli

fit·ter ['fɪtə(r)] *n* assemblatore *m*, -trice *f*

fit·ting ['fɪtɪŋ] *adj* appropriato

fit·tings ['fɪtɪŋz] *npl* equipaggiamento *msg*

five [faɪv] cinque

fiv·er ['faɪvə(r)] F banconota *f* da cinque sterline

fix [fɪks] **1** *n (solution)* soluzione *f*; *be in a* ~ F essere nei casini F **2** *v/t (attach)* fissare; *(repair)* aggiustare; *(arrange: meeting etc)* fissare; *lunch* preparare; *dishonestly: match etc* manipolare; ~ *sth onto sth* attaccare qc a qc; *I'll* ~ *you a drink* ti preparo da bere

♦ **fix up** *v/t meeting* fissare; *it's all fixed up* è tutto stabilito

fixed [fɪkst] *adj in one position* fisso; *timescale, exchange rate* stabilito

fix·tures ['fɪkstʃəz] *npl in room* installazioni *fpl fisse*; SP incontro *m*

♦ **fiz·zle out** ['fɪzl] *v/i* F sfumare F

fiz·zy ['fɪzɪ] *adj drink* gassato

flab [flæb] *on body* ciccia *f*

flab·ber·gast ['flæbəɡɑːst] *v/t* F: *be* ~*ed* cadere dalle nuvole

flab·by ['flæbɪ] *adj muscles, stomach* flaccido

flag[1] [flæɡ] *n* bandiera *f*

flag[2] [flæɡ] *v/i (pret & pp -ged) (tire)* soccorrere

'flag·pole asta *f*

fla·grant ['fleɪɡrənt] *adj* flagrante

'flag·ship *fig* cavallo *m* di battaglia

'flag·staff asta *f*

'flag·stone lastra *f* di pietra

flair [fleə(r)] *n (talent)* talento *m*; *(style)* stile *m*

flake [fleɪk] *n of snow* fiocco *m*; *of paint, plaster* scaglia *f*

♦ **flake off** *v/i* squamarsi

flak·y ['fleɪkɪ] *adj* squamato

flak·y 'pas·try pasta *f* sfoglia

flam·boy·ant [flæm'bɔɪənt] *adj personality* esuberante

flam·boy·ant·ly [flæm'bɔɪəntlɪ] *adv dressed in modo vistoso*

flame [fleɪm] *n* fiamma *f*; *go up in* ~*s* incendiarsi

flam·ma·ble ['flæməbl] *adj* infiammabile

flan [flæn] sformato *m*

flank [flæŋk] **1** *n* fianco *m* **2** *v/t*: *be* ~*ed by* essere affiancato da

flan·nel ['flænl] *n for washing* guanto *m* di spugna

flap [flæp] **1** *n of envelope, pocket* falda *f*; *of table* ribalta *f*; *be in a* ~ F essere in fibrillazione F **2** *v/t (pret & pp -ped) wings* sbattere **3** *v/i (pret & pp -ped) of flag etc* sventolare; *(panic)* andare in fibrillazione F

flare [fleə(r)] **1** *n (distress signal)* razzo *m*; *in dress* svasatura *f*; ~*s trousers* pantaloni *mpl* a zampa di elefante **2** *v/t nostrils* allargare

♦ **flare up** *v/i of violence, illness, temper* esplodere; *of fire* divampare

flash [flæʃ] **1** *n of light* lampo *m*; PHOT flash *m inv*; *in a* ~ F in un istante; *have a* ~ *of inspiration* avere un lampo di genio; ~ *of lightning* lampo *m* **2** *v/i of light* lampeggiare **3** *v/t*: ~ *one's headlights* lampeggiare

'flash·back *in film* flashback *m inv*

flash·er ['flæʃə(r)] MOT freccia *f*; F *person* esibizionista *m*

'flash·light *esp Am* pila *f*; PHOT flash *m inv*

flash·y ['flæʃɪ] *adj pej* appariscente

flask [flɑːsk] *(vacuum* ~*)* termos *m inv*

flat[1] [flæt] **1** *adj surface, land, tone* piatto; *beer* sgassato; *battery, tyre* a terra; *shoes* basso; *A*/*B* – MUS la/si bemolle; *and that's* ~ F punto e

basta F **2** *adv* MUS sotto tonalità; ~ *out work, run, drive* a tutto gas **3** *n* gomma *f* a terra

flat² [flæt] *n Br* (*apartment*) appartamento *m*

flat-chest·ed [flæt'tʃestɪd] *adj* piatto

flat·ly ['flætlɪ] *adv refuse, deny* risolutamente

'**flat·mate** persona *f* con cui si divide la casa

'**flat rate** tariffa *f* forfettaria

flat·ten ['flætn] *v/t land, road* livellare; *by bombing, demolition* radere al suolo

flat·ter ['flætə(r)] *v/t* adulare

flat·ter·er ['flætərə(r)] adulatore *m*, -trice *f*

flat·ter·ing ['flætərɪŋ] *adj comments* lusinghiero; *Jane's dress is very ~* il vestito di Jane le dona molto

flat·ter·y ['flætərɪ] adulazione *f*

flat·u·lence ['flætjʊləns] flatulenza *f*

flat·ware ['flætweər] *Am* stoviglie *fpl*

flau·tist ['flɔːtɪst] flautista *m/f*

fla·vor *etc Am* → **flavour** *etc*

fla·vour ['fleɪvə(r)] **1** *n* gusto *m* **2** *v/t food* insaporire

fla·vour·ing ['fleɪvərɪŋ] *n* aroma *m*

flaw [flɔː] *n* difetto *m*

flaw·less ['flɔːlɪs] *adj* perfetto

flea [fliː] *n* pulce *f*

fleck [flek] puntino *m*

fled [fled] *pret & pp* → **flee**

flee [fliː] *v/i* (*pret & pp* **fled**) scappare

fleece [fliːs] *v/t* F fregare F

fleet [fliːt] *n* NAUT flotta *f*; *of taxis, trucks* parco *m* macchine

fleet·ing ['fliːtɪŋ] *adj visit etc* di sfuggita; *catch a ~ glimpse of* vedere di sfuggita

flesh [fleʃ] carne *f*; *of fruit* polpa *f*; *meet / see a person in the ~* incontrare / vedere una persona in carne e ossa

flex [fleks] **1** *v/t muscles* flettere **2** *n* ELEC cavo *m*

flex·i·bil·i·ty [fleksə'bɪlətɪ] flessibilità *f*

flex·i·ble ['fleksəbl] *adj* flessibile; *I'm quite ~ about arrangements, timing* sono abbastanza flessibile

flex·(i)·time ['fleks(ɪ)taɪm] orario *m* flessibile

flew [fluː] *pret* → **fly**

flick [flɪk] *v/t tail* agitare; *he ~ed a fly off his hand* ha cacciato via una mosca dalla mano; *she ~ed her hair out of her eyes* si è tolta i capelli dagli occhi con un gesto

◆ **flick through** *v/t book, magazine* sfogliare

flick·er ['flɪkə(r)] *v/i of light* tremolare

'**flick-knife** coltello *m* a scatto

fli·er ['flaɪə(r)] (*circular*) volantino *m*

flies [flaɪz] *npl on trousers* patta *f*

flight [flaɪt] *n* volo *m*; (*fleeing*) fuga *f*; ~ (*of stairs*) rampa *f* (di scale)

'**flight at·tend·ant** assistente *m/f* di volo; '**flight crew** equipaggio *m* di volo; '**flight deck** *in aeroplane* cabina *f* di pilotaggio; *of aircraft carrier* ponte *m* di decollo; '**flight num·ber** numero *m* di volo; '**flight path** rotta *f* (di volo); '**flight re·cord·er** registratore *m* di volo; '**flight time** *departure* orario *m* di volo; *duration* durata *f* di volo

flight·y ['flaɪtɪ] *adj* volubile

flim·sy ['flɪmzɪ] *adj structure, furniture* leggero; *dress, material* sottile; *excuse* debole

flinch [flɪntʃ] *v/i* sobbalzare

fling [flɪŋ] **1** *v/t* (*pret & pp* **flung**) scagliare; *~ o.s. into a chair* buttarsi su una sedia **2** *n* F (*affair*) avventura *f*

◆ **flip through** [flɪp] *v/t* (*pret & pp* **-ped**) *book, magazine* sfogliare

flip·per ['flɪpə(r)] *for swimming* pinna *f*

flirt [flɜːt] **1** *v/i* flirtare **2** *n* flirt *m* inv

flir·ta·tious [flɜː'teɪʃəs] *adj* civettuolo

float [fləʊt] *v/i* galleggiare; FIN fluttuare

float·ing vot·er ['fləʊtɪŋ] elettore che cambia spesso opinione

flock [flɒk] **1** *n of sheep* gregge *m* **2** *v/i* accorrere in massa

flog [flɒg] *v/t* (*pret & pp* **-ged**) (*whip*) fustigare; F (*sell*) vendere

flood [flʌd] **1** *n* inondazione *f* **2** *v/t of river* inondare; **~ its banks** *of river* straripare
♦ **flood in** *v/i* affluire

flood·ing ['flʌdɪŋ] inondazione *f*

'**flood·light** *n* riflettore *m*

flood·lit ['flʌdlɪt] *adj match* illuminato da riflettori

flood wa·ters ['flʌdwɔːtəz] *npl* acque *fpl* dell'inondazione

floor [flɔː(r)] *n* pavimento *m*; *(storey)* piano *m*

'**floor·board** asse *f* del pavimento; '**floor cloth** straccio *m* per lavare per terra; '**floor·lamp** *Am* lampada *f* a stelo

flop [flɒp] **1** *v/i* (*pret & pp* **-ped**) crollare; F (*fail*) fare fiasco **2** *n* F (*failure*) fiasco *m*

flop·py ['flɒpɪ] *adj not stiff* floscio; *(weak)* moscio

flop·py ('**disk**) floppy *m inv*, floppy disk *m inv*

Flor·ence ['flɒrəns] Firenze

Flor·en·tine ['flɒrəntaɪn] **1** *adj* fiorentino **2** *n* fiorentino *m*, -a *f*

flor·ist ['flɒrɪst] fiorista *m/f*

floss [flɒs] **1** *n for teeth* filo *m* interdentale **2** *v/t:* **~ one's teeth** passare il filo interdentale

flour ['flaʊə(r)] farina *f*

flour·ish ['flʌrɪʃ] *v/i* fiorire; *of business, civilization* prosperare

flour·ish·ing ['flʌrɪʃɪŋ] *adj business, trade* prospero

flow [fləʊ] **1** *v/i of river, traffic, current* scorrere; *of work* procedere **2** *n of river, ideas* flusso *m*

'**flow·chart** diagramma *m* (di flusso)

flow·er ['flaʊə(r)] **1** *n* fiore *m* **2** *v/i* fiorire

'**flow·er·bed** aiuola *f*; '**flow·er·pot** vaso *m* per fiori; '**flow·er show** esposizione *f* floreale

flow·er·y ['flaʊərɪ] *adj pattern* a fiori; *style of writing* fiorito

flown [fləʊn] *pp* → **fly**

flu [fluː] influenza *f*

fluc·tu·ate ['flʌktjʊeɪt] *v/i* oscillare

fluc·tu·a·tion [flʌktjʊ'eɪʃn] oscillazione *f*

flu·en·cy ['fluːənsɪ] *in a language* scioltezza *f*

flu·ent ['fluːənt] *adj* fluente; **he speaks ~ Spanish** parla correntemente lo spagnolo

flu·ent·ly ['fluːəntlɪ] *adv speak, write* correntemente

fluff [flʌf] *material* lanugine *f*; **a bit of ~** un po' di lanugine

fluff·y ['flʌfɪ] *adj material, hair* lanuginoso; *clouds* soffice; **~ toy** peluche *m inv*

fluid ['fluːɪd] *n* fluido *m*

flung [flʌŋ] *pret & pp* → **fling**

flunk [flʌŋk] *v/t Am* F essere bocciato a

flu·o·res·cent [fluə'resnt] *adj light* fluorescente

flur·ry ['flʌrɪ] *of snow* raffica *f*

flush [flʌʃ] **1** *v/t toilet* tirare l'acqua di; **~ sth down the toilet** buttare qc giù dal water **2** *v/i (go red in the face)* diventare rosso; **the toilet won't ~** lo sciacquone del bagno non funziona **3** *adj (level)* a filo; **be ~ with ...** a filo con ...
♦ **flush away** *v/t down toilet* buttare giù dal water
♦ **flush out** *v/t rebels etc* scovare

flus·ter ['flʌstə(r)] *v/t* mettere in agitazione; **get ~ed** mettersi in agitazione

flute [fluːt] MUS flauto *m* traverso; *glass* flute *m inv*

flut·ter ['flʌtə(r)] **1** *v/i of bird* sbattere le ali; *of wings* sbattere; *of flag* sventolare; *of heart* battere forte **2** *n* F (*bet*) piccola scommessa *f*

fly[1] [flaɪ] *n insect* mosca *f*

fly[2] [flaɪ] *n on trousers* patta *f*

fly[3] [flaɪ] (*pret* **flew**, *pp* **flown**) **1** *v/i* volare; *of flag* sventolare; *(rush)* precipitarsi; **~ into a rage** perdere le staffe **2** *v/t aeroplane* pilotare; *airline* volare con; *(transport by air)* spedire per via aerea
♦ **fly away** *v/i of bird, plane* volare via
♦ **fly back** *v/i (travel back)* ritornare (in aereo)
♦ **fly in 1** *v/i of plane, passengers* arrivare **2** *v/t supplies etc* mandare per

via aerea

♦**fly off** v/i of hat etc volare via

♦**fly out** v/i partire in aereo

♦**fly past** v/i in formation volare in formazione; of time volare

fly·ing ['flaɪɪŋ] n volare m

fly·ing 'sau·cer disco m volante

'**fly·o·ver** MOT cavalcavia m inv

foam [fəʊm] n on liquid schiuma f

foam 'rub·ber gommapiuma® f

FOB [efəʊ'biː] abbr (= **free on board**) FOB

fo·cus ['fəʊkəs] **1** n of attention centro m; PHOT fuoco m; **be in- / be out of -** PHOT essere a fuoco / non essere a fuoco **2** v/t: **- one's attention on** focalizzare l'attenzione su **3** v/i mettere a fuoco

♦**focus on** v/t problem, issue focalizzare l'attenzione su; PHOT mettere a fuoco

fod·der ['fɒdə(r)] foraggio m

foe·tal ['fiːtl] adj → **fetal**

foe·tus ['fiːtəs] → **fetus**

fog [fɒg] nebbia f

♦**fog up** v/i (pret & pp **-ged**) appannarsi

'**fog·bound** adj bloccato dalla nebbia

fog·gy ['fɒgɪ] adj nebbioso; **I haven't the foggiest (idea)** non ne ho la più pallida idea

foi·ble ['fɔɪbl] fisima f

foil[1] [fɔɪl] n carta f stagnola

foil[2] [fɔɪl] v/t (thwart) sventare

fold[1] [fəʊld] **1** v/t paper etc piegare; **- one's arms** incrociare le braccia **2** v/i of business chiudere i battenti **3** n in cloth etc piega f

♦**fold up 1** v/t chairs etc chiudere; clothes piegare **2** v/i of chair, table chiudere

fold[2] [fəʊld] n for sheep etc ovile m

fold·er ['fəʊldə(r)] for documents cartellina f; COMPUT directory f inv

fold·ing ['fəʊldɪŋ] adj pieghevole; **- chair** sedia f pieghevole

fo·li·age ['fəʊlɪɪdʒ] fogliame m

folk [fəʊk] (people) gente f; **my -** (family) i miei parenti; **come in, -s** entrate, gente

'**folk dance** danza f popolare; '**folk mu·sic** musica f folk; '**folk sing·er** cantante m/f folk; '**folk song** canzone f popolare

fol·low ['fɒləʊ] **1** v/t (also understand) seguire **2** v/i seguire; logically quadrare; **it -s from this that ...** ne consegue che ...; **as -s** quanto segue

♦**follow up** v/t letter, inquiry dare seguito a

fol·low·er ['fɒləʊə(r)] of politician etc seguace m/f; of football team tifoso m, -a f; **are you a - of ...?** of TV programme segui ...?

fol·low·ing ['fɒləʊɪŋ] **1** adj seguente **2** n people seguito m; **the -** quanto segue

'**fol·low-up meet·ing** riunione f ulteriore

'**fol·low-up vis·it** to doctor etc visita f successiva

fol·ly ['fɒlɪ] (madness) follia f

fond [fɒnd] adj (loving) affezionato; memory caro; **he is - of travel** gli piace viaggiare

fon·dle ['fɒndl] v/t accarezzare

fond·ness ['fɒndnɪs] for person affetto m; for wine, food gusto m

font [fɒnt] for printing carattere m; in church fonte f battesimale

food [fuːd] cibo m; **I like Italian -** mi piace la cucina italiana; **there's no - in the house** non c'è niente da mangiare in casa

'**food chain** catena f alimentare

food·ie ['fuːdɪ] F buongustaio m, -a f

'**food mix·er** mixer m inv

food poi·son·ing ['fuːdpɔɪznɪŋ] intossicazione f alimentare

fool [fuːl] **1** n pazzo m, -a f; **make a - of o.s.** rendersi ridicolo **2** v/t ingannare; **- s.o. into believing that ...** far credere a qu che ...

♦**fool about, fool around** v/i fare lo sciocco; sexually avere l'amante

♦**fool around with** v/t knife, drill etc trastullarsi con; s.o.'s wife avere una relazione con

'**fool·har·dy** adj temerario

fool·ish ['fuːlɪʃ] adj sciocco

fool·ish·ly ['fuːlɪʃlɪ] *adv* scioccamente

'fool·proof *adj* a prova di idiota

foot [fʊt] (*pl* **feet** [fiːt]) *also measurement* piede *m*; **on** ~ a piedi; *I've been on my feet all day* sono stato in piedi tutto il giorno; *be back on one's feet* essere di nuovo in piedi; *at the* ~ *of the page* a piè di pagina; *at the* ~ *of the hill* ai piedi della collina; *put one's* ~ *in it* F fare una gaffe

foot·age ['fʊtɪdʒ] pellicola *f* cinematografica

'foot·ball (*soccer*) calcio *m*; *American style* football *m* americano; (*ball*) pallone *m* da calcio; *for American football* pallone *m* da football americano

foot·bal·ler ['fʊtbɔːlə(r)] calciatore *m*, -trice *f*

'foot·ball hoo·li·gan teppista *m* del calcio; **'foot·ball pitch** campo *m* da calcio; **'foot·ball play·er** *soccer* calciatore *m*, -trice *f*; *American style* giocatore *m* di football americano; **'foot·bridge** passerella *f*

foot·er ['fʊtə(r)] COMPUT piè *m* di pagina

foot·hills ['fʊthɪlz] *npl* colline *fpl* pedemontane

'foot·hold *in climbing* punto *m* d'appoggio; *gain a* ~ *fig* conquistarsi uno spazio

foot·ing ['fʊtɪŋ] (*basis*) presupposti *mpl*; *lose one's* ~ perdere il punto d'appoggio; *be on the same* ~/*a different* ~ essere sullo stesso piano/su un piano diverso; *be on a friendly* ~ *with ...* avere rapporti amichevoli con ...

foot·lights ['fʊtlaɪts] *npl* luci *fpl* della ribalta; **'foot·mark** impronta *f* di piede; **'foot·note** nota *f* a piè di pagina; **'foot·path** sentiero *m*; **'foot·print** impronta *f* di piede; **'foot·step** passo *m*; *follow in s.o.'s* ~*s* seguire i passi di qu; **'foot·stool** sgabello *m* per i piedi; **'foot·wear** calzatura *f*

for [fə(r)], [fɔː(r)] *prep* ◊ *purpose,* *destination etc* per; *a train* ~ *...* un treno per ...; *clothes* ~ *children* abbigliamento *m* per bambini; *it's too big/small* ~ *you* è troppo grande/piccolo per te; *here's a letter* ~ *you* c'è una lettera per te; *this is* ~ *you* questo è per te; *what is there* ~ *lunch?* cosa c'è per pranzo?; *the steak is* ~ *me* la bistecca è per me; *what is this* ~? a cosa serve?; *what* ~? a che scopo?, perché?; ◊ *time* per; ~ *three days/two hours* per tre giorni/due ore; *I have been waiting* ~ *an hour* ho aspettato (per) un'ora; *please get it done* ~ *Monday* per favore, fallo per lunedì; ◊ *distance* per; *I walked* ~ *a mile* ho camminato per un miglio; *it stretches* ~ *100 miles* si estende per 100 miglia; ◊ (*in favour of*) per; *campaign* ~ fare una campagna per; *I am* ~ *the idea* sono a favore dell'idea; ◊ (*instead of, on behalf of*) per; *let me do that* ~ *you* lascia che te lo faccia io, lascia che faccia questo per te; *we are agents* ~ *...* siamo rappresentanti di ...; ◊ (*in exchange for*) per; *I bought it* ~ *£25* l'ho comprato per 25 sterline; *how much did you sell it* ~? a quanto l'hai venduto?

for·bade [fə'bæd] *pret* → **forbid**

for·bid [fə'bɪd] *v/t* (*pret* **forbade**, *pp* **forbidden**) vietare, proibire; ~ *s.o. to do sth* vietare o proibire a qu di fare qc

for·bid·den [fə'bɪdn] **1** *adj* vietato, proibito; *smok·ing* ~ vietato fumare; *park·ing* ~ divieto di sosta **2** *pp* → **forbid**

for·bid·ding [fə'bɪdɪŋ] *adj* ostile

force [fɔːs] **1** *n* (*violence*) forza *f*; *come into* ~ *of law etc* entrare in vigore; *the* ~*s* MIL le forze armate **2** *v/t door, lock* forzare; ~ *s.o. to do sth* forzare o costringere qu a fare qc; ~ *sth open* aprire qc con la forza ◆ *force back v/t tears etc* trattenere

forced [fɔːst] *adj laugh, smile* forzato

forced 'land·ing atterraggio *m* d'emergenza

force·ful ['fɔːsfʊl] *adj argument, speaker* convincente; *character* energico

force·ful·ly ['fɔːsflɪ] *adv* in modo energico

for·ceps ['fɔːseps] *npl* MED forcipe *f*

for·ci·ble ['fɔːsəbl] *adj entry* forzato; *argument* convincente

for·ci·bly ['fɔːsəblɪ] *adv restrain* con la forza

ford [fɔːd] *n* guado *m*

fore [fɔː(r)] *n*: **come to the ~** salire alla ribalta

'**fore·arm** avambraccio *m*; **fore·bears** ['fɔːbeəz] *npl* antenati *mpl*; **fore·bod·ing** [fə'bəʊdɪŋ] presentimento *m*; '**fore·cast 1** *n* previsione *f* **2** *v/t (pret & pp forecast)* prevedere; '**fore·court** *of garage* area *f* di rifornimento; **fore·fa·thers** ['fɔːfɑːðəz] *npl* antenati *mpl*; '**fore·fin·ger** indice *m*; '**fore·front: be in the ~ of** essere all'avanguardia in; '**fore·gone** *adj*: **that's a ~ con·clusion** è una conclusione scontata; '**fore·ground** primo piano *m*; '**fore·hand** *in tennis* diritto *m*; '**fore·head** fronte *f*

for·eign ['fɒrən] *adj* straniero; *trade, policy* estero

for·eign af·fairs *npl* affari *mpl* esteri; **for·eign 'aid** aiuti *mpl* ad altri paesi; **for·eign 'bod·y** corpo *m* estraneo; **for·eign 'cur·ren·cy** valuta *f* estera

for·eign·er ['fɒrənə(r)] straniero *m*, -a *f*

for·eign ex'change cambio *m* valutario; **for·eign 'lan·guage** lingua *f* straniera; '**For·eign Of·fice** *in UK* Ministero *m* degli esteri; **for·eign 'pol·i·cy** politica *f* estera; **For·eign 'Sec·re·ta·ry** *in UK* ministro *m* degli esteri

'**fore·man** caposquadra *m*

'**fore·most 1** *adv (uppermost)* soprattutto **2** *adj (leading)* principale

fo·ren·sic 'medi·cine [fə'renzɪk] medicina *f* legale

fo·ren·sic 'scien·tist medico *m* legale

'**fore·run·ner** precursore *m*; **fore·'saw** *pret* → **foresee**; **fore·'see** *v/t (pret foresaw, pp foreseen)* prevedere; **fore·see·a·ble** [fə'siːəbl] *adj* prevedibile; **in the ~ future** per quanto si possa prevedere in futuro; **fore·'seen** *pp* → **foresee**; '**fore·sight** lungimiranza *f*

for·est ['fɒrɪst] foresta *f*

for·est·er ['fɒrɪstə(r)] guardaboschi *m/f*

for·est·ry ['fɒrɪstrɪ] scienze *fpl* forestali

'**fore·taste** anteprima *m*, assaggio *m*

fore·'tell *v/t (pret & pp foretold)* predire

fore·'told *pret & pp* → **foretell**

for·ev·er [fə'revə(r)] *adv* per sempre; **it is ~ raining here** piova continuamente qui

for·gave [fə'geɪv] *pret* → **forgive**

fore·word ['fɔːwɜːd] prefazione *f*

for·feit ['fɔːfɪt] *v/t right, privilege etc* perdere

forge [fɔːdʒ] *v/t (counterfeit)* contraffare; *signature* falsificare

♦ **forge ahead** *v/i* prendere il sopravvento

forg·er ['fɔːdʒə(r)] falsario *m*, -a *f*

forg·er·y ['fɔːdʒərɪ] *(banknote)* falsificazione *f*; *(document)* falso *m*

for·get [fə'get] *v/t (pret forgot, pp forgotten)* dimenticare; **~ him, he's a waste of time** lascialo perdere, ti fa solo perdere tempo

for·get·ful [fə'getfʊl] *adj* smemorato

for·get-me-not non-ti-scordar-di-me *m inv*

for·give [fə'gɪv] *v/t & v/i (pret forgave, pp forgiven)* perdonare

for·giv·en [fə'gɪvn] *pp* → **forgive**

for·give·ness [fə'gɪvnɪs] perdono *m*

for·got [fə'gɒt] *pret* → **forget**

for·got·ten [fə'gɒtn] *pp* → **forget**

fork [fɔːk] *n for eating* forchetta *f*; *for gardening* forca *f*; *in road* biforcazione *f*

♦ **fork out** *v/t & v/i F (pay)* sborsare F

fork·lift 'truck muletto *m*

form [fɔːm] **1** *n (shape)* forma *f*; *(document)* modulo *m*; *in school* classe *f*; **be on / off** ~ essere in / fuori forma; **in the ~ of** sotto forma di 2 *v/t in clay etc* modellare; *friendship* creare; *opinion* formarsi; *past tense etc* formare; (*constitute*) costituire 3 *v/i* (*take shape, develop*) formarsi

form·al ['fɔ:ml] *adj* formale

for·mal·i·ty [fə'mælətɪ] formalità *f inv*; **it's just a** ~ è solo una formalità; **the formalities** le formalità

for·mal·ly ['fɔ:məlɪ] *adv* formalmente

for·mat ['fɔ:mæt] 1 *v/t* (*pret & pp* **-ted**) *diskette* formattare; *document* impaginare 2 *n* (*size: of magazine etc*) formato *m*; (*makeup: of programme*) formula *f*

for·ma·tion [fɔ:'meɪʃn] formazione *f*

for·ma·tive ['fɔ:mətɪv] *adj* formativo; **in his ~ years** nei suoi anni formativi

for·mer ['fɔ:mə(r)] *adj wife, president* ex *inv*; *statement, arrangement* precedente; **the** ~ quest'ultimo

for·mer·ly ['fɔ:məlɪ] *adv* precedentemente

for·mi·da·ble ['fɔ:mɪdəbl] *adj* imponente

for·mu·la ['fɔ:mjʊlə] formula *f*

for·mu·late ['fɔ:mjʊleɪt] *v/t* (*express*) formulare

for·ni·cate ['fɔ:nɪkeɪt] *v/i fml* fornicare

for·ni·ca·tion [fɔ:nɪ'keɪʃn] *fml* fornicazione *f*

fort [fɔ:t] MIL forte *m*

forth [fɔ:θ] *adv*: **back and** ~ avanti e indietro; **and so** ~ eccetera; **from that day** ~ da quel giorno in poi

forth·com·ing ['fɔ:θkʌmɪŋ] *adj* (*future*) prossimo; *personality* comunicativo

'forth·right *adj* schietto

for·ti·eth ['fɔ:tɪɪθ] *n & adj* quarantesimo, -a

fort·night ['fɔ:tnaɪt] due settimane

for·tress ['fɔ:trɪs] MIL fortezza *f*

for·tu·nate ['fɔ:tʃʊnət] *adj* fortunato

for·tu·nate·ly ['fɔ:tʃʊnətlɪ] *adv* fortunatamente

for·tune ['fɔ:tʃu:n] sorte *f*; (*lot of money*) fortuna *f*; **tell s.o.'s** ~ predire il futuro a qu

'for·tune-tell·er chiromante *m/f*

for·ty ['fɔ:tɪ] quaranta; **have ~ winks** F fare un pisolino F

Fo·rum ['fɔ:rəm] *Roman* foro *m*

fo·rum ['fɔ:rəm] *fig* foro *m*

for·ward ['fɔ:wəd] 1 *adv* avanti 2 *adj pej: person* diretto 3 *n* SP attaccante *m* 4 *v/t letter* inoltrare

'for·ward·ing ad·dress ['fɔ:wədɪŋ] recapito *m*

'for·ward·ing a·gent COM spedizioniere *m*

'for·ward-look·ing *adj* progressista

fos·sil ['fɒsəl] fossile *m*

fos·sil·ized ['fɒsəlaɪzd] *adj* fossilizzato

fos·ter ['fɒstə(r)] *v/t child* avere in affidamento; *attitude, belief* incoraggiare

'fos·ter child figlio *m*, -a *f* in affidamento

'fos·ter home famiglia *f* di accoglienza

'fos·ter par·ents *npl* genitori *mpl* con affidamento

fought [fɔ:t] *pret & pp* → **fight**

foul [faʊl] 1 *n* SP fallo *m* 2 *adj smell, taste* pessimo; *weather* orribile 3 *v/t* SP fare un fallo contro

found¹ [faʊnd] *v/t school etc* fondare

found² [faʊnd] *pret & pp* → **find**

foun·da·tion [faʊn'deɪʃn] *of theory etc* fondamenta *fpl*; (*organization*) fondazione *f*; *make-up* fondotinta *m*

foun·da·tions [faʊn'deɪʃnz] *npl of building* fondamenta *fpl*

found·er ['faʊndə(r)] *n* fondatore *m*, -trice *f*

found·ing ['faʊndɪŋ] *n* fondazione *f*

foun·dry ['faʊndrɪ] fonderia *f*

foun·tain ['faʊntɪn] fontana *f*

'foun·tain pen penna *f* stilografica

four [fɔ:(r)] 1 *adj* quattro 2 *n*: **on all ~s** a quattro zampe

four-let·ter 'word parolaccia *f*; **four-post·er** ('bed) letto *m* a baldacchino; **'four-star** *adj hotel etc* a quattro stelle; **four-star** ('**pet·rol**) super *f*

four·teen [fɔːˈtiːn] quattordici

four·teenth [ˈfɔːtiːnθ] *n* & *adj* quattordicesimo, -a

fourth [fɔːθ] *n* & *adj* quarto, -a

four-wheel '**drive** MOT quattro per
quattro *m inv*

fowl [faul] pollame *m*

fox [fɒks] **1** *n* volpe *f* **2** *v/t* (*puzzle*)
mettere in difficoltà

foy·er [ˈfɔɪeɪ] atrio *m*

frac·tion [ˈfrækʃn] frazione *f*

frac·tion·al·ly [ˈfrækʃnəlɪ] *adv* lieve-
mente

frac·ture [ˈfræktʃə(r)] **1** *n* frattura *f*
2 *v/t* fratturare

fra·gile [ˈfrædʒaɪl] *adj* fragile

frag·ment [ˈfrægmənt] *n* frammento
m

frag·men·tar·y [frægˈmentərɪ] *adj*
frammentario

fra·grance [ˈfreɪgrəns] fragranza *f*

fra·grant [ˈfreɪgrənt] *adj* profumato

frail [freɪl] *adj* gracile

frame [freɪm] **1** *n* of picture, window
cornice *f*; of glasses montatura *f*; of
bicycle telaio *m*; **~ of mind** stato *m*
d'animo **2** *v/t* picture incorniciare; F
person incastrare F

'**frame-up** F montatura *f*

'**frame·work** struttura *f*

France [frɑːns] Francia *f*

fran·chise [ˈfræntʃaɪz] *n* for business
concessione *f*

frank [fræŋk] *adj* franco

frank·furt·er [ˈfræŋkfɜːtə(r)] wurstel
m inv

frank·ly [ˈfræŋklɪ] *adv* francamente

frank·ness [ˈfræŋknɪs] franchezza *f*

fran·tic [ˈfræntɪk] *adj* search, attempt
frenetico; (*worried*) agitatissimo

fran·ti·cal·ly [ˈfræntɪklɪ] *adv* freneti-
camente

fra·ter·nal [frəˈtɜːnl] *adj* fraterno

fraud [frɔːd] frode *f*; person impostore *m*, -trice *f*

fraud·u·lent [ˈfrɔːdjʊlənt] *adj* fraudolento

fraud·u·lent·ly [ˈfrɔːdjʊləntlɪ] *adv* in
modo fraudolento

frayed [freɪd] *adj cuffs* liso

freak [friːk] **1** *n unusual event* fenomeno *m* anomalo; *two-headed per-
son, animal etc* scherzo *m* di natura;
F *strange person* tipo *m*, -a *f* strambo,
-a; *movie* / *jazz* ~ F (*fanatic*) fanatico *m*, -a *f* del cinema / del jazz **2** *adj
wind, storm etc* violento

freck·le [ˈfrekl] lentiggine *f*

free [friː] **1** *adj* (at *liberty*, not occupied) libero; (no *cost*) gratuito; **are
you ~ this afternoon?** sei libero
oggi pomeriggio?; **~ and easy** spensierato; **for ~** travel, get sth gratis **2**
v/t prisoners liberare

free·bie [ˈfriːbɪ] F omaggio *m*

free·dom [ˈfriːdəm] libertà *f*

free·dom of '**speech** libertà *f* di parola

free·dom of the '**press** libertà *f* di
stampa

free '**en·ter·prise** liberalismo *m* economico; **free** '**kick** in soccer calcio *m*
di punizione; **free·lance** [ˈfriːlɑːns]
1 *adj* free lance inv **2** *adv* work free
lance inv; **free·lanc·er** [ˈfriːlɑːns-
ə(r)] free lance *m/f inv*

free·ly [ˈfriːlɪ] *adv* admit apertamente

free mar·ket e'**con·o·my** economia
f del libero mercato; **free-range**
'**chick·en** pollo *m* ruspante; **free-
range** '**eggs** *npl* uova *fpl* di galline
ruspanti; **free** '**sam·ple** campione
m gratuito; **free** '**speech** libertà *f* di
espressione; '**free·way** Am autostrada *f*; **free**'**wheel** *v/i* on bicycle
andare a ruota libera

freeze [friːz] (pret **froze**, pp **frozen**)
1 *v/t* food, river gelare; wages, account congelare; video bloccare **2** *v/i*
of water gelare

♦**freeze over** *v/i* of river gelare

'**freeze-dried** *adj* liofilizzato

freez·er [ˈfriːzə(r)] freezer *m inv*,
congelatore *m*

freez·ing [ˈfriːzɪŋ] **1** *adj* gelato; *it's ~
out here* si gela qui fuori; *it's ~
(cold)* of weather si gela; of water è
gelata; *I'm ~ (cold)* sono congelato
2 *n*: **10 below ~** 10 gradi sotto
zero

'**freez·ing com·part·ment** freezer
m inv

'**freez·ing point** punto *m* di congelamento

freight [freɪt] *n* carico *m*; *costs* trasporto *m*

freight·er ['freɪtə(r)] *ship* nave *f* da
carico; *aeroplane* aereo *f* da carico

French [frentʃ] **1** *adj* francese **2** *n*
(*language*) francese *m*; *the* ~ i francesi

French 'bread baguette *fpl*; '**French
fries** *npl* patate *fpl* fritte; '**Frenchman** francese *m*; **French 'stick**
baguette *f inv*; **French 'win·dows**
npl vetrata *f*; '**French·wom·an**
francese *f*

fren·zied ['frenzɪd] *adj attack, activity*
frenetico; *mob* impazzito

fren·zy ['frenzɪ] frenesia *f*

fre·quen·cy ['friːkwənsɪ] frequenza
f

fre·quent¹ ['friːkwənt] *adj* frequente

fre·quent² [frɪ'kwent] *v/t bar etc* frequentare

fre·quent·ly ['friːkwəntlɪ] *adv* fre-
quentemente

fres·co ['freskəʊ] affresco *m*

fresh [freʃ] *adj fruit, meat etc*, (*cold*)
fresco; (*new: start*) nuovo

fresh 'air aria *f* fresca

fresh·en ['freʃn] *v/i of wind* rinfrescare
♦ **freshen up 1** *v/i* rinfrescarsi **2** *v/t
room, paintwork* rinfrescare

'**fresh·er** ['freʃə(r)] matricola *f*

fresh·ly ['freʃlɪ] *adv* appena

fresh·ness ['freʃnɪs] *of fruit, meat,
climate* freschezza *f*; *of style, approach* novità *f*

fresh 'or·ange spremuta *f* d'arancia

'**fresh·wa·ter** *adj* d'acqua dolce

fret [fret] *v/i* (*pret & pp* -**ted**) agitarsi

Freud·i·an ['frɔɪdɪən] *adj* freudiano

fric·tion ['frɪkʃn] PHYS frizione *f*;
between people attrito *m*

Fri·day ['fraɪdeɪ] venerdì *m inv*

fridge [frɪdʒ] frigo *m*

fried 'egg [fraɪd] uovo *m* fritto

fried po'ta·toes *npl* patate *fpl* salta-
te

friend [frend] amico *m*, -a *f*; *make* ~s
fare amicizia; *make* ~s *with s.o.*
fare amicizia con qu

friend·li·ness ['frendlɪnɪs] amiche-
volezza *f*

friend·ly ['frendlɪ] **1** *adj* amichevole;
(*easy to use*) facile da usare; *be* ~
with s.o. (*be friends*) essere in rapporti d'amicizia con qu; *they're
very* ~ *with each other* sono molto in
confidenza; *he started getting too*
~ ha cominciato a prendersi troppa
confidenza **2** *n* SP amichevole *f*

'**friend·ship** ['frendʃɪp] amicizia *f*

fries [fraɪz] *npl* patate *fpl* fritte

fright [fraɪt] paura *f*; *give s.o. a* ~ far
paura a qu

fright·en ['fraɪtn] *v/t* spaventare; *be
~ed (of)* aver paura (di); *don't be
~ed* non aver paura
♦ **frighten away** *v/t* far scappare

fright·en·ing ['fraɪtnɪŋ] *adj* spaventoso

fri·gid ['frɪdʒɪd] *adj sexually* frigido

frill [frɪl] *on dress etc* volant *m inv*; ~s
(*fancy extras*) fronzoli *mpl*

frill·y ['frɪlɪ] *adj* pieno di volant

fringe [frɪndʒ] frangia *f*; (*edge*) mar-
gini *mpl*

fringe ben·e·fits *npl* benefici *mpl*
accessori

frisk [frɪsk] *v/t* F frugare F

frisk·y ['frɪskɪ] *adj puppy etc* vivace
♦ **fritter away** ['frɪtə(r)] *v/t time, fortune* sprecare

fri·vol·i·ty [frɪ'vɒlətɪ] frivolezza *f*

friv·o·lous ['frɪvələs] *adj person,
pleasures* frivolo

frizz·y ['frɪzɪ] *adj hair* crespo

frog [frɒg] rana *f*

'**frog·man** sommozzatore *m*, -trice *f*

from [frɒm] *prep* ◊ *in time* da; ~ *9 to 5
(o'clock)* dalle 9 alle 5; ~ *the 18th
century* dal XVIII secolo; ~ *today
on* da oggi in poi; ~ *next Tuesday*
da martedì della prossima settimana ◊ *in space* da; ~ *here to there* da
qui a lì; *we drove here* ~ *Paris* siamo venuti qui in macchina da Parigi
◊ *origin* di; *a letter* ~ *Jo* una lettera
di Jo; *a gift* ~ *the management* un

regalo della direzione; *it doesn't say who it's* ~ non c'è scritto di chi è; *I am* ~ *Liverpool* sono di Liverpool; *made* ~ *bananas* fatto di banane ◊ *(because of)* di; *tired* ~ *the journey* stanco del viaggio; *it's* ~ *overeating* è a causa del troppo mangiare

front [frʌnt] **1** *n of building* lato *m* principale; *of car, statue* davanti *m inv*; *of book* copertina *f*; *(cover organization)* facciata *f*; MIL, *of weather* fronte *m*; *in* ~ davanti; *in* ~ *of* davanti a; *at the* ~ davanti; *at the* ~ *of of bus etc* nella parte anteriore di **2** *adj wheel, seat* anteriore **3** *v/t TV programme* presentare

front 'bench POL *principali esponenti mpl del governo e dell'opposizione nel Parlamento*; front 'cov·er copertina *f*; front 'door porta *f* principale; front 'en·trance entrata *f* principale

fron·tier ['frʌntɪə(r)] *also fig* frontiera *f*

'front 'line MIL fronte *m*; front 'page *of newspaper* prima pagina *f*; front page 'news *nsg* notizia *f* di prima pagina; front 'row prima fila *f*; front seat 'pas·sen·ger *in car* passeggero *m* davanti; front-wheel 'drive trazione *f* anteriore

frost [frɒst] *n* brina *f*

'frost·bite congelamento *m*

'frost·bit·ten *adj* congelato

frosted glass ['frɒstɪd] vetro *m* smerigliato

frost·y ['frɒstɪ] *adj also fig* gelido

froth [frɒθ] *n* spuma *f*

froth·y ['frɒθɪ] *adj cream etc* spumoso

frown [fraʊn] **1** *n* cipiglio *m* **2** *v/i* aggrottare le sopracciglia

froze [frəʊz] *pret* → freeze

fro·zen ['frəʊzn] **1** *adj* gelato; *wastes* gelido; *food* surgelato; *I'm* ~ F sono congelato F **2** *pp* → freeze

fro·zen 'food cibi *mpl* surgelati

fruit [fruːt] frutto *m*; *collective* frutta *f*

'fruit cake *dolce f con frutta candita*

fruit·ful ['fruːtfʊl] *adj discussions etc* fruttuoso

'fruit juice succo *m* di frutta; 'fruit ma·chine slot machine *f inv*; fruit 'sal·ad macedonia *f*

frus·trate [frʌ'streɪt] *v/t person* frustrare; *plans* scombussolare

frus·trat·ed [frʌ'streɪtɪd] *adj look, sigh* frustrato

frus·trat·ing [frʌ'streɪtɪŋ] *adj* frustrante

frus·trat·ing·ly [frʌ'streɪtɪŋlɪ] *adv slow, hard* in modo frustrante

frus·tra·tion [frʌ'streɪʃn] frustrazione *f*; *sexual* ~ insoddisfazione *f* sessuale; *the* ~*s of modern life* le frustrazioni della vita moderna

fry [fraɪ] *v/t* (*pret & pp* *-ied*) friggere

'fry·ing pan ['fraɪɪŋ] padella *f*

fuck [fʌk] *v/t* V scopare V; ~*!* cazzo!

♦fuck off *v/i* V andare affanculo V; *fuck off!* vaffanculo!

fuck·ing ['fʌkɪŋ] **1** *adj* V del cazzo V **2** *adv* V; *I'm* ~ *late!* V sono in ritardo, cazzo!; *I'm* ~ *tired* cazzo, come sono stanco

fu·el ['fjuːəl] **1** *n* carburante *m* **2** *v/t fig* alimentare

fu·gi·tive ['fjuːdʒətɪv] *n* fuggiasco *m*, -a *f*

ful·fil, *Am* ful·fill [fʊl'fɪl] *v/t* (*pret & pp* *-led*) *dreams* realizzare; *needs, expectations* soddisfare; *contract* eseguire; *requirements* corrispondere a; *feel* ~*led in job, life* sentirsi soddisfatto

ful·fil·ment, *Am* ful·fill·ment [fʊl'fɪlmənt] *of contract* esecuzione *f*; *of dreams* realizzazione *f*; *moral, spiritual* soddisfazione *f*

full [fʊl] *adj* pieno (*of* di); *account, report* esauriente; *life* intenso; ~ *up hotel, with food* pieno; *in* ~ *write* per intero; *pay in* ~ saldare il conto

full 'board pensione *f* completa; 'full-grown *adj* adulto; ~ *adult person* adulto in età matura; *animal* adulto completamente sviluppato; 'full-length *adj dress* lungo; ~ *film* lungometraggio *m*; full 'moon luna *f* piena; full 'stop punto *m* fermo; full-'time *adj & adv worker, job* a tempo pieno

ful·ly ['fʊlɪ] *adv booked, recovered* completamente; *understand, explain* perfettamente; *describe* ampiamente

fum·ble ['fʌmbl] *v/t catch* farsi sfuggire

♦ **fumble about** *v/i in bags, pockets* frugare; *move in the dark* andare a tastoni; *search in the dark* cercare a tastoni

fume [fjuːm] *v/i*: **be fuming** F (*be very angry*) essere nero F

fumes [fjuːmz] *npl* esalazioni *fpl*

fun [fʌn] *n* divertimento *m*; **it was great ~** era molto divertente; **bye, have ~!** ciao, divertiti!; **for ~** per divertirsi; (*joking*) per scherzo; **make ~ of** prendere in giro

func·tion ['fʌŋkʃn] **1** *n* (*purpose*) funzione *f*; (*reception etc*) cerimonia *f* **2** *v/i* funzionare; **~ as** servire da

func·tion·al ['fʌŋkʃnl] *adj* funzionale

fund [fʌnd] **1** *n* fondo *m* **2** *v/t project etc* finanziare

fun·da·men·tal [fʌndə'mentl] *adj* fondamentale

fun·da·men·tal·ist [fʌndə'mentlɪst] *n* fondamentalista *m/f*

fun·da·men·tal·ly [fʌndə'mentlɪ] *adv* fondamentalmente

fund·ing ['fʌndɪŋ] *money* fondi *mpl*

fu·ne·ral ['fjuːnərəl] *funerale m*

'fu·ne·ral di·rec·tor impresario *m* delle pompe funebri

'fu·ne·ral home *Am*, **'fu·ne·ral par·lour** obitorio *m*

'fun·fair luna park *m inv*

fun·gus ['fʌŋɡəs] fungo *m*

fu·nic·u·lar ('rail·way) [fjuː'nɪkjʊlə(r)] funicolare *f*

fun·nel ['fʌnl] *n of ship* imbuto *m*

fun·ni·ly ['fʌnɪlɪ] *adv* (*oddly*) stranamente; (*comically*) in modo divertente; **~ enough** per quanto strano

fun·ny ['fʌnɪ] *adj* (*comical*) divertente; (*odd*) strano

'fun·ny bone osso *m* del gomito

fur [fɜː(r)] pelliccia *f*; *on animal* pelo *m*

fu·ri·ous ['fjʊərɪəs] *adj* (*angry*) furioso; (*intense*) spaventoso; **at a ~ pace** a tutta velocità

fur·nace ['fɜːnɪs] forno *m*

fur·nish ['fɜːnɪʃ] *v/t room* arredare; (*supply*) fornire

fur·ni·ture ['fɜːnɪtʃə(r)] mobili *mpl*; **a piece of ~** un mobile

fur·ry ['fɜːrɪ] *adj animal* coperto di pelliccia

fur·ther ['fɜːðə(r)] **1** *adj* (*additional*) ulteriore; (*more distant*) più lontano; **until ~ notice** fino a nuovo avviso; **have you anything ~ to say?** ha qualcosa da aggiungere? **2** *adv walk, drive* oltre; **~, I want to say ...** inoltre, volevo dire ...; **two miles ~ (on)** due miglia più avanti **3** *v/t cause etc* favorire

fur·ther ed·u·ca·tion istruzione *f* universitaria o para-universitaria

fur·ther·more *adv* inoltre

fur·thest ['fɜːðɪst] **1** *adj* più lontano **2** *adv*: **this is the ~ north** è il punto più a nord; **the ~ man has travelled in space** il punto più lontano che si è raggiunto nello spazio

fur·tive ['fɜːtɪv] *adj glance* furtivo

fur·tive·ly ['fɜːtɪvlɪ] *adv* furtivamente

fu·ry ['fjʊərɪ] (*anger*) furore *m*

fuse [fjuːz] **1** *n* ELEC fusibile *m* **2** *v/i* ELEC bruciarsi **3** *v/t* ELEC bruciare

'fuse·box scatola *f* dei fusibili

fu·se·lage ['fjuːzəlɑːʒ] fusoliera *f*

'fuse wire filo *m* per fusibili

fu·sion ['fjuːʒn] fusione *f*

fuss [fʌs] *n* agitazione *f*; *about film, event* scalpore *m*; **make a ~ complain** fare storie; *behave in exaggerated way* agitarsi; **make a ~ of** *very attentive to* colmare qu di attenzioni

fuss·y ['fʌsɪ] *adj person* difficile; *design etc* complicato; **be a ~ eater** essere schizzinoso nel mangiare

fu·tile ['fjuːtaɪl] *adj* futile

fu·til·i·ty [fjuː'tɪlɪtɪ] futilità *f inv*

fu·ture ['fjuːtʃə(r)] **1** *n* futuro *m*; **in ~** in futuro **2** *adj* futuro

411 gap year

fu·tures ['fjuːtʃəz] *npl* FIN titoli *mpl* a termine

'fu·tures mar·ket FIN mercato *m* dei titoli a termine

fu·tur·is·tic [fjuːtʃə'rɪstɪk] *adj design* futuristico

fuzz·y ['fʌzɪ] *adj hair* crespo; *(out of focus)* sfuocato

G

gab [gæb] *n*: *have the gift of the ~* F avere la parlantina F

gab·ble ['gæbl] *v/i* parlare troppo in fretta

♦ **gad about** [gæd] *v/i (pret & pp -ded)* andarsene in giro

gad·get ['gædʒɪt] congegno *m*

Gael·ic ['geɪlɪk] *n language* gaelico *m*

gaffe [gæf] gaffe *f inv*

gag [gæg] **1** *n* bavaglio *m*; *(joke)* battuta *f* **2** *v/t (pret & pp -ged) person* imbavagliare; *the press* azzittire

gai·ly ['geɪlɪ] *adv (blithely)* allegramente

gain [geɪn] *v/t (acquire)* acquisire, acquistare; *~ speed* acquistare velocità; *~ 10 pounds* aumentare di 10 libbre

ga·la ['gɑːlə] *concert etc* serata *f* di gala

gal·ax·y ['gæləksɪ] AST galassia *f*

gale [geɪl] bufera *f*

gal·lant ['gælənt] *adj* galante

gall blad·der ['gɔːlblædə(r)] cistifellea *f*

gal·le·ry ['gælərɪ] galleria *f*

gal·ley ['gælɪ] *on ship* cambusa *f*

♦ **gal·li·vant around** ['gælɪvænt] *v/i* andarsene a spasso

gal·lon ['gælən] gallone *m*; *~s of tea* F litri *mpl* di tè

gal·lop ['gæləp] *v/i* galoppare

gal·lows ['gæləʊz] *npl* forca *fsg*

gall·stone ['gɔːlstəʊn] calcolo *m* biliare

ga·lore [gə'lɔː(r)] *adj*: *apples / novels ~* mele / romanzi a iosa

gal·va·nize ['gælvənaɪz] *v/t* TECH

galvanizzare; *fig* stimolare

gam·ble ['gæmbl] *v/i* giocare (d'azzardo)

gam·bler ['gæmblə(r)] giocatore *m*, -trice *f* (d'azzardo)

gam·bling ['gæmblɪŋ] *n* gioco *m* (d'azzardo)

game [geɪm] *n* gioco *m*; *(match, in tennis)* partita *f*

'game·keep·er guardacaccia *m/f inv*

'game re·serve riserva *f* di caccia

gam·mon ['gæmən] coscia *f* di maiale affumicata

gang [gæŋ] banda *f*

♦ **gang up on** *v/t* mettersi contro

'gang rape 1 *n* stupro *m* collettivo **2** *v/t* stuprare in massa

gan·grene ['gæŋgriːn] MED cancrena *f*

gang·ster ['gæŋstə(r)] malvivente *m*, gangster *m inv*

'gang war·fare guerra *f* tra bande

'gang·way passaggio *m*; *for ship* passerella *f*

gaol [dʒeɪl] → *jail*

gap [gæp] *in wall, for parking* buco *m*; *in conversation, life* vuoto *m*; *in time* intervallo *m*; *in story, education* lacuna *f*; *between two people's characters* scarto *m*

gape [geɪp] *v/i of person* rimanere a bocca aperta; *of hole* spalancarsi

♦ **gape at** *v/t* guardare a bocca aperta

gap·ing ['geɪpɪŋ] *adj hole* spalancato

'gap year anno *m* tra la fine del liceo e l'inizio dell'università dedicato ad altre attività

gar·age ['gærɪdʒ] *n for parking* garage *m inv*; *for petrol* stazione *f* di servizio; *for repairs* officina *f*

gar·bage ['gɑːbɪdʒ] *n* rifiuti *mpl*; (*fig: nonsense*) idiozie *fpl*

gar·bled ['gɑːbld] *adj message* ingarbugliato

gar·den ['gɑːdn] giardino *m*; *for vegetables* orto *m*

'gar·den cen·ter *Am*, **'gar·den cen·tre** centro *m* per il giardinaggio

gar·den·er ['gɑːdnə(r)] giardiniere *m*, -a *f*

gar·den·ing ['gɑːdnɪŋ] giardinaggio *m*

gar·gle ['gɑːgl] *v/i* fare i gargarismi

gar·goyle ['gɑːgɔɪl] ARCHI gargouille *f inv*

gar·ish ['geərɪʃ] *adj* sgargiante

gar·land ['gɑːlənd] *n* ghirlanda *f*

gar·lic ['gɑːlɪk] aglio *m*

gar·lic 'bread pane *m* all'aglio

gar·ment ['gɑːmənt] capo *m* d'abbigliamento

gar·nish ['gɑːnɪʃ] *v/t* guarnire

gar·ret ['gærɪt] soffitta *f*

gar·ri·son ['gærɪsn] *n* guarnigione *f*

gar·ter ['gɑːtə(r)] giarrettiera *f*

gas [gæs] *n* gas *m inv*; (*esp Am: gasoline*) benzina *f*

'gas bill bolletta *f* del gas

gash [gæʃ] *n* taglio *m*

gas·ket ['gæskɪt] guarnizione *f*

'gas man impiegato *m* del gas

'gas me·ter contatore *m* del gas

gas·o·line ['gæsəliːn] *Am* benzina *f*

gasp [gɑːsp] **1** *n* sussulto *m* **2** *v/i* rimanere senza fiato; **~ for breath** essere senza fiato; **he collapsed ~ing for breath** si è accasciato senza fiato

'gas ped·al *Am* acceleratore *m*; **'gas pipe·line** gasdotto *m*; **'gas sta·tion** *Am* stazione *f* di rifornimento; **'gas stove** cucina *f* a gas

gas·tric ['gæstrɪk] *adj* MED gastrico

gas·tric 'flu MED influenza *f* intestinale; **gas·tric 'juices** *npl* succhi *mpl* gastrici; **gas·tric 'ul·cer** MED ulcera *f* gastrica

gate [geɪt] cancello *m*; *of city, castle, at airport* porta *f*

ga·teau ['gætəʊ] torta *f*

'gate·crash *v/t* intrufolarsi in

'gate·way ingresso *m*; *fig* via *f* d'accesso

gath·er ['gæðə(r)] **1** *v/t facts, information* raccogliere; **~ speed** acquistare velocità; **am I to ~ that ...?** (*understand*) devo dedurre che ...? **2** *v/i* (*understand*) dedurre

♦ **gather up** *v/t possessions* radunare

gath·er·ing ['gæðərɪŋ] *n* (*group of people*) raduno *m*

gau·dy ['gɔːdɪ] *adj* pacchiano

gauge [geɪdʒ] **1** *n* indicatore *m* **2** *v/t pressure* misurare; *opinion* valutare

gaunt [gɔːnt] *adj* smunto

gauze [gɔːz] garza *f*

gave [geɪv] *pret* → **give**

gaw·ky ['gɔːkɪ] *adj* impacciato

gawp [gɔːp] *v/i* F fissare come un ebete F; **~ at sth** fissare qc con aria inebetita

gay [geɪ] **1** *n* (*homosexual*) omosessuale *m/f* **2** *adj* omosessuale; *club* gay *inv*

gaze [geɪz] **1** *n* sguardo *m* **2** *v/i* fissare

♦ **gaze at** *v/t* fissare

GB [dʒiː'biː] *abbr* (= **Great Britain**) GB (= Gran Bretagna *f*)

GDP [dʒiːdiː'piː] *abbr* (= **gross domestic product**) PIL *m* (= prodotto *m* interno lordo)

gear [gɪə(r)] *n* (*equipment*) equipaggiamento *m*; *in vehicles* marcia *f*

'gear·box MOT scatola *f* del cambio

'gear le·ver, **'gear shift** MOT leva *f* del cambio

geese [giːs] *pl* → **goose**

gel [dʒel] *for hair, shower* gel *m inv*

gel·a·tine ['dʒelətiːn] gelatina *f*

gel·ig·nite ['dʒelɪgnaɪt] gelignite *f*

gem [dʒem] gemma *f*; *fig: book etc* capolavoro *m*; *person* perla *f* rara

Gem·i·ni ['dʒemɪnaɪ] ASTR Gemelli *mpl*

gen·der ['dʒendə(r)] genere *m*

gene [dʒiːn] gene *m*; **it's in his ~s** è una sua caratteristica innata

gen·e·ral ['dʒenrəl] **1** *n* MIL generale *m*; **in ~** in generale **2** *adj* generale

gen·e·ral e'lec·tion elezioni *fpl* politiche

gen·er·al·i·za·tion [dʒenrəlaɪˈzeɪʃn] generalizzazione *f*

gen·er·al·ize ['dʒenrəlaɪz] *v/i* generalizzare

gen·er·al·ly ['dʒenrəlɪ] *adv* generalmente; **~ speaking** in generale

gen·e·ral prac'ti·tion·er medico *m* generico

gen·e·rate ['dʒenəreɪt] *v/t* generare; *in linguistics* formare

gen·e·ra·tion [dʒenəˈreɪʃn] generazione *f*

gen·e·ra·tion gap scarto *m* generazionale

gen·e·ra·tor ['dʒenəreɪtə(r)] ELEC generatore *m*

ge·ner·ic drug [dʒəˈnerɪk] MED *medicina f senza una marca specifica*

gen·e·ros·i·ty [dʒenəˈrɒsɪtɪ] generosità *f*

gen·e·rous ['dʒenərəs] *adj* generoso

ge·net·ic [dʒɪˈnetɪk] *adj* genetico

ge·net·i·cal·ly [dʒɪˈnetɪklɪ] *adv* geneticamente; **~ modified** transgenico

ge·net·ic 'code codice *m* genetico; **ge·net·ic en·gi·neer·ing** ingegneria *f* genetica; **ge·net·ic 'fin·ger·print** esame *m* del DNA

ge·net·i·cist [dʒɪˈnetɪsɪst] genetista *m/f*

ge·net·ics [dʒɪˈnetɪks] genetica *f*

ge·ni·al ['dʒiːnɪəl] *adj person, company* gioviale

gen·i·tals ['dʒenɪtlz] *npl* genitali *mpl*

ge·ni·us ['dʒiːnɪəs] genio *m*

Gen·o·a ['dʒenəʊə] Genova *f*

gen·o·cide ['dʒenəsaɪd] genocidio *m*

gen·tle ['dʒentl] *adj* delicato; *breeze, slope* dolce

gen·tle·man ['dʒentlmən] signore *m*; **he's a real ~** è un vero gentleman

gen·tle·ness ['dʒentlnɪs] delicatezza *f*; *of breeze, slope* dolcezza *f*

gen·tly ['dʒentlɪ] *adv* delicatamente; *blow, slope* dolcemente

gents [dʒents] *toilet* bagno *m* degli uomini

gen·u·ine ['dʒenjʊɪn] *adj* autentico; *(sincere)* sincero

gen·u·ine·ly ['dʒenjʊɪnlɪ] *adv* sinceramente

ge·o·graph·i·cal [dʒɪəˈgræfɪkl] *adj* geografico

ge·og·ra·phy [dʒɪˈɒgrəfɪ] geografia *f*

ge·o·log·i·cal [dʒɪəˈlɒdʒɪkl] *adj* geologico

ge·ol·o·gist [dʒɪˈɒlədʒɪst] geologo *m*, -a *f*

ge·ol·o·gy [dʒɪˈɒlədʒɪ] geologia *f*

ge·o·met·ric, ge·o·met·ri·cal [dʒɪəˈmetrɪk(l)] *adj* geometrico

ge·om·e·try [dʒɪˈɒmətrɪ] geometria *f*

ge·ra·ni·um [dʒəˈreɪnɪəm] geranio *m*

ger·i·at·ric [dʒerɪˈætrɪk] **1** *adj* geriatrico **2** *n* anziano *m*, -a *f*

germ [dʒɜːm] *also fig* germe *m*

Ger·man ['dʒɜːmən] **1** *adj* tedesco **2** *n person* tedesco *m*, -a *f*; *language* tedesco *m*

Ger·man 'mea·sles *nsg* rosolia *f*

Ger·man 'shep·herd pastore *m* tedesco

Ger·ma·ny ['dʒɜːmənɪ] Germania *f*

ger·mi·nate ['dʒɜːmɪneɪt] *v/i of seed* germogliare

germ 'war·fare guerra *f* batteriologica

ges·tic·u·late [dʒeˈstɪkjʊleɪt] *v/i* gesticolare

ges·ture ['dʒestʃə(r)] *n also fig* gesto *m*

get [get] *v/t* (*pret & pp* **got**) *(obtain)* prendere; *(fetch)* andare a prendere; *(receive: letter)* ricevere; *(receive: knowledge, respect etc)* ottenere; *(catch: bus, train, flu)* prendere; *(become)* diventare; *(arrive)* arrivare; *(understand)* afferrare; **~ sth done** *causative* farsi fare qc; **~ s.o. to do sth** far fare qc a qu; **I'll ~ him to do it** glielo faccio fare; **~ to do sth** *have opportunity* avere occasione di fare qc; **~ one's hair cut** tagliarsi i capelli; **~ sth ready** preparare qc; **~**

going (*leave*) andare via; *I have got to study / see him* devo studiare / vederlo; *I don't want to, but I've got to* non voglio, ma devo; *~ to know* venire a sapere

♦ **get about** *v/i* (*travel*) andare in giro; (*be mobile*) muoversi

♦ **get along** *v/i* (*progress*) procedere; *how is he getting along at school?* come se la cava a scuola?; *come to party etc* venire; *with s.o.* andare d'accordo

♦ **get at** *v/t* (*criticize*) prendersela con; (*imply, mean*) volere arrivare a; *I don't understand what you're getting at* non capisco dove vuoi arrivare

♦ **get away 1** *v/i* (*leave*) andare via **2** *v/t*: *get sth away from s.o.* togliere qc a qu

♦ **get away with** *v/t* cavarsela per

♦ **get back 1** *v/i* (*return*) ritornare; *I'll get back to you on that* ti faccio sapere **2** *v/t* (*obtain again*) recuperare

♦ **get by** *v/i* (*pass*) passare; *financially* tirare avanti

♦ **get down 1** *v/i from ladder etc* scendere; (*duck etc*) abbassarsi **2** *v/t* (*depress*) buttare giù

♦ **get down to** *v/t* (*start: work*) mettersi a; (*reach: real facts*) arrivare a; *let's get down to business* parliamo d'affari

♦ **get in 1** *v/i* (*arrive: of train, plane*) arrivare; (*come home*) arrivare a casa; *to car* salire; *how did they get in?* of thieves, mice etc come sono entrati? **2** *v/t to suitcase etc* far entrare

♦ **get off 1** *v/i from bus etc* scendere; (*finish work*) finire; (*not be punished*) cavarsela **2** *v/t* (*remove*) togliere; *clothes, hat, footgear* togliersi; *get off the grass!* togliti dal prato!

♦ **get off with** *v/t* F *sexually* rimorchiare F; *get off with a small fine* cavarsela con una piccola multa

♦ **get on 1** *v/i to bike, bus, train* salire; (*be friendly*) andare d'accordo; (*advance: of time*) farsi tardi; (*become*

old) invecchiare; (*make progress*) procedere; *he's getting on well at school* se la sta cavando bene a scuola; *it's getting on getting late* si sta facendo tardi; *he's getting on getting old* sta invecchiando; *he's getting on for 50* va per i 50 anni **2** *v/t*: *get on the bus / one's bike* salire sull'autobus / sulla bici; *get one's hat on* mettersi il cappello; *I can't get these trousers on* non riesco a mettermi questi pantaloni

♦ **get out 1** *v/i of car etc* scendere; *of prison* uscire; *get out!* fuori!; *let's get out of here* usciamo da qui; *I don't get out much these days* non esco molto in questi giorni **2** *v/t* (*extract: nail, something jammed*) tirare fuori; (*remove: stain*) mandare via; (*pull out: gun, pen*) tirare fuori

♦ **get over** *v/t fence, disappointment etc* superare; *lover etc* dimenticare

♦ **get over with** *v/t* togliersi; *let's get it over with* togliamocelo

♦ **get through** *v/i on telephone* prendere la linea; (*make self understood*) farsi capire; *get through to s.o.* (*make self understood*) farsi capire da qu; *I called you all day but I didn't manage to get through* ti ho chiamato tutto il giorno, ma era sempre occupato

♦ **get up 1** *v/i of person, wind* alzarsi **2** *v/t* (*climb: hill*) salire su

'get·a·way *from robbery* fuga *f*

'get·a·way car macchina *f* per la fuga

'get-to·geth·er ritrovo *m*

ghast·ly ['gɑːstlɪ] *adj colour, experience, person etc* orrendo; *you look ~* hai un aspetto orribile

gher·kin ['gɜːkɪn] cetriolino *m* sotto aceto

ghet·to ['getəʊ] ghetto *m*

ghost [gəʊst] fantasma *m*, spettro *m*

ghost·ly ['gəʊstlɪ] *adj* spettrale

'ghost town città *f inv* fantasma

ghoul [guːl] persona *f* morbosa

ghoul·ish ['guːlɪʃ] *adj* macabro

gi·ant ['dʒaɪənt] **1** *n* gigante *m* **2** *adj* gigante

gib·ber·ish ['dʒɪbərɪʃ] F bestialità fpl F

gibe [dʒaɪb] n frecciatina f

gib·lets ['dʒɪblɪts] npl frattaglie fpl (di volatili)

gid·di·ness ['gɪdɪnɪs] giramenti mpl di testa

gid·dy ['gɪdɪ] adj: **I feel ~** mi gira la testa

gift [gɪft] regalo m

gift·ed ['gɪftɪd] adj dotato

'gift to·ken, **'gift voucher** buono m d'acquisto

'gift·wrap 1 n carta f da regalo **2** v/t (pret & pp **-ped**) impacchettare; **would you like it ~ped?** le faccio un pacco regalo?

gig [gɪg] F concerto m

gi·ga·byte ['gɪgəbaɪt] COMPUT gigabyte m inv

gi·gan·tic [dʒaɪ'gæntɪk] adj gigante

gig·gle ['gɪgl] **1** v/i ridacchiare **2** n risatina f

gig·gly ['gɪglɪ] adj ridacchiante

gill [gɪl] of fish branchia f

gilt [gɪlt] n doratura f; **~s** FIN titoli mpl obbligazionari

gim·mick ['gɪmɪk] trovata f

gim·mick·y ['gɪmɪkɪ] adj appariscente

gin [dʒɪn] gin m inv; **~ and tonic** gin and tonic m inv

gin·ger ['dʒɪndʒə(r)] **1** n spice zenzero m **2** adj hair rosso carota; cat rosso

gin·ger 'beer bibita f allo zenzero

'gin·ger·bread pan m di zenzero

gin·ger·ly ['dʒɪndʒəlɪ] adv con cautela

gip·sy ['dʒɪpsɪ] zingaro m, -a f

gi·raffe [dʒɪ'rɑːf] giraffa f

gir·der ['gɜːdə(r)] n trave f

girl [gɜːl] ragazza f

'girl·friend of boy ragazza f; of girl amica f

girl 'guide giovane esploratrice f

girl·ie ['gɜːlɪ] adj F da femminuccia F

'girl·ie mag·a·zine pornographic rivista f per soli uomini

girl·ish ['gɜːlɪʃ] adj tipicamente femminile

gi·ro ['dʒaɪərəʊ] bonifico m

gist [dʒɪst] sostanza f

give [gɪv] v/t (pret **gave**, pp **given**) dare; present fare; (supply: electricity etc) fornire; talk, groan fare; party dare; pain, appetite far venire; **~ her my love** salutala da parte mia

♦ **give away** v/t as present regalare; (betray) tradire; **give o.s. away** tradirsi

♦ **give back** v/t restituire

♦ **give in 1** v/i surrender arrendersi **2** v/t (hand in) consegnare

♦ **give off** v/t smell, fumes emettere

♦ **give onto** v/t (open onto) dare su

♦ **give out 1** v/t leaflets etc distribuire **2** v/i of supplies, strength esaurirsi

♦ **give up 1** v/t smoking etc rinunciare a; **he gave up smoking** ha smesso di fumare; **give o.s. up to the police** consegnarsi alla polizia **2** v/i (cease habit) smettere; (stop making effort) lasciar perdere

♦ **give way** v/i of bridge etc cedere; MOT dare la precedenza

give-and-'take concessioni fpl reciproche

giv·en ['gɪvn] pp → **give**

'giv·en name nome m di battesimo

gla·ci·er ['glæsɪə(r)] ghiacciaio m

glad [glæd] adj contento

glad·ly ['glædlɪ] adv volentieri

glam·or Am → **glamour**

glam·or·ize ['glæməraɪz] v/t esaltare

glam·or·ous ['glæmərəs] adj affascinante

glam·our ['glæmə(r)] fascino m

glance [glɑːns] **1** n sguardo m; **at first ~** a prima vista **2** v/i dare un'occhiata o uno sguardo

♦ **glance at** v/t dare un'occhiata o uno sguardo a

gland [glænd] ghiandola f

glan·du·lar fe·ver ['glændjʊlə(r)] mononucleosi f

glare [gleə(r)] **1** n of sun, headlights luce f abbagliante **2** v/i of sun, headlights splendere di luce abbagliante

♦ **glare at** v/t guardare di storto

glar·ing ['gleərɪŋ] *adj mistake* lampante

glar·ing·ly ['gleərɪŋlɪ] *adv:* **be ~ obvious** essere più che ovvio

glass [glɑːs] *material* vetro *m*; *for drink* bicchiere *m*

glass 'case teca *f*

glasses *npl* occhiali *mpl*

'**glass·house** serra *f*

glaze [gleɪz] *n* smalto *m* trasparente

♦ **glaze over** *v/i of eyes* appannarsi

glazed [gleɪzd] *adj expression* assente

gla·zi·er ['gleɪzɪə(r)] vetraio *m*

glaz·ing ['gleɪzɪŋ] vetri *mpl*

gleam [gliːm] **1** *n* luccichio *m* **2** *v/i* luccicare

glee [gliː] allegria *f*

glee·ful ['gliːfʊl] *adj* allegro

glib [glɪb] *adj* poco convincente

glib·ly ['glɪblɪ] *adv* in modo poco convincente

glide [glaɪd] *v/i of skier, boat* scivolare; *of bird, plane* planare

glid·er ['glaɪdə(r)] aliante *m*

glid·ing ['glaɪdɪŋ] *n* SP volo *m* planato

glim·mer ['glɪmə(r)] **1** *n of light* barlume *m*; **~ of hope** barlume *m* di speranza **2** *v/i* emettere un barlume

glimpse [glɪmps] **1** *n* occhiata *f*; **catch a ~ of** intravedere **2** *v/t* intravedere

glint [glɪnt] **1** *n* luccichio *m* **2** *v/i of light, eyes* luccicare

glis·ten ['glɪsn] *v/i* scintillare

glit·ter ['glɪtə(r)] *v/i* brillare

glit·ter·ati *npl:* **the ~** il bel mondo

gloat [gləʊt] *v/i* gongolare

♦ **gloat over** *v/t* compiacersi di

glo·bal ['gləʊbl] *adj* (*worldwide*) mondiale; *without exceptions* globale

glo·bal e'con·o·my economia *f* mondiale

glo·bal 'mar·ket mercato *m* mondiale

glo·bal 'warm·ing effetto *m* serra

globe [gləʊb] globo *m*; *model of earth* mappamondo *m*

gloom [gluːm] (*darkness*) penombra

f; *mood* tristezza *f*

gloom·i·ly ['gluːmɪlɪ] *adv* tristemente

gloom·y ['gluːmɪ] *adj room* buio; *mood, person* triste; *day* grigio

glo·ri·ous ['glɔːrɪəs] *adj weather, day* splendido; *victory* glorioso

glo·ry ['glɔːrɪ] *n* gloria *f*; (*beauty*) splendore *m*

gloss [glɒs] *n* (*shine*) lucido *m*; (*general explanation*) glossa *f*

♦ **gloss over** *v/t* sorvolare su

glos·sa·ry ['glɒsərɪ] glossario *m*

'**gloss paint** vernice *f* lucida

gloss·y ['glɒsɪ] **1** *adj paper* patinato **2** *n magazine* rivista *f* femminile

glove [glʌv] guanto *m*

'**glove com·part·ment** *in car* cruscotto *m*

'**glove pup·pet** burattino *m*

glow [gləʊ] **1** *n of light, fire* bagliore *m*; *in cheeks* colorito *m* vivo; *of candle* luce *f* fioca **2** *v/i of light* brillare; *her cheeks* **~ed** è diventata rossa

glow·er ['glaʊə(r)] *v/i:* **~ at s.o.** guardare qu in cagnesco

glow·ing ['gləʊɪŋ] *adj description* entusiastico

glu·cose ['gluːkəʊs] glucosio *m*

glue [gluː] **1** *n* colla *f* **2** *v/t:* **~ sth to sth** incollare qc a qc; **be ~d to the TV** F essere incollato alla TV F

glum [glʌm] *adj* triste

glum·ly ['glʌmlɪ] *adv* tristemente

glut [glʌt] *n* eccesso *m*

glut·ton ['glʌtən] ghiottone *m*, -a *f*

glut·ton·y ['glʌtənɪ] ghiottoneria *f*

GMT [dʒiːem'tiː] *abbr* (= **Greenwich Mean Time**) ora *f* di Greenwich

gnarled [nɑːld] *adj branch, hands* nodoso

gnat [næt] moscerino *m*

gnaw [nɔː] *v/t bone* rosicchiare

GNP [dʒiːen'piː] *abbr* (= **gross national product**) PNL *m* (= prodotto *m* nazionale lordo)

go [gəʊ] **1** *n* (*try*) tentativo *m*; *it's my* **~** tocca a me, è il mio turno; **have a ~ at sth** (*try*) fare un tentativo in qc; (*complain about*) lamentarsi di qc;

be on the ~ essere indaffarato; **in one ~** *drink, write etc* tutto in una volta **2** *v/i* ◊ (*pret* **went**, *pp* **gone**) andare; (*leave: of train, plane*) partire; (*leave: of people*) andare via; (*work, function*) funzionare; (*become*) diventare; (*come out of: stain etc*) andare via; (*cease: of pain etc*) sparire; (*match: of colours etc*) stare bene insieme; ~ **shopping / jogging** andare a fare spese / andare a correre; **I must be ~ing** devo andare; **let's ~!** andiamo!; ~ **for a walk** andare a fare una passeggiata; ~ **to bed** andare a letto; ~ **to school** andare a scuola; **how's the work ~ing?** come va il lavoro?; **they're ~ing for £50** (*being sold at*) li vendono a £50; **be all gone** (*finished*) essere finito; **I've gone 15 miles** ho fatto 15 miglia; **there are two days to ~ before ...** mancano due giorni a ...; **the story ~es that ...** la storia dice che ...; **to ~** *Am food* da asporto ◊ *future* **I'm ~ing to meet him tomorrow** lo incontrerò domani; **it's ~ing to snow** sta per nevicare

♦ **go ahead** *v/i and do sth* andare avanti; **go ahead!** (*on you go*) fai pure!

♦ **go ahead with** *v/t plans etc* andare avanti con

♦ **go along with** *v/t suggestion* concordare con

♦ **go at** *v/t* (*attack*) scagliarsi contro

♦ **go away** *v/i of person, pain* andare via; *of rain* smettere

♦ **go back** *v/i* (*return*) ritornare; (*date back*) rimontare; **we go back a long way** ci conosciamo da una vita; **go back to sleep** tornare a dormire

♦ **go by** *v/i of car, people, time* passare

♦ **go down** *v/i* scendere; *of sun, ship* tramontare; *of ship* affondare; *of swelling* diminuire; **will it go down well with them?** la prenderanno bene?

♦ **go for** *v/t* (*attack*) attaccare; **I don't much go for gin** non vado matto per il gin; **she really goes for him** le

piace davvero

♦ **go in** *v/i to room, house* entrare; *of sun* andare via; (*fit: of part etc*) andare

♦ **go in for** *v/t competition, race* iscriversi a; (*like, take part in*) dedicarsi a

♦ **go off 1** *v/i* (*leave*) andarsene; *of bomb* esplodere; *of gun* sparare; *of alarm* scattare; *of light* spegnersi; *of milk etc* andare a male **2** *v/t* (*stop liking*) stufarsi di

♦ **go on** *v/i* (*continue*) andare avanti; (*happen*) succedere; **go on, do it!** encouraging dai, fallo!; **what's going on?** cosa sta succedendo?

♦ **go on at** *v/t* (*nag*) sgridare

♦ **go out** *v/i of person* uscire; *of light, fire* spegnersi

♦ **go out with** *v/t romantically* uscire con

♦ **go over** *v/t* (*check*) esaminare; (*do again*) rifare

♦ **go through** *v/t illness, hard times* passare; (*check*) controllare; (*read through*) leggere

♦ **go under** *v/i* (*sink*) affondare; *of company* fallire

♦ **go up** *v/i* salire

♦ **go without 1** *v/t food etc* fare a meno di **2** *v/i* farne a meno

goad [gəʊd] *v/t* spronare

'**go-a·head 1** *n* via libera *m*; **get the ~** avere il via libera **2** *adj* (*enterprising, dynamic*) intraprendente

goal [gəʊl] (*sport: target*) rete *f*; (*sport: points*) gol *m inv*; (*objective*) obiettivo *m*

goal·ie ['gəʊlɪ] F portiere *m*

'**goal·keep·er** portiere *m*; '**goal kick** rimessa *f*; '**goal·mouth** area *f* di porta; '**goal·post** palo *m*

goat [gəʊt] capra *f*

gob·ble ['gɒbl] *v/t* tranguggiare

♦ **gobble up** *v/t* tranguggiare

gob·ble·dy·gook ['gɒbldɪguːk] F linguaggio *m* incomprensibile

'**go-be·tween** mediatore *m*, -trice *f*

gob·smacked ['gɒbsmækt] *adj* P sbigottito

god [gɒd] dio *m*; **thank God!** grazie a Dio!; **oh God!** Dio mio!

'god·child figlioccio *m*, -a *f*

'god·daugh·ter figliaccia *f*

god·dess ['gɒdɪs] dea *f*

'god·fa·ther *also in mafia* padrino *m*;

'god·for·sak·en ['gɒdfəseɪkən] *adj place, town* dimenticato da Dio;

'god·moth·er madrina *f*; **'god·pa·rent** *man* padrino *m*; *woman* madrina *f*; **'god·send** benedizione *f*; **'god·son** figlioccio *m*

go·fer ['gəʊfə(r)] F galoppino *m*, -a *f* F

gog·gles ['gɒglz] *npl* occhialini *mpl*

go·ing ['gəʊɪŋ] *adj price etc* corrente; **~ concern** azienda *f* florida

go·ings-on [gəʊɪŋz'ɒn] *npl* vicende *fpl*

gold [gəʊld] **1** *n* oro *m* **2** *adj* d'oro

gold·en ['gəʊldn] *adj sky, hair* dorato

gold·en 'hand·shake buonuscita *f*

gold·en 'wed·ding (an·ni·ver·sa·ry) nozze *fpl* d'oro

'gold·fish pesce *m* rosso; **'gold mine** *fig* miniera *f* d'oro; **'gold·smith** orefice *m/f*

golf [gɒlf] golf *m*

golf ball palla *f* da golf; **'golf club** *organization* club *m inv* di golf; *stick* mazza *f* da golf; **'golf course** campo *m* di golf

golf·er ['gɒlfə(r)] giocatore *m*, -trice di golf

gon·do·la ['gɒndələ] gondola *f*

gon·do·lier [gɒndə'lɪə(r)] gondoliere *m*

gone [gɒn] *pp* → **go**

gong [gɒŋ] gong *m inv*

good [gʊd] **1** *adj* buono; *weather, film* bello; *actor, child* bravo; **a ~** many un bel po' (di); **be ~ at** essere bravo in; **be ~ for s.o.** fare bene a qu; **be ~ for sth** andare bene per qc; **~!** bene!; *it's ~ to see you* è bello vederti **2** *n* bene *m*; *it did him no ~* non gli ha fatto bene; *it did him a lot of ~* gli ha fatto molto bene; *what ~ is that to me?* a che cosa mi serve?; *the ~* il buono; *people* i buoni

good·bye [gʊd'baɪ] arrivederci; *say* **~ to s.o., wish s.o. ~** salutare qu

'good-for-nothing *n* buono *m*, -a *f* a nulla; **Good 'Fri·day** venerdì *m inv* santo; **good-hu·mored** *Am*, **good-hu·moured** [gʊd'hju:məd] *adj* di buon umore; **good-'look·ing** [gʊd'lʊkɪŋ] *adj* attraente; **good-na·tured** [gʊd'neɪtʃəd] di buon cuore

good·ness ['gʊdnɪs] bontà *f*; *thank* **~!** grazie al cielo

goods [gʊdz] *npl* COM merce *fsg*

good·will buona volontà *f*

good·y-good·y ['gʊdɪgʊdɪ] *n* F santarellino *m*, -a *f* F

goo·ey ['gu:ɪ] *adj* appiccicoso

goof [gu:f] *v/i* F fare una gaffe

goose [gu:s] (*pl* **geese** [gi:s]) oca *f*

goose·ber·ry ['gʊzbərɪ] uva *f* spina

'goose pim·ples *npl* pelle *f* d'oca

gorge [gɔ:dʒ] **1** *n* gola *f* **2** *v/t*: **~ o.s. on sth** strafogarsi di qc

gor·geous ['gɔ:dʒəs] *adj* stupendo; *smell* ottimo

go·ril·la [gə'rɪlə] gorilla *m*

gosh [gɒʃ] *int* caspita

go-'slow sciopero *m* bianco

Gos·pel ['gɒspl] *in Bible* vangelo *m*

'gos·pel truth sacrosanta verità *f inv*

gos·sip ['gɒsɪp] **1** *n* pettegolezzo *m*; *person* pettegolo *m*, -a *f* **2** *v/i* spettegolare

'gos·sip col·umn cronaca *f* rosa

'gos·sip col·umn·ist giornalista *m/f* di cronaca rosa

gossipy ['gɒsɪpɪ] *adj letter* pieno di chiacchiere

got [gɒt] *pret & pp* → **get**

gour·met ['gʊəmeɪ] *n* buongustaio *m*, -a *f*

gov·ern ['gʌvn] *v/t country* governare

gov·ern·ment ['gʌvnmənt] governo *m*

gov·er·nor ['gʌvənə(r)] governatore *m*

gown [gaʊn] (*long dress*) abito *m* lungo; (*wedding dress*) abito *m* da sposa; *of academic, judge* toga *f*; *of surgeon* camice *m*

grate

GP [dʒiː'piː] *abbr* (= *General Practitioner*) medico *m* generico

grab [græb] *v/t* (*pret & pp -bed*) afferrare; *~ a bite to eat* fare uno spuntino rapido; *~ some sleep* farsi una dormita

grace [greɪs] *of dancer etc* grazia *f*; *before meals* preghiera *f* (prima di un pasto)

grace·ful ['greɪsfʊl] *adj* aggraziato

grace·ful·ly ['greɪsfʊlɪ] *adv move* con grazia

gra·cious ['greɪʃəs] *adj person* cortese; *style* elegante; *living* agiato; *good ~!* santo cielo!

grade [greɪd] **1** *n* (*quality*) qualità *f inv*; EDU voto *m* **2** *v/t* classificare

'grade school *Am* scuola *f* elementare

gra·di·ent ['greɪdɪənt] pendenza *f*

grad·u·al ['grædʒʊəl] *adj* graduale

grad·u·al·ly ['grædʒʊəlɪ] *adv* gradualmente

grad·u·ate ['grædʒʊət] **1** *n* laureato *m*, -a *f* **2** *v/i from university* laurearsi

grad·u·a·tion [grædʒʊ'eɪʃn] laurea *f*; *ceremony* cerimonia *f* di laurea

graf·fi·ti [grə'fiːtiː] graffiti *mpl*

graft [grɑːft] **1** *n* BOT innesto *m*; MED trapianto *m*; F (*hard work*) duro lavoro *m* **2** *v/t* BOT innestare; MED trapiantare

grain [greɪn] cereali *mpl*; *seed* granello *m*; *of rice, wheat* chicco *m*; *in wood* venatura *f*; *go against the ~* essere contro natura

gram [græm] grammo *m*

gram·mar ['græmə(r)] grammatica *f*

'gram·mar school liceo *m*

gram·mat·i·cal [grə'mætɪkl] *adj* grammaticale

gram·mat·i·cal·ly *adv* grammaticalmente

grand [grænd] **1** *adj* grandioso; F (*very good*) eccezionale **2** *n* F (*£1000*) mille sterline *fpl*

'grand·dad ['grændæd] nonno *m*

'grand·child nipote *m/f*

'grand·daugh·ter nipote *f*

gran·deur ['grændʒə(r)] grandiosità *f*

'grand·fa·ther nonno *m*

'grand·fa·ther clock pendolo *m*

gran·di·ose ['grændɪəʊs] *adj* grandioso

'grand·ma F nonna *f*; **'grand·moth·er** nonna *f*; **'grand·pa** F nonno *m*; **'grand·par·ents** *npl* nonni *mpl*; **grand pi'an·o** pianoforte *m* a coda; **grand 'slam** grande slam *m inv*; **'grand·son** nipote *m*; **'grand·stand** tribuna *f*

gran·ite ['grænɪt] granito *m*

gran·ny ['grænɪ] F nonna *f*

'gran·ny flat appartamento *m* annesso

grant [grɑːnt] **1** *n money* sussidio *m*; *for university* borsa *f* di studio **2** *v/t visa* assegnare; *permission* concedere; *request, wish* esaudire; *take sth for ~ed* dare qc per scontato; *he takes his wife for ~ed* considera quello che fa sua moglie come dovuto

gran·ule ['grænjuːl] granello *m*

grape [greɪp] acino *m* d'uva; *~s* uva *fsg*

'grape·fruit pompelmo *m*; **'grape·fruit juice** succo *m* di pompelmo; **'grape·vine**: *I heard on the ~ that ...* ho sentito dire che ...

graph [grɑːf] grafico *m*

graph·ic ['græfɪk] **1** *adj* grafico; (*vivid*) vivido **2** *n* COMPUT grafico *m*; *~s* grafica *f*

graph·i·cal·ly ['græfɪklɪ] *adv describe* in modo vivido

graph·ic de'sign·er grafico *m*, -a *f*

♦ **grap·ple with** ['græpl] *v/t attacker* lottare con; *problem etc* essere alle prese con

grasp [grɑːsp] **1** *n physical* presa *f*; *mental* comprensione *f* **2** *v/t physically, mentally* afferrare

grass [grɑːs] *n* erba *f*

'grass·hop·per cavalletta *f*; **grass roots** *npl people* massa *f* popolare; **grass 'wid·ow** donna *f* il cui marito è spesso assente; **grass 'wid·ow·er** uomo *m* la cui moglie è spesso assente

gras·sy ['grɑːsɪ] *adj* erboso

grate¹ [greɪt] *n metal* grata *f*

grate² [greɪt] **1** v/t in cooking grattugiare **2** v/i of sounds stridere

grate·ful ['greɪtfʊl] adj grato; **be ~ to s.o.** essere grato a qu

grate·ful·ly ['greɪtfʊlɪ] adv con gratitudine

grat·er ['greɪtə(r)] grattugia f

grat·i·fy ['grætɪfaɪ] v/t (pret & pp **-ied**) soddisfare

grat·ing ['greɪtɪŋ] **1** n grata f **2** adj sound, voice stridente

grat·i·tude ['grætɪtjuːd] gratitudine f

gra·tu·i·tous [grə'tjuːɪtəs] adj gratuito

gra·tu·i·ty [grə'tjuːətɪ] (tip) mancia f

grave¹ [greɪv] n tomba f

grave² [greɪv] adj (serious) grave

grav·el ['grævl] n ghiaia f

'grave·stone lapide f

'grave·yard cimitero m

◆ **grav·i·tate towards** ['grævɪteɪt] v/t gravitare intorno a

grav·i·ty ['grævətɪ] PHYS forza f di gravità

gra·vy ['greɪvɪ] sugo m della carne

gray Am → **grey**

graze¹ [greɪz] v/i of cow, horse brucare

graze² [greɪz] **1** v/t arm etc graffiare **2** n graffio m

grease [griːs] n grasso m

grease-proof 'pa·per carta f oleata

greas·y ['griːsɪ] adj food, hair, skin grasso; hands, plate unto

great [greɪt] adj grande; F (very good) fantastico; **~ to see you!** sono contento di vederti!

Great 'Brit·ain Gran Bretagna f; **great-'grand·child** pronipote m/f; **great-'grand·daugh·ter** pronipote f; **great-'grand·fa·ther** bisnonno m; **great-'grand·moth·er** bisnonna f; **great-'grand·par·ents** npl bisnonni mpl; **great-'grand·son** pronipote m

great·ly ['greɪtlɪ] adv molto

great·ness ['greɪtnɪs] grandezza f

Greece [griːs] Grecia f

greed [griːd] avidità f; for food ingordigia f

greed·i·ly ['griːdɪlɪ] adv con avidità; eat con ingordigia

greed·y ['griːdɪ] adj avido; for food ingordo

Greek [griːk] **1** n greco m, -a f; language greco m **2** adj greco

green [griːn] adj verde; environmentally ecologico; **the Greens** POL i verdi

green 'beans npl fagiolini mpl; **'green belt** zona f verde tutt'intorno ad una città; **'green card** driving insurance carta f verde; **green 'fin·gers: have ~** avere il pollice verde; **'green·gro·cer** fruttivendolo m, -a f; **'green·horn** F pivello m, -a f F; **'green·house** serra f; **'green·house ef·fect** effetto m serra; **'green·house gas** gas m inv inquinante; **green 'pep·per** vegetable peperone m

greens [griːnz] npl verdura f

greet [griːt] v/t salutare

greet·ing ['griːtɪŋ] saluto m

'greet·ings card biglietto m d'auguri

gre·gar·i·ous [grɪ'geərɪəs] adj person socievole

gre·nade [grɪ'neɪd] granata f

grew [gruː] pret → **grow**

grey [greɪ] adj grigio; hair bianco; **be going ~** cominciare ad avere i capelli grigi

grey-haired [greɪ'heəd] adj con i capelli bianchi

'grey·hound levriero m

grid [grɪd] grata f; on map reticolato m

'grid·lock in traffic ingorgo m

grief [griːf] dolore m

grief-strick·en ['griːfstrɪkn] adj addolorato

griev·ance ['griːvəns] rimostranza f

grieve [griːv] v/i essere addolorato; **~ for s.o.** essere addolorato per qu

grill [grɪl] **1** n for cooking grill m inv; metal frame griglia f; dish grigliata f; on window grata f **2** v/t food fare alla griglia; (interrogate) mettere sotto torchio

grille [grɪl] grata f

grim [grɪm] *adj* cupo; *determination* accanito

gri·mace ['grɪməs] *n* smorfia *f*

grime [graɪm] sporcizia *f*

grim·ly ['grɪmlɪ] *adv* con aria grave

grim·y ['graɪmɪ] *adj* sudicio

grin [grɪn] **1** *n* sorriso *m* **2** *v/i* (*pret & pp -ned*) sorridere

grind [graɪnd] *v/t* (*pret & pp ground*) *coffee, meat* macinare; **~ one's teeth** digrignare i denti

grip [grɪp] **1** *n on rope etc* presa *f*; *he's losing his* ~ *losing skills* sta perdendo dei colpi; *get to* ~*s with sth* affrontare qc **2** *v/t* (*pret & pp -ped*) afferrare; *of brakes* fare presa su; *be* ~*ped by sth* *by panic* essere preso da qc

gripe [graɪp] **1** *n* lamentela *f* **2** *v/i* lamentarsi

grip·ping ['grɪpɪŋ] *adj* avvincente

gris·tle ['grɪsl] cartilagine *f*

grit [grɪt] **1** *n* (*dirt*) granelli *mpl*; *for roads* sabbia *f* **2** *v/t* (*pret & pp -ted*): ~ *one's teeth* stringere i denti

grit·ty ['grɪtɪ] *adj* F *book, film etc* realistico

groan [grəʊn] **1** *n* gemito *m* **2** *v/i* gemere

gro·cer ['grəʊsə(r)] droghiere *m*; *at the* ~*'s* (*shop*) dal droghiere

gro·cer·ies ['grəʊsərɪz] *npl* generi *mpl* alimentari

gro·cer·y store ['grəʊsərɪ] drogheria *f*

grog·gy ['grɒgɪ] *adj* F intontito

groin [grɔɪn] ANAT inguine *m*

groom [gruːm] **1** *n for bride* sposo *m*; *for horse* stalliere *m* **2** *v/t horse* strigliare; (*train, prepare*) preparare; *well* ~*ed in appearance* ben curato

groove [gruːv] scanalatura *f*

grope [grəʊp] **1** *v/i in the dark* brancolare **2** *v/t sexually* palpeggiare
♦ **grope for** *v/t door handle* cercare a tastoni; *the right word* cercare di trovare

gross [grəʊs] *adj* (*coarse, vulgar*) volgare; *exaggeration* madornale; FIN lordo

gross do·mes·tic 'prod·uct pro-

dotto *m* interno lordo

gross na·tion·al 'prod·uct prodotto *m* nazionale lordo

grot·ty ['grɒtɪ] *adj* F *street, flat* squallido; *I feel* ~ sto da schifo F

ground¹ [graʊnd] **1** *n* suolo *m*; (*area, for sport*) terreno *m*; (*reason*) motivo *m*, ragione *f*; ELEC terra *f*; *on the* ~ per terra; *on the* ~*s of* a causa di **2** *v/t* ELEC mettere a terra

ground² [graʊnd] *pret & pp → grind*

'ground con·trol controllo *m* da terra; '**ground crew** personale *m* di terra; '**ground floor** pianoterra *m inv*

ground·ing ['graʊndɪŋ] *in subject* basi *fpl*; *have a good* ~ *in* avere delle buone basi di

ground·less ['graʊndlɪs] *adj* infondato; '**ground plan** pianta *f* del piano terra; '**ground staff** SP personale *m* addetto alla manutenzione dei campi sportivi; *at airport* personale *m* di terra; '**ground·work** lavoro *m* di preparazione

group [gruːp] **1** *n* gruppo *m* **2** *v/t* raggruppare

group·ie ['gruːpɪ] F *ragazza f che segue un gruppo o cantante rock in tutti i concerti*

group 'ther·a·py terapia *f* di gruppo

grouse¹ [graʊs] (*pl grouse*) *bird* gallo *m* cedrone

grouse² [graʊs] **1** *n* F lamentela *f* **2** *v/i* F brontolare

grov·el ['grɒvl] *v/i fig* umiliarsi

grow [grəʊ] (*pret grew, pp grown*) **1** *v/i of child, animal, plant* crescere; *of number, amount* aumentare; *of business* svilupparsi; *let one's hair* ~ farsi crescere i capelli; ~ *old / tired* invecchiare / stancarsi; ~ *into sth* diventare qc **2** *v/t flowers* coltivare
♦ **grow up** *of person* crescere; *of city* svilupparsi; *grow up!* comportati da adulto!

growl [graʊl] **1** *n* grugnito *m* **2** *v/i* ringhiare

grown [grəʊn] *pp → grow*

grown-up ['grəʊnʌp] **1** *n* adulto *m*, -a *f* **2** *adj* adulto

growth [grəʊθ] *of person* crescita *f*; *of company* sviluppo *m*; (*increase*) aumento *m*; MED tumore *m*

grub[1] [grʌb] *of insect* larva *f*

grub[2] [grʌb] F (*food*) mangiare *m*

grub·by ['grʌbɪ] *adj* sporco

grudge [grʌdʒ] **1** *n* rancore *m*; **bear s.o. a ~** portare rancore a qu **2** *v/t* dare a malincuore; **~ s.o. sth** invidiare qc a qu

grudg·ing ['grʌdʒɪŋ] *adj* riluttante

grudg·ing·ly ['grʌdʒɪŋlɪ] *adv* a malincuore

gru·el·ing *Am*, **gru·el·ling** ['gruːəlɪŋ] *adj climb, task* estenuante

gruff [grʌf] *adj* burbero

grum·ble ['grʌmbl] *v/i* brontolare

grum·bler ['grʌmblə(r)] brontolone *m*, -a *f*

grump·y ['grʌmpɪ] *adj* scontroso

grunt [grʌnt] **1** *n* grugnito *m* **2** *v/i* grugnire

guar·an·tee [gærən'tiː] **1** *n* garanzia *f*; **~ period** periodo *m* di garanzia **2** *v/t* garantire

guar·an·tor [gærən'tɔː(r)] garante *m*

guard [gɑːd] **1** *n* guardia *m*; **be on one's ~ against** stare in guardia contro **2** *v/t* fare la guardia a

◆ **guard against** *v/t* guardarsi da

'guard dog cane *m* da guardia

guard·ed ['gɑːdɪd] *adj reply* cauto

guard·i·an ['gɑːdɪən] LAW tutore *m*, -trice *f*

guard·i·an 'an·gel angelo *m* custode

guer·ril·la [gə'rɪlə] guerrigliero *m*, -a *f*

guer·ril·la 'war·fare guerriglia *f*

guess [ges] **1** *n* supposizione *f*; *I give you three ~es* ti do tre possibilità di indovinare **2** *v/t the answer* indovinare; *I ~ so* suppongo di sì; *I ~ not* suppongo di no **3** *v/i correctly* indovinare; *I was just ~ing* ho tirato a indovinare

'guess·work congettura *f*

guest [gest] ospite *m/f*

'guest·house pensione *f*

'guest·room camera *f* degli ospiti

guf·faw [gʌ'fɔː] **1** *n* sghignazzata *f* **2** *v/i* sghignazzare

guid·ance ['gaɪdəns] consigli *mpl*

guide [gaɪd] **1** *n person, book* guida *f* **2** *v/t* guidare

'guide·book guida *f* turistica

guid·ed 'mis·sile ['gaɪdɪd] missile *m* guidato

'guide dog cane *m* per ciechi

guid·ed 'tour visita *f* guidata

'guide·lines ['gaɪdlaɪnz] *npl* direttive *fpl*

guilt [gɪlt] colpa *f*; LAW colpevolezza *f*

guilt·y ['gɪltɪ] *adj also* LAW colpevole; *have a ~ conscience* avere la coscienza sporca

guin·ea pig ['gɪnɪpɪg] porcellino *m* d'india; *for experiments, fig* cavia *f*

guise [gaɪz]: *under the ~ of* dietro la maschera di

gui·tar [gɪ'tɑː(r)] chitarra *f*

gui'tar case custodia *f* della chitarra

gui·tar·ist [gɪ'tɑːrɪst] chitarrista *m/f*

gui'tar play·er chitarrista *m/f*

gulf [gʌlf] golfo *m*; *fig* divario *m*; **the Gulf** il Golfo

gull [gʌl] *n bird* gabbiano *m*

gul·let ['gʌlɪt] ANAT esofago *m*

gul·li·ble ['gʌlɪbl] *adj* credulone

gulp [gʌlp] **1** *n of water* sorso *m*; *of air* boccata *f* **2** *v/i in surprise* deglutire

◆ **gulp down** *v/t drink* ingoiare; *food* trangugiare

gum[1] [gʌm] *in mouth* gengiva *f*

gum[2] [gʌm] *n* (*glue*) colla *f*; (*chewing gum*) gomma *f*

gump·tion ['gʌmpʃn] F sale *m* in zucca F

gun [gʌn] *pistol, revolver, rifle* arma *f* da fuoco; (*cannon*) cannone *m*

◆ **gun down** *v/t* (*pret & pp* -**ned**) sparare a morte a

'gun·fire spari *mpl*; **'gun·man** uomo *m* armato; *robber* rapinatore *m*; **'gun·point**: *at ~* con un'arma puntata addosso; **'gun·shot** sparo *m*; **'gun·shot wound** ferita *f* da arma da fuoco

gur·gle ['gɜːgl] *v/i of baby, drain* gorgogliare

gu·ru ['guru] *fig* guru *m inv*

gush [gʌʃ] *v/i of liquid* sgorgare

gush·y ['gʌʃɪ] *adj* F (*enthusiastic*)

iper-entusiastico

gust [gʌst] raffica *f*

gus·to ['gʌstəu]: **with ~** con slancio

gust·y ['gʌstɪ] *of weather* ventoso; *~ wind* vento a raffiche

gut [gʌt] **1** *n* intestino *m*; F *(stomach)* pancia *f* **2** *v/t* (*pret & pp* **-ted**) *(destroy)* sventrare

guts [gʌts] *npl* F *(courage)* fegato *m* F

guts·y ['gʌtsɪ] *adj* F *person* che ha fegato; F *thing to do* che richiede fegato

gut·ter ['gʌtə(r)] *on pavement* canaletto *m* di scolo; *on roof* grondaia *f*

'**gut·ter-press** *pej* stampa *f* scandalistica

guv [gʌv] F capo *m*, -a *f* F

guy [gaɪ] F tipo *m* F; *hey, you ~s* ei, gente

guz·zle ['gʌzl] *v/t* ingozzarsi di

gym [dʒɪm] palestra *f*; *(activity)* ginnastica *f*

'**gym class** educazione *f* fisica

gym·na·si·um [dʒɪm'neɪzɪəm] palestra *f*

gym·nast ['dʒɪmnæst] ginnasta *m/f*

gym·nas·tics [dʒɪm'næstɪks] *nsg* ginnastica *f*

'**gym shoes** *npl* scarpe *fpl* da ginnastica

'**gym teacher** insegnante *m/f* di educazione fisica

gy·ne·col·o·gy *etc* Am → **gynaecology** *etc*

gy·nae·col·o·gy [gaɪnɪ'kɒlədʒɪ] ginecologia *f*

gy·nae·col·o·gist [gaɪnɪ'kɒlədʒɪst] ginecologo *m*, -a *f*

gyp·sy ['dʒɪpsɪ] zingaro *m*, -a *f*

H

hab·it ['hæbɪt] abitudine *f*; *get into the ~ of doing sth* prendere l'abitudine di fare qc

hab·it·a·ble ['hæbɪtəbl] *adj* abitabile

hab·i·tat ['hæbɪtæt] habitat *m inv*

ha·bit·u·al [hə'bɪtjʊəl] *adj* solito; *smoker, drinker* incallito

hack [hæk] *n (poor writer)* scribacchino *m*

hack·er ['hækə(r)] COMPUT hacker *m/f inv*

hack·neyed ['hæknɪd] *adj* trito

had [hæd] *pret & pp* → **have**

had·dock ['hædək] haddock *m inv*

haem·or·rhage ['hemərɪdʒ] **1** *n* emorragia *f* **2** *v/i* avere un'emorragia

hag·gard ['hægəd] *adj* tirato

hag·gle ['hægl] *v/i* contrattare

hail [heɪl] *n* grandine *f*

'**hail·stone** chicco *m* di grandine

'**hail·storm** grandinata *f*

hair [heə(r)] capelli *mpl*; *single* capello *m*; *on body, of animal* pelo *m*

'**hair·brush** spazzola *f* per capelli; '**hair·cut** taglio *m* di capelli; '**hair·do** F pettinatura *f*; '**hair·dress·er** parrucchiere *m*, -a *f*; *at the ~'s* dal parrucchiere; '**hair·dri·er**, '**hair·dry·er** fon *m inv*

hair·less ['heəlɪs] *adj* glabro

'**hair·pin** forcina *f*; **hair·pin 'bend** tornante *m*; **hair-rais·ing** ['heəreɪzɪŋ] *adj* terrificante; **hair re·mov·er** [heərɪ'muːvə(r)] crema *f* depilatoria

'**hair's breadth** *fig: by a ~* per un pelo

hair-split·ting ['heəsplɪtɪŋ] *n* pedanteria *f*; '**hair spray** lacca *f* per capelli; '**hair·style** acconciatura *f*; '**hair·styl·ist** parrucchiere *m*, -a *f*

hair·y ['heərɪ] *adj arm, animal* peloso; F *(frightening)* preoccupante

half [hɑːf] **1** *n* (*pl* **halves** [hɑːvz])

metà f inv, mezzo m; **~ past ten** le dieci e mezza; **~ an hour** mezz'ora; **~ a pound** mezza libbra; **go halves with s.o. on sth** fare a metà di qc con qu **2** adj mezzo **3** adv a metà

half-heart·ed [hɑːfˈhɑːtɪd] adj poco convinto; **half 'term** vacanza f a metà trimestre; **half 'time 1** n SP intervallo m **2** adj: **~job** lavoro a metà giornata; **~score** risultato alla fine del primo tempo; **half'way 1** adj stage, point intermedio **2** adv also fig a metà strada; **~finished** fatto a metà

hall [hɔːl] large room sala f; hallway in house ingresso m

Hal·low·e·en [hæləʊiːn] vigilia f d'Ognissanti

halo ['heɪləʊ] aureola f

halt [hɔːlt] **1** v/i fermarsi **2** v/t fermare **3** n: **come to a ~** arrestarsi

halve [hɑːv] v/t dimezzare

ham [hæm] prosciutto m

ham·burg·er [ˈhæmbɜːɡə(r)] hamburger m inv

ham·mer ['hæmə(r)] **1** n martello m **2** v/i martellare; **~ at the door** picchiare alla porta

ham·mock [ˈhæmək] amaca f

ham·per[1] [ˈhæmpə(r)] n for food cestino m

ham·per[2] [ˈhæmpə(r)] v/t (obstruct) ostacolare

ham·ster [ˈhæmstə(r)] criceto m

hand [hænd] n mano m; of clock lancetta f; (worker) operaio m; **at ~, to ~** a portata di mano; **at first ~** di prima mano; **by ~** a mano; **on the one ~ ..., on the other ~ ...** da un lato ..., dall'altro ...; **in ~** (being done) in corso; **on your right ~** sulla tua destra; **~s off!** giù le mani!; **~s up!** mani in alto!; **change ~s** cambiare di mano; **give s.o. a ~** dare una mano a qu
♦ **hand down** v/t passare
♦ **hand in** v/t consegnare
♦ **hand on** v/t passare
♦ **hand out** v/t distribuire
♦ **hand over** v/t consegnare; child to parent etc dare

'hand·bag borsetta f; **'hand·book** manuale m; **'hand·brake** freno m a mano; **'hand·cuff** v/t ammanettare; **hand·cuffs** [ˈhæn(d)kʌfs] npl manette fpl

hand·i·cap [ˈhændɪkæp] handicap m inv

hand·i·capped [ˈhændɪkæpt] adj also fig handicappato

hand·i·craft [ˈhændɪkrɑːft] artigianato m

hand·i·work [ˈhændɪwɜːk] opera f

hand·ker·chief [ˈhæŋkətʃɪf] fazzoletto m

han·dle [ˈhændl] **1** n maniglia f **2** v/t goods maneggiare; case, deal trattare; difficult person prendere; **let me ~ this** lascia fare a me; **be able to ~ s.o.** saperci fare con qu

han·dle·bars [ˈhændlbɑːz] npl manubrio msg

'hand lug·gage bagaglio m a mano; **hand·made** [hæn(d)ˈmeɪd] adj fatto a mano; **'hand·rail** corrimano m inv; **'hand·shake** stretta f di mano

hands-off [hændzˈɒf] adj approach teorico; **he has a ~ style of management** non partecipa direttamente agli aspetti pratici della gestione

hand·some [ˈhænsəm] adj bello

hands-on [hændzˈɒn] adj experience pratico; **he has a ~ style of management** partecipa direttamente agli aspetti pratici della gestione

'hand·writ·ing calligrafia f

hand·writ·ten [ˈhændrɪtn] adj scritto a mano

hand·y [ˈhændɪ] adj tool, device pratico; **it's ~ for the shops** è comodo per i negozi; **it might come in ~** potrebbe tornare utile

hang [hæŋ] **1** v/t (pret & pp hung) picture appendere; person (pret & pp hanged) impiccare **2** v/i (pret & pp hung) of dress, hair cadere; **his coat was ~ing behind the door** il suo cappotto era appeso dietro la porta **3** n: **get the ~ of** F capire
♦ **hang about** v/i on streets gironzolare; **hang about a minute!** F un attimo!

◆ hang on v/i (wait) aspettare

◆ hang on to v/t (keep) tenere

◆ hang up v/i TELEC riattaccare

han·gar ['hæŋə(r)] hangar m inv

hang·er ['hæŋə(r)] for clothes gruccia f

hang glid·er ['hæŋglaɪdə(r)] deltaplano m

hang glid·ing ['hæŋglaɪdɪŋ] deltaplano m

'hang·o·ver postumi mpl della sbornia

◆ hanker after ['hæŋkə(r)] v/t desiderare

han·kie, han·ky ['hæŋkɪ] F fazzoletto m

hap·haz·ard [hæp'hæzəd] adj a casaccio

hap·pen ['hæpn] v/i succedere; if you ~ to see him se ti capita di vederlo; what has ~ed to you? cosa ti è successo?

◆ happen across v/t trovare per caso

hap·pen·ing ['hæpnɪŋ] avvenimento m

hap·pi·ly ['hæpɪlɪ] adv allegramente; (gladly) volentieri; (luckily) per fortuna

hap·pi·ness ['hæpɪnɪs] felicità f inv

hap·py ['hæpɪ] adj felice

hap·py-go-'luck·y adj spensierato

'hap·py hour orario m in cui le consumazioni costano meno

har·ass [hə'ræs] v/t tormentare; sexually molestare

har·assed [hər'æst] adj stressato

har·ass·ment [hə'ræsmənt] persecuzione f; sexual ~ molestie fpl sessuali

har·bor Am, har·bour ['haːbə(r)] 1 n porto m 2 v/t criminal dar rifugio a; grudge covare

hard [haːd] adj duro; (difficult) difficile; facts, evidence concreto; drug pesante; ~ of hearing duro d'orecchio

'hard·back n libro m con copertina rigida; hard-boiled [haːd'bɔɪld] adj egg sodo; 'hard cop·y copia f stampata; 'hard core n (pornography)

pornografia f hard-core; hard 'cur·ren·cy valuta f forte; hard 'disk hard disk m inv

hard·en ['haːdn] 1 v/t indurire 2 v/i of glue indurirsi; of attitude irrigidirsi

'hard hat casco m; (construction worker) muratore m; hard·head·ed [haːd'hedɪd] adj pratico; hard-heart·ed [haːd'haːtɪd] adj dal cuore duro; hard 'line linea f dura; hard-'lin·er sostenitore m, -trice f della linea dura

hard·ly ['haːdlɪ] adv a malapena; ~ ever quasi mai; you can ~ expect him to ... non puoi certo aspettarti che lui ...; ~/ ci crederebbe!

hard·ness ['haːdnɪs] durezza f; (difficulty) difficoltà f inv

hard·'sell tecnica f aggressiva di vendita

hard·ship ['haːdʃɪp] difficoltà fpl economiche

hard 'shoul·der corsia f di emergenza; hard 'up adj al verde; 'hard·ware ferramenta fpl; COMPUT hardware m inv; 'hard·ware store negozio m di ferramenta; hard·work·ing [haːd'wəːkɪŋ] adj che lavora duro

har·dy ['haːdɪ] adj resistente

hare [heə(r)] lepre f

hare·brained ['heəbreɪnd] adj pazzo

harm [haːm] 1 n danno m; it wouldn't do any ~ to ... non sarebbe una cattiva idea ... 2 v/t danneggiare

harm·ful ['haːmfʊl] adj dannoso

harm·less ['haːmlɪs] adj innocuo

har·mo·ni·ous [haː'məʊnɪəs] adj armonioso

har·mo·nize ['haːmənaɪz] v/i armonizzare

har·mo·ny ['haːmənɪ] armonia f

harp [haːp] n arpa f

◆ harp on about v/t F menarsela su F

har·poon [haː'puːn] arpione m

harsh [haːʃ] adj criticism, words duro; colour, light troppo forte

harsh·ly ['haːʃlɪ] adv duramente

har·vest ['haːvɪst] n raccolto m

H

hash [hæʃ] n F: **make a ~ of** fare un pasticcio di

hash·ish [ˈhæʃiːʃ] hashish m inv

'hash mark cancelletto m

haste [heɪst] n fretta f

has·ten [ˈheɪsn] v/i: **to do sth** affrettarsi a fare qc

hast·i·ly [ˈheɪstɪlɪ] adv in fretta

hast·y [ˈheɪstɪ] adj frettoloso

hat [hæt] cappello m

hatch [hætʃ] n for serving food passa-vivande m inv; on ship boccaporto m

♦ hatch out v/i of eggs schiudersi

hatch·et [ˈhætʃɪt] ascia f; **bury the ~** seppellire l'ascia di guerra

hate [heɪt] 1 n odio m 2 v/t odiare

ha·tred [ˈheɪtrɪd] odio m

haugh·ty [ˈhɔːtɪ] adj altezzoso

haul [hɔːl] 1 n of fish pescata f 2 v/t (pull) trascinare

haul·age [ˈhɔːlɪdʒ] autotrasporto m

'haul·age com·pa·ny impresa f di autotrasporto

haul·i·er [ˈhɔːlɪə(r)] autotrasporta-tore m

haunch [hɔːntʃ] anca f

haunt [hɔːnt] 1 v/t: this place is ~ed questo posto è infestato dai fanta-smi 2 n ritrovo m

haunt·ing [ˈhɔːntɪŋ] adj tune indi-menticabile

have [hæv] (pret & pp had) 1 v/t ◊ avere; breakfast, shower fare; **can I ~ ...?** posso avere ...?; **I'll ~ a coffee** prendo un caffè; **~ lunch/dinner** pranzare/cenare; **do you ~ ...?** ha ...? ◊ must: ~ (got) to dovere; **I ~ (got) to go** devo andare ◊ causative: **~ sth done** far fare qc; **I had the printer fixed** ho fatto riparare la stampante; **I had my hair cut** mi sono tagliata i capelli 2 v/aux avere; with verbs of motion essere; **~ you seen her?** l'hai vista?; **I ~ come** sono venuto

♦ have back v/t: when can I have it back? quando posso riaverlo?

♦ have on v/t (wear) portare, indos-sare; **do you have anything on tonight?** (have planned) hai pro-grammi per stasera?

ha·ven [ˈheɪvn] fig oasi f inv

hav·oc [ˈhævək] caos m inv; **play ~ with** scombussolare

hawk [hɔːk] also fig falco m

hay [heɪ] fieno m

'hay fe·ver raffreddore m da fieno

hay stack pagliaio m

haz·ard [ˈhæzəd] n rischio m

'haz·ard lights npl MOT luci fpl di emergenza

haz·ard·ous [ˈhæzədəs] adj rischioso

haze [heɪz] foschia f

ha·zel [ˈheɪzl] n (tree) nocciolo m

'ha·zel·nut nocciola f

haz·y [ˈheɪzɪ] adj view, image indistin-to; memories vago; **I'm a bit ~ about it** non ne sono certo

he [hiː] pron lui; ~'s French è france-se; you're funny, ~'s not tu sei spiri-toso, lui no; there ~ is eccolo

head [hed] 1 n testa f; (boss, leader) capo m; of primary school direttore m, -trice f; of secondary school presi-de m/f; on beer schiuma f; of nail capocchia f; of queue, line inizio m; of tape recorder testina f; **£15 a ~** 15 sterline a testa; **~s or tails?** testa o croce?; **at the ~ of the list** in cima alla lista; **~ over heels** fall a capofit-to; **~ over heels in love** pazzamente innamorato; lose one's ~ (go crazy) perdere la testa 2 v/t (lead) essere a capo di; ball colpire di testa

'head·ache mal m di testa

'head·band fascia f per i capelli

head·er [ˈhedə(r)] in soccer colpo m di testa; in document intestazione f

'head·hunt v/t COM: be ~ed essere selezionato da un cacciatore di te-ste

'head·hunt·er COM cacciatore m di teste

head·ing [ˈhedɪŋ] in list titolo m

'head·lamp fanale m; 'head·land promontorio m; 'head·light fanale m; 'head·line n in newspaper titolo; make the ~s fare titolo; 'head·long adv fall a testa in giù; 'head·mas·ter in primary school di-rettore m; in secondary school presi-de m; 'head·mis·tress in primary

school direttrice *f*, *in secondary school* preside *f*; **head 'of·fice** *of company* sede *f* centrale; **head-'on 1** *adv* crash frontalmente **2** *adj* crash frontale; **'head·phones** *npl* cuffie *fpl*; **'head·quar·ters** *npl* sede *fsg*; MIL quartier *msg* generale; **'head·rest** poggiatesta *m inv*; **'head·room** *for vehicle under bridge* altezza *f* utile; *in car* altezza *f* dell'abitacolo; **'head·scarf** foulard *m inv*; **'head·strong** *adj* testardo; **head 'teach·er** *in primary school* direttore *m*, -trice *f*; *in secondary school* preside *m/f*; **head 'wait·er** capocameriere *m*; **'head·wind** vento *m* di prua

head·y ['hedɪ] *adj drink, wine etc* inebriante

heal [hiːl] *v/t v/i* guarire

♦ **heal up** *v/i* cicatrizzarsi

health [helθ] *n* salute *f*; (*public ~*) sanità *f inv*; **your ~!** (alla) salute!

'health care assistenza *f* sanitaria

'health farm beauty farm *f inv*; **'health food** alimenti *mpl* macrobiotici; **'health food store** negozio *m* di macrobiotica; **'health in·sur·ance** assicurazione *f* contro le malattie; **'health re·sort** stazione *f* termale

health·y ['helθɪ] *adj also fig* sano

heap [hiːp] *n* mucchio *m*

♦ **heap up** *v/t* ammucchiare

hear [hɪə(r)] *v/t & v/i* (*pret & pp* **heard**) sentire

♦ **hear about** *v/t* sapere di

♦ **hear from** *v/t* (*have news from*) avere notizie di

heard [hɜːd] *pret & pp* → **hear**

hear·ing ['hɪərɪŋ] udito *m*; LAW udienza *f*; **be within / out of ~** essere / non essere a portata di voce

'hear·ing aid apparecchio *m* acustico

'hear·say diceria *f*; **by ~** per sentito dire

hearse [hɜːs] carro *m* funebre

heart [hɑːt] cuore *m*; *of problem etc* nocciolo *m*; **know sth by ~** sapere qc a memoria

'heart at·tack infarto *m*; **'heart·beat** battito *m* cardiaco; **'heart-break·ing** *adj* straziante; **'heart·brok·en** *adj* affranto; **'heart·burn** bruciore *m* di stomaco; **'heart fail·ure** infarto *m*; **'heart·felt** ['hɑːtfelt] *adj sympathy* sentito

hearth [hɑːθ] focolare *m*

heart·less ['hɑːtlɪs] *adj* spietato

heart-rend·ing ['hɑːtrendɪŋ] *adj plea, sight* straziante

hearts [hɑːts] *npl in cards* cuori *mpl*

'heart throb F idolo *m*

'heart trans·plant trapianto *m* cardiaco

heart·y ['hɑːtɪ] *adj appetite* robusto; *meal* sostanzioso; *person* gioviale

heat [hiːt] calore *m*; (*hot weather*) caldo *m*

♦ **heat up** *v/t* riscaldare

heat·ed ['hiːtɪd] *adj swimming pool* riscaldato; *discussion* animato

heat·er ['hiːtə(r)] *radiator* termosifone *m*; *electric, gas* stufa *f*; *in car* riscaldamento *m*

heath [hiːθ] brughiera *f*

hea·then ['hiːðn] *n* pagano *m*, -a *f*

heath·er ['heðə(r)] erica *f*

heat·ing ['hiːtɪŋ] riscaldamento *m*

'heat·proof, **'heat-re·sis·tant** *adj* termoresistente; **'heat·stroke** colpo *m* di calore; **'heat·wave** ondata *f* di caldo

heave [hiːv] *v/t* (*lift*) sollevare

heav·en ['hevn] paradiso *m*; **good ~s!** santo cielo!

heav·en·ly ['hevnlɪ] *adj* F divino

heav·y ['hevɪ] *adj* pesante; *cold, rain, accent* forte; *traffic* intenso; *food* pesante; *smoker* accanito; *drinker* forte; *financial loss, casualties* ingente; **be a ~ sleeper** avere il sonno pesante

heav·y·-'du·ty *adj* resistente

'heav·y·weight *adj* SP di pesi massimi

heck·le ['hekl] *v/t* interrompere di continuo

hec·tic ['hektɪk] *adj* frenetico

hedge [hedʒ] *n* siepe *f*

hedge·hog ['hedʒhɒg] riccio *m*

hedge·row ['hedʒrəʊ] siepe *f*

heed [hiːd] *v/t*: **pay ~ to ...** ascoltare ...

heel [hiːl] *of foot* tallone *m*, calcagno *m*; *of shoe* tacco *m*

'heel bar calzoleria *f* istantanea

hef·ty ['heftɪ] *adj* massiccio

height [haɪt] altezza *f*; *of aeroplane* altitudine *f*; **at the ~ of summer** nel pieno dell'estate

height·en ['haɪtn] *v/t effect, tension* aumentare

heir [eə(r)] erede *m*

heir·ess ['eərɪs] ereditiera *f*

held [held] *pret & pp* → **hold**

hel·i·cop·ter ['helɪkɒptə(r)] elicottero *m*

hell [hel] inferno *m*; **what the ~ are you doing / do you want?** F che diavolo fai / vuoi?; F; **go to ~!** F va' all'inferno!; F; **a ~ of a lot** F un casino F; **one ~ of a nice guy** F un tipo in gambissima

hel·lo [hə'ləʊ] *int informal* ciao; *more formal* buongiorno; buona sera; TELEC pronto; **say ~ to s.o.** salutare qu

helm [helm] NAUT timone *m*

hel·met ['helmɪt] *of motorcyclist* casco *m*; *of soldier* elmetto *m*

help [help] **1** *n* aiuto *m* **2** *v/t* aiutare; **~ o.s.** *to food* servirsi; **I can't ~ it** non ci posso far niente; **I couldn't ~ laughing** non ho potuto fare a meno di ridere

help·er ['helpə(r)] aiutante *m/f*

help·ful ['helpfʊl] *adj person* di aiuto; *advice* utile; **he was very ~** mi è stato di grande aiuto

help·ing ['helpɪŋ] *of food* porzione *f*

help·less ['helplɪs] *adj (unable to cope)* indifeso; *(powerless)* impotente

help·less·ly ['helplɪslɪ] *adv*: **we watched ~** guardavamo impotenti

help·less·ness ['helplɪsnɪs] impotenza *f*

'help me·nu COMPUT menu *m inv* della guida in linea

hem [hem] *n of dress etc* orlo *m*

hem·i·sphere ['hemɪsfɪə(r)] emisfero *m*

'hem·line orlo *m*

hen [hen] gallina *f*

hench·man ['hentʃmən] *pej* scagnozzo *m*

'hen par·ty equivalente *m* al femminile della festa d'addio al celibato

hen·pecked ['henpekt] *adj*: **~ husband** marito *m* succube della moglie

hep·a·ti·tis [hepə'taɪtɪs] epatite *f*

her [hɜː(r)] **1** *adj* suo *m*, la sua *f*, i suoi *mpl*, le sue *fpl*; **~ ticket** il suo biglietto; **~ brother / sister** suo fratello / sua sorella **2** *pron direct object* la; *indirect object* le; *after prep* lei; **I know ~** la conosco; **I gave ~ the keys** le ho dato le chiavi; **this is for ~** questo è per lei; **who? - ~** chi? - lei

herb [hɜːb] *for medicines* erba *f* medicinale; *for flavouring* erba *f* aromatica

herb(al) tea ['hɜːb(əl)] tisana *f*

herd [hɜːd] *n* mandria *f*

here [hɪə(r)] *adv* qui, qua; **~'s to you!** *as toast* salute!; **~ you are** *giving sth* ecco qui; **~!** *in roll-call* presente!

he·red·i·ta·ry [hə'redɪtərɪ] *adj disease* ereditario

he·red·i·ty [hə'redɪtɪ] ereditarietà *f inv*

her·i·tage ['herɪtɪdʒ] patrimonio *m*

her·mit ['hɜːmɪt] eremita *m/f*

her·ni·a ['hɜːnɪə] MED ernia *f*

he·ro ['hɪərəʊ] eroe *m*

he·ro·ic [hɪ'rəʊɪk] *adj* eroico

he·ro·i·cal·ly [hɪ'rəʊɪklɪ] *adv* eroicamente

her·o·in ['herəʊɪn] eroina *f*

'her·o·in ad·dict eroinomane *m/f*

her·o·ine ['herəʊɪn] eroina *f*

her·o·ism ['herəʊɪzm] eroismo *m*

her·on ['herən] airone *m*

her·pes ['hɜːpiːz] MED herpes *m*

her·ring ['herɪŋ] aringa *f*

hers [hɜːz] *pron* il suo *m*, la sua *f*, i suoi *mpl*, le sue *fpl*; **a friend of ~** un suo amico

her·self [hɜː'self] *pron reflexive* si;

emphatic se stessa; *after prep* sé, se stessa; *she must be proud of ~* dev'essere fiera di sé *o* se stessa; *she hurt ~* si è fatta male; *she told me so ~* me l'ha detto lei stessa; *by ~* da sola

hes·i·tant ['hezɪtənt] *adj* esitante

hes·i·tant·ly ['hezɪtəntlɪ] *adv* con esitazione

hes·i·tate ['hezɪteɪt] *v/i* esitare

hes·i·ta·tion [hezɪ'teɪʃn] esitazione *f*

het·er·o·sex·u·al [hetərəʊ'seksjuəl] *adj* eterosessuale

hey·day ['heɪdeɪ] tempi *mpl* d'oro

hi [haɪ] *int* ciao

hi·ber·nate ['haɪbəneɪt] *v/i* andare in letargo

hic·cup ['hɪkʌp] *n* singhiozzo *m*; *(minor problem)* intoppo *m*; *have the ~s* avere il singhiozzo

hid [hɪd] *pret* → **hide**

hid·den ['hɪdn] **1** *adj* nascosto **2** *pp* → **hide**

hidden a'gen·da *fig* secondo fine *m*

hide¹ [haɪd] *(pret* **hid**, *pp* **hidden)* **1** *v/t* nascondere **2** *v/i* nascondersi

hide² [haɪd] *n* of animal pelle *f*

hide-and-'seek nascondino *m*

'hide·a·way rifugio *m*

hid·e·ous ['hɪdɪəs] *adj* face, weather orrendo; *crime* atroce

hid·ing¹ ['haɪdɪŋ] *(beating)* batosta *f*

hid·ing² ['haɪdɪŋ] *n*: *be in ~* tenersi nascosto; *go into ~* darsi alla macchia

'hid·ing place nascondiglio *m*

hi·er·ar·chy ['haɪərɑːkɪ] gerarchia *f*

hi-fi ['haɪfaɪ] hi-fi *m inv*

high [haɪ] **1** *adj* building, price, mountain, note, temperature, salary alto; *wind, speed* forte; *quality, hopes* buono; *(on drugs)* fatto F; *~ in the sky* in alto nel cielo; *have a very ~ opinion of …* stimare molto …; *it is ~ time he left* sarebbe ora che se ne andasse **2** *n* in statistics livello *m* record **3** *adv* in alto

'high·brow *adj* intellettuale; **'high·chair** seggiolone *m*; **high·'class** *adj* di (prima) classe; **High 'Court** Corte *f* Suprema; **high 'div·ing** tuffo *m*;

high-'fre·quen·cy *adj* ad alta frequenza; **high-'grade** *adj* di buona qualità; **high-hand·ed** [haɪ'hænd-ɪd] *adj* autoritario; **high-heeled** [haɪ'hiːld] *adj* col tacco alto; **'high jump** salto *m* in alto; **high-'lev·el** *adj* ad alto livello; **'high life** bella vita *f*; **'high·light 1** *n (main event)* clou *m inv*; *in hair* colpo *m* di sole **2** *v/t with pen* evidenziare; COMPUT selezionare; **'high·light·er** *pen* evidenziatore *m*

high·ly ['haɪlɪ] *adv desirable, likely* molto; *be ~ paid* essere pagato profumatamente; *think ~ of s.o.* stimare molto qu

high·ly 'strung *adj* nervoso

high per'form·ance *adj drill, battery* ad alto rendimento; **high-pitched** [haɪ'pɪtʃt] *adj* acuto; **'high point** clou *m inv*; **high-pow·ered** [haɪ-'paʊəd] *adj engine* potente; *intellectual* di prestigio; **high 'pres·sure 1** *n weather* alta pressione *f* **2** *adj* TECH ad alta pressione; *salesman* aggressivo; **high 'priest** gran sacerdote *m*; **'high-rise** palazzone *m*; **'high school** scuola *f* superiore; **high so'ci·e·ty** alta società *f inv*; **high-speed 'train** treno *m* ad alta velocità; **'high street** via *f* principale; **high 'tech 1** *n* high-tech *m inv* **2** *adj* high tech; **high 'tide** alta marea *f*; **high-'volt·age** alta tensione *f*; **high 'wa·ter** alta marea *f*; **High·way 'Code** Codice *m* stradale

hi·jack ['haɪdʒæk] **1** *v/t* dirottare **2** *n* dirottamento *m*

hi·jack·er ['haɪdʒækə(r)] dirottatore *m*, -trice *f*

hike¹ [haɪk] **1** *n* camminata *f* **2** *v/i* fare camminate

hike² [haɪk] *n in prices* aumento *m*

hik·er ['haɪkə(r)] escursionista *m/f*

hik·ing ['haɪkɪŋ] escursionismo *m*

'hik·ing boots *npl* scarponcini *mpl* da camminata

hi·lar·i·ous [hɪ'leərɪəs] *adj* divertentissimo

hill [hɪl] collina *f*; *(slope)* altura *f*

hill·side ['hɪlsaɪd] pendio *m*

hill·top ['hɪltɒp] cima *f* della collina

hill·y ['hɪlɪ] *adj* collinoso

hilt [hɪlt] impugnatura *f*

him [hɪm] *pron direct object* lo; *indirect object* gli; *after prep* lui; *I know ~* lo conosco; *I gave ~ the keys* gli ho dato le chiavi; *this is for ~* questo è per lui; *who? – ~* chi? – lui

him·self [hɪm'self] *pron* se stesso; *after prep* sé, se stesso; *he must be proud of ~* dev'essere fiero di sé *o* se stesso; *he hurt ~* si è fatto male; *he told me so* me l'ha detto lui stesso; *by ~* da solo

hind [haɪnd] *adj* posteriore

hin·der ['hɪndə(r)] *v/t* intralciare

hin·drance ['hɪndrəns] intralcio *m*

hind·sight ['haɪndsaɪt]: *with ~* con il senno di poi

hinge [hɪndʒ] cardine *m*

◆ **hinge on** *v/t* dipendere da

hint [hɪnt] *n* (*clue*) accenno *m*; (*piece of advice*) consiglio *m*; (*implied suggestion*) allusione *f*; *of red, sadness etc* punta *f*

hip [hɪp] *n* fianco *m*

hip 'pock·et tasca *f* posteriore

hip·po·pot·a·mus [hɪpə'pɒtəməs] ippopotamo *m*

hire ['haɪə(r)] *v/t room, hall* affittare; *workers, staff* assumere; *conjuror etc* ingaggiare

hire 'pur·chase acquisto *m* rateale

his [hɪz] **1** *adj* il suo *m*, la sua *f*, i suoi *mpl*, le sue *fpl*; *~ bag* la sua valigia; *~ brother / sister* suo fratello / sua sorella **2** *pron* il suo *m*, la sua *f*, i suoi *mpl*, le sue *fpl*; *a friend of ~* un suo amico

hiss [hɪs] *v/i* sibilare

his·to·ri·an [hɪ'stɔːrɪən] storico *m*, -a *f*

his·tor·ic [hɪ'stɒrɪk] *adj* storico

his·tor·i·cal [hɪ'stɒrɪkl] *adj* storico

his·to·ry ['hɪstərɪ] storia *f*

hit [hɪt] **1** *v/t* (*pret & pp hit*) colpire; (*collide with*) sbattere contro; *I ~ my knee* ho battuto il ginocchio; *he was ~ by a bullet* è stato colpito da un proiettile; *it suddenly ~ me* (*I realized*) improvvisamente ho realizzato; *~ town* (*arrive*) arrivare (in città) **2** *n* (*blow*) colpo *m*; (*success*) successo *m*

◆ **hit back** *v/i* reagire

◆ **hit on** *v/t idea* trovare

◆ **hit out at** *v/t* (*criticize*) attaccare

hit-and-run *adj*: *~ accident* incidente *m* con omissione di soccorso

hitch [hɪtʃ] **1** *n* (*problem*) contrattempo *m*; *without a ~* senza contrattempi **2** *v/t*: *~ sth to sth* legare qc a qc; *with hook* agganciare qc a qc; *~ a lift* chiedere un passaggio **3** *v/i* (*hitchhike*) fare l'autostop

◆ **hitch up** *v/t wagon, trailer* attaccare

hitch·hike *v/i* fare l'autostop

hitch·hik·er autostoppista *m/f*

hitch·hik·ing autostop *m inv*

hi-'tech 1 *n* high-tech *m inv* **2** *adj* high tech

hit·list libro *m* nero; **hit·man** sicario *m*; **hit-or-'miss** *adj*: *on a ~ basis* affidandosi al caso; **hit squad** commando *m*

HIV [eɪtʃaɪ'viː] *abbr* (= *human immunodeficiency virus*) HIV *m*

hive [haɪv] *for bees* alveare *m*

◆ **hive off** *v/t* (COM: *separate off*) separare

HIV-'pos·i·tive sieropositivo

hoard [hɔːd] **1** *n* provvista *f*; *~ of money* gruzzolo *m* **2** *v/t* accumulare

hoard·er ['hɔːdə(r)] persona *f* che non butta mai niente

hoarse [hɔːs] *adj* rauco

hoax [həʊks] *n* scherzo *m*; *malicious* falso allarme *m*

hob [hɒb] *on cooker* piano *m* di cottura

hob·ble ['hɒbl] *v/i* zoppicare

hob·by ['hɒbɪ] hobby *m inv*

hock·ey ['hɒkɪ] hockey *m* (su prato)

hoist [hɔɪst] **1** *n* montacarichi *m inv* **2** *v/t* (*lift*) sollevare; *flag* issare

hold [həʊld] *v/t* (*pret & pp held*) *in hand* tenere; (*support, keep in place*) reggere; *passport, licence* avere; *prisoner, suspect* trattenere; (*contain*) contenere; *job, post* occupare; *course* tenere; **~ hands** tenersi per mano; **~ one's breath** trattenere il fiato; *he can* **~ his drink** regge bene l'alcol; **~ s.o. responsible** ritenere qu responsabile; **~ that ...** (believe, maintain) sostenere che ...; **~ the line** TELEC resti in linea **2** *n in ship, plane* stiva *f*; **catch ~ of sth** afferrare qc; *lose one's ~ on sth on rope etc* perdere la presa su qc

♦ **hold against** v/t: **hold sth against s.o.** volerne a qu per qc

♦ **hold back 1** v/t *crowds* contenere; *facts* nascondere **2** v/i (hesitate) esitare; *he's holding back not telling all* non sta dicendo tutta la verità

♦ **hold on** v/i (wait) attendere; TELEC restare in linea; *now hold on a minute!* aspetta un attimo!

♦ **hold on to** v/t (keep) tenere; *belief* aggrapparsi a

♦ **hold out 1** v/t *hand* tendere; *prospect* offrire **2** v/i *of supplies* durare; *of trapped miners etc* resistere

♦ **hold up 1** v/t *hand* alzare; *bank etc* rapinare; (make late) trattenere; *hold sth up as an example* portare qc ad esempio

♦ **hold with** v/t (approve of) essere d'accordo con

'**hold·all** borsone *m*

hold·er ['həʊldə(r)] (container) contenitore *m*; *of passport* titolare *m*; *of ticket* possessore *m*; *of record* detentore *m*, -trice *f*

'**hold·ing com·pa·ny** holding *f inv*

'**hold·up** (robbery) rapina *f*; (delay) ritardo *m*

hole [həʊl] buco *m*

hol·i·day ['hɒlədeɪ] vacanza *f*; *public* giorno *m* festivo; (day off) giorno *m* di ferie; **go on ~** andare in vacanza

hol·i·day·mak·er ['hɒlədeɪmeɪkə(r)] vacanziere *m*, -a *f*

Hol·land ['hɒlənd] Olanda *f*

hol·low ['hɒləʊ] adj *object* cavo, vuoto; *cheeks* infossato

hol·ly ['hɒlɪ] agrifoglio *m*

hol·o·caust ['hɒləkɔːst] olocausto *m*

hol·o·gram ['hɒləɡræm] ologramma *m*

hol·ster ['həʊlstə(r)] fondina *f*

ho·ly ['həʊlɪ] adj santo

Ho·ly 'Spir·it Spirito *m* Santo

'**Ho·ly Week** settimana *f* santa

home [həʊm] **1** *n* casa *f*; (native country) patria *f*; *for old people* casa *f* di riposo; *for children* istituto *m*; **at ~** a casa; **make yourself at ~** fai come a casa tua; **at ~** SP in casa; **work from ~** lavorare da casa **2** *adv* a casa; **go ~** andare a casa; *is she* **~ yet?** è tornata?

home ad·dress indirizzo *m* di casa; **home 'bank·ing** home-banking *m inv*; '**home·com·ing** ritorno *m*; **home com'put·er** computer *m inv* (per casa)

home·less ['həʊmlɪs] adj senza tetto; **the ~** i senzacasa

'**home·lov·ing** adj casalingo

home·ly ['həʊmlɪ] adj semplice; (welcoming) accogliente

home'made adj fatto in casa, casalingo; '**home match** incontro *m* casalingo; **home 'mov·ie** filmino *m* (casalingo); '**Home Of·fice** Ministero *m* degli Interni

ho·me·op·a·thy [həʊmɪ'ɒpəθɪ] omeopatia *f*

'**home page** home page *f*; **Home 'Sec·ret·ar·y** Ministro *m* degli Interni; '**home·sick** adj: **be ~** avere nostalgia di casa; '**home town** città *f inv* natale

home·ward ['həʊmwəd] adv verso casa

'**home·work** EDU compiti *mpl* a casa

'**home·work·ing** COM telelavoro *m inv*

hom·i·cide ['hɒmɪsaɪd] *crime* omicidio *m*; *Am: police department* (squadra *f*) omicidi *f*

hom·o·graph ['hɒməɡræf] omografo *m*

ho·mo·pho·bi·a [hɒmə'fəʊbɪə] omofobia *f*

ho·mo·sex·u·al [hɒmə'seksjʊəl] **1** adj omosessuale **2** *n* omosessuale *m/f*

hon·est ['ɒnɪst] *adj* onesto

hon·est·ly ['ɒnɪstlɪ] *adv* onestamente; *~!* ma insomma!

hon·es·ty ['ɒnɪstɪ] onestà *f inv*

hon·ey ['hʌnɪ] miele *m*; F *(darling)* tesoro *m*

'hon·ey·comb favo *m*

'hon·ey·moon *n* luna *f* di miele

honk [hɒŋk] *v/t horn* suonare

hon·or *etc Am* → **honour** *etc*

hon·our ['ɒnə(r)] **1** *n* onore *m* **2** *v/t* onorare

hon·our·a·ble ['ɒnərəbl] *adj* onorevole

hood [hʊd] *over head* cappuccio *m*; *over cooker* cappa *f*; MOT: *on convertible* capote *f inv*

hood·lum ['huːdləm] gangster *m inv*

hoof [huːf] zoccolo *m*

hook [hʊk] gancio *m*; *for fishing* amo *m*; *off the ~* TELEC staccato

hooked [hʊkt] *adj*: *be ~ on s.o. / sth* essere fanatico di qu / qc; *be ~ on sth on drugs* essere assuefatto a qc

hook·er ['hʊkə(r)] F prostituta *f*; *in rugby* tallonatore *m*

hoo·li·gan ['huːlɪɡən] teppista *m/f*

hoo·li·gan·ism ['huːlɪɡənɪzm] teppismo *m*

hoop [huːp] cerchio *m*

hoot [huːt] **1** *v/t horn* suonare **2** *v/i of car* suonare il clacson; *of owl* gufare

hoo·ver® ['huːvə(r)] **1** *n* aspirapolvere *m* **2** *v/t carpets, room* pulire con l'aspirapolvere

hop¹ [hɒp] *n plant* luppolo *m*

hop² [hɒp] *v/i (pret & pp -ped)* saltare

hope [həʊp] **1** *n* speranza *f*; *there's no ~ of that* non farci conto **2** *v/i* sperare; *~ for sth* augurarsi qc; *I ~ so* spero di sì; *I ~ not* spero di no **3** *v/t*: *I ~ you like it* spero che ti piaccia

hope·ful ['həʊpfʊl] *adj person* ottimista; *(promising)* promettente

hope·ful·ly ['həʊpflɪ] *adv say, wait* con ottimismo; *(I / we hope)* si spera

hope·less ['həʊplɪs] *adj position, prospect* senza speranza; *(useless: person)* negato F

ho·ri·zon [hə'raɪzn] orizzonte *m*

hor·i·zon·tal [hɒrɪ'zɒntl] *adj* orizzontale

hor·mone ['hɔːməʊn] ormone *m*

horn [hɔːn] *of animal* corno *m*; MOT clacson *m inv*

hor·net ['hɔːnɪt] calabrone *m*

horn-rimmed 'spec·ta·cles [hɔːn·rɪmd] *npl* occhiali *mpl* con montatura di tartaruga

horn·y ['hɔːnɪ] *adj* F *sexually* arrapato P

hor·o·scope ['hɒrəskəʊp] oroscopo *m*

hor·ri·ble ['hɒrɪbl] *adj* orribile

hor·ri·fy ['hɒrɪfaɪ] *v/t (pret & pp -ied)* inorridire; *I was horrified* ero scioccato

hor·ri·fy·ing ['hɒrɪfaɪɪŋ] *adj experience* terrificante; *idea, prices* allucinante

hor·ror ['hɒrə(r)] orrore *m*; *the ~s of war* le atrocità della guerra

'hor·ror mov·ie film *m* dell'orrore

hors d'oeu·vre [ɔː'dɜːvr] antipasto *m*

horse [hɔːs] cavallo *m*

'horse·back *n*: *on ~* a cavallo; *of TV programme* ippocastano *m*; **'horse·pow·er** cavallo-vapore *m*; **'horse·shoe** ferro *m* di cavallo

hor·ti·cul·ture ['hɔːtɪkʌltʃə(r)] orticoltura *f*

hose [həʊz] *n* tubo *m* di gomma

hos·pice ['hɒspɪs] ospedale *m* per i malati terminali

hos·pi·ta·ble [hɒ'spɪtəbl] *adj* ospitale

hos·pi·tal ['hɒspɪtl] ospedale *m*; *go into ~* essere ricoverato (in ospedale)

hos·pi·tal·i·ty [hɒspɪ'tælətɪ] ospitalità *f inv*

host [həʊst] *n at party, reception* padrone *m* di casa; *of TV programme* presentatore *m*, -trice *f*

hos·tage ['hɒstɪdʒ] ostaggio *m*; *be taken ~* essere preso in ostaggio

hos·tel ['hɒstl] *for students* pensionato *m*; *(youth ~)* ostello *m* (della gioventù)

hos·tess ['həʊstɪs] *at party, reception*

padrona *f* di casa; *on aeroplane* hostess *f inv*

hos·tile ['hɒstaɪl] *adj* ostile

hos·til·i·ty [hɒ'stɪlətɪ] ostilità *f inv*

hot [hɒt] *adj weather, water* caldo; *(spicy)* piccante; F *(good)* bravo (**at sth** in qc); *it's* ~ fa caldo; *I'm* ~ ho caldo

'hot dog hot dog *m inv*

ho·tel [həʊ'tel] albergo *m*

'hot·plate piastra *f* riscaldante

'hot spot *military, political* zona *f* calda

hour ['aʊə(r)] ora *f*

hour·ly ['aʊəlɪ] *adj pay, rate* a ora; *at* ~ *intervals* ad ogni ora

house [haʊs] **1** *n* casa *f*; POL camera *f*; THEA sala *f*; *at your* ~ a casa tua, da te **2** *v/t* [haʊz] alloggiare

'house·boat house boat *f inv*; 'house·break·ing furto *m* con scasso; 'house·hold famiglia *f*; house·hold 'name nome *m* conosciuto; 'house hus·band casalingo *m*; 'house·keep·er governante *f*; 'house·keep·ing *activity* governo *m* della casa; *money* soldi *mpl* per le spese di casa; house·warm·ing (party) ['haʊswɔ:mɪŋ] *festa f* per inaugurare la nuova casa; 'house·wife casalinga *f*; 'house·work lavori *mpl* domestici

hous·ing ['haʊzɪŋ] alloggi *mpl*; TECH alloggiamento *m*

hov·el ['hɒvl] tugurio *m*

hov·er ['hɒvə(r)] *v/i* librarsi

'hov·er·craft hovercraft *m inv*

how [haʊ] *adv* come; ~ *are you?* come stai?; ~ *about ...?* che ne dici di ...?; ~ *much?* quanto?; ~ *much is it? of cost* quant'è?; ~ *many?* quanti?; ~ *often?* ogni quanto?; ~ *odd / lovely!* che strano / bello!

how·ev·er *adv* comunque; ~ *big / rich they are* per quanto grandi / ricchi siano

howl [haʊl] *v/i of dog* ululare; *of person in pain* urlare; ~ *with laughter* sbellicarsi dalle risate

howl·er ['haʊlə(r)] *mistake* strafalcione *m*

hub [hʌb] *of wheel* mozzo *m*

'hub·cap coprimozzo *m*

♦ hud·dle to·geth·er ['hʌdl] *v/i* stringersi l'un l'altro

hue [hju:] tinta *f*

huff [hʌf]: *be in a* ~ essere imbronciato

hug [hʌg] **1** *v/t (pret & pp -ged)* abbracciare **2** *n* abbraccio *m*

huge [hju:dʒ] *adj* enorme

hull [hʌl] scafo *m*

hul·la·ba·loo [hʌləbə'lu:] baccano *m*

hum [hʌm] *(pret & pp -med)* **1** *v/t song, tune* canticchiare **2** *v/i of person* canticchiare; *of machine* ronzare

hu·man ['hju:mən] **1** *n* essere *m* umano **2** *adj* umano; ~ *error* errore *m* umano

hu·man 'be·ing essere *m* umano

hu·mane [hju:'meɪn] *adj* umano

hu·man·i·tar·i·an [hju:mænɪ'teərɪən] *adj* umanitario

hu·man·i·ty [hju:'mænətɪ] umanità *f inv*

hu·man 'race genere *m* umano

hu·man re'sourc·es *npl* risorse *fpl* umane

hum·ble ['hʌmbl] *adj origins, person* umile; *house* modesto

hum·drum ['hʌmdrʌm] *adj* monotono

hu·mid ['hju:mɪd] *adj* umido

hu·mid·i·fi·er [hju:'mɪdɪfaɪə(r)] umidificatore *m*

hu·mid·i·ty [hju:'mɪdətɪ] umidità *f inv*

hu·mil·i·ate [hju:'mɪlɪeɪt] *v/t* umiliare

hu·mil·i·at·ing [hju:'mɪlɪeɪtɪŋ] *adj* umiliante

hu·mil·i·a·tion [hju:mɪlɪ'eɪʃn] umiliazione *f*

hu·mil·i·ty [hju:'mɪlɪtɪ] umiltà *f inv*

hu·mor *Am → humour*

hu·mor·ous ['hju:mərəs] *adj person* spiritoso; *story* umoristico

hu·mour ['hju:mə(r)] umorismo *m*; *(mood)* umore *m*; *sense of* ~ senso dell'umorismo

hump [hʌmp] **1** *n of camel, person* gobba *f*; *on road* dosso *m* **2** *v/t* F

H

hunch [hʌntʃ] (*idea*) impressione *f*; *of detective* intuizione *f*

hun·dred ['hʌndrəd] cento *m*; **a ~ ...** cento ...

hun·dredth ['hʌndrəθ] *n & adj* centesimo, -a

'hun·dred·weight cinquanta chili (*circa*)

hung [hʌŋ] *pret & pp* → **hang**

Hun·gar·i·an [hʌŋ'geəriən] **1** *adj* ungherese **2** *n person* ungherese *m/f*; *language* ungherese *m*

Hun·ga·ry ['hʌŋgəri] Ungheria *f*

hun·ger ['hʌŋgə(r)] fame *f*

hung-o·ver [hʌŋ'əʊvə(r)] *adj*: **feel ~** avere i postumi della sbornia

hun·gry ['hʌŋgri] *adj* affamato; **I'm ~** ho fame

hunk [hʌŋk] *n* tocco *m*; F (*man*) fusto *m* F

hun·ky-do·ry [hʌŋkı'dɔːrı] *adj* F: **everything's ~** tutto va a meraviglia

hunt [hʌnt] **1** *n for animals* caccia *f*; *for job, house, missing child* ricerca *f* **2** *v/t animal* cacciare

♦ **hunt for** *v/t* cercare

hunt·er ['hʌntə(r)] cacciatore *m*, -trice *f*

hunt·ing ['hʌntɪŋ] caccia *f*

hur·dle ['hɜːdl] *also fig* ostacolo *m*

hur·dler ['hɜːdlə(r)] SP ostacolista *m/f*

hur·dles *npl* SP: **100 metres ~** i cento metri a ostacoli

hurl [hɜːl] *v/t* scagliare

hur·ray [hʊ'reɪ] *int* urrà!

hur·ri·cane ['hʌrıkən] uragano *m*

hur·ried ['hʌrɪd] *adj* frettoloso

hur·ry ['hʌrɪ] **1** *n* fretta *f*; **be in a ~** avere fretta **2** *v/i* (*pret & pp -ied*) sbrigarsi

♦ **hurry up 1** *v/i* sbrigarsi; **hurry up!** sbrigati! **2** *v/t* fare fretta a

hurt [hɜːt] (*pret & pp* **hurt**) **1** *v/i* far male; **does it ~?** ti fa male? **2** *v/t physically* far male a; *emotionally* ferire

hus·band ['hʌzbənd] marito *m*

hush [hʌʃ] *n* silenzio *m*; **~!** silenzio!

♦ **hush up** *v/t scandal etc* mettere a tacere

husk [hʌsk] pula *m*

hus·ky ['hʌski] *adj voice* roco

hus·tle ['hʌsl] **1** *n*: **~ and bustle** trambusto *m* **2** *v/t person* spingere

hut [hʌt] capanno *m*

hy·a·cinth ['haɪəsɪnθ] giacinto *m*

hy·brid ['haɪbrɪd] *n plant, animal* ibrido *m*

hy·drant ['haɪdrənt] idrante *m*

hy·drau·lic [haɪ'drɔːlɪk] *adj* idraulico

hy·dro·e·lec·tric [haɪdrəʊɪ'lektrɪk] *adj* idroelettrico

'hy·dro·foil ['haɪdrəfɔɪl] *boat* aliscafo *m*

hy·dro·gen ['haɪdrədʒən] idrogeno *m*

'hy·dro·gen bomb bomba *f* H

hy·giene ['haɪdʒiːn] igiene *f*

hy·gien·ic [haɪ'dʒiːnɪk] *adj* igienico

hymn [hɪm] *n* inno *m* (sacro)

hype [haɪp] *n* pubblicità *f inv*

hy·per·ac·tive [haɪpər'æktɪv] *adj* iperattivo

hy·per·mar·ket ['haɪpəmɑːkɪt] ipermercato *m*

hy·per·sen·si·tive [haɪpə'sensɪtɪv] *adj* ipersensibile

hy·per·ten·sion [haɪpə'tenʃn] ipertensione *f*

hy·per·text ['haɪpətekst] COMPUT ipertesto *m*

hy·phen ['haɪfn] trattino *m*

hyp·no·sis [hɪp'nəʊsɪs] ipnosi *f*

hyp·no·ther·a·py [hɪpnəʊ'θerəpɪ] ipnoterapia *f*

hyp·no·tize ['hɪpnətaɪz] *v/t* ipnotizzare

hy·po·chon·dri·ac [haɪpə'kɒndriæk] *n* ipocondriaco *m*, -a *f*

hy·poc·ri·sy [hɪ'pɒkrəsɪ] ipocrisia *f*

hyp·o·crite ['hɪpəkrɪt] ipocrita *m/f*

hyp·o·crit·i·cal [hɪpə'krɪtɪkl] *adj* ipocrita

hy·po·ther·mi·a [haɪpəʊ'θɜːmɪə] ipotermia *f*

hy·poth·e·sis [haɪ'pɒθəsɪs] (*pl* **hypotheses** [haɪ'pɒθəsiːz]) ipotesi *f inv*

hy·po·thet·i·cal [haɪpə'θetɪkl] *adj* ipotetico

hys·ter·ec·to·my [hɪstə'rektəmɪ] isterectomia *f*

hys·te·ri·a [hɪ'stɪərɪə] isteria *f*

hys·ter·i·cal [hɪ'sterɪkl] *adj person,* *laugh* isterico; F (*very funny*) buffissimo; ***become*** ~ avere una crisi isterica

hys·ter·ics [hɪ'sterɪks] *npl laughter* attacco *m* di risa; MED crisi *f* isterica

I

I [aɪ] *pron* io; ~ **am English** sono inglese; **you're crazy,** ~'**m not** tu sei pazzo, io no

ice [aɪs] ghiaccio *m*; **break the** ~ *fig* rompere il ghiaccio

♦ **ice up** *v/i of engine, wings* ghiacciarsi

ice·berg ['aɪsbɜːg] iceberg *m inv*; '**ice-box** *Am* frigo *m*; '**ice-break·er** *ship* rompighiaccio *m inv*; '**ice cream** gelato *m*; '**ice cream par·lor** *Am*, '**ice cream par·lour** gelateria *f*; '**ice cube** cubetto *m* di ghiaccio

iced [aɪst] *adj drink* ghiacciato; *cake* glassato

iced 'cof·fee caffè *m inv* freddo

'**ice hock·ey** hockey *m inv* sul ghiaccio; '**ice lol·ly** ghiacciolo *m*; '**ice rink** pista *f* di pattinaggio; '**ice skate** pattinare (sul ghiaccio); '**ice skat·ing** pattinaggio *m* (sul ghiaccio)

i·ci·cle ['aɪsɪkl] ghiacciolo *m*

i·cing ['aɪsɪŋ] glassa *f*

i·con ['aɪkɒn] *cultural* mito *m*; COMPUT icona *f*

icy ['aɪsɪ] *adj road, surface* ghiacciato; *welcome* glaciale

ID [aɪ'diː] *abbr* (= *identity*): **have you got any** ~ **on you?** ha un documento d'identità?

idea [aɪ'dɪə] idea *f*; **good** ~! ottima idea!; **I have no** ~ non ne ho la minima idea; **it's not a good** ~ **to ...** non è una buona idea ...

i·deal [aɪ'dɪəl] *adj* (*perfect*) ideale; **it's not** ~ **but we'll take it** non è l'ideale ma lo prendiamo lo stesso

i·deal·is·tic [aɪdɪə'lɪstɪk] *adj person* idealista; *views* idealistico

i·deal·ly [aɪ'dɪəlɪ] *adv*: **the hotel is** ~ **situated** l'albergo si trova in una posizione ideale; ~, **we would do it like this** l'ideale sarebbe farlo così

i·den·ti·cal [aɪ'dentɪkl] *adj* identico; ~ **twins** gemelli *mpl* monozigotici

i·den·ti·fi·ca·tion [aɪdentɪfɪ'keɪʃn] identificazione *f*, riconoscimento *m*; *papers etc* documento *m* di riconoscimento *o* d'identità

i·den·ti·fy [aɪ'dentɪfaɪ] *v/t* (*pret & pp -ied*) (*recognize*) identificare, riconoscere; (*point out*) individuare

i·den·ti·ty [aɪ'dentətɪ] identità *f inv*; ~ **card** carta *f* d'identità; **a case of mistaken** ~ uno scambio di persona

i·de·o·log·i·cal [aɪdɪə'lɒdʒɪkl] *adj* ideologico

i·de·ol·o·gy [aɪdɪ'ɒlədʒɪ] ideologia *f*

id·i·om ['ɪdɪəm] (*saying*) locuzione *f* idiomatica

id·i·o·mat·ic [ɪdɪə'mætɪk] *adj* naturale

id·i·o·syn·cra·sy [ɪdɪə'sɪŋkrəsɪ] piccola mania *f*

id·i·ot ['ɪdɪət] idiota *m/f*

id·i·ot·ic [ɪdɪ'ɒtɪk] *adj* idiota

i·dle ['aɪdl] **1** *adj person* disoccupato; *threat* vuoto; *machinery* inattivo; **in an** ~ **moment** in un momento libero **2** v/i of engine girare al minimo

♦ **idle away** v/t *the time etc* trascorrere oziando

i·dol ['aɪdl] idolo *m*

i·dol·ize ['aɪdəlaɪz] v/t idolatrare

i·dyl·lic [ɪ'dɪlɪk] adj idilli(a)co

if [ɪf] conj se; ~ **only you had told me** se (solo) me l'avessi detto

ig·nite [ɪg'naɪt] v/t dar fuoco a

ig·ni·tion [ɪg'nɪʃn] in car accensione f; ~ **key** chiave f dell'accensione

ig·no·rance ['ɪgnərəns] ignoranza f

ig·no·rant ['ɪgnərənt] adj (rude) cafone; **be ~ of sth** ignorare qc

ig·nore [ɪg'nɔː(r)] v/t ignorare

ill [ɪl] adj ammalato; **fall ~, be taken ~** ammalarsi; **feel ~** sentirsi male; **look ~** avere una brutta cera; **feel ~ at ease** sentirsi a disagio

il·le·gal [ɪ'liːgl] adj illegale

il·le·gi·ble [ɪ'ledʒəbl] adj illeggibile

il·le·git·i·mate [ɪlɪ'dʒɪtɪmət] adj child illegittimo

ill-fat·ed [ɪl'feɪtɪd] adj sfortunato

il·li·cit [ɪ'lɪsɪt] adj copy, imports illegale; pleasure, relationship illecito

il·lit·e·rate [ɪ'lɪtərət] adj analfabeta

ill-man·nered [ɪl'mænəd] adj maleducato

ill-na·tured [ɪl'neɪtʃəd] adj d'indole cattiva

ill·ness ['ɪlnɪs] malattia f

il·log·i·cal [ɪ'lɒdʒɪkl] adj illogico

ill-tem·pered [ɪl'tempəd] adj irascibile

ill'treat v/t maltrattare

il·lu·mi·nate [ɪ'luːmɪneɪt] v/t building etc illuminare

il·lu·mi·nat·ing [ɪ'luːmɪneɪtɪŋ] adj remarks etc chiarificatore

il·lu·sion [ɪ'luːʒn] illusione f

il·lus·trate ['ɪləstreɪt] v/t illustrare

il·lus·tra·tion [ɪlə'streɪʃn] (picture) illustrazione f; with examples esemplificazione f

il·lus·tra·tor [ɪlə'streɪtə(r)] illustratore m, -trice f

ill 'will rancore m

im·age ['ɪmɪdʒ] immagine f; (exact likeness) ritratto m

'im·age-con·scious adj attento all'immagine

i·ma·gi·na·ble [ɪ'mædʒɪnəbl] adj immaginabile; **the biggest / smallest size** ~ la misura più grande / piccola che si possa immaginare

i·ma·gi·na·ry [ɪ'mædʒɪnərɪ] adj immaginario

i·ma·gi·na·tion [ɪmædʒɪ'neɪʃn] immaginazione f, fantasia f; **it's all in your** ~ è tutto frutto della tua immaginazione

i·ma·gi·na·tive [ɪ'mædʒɪnətɪv] adj fantasioso

i·ma·gine [ɪ'mædʒɪn] v/t immaginare; **I can just** ~ **it** me l'immagino; **you're imagining things** è frutto della tua immaginazione

im·be·cile ['ɪmbəsiːl] ebete m/f

IMF [aɪem'ef] abbr (= **International Monetary Fund**) FMI m (= Fondo m Monetario Internazionale)

im·i·tate ['ɪmɪteɪt] v/t imitare

im·i·ta·tion [ɪmɪ'teɪʃn] imitazione f; **learn by** ~ imparare copiando

im·mac·u·late [ɪ'mækjʊlət] adj immacolato

im·ma·te·ri·al [ɪmə'tɪərɪəl] adj (not relevant) irrilevante

im·ma·ture [ɪmə'tʃʊə(r)] adj immaturo

im·me·di·ate [ɪ'miːdɪət] adj immediato; **the ~ family** i familiari più stretti; **the ~ problem** il problema più immediato; **in the ~ neighbourhood** nelle immediate vicinanze

im·me·di·ate·ly [ɪ'miːdɪətlɪ] adv immediatamente; ~ **after the bank / church** subito dopo la banca / chiesa

im·mense [ɪ'mens] adj immenso

im·merse [ɪ'mɜːs] v/t immergere; ~ **o.s. in** immergersi in

im·mer·sion heat·er [ɪ'mɜːʃn] scaldabagno m elettrico

im·mi·grant ['ɪmɪgrənt] n immigrato m, -a f

im·mi·grate ['ɪmɪgreɪt] v/i immigrare

im·mi·gra·tion [ɪmɪ'greɪʃn] act immigrazione f; **Immigration** government ment department ufficio m stranieri

im·mi·nent ['ɪmɪnənt] adj imminente

im·mo·bi·lize [ɪ'məʊbɪlaɪz] v/t factory, person, car immobilizzare

im·mo·bi·liz·er [ɪ'məʊbɪlaɪzə(r)] on car immobilizzatore m

im·mod·e·rate [ɪ'mɒdərət] adj smodato

im·mor·al [ɪ'mɒrəl] adj immorale

im·mor·al·i·ty [ɪmɒ'rælɪtɪ] immoralità f inv

im·mor·tal [ɪ'mɔːtl] adj immortale

im·mor·tal·i·ty [ɪmɔː'tælɪtɪ] immortalità f inv

im·mune [ɪ'mjuːn] adj to illness, infection immune; from ruling, requirement esente

im·mune sys·tem MED sistema m immunitario

im·mu·ni·ty [ɪ'mjuːnətɪ] to infection immunità f inv; from ruling esenzione f; **diplomatic ~** immunità f inv diplomatica

im·pact ['ɪmpækt] n of meteorite, vehicle urto m; of new manager etc impatto m; (effect) effetto m

im·pair [ɪm'peə(r)] v/t danneggiare

im·paired [ɪm'peəd] adj danneggiato

im·par·tial [ɪm'pɑːʃl] adj imparziale

im·pass·a·ble [ɪm'pɑːsəbl] adj road impraticabile

im·passe ['æmpɑːs] in negotiations etc impasse m inv

im·pas·sioned [ɪm'pæʃnd] adj speech, plea appassionato

im·pas·sive [ɪm'pæsɪv] adj impassibile

im·pa·tience [ɪm'peɪʃəns] impazienza f

im·pa·tient [ɪm'peɪʃənt] adj impaziente

im·pa·tient·ly [ɪm'peɪʃəntlɪ] adv con impazienza

im·peach [ɪm'piːtʃ] v/t President mettere in stato d'accusa

im·pec·ca·ble [ɪm'pekəbl] adj impeccabile

im·pec·ca·bly [ɪm'pekəblɪ] adv impeccabilmente

im·pede [ɪm'piːd] v/t ostacolare

im·ped·i·ment [ɪm'pedɪmənt] in speech difetto m

im·pend·ing [ɪm'pendɪŋ] adj imminente

im·pen·e·tra·ble [ɪm'penɪtrəbl] adj impenetrabile

im·per·a·tive [ɪm'perətɪv] **1** adj essenziale **2** n GRAM imperativo m

im·per·cep·ti·ble [ɪmpɜː'septɪbl] adj impercettibile

im·per·fect [ɪm'pɜːfekt] **1** adj imperfetto **2** n GRAM imperfetto m

im·pe·ri·al [ɪm'pɪərɪəl] adj imperiale

im·per·son·al [ɪm'pɜːsənl] adj impersonale

im·per·so·nate [ɪm'pɜːsəneɪt] v/t as a joke imitare; illegally fingersi

im·per·ti·nence [ɪm'pɜːtɪnəns] impertinenza f

im·per·ti·nent [ɪm'pɜːtɪnənt] adj impertinente

im·per·tur·ba·ble [ɪmpə'tɜːbəbl] adj imperturbabile

im·per·vi·ous [ɪm'pɜːvɪəs] adj: **~ to** indifferente a

im·pe·tu·ous [ɪm'petjʊəs] adj impetuoso

im·pe·tus ['ɪmpɪtəs] of campaign etc impeto m

im·ple·ment ['ɪmplɪmənt] **1** n utensile m **2** v/t implementare; measures attuare, implementare

im·pli·cate ['ɪmplɪkeɪt] v/t implicare; **~ s.o. in sth** implicare qu in qc

im·pli·ca·tion [ɪmplɪ'keɪʃn] conseguenza f possibile; **by ~** implicitamente

im·pli·cit [ɪm'plɪsɪt] adj implicito; trust assoluto

im·plore [ɪm'plɔː(r)] v/t implorare

im·ply [ɪm'plaɪ] v/t (pret & pp **-ied**) implicare; **are you ~ing I was lying?** stai insinuando che ho mentito?

im·po·lite [ɪmpə'laɪt] adj maleducato

im·port ['ɪmpɔːt] **1** n importazione f; item articolo m d'importazione **2** v/t importare

im·por·tance [ɪm'pɔːtəns] importanza f

im·por·tant [ɪm'pɔːtənt] adj importante

im·por·ter [ɪm'pɔːtə(r)] importatore m, -trice f

im·pose [ɪm'pəʊz] v/t tax imporre; ~ o.s. on s.o. disturbare qu

im·pos·ing [ɪm'pəʊzɪŋ] imponente

im·pos·si·bil·i·ty [ɪmpɒsɪ'bɪlɪtɪ] impossibilità f inv

im·pos·si·ble [ɪm'pɒsɪbəl] adj impossibile

im·pos·tor [ɪm'pɒstə(r)] impostore m, -a f

im·po·tence ['ɪmpətəns] impotenza f

im·po·tent ['ɪmpətənt] adj impotente

im·pov·e·rished [ɪm'pɒvərɪʃt] adj impoverito

im·prac·ti·cal [ɪm'præktɪkəl] adj person senza senso pratico; suggestion poco pratico

im·press [ɪm'pres] v/t fare colpo su; be ~ed by s.o. / sth essere colpito da qu / qc; $500 an hour? – I'm ~ed 500 dollari all'ora? – però!; terrible work, I'm not ~ed pessimo lavoro, vergogna

im·pres·sion [ɪm'preʃn] impressione f; (impersonation) imitazione f; make a good / bad ~ on s.o. fare buona / cattiva impressione su qu; I get the ~ that … ho l'impressione che …

im·pres·sion·a·ble [ɪm'preʃənəbl] adj impressionabile

im·pres·sive [ɪm'presɪv] adj notevole

im·print ['ɪmprɪnt] n of credit card impressione f

im·pris·on [ɪm'prɪzn] v/t incarcerare

im·pris·on·ment [ɪm'prɪznmənt] carcerazione f; 15 years' ~ 15 anni di carcere o reclusione

im·prob·a·ble [ɪm'prɒbəbəl] adj improbabile

im·prop·er [ɪm'prɒpə(r)] adj behaviour sconveniente; use improprio

im·prove [ɪm'pruːv] v/t & v/i migliorare

im·prove·ment [ɪm'pruːvmənt] miglioramento m

im·pro·vise ['ɪmprəvaɪz] v/i improvvisare

im·pulse ['ɪmpʌls] impulso m; do sth on an ~ fare qc d'impulso

'impulse buy acquisto m d'impulso

im·pul·sive [ɪm'pʌlsɪv] adj impulsivo

im·pu·ni·ty [ɪm'pjuːnətɪ]: with ~ impunemente

im·pure [ɪm'pjʊə(r)] adj impuro

in [ɪn] 1 prep ◊ ~ Birmingham / Milan a Birmingham / Milano; ~ the street per strada; ~ the box nella scatola; put it ~ your pocket mettitelo in tasca; wounded ~ the leg / arm ferito alla gamba / al braccio ◊ ~ 1999 nel 1999; ~ two hours from now tra due ore; over period of in due ore; ~ the morning la mattina; ~ the summer d'estate; ~ September a o in settembre ◊ ~ English / Italian in inglese / italiano; ~ a loud voice a voce alta; ~ his style nel suo stile; ~ yellow di giallo ◊ ~ crossing the road (while) mentre attraversava la strada; ~ agreeing to this (by virtue of) accettando questo ◊ ~ his first novel nel suo primo romanzo; ~ Dante in Dante ◊ three ~ all tre in tutto; one ~ ten uno su dieci 2 adv: be ~ at home essere a casa; in the building etc esserci; arrived: of train essere arrivato; in its position essere dentro; is she ~? c'è?; ~ here / there qui / lì (dentro) 3 adj (fashionable, popular), in, di moda

in·a·bil·i·ty [ɪnə'bɪlɪtɪ] incapacità f inv

in·ac·ces·si·ble [ɪnək'sesɪbl] adj inaccessibile

in·ac·cu·rate [ɪn'ækjʊrət] adj inaccurato

in·ac·tive [ɪn'æktɪv] adj inattivo

in·ad·e·quate [ɪn'ædɪkwət] adj inadeguato

in·ad·vis·a·ble [ɪnəd'vaɪzəbl] adj sconsigliabile

in·an·i·mate [ɪn'ænɪmət] *adj* inanimato

in·ap·pro·pri·ate [ɪnə'prəʊprɪət] *adj* inappropriato

in·ar·tic·u·late [ɪnɑː'tɪkjʊlət] *adj* che si esprime male

in·at·ten·tive [ɪnə'tentɪv] *adj* disattento

in·au·di·ble [ɪn'ɔːdɪbl] *adj* impercettibile

in·au·gu·ral [ɪ'nɔːgjʊrəl] *adj speech* inaugurale

in·au·gu·rate [ɪ'nɔːgjʊreɪt] *v/t* inaugurare

in·born ['ɪnbɔːn] *adj* innato

in·breed·ing ['ɪnbriːdɪŋ] unioni *fpl* tra consanguinei

in·cal·cul·a·ble [ɪn'kælkjʊləbl] *adj damage* incalcolabile

in·ca·pa·ble [ɪn'keɪpəbl] *adj* incapace; *be ~ of doing sth* essere incapace di fare qc

in·cen·di·a·ry de·vice [ɪn'sendɪərɪ] ordigno *m* incendiario

in·cense¹ ['ɪnsens] *n* incenso *m*

in·cense² [ɪn'sens] *v/t* fare infuriare

in·cen·tive [ɪn'sentɪv] incentivo *m*

in·ces·sant [ɪn'sesnt] *adj* incessante

in·ces·sant·ly [ɪn'sesntlɪ] *adv* incessantemente

in·cest ['ɪnsest] incesto *m*

inch [ɪntʃ] pollice *m*

in·ci·dent ['ɪnsɪdənt] incidente *m*

in·ci·den·tal [ɪnsɪ'dentl] *adj* casuale; *~ expenses* spese accessorie

in·ci·den·tal·ly [ɪnsɪ'dentlɪ] *adv (by the way)* a proposito

in·cin·e·ra·tor [ɪn'sɪnəreɪtə(r)] inceneritore *m*

in·ci·sion [ɪn'sɪʒn] incisione *f*

in·ci·sive [ɪn'saɪsɪv] *adj mind, analysis* acuto

in·cite [ɪn'saɪt] *v/t* incitare; *~ s.o. to do sth* istigare qu a fare qc

in·clem·ent [ɪn'klemənt] *adj weather* inclemente

in·cli·na·tion [ɪnklɪ'neɪʃn] *tendency, liking* inclinazione *f*

in·cline [ɪn'klaɪn] *v/t: be ~d to believe sth* essere propenso a credere qc; *be ~d to do sth* avere la tendenza di fare qc

in·close, in·clos·ure → enclose, enclosure

in·clude [ɪn'kluːd] *v/t* includere, comprendere

in·clud·ing [ɪn'kluːdɪŋ] *prep* compreso, incluso

in·clu·sive [ɪn'kluːsɪv] **1** *adj price* tutto compreso **2** *prep:* ~ *of VAT* IVA compresa **3** *adv: from Monday to Thursday* ~ dal lunedì al giovedì compreso

in·co·her·ent *adj* incoerente

in·come ['ɪnkəm] reddito *m*

'in·come tax imposta *f* sul reddito

in·com·ing ['ɪnkʌmɪŋ] *adj flight, phonecall, mail* in arrivo; *tide* montante; *president* entrante

in·com·pa·ra·ble [ɪn'kɒmprəbl] *adj* incomparabile

in·com·pat·i·bil·i·ty [ɪnkəmpætɪ'bɪlɪtɪ] incompatibilità *f inv*

in·com·pat·i·ble [ɪnkəm'pætɪbl] *adj* incompatibile

in·com·pe·tence [ɪn'kɒmpɪtəns] incompetenza *f*

in·com·pe·tent [ɪn'kɒmpɪtənt] *adj* incompetente

in·com·plete [ɪnkəm'pliːt] *adj* incompleto

in·com·pre·hen·si·ble [ɪnkɒmprɪ'hensɪbl] *adj* incomprensibile

in·con·cei·va·ble [ɪnkən'siːvəbl] *adj* inconcepibile

in·con·clu·sive [ɪnkən'kluːsɪv] *adj* inconcludente

in·con·gru·ous [ɪn'kɒŋgrʊəs] *adj* fuori luogo

in·con·sid·er·ate [ɪnkən'sɪdərət] *adj* poco gentile

in·con·sis·tent [ɪnkən'sɪstənt] *adj* incoerente

in·con·so·la·ble [ɪnkən'səʊləbl] *adj* inconsolabile

in·con·spic·u·ous [ɪnkən'spɪkjʊəs] *adj* poco visibile; *make o.s.* ~ passare inosservato

in·con·ve·ni·ence [ɪnkən'viːnɪəns] *n* inconveniente *m*

in·con·ve·ni·ent [ɪnkən'viːnɪənt] *adj*

scomodo; *time* poco opportuno

in·cor·po·rate [ɪnˈkɔːpəreɪt] *v/t* includere

in·cor·rect [ɪnkəˈrekt] *adj answer* errato; *behaviour* scorretto; **am I ~ in thinking …?** sbaglio a pensare che …?

in·cor·rect·ly [ɪnkəˈrektlɪ] *adv* in modo errato

in·cor·ri·gi·ble [ɪnˈkɒrɪdʒəbl] *adj* incorreggibile

in·crease [ɪnˈkriːs] **1** *v/t & v/i* aumentare **2** *n* [ˈɪnkriːs] aumento *m*; **on the ~** in aumento

in·creas·ing [ɪnˈkriːsɪŋ] *adj* crescente

in·creas·ing·ly [ɪnˈkriːsɪŋlɪ] *adv* sempre più

in·cred·i·ble [ɪnˈkredɪbl] *adj* (*amazing, very good*) incredibile

in·crim·i·nate [ɪnˈkrɪmɪneɪt] *v/t* compromettere; **~ o.s.** compromettersi

in·cu·ba·tor [ˈɪŋkjʊbeɪtə(r)] incubatrice *f*

in·cur [ɪnˈkɜː(r)] *v/t* (*pret & pp* **-red**) *costs* affrontare; *debts* contrarre; *s.o.'s anger* esporsi a

in·cu·ra·ble [ɪnˈkjʊrəbl] *adj* incurabile

in·debt·ed [ɪnˈdetɪd] *adj*: **be ~ to s.o.** essere (molto) obbligato a qu

in·de·cent [ɪnˈdiːsnt] *adj* indecente

in·de·ci·sive [ɪndɪˈsaɪsɪv] *adj* indeciso

in·de·ci·sive·ness [ɪndɪˈsaɪsɪvnɪs] indecisione *f*

in·deed [ɪnˈdiːd] *adv* (*in fact*) in effetti; (*yes, agreeing*) esatto; **very much ~** moltissimo; **thank you very much ~** grazie mille

in·de·fi·na·ble [ɪndɪˈfaɪnəbl] *adj* indefinibile

in·def·i·nite [ɪnˈdefɪnɪt] *adj* indeterminato; **~ article** GRAM articolo *m* indeterminativo

in·def·i·nite·ly [ɪnˈdefɪnɪtlɪ] *adv* a tempo indeterminato

in·del·i·cate [ɪnˈdelɪkət] *adj* indelicato

in·dent [ˈɪndent] **1** *n in text* rientro *m* a margine **2** *v/t* [ɪnˈdent] *line*

rientrare il margine di

in·de·pen·dence [ɪndɪˈpendəns] indipendenza *f*

in·de·pen·dent [ɪndɪˈpendənt] *adj* indipendente

in·de·pen·dent·ly [ɪndɪˈpendəntlɪ] *adv* indipendentemente; **~ of** indipendentemente da

in·de·scri·ba·ble [ɪndɪˈskraɪbəbl] *adj* indescrivibile

in·de·scrib·a·bly [ɪndɪˈskraɪbəblɪ] *adv*: **~ beautiful** di una bellezza indescrivibile; **~ bad** pessimo

in·de·struc·ti·ble [ɪndɪˈstrʌktəbl] *adj* indistruttibile

in·de·ter·mi·nate [ɪndɪˈtɜːmɪnət] *adj* indeterminato

in·dex [ˈɪndeks] indice *m*

'in·dex card scheda *f*; 'in·dex fin·ger indice *m*; in·dex-'linked *adj* indicizzato

In·di·a [ˈɪndɪə] India *f*

In·di·an [ˈɪndɪən] **1** *adj* indiano **2** *n person* indiano *m*, -a *f*; *American* indiano *m*, -a *f* d'America

In·di·an 'sum·mer estate *f* di San Martino

in·di·cate [ˈɪndɪkeɪt] **1** *v/t* indicare **2** *v/i when driving* segnalare (il cambiamento di direzione)

in·di·ca·tion [ɪndɪˈkeɪʃn] indicazione *f*

in·di·ca·tor [ˈɪndɪkeɪtə(r)] *on car* indicatore *m* di direzione, freccia *f* F

in·dict [ɪnˈdaɪt] *v/t* incriminare

in·dif·fer·ence [ɪnˈdɪfrəns] indifferenza *f*

in·dif·fer·ent [ɪnˈdɪfrənt] *adj* indifferente; (*mediocre*) mediocre

in·di·ges·ti·ble [ɪndɪˈdʒestɪbl] *adj* indigesto

in·di·ges·tion [ɪndɪˈdʒestʃn] indigestione *f*

in·dig·nant [ɪnˈdɪgnənt] *adj* indignato

in·dig·na·tion [ɪndɪgˈneɪʃn] indignazione *f*

in·di·rect [ɪndɪˈrekt] *adj* indiretto

in·di·rect·ly [ɪndɪˈrektlɪ] *adv* indirettamente

in·dis·creet [ɪndɪˈskriːt] adj indiscreto

in·dis·cre·tion [ɪndɪˈskreʃn] indiscrezione f; sexual scappatella f

in·dis·crim·i·nate [ɪndɪˈskrɪmɪnət] adj indiscriminato

in·dis·pen·sa·ble [ɪndɪˈspensəbl] adj indispensabile

in·dis·posed [ɪndɪˈspəʊzd] adj (not well) indisposto

in·dis·pu·ta·ble [ɪndɪˈspjuːtəbl] adj indiscutibile

in·dis·pu·ta·bly [ɪndɪˈspjuːtəbli] adv indiscutibilmente

in·dis·tinct [ɪndɪˈstɪŋkt] adj indistinto

in·dis·tin·guish·a·ble [ɪndɪˈstɪŋgwɪʃəbl] adj indistinguibile

in·di·vid·u·al [ɪndɪˈvɪdjʊəl] **1** n individuo m **2** adj (separate) singolo; (personal) individuale

in·di·vid·u·a·list [ɪndɪˈvɪdjʊəlɪst] adj individualista

in·di·vid·u·al·ly [ɪndɪˈvɪdjʊəli] adv individualmente

in·di·vis·i·ble [ɪndɪˈvɪzɪbl] adj indivisibile

in·doc·tri·nate [ɪnˈdɒktrɪneɪt] v/t indottrinare

in·do·lence [ˈɪndələns] indolenza f

in·do·lent [ˈɪndələnt] adj indolente

In·do·ne·sia [ɪndəˈniːʒə] Indonesia f

In·do·ne·sian [ɪndəˈniːʒən] **1** adj indonesiano **2** n person indonesiano m, -a f

in·door [ˈɪndɔː(r)] adj activities, games al coperto; arena, swimming pool coperto

in·doors [ɪnˈdɔːz] adv in building all'interno; at home in casa

in·duc·tion course [ɪnˈdʌkʃn] corso m d'avviamento

in·dulge [ɪnˈdʌldʒ] **1** v/t o.s., one's tastes soddisfare **2** v/i: ~ **in sth** lasciarsi andare a qc; in joke permettersi qc

in·dul·gence [ɪnˈdʌldʒəns] of tastes, appetite etc soddisfazione f; (laxity) indulgenza f

in·dul·gent [ɪnˈdʌldʒənt] adj (not strict enough) indulgente

in·dus·tri·al [ɪnˈdʌstrɪəl] adj industriale

in·dus·tri·al 'ac·tion agitazione f sindacale

in·dus·tri·al dis'pute vertenza f sindacale

in·dus·tri·al es'tate zona f industriale

in·dus·tri·al·ist [ɪnˈdʌstrɪəlɪst] industriale m

in·dus·tri·al·ize [ɪnˈdʌstrɪəlaɪz] **1** v/t industrializzare **2** v/i industrializzarsi

in·dus·tri·al 'waste scorie fpl industriali

in·dus·tri·ous [ɪnˈdʌstrɪəs] adj diligente

in·dus·try [ˈɪndəstri] industria f

in·ef·fec·tive [ɪnɪˈfektɪv] adj inefficace

in·ef·fec·tu·al [ɪnɪˈfektʃʊəl] adj person inetto

in·ef·fi·cient [ɪnɪˈfɪʃənt] adj inefficiente

in·el·i·gi·ble [ɪnˈelɪdʒɪbl] adj: **be ~ for sth** non avere diritto a qc

in·ept [ɪˈnept] adj inetto

in·e·qual·i·ty [ɪnɪˈkwɒlɪti] disuguaglianza f

in·es·ca·pa·ble [ɪnɪˈskeɪpəbl] adj inevitabile

in·es·ti·ma·ble [ɪnˈestɪməbl] adj inestimabile

in·ev·i·ta·ble [ɪnˈevɪtəbl] adj inevitabile: **the ~ bottle of ...** l'immancabile bottiglia di ...

in·ev·i·ta·bly [ɪnˈevɪtəbli] adv inevitabilmente

in·ex·cu·sa·ble [ɪnɪkˈskjuːzəbl] adj imperdonabile

in·ex·haus·ti·ble [ɪnɪgˈzɔːstəbl] adj supply inesauribile

in·ex·pen·sive [ɪnɪkˈspensɪv] adj poco costoso, economico

in·ex·pe·ri·enced [ɪnɪkˈspɪərɪənst] adj inesperto

in·ex·pli·ca·ble [ɪnɪkˈsplɪkəbl] adj inspiegabile

in·ex·pres·si·ble [ɪnɪkˈspresɪbl] adj inesprimibile

in·fal·li·ble [ɪnˈfælɪbl] adj infallibile

in·fa·mous [ˈɪnfəməs] *adj* famigerato

in·fan·cy [ˈɪnfənsɪ] *of person* infanzia *f*; *of state, institution* stadio *m* iniziale

in·fant [ˈɪnfənt] bambino *m* piccolo, bambina *f* piccola

in·fan·tile [ˈɪnfəntaɪl] *adj pej* infantile

in·fan·try [ˈɪnfəntrɪ] fanteria *f*

in·fan·try 'sol·dier fante *m*

'in·fant school scuola *f* elementare

in·fat·u·at·ed [ɪnˈfætʃʊeɪtɪd] *adj*: **be ~ with s.o.** essere infatuato di qu

in·fect [ɪnˈfekt] *v/t of person* contagiare; *food, water* contaminare; **become ~ed** *of wound* infettarsi; *of person* contagiarsi

in·fec·tion [ɪnˈfekʃn] infezione *f*

in·fec·tious [ɪnˈfekʃəs] *disease* infettivo, contagioso; *fig: laughter* contagioso

in·fer [ɪnˈfɜː(r)] *v/t* (*pret & pp* **-red**): **~ sth from sth** dedurre qc da qc

in·fe·ri·or [ɪnˈfɪərɪə(r)] *adj quality, workmanship* inferiore; *in rank* subalterno

in·fe·ri·or·i·ty [ɪnfɪərɪˈɒrətɪ] *in quality* inferiorità *f inv*

in·fe·ri·or·i·ty com·plex complesso *m* d'inferiorità

in·fer·tile [ɪnˈfɜːtaɪl] *adj* sterile

in·fer·til·i·ty [ɪnfɜːˈtɪlɪtɪ] sterilità *f inv*

in·fi·del·i·ty [ɪnfɪˈdelɪtɪ] infedeltà *f inv*

in·fil·trate [ˈɪnfɪltreɪt] *v/t* infiltrare

in·fi·nite [ˈɪnfɪnət] *adj* infinito

in·fin·i·tive [ɪnˈfɪnɪtɪv] GRAM infinito *m*

in·fin·i·ty [ɪnˈfɪnɪtɪ] infinito *m*

in·firm [ɪnˈfɜːm] *adj* infermo

in·fir·ma·ry [ɪnˈfɜːmərɪ] infermeria *f*

in·fir·mi·ty [ɪnˈfɜːmətɪ] infermità *f inv*

in·flame [ɪnˈfleɪm] *v/t passions* accendere

in·flam·ma·ble [ɪnˈflæməbl] *adj* infiammabile

in·flam·ma·tion [ɪnfləˈmeɪʃn] MED infiammazione *f*

in·flat·a·ble [ɪnˈfleɪtəbl] *adj dinghy* gonfiabile

in·flate [ɪnˈfleɪt] *v/t tyre, dinghy* gonfiare; *economy* inflazionare

in·fla·tion [ɪnˈfleɪʃən] inflazione *f*

in·fla·tion·a·ry [ɪnˈfleɪʃənərɪ] *adj* inflazionistico

in·flec·tion [ɪnˈflekʃn] *of voice* intonazione *f*

in·flex·i·ble [ɪnˈfleksɪbl] *adj attitude, person* inflessibile

in·flict [ɪnˈflɪkt] *v/t*: **~ sth on s.o.** *punishment* infliggere qc a qu; *wound, suffering* procurare qc a qu

'in-flight *adj*: **~ entertainment** intrattenimento a bordo

in·flu·ence [ˈɪnfluəns] **1** *n* influenza *f*; **be a good / bad ~ on s.o.** avere una buona / cattiva influenza su qu; **people who have ~** persone influenti; **who were your main ~s?** chi si è ispirato principalmente? **2** *v/t s.o.'s thinking* esercitare un'influenza su; *decision* influenzare

in·flu·en·tial [ɪnfluˈenʃl] *adj writer, philosopher, film-maker* autorevole; **she knows ~ people** conosce gente influente

in·flu·en·za [ɪnfluˈenzə] influenza *f*

in·form [ɪnˈfɔːm] **1** *v/t* informare; **~ s.o. about sth** informare qu di qc; **please keep me ~ed** tienimi informato **2** *v/i* denunciare; **~ on s.o.** denunciare qu

in·for·mal [ɪnˈfɔːml] *adj* informale

in·for·mal·i·ty [ɪnfɔːˈmælɪtɪ] informalità *f inv*

in·form·ant [ɪnˈfɔːmənt] informatore *m*, -trice *f*

in·for·ma·tion [ɪnfəˈmeɪʃn] informazione *f*; **a bit of ~** un'informazione

in·for·ma·tion 'sci·ence informatica *f*

in·for·ma·tion 'sci·en·tist informatico *m*, -a *f*

in·for·ma·tion tech'nol·o·gy informatica *f*

in·for·ma·tive [ɪnˈfɔːmətɪv] *adj article etc* istruttivo; **he wasn't very ~** non è stato di grande aiuto

in·form·er [ɪnˈfɔːmə(r)] informatore *m*, -trice *f*

in·fra·red [ɪnfrəˈred] *adj* infrarosso

in·fra·struc·ture [ˈɪnfrəstrʌktʃə(r)] infrastruttura f

in·fre·quent [ɪnˈfriːkwənt] adj raro

in·fu·ri·ate [ɪnˈfjʊərɪeɪt] v/t far infuriare

in·fu·ri·at·ing [ɪnˈfjʊərɪeɪtɪŋ] adj esasperante

in·fuse [ɪnˈfjuːz] v/i: let the tea ~ lasciare in infusione il tè

in·fu·sion [ɪnˈfjuːʒn] (herb tea) infuso m

in·ge·ni·ous [ɪnˈdʒiːnɪəs] adj ingegnoso

in·ge·nu·i·ty [ɪndʒɪˈnjuːətɪ] ingegnosità f inv

in·got [ˈɪŋɡət] lingotto m

in·gra·ti·ate [ɪnˈɡreɪʃɪeɪt] v/t: ~ o.s. with s.o. ingraziarsi qu

in·grat·i·tude [ɪnˈɡrætɪtjuːd] ingratitudine f

in·gre·di·ent [ɪnˈɡriːdɪənt] for cooking ingrediente m; fig: for success elemento m

in·hab·it [ɪnˈhæbɪt] v/t abitare

in·hab·it·a·ble [ɪnˈhæbɪtəbl] adj abitabile

in·hab·i·tant [ɪnˈhæbɪtənt] abitante m/f

in·hale [ɪnˈheɪl] 1 v/t inalare 2 v/i when smoking aspirare

in·ha·ler [ɪnˈheɪlə(r)] inalatore m

in·her·it [ɪnˈherɪt] v/t ereditare

in·her·i·tance [ɪnˈherɪtəns] eredità f inv

in·hib·it [ɪnˈhɪbɪt] v/t growth, conversation etc inibire

in·hib·it·ed [ɪnˈhɪbɪtɪd] adj inibito

in·hi·bi·tion [ɪnhɪˈbɪʃn] inibizione f

in·hos·pi·ta·ble [ɪnhɒˈspɪtəbl] adj inospitale

'in-house 1 adj aziendale 2 adv work all'interno dell'azienda

in·hu·man [ɪnˈhjuːmən] adj disumano

i·ni·tial [ɪˈnɪʃl] 1 adj iniziale 2 n iniziale f 3 v/t (write initials on) siglare (con le iniziali)

i·ni·tial·ly [ɪˈnɪʃlɪ] adv inizialmente

i·ni·ti·ate [ɪˈnɪʃɪeɪt] v/t avviare

i·ni·ti·a·tion [ɪnɪʃɪˈeɪʃn] avviamento m

i·ni·tia·tive [ɪˈnɪʃətɪv] iniziativa f; do sth on one's own ~ fare qc di propria iniziativa; take the ~ prendere l'iniziativa

in·ject [ɪnˈdʒekt] v/t medicine, drug, fuel iniettare; capital investire

in·jec·tion [ɪnˈdʒekʃn] MED, of fuel iniezione f; of capital investimento m

'in-joke: it's an ~ è una battuta tra di noi/loro

in·jure [ˈɪndʒə(r)] v/t ferire; ~ o.s. ferirsi

in·jured [ˈɪndʒəd] 1 adj leg ferito; feelings offeso 2 npl feriti mpl

in·ju·ry [ˈɪndʒərɪ] ferita f

'in·ju·ry time SP minuti mpl di recupero

in·jus·tice [ɪnˈdʒʌstɪs] ingiustizia f

ink [ɪŋk] inchiostro m

'ink·jet ('prin·ter) stampante f a getto d'inchiostro

in·land [ˈɪnlənd] adj areas dell'interno; mail nazionale; sea interno

In·land 'Rev·e·nue fisco m

in-laws [ˈɪnlɔːz] npl famiglia fsg della moglie/del marito; (wife's/husband's parents) suoceri mpl

in·lay [ˈɪnleɪ] n intarsio m

in·let [ˈɪnlet] of sea insenatura f; in machine presa f

in·mate [ˈɪnmeɪt] of prison detenuto m, -a f; of mental hospital ricoverato m, -a f

inn [ɪn] locanda f

in·nate [ɪˈneɪt] adj innato

in·ner [ˈɪnə(r)] adj interno

in·ner 'cit·y centro m in degrado di una zona urbana; ~ decay degrado del centro urbano

'in·ner·most adj thoughts etc più intimo

in·ner 'tube camera f d'aria

in·nings [ˈɪnɪŋz] nsg in cricket turno m di battuta

in·no·cence [ˈɪnəsəns] innocenza f

in·no·cent [ˈɪnəsənt] adj innocente

in·noc·u·ous [ɪˈnɒkjʊəs] adj innocuo

in·no·va·tion [ɪnəˈveɪʃn] innovazione f

in·no·va·tive ['ɪnəvətɪv] adj innovativo

in·no·va·tor ['ɪnəveɪtə(r)] innovatore m, -trice f

in·nu·me·ra·ble [ɪ'nju:mərəbl] adj innumerevole

i·noc·u·late [ɪ'nɒkjuleɪt] v/t vaccinare

i·noc·u·la·tion [ɪ'nɒkju'leɪʃn] vaccinazione f

in·of·fen·sive [ɪnə'fensɪv] adj inoffensivo

in·or·gan·ic [ɪnɔː'gænɪk] adj inorganico

'in·pa·tient degente m/f

in·put ['ɪnput] 1 n contributo m; COMPUT input m inv 2 v/t (pret & pp -ted or input) into project contribuire con; COMPUT inserire

in·quest ['ɪnkwest] inchiesta f giudiziaria

in·quire [ɪn'kwaɪə(r)] v/i domandare; ~ into sth svolgere indagini su qc

in·quir·y [ɪn'kwaɪərɪ] richiesta f di informazioni; (public ~) indagine f

in·quis·i·tive [ɪn'kwɪzətɪv] adj curioso

in·sane [ɪn'seɪn] adj pazzo

in·san·i·ta·ry [ɪn'sænɪtrɪ] adj antigienico

in·san·i·ty [ɪn'sænɪtɪ] infermità f mentale

in·sa·tia·ble [ɪn'seɪʃəbl] adj insaziabile

in·scrip·tion [ɪn'skrɪpʃn] iscrizione f

in·scru·ta·ble [ɪn'skru:təbl] adj imperscrutabile

in·sect ['ɪnsekt] insetto m

in·sec·ti·cide [ɪn'sektɪsaɪd] insetticida m

'in·sect re·pel·lent insettifugo m

in·se·cure [ɪnsɪ'kjuə(r)] adj insicuro

in·se·cu·ri·ty [ɪnsɪ'kjuərɪtɪ] insicurezza f

in·sen·si·tive [ɪn'sensɪtɪv] adj insensibile

in·sen·si·tiv·i·ty [ɪnsensɪ'tɪvɪtɪ] insensibilità f inv

in·sep·a·ra·ble [ɪn'sepərəbl] adj two issues inscindibile; two people inseparabile

in·sert ['ɪnsɜːt] 1 n in magazine etc inserto m 2 v/t [ɪn'sɜːt] inserire; ~ sth into sth inserire qc in qc

in·ser·tion [ɪn'sɜːʃn] (act) inserimento m

in·side [ɪn'saɪd] 1 n of house, box interno m; of road destra f; sinistra f; someone on the ~ at Lloyds qualcuno che lavora ai Lloyds; ~ out a rovescio; turn sth ~ out rivoltare qc; know sth ~ out sapere qc a menadito 2 prep dentro; ~ of 2 hours in meno di due ore 3 adv stay, remain, go, carry dentro; I've never been ~ non sono mai entrato 4 adj interno; ~ information informazioni riservate; ~ lane SP corsia f interna; on road corsia f di marcia; ~ pocket tasca f interna

in·sid·er [ɪn'saɪdə(r)]: an ~ from the Department ... un impiegato del Ministero ...

in·sid·er 'deal·ing FIN insider trading m inv

in·sides [ɪn'saɪdz] npl pancia fsg; intestines budella fpl

in·sid·i·ous [ɪn'sɪdɪəs] adj insidioso

in·sight ['ɪnsaɪt]: it offers an ~ into ... permette di capire ...; full of ~ molto intuitivo

in·sig·nif·i·cant [ɪnsɪg'nɪfɪkənt] adj insignificante

in·sin·cere [ɪnsɪn'sɪə(r)] adj falso

in·sin·cer·i·ty [ɪnsɪn'serɪtɪ] falsità f inv

in·sin·u·ate [ɪn'sɪnjueɪt] v/t (imply) insinuare

in·sist [ɪn'sɪst] v/i insistere; please keep it, I ~ tienilo, ci tengo!

♦insist on v/t esigere; insist on doing sth insistere per fare qc

in·sis·tent [ɪn'sɪstənt] adj insistente

in·so·lent ['ɪnsələnt] adj insolente

in·sol·u·ble [ɪn'sɒljubl] adj problem insolvibile; substance insolubile

in·sol·vent [ɪn'sɒlvənt] adj insolvente

in·som·ni·a [ɪn'sɒmnɪə] insonnia f

in·som·ni·ac [ɪn'sɒmnɪæk] persona f che soffre di insonnia

in·spect [ɪn'spekt] v/t work, tickets,

baggage controllare; *building, factory, school* ispezionare

in·spec·tion [ɪnˈspekʃn] *of work, tickets, baggage* controllo *m*; *of building, factory, school* ispezione *f*

in·spec·tor [ɪnˈspektə(r)] *in factory* ispettore *m*, -trice *f*; *on buses* controllore *m*; *of police* ispettore *m*

in·spi·ra·tion [ɪnspəˈreɪʃn] ispirazione *f*; *(very good idea)* lampo *m* di genio

in·spire [ɪnˈspaɪə(r)] *v/t respect etc* suscitare; **be ~d by s.o. / sth** essere ispirato da qu / qc

in·sta·bil·i·ty [ɪnstəˈbɪlɪtɪ] *of character, economy* instabilità *f inv*

in·stall [ɪnˈstɔːl] *v/t computer, telephones, software* installare

in·stal·la·tion [ɪnstəˈleɪʃn] *of new equipment, software* installazione *f*; *military* ~ struttura *f* militare

in·stal·ment, **in·stall·ment** *Am* [ɪnˈstɔːlmənt] *of story, TV drama etc* puntata *f*; *(payment)* rata *f*

in·stance [ˈɪnstəns] *(example)* esempio *m*; **for** ~ per esempio

in·stant [ˈɪnstənt] **1** *adj* immediato **2** *n* istante *m*; **in an** ~ in un attimo

in·stan·ta·ne·ous [ɪnstənˈteɪnɪəs] *adj* immediato

in·stant ˈcof·fee caffè *m inv* istantaneo *o* solubile

in·stant·ly [ˈɪnstəntlɪ] *adv* istantaneamente

in·stead [ɪnˈsted] *adv* invece; ~ **of** invece di

in·step [ˈɪnstep] collo *m* del piede

in·stinct [ˈɪnstɪŋkt] istinto *m*

in·stinc·tive [ɪnˈstɪŋktɪv] *adj* istintivo

in·sti·tute [ˈɪnstɪtjuːt] **1** *n* istituto *m* **2** *v/t new law* introdurre; *enquiry* avviare

in·sti·tu·tion [ɪnstɪˈtjuːʃn] *governmental* istituto *m*; *sth traditional* istituzione *f*; *(setting up)* avviamento *m*

in·struct [ɪnˈstrʌkt] *v/t (order)* dare istruzioni a; *(teach)* istruire; ~ **s.o. to do sth** *(order)* dare istruzioni a qu di fare qc

in·struc·tion [ɪnˈstrʌkʃn] istruzione

f, ~**s for use** istruzioni per l'uso

in·struc·tion man·u·al libretto *m* d'istruzioni

in·struc·tive [ɪnˈstrʌktɪv] *adj* istruttivo

in·struc·tor [ɪnˈstrʌktə(r)] istruttore *m*, -trice *f*

in·stru·ment [ˈɪnstrʊmənt] strumento *m*

in·sub·or·di·nate [ɪnsəˈbɔːdɪnət] *adj* insubordinato

in·suf·fi·cient [ɪnsəˈfɪʃnt] *adj* insufficiente

in·su·late [ˈɪnsjuleɪt] *v/t* ELEC isolare; *against cold* isolare termicamente

in·su·lat·ing tape nastro *m* isolante

in·su·la·tion [ɪnsjʊˈleɪʃn] ELEC isolamento *m*; *against cold* isolamento *m* termico

in·su·lin [ˈɪnsjʊlɪn] insulina *f*

in·sult [ˈɪnsʌlt] **1** *n* insulto *m* **2** *v/t* [ɪnˈsʌlt] insultare

in·sur·ance [ɪnˈʃʊərəns] assicurazione *f*

in·sur·ance com·pa·ny compagnia *f* di assicurazioni; **in·sur·ance pol·i·cy** polizza *f* di assicurazione; **in·sur·ance prem·i·um** premio *m* assicurativo

in·sure [ɪnˈʃʊə(r)] *v/t* assicurare

in·sured [ɪnˈʃʊəd] **1** *adj* assicurato; **be ~ed** essere assicurato **2** *n*: **the** ~ l'assicurato

in·sur·moun·ta·ble [ɪnsəˈmaʊntəbl] *adj* insormontabile

in·tact [ɪnˈtækt] *adj (not damaged)* intatto

in·take [ˈɪnteɪk] *of college etc* (numero *m* di) iscrizioni *fpl*

in·te·grate [ˈɪntɪgreɪt] *v/t* integrare

in·te·grat·ed ˈcir·cuit [ˈɪntɪgreɪtɪd] *adj* circuito *m* integrato

in·teg·ri·ty [ɪnˈtegrətɪ] integrità *f inv*

in·tel·lect [ˈɪntəlekt] intelletto *m*

in·tel·lec·tual [ɪntəˈlektjʊəl] **1** *adj* intellettuale **2** *n* intellettuale *m/f*

in·tel·li·gence [ɪnˈtelɪdʒəns] intelligenza *f*; *(information)* informazioni *fpl*

in·tel·li·gence of·fi·cer agente *m/f*

dei servizi segreti

in·tel·li·gence ser·vice servizi *mpl* segreti

in·tel·li·gent [ɪn'telɪdʒənt] *adj* intelligente

in·tel·li·gi·ble [ɪn'telɪdʒəbl] *adj* intelligibile

in·tend [ɪn'tend] *v/i*: **~ to do sth** (*do on purpose*) volere fare qc; (*plan to do*) avere intenzione di fare qc; *that's not what I ~ed* non è quello che intendevo

in·tense [ɪn'tens] *adj pleasure, heat, pressure* intenso; *concentration* profondo; *he's too ~* è troppo serio

in·ten·si·fy [ɪn'tensɪfaɪ] (*pret & pp -ied*) **1** *v/t effect, pressure* intensificare **2** *v/i of pain* acuirsi; *of fighting* intensificarsi

in·ten·si·ty [ɪn'tensətɪ] intensità *f inv*

in·ten·sive [ɪn'tensɪv] *adj* intensivo

in·ten·sive 'care (**u·nit**) MED (reparto *m* di) terapia *f* intensiva

in·ten·sive 'course corso *m* intensivo

in·tent [ɪn'tent] *adj* **be ~ on doing sth** (*determined to do*) essere deciso a fare qc; (*concentrating on*) essere intento a fare qc

in·ten·tion [ɪn'tenʃn] intenzione *f*; *I have no ~ of ...* (*refuse to*) non ho intenzione di ...

in·ten·tion·al [ɪn'tenʃənl] *adj* intenzionale

in·ten·tion·al·ly [ɪn'tenʃnlɪ] *adv* intenzionalmente

in·ter·ac·tion [ɪntər'ækʃn] interazione *f*

in·ter·ac·tive [ɪntər'æktɪv] *adj* interattivo

in·ter·cede [ɪntə'siːd] *v/i* intercedere

in·ter·cept [ɪntə'sept] *v/t* intercettare

in·ter·change ['ɪntətʃeɪndʒ] *Am* MOT interscambio *m*

in·ter·change·a·ble [ɪntə'tʃeɪndʒəbl] *adj* interscambiabile

in·ter·com ['ɪntəkɒm] citofono *m*

in·ter·course ['ɪntəkɔːs] *sexual* rapporto *m* sessuale

in·ter·de·pend·ent [ɪntədɪ'pendənt] *adj* interdipendente

in·ter·est ['ɪntrəst] **1** *n* interesse *m*; FIN: *rate* interesse *m*; *money paid / received* interessi *mpl*; **take an ~ in sth** interessarsi di qc **2** *v/t* interessare; *does that offer ~ you?* t'interessa l'offerta?

in·ter·est·ed ['ɪntrəstɪd] *adj* interessato; **be ~ in sth** interessarsi di qc; *thanks, but I'm not ~* grazie, non mi interessa

in·ter·est-free 'loan prestito *m* senza interessi

in·ter·est·ing ['ɪntrəstɪŋ] *adj* interessante

'in·ter·est rate FIN tasso *m* d'interesse

interface ['ɪntəfeɪs] **1** *n* interfaccia *f* **2** *v/i* interfacciarsi

in·ter·fere [ɪntə'fɪə(r)] *v/i* interferire
◆ **interfere with** *v/t* manomettere; *plans* intralciare

in·ter·fer·ence [ɪntə'fɪərəns] interferenza *f*; *on radio* interferenze *fpl*

in·te·ri·or [ɪn'tɪərɪə(r)] **1** *adj* interno **2** *n of house* interno *m*; *of country* entroterra *m*

in·te·ri·or 'dec·o·ra·tor arredatore *m*, -trice *f*; **in·te·ri·or de'sign** architettura *f* d'interni; **in·te·ri·or de'sign·er** architetto *m* d'interni

in·ter·lude ['ɪntəluːd] *at theatre, concert* intervallo *m*; (*period*) parentesi *f*

in·ter·mar·ry [ɪntə'mærɪ] *v/i* (*pret & pp -ied*) fare matrimoni misti

in·ter·me·di·a·ry [ɪntə'miːdɪərɪ] *n* intermediario *m*, -a *f*

in·ter·me·di·ate [ɪntə'miːdɪət] *adj* intermedio

in·ter·mis·sion [ɪntə'mɪʃn] *in theatre, cinema* intervallo *m*

in·tern [ɪn'tɜːn] *v/t* internare

in·ter·nal [ɪn'tɜːnl] *adj* interno

in·ter·nal com'bus·tion en·gine motore *m* a scoppio

in·ter·nal·ly [ɪn'tɜːnəlɪ] *adv*: *he's bleeding ~* ha un'emorragia interna; *not to be taken ~* per uso esterno

in·ter·na·tion·al [ɪntə'næʃnl] **1** *adj*

in·ter·na·tion·ale 2 *n match* partita *f* internazionale; *player* giocatore *m*, -trice *f* della nazionale

In·ter·na·tion·al Court of 'Jus·tice Corte *f* Internazionale di Giustizia

in·ter·na·tion·al·ly [ɪntə'næʃnəlɪ] *adv* a livello internazionale

In·ter·na·tion·al 'Mon·e·tar·y Fund Fondo *m* Monetario Internazionale

In·ter·net ['ɪntənet] Internet *m inv*; **on the ~** su Internet; **~ service provider** provider *m inv* di servizi Internet

in·ter·pret [ɪn'tɜːprɪt] 1 *v/t linguistically* tradurre; *piece of music, comment etc* interpretare 2 *v/i* fare da interprete

in·ter·pre·ta·tion [ɪntɜːprɪ'teɪʃn] *linguistic* traduzione *f*; *of piece of music, meaning* interpretazione *f*

in·ter·pret·er [ɪn'tɜːprɪtə(r)] interprete *m/f*

in·ter·re·lat·ed [ɪntərɪ'leɪtɪd] *adj* correlato

in·ter·ro·gate [ɪn'terəgeɪt] *v/t* interrogare

in·ter·ro·ga·tion [ɪntərə'geɪʃn] interrogatorio *m*

in·ter·rog·a·tive [ɪntə'rɒgətɪv] *n* GRAM forma *f* interrogativa

in·ter·ro·ga·tor [ɪntərə'geɪtə(r)] interrogante *m/f*

in·ter·rupt [ɪntə'rʌpt] *v/t & v/i* interrompere

in·ter·rup·tion [ɪntə'rʌpʃn] interruzione *f*

in·ter·sect [ɪntə'sekt] 1 *v/t* intersecare 2 *v/i* intersecarsi

in·ter·sec·tion ['ɪntəsekʃn] (*crossroads*) incrocio *m*

in·ter·val ['ɪntəvl] intervallo *m*; **sunny ~s** schiarite

in·ter·vene [ɪntə'viːn] *v/i of person, police etc* intervenire; *of time* trascorrere

in·ter·ven·tion [ɪntə'venʃn] intervento *m*

in·ter·view ['ɪntəvjuː] 1 *n on TV, in paper* intervista *f*; *for job* intervista *f* d'assunzione, colloquio *m* di lavoro 2 *v/t on TV, for paper* intervistare; *for*

job sottoporre a intervista

in·ter·view·ee [ɪntəvjuː'iː] *on TV* intervistato *m*, -a *f*; *for job* candidato *m*, -a *f*

in·ter·view·er ['ɪntəvjuːə(r)] *on TV, for paper* intervistatore *m*, -trice *f*; (*for job*) persona *f* che conduce un'intervista d'assunzione

in·tes·tine [ɪn'testɪn] intestino *m*

in·ti·ma·cy ['ɪntɪməsɪ] intimità *f inv*

in·ti·mate ['ɪntɪmət] *adj friend, thoughts* intimo; **be ~ with s.o.** *sexually* avere rapporti intimi con qu

in·tim·i·date [ɪn'tɪmɪdeɪt] *v/t* intimidire

in·tim·i·da·tion [ɪntɪmɪ'deɪʃn] intimidazione *f*

in·to ['ɪntʊ] *prep* in; **he put it ~ his suitcase** l'ha messo in valigia; **translate ~ English** tradurre in inglese; **be ~ sth** *F* (*like*) amare qc; (*be involved with*) interessarsi di qc; **be ~ drugs** fare uso di droga; **when you're ~ the job** quando sei pratico del lavoro

in·tol·e·ra·ble [ɪn'tɒlərəbl] *adj* intollerabile

in·tol·e·rant [ɪn'tɒlərənt] *adj* intollerante

in·tox·i·cat·ed [ɪn'tɒksɪkeɪtɪd] *adj* ubriaco

in·tran·si·tive [ɪn'trænsɪtɪv] *adj* intransitivo

in·tra·ve·nous [ɪntrə'viːnəs] *adj* endovenoso

in·trep·id [ɪn'trepɪd] *adj* intrepido

in·tri·cate ['ɪntrɪkət] *adj* complicato

in·trigue ['ɪntriːg] 1 *n* intrigo *m* 2 *v/t* [ɪn'triːg] intrigare; **I would be ~d to know …** m'interesserebbe molto sapere …

in·tri·gu·ing [ɪn'triːgɪŋ] *adj* intrigante

in·tro·duce [ɪntrə'djuːs] *v/t person* presentare; *new technique etc* introdurre; **may I ~ …?** permette che le presenti …?

in·tro·duc·tion [ɪntrə'dʌkʃn] *to person* presentazione *f*; *to a new food, sport etc* approccio *m*; *in book, of new technique* introduzione *f* in·tro·vert ['ɪntrəvɜːt] introverso m, -a f

in·trude [ɪn'truːd] v/i importunare

in·trud·er [ɪn'truːdə(r)] intruso m, -a f

in·tru·sion [ɪn'truːʒn] intrusione f

in·tu·i·tion [ɪntjuː'ɪʃn] intuito m

in·vade [ɪn'veɪd] v/t invadere

in·val·id¹ [ɪn'vælɪd] adj non valido

in·va·lid² ['ɪnvəlɪd] n MED invalido m, -a f

in·val·i·date [ɪn'vælɪdeɪt] v/t claim, theory invalidare

in·val·u·a·ble [ɪn'væljʊbl] adj help, contributor prezioso

in·var·i·a·bly [ɪn'veɪrɪəblɪ] adv (always) invariabilmente

in·va·sion [ɪn'veɪʒn] invasione f

in·vent [ɪn'vent] v/t inventare

in·ven·tion [ɪn'venʃn] invenzione f

in·ven·tive [ɪn'ventɪv] adj fantasioso

in·ven·tor [ɪn'ventə(r)] inventore m, -trice f

in·ven·to·ry ['ɪnvəntrɪ] inventario m

in·verse [ɪn'vɜːs] adj order inverso

in·vert [ɪn'vɜːt] v/t invertire

in·vert·ed 'com·mas [ɪn'vɜːtɪd] npl virgolette fpl

in·ver·te·brate [ɪn'vɜːtɪbrət] n invertebrato m

invest [ɪn'vest] v/t & v/i investire

in·ves·ti·gate [ɪn'vestɪgeɪt] v/t indagare su

in·ves·ti·ga·tion [ɪnvestɪ'geɪʃn] indagine f

in·ves·ti·ga·tive 'jour·nal·ism [ɪn'vestɪgətɪv] giornalismo m investigativo

in·vest·ment [ɪn'vestmənt] investimento m

in·ves·tor [ɪn'vestə(r)] investitore m, -trice

in·vig·or·at·ing [ɪn'vɪgəreɪtɪŋ] adj climate tonificante

in·vin·ci·ble [ɪn'vɪnsəbl] adj invincibile

in·vis·i·ble [ɪn'vɪzɪbl] adj invisibile

in·vi·ta·tion [ɪnvɪ'teɪʃn] invito m

in·vite [ɪn'vaɪt] v/t invitare; can I ~ you for a meal? posso invitarti a pranzo?

♦ invite in v/t invitare a entrare

in·voice ['ɪnvɔɪs] 1 n fattura f 2 v/t customer fatturare

in·vol·un·ta·ry [ɪn'vɒləntrɪ] adj involontario

in·volve [ɪn'vɒlv] v/t hard work, expense comportare; (concern) riguardare; what does it ~? che cosa comporta?; get ~d with sth entrare a far parte di qc; get ~d with s.o. emotionally, romantically legarsi a qu

in·volved [ɪn'vɒlvd] adj (complex) complesso

in·volve·ment [ɪn'vɒlvmənt] in a project etc partecipazione f; in a crime, accident coinvolgimento m

in·vul·ne·ra·ble [ɪn'vʌlnərəbl] adj invulnerabile

in·ward ['ɪnwəd] 1 adj direction verso l'interno; feeling, thoughts intimo 2 adv verso l'interno

in·ward·ly ['ɪnwədlɪ] adv dentro di sé

i·o·dine ['aɪədiːn] iodio m

IOU [aɪəʊ'juː] abbr (= I owe you) pagherò m

IQ [aɪ'kjuː] abbr (= intelligence quotient) quoziente m d'intelligenza

I·ran [ɪ'rɑːn] Iran m

I·ra·ni·an [ɪ'reɪnɪən] 1 adj iraniano 2 n person iraniano m, -a f

I·raq [ɪ'rɑːk] Iraq m

I·ra·qi [ɪ'rɑːkɪ] 1 adj iracheno 2 n person iracheno m, -a f

Ire·land ['aɪələnd] Irlanda f

i·ris ['aɪrɪs] of eye iride f; flower iris m inv

I·rish ['aɪrɪʃ] adj irlandese

'I·rish·man irlandese m

'I·rish·wom·an irlandese f

i·ron ['aɪən] 1 n substance ferro m; for clothes ferro m da stiro 2 v/t shirts etc stirare

i·ron·ic(al) [aɪ'rɒnɪk(l)] adj ironico

i·ron·ing ['aɪənɪŋ]: do the ~ stirare

'i·ron·ing board asse m da stiro

'i·ron·works stabilimento m siderurgico

i·ron·y ['aɪərənɪ] ironia f

ir·ra·tion·al [ɪ'ræʃənl] adj irrazionale

ir·rec·on·ci·la·ble [ɪrekən'saɪləbl] *adj* inconciliabile

ir·re·cov·er·a·ble [ɪrɪ'kʌvərəbl] *adj* irrecuperabile

ir·reg·u·lar [ɪ'regjʊlə(r)] *adj* irregolare

ir·rel·e·vant [ɪ'reləvənt] *adj* non pertinente

ir·rep·a·ra·ble [ɪ'repərəbl] *adj* irreparabile

ir·re·place·a·ble [ɪrɪ'pleɪsəbl] *adj object, person* insostituibile

ir·re·pres·si·ble [ɪrɪ'presəbl] *adj sense of humour* incontenibile; *person* che non si lascia abbattere

ir·re·proa·cha·ble [ɪrɪ'prəʊtʃəbl] *adj* irreprensibile

ir·re·sis·ti·ble [ɪrɪ'zɪstəbl] *adj* irresistibile

ir·re·spec·tive [ɪrɪ'spektɪv] *adj*: ~ of a prescindere da

ir·re·spon·si·ble [ɪrɪ'spɒnsəbl] *adj* irresponsabile

ir·re·trie·va·ble [ɪrɪ'triːvəbl] *adj* irrecuperabile

ir·rev·e·rent [ɪ'revərənt] *adj* irriverente

ir·rev·o·ca·ble [ɪ'revəkəbl] *adj* irrevocabile

ir·ri·gate ['ɪrɪgeɪt] *v/t* irrigare

ir·ri·ga·tion [ɪrɪ'geɪʃn] irrigazione *f*

ir·ri·ga·tion ca·nal canale *m* d'irrigazione

ir·ri·ta·ble ['ɪrɪtəbl] *adj* irritabile

ir·ri·tate ['ɪrɪteɪt] *v/t* irritare

ir·ri·tat·ing ['ɪrɪteɪtɪŋ] *adj* irritante

ir·ri·ta·tion [ɪrɪ'teɪʃn] irritazione *f*

Is·lam ['ɪzlɑːm] Islam *m*

Is·lam·ic [ɪz'læmɪk] *adj* islamico

is·land ['aɪlənd] isola *f*; (*traffic*) ~ isola *f* spartitraffico

is·land·er ['aɪləndə(r)] isolano *m*, -a *f*

i·so·late ['aɪsəleɪt] *v/t* isolare

i·so·lat·ed ['aɪsəleɪtɪd] *adj house, occurrence* isolato

i·so·la·tion [aɪsə'leɪʃn] *of a region* isolamento *m*; *in ~ taken etc* da solo

i·so·la·tion ward reparto *m* d'isola-

mento

ISP [aɪes'piː] *abbr* (= *Internet service provider*) provider *m inv* di servizi Internet

Is·rael ['ɪzreɪl] Israele *m*

Is·rae·li [ɪz'reɪlɪ] **1** *adj* israeliano **2** *n person* israeliano *m*, -a *f*

is·sue ['ɪʃuː] **1** *n* (*matter*) questione *f*; (*result*) risultato *m*; *of magazine* numero *m*; **the point at** ~ il punto in discussione; **take** ~ **with s.o./sth** prendere posizione contro qu/qc **2** *v/t passports, visa* rilasciare; *supplies* distribuire; *coins* emettere; *warning* dare

IT [aɪ'tiː] *abbr* (= *information technology*) IT *f*

it [ɪt] *pron* ◊ *as subject*: **what colour is** ~? – ~ **is red** di che colore è? – è rosso; ~**'s raining** piove; ~**'s me/him** sono io/è lui; ~**'s Charlie here** TELEC sono Charlie; **that's** ~! (*that's right*) proprio così!; (*finished*) finito! ◊ *as object* lo *m*, la *f*; **I broke** ~ l'ho rotto, -a; **I can't eat** ~ **all** non posso mangiarla tutta

I·tal·i·an [ɪ'tæljən] **1** *adj* italiano **2** *n person* italiano *m*, -a *f*; *language* italiano *m*

i·tal·ic [ɪ'tælɪk] *adj* in corsivo

I·ta·ly ['ɪtəlɪ] Italia *f*

itch [ɪtʃ] **1** *n* prurito *m* **2** *v/i* prudere

i·tem ['aɪtəm] *on agenda* punto *m* (all'ordine del giorno); *on shopping list* articolo *m*; *in accounts* voce *f*; *news* ~ notizia *f*; ~ **of clothing** capo *m* di vestiario

i·tem·ize ['aɪtəmaɪz] *v/t invoice* dettagliare

i·tin·e·ra·ry [aɪ'tɪnərərɪ] itinerario *m*

its [ɪts] *adj* il suo *m*, la sua *f*, i suoi *mpl*, le sue *fpl*

it's [ɪts] → *it is*; *it has*

it·self [ɪt'self] *pron reflexive* si; *emphatic* di per sé; *by* ~ (*alone*) da solo; (*automatically*) da sé

i·vo·ry ['aɪvərɪ] avorio *m*

i·vy ['aɪvɪ] edera *f*

J

jab [dʒæb] v/t (*pret & pp* **-bed**) conficcare

jab·ber ['dʒæbə(r)] v/i parlare fitto fitto

jack [dʒæk] n MOT cric m inv; *in cards* fante m

♦ **jack up** v/t MOT sollevare con il cric

jack·et ['dʒækɪt] n giacca f; *of book* copertina f

jack·et po'ta·to patata f al forno con la buccia

'jack·knife 1 n coltello m a serramanico **2** v/i: **the lorry ~d** il rimorchio dell'articolato si è messo di traverso

'jack·pot primo premio m; **hit the ~** vincere il primo premio; *fig* fare un terno al lotto

jade [dʒeɪd] giada f

jad·ed ['dʒeɪdɪd] *adj* spossato

jag·ged ['dʒægɪd] *adj* frastagliato

jail [dʒeɪl] n prigione f

jam[1] [dʒæm] *for bread* marmellata f

jam[2] [dʒæm] **1** n MOT ingorgo m; **be in a ~** F (*difficulty*) essere in difficoltà **2** v/t (*pret & pp* **-med**) (*ram*) ficcare; (*cause to stick*) bloccare; *broadcast* disturbare; **be ~med** *of roads* essere congestionato; *of door, window* essere bloccato **3** v/i (*pret & pp* **-med**) (*stick*) bloccarsi; (*squeeze*) stiparsi

♦ **jam on** v/t: **jam on the brakes** inchiodare

jam-'packed *adj* F pieno zeppo

jan·i·tor ['dʒænɪtə(r)] custode m

Jan·u·a·ry ['dʒænjʊərɪ] gennaio m

Ja·pan [dʒəˈpæn] Giappone m

Jap·a·nese [dʒæpəˈniːz] **1** *adj* giapponese **2** n *person* giapponese m/f; *language* giapponese m

jar[1] [dʒɑː(r)] n *container* barattolo m

jar[2] [dʒɑː(r)] v/i (*pret & pp* **-red**) *of noise* stridere; **~ on** dar fastidio a

jar·gon ['dʒɑːgən] gergo m

jaun·dice ['dʒɔːndɪs] itterizia f

jaun·diced ['dʒɔːndɪst] *adj fig* cinico

jaunt [dʒɔːnt] gita f

jaun·ty ['dʒɔːntɪ] *adj* sbarazzino

jav·e·lin ['dʒævlɪn] (*spear*) giavellotto m; *event* lancio m del giavellotto

jaw [dʒɔː] n mascella f

jay·walk·er ['dʒeɪwɔːkə(r)] pedone m indisciplinato

jazz [dʒæz] jazz m inv

♦ **jazz up** v/t F ravvivare

jeal·ous ['dʒeləs] *adj* geloso; **be ~ of ...** essere geloso di ...

jeal·ous·ly ['dʒeləslɪ] *adv* gelosamente

jeal·ous·y ['dʒeləsɪ] gelosia f

jeans [dʒiːnz] *npl* jeans *mpl*

jeep [dʒiːp] jeep f inv

jeer [dʒɪə(r)] **1** n scherno m **2** v/i schernire; **~ at** schernire

jel·ly ['dʒelɪ] gelatina f

'jel·ly ba·by bonbon m inv di gelatina; **'jel·ly bean** bonbon m inv di gelatina; **'jel·ly·fish** medusa f

jeop·ar·dize ['dʒepədaɪz] v/t mettere in pericolo

jeop·ar·dy ['dʒepədɪ]: **be in ~** essere in pericolo

jerk[1] [dʒɜːk] **1** n scossone m **2** v/t dare uno strattone

jerk[2] [dʒɜːk] F idiota m/f

jerk·y ['dʒɜːkɪ] *adj movement* a scatti

jer·sey ['dʒɜːzɪ] (*sweater*) maglia f; *fabric* jersey m inv

jest [dʒest] **1** n scherzo m; **in ~** per scherzo **2** v/i scherzare

Je·sus ['dʒiːzəs] Gesù m

jet [dʒet] **1** n *of water* zampillo m; (*nozzle*) becco m; *airplane* jet m inv **2** v/i (*pret & pp* **-ted**) *travel* volare

jet-'black *adj* (nero) corvino; **'jet en·gine** motore m a reazione; **'jet·lag** jet-lag m inv

jet·ti·son ['dʒetɪsn] v/t gettare; fig abbandonare

jet·ty ['dʒetɪ] molo m

Jew [dʒuː] ebreo m, -a f

jew·el ['dʒuːəl] gioiello m; fig: person perla f

jew·el·er Am, **jew·el·ler** ['dʒuːlə(r)] gioielliere m

jew·el·lery, jew·el·ry Am ['dʒuːlrɪ] gioielli mpl

Jew·ish ['dʒuːɪʃ] adj ebraico; people ebreo

jif·fy ['dʒɪfɪ] F: **in a ~** in un batter d'occhio, in un attimo

jig·saw (puzzle) ['dʒɪgsɔː] puzzle m inv

jilt [dʒɪlt] v/t piantare

jin·gle ['dʒɪŋgl] **1** n song jingle m inv **2** v/i of keys, coins tintinnare

jinx [dʒɪŋks] n person iettatore m, -trice f; (bad luck) **there's a ~ on this project** questo progetto è iellato

jit·ters ['dʒɪtəz] npl F: **get the ~** avere fifa F

jit·ter·y ['dʒɪtərɪ] adj F nervoso

job [dʒɒb] n (employment) lavoro m; (task) compito m; **out of a ~** senza lavoro; **it's a good ~ you ...** meno male che tu ...; **you'll have a ~** (it'll be difficult) sarà un'impresa

'job cen·tre Br ufficio m di collocamento; **'job de·scrip·tion** elenco m delle mansioni; **'job hunt: be ~ing** cercare lavoro

job·less ['dʒɒblɪs] adj disoccupato

job sat·is·fac·tion soddisfazione f nel lavoro

jock·ey ['dʒɒkɪ] n fantino m

jog [dʒɒg] **1** n corsa f; **go for a ~** andare a fare footing **2** v/i (pret & pp **-ged**) as exercise fare footing **3** v/t (pret & pp **-ged**) elbow etc urtare; **~ s.o.'s memory** rinfrescare la memoria a qu

♦ **jog along** v/i F procedere

jog·ger ['dʒɒgə(r)] person persona f che fa footing; Am shoe scarpa f da ginnastica

jog·ging ['dʒɒgɪŋ] footing m inv; **go ~** fare footing

'jog·ging suit tuta f da ginnastica

join [dʒɔɪn] **1** n giuntura f **2** v/i of roads, rivers unirsi; (become a member) iscriversi **3** v/t (connect) unire; person unirsi a; club iscriversi a; (go to work for) entrare in; of road congiungersi a

♦ **join in** v/i partecipare

♦ **join up** v/i MIL arruolarsi

join·er ['dʒɔɪnə(r)] n falegname m

joint [dʒɔɪnt] **1** n ANAT articolazione f; in woodwork giunto m; of meat arrosto m; F place locale m; of cannabis spinello m **2** adj (shared) comune

joint ac·count conto m comune

joint 'ven·ture joint venture f inv

joke [dʒəʊk] **1** n story barzelletta f; (practical ~) scherzo m; **play a ~ on** fare uno scherzo a; **it's no ~** non è uno scherzo **2** v/i (pretend) scherzare

jok·er ['dʒəʊkə(r)] in cards jolly m inv; F burlone m, -a f

jok·ing ['dʒəʊkɪŋ]: **~ apart** scherzi a parte

jok·ing·ly ['dʒəʊkɪŋlɪ] adv scherzosamente

jol·ly ['dʒɒlɪ] adj allegro; **~ good** benissimo

jolt [dʒəʊlt] **1** n (jerk) scossone m **2** v/t (push) urtare

jos·tle ['dʒɒsl] v/t spintonare

♦ **jot down** [dʒɒt] v/t (pret & pp **-ted**) annotare

jour·nal ['dʒɜːnl] magazine rivista f; diary diario m

jour·nal·is·m ['dʒɜːnəlɪzm] giornalismo m

jour·nal·ist ['dʒɜːnəlɪst] giornalista m/f

jour·ney ['dʒɜːnɪ] n viaggio m

jo·vi·al ['dʒəʊvɪəl] adj gioviale

joy [dʒɔɪ] gioia f

'joy·stick COMPUT joystick m inv

ju·bi·lant ['dʒuːbɪlənt] adj esultante

ju·bi·la·tion [dʒuːbɪ'leɪʃn] giubilo m

judge [dʒʌdʒ] **1** n giudice m **2** v/t giudicare; competition fare da giudice a **3** v/i giudicare

judg(e)·ment ['dʒʌdʒmənt] n

giudizio m; **I agreed, against my better** ~ ho accettato, pur pensando che fosse sbagliato; **an error of** ~ un errore di valutazione

'**Judg(e)·ment Day** il giorno m del giudizio

ju·di·cial [dʒuːˈdɪʃl] adj giudiziario

ju·di·cious [dʒuːˈdɪʃəs] adj giudizioso

ju·do [ˈdʒuːdəʊ] judo m inv

jug [dʒʌg] brocca f

jug·ger·naut [ˈdʒʌgənɔːt] bisonte m della strada F

jug·gle [ˈdʒʌgl] v/t fare giochi di destrezza con; fig: conflicting demands destreggiarsi fra; figures manipolare

jug·gler [ˈdʒʌglə(r)] giocoliere m

juice [dʒuːs] succo m

juic·y [ˈdʒuːsɪ] adj succoso; news, gossip piccante

juke·box [ˈdʒuːkbɒks] juke-box m inv

Ju·ly [dʒuːˈlaɪ] luglio m

jum·ble [ˈdʒʌmbl] mucchio m

♦ **jumble up** v/t mescolare

'**jum·ble sale** vendita f di beneficenza

jum·bo (jet) [ˈdʒʌmbəʊ] jumbo m (jet)

'**jum·bo-sized** adj gigante

jump [dʒʌmp] **1** n salto m; (increase) impennata f; **give a** ~ **of surprise** sobbalzare **2** v/i saltare; (increase) aumentare rapidamente, avere un'impennata; in surprise sobbalzare; ~ **to one's feet** balzare in piedi; ~ **to conclusions** arrivare a conclusioni affrettate **3** v/t fence etc saltare; F (attack) aggredire; ~ **the queue** non rispettare la fila; ~ **the lights** passare col rosso

♦ **jump at** opportunity prendere al balzo, cogliere al volo

jump·er¹ [ˈdʒʌmpə(r)] golf m inv

jump·er² [ˈdʒʌmpə(r)] SP saltatore m, -trice f

jump·y [ˈdʒʌmpɪ] adj nervoso

junc·tion [ˈdʒʌŋkʃn] of roads incrocio m

junc·ture [ˈdʒʌŋktʃə(r)] fml: **at this** ~ in questo frangente

June [dʒuːn] giugno m

jun·gle [ˈdʒʌŋgl] giungla f

ju·ni·or [ˈdʒuːnɪə(r)] **1** adj (subordinate) subalterno; (younger) giovane **2** n in rank subalterno m, -a f; **she is ten years my** ~ ha dieci anni meno di me

'**ju·ni·or school** scuola f elementare

junk [dʒʌŋk] (rubbish) robaccia f

'**junk food** alimenti mpl poco sani

junk·ie [ˈdʒʌŋkɪ] n F tossico m, -a f F

'**junk mail** posta f spazzatura; '**junk shop** negozio m di chincaglierie; '**junk·yard** deposito m di robivecchi

ju·ris·dic·tion [dʒʊərɪsˈdɪkʃn] LAW giurisdizione f

ju·ror [ˈdʒʊərə(r)] n giurato m, -a f

ju·ry [ˈdʒʊərɪ] n giuria f

just [dʒʌst] **1** adj giusto **2** adv (barely) appena; (exactly) proprio; (only) solo; **I've ~ seen her** l'ho appena vista; ~ **about** (almost) quasi; **I was ~ about to leave when ...** stavo proprio per andarmene quando ...; **a house ~ like that** una casa proprio così; **he left her ~ like that** l'ha lasciata così, senza spiegazioni; **he agreed ~ like that** l'ha accettato così, senza pensarci due volte; ~ **now** (a few moments ago) proprio ora; (at the moment) al momento; ~ **you wait!** aspetta un po'!; ~ **be quiet!** fai silenzio!; ~ **as rich** altrettanto ricco

jus·tice [ˈdʒʌstɪs] giustizia f

jus·ti·fi·a·ble [dʒʌstɪˈfaɪəbl] adj giustificabile

jus·ti·fi·a·bly [dʒʌstɪˈfaɪəblɪ] adv a ragione

jus·ti·fi·ca·tion [dʒʌstɪfɪˈkeɪʃn] giustificazione f

jus·ti·fy [ˈdʒʌstɪfaɪ] v/t (pret & pp -ied) also text giustificare

just·ly [ˈdʒʌstlɪ] adv giustamente

♦ **jut out** [dʒʌt] v/i (pret & pp -ted) sporgere

ju·ve·nile [ˈdʒuːvənaɪl] **1** adj minorile; pej puerile **2** n fml minore m/f

ju·ve·nile de·lin·quen·cy delinquenza *f* minorile

ju·ve·nile de·lin·quent delinquente
m/f minorile

K

k [keɪ] *abbr* (= *kilobyte*) k (=kilobyte
m inv); (= *thousand*) mille; *earn
25K* guadagnare 25 mila sterline
kan·ga·roo [kæŋgəˈruː] canguro *m*
ka·ra·te [kəˈrɑːtɪ] karate *m inv*
ka·ra·te chop colpo *m* di karate
ke·bab [kɪˈbæb] spiedino *m* di carne
keel [kiːl] NAUT chiglia *f*
♦ keel over *v/i of boat* capovolgersi;
of structure crollare; *of person* cascare per terra; *faint* svenire
keen [kiːn] *adj person* entusiasta;
interest, competition vivo; *be ~ on
sth* essere appassionato di qc; *I'm
not ~ on the idea* l'idea non mi va
tanto; *he's ~ on her* lei gli piace
molto; *be ~ to do sth* aver molta
voglia di fare qc
keep [kiːp] 1 *n* (*maintenance*) vitto e
alloggio *m*; *for ~s* F per sempre 2 *v/t*
(*pret & pp* **kept**) tenere; (*not lose*)
mantenere; (*detain*) trattenere;
family mantenere; *animals* allevare;
~ a promise mantenere una promessa; *~ s.o. company* tenere compagnia a qu; *~ s.o. waiting* far
aspettare qu; *~ sth to o.s.* (*not tell*)
tenere qc per sé; *~ sth from s.o.* nascondere qc a qu; *~ s.o. from doing
sth* impedire a qu di fare qc; *~
trying!* continua a provare!; *don't ~
interrupting!* non interrompere in
continuazione! 3 *v/i* (*pret & pp
kept*) (*remain*) rimanere; *of food,
milk* conservarsi; *~ left* tenere la sinistra; *~ straight on* vai sempre
dritto; *~ still* stare fermo
♦ keep away 1 *v/i* stare alla larga;
keep away from ... stai alla larga
da ... 2 *v/t* tenere lontano; *keep s.o.*

away from sth tenere qu lontano
da qc
♦ keep back *v/t* (*hold in check*) trattenere; *information* nascondere
♦ keep down *v/t voice* abbassare;
costs, inflation etc contenere; *food*
trattenere; *keep the noise down,
will you?* fate meno rumore!
♦ keep in *v/t in hospital* trattenere;
keep a pupil in punire uno studente
trattenendolo oltre l'orario scolastico
♦ keep off 1 *v/t* (*avoid*) evitare; *keep
off the grass* non calpestare l'erba
2 *v/i*: *if the rain keeps off* se non
piove
♦ keep on 1 *v/i* continuare; *keep on
doing sth* continuare a fare qc 2 *v/t*
employee, coat tenere
♦ keep on at *v/t* (*nag*) assillare
♦ keep out 1 *v/t the cold* proteggere
da; *person* escludere 2 *v/i of room*
non entrare (*of* in); *of argument etc*
non immischiarsi (*of* in); *keep out
as sign* vietato l'ingresso; *you keep
out of this!* non immischiarti!
♦ keep to *v/t path, rules* seguire; *keep
to the point* non divagare
♦ keep up 1 *v/i when walking, running etc* tener dietro 2 *v/t pace, payments* stare dietro a; *bridge, pants*
reggere
♦ keep up *v/t* stare al passo con;
(*stay in touch with*) mantenere i rapporti con
keep·ing [ˈkiːpɪŋ]: *be in ~ with* essere in armonia con
'keep·sake ricordo *m*
keg [keg] barilotto *m*
ken·nel [ˈkenl] canile *m*
ken·nels [ˈkenlz] *npl* canile *m*

kept [kept] *pret & pp* → **keep**

kerb [kɜːb] orlo *m* del marciapiede

ker·nel ['kɜːnl] nocciolo *m*

ketch·up ['ketʃʌp] ketchup *m inv*

ket·tle ['ketl] bollitore *m*

key [kiː] **1** *n* to door, drawer, MUS chiave *f*; on keyboard tasto *m* **2** *adj* (vital) chiave **3** *v/t* COMPUT battere

♦ **key in** *v/t* data immettere

'key·board COMPUT, MUS tastiera *f*; **'key·board·er** COMPUT, MUS tastierista *m/f*; **'key·card** tessera *f* magnetica

keyed-up [kiːd'ʌp] *adj* agitato

'key·hole buco *m* della serratura; **key·note** 'speech discorso *m* programmatico; **'key·ring** portachiavi *m inv*

kha·ki ['kɑːkɪ] *adj colour* cachi *inv*

kick [kɪk] **1** *n* calcio *m*; F (thrill) gusto *m*; (just) for ~s F (solo) per il gusto di farlo **2** *v/t* dare un calcio a; F habit liberarsi da F dare calci; SP calciare; of horse scalciare

♦ **kick around** *v/t* (treat harshly) maltrattare; F (discuss) discutere di; **kick a ball around** giocare a pallone

♦ **kick in** *v/i* P (start to operate) entrare in funzione

♦ **kick off** *v/i* F (start) iniziare; of player dare il calcio d'inizio

♦ **kick out** *v/t* buttar fuori; **be kicked out of the company / army** essere buttato fuori dalla ditta / dall'esercito

♦ **kick up** *v/t*: **kick up a fuss** fare una scenata

'kick·back F (bribe) tangente *f*

'kick-off SP calcio *m* d'inizio

kid [kɪd] **1** *n* F (child) bambino *m*, -a *f*; F (young person) ragazzo *m*, -a *f*; ~ **brother / sister** fratello / sorella minore **2** *v/t* (pret & pp **-ded**) F prendere in giro **3** *v/i* (pret & pp **-ded**) F scherzare; **I was only ~ding** stavo solo scherzando

kid·der ['kɪdə(r)] F burlone *m*, -a *f*

kid 'gloves: handle s.o. with ~ trattare qu coi guanti

kid·nap ['kɪdnæp] *v/t* (pret & pp **-ped**) rapire, sequestrare

kid·nap·per ['kɪdnæpə(r)] rapitore *m*, -trice *f*, sequestratore *m*, -trice *f*

'kid·nap·ping ['kɪdnæpɪŋ] rapimento *m*, sequestro *m* (di persona)

kid·ney ['kɪdnɪ] ANAT rene *m*; in cooking rognone *m*

'kid·ney bean fagiolo *m* comune

'kid·ney ma·chine MED rene *m* artificiale

kill [kɪl] *v/t* uccidere; plant, time ammazzare; **be ~ed in an accident** morire in un incidente; ~ **o.s.** suicidarsi; ~ **o.s. laughing** F morire dalle risate

kil·ler ['kɪlə(r)] (murderer) assassino *m*, -a *f*; (hired ~) killer *m/f inv*; **flu can be a ~** si può morire di influenza

kil·ling ['kɪlɪŋ] omicidio *m*; **make a ~** F (lots of money) fare un pacco di soldi F

kil·ling·ly ['kɪlɪŋlɪ] *adv* F: ~ **funny** divertentissimo

kiln [kɪln] fornace *f*

ki·lo ['kiːləʊ] chilo *m*

ki·lo·byte ['kɪləʊbaɪt] COMPUT kilobyte *m inv*

ki·lo·gram ['kɪləʊgræm] chilogrammo *m*

ki·lo·me·ter *Am*, **ki·lo·me·tre** [kɪ'lɒmɪtə(r)] chilometro *m*

kilt [kɪlt] kilt *m inv*

kind[1] [kaɪnd] *adj* gentile

kind[2] [kaɪnd] *n* (sort) tipo *m*; (make, brand) marca *f*; **all ~s of people** gente di tutti i tipi; **nothing of the ~!** niente affatto!; ~ **of sad / strange** F un po' triste / strano

kin·der·gar·ten ['kɪndəgɑːtn] asilo *m*

kind-heart·ed [kaɪnd'hɑːtɪd] *adj* di buon cuore

kind·ly ['kaɪndlɪ] **1** *adj* gentile **2** *adv* gentilmente; (please) per cortesia

kind·ness ['kaɪndnɪs] *n* gentilezza *f*

king [kɪŋ] re *m inv*

king·dom ['kɪŋdəm] regno *m*

'king-size(d) *adj bed* matrimoniale grande; cigarettes lungo kink [kɪŋk] *in hose etc* attorcigliamento *m*

kink·y ['kɪŋkɪ] *adj* F particolare F

kiosk ['kiːɒsk] edicola *f*

kip [kɪp] P pisolino *m*

kip·per ['kɪpə(r)] aringa *f* affumicata

kiss [kɪs] **1** *n* bacio *m* **2** *v/t* baciare **3** *v/i* baciarsi

kiss of 'life respirazione *f* bocca a bocca

kit [kɪt] kit *m inv*; (*equipment*) attrezzatura *f*; *for assembly* kit *m inv* di montaggio

kitch·en ['kɪtʃɪn] cucina *f*

kitch·en·ette [kɪtʃɪ'net] cucinino *m*

kitch·en 'sink: *she packs everything but the ~* F si porta dietro tutta la casa

kite [kaɪt] aquilone *m*

kit·ten ['kɪtn] gattino *m*

kit·ty ['kɪtɪ] *money* cassa *f* comune

knack [næk] capacità *f inv*; *there's a ~ to it* bisogna saperlo fare

knead [niːd] *v/t dough* lavorare

knee [niː] *n* ginocchio *m*

'knee·cap *n* rotula *f*

kneel [niːl] *v/i* (*pret & pp* knelt) inginocchiarsi

'knee-length *adj* al ginocchio

knelt [nelt] *pret & pp → kneel*

knew [njuː] *pret → know*

knick·ers ['nɪkəz] *npl* mutandine *fpl*; *get one's ~ in a twist* P agitarsi

knick-knacks ['nɪknæks] *npl* F ninnoli *mpl*

knife [naɪf] **1** *n* (*pl knives* [naɪvz]) coltello *m* **2** *v/t* accoltellare

knight [naɪt] *n* cavaliere *m*

knit [nɪt] (*pret & pp -ted*) **1** *v/t* fare a maglia **2** *v/i* lavorare a maglia

♦knit together *v/i of broken bone* saldarsi

knit·ting ['nɪtɪŋ] *sth being knitted* lavoro *m* a maglia; *activity* il lavorare *m* a maglia

'knit·ting nee·dle ferro *m* (da calza)

'knit·wear maglieria *f*

knob [nɒb] *on door* pomello *m*; *of butter* noce *f*

knock [nɒk] **1** *n on door* colpo *m*; (*blow*) botta *f* **2** *v/t* (*hit*) colpire; *head, knee* battere; F (*criticize*) criticare **3** *v/i at the door* bussare (*at* a); *I ~ed my head* ho battuto la testa

♦knock around **1** *v/t* F (*beat*) picchiare **2** *v/i* F (*travel*) vagabondare

♦knock down *v/t of car* investire; *object, building etc* buttar giù; F (*reduce the price of*) scontare

♦knock off **1** *v/t* F (*steal*) fregare P **2** *v/i* F (*stop work for the day*) smontare F

♦knock out *v/t* (*make unconscious*) mettere K.O. F; *power lines etc* mettere fuori uso; (*eliminate*) eliminare

♦knock over *v/t* far cadere; *of car* investire

'knock·down *adj*: *a ~ price* un prezzo stracciato

knock·er ['nɒkə(r)] *on door* battente *m*

knock-kneed [nɒk'niːd] *adj* con le gambe storte

'knock·out *in boxing* K.O. *m inv*

knot [nɒt] **1** *n* nodo *m* **2** *v/t* (*pret & pp -ted*) annodare

'knot·ty ['nɒtɪ] *adj problem* spinoso

know [nəʊ] **1** *v/t* (*pret knew, pp known*) sapere; *person, place* conoscere; (*recognize*) riconoscere; *~ how to waltz* saper ballare il valzer **2** *v/i* (*pret knew, pp known*) sapere; *I don't ~* non so; *yes, I ~* sì, lo so **3** *n*: *be in the ~* F essere beninformato

'know-all F sapientone *m*, -a *f*

'know-how F know-how *m inv*

know·ing ['nəʊɪŋ] *adj* d'intesa

know·ing·ly ['nəʊɪŋlɪ] *adv* (*wittingly*) deliberatamente; *smile etc* con aria d'intesa

knowl·edge ['nɒlɪdʒ] conoscenza *f*; *to the best of my ~* per quanto io sappia; *have a good ~ of ...* avere una buona conoscenza di ...

knowl·edge·a·ble ['nɒlɪdʒəbl] *adj* ferrato

known [nəʊn] *pp → know*

knuck·le ['nʌkl] nocca *f*

♦knuckle down *v/i* F impegnarsi

♦knuckle under *v/i* F cedere

KO [keɪ'əʊ] (*knockout*) K.O. *m inv*

K

Ko·ran [kəˈrɑːn] Corano *m*
Ko·re·a [kəˈriːə] Corea *f*
Ko·re·an [kəˈriːən] **1** *adj* coreano **2** *n* coreano *m*, -a *f*; *language* coreano *m*

ko·sher [ˈkəʊʃə(r)] *adj* REL kasher; F a posto
kow·tow [ˈkaʊtaʊ] *v/i* F prostrarsi
ku·dos [ˈkjuːdɒs] gloria *f*

L

lab [læb] laboratorio *m*
la·bel [ˈleɪbl] **1** *n* etichetta *f* **2** *v/t baggage* mettere l'etichetta su
la·bo·ra·to·ry [ləˈbɒrətri] laboratorio *m*
la·bo·ra·to·ry tech·ni·cian tecnico *m* di laboratorio
la·bor *etc Am* → **labour** *etc*
la·bo·ri·ous [ləˈbɔːrɪəs] *adj* laborioso
'la·bor u·ni·on *Am* sindacato *m*
la·bour [ˈleɪbə(r)] *n* (*work*) lavoro *m*; *in pregnancy* travaglio *m*; **be in ~** avere le doglie *fpl*
la·boured [ˈleɪbəd] *adj style, speech* pesante
la·bour·er [ˈleɪbərə(r)] manovale *m*
'La·bour Par·ty partito *m* laburista
'la·bour ward MED sala *f* travaglio
lace [leɪs] *n material* pizzo *m*; *for shoe* laccio *m*
◆ **lace up** *v/t shoes* allacciare
lack [læk] **1** *n* mancanza *f* **2** *v/t* mancare di **3** *v/i*: **be ~ing** mancare
lac·quer [ˈlækə(r)] *n for hair* lacca *f*
lad [læd] ragazzo *m*
lad·der [ˈlædə(r)] scala *f* (a pioli); *Br*: *in tights* sfilatura *f*
'lad·der·proof *adj Br* indemagliabile
la·den [ˈleɪdn] *adj* carico
la·dies (room) [ˈleɪdiːz] bagno *m* per donne
la·dle [ˈleɪdl] *n* mestolo *m*
la·dy [ˈleɪdɪ] signora *f*
'la·dy·bird coccinella *f*
'la·dy·like da signora; **she's not very ~** non è certo una signora
lag [læg] *v/t* (*pret & pp* **-ged**) *pipes* isolare

◆ **lag behind** *v/i* essere indietro
la·ger [ˈlɑːɡə(r)] birra *f* (bionda)
la·goon [ləˈɡuːn] laguna *f*
laid [leɪd] *pret & pp* → **lay**
laid-back [leɪdˈbæk] *adj* rilassato
lain [leɪn] *pp* → **lie**
lake [leɪk] lago *m*
lamb [læm] *animal, meat* agnello *m*
lame [leɪm] *adj person* zoppo; *excuse* zoppicante
la·ment [ləˈment] **1** *n* lamento *m* **2** *v/t* piangere
lam·en·ta·ble [ˈlæməntəbl] *adj* deplorevole
lam·i·nat·ed [ˈlæmɪneɪtɪd] *adj surface* laminato; *paper* plastificato
lam·i·nat·ed 'glass vetro *m* laminato
lamp [læmp] lampada *f*
'lamp·post lampione *m*
'lamp·shade paralume *m*
land [lænd] **1** *n* terreno *m* (*shore*) terra *f* (*country*) paese *m*; **by ~** per via di terra; **on ~** sulla terraferma; **work on the ~** *as farmer* lavorare la terra **2** *v/t aeroplane* far atterrare; *job* accaparrarsi **3** *v/i of aeroplane* atterrare; *of ball, sth thrown* cadere, finire
land·ing [ˈlændɪŋ] *n of aeroplane* atterraggio *m*; *top of staircase* pianerottolo *m*
'land·ing field terreno *m* d'atterraggio; **'land·ing gear** carrello *m* d'atterraggio; **'land·ing strip** pista *f* d'atterraggio
'land·la·dy *of bar* proprietaria *f*; *of rented room* padrona *f* di casa;
'land·lord *of bar* proprietario *m*; *of*

rented room padrone *m* di casa;
'**land·mark** punto *m* di riferimento;
fig pietra *f* miliare; '**land own·er**
proprietario *m*, -a *f* terriero, -a;
land·scape ['lændskeɪp] **1** *n* paesaggio *m* **2** *adv print* landscape, orizzontale

'**land·slide** frana *f*

land·slide '**vic·to·ry** vittoria *f*
schiacciante

lane [leɪn] *in country* viottolo *m*;
(alley) vicolo *m*; MOT corsia *f*

lan·guage ['læŋgwɪdʒ] lingua *f*;
(speech, style) linguaggio *m*

'**lan·guage lab** laboratorio *m* linguistico

lank [læŋk] *adj pej: hair* diritto

lank·y ['læŋkɪ] *adj person* allampanato

lan·tern ['læntən] lanterna *f*

lap[1] [læp] *n of track* giro *m* (di pista)

lap[2] [læp] *n of water* sciabordio *m*

♦ **lap up** *v/t* (*pret & pp* -**ped**) *drink, milk* leccare; *flattery* compiacersi di

lap[3] [læp] *n of person* grembo *m*

la·pel [lə'pel] bavero *m*

lapse [læps] **1** *n (mistake, slip)* mancanza *f*; *of time* intervallo *m*; ~ *of memory* vuoto *m* di memoria; ~ *of taste* caduta *f* di tono **2** *v/i* scadere; ~ *into* cadere in

'**lap·top** COMPUT laptop *m inv*

lar·ce·ny ['lɑːsənɪ] furto *m*

lard [lɑːd] lardo *m*

lar·der ['lɑːdə(r)] dispensa *f*

large [lɑːdʒ] *adj* grande; *at* ~ in libertà

large·ly ['lɑːdʒlɪ] *adv (mainly)* in gran parte

lark [lɑːk] *bird* allodola *f*

lar·va ['lɑːvə] larva *f*

lar·yn·gi·tis [lærɪn'dʒaɪtɪs] laringite *f*

lar·ynx ['lærɪŋks] laringe *f*

la·ser ['leɪzə(r)] laser *m inv*

'**la·ser beam** raggio *m* laser

'**la·ser print·er** stampante *f* laser

lash[1] [læʃ] *v/t with whip* frustare

lash[2] [læʃ] *n (eyelash)* ciglio *m*

♦ **lash down** *v/t with rope* assicurare

♦ **lash out** *v/i with fists, words* menare
colpi

lass [læs] ragazza *f*

last[1] [lɑːst] **1** *adj in series* ultimo;
(preceding) precedente; ~ *but one*
penultimo; ~ *night* ieri sera; ~ *year*
l'anno scorso **2** *adv he finished* ~
ha finito per ultimo; *in race* è arrivato ultimo; *when I* ~ *saw him* l'ultima volta che l'ho visto; ~ *but not
least* per finire; *at* ~ finalmente

last[2] [lɑːst] *v/i* durare

last·ing ['lɑːstɪŋ] *adj* duraturo

last·ly ['lɑːstlɪ] *adv* per finire

latch [lætʃ] chiavistello *m*

late [leɪt] **1** *adj (behind time)* in ritardo; *in day* tardi; *it's getting* ~ si sta
facendo tardi; *of* ~ recentemente;
the ~ *19th century* il tardo XIX secolo **2** *adv* tardi

late·ly ['leɪtlɪ] *adv* recentemente

lat·er ['leɪtə(r)] *adv* più tardi; *see
you* ~! a più tardi; ~ *on* più tardi

lat·est ['leɪtɪst] *adj* ultimo, più recente **2** *n: at the* ~ al più tardi

lathe [leɪð] *n* tornio *m*

la·ther ['lɑːðə(r)] *from soap* schiuma
f; *the horse is in a* ~ il cavallo è sudato

Lat·in ['lætɪn] **1** *adj* latino **2** *n* latino
m

Lat·in A'mer·i·ca America *f* Latina

La·tin A'mer·i·can 1 *n* latino-americano *m*, -a *f* **2** *adj* latino-americano

lat·i·tude ['lætɪtjuːd] *geographical* latitudine *f*; *(freedom to act)* libertà *f
inv* d'azione

lat·ter ['lætə(r)] *adj: the* ~ quest'ultimo

laugh [lɑːf] **1** *n* risata *f*; *it was a* ~ ci
siamo divertiti **2** *v/i* ridere

♦ **laugh at** *v/t* ridere di

'**laugh·ing stock** zimbello *m*; *become a* ~ rendersi ridicolo

laugh·ter ['lɑːftə(r)] risata *f*; *sounds
of* ~ delle risate

launch [lɔːntʃ] **1** *n boat* lancia *f*; *of
rocket, product* lancio *m*; *of ship* varo
m **2** *v/t rocket, product* lanciare; *ship*
varare

'**launch cer·e·mo·ny** cerimonia *f* di
lancio

launch·(ing) pad rampa *f* di lancio

laun·der ['lɔːndə(r)] v/t *clothes* lavare e stirare; **~ money** riciclare denaro sporco

laun·derette [lɔːn'dret] lavanderia *f* automatica

laun·dry ['lɔːndrɪ] *place* lavanderia *f*; *clothes* bucato *m*

lau·rel ['lɒrəl] alloro *m*

lav·a·to·ry ['lævətrɪ] gabinetto *m*

lav·en·der ['lævəndə(r)] lavanda *f*

lav·ish ['lævɪʃ] *adj meal* lauto; *reception, lifestyle* sontuoso

law [lɔː] legge *f*; **criminal** / **civil ~** diritto *m* penale / civile; **against the ~** contro la legge; **forbidden by ~** vietato dalla legge

law-a·bid·ing ['lɔːəbaɪdɪŋ] *adj* che rispetta la legge

'law court tribunale *m*

law·ful ['lɔːful] *adj* legale

law·less ['lɔːlɪs] *adj* senza legge

lawn [lɔːn] prato *m* all'inglese; **play on the ~** giocare sul prato

'lawn mow·er tagliaerba *m inv*

'law·suit azione *f* legale

law·yer ['lɔːjə(r)] avvocato *m*

lax [læks] *adj* permissivo

lax·a·tive ['læksətɪv] *n* lassativo *m*

lay¹ [leɪ] *pret* → **lie**

lay² [leɪ] v/t (*pret & pp* **laid**) (*put down*) posare; *eggs* deporre; V (*sexually*) scopare V

♦ **lay into** v/t (*attack*) aggredire

♦ **lay off** v/t *workers* licenziare; *temporarily* mettere in cassa integrazione

♦ **lay on** v/t (*provide*) offrire

♦ **lay out** v/t *objects* disporre; *page* impaginare

'lay·a·bout F scansafatiche *m/f inv*

'lay-by *on road* piazzola *f* di sosta

lay·er ['leɪə(r)] strato *m*

'lay·man laico *m*

'lay-off licenziamento *m*; **there have been 50 ~s** *temporary* 50 operai sono stati messi in cassa integrazione

♦ **laze around** [leɪz] v/i oziare

la·zy ['leɪzɪ] *adj person* pigro; *day* passato a oziare

lb *abbr* (= **pound**) libbra *f*

LCD [elsiː'diː] *abbr* (= **liquid crystal display**) display *m inv* a cristalli liquidi

lead¹ [liːd] **1** v/t (*pret & pp* **led**) *procession, race* essere in testa a; *company, team* essere a capo di; (*guide, take*) condurre **2** v/i (*pret & pp* **led**) *in race, competition* essere in testa; (*provide leadership*) dirigere; **a street ~ing off the square** una strada che parte dalla piazza; **a street ~ing into the square** una strada che sbocca sulla piazza; **where is this ~ing?** dove vuoi andare a parare? **3** *n in race* posizione *f* di testa; **be in the ~** essere in testa; **take the ~** passare in testa

♦ **lead on** v/i (*go in front*) guidare

♦ **lead up to** v/t preludere

lead² [liːd] *for dog* guinzaglio *m*

lead³ [led] *substance* piombo *m*

lead·ed ['ledɪd] *adj petrol* con piombo

lead·er ['liːdə(r)] *person* capo *m*; *in race, on market* leader *m/f inv*; *in newspaper* editoriale *m*

lead·er·ship ['liːdəʃɪp] *of party etc* direzione *f*, leadership *f inv*; **under his ~** sotto la sua direzione; **~ skills** capacità *f* di comando; **~ contest** lotta *f* per la direzione

lead-free ['ledfriː] *adj petrol* senza piombo

lead·ing ['liːdɪŋ] *adj runner* in testa; *company, product* leader *inv*

'lead·ing-edge *adj company, technology* all'avanguardia

leaf [liːf] (*pl* **leaves** [liːvz]) foglia *f*

♦ **leaf through** v/t sfogliare

leaf·let ['liːflət] dépliant *m inv*

league [liːg] lega *f*; SP campionato *m*

leak [liːk] **1** *n of water* perdita *f*; *of gas* fuga *f*; **there's been a ~ of information** c'è stata una fuga di notizie **2** v/i *of pipe* perdere; *of boat* far acqua

♦ **leak out** v/i *of air, gas* fuoriuscire; *of news* trapelare

leak·y ['liːkɪ] *adj pipe* che perde; *boat* che fa acqua

lean¹ [liːn] **1** v/i *be at an angle* pendere; **~ against sth** appoggiarsi a qc

2 *v/t* appoggiare; **~ sth against sth** appoggiare qc a qc

lean² [li:n] *adj meat* magro;*style, prose* asciutto

leap [li:p] **1** *n* salto *m*; **a great ~ forward** un grande balzo in avanti **2** *v/i* saltare

'leap year anno *m* bisestile

learn [lɜːn] **1** *v/t* imparare; *(hear)* apprendere; **~ how to do sth** imparare a fare qc **2** *v/i* imparare

learn·er [ˈlɜːnə(r)] principiante *m/f*

'learn·ing driv·er principiante *m/f* (alla guida)

learn·ing [ˈlɜːnɪŋ] *n (knowledge)* sapere *m*; *(act)* apprendimento *m*

'learn·ing curve processo *m* di apprendimento; **be constantly on the ~** non finire mai di imparare

lease [li:s] **1** *n* (contratto *m* di) affitto *m* **2** *v/t flat, equipment* affittare

♦ **lease out** *v/t flat, equipment* dare in affitto

lease 'pur·chase acquisto *m* in leasing

leash [li:ʃ] *for dog* guinzaglio *m*

least [li:st] **1** *adj (slightest)* minimo; **I've the ~ debt** io ho il debito minore **2** *adv* meno **3** *n* minimo *m*; **not in the ~ suprised / disappointed** per niente sorpreso / deluso; **at ~** almeno

leath·er [ˈleðə(r)] **1** *n* pelle *f*, cuoio *m* **2** *adj* di pelle, di cuoio

leave [li:v] **1** *n (holiday)* congedo *m*; MIL licenza *f*; **on ~** in congedo, in licenza **2** *v/t (pret & pp left)* lasciare; *room, house, office* uscire da;*station, airport* partire da; *(forget)* dimenticare; **~ school** finire gli studi; **let's ~ things as they are** lasciamo le cose come stanno; **how did you ~ things with him?** come sei rimasto d'accordo con lui?; **~ s.o. / sth alone** lasciare stare qu / qc; **be left** rimanere; **there is nothing left** non è rimasto niente **3** *v/i (pret & pp left) of person, plane, bus* partire; **he's just left** è appena uscito

♦ **leave behind** *v/t intentionally*

lasciare; *(forget)* dimenticare

♦ **leave on** *v/t hat, coat* non togliersi; *TV, computer* lasciare acceso

♦ **leave out** *v/t word, figure* omettere; *(not put away)* lasciare in giro; **leave me out of this** non mi immischiare in questa faccenda

'leav·ing par·ty festa *f* d'addio

lec·ture [ˈlektʃə(r)] **1** *n* lezione *f* **2** *v/i at university* insegnare

'lec·ture hall aula *f* magna

lec·tur·er [ˈlektʃərə(r)] professore *m*, -essa universitaria, -a

LED [eliːˈdiː] *abbr (= light-emitting diode)* LED *m inv*

led [led] *pret & pp* → **lead¹**

ledge [ledʒ] *of window* davanzale *m*; *on rock face* sporgenza *f*

ledg·er [ˈledʒə(r)] COM libro *m* mastro

leek [li:k] porro *m*

leer [lɪə(r)] *n sexual* sguardo *m* libidinoso; *evil* sguardo *m* malvagio

left¹ [left] **1** *adj* sinistro; POL di sinistra **2** *n* sinistra *f*; **on the ~** a sinistra; **on the ~ of sth** a sinistra di qc; **to the ~** *turn, look* a sinistra **3** *adv turn, look* a sinistra

left² [left] *pret & pp* → **leave**

'left-hand *adj* sinistro; **left-hand 'drive** guida *f* a sinistra; **left-'handed** *adj* mancino; **left 'lug·gage (office)** deposito *m* bagagli; **'left-overs** *npl food* avanzi *mpl*; **'left-wing** *adj* POL di sinistra

leg [leg] *of person* gamba *f*; *of animal* zampa *f*; *of turkey, chicken* coscia *f*; *of lamb* cosciotto *m*; *of journey* tappa *f*; *of competition* girone *m*; **pull s.o.'s ~** prendere in giro qu

leg·a·cy [ˈlegəsɪ] eredità *f inv*

le·gal [ˈliːgl] *adj* legale

le·gal ad·vis·er consulente *m/f* legale

le·gal·i·ty [lɪˈgælətɪ] legalità *f inv*

le·gal·ize [ˈliːgəlaɪz] *v/t* legalizzare

le·gend [ˈledʒənd] leggenda *f*

le·gen·da·ry [ˈledʒəndrɪ] *adj* leggendario

le·gi·ble [ˈledʒəbl] *adj* leggibile

le·gis·late [ˈledʒɪsleɪt] *v/i* legiferare

L

le·gis·la·tion [ledʒɪs'leɪʃn] legislazione f

le·gis·la·tive ['ledʒɪslətɪv] adj legislativo

le·gis·la·ture ['ledʒɪslətʃə(r)] POL legislatura f

le·git·i·mate [lɪ'dʒɪtɪmət] adj legittimo

'leg room spazio m per le gambe

lei·sure ['leʒə(r)] svago m; **at your ~** con comodo

'lei·sure cen·ter Am, 'lei·sure cen·tre centro m sportivo e ricreativo

lei·sure·ly ['leʒəlɪ] adj pace, lifestyle tranquillo

'lei·sure time tempo m libero

le·mon ['lemən] limone m

le·mon·ade [lemə'neɪd] fizzy gazzosa f; made from lemon juice limonata f

'le·mon juice succo m di limone

le·mon 'tea tè m inv al limone

lend [lend] v/t (pret & pp **lent**) prestare; **~ s.o. sth** prestare qc a qu

length [leŋθ] lunghezza f; piece: of material taglio m; **at ~** describe, explain a lungo; (eventually) alla fine

length·en ['leŋθən] v/t allungare

length·y ['leŋθɪ] adj speech, stay lungo

le·ni·ent ['liːnɪənt] adj indulgente

lens [lenz] of camera obiettivo m; of spectacles lente f; of eye cristallino m

'lens cov·er of camera copriobiettivo m

Lent [lent] REL Quaresima f

lent [lent] pret & pp → **lend**

len·til ['lentl] lenticchia f

len·til 'soup minestra f di lenticchie

Leo ['liːəʊ] ASTR Leone m

leop·ard ['lepəd] leopardo m

le·o·tard ['liːətɑːd] body m inv

les·bi·an ['lezbɪən] **1** n lesbica f **2** adj di / per lesbiche

less [les] adv (di) meno; **eat / talk ~** parlare / mangiare (di) meno; **~ interesting / serious** meno interessante / serio; **it costs ~** costa (di) meno; **~ than £200** meno di £200

less·en ['lesn] v/t & v/i diminuire

les·son ['lesn] lezione f

let [let] v/t (pret & pp **let**) (allow) lasciare; (rent) affittare; **~ s.o. do sth** lasciar fare qc a qu; **~ me go!** lasciami andare!; **~ him come in!** fallo entrare!; **~'s go / stay** andiamo / restiamo; **~'s not argue** non litighiamo; **~ alone** tanto meno; **~ go of sth** of rope, handle mollare qc

♦ **let down** v/t hair sciogliersi; blinds abbassare; (disappoint) deludere; dress, trousers allungare

♦ **let in** v/t to house far entrare

♦ **let off** v/t not punish perdonare; from car far scendere

♦ **let out** v/t of room, building far uscire; jacket etc allargare; groan, yell emettere

♦ **let up** v/i (stop) smettere

le·thal ['liːθl] mortale

leth·ar·gic [lɪ'θɑːdʒɪk] adj fiacco

leth·ar·gy ['leθədʒɪ] fiacchezza f

let·ter ['letə(r)] lettera f

'let·ter·box on street buca f delle lettere; in door cassetta f della posta; 'let·ter·head heading intestazione f; (headed paper) carta f intestata; let·ter of 'cred·it COM lettera f di credito

let·tuce ['letɪs] lattuga f

'let·up: without a ~ senza sosta

leu·ke·mi·a [luː'kiːmɪə] leucemia f

lev·el ['levl] **1** adj field, surface piano; in competition, scores pari; **draw ~ with s.o.** in match pareggiare; **he drew ~ with the leading car** ha raggiunto l'auto in testa **2** n livello m; **on the ~** F (honest) onesto

lev·el 'cross·ing Br passaggio m a livello

lev·el-head·ed [levl'hedɪd] adj posato

le·ver ['liːvə(r)] **1** n leva f **2** v/t: **~ sth up / off** sollevare / togliere qc con una leva; **~ sth open** aprire qc facendo leva

lev·er·age ['liːvrɪdʒ] forza f, (influence) influenza f

lev·y ['levɪ] v/t (pret & pp **-ied**) taxes imporre

lewd [luːd] adj osceno

lighter

li·a·bil·i·ty [laɪə'bɪlətɪ] (*responsibility*) responsabilità *f inv*; F *person* peso *m* morto; F *thing* peso *m*

li·a·ble ['laɪəbl] *adj* (*answerable*) responsabile; **it's ~ to break** (*likely*) è probabile che si rompa

♦ liaise with [lɪ'eɪz] *v/t* tenere i contatti con

li·ai·son [lɪ'eɪzɒn] (*contacts*) contatti *mpl*

li·ar ['laɪə(r)] bugiardo *m*, -a *f*

li·bel ['laɪbl] **1** *n* diffamazione *f* **2** *v/t* diffamare

lib·e·ral ['lɪbrəl] *adj* (*broad-minded*), POL liberale; *portion etc* abbondante

lib·e·rate ['lɪbəreɪt] *v/t* liberare

lib·e·rat·ed ['lɪbəreɪtɪd] *adj woman* emancipato

lib·e·ra·tion [lɪbə'reɪʃn] liberazione *f*

lib·er·ty ['lɪbətɪ] libertà *f inv*; **at ~** *of prisoner etc* in libertà; **be at ~ to do sth** poter fare qc

Libra ['liːbrə] ASTR Bilancia *f*

li·brar·i·an [laɪ'breərɪən] bibliotecario *m*, -a *f*

li·bra·ry ['laɪbrərɪ] biblioteca *f*

Lib·y·a ['lɪbɪə] Libia *f*

Lib·y·an ['lɪbɪən] **1** *adj* libico **2** *n person* libico *m*, -a *f*

lice [laɪs] *pl* → **louse**

li·cence ['laɪsns] (*driving ~*) patente *f*; (*road tax ~*) bollo *m* (auto); *for TV* canone *m* (televisivo); *for gun* porto *m* d'armi; *for imports/exports* licenza *f*; *for dog* tassa *f*

li·cense ['laɪsns] **1** *v/t issue ~* rilasciare la licenza a; **be ~d** *to sell alcohol* essere autorizzato alla vendita di alcolici; **the car isn't ~d** la macchina non ha il bollo **2** *n Am* → **licence**

'li·cense plate *Am* targa *f*

lick [lɪk] **1** *n* leccata *f*; **a ~ of paint** una passata di vernice **2** *v/t* leccare; **one's lips** leccarsi i baffi

lick·ing ['lɪkɪŋ] F (*defeat*): **get a ~** prendere una batosta

lid [lɪd] coperchio *m*

lie¹ [laɪ] **1** *n* bugia *f*; **tell ~s** dire bugie **2** *v/i* mentire

lie² [laɪ] *v/i* (*pret* **lay**, *pp* **lain**) *of person* sdraiarsi; *of object* stare; (*be situated*) trovarsi

♦ lie down *v/i* sdraiarsi

'lie-in: **have a ~** restare a letto fino a tardi

lieu [ljuː] *n*: **in ~ of** invece di

lieu·ten·ant [lef'tenənt] tenente *m*

life [laɪf] (*pl* **lives** [laɪvz]) vita *f*; *of machine* durata *f*; *of battery* autonomia *f*; **all her ~** tutta la vita; **that's ~!** così è la vita!

'life as·sur·ance *Br* assicurazione *f* sulla vita; 'life belt salvagente *m inv*; 'life·boat lancia *f* di salvataggio; 'life ex·pect·an·cy aspettativa *f* di vita; 'life·guard bagnino *m*, -a *f*; 'life his·to·ry ciclo *m* vitale; 'life im·pris·on·ment ergastolo *m*; 'life in·sur·ance assicurazione *f* sulla vita; 'life jack·et giubbotto *m* di salvataggio

life·less ['laɪflɪs] *adj* senza vita

life·like ['laɪflaɪk] *adj* fedele

'life·long *adj* di vecchia data; 'life-sav·ing *adj drug* salvavita; 'life·sized *adj* a grandezza naturale; 'life-threat·en·ing *adj* mortale; 'life·time *n*: **in my ~** in vita mia

lift [lɪft] **1** *v/t* sollevare **2** *v/i of fog* diradarsi **3** *n Br*: *in building* ascensore *m*; *in car* passaggio *m*; **give s.o. a ~** dare un passaggio a qu

♦ lift off *v/i of rocket* decollare

'lift-off *of rocket* decollo *m*

lig·a·ment ['lɪgəmənt] legamento *m*

light¹ [laɪt] **1** *n* luce *f*; **in the ~ of** alla luce di; **have you got a ~?** hai da accendere? **2** *v/t* (*pret & pp* **lit**) *fire, cigarette* accendere; (*illuminate*) illuminare **3** *adj not dark* chiaro

light² [laɪt] **1** *adj not heavy* leggero **2** *adv*: **travel ~** viaggiare leggero

♦ light up **1** *v/t* (*illuminate*) illuminare **2** *v/i* (*start to smoke*) accendersi una sigaretta

'light bulb lampadina *f*

light·en¹ ['laɪtn] *v/t colour* schiarire

light·en² ['laɪtn] *v/t load* alleggerire

♦ lighten up *v/i of person* rilassarsi

light·er ['laɪtə(r)] *for cigarettes* accendino *m*

L

light-head·ed [laɪt'hedɪd] *adj* (*dizzy*) stordito; **light-'heart·ed** [laɪt'hɑːtɪd] *adj film* leggero; **'light-house** faro *m*

light·ing ['laɪtɪŋ] illuminazione *f*

light·ly ['laɪtlɪ] *adv touch* leggermente; **get off** ~ cavarsela con poco

light·ness ['laɪtnɪs] leggerezza *f*

light·ning ['laɪtnɪŋ] fulmine *m*

'light·ning con·duc·tor parafulmine *m*

'light pen penna *f* luminosa

'light·weight *in boxing* peso *m* leggero

'light year anno *m* luce

like¹ [laɪk] **1** *prep* come; ~ **this / that** così; **what is she** ~? *in looks, character* com'è?; **it's not** ~ **him** not his character non è da lui; **look** ~ **s.o.** assomigliare a qu **2** *conj* F (*as*) come; ~ **I said** come ho già detto

like² [laɪk] *v/t*: **I** ~ **it / her** mi piace; **I would** ~ ... vorrei ...; **I would** ~ **to** ... vorrei ...; **would you** ~ ...? ti va ...?; **would you** ~ **to** ...? ti va di ...?; **he** ~**s swimming** gli piace nuotare; **if you** ~ se vuoi

like·a·ble ['laɪkəbl] *adj* simpatico

like·li·hood ['laɪklɪhʊd] probabilità *f inv*; **in all** ~ molto probabilmente

like·ly ['laɪklɪ] *adj* (*probable*) probabile; **not** ~! difficile!

like·ness ['laɪknɪs] (*resemblance*) somiglianza *f*

'like·wise ['laɪkwaɪz] *adv* altrettanto

lik·ing ['laɪkɪŋ] predilizione *f*; **is it to your** ~? *fml* è di tuo gradimento?; **take a** ~ **to s.o.** prendere qu in simpatia

li·lac ['laɪlək] *flower* lillà *m inv*; *colour* lilla *m inv*

li·ly ['lɪlɪ] giglio *m*

li·ly of the 'val·ley mughetto *m*

limb [lɪm] arto *m*

lime¹ [laɪm] *fruit* limetta *f*

lime² [laɪm] *substance* calce *f*

lime'green *adj* verde *m* acido

'lime·light *n*: **be in the** ~ essere in vista

lim·it ['lɪmɪt] **1** *n* limite *m*; **within** ~**s** entro certi limiti; **off** ~**s** off-limits; **that's the** ~! F è il colmo! **2** *v/t* limitare

lim·i·ta·tion [lɪmɪ'teɪʃn] limite *m*

lim·it·ed 'com·pa·ny società *f inv* a responsabilità limitata

li·mo ['lɪməʊ] F limousine *f inv*

lim·ou·sine ['lɪməziːn] limousine *f inv*

limp¹ [lɪmp] *adj* floscio

limp² [lɪmp] *n*: **he has a** ~ zoppica

line¹ [laɪn] *n on paper, road* linea *f*; *of people, trees* fila *f*; *of text* riga *f*; (*cord*) filo *m*; *of business* settore *m*; TELEC linea *f*; **the** ~ **is busy** è occupato; **hold the** ~ rimanga in linea; **draw the** ~ **at sth** non tollerare qc; ~ **of inquiry** pista *f*; ~ **of reasoning** filo *m* del ragionamento; **stand in** ~ *esp Am* fare la fila; **in** ~ **with** ... (*conforming with*) in linea con ...

line² [laɪn] *v/t* foderare

♦ **line up** *v/i* mettersi in fila

lin·e·ar ['lɪnɪə(r)] *adj* lineare

lin·en ['lɪnɪn] *material* lino *m*; *sheets etc* biancheria *f*

lin·er ['laɪnə(r)] *ship* transatlantico *m*

lines·man ['laɪnzmən] SP guardalinee *m inv*

lin·ger ['lɪŋgə(r)] *v/i of person* attardarsi; *of smell, pain* persistere

lin·ge·rie ['lænʒərɪ] lingerie *f inv*

lin·guist ['lɪŋgwɪst] *professional* linguista *m/f*; *person good at languages* poliglotta *m/f*

lin·guis·tic [lɪŋ'gwɪstɪk] *adj* linguistico

lin·ing ['laɪnɪŋ] *of clothes* fodera *f*; *of brakes* guarnizione *f*

link [lɪŋk] **1** *n* (*connection*) legame *m*; *in chain* anello *m* **2** *v/t* collegare

♦ **link up** *v/i* riunirsi; TV collegarsi

li·on ['laɪən] leone *m*

li·on·ess ['laɪənes] leonessa *f*

lip [lɪp] labbro *m*; ~**s** labbra

'lip·read *v/i* (*pret & pp* -**read** [red]) leggere le labbra

'lip·stick rossetto *m*

li·queur [lɪ'kjʊə(r)] liquore *m*

liq·uid ['lɪkwɪd] **1** *n* liquido *m* **2** *adj* liquido

liq·ui·date ['lɪkwɪdeɪt] *v/t* liquidare

L

liq·ui·da·tion [lɪkwɪˈdeɪʃn] liquidazione f; *go into* ~ andare in liquidazione

liq·ui·di·ty [lɪˈkwɪdɪtɪ] FIN liquidità f inv

liq·uid·ize [ˈlɪkwɪdaɪz] v/t frullare

liq·uid·iz·er [ˈlɪkwɪdaɪzə(r)] frullatore m

liq·uor [ˈlɪkə(r)] superalcolici mpl

liq·uo·rice [ˈlɪkərɪs] liquirizia f

lisp [lɪsp] **1** n lisca f **2** v/i parlare con la lisca

list [lɪst] **1** n elenco m, lista f **2** v/t elencare

lis·ten [ˈlɪsn] v/i ascoltare

♦ **listen in** v/i ascoltare (di nascosto)

♦ **listen to** v/t radio, person ascoltare

lis·ten·er [ˈlɪsnə(r)] to radio ascoltatore m, -trice f; *he's a good* ~ sa ascoltare

list·ings mag·a·zine [ˈlɪstɪŋz] guida f dei programmi radio / TV

list·less [ˈlɪstlɪs] adj apatico

lit [lɪt] pret & pp → *light*

lit·e·ral [ˈlɪtərəl] adj letterale

lit·e·ral·ly [ˈlɪtərəlɪ] adv letteralmente

lit·e·ra·ry [ˈlɪtərərɪ] adj letterario

lit·e·rate [ˈlɪtərət] adj: *be* ~ saper leggere e scrivere

lit·e·ra·ture [ˈlɪtrətʃə(r)] letteratura f; F (*leaflets*) opuscoli mpl

li·tre [ˈliːtə(r)] litro m

lit·ter [ˈlɪtə(r)] rifiuti mpl; of animal cucciolata f

lit·ter bas·ket cestino m dei rifiuti

lit·ter bin bidone m dei rifiuti

lit·tle [ˈlɪtl] **1** adj piccolo; *the* ~ *ones* i piccoli **2** n: *the* ~ il poco che so; *a* ~ un po'; *a* ~ *bread/wine* un po' di pane / vino; *a* ~ *is better than nothing* meglio poco che niente **3** adv: *by* ~ (a) poco a poco; *a* ~ *better/bigger* un po' meglio / più grande; *a* ~ *before 6* un po' prima delle 6

live¹ [lɪv] v/i (*reside*) abitare; (*be alive*) vivere

♦ **live on 1** v/t rice, bread vivere di **2** v/i continue living sopravvivere

♦ **live up**: *live it up* fare la bella vita

♦ **live up to** v/t essere all'altezza di

♦ **live with** v/t vivere con

live² [laɪv] **1** adj broadcast dal vivo **2** adv broadcast in diretta; record dal vivo; ammunition carico

live·li·hood [ˈlaɪvlɪhʊd] mezzi mpl di sostentamento; *earn one's* ~ guadagnarsi da vivere

live·li·ness [ˈlaɪvlɪnɪs] vivacità f inv

live·ly [ˈlaɪvlɪ] adj vivace

liv·er [ˈlɪvə(r)] fegato m

live·stock [ˈlaɪvstɒk] bestiame m

liv·id [ˈlɪvɪd] adj (*angry*) furibondo

liv·ing [ˈlɪvɪŋ] **1** adj in vita **2** n: *earn one's* ~ guadagnarsi da vivere; *what do you do for a* ~? che lavoro fai?; *standard of* ~ tenore m di vita

liv·ing room salotto m, soggiorno m

liz·ard [ˈlɪzəd] lucertola f

load [ləʊd] **1** n carico m; ~*s of* F un sacco di **2** v/t caricare; ~ *sth onto sth* caricare qc su qc

load·ed [ˈləʊdɪd] adj F (*very rich*) ricco sfondato

loaf [ləʊf] n (pl *loaves* [ləʊvz]): *a* ~ *of bread* una pagnotta

♦ **loaf about** v/i F oziare

loaf·er [ˈləʊfə(r)] shoe mocassino m

loan [ləʊn] **1** n prestito m; *on* ~ in prestito **2** v/t: ~ *s.o. sth* prestare qc a qu

loathe [ləʊð] v/t detestare

loath·ing [ˈləʊðɪŋ] disgusto m

lob·by [ˈlɒbɪ] in hotel, theatre atrio m; POL lobby f inv

lobe [ləʊb] of ear lobo m

lob·ster [ˈlɒbstə(r)] aragosta f

lo·cal [ˈləʊkl] **1** adj people, bar del posto; produce locale; *I'm not* ~ non sono del posto **2** n persona f del posto; *are you a* ~? sei del posto?

lo·cal call TELEC telefonata f urbana; **lo·cal e'lec·tions** npl elezioni fpl amministrative; **lo·cal 'gov·ern·ment** amministrazione f locale

lo·cal·i·ty [ləʊˈkælətɪ] località f inv

lo·cal·ly [ˈləʊkəlɪ] adv live, work nella zona

lo·cal 'pro·duce prodotti mpl locali

lo·cal time ora f locale

lo·cate [ləʊ'keɪt] v/t *new factory etc* situare; *identify position of* localizzare; **be ~d** essere situato

lo·ca·tion [ləʊ'keɪʃn] (*siting*) ubicazione f; *identifying position of* localizzazione f; **on ~** *film* in esterni; **the film was shot on ~ in ...** gli esterni del film sono stati girati in ...

loch lago m

lock¹ [lɒk] *of hair* ciocca f

lock² [lɒk] **1** n *on door* serratura f **2** v/t *door* chiudere a chiave; **~ sth in position** bloccare qc

◆**lock away** v/t mettere sottochiave

◆**lock in** v/t *person* chiudere dentro

◆**lock out** v/t *of house* chiudere fuori

◆**lock up** v/t *in prison* mettere dentro

lock·er ['lɒkə(r)] armadietto m

'lock·er room spogliatoio m

lock·et ['lɒkɪt] medaglione m

lock·smith ['lɒksmɪθ] fabbro m ferraio

lo·cust ['ləʊkəst] locusta f

lodge [lɒdʒ] **1** v/t *complaint* presentare **2** v/i *of bullet* conficcarsi

lodg·er ['lɒdʒə(r)] pensionante m/f

loft [lɒft] soffitta f

loft·y ['lɒftɪ] adj *peak* alto; *ideals* nobile

log [lɒg] *wood* ceppo m; *written record* giornale m

◆**log off** v/i (*pret & pp* **-ged**) disconnettersi (**from** da)

◆**log on** v/i connettersi

◆**log on to** v/t connettersi a

'log·book giornale m di bordo

log 'cab·in casetta f di legno

log·ger·heads ['lɒgəhedz]: **be at ~** essere ai ferri corti

lo·gic ['lɒdʒɪk] logica f

lo·gic·al ['lɒdʒɪkl] adj logico

lo·gic·al·ly ['lɒdʒɪklɪ] adv a rigor di logica; *arrange* in modo logico

lo·gis·tics [lə'dʒɪstɪks] npl logistica f

lo·go ['ləʊgəʊ] logo m inv

loi·ter ['lɔɪtə(r)] v/i gironzolare

lol·li·pop ['lɒlɪpɒp] lecca lecca m inv

'lol·li·pop man/wo·man Br uomo/ donna che aiuta i bambini ad attraversare la strada

lol·ly ['lɒlɪ] (*ice lolly*) ghiacciolo m; F

(*money*) grana f F

Lon·don ['lʌndən] Londra f

lone·li·ness ['ləʊnlɪnɪs] solitudine f

lone·ly ['ləʊnlɪ] adj *person* solo; *place* isolato

lon·er ['ləʊnə(r)] persona f solitaria

long¹ [lɒŋ] **1** adj lungo; **it's a ~ way** è lontano **2** adv: **don't be ~** torna presto **5 weeks is too ~** 5 settimane è troppo; **will it take ~?** ci vorrà tanto?; **that was ~ ago** è stato tanto tempo fa; **~ before then** molto prima di allora; **before ~** poco tempo dopo; **we can't wait any ~er** non possiamo attendere oltre; **he no ~er works here** non lavora più qui; **so ~ as** (*provided*) sempre che; **so ~!** arrivederci!

long² [lɒŋ] v/i: **~ for sth** desiderare ardentemente qc; **be ~ing to do sth** desiderare ardentemente fare qc

long-'dis·tance adj *phonecall* interurbano; *race* di fondo; *flight* intercontinentale

lon·gev·i·ty [lɒn'dʒevɪtɪ] longevità f inv

long·ing ['lɒŋɪŋ] n desiderio m

lon·gi·tude ['lɒŋgɪtjuːd] longitudine f

'long jump salto m in lungo; **long-'life milk** latte m a lunga conservazione; **'long-range** *missile* a lunga gittata; *forecast* a lungo termine; **long-'sight·ed** [lɒŋ'saɪtɪd] adj presbite; **long-'sleeved** [lɒŋ'sliːvd] adj a maniche lunghe; **long-'stand·ing** adj di vecchia data; **'long-term** adj *plans*, *investment* a lunga scadenza; *relationship* stabile; **'long wave** RAD onde fpl lunghe

long-'wind·ed [lɒŋ'wɪndɪd] adj prolisso

loo [luː] F gabinetto m

look [lʊk] **1** n (*appearance*) aspetto m; (*glance*) sguardo m; **give s.o./ sth a ~** dare uno sguardo a qu/qc; **have a ~ at sth** examine dare un'occhiata a qc; **can I have a ~ around?** *in shop etc* posso dare un'occhiata?; **~s** (*beauty*) bellezza f **2** v/i guardare; (*search*) cercare;

(seem) sembrare; **you ~ tired / different** sembri stanco / diverso

♦ **look after** v/t badare a

♦ **look ahead** v/i *fig* pensare al futuro

♦ **look around** v/i *in shop etc* dare un'occhiata in giro; *(look back)* guardarsi indietro

♦ **look at** v/t guardare; *(consider)* considerare

♦ **look back** v/i guardare indietro

♦ **look down on** v/t disprezzare

♦ **look for** v/t cercare

♦ **look forward to** v/t: **look forward to doing sth** non veder l'ora di fare qc; **I'm looking forward to the holidays** non vedo l'ora che arrivino le vacanze; **I'm not looking forward to it** non ne ho proprio voglia

♦ **look in on** v/t *(visit)* passare a trovare

♦ **look into** v/t *(investigate)* esaminare

♦ **look on 1** v/i *(watch)* rimanere a guardare **2** v/t: **I look on you as a friend** *(consider)* ti considero un amico

♦ **look onto** v/t *garden, street* dare su

♦ **look out** v/i *of window etc* guardare fuori; *(pay attention)* fare attenzione; **look out!** attento!

♦ **look out for** v/t cercare; *(be on guard against)* fare attenzione a

♦ **look out of** v/t *window* guardare da

♦ **look over** v/t *house, translation* esaminare

♦ **look round** v/t *museum, city* visitare

♦ **look through** v/t *magazine, notes* scorrere

♦ **look to** v/t *(rely on)* contare su

♦ **look up 1** v/i *from paper etc* sollevare lo sguardo; *(improve)* migliorare **2** v/t *word, phone number* cercare; *(visit)* andare a trovare

♦ **look up to** v/t *(respect)* avere rispetto per

lookout n *person* sentinella f; *place* posto m di guardia; **be on the ~** stare all'erta; **be on the ~ for** *accommodation etc* cercare di trovare; *new staff etc* essere alla ricerca di

♦ **loom up** [luːm] v/i apparire

loon·y ['luːnɪ] **1** n F matto m, -a f **2** adj F matto

loop [luːp] n cappio m

'loop·hole *in law etc* scappatoia f

loose [luːs] adj *wire, button* allentato; *clothes* ampio; *tooth* che tentenna; *morals* dissoluto; *wording* vago; **~ change** spiccioli mpl; **~ ends** of problem, discussion aspetti mpl da esaminare

loose·ly ['luːslɪ] adv *tied* senza stringere; *worded* vagamente

loos·en ['luːsn] v/t *collar, knot* allentare

loot [luːt] **1** n bottino m **2** v/t & v/i saccheggiare

loot·er ['luːtə(r)] saccheggiatore m, -trice f

♦ **lop off** [lɒp] v/t *(pret & pp -ped)* tagliar via

lop·sid·ed [lɒp'saɪdɪd] adj sbilenco

Lord [lɔːd] *(God)* Signore m; **the (House of) ~s** la camera dei Lord

Lord's 'Prayer il Padrenostro m

lor·ry ['lɒrɪ] *Br* camion m inv

lose [luːz] *(pret & pp lost)* **1** v/t *object* perdere **2** v/i SP perdere; *of clock* andare indietro; **I'm lost** mi sono perso; **get lost!** F sparisci!

♦ **lose out** v/i rimetterci

los·er ['luːzə(r)] *in contest* perdente m/f; F *in life* sfigato m, -a f

loss [lɒs] perdita f; **make a ~** subire una perdita; **be at a ~** essere perplesso

lost [lɒst] **1** adj perso **2** pret & pp → **lose**

lost and 'found *Am*, **lost 'prop·er·ty of·fice** *Br* ufficio m oggetti smarriti

lot [lɒt] n: **the ~** tutto; **a ~, ~s** molto; **a ~ of ice cream, ~s of ice cream** molto gelato; **a ~ of ice creams, ~s of ice creams** molti gelati; **a ~ better / easier** molto meglio / più facile

lo·tion ['ləʊʃn] lozione f

lot·te·ry ['lɒtərɪ] lotteria f

loud [laʊd] adj *music, voice, noise* forte; *colour* sgargiante

loud'speak·er altoparlante *m*; *for stereo* cassa *f* dello stereo

lounge [laʊndʒ] *in house* soggiorno *m*; *in hotel* salone *m*; *at airport* sala *f* partenze

♦ **lounge about** *v/i* poltrire

'**lounge suit** completo *m* da uomo

louse [laʊs] (*pl* **lice** [laɪs]) pidocchio *m*

lous·y ['laʊzɪ] *adj* schifoso F; *I feel ~* mi sento uno schifo

lout [laʊt] teppista *m/f*

lov·a·ble ['lʌvəbl] *adj* adorabile

love [lʌv] **1** *n* amore *m*; *in tennis* zero *m*; *be in ~* essere innamorato; *fall in ~* innamorarsi; *make ~* fare l'amore; *make ~ to* fare l'amore con; *yes, my ~* sì, tesoro **2** *v/t person, country, wine* amare; *~ doing sth* amare fare qc

'**love af·fair** relazione *f*, '**love·life** vita *f* sentimentale; '**love let·ter** lettera *f* d'amore

love·ly ['lʌvlɪ] *adj face, colour, holiday* bello; *meal, smell* buono; *we had a ~ time* siamo stati benissimo

lov·er ['lʌvə(r)] amante *m/f*

lov·ing ['lʌvɪŋ] *adj* affettuoso

lov·ing·ly ['lʌvɪŋlɪ] *adv* amorosamente

low [ləʊ] **1** *adj bridge, price, voice* basso; *quality* scarso; *be feeling ~* sentirsi giù; *be ~ on petrol* avere poca benzina **2** *n in weather* depressione *f*; *in sales, statistics* minimo *m*

low·brow ['ləʊbraʊ] *adj* di scarso spessore culturale; **low-'cal·o·rie** *adj* ipocalorico; '**low-cut** *adj dress* scollato

low·er ['ləʊə(r)] *v/t boat, sth to the ground* calare; *flag, hemline* ammainare; *pressure, price* abbassare

'**low-fat** *adj* magro

'**low·key** *adj* discreto; '**low·lands** *npl* bassopiano *m*; **low-'pres·sure ar·e·a** area *f* di bassa pressione; '**low sea·son** bassa stagione *f*; '**low tide** bassa marea *f*

loy·al ['lɔɪəl] *adj* leale

loy·al·ly ['lɔɪəlɪ] *adv* lealmente

loy·al·ty ['lɔɪəltɪ] lealtà *f inv*

loz·enge ['lɒzɪndʒ] *shape* rombo *m*; *tablet* pastiglia *f*

LP [el'piː] *abbr* (= **long-playing record**) LP *m inv* (= long-playing *m inv*)

Ltd *abbr* (= **limited**) s.r.l. (= società *f inv* a responsabilità limitata)

lu·bri·cant ['luːbrɪkənt] lubrificante *m*

lu·bri·cate ['luːbrɪkeɪt] *v/t* lubrificare

lu·bri·ca·tion [luːbrɪ'keɪʃn] lubrificazione *f*

lu·cid ['luːsɪd] *adj* (*clear*) chiaro; (*sane*) lucido

luck [lʌk] fortuna *f*; *bad ~* sfortuna; *hard ~!* che sfortuna!; *good ~* fortuna *f*; *good ~!* buona fortuna!

luck·i·ly ['lʌkɪlɪ] *adv* fortunatamente

luck·y ['lʌkɪ] *adj* fortunato; *you were ~* hai avuto fortuna; *he's ~ to be alive* è vivo per miracolo; *that's ~!* che fortuna!

lu·cra·tive ['luːkrətɪv] *adj* redditizio

lu·di·crous ['luːdɪkrəs] *adj* ridicolo

lug [lʌg] *v/t* (*pret & pp* **-ged**) F trascinare

lug·gage ['lʌgɪdʒ] bagagli *mpl*

'**lug·gage rack** *in train* portabagagli *m inv*

luke·warm ['luːkwɔːm] *adj* tiepido

lull [lʌl] **1** *n in fighting* momento *m* di calma; *in conversation* pausa *f* **2** *v/t*: *~ s.o. into a false sense of security* illudersi che tutto vada bene

lul·la·by ['lʌləbaɪ] ninnananna *f*

lum·ba·go [lʌmˈbeɪgəʊ] lombaggine *f*

lum·ber ['lʌmbə(r)] (*timber*) legname *m*

lu·mi·nous ['luːmɪnəs] *adj* luminoso

lump [lʌmp] *of sugar* zolletta *f*; (*swelling*) nodulo *m*

♦ **lump together** *v/t* mettere insieme

lump 'sum pagamento *m* unico

lump·y ['lʌmpɪ] *adj sauce* grumoso; *mattress* pieno di buchi

lu·na·cy ['luːnəsɪ] pazzia *f*

lu·nar ['luːnə(r)] *adj* lunare

lu·na·tic ['luːnətɪk] *n* pazzo *m*, -a *f*

lunch [lʌntʃ] pranzo *m*; *have ~* pranzare

maggot

'lunch box cestino *m* del pranzo;
'lunch break pausa *f* pranzo;
'lunch hour pausa *f* pranzo;
'lunch·time ora *f* di pranzo

lung [lʌŋ] polmone *m*

'lung can·cer cancro *m* al polmone

♦ lunge at [lʌndʒ] *v/t* scagliarsi contro

lurch [lɜːtʃ] *v/i* barcollare

lure [luə(r)] **1** *n* attrattiva *f* **2** *v/t* attirare; **~ s.o. into a trap** far cadere qu in trappola

lu·rid ['luərɪd] *adj colour* sgargiante; *details* scandaloso

lurk [lɜːk] *v/i of person* appostarsi; *of doubt* persistere

lus·cious ['lʌʃəs] *adj* sensuale

lush [lʌʃ] *adj vegetation* lussureggiante

lust [lʌst] *n* libidine *f*

lux·u·ri·ous [lʌgˈʒuərɪəs] *adj* lussuoso

lux·u·ri·ous·ly [lʌgˈʒuərɪəslɪ] *adv* lussuosamente

lux·u·ry ['lʌkʃərɪ] **1** *n* lusso *m* **2** *adj* di lusso

LV *abbr* (= **luncheon voucher**) buono *m* pasto

lymph gland ['lɪmfglænd] ghiandola *f* linfatica

lynch [lɪntʃ] *v/t* linciare

lyr·i·cist ['lɪrɪsɪst] paroliere *m*

lyr·ics ['lɪrɪks] *npl* parole *fpl*, testi *mpl*

M

M [em] *abbr* (= **medium**) M (= medio)

MA [emˈeɪ] *abbr* (= **Master of Arts**) master *m inv*

ma'am [mæm] *Am* signora *f*

mac [mæk] F (*mackintosh*) impermeabile *m*

ma·chine [məˈʃiːn] **1** *n* macchina *f* **2** *v/t with sewing machine* cucire a macchina; TECH lavorare a macchina

ma'chine gun mitragliatrice *f*

ma·chine-'read·a·ble *adj* leggibile dalla macchina

ma·chin·e·ry [məˈʃiːnərɪ] (*machines*) macchinario *m*

ma·chine trans·la·tion traduzione *f* fatta dal computer

ma·chis·mo [məˈkɪzməʊ] machismo *m*

mach·o ['mætʃəʊ] *adj* macho *m*

mack·in·tosh ['mækɪntɒʃ] impermeabile *m*

mac·ro ['mækrəʊ] COMPUT macro *f*

mad [mæd] *adj* (*insane*) pazzo *m*; F (*angry*) furioso; **be ~ about** F andar matto per; **drive s.o. ~** far impazzire qu; **go ~** (*become insane*) impazzire; F *with enthusiasm* impazzire; **like ~** F *run, work* come un matto

mad·am ['mædəm] signora *f*

mad 'cow dis·ease F morbo *m* della mucca pazza

mad·den ['mædən] *v/t* (*infuriate*) esasperare

mad·den·ing ['mædnɪŋ] *adj* esasperante

made [meɪd] *pret & pp* → **make**

made-to-'meas·ure *adj* su misura

'mad·house *fig* manicomio *m*

mad·ly ['mædlɪ] *adv* come un matto; **~ in love** pazzamente innamorato

'mad·man pazzo *m*

mad·ness ['mædnɪs] pazzia *f*

Ma·don·na [məˈdɒnə] Madonna *f*

Ma·fi·a ['mæfɪə] Mafia *f*

mag·a·zine [mægəˈziːn] *printed* rivista *f*

mag·got ['mægət] verme *m*

Ma·gi ['meɪdʒaɪ] REL Re Magi *mpl*

ma·gic ['mædʒɪk] **1** *n* magia *f*; *tricks* giochi *mpl* di prestigio; *like ~* come per magia **2** *adj* magico

mag·i·cal ['mædʒɪkl] *adj powers, moment* magico

ma·gi·cian [mə'dʒɪʃn] *performer* mago *m*, -a *f*

ma·gic 'spell incantesimo *m*; **ma·gic 'trick** gioco *m* di prestigio; **mag·ic 'wand** bacchetta *f* magica

mag·is·trate ['mædʒɪstreɪt] magistrato *m*

mag·nan·i·mous [mæg'nænɪməs] *adj* magnanimo

mag·net ['mægnɪt] calamita *f*, magnete *m*

mag·net·ic [mæg'netɪk] *adj* calamitato; *also fig* magnetico

mag·net·ic 'stripe striscia *f* magnetizzata

mag·net·ism [mæg'netɪzm] *of person* magnetismo *m*

mag·nif·i·cence [mæg'nɪfɪsəns] magnificenza *f*

mag·nif·i·cent [mæg'nɪfɪsənt] *adj* magnifico

mag·ni·fy ['mægnɪfaɪ] *v/t* (*pret & pp -ied*) ingrandire; *difficulties* ingigantire

'mag·ni·fy·ing glass lente *f* d'ingrandimento

mag·ni·tude ['mægnɪtjuːd] *of problem* portata *f*; AST magnitudine *f*

ma·hog·a·ny [mə'hɒgənɪ] mogano *m*

maid [meɪd] *servant* domestica *f*; *in hotel* cameriera *f*

maid·en name ['meɪdn] nome *m* da ragazza; **maid·en 'speech** discorso *m* inaugurale; **maid·en 'voy·age** viaggio *m* inaugurale

mail [meɪl] **1** *n* posta *f*; *put sth in the ~* spedire qc **2** *v/t letter* spedire; *person* spedire a

'mail·box *Am* buca *f* delle lettere; *Am: of house* cassetta *f* delle lettere; COMPUT casella *f* postale

'mail·ing list mailing list *m inv*

'mail·man *Am* postino *m*; **mail·'or·der cat·a·log** *Am*, **mail·'or·der**

cat·a·logue catalogo *m* di vendita per corrispondenza; **mail·'or·der firm** ditta *f* di vendita per corrispondenza; **'mail·shot** mailing *m inv*

maim [meɪm] *v/t* mutilare

main [meɪn] *adj* principale

'main course piatto *m* principale; **main 'en·trance** entrata *f* principale; **'main·frame** mainframe *m inv*; **'main·land** terraferma *f*, continente *m*; *on the ~* sul continente

main·ly ['meɪnlɪ] *adv* principalmente

main 'road strada *f* principale

'main street corso *m*

main·tain [meɪn'teɪn] *v/t* mantenere; *pace, speed; relationship; machine, house; family; innocence, guilt* sostenere; *~ that* sostenere che

main·te·nance ['meɪntənəns] *of machine, house* manutenzione *f*; *money* alimenti *mpl*; *of law and order* mantenimento *m*

'main·te·nance costs *npl* spese *fpl* di manutenzione

'main·te·nance staff addetti *mpl* alla manutenzione

ma·jes·tic [mə'dʒestɪk] *adj* maestoso

maj·es·ty ['mædʒəstɪ] (*grandeur*) maestà *f inv*; *Her Majesty* Sua Maestà

ma·jor ['meɪdʒə(r)] **1** *adj* (*significant*) importante, principale; *in C ~* MUS in Do maggiore **2** *n* MIL maggiore *m*

ma·jor·i·ty [mə'dʒɒrətɪ] *also* POL maggioranza *f*; maggioranza *f*; *be in the ~* essere in maggioranza

make [meɪk] **1** *n brand* marca *f* **2** *v/t* (*pret & pp made*) *decision* prendere; (*earn*) guadagnare; MATH fare; *~ s.o. do sth* (*force to*) far fare qc a qu; (*cause to*) spingere qu a fare qc; *you can't ~ me do it!* non puoi costringermi a farlo!; *~ s.o. happy / angry* far felice / arrabbiare qu; *~ s.o. happy / sad* rendere felice / triste qu; *~ a decision* prendere una decisione; *~ a telephone call* fare una telefonata; *made in Japan* made in Japan; *~ it catch bus, train,* come, succeed, survive farcela; **what time do you ~ it?** che ore fai?; ~ **believe** far finta; ~ **do with** arrangiarsi con; **what do you ~ of it?** cosa ne pensi?

♦ **make for** v/t (go towards) dirigersi verso

♦ **make off** v/i svignarsela

♦ **make off with** v/t (steal) svignarsela con

♦ **make out** v/t list fare; cheque compilare; (see) distinguere; (imply) far capire; **who shall I make the cheque out to?** a chi devo intestare l'assegno?

♦ **make over**: **make sth over to s.o.** cedere qc a qu

♦ **make up 1** v/i of woman, actor truccarsi; after quarrel fare la pace **2** v/t story, excuse inventare; face truccare; (constitute) costituire; **be made up of** essere composto da; **make up one's mind** decidersi; **make it up** after quarrel fare la pace

♦ **make up for** v/t compensare; **I'll make up for forgetting your birthday** mi farò perdonare di essermi scordato del tuo compleanno

'**make-be·lieve** n finta f

mak·er ['meɪkə(r)] manufacturer fabbricante m

make·shift ['meɪkʃɪft] adj improvvisato

make-up ['meɪkʌp] (cosmetics) trucco m

'**make-up bag** trousse f inv da trucco

mal·ad·just·ed [mælə'dʒʌstɪd] adj disadattato

male [meɪl] **1** adj (masculine) maschile; animal, bird, fish maschio **2** n man uomo m; animal, bird, fish maschio m

male 'chau·vin·ism maschilismo m; **male chau·vin·ist 'pig** maschilista m; **male 'nurse** infermiere m

ma·lev·o·lent [mə'levələnt] adj malevolo

mal·func·tion [mæl'fʌŋkʃn] **1** n cattivo m funzionamento **2** v/i funzionare male

mal·ice ['mælɪs] cattiveria f, malvagità f

ma·li·cious [mə'lɪʃəs] adj cattivo, malvagio

ma·lig·nant [mə'lɪgnənt] adj tumour maligno

mall [mæl] (shopping ~) centro m commerciale

mal·nu·tri·tion [mælnjuː'trɪʃn] denutrizione f

mal·prac·tice [mæl'præktɪs] negligenza f

malt ('whis·ky) [mɔːlt] whisky m inv di malto

mal·treat [mæl'triːt] v/t maltrattare

mal·treat·ment [mæl'triːtmənt] maltrattamento m

mam·mal ['mæml] mammifero m

mam·moth ['mæməθ] adj (enormous) colossale

man [mæn] **1** n (pl men [men]) person, human being uomo m; (human being) uomo m; (humanity) umanità f inv; in draughts pedina f **2** v/t (pret & pp -ned) telephones, front desk essere di servizio a; **it was ~ned by a crew of three** aveva un equipaggio di tre uomini

man·age ['mænɪdʒ] **1** v/t business, money gestire; money; suitcase; **can you ~ the suitcase?** ce la fai a portare la valigia?; ~ **to** ... riuscire a ... **2** v/i cope, financially tirare avanti; (financially); **can you ~?** ce la fai?

man·age·a·ble ['mænɪdʒəbl] adj suitcase etc maneggevole; hair docile; able to be done fattibile

man·age·ment ['mænɪdʒmənt] (managing) gestione f; (managers) direzione f; **under his ~** durante la sua gestione

man·age·ment 'buy-out acquisizione f di un'impresa da parte dei suoi dirigenti; **man·age·ment con'sult·ant** consulente m/f di gestione aziendale; '**man·age·ment stud·ies** corso m di formazione manageriale; '**man·age·ment team** team m inv manageriale

man·ag·er ['mænɪdʒə(r)] manager

M

m/f inv, direttore *m*, -trice *f*

man·a·ge·ri·al [mænɪ'dʒɪərɪəl] *adj* managerial

man·ag·ing di'rec·tor direttore *m* generale

man·da·rin 'or·ange [mændərɪn] mandarino *m*

man·date ['mændeɪt] (*authority, task*) mandato *m*

man·da·to·ry ['mændətrɪ] *adj* obbligatorio

mane [meɪn] *of horse* criniera *f*

ma·neu·ver *Am* → **manoeuvre**

man·gle ['mæŋgl] *v/t* (*crush*) stritolare

man·han·dle ['mænhændl] *v/t person* malmenare; *object* caricare

man·hood ['mænhʊd] *maturity* età *f inv* adulta; (*virility*) virilità *f inv*

'man·hour ora *f* lavorativa

'man·hunt caccia *f* all'uomo

ma·ni·a ['meɪnɪə] (*craze*) mania *f*

ma·ni·ac ['meɪnɪæk] F pazzo *m*, -a *f*

man·i·cure ['mænɪkjʊə(r)] *n* manicure *f inv*

man·i·fest ['mænɪfest] **1** *adj* palese **2** *v/t* manifestare; **~ itself** manifestarsi

ma·nip·u·late [mə'nɪpjʊleɪt] *v/t person, bones* manipolare; *equipment* maneggiare

ma·nip·u·la·tion [mənɪpjʊ'leɪʃn] *of person, bones* manipolazione *f*; *of bones*

ma·nip·u·la·tive [mə'nɪpjʊlətɪv] *adj* manipolatore

man'kind umanità *f inv*

man·ly ['mænlɪ] *adj* virile

'man-made *adj* sintetico

man·ner ['mænə(r)] *of doing sth* maniera *f*, modo *m*; (*attitude*) modo *m* di fare

man·ners ['mænəz] *npl*: *good / bad ~* buone / cattive maniere *fpl*; *have no ~* essere maleducato

ma·noeu·vre [mə'nuːvə(r)] **1** *n* manovra *f* **2** *v/t* manovrare

man·or ['mænə(r)] maniero *m*

'man·pow·er manodopera *f*, personale *m*

man·sion ['mænʃn] villa *f*

'man·slaugh·ter omicidio *m* colposo

man·tel·piece ['mæntlpiːs] mensola *f* del caminetto

man·u·al ['mænjʊəl] **1** *adj* manuale **2** *n* manuale *m*

man·u·al·ly ['mænjʊəlɪ] *adv* manualmente

man·u·fac·ture [mænjʊ'fæktʃə(r)] **1** *n* manifattura *f* **2** *v/t equipment* fabbricare

man·u·fac·tur·er [mænjʊ'fæktʃər·ə(r)] fabbricante *m/f*

man·u·fac·tur·ing [mænjʊ'fæktʃər·ɪŋ] *adj industry* manifatturiero

ma·nure [mə'njʊə(r)] letame *m*

man·u·script ['mænjʊskrɪpt] manoscritto *m*; *typed* dattiloscritto *m*

man·y ['menɪ] **1** *adj* molti; *~ times* molte volte; *not ~ people / taxis* poche persone / pochi taxi; *too ~ problems / beers* troppi problemi / troppe birre **2** *pron* molti *m*, molte *f*; *a great ~, a good ~* moltissimi; *how ~ do you need?* quanti ne servono?; *as ~ as 200* ben 200

'man-year anno / uomo *m*

map [mæp] *n* cartina *f*; (*street* ~) pianta *f*, piantina *f*

♦ **map out** *v/t* (*pret & pp* **-ped**) pianificare

ma·ple ['meɪpl] acero *m*

mar [mɑː(r)] *v/t* (*pret & pp* **-red**) guastare

mar·a·thon ['mærəθən] *race* maratona *f*

mar·ble ['mɑːbl] *material* marmo *m*

March [mɑːtʃ] marzo *m*

march [mɑːtʃ] **1** *n* marcia *f*; (*demonstration*) dimostrazione *f*, manifestazione *f* **2** *v/i* marciare; *in protest* dimostrare, manifestare; *~ from A to B in protest* sfilare in corteo da A a B

march·er ['mɑːtʃə(r)] dimostrante *m/f*, manifestante *m/f*

mare [meə(r)] cavalla *f*, giumenta *f*

mar·ga·rine [mɑːdʒə'riːn] margarina *f*

mar·gin ['mɑːdʒɪn] *of page* margine *m*; (COM: *profit margin*) margine *m* di guadagno; **by a narrow ~** di stretta misura

mar·gin·al ['mɑ:dʒɪnl] *adj (slight)* leggero

mar·gin·al·ly ['mɑ:dʒɪnlɪ] *adv (slightly)* leggermente

mar·i·hua·na, mar·i·jua·na [mærɪ'hwɑːnə] marijuana *f*

ma·ri·na [mə'riːnə] porticciolo *m*

mar·i·nade [mærɪ'neɪd] *n* marinata *f*

mar·i·nate ['mærɪneɪt] *v/t* marinare

ma·rine [mə'riːn] **1** *adj* marino **2** *n* MIL marina *f* militare

mar·i·tal ['mærɪtl] *adj* coniugale

mar·i·tal 'sta·tus stato *m* civile

mar·i·time ['mærɪtaɪm] *adj* marittimo

mar·jo·ram ['mɑ:dʒərəm] maggiorana *f*

mark¹ [mɑːk] FIN marco *m*

mark² [mɑːk] **1** *n (stain)* macchia *f*; *(sign, token)* segno *m*; *(trace)*; EDU voto *m*; **leave one's ~** lasciare un segno *v/t (stain)* macchiare; EDU correggere; *(indicate)* indicare; *(commemorate)* celebrare; **your essays will be ~ed out of ten** ai temi sarà assegnata una votazione da 1 a 10 **3** *v/i of fabric* macchiarsi

♦ **mark down** *v/t goods* ribassare

♦ **mark out** *v/t with a line etc* delimitare; *(fig: set apart)* distinguere

♦ **mark up** *v/t price* aumentare; *goods* aumentare il prezzo di

marked [mɑːkt] *adj (definite)* spiccato

mark·er ['mɑːkə(r)] *(highlighter)* evidenziatore *m*

mar·ket ['mɑːkɪt] **1** *n* mercato *m*; *for particular commodity*; *(stock ~)* mercato *m* azionario; **on the ~** sul mercato **2** *v/t* vendere

mar·ket·a·ble ['mɑːkɪtəbl] *adj* commercializzabile

mar·ket e'con·o·my economia *f* di mercato

'**mar·ket for·ces** *npl* forze *fpl* di mercato

mar·ket·ing ['mɑːkɪtɪŋ] marketing *m inv*

'**mar·ket·ing cam·paign** campagna

f di marketing; '**mar·ket·ing de·part·ment** reparto *m* marketing; '**mar·ket·ing mix** marketing mix *m inv*; '**mar·ket·ing strat·e·gy** strategia *f* di marketing

mar·ket 'lead·er leader *m inv* del mercato; '**mar·ket·place** *in town* piazza *f* del mercato; *for commodities* piazza *f*, mercato *m*; **mar·ket re'search** ricerca *f* di mercato; **mar·ket 'share** quota *f* di mercato

mark-up ['mɑːkʌp] ricarico *m*

mar·ma·lade ['mɑːməleɪd] marmellata *f* d'arance

mar·quee [mɑː'kiː] padiglione *f*

mar·riage ['mærɪdʒ] matrimonio *m*; *event* nozze *fpl*

'**mar·riage cer·tif·i·cate** certificato *m* di matrimonio

mar·riage 'guid·ance coun·sel·lor consulente *m/f* matrimoniale

mar·ried ['mærɪd] *adj* sposato; **be ~ to ...** essere sposato con ...

mar·ried 'life vita *f* coniugale

mar·ry ['mærɪ] *v/t (pret & pp -ied)* sposare; *of priest* unire in matrimonio; **get married** sposarsi

marsh [mɑːʃ] palude *f*

mar·shal ['mɑːʃl] *official* membro *m* del servizio d'ordine

marsh·mal·low [mɑːʃ'mæləʊ] *caramella f soffice e gommosa*

marsh·y ['mɑːʃɪ] *adj* paludoso

mar·tial arts [mɑːʃl'ɑːts] *npl* arti *fpl* marziali

mar·tial 'law legge *f* marziale

mar·tyr ['mɑːtə(r)] martire *m/f*

mar·tyred ['mɑːtəd] *adj fig* da martire

mar·vel ['mɑːvl] meraviglia *f*

♦ **marvel at** *v/t* meravigliarsi di

mar·ve·lous *Am*, **mar·vel·lous** ['mɑːvələs] *adj* meraviglioso

Marx·ism ['mɑːksɪzm] marxismo *m*

Marx·ist ['mɑːksɪst] **1** *adj* marxista **2** *n* marxista *m/f*

mar·zi·pan ['mɑːzɪpæn] marzapane *m*

mas·ca·ra [mæ'skɑːrə] mascara *m inv*

mas·cot ['mæskət] mascotte *f inv*

mas·cu·line ['mæskjʊlɪn] *adj* maschile

mas·cu·lin·i·ty [mæskjʊ'lɪnətɪ] (*virility*) virilità *f inv*

mash [mæʃ] *v/t* passare, schiacciare

mashed po·ta·toes [mæʃt] *npl* purè *m inv* di patate

mask [mɑːsk] **1** *n* maschera *f* **2** *v/t feelings* mascherare

'mask·ing tape nastro *m* adesivo di carta

mas·och·ism ['mæsəkɪzm] masochismo *m*

mas·och·ist ['mæsəkɪst] masochista *m/f*

ma·son ['meɪsn] scalpellino *m*

ma·son·ry ['meɪsnrɪ] muratura *f*

mas·que·rade [mæskə'reɪd] **1** *n fig* messinscena *f* **2** *v/i:* **~ as** farsi passare per

mass¹ [mæs] **1** *n great amount* massa *f*; **the ~es** le masse; **~es of** F un sacco di F **2** *v/i* radunarsi

mass² [mæs] REL messa *f*

mas·sa·cre ['mæsəkə(r)] **1** *n also fig* massacro *m* **2** *v/t also fig* massacrare

mas·sage ['mæsɑːʒ] **1** *n* massaggio *m* **2** *v/t* massaggiare; *figures* manipolare

'mas·sage par·lor *Am*, **'mas·sage par·lour** *euph* casa *f* d'appuntamenti

mas·seur [mæ'sɜː(r)] massaggiatore *m*

mas·seuse [mæ'sɜːz] massaggiatrice *f*

mas·sive ['mæsɪv] *adj* enorme; *heart attack* grave

mass 'me·di·a *npl* mass media *mpl*; **mass-pro'duce** *v/t* produrre in serie; **mass pro'duc·tion** produzione *f* in serie

mast [mɑːst] *of ship* albero *m*; *for radio signal* palo *m* dell'antenna

mas·ter ['mɑːstə(r)] **1** *n of dog* padrone *m*; *of ship* capitano *m*; **be a ~ of** essere un maestro di **2** *v/t skill, language* avere completa padronanza di; *situation* dominare

'mas·ter bed·room camera *f* da letto principale

'mas·ter key passe-partout *m inv*

mas·ter·ly ['mɑːstəlɪ] *adj* magistrale

'mas·ter·mind 1 *n fig* cervello *m* **2** *v/t* ideare; **Mas·ter of 'Arts** master *m inv*; **mas·ter of 'cer·e·mo·nies** maestro *m* di cerimonie; **'mas·ter·piece** capolavoro *m*; **'mas·ter's (de·gree)** master *m inv*

mas·ter·y ['mɑːstərɪ] padronanza *f*

mas·tur·bate ['mæstəbeɪt] *v/i* masturbarsi

mat [mæt] *for floor* tappetino *m*; SP tappeto *m*; *for table* tovaglietta *f* all'americana

match¹ [mætʃ] *for cigarette* fiammifero *m*; *wax* cerino *m*

match² [mætʃ] **1** *n (competition)* partita *f*; **be no ~ for s.o.** non poter competere con qu; **meet one's ~** trovare pane per i propri denti **2** *v/t (be the same as)* abbinare; *(equal)* uguagliare **3** *v/i of colours, patterns* intonarsi

'match·box scatola *f* di fiammiferi

match·ing ['mætʃɪŋ] *adj* abbinato

'match stick fiammifero *m*

mate [meɪt] **1** *n of animal* compagno *m*, -a *f*, NAUT secondo *m*; F *friend* amico *m*, -a *f* **2** *v/i* accoppiarsi

ma·te·ri·al [mə'tɪərɪəl] **1** *n fabric* stoffa *f*, tessuto *m*; *substance* materia *f*; **~s** occorrente *m* **2** *adj* materiale

ma·te·ri·al·ism [mə'tɪərɪəlɪzm] materialismo *m*

ma·te·ri·al·ist [mətɪərɪə'lɪst] materialista *m/f*

ma·te·ri·al·is·tic [mətɪərɪə'lɪstɪk] *adj* materialistico

ma·te·ri·al·ize [mə'tɪərɪəlaɪz] *v/i* materializzarsi

ma·ter·nal [mə'tɜːnl] *adj* materno

ma·ter·ni·ty [mə'tɜːnətɪ] maternità *f inv*

ma'ter·ni·ty dress vestito *m* premaman; **ma'ter·ni·ty leave** congedo *m* per maternità; **ma·'ter·ni·ty ward** reparto *m* maternità

math *Am* → **maths**

math·e·mat·i·cal [mæθə'mætɪkl] *adj* matematico

math·e·ma·ti·cian [mæθmə'tɪʃn]

matematico *m*, -a *f*

math·e·mat·ics [mæθ'mætɪks] matematica *f*

maths [mæθs] matematica *f*

mat·i·née ['mætɪneɪ] matinée *f inv*

ma·tri·arch ['meɪtrɪɑːk] matriarca *f*

ma·tri·arch·al [meɪtrɪ'ɑːkl] *adj* matriarcale

mat·ri·mo·ny ['mætrɪmənɪ] matrimonio *m*

matt [mæt] *adj* opaco

mat·ter ['mætə(r)] **1** *n* (*affair*) questione *f*, faccenda *f*; PHYS materia *f*; **as a ~ of course** per abitudine; **as a ~ of fact** a dir la verità; **what's the ~?** cosa c'è?; **no ~ what she says** qualsiasi cosa dica **2** *v/i* importare; **it doesn't ~** non importa

mat·ter-of-'fact *adj* distaccato

mat·tress ['mætrɪs] materasso *m*

ma·ture [mə'tjʊə(r)] **1** *adj* maturo **2** *v/i of person, insurance policy etc* maturare; *of wine* invecchiare

ma·tu·ri·ty [mə'tjʊrətɪ] maturità *f inv*

maul [mɔːl] *v/t also fig* sbranare

max·i·mize ['mæksɪmaɪz] *v/t* massimizzare

max·i·mum ['mæksɪməm] **1** *adj* massimo **2** *n* massimo *m*

May [meɪ] maggio *m*

may [meɪ] *v/aux* ◊ (*possibility*): **it ~ rain** potrebbe piovere, può darsi che piova; **you ~ be right** potresti aver ragione, può darsi che abbia ragione; **it ~ not happen** magari non succederà, può darsi che non succeda ◊ (*permission*): **~ I help/ smoke?** posso aiutare/fumare?; **you ~ if you like** puoi farlo se vuoi

may·be ['meɪbiː] *adv* forse

'**May Day** il primo maggio

may·on·naise [meɪə'neɪz] maionese *f*

may·or ['meə(r)] sindaco *m*

maze [meɪz] *also fig* dedalo *m*, labirinto *m*

MB *abbr* (= **megabyte**) MB *m* (= megabyte *m inv*)

MBA [embiː'eɪ] *abbr* (= **master of business administration**) master

m inv in amministrazione aziendale

MBO [embiː'əʊ] *abbr* (= **management buyout**) acquisizione *f* di un'impresa da parte dei suoi dirigenti

MC [em'siː] *abbr* (= **master of ceremonies**) maestro *m* di cerimonie

MD [em'diː] *abbr* (= **Doctor of Medicine**) dottore *m* in medicina

me [miː] *pron direct & indirect object* mi; *after prep, stressed* me; **she knows ~** mi conosce; **she spoke to ~** mi ha parlato; **she spoke to ~ but not to him** ha parlato a me ma non a lui; **without ~** senza di me; **it's ~** sono io; **who? ~?** chi? io?

mead·ow ['medəʊ] prato *m*

mea·ger *Am*, **mea·gre** ['miːgə(r)] *adj* scarso

meal [miːl] pranzo *m*, pasto *m*; **enjoy your ~!** buon appetito!

'**meal·time** ora *f* di pranzo

mean¹ [miːn] *adj with money* avaro; (*nasty*) cattivo

mean² [miːn] (*pret & pp* **meant**) **1** *v/t* (*signify*) significare, voler dire; **do you ~ it?** (*intend*) dici sul serio?; **~ to do sth** avere l'intenzione di fare qc; **be ~t for** essere destinato a; *of remark* essere diretto a; **doesn't it ~ anything to you?** (*doesn't it matter?*) non conta niente per te? **2** *v/i*: **~ well** avere buone intenzioni

mean·ing ['miːnɪŋ] *of word* significato *m*

mean·ing·ful ['miːnɪŋfʊl] *adj* (*comprehensible*) comprensibile; (*constructive*) costruttivo; *glance* eloquente

mean·ing·less ['miːnɪŋlɪs] *adj sentence etc* senza senso; *gesture* vuoto

means [miːnz] *npl financial* mezzi *mpl*; (*nsg: way*) modo *m*; **~ of transport** mezzo *m* di trasporto; **by all ~** (*certainly*) certamente; **by no ~ rich/poor** lungi dall'essere ricco/povero; **by ~ of** per mezzo di

meant [ment] *pret & pp* → **mean²**

mean-time ['miːntaɪm] **1** *adv* intanto **2** *n*: **in the ~** nel frattempo

mean·while ['miːnwaɪl] **1** *adv* intan-

M

to **2** *n*: *in the* ~ nel frattempo

mea·sles ['mi:zlz] *nsg* morbillo *m*

mea·sure ['meʒə(r)] **1** *n* (*step*) misura *f*, provvedimento *m*; *a* ~ *of success certain amount* un certo successo **2** *v/t* prendere le misure di **3** *v/i* misurare

♦ **measure out** *v/t amount* dosare; *area* misurare

♦ **measure up to** *v/t* dimostrarsi all'altezza di

mea·sure·ment ['meʒəmənt] *action* misurazione *f*; (*dimension*) misura *f*; *system of* ~ sistema *m* di misura

meas·ur·ing jug ['meʒərɪŋ] misurino *m*

'mea·sur·ing tape metro *m* a nastro

meat [mi:t] carne *f*

'meat·ball polpetta *f*

'meat·loaf polpettone *m*

me·chan·ic [mɪ'kænɪk] meccanico *m*

me·chan·i·cal [mɪ'kænɪkl] *adj also fig* meccanico

me·chan·i·cal en·gi·neer ingegnere *m* meccanico

me·chan·i·cal en·gi·neer·ing ingegneria *f* meccanica

me·chan·i·cal·ly [mɪ'kænɪklɪ] *adv also fig* meccanicamente

mech·a·nism ['mekənɪzm] meccanismo *m*

mech·a·nize ['mekənaɪz] *v/t* meccanizzare

med·al ['medl] medaglia *f*

med·a·list *Am*, **med·al·list** ['medəlɪst] vincitore *m*, -trice *f* di una medaglia

med·dle ['medl] *v/i* (*interfere*) immischiarsi; ~ *with* (*tinker*) mettere le mani in

me·di·a ['mi:dɪə] *npl*: *the* ~ i mass media *mpl*

'me·di·a cov·er·age: *it was given a lot of* ~ gli è stato dato molto spazio in tv e sui giornali; *an event that got a lot of* ~ un avvenimento di grande risonanza

med·i·ae·val [medɪ'i:vl] → **medieval**

'me·di·a e·vent spettacolo *m* sensazionale; **me·di·a 'hype** montatura *f* della stampa; **'me·di·a stud·ies** scienze *fpl* delle comunicazioni

me·di·ate ['mi:dɪeɪt] *v/i* fare da mediatore *m*, -trice *f*

me·di·a·tion [mi:dɪ'eɪʃn] mediazione *f*

me·di·a·tor ['mi:dɪeɪtə(r)] mediatore *m*, -trice *f*

med·i·cal ['medɪkl] **1** *adj* medico **2** *n* visita *f* medica

'med·i·cal cer·tif·i·cate certificato *m* medico; **'med·i·cal ex·am·i·na·tion** visita *f* medica; **'med·i·cal his·to·ry** anamnesi *f inv*; **'med·i·cal pro·fes·sion** professione *f* medica; corpo *m* medico; **'med·i·cal re·cord** cartella *f* clinica

med·i·cat·ed ['medɪkeɪtɪd] *adj* medicato

med·i·ca·tion [medɪ'keɪʃn] medicina *f*

me·di·ci·nal [mɪ'dɪsɪnl] *adj* medicinale

med·i·cine ['medsən] medicina *f*

'med·i·cine cab·i·net armadietto *m* dei medicinali

med·i·e·val [medɪ'i:vl] *adj* medievale

me·di·o·cre [mi:dɪ'əʊkə(r)] *adj* mediocre

me·di·oc·ri·ty [mi:dɪ'ɒkrətɪ] mediocrità *f inv*

med·i·tate ['medɪteɪt] *v/i* meditare

med·i·ta·tion [medɪ'teɪʃn] meditazione *f*

Med·i·ter·ra·ne·an [medɪtə'reɪnɪən] **1** *adj* mediterraneo **2** *n*: *the* ~ il Mar Mediterraneo; *area* i paesi mediterranei

me·di·um ['mi:dɪəm] **1** *adj* (*average*) medio; *steak* cotto al punto giusto **2** *n in size* media *f*; (*vehicle*) strumento *m*; (*spiritualist*) medium *m/f inv*

me·di·um-sized ['mi:dɪəmsaɪzd] *adj* di grandezza media; **me·di·um 'term**: *in the* ~ a medio termine; **'me·di·um wave** RAD onde *fpl* medie

med·ley ['medlɪ] (*assortment*) misto *m*

meek [mi:k] *adj* mite

meet [mi:t] **1** *v/t* (*pret & pp* **met**) incontrare; (*get to know*) conoscere; (*collect*) andare *o* venire a prendere; *in competition* affrontare; *of eyes* incrociare; (*satisfy*) soddisfare; *I'll ~ you there* ci vediamo lì **2** *v/i* (*pret & pp* **met**) incontrarsi; *in competition* affrontarsi; *of eyes* incrociarsi; *of committee etc* riunirsi; *have you two met?* (*do you know each other?*) vi conoscete? **3** *n Am* SP raduno *m* sportivo

♦**meet with** *v/t person* avere un incontro con; *opposition, approval etc* incontrare; *it met with success / failure* ha avuto successo / è fallito

meet·ing ['mi:tɪŋ] incontro *m*; *of committee, in business* riunione *f*; appuntamento *m*; *he's in a ~* è in riunione

'**meet·ing place** luogo *m* d'incontro

meg·a·byte ['megəbaɪt] COMPUT megabyte *m inv*

mel·an·chol·y ['melənkəlɪ] *adj* malinconia *f*

mel·low ['meləʊ] **1** *adj* maturo **2** *v/i of person* addolcirsi

me·lo·di·ous [mɪ'ləʊdɪəs] *adj* melodioso

mel·o·dra·mat·ic [melədrə'mætɪk] *adj* melodrammatico

mel·o·dy ['melədɪ] melodia *f*

mel·on ['melən] melone *m*

melt [melt] **1** *v/i* sciogliersi **2** *v/t* sciogliere

♦**melt away** *v/i fig* svanire

♦**melt down** *v/t metal* fondere

melt·ing pot ['meltɪŋpɒt] *fig* crogiolo *m* di culture

mem·ber ['membə(r)] *of family* componente *m/f*; *of club* socio *m*; *of organization* membro *m*

Mem·ber of 'Par·lia·ment deputato *m*

mem·ber·ship ['membəʃɪp] iscrizione *f*; *number of members* numero *m* dei soci

'**mem·ber·ship card** tessera *f* d'iscrizione

mem·brane ['membreɪn] membrana *f*

me·men·to [me'mentəʊ] souvenir *m inv*

mem·o ['meməʊ] circolare *f*

mem·oirs ['memwɑːz] *npl* memorie *fpl*

'**mem·o pad** blocco *m* notes

mem·o·ra·ble ['memərəbl] *adj* memorabile

me·mo·ri·al [mɪ'mɔːrɪəl] **1** *adj* commemorativo **2** *n also fig* memorial *m inv*

mem·o·rize ['meməraɪz] *v/t* memorizzare

mem·o·ry ['memərɪ] (*recollection*) ricordo *m*; *power of recollection* memoria *f*; COMPUT memoria *f*; *in ~ of* in memoria di

men [men] *pl →* **man**

men·ace ['menɪs] **1** *n* (*threat*) minaccia *f*; *person* pericolo *m* pubblico; (*nuisance*) peste *f* **2** *v/t* minacciare

men·ac·ing ['menɪsɪŋ] minaccioso

mend [mend] **1** *v/t* riparare **2** *n*: *be on the ~ after illness* essere in via di guarigione

me·ni·al ['mi:nɪəl] *adj* umile

men·in·gi·tis [menɪn'dʒaɪtɪs] meningite *f*

men·o·pause ['menəpɔːz] menopausa *f*

'**men's room** *Am* bagno *m* (degli uomini)

men·stru·ate ['menstrʊeɪt] *v/i* avere le mestruazioni

men·stru·a·tion [menstrʊ'eɪʃn] mestruazione *f*

men·tal ['mentl] *adj* mentale; F (*crazy*) pazzo

men·tal a'rith·me·tic calcolo *m* mentale; **men·tal 'cru·el·ty** crudeltà *f inv* mentale; '**men·tal hos·pi·tal** ospedale *m* psichiatrico; **men·tal 'ill·ness** malattia *f* mentale

men·tal·i·ty [men'tælətɪ] mentalità *f inv*

men·tal·ly ['mentəlɪ] *adv inwardly* mentalmente; *calculate etc* a mente

M

men·tal·ly 'hand·i·capped *adj* handicappato mentale

men·tal·ly 'ill *adj* malato di mente

men·tion ['menʃn] **1** *n* cenno *m*; **he made no ~ of it** non ne ha fatto cenno **2** *v/t* accennare a; **she ~ed that ...** ha accennato al fatto che ...; **don't ~ it** (*you're welcome*) non c'è di che

men·tor ['mentɔː(r)] guida *f* spirituale

men·u ['menjuː] *also* COMPUT menu *m inv*

MEP [emiːˈpiː] *abbr* (= **Member of the European Parliament**) eurodeputato *m*

mer·ce·na·ry ['mɜːsɪnərɪ] **1** *adj* mercenario **2** *n* MIL mercenario *m*

mer·chan·dise ['mɜːtʃəndaɪz] merce *f*

mer·chant ['mɜːtʃənt] commerciante *m/f*

mer·chant 'bank banca *f* d'affari

mer·chant 'bank·er banchiere *m* d'affari

mer·ci·ful ['mɜːsɪfʊl] *adj* misericordioso

mer·ci·ful·ly ['mɜːsɪflɪ] *adv* (*thankfully*) per fortuna

mer·ci·less ['mɜːsɪlɪs] *adj* spietato

mer·cu·ry ['mɜːkjʊrɪ] mercurio *m*

mer·cy ['mɜːsɪ] misericordia *f*; **be at s.o.'s ~** essere alla mercé di qu

mere [mɪə(r)] *adj* semplice; **he's a ~ child** è solo un bambino

mere·ly ['mɪəlɪ] *adv* soltanto

merge [mɜːdʒ] *v/i of two lines etc* unirsi; *of companies* fondersi

merg·er ['mɜːdʒə(r)] COM fusione *f*

mer·it ['merɪt] **1** *n* (*worth*) merito *m*; (*advantage*) vantaggio *m* **2** *v/t* meritare

mer·ri·ment ['merɪmənt] ilarità *f inv*

mer·ry ['merɪ] *adj* allegro; **Merry Christmas!** Buon Natale!

'mer·ry-go-round giostra *f*

mesh [meʃ] *in net* maglia *f*

mess [mes] (*untidiness*) disordine *m*; (*trouble*) pasticcio *m*; **be a ~ of** *room, desk, hair* essere in disordine; *of situation, s.o.'s life* essere un pasticcio

♦ **mess about, mess around 1** *v/i* (*waste time*) trastullarsi **2** *v/t person* menare per il naso

♦ **mess around with** *v/t* (*play with*) giocare con; (*interfere with*) armeggiare con; *s.o.'s wife* avere una relazione con

♦ **mess up** *v/t room, papers* mettere sottosopra; *task, plans, marriage* rovinare

mes·sage ['mesɪdʒ] *also fig* messaggio *m*

mes·sen·ger ['mesɪndʒə(r)] (*courier*) fattorino *m*, -a *f*

Mes·si·ah [me'saɪə] Messia *m*

mess·y ['mesɪ] *adj room* in disordine; *person* disordinato; *job* sporco; *divorce, situation* antipatico

met [met] *pret & pp* → **meet**

met·a·bol·ic [metə'bɒlɪk] *adj* metabolico

me·tab·o·lis·m [mətæ'bəlɪzm] metabolismo *m*

met·al ['metl] **1** *adj* in *o* di metallo **2** *n* metallo *m*

me·tal·lic [mɪ'tælɪk] *adj* metallico

met·a·phor ['metəfə(r)] metafora *f*

me·te·or ['miːtɪə(r)] meteora *f*

me·te·or·ic [miːtɪ'ɒrɪk] *adj fig* fulmineo

me·te·or·ite ['miːtɪəraɪt] meteorite *m o f*

me·te·or·o·log·i·cal [miːtɪərə'lɒdʒɪkl] *adj* meteorologico

me·te·or·ol·o·gist [miːtɪə'rɒlədʒɪst] meteorologo *m*, -a *f*

me·te·o·rol·o·gy [miːtɪə'rɒlədʒɪ] meteorologia *f*

me·ter ['miːtə(r)] *for gas etc* contatore *m*; (*parking ~*) parchimetro *m*; *Am: length* metro *m*

'me·ter read·ing lettura *f* del contatore

meth·od ['meθəd] metodo *m*

me·thod·i·cal [mɪ'θɒdɪkl] *adj* metodico

me·thod·i·cal·ly [mɪ'θɒdɪklɪ] *adv* metodicamente

me·tic·u·lous [mɪ'tɪkjʊləs] *adj* meticoloso

me·tic·u·lous·ly [mɪ'tɪkjʊləslɪ] *adv* meticolosamente

me·tre ['miːtə(r)] metro *m*

met·ric ['metrɪk] *adj* metrico

me·trop·o·lis [mɪ'trɒpəlɪs] metropoli *f inv*

met·ro·pol·i·tan [metrə'pɒlɪtən] *adj* metropolitano

mew [mjuː] *n & v/i* → *miaow*

Mex·i·can ['meksɪkən] **1** *adj* messicano **2** *n* messicano *m*, -a *f*

Mex·i·co ['meksɪkəʊ] Messico *m*

mez·za·nine (floor) ['mezəniːn] mezzanino *m*

mi·aow [mɪaʊ] **1** *n* miao *m* **2** *v/i* miagolare

mice [maɪs] *pl* → *mouse*

mick·ey mouse [mɪkɪ'maʊs] *adj* P *course, qualification* del piffero F

mi·cro·bi·ol·o·gy ['maɪkrəʊ] microbiologia *f*; **'mi·cro·chip** microchip *m inv*; **'mi·cro·cli·mate** microclima *m*; **mi·cro·cosm** ['maɪkrəʊkɒzm] microcosmo *m*; **'mi·cro·e·lec·tron·ics** microelettronica *f*; **'mi·cro·film** microfilm *m inv*; **'mi·cro·or·gan·ism** microrganismo *m*; **'mi·cro·phone** microfono *m*; **mi·cro·pro·ces·sor** microprocessore *m*; **'mi·cro·scope** microscopio *m*; **mi·cro·scop·ic** [maɪkrə'skɒpɪk] *adj* microscopico; **'mi·cro·wave** oven forno *m* a microonde

mid-air [mɪd'eə(r)]: *in* ~ a mezz'aria

mid·day [mɪd'deɪ] mezzogiorno *m*

mid·dle ['mɪdl] **1** *adj* di mezzo **2** *n* mezzo *m*; *in the ~ of* *of floor, room* nel centro di, in mezzo a; *of period of time* a metà di; *be in the ~ of doing sth* stare facendo qc

'mid·dle-aged *adj* di mezz'età; **'Mid·dle Ages** *npl* Medioevo *m*; **mid·dle 'class** *adj* borghese; **the ~ class(es)** *npl* la borghesia *f*; **Mid·dle 'East** Medio Oriente *m*; **'mid·dle·man** intermediario *m*; **'man·age·ment** quadri *mpl* intermedi; **mid·dle 'name** secondo nome *m*; **'mid·dle·weight** boxer peso *m* medio

mid·dling ['mɪdlɪŋ] *adj* medio

mid·field·er [mɪd'fiːldə(r)] centrocampista *m*

midge [mɪdʒ] moscerino *m*

midg·et ['mɪdʒɪt] *adj* di dimensioni ridotte

'Mid·lands *npl* regione *f* nell'Inghilterra centrale

'mid·night ['mɪdnaɪt] mezzanotte *f*; *at* ~ a mezzanotte; **'mid·sum·mer** piena estate *f*; **'mid·way** *adv* a metà strada; ~ *through* a metà di; **'mid·week** *adv* a metà settimana; **'Mid·west** regione *f* medio-occidentale degli USA; **'mid·wife** ostetrica *f*; **'mid·win·ter** pieno inverno *m*

might¹ [maɪt] *v/aux*: *I – be late* potrei far tardi; *it ~ rain* magari piove; *it ~ never happen* potrebbe non succedere mai; *I ~ have lost it* perhaps I did forse l'ho perso; *it would have been possible* avrei potuto perderlo; *he ~ have left* forse se n'è andato; *you ~ as well spend the night here* tanto vale che passi la notte qui; *you ~ have told me!* potevi dirmelo!

might² [maɪt] (*power*) forze *fpl*

might·y ['maɪtɪ] **1** *adj* potente **2** *adv* F (*extremely*) molto

mi·graine ['miːgreɪn] emicrania *f*

mi·grant work·er ['maɪgrənt] emigrante *m/f*

mi·grate [maɪ'greɪt] *v/i* emigrare; *of birds* migrare

mi·gra·tion [maɪ'greɪʃn] emigrazione *f*; *of birds* migrazione *f*

mike [maɪk] F microfono *m*

Milan [mɪ'læn] Milano *f*

mild [maɪld] *adj* weather mite; *cheese, person* dolce; *curry* poco piccante; *punishment, sedative* leggero

mil·dew ['mɪldjuː] muffa *f*

mild·ly ['maɪldlɪ] *adv* gentilmente; (*slightly*) moderatamente; *to put it* ~ a dir poco

mild·ness ['maɪldnɪs] *of weather* mitezza *f*; *of person, voice* dolcezza *f*

mile [maɪl] miglio *m*; **~s better / easier** F molto meglio / più facile

mile·age ['maɪlɪdʒ] chilometraggio *m*

'mile·stone *also fig* pietra *f* miliare

mil·i·tant ['mɪlɪtənt] **1** *adj* militante **2** *n* militante *m/f*

mil·i·ta·ry ['mɪlɪtrɪ] **1** *adj* militare **2** *n*: **the** ~ l'esercito *m*, le forze *fpl* armate; **it's run by the** ~ è in mano ai militari

mil·i·ta·ry a'cad·e·my accademia *f* militare; **mil·i·ta·ry po'lice** polizia *f* militare; **mil·i·ta·ry 'serv·ice** servizio *m* militare

mi·li·tia [mɪ'lɪʃə] milizia *f*

milk [mɪlk] **1** *n* latte *m* **2** *v/t* mungere

'milk bot·tle bottiglia *f* del latte; milk 'choc·o·late cioccolato *m* al latte; 'milk float furgone *m* del latte; 'milk jug bricco *m* del latte; 'milk·man lattaio *m*; milk of mag'ne·sia latte *m* di magnesia; 'milk·shake frappé *m inv*

'milk·y ['mɪlkɪ] *adj* con tanto latte

Milk·y 'Way Via *f* Lattea

mill [mɪl] *for grain* mulino *m*; *for textiles* fabbrica *f*

♦ mill about, mill around *v/i* brulicare

mil·len·ni·um [mɪ'lenɪəm] millennio *m*

mil·li·gram ['mɪlɪgræm] milligrammo *m*

mil·li·me·ter *Am*, mil·li·me·tre ['mɪlɪmiːtə(r)] millimetro *m*

mil·lion ['mɪljən] milione *m*

mil·lion·aire [mɪljə'neə(r)] miliardario *m*, -a *f*

mime [maɪm] *v/t* mimare

mim·ic ['mɪmɪk] **1** *n* imitatore *m*, -trice *f* **2** *v/t* (*pret & pp -ked*) imitare

mince [mɪns] *v/t meat* carne *f* tritata

'mince·meat *frutta f secca tritata*

mince 'pie *pasticcino m ripieno di frutta secca tritata*

mind [maɪnd] **1** *n* mente *f*, cervello *m*; **it's all in your** ~ è solo la tua immaginazione; **be out of one's** ~ essere matto; **keep sth in** ~ tenere presente qc; **I've a good** ~ **to ...** ho proprio voglia di ...; **change one's** ~ cambiare idea; **it didn't enter my** ~ non

mi è passato per la testa; **give s.o. a piece of one's** ~ cantarne quattro a qu; **make up one's** ~ decidersi; **have sth on one's** ~ essere preoccupato per qc; **keep one's** ~ **on sth** concentrarsi su qc **2** *v/t* (*look after*) tenere d'occhio; *children* badare a; (*heed*) fare attenzione a; **I don't** ~ **tea if that's all you've got** (*object to*) il tè va bene se non hai altro; **I don't** ~ **what we do** non importa cosa facciamo; **do you** ~ **if I smoke?, do you** ~ **my smoking?** le dispiace se fumo?; **would you** ~ **opening the window?** le dispiace aprire la finestra?; ~ **the step!** attento al gradino!; ~ **your own business!** fatti gli affari tuoi! **3** *v/i*: ~! (*be careful*) attenzione!; **never** ~! non farci caso!; **I don't** ~ è uguale *o* indifferente

mind-bog·gling ['maɪndbɒglɪŋ] *adj* incredibile

mind·less ['maɪndlɪs] *adj violence* insensato

mine¹ [maɪn] *pron* il mio *m*, la mia *f*, i miei *mpl*, le mie *fpl*; **a cousin of** ~ un mio cugino

mine² [maɪn] **1** *n for coal etc* miniera *f* **2** *v/i*: ~ **for** estrarre

mine³ [maɪn] **1** *n explosive* mina *f* **2** *v/t* minare

'mine·field *also fig* campo *m* minato

min·er ['maɪnə(r)] minatore *m*

min·e·ral ['mɪnərəl] *n* minerale *m*

'min·e·ral wa·ter acqua *f* minerale

'mine·sweep·er NAUT dragamine *m inv*

min·gle ['mɪŋgl] *v/i of sounds, smells* mischiarsi; *at party* mescolarsi

min·i ['mɪnɪ] *skirt* mini *f inv*

min·i·a·ture ['mɪnɪtʃə(r)] *adj* in miniatura

'min·i·bus minibus *m inv*

'min·i·cab radiotaxi *m inv*

min·i·mal ['mɪnɪməl] *adj* minimo

min·i·mal·ism ['mɪnɪməlɪzm] minimalismo *m*

min·i·mize ['mɪnɪmaɪz] *v/t* minimizzare

min·i·mum ['mɪnɪməm] **1** *adj* minimo **2** *n* minimo *m*

min·i·mum 'wage salario *m* minimo garantito

min·ing ['maɪnɪŋ] industria *f* mineraria

'**min·i·se·ries** TV miniserie *f inv*

'**min·i·skirt** minigonna *f*

min·is·ter ['mɪnɪstə(r)] POL ministro *m*; REL pastore *m*

min·is·te·ri·al [mɪnɪ'stɪərɪəl] *adj* ministeriale

min·is·try ['mɪnɪstrɪ] POL ministero *m*

mink [mɪŋk] **1** *adj fur* di visone **2** *n coat* visone *m*

mi·nor ['maɪnə(r)] **1** *adj* piccolo; **in D ~** MUS in Re minore **2** *n* LAW minorenne *m/f*

mi·nor·i·ty [maɪ'nɒrətɪ] minoranza *f*; **be in the ~** essere in minoranza

mint [mɪnt] *n herb* menta *f*; *chocolate* cioccolato *m* alla menta; *sweet* mentina *f*

mi·nus ['maɪnəs] **1** *n* (~ *sign*) meno *m* **2** *prep* meno; **~ 10 degrees** 10 gradi sotto zero

mi·nus·cule ['mɪnəskjuːl] *adj* minuscolo

min·ute¹ ['mɪnɪt] *of time* minuto *m*; **in a ~** (*soon*) in un attimo; **just a ~** un attimo

mi·nute² [maɪ'njuːt] *adj* (*tiny*) piccolissimo; (*detailed*) minuzioso; **in ~ detail** minuziosamente

'**mi·nute hand** lancetta *f* dei minuti

mi·nute·ly [maɪ'njuːtlɪ] *adv* (*in detail*) minuziosamente; (*very slightly*) appena

min·utes ['mɪnɪts] *npl of meeting* verbale *m*

mir·a·cle ['mɪrəkl] miracolo *m*

mi·rac·u·lous [mɪ'rækjʊləs] *adj* miracoloso

mi·rac·u·lous·ly [mɪ'rækjʊləslɪ] *adv* miracolosamente

mi·rage ['mɪrɑːʒ] miraggio *m*

mir·ror ['mɪrə(r)] **1** *n* specchio *m*; MOT specchietto *m* **2** *v/t* riflettere; **be ~ed in sth** *in water etc* specchiarsi in qc; *fig* rispecchiarsi in qc

mirth [mɜːθ] ilarità *f inv*

mis·an·thro·pist [mɪ'zænθrəpɪst] misantropo *m*

mis·ap·pre·hen·sion [mɪsæprɪ'henʃn]: **be under a ~** sbagliarsi

mis·be·have [mɪsbə'heɪv] *v/i* comportarsi male

mis·be·hav·ior *Am,* **mis·be·hav·iour** [mɪsbə'heɪvjə(r)] comportamento *m* scorretto

mis·cal·cu·late [mɪs'kælkjʊleɪt] *v/t & v/i* calcolare male

mis·cal·cu·la·tion [mɪs'kælkjʊleɪʃn] errore *m* di calcolo

mis·car·riage ['mɪskærɪdʒ] MED aborto *m* spontaneo; **~ of justice** errore *m* giudiziario

mis·car·ry ['mɪskærɪ] *v/i* (*pret & pp -ied*) *of plan* fallire

mis·cel·la·ne·ous [mɪsə'leɪnɪəs] *adj* eterogeneo

mis·chief ['mɪstʃɪf] (*naughtiness*) birichinate *fpl*

mis·chie·vous ['mɪstʃɪvəs] *adj* (*naughty*) birichino; (*malicious*) perfido

mis·con·cep·tion [mɪskən'sepʃn] idea *f* sbagliata

mis·con·duct [mɪs'kɒndʌkt] reato *m* professionale

mis·con·strue [mɪskən'struː] *v/t* interpretare male

mis·de·mea·nor *Am,* **mis·de·mea·nour** [mɪsdə'miːnə(r)] infrazione *f*

mi·ser ['maɪzə(r)] avaro *m*, -a *f*

mis·e·ra·ble ['mɪzrəbl] *adj* (*unhappy*) infelice; *weather, performance* deprimente

mi·ser·ly ['maɪzəlɪ] *adj person* avaro; *amount* misero

mis·e·ry ['mɪzərɪ] (*unhappiness*) tristezza *f*; (*wretchedness*) miseria *f*

mis·fire [mɪs'faɪə(r)] *v/i of joke, scheme* far cilecca; *of engine* perdere colpi

mis·fit ['mɪsfɪt] *in society* disadattato *m*, -a *f*

mis·for·tune [mɪs'fɔːtʃən] sfortuna *f*

mis·giv·ings [mɪs'gɪvɪŋz] *npl* dubbi *mpl*

mis·guid·ed [mɪs'gaɪdɪd] *adj* at-

M

tempts, theory sbagliato; **he was ~ in maintaining that ...** sbagliava a sostenere che ...

mis·han·dle [mɪs'hændl] v/t situation gestire male

mis·hap ['mɪshæp] incidente m

mis·in·form [mɪsɪn'fɔːm] v/t informare male

mis·in·ter·pret [mɪsɪn'tɜːprɪt] v/t interpretare male

mis·in·ter·pre·ta·tion [mɪsɪntɜːprɪ-'teɪʃn] interpretazione f errata

mis·judge [mɪs'dʒʌdʒ] v/t person, situation giudicare male

mis·lay [mɪs'leɪ] v/t (pret & pp **-laid**) smarrire

mis·lead [mɪs'liːd] v/t (pret & pp **-led**) trarre in inganno

mis·lead·ing [mɪs'liːdɪŋ] adj fuorviante

mis·man·age [mɪs'mænɪdʒ] v/t gestire male

mis·man·age·ment [mɪs'mænɪdʒ-mənt] cattiva gestione f

mis·match ['mɪsmætʃ] discordanza f

mis·placed ['mɪspleɪst] adj loyalty, enthusiasm malriposto

mis·print ['mɪsprɪnt] refuso m

mis·pro·nounce [mɪsprə'naʊns] v/t pronunciare male

mis·pro·nun·ci·a·tion [mɪsprənʌn-sɪ'eɪʃn] errore m di pronuncia

mis·read [mɪs'riːd] v/t (pret & pp **-read** [red]) word, figures leggere male; situation interpretare male

mis·rep·re·sent [mɪsreprɪ'zent] v/t facts, truth travisare; **I've been ~ed** hanno travisato quello che ho detto

miss¹ [mɪs]: **Miss Smith** signorina Smith; **~!** signorina!

miss² [mɪs] **1** n: **give the meeting / party a ~** non andare alla riunione / festa **2** v/t (not hit) mancare; emotionally sentire la mancanza di; bus, train, plane perdere; (not be present at) mancare a; **I ~ you** mi manchi; **you've just ~ed him** he's just gone è appena uscito; **we must have ~ed the turnoff** ci dev'essere

sfuggito lo svincolo **3** v/i fallire

mis·shap·en [mɪs'ʃeɪpən] adj deforme

mis·sile ['mɪsaɪl] (rocket) missile m

miss·ing ['mɪsɪŋ] adj scomparso; **be ~ of** person, plane essere disperso; **there's a piece ~** manca un pezzo

mis·sion ['mɪʃn] (task, people) missione f

mis·sion·a·ry ['mɪʃənrɪ] REL missionario m, -a f

mis·spell [mɪs'spel] v/t scrivere male

mist [mɪst] foschia f

♦ **mist over** v/i of eyes velarsi di lacrime

♦ **mist up** v/i of mirror, window appannarsi

mis·take [mɪ'steɪk] **1** n errore m, sbaglio m; **make a ~** fare un errore, sbagliarsi; **by ~** per errore **2** v/t (pret **mistook**, pp **mistaken**) sbagliare; **~ sth for sth** scambiare qc per qc

mis·tak·en [mɪ'steɪkən] **1** adj sbagliato; **be ~** sbagliarsi **2** pp → **mistake**

mis·ter ['mɪstə(r)] → **Mr**

mis·tress ['mɪstrɪs] lover amante f; of servant, of dog padrona f

mis·trust [mɪs'trʌst] **1** n diffidenza f **2** v/t diffidare di

mist·y ['mɪstɪ] adj weather nebbioso; eyes velato

mis·un·der·stand [mɪsʌndə'stænd] v/t (pret & pp **-stood**) fraintendere

mis·un·der·stand·ing [mɪsʌndə-'stændɪŋ] mistake malinteso m, equivoco m; argument dissapore m

mis·use [mɪs'juːs] **1** n uso m improprio **2** v/t [mɪs'juːz] usare impropriamente

miti·ga·ting cir·cum·stances ['mɪtɪɡeɪtɪŋ] npl circostanze fpl attenuanti

mit·ten ['mɪtən] muffola f

mix [mɪks] **1** n (mixture) mescolanza f; in cooking miscuglio m; in cooking: ready to use preparato m **2** v/t mescolare **3** v/i socially socializzare

♦ **mix up** v/t confondere; **mix sth up with sth** scambiare qc per qc; **be mixed up** emotionally avere disturbi emotivi; *of figures, papers* essere in disordine; **be mixed up in** essere coinvolto in; **get mixed up with** avere a che fare con

♦**mix with** *v/t (associate with)* frequentare

mixed [mɪkst] *adj* misto; *reactions, reviews* contrastante; **I've got ~ feelings** sono combattuto

mixed 'mar·riage matrimonio *m* misto

mix·er ['mɪksə(r)] *for food* mixer *m inv*; *drink* bibita *f da mischiare a un superalcolico*; **she's a good ~** è molto socievole

mix·ture ['mɪkstʃə(r)] miscuglio *m; medicine* sciroppo *m*

mix-up ['mɪksʌp] confusione *f*

moan [məʊn] **1** *n of pain* lamento *m*, gemito *m; (complaint)* lamentela *f* **2** *v/i in pain* lamentarsi, gemere; *(complain)* lamentarsi

mob [mɒb] **1** *n* folla *f* **2** *v/t (pret & pp -bed)* prendere d'assalto

mo·bile ['məʊbaɪl] **1** *adj that can be moved* mobile; **she's less ~ now** non si può muovere tanto, ora **2** *n for decoration* mobile *m inv; phone* telefonino *m*

mo·bile 'home casamobile *f*

mo·bile 'phone telefono *m* cellulare

mo·bil·i·ty [mə'bɪlətɪ] mobilità *f inv*

mob·ster ['mɒbstə(r)] gangster *m inv*

mock [mɒk] **1** *adj* finto; *exam, election* simulato; **a ~-Tudor house** una casa in stile Tudor **2** *v/t* deridere

mock·e·ry ['mɒkərɪ] *(derision)* scherno *m; (travesty)* farsa *f*

mock-up ['mɒkʌp] *(model)* modello *m*

mod cons [mɒd'kɒnz] *npl*: **with all ~** con tutti i comfort

mode [məʊd] *form* mezzo *m*; COMPUT modalità *f inv*

mod·el ['mɒdl] **1** *adj employee, husband* modello; *boat, plane in miniatura* **2** *n (miniature)* modellino *m; (pattern)* modello *m; (fashion ~)* indossatrice *f;* **male =** indossatore *m* **3** *v/t* indossare **4** *v/i for designer* fare

l'indossatore / -trice; *for artist, photographer* posare

mo·dem ['məʊdem] modem *m inv*

mod·e·rate ['mɒdərət] **1** *adj* moderato **2** *n* POL moderato *m*, -a *f* **3** *v/t* ['mɒdəreɪt] moderare **4** *v/i* calmarsi

mod·e·rate·ly ['mɒdərətlɪ] *adv* abbastanza

mod·e·ra·tion [mɒdə'reɪʃn] *(restraint)* moderazione *f;* **in ~** con moderazione

mod·ern ['mɒdn] *adj* moderno

mod·ern·i·za·tion [mɒdənaɪ'zeɪʃn] modernizzazione *f*

mod·ern·ize ['mɒdənaɪz] **1** *v/t* modernizzare **2** *v/i of business, country* modernizzarsi

mod·ern 'lan·guag·es lingue *fpl* moderne

mod·est ['mɒdɪst] *adj* modesto

mod·es·ty ['mɒdɪstɪ] modestia *f*

mod·i·fi·ca·tion [mɒdɪfɪ'keɪʃn] modifica *f*

mod·i·fy ['mɒdɪfaɪ] *v/t (pret & pp -ied)* modificare

mod·u·lar ['mɒdjʊlə(r)] *adj furniture* modulare

mod·ule ['mɒdjuːl] modulo *m; (space ~)* modulo *m* spaziale

moist [mɔɪst] *adj* umido

moist·en ['mɔɪsn] *v/t* inumidire

mois·ture ['mɔɪstʃə(r)] umidità *f inv*

mois·tur·iz·er ['mɔɪstʃəraɪzə(r)] *for skin* idratante *m*

mo·lar ['məʊlə(r)] molare *m*

mold *etc Am* → **mould** *etc*

mole [məʊl] *on skin* neo *m; animal, spy* talpa *f*

mo·lec·u·lar [mə'lekjʊlə(r)] *adj* molecolare

mol·e·cule ['mɒlɪkjuːl] molecola *f*

mo·lest [mə'lest] *v/t child, woman* molestare

mol·ly·cod·dle ['mɒlɪkɒdl] *v/t* F coccolare

mol·ten ['məʊltən] *adj* fuso

mo·ment ['məʊmənt] attimo *m*, istante *m;* **at the ~** al momento; **for the ~** per il momento

mo·men·tar·i·ly [məʊmən'teərɪlɪ] *adv (for a moment)* per un momento; (*Am: in a moment*) da un momento all'altro

mo·men·ta·ry ['məʊməntrɪ] *adj* momentaneo

mo·men·tous [mə'mentəs] *adj* importante

mo·men·tum [mə'mentəm] impeto *m*

mon·arch ['mɒnək] monarca *m*

mon·ar·chy ['mɒnəkɪ] monarchia *f*

mon·as·tery ['mɒnəstrɪ] monastero *m*

mo·nas·tic [mə'næstɪk] *adj* monastico

Mon·day ['mʌndeɪ] lunedì *m inv*

mon·e·ta·ry ['mʌnɪtrɪ] *adj* monetario

mon·ey ['mʌnɪ] denaro *m*, soldi *mpl*

'**mon·ey belt** marsupio *m*; '**mon·ey mar·ket** mercato *m* monetario; '**mon·ey or·der** vaglia *m*

mon·grel ['mʌŋgrəl] cane *m* bastardo

mon·i·tor ['mɒnɪtə(r)] **1** *n* COMPUT monitor *m inv* **2** *v/t* osservare

monk [mʌŋk] frate *m*, monaco *m*

mon·key ['mʌŋkɪ] scimmia *f*; F (*child*) diavoletto *m*

♦ **monkey about with** *v/t* F armeggiare con

'**mon·key wrench** chiave *f* a rullino

mon·o·gram ['mɒnəgræm] monogramma *m*

mon·o·grammed ['mɒnəgræmd] con il monogramma

mon·o·log *Am*, **mon·o·logue** ['mɒnəlɒg] monologo *m*

mo·nop·o·lize [mə'nɒpəlaɪz] *v/t also fig* monopolizzare

mo·nop·o·ly [mə'nɒpəlɪ] monopolio *m*

mo·not·o·nous [mə'nɒtənəs] *adj* monotono

mo·not·o·ny [mə'nɒtənɪ] monotonia *f*

mon·soon [mɒn'suːn] monsone *m*

mon·ster ['mɒnstə(r)] mostro *m*

mon·stros·i·ty [mɒn'strɒsətɪ] obbrobrio *m*

mon·strous ['mɒnstrəs] *adj* mostruoso

month [mʌnθ] mese *m*

month·ly ['mʌnθlɪ] **1** *adj* mensile **2** *adv* mensilmente **3** *n magazine* mensile *m*

mon·u·ment ['mɒnjʊmənt] monumento *m*

mon·u·men·tal [mɒnjʊ'mentl] *adj fig* monumentale

moo [muː] *v/i* muggire

mood [muːd] (*frame of mind*) umore *m*; (*bad ~*) malumore *m*; *of meeting, country* clima *m*; **be in a good** / **bad ~** essere di cattivo / buon umore; **be in the ~ for** aver voglia di

mood·y ['muːdɪ] *adj* lunatico; (*bad-tempered*) di cattivo umore

moon [muːn] luna *f*

'**moon·light 1** *n* chiaro *m* di luna **2** *v/i* F lavorare in nero; '**moon·lit** *adj* night di luna piena

moor [mʊə(r)] *v/t boat* ormeggiare

moor·ings ['mʊərɪŋz] *npl* ormeggio *m*

moose [muːs] alce *m*

mop [mɒp] **1** *n for floor* mocio® *m*; *for dishes* spazzolino per i piatti **2** *v/t* (*pret & pp -ped*) *floor* lavare; *eyes, face* asciugare

♦ **mop up** *v/t* raccogliere; MIL eliminare

mope [məʊp] *v/i* essere depresso

mo·ped ['məʊped] motorino *m*

mor·al ['mɒrəl] **1** *adj* morale; *person* di saldi principi morali **2** *n of story* morale *f*; **~s** principi *mpl* morali

mo·rale [mə'rɑːl] morale *m*

mo·ral·i·ty [mə'rælətɪ] moralità *f inv*

mor·bid ['mɔːbɪd] *adj* morboso

more [mɔː(r)] **1** *adj* più, altro; **some ~ tea?** dell'altro tè?; **a few ~ sandwiches** qualche altro tramezzino; **for ~ information** per maggiori informazioni; **~ and students** / **time** sempre più studenti / tempo; **there's no ~ ...** non c'è più ... **2** *adv* più; *with verbs* di più; **~ important** più importante; **~ often** più spesso; **~ and ~** sempre di più; **~ or less** più o meno; **once ~** ancora una volta; **~ than 100** oltre 100; **I don't live**

there any ~ non abito più lì **3** *pron*: *do you want some* ~? ne vuoi ancora?, ne vuoi dell'altro; *a little* ~ un altro po'

more·o·ver [mɔːˈrəʊvə(r)] *adv* inoltre

morgue [mɔːg] obitorio *m*

morn·ing [ˈmɔːnɪŋ] mattino *m*, mattina *f*; *in the* ~ di mattina; (*tomorrow*) domattina; *this* ~ stamattina; *tomorrow* ~ domani mattina; *good* ~ buongiorno

morn·ing 'sick·ness nausee *fpl* mattutine

mo·ron [ˈmɔːrɒn] F idiota *m/f*

mo·rose [məˈrəʊs] *adj* imbronciato

mor·phine [ˈmɔːfiːn] morfina *f*

mor·sel [ˈmɔːsl] pezzetto *m*

mor·tal [ˈmɔːtl] **1** *adj* mortale **2** *n* mortale *m/f*

mor·tal·i·ty [mɔːˈtælətɪ] mortalità *f inv*

mor·tar¹ [ˈmɔːtə(r)] MIL mortaio *m*

mor·tar² [ˈmɔːtə(r)] *cement* malta *f*

mort·gage [ˈmɔːgɪdʒ] **1** *n* mutuo *m* ipotecario *m/t* ipotecare

mor·tu·a·ry [ˈmɔːtjʊərɪ] camera *f* mortuaria

mo·sa·ic [məʊˈzeɪɪk] mosaico *m*

Mos·cow [ˈmɒskəʊ] Mosca *f*

Mos·lem [ˈmʊzlɪm] **1** *adj* islamico **2** *n* musulmano *m*, -a *f*

mosque [mɒsk] moschea *f*

mos·qui·to [mɒsˈkiːtəʊ] zanzara *f*

moss [mɒs] muschio *m*

moss·y [ˈmɒsɪ] *adj* coperto di muschio

most [məʊst] **1** *adj* la maggior parte di; ~ *Saturdays* quasi tutti i sabati **2** *adv* (*very*) estremamente; *the* ~ *beautiful / interesting* il più bello / interessante; *that's the one I like* ~ è quello che mi piace di più; ~ *of all* soprattutto **3** *pron* la maggior parte (*of* di); *at* (*the*) ~ al massimo; *make the* ~ *of* approfittare (al massimo) di

most·ly [ˈməʊstlɪ] *adv* per lo più

MOT [eməʊˈtiː] Br revisione *f* annuale obbligatoria dei veicoli

mo·tel [məʊˈtel] motel *m inv*

moth [mɒθ] falena *f*; (*clothes* ~) tarma *f*

'moth·ball naftalina *f*

moth·er [ˈmʌðə(r)] **1** *n* madre *f* **2** *v/t* fare da mamma a

'moth·er·board COMPUT scheda *f* madre

'moth·er·hood maternità *f inv*

Moth·er·ing 'Sun·day → *Mother's Day*

'moth·er-in-law (*pl* **mothers-in-law**) suocera *f*

moth·er·ly [ˈmʌðəlɪ] *adj* materno

moth·er-of-'pearl madreperla *f*;

'Moth·er's Day Festa *f* della mamma; **'moth·er tongue** madrelingua *f*

mo·tif [məʊˈtiːf] *n* motivo *m*

mo·tion [ˈməʊʃn] **1** *n* (*movement*) moto *m*; (*proposal*) mozione *f*; *set things in* ~ metter in moto le cose **2** *v/t*: *he* ~*ed me forward* mi ha fatto cenno di avvicinarmi

mo·tion·less [ˈməʊʃnlɪs] *adj* immobile

mo·ti·vate [ˈməʊtɪveɪt] *v/t person* motivare

mo·ti·va·tion [məʊtɪˈveɪʃn] motivazione *f*

mo·tive [ˈməʊtɪv] motivo *m*

mo·tor [ˈməʊtə(r)] motore *m*; Br F *car* macchina *f*

'mo·tor·bike moto *f*; **'mo·tor·boat** motoscafo *m*; **mo·tor·cade** [ˈməʊtəkeɪd] corteo *m* di auto; **'mo·tor·cy·cle** motocicletta *f*; **'mo·tor·cy·clist** motociclista *m/f*; **'mo·tor home** casamobile *f*

mo·tor·ist [ˈməʊtərɪst] automobilista *m/f*

'mo·tor me·chan·ic meccanico *m*; **'mo·tor rac·ing** automobilismo *m*; **'mo·tor·scoot·er** scooter *m inv*; **'mo·tor show** salone *m* dell'automobile; **'mo·tor ve·hi·cle** autoveicolo *m*; **'mo·tor·way** Br autostrada *f*

mot·to [ˈmɒtəʊ] motto *m*

mould¹ [məʊld] *on food* muffa *f*

mould² [məʊld] **1** *n* stampo *m* **2** *v/t also fig* plasmare

mould·y ['məʊldɪ] *adj food* ammuffito

mound [maʊnd] (*hillock*) collinetta *f*; *in baseball* pedana *f* del lanciatore; (*pile*) mucchio *m*

mount [maʊnt] **1** *n* (*horse*) cavalcatura *f*; **Mount McKinlay** il Monte McKinlay **2** *v/t steps* salire; *horse* montare a; *bicycle* montare in; *campaign* organizzare; *jewel* montare; *photo*, *painting* incorniciare **3** *v/i* (*increase*) aumentare

♦ **mount up** *v/i* accumularsi

moun·tain ['maʊntɪn] montagna *f*

'moun·tain bike mountain bike *f inv*

moun·tain·eer [maʊntɪ'nɪə(r)] alpinista *m/f*

moun·tain·eer·ing [maʊntɪ'nɪərɪŋ] alpinismo *m*

moun·tain·ous ['maʊntɪnəs] *adj* montuoso

moun·tain 'res·cue serv·ice soccorso *m* alpino

mount·ed po'lice ['maʊntɪd] polizia *f* a cavallo

mourn [mɔːn] **1** *v/t* piangere **2** *v/i*: ~ **for** piangere la morte di

mourn·er ['mɔːnə(r)] persona *f* che partecipa a un corteo funebre

mourn·ful ['mɔːnfʊl] *adj* triste

mourn·ing ['mɔːnɪŋ] lutto *m*; **be in** ~ essere in lutto; **wear** ~ portare il lutto

mouse [maʊs] (*pl* **mice** [maɪs]) topo *m*; COMPUT mouse *m inv*

'mouse mat COMPUT tappetino *m* del mouse

mous·tache [mə'stɑː(r)ʃ] baffi *mpl*

mouth [maʊθ] *of person* bocca *f*; *of river* foce *f*

mouth·ful ['maʊθfʊl] *of food* boccone *m*; *of drink* sorsata *f*

'mouth·or·gan armonica *f* a bocca; **'mouth·piece** *of instrument* bocchino *m*; (*spokesperson*) portavoce *m/f*; **'mouth·wash** collettorio *m*; **'mouth·wa·ter·ing** *adj* che fa venire l'acquolina

move [muːv] **1** *n* (*step*, *action*) mossa *f*; *change of house* trasloco *m*; **get a ~ on!** F spicciati!; **don't make a ~!** non

ti muovere! **2** *v/t object* spostare, muovere; (*transfer*) trasferire; *emotionally* commuovere; ~ **house** traslocare **3** *v/i* muoversi, spostarsi; (*transfer*) trasferirsi

♦ **move around** *v/i in room* muoversi; *from place to place* spostarsi

♦ **move away** *v/i* allontanarsi; *move house* traslocare

♦ **move in** *v/i* trasferirsi

♦ **move on** *v/i* ripartire; *in discussion* andare avanti; **move on to sth** passare a qc

♦ **move out** *v/i of house* andare via; *of troops* ritirarsi

♦ **move up** *v/i in league* avanzare; (*make room*) spostarsi

♦ **move·ment** ['muːvmənt] movimento *m*

mov·ie ['muːvɪ] film *m inv*; **go to a ~ / the ~s** andare al cinema

'mov·ie thea·ter *Am* cinema *m inv*

mov·ing ['muːvɪŋ] *adj which can move* mobile; *emotionally* commovente

mow [məʊ] *v/t grass* tagliare, falciare

♦ **mow down** *v/t* falciare

mow·er ['məʊə(r)] tosaerba *m inv*

MP [em'piː] *abbr* (= **Member of Parliament**) deputato *m*; (= **Military Policeman**) polizia *f* militare

mph [empiː'eɪtʃ] *abbr* (= **miles per hour**) miglia *fpl* orarie

Mr ['mɪstə(r)] signor

Mrs ['mɪsɪz] signora

Ms [mɪz] signora *appellativo m usato sia per donne sposate che nubili*

Mt *abbr* (= **Mount**) M. (= monte *m*)

much [mʌtʃ] **1** *adj* molto; **so ~ money** tanti soldi; **how ~ sugar?** quanto zucchero?; **as ~ ... as ...** tanto ... quanto ... **2** *adv* molto; **very ~** moltissimo; **too ~** troppo; **as ~ as ...** tanto quanto ...; **as ~ as a million dollars** addirittura un milione di dollari; **I thought as ~** me l'aspettavo **3** *pron* molto; **nothing ~** niente di particolare; **there's not ~ left** non ne è rimasto, -a molto, -a

muck [mʌk] (*dirt*) sporco *m*

mu·cus ['mjuːkəs] muco *m*

mud [mʌd] fango *m*

mud·dle ['mʌdl] **1** *n* disordine *m*; *I'm in a ~* sono confuso **2** *v/t* confondere

♦ **muddle up** *v/t* (*mess up*) mettere in disordine; (*confuse*) confondere

mud·dy ['mʌdɪ] *adj* fangoso *m*; *hands, boots* sporco di fango

mues·li ['muːzlɪ] müsli *m inv*

muf·fle ['mʌfl] *v/t sound* attutire; *voice* camuffare

muf·fler ['mʌflər] *Am* MOT marmitta *f*

♦ **muffle up** *v/i* coprirsi bene

mug¹ [mʌg] *for tea, coffee* tazzone *m*; F (*face*) faccia *f*

mug² [mʌg] *v/t* (*pret & pp* **-ged**) *attack* aggredire

mug·ger ['mʌgə(r)] aggressore *m*

mug·ging ['mʌgɪŋ] aggressione *f*

mug·gy ['mʌgɪ] *adj* afoso

mule [mjuːl] *animal* mulo *m*; (*slipper*) mule *f inv*

♦ **mull over** [mʌl] *v/t* riflettere su

mul·ti·lat·e·ral [mʌltɪ'lætərəl] *adj* POL multilaterale

mul·ti·lin·gual [mʌltɪ'lɪŋgwəl] *adj* multilingue *inv*

mul·ti·me·di·a [mʌltɪ'miːdɪə] **1** *adj* multimediale **2** *n* multimedialità *f inv*

mul·ti·na·tion·al [mʌltɪ'næʃnl] **1** *adj* multinazionale **2** *n* COM multinazionale *f*

mul·ti·ple ['mʌltɪpl] *adj* multiplo

mul·ti·ple 'choice ques·tion esercizio *m* a scelta multipla

mul·ti·ple scle·ro·sis sclerosi *f* multipla

'mul·ti·plex ('cin·e·ma) cinema *m inv* multisale

mul·ti·pli·ca·tion [mʌltɪplɪ'keɪʃn] moltiplicazione *f*

mul·ti·ply ['mʌltɪplaɪ] (*pret & pp* **-ied**) **1** *v/t* moltiplicare **2** *v/i* moltiplicarsi

mul·ti-sto·rey (car park) [mʌltɪ'stɔːrɪ] parcheggio *m* a più piani

mum [mʌm] mamma *f*

mum·ble ['mʌmbl] **1** *n* borbottio *m* **2** *v/t & v/i* borbottare

mum·my ['mʌmɪ] mamma *f*

mumps [mʌmps] *nsg* orecchioni *mpl*

munch [mʌntʃ] *v/t & v/i* sgranocchiare

mu·ni·ci·pal [mjuː'nɪsɪpl] *adj* municipale

mu·ral ['mjʊərəl] murale *m*

mur·der ['mɜːdə(r)] **1** *n* omicidio *m* **2** *v/t person* uccidere; *song* rovinare

mur·der·er ['mɜːdərə(r)] omicida *m/f*

mur·der·ous ['mɜːdrəs] *adj rage, look* omicida

murk·y ['mɜːkɪ] *adj also fig* torbido

mur·mur ['mɜːmə(r)] **1** *n* mormorio *m* **2** *v/t* mormorare

mus·cle ['mʌsl] muscolo *m*

mus·cu·lar ['mʌskjʊlə(r)] *adj pain, strain* muscolare; *person* muscoloso

muse [mjuːz] *v/i* riflettere

mu·se·um [mjuː'zɪəm] museo *m*

mush·room ['mʌʃrʊm] **1** *n* fungo *m* **2** *v/i* crescere rapidamente

mu·sic ['mjuːzɪk] musica *f*; *in written form* spartito *m*

mu·sic·al ['mjuːzɪkl] **1** *adj* musicale; *person* portato per la musica; *voice* melodioso **2** *n* musical *m inv*

'mu·sic(·al) box carillon *m inv*

mu·sic·al 'in·stru·ment strumento *m* musicale

mu·si·cian [mjuː'zɪʃn] musicista *m/f*

mus·sel ['mʌsl] cozza *f*

must [mʌst] *v/aux* ◊ (*necessity*): *I ~ be on time* devo arrivare in orario; *I ~* devo; *I ~n't be late* non devo far tardi ◊ (*probability*): *it ~ be about 6 o'clock* devono essere circa le sei; *they ~ have arrived by now* ormai devono essere arrivati

mus·tache *Am* → **moustache**

mus·tard ['mʌstəd] senape *f*

must·y ['mʌstɪ] *adj smell* di stantio; *room* che sa di stantio

mute [mjuːt] *adj* muto

mut·ed ['mjuːtɪd] *adj* tenue

mu·ti·late ['mjuːtɪleɪt] *v/t* mutilare

mu·ti·ny ['mjuːtɪnɪ] **1** *n* ammutinamento *m* **2** *v/i* (*pret & pp* **-ied**) ammutinarsi

M

mut·ter['mʌtə(r)] v/t & v/i farfugliare

mut·ton['mʌtn] montone *m*

mu·tu·al ['mju:tjʊəl] *adj* admiration reciproco; *friend* in comune

muz·zle ['mʌzl] **1** *n of animal* muso *m*; *for dog* museruola *f* **2** v/t: ~ **the press** imbavagliare la stampa

my[maɪ] *adj* il mio *m*, la mia *f*, i miei *mpl*, le mie *fpl*; ~ **bag** said by man/ *woman* la mia valigia; ~ **sister/ brother** mia sorella/mio fratello

my·op·ic[maɪ'ɒpɪk] *adj* miope

my·self [maɪ'self] *pron reflexive* mi; *emphatic* io stesso; *after prep* me

stesso; *I've hurt* ~ mi sono fatto male; ~, *I'd prefer …* quanto a me, preferirei …; *by* ~ da solo

mys·te·ri·ous [mɪ'stɪərɪəs] *adj* misterioso

mys·te·ri·ous·ly [mɪ'stɪərɪəslɪ] *adv* misteriosamente

mys·te·ry ['mɪstərɪ] mistero *m*

mys·tic ['mɪstɪk] *adj* mistico

mys·ti·fy ['mɪstɪfaɪ] v/t (*pret & pp -ied*) lasciare perplesso

myth[mɪθ] *also fig* mito *m*

myth·i·cal['mɪθɪkl] *adj* mitico

my·thol·o·gy[mɪ'θɒlədʒɪ] mitologia *f*

N

nab[næb] v/t (*pret & pp -bed*) F take for o.s. prendere

nag[næg] (*pret & pp -ged*) **1** v/i of person brontolare di continuo **2** v/t assillare; ~ *s.o. to do sth* assillare qu perché faccia qc

nag·ging['nægɪŋ] *adj person* brontolone; *doubt, pain* assillante

nail[neɪl] *for wood* chiodo *m*; *on finger, toe* unghia *f*

'**nail clip·pers** *npl* tagliaunghie *m inv*; '**nail file** limetta *f* per unghie; '**nail pol·ish** smalto *m* per unghie; '**nail pol·ish re·mov·er** solvente *m* per unghie; '**nail scis·sors** *npl* forbicine *fpl* per unghie; '**nail var·nish** smalto *m* per unghie

na·ive[naɪ'i:v] *adj* ingenuo

naked ['neɪkɪd] *adj* nudo; *to the* ~ *eye* a occhio nudo

name [neɪm] **1** *n* nome *m*; *what's your* ~? come ti chiami?; *call s.o.* ~*s* insultare qu; *make a* ~ *for o.s.* farsi un nome **2** v/t chiamare

♦ **name after** v/t: *they named him after his grandfather* gli hanno messo il nome del nonno.

♦ **name for** *Am* → *name after*

name·ly['neɪmlɪ] *adv* cioè

'**name·sake**omonimo *m*, -a *f*

'**name·tag**on clothing etc targhetta *f* col nome

nan·ny['nænɪ] bambinaia *f*

nap[næp] *n* sonnellino *m*; *have a* ~ farsi un sonnellino

nape[neɪp]: ~ *of the neck* nuca *f*

nap·kin['næpkɪn] (*table* ~) tovagliolo *m*; *Am* (*sanitary* ~) assorbente *m*

Na·ples['neɪpəlz] Napoli *f*

nap·py['næpɪ] pannolino *m*

nar·cot·ic[nɑː'kɒtɪk] *n* narcotico *m*

nar·rate[nə'reɪt] v/t raccontare, narrare

nar·ra·tion[nə'reɪʃn] narrazione *f*

nar·ra·tive['nærətɪv] **1** *n story* racconto **2** *adj poem, style* narrativo

nar·ra·tor[nə'reɪtə(r)] narratore *m*, -trice *f*

nar·row ['nærəʊ] *adj street, bed* stretto; *views, mind* ristretto; *victory* di stretta misura

nar·row·ly['nærəʊlɪ] *adv win* di stretta misura; ~ *escape sth* scampare a qc per un pelo F nar·row-mind·ed [nærəʊ'maɪndɪd] *adj* di idee ristrette

na·sal['neɪzl] *adj voice* nasale

nas·ty['nɑːstɪ] *adj person, thing to say, smell, weather* cattivo; *cut, wound, disease* brutto

na·tion['neɪʃn] nazione *f*

na·tion·al ['næʃənl] **1** *adj* nazionale **2** *n* cittadino *m*, -a *f*

na·tion·al 'an·them inno *m* nazionale

na·tion·al 'debtdebito *m* pubblico

na·tion·al·ism ['næʃənəlɪzm] nazionalismo *m*

na·tion·al·i·ty [næʃə'nælətɪ] nazionalità *f inv*

na·tion·al·ize ['næʃənəlaɪz] *v/t industry etc* nazionalizzare

na·tion·al 'park parco *m* nazionale

na·tive ['neɪtɪv] **1** *adj* indigeno; **~ language** madrelingua *f* **2** *n (tribesman)* indigeno *m*, -a *f*; **she's a ~ of New York** è originaria di New York; **she speaks Chinese like a ~** parla cinese come una madrelingua

na·tive 'coun·trypatria *f*

na·tive 'speak·er, *English* ~ persona *f* di madrelingua inglese

NATO['neɪtəʊ] *abbr* (= **North Atlantic Treaty Organization**) NATO *f*

nat·u·ral['næʧrəl] *adj* naturale

nat·u·ral 'gasgas *m inv* naturale

nat·u·ral·ist ['næʧrəlɪst] naturalista *m/f*

nat·u·ral·ize ['næʧrəlaɪz] *v/t*: **become ~d** naturalizzarsi

nat·u·ral·ly ['næʧərəlɪ] *adv (of course)* naturalmente; *behave, speak* con naturalezza; *(by nature)* per natura

nat·u·ral 'sci·encescienze *fpl* naturali

nat·u·ral 'sci·en·tiststudioso *m*, -a *f* di scienze naturali

na·ture['neɪʧə(r)] natura *f*

na·ture re'serveriserva *f* naturale

naugh·ty['nɔːtɪ] *adj* cattivo; *photograph, word etc* spinto

nau·se·a['nɔːzɪə] nausea *f*

nau·se·ate ['nɔːzɪeɪt] *v/t (fig: disgust)* disgustare

nau·se·at·ing['nɔːzɪeɪtɪŋ] *adj smell, taste* nauseante; *person* disgustoso

nau·seous ['nɔːzɪəs] *adj*: **feel ~** avere la nausea

nau·ti·cal ['nɔːtɪkl] *adj* nautico

'nau·ti·cal mile miglio *m* nautico

na·val ['neɪvl] *adj* navale; *officer, uniform* della marina

'na·val basebase *f* navale

na·vel['neɪvl] ombelico *m*

nav·i·ga·ble['nævɪgəbl] *adj river* navigabile

nav·i·gate['nævɪgeɪt] *v/i in ship, in aeroplane* navigare; *in car* fare da navigatore /-trice; COMPUT navigare

nav·i·ga·tion [nævɪ'geɪʃn] navigazione *f*

nav·i·ga·tor['nævɪgeɪtə(r)] *on ship, in aeroplane* ufficiale *m* di rotta; *in car* navigatore *m*, -trice *f*

na·vy['neɪvɪ] marina *f* militare

na·vy 'blue1 *n* blu *m inv* scuro 2 *adj* blu scuro

near[nɪə(r)] **1** *adv* vicino **2** *prep* vicino a; **~ the bank** vicino alla banca; **do you go ~ the bank?** va dalle parti della banca? **3** *adj* vicino; **the ~est stop** la fermata più vicina; **in the ~ future** nel prossimo futuro

near·by[nɪə'baɪ] *adv live* vicino

near·ly['nɪəlɪ] *adv* quasi

near-sight·ed[nɪə'saɪtɪd] *adj* miope

neat[niːt] *adj room, desk, person* ordinato; *whisky* liscio; *solution* efficace; F *(terrific)* fantastico

ne·ces·sar·i·ly ['nesəserəlɪ] *adv* necessariamente

ne·ces·sa·ry['nesəserɪ] *adj* necessario; **it is ~ to …** è necessario …, bisogna …

ne·ces·si·tate[nɪ'sesɪteɪt] *v/t* rendere necessario

ne·ces·si·ty[nɪ'sesɪtɪ] necessità *f inv*

neck[nek] collo *m*

neck·lace['neklɪs] collana *f*

'neck·lineof dress scollo *m*

née[neɪ] *adj*: **Lisa Higgins ~ Smart** Lisa Higgins nata Smart

need[niːd] **1** *n* bisogno *m*; **if ~ be** se necessario; **be in ~** *(be needy)* essere

N

bisognoso; **be in ~ of sth** aver bisogno di qc; **there's no ~ to be rude / upset** non c'è bisogno di essere maleducato / triste **2** *v/t* avere bisogno di; **you'll ~ to buy one** dovrai comprarne uno; **you don't ~ to wait** non c'è bisogno che aspetti; **I ~ to talk to you** ti devo parlare; **~ I say more?** devo aggiungere altro?

nee·dle ['ni:dl] *for sewing, on dial* ago *m*; *on record player* puntina *f*

'nee·dle·work cucito *m*

need·y ['ni:dɪ] *adj* bisognoso

neg·a·tive ['negətɪv] **1** *adj* negativo **2** *n* ELEC polo *m* negativo; PHOT negativa *f*; **answer in the ~** rispondere negativamente

ne·glect [nɪ'glekt] **1** *n* trascuratezza *f* **2** *v/t garden, one's health* trascurare; **~ to do sth** trascurare di fare qc

ne·glect·ed [nɪ'glektɪd] *adj gardens, author* trascurato; **feel ~** sentirsi trascurato

neg·li·gence ['neglɪdʒəns] negligenza *f*

neg·li·gent ['neglɪdʒənt] *adj* negligente

neg·li·gi·ble ['neglɪdʒəbl] *adj quantity, amount* trascurabile

ne·go·ti·a·ble [nɪ'gəʊʃəbl] *adj salary, contract* negoziabile

ne·go·ti·ate [nɪ'gəʊʃɪeɪt] **1** *v/i* trattare **2** *v/t deal, settlement* negoziare; *obstacles* superare; *bend in road* affrontare

ne·go·ti·a·tion [nɪgəʊʃɪ'eɪʃn] negoziato *m*, trattativa *f*

ne·go·ti·a·tor [nɪ'gəʊʃɪeɪtə(r)] negoziatore *m*, -trice *f*

neigh [neɪ] *v/i* nitrire

neigh·bor *etc Am* → **neighbour** *etc*

neigh·bour ['neɪbə(r)] vicino *m*, -a *f*

neigh·bour·hood ['neɪbəhʊd] *in town* quartiere *m*; **in the ~ of** *fig* intorno a

neigh·bour·ing ['neɪbərɪŋ] *adj house, state* confinante

neigh·bour·ly ['neɪbəlɪ] *adj* amichevole

nei·ther ['naɪðə(r)] **1** *adj*: **~ player** nessuno dei due giocatori **2** *pron*

nessuno *m* dei due, nessuna *f* delle due, né l'uno né l'altro, né l'una né l'altra **3** *adv*: **~ ... nor ...** né ... né ... **4** *conj* neanche; **~ do I** neanch'io

ne·on light ['ni:ɒn] luce *f* al neon

neph·ew ['nevju:] nipote *m* (di zii)

nerd [nɜ:d] P fesso *m*, -a *f* P; *in style* tamarro *m* P

nerve [nɜ:v] nervo *m*; *(courage)* coraggio *m*; *(impudence)* faccia *f* tosta; **it's bad for my ~s** mi mette in agitazione; **get on s.o.'s ~s** dare sui nervi a qu

nerve-rack·ing ['nɜ:vrækɪŋ] *adj* snervante

nerv·ous ['nɜ:vəs] *adj* nervoso; **be ~ about doing sth** essere ansioso all'idea di fare qc

nerv·ous 'break·down esaurimento *m* nervoso

nerv·ous 'en·er·gy: be full of ~ essere sovraeccitato

nerv·ous·ness ['nɜ:vəsnɪs] nervosismo *m*

nerv·ous 'wreck: be a ~ avere i nervi a pezzi

nest [nest] *n* nido *m*

nes·tle ['nesl] *v/i* rannicchiarsi

net¹ [net] *for fishing* retino *m*; *for tennis* rete *f*

net² [net] *adj* COM netto

net 'cur·tain tenda *f* di tulle

net 'pro·fit guadagno *m o* utile *m* netto

net·tle ['netl] ortica *f*

'net·work *of contacts, cells* rete *f*; COMPUT network *m inv*

neu·rol·o·gist [njʊə'rɒlədʒɪst] neurologo *m*, -a *f*

neu·ro·sis [njʊə'rəʊsɪs] nevrosi *f inv*

neu·rot·ic [njʊ'rɒtɪk] *adj* nevrotico

neu·ter ['nju:tə(r)] *v/t animal* sterilizzare

neu·tral ['nju:trl] **1** *adj country* neutrale; *colour* neutro **2** *n gear* folle *m*; **in ~** in folle

neu·tral·i·ty [nju:'trælətɪ] neutralità *f inv*

neu·tral·ize ['nju:trəlaɪz] *v/t* neutralizzare

nev·er ['nevə(r)] *adv* mai; **~! in**

disbelief ma va'!; *you're ~ going to believe this* non ci crederesti mai; *you ~ promised, did you?* non l'avrai promesso, spero!

nev·er-'end·ing *adj* senza fine

nev·er·the·less [nevəðə'les] *adv* comunque, tuttavia

new [njuː] *adj* nuovo; *this system is still ~ to me* non sono ancora abituato al sistema; *I'm ~ on the job* sono nuovo del mestiere; *that's nothing ~* non è una novità

'new-born *adj* neonato

new·com·er ['njuːkʌmə(r)] nuovo arrivato *m*, nuova arrivata *f*

new·ly ['njuːlɪ] *adv* (*recently*) recentemente

'new·ly weds [wedz] *npl* sposini *mpl*

new 'moon luna *f* nuova

news [njuːz] notizia *f*; *on TV, radio* notiziario *m*; novità *f inv*; *any ~?* ci sono novità?; *that's ~ to me* mi giunge nuovo

'news a·gen·cy agenzia *f* di stampa; **'news·a·gent** giornalaio *m*; **'news·cast** telegiornale *m*; **'news·cast·er** giornalista *m/f* televisivo, -a; **'news flash** notizia *f* flash; **'news·pa·per** giornale *m*; **'news·read·er** giornalista *m/f* radiotelevisivo, -a; **'news re·port** notiziario *m*; **'news·stand** edicola *f*; **'news·ven·dor** edicolante *m/f*

new 'year anno *m* nuovo; *Happy New Year!* buon anno!; **New Year's 'Day** capodanno *m*; **New Year's 'Eve** San Silvestro *m*; **New Zea·land** ['ziːlənd] Nuova Zelanda *f*; **New Zea·land·er** ['ziːləndə(r)] neozelandese *m/f*

next [nekst] **1** *adj in time* prossimo; *in space* vicino; *the ~ week / month he came back again* la settimana / il mese dopo ritornò; *who's ~?* a chi tocca? **2** *adv* dopo; *~ to* (*beside*) accanto a; (*in comparison with*) a paragone di

next 'door 1 *adj*: *~ neighbour* vicino *m*, -a *f* di casa **2** *adv* live nella casa accanto

next of 'kin parente *m/f* prossimo

nib·ble ['nɪbl] *v/t* mordicchiare

nice [naɪs] *adj person* carino, gentile; *day, weather, party* bello; *meal, food* buono; *be ~ to your sister!* sii carino con tua sorella!; *that's very ~ of you* molto gentile da parte tua!

nice·ly ['naɪslɪ] *adv written, presented* bene

nice·ties ['naɪsətɪz] *npl*: *social ~* convenevoli *mpl*

niche [niːʃ] *in market* nicchia *f* (di mercato); *special position* nicchia *f*

nick [nɪk] *n cut* taglietto *m*; *in the ~ of time* appena in tempo

nick·el ['nɪkl] *material* nichel *m inv*; (*Am: coin*) moneta *f* da 5 centesimi di dollaro

'nick·name *n* soprannome *m*

niece [niːs] nipote *f* (di zii)

nig·gard·ly ['nɪgədlɪ] *adj amount* misero; *person* tirchio

night [naɪt] notte *f*; (*evening*) sera *f*; *at ~* di notte / di sera; *last ~* ieri notte / ieri sera; *travel by ~* viaggiare di notte; *during the ~* durante la notte; *stay the ~* rimanere a dormire; *a room for 2 ~s* una stanza per due notti; *work ~s* fare il turno di notte; *good ~* buona notte; *in the middle of the ~* a notte fonda

'night·cap (*drink*) bicchierino *m* bevuto prima di andare a letto; **'night·club** night(-club) *m inv*; **'night·dress** camicia *f* da notte; **'night·fall**: *at ~* al calar della notte; **'night flight** volo *m* notturno; **'night·gown** camicia *f* da notte

night·ie ['naɪtɪ] F camicia *f* da notte

nigh·tin·gale ['naɪtɪŋgeɪl] usignolo *m*

'night·life vita *f* notturna

night·ly ['naɪtlɪ] *adj & adv* ogni sera; *late at night* ogni notte

'night·mare *also fig* incubo *m*; **'night por·ter** portiere *m* notturno; **'night school** scuola *f* serale; **'night shift** turno *m* di notte; **'night·shirt** camicia *f* da notte (*da uomo*); **'night·spot** locale *m* notturno; **'night·time**: *at ~, in the ~* di notte, la notte

nil [nɪl] SP zero *m*

N

nim·ble ['nɪmbl] *adj* agile

nine [naɪn] nove

nine·teen [naɪn'tiːn] diciannove

nine·teenth [naɪn'tiːnθ] *n & adj* diciannovesimo, -a

nine·ti·eth ['naɪntɪɪθ] *n & adj* novantesimo, -a

nine·ty ['naɪntɪ] novanta

ninth [naɪnθ] *n & adj* nono

nip [nɪp] (*pinch*) pizzico *m*; (*bite*) morso *m*

nip·ple ['nɪpl] capezzolo *m*

ni·tro·gen ['naɪtrədʒn] azoto *m*

no [nəʊ] **1** *adv* no **2** *adj* nessuno; **there's ~ coffee / tea left** non c'è più caffè / tè; **I have ~ family / money** non ho famiglia / soldi; **I'm ~ linguist / expert** non sono un linguista / esperto; **~ parking** sosta vietata; **~ smoking** vietato fumare

no·bil·i·ty [nəʊ'bɪlətɪ] nobiltà *f inv*

no·ble ['nəʊbl] *adj* nobile

no·bod·y ['nəʊbɑdɪ] *pron* nessuno; **~ knows** nessuno lo sa; **there was ~ at home** non c'era nessuno in casa

nod [nɒd] **1** *n* cenno *m* del capo **2** *v/i* (*pret & pp* **-ded**) fare un cenno col capo; **~ in agreement** annuire

♦ **nod off** *v/i* (*fall asleep*) appisolarsi

no-hop·er [nəʊ'həʊpə(r)] F buono *m*, -a *f* a nulla

noise [nɔɪz] (*sound*) rumore *m*; *loud, unpleasant* chiasso *m*

nois·y ['nɔɪzɪ] *adj* rumoroso; *children, party* chiassoso; **don't be so ~** non fate tanto rumore

nom·i·nal ['nɒmɪnl] *adj amount* simbolico

nom·i·nate ['nɒmɪneɪt] *v/t* (*appoint*) designare; **~ s.o. for a post** proporre qu come candidato per una posizione

nom·i·na·tion [nɒmɪ'neɪʃn] (*appointing*) nomina *f*; (*proposal*) candidatura *f*; *person proposed* candidato *m*, -a *f*

nom·i·nee [nɒmɪ'niː] candidato *m*, -a *f*

non ... [nɒn] non ...

non·al·co·hol·ic *adj* analcolico

non·a·ligned *adj* non allineato

non·cha·lant ['nɒnʃələnt] *adj* noncurante

non·com·mis·sioned 'of·fi·cer sottufficiale *m*

non·com'mit·tal *adj person, response* evasivo

non·de·script ['nɒndɪskrɪpt] *adj* ordinario

none [nʌn] *pron* nessuno *m*, -a *f*; **~ of the students** nessuno degli studenti; **~ of this money is mine** neanche una lira di questi soldi è mia; **there are ~ left** non ne sono rimasti; **there is ~ left** non ne è rimasto, non ne è rimasto niente

non'en·ti·ty nullità *f inv*

none·the·less [nʌnðə'les] *adv* nondimeno

non·ex'ist·ent *adj* inesistente

non'fic·tion opere *fpl* non di narrativa

non·(in)'flam·ma·ble *adj* non infiammabile

non·in·ter'fer·ence, non·in·ter'ven·tion non intervento *m*

non-'i·ron *adj shirt* che non si stira

'no-no *that's a ~* F non si fa

no-'non·sense *adj approach* pragmatico

non'pay·ment mancato pagamento *m*

non·pol'lut·ing *adj* non inquinante

non'res·i·dent *n in country* non residente *m/f*; (*in hotel*) persona *f* chi non è cliente di un albergo

non·re·turn·a·ble [nɒnrɪ'tɜːnəbl] *adj* a fondo perduto

non'sense ['nɒnsəns] sciocchezze *fpl*; **don't talk ~** non dire sciocchezze; **~, it's easy!** sciocchezze, è facile!

non'skid *adj tyres* antisdrucciolevole

non'slip *adj surface* antiscivolo *inv*

non'smok·er *person* non fumatore *m*, -trice *f*

non'stand·ard *adj* fuori standard, non di serie; *use of a word* che fa eccezione

non'stick *adj pans* antiaderente

non'stop 1 *adj flight, train* diretto; *chatter* continuo **2** *adv fly, travel* senza scalo; *chatter, argue* di continuo

non'swim·mer *persona f chi non sa nuotare*

non'u·nion *adj* non appartenente al sindacato

non'vi·o·lence non violenza *f*

non'vi·o·lent *adj* non violento

noo·dles ['nu:dlz] *npl* spaghetti *mpl* cinesi

nook [nʊk] angolino *m*

noon [nu:n] mezzogiorno *m*; **at ~** a mezzogiorno

noose [nu:s] cappio *m*

nor [nɔ:(r)] *adv conj* né; **~ do I** neanch'io, neanche a me

norm [nɔ:m] norma *f*

nor·mal ['nɔ:ml] *adj* normale

nor·mal·i·ty [nɔ:'mæləti] normalità *f inv*

nor·mal·ize ['nɔ:məlaɪz] *v/t relationships* normalizzare

nor·mal·ly ['nɔ:məli] *adv* (*usually*) di solito; *in a normal way* normalmente

north [nɔ:θ] **1** *n* nord *m*; **to the ~ of** a nord di **2** *adj* settentrionale, nord *inv* **3** *adv travel* verso nord; **~ of** a nord di

North Am'er·i·ca America *f* del Nord; **North Am'er·i·can 1** *n* nordamericano *m*, -a **2** *adj* nordamericano; **north'east** *n* nordest

nor·ther·ly ['nɔ:ðəli] *adj wind* settentrionale; *direction* nord *inv*

nor·thern ['nɔ:ðən] *adj* settentrionale

nor·thern·er ['nɔ:ðənə(r)] settentrionale *m/f*

North Ko're·a Corea *f* del Nord; **North Ko're·an 1** *adj* nordcoreano **2** *n* nordcoreano *m*, -a *f*; **North 'Pole** polo *m* nord

north·wards ['nɔ:ðwədz] *adv travel* verso nord

north·west [nɔ:ð'west] *n* nordovest *m*

Nor·way ['nɔ:wei] Norvegia *f*

Nor·we·gian [nɔ:'wi:dʒn] **1** *adj* norvegese **2** *n person* norvegese *m/f*; *language* norvegese *m*

nose [nəʊz] naso *m*; **right under my**

~! proprio sotto il naso!

◆**nose about** *v/i* F curiosare

'nose·bleed emorragia *f* nasale

nos·tal·gia [nɒ'stældʒɪə] nostalgia *f*

nos·tal·gic [nɒ'stældʒɪk] *adj* nostalgico

nos·tril ['nɒstrəl] narice *f*

nos·y ['nəʊzi] *adj* F curioso

not [nɒt] *adv* non; **~ this one, that one** non questo, quello; **~ a lot** non molto; **I hope ~** spero di no; **I don't know** non so; **I am ~ American** non sono americano; **he didn't help** non ha aiutato; **~ me** io no

no·ta·ble ['nəʊtəbl] *adj* notevole

no·ta·ry ['nəʊtəri] notaio *m*

notch [nɒtʃ] tacca *f*

note [nəʊt] *n short letter* biglietto *m*; MUS nota *f; memo to self* appunto *m*; *comment on text* nota *f*; **take ~s** prendere appunti; **take ~ of sth** prendere nota di qc

◆**note down** *v/t* annotare

'note·book taccuino *m*; COMPUT notebook *m inv*

not·ed ['nəʊtɪd] *adj* noto

'note·pad bloc-notes *m inv*

'note·pa·per carta *f* da lettere

noth·ing ['nʌθɪŋ] *pron* niente; **~ but** nient'altro che; **~ much** niente di speciale; **for ~** (*for free*) gratis; (*for no reason*) per un nonnulla; **I'd like ~ better** non chiedo di meglio

no·tice ['nəʊtɪs] **1** *n on notice board, in street* avviso *m*; (*advance warning*) preavviso *m*; *in newspaper* annuncio *m*; *to leave job* preavviso *m*; *to leave house* disdetta *f*; **at short ~** con un breve preavviso; **until further ~** fino a nuovo avviso; **give s.o. his / her ~** *to quit job* dare il preavviso a qu; *to leave house* dare la disdetta a qu; **hand in one's ~** *to employer* presentare le dimissioni; **four weeks' ~** quattro settimane di preavviso; **take ~ of sth** fare caso a qc; **take no ~ of s.o. / sth** non fare caso a qu / qc **2** *v/t* notare

no·tice·a·ble ['nəʊtɪsəbl] *adj* sensibile

'notice board bacheca *f*

no·ti·fy ['nəʊtɪfaɪ] *v/t* (*pret & pp -ied*) informare

no·tion ['nəʊʃn] idea *f*

no·to·ri·ous [nəʊ'tɔːrɪəs] *adj* famigerato

nou·gat ['nuːgɑː] torrone *m*

nought [nɔːt] zero *m*

noun [naʊn] nome *m*, sostantivo *m*

nour·ish·ing ['nʌrɪʃɪŋ] *adj* nutriente

nour·ish·ment ['nʌrɪʃmənt] nutrimento *m*

nov·el ['nɒvl] *n* romanzo *m*

nov·el·ist ['nɒvlɪst] romanziere *m*, -a *f*

nov·el·ty ['nɒvltɪ] novità *f inv*

No·vem·ber [nəʊ'vembə(r)] novembre *m*

nov·ice ['nɒvɪs] principiante *m/f*

now [naʊ] *adv* ora, adesso; **~ and again**, **~ and then** ogni tanto; **by ~** ormai; **from ~ on** d'ora in poi; **right ~** subito; **just ~** (*proprio*) adesso; **~, ~!** su, su!; **~, where did I put it?** dunque, dove l'ho messo?

now·a·days ['naʊədeɪz] *adv* oggigiorno

no·where ['nəʊweə(r)] *adv* da nessuna parte; **there's ~ to sit** non c'è posto; **it's ~ near finished** è ben lontano dall'essere terminato

noz·zle ['nɒzl] bocchetta *f*

nu·cle·ar ['njuːklɪə(r)] *adj* nucleare; **nu·cle·ar 'en·er·gy** energia *f* nucleare; **nu·cle·ar 'fis·sion** fissione *f* nucleare; **'nu·cle·ar-free** *adj* denuclearizzato; **nu·cle·ar 'phys·ics** fisica *f* nucleare; **nu·cle·ar 'pow·er** energia *f* nucleare; POL potenza *f* nucleare; **nu·cle·ar 'pow·er sta·tion** centrale *f* nucleare; **nu·cle·ar re'ac·tor** reattore *m* nucleare; **nu·cle·ar 'waste** scorie *fpl* radioattive; **nu·cle·ar 'weap·on** arma *f* nucleare

nude [njuːd] **1** *adj* nudo **2** *n painting* nudo *m*; **in the ~** nudo

nudge [nʌdʒ] *v/t* dare un colpetto di gomito a

nud·ist ['njuːdɪst] *n* nudista *m/f*

nui·sance ['njuːsns] seccatura *f*;

make a ~ of o.s. dare fastidio; **what a ~!** che seccatura!

nuke [njuːk] *v/t* F distruggere con armi atomiche

null and 'void [nʌl] *adj* nullo

numb [nʌm] *adj* intirizzito; *emotionally* impietrito

num·ber ['nʌmbə(r)] **1** *n* (*figure*) numero *m*, cifra *f*; (*quantity*) quantità *f inv*; *of hotel room, house, phone number etc* numero *m* **2** *v/t* put a number on contare

'number plate MOT targa *f*

numeral ['njuːmərəl] numero *m*

nu·me·rate ['njuːmərət] *adj*: **be ~** avere buone basi in matematica; *of children* saper contare

nu·me·rous ['njuːmərəs] *adj* numeroso

nun [nʌn] suora *f*

nurse [nɜːs] infermiere *m*, -a *f*

nur·se·ry ['nɜːsərɪ] *school* asilo *m*; *in house* stanza *f* dei bambini; *for plants* vivaio *m*

'nur·se·ry rhyme filastrocca *f*; **'nur·se·ry school** scuola *f* materna; **'nur·se·ry school teach·er** insegnante *m/f* di scuola materna

nurs·ing ['nɜːsɪŋ] professione *f* d'infermiere; **she went into ~** è diventata infermiera

'nurs·ing home *for old people* casa *f* di riposo

nut [nʌt] noce *f*; *for bolt* dado *m*; **~s** F (*testicles*) palle *fpl*

'nut·crack·ers *npl* schiaccianoci *m inv*

nu·tri·ent ['njuːtrɪənt] *n* sostanza *f* nutritiva

nu·tri·tion [njuː'trɪʃn] alimentazione *f*

nu·tri·tious [njuː'trɪʃəs] *adj* nutriente

nuts [nʌts] *adj* F (*crazy*) svitato; **be ~ about s.o.** essere pazzo di qu

'nut·shell: **in a ~** in poche parole

nut·ty ['nʌtɪ] *adj taste* di noce; F (*crazy*) pazzo

ny·lon ['naɪlɒn] **1** *n* nylon *m inv* **2** *adj* di nylon

O

oak [əʊk] *tree* quercia *f*; *wood* rovere *m*

OAP [əʊeɪ'pi:] *abbr* (= **old age pensioner**) pensionato *m*, -a *f*

oar [ɔː(r)] remo *m*

o·a·sis [əʊ'eɪsɪs] (*pl* **oases** [əʊ'eɪsi:z]) *also fig* oasi *f inv*

oath [əʊθ] LAW giuramento *m*; (*swearword*) imprecazione *f*; **on ~** sotto giuramento

'**oat·meal** farina *f* d'avena

oats [əʊts] *npl* avena *f*

o·be·di·ence [ə'bi:dɪəns] ubbidienza *f*

o·be·di·ent [ə'bi:dɪənt] *adj* ubbidiente

o·be·di·ent·ly [ə'bi:dɪəntlɪ] *adv* docilmente

o·bese [əʊ'bi:s] *adj* obeso

o·bes·i·ty [əʊ'bi:sɪtɪ] obesità *f inv*

o·bey [ə'beɪ] *v/t parents* ubbidire a; *law* osservare

o·bit·u·a·ry [ə'bɪtjʊərɪ] *n* necrologio *m*

ob·ject¹ ['ɒbdʒɪkt] *n* (*thing*) oggetto *m*; (*aim*) scopo *m*; GRAM complemento *m*

ob·ject² [əb'dʒekt] *v/i* avere da obiettare

♦ **object to** *v/t* essere contrario a

ob·jec·tion [əb'dʒekʃn] obiezione *f*

ob·jec·tio·na·ble [əb'dʒekʃnəbl] *adj* (*unpleasant*) antipatico

ob·jec·tive [əb'dʒektɪv] **1** *adj* obiettivo **2** *n* obiettivo *m*

ob·jec·tive·ly [əb'dʒektɪvlɪ] *adv* obiettivamente

ob·jec·tiv·i·ty [əb'dʒektɪvətɪ] obiettività *f inv*

ob·li·ga·tion [ɒblɪ'geɪʃn] obbligo *m*; **be under an ~ to s.o.** essere in debito con qu

ob·lig·a·to·ry [ə'blɪgətrɪ] *adj* obbligatorio

o·blige [ə'blaɪdʒ] *v/t*: **much ~d!** grazie mille!

o·blig·ing [ə'blaɪdʒɪŋ] *adj* servizievole

o·blique [ə'bli:k] **1** *adj reference* indiretto **2** *n in punctuation* barra *f*

o·blit·er·ate [ə'blɪtəreɪt] *v/t city* annientare; *memory* cancellare

o·bliv·i·on [ə'blɪvɪən] oblio *m*; **fall into ~** cadere in oblio

o·bliv·i·ous [ə'blɪvɪəs] *adj*: **be ~ of sth** essere ignaro di qc

ob·long ['ɒblɒŋ] **1** *adj* rettangolare **2** *n* rettangolo *m*

ob·nox·ious [əb'nɒkʃəs] *adj* offensivo; *smell* sgradevole

ob·scene [əb'si:n] *adj* osceno; *salary, poverty* vergognoso

ob·scen·i·ty [əb'senətɪ] oscenità *f inv*

ob·scure [əb'skjʊə(r)] *adj* oscuro

ob·scu·ri·ty [əb'skjʊərətɪ] oscurità *f inv*

ob·ser·vance [əb'zɜːvns] osservanza *f*

ob·ser·vant [əb'zɜːvnt] *adj* osservante

ob·ser·va·tion [ɒbzə'veɪʃn] osservazione *f*

ob·ser·va·to·ry [əb'zɜːvətrɪ] osservatorio *m*

ob·serve [əb'zɜːv] *v/t* osservare

ob·serv·er [əb'zɜːvə(r)] osservatore *m*, -trice *f*

ob·sess [əb'ses] *v/t*: **be ~ed by / with** essere fissato con

ob·ses·sion [əb'seʃn] fissazione *f*

ob·ses·sive [əb'sesɪv] *adj person, behaviour* ossessivo

ob·so·lete ['ɒbsəli:t] *adj model* obsoleto; *word* disusato, antiquato

ob·sta·cle ['ɒbstəkl] *also fig* ostacolo *m*

ob·ste·tri·cian [ɒbstə'trɪʃn] ostetrico *m*, -a *f*

ob·stet·rics [ɒbˈstetrɪks] ostetricia f

ob·sti·na·cy [ˈɒbstɪnəsɪ] ostinazione f

ob·sti·nate [ˈɒbstɪnət] adj ostinato

ob·sti·nate·ly [ˈɒbstɪnətlɪ] adv ostinatamente

ob·struct [əbˈstrʌkt] v/t road, passage ostruire; investigation, police ostacolare

ob·struc·tion [əbˈstrʌkʃn] on road etc ostruzione f

ob·struc·tive [əbˈstrʌktɪv] adj behaviour, tactics ostruzionista

ob·tru·sive [əbˈtruːsɪv] adj music invadente; colour stonato

ob·tain [əbˈteɪn] v/t ottenere

ob·tain·a·ble [əbˈteɪnəbl] adj products reperibile

ob·tuse [əbˈtjuːs] adj fig ottuso

ob·vi·ous [ˈɒbvɪəs] adj ovvio, evidente

ob·vi·ous·ly [ˈɒbvɪəslɪ] adv ovviamente, evidentemente; ~! ovviamente!

oc·ca·sion [əˈkeɪʒn] occasione f

oc·ca·sion·al [əˈkeɪʒənl] adj sporadico; I like the ~ whisky bevo un whisky ogni tanto

oc·ca·sion·al·ly [əˈkeɪʒnlɪ] adv ogni tanto

oc·cult [ɒˈkʌlt] 1 adj occulto 2 n: the ~ l'occulto m

oc·cu·pant [ˈɒkjʊpənt] of vehicle occupante m/f; of building, flat abitante m/f

oc·cu·pa·tion [ɒkjʊˈpeɪʃn] (job) professione f; of country occupazione f

oc·cu·pa·tion·al ther·a·pist [ɒkjʊˈpeɪʃnl] ergoterapeuta m/f

oc·cu·pa·tion·al ther·a·py ergoterapia f

oc·cu·py [ˈɒkjʊpaɪ] v/t (pret & pp -ied) occupare

oc·cur [əˈkɜː(r)] v/i (pret & pp -red) accadere; it ~red to me that ... mi è venuto in mente che ...

oc·cur·rence [əˈkʌrəns] evento m

o·cean [ˈəʊʃn] oceano m

o·ce·a·nog·ra·pher [əʊʃnˈɒgrəfə(r)] oceanografo m, -a f

o·ce·a·nog·ra·phy [əʊʃnˈɒgrəfɪ] oceanografia f

o'clock [əˈklɒk]: at five / six ~ alle cinque / sei; it's one ~ è l'una; it's three ~ sono le tre

Oc·to·ber [ɒkˈtəʊbə(r)] ottobre m

oc·to·pus [ˈɒktəpəs] polpo m

OD [əʊˈdiː] v/i: F ~ on drug fare un'overdose di

odd [ɒd] adj (strange) strano; (not even) dispari; the ~ one out l'eccezione f; 50 ~ 50 e rotti

'odd·ball F persona f stramba; he's an ~ è un tipo strambo

odds [ɒdz] npl: be at ~ with essere in disaccordo con; the ~ are 10 to one le probabilità sono 10 contro una; the ~ are that ... è probabile che ...; against all the ~ contro ogni aspettativa

odds and 'ends npl objects cianfrusaglie fpl; things to do cose fpl

'odds-on adj: the ~ favourite il favorito; it's ~ that ... è praticamente scontato che ...

o·di·ous [ˈəʊdɪəs] adj odioso

o·dor Am, **o·dour** [ˈəʊdə(r)] odore m

of [ɒv], [əv] prep di; the works ~ Dickens le opere di Dickens; it's made ~ steel è di acciaio; die ~ cancer morire di cancro; a friend ~ mine un mio amico; very nice ~ him molto gentile da parte sua; ~ the three this is ... dei tre questo è ...

off [ɒf] 1 prep: a lane ~ the main road not far from un sentiero poco lontano dalla strada principale; leading off un sentiero che parte dalla strada principale; £20 ~ the price 20 sterline di sconto; he's ~ his food ha perso l'appetito 2 adv: be ~ of light, TV etc essere spento; of gas, tap essere chiuso; (cancelled) essere annullato; of food essere finito; she was ~ today not at work oggi non era al lavoro; you've left the lid ~ non hai messo il coperchio; we're ~ tomorrow leaving partiamo domani; I'm ~ to New York vado a New York; I must be ~ devo andare;

with his trousers / hat ~ senza pantaloni / cappello; *take a day* ~ prendere un giorno libero; *it's 3 miles* ~ dista 3 miglia; *it's a long way* ~ è molto lontano; *drive* ~ partire (in macchina); *walk* ~ allontanarsi; ~ *and on* ogni tanto 3 *adj food* andato a male; ~ *switch* interruttore *m* di spegnimento

of·fal ['ɒfl] frattaglie *fpl*

of·fence [ə'fens] LAW reato *m*; *take* ~ *at sth* offendersi per qc

of·fend [ə'fend] *v/t* (*insult*) offendere

of·fend·er [ə'fendə(r)] LAW delinquente *m/f*; ~s *will be prosecuted* i trasgressori saranno perseguiti a norma di legge

of·fense *Am* → *offence*

of·fen·sive [ə'fensɪv] 1 *adj* behaviour, remark, offensivo; smell sgradevole 2 *n* (MIL: attack) offensiva *f*; *go onto the* ~ passare all'offensiva

of·fer ['ɒfə(r)] 1 *n* offerta *f* 2 *v/t* offrire; ~ *s.o. sth* offrire qc a qu

off·hand *adj attitude* disinvolto

of·fice ['ɒfɪs] ufficio *m*; (*position*) carica *f*

'of·fice block complesso *m* di uffici

'of·fice hours *npl* orario *m* d'ufficio

of·fi·cer ['ɒfɪsə(r)] MIL ufficiale *m*; in police agente *m/f*

of·fi·cial [ə'fɪʃl] 1 *adj* ufficiale 2 *n* funzionario *m*, -a *f*

of·fi·cial·ly [ə'fɪʃlɪ] *adv* ufficialmente

of·fi·ci·ate [ə'fɪʃɪeɪt] *v/i* officiare

of·fi·cious [ə'fɪʃəs] *adj* invadente

'off-li·cence *Br* negozio *m* di alcolici

'off-line *adj & adv* off-line

'off-peak *adj rates* ridotto; ~ *electricity* elettricità *f* a tariffa ridotta

'off-sea·son 1 *adj rates* di bassa stagione 2 *n* bassa stagione *f*

'off·set *v/t* (*pret & pp* -*set*) losses, disadvantage compensare

'off·shore *adj drilling rig, investment* off-shore *inv*

'off·side 1 *adj wheel etc* destro; on the left sinistro 2 *adv* SP in fuorigioco

'off·spring figli *mpl*; of animal piccoli *mpl*

off-the-'rec·ord *adj* ufficioso

'off-white *adj* bianco sporco

of·ten ['ɒfn] *adv* spesso

oil [ɔɪl] 1 *n* olio *m*; petroleum petrolio *m*; for central heating nafta *f* 2 *v/t* hinges, bearings oliare

'oil change cambio *m* dell'olio; 'oil·cloth tela *f* cerata; 'oil com·pa·ny compagnia *f* petrolifera; 'oil·field giacimento *m* petrolifero; 'oil-fired *adj* central heating a nafta; 'oil paint·ing quadro *m* a olio; 'oil-pro·duc·ing coun·try paese *m* produttore di petrolio; 'oil re·fin·e·ry raffineria *f* di petrolio; 'oil rig piattaforma *f* petrolifera; 'oil-skins *npl* abiti *mpl* di tela cerata; 'oil slick chiazza *f* di petrolio; 'oil tank·er petroliera *f*; 'oil well pozzo *m* petrolifero

oil·y ['ɔɪlɪ] *adj* unto

oint·ment ['ɔɪntmənt] pomata *f*

ok [əʊ'keɪ] *adj, adv* F: *is it* ~ *with you if …?* ti va bene se …?; *does that look* ~? ti sembra che vada bene?; *that's* ~ *by me* per me va bene; *are you* ~? well, not hurt stai bene?; *are you* ~ *for Friday?* ti va bene venerdì?; *he's* ~ (*is a good guy*) è in gamba

old [əʊld] *adj* vecchio; (*previous*) precedente; *how* ~ *are you / is he?* quanti anni hai / ha?; *he's getting* ~ sta invecchiando

old 'age vecchiaia *f*

old age 'pen·sion pensione *f* di anzianità

old-age 'pen·sion·er pensionato *m*, -a *f*

old 'peo·ple's home casa *f* di riposo (per anziani)

old-'fash·ioned *adj* antiquato

ol·ive ['ɒlɪv] oliva *f*

'ol·ive oil olio *m* d'oliva

O·lym·pic 'Games [ə'lɪmpɪk] *npl* Olimpiadi *fpl*, giochi *mpl* olimpici

om·e·let *Am*, om·e·lette ['ɒmlɪt] frittata *f*

om·i·nous ['ɒmɪnəs] *adj* sinistro

o·mis·sion [ə'mɪʃn] omissione *f*; on purpose esclusione *f*

o·mit [ə'mɪt] *v/t* (*pret & pp -ted*) omettere; *on purpose* escludere; *~ to do sth* tralasciare di fare qc

om·nip·o·tent [ɒm'nɪpətənt] *adj* onnipotente

om·nis·ci·ent [ɒm'nɪsɪənt] *adj* onnisciente

on [ɒn] **1** *prep* su; *~ the table/wall* sul tavolo/muro; *~ the bus/train* in autobus/treno; *get ~ the bus/train* salire sull'autobus/sul treno; *~ TV/the radio* alla tv/radio; *~ Sunday* domenica; *~ Sundays* di domenica; *~ the 1st of June* il primo di giugno; *be ~ holiday/sale/offer* essere in vacanza/vendita/offerta; *I'm ~ antibiotics* sto prendendo antibiotici; *this is ~ me* (*I'm paying*) offro io; *have you any money ~ you?* hai dei soldi con te?; *~ his arrival/departure* al suo arrivo/alla sua partenza; *~ hearing this* al sentire queste parole **2** *adv*: *be ~ of light, TV etc* essere acceso; *of gas, tap* essere aperto; *of machine* essere in funzione; *of handbrake* essere inserito; *it's ~ after the news of programme* è dopo il notiziario; *the meeting is ~ scheduled to happen* la riunione si fa; *put the lid ~* metti il coperchio; *with his jacket/hat ~* con la giacca/il cappello; *what's ~ tonight? on TV etc* cosa c'è stasera?; *I've got something ~ tonight planned* stasera ho un impegno; *you're ~ I accept your offer etc* d'accordo; *that's not ~* (*not allowed, not fair*) non è giusto; *~ you go* (*go ahead*) fai pure; *walk/talk ~* continuare a parlare/camminare; *and so ~* e così via; *~ and ~ talk etc* senza sosta **3** *adj*: *the ~ switch* l'interruttore *m* d'accensione

once [wʌns] **1** *adv* (*one time*) una volta; (*formerly*) un tempo; *~ again, ~ more* ancora una volta; *at ~* (*immediately*) subito; *all at ~* (*suddenly*) improvvisamente; (*all*) *at ~* (*together*) contemporaneamente; *~ upon a time there was ...* c'era una volta ...; *~ in a while* ogni tanto; *~*

and for all una volta per tutte; *for ~* per una volta **2** *conj* non appena; *~ you have finished* non appena hai finito

one [wʌn] **1** *n* (*number*) uno *m* **2** *adj* uno, -a; *~ day* un giorno **3** *pron* uno *m*, -a *f*; *which ~? quale?*; *that ~* quello *m*, -a *f*; *this ~* questo *m*, -a *f*; *by ~ enter, deal with* uno alla volta; *~ another* l'un l'altro, a vicenda; *what can ~ say/do?* cosa si può dire/fare?; *~ would have thought that ...* si sarebbe pensato che ...; *the more ~ thinks about it ...* più ci si pensa ...; *the little ~s* i piccoli; *I for ~* per quanto mi riguarda

one-'off 1 *n* fatto *m* eccezionale; *person* persona *f* eccezionale **2** *adj* unico

one-par·ent *fam·i·ly* famiglia *f* monogenitore

one'self *pron reflexive* si; *after prep* se stesso *m*, -a *f*, sé; *cut ~* tagliarsi; *do sth ~* fare qc da sé; *do sth by ~* fare qc da solo

one-sid·ed [wʌn'saɪdɪd] *adj* unilaterale

one-track 'mind *hum*: *have a ~* essere fissato col sesso

'one-way street strada *f* a senso unico

'one-way tick·et biglietto *m* di sola andata

on·ion ['ʌnjən] cipolla *f*

'on-line *adj & adv* on-line *inv*

'on-line serv·ice COMPUT servizio *m* on-line

on·look·er ['ɒnlʊkə(r)] astante *m*

on·ly ['əʊnlɪ] **1** *adv* solo; *not ~ X but also Y* non solo X ma anche Y; *~ just* a malapena **2** *adj* unico; *~ son* unico figlio maschio

'on·set inizio *m*

'onside *adv* SP non in fuorigioco

on-the-job 'train·ing training *m inv* sul lavoro

on·to ['ɒntu:] *prep*: *put sth ~ sth* mettere qc sopra qc

on·wards ['ɒnwədz] *adv* in avanti; *from ... ~* da ... in poi

ooze [u:z] **1** *v/i of liquid, mud* colare

2 v/t: **he ~s charm** è di una gentilezza esagerata

o·paque [əʊˈpeɪk] *glass* opaco

OPEC [ˈəʊpek] *abbr* (= *Organization of Petroleum Exporting Countries*) OPEC *f*

o·pen [ˈəʊpən] **1** *adj* aperto; *flower* sbocciato; (*honest, frank*) aperto, franco; **in the ~ air** all'aria aperta **2** v/t aprire **3** v/i *of door, shop* aprirsi; *of flower* sbocciare

♦ **open up** v/i *of person* aprirsi

o·pen-'air *adj meeting, concert* all'aperto; *pool* scoperto; **'o·pen day** giornata *f* di apertura al pubblico; **o·pen·'end·ed** *adj contract etc* aperto

o·pen·ing [ˈəʊpənɪŋ] *in wall etc* apertura *f*; *of film, novel etc* inizio *m*; (*job going*) posto *m* vacante

'o·pen·ing hours *npl* orario *m* d'apertura

o·pen·ly [ˈəʊpənlɪ] *adv* (*honestly, frankly*) apertamente

o·pen-mind·ed [əʊpənˈmaɪndɪd] *adj* aperto; **o·pen 'plan of·fice** open space *m inv*; **'o·pen tick·et** biglietto *m* aperto

op·e·ra [ˈɒpərə] lirica *f*, opera *f*

'op·e·ra glass·es *npl* binocolo *m* da teatro; **'op·e·ra house** teatro *m* dell'opera; **'op·e·ra sing·er** cantante lirico *m*, -a *f*

op·e·rate [ˈɒpəreɪt] **1** v/i *of company* operare; *of airline, bus service* essere in servizio; *of machine* funzionare; MED aprire, intervenire **2** v/t *machine* far funzionare

♦ **operate on** v/t MED operare

'op·e·rat·ing in·struc·tions *npl* istruzioni *fpl* per l'uso

'op·e·rat·ing sys·tem COMPUT sistema *m* operativo

op·e·ra·tion [ɒpəˈreɪʃn] operazione *f*; MED intervento *m* (chirurgico), operazione *f*; *of machine* funzionamento *m*; **~s** *of company* operazioni *fpl*; **have an ~** MED subire un intervento (chirurgico)

op·e·ra·tor [ˈɒpəreɪtə(r)] TELEC centralinista *m/f*; *of machine* operatore

m, -trice *f*; (*tour ~*) operatore *m* turistico

o·pin·ion [əˈpɪnjən] opinione *f*, parere *m*; **in my ~** a mio parere

o·pin·ion poll sondaggio *m* d'opinione

op·po·nent [əˈpəʊnənt] avversario *m*, -a *f*

op·por·tune [ˈɒpətjuːn] *adj fml* opportuno

op·por·tu·nist [ɒpəˈtjuːnɪst] opportunista *m/f*

op·por·tu·ni·ty [ɒpəˈtjuːnətɪ] opportunità *f inv*

op·pose [əˈpəʊz] v/t opporsi a; **be ~d to ...** essere contrario a ...; **as ~d to ...** piuttosto che ...

op·po·site [ˈɒpəzɪt] **1** *adj direction* opposto; *meaning, views* contrario; *house* di fronte; **the ~ side of the road** l'altro lato della strada; **the ~ sex** l'altro sesso **2** *n* contrario *m*

op·po·site 'num·ber omologo *m*

op·po·si·tion [ɒpəˈzɪʃn] opposizione *f*

op·press [əˈpres] v/t *the people* opprimere

op·pres·sive [əˈpresɪv] *adj rule, dictator* oppressivo; *weather* opprimente

opt [ɒpt] v/t: **~ to do sth** optare per fare qc

op·ti·cal il·lu·sion [ˈɒptɪkl] illusione *f* ottica

op·ti·cian [ɒpˈtɪʃn] *dispensing* ottico *m*, -a *f*; *ophthalmic* optometrista *m/f*

op·ti·mism [ˈɒptɪmɪzm] ottimismo *m*

op·ti·mist [ˈɒptɪmɪst] ottimista *m/f*

op·ti·mist·ic [ɒptɪˈmɪstɪk] *adj attitude, view* ottimistico; *person* ottimista

op·ti·mist·ic·al·ly [ɒptɪˈmɪstɪklɪ] *adv* ottimisticamente

op·ti·mum [ˈɒptɪməm] **1** *adj* ottimale **2** *n* optimum *m inv*

op·tion [ˈɒpʃn] possibilità *f inv*, opzione *f*; **he had no other ~** non ha avuto scelta

op·tion·al [ˈɒpʃnl] *adj* facoltativo

op·tion·al 'ex·tras *npl* optional *m inv*

or [ɔː(r)] *conj* o; **he can't hear ~ see** non può né sentire né vedere; **~ else!** o guai a te!

o·ral ['ɔːrəl] *adj* orale

or·ange ['ɒrɪndʒ] **1** *adj colour* arancione **2** *n fruit* arancia *f*; *colour* arancione *m*

or·ange·ade ['ɒrɪndʒeɪd] aranciata *f*

'or·ange juice succo *m* d'arancia

or·ange 'squash aranciata *f* non gasata

or·a·tor ['ɒrətə(r)] oratore *m*, -trice *f*

or·bit ['ɔːbɪt] **1** *n of earth* orbita *f*; **send sth into ~** lanciare in orbita qc **2** *v/t the earth* orbitare intorno a

or·chard ['ɔːtʃəd] frutteto *m*

or·ches·tra ['ɔːkɪstrə] orchestra *f*

or·chid ['ɔːkɪd] orchidea *f*

or·dain [ɔː'deɪn] *v/t priest* ordinare

or·deal [ɔː'diːl] esperienza *f* traumatizzante

or·der ['ɔːdə(r)] **1** *n* ordine *m*; *for goods, in restaurant* ordinazione *f*; **in ~ to do sth** così da fare qc; **he stood down in ~ that she could get the job** si è ritirato, così che lei potesse avere il lavoro; **out of ~** (*not functioning*) fuori servizio; (*not in sequence*) fuori posto; **he's out of ~** (*not doing the proper thing*) si sta comportando in modo scorretto **2** *v/t* ordinare; **~ s.o. to do sth** ordinare a qu di fare qc **3** *v/i* ordinare

or·der·ly ['ɔːdəlɪ] **1** *adj room, mind* ordinato; *crowd* disciplinato **2** *n in hospital* inserviente *m/f*

or·di·nal num·ber ['ɔːdɪnl] numero *m* ordinale

or·di·nar·i·ly [ɔːdɪ'neərɪlɪ] *adv* (*as a rule*) normalmente

or·di·nary ['ɔːdɪnərɪ] *adj* normale; *pej* ordinario; **nothing out of the ~** niente di straordinario

ore [ɔː(r)] minerale *m* grezzo

or·gan ['ɔːgən] ANAT, MUS organo *m*

or·gan·ic [ɔː'gænɪk] *adj food, fertilizer* biologico

or·gan·i·cal·ly [ɔː'gænɪklɪ] *adv grown* biologicamente

or·gan·ism ['ɔːgənɪzm] organismo *m*

or·gan·i·za·tion [ɔːgənaɪ'zeɪʃn] organizzazione *f*

or·gan·ize ['ɔːgənaɪz] *v/t* organizzare

or·gan·ized 'crime criminalità *f inv* organizzata

or·gan·iz·er ['ɔːgənaɪzə(r)] *person* organizzatore *m*, -trice *f*

or·gas·m ['ɔːgæzm] orgasmo *m*

O·ri·ent ['ɔːrɪənt] Oriente *m*

O·ri·en·tal [ɔːrɪ'entl] **1** *adj* orientale **2** *n* orientale *m/f*

o·ri·en·tate ['ɔːrɪənteɪt] *v/t* (*direct*) orientare; **~ o.s.** (*get bearings*) orientarsi

or·i·gin ['ɒrɪdʒɪn] origine *f*; **of Chinese ~** di origine cinese

o·rig·i·nal [ə'rɪdʒənl] **1** *adj* originale **2** *n painting etc* originale *m*

o·rig·i·nal·i·ty [ərɪdʒɪn'ælətɪ] originalità *f inv*

o·rig·i·nal·ly [ə'rɪdʒənəlɪ] *adv* (*at first*) in origine; **~ he comes from France** è di origini francesi

o·rig·i·nate [ə'rɪdʒɪneɪt] **1** *v/t scheme, idea* dare origine a **2** *v/i of idea, belief* avere origine

o·rig·i·na·tor [ə'rɪdʒɪneɪtə(r)] *of scheme etc* ideatore *m*, -trice *f*

or·na·ment ['ɔːnəmənt] soprammobile *m*

or·na·men·tal [ɔːnə'mentl] *adj* ornamentale

or·nate [ɔː'neɪt] *adj style, architecture* ornato

or·phan ['ɔːfn] *n* orfano *m*, -a *f*

or·phan·age ['ɔːfənɪdʒ] orfanotrofio *m*

or·tho·dox ['ɔːθədɒks] *adj also fig* ortodosso

or·tho·pe·dic [ɔːθə'piːdɪk] *adj* ortopedico

os·ten·si·bly [ɒ'stensəblɪ] *adv* apparentemente

os·ten·ta·tion [ɒsten'teɪʃn] ostentazione *f*

os·ten·ta·tious [ɒsten'teɪʃəs] *adj* ostentato

os·ten·ta·tious·ly [ɒsten'teɪʃəslɪ]

adv con ostentazione

os·tra·cize ['ɒstrəsaɪz] *v/t* ostracizzare

oth·er ['ʌðə(r)] **1** *adj* altro; *the ~ day* l'altro giorno; *every ~ day* a giorni alterni; *every ~ person* una persona su due **2** *n* l'altro *m*, -a *f*; *the ~s* gli altri

oth·er·wise ['ʌðəwaɪz] *adv* altrimenti; *(differently)* diversamente

OTT [əʊtiː'tiː] *abbr* F (= *over the top*) esagerato

ot·ter ['ɒtə(r)] lontra *f*

ought [ɔːt] *v/aux*: *I/you ~ to know* dovrei/dovresti saperlo; *you ~ to have done it* avresti dovuto farlo

ounce [aʊns] oncia *f*

our ['aʊə(r)] *adj* il nostro *m*, la nostra *f*, i nostri *mpl*, le nostre *fpl*; *~ brother/sister* nostro fratello/nostra sorella

ours ['aʊəz] *pron* il nostro *m*, la nostra *f*, i nostri *mpl*, le nostre *fpl*

our·selves [aʊə'selvz] *pron reflexive* ci; *emphatic* noi stessi/noi stesse; *after prep* noi; *we did it ~* l'abbiamo fatto noi (stessi/stesse); *we talked about ~* abbiamo parlato di noi; *by ~* da soli

oust [aʊst] *v/t from office* esautorare

out [aʊt]: *be ~ of light, fire* essere spento; *of flower* essere sbocciato; *of sun* splendere; *not at home, not in building* essere fuori; *of calculations* essere sbagliato; *(be published)* essere uscito; *of secret* essere svelato; *no longer in competition* essere eliminato; *of workers* essere in sciopero; *(no longer in fashion)* essere out; *~ here in Dallas* qui a Dallas; *he's ~ in the garden* è in giardino; *(get) ~!* fuori!; *(get) ~ of my room!* fuori dalla mia stanza!; *that's ~!* (out of the question) è fuori discussione!; *he's ~ to win* fully intends to è deciso a vincere

out·board '**mo·tor** motore *m* fuoribordo

'**out·break** *of war, disease* scoppio *m*

'**out·build·ing** annesso *m*

'**out·burst** *emotional* reazione *f* violenta; *~ of anger* esplosione *f* di rabbia

'**out·cast** *n* emarginato *m*, -a *f*

'**out·come** risultato *m*

'**out·cry** protesta *f*

out'**dat·ed** *adj* sorpassato

out'**do** *v/t* (*pret* -*did*, *pp* -*done*) superare

'**out·door** *adj toilet, activities, life* all'aperto; *swimming pool* scoperto

out'**doors** *adv* all'aperto

out·er ['aʊtə(r)] *adj wall etc* esterno

out·er '**space** spazio *m* intergalattico

'**out·fit** *(clothes)* completo *m*; *(company, organization)* organizzazione *f*

'**out·go·ing** *adj flight, mail* in partenza; *personality* estroverso

out'**grow** *v/t* (*pret* -*grew*, *pp* -*grown*) *bad habits, interests* perdere

out·ing ['aʊtɪŋ] *(trip)* gita *f*

out'**last** *v/t* sopravvivere a

'**out·let** *of pipe* scarico *m*; *for sales* punto *m* di vendita

'**out·line 1** *n of person, building etc* profilo *m*; *of plan, novel* abbozzo *m* **2** *v/t plans etc* abbozzare

out'**live** *v/t* sopravvivere a

'**out·look** *(prospects)* prospettiva *f*

'**out·ly·ing** *adj areas* periferico

out'**num·ber** *v/t* superare numericamente

out of *prep* (*motion*) fuori; *fall ~ the window* cadere dalla finestra ◊ (*position*) da **20 miles** ~ **Newcastle** 20 miglia da Newcastle ◊ (*cause*) per; ~ *jealousy/curiosity* per gelosia/curiosità ◊ (*without*) senza; *we're ~ petrol/beer* siamo senza benzina/birra ◊ *from a group* su **5** ~ **10** 5 su 10

out-of-'**date** *adj passport* scaduto; *values* superato

out-of-the-'**way** *adj* fuori mano

'**out·pa·tient** paziente *m/f* esterno, -a

'**out·pa·tients**' (*clin·ic*) ambulatorio *m*

out·per'**form** *v/t of machine, investment* rendere meglio di; *of company, economy* andare meglio di

'**out·put 1** *n of factory* produzione *f*;

O

COMPUT output *m inv* **2** *v/t* (*pret & pp* **-ted** *or* **output**) (*produce*) produrre; COMPUT: *signal* emettere

'**out·rage 1** *n feeling* sdegno *m*; *act* atrocità *f inv* **2** *v/t* indignare

out·ra·geous [aʊtˈreɪdʒəs] *adj acts* scioccante; *prices* scandaloso

'**out·right 1** *adj winner* assoluto **2** *adv win* nettamente; *kill* sul colpo

out'run *v/t* (*pret* **-ran**, *pp* **-run**) *also fig* superare; *run faster than* correre più veloce di

'**out·set** *n*: **at / from the ~** all' / dall'inizio

out'shine *v/t* (*pret & pp* **-shone**) eclissare

'**out·side 1** *adj surface, wall, lane* esterno **2** *adv sit, go* fuori **3** *prep* fuori da; *(apart from)* al di fuori di **4** *n of building, case etc* esterno *m*; **at the ~** al massimo

out·side 'broad·cast trasmissione *f* in esterni

out·sid·er [aʊtˈsaɪdə(r)] estraneo *m*, -a *f*; *in election, race* outsider *m inv*

'**out·size** *adj clothing* di taglia forte

'**out·skirts** *npl* periferia *f*

out'smart → **outwit**

out'stand·ing *adj success, writer* eccezionale; FIN: *invoice, sums* da saldare

out·stretched [ˈaʊtstretʃt] *adj hands* teso

out'vote *v/t* mettere in minoranza

out·ward [ˈaʊtwəd] *adj appearance* esteriore; **~ journey** viaggio *m* d'andata

'**out·ward·ly** [ˈaʊtwədlɪ] *adv* esteriormente

out'weigh *v/t* contare più di

out'wit *v/t* (*pret & pp* **-ted**) riuscire a gabbare

o·val [ˈəʊvl] *adj* ovale

o·va·ry [ˈəʊvərɪ] ovaia *f*

o·va·tion [əʊˈveɪʃn] ovazione *f*; **she was given a standing ~** il pubblico s'è alzato in piedi per applaudirla

ov·en [ˈʌvn] *in kitchen* forno *m*; *in factory* fornace *f*

'**ov·en glove**, '**ov·en mitt** guanto *m*

da forno; '**ov·en-proof** *adj* pirofilo; '**ov·en-read·y** *adj* pronto da mettere al forno

o·ver [ˈəʊvə(r)] **1** *prep (above)* sopra, su; *(across)* dall'altra parte; *(more than)* oltre; *(during)* nel corso di; **~ the phone** al telefono; **travel all ~ Brazil** girare tutto il Brasile; **you find them all ~ Brazil** si trovano dappertutto in Brasile; **let's talk ~ a meal** parliamone a pranzo; **we're ~ the worst** il peggio è passato; **~ and above** oltre a **2** *adv*: **be ~** (*finished*) essere finito; *(left)* essere rimasto; **~ to you** (*your turn*) tocca a te; **~ in Japan** in Giappone; **~here / there** qui / lì; **it hurts all ~** mi fa male dappertutto; **painted white all ~** tutto dipinto di bianco; **it's all ~** è finito; **I've told you ~ and ~ again** te l'ho detto mille volte; **do sth ~ again** rifare qc

o·ver·all [ˈəʊvərɔːl] **1** *adj length* totale **2** *adv measure* complessivamente; *(in general)* nell'insieme

o·ver·alls [ˈəʊvərɔːlz] *npl* tuta *f* da lavoro

o·ver'awe *v/t* intimidire; **be ~d by s.o. / sth** essere intimidito da qu / qc

o·ver'bal·ance *v/i* perdere l'equilibrio

o·ver'bear·ing *adj* autoritario

'o·ver·board *adv*: **man ~!** uomo in mare!; **go ~ for s.o. / sth** entusiasmarsi per qu / qc

'o·ver·cast *adj day, sky* nuvoloso

o·ver'charge *v/t customer* far pagare più del dovuto a

'o·ver·coat cappotto *m*

o·ver'come *v/t* (*pret* **-came**, *pp* **-come**) *difficulties, shyness* superare; **be ~ by emotion** essere sopraffatto dall'emozione

o·ver'crowd·ed *adj* sovraffollato

o·ver'do *v/t* (*pret* **-did**, *pp* **-done**) *(exaggerate)* esagerare; *in cooking* stracuocere; **you're ~ing things** *taking on too much* ti stai strapazzando

o·ver'done *adj meat* stracotto

'o·ver·dose *n* overdose *f inv*

'o·ver·draft scoperto *m* (di conto); **have an ~** avere il conto scoperto

o·ver'draw *v/t* (*pret* **-drew**, *pp* **-drawn**): **~ one's account** andare allo scoperto; **be £800 ~n** essere (allo) scoperto di 800 sterline

o·ver'dressed *adj* troppo elegante

'o·ver·drive MOT overdrive *m inv*

o·ver'due *adj* bill, rent arretrato; train, baby in ritardo

o·ver·es·ti·mate *v/t* abilities, value sovrastimare

o·ver·ex'pose *v/t* photograph sovraesporre

'o·ver·flow[1] *n* pipe troppopieno *m*

o·ver'flow[2] *v/i* of water traboccare; of river straripare

o·ver'grown *adj* garden coperto d'erbacce; **he's an ~ baby** è un bambinone

o·ver'haul *v/t* engine revisionare; plans rivedere

'o·ver·head[1] *adj* lights, cables in alto, aereo; railway soprelevato

'o·ver·head[2] Am *nsg*, 'over·heads *npl* FIN costi *mpl* di gestione; **travel ~** spese *fpl* di viaggio

o·ver·head pro·jec·tor lavagna *f* luminosa

o·ver'hear *v/t* (*pret & pp* **-heard**) sentire per caso

o·ver'heat·ed *adj* room, engine surriscaldato

o·ver'joyed [əʊvə'dʒɔɪd] *adj* felicissimo

'o·ver·kill: **that's ~** è un'esagerazione

'o·ver·land *adj & adv* via terra

o·ver'lap *v/i* (*pret & pp* **-ped**) (partly cover) sovrapporsi; (partly coincide) coincidere

o·ver'leaf: **see ~** a tergo

o·ver'load *v/t* sovraccaricare

o·ver'look *v/t* of tall building etc dominare, dare su; deliberately chiudere un occhio su; accidentally non notare; **the room ~s the garden** la stanza dà sul giardino

o·ver·ly ['əʊvəlɪ] *adv* troppo; **not ~ ...** non particolarmente ...

'o·ver·night *adv* travel di notte; stay

per la notte

o·ver·night 'bag piccola borsa *f* da viaggio

o·ver'paid *adj* strapagato

o·ver·pop·u·lat·ed [əʊvə'pɒpjʊleɪtɪd] *adj* sovrappopolato

o·ver'pow·er *v/t* physically sopraffare

o·ver'pow·er·ing [əʊvə'paʊrɪŋ] *adj* smell asfissiante; sense of guilt opprimente

o·ver'priced [əʊvə'praɪst] *adj* troppo caro

o·ver'rat·ed [əʊvə'reɪtɪd] *adj* sopravvalutato

o·ver·re'act *v/i* reagire in modo eccessivo

o·ver'ride *v/t* (*pret* **-rode**, *pp* **-ridden**) annullare; person annullare la decisione di; (be more important than) prevalere su

o·ver'rid·ing *adj* concern principale

o·ver'rule *v/t* decision annullare

o·ver'run *v/t* (*pret* **-ran**, *pp* **-run**) country invadere; time sforare; **be ~ with** essere invaso da

o·ver'seas *adv & adj* all'estero

o·ver'see *v/t* (*pret* **-saw**, *pp* **-seen**) sorvegliare

o·ver'shad·ow *v/t* fig eclissare

'o·ver·sight svista *f*

o·ver·sim·pli·fi·ca·tion semplificazione *f* eccessiva

o·ver'sim·pli·fy *v/t* (*pret & pp* **-ied**) semplificare troppo

o·ver'sleep *v/i* (*pret & pp* **-slept**) non svegliarsi in tempo

o·ver'state *v/t* esagerare

o·ver'state·ment esagerazione *f*

o·ver'step *v/t* (*pret & pp* **-ped**): fig **~ the mark** passare il segno

o·ver'take *v/t* (*pret* **-took**, *pp* **-taken**) in work, development superare; MOT sorpassare

o·ver'throw[1] *v/t* (*pret* **-threw**, *pp* **-thrown**) government rovesciare

'o·ver·throw[2] *n* of government rovesciamento *m*

'o·ver·time Br **1** *n* straordinario *m* **2** *adv*: **work ~** fare lo straordinario

'o·ver·ture ['əʊvətjʊə(r)] MUS ouverture *f inv*; **make ~s to** fare approcci a

o·ver'turn 1 *v/t vehicle, object* ribaltare; *government* rovesciare **2** *v/i of vehicle* ribaltarsi

'o·ver·view visione *f* d'insieme

o·ver'weight *adj* sovrappeso

o·ver'whelm [əʊvə'welm] *v/t with work* oberare; *with emotion* sopraffare; **be ~ed by** *response* essere colpito da

o·ver'whelm·ing [əʊvə'welmɪŋ] *adj feeling* profondo; *majority* schiacciante

o·ver'work 1 *n* lavoro *m* eccessivo **2** *v/i* lavorare troppo **3** *v/t* far lavorare troppo

owe [əʊ] *v/t* dovere; **~ s.o. £500** dovere £500 a qu; **~ s.o. an apology** dovere delle scuse a qu; **how much**

do I ~ you? quanto le devo?

ow·ing to ['əʊɪŋ] *prep* a causa di

owl [aʊl] gufo *m*

own¹ [əʊn] *v/t* possedere

own² [əʊn] **1** *adj* proprio; **my ~ car** la mia macchina; **my very ~ mother** proprio mia madre **2** *pron*: **a car of my ~** un'auto tutta mia; **on my / his ~ da** solo

♦ **own up** *v/i* confessare

own·er ['əʊnə(r)] proprietario *m*, -a *f*

own·er·ship ['əʊnəʃɪp] proprietà *f inv*

ox [ɒks] bue *m*

ox·ide ['ɒksaɪd] ossido *m*

ox·y·gen ['ɒksɪdʒən] ossigeno *m*

oy·ster ['ɔɪstə(r)] ostrica *f*

oz *abbr* (= **ounce(s)**) oncia *f*

o·zone ['əʊzəʊn] ozono *m*

'o·zone lay·er fascia *f* o strato *m* d'ozono

P

p [pi:] *abbr* (= **penny**; **pence**) penny *m inv*

PA [pi:'eɪ] *abbr* (= **personal assistant**) assistente *m/f* personale

pace [peɪs] **1** *n* (*step*) passo *m*; (*speed*) ritmo *m* **2** *v/i*: **~ up and down** camminare su e giù

'pace·mak·er MED pacemaker *m inv*; SP battistrada *m inv*

Pa·cif·ic [pə'sɪfɪk]: **the ~ (Ocean)** il Pacifico

pac·i·fism ['pæsɪfɪzm] pacifismo *m*

pac·i·fist ['pæsɪfɪst] *n* pacifista *m/f*

pac·i·fy ['pæsɪfaɪ] *v/t* (*pret & pp -ied*) placare

pack [pæk] **1** *n* (*back~*) zaino *m*; *of cereal, food* confezione *f*; *of cigarettes* pacchetto *m*; *of peas etc* confezione *f*; *of cards* mazzo *m* **2** *v/t bag* fare; *item of clothing etc* mettere in valigia; *goods* imballare; *groceries* imbu-

stare **3** *v/i* fare la valigia / le valigie

pack·age ['pækɪdʒ] **1** *n* (*parcel*) pacco *m*; *of offers etc* pacchetto *m* **2** *v/t* confezionare

'pack·age deal *for holiday* offerta *f* tutto compreso

'pack·age tour viaggio *m* organizzato

pack·ag·ing ['pækɪdʒɪŋ] *also fig* confezione *f*

packed [pækt] *adj* (*crowded*) affollato

pack·et ['pækɪt] confezione *f*; *of cigarettes, crisps* pacchetto *m*

pact [pækt] patto *m*

pad¹ [pæd] **1** *n piece of cloth etc* tampone *m*; *for writing* blocchetto *m* **2** *v/t* (*pret & pp -ded*) *with material* imbottire; *speech, report* farcire

pad² [pæd] *v/i* (*move quietly*) camminare a passi felpati

pad·ded ['pædɪd] *adj jacket, shoulders* imbottito

pad·ding ['pædɪŋ] *material* imbottitura *f*; *in speech etc* riempitivo *m*

pad·dle ['pædl] **1** *for canoe* pagaia *f* **2** *v/i in canoe* pagaiare; *in water* sguazzare

pad·dling pool ['pædlɪŋpu:l] piscinetta *f* per bambini

pad·dock ['pædək] paddock *m inv*

pad·lock ['pædlɒk] **1** *n* lucchetto *m* **2** *v/t gate* chiudere col lucchetto; **~ X to Y** fissare col lucchetto X a Y

paed·i·at·ric *etc* → **pediatric** *etc*

page¹ [peɪdʒ] *n of book etc* pagina *f*

page² [peɪdʒ] *v/t (call)* chiamare con l'altoparlante; *with pager* chiamare col cercapersone

pag·er ['peɪdʒə(r)] cercapersone *m inv*

paid [peɪd] *pret & pp* → **pay**

paid em·ploy·ment occupazione *f* rimunerata

pail [peɪl] secchio *m*

pain [peɪn] dolore *m*; **be in ~** soffrire; **take ~s to ...** fare il possibile per ...; **a ~ in the neck** F una rottura *f* di scatole F

pain·ful ['peɪnfʊl] *adj (distressing)* doloroso; *(laborious)* difficile; **my leg is still ~** la gamba mi fa ancora male; **it is my ~ duty to inform you ...** siamo addolorati di comunicarle ...

pain·ful·ly ['peɪnflɪ] *adv (extremely, acutely)* estremamente

pain·kill·er ['peɪnkɪlə(r)] analgesico *m*

pain·less ['peɪnlɪs] *adj* indolore

pains·tak·ing ['peɪnzteɪkɪŋ] *adj* accurato

paint [peɪnt] **1** *n for wall, car* vernice *f*; *for artist* colore *m* **2** *v/t wall etc* pitturare; *picture* dipingere **3** *v/i as art form* dipingere

paint·brush ['peɪntbrʌʃ] pennello *m*

paint·er ['peɪntə(r)] *decorator* imbianchino *m*; *artist* pittore *m*, -trice *f*

paint·ing ['peɪntɪŋ] *activity* pittura *f*; *(picture)* quadro *m*

paint·work ['peɪntwɜ:k] vernice *f*

pair [peə(r)] *of objects* paio *m*; *of animals, people* coppia *f*; **a ~ of shoes** un paio di scarpe

pa·ja·mas *Am* → **pyjamas**

Pa·ki·stan [pɑ:kɪ'stɑ:n] Pakistan *m*

Pa·ki·sta·ni [pɑ:kɪ'stɑ:nɪ] **1** *n* pakistano *m*, -a *f* **2** *adj* pakistano

pal [pæl] F *(friend)* amico *m*, -a *f*

pal·ace ['pælɪs] palazzo *m* signorile

pal·ate ['pælət] palato *m*

pa·la·tial [pə'leɪʃl] *adj* sfarzoso

pale [peɪl] *adj person* pallido; **~ pink / blue** rosa / celeste pallido

Pal·e·stine ['pæləstaɪn] Palestina *f*

Pal·e·stin·i·an [pælə'stɪnɪən] **1** *n* palestinese *m/f* **2** *adj* palestinese

pal·let ['pælɪt] pallet *m inv*

pal·lor ['pælə(r)] pallore *m*

palm¹ [pɑ:m] *of hand* palma *f*

palm² [pɑ:m] *tree* palma *f*

pal·pi·ta·tions [pælpɪ'teɪʃnz] *npl* MED palpitazioni *fpl*

pal·try ['pɔ:ltrɪ] *adj* irrisorio

pam·per ['pæmpə(r)] *v/t* viziare

pam·phlet ['pæmflɪt] volantino *m*

pan [pæn] **1** *n for cooking* pentola *f*; *for frying* padella *f* **2** *v/t (pret & pp -ned)* F *(criticize)* stroncare F

♦ **pan out** *v/i (develop)* svilupparse

pan·cake ['pænkeɪk] crêpe *f inv*

pan·da ['pændə] panda *m inv*

pan·de·mo·ni·um [pændɪ'məʊnɪəm] pandemonio *m*

♦ **pan·der to** ['pændə(r)] *v/t* assecondare

pane [peɪn]: **~ (of glass)** vetro *m*

pan·el ['pænl] pannello *m*; *of experts* gruppo *m*; *of judges* giuria *f*

pan·el·ling ['pænəlɪŋ] rivestimento *m* a pannelli

pang [pæŋ] *of remorse* fitta *f*; **~s of hunger** morsi *mpl* della fame

pan·ic ['pænɪk] **1** *n* panico *m* **2** *v/i (pret & pp -ked)*: **don't ~** non farti prendere dal panico

'pan·ic buy·ing FIN acquisto *m* motivato dal panico; **'pan·ic sel·ling** FIN vendita *f* motivata dal panico; **'pan·ic-strick·en** *adj* in preda al panico

pan·o·ra·ma [pænə'rɑ:mə] panorama *m*

P

pa·no·ra·mic [pænə'ræmɪk] *adj* view panoramico

pan·sy ['pænzɪ] *flower* viola *f* del pensiero

pant [pænt] *v/i* ansimare

pan·ties ['pæntɪz] *npl* mutandine *fpl*

pants [pænts] *npl* (*underpants*) mutande *fpl*; *esp Am* (*trousers*) pantaloni *mpl*

pan·ty·hose ['pæntɪhəʊz] *Am* collant *mpl*

pa·pal ['peɪpəl] *adj* pontificio

pa·per ['peɪpə(r)] **1** *n material* carta *f*; (*news~*) giornale *m*; (*wall~*) carta *f* da parati; *academic* relazione *f*; (*examination ~*) esame *m*; **~s** (*identity ~s, documents*) documenti *mpl*; *a piece of ~* un pezzo di carta **2** *adj* di carta **3** *v/t room, walls* tappezzare

'**paperback** tascabile *m*; **paper 'bag** sacchetto *m* di carta; '**paper boy** ragazzo *m* che recapita i giornali a domicilio; '**paper clip** graffetta *f*; '**paper cup** bicchiere *m* di carta; '**paperwork** disbrigo *m* delle pratiche

par [pɑː (r)] *in golf* par *m inv*; *be on a ~ with* essere allo stesso livello di; *feel below ~* non sentirsi bene

par·a·chute ['pærəʃuːt] **1** *n* paracadute *m inv* **2** *v/i* paracadutarsi **3** *v/t troops, supplies* paracadutare

par·a·chut·ist ['pærəʃuːtɪst] paracadutista *m/f*

pa·rade [pə'reɪd] **1** *n* (*procession*) sfilata *f* **2** *v/i* sfilare **3** *v/t knowledge, new car* fare sfoggio di

par·a·dise ['pærədaɪs] paradiso *m*

par·a·dox ['pærədɒks] paradosso *m*

par·a·dox·i·cal [pærə'dɒksɪkl] *adj* paradossale

par·a·dox·i·cal·ly [pærə'dɒksɪklɪ] *adv* paradossalmente

par·a·graph ['pærəgrɑːf] paragrafo *m*

par·al·lel ['pærəlel] **1** *n* (*in geometry*) parallela *f*, GEOG, *fig* parallelo *m*; *do two things in ~* fare due cose in parallelo **2** *adj also fig* parallelo **3** *v/t* (*match*) uguagliare

par·a·lyse ['pærəlaɪz] *v/t also fig* paralizzare

pa·ral·y·sis [pə'ræləsɪs] *also fig* paralisi *f inv*

par·a·med·ic [pærə'medɪk] *n* paramedico *m*, -a *f*

pa·ram·e·ter [pə'ræmɪtə(r)] parametro *m*

par·a·mil·i·tar·y [pærə'mɪlɪtrɪ] **1** *adj* paramilitare **2** *n appartenente m/f ad un'organizzazione paramilitare*

par·a·mount ['pærəmaʊnt] *adj* vitale; *be ~* essere di vitale importanza

par·a·noi·a [pærə'nɔɪə] paranoia *f*

par·a·noid ['pærənɔɪd] *adj* paranoico

par·a·pher·na·li·a [pærəfə'neɪlɪə] armamentario *m*

par·a·phrase ['pærəfreɪz] *v/t* parafrasare

par·a·pleg·ic [pærə'pliːdʒɪk] *n* paraplegico *m*, -a *f*

par·a·site ['pærəsaɪt] *also fig* parassita *m*

par·a·sol ['pærəsɒl] parasole *m*

par·a·troop·er ['pærətruːpə(r)] MIL paracadutista *m*

par·cel ['pɑːsl] *n* pacco *m*

♦ **parcel up** *v/t* impacchettare

parch [pɑːtʃ] *v/t* riardere; *be ~ed* F of person essere assetato

par·don ['pɑːdn] **1** *n* LAW grazia *f*; *I beg your ~?* (*what did you say*) prego?; *I beg your ~* (*I'm sorry*) scusi **2** *v/t* scusare; LAW graziare

pare [peə(r)] *v/t* (*peel*) pelare

par·ent ['peərənt] genitore *m*

pa·ren·tal [pə'rentl] *adj* dei genitori

'**parent company** società *f inv* madre

parent-'teacher association organizzazione *f* composta da genitori e insegnanti

par·ish ['pærɪʃ] parrocchia *f*

park[1] [pɑːk] *n* parco *m*

park[2] [pɑːk] *v/t & v/i* MOT parcheggiare

par·ka ['pɑːkə] parka *m inv*

par·king ['pɑːkɪŋ] MOT parcheggio *m*; *no ~* sosta *f* vietata

'**parking brake** *Am* freno *m* a mano;

'par·king disc disco *m* orario; **'par·king lot** *Am* parcheggio *m*; **'park·ing me·ter** parchimetro *m*; **'park·ing place** parcheggio *m*; **'park·ing tick·et** multa *f* per sosta vietata

par·lia·ment ['pɑːləmənt] parlamento *m*

par·lia·men·ta·ry [pɑːljəˈmentərɪ] *adj* parlamentare

pa·role [pəˈrəul] **1** *n* libertà *f inv* vigilata; **be out on ~** essere rimesso in libertà vigilata **2** *v/t* concedere la libertà vigilata a

par·rot ['pærət] pappagallo *m*

pars·ley ['pɑːslɪ] prezzemolo *m*

part [pɑːt] **1** *n* parte *f*; *of machine* pezzo *m*; *Am*: *in hair* riga *f*; **take ~ in** prendere parte in **2** *adv* (*partly*) in parte **3** *v/i* separarsi **4** *v/t*: **~ one's hair** farsi la riga

♦ **part with** *v/t* separarsi da

'part ex·change permuta *f*; **take sth in ~ exchange** prendere qc in permuta

par·tial ['pɑːʃl] *adj* (*incomplete*) parziale; **be ~ to** avere un debole per

par·tial·ly ['pɑːʃəlɪ] *adv* parzialmente

par·ti·ci·pant [pɑːˈtɪsɪpənt] partecipante *m/f*

par·ti·ci·pate [pɑːˈtɪsɪpeɪt] *v/i* partecipare; **~ in sth** partecipare a qc

par·ti·ci·pa·tion [pɑːtɪsɪˈpeɪʃn] partecipazione *f*

par·ti·cle ['pɑːtɪkl] PHYS particella *f*; *small amount* briciolo *m*

par·tic·u·lar [pəˈtɪkjʊlə(r)] *adj* (*specific*) particolare; (*fussy*) pignolo; **in ~** in particolare

par·tic·u·lar·ly [pəˈtɪkjʊləlɪ] *adv* particolarmente

part·ing ['pɑːtɪŋ] *of people* separazione *f*; *in hair* riga *f*

par·ti·tion [pɑːˈtɪʃn] **1** *n* (*screen*) tramezzo *m*; (*of country*) suddivisione *f* **2** *v/t country* suddividere

♦ **partition off** *v/t* tramezzare

part·ly ['pɑːtlɪ] *adv* in parte

part·ner ['pɑːtnə(r)] COM socio *m*, -a *f*; *in relationship* partner *m/f inv*; *in particular activity* compagno *m*, -a *f*

part·ner·ship ['pɑːtnəʃɪp] COM società *f inv*; *in particular activity* sodalizio *m*

part of 'speech GRAM parte *f* del discorso; **'part own·er** comproprietario *m*, -a *f*, **part-time** *adj & adv* part-time; **part·'tim·er** lavoratore *m*, -trice *f* part-time

par·ty ['pɑːtɪ] **1** *n* (*celebration*) festa *f*; POL partito *m*; (*group*) gruppo *m*; **be a ~ to** essere coinvolto in **2** *v/i* (*pret & pp -ied*) F far baldoria

pass [pɑːs] **1** *n for getting into a place* passi *m inv*; SP passaggio *m*; *in mountains* passo *m*; **make a ~ at** fare avances a **2** *v/t* (*hand*) passare; (*go past*) passare davanti a; (*overtake*) sorpassare; (*go beyond*) superare; (*approve*) approvare; SP passare; **~ an exam** superare un esame; **~ sentence** LAW emanare la sentenza; **~ the time** passare il tempo **3** *v/i* passare; *in exam* essere promosso

♦ **pass around** *v/t* far circolare

♦ **pass away** *v/i euph* spegnersi *euph*

♦ **pass by 1** *v/t* (*go past*) passare davanti a **2** *v/i* (*go past*) passare

♦ **pass on 1** *v/t information, book, savings* passare (**to** a) **2** *v/i* (*euph: die*) mancare *euph*

♦ **pass out** *v/i* (*faint*) svenire

♦ **pass through** *v/t town* passare per

♦ **pass up** *v/t opportunity* lasciarsi sfuggire

pass·a·ble ['pɑːsəbl] *adj road* transitabile; (*acceptable*) passabile

pas·sage ['pæsɪdʒ] (*corridor*) passaggio *m*; *from poem, book* passo *m*; **the ~ of time** il passare del tempo

pas·sage·way ['pæsɪdʒweɪ] corridoio *m*

pas·sen·ger ['pæsɪndʒə(r)] passeggero *m*, -a *f*

'pas·sen·ger seat sedile *m* del passeggero

pas·ser-by [pɑːsəˈbaɪ] (*pl passers-by*) passante *m/f*

pas·sion ['pæʃn] passione *f*

pas·sion·ate ['pæʃnət] adj appassionato

pas·sive ['pæsɪv] 1 adj passivo 2 n GRAM passivo m; *in the ~* al passivo

'pass mark EDU voto m sufficiente

Pass·o·ver ['pɑːsəʊvə(r)] REL Pasqua f ebraica

pass·port ['pɑːspɔːt] passaporto m

'pass·port control controllo m passaporti

pass·word ['pɑːswɜːd] parola f d'ordine; COMPUT password f inv

past [pɑːst] 1 adj (former) precedente; *in the ~ few days* nei giorni scorsi; *that's all ~ now* è acqua passata ormai 2 n passato m; *in the ~* nel passato 3 prep in position oltre; *it's half ~ two* sono le due e mezza; *it's ~ seven o'clock* sono le sette passate 4 adv: *run ~* passare di corsa

pas·ta ['pæstə] pasta f

paste [peɪst] 1 n (adhesive) colla f 2 v/t (stick) incollare

pas·tel ['pæstl] 1 n pastello m 2 adj pastello

pas·time ['pɑːstaɪm] passatempo m

past par·ti·ci·ple GRAM participio m passato

pas·tra·mi [pæ'strɑːmɪ] affettato m di carne di manzo speziata

pas·try ['peɪstrɪ] for pie pasta f (sfoglia); (small cake) pasticcino m

'past tense GRAM passato m

pas·ty [peɪstɪ] adj complexion smorto

pat [pæt] 1 n colpetto m; affectionate buffetto m; *give s.o. a ~ on the back* fig dare una pacca sulla spalla a qu 2 v/t (pret & pp -ted) dare un colpetto a; affectionately dare un buffetto a

patch [pætʃ] 1 n on clothing pezza f; (period of time) periodo m; (area) zona f; *go through a bad ~* attraversare un brutto periodo; *~es of fog* banchi mpl di nebbia; *be not a ~ on* fig non essere niente a paragone di 2 v/t clothing rattoppare

♦ **patch up** v/t (repair temporarily) riparare alla meglio; quarrel risolvere

patch·work ['pætʃwɜːk] 1 n patchwork m inv 2 adj quilt patchwork inv

patch·y ['pætʃɪ] adj quality irregolare; work, performance discontinuo, disuguale

pâ·té ['pæteɪ] pâté m inv

pa·tent ['peɪtnt] 1 adj palese 2 n for invention brevetto m 3 v/t invention brevettare

pa·tent 'leath·er vernice f

pa·tent·ly ['peɪtntlɪ] adv (clearly) palesemente

pa·ter·nal [pə'tɜːnl] adj paterno

pa·ter·nal·ism [pə'tɜːnlɪzm] paternalismo m

pa·ter·nal·is·tic [pətɜːnl'ɪstɪk] adj paternalistico

pa·ter·ni·ty [pə'tɜːnɪtɪ] paternità f inv

path [pɑːθ] sentiero m; fig strada f

pa·thet·ic [pə'θetɪk] adj invoking pity patetico; F (very bad) penoso

path·o·log·i·cal [pæθə'lɒdʒɪkl] adj patologico

pa·thol·o·gy [pə'θɒlədʒɪ] patologia f

pa·thol·o·gist [pə'θɒlədʒɪst] patologo m, -a f

pa·tience ['peɪʃns] pazienza f; Br. card game solitario m

pa·tient ['peɪʃnt] 1 n paziente m/f 2 adj paziente; *just be ~!* abbi pazienza!

pa·tient·ly ['peɪʃntlɪ] adv pazientemente

pat·i·o ['pætɪəʊ] terrazza f

pat·ri·ot ['peɪtrɪət] patriota m/f

pat·ri·ot·ic [peɪtrɪ'ɒtɪk] adj patriottico

pa·tri·ot·ism ['peɪtrɪətɪzm] patriottismo m

pa·trol [pə'trəʊl] 1 n pattuglia f; *be on ~* essere di pattuglia 2 v/t (pret & pp -led) streets, border pattugliare

pa'trol car autopattuglia f

pa'trol·man agente m/f di pattuglia

pa·tron ['peɪtrən] of artist patrocinatore m, -trice f; of charity patrono m, -essa f; of shop, cinema cliente m/f

pa·tron·age ['peɪtrənɪdʒ] of artist patronato m; of charity patrocinio m

pa·tron·ize ['pætrənaɪz] v/t shop essere cliente di; *person* trattare con condiscendenza

pa·tron·iz·ing ['pætrənaɪzɪŋ] *adj* condiscendente

pa·tron 'saint patrono *m*, -a *f*

pat·ter ['pætə(r)] **1** *n of rain etc* picchiettio *m*; F *of salesman* imbonimento *m* **2** *v/i* picchiettare

pat·tern ['pætn] *n on wallpaper, fabric* motivo *m*, disegno *m*; *for knitting, sewing* (carta) modello *m*; *in behaviour, events* schema *m*

pat·terned ['pætənd] *adj* fantasia *inv*

paunch [pɔːnʧ] pancia *f*

pause [pɔːz] **1** *n* pausa *f* **2** *v/i* fermarsi **3** *v/t tape* fermare

pave [peɪv] *v/t* pavimentare; **~ the way for** *fig* aprire la strada a

pave·ment ['peɪvmənt] *Br* marciapiede *m*

pav·ing stone ['peɪvɪŋ] lastra *f* di pavimentazione

paw [pɔː] **1** *n of animal*, F *(hand)* zampa *f* **2** *v/t* F palpare

pawn¹ [pɔːn] *n in chess* pedone *m*; *fig* pedina *f*

pawn² [pɔːn] *v/t* impegnare

'pawn·bro·ker prestatore *m*, -trice *f* su pegno

'pawn·shop monte *m* di pietà

pay [peɪ] **1** *n* paga *f*; **in the ~ of** al soldo di **2** *v/t (pret & pp paid)* pagare; **~ attention** fare attenzione; **~ s.o. a compliment** fare un complimento a qu **3** *v/i (pret & pp paid)* pagare; *(be profitable)* rendere; **it doesn't ~ to ...** non conviene ...; **~ for** *purchase* pagare; **you'll ~ for this!** *fig* la pagherai!

♦ **pay back** *v/t person* restituire i soldi a; *loan* restituire; *(get revenge on)* farla pagare a

♦ **pay in** *v/t to bank* versare

♦ **pay off** **1** *v/t debt* estinguere; *workers* liquidare; *corrupt official* comprare **2** *v/i (be profitable)* dare frutti

♦ **pay up** *v/i* pagare

pay·a·ble ['peɪəbl] *adj* pagabile

'pay·day giorno *m* di paga

pay·ee [peɪ'iː] beneficiario *m*, -a *f*

pay·er ['peɪə(r)] pagatore *m*, -trice *f*

pay·ment ['peɪmənt] pagamento *m*

'pay pack·et busta *f* paga; **'pay phone** telefono *m* pubblico; **'pay·roll** *money* stipendi *mpl*; *employees* personale *m*; **be on the ~** essere sul libro paga; **'pay·slip** busta *f* paga

PC [piː'siː] *abbr* (= **personal computer**) PC *m inv*; (= **politically correct**) politicamente corretto; (= **police constable**) agente *m* di polizia

pea [piː] pisello *m*

peace [piːs] pace *f*

peace·a·ble ['piːsəbl] *adj person* pacifico

peace·ful ['piːsfʊl] *adj* tranquillo; *demonstration* pacifico

peace·ful·ly ['piːsflɪ] *adv* tranquillamente; *demonstrate* pacificamente

peach [piːʧ] pesca *f*; *tree* pesco *m*

pea·cock ['piːkɒk] pavone *m*

peak [piːk] **1** *n* vetta *f*; *fig* apice *m* **2** *v/i* raggiungere il livello massimo

'peak con·sump·tion periodo *m* di massimo consumo; **'peak hours** *npl* ore *fpl* di punta; **peak 'view·ing hours** *npl* prima serata *f*

pea·nut ['piːnʌt] arachide *f*; **get paid ~s** F essere pagati una miseria F; **that's ~s to him** F sono briciole per lui

pea·nut 'but·ter burro *m* d'arachidi

pear [peə(r)] pera *f*; *tree* pero *m*

pearl [pɜːl] perla *f*

peas·ant ['peznt] contadino *m*, -a *f*

peb·ble ['pebl] ciottolo *m*

peck [pek] **1** *n (bite)* beccata *f*; *(kiss)* bacetto *m* **2** *v/t (bite)* beccare; *(kiss)* dare un bacetto

pe·cu·li·ar [pɪ'kjuːlɪə(r)] *adj (strange)* strano; **~ to** *(special)* caratteristico di

pe·cu·li·ar·i·ty [pɪkjuːlɪ'ærətɪ] *(strangeness)* stranezza *f*; *(special feature)* caratteristica *f*

ped·al ['pedl] **1** *n of bike* pedale *m* **2** *v/i turn ~s* pedalare; *(cycle)* andare in bicicletta

pe·dan·tic [pɪ'dæntɪk] *adj* pedante

ped·dle ['pedl] *v/t drugs* spacciare

ped·es·tal ['pedɪstl] *for statue* piedistallo *m*

P

pe·des·tri·an [pɪ'destrɪən] n pedone m

pe·des·tri·an 'cros·sing passaggio m pedonale

pe·des·tri·an 'pre·cinct zona f pedonale

pe·di·at·ric [piːdɪ'ætrɪk] adj pediatrico

pe·di·a·tri·cian [piːdɪə'trɪʃn] pediatra m/f

pe·di·at·rics [piːdɪ'ætrɪks] pediatria f

ped·i·cure ['pedɪkjʊə(r)] pedicure f inv

ped·i·gree ['pedɪgriː] 1 n pedigree m inv 2 adj di razza pura

pee [piː] v/i F fare pipì F

peek [piːk] 1 n sbirciata F 2 v/i sbirciare F

peel [piːl] 1 n buccia f; of citrus fruit scorza f 2 v/t fruit, vegetables sbucciare 3 v/i of nose, shoulders spellarsi; of paint scrostarsi

◆ peel off 1 v/t wrapper etc togliere 2 v/i of wrapper venir via

peep [piːp] → peek

peep·hole ['piːphəʊl] spioncino m

peer¹ [pɪə(r)] n (equal) pari m/f inv

peer² [pɪə(r)] v/i guardare; ~ through the mist guardare attraverso la foschia; ~ at scrutare

peeved [piːvd] adj F seccato

peg [peg] n for coat attaccapanni m inv; for tent picchetto m; off the ~ prêt-à-porter

pe·jo·ra·tive [pɪ'dʒɒrətɪv] adj peggiorativo

pel·let ['pelɪt] pallina f; (bullet) pallino m

pelt [pelt] 1 v/t: ~ s.o. with sth tirare qc a qu 2 v/i: they ~ed along the road F sono sfrecciati per strada; it's ~ing down F piove a dirotto

pel·vis ['pelvɪs] pelvi f inv

pen¹ [pen] n penna f

pen² [pen] (enclosure) recinto m

pe·nal·ize ['piːnəlaɪz] v/t penalizzare

pen·al·ty ['penəltɪ] ammenda f; in soccer rigore m; in rugby punizione f; take the ~ battere il rigore / la punizione

'pen·al·ty ar·e·a SP area f di rigore;
'pen·al·ty clause LAW penale f;
'pen·al·ty kick in soccer calcio m di rigore; in rugby calcio m di punizione; pen·al·ty 'shoot·out rigori mpl;
'pen·al·ty spot dischetto m di rigore

pence [pens] npl penny m inv

pen·cil ['pensɪl] matita f

pen·cil 'sharp·en·er temperamatite m inv

pen·dant ['pendənt] necklace pendaglio m

pend·ing ['pendɪŋ] 1 prep in attesa di 2 adj: be ~ essere in sospeso

pen·e·trate ['penɪtreɪt] v/t penetrare in

pen·e·trat·ing ['penɪtreɪtɪŋ] adj stare, scream penetrante; analysis perspicace

pen·e·tra·tion [penɪ'treɪʃn] penetrazione f

'pen friend amico m, -a f di penna

pen·guin ['peŋgwɪn] pinguino m

pen·i·cil·lin [penɪ'sɪlɪn] penicillina f

pe·nin·su·la [pə'nɪnsjʊlə] penisola f

pe·nis ['piːnɪs] pene m

pen·i·tence ['penɪtəns] penitenza f

pen·i·tent ['penɪtənt] adj pentito

pen·knife ['pennaɪf] temperino m

'pen name pseudonimo m

pen·nant ['penənt] gagliardetto m

pen·ni·less ['penɪlɪs] adj al verde

pen·ny ['penɪ] penny m inv

'pen pal amico m, -a f di penna

pen·sion ['penʃn] pensione f

◆ pension off v/t mandare in pensione

pen·sion·er ['penʃnə(r)] pensionato m, -a f

'pen·sion fund fondo m pensioni
'pen·sion scheme schema m pensionistico

pen·sive ['pensɪv] adj pensieroso

Pen·ta·gon ['pentəgɒn]: the ~ il Pentagono

pen·tath·lon [pen'tæθlən] pentathlon m inv

Pen·te·cost ['pentɪkɒst] Pentecoste f

pent·house ['penthaʊs] attico m

pent-up ['pentʌp] *adj* represso

pe·nul·ti·mate [pe'nʌltɪmət] *adj* penultimo

peo·ple ['piːpl] *npl* gente *f*, persone *fpl*; *(nsg: race, tribe)* popolazione *f*; **the ~** *(the citizens)* il popolo; **the American ~** gli americani; **~ say ...** si dice che ...

pep·per ['pepə(r)] *spice* pepe *m*; *vegetable* peperone *m*

pep·per·mint *sweet* mentina *f*; *flavouring* menta *f*

pep talk ['peptɔːk] discorso *m* d'incoraggiamento

per [pɜː(r)] *prep* a; **100 km ~ hour** 100 km all'ora; **£50 ~ night** 50 sterline a notte; **~ annum** all'anno

per·ceive [pə'siːv] *v/t with senses* percepire; *(view, interpret)* interpretare

per·cent [pə'sent] per cento

per·cen·tage [pə'sentɪdʒ] percentuale *f*

per·cep·ti·ble [pə'septəbl] *adj* percettibile

per·cep·ti·bly [pə'septəbli] *adv* percettibilmente

per·cep·tion [pə'sepʃn] *through senses* percezione *f*; *(insight)* sensibilità *f inv*

per·cep·tive [pə'septɪv] *adj person, remark* perspicace

perch [pɜːtʃ] **1** *n for bird* posatoio *m* **2** *v/i of bird* posarsi; *of person* appollaiarsi

per·co·late ['pɜːkəleɪt] *v/i of coffee* filtrare

per·co·la·tor ['pɜːkəleɪtə(r)] caffettiera *f* a filtro

per·cus·sion [pə'kʌʃn] percussioni *fpl*

per·cus·sion in·stru·ment strumento *m* a percussione

pe·ren·ni·al [pə'renɪəl] *n* BOT pianta *f* perenne

per·fect ['pɜːfɪkt] **1** *n* GRAM passato *m* prossimo **2** *adj* perfetto **3** *v/t* [pə'fekt] perfezionare

per·fec·tion [pə'fekʃn] perfezione *f*; **to ~** alla perfezione

per·fec·tion·ist [pə'fekʃnɪst] perfezionista *m/f*

per·fect·ly ['pɜːfɪktli] *adv* perfettamente

per·fo·rat·ed ['pɜːfəreɪtɪd] *adj* line perforato

per·fo·ra·tions [pɜːfə'reɪʃnz] *npl* linea *fsg* perforata

per·form [pə'fɔːm] **1** *v/t (carry out)* eseguire; *of actors* rappresentare; *of musician* eseguire **2** *v/i of actor, musician, dancer* esibirsi; *of actor* recitare; **the car ~s well** la macchina dà ottime prestazioni

per·form·ance [pə'fɔːməns] *by actor* rappresentazione *f*; *by musician* esecuzione *f*; *(show)* spettacolo *m*; *of employee, company etc* rendimento *m*; *of machine* prestazioni *fpl*

per·form·ance car auto *f inv* di alte prestazioni

per·form·er [pə'fɔːmə(r)] artista *m/f*

per·fume ['pɜːfjuːm] profumo *m*

per·func·to·ry [pə'fʌŋktəri] *adj* superficiale

per·haps [pə'hæps] *adv* forse

per·il ['perəl] pericolo *m*

per·il·ous ['perələs] *adj* pericoloso

pe·rim·e·ter [pə'rɪmɪtə(r)] perimetro *m*

pe·rim·e·ter fence recinzione *f*

pe·ri·od ['pɪərɪəd] *time* periodo *m*; *(menstruation)* mestruazioni *fpl*; **I don't want to, ~!** *Am* non voglio, punto e basta!

pe·ri·od·ic [pɪərɪ'ɒdɪk] *adj* periodico

pe·ri·od·i·cal [pɪərɪ'ɒdɪkl] *n* periodico *m*

pe·ri·od·i·cal·ly [pɪərɪ'ɒdɪkli] *adv* periodicamente

pe·riph·e·ral [pə'rɪfərəl] **1** *adj not crucial* marginale **2** *n* COMPUT periferica *f*

pe·riph·e·ry [pə'rɪfəri] periferia *f*

per·ish ['perɪʃ] *v/i of rubber* deteriorarsi; *of person* perire

per·ish·a·ble ['perɪʃəbl] *adj food* deteriorabile

per·ish·ing ['perɪʃɪŋ] *adj* F: **it's ~** fa un freddo da cane F

per·jure ['pɜːdʒə(r)] *v/r*: **~ o.s.** spergiurare

per·ju·ry ['pɜːdʒərɪ] falso giuramento *m*

perk [pɜːk] *n of job* vantaggio *m*

♦ **perk up 1** *v/t* F tirare su di morale **2** *v/i* F animarsi

perk·y ['pɜːkɪ] *adj* F (*cheerful*) allegro

perm [pɜːm] **1** *n* permanente *f* **2** *v/t* fare la permanente a

per·ma·nent ['pɜːmənənt] *adj* permanente; *job, address* fisso

per·ma·nent·ly ['pɜːmənəntlɪ] *adv* permanentemente

per·me·a·ble ['pɜːmɪəbl] *adj* permeabile

per·me·ate ['pɜːmɪeɪt] *v/t* permeare

per·mis·si·ble [pə'mɪsəbl] *adj* permesso, ammissibile

per·mis·sion [pə'mɪʃn] permesso *m*

per·mis·sive [pə'mɪsɪv] *adj* permissivo

per·mis·sive so'ci·e·ty società *f inv* permissiva

per·mit ['pɜːmɪt] **1** *n* permesso *m* **2** *v/t* [pə'mɪt] (*pret & pp* **-ted**) permettere; **~ s.o. to do sth** permettere a qu di fare qc

per·pen·dic·u·lar [pɜːpən'dɪkjulə(r)] *adj* perpendicolare

per·pet·u·al *adj* perenne

per·pet·u·al·ly [pə'petjuəlɪ] *adv* perennemente

per·pet·u·ate [pə'petjueɪt] *v/t* perpetuare

per·plex [pə'pleks] *v/t* lasciare perplesso

per·plexed [pə'plekst] *adj* perplesso

per·plex·i·ty [pə'pleksɪtɪ] perplessità *f inv*

per·se·cute ['pɜːsɪkjuːt] *v/t* perseguitare

per·se·cu·tion [pɜːsɪ'kjuːʃn] persecuzione *f*

per·se·cu·tor [pɜːsɪ'kjuːtə(r)] persecutore *m*, -trice *f*

per·se·ver·ance [pɜːsɪ'vɪərəns] perseveranza *f*

per·se·vere [pɜːsɪ'vɪə(r)] *v/i* perseverare

per·sist [pə'sɪst] *v/i* persistere; **~ in** persistere in

per·sis·tence [pə'sɪstəns] (*perseverance*) perseveranza *f*; (*continuation*) persistere *m*

per·sis·tent [pə'sɪstənt] *adj person, questions* insistente; *rain, unemployment etc* continuo

per·sis·tent·ly [pə'sɪstəntlɪ] *adv* (*continually*) continuamente

per·son ['pɜːsn] persona *f*; **in ~** di persona

per·son·al ['pɜːsnl] *adj* personale; **don't make ~ remarks** non fare commenti personali

per·son·al as'sist·ant assistente *m/f* personale; **'per·son·al col·umn** annunci *mpl* personali; **per·son·al com'put·er** personal computer *m inv*; **per·son·al 'hy·giene** igiene *f* personale

per·son·al·i·ty [pɜːsə'nælətɪ] personalità *f inv*

per·son·al·ly ['pɜːsənəlɪ] *adv* personalmente; **don't take it ~** non offenderti

per·son·al 'or·gan·iz·er agenda *f* elettronica; **per·son·al 'pro·noun** pronome *m* personale; **per·son·al 'ster·e·o** Walkman® *m inv*

per·son·i·fy [pə'sɒnɪfaɪ] *v/t* (*pret & pp* **-ied**) *of person* personificare

per·son·nel [pɜːsə'nel] *employees* personale *m*; *department* ufficio *m* del personale

per·son'nel man·a·ger direttore *m*, -trice *f* del personale

per·spec·tive [pə'spektɪv] PAINT prospettiva *f*; **get sth into ~** vedere qc nella giusta prospettiva

per·spi·ra·tion [pɜːspɪ'reɪʃn] traspirazione *f*

per·spire [pə'spaɪə(r)] *v/i* sudare

per·suade [pə'sweɪd] *v/t* persuadere, convincere; **~ s.o. to do sth** persuadere *o* convincere qu a fare qc

per·sua·sion [pə'sweɪʒn] persuasione *f*

per·sua·sive [pə'sweɪsɪv] *adj* persuasivo

per·ti·nent ['pɜːtɪnənt] *adj fml* pertinente

per·turb [pəˈtɜːb] *v/t* inquietare
per·turb·ing [pəˈtɜːbɪŋ] *adj* inquietante
pe·ruse [pəˈruːz] *v/t fml* leggere
per·va·sive [pəˈveɪsɪv] *adj influence, ideas* diffuso
per·verse [pəˈvɜːs] *adj* ostinato, irragionevole; *sexually* pervertito; **be ~** *(awkward)* essere un bastian contrario; **take a ~ delight in doing sth** provare un piacere perverso a fare qc
per·ver·sion [pəˈvɜːʃn] *n sexual* perversione *f*
per·vert [ˈpɜːvɜːt] *n sexual* pervertito *m*, -a *f*
pes·si·mis·m [ˈpesɪmɪzm] pessimismo *m*
pes·si·mist [ˈpesɪmɪst] pessimista *m/f*
pes·si·mis·tic [pesɪˈmɪstɪk] *adj attitude, view* pessimistico; *person* pessimista
pest [pest] *animale / insetto m* nocivo; *F person* peste *f*
pes·ter [ˈpestə(r)] *v/t* assillare; **~ s.o. to do sth** assillare qu perché faccia qc
pes·ti·cide [ˈpestɪsaɪd] pesticida *m*
pet [pet] **1** *n animal* animale *m* domestico; *(favourite)* favorito *m*, -a *f* **2** *adj* preferito **3** *v/t (pret & pp -ted) animal* accarezzare **4** *v/i (pret & pp -ted) of couple* pomiciare F
pet·al [ˈpetl] petalo *m*
♦**pe·ter out** [ˈpiːtə(r)] *v/i of rebellion, rain* cessare; *of path* finire
pe·tite [pəˈtiːt] *adj* minuta
pe·ti·tion [pəˈtɪʃn] *n* petizione *f*
'pet name nomignolo *m*
pet·ri·fied [ˈpetrɪfaɪd] *adj* terrorizzato
pet·ri·fy [ˈpetrɪfaɪ] *v/t (pret & pp -ied)* terrorizzare
pet·ro·chem·i·cal [petrəʊˈkemɪkl] *adj* petrolchimico
pet·rol [ˈpetrl] benzina *f*
pe·tro·le·um [pɪˈtrəʊlɪəm] petrolio *m*
'pet·rol gauge spia *f* della benzina; **'pet·rol pump** pompa *f* della benzina; **'pet·rol sta·tion** stazione *f* di servizio
pet·ting [ˈpetɪŋ] petting *m inv*
pet·ty [ˈpetɪ] *adj person, behaviour* meschino; *details, problem* insignificante
pet·ty 'cash piccola cassa *f*
pet·u·lant [ˈpetjʊlənt] *adj* petulante
pew [pjuː] banco *m* (di chiesa)
pew·ter [ˈpjuːtə(r)] peltro *m*
phar·ma·ceu·ti·cal [fɑːməˈsjuːtɪkl] *adj* farmaceutico
phar·ma·ceu·ti·cals [fɑːməˈsjuːtɪklz] *npl* farmaceutici *mpl*
phar·ma·cist [ˈfɑːməsɪst] farmacista *m/f*
phar·ma·cy [ˈfɑːməsɪ] farmacia *f*
phase [feɪz] fase *f*
♦**phase in** *v/t* introdurre gradualmente
♦**phase out** *v/t* eliminare gradualmente
PhD [piːeɪtʃˈdiː] *abbr (= **Doctor of Philosophy**)* dottorato *m* di ricerca
phe·nom·e·nal [fɪˈnɒmɪnl] *adj* fenomenale
phe·nom·e·nal·ly [fɪˈnɒmɪnlɪ] *adv* straordinariamente
phe·nom·e·non [fɪˈnɒmɪnɒn] fenomeno *m*
phil·an·throp·ic [fɪlənˈθrɒpɪk] *adj* filantropico
phi·lan·thro·pist [fɪˈlænθrəpɪst] filantropo *m*, -a *f*
phi·lan·thro·py [fɪˈlænθrəpɪ] filantropia *f*
Phil·ip·pines [ˈfɪlɪpiːnz] *npl:* **the ~** le Filippine *fpl*
phil·is·tine [ˈfɪlɪstaɪn] *n* ignorante *m/f*
phi·los·o·pher [fɪˈlɒsəfə(r)] filosofo *m*, -a *f*
phil·o·soph·i·cal [fɪləˈsɒfɪkl] *adj* filosofico
phi·los·o·phy [fɪˈlɒsəfɪ] filosofia *f*
pho·bi·a [ˈfəʊbɪə] fobia *f*
phone [fəʊn] **1** *n* telefono *m*; **be on the ~** *have one* avere il telefono; *be talking* essere al telefono **2** *v/t* telefonare a **3** *v/i* telefonare
'phone book guida *f* telefonica,

P

elenco telefonico *m*; '**phone booth** cabina *f* telefonica; '**phone box** cabina *f* telefonica; '**phone call** telefonata *f*; '**phone card** scheda *f* telefonica; '**phone num·ber** numero *m* di telefono

pho·net·ics [fəˈnetɪks] fonetica *f*

pho·n(e)y [ˈfəʊnɪ] *adj* F falso

pho·to [ˈfəʊtəʊ] *n* foto *f*

'**pho·to al·bum** album *m* fotografico; '**pho·to·cop·i·er** fotocopiatrice *f*; '**pho·to·cop·y 1** *n* fotocopia *f* **2** *v/t* (*pret & pp* **-ied**) fotocopiare

pho·to·gen·ic [fəʊtəʊˈdʒenɪk] *adj* fotogenico

pho·to·graph [ˈfəʊtəgrɑːf] **1** *n* fotografia *f* **2** *v/t* fotografare

pho·tog·ra·pher [fəˈtɒgrəfə(r)] fotografo *m*, -a *f*

pho·tog·ra·phy [fəˈtɒgrəfɪ] fotografia *f*

phrase [freɪz] **1** *n* frase *f* **2** *v/t* esprimere

'**phrase·book** vocabolarietto *m* di frasi utili

phys·i·cal [ˈfɪzɪkl] **1** *adj* fisico **2** *n* MED visita *f* medica

phys·i·cal 'hand·i·cap *adj* handicap *m inv* fisico

phys·i·cal·ly [ˈfɪzɪklɪ] *adv* fisicamente

phys·i·cal·ly 'hand·i·cap·ped *adj:* **be ~** essere portatore *m*, -trice *f* di handicap fisico

phy·si·cian [fɪˈzɪʃn] medico *m*

phys·i·cist [ˈfɪzɪsɪst] fisico *m*, -a *f*

phys·ics [ˈfɪzɪks] fisica *f*

phys·i·o·ther·a·pist [fɪzɪəʊˈθerəpɪst] fisioterapeuta *m/f*

phys·i·o·ther·a·py [fɪzɪəʊˈθerəpɪ] fisioterapia *f*

phy·sique [fɪˈziːk] fisico *m*

pi·a·nist [ˈpɪənɪst] pianista *m/f*

pi·an·o [pɪˈænəʊ] piano *m*

pick [pɪk] **1** *n:* **take your ~** scegli quello che vuoi **2** *v/t* (*choose*) scegliere; *flowers, fruit* raccogliere; **~ one's nose** mettersi le dita nel naso **3** *v/i:* **~ and choose** fare i difficili

♦ **pick at** *v/t:* **pick at one's food** man-

giucchiare poco

♦ **pick on** *v/t* treat *unfairly* prendersela con; (*select*) scegliere

♦ **pick out** *v/t* (*identify*) riconoscere

♦ **pick up 1** *v/t* prendere; *phone* sollevare; *baby* prendere in braccio; *from ground* raccogliere; (*collect*) andare/venire a prendere; *information* raccogliere; *in car* far salire; *man, woman* rimorchiare F; *language, skill* imparare; *habit, illness* prendere; (*buy*) trovare; *criminal* arrestare; **pick up the tab** F pagare (il conto) **2** *v/i* (*improve*) migliorare

pick·et [ˈpɪkɪt] **1** *n* of strikers picchetto *m* **2** *v/t* picchettare

'**pick·et line** cordone *m* degli scioperanti

pick·le [ˈpɪkl] *v/t* conservare sott'aceto

pick·les [ˈpɪklz] *npl* sottaceti *mpl*

'**pick·pock·et** borseggiatore *m*, -trice *f*

pick·y [ˈpɪkɪ] *adj* F difficile (da accontentare)

pic·nic [ˈpɪknɪk] **1** *n* picnic *m inv* **2** *v/i* (*pret & pp* **-ked**) fare un picnic

pic·ture [ˈpɪktʃə(r)] **1** *n* photo foto *f*; *painting* quadro *m*; *illustration* figura *f*; *film* film *m inv*; *put/keep s.o. in the ~* mettere/tenere al corrente qu **2** *v/t* immaginare

'**pic·ture book** libro *m* illustrato

pic·ture 'post·card cartolina *f* illustrata

pic·tures [ˈpɪktʃəz] *npl* cinema *m*

pic·tur·esque [pɪktʃəˈresk] *adj* pittoresco

pie [paɪ] *sweet* torta *f*; *savoury* pasticcio *m*

piece [piːs] pezzo *m*; **a ~ of pie/ bread** una fetta di torta/pane; **a ~ of advice** un consiglio; **go to ~s** crollare; **take to ~s** smontare

♦ **piece together** *v/t* broken *plate* rimettere insieme; *facts, evidence* ricostruire

piece·meal [ˈpiːsmiːl] *adv* poco alla volta

piece·work [ˈpiːswɜːk] *n* lavoro *m* a cottimo

pier [pɪə(r)] *at seaside* pontile *m*

pierce [pɪəs] *v/t (penetrate)* trapassare; *ears* farsi i buchi in

pierc·ing [ˈpɪəsɪŋ] *noise* lacerante; *eyes* penetrante; *wind* pungente

pig [pɪɡ] *also fig* maiale *m*

pi·geon [ˈpɪdʒɪn] piccione *m*

ˈpi·geon·hole **1** *n* casella *f* **2** *v/t person* etichettare; *proposal* archiviare

ˈpig·gy·bank [ˈpɪɡɪbæŋk] salvadanaio *m*

pig·head·ed [pɪɡˈhedɪd] *adj* testardo

ˈpig·skin pelle *f* di cinghiale; ˈpig·sty *also fig* porcile *m*; ˈpig·tail *plaited* treccina *f*

pile [paɪl] mucchio *m*; F **a ~ of work** un sacco di lavoro F

♦ pile up **1** *v/i of work, bills* accumularsi **2** *v/t* ammucchiare

piles [paɪlz] *nsg* MED emorroidi *fpl*

pile-up [ˈpaɪlʌp] MOT tamponamento *m* a catena

pil·fer·ing [ˈpɪlfərɪŋ] piccoli furti *mpl*

pil·grim [ˈpɪlɡrɪm] pellegrino *m*, -a *f*

pil·grim·age [ˈpɪlɡrɪmɪdʒ] pellegrinaggio *m*

pill [pɪl] pastiglia *f*; **the ~** la pillola; **be on the ~** prendere la pillola

pil·lar [ˈpɪlə(r)] colonna *f*

ˈpil·lar box buca *f* delle lettere (a colonnina)

pil·lion [ˈpɪljən] *of motor bike* sellino *m* posteriore

pil·low [ˈpɪləʊ] *n* guanciale *m*

ˈpil·low·case, ˈpil·low·slip federa *f*

pi·lot [ˈpaɪlət] **1** *n of aeroplane* pilota *m/f* **2** *v/t aeroplane* pilotare

ˈpi·lot plant stabilimento *m* pilota

ˈpi·lot scheme progetto *m* pilota

pimp [pɪmp] *n* ruffiano *m*

pim·ple [ˈpɪmpl] brufolo *m*

pin [pɪn] **1** *n for sewing* spillo *m*; *in bowling* birillo *m*; *(badge)* spilla *f*; ELEC spinotto *m* **2** *v/t (pret & pp -ned) (hold down)* immobilizzare; *(attach)* attaccare; *on lapel* appuntare

♦ pin down *v/t*: **pin s.o. down to a date** far fissare una data a qu

♦ pin up *v/t notice* appuntare

PIN [pɪn] *abbr (= **personal identification number**)* numero *m* di codice personale

pin·cers [ˈpɪnsəz] *npl tool* tenaglie *fpl*; *of crab* chele *fpl*

pinch [pɪntʃ] **1** *n* pizzico *m*; **at a ~** al massimo **2** *v/t* pizzicare **3** *v/i of shoes* stringere

pine¹ [paɪn] *n* pino *m*; **~ furniture** mobili *mpl* di pino

pine² [paɪn] *v/i*: **~ for** soffrire per la mancanza di

pine·ap·ple [ˈpaɪnæpl] ananas *m inv*

ping [pɪŋ] **1** *n* suono *m* metallico **2** *v/i* fare un suono metallico

ping-pong [ˈpɪŋpɒŋ] ping-pong *m inv*

pink [pɪŋk] *adj* rosa *inv*

pin·na·cle [ˈpɪnəkl] *fig* apice *m*

ˈpin·point *v/t* indicare con esattezza

ˈpins and ˈnee·dles *npl* formicolio *m*

ˈpin·stripe *adj* gessato

pint [paɪnt] pinta *f*

ˈpin-up *(girl)* pin-up *f inv*

pi·o·neer [paɪəˈnɪə(r)] **1** *n fig* pioniere *m*, -a *f* **2** *v/t* essere il/la pioniere di

pi·o·neer·ing [paɪəˈnɪərɪŋ] *adj work* pionieristico

pi·ous [ˈpaɪəs] *adj* pio

pip [pɪp] *n of fruit* seme *m*

pipe [paɪp] **1** *n for smoking* pipa *f*; *for water, gas, sewage* tubo *m* **2** *v/t* trasportare con condutture

♦ pipe down *v/i* F far silenzio

piped mu·sic [paɪptˈmjuːzɪk] musica *f* di sottofondo

pipe·line conduttura *f*; **in the ~** *fig* in arrivo

pip·ing hot [paɪpɪŋˈhɒt] *adj* caldissimo

pi·rate [ˈpaɪərət] *v/t software* piratare

Pis·ces [ˈpaɪsiːz] ASTR Pesci *m/f inv*

piss [pɪs] **1** *v/i* P *(urinate)* pisciare P **2** *n (urine)* piscio *m* P; **take the ~out of s.o.** P prendere qu per il culo P

♦ piss off *v/i* P sparire; **piss off!** levati dalle palle! P

pissed [pɪst] *adj* P *(drunk)* sbronzo F; *Am (annoyed)* seccato

pis·tol [ˈpɪstl] pistola *f*

pis·ton ['pɪstən] pistone *m*

pit [pɪt] *n* (*hole*) buca *f*; (*coal mine*) miniera *f*

pitch¹ [pɪtʃ] *n* MUS intonazione *f*

pitch² [pɪtʃ] *v/t* tent piantare; *ball* lanciare

'pitch black *adj* buio pesto

pitch·er ['pɪtʃə(r)] *container* brocca *f*

pit·e·ous ['pɪtɪəs] *adj* pietoso

pit·fall ['pɪtfɔːl] tranello *m*

pith [pɪθ] *of citrus fruit* parte *f* bianca della scorza

pit·i·ful ['pɪtɪful] *adj sight* pietoso; *excuse, attempt* penoso

pit·i·less ['pɪtɪləs] *adj* spietato

pits [pɪts] *npl in motor racing* box *m inv*

'pit stop *in motor racing* sosta *f* ai box

pit·tance ['pɪtns] miseria *f*

pit·y ['pɪtɪ] **1** *n* pietà *f inv*; *it's a ~ that* è un peccato che; *what a ~!* che peccato!; *take ~ on* avere pietà di **2** *v/t* (*pret & pp -ied*) *person* avere pietà di

piv·ot ['pɪvət] *v/i* ruotare

piz·za ['piːtsə] pizza *f*

plac·ard ['plækɑːd] cartello *m*

place [pleɪs] **1** *n* posto *m*; *flat, house* casa *f*; *I've lost my ~ in book* ho perso il segno; *at my / his ~* a casa mia / sua; *in ~ of* invece di; *feel out of ~* sentirsi fuori posto; *take ~* aver luogo; *in the first ~* (*firstly*) in primo luogo **2** *v/t* (*put*) piazzare; *I can't quite ~ you* non mi ricordo dove ci siamo conosciuti; *~ an order* fare un'ordinazione

'place mat tovaglietta *f* all'americana

plac·id ['plæsɪd] *adj* placido

pla·gia·rism ['pleɪdʒərɪzm] plagio *m*

pla·gia·rize ['pleɪdʒəraɪz] *v/t* plagiare

plague [pleɪg] **1** *n* peste *f* **2** *v/t* (*bother*) tormentare

plain¹ [pleɪn] *n* pianura *f*

plain² [pleɪn] **1** *adj* (*clear, obvious*) chiaro; *not fancy* semplice; *not pretty* scialbo; *not patterned* in tinta unita; (*blunt*) franco; *~ chocolate*

cioccolato *m* fondente **2** *adv* semplicemente; *it's ~ crazy* è semplicemente matto

'plain-clothes: in ~ in borghese

plain·ly ['pleɪnlɪ] *adv* (*clearly*) chiaramente; (*bluntly*) francamente; (*simply*) semplicemente

plain-'spo·ken *adj* franco

plain·tiff ['pleɪntɪf] LAW attore *m*, -trice *f*

plain·tive ['pleɪntɪv] *adj* lamentoso

plait [plæt] **1** *n in hair* treccia *f* **2** *v/t hair* intrecciare

plan [plæn] **1** *n* (*project, intention*) piano *m*; (*drawing*) progetto *m* **2** *v/t* (*pret & pp -ned*) (*prepare*) organizzare; (*design*) progettare; *~ to do, ~ on doing* avere in programma di **3** *v/i* (*pret & pp -ned*) pianificare

plane¹ [pleɪn] *n* (*aeroplane*) aereo *m*

plane² [pleɪn] *tool* pialla *f*

plan·et ['plænɪt] pianeta *m*

plank [plæŋk] *of wood* asse *f*; *fig: of policy* punto *m*

plan·ning ['plænɪŋ] pianificazione *f*; *at the ~ stage* allo stadio di progettazione

plant¹ [plɑːnt] **1** *n* pianta *f* **2** *v/t* piantare

plant² [plɑːnt] *n* (*factory*) stabilimento *m*; (*equipment*) impianto *m*

plan·ta·tion [plæn'teɪʃn] piantagione *f*

plaque [plæk] *on wall, teeth* placca *f*

plas·ter ['plɑːstə(r)] **1** *n on wall, ceiling* intonaco *m* **2** *v/t wall, ceiling* intonacare; *be ~ed with* essere ricoperto di

plas·ter cast ingessatura *f*

plas·tic ['plæstɪk] **1** *n* plastica *f*; F (*money*) carte *fpl* di credito **2** *adj made of ~* di plastica

plas·tic 'bag sacchetto *m* di plastica; **'plas·tic mon·ey** carte *fpl* di credito; **plas·tic 'sur·geon** chirurgo *m* plastico; **plas·tic 'sur·ge·ry** chirurgia *f* plastica

plate [pleɪt] *n for food* piatto *m*; *sheet of metal* lastra *f*

pla·teau ['plætəʊ] altopiano *m*

plat·form ['plætfɔːm] (*stage*) palco

m; of railway station binario *m; fig:
political* piattaforma *f*
plat·i·num ['plætɪnəm] **1** *n* platino *m*
2 *adj* di platino
plat·i·tude ['plætɪtjuːd] banalità *f inv*
pla·ton·ic [plə'tɒnɪk] *adj relationship*
platonico
pla·toon [plə'tuːn] *of soldiers* ploto-
ne *m*
plat·ter ['plætə(r)] *for meat, fish* vassoio *m*
plau·si·ble ['plɔːzəbl] *adj* plausibile
play [pleɪ] **1** *n in theatre, on TV* commedia *f; of children,* TECH, SP gioco *m*
2 *v/i of children,* SP giocare; *of
musician* suonare **3** *v/t* MUS suonare;
game giocare a; *opponent* giocare
contro; (*perform: Macbeth etc*) rappresentare; *particular role* interpretare; ~ *a joke on* fare uno scherzo a
♦ **play around** *v/i* F (*be unfaithful*):
his wife's been playing around
sua moglie lo ha tradito; *her
husband was playing around
with his secretary* suo marito aveva una relazione con la segretaria
♦ **play down** *v/t* minimizzare
♦ **play up** *v/i of machine* dare noie; *of
child* fare i capricci; *of tooth, bad
back etc* fare male
play·act ['pleɪækt] *v/i* (*pretend*) fare
la commedia
play·back ['pleɪbæk] playback *m inv*
play·boy ['pleɪbɔɪ] playboy *m inv*
play·er ['pleɪə(r)] SP giocatore *m*,
-trice *f; musician* musicista *m/f; actor*
attore *m*, -trice *f*
play·ful ['pleɪfʊl] *adj punch, mood*
scherzoso; *puppy* giocherellone
play·ground ['pleɪɡraʊnd] *in school*
cortile *m* per la ricreazione; *in park*
parco *m* giochi
'play·group asilo *m*
play·ing card ['pleɪɪŋkɑːd] carta *f* da
gioco
play·ing field ['pleɪɪŋfiːld] campo *m*
sportivo
play·mate ['pleɪmeɪt] compagno *m*,
-a *f* di gioco
play·wright ['pleɪraɪt] commediografo *m*, -a *f*

plc [piːel'siː] *abbr* (= **public limited
company**) società *f inv* a responsabilità limitata quotata in borsa
plea [pliː] **1** *n* appello *m*
plead **2** *v/i:* ~ *for* supplicare; ~ *guilty /
not guilty* dichiararsi colpevole /
innocente; *with* supplicare
pleas·ant ['pleznt] *adj* piacevole
please [pliːz] **1** *adv* per favore; *more
tea? – yes,* ~ ancora tè? – sì, grazie
; ~ *do* fai pure, prego **2** *v/t* far piacere
a; ~ *yourself* fai come ti pare
pleased [pliːzd] *adj* contento; ~ *to
meet you* piacere!
pleas·ing ['pliːzɪŋ] *adj* piacevole
pleas·ure ['pleʒə(r)] (*happiness, satisfaction*) contentezza *f;* (*as opposed
to work*) piacere *m;* (*delight*) gioia *f;
it's a* ~ (*you're welcome*) è un piacere; *with* ~ con vero piacere
pleat [pliːt] *n in skirt* piega *f*
pleat·ed skirt ['pliːtɪd] gonna *f* a pieghe
pledge [pledʒ] **1** *n* (*promise*) promessa *f* **2** *v/t* (*promise*) promettere
plen·ti·ful ['plentɪfʊl] *adj* abbondante
plen·ty ['plentɪ] (*abundance*) abbondanza *f;* ~ *of* molto; *that's* ~ basta
così; *there's* ~ *for everyone* ce n'è
per tutti
pli·a·ble *adj* flessibile
pli·ers *npl* pinze *fpl; a pair of* ~ un
paio di pinze
plight [plaɪt] situazione *f* critica
plod [plɒd] *v/i* (*pret & pp* **-ded**) *walk*
trascinarsi
♦ **plod on** *v/i with a job* sgobbare
plod·der ['plɒdə(r)] *at work, school*
sgobbone *m*, -a *f*
plot¹ [plɒt] *n land* appezzamento *m*
plot² [plɒt] **1** *n* (*conspiracy*) complotto *m; of novel* trama *f* **2** *v/t & v/i* (*pret
& pp* **-ted**) complottare
plot·ter ['plɒtə(r)] cospiratore *m*,
-trice *f;* COMPUT plotter *m inv*
plough, plow *Am* [plaʊ] **1** *n* aratro *m*
2 *v/t & v/i* arare
♦ **plough back** *v/t profits* reinvestire
pluck [plʌk] *v/t eyebrows* pinzare;
chicken spennare

P

♦ **pluck up** v/t: **pluck up courage** trovare il coraggio

plug [plʌg] **1** n for sink, bath tappo m; electrical spina f; (spark ~) candela f; for new book etc pubblicità f inv **2** v/t (pret & pp **-ged**) tappare; new book etc fare pubblicità a

♦ **plug away** v/i F sgobbare

♦ **plug in** v/t attaccare (alla presa)

plum [plʌm] **1** n susina f **2** adj: ~ **job** F un lavoro favoloso

plum·age ['pluːmɪdʒ] piumaggio m

plumb [plʌm] adj a piombo

♦ **plumb in** v/t washing machine collegare all'impianto idraulico

plumb·er ['plʌmə(r)] idraulico m

plumb·ing ['plʌmɪŋ] pipes impianto m idraulico

plume [pluːm] n piuma f

plum·met ['plʌmɪt] v/i of aeroplane precipitare; of share prices crollare

plump [plʌmp] adj person, chicken in carne; hands, feet, face paffuto

♦ **plump for** v/t scegliere

plunge [plʌndʒ] **1** n caduta f; in prices crollo m; **take the ~** fare il gran passo **2** v/i precipitare; of prices crollare **3** v/t knife conficcare; tomatoes immergere; **the city was ~d into darkness** la città fu immersa nel buio; **the news ~d him into despair** la notizia lo gettò nella disperazione

plung·ing ['plʌndʒɪŋ] adj neckline profondo

plu·per·fect ['pluːpɜːfɪkt] n GRAM piuccheperfetto m

plu·ral ['plʊərəl] **1** n plurale m **2** adj plurale

plus [plʌs] **1** prep più **2** adj: **£500 ~** oltre 500 sterline **3** n symbol più m inv; (advantage) vantaggio m **4** conj (moreover, in addition) per di più

plush [plʌʃ] adj di lusso

'plus sign segno m più

ply·wood ['plaɪwʊd] compensato m

PM [piː'em] abbr (= **Prime Minister**) primo ministro m

p.m. [piː'em] abbr (= **post meridiem**): **at 2 ~** alle 2 del pomeriggio; **at 10.30 ~** alle 10.30 di sera

pneu·mat·ic [njuː'mætɪk] adj pneumatico

pneu·mat·ic 'drill martello m pneumatico

pneu·mo·ni·a [njuː'məʊnɪə] polmonite f

poach[1] [pəʊtʃ] v/t cook bollire; egg fare in camicia

poach[2] [pəʊtʃ] **1** v/i for game cacciare di frodo; for fish pescare di frodo **2** v/t cacciare/pescare di frodo

poached egg [pəʊtʃt'eg] uovo m in camicia

poach·er ['pəʊtʃə(r)] of salmon, game cacciatore/pescatore m di frodo

P.O. Box [piː'əʊbɒks] casella f postale

pock·et ['pɒkɪt] **1** n tasca f; **line one's ~s** arricchirsi; **be out of ~** rimetterci **2** adj (miniature) in miniatura **3** v/t intascare

pock·et 'cal·cu·la·tor calcolatrice f tascabile

'pocket book Am (wallet) portafoglio m; (handbag) borsetta f

po·di·um ['pəʊdɪəm] podio m

po·em ['pəʊɪm] poesia f

po·et ['pəʊɪt] poeta m, -essa f

po·et·ic [pəʊ'etɪk] adj person, description poetico

po·et·ic 'jus·tice giustizia f divina

po·et·ry ['pəʊɪtrɪ] poesia f

poign·ant ['pɔɪnjənt] adj commovente

point [pɔɪnt] **1** n of pencil, knife punta f; in competition, exam punto m; (purpose) senso m; (moment) punto m; in argument, discussion punto m; in decimals virgola f; **that's beside the ~** non c'entra; **be on the ~ of** stare giusto per; **get to the ~** venire al dunque; **that's a ~** questo, in effetti, è vero; **the ~ is ...** il fatto è che ...; **you've got a ~ there** su questo, hai ragione; **I take your ~** su questo, ti do ragione; **there's no ~ in waiting/trying** non ha senso aspettare/tentare **2** v/i indicare **3** v/t gun puntare (**at** contro)

♦ **point at** v/t with finger indicare col dito

◆ **point out** v/t sights, advantages indicare

◆ **point to** v/t with finger additare; (fig: indicate) far presupporre

'point-blank 1 adj refusal, denial categorico; **at ~ range** a bruciapelo **2** adv refuse, deny categoricamente

point·ed ['pɔɪntɪd] adj remark, question significativo

point·er ['pɔɪntə(r)] for teacher bacchetta f; (hint) consiglio m; (sign, indication) indizio m

point·less ['pɔɪntləs] adj inutile; **it's ~ trying** è inutile tentare

'point of sale punto m vendita

'point of view punto m di vista

poise [pɔɪz] padronanza f di sé

poised [pɔɪzd] adj person posato

poi·son ['pɔɪzn] **1** n veleno m **2** v/t avvelenare

poi·son·ous ['pɔɪznəs] adj velenoso

poke [pəʊk] **1** n colpetto m **2** v/t (prod) dare un colpetto a; (stick) ficcare; **~ fun at** prendere in giro; **~ one's nose into** ficcare il naso in

◆ **poke around** v/i F curiosare

pok·er ['pəʊkə(r)] card game poker m inv

pok·y ['pəʊkɪ] adj F (cramped) angusto

Po·land ['pəʊlənd] Polonia f

po·lar ['pəʊlə(r)] adj polare

po·lar bear orso m polare

po·lar·ize ['pəʊləraɪz] v/t polarizzare

Pole [pəʊl] polacco m, -a f

pole[1] [pəʊl] of wood, metal paletto m

pole[2] [pəʊl] of earth polo m

'pole star stella f polare; **'pole·vault** salto m con l'asta; **'pole-vault·er** saltatore m, -trice f con l'asta

po·lice [pə'li:s] n polizia f

po·lice car auto f della polizia; **po·lice·man** poliziotto m; **po·lice state** stato m di polizia; **po·lice sta·tion** commissariato m di polizia; **po·lice·wo·man** donna f poliziotto

pol·i·cy[1] ['pɒlɪsɪ] politica f

pol·i·cy[2] ['pɒlɪsɪ] (insurance ~) polizza f

po·li·o ['pəʊlɪəʊ] polio f

Pol·ish ['pəʊlɪʃ] **1** adj polacco **2** n polacco m

pol·ish ['pɒlɪʃ] **1** n product lucido m; (nail ~) smalto m **2** v/t lucidare; speech rifinire

◆ **polish off** v/t food spazzolare F

◆ **polish up** v/t skill perfezionare

pol·ished ['pɒlɪʃt] adj performance impeccabile

po·lite [pə'laɪt] adj cortese

po·lite·ly [pə'laɪtlɪ] adv cortesemente

po·lite·ness [pə'laɪtnɪs] cortesia f

po·lit·i·cal [pə'lɪtɪkl] adj politico

po·lit·i·cal·ly cor·rect [pə'lɪtɪklɪ kə'rekt] adj politicamente corretto

po·li·ti·cian [pɒlɪ'tɪʃn] uomo m politico, donna f politica

pol·i·tics ['pɒlətɪks] politica f; **what are his ~?** di che tendenze politiche è?

poll [pəʊl] **1** n (survey) sondaggio m; **the ~s** (election) le elezioni fpl; **go to the ~s** (vote) andare alle urne **2** v/t people fare un sondaggio tra; votes guadagnare

pol·len ['pɒlən] polline m

'pol·len count concentrazione f di polline

'poll·ing booth ['pəʊlɪŋ] cabina f elettorale; **'poll·ing day** giorno m delle elezioni; **'poll·ing sta·tion** seggio m elettorale

poll·ster ['pɒlstə(r)] esperto m, -a f di sondaggi

pol·lu·tant [pə'lu:tənt] sostanza f inquinante

pol·lute [pə'lu:t] v/t inquinare

pol·lu·tion [pə'lu:ʃn] inquinamento m

po·lo ['pəʊləʊ] SP polo m

'po·lo neck adj sweater a dolcevita

'po·lo shirt polo f inv

pol·y·es·ter [pɒlɪ'estə(r)] poliestere m

pol·y·sty·rene [pɒlɪ'staɪri:n] polistirolo m

pol·y·thene ['pɒlɪθi:n] polietilene m

pol·y·thene 'bag sacchetto m di plastica

P

pol·y·un·sat·u·rat·ed [pɒlɪʌn'sætjə-reɪtɪd] *adj* polinsaturo

pom·pous ['pɒmpəs] *adj* pomposo

pond [pɒnd] stagno *m*

pon·der ['pɒndə(r)] *v/i* riflettere

pon·tiff ['pɒntɪf] pontefice *m*

pon·y ['pəʊnɪ] pony *m inv*

'pon·y·tail coda *f* (di cavallo)

poo·dle ['puːdl] barboncino *m*

pool[1] [puːl] (*swimming ~*) piscina *f*; *of water*, *blood* pozza *f*

pool[2] [puːl] *game* biliardo *m*

pool[3] [puːl] **1** *n common fund* cassa *f* comune **2** *v/t resources* mettere insieme

'pool hall sala *f* da biliardo

pools [puːlz] *npl* totocalcio *m*; **do the ~** giocare al totocalcio

'pool table tavolo *m* da biliardo

poop·ed [puːpt] *adj* F stanco morto

poor [pʊə(r)] **1** *adj not wealthy, unfortunate* povero; *not good* misero; *be in ~ health* essere in cattiva salute; *~ old Tony!* povero Tony! **2** *n: the ~* i poveri

poor·ly ['pʊəlɪ] **1** *adv* male **2** *adj* (*unwell*) indisposto

pop[1] [pɒp] **1** *n noise* schiocco *m* **2** *v/i* (*pret & pp -ped*) *of balloon etc* scoppiare **3** *v/t* (*pret & pp -ped*) *cork* stappare; *balloon* far scoppiare

pop[2] [pɒp] **1** *n* MUS pop *m inv* **2** *adj* pop *inv*

pop[3] [pɒp] *v/t* (*pret & pp -ped*) F (*put*) ficcare F; *~ one's head around the door* sbucare con la testa dalla porta

♦ **pop in** *v/i* F (*make a brief visit*) entrare un attimo

♦ **pop out** *v/i* F (*go out for a short time*) fare un salto fuori

♦ **pop up** *v/i* F (*appear suddenly*) saltare fuori

'pop con·cert concerto *m* pop

pop·corn ['pɒpkɔːn] popcorn *m inv*

pope [pəʊp] papa *m*

'pop group gruppo *m* pop

pop·py ['pɒpɪ] papavero *m*

'pop song canzone *f* pop

pop·u·lar ['pɒpjʊlə(r)] *adj* popolare; *belief, support* diffuso

pop·u·lar·i·ty [pɒpjʊ'lærətɪ] popolarità *f inv*

pop·u·late ['pɒpjʊleɪt] *v/t* popolare

pop·u·la·tion [pɒpjʊ'leɪʃn] popolazione *f*

porce·lain ['pɔːsəlɪn] **1** *n* porcellana *f* **2** *adj* di porcellana

porch [pɔːtʃ] porticato *m*; *Am* veranda *f*

por·cu·pine ['pɔːkjʊpaɪn] porcospino *m*

pore [pɔː(r)] *of skin* poro *m*

♦ **pore over** *v/t* studiare attentamente

pork [pɔːk] maiale *m*

porn [pɔːn] *n* F porno *m* F

porn(o) [pɔːn, 'pɔːnəʊ] *adj* F porno *inv* F

por·no·graph·ic [pɔːnə'græfɪk] *adj* pornografico

porn·og·ra·phy [pɔː'nɒgrəfɪ] pornografia *f*

po·rous ['pɔːrəs] *adj* poroso

port[1] [pɔːt] *n* (*harbour, drink*) porto *m*

port[2] [pɔːt] *adj* (*left-hand*) babordo; *on the ~ side* a babordo

por·ta·ble ['pɔːtəbl] **1** *adj* portatile **2** *n* portatile *m*

por·ter ['pɔːtə(r)] portiere *m*

port·hole ['pɔːthəʊl] NAUT oblò *m inv*

por·tion ['pɔːʃn] *n* parte *f*; *of food* porzione *f*

por·trait ['pɔːtreɪt] **1** *n* ritratto *m* **2** *adv print* verticale

por·tray [pɔː'treɪ] *v/t of artist, photographer* ritrarre; *of actor* interpretare; *of author* descrivere

por·tray·al [pɔː'treɪəl] *by actor* rappresentazione *f*; *by author* descrizione *f*

Por·tu·gal ['pɔːtjʊgl] Portogallo *m*

Por·tu·guese [pɔːtjʊ'giːz] **1** *adj* portoghese **2** *n person* portoghese *m/f*; *language* portoghese *m*

pose [pəʊz] **1** *n* (*pretence*) posa *f* **2** *v/i for artist, photographer* posare; *~ as* farsi passare per **3** *v/t: ~ a problem / a threat* creare un problema / una minaccia

posh [pɒʃ] *adj* F elegante; *pej* snob

po·si·tion [pəˈzɪʃn] **1** *n* posizione *f*; *what would you do in my ~?* cosa faresti al mio posto? **2** *v/t* sistemare, piazzare

pos·i·tive [ˈpɒzətɪv] *adj* positivo; *be ~ (sure)* essere certo

pos·i·tive·ly [ˈpɒzətɪvlɪ] *adv* (*downright*) decisamente; (*definitely*) assolutamente; *think* in modo positivo

pos·sess [pəˈzes] *v/t* possedere

pos·ses·sion [pəˈzeʃn] (*ownership*) possesso *m*; *thing owned* bene *m*; *~s* averi *mpl*

pos·ses·sive [pəˈzesɪv] *adj also* GRAM possessivo

pos·si·bil·i·ty [pɒsəˈbɪlətɪ] possibilità *f inv*

pos·si·ble [ˈpɒsəbl] *adj* possibile; *the shortest / quickest ~ ...* la ... più breve / veloce possibile; *the best ~ ...* la miglior ... possibile

pos·si·bly [ˈpɒsəblɪ] *adv* (*perhaps*) forse; *that can't ~ be right* non è possibile che sia giusto; *could you ~ tell me ...?* potrebbe per caso dirmi ...?

post¹ [pəʊst] **1** *n of wood, metal* palo *m* **2** *v/t notice* affiggere; *profits* annunciare; *keep s.o. ~ed* tenere informato qu

post² [pəʊst] **1** *n* (*place of duty*) posto *m* **2** *v/t soldier, employee* assegnare; *guards* piazzare

post³ [pəʊst] **1** *n* (*mail*) posta *f*; *by ~* per posta **2** *v/t letter* spedire (per posta); (*put in the mail*) imbucare

post·age [ˈpəʊstɪdʒ] affrancatura *f*

'**post·age stamp** *fml* francobollo *m*

post·al [ˈpəʊstl] *adj* postale

'**post·al or·der** vaglia *m* postale

'**post·box** buca *f* delle lettere; '**post·card** cartolina *f*; '**post·code** codice *m* di avviamento postale; '**post·date** *v/t* postdatare

post·er [ˈpəʊstə(r)] *n* manifesto *m*; *for decoration* poster *m inv*

pos·te·ri·or [pɒˈstɪərɪə(r)] *n* (*hum: buttocks*) posteriore *m*

pos·ter·i·ty [pɒˈsterətɪ] posteri *mpl*

post·grad·u·ate [ˈpəʊstɡrædjʊət]

1 *n studente m / studentessa f di un corso post-universitario* **2** *adj* post-universitario

post·hu·mous [ˈpɒstjʊməs] *adj* postumo

post·hu·mous·ly [ˈpɒstjʊməslɪ] *adv* dopo la sua morte; *it was published ~* è stato pubblicato postumo

post·ing [ˈpəʊstɪŋ] (*assignment*) incarico *m*

post·man [ˈpəʊstmən] postino *m*

post·mark [ˈpəʊstmɑːk] timbro *m* postale

post·mor·tem [pəʊstˈmɔːtəm] autopsia *f*

'**post of·fice** ufficio *m* postale

post·pone [pəʊstˈpəʊn] *v/t* rinviare

post·pone·ment [pəʊstˈpəʊnmənt] rinvio *m*

pos·ture [ˈpɒstʃə(r)] posizione *f*

'**post·war** *adj* del dopoguerra

pot¹ [pɒt] *n for cooking* pentola *f*; *for coffee* caffettiera *f*; *for tea* teiera *f*; *for plant* vaso *m*

pot² [pɒt] F (*marijuana*) erba *f* F

po·ta·to [pəˈteɪtəʊ] patata *f*

po·ta·to chips *Am*, **po·ta·to crisps** *Br npl* patatine *fpl*

'**pot·bel·ly** [ˈpɒtbelɪ] pancetta F

po·tent [ˈpəʊtənt] *adj* potente

po·ten·tial [pəˈtenʃl] **1** *adj* potenziale **2** *n* potenziale *m*

po·ten·tial·ly [pəˈtenʃəlɪ] *adv* potenzialmente

pot·hole [ˈpɒthəʊl] *n in road* buca *f*

pot·ter [ˈpɒtə(r)] *n* vasaio *m*, -a *f*

pot·ter·y [ˈpɒtərɪ] *n activity* ceramica *f*; *items* vasellame *m*; *place* laboratorio *m* di ceramica

pot·ty [ˈpɒtɪ] *n for baby* vasino *m*

pouch [paʊtʃ] (*bag*) borsa *f*

poul·try [ˈpəʊltrɪ] *birds* volatili *mpl*; *meat* pollame *m*

pounce [paʊns] *v/i of animal* balzare; *fig* piombare

pound¹ [paʊnd] *n weight* libbra *f*; FIN sterlina *f*

pound² [paʊnd] *for strays* canile *m* municipale; *for cars* deposito *m* auto

pound³ [paʊnd] *v/i of heart* battere

P

forte; **~ on** (*hammer on*) picchiare su

pound 'ster·ling sterlina *f*

pour [pɔː(r)] **1** *v/t liquid* versare **2** *v/i*: **it's ~ing (with rain)** sta diluviando

♦ **pour out** *v/t liquid* versare; *troubles* sfogarsi raccontando

pout [paʊt] *v/i* fare il broncio

pov·er·ty ['pɒvətɪ] povertà *f inv*

pov·er·ty-strick·en ['pɒvətɪstrɪkn] *adj* poverissimo

pow·der ['paʊdə(r)] **1** *n* polvere *f*; *for face* cipria *f* **2** *v/t*: **~ one's face** mettersi la cipria

'pow·der room F toilette *f inv* per signore

pow·er ['paʊə(r)] **1** *n* (*strength*) forza *f*; *of engine* potenza *f*; (*authority*) potere *m*; (*energy*) energia *f*; (*electricity*) elettricità *f inv*; **in ~** POL al potere; **fall from ~** POL perdere il potere **2** *v/t*: **~ed by atomic energy** a propulsione atomica

'pow·er-as·sist·ed steer·ing servosterzo *m*; **'pow·er cut** interruzione *f* di corrente; **'pow·er fail·ure** guasto *m* alla linea elettrica

pow·er·ful ['paʊəfʊl] *adj* potente

pow·er·less ['paʊəlɪs] *adj* impotente; **be ~ to ...** non poter far niente per ...

'pow·er line linea *f* elettrica; **'pow·er sta·tion** centrale *f* elettrica; **'pow·er steer·ing** servosterzo *m*; **'pow·er u·nit** alimentatore *m*

PR [piːˈɑː(r)] *abbr* (= **public relations**) relazioni *fpl* pubbliche

prac·ti·cal ['præktɪkl] *adj* pratico

prac·ti·cal 'joke scherzo *m*

prac·ti·cal·ly ['præktɪklɪ] *adv behave, think* in modo pratico; (*almost*) praticamente

prac·tice ['præktɪs] **1** *n* pratica *f*; (*training*) esercizio *m*; (*rehearsal*) prove *fpl*; (*custom*) consuetudine *f*; **in ~** (*in reality*) in pratica; **be out of ~** essere fuori allenamento **2** *v/t & v/i Am →* **practise**

prac·tise ['præktɪs] **1** *v/t* esercitarsi in; *law, medicine* esercitare **2** *v/i* esercitarsi

prag·mat·ic [præg'mætɪk] *adj* pragmatico

prag·ma·tism ['prægmətɪzm] pragmatismo *m*

prai·rie ['preərɪ] prateria *f*

praise [preɪz] **1** *n* lode *f* **2** *v/t* lodare

praise·wor·thy ['preɪzwɜːðɪ] *adj* lodevole

pram [præm] carrozzina *f*

prank [præŋk] *n* birichinata *f*

prat·tle ['prætl] *v/i* cianciare

prawn [prɔːn] gamberetto *m*

pray [preɪ] *v/i* pregare

prayer [preə(r)] preghiera *f*

preach [priːtʃ] **1** *v/i* predicare **2** *v/t sermon* predicare

preach·er ['priːtʃə(r)] predicatore *m*, -trice *f*

pre·am·ble [priːˈæmbl] preambolo *m*

pre·car·i·ous [prɪˈkeərɪəs] *adj* precario

pre·car·i·ous·ly [prɪˈkeərɪəslɪ] *adv* precariamente

pre·cau·tion [prɪˈkɔːʃn] precauzione *f*

pre·cau·tion·a·ry [prɪˈkɔːʃnrɪ] *adj measure* di precauzione

pre·cede [prɪˈsiːd] *v/t* precedere

pre·ce·dence ['presɪdəns] precedenza *f*; **take ~ over ...** avere la precedenza su ...

pre·ce·dent ['presɪdənt] *n* precedente *m*

pre·ce·ding [prɪˈsiːdɪŋ] *adj* precedente

pre·cinct ['priːsɪŋkt] (*Am: district*) distretto *m*

pre·cious ['preʃəs] *adj* prezioso

pre·cip·i·tate [prɪˈsɪpɪteɪt] *v/t crisis* accelerare

pre·cip·i·ta·tion [prɪsɪpɪˈteɪʃn] *fml* precipitazione *f*

pré·cis ['preɪsiː] *n* riassunto *m*

pre·cise [prɪˈsaɪs] *adj* preciso

pre·cise·ly [prɪˈsaɪslɪ] *adv* precisamente

pre·ci·sion [prɪˈsɪʒn] precisione *f*

pre·co·cious [prɪˈkəʊʃəs] *adj child* precoce

pre·con·ceived [priːkənˈsiːvd] *adj*

idea preconcetto

pre·con·di·tion [priːkənˈdɪʃn] condizione *f* indispensabile

pred·a·tor [ˈpredətə(r)] *animal* predatore *m*, -trice *f*

pred·a·to·ry [ˈpredətrɪ] *adj* rapace

pre·de·ces·sor [ˈpriːdɪsesə(r)] predecessore *m*

pre·des·ti·na·tion [priːdestɪˈneɪʃn] predestinazione *f*

pre·des·tined [priːˈdestɪnd] *adj*: **be ~ to** essere predestinato a

pre·dic·a·ment [prɪˈdɪkəmənt] situazione *f* difficile

pre·dict [prɪˈdɪkt] *v/t* predire

pre·dict·a·ble [prɪˈdɪktəbl] *adj* prevedibile

pre·dic·tion [prɪˈdɪkʃn] predizione *f*

pre·dom·i·nant [prɪˈdɒmɪnənt] *adj* predominante

pre·dom·i·nant·ly [prɪˈdɒmɪnəntlɪ] *adv* prevalentemente

pre·dom·i·nate [prɪˈdɒmɪneɪt] *v/i* predominare

preen [priːn] *v/t*: **~ o.s.** *fig* farsi bello

pre·fab·ri·cat·ed [priːˈfæbrɪkeɪtɪd] *adj* prefabbricato

pref·ace [ˈprefɪs] *n* prefazione *f*

pre·fect [ˈpriːfekt] EDU *studente m / studentessa f* dell'ultimo anno di liceo con responsabilità disciplinari

pre·fer [prɪˈfɜː(r)] *v/t* (*pret & pp -red*) preferire; **~ X to Y** preferire X a Y; **~ to do** preferire fare

pref·e·ra·ble [ˈprefərəbl] *adj* preferibile

pref·e·ra·bly [ˈprefərəblɪ] *adv* preferibilmente

pref·e·rence [ˈprefərəns] preferenza *f*; **give ~ to** dare *o* accordare la preferenza a

pref·er·en·tial [prefəˈrenʃl] *adj* preferenziale

pre·fix [ˈpriːfɪks] prefisso *m*

preg·nan·cy [ˈpregnənsɪ] gravidanza *f*

preg·nant [ˈpregnənt] *adj* incinta; **get ~** restare incinta

pre·heat [ˈpriːhiːt] *v/t oven* far riscaldare

pre·his·tor·ic [priːhɪsˈtɒrɪk] *adj* preistorico

pre·judge [priːˈdʒʌdʒ] *v/t* giudicare a priori

prej·u·dice [ˈpredʒʊdɪs] **1** *n* pregiudizio *m* **2** *v/t person* influenzare; *chances* pregiudicare

prej·u·diced [ˈpredʒʊdɪst] *adj* prevenuto

prej·u·di·cial [predʒʊˈdɪʃl] *adj*: **be ~ to** essere pregiudizievole a

pre·lim·i·na·ry [prɪˈlɪmɪnərɪ] *adj* preliminare

prel·ude [ˈpreljuːd] preludio *m*

pre·mar·i·tal [priːˈmærɪtl] *adj* prematrimoniale

pre·ma·ture [ˈpremətjʊə(r)] *adj* prematuro

pre·med·i·tat·ed [priːˈmedɪteɪtɪd] *adj* premeditato

prem·i·er [ˈpremɪə(r)] *n* (*Prime Minister*) premier *m inv*

prem·i·ère [ˈpremɪeə(r)] *n* premiere *f inv*, prima *f*

prem·is·es [ˈpremɪsɪz] *npl* locali *mpl*

pre·mi·um [ˈpriːmɪəm] *n in insurance* premio *m*

pre·mo·ni·tion [premə'nɪʃn] premonizione *f*

pre·oc·cu·pied [priːˈɒkjʊpaɪd] *adj* preoccupato

pre·paid [ˈpriːpeɪd] *adj* prepagato

prep·a·ra·tion [prepəˈreɪʃn] preparazione *f*; **in ~ for** in vista di; **~s** preparativi *mpl*

pre·pare [prɪˈpeə(r)] **1** *v/t* preparare; **be ~d to do sth** (*willing*) essere preparato a fare qc; **be ~d for sth** (*be expecting*) essere preparato per qc **2** *v/i* prepararsi

prep·o·si·tion [prepə'zɪʃn] preposizione *f*

pre·pos·sess·ing [priːpə'zesɪŋ] *adj* attraente

pre·pos·ter·ous [prɪˈpɒstərəs] *adj* ridicolo

prep school [ˈprepskuːl] *scuola f privata di preparazione alla scuola superiore*

pre·req·ui·site [priːˈrekwɪzɪt] condizione *f* indispensabile

P

pre·rog·a·tive [prɪˈrɒgətɪv] prerogativa f

pre·scribe [prɪˈskraɪb] v/t of doctor prescrivere

pre·scrip·tion [prɪˈskrɪpʃn] MED ricetta f medica

pres·ence [ˈprezns] presenza f; **in the ~ of** in presenza di

pres·ence of ˈmind presenza f di spirito

pres·ent¹ [ˈpreznt] **1** adj (current) attuale; **be ~** essere presente **2** n: **the ~** also GRAM il presente; **at ~** al momento

pres·ent² [ˈpreznt] n (gift) regalo m

pre·sent³ [prɪˈzent] v/t award consegnare; bouquet offrire; programme presentare; **~ s.o. with sth, ~ sth to s.o.** offrire qc a qu

pre·sen·ta·tion [prezn'teɪʃn] presentazione f

pres·ent-day [preznt'deɪ] adj di oggi

pre·sent·er [prɪˈzentə(r)] presentatore m, -trice f

pres·ent·ly [ˈprezntlɪ] adv (at the moment) attualmente; (soon) tra breve

ˈpres·ent tense presente m

pres·er·va·tion [prezə'veɪʃn] of food conservazione f; of standards, peace etc mantenimento m

pre·ser·va·tive [prɪˈzɜːvətɪv] n for wood; in food conservante m

pre·serve [prɪˈzɜːv] **1** n (domain) dominio m **2** v/t standards, peace etc mantenere; wood etc proteggere; food conservare

pre·serves [prɪˈzɜːvz] npl conserve fpl

pre·side [prɪˈzaɪd] v/i at meeting presiedere; **~ over** meeting presiedere a

pres·i·den·cy [ˈprezɪdənsɪ] presidenza f

pres·i·dent [ˈprezɪdnt] presidente m

pres·i·den·tial [prezɪ'denʃl] adj presidenziale

press [pres] **1** n: **the ~** la stampa **2** v/t button premere; (urge) far pressione su; (squeeze) stringere; clothes stirare; grapes, olives spremere **3** v/i: **~ for** fare pressioni per ottenere

ˈpress a·gen·cy agenzia f di stampa

ˈpress con·fer·ence conferenza f stampa

press·ing [ˈpresɪŋ] adj urgente

press-stud [ˈpresstʌd] (bottone m) automatico

press-up [ˈpresʌp] flessione f sulle braccia

pres·sure [ˈpreʃə(r)] **1** n pressione f; **be under ~ (to do)** essere sotto pressione (per fare) **2** v/t fare delle pressioni su

ˈpres·sure cook·er pentola f a pressione

ˈpres·sur·ize [ˈpreʃəraɪz] v/t person fare delle pressioni su

pres·tige [preˈstiːʒ] prestigio m

pres·ti·gious [preˈstɪdʒəs] adj prestigioso

pre·sum·a·ble [prɪˈzjuːməbl] adj presumibile

pre·su·ma·bly [prɪˈzjuːməblɪ] adv presumibilmente

pre·sume [prɪˈzjuːm] v/i presumere; **~ to do** fml permettersi di fare

pre·sump·tion [prɪˈzʌmpʃn] of innocence, guilt presunzione f

pre·sump·tu·ous [prɪˈzʌmptjʊəs] adj impertinente

pre·sup·pose [priːsə'pəʊs] v/t presupporre

pre-tax [ˈpriːtæks] adj al lordo d'imposta

pre·tence [prɪˈtens] finta f

pre·tend [prɪˈtend] **1** v/t fingere **2** v/i fare finta

pre·tense Am → pretence

pre·ten·tious [prɪˈtenʃəs] adj pretenzioso

pre·text [ˈpriːtekst] pretesto m

pret·ty [ˈprɪtɪ] **1** adj carino **2** adv (quite) piuttosto

pre·vail [prɪˈveɪl] v/i (triumph) prevalere

pre·vail·ing [prɪˈveɪlɪŋ] adj prevalente

pre·var·i·cate [prɪˈværɪkeɪt] v/i tergiversare

pre·vent [prɪˈvent] v/t prevenire; **~ s.o. (from) doing sth** impedire a qu di fare qc

pre·ven·tion [prɪ'venʃn] prevenzione f

pre·ven·tive [prɪ'ventɪv] adj preventivo

pre·view ['priːvjuː] n of film, exhibition anteprima f

pre·vi·ous ['priːvɪəs] adj precedente; ~ **to** prima di

pre·vi·ous·ly ['priːvɪəslɪ] adv precedentemente

pre-war ['priːwɔː(r)] adj dell'anteguerra

prey [preɪ] n preda f
♦ **prey on** v/t far preda di; fig: of conman etc approfittarsi di; **prey on s.o.'s mind** preoccupare qu

price [praɪs] 1 n prezzo m 2 v/t COM fissare il prezzo di

price·less ['praɪslɪs] adj (valuable) di valore inestimabile

'**price tag** cartellino m del prezzo

'**price war** guerra f dei prezzi

price·y ['praɪsɪ] adj F caro

prick[1] [prɪk] 1 n pain puntura f 2 v/t (jab) pungere

prick[2] [prɪk] n V (penis) cazzo m V; person testa f di cazzo V
♦ **prick up** v/t: **prick up one's ears** also fig drizzare le orecchie

prick·le ['prɪkl] on plant spina f

prick·ly ['prɪklɪ] adj plant spinoso; beard ispido; (irritable) permaloso

pride [praɪd] 1 n in person, achievement orgoglio m; (self-respect) amor m proprio 2 v/t: ~ **o.s. on** vantarsi di

priest [priːst] n prete m

pri·ma·ri·ly [praɪ'meərɪlɪ] adv principalmente

pri·ma·ry ['praɪmərɪ] adj principale

'**pri·ma·ry school** scuola f elementare

prime [praɪm] 1 n: **be in one's** ~ essere nel fiore degli anni 2 adj example, reason principale; (very good) ottimo; **of** ~ **importance** della massima importanza

prime 'min·is·ter primo ministro m

'**prime time TV** TV programmi mpl di prima serata

prim·i·tive ['prɪmɪtɪv] adj also fig primitivo

prim·rose ['prɪmrəʊz] primula f

prince [prɪns] principe m

prin·cess [prɪn'ses] principessa f

prin·ci·pal ['prɪnsəpl] 1 adj principale 2 n of school preside m/f

prin·ci·pal·i·ty [prɪnsɪ'pælətɪ] principato m

prin·ci·pal·ly ['prɪnsəplɪ] adv principalmente

prin·ci·ple ['prɪnsəpl] principio m; **on** ~ per principio; **in** ~ in linea di principio

print [prɪnt] 1 n in book, newspaper etc caratteri mpl; photograph stampa f; mark impronta f; **out of** ~ esaurito 2 v/t stampare; (use block capitals) scrivere in stampatello
♦ **print out** v/t stampare

print·ed mat·ter ['prɪntɪdmætə(r)] stampe fpl

print·er ['prɪntə(r)] person tipografo m; machine stampante f

print·ing press ['prɪntɪŋpres] pressa f tipografica

'**print·out** stampato m

pri·or ['praɪə(r)] 1 adj precedente 2 prep: ~ **to** prima di

pri·or·i·tize [praɪ'ɒrətaɪz] v/t (put in order of priority) classificare in ordine d'importanza; (give priority to) dare precedenza a

pri·or·i·ty [praɪ'ɒrətɪ] priorità f inv; **have** ~ avere la precedenza

pris·on ['prɪzn] prigione f

pris·on·er ['prɪznə(r)] prigioniero m, -a f; **take s.o.** ~ fare prigioniero qu

pris·on·er of 'war prigioniero m di guerra

priv·a·cy ['prɪvəsɪ] privacy f inv

pri·vate ['praɪvət] 1 adj privato 2 n MIL soldato m semplice; **in** ~ in privato

pri·vate 'en·ter·prise iniziativa f privata

pri·vate·ly ['praɪvətlɪ] adv (in private) in privato; (inwardly) dentro di sé; ~ **funded** finanziato da privati; ~ **owned** privato

'**pri·vate sec·tor** settore m privato

pri·va·ti·za·tion [praɪvətaɪ'zeɪʃn] privatizzazione f

P

pri·va·tize ['praɪvətaɪz] v/t privatizzare

priv·i·lege ['prɪvɪlɪdʒ] *special treatment* privilegio m; (*honour*) onore m

priv·i·leged ['prɪvɪlɪdʒd] *adj* privilegiato; (*honoured*) onorato

prize [praɪz] **1** n premio m **2** v/t dare molto valore a

prize·win·ner ['praɪzwɪnə(r)] vincitore m, -trice f

prize·win·ning ['praɪzwɪnɪŋ] *adj* vincente

pro[1] [prəʊ] n: **the ~s and cons** i pro e i contro

pro[2] [prəʊ] → **professional**

pro[3] [prəʊ] *prep:* **be ~ ...** (*in favour of*) essere a favore di ...

prob·a·bil·i·ty [prɒbə'bɪlətɪ] probabilità f *inv*

prob·a·ble ['prɒbəbl] *adj* probabile

prob·a·bly ['prɒbəblɪ] *adv* probabilmente

pro·ba·tion [prə'beɪʃn] *in job* periodo m di prova; LAW libertà f inv vigilata; **on ~** *in job* in prova

pro·ba·tion of·fi·cer *funzionario m che sorveglia i vigilati*

pro·ba·tion pe·ri·od *in job* periodo m di prova

probe [prəʊb] **1** n (*investigation*) indagine f; *scientific* sonda f **2** v/t esplorare; (*investigate*) investigare

prob·lem ['prɒbləm] problema m; **no ~** non c'è problema

pro·ce·dure [prə'siːdʒə(r)] procedura f

pro·ceed [prə'siːd] **1** v/i *of people* proseguire; *of work etc* procedere **2** v/t: **~ to do sth** cominciare a fare qc

pro·ceed·ings [prə'siːdɪŋz] *npl* (*events*) avvenimenti *mpl*

pro·ceeds ['prəʊsiːdz] *npl* ricavato m

pro·cess ['prəʊses] **1** n processo m; **in the ~** *while doing it* nel far ciò **2** v/t *food, raw materials* trattare; *data* elaborare; *application etc* sbrigare; **~ed cheese** formaggio m fuso

pro·ces·sion [prə'seʃn] processione f

pro·claim [prə'kleɪm] v/t proclamare

proc·la·ma·tion [prɒklə'meɪʃn] proclamazione f

prod [prɒd] **1** n colpetto m **2** v/t (*pret & pp* **-ded**) dare un colpetto a

pro·di·gious [prə'dɪdʒəs] *adj* straordinario

prod·i·gy ['prɒdɪdʒɪ]: (*infant*) **~** bambino m, -a f prodigio

prod·uce[1] ['prɒdjuːs] n prodotti *mpl*

pro·duce[2] [prə'djuːs] v/t produrre; (*bring about*) dare origine a; (*bring out*) tirar fuori; *play, play* mettere in scena

pro·duc·er [prə'djuːsə(r)] produttore m, -trice f; *of play* regista m/f

prod·uct ['prɒdʌkt] prodotto m; (*result*) risultato m

pro·duc·tion [prə'dʌkʃn] produzione f; *of play* regia f; **a new ~ of ...** una nuova messa in scena di ...

pro·duc·tion ca·pac·i·ty capacità f *inv* produttiva

pro·duc·tion costs *npl* costi *mpl* di produzione

pro·duc·tive [prə'dʌktɪv] *adj* produttivo

pro·duc·tiv·i·ty [prɒdʌk'tɪvətɪ] produttività f *inv*

pro·fane [prə'feɪn] *adj language* sacrilego

pro·fan·i·ty [prə'fænətɪ] (*swearword*) imprecazione f

pro·fess [prə'fes] v/t dichiarare

pro·fes·sion [prə'feʃn] professione f

pro·fes·sion·al [prə'feʃnl] **1** *adj not amateur* professionale; *advice, help* di un esperto; *piece of work* da professionista; **turn ~** passare al professionismo **2** n professionista m/f

pro·fes·sion·al·ly [prə'feʃnlɪ] *adv play sport* a livello professionistico; (*well, skilfully*) in modo professionale

pro·fes·sor [prə'fesə(r)] professore m (universitario)

pro·fi·cien·cy [prə'fɪʃnsɪ] competenza f

pro·fi·cient [prə'fɪʃnt] *adj* competente

pro·file ['prəʊfaɪl] profilo *m*

prof·it ['prɒfɪt] **1** *n* profitto *m* **2** *v/i*: ~ **by**, ~ **from** trarre profitto da

prof·it·a·bil·i·ty [prɒfɪtə'bɪlətɪ] redditività *f inv*

prof·it·a·ble ['prɒfɪtəbl] *adj* redditizio

'**prof·it cen·ter** *Am*, '**prof·it cen·tre** centro *m* di profitto

'**prof·it mar·gin** margine *m* di profitto

pro·found [prə'faʊnd] *adj* profondo

pro·found·ly [prə'faʊndlɪ] *adv* profondamente

pro·fuse [prə'fjuːs] abbondante

pro·fuse·ly [prə'fjuːslɪ] *adv* thank con grande effusione; bleed copiosamente

prog·no·sis [prɒg'nəʊsɪs] prognosi *f inv*

pro·gram ['prəʊgræm] **1** *n* COMPUT programma *m* **2** *v/t* (pret & pp -med) COMPUT programmare

pro·gram *Am*, **pro·gramme** ['prəʊgræm] **1** *n* programma *m* **2** *v/t* programmare

pro·gram·mer ['prəʊgræmə(r)] COMPUT programmatore *m*, -trice *f*

pro·gress ['prəʊgres] **1** *n* progresso *m*; make ~ fare progressi; in ~ in corso **2** *v/i* [prə'gres] (advance in time) procedere; (move on) avanzare; (make progress) fare progressi; how is the work ~ing? come procede il lavoro?

pro·gres·sive [prə'gresɪv] *adj* (enlightened) progressista; which progresses progressivo

pro·gres·sive·ly [prə'gresɪvlɪ] *adv* progressivamente

pro·hib·it [prə'hɪbɪt] *v/t* proibire

pro·hi·bi·tion [prəʊhɪ'bɪʃn] proibizione *f*; **Prohibition** il Proibizionismo

pro·hib·i·tive [prə'hɪbɪtɪv] *adj* prices proibitivo

proj·ect¹ ['prɒdʒekt] *n* (plan) piano *m*; (undertaking) progetto *m*; EDU ricerca *f*

pro·ject² [prə'dʒekt] **1** *v/t* figures, sales fare una proiezione di; film

proiettare **2** *v/i* (stick out) sporgere in fuori

pro·jec·tion [prə'dʒekʃn] (forecast) proiezione *f*

pro·jec·tor [prə'dʒektə(r)] for slides proiettore *m*

pro·lif·ic [prə'lɪfɪk] *adj* writer, artist prolifico

pro·log *Am*, **pro·logue** ['prəʊlɒg] prologo *m*

pro·long [prə'lɒŋ] *v/t* prolungare

prom·i·nent ['prɒmɪnənt] *adj* nose, chin sporgente; (significant) prominente

prom·is·cu·i·ty [prɒmɪ'skjuːətɪ] promiscuità *f inv*

prom·is·cu·ous [prə'mɪskjʊəs] *adj* promiscuo

prom·ise ['prɒmɪs] **1** *n* promessa *f* **2** *v/t* promettere; ~ to ... promettere di ...; ~ sth to s.o. promettere qc a qu **3** *v/i* promettere; I ~ lo prometto

prom·is·ing ['prɒmɪsɪŋ] *adj* promettente

pro·mote [prə'məʊt] *v/t* promuovere

pro·mot·er [prə'məʊtə(r)] of sports event promoter *m/f inv*

pro·mo·tion [prə'məʊʃn] promozione *f*; get ~ essere promosso

prompt [prɒmpt] **1** *adj* (on time) puntuale; (speedy) tempestivo **2** *adv*: at two o'clock ~ alle due in punto **3** *v/t* (cause) causare; actor dare l'imbeccata a **4** *n* COMPUT prompt *m inv*

prompt·ly ['prɒmptlɪ] *adv* (on time) puntualmente; (immediately) prontamente

prone [prəʊn] *adj*: be ~ to essere soggetto a

prong [prɒŋ] dente *m*

pro·noun ['prəʊnaʊn] pronome *m*

pro·nounce [prə'naʊns] *v/t* word pronunciare; (declare) dichiarare

pro·nounced [prə'naʊnst] *adj* accent spiccato; views preciso

pron·to ['prɒntəʊ] *adv* F immediatamente

pro·nun·ci·a·tion [prənʌnsɪ'eɪʃn] pronuncia *f*

proof [pruːf] *n* prova *f*; of book bozza *f*

prop [prɒp] **1** v/t (*pret & pp* **-ped**) appoggiare **2** n THEA materiale m di scena

♦ **prop up** v/t *also fig* sostenere

prop·a·gan·da [prɒpə'gændə] propaganda f

pro·pel [prə'pel] v/t (*pret & pp* **-led**) spingere; *of engine, fuel* azionare

pro·pel·lant [prə'pelənt] *in aerosol* propellente m

pro·pel·ler [prə'pelə(r)] elica f

prop·er ['prɒpə(r)] adj (*real*) vero e proprio; (*correct*) giusto; (*fitting*) appropriato

prop·er·ly ['prɒpəlɪ] adv (*correctly*) correttamente; (*fittingly*) in modo appropriato

'prop·er noun nome m proprio

prop·er·ty ['prɒpətɪ] proprietà f inv

prop·er·ty de·vel·op·er impresario m edile

proph·e·cy ['prɒfəsɪ] profezia f

proph·e·sy ['prɒfəsaɪ] v/t (*pret & pp* **-ied**) profetizzare

pro·por·tion [prə'pɔːʃn] proporzione f

pro·por·tion·al [prə'pɔːʃnl] adj proporzionale

pro·por·tion·al rep·re·sen'ta·tion POL rappresentanza f proporzionale

pro·pos·al [prə'pəʊzl] proposta f

pro·pose [prə'pəʊz] **1** v/t (*suggest*) proporre; ~ **to do sth** (*plan*) proporsi di fare qc **2** v/i *make offer of marriage* fare una proposta di matrimonio

prop·o·si·tion [prɒpə'zɪʃn] **1** n proposta f **2** v/t *woman* fare proposte sessuali a

pro·pri·e·tor [prə'praɪətə(r)] proprietario m, -a f

pro·pri·e·tress [prə'praɪətrɪs] proprietaria f

prose [prəʊz] prosa f

pros·e·cute ['prɒsɪkjuːt] v/t LAW intentare azione legale contro; *of lawyer* sostenere l'accusa contro

pros·e·cu·tion [prɒsɪ'kjuːʃn] LAW azione f giudiziaria; (*lawyers*) accusa f

pros·pect ['prɒspekt] **1** n (*chance, likelihood*) probabilità f inv; *thought of something in the future* prospettiva f; ~**s** *for company, in job* prospettive fpl **2** v/i: ~ **for** gold cercare

pro·spec·tive [prə'spektɪv] adj potenziale; MP aspirante

pros·per ['prɒspə(r)] v/i prosperare

pros·per·i·ty [prɒ'sperətɪ] prosperità f inv

pros·per·ous ['prɒspərəs] adj prospero

pros·ti·tute ['prɒstɪtjuːt] n prostituta f; **male ~** prostituto m

pros·ti·tu·tion [prɒstɪ'tjuːʃn] prostituzione f

pros·trate ['prɒstreɪt] adj: **be ~ with grief** essere abbattuto dal dolore

pro·tect [prə'tekt] v/t proteggere

pro·tec·tion [prə'tekʃn] protezione f

pro'tec·tion mon·ey pizzo m F

pro·tec·tive [prə'tektɪv] adj protettivo

pro·tec·tive 'cloth·ing indumenti mpl protettivi

pro·tec·tor [prə'tektə(r)] protettore m, -trice f

pro·tein ['prəʊtiːn] proteina f

pro·test ['prəʊtest] **1** n protesta f **2** v/t [prə'test] protestare **3** v/i protestare; POL manifestare, protestare

Prot·es·tant ['prɒtɪstənt] **1** n protestante m/f **2** adj protestante

pro·test·er [prə'testə(r)] dimostrante m/f, manifestante m/f

pro·to·col ['prəʊtəkɒl] protocollo m

pro·to·type ['prəʊtətaɪp] prototipo m

pro·tract·ed [prə'træktɪd] adj prolungato

pro·trude [prə'truːd] v/i sporgere

pro·trud·ing [prə'truːdɪŋ] adj sporgente

proud [praʊd] adj orgoglioso, fiero; **be ~ of** essere fiero di

proud·ly ['praʊdlɪ] adv con orgoglio

prove [pruːv] v/t dimostrare

prov·erb ['prɒvɜːb] proverbio m

pro·vide [prə'vaɪd] v/t money, food fornire; *opportunity* offrire; ~ **s.o. with sth** fornire qu di qc

♦ **provide for** v/t family provvedere a; of law etc contemplare

pro·vi·ded [prə'vaɪdɪd] conj: ~ **(that)** (on condition that) a condizione che

prov·ince ['prɒvɪns] provincia f

pro·vin·cial [prə'vɪnʃl] adj also pej provinciale

pro·vi·sion [prə'vɪʒn] (supply) fornitura f; of law, contract disposizione f

pro·vi·sion·al [prə'vɪʒnl] adj provvisorio

pro·vi·so [prə'vaɪzəʊ] condizione f

prov·o·ca·tion [prɒvə'keɪʃn] provocazione f

pro·voc·a·tive [prə'vɒkətɪv] adj provocatorio; sexually provocante

pro·voke [prə'vəʊk] v/t (cause) causare; (annoy) provocare

prow [praʊ] NAUT prua f

prow·ess ['praʊɪs] abilità f inv

prowl [praʊl] v/i aggirarsi

prowl·er ['praʊlə(r)] tipo m sospetto

prox·im·i·ty [prɒk'sɪmɪtɪ] prossimità f inv

prox·y ['prɒksɪ] (authority) procura f; person procuratore m, -trice f, mandatario m, -a f

prude [pruːd]: **be a ~** scandalizzarsi facilmente

pru·dence ['pruːdns] prudenza f

pru·dent ['pruːdnt] adj prudente

prud·ish ['pruːdɪʃ] adj che si scandalizza facilmente

prune[1] [pruːn] n prugna f

prune[2] [pruːn] v/t plant potare; fig ridurre

pry [praɪ] v/i (pret & pp **-ied**) essere indiscreto

♦ **pry into** v/t ficcare il naso in

PS ['piːes] abbr (= **postscript**) P.S. (= post scriptum m inv)

pseu·do·nym ['sjuːdənɪm] pseudonimo m

psy·chi·at·ric [saɪkɪ'ætrɪk] adj psichiatrico

psy·chi·a·trist [saɪ'kaɪətrɪst] psichiatra m/f

psy·chi·a·try [saɪ'kaɪətrɪ] psichiatria f

psy·chic ['saɪkɪk] adj psichico; **I'm not ~!** non sono un indovino!

psy·cho·an·a·lyse [saɪkəʊ'ænəlaɪz] v/t psicanalizzare

psy·cho·a·nal·y·sis [saɪkəʊən'æləsɪs] psicanalisi f

psy·cho·an·a·lyst [saɪkəʊ'ænəlɪst] psicanalista m/f

psy·cho·log·i·cal [saɪkə'lɒdʒɪkl] adj psicologico

psy·cho·log·i·cal·ly [saɪkə'lɒdʒɪklɪ] adv psicologicamente

psy·chol·o·gist [saɪ'kɒlədʒɪst] psicologo m, -a f

psy·chol·o·gy [saɪ'kɒlədʒɪ] psicologia f

psy·cho·path ['saɪkəpæθ] psicopatico m, -a f

psy·cho·so·mat·ic [saɪkəʊsə'mætɪk] adj psicosomatico

PT [piː'tiː] abbr (= **physical training**) educazione f fisica

PTO [piːtiː'əʊ] abbr (= **please turn over**) vedi retro

pub [pʌb] pub m inv

pu·ber·ty ['pjuːbətɪ] pubertà f inv

pu·bic hair [pjuː'bɪk'heə(r)] peli mpl del pube

pub·lic ['pʌblɪk] **1** adj pubblico **2** n: **the ~** il pubblico; **in ~** in pubblico

pub·li·ca·tion [pʌblɪ'keɪʃn] pubblicazione f

pub·lic 'hol·i·day giorno m festivo

pub·lic·i·ty [pʌb'lɪsətɪ] pubblicità f inv

pub·li·cize ['pʌblɪsaɪz] v/t make known far sapere in giro; COM reclamizzare

pub·lic 'li·bra·ry biblioteca f pubblica

pub·lic lim·it·ed 'com·pa·ny società f inv a responsabilità limitata quotata in borsa

pub·lic·ly ['pʌblɪklɪ] adv pubblicamente

pub·lic 'pros·e·cu·tor pubblico ministero m; **pub·lic re'la·tions** npl relazioni fpl pubbliche; **'pub·lic school** Br scuola f privata; **'pub·lic sec·tor** settore m pubblico; **pub·lic 'trans·port** mezzi mpl pubblici

pub·lish ['pʌblɪʃ] v/t pubblicare

pub·lish·er ['pʌblɪʃə(r)] editore m

P

pub·lish·ing ['pʌblɪʃɪŋ] editoria f

'pub·lish·ing com·pa·ny casa f editrice

pud·ding ['pudɪŋ] *dish* budino m; *part of meal* dolce m

pud·dle ['pʌdl] n pozzanghera f

puff [pʌf] **1** n *of wind, smoke* soffio m **2** v/i (*pant*) ansimare; **~ on a cigarette** tirare boccate da una sigaretta

puff·y ['pʌfɪ] *adj eyes, face* gonfio

puke [pjuːk] v/i F vomitare

pull [pul] **1** n *on rope* tirata f; F (*appeal*) attrattiva f; F (*influence*) influenza f **2** v/t (*drag*) tirare; (*tug*) dare uno strappo a; *tooth* togliere **3** v/i tirare; **~ a muscle** farsi uno strappo muscolare

♦ **pull ahead** v/i *in race, competition* portarsi in testa

♦ **pull apart** v/t (*separate*) separare

♦ **pull away** v/t spostare

♦ **pull down** v/t (*lower*) tirar giù; (*demolish*) demolire

♦ **pull in** v/i *of bus, train* arrivare

♦ **pull off** v/t togliere; F *deal etc* portare a termine

♦ **pull out 1** v/t tirar fuori; *troops* (*far*) ritirare **2** v/i *of agreement, competition*, MIL ritirarsi; *of ship* partire

♦ **pull over** v/i *of driver* accostarsi

♦ **pull through** v/i *from an illness* farcela F

♦ **pull together 1** v/i (*cooperate*) cooperare **2** v/t: **pull o.s. together** darsi una mossa F

♦ **pull up 1** v/t (*raise*) tirar su; *plant, weeds* strappare **2** v/i *of car etc* fermarsi

pul·ley ['pulɪ] puleggia f

pull·o·ver ['puləuvə(r)] pullover m inv

pulp [pʌlp] *soft mass* poltiglia f; *of fruit* polpa f; *for paper-making* pasta f

pul·pit ['pulpɪt] pulpito m

pul·sate [pʌl'seɪt] v/i *of heart, blood* pulsare; *of rhythm* vibrare

pulse [pʌls] polso m

pul·ver·ize ['pʌlvəraɪz] v/t polveriz-

zare

pump [pʌmp] **1** n pompa f **2** v/t pompare

♦ **pump up** v/t gonfiare

pump·kin ['pʌmpkɪn] zucca f

pun [pʌn] gioco m di parole

punch [pʌntʃ] **1** n *blow* pugno m; *implement* punzonatrice f **2** v/t *with a fist* dare un pugno a; *hole* perforare; *ticket* forare

'punch line finale m

punc·tu·al ['pʌŋktjuəl] *adj* puntuale

punc·tu·al·i·ty [pʌŋktju'ælətɪ] puntualità f inv

punc·tu·al·ly ['pʌŋktjuəlɪ] *adv* puntualmente

punc·tu·ate ['pʌŋktjueɪt] v/t mettere la punteggiatura in

punc·tu·a·tion ['pʌŋktju'eɪʃn] punteggiatura f

punc·tu·a·tion mark segno m d'interpunzione

punc·ture ['pʌŋktʃə(r)] **1** n foratura f **2** v/t forare

pun·gent ['pʌndʒənt] *adj* acre; *taste* aspro

pun·ish ['pʌnɪʃ] v/t *person* punire

pun·ish·ing ['pʌnɪʃɪŋ] *adj pace, schedule* estenuante

pun·ish·ment ['pʌnɪʃmənt] punizione f

punk (rock) ['pʌŋkrɒk] MUS punk m inv

pu·ny ['pjuːnɪ] *adj person* gracile

pup [pʌp] cucciolo m

pu·pil[1] ['pjuːpl] *of eye* pupilla f

pu·pil[2] ['pjuːpl] (*student*) allievo m, -a f

pup·pet ['pʌpɪt] burattino m; *with strings* marionetta f

'pup·pet gov·ern·ment governo m fantoccio

pup·py ['pʌpɪ] cucciolo m

pur·chase[1] ['pɜːtʃəs] **1** n acquisto m **2** v/t acquistare

pur·chase[2] ['pɜːtʃəs] (*grip*) presa f

pur·chas·er ['pɜːtʃəsə(r)] acquirente m/f

pure [pjuə(r)] *adj* puro; **~ new wool** pura lana f vergine

pure·ly ['pjuəlɪ] *adv* puramente

pur·ga·to·ry ['pɜːgətrɪ] purgatorio *m*

purge [pɜːdʒ] **1** *n of political party* epurazione *f* **2** *v/t* epurare

pu·ri·fy ['pjʊərɪfaɪ] *v/t* (*pret & pp -ied*) *water* purificare

pu·ri·tan ['pjʊərɪtən] puritano *m*, -a *f*

pu·ri·tan·i·cal [pjʊərɪ'tænɪkl] *adj* puritano

pu·ri·ty ['pjʊərɪtɪ] purezza *f*

pur·ple ['pɜːpl] *adj* viola *inv*

pur·pose ['pɜːpəs] (*aim*, *object*) scopo *m*; **on** ~ di proposito

pur·pose·ful ['pɜːpəsfʊl] *adj* risoluto

pur·pose·ly ['pɜːpəslɪ] *adv* di proposito

purr [pɜː(r)] *v/i of cat* far le fusa

purse [pɜːs] *n for money* borsellino *m*; *Am* (*handbag*) borsetta *f*

pur·sue [pə'sjuː] *v/t person* inseguire; *career* intraprendere; *course of action* proseguire

pur·su·er [pə'sjuːə(r)] inseguitore *m*, -trice *f*

pur·suit [pə'sjuːt] (*chase*) inseguimento *m*; *of happiness etc* ricerca *f*; *activity* occupazione *f*; **those in** ~ gli inseguitori

pus [pʌs] pus *m inv*

push [pʊʃ] **1** *n* (*shove*) spinta *f*; **at the ~ of a button** premendo un pulsante **2** *v/t* (*shove*) spingere; *button* premere; (*pressurize*) far pressioni su; *F drugs* spacciare; **be ~ed for** F essere a corto di; **be ~ing 40** F essere sulla quarantina **3** *v/i* spingere

♦ **push ahead** *v/i* andare avanti

♦ **push along** *v/t cart etc* spingere

♦ **push away** *v/t* respingere

♦ **push off 1** *v/t lid* spingere via **2** *v/i* F (*leave*) andarsene; **push off!** sparisci! F

♦ **push on** *v/i* (*continue*) continuare

♦ **push up** *v/t prices* far salire

push-but·ton ['pʊʃbʌtn] *adj* a tastiera

'push·chair passeggino *m*

push·er ['pʊʃə(r)] F *of drugs* spacciatore *m*, -trice *f*

push-up ['pʊʃʌp] flessione *f* sulle braccia

push·y ['pʊʃɪ] *adj* F troppo intraprendente

puss, pus·sy (cat) [pʊs, 'pʊsɪ (kæt)] F micio *m*, -a *f*

♦ **pussyfoot about** ['pʊsɪfʊt] *v/i* F tentennare

put [pʊt] *v/t* (*pret & pp* **put**) mettere; *question* porre; ~ **the cost at ...** stimare il costo intorno a ...

♦ **put across** *v/t ideas etc* trasmettere

♦ **put aside** *v/t* mettere da parte

♦ **put away** *v/t in cupboard etc* mettere via; *in institution* rinchiudere; (*consume*) far fuori; *money* mettere da parte

♦ **put back** *v/t* (*replace*) rimettere a posto

♦ **put by** *v/t money* mettere da parte

♦ **put down** *v/t* mettere giù; *deposit* versare; *rebellion* reprimere; *animal* abbattere; (*belittle*) sminuire; *in writing* scrivere; **put one's foot down** *in car* accelerare; (*be firm*) farsi valere; **put X down to Y** (*attribute*) attribuire X a Y

♦ **put forward** *v/t idea etc* avanzare

♦ **put in** *v/t* inserire; *overtime* fare; *time, effort* dedicare; *request, claim* presentare

♦ **put in for** *v/t* (*apply for*) fare domanda per

♦ **put off** *v/t light, radio, TV* spegnere; (*postpone*) rimandare; (*deter*) scoraggiare; (*repel*) disgustare; **the accident put me off driving** l'incidente mi ha fatto passare la voglia di guidare

♦ **put on** *v/t light, radio, TV* accendere; *tape, music* mettere su; *jacket, shoes, glasses* mettersi; *makeup* mettere; (*perform*) mettere in scena; (*assume*) affettare; **put on the brakes** frenare; **put on weight** ingrassare; **she's just putting it on** sta solo fingendo

♦ **put out** *v/t hand* allungare; *fire, light* spegnere

♦ **put through** *v/t*: **I'll put you through (to him)** glielo passo; **I'll put you through to sales** le passo l'ufficio vendite

P

♦ **put together** v/t (*assemble*) montare; (*organize*) organizzare

♦ **put up** v/t *hand* alzare; *person* ospitare; (*erect*) costruire; *prices* aumentare; *poster, notice* affiggere; *money* fornire; **put up for sale** mettere in vendita

♦ **put up with** v/t (*tolerate*) sopportare

putt [pʌt] v/t & v/i SP pattare

put·ty ['pʌtɪ] mastice m

puz·zle ['pʌzl] **1** n (*mystery*) mistero m; *game* rebus m inv; *jigsaw* puzzle m inv; *crossword* cruciverba m inv **2** v/t lasciar perplesso

puz·zling ['pʌzlɪŋ] adj inspiegabile

PVC [piːviːˈsiː] abbr (= **polyvinyl chloride**) PVC m inv (= polivinilcloruro m)

py·ja·mas [pəˈdʒɑːməz] npl pigiama m

py·lon ['paɪlən] pilone m

Q

quack¹ [kwæk] **1** n *of duck* qua qua m inv **2** v/i fare qua qua

quack² [kwæk] F (*bad doctor*) ciarlatano m, -a f; **I'm going to see the ~** vado dal dottore

quad·ran·gle ['kwɒdræŋgl] *figure* quadrilatero m; *courtyard* cortile m

quad·ru·ped ['kwɒdruped] quadrupede m

quad·ru·ple ['kwɒdrupl] v/i quadruplicare

quad·ru·plets ['kwɒdruplɪts] npl quattro gemelli mpl

quads [kwɒdz] npl F quattro gemelli mpl

quag·mire ['kwɒgmaɪə(r)] fig ginepraio m

quail [kweɪl] v/i perdersi d'animo

quaint [kweɪnt] adj *pretty* pittoresco; *slightly eccentric: ideas etc* curioso

quake [kweɪk] **1** n (*earthquake*) terremoto m **2** v/i also fig tremare

qual·i·fi·ca·tion [kwɒlɪfɪˈkeɪʃn] *from university* titolo m di studio; *of remark etc* riserva f; **have the right ~s for a job** skills avere tutti i requisiti per un lavoro

qual·i·fied ['kwɒlɪfaɪd] adj *doctor, engineer etc* abilitato; (*restricted*) con riserva; **I am not ~ to judge** non sono in grado di valutare

qual·i·fy ['kwɒlɪfaɪ] (*pret & pp* **-ied**) **1** v/t *of degree, course etc* abilitare; *remark etc* precisare **2** v/i (*get certificate etc*) ottenere la qualifica (**as** di); *in competition* qualificarsi; **our team has qualified for the semi-final** la nostra squadra è entrata in semifinale; **that doesn't ~ as ...** non può essere considerato ...

qual·i·ty ['kwɒlɪtɪ] qualità f inv

qual·i·ty con'trol controllo m (di) qualità

qualm [kwɑːm]: **have no ~s about ...** non aver scrupoli a ...

quan·da·ry ['kwɒndərɪ] n dilemma m; **be in a ~** avere un dilemma

quan·ti·fy ['kwɒntɪfaɪ] v/t (*pret & pp* **-ied**) quantificare

quan·ti·ty ['kwɒntətɪ] quantità f inv

quan·tum 'phys·ics ['kwɒntəm] teoria f fisica dei quanti

quar·an·tine ['kwɒrəntiːn] n quarantena f

quar·rel ['kwɒrəl] **1** n litigio m **2** v/i (*pret & pp* **-led**, Am **-ed**) litigare

quar·rel·some ['kwɒrəlsʌm] adj litigioso

quar·ry¹ ['kwɒrɪ] *in hunt* preda f

quar·ry² ['kwɒrɪ] *for mining* cava f

quart [kwɔːt] quarto m di gallone

quar·ter ['kwɔːtə(r)] **1** n quarto m;

part of town quartiere m; **a ~ of an hour** un quarto d'ora; (a) **~ to 5** le cinque meno un quarto; (a) **~ past 5** le cinque e un quarto **2** v/t dividere in quattro parti

quar·ter-'fi·nal partita f dei quarti mpl di finale

quar·ter-'fi·nal·ist concorrente m/f dei quarti di finale

quar·ter·ly ['kwɔːtəlɪ] **1** adj trimestrale **2** adv trimestralmente

quar·ters ['kwɔːtəz] npl MIL quartieri mpl

quar·tet [kwɔːˈtet] MUS quartetto m

quartz [kwɔːts] quarzo m

quash [kwɒʃ] v/t rebellion reprimere; court decision annullare

qua·ver ['kweɪvə(r)] **1** n in voice tremolio m; MUS croma f **2** v/i of voice tremolare

quay [kiː] banchina f

'quay·side banchina f

quea·sy ['kwiːzɪ] adj nauseato

queen [kwiːn] regina f

queen 'bee ape f regina

queer [kwɪə(r)] adj (peculiar) strano

queer·ly ['kwɪə(r)lɪ] adv stranamente

quell [kwel] v/t soffocare

quench [kwentʃ] v/t also fig spegnere

que·ry ['kwɪərɪ] **1** n interrogativo m **2** v/t (pret & pp **-ied**) express doubt about contestare; check controllare

quest [kwest] n ricerca f

ques·tion ['kwestʃn] **1** n domanda f; matter questione f; **in ~** (being talked about) in questione; (in doubt) in dubbio; **it's a ~ of money / time** è questione di soldi / tempo; **that's out of the ~** è fuori discussione **2** v/t person interrogare; (doubt) dubitare di; **that's not being ~ed** nessuno lo mette in dubbio

ques·tion·a·ble ['kwestʃnəbl] adj discutibile; (dubious) dubbio

ques·tion·er ['kwestʃnə(r)] n interrogatore m, -trice f

ques·tion·ing ['kwestʃnɪŋ] **1** adj look, tone interrogativo **2** n interrogatorio m

'ques·tion mark punto m interrogativo

'ques·tion mas·ter presentatore m, -trice f di quiz

ques·tion·naire [kwestʃəˈneə(r)] n questionario m

queue [kjuː] **1** n coda f, fila f **2** v/i fare la fila o la coda

queue-jump·er ['kjuːdʒʌmpə(r)] persona f che non rispetta la coda

quib·ble ['kwɪbl] v/i cavillare

quick [kwɪk] adj person svelto; reply, change veloce; **be ~!** fai presto!, fai in fretta!; **let's have a ~ drink** beviamo qualcosina?; **can I have a ~ look?** posso dare un'occhiatina?; **that was ~!** già fatto?

quick·ie ['kwɪkɪ] F: **have a ~** quick drink bere qualcosina

quick·ly ['kwɪklɪ] adv rapidamente, in fretta

'quick·sand sabbie fpl mobili; **'quick·sil·ver** mercurio m; **quick-wit·ted** [kwɪkˈwɪtɪd] adj sveglio

quid [kwɪd] F sterlina f; **50 ~** 50 sterline

qui·et ['kwaɪət] adj voice, music basso; engine silenzioso; street, life, town tranquillo; **keep ~ about sth** tenere segreto qc; **~!** silenzio!, stai zitto!

♦ **quieten down** ['kwaɪətn] **1** v/t calmare **2** v/i calmarsi

quiet·ly ['kwaɪətlɪ] adv not loudly silenziosamente, senza far rumore; (without fuss) semplicemente; (peacefully) tranquillamente

quiet·ness ['kwaɪətnɪs] of night, street tranquillità f, calma f; of voice dolcezza f

quilt [kwɪlt] on bed piumino m

quilt·ed ['kwɪltɪd] adj trapuntato

quin·ine ['kwɪniːn] chinino m

quin·tet [kwɪnˈtet] MUS quintetto m

quip [kwɪp] **1** n battuta f (di spirito) **2** v/i (pret & pp **-ped**) scherzare

quirk [kwɜːk] bizzarria f

quirk·y ['kwɜːkɪ] adj bizzarro

quit [kwɪt] (pret & pp **quit**) **1** v/t job mollare F; **~ doing sth** smettere di fare qc **2** v/i (leave job) licenziarsi;

Q

COMPUT uscire; **get one's notice to ~ from landlord** ricevere la disdetta

quite [kwaɪt] *adv* (*fairly*) abbastanza; (*completely*) completamente; **not ~ ready** non ancora pronto; **I didn't ~ understand** non ho capito bene; **is that right? – not ~** giusto? – non esattamente; **~!** esatto!; **~ a lot drink**, *change* parecchio; **~ a lot better** molto meglio; **~ a few** un bel po'; **it was ~ a surprise / change** è stata una bella sorpresa / un bel cambiamento

quits [kwɪts] *adj*: **be ~ with s.o.** essere pari con qu

quit·ter ['kwɪtə(r)] F rinunciatario *m*, -a *f*

quiv·er ['kwɪvə(r)] *v/i* tremare

quiz [kwɪz] **1** *n* quiz *m inv* **2** *v/t* (*pret & pp* **-zed**) interrogare

'quiz mas·ter conduttore *m*, -trice *f* (di gioco a quiz)

'quiz pro·gram *Am*, **'quiz pro·gramme** gioco *m* a quiz

quo·ta ['kwəʊtə] quota *f*

quo·ta·tion [kwəʊ'teɪʃn] *from author* citazione *f*; *price* preventivo *m*; **give s.o. a ~ for sth** fare un preventivo a qu per qc

quo·ta·tion marks *npl* virgolette *fpl*

quote [kwəʊt] **1** *n from author* citazione *f*; *price* preventivo *m*; (*quotation mark*) virgoletta *f*; **in ~s** tra virgolette **2** *v/t text* citare; *price* stimare; **~d on the Stock Exchange** quotato in Borsa **3** *v/i*: **~ from an author** citare un autore

---

R

rab·bi ['ræbaɪ] rabbino *m*

rab·bit ['ræbɪt] coniglio *m*

♦ **rabbit on** *v/i* P blaterare

rab·ble ['ræbl] marmaglia *f*

rab·ble-rous·er ['ræblraʊzə(r)] agitatore *m*, -trice *f*

ra·bies ['reɪbiːz] *nsg* rabbia *f*, idrofobia *f*

race[1] [reɪs] *n of people* razza *f*

race[2] [reɪs] **1** *n* SP gara *f*; **the ~s** (*horse races*) le corse **2** *v/i* (*run fast*) correre; **he ~d against the world champion** ha gareggiato contro il campione del mondo **3** *v/t*: **I'll ~ you** facciamo una gara

'race·course ippodromo *m*; **'race·horse** cavallo *m* da corsa; **'race re·la·tions** *npl* rapporti *mpl* interrazziali; **'race riot** scontri *mpl* razziali; **'race·track** pista *f*; *for horses* ippodromo *m*

ra·cial ['reɪʃl] *adj* razziale; **~ equality** parità *f inv* razziale

rac·ing ['reɪsɪŋ] corse *fpl*

'rac·ing car auto *f inv* da corsa

'rac·ing driv·er pilota *m* automobilistico

ra·cis·m ['reɪsɪzm] razzismo *m*

ra·cist ['reɪsɪst] **1** *n* razzista *m/f* **2** *adj* razzista

rack [ræk] **1** *n* for parking bikes rastrelliera *f*; *for bags on train* portabagagli *m inv*; *for CDs* porta-CD *m inv* **2** *v/t*: **~ one's brains** scervellarsi

rack·et[1] ['rækɪt] SP racchetta *f*

rack·et[2] ['rækɪt] (*noise*) baccano *m*; *criminal activity* racket *m inv*

ra·dar ['reɪdɑː(r)] radar *m inv*

'ra·dar screen schermo *m* radar

'ra·dar trap autovelox® *m*

ra·di·al 'tire *Am*, **ra·di·al 'tyre** ['reɪdɪəl] pneumatico *m* radiale

ra·di·ance ['reɪdɪəns] splendore *m*

ra·di·ant ['reɪdɪənt] *adj smile* splendente; *appearance* raggiante

ra·di·ate ['reɪdɪeɪt] *v/i of heat, light etc* diffondersi

ra·di·a·tion [reɪdɪ'eɪʃn] PHYS radiazione *f*

ra·di·a·tor ['reɪdɪeɪtə(r)] *in room* termosifone *m*; *in car* radiatore *m*

rad·i·cal ['rædɪkl] **1** *adj* radicale **2** *n* radicale *m/f*

rad·i·cal·ism ['rædɪkəlɪzm] POL radicalismo *m*

rad·i·cal·ly ['rædɪklɪ] *adv* radicalmente

ra·di·o ['reɪdɪəʊ] radio *f inv*; **on the ~** alla radio; **by ~** via radio

ra·di·o·ac·tive [reɪdɪəʊ'æktɪv] *adj* radioattivo; **ra·di·o·ac·tive 'waste** scorie *fpl* radioattive; **ra·di·o·ac·tiv·i·ty** [reɪdɪəʊæk'tɪvətɪ] radioattività *f inv*; **ra·di·o a'larm** radiosveglia *f*

ra·di·og·ra·pher [reɪdɪ'ɒgrəfə(r)] radiologo *m*, -a *f*

ra·di·og·ra·phy [reɪdɪ'ɒgrəfɪ] radiografia *f*

'ra·di·o sta·tion stazione *f* radiofonica, radio *f inv*; **'ra·di·o tax·i** radiotaxi *m inv*; **ra·di·o·ther·a·py** radioterapia *f*

rad·ish ['rædɪʃ] ravanello *m*

ra·di·us ['reɪdɪəs] raggio *m*

raf·fle ['ræfl] *n* lotteria *f*

raft [rɑːft] zattera *f*

raf·ter ['rɑːftə(r)] travicello *m*

rag [ræg] *n for cleaning etc* straccio *m*; **dressed in ~s** vestito di stracci

rage [reɪdʒ] **1** *n* rabbia *f*, collera *f*; **be in a ~** essere furioso; **be all the ~** essere di moda **2** *v/i of person* infierire; *of storm* infuriare

rag·ged ['rægɪd] *adj* stracciato

raid [reɪd] **1** *n* raid *m inv* **2** *v/t of police, robbers* fare un raid in; *fridge, orchard* fare razzia in

raid·er ['reɪdə(r)] *on bank etc* rapinatore *m*, -trice *f*

rail [reɪl] *n on track* rotaia *f*; (*hand~*) corrimano *m*; (*barrier*) parapetto *m*; **curtain ~** bastone *m* per tende; **towel ~** portasciugamano *m inv*; **by ~** in treno

rail·ings ['reɪlɪŋz] *npl around park*

inferriata *f*

'rail·road *etc Am* → **railway** *etc*

rail·way ['reɪlweɪ] ferrovia *f*

'rail·way line linea *f* ferroviaria

'rail·way sta·tion stazione *f* ferroviaria

rain [reɪn] **1** *n* pioggia *f*; **in the ~** sotto la pioggia **2** *v/i* piovere; **it's ~ing** sta piovendo

'rain·bow arcobaleno *m*; **'rain·coat** impermeabile *m*; **'rain·drop** goccia *f* di pioggia; **'rain·fall** piovosità *f inv*; **'rain for·est** foresta *f* pluviale; **'rain·proof** *adj fabric* impermeabile; **'rain·storm** temporale *m*

rain·y ['reɪnɪ] *adj day* di pioggia; *weather* piovoso; **it's ~** piove molto

raise [reɪz] **1** *n esp Am: in salary* aumento *m* **2** *v/t shelf, question* sollevare; *offer* aumentare; *children* allevare; *money* raccogliere

rai·sin ['reɪzn] uva *f* passa

rake [reɪk] *n for garden* rastrello *m*

♦ **rake up** *v/t leaves* rastrellare; *fig* rivangare

ral·ly ['rælɪ] *n meeting* raduno *m*; MOT rally *m inv*; *in tennis* scambio *m*

♦ **rally round** (*pret & pp* **-ied**) **1** *v/i* offrire aiuto **2** *v/t*: **rally round s.o.** aiutare qu

RAM [ræm] *abbr* COMPUT (= *random access memory*) RAM *f inv*

ram [ræm] **1** *n* montone *m* **2** *v/t* (*pret & pp* **-med**) *ship, car* sbattere contro

ram·ble ['ræmbl] **1** *n walk* escursione *f* **2** *v/i walk* fare passeggiate; *in speaking* divagare; *talk incoherently* vaneggiare

ram·bler ['ræmblə(r)] *walker* escursionista *m/f*

ram·bling ['ræmblɪŋ] *adj speech* sconnesso

ramp [ræmp] rampa *f*; *for raising vehicle* ponte *m* idraulico

ram·page ['ræmpeɪdʒ] **1** *v/i* scatenarsi **2** *n*: **go on the ~** scatenarsi

ram·pant ['ræmpənt] *adj inflation* dilagante

ram·part ['ræmpɑːt] bastione *m*

ram·shack·le ['ræmʃækl] *adj* sgangherato

ran [ræn] *pret* → **run**

ranch [rɑːntʃ] ranch *m inv*

ran·cid ['rænsɪd] *adj* rancido

ran·cour ['ræŋkə(r)] rancore *m*

R&D [ɑːrən'diː] *abbr* (= *research and development*) ricerca *f* e sviluppo *m*

ran·dom ['rændəm] **1** *adj* casuale; ~ *sample* campione *m* casuale; *take a ~ sample* prendere un campione a caso **2** *n*: *at* ~ a caso

ran·dy ['rændɪ] *adj* F arrapato F

range [reɪndʒ] **1** *n of products* gamma *f*; *of missile, gun* gittata *f*; *of salary* scala *f*; *of voice* estensione *f*; *of mountains* catena *f*, (*shooting* ~) poligono *m* (di tiro); *at close* ~ a distanza ravvicinata **2** *v/i*: ~ *from X to Y* variare da X a Y

rank [ræŋk] **1** *n* MIL grado *m*; *in society* rango *m*; *the* ~*s* MIL la truppa **2** *v/t* classificare
  ♦ **rank among** *v/t* classificarsi tra

ran·kle ['ræŋkl] *v/i* bruciare

ran·sack ['rænsæk] *v/t* saccheggiare

ran·som ['rænsəm] *n* riscatto *m*; *hold s.o. to* ~ tenere in ostaggio qu

'**ran·som mon·ey** (soldi *mpl* del) riscatto *m*

rant [rænt] *v/i*: ~ *and rave* inveire

rap [ræp] **1** *n at door etc* colpo *m*; MUS rap *m inv* **2** *v/t* (*pret & pp* -*ped*) *table etc* battere
  ♦ **rap at** *v/t window etc* bussare a

rape[1] [reɪp] **1** *n* stupro *m* **2** *v/t* violentare

rape[2] [reɪp] *n* BOT colza *f*

'**rape vic·tim** vittima *f* stupro

rap·id ['ræpɪd] *adj* rapido

ra·pid·i·ty [rə'pɪdətɪ] rapidità *f inv*

rap·id·ly ['ræpɪdlɪ] *adv* rapidamente

rap·ids ['ræpɪdz] *npl* rapide *fpl*

rap·ist ['reɪpɪst] violentatore *m*

rap·port [ræ'pɔː(r)] rapporto *m*

rap·ture ['ræptʃə(r)] *n*: *go into* ~*s over* andare in estasi per

rap·tur·ous ['ræptʃərəs] *adj* entusiastico

rare [reə(r)] *adj* raro; *steak* al sangue

rare·ly ['reəlɪ] *adv* raramente

rar·i·ty ['reərətɪ] rarità *f inv*

ras·cal ['rɑːskl] birbante *m/f*

rash[1] [ræʃ] *n* MED orticaria *f*

rash[2] [ræʃ] *adj* action, behaviour avventato

rash·er ['ræʃə(r)] fettina *f*

rash·ly ['ræʃlɪ] *adv* avventatamente

rasp·ber·ry ['rɑːzbərɪ] lampone *m*

rat [ræt] *n* ratto *m*

rate [reɪt] **1** *n of exchange* tasso *m*; *of pay, pricing* tariffa *f*; (*speed*) ritmo *m*; ~ *of interest* FIN tasso *m* d'interesse; *at this* ~ (*at this speed*) di questo passo; *at any* ~ in ogni modo **2** *v/t* (*consider, rank*) reputare

rath·er ['rɑːðə(r)] *adv* piuttosto; *I would* ~ *stay here* preferirei stare qui; *or would you* ~ ...? o preferiresti ...?

rat·i·fi·ca·tion [rætɪfɪ'keɪʃn] ratifica *f*

rat·i·fy ['rætɪfaɪ] *v/t* (*pret & pp* -*ied*) ratificare

rat·ings ['reɪtɪŋz] *npl* indice *m* d'ascolto

ra·tio ['reɪʃɪəʊ] proporzione *f*

ra·tion ['ræʃn] **1** *n* razione *f* **2** *v/t supplies* razionare

ra·tion·al ['ræʃənl] *adj* razionale

ra·tion·al·i·ty [ræʃə'nælɪtɪ] razionalità *f inv*

ra·tion·al·i·za·tion [ræʃənəlaɪ'zeɪʃn] razionalizzazione *f*

ra·tion·al·ize ['ræʃənəlaɪz] *v/t & v/i* razionalizzare

ra·tion·al·ly ['ræʃənlɪ] *adv* razionalmente

'**rat race** corsa *f* al successo

rat·tle ['rætl] **1** *n* noise rumore *m*; *toy* sonaglio *m* **2** *v/t* scuotere **3** *v/i* far rumore
  ♦ **rattle off** *v/t poem, list of names* snocciolare
  ♦ **rattle through** *v/t* fare di gran carriera

'**rat·tle·snake** serpente *m* a sonagli

rau·cous ['rɔːkəs] *adj* sguaiato

rav·age ['rævɪdʒ] **1** *n*: *the* ~*s of time* le ingiurie del tempo **2** *v/t*: ~*d by*

war devastato dalla guerra

rave [reɪv] **1** *v/i* delirare; **~ about sth** be very enthusiastic entusiasmarsi per qc **2** *n* party rave *m inv*

ra·ven ['reɪvn] corvo *m*

rav·e·nous ['rævənəs] *adj* famelico

rav·e·nous·ly ['rævənəslɪ] *adv* voracemente

rave re·view recensione *f* entusiastica

ra·vine [rə'viːn] burrone *m*

rav·ing ['reɪvɪŋ] *adv*: **~ mad** matto da legare

ra·vi·o·li ['rævɪəʊlɪ] *nsg* ravioli *mpl*

rav·ish·ing ['rævɪʃɪŋ] *adj* incantevole

raw [rɔː] *adj* meat, vegetable crudo; sugar, iron grezzo

raw ma·te·ri·al materia *f* prima

ray [reɪ] raggio *m*; **a ~ of hope** un raggio di speranza

raze [reɪz] *v/t*: **~ to the ground** radere al suolo

ra·zor ['reɪzə(r)] rasoio *m*

'ra·zor blade lametta *f* da barba

re [riː] *prep* COM con riferimento a

reach [riːtʃ] **1** *n*: **within ~** vicino (**of** a); *within arm's reach* a portata (di mano); **out of ~** non a portata (**of** di); **keep out of ~ of children** tenere lontano dalla portata dei bambini **2** *v/t* city etc arrivare a; decision, agreement, conclusion raggiungere; **can you ~ it?** ci arrivi?

◆ **reach out** *v/i* allungare la mano

re·act [rɪ'ækt] *v/i* reagire

re·ac·tion [rɪ'ækʃn] reazione *f*

re·ac·tion·a·ry [rɪ'ækʃnrɪ] **1** *n* POL reazionario *m*, -a *f* **2** *adj* POL reazionario

re·ac·tor [rɪ'æktə(r)] nuclear reattore *m*

read [riːd] (*pret & pp* **read** [red]) **1** *v/i* leggere; **~ to s.o.** leggere a qu **2** *v/t* leggere; (study) studiare

◆ **read out** *v/t* aloud leggere a voce alta

◆ **read up on** *v/t* documentarsi su

rea·da·ble ['riːdəbl] *adj* handwriting leggibile; book di piacevole lettura

read·er ['riːdə(r)] person lettore *m*, -trice *f*

read·i·ly ['redɪlɪ] *adv* (willingly) volentieri; (easily) facilmente

read·i·ness ['redɪnɪs] for action disponibilità *f inv*; to agree prontezza *f*

read·ing ['riːdɪŋ] also from meter lettura *f*

'read·ing mat·ter roba *f* da leggere

re·ad·just [riːə'dʒʌst] **1** *v/t* equipment, controls regolare **2** *v/i* to conditions riadattarsi

read-'on·ly file COMPUT file *m inv* di sola lettura

read-'on·ly mem·o·ry COMPUT memoria *f* di sola lettura

read·y ['redɪ] *adj* pronto; **get (o.s.) ~** prepararsi; **get sth ~** preparare qc

read·y 'cash contanti *mpl*; **read·y-made** *adj* stew etc precotto; solution bell'e pronto; **read·y-to-wear** *adj* confezionato

real [riːl] *adj* vero

real es·tate proprietà *fpl* immobiliari

re·al·ism ['rɪəlɪzm] realismo *m*

re·al·ist ['rɪəlɪst] realista *m/f*

re·al·is·tic [rɪə'lɪstɪk] *adj* realistico

re·al·is·tic·al·ly [rɪə'lɪstɪklɪ] *adv* realisticamente

re·al·i·ty [rɪ'ælətɪ] realtà *f inv*

re·a·li·za·tion [rɪəlaɪ'zeɪʃn] realizzazione *f*

re·a·lize ['rɪəlaɪz] *v/t* rendersi conto di, realizzare; FIN realizzare; **I ~ now that ...** ora capisco che ...

real·ly ['rɪəlɪ] *adv* veramente; **~?** davvero?; **not ~** (not much) non proprio

real 'time *n* COMPUT tempo *m* reale

real-time *adj* COMPUT in tempo reale

reap [riːp] *v/t* mietere

re·ap·pear [riːə'pɪə(r)] *v/i* riapparire

re·ap·pear·ance [riːə'pɪərəns] ricomparsa *f*

rear [rɪə(r)] **1** *n* of building retro *m*; of train parte *f* posteriore **2** *adj* posteriore

rear 'end F of person posteriore *m*

rear-'end *v/t*: **be ~ed** F essere tamponato

R

rear 'light *of car* fanalino *m* posteriore

re·arm [riː'ɑːm] **1** *v/t* riarmare **2** *v/i* riarmarsi

'rear·most *adj* ultimo

re·ar·range [riːə'reɪnʒ] *v/t furniture* spostare; *schedule* cambiare

rear-view 'mir·ror specchietto *m* retrovisore

rea·son ['riːzn] **1** *n faculty* ragione *f*; (*cause*) motivo *m*; *see / listen to ~* ascoltare ragione **2** *v/i*: *~ with s.o.* far ragionare con qu

rea·so·na·ble ['riːznəbl] *adj person, price* ragionevole; *weather, health* discreto; *a ~ number of people* un discreto numero di persone

rea·so·na·bly ['riːznəblɪ] *adv act, behave* ragionevolmente; (*quite*) abbastanza

rea·son·ing ['riːznɪŋ] ragionamento *m*

re·as·sure [riːə'ʃʊə(r)] *v/t* rassicurare

re·as·sur·ing [riːə'ʃʊərɪŋ] *adj* rassicurante

re·bate ['riːbeɪt] *money back* rimborso *m*

reb·el ['rebl] **1** *n* ribelle *m/f*; *~ forces* forze *fpl* ribelli **2** *v/i* [rɪ'bel] (*pret & pp* **-led**) ribellarsi

reb·el·lion [rɪ'belɪən] ribellione *f*

reb·el·lious [rɪ'belɪəs] *adj* ribelle

reb·el·lious·ly [rɪ'belɪəslɪ] *adv* con atteggiamento ribelle

reb·el·lious·ness [rɪ'belɪəsnɪs] spirito *m* di ribellione

re·boot [riː'buːt] *v/t & v/i* COMPUT riavviare

re·bound [rɪ'baʊnd] *v/i of ball etc* rimbalzare

re·buff [rɪ'bʌf] *n* secco rifiuto *m*

re·build ['riːbɪld] *v/t* (*pret & pp* **-built**) ricostruire

re·buke [rɪ'bjuːk] *v/t* rimproverare

re·call [rɪ'kɔːl] *v/t* richiamare; (*remember*) ricordare

re·cap ['riːkæp] *v/i* (*pret & pp* **-ped**) F ricapitolare

re·cap·ture [riː'kæptʃə(r)] *v/t criminal* ricatturare; *town* riconquistare

re·cede [rɪ'siːd] *v/i of flood waters* abbassarsi

re·ced·ing [rɪ'siːdɪŋ] *adj forehead, chin* sfuggente; *have a ~ hairline* essere stempiato

re·ceipt [rɪ'siːt] *for purchase* ricevuta *f*, scontrino *m*; *acknowledge ~ of sth* accusare ricevuta di qc; *~s* FIN introiti *mpl*

re·ceive [rɪ'siːv] *v/t* ricevere

re·ceiv·er [rɪ'siːvə(r)] *of letter* destinatario *m*, -a *f*; TELEC ricevitore *m*; *radio* apparecchio *m* ricevente

re·ceiv·er·ship [rɪ'siːvəʃɪp]: *be in ~* essere in amministrazione controllata

re·cent ['riːsnt] *adj* recente

re·cent·ly ['riːsntlɪ] *adv* recentemente

re·cep·tion [rɪ'sepʃn] *in hotel, company* reception *f inv*; *formal party* ricevimento *m*; (*welcome*) accoglienza *f*; *on radio, mobile phone* ricezione *f*

re·cep·tion desk banco *m* della reception

re·cep·tion·ist [rɪ'sepʃnɪst] receptionist *m/f inv*

re·cep·tive [rɪ'septɪv] *adj*: *be ~ to sth* essere ricettivo verso qc

re·cess ['riːses] *in wall etc* rientranza *f*; *of parliament* vacanza *f*

re·ces·sion [rɪ'seʃn] *economic* recessione *f*

re·charge [riː'tʃɑːdʒ] *v/t battery* ricaricare

re·ci·pe ['resəpɪ] ricetta *f*

're·ci·pe book ricettario *m*

re·cip·i·ent [rɪ'sɪpɪənt] destinatario *m*, -a *f*

re·cip·ro·cal [rɪ'sɪprəkl] *adj* reciproco

re·cit·al [rɪ'saɪtl] MUS recital *m inv*

re·cite [rɪ'saɪt] *v/t poem* recitare; *details, facts* enumerare

reck·less ['reklɪs] *adj* spericolato

reck·less·ly ['reklɪslɪ] *adv behave, drive* in modo spericolato; *spend* avventatamente

reck·on ['rekən] *v/i* (*think, consider*) pensare

R

♦**reckon on** v/t contare su

♦**reckon with** v/t: **have s.o. / sth to reakon with** dover fare i conti con qu / qc

reck·on·ing ['rekənɪŋ] calcoli mpl

re·claim [rɪ'kleɪm] v/t land bonificare

re·cline [rɪ'klaɪn] v/i sdraiarsi

re·clin·er [rɪ'klaɪnə(r)] chair poltrona f reclinabile

re·cluse [rɪ'klu:s] eremita m/f

rec·og·ni·tion [rekəg'nɪʃn] of state, s.o.'s achievements riconoscimento m; **have changed beyond ~** essere irriconoscibile

rec·og·niz·a·ble [rekəg'naɪzəbl] adj riconoscibile

rec·og·nize ['rekəgnaɪz] v/t riconoscere; **it can be ~d by ...** si riconosce da ...

re·coil [rɪ'kɔɪl] v/i indietreggiare

rec·ol·lect [rekə'lekt] v/t rammentare

rec·ol·lec·tion [rekə'lekʃn] ricordo m

rec·om·mend [rekə'mend] v/t consigliare

rec·om·men·da·tion [rekəmen'deɪʃn] consiglio m

rec·om·pense ['rekəmpens] n fml ricompensa f; LAW risarcimento m

rec·on·cile ['rekənsaɪl] v/t people, differences riconciliare; facts conciliare; **~ o.s. to ...** rassegnarsi a ...; **they are now ~d** si sono riconciliati

rec·on·cil·i·a·tion [rekənsɪlɪ'eɪʃn] of people, differences riconciliazione f; of facts conciliazione f

re·con·di·tion [ri:kən'dɪʃn] v/t ricondizionare

re·con·nais·sance [rɪ'kɒnɪsns] MIL ricognizione f

re·con·sid·er [ri:kən'sɪdə(r)] **1** v/t offer, one's position riconsiderare **2** v/i ripensare

re·con·struct [ri:kən'strʌkt] v/t city, crime, life ricostruire

rec·ord¹ ['rekɔːd] n MUS disco m; etc record m inv, primato m; written document etc nota f; in database record m inv; **~s** archivio m; **say sth off the ~** dire qc ufficiosamente;

have a criminal ~ avere precedenti penali; **he has a good ~ for punctuality / reliability** è sempre stato puntuale / affidabile

record² [rɪ'kɔːd] v/t electronically registrare; in writing annotare

'rec·ord-break·ing adj da record

re·cor·der [rɪ'kɔːdə(r)] MUS flauto m dolce

'rec·ord hold·er primatista m/f

re·cord·ing [rɪ'kɔːdɪŋ] registrazione f

re'cord·ing stu·di·o sala f di registrazione

rec·ord play·er ['rekɔːd] giradischi m inv

re·count [rɪ'kaʊnt] v/t (tell) raccontare

re·count ['ri:kaʊnt] **1** n of votes nuovo conteggio m **2** v/t (count again) ricontare

re·coup [rɪ'ku:p] v/t financial losses rifarsi di

re·cov·er [rɪ'kʌvə(r)] **1** v/t stolen goods recuperare **2** v/i from illness rimettersi

re·cov·er·y [rɪ'kʌvərɪ] of stolen goods recupero m; from illness guarigione f; **he has made a speedy ~** è guarito in fretta

rec·re·a·tion [rekrɪ'eɪʃn] ricreazione f

rec·re·a·tion·al [rekrɪ'eɪʃnl] adj done for pleasure ricreativo

re·cruit [rɪ'kru:t] **1** n MIL recluta f; to company neoassunto m, -a f **2** v/t new staff assumere; members arruolare

re·cruit·ment [rɪ'kru:tmənt] assunzione f; MIL, POL reclutamento m

re'cruit·ment drive campagna f di arruolamento

rec·tan·gle ['rektæŋgl] rettangolo m

rec·tan·gu·lar [rek'tæŋgjʊlə(r)] adj rettangolare

rec·ti·fy ['rektɪfaɪ] v/t (pret & pp -ied) (put right) rettificare

re·cu·pe·rate [rɪ'kju:pəreɪt] v/i recuperare

re·cur [rɪ'kɜː(r)] (pret & pp -red) v/i

R

of error, event ripetersi; *of symptoms* ripresentarsi

re·cur·rent[rɪ'kʌrənt] *adj* ricorrente

re·cy·cla·ble [riː'saɪkləbl] *adj* riciclabile

re·cy·cle[riː'saɪkl] *v/t* riciclare

re·cy·cling[riː'saɪklɪŋ] riciclo *m*

red[red] *adj* rosso; **in the ~** FIN in rosso

Red 'Cross Croce *f* Rossa

red·den['redn] *v/i* (*blush*) arrossire

re·dec·o·rate [riː'dekəreɪt] *v/t* ritinteggiare; *change wallpaper* ritapezzare

re·deem[rɪ'diːm] *v/t debt* estinguere; *sinners* redimere

re·deem·ing [rɪ'diːmɪŋ]: **~ feature** aspetto *m* positivo

re·demp·tion [rɪ'dempʃn] REL redenzione *f*

re·de·vel·op [riːdɪ'veləp] *v/t part of town* risanare

red-'hand·ed [red'hændɪd] *adj*: **catch s.o. ~** cogliere qu in flagrante; 'red·head rosso *m*, -a *f*; red-'hot *adj* rovente; red-'let·ter day giorno *m* memorabile; red 'light *at traffic lights* rosso *m*; red 'light dis·trict quartiere *m* a luci rosse; red 'meat carni *fpl* rosse

re·dou·ble [riː'dʌbl] *v/t*: **~ one's efforts** intensificare gli sforzi

red 'pep·per peperone *m* rosso

red 'tape F burocrazia *f*

re·duce[rɪ'djuːs] *v/t* ridurre

re·duc·tion [rɪ'dʌkʃn] riduzione *f*

re·dun·dan·cy [rɪ'dʌndənsɪ] Br *at work* licenziamento *m*

re'dun·dan·cy no·tice Br avviso *m* di licenziamento

re·'dun·dan·cy pay·ment Br indennità *f inv* di licenziamento

re·dun·dant[rɪ'dʌndənt] *adj* (*unnecessary*) superfluo; Br **be made ~ at work** essere licenziato; Br **make s.o. ~** licenziare qu

reed[riːd] BOT canna *f*

reef[riːf] *in sea* scogliera *f*

'reef knot nodo *m* piano

reek[riːk] *v/i* puzzare; **~ of ...** puzzare di ...

reel[riːl] *n of film* rullino *m*; *of thread* rocchetto *m*; *of tape* bobina *f*; *of fishing line* mulinello *m*

♦ reel off *v/t* snocciolare

re-e'lect *v/t* rieleggere

re-e'lec·tion rielezione *f*

re-'en·try *of spacecraft* rientro *m*

ref[ref] F arbitro *m*

re·fer [rɪ'fɜː(r)] **1** *v/t* (*pret & pp* **-red**): **~ a decision / problem to s.o.** rinviare una decisione / un problema a qu **2** *v/i*: **~ to ...** (*allude to*) riferirsi a ...; *dictionary etc* consultare ...

ref·er·ee [refə'riː] SP arbitro *m*; *for job* referenza *f*

ref·er·ence ['refərəns] (*allusion*) allusione *f*; *for job* referenza *f*; (**~ number**) (numero *m* di) riferimento *m*; **with ~ to** con riferimento a

'ref·er·ence book opera *f* di consultazione; 'ref·er·ence li·bra·ry biblioteca *f* di consultazione; 'ref·er·ence num·ber numero *m* di riferimento

ref·er·en·dum [refə'rendəm] referendum *m inv*

re·fill['riːfɪl] *v/t glass* riempire

re·fine[rɪ'faɪn] *v/t* raffinare

re·fined [rɪ'faɪnd] *adj manners, language* raffinato

re·fine·ment[rɪ'faɪnmənt] *to process, machine* miglioramento *m*

re·fin·e·ry [rɪ'faɪnərɪ] raffineria *f*

re·fla·tion['riː'fleɪʃn] reflazione *f*

reflect[rɪ'flekt] **1** *v/t light* riflettere; **be ~ed in ...** riflettersi in ... **2** *v/i* (*think*) riflettere

re·flec·tion[rɪ'flekʃn] *in water, glass etc* riflesso *m*; (*consideration*) riflessione *f*; **on ~** dopo averci riflettuto

re·flex['riːfleks] *in body* riflesso *m*

re·flex re'ac·tion riflesso *m*

re·form [rɪ'fɔːm] **1** *n* riforma *f* **2** *v/t* riformare

re·form·er [rɪ'fɔːmə(r)] riformatore *m*, -trice *f*

re·frain¹ [rɪ'freɪn] *v/i fml*: **please ~ from smoking** si prega di non fumare

re·frain²[rɪˈfreɪn] *n in song* ritornello *m*

re·fresh[rɪˈfreʃ] *v/t person* ristorare; **feel ~ed** sentirsi ristorato

refresh·er course[rɪˈfreʃə(r)] corso *m* di aggiornamento

re·fresh·ing[rɪˈfreʃɪŋ] *adj drink* rinfrescante; *experience* piacevole

re·fresh·ments [rɪˈfreʃmənts] *npl* rinfreschi *mpl*

re·fri·ge·rate[rɪˈfrɪdʒəreɪt] *v/t*: **keep ~d** conservare in frigo

re·fri·ge·ra·tor[rɪˈfrɪdʒəreɪtə(r)] frigorifero *m*

re·fu·el[riːˈfjuːəl] **1** *v/t aeroplane* rifornire di carburante **2** *v/i of aeroplane, car* fare rifornimento

ref·uge[ˈrefjuːdʒ] rifugio *m*; **take ~ from storm etc** ripararsi

ref·u·gee[refjʊˈdʒiː] rifugiato *m*, -a *f*, profugo *m*, -a *f*

re·fund 1 [ˈriːfʌnd] rimborso *m* **2** [rɪˈfʌnd] rimborsare

re·fus·al[rɪˈfjuːzl] rifiuto *m*

re·fuse¹[rɪˈfjuːz] *v/t & v/i* rifiutare; **~ to do sth** rifiutare di fare qc

ref·use² [ˈrefjuːs] (*garbage*) rifiuti *mpl*

'ref·use col·lec·tion raccolta *f* dei rifiuti

'ref·use dumpdiscarica *f* (dei rifiuti)

re·fute[rɪˈfjuːt] *v/t* confutare

re·gain [rɪˈgeɪn] *v/t control, lost territory, the lead* riconquistare

re·gal[ˈriːgl] *adj* regale

re·gard [rɪˈgɑːd] **1** *n*: **have great ~ for s.o.** avere molta stima di qu; **in this ~** a questo riguardo; **with ~ to** riguardo a; (*kind*) **~s** cordiali saluti; **give my ~s to Paola** saluti a Paola; **with no ~ for ...** senza alcun riguardo per ... **2** *v/t*: **s.o. / sth as sth** considerare qu/qc come qc; **as ~s ...** riguardo a ...

re·gard·ing[rɪˈgɑːdɪŋ] *prep* riguardo a

re·gard·less [rɪˈgɑːdlɪs] *adv* lo stesso; **~ of** senza tener conto di

re·gime[reɪˈʒiːm] (*government*) regime *m*

re·gi·ment[ˈredʒɪmənt] *n* reggimento *m*

re·gion[ˈriːdʒən] regione *f*; **in the ~ of** intorno a

re·gion·al[ˈriːdʒənl] *adj* regionale

re·gis·ter [ˈredʒɪstə(r)] **1** *n* registro *m* **2** *v/t birth, death: by individual* denunciare; *by authorities* registrare; *vehicle* iscrivere; *letter* assicurare; *emotion* mostrare; **send a letter ~ed** spedire una lettera assicurata **3** *v/i at university* iscriversi; **I'm ~ed with Dr Lee** il mio medico è il dottor Lee

re·gis·tered let·ter[ˈredʒɪstəd] (lettera *f*) assicurata *f*

reg·is·trar [redʒɪˈstrɑː(r)] *of births etc* ufficiale *m* di stato civile

re·gis·tra·tion[redʒɪˈstreɪʃn] *Br* (*vehicle number*) numero *m* di targa; *at university* iscrizione *f*

re·gis·tra·tion num·ber *Br* MOT numero *m* di targa

re·gis·try of·fice [ˈredʒɪstrɪ] ufficio *m* di stato civile

re·gret [rɪˈgret] **1** *v/t* (*pret & pp* **-ted**) rammaricarsi di; *missed opportunity* rimpiangere; **we ~ to inform you that ...** siamo spiacenti di informarla che ... **2** *n* rammarico *m*

re·gret·ful[rɪˈgretfəl] *adj* di rammarico

re·gret·ful·ly [rɪˈgretfəlɪ] *adv* con rammarico

re·gret·ta·ble[rɪˈgretəbl] *adj* deplorevole

re·gret·ta·bly [rɪˈgretəblɪ] *adv* purtroppo

reg·u·lar[ˈregjʊlə(r)] **1** *adj* regolare; (*esp Am: ordinary*) normale **2** *n at bar etc* cliente *m/f* abituale

reg·u·lar·i·ty[regjʊˈlærətɪ] regolarità *f inv*

reg·u·lar·ly[ˈregjʊlərlɪ] *adv* regolarmente

reg·u·late [ˈregʊleɪt] *v/t* regolare

reg·u·la·tion[regʊˈleɪʃn] (*rule*) regolamento *m*; *control* controllo *m*

re·hab[ˈriːhæb] F riabilitazione *f*

re·ha·bil·i·tate [riːhəˈbɪlɪteɪt] *v/t ex-criminal* riabilitare

R

re·hears·al [rɪ'hɜːsl] prova *f*
re·hearse [rɪ'hɜːs] *v/t & v/i* provare
reign [reɪn] **1** *n* regno *m* **2** *v/i* regnare
re·im·burse [riːɪm'bɜːs] *v/t* rimborsare
rein [reɪn] redine *f*
re·in·car·na·tion [riːɪnkɑː'neɪʃn] reincarnazione *f*
re·in·force [riːɪn'fɔːs] *v/t* rinforzare
re·in·forced con·crete [riːɪn'fɔːst] cemento *m* armato
re·in·force·ments [riːɪn'fɔːsmənts] *npl* MIL rinforzi *mpl*
re·in·state [riːɪn'steɪt] *v/t* reintegrare
re·it·e·rate [riː'ɪtəreɪt] *v/t fml* ripetere
re·ject [rɪ'dʒekt] *v/t* respingere
re·jec·tion [rɪ'dʒekʃn] rifiuto *m*
re·lapse ['riːlæps] *n* MED ricaduta *f*; **have a ~** avere una ricaduta
re·late [rɪ'leɪt] **1** *v/t story* raccontare; **~ sth to sth** collegare qc a qc **2** *v/i:* **~ to …** be connected with riferirsi a …; **he doesn't ~ to people** non sa stabilire un rapporto con gli altri
re·lat·ed [rɪ'leɪtɪd] *adj by family* imparentato; *events, ideas etc* collegato
re·la·tion [rɪ'leɪʃn] *in family* parente *m/f*; *(connection)* rapporto *m*; **business/diplomatic ~s** rapporti d'affari/diplomatici
re·la·tion·ship [rɪ'leɪʃnʃɪp] rapporto *m*
rel·a·tive ['relətɪv] **1** *n* parente *m/f* **2** *adj* relativo; **X is ~ to Y** X è legato a Y
rel·a·tive·ly ['relətɪvlɪ] *adv* relativamente
re·lax [rɪ'læks] **1** *v/i* rilassarsi; **~!, don't get angry** rilassati! non te la prendere **2** *v/t* rilassare
re·lax·a·tion [riːlæk'seɪʃn] relax *m inv*; *of rules etc* rilassamento *m*
re·laxed [rɪ'lækst] *adj* rilassato
re·lax·ing [rɪ'læksɪŋ] *adj* rilassante
re·lay [riː'leɪ] **1** *v/t* trasmettere **2** *n:* **~ (race)** *(corsa f a)* staffetta *f*
re·lease [rɪ'liːs] **1** *n from prison* rilascio *m*; *of CD etc* uscita *f*; *of software* versione *f*; **this film is a new ~** è un

film appena uscito **2** *v/t prisoner* rilasciare; *handbrake* togliere; *film, record* far uscire; *information* rendere noto
rel·e·gate ['relɪgeɪt] *v/t* relegare; **be ~d** SP essere retrocesso
rel·e·ga·tion [relɪ'geɪʃn] SP retrocessione *f*
re·lent [rɪ'lent] *v/i* cedere
re·lent·less [rɪ'lentlɪs] *adj* incessante, implacabile
re·lent·less·ly [rɪ'lentlɪslɪ] *adv* incessantemente
rel·e·vance ['reləvəns] pertinenza *f*
rel·e·vant ['reləvənt] *adj* pertinente
re·li·a·bil·i·ty [rɪlaɪə'bɪlətɪ] affidabilità *f inv*
re·li·a·ble [rɪ'laɪəbl] *adj* affidabile
re·li·a·bly [rɪ'laɪəblɪ] *adv:* **I am ~ informed that …** so da fonte certa che …
re·li·ance [rɪ'laɪəns] dipendenza *f*; **~ on s.o./sth** dipendenza da qu/qc
re·li·ant [rɪ'laɪənt] *adj:* **be ~ on** dipendere da
rel·ic ['relɪk] reliquia *f*
re·lief [rɪ'liːf] sollievo *m*; **that's a ~** che sollievo; **in ~ in art** in rilievo
re·lieve [rɪ'liːv] *v/t pressure, pain* alleviare; *(take over from)* dare il cambio a; **be ~d at** *news etc* essere sollevato
re·li·gion [rɪ'lɪdʒən] religione *f*
re·li·gious [rɪ'lɪdʒəs] *adj* religioso
re·li·gious·ly [rɪ'lɪdʒəslɪ] *adv (conscientiously)* religiosamente
re·lin·quish [rɪ'lɪŋkwɪʃ] *v/t* rinunciare a
rel·ish ['relɪʃ] **1** *n sauce* salsa *f*; *(enjoyment)* gusto *m* **2** *v/t idea, prospect* gradire
re·live [riː'lɪv] *v/t* rivivere
re·lo·cate [riːlə'keɪt] *v/i of business, employee* trasferirsi
re·lo·ca·tion [riːlə'keɪʃn] *of business, employee* trasferimento *m*
re·luc·tance [rɪ'lʌktəns] riluttanza *f*
re·luc·tant [rɪ'lʌktənt] *adj* riluttante; **be ~ to do sth** essere restio a fare qc
re·luc·tant·ly [rɪ'lʌktəntlɪ] *adv* a malincuore

♦ **re·ly on** [rɪ'laɪ] *v/t* (*pret & pp -ied*) contare su; *rely on s.o. to do sth* contare su qu perché faccia qc

re·main [rɪ'meɪn] *v/i* rimanere

re·main·der [rɪ'meɪndə(r)] **1** *n also* MATH resto *m* **2** *v/t* svendere

re·main·ing [rɪ'meɪnɪŋ] *adj* restante

re·mains [rɪ'meɪnz] *npl of body* resti *mpl*

re·make ['riːmeɪk] *n of film* remake *m inv*

re·mand [rɪ'mɑːnd] **1** *v/t*: ~ *s.o. in custody* ordinare la custodia cautelare di qu **2** *n*: *be on* ~ essere in attesa di giudizio

re·mark [rɪ'mɑːk] **1** *n* commento *m* **2** *v/t* osservare

re·mar·ka·ble [rɪ'mɑːkəbl] *adj* notevole

re·mark·a·bly [rɪ'mɑːkəblɪ] *adv* notevolmente

re·mar·ry [riː'mærɪ] *v/i* (*pret & pp -ied*) risposarsi

rem·e·dy ['remədɪ] *n* rimedio *m*

re·mem·ber [rɪ'membə(r)] **1** *v/t* ricordare; ~ *to lock the door* ricordati di chiudere la porta a chiave; ~ *me to her* dalle i miei saluti **2** *v/i* ricordare, ricordarsi

Re·mem·brance Day [rɪ'membrəns] *11 novembre, commemorazione f dei caduti in guerra*

re·mind [rɪ'maɪnd] *v/t*: ~ *s.o. of s.o. / sth* ricordare qu / qc a qu

re·mind·er [rɪ'maɪndə(r)] promemoria *m*; COM: *for payment* sollecito *m*

rem·i·nisce [remɪ'nɪs] *v/i* rievocare il passato

rem·i·nis·cent [remɪ'nɪsənt] *adj*: *be ~ of sth* far venire in mente qc

re·miss [rɪ'mɪs] *adj fml* negligente

re·mis·sion [rɪ'mɪʃn] remissione *f*

rem·nant ['remnənt] resto *m*; *of fabric* scampolo *m*

re·morse [rɪ'mɔːs] rimorso *m*

re·morse·less [rɪ'mɔːslɪs] *adj* spietato

re·mote 'ac·cess COMPUT accesso *m* remoto

re·mote con'trol telecomando *m*

re·mote·ly [rɪ'məʊtlɪ] *adv related, connected* lontanamente; *just ~ possible* vagamente possibile

re·mote·ness [rɪ'məʊtnəs] isolamento *m*

re·mov·a·ble [rɪ'muːvəbl] *adj* staccabile

re·mov·al [rɪ'muːvl] rimozione *f*; *from home* trasloco *m*

re'mov·al firm ditta *f* di traslochi

re'mov·al van furgone *m* dei traslochi

re·move [rɪ'muːv] *v/t top, lid* togliere; MED asportare; *doubt, suspicion* eliminare

re·mu·ner·a·tion [rɪmjuːnə'reɪʃn] rimunerazione *f*

re·mu·ner·a·tive [rɪ'mjuːnərətɪv] *adj* rimunerativo

Re·nais·sance [rɪ'neɪsəns] Rinascimento *m*

re·name [riː'neɪm] *v/t* ribattezzare; *file* rinominare

ren·der ['rendə(r)] *v/t service* rendere; ~ *s.o. helpless* rendere infermo qu

ren·der·ing ['rendərɪŋ] *of piece of music* interpretazione *f*

ren·dez·vous ['rɒndeɪvuː] (*meeting*) incontro *m*

re·new [rɪ'njuː] *v/t contract, licence* rinnovare; *feel ~ed* sentirsi rinato

re·new·al [rɪ'njuːəl] *of contract etc* rinnovo *m*

re·nounce [rɪ'naʊns] *v/t title, rights* rinunciare a

ren·o·vate ['renəveɪt] *v/t* ristrutturare

ren·o·va·tion [renə'veɪʃn] ristrutturazione *f*

re·nown [rɪ'naʊn] fama *f*

re·nowned [rɪ'naʊnd] *adj* famoso

rent [rent] **1** *n* affitto *m*; *for ~* affittasi **2** *v/t flat* affittare; *car equipment*, noleggiare; (~ *out*) affittare

rent·al ['rentl] *for flat* affitto *m*; *for car* noleggio *m*; *for TV, phone* canone *m*

R

'rent·al a·gree·ment contratto *m* di noleggio

rent-'free *adv* gratis

re·o·pen [riː'əʊpn] *v/t & v/i* riaprire

re·or·gan·i·za·tion [riːɔːɡənaɪz'eɪʃn] riorganizzazione *f*

re·or·gan·ize [riː'ɔːɡənaɪz] *v/t* riorganizzare

rep [rep] COM rappresentante *m/f*

re·paint [riː'peɪnt] *v/t* ridipingere

re·pair [rɪ'peə(r)] **1** *v/t* riparare **2** *n: in a good / bad state of ~* in buono / cattivo stato; **~s** riparazioni *fpl*

re'pair·man tecnico *m*

re·pa·tri·ate [riː'pætrɪeɪt] *v/t* rimpatriare

re·pa·tri·a·tion [riː'pætrɪ'eɪʃn] rimpatrio *m*

re·pay [riː'peɪ] *v/t* (*pret & pp* **-paid**) *money* restituire; *person* ripagare

re·pay·ment [riː'peɪmənt] pagamento *m*

re·peal [rɪ'piːl] *v/t law* abrogare

re·peat [rɪ'piːt] **1** *v/t* ripetere; *am I ~ing myself?* l'ho già detto? **2** *n programme* replica *f*

re·peat 'busi·ness COM ulteriori ordini *mpl*

re·peat·ed [rɪ'piːtɪd] *adj* ripetuto

re·peat·ed·ly [rɪ'piːtɪdlɪ] *adv* ripetutamente

re·peat 'or·der COM ulteriore ordine *m*

re·pel [rɪ'pel] *v/t* (*pret & pp* **-led**) *invaders, attack* respingere; (*disgust*) ripugnare

re·pel·lent [rɪ'pelənt] **1** *n* (*insect ~*) insettifugo *m* **2** *adj* ripugnante

re·pent [rɪ'pent] *v/i* pentirsi

re·per·cus·sions [riːpə'kʌʃnz] *npl* ripercussioni *fpl*

rep·er·toire ['repətwɑː(r)] repertorio *m*

rep·e·ti·tion [repɪ'tɪʃn] ripetizione *f*

rep·e·ti·tive [rɪ'petɪtɪv] *adj* ripetitivo

re·place [rɪ'pleɪs] *v/t* (*put back*) mettere a posto *v/t* (*take the place of*) sostituire

re·place·ment [rɪ'pleɪsmənt] *person* sostituto *m*, -a *f*; *act* sostituzione *f*; *this is the ~ for the old model* questo è il modello che sostituisce il vecchio

re·place·ment 'part pezzo *m* di ricambio

re·play ['riːpleɪ] **1** *n recording* replay *m inv*; *match* spareggio *m* **2** *v/t match* rigiocare

re·plen·ish [rɪ'plenɪʃ] *v/t container* riempire; *supplies* rifornire

rep·li·ca ['replɪkə] copia *f*

re·ply [rɪ'plaɪ] **1** *n* risposta *f* **2** *v/t & v/i* (*pret & pp* **-ied**) rispondere

re·port [rɪ'pɔːt] **1** *n* (*account*) resoconto *m*; *by journalist* servizio *m*; EDU pagella *f* **2** *v/t facts* fare un servizio su; *to authorities* denunciare; *~ one's findings to s.o.* riferire sulle proprie conclusioni a qu; *~ a person to the police* denunciare qualcuno alla polizia; *he is ~ed to be in London* si dice che sia a Londra **3** *v/i of journalist* fare un reportage; (*present o.s.*) presentarsi ♦ *report to v/t in business* rendere conto a

re·port·er [rɪ'pɔːtə(r)] giornalista *m/f*

re·pos·sess [riːpə'zes] *v/t* COM riprendersi

rep·re·hen·si·ble [reprɪ'hensəbl] *adj* riprovevole

rep·re·sent [reprɪ'zent] *v/t* rappresentare

rep·re·sen·ta·tive [reprɪ'zentətɪv] **1** *n* rappresentante *m/f* **2** *adj* (*typical*) rappresentativo

re·press [rɪ'pres] *v/t* reprimere

re·pres·sion [rɪ'preʃn] POL repressione *f*

re·pres·sive [rɪ'presɪv] *adj* POL repressivo

re·prieve [rɪ'priːv] **1** *n* LAW sospensione *f* della pena capitale; *fig* proroga *f* **2** *v/t prisoner* sospendere l'esecuzione di

rep·ri·mand ['reprɪmɑːnd] *v/t* ammonire

re·print ['riːprɪnt] **1** *n* ristampa *f* **2** *v/t* ristampare

re·pri·sal [rɪ'praɪzl] rappresaglia *f*; *take ~s* fare delle rappresaglie; *in ~*

for per rappresaglia contro

re·proach [rɪ'prəʊtʃ] **1** n rimprovero m; **be beyond ~** essere irreprensibile **2** v/t rimproverare

re·proach·ful [rɪ'prəʊtʃfʊl] adj di rimprovero

re·proach·ful·ly [rɪ'prəʊtʃfʊlɪ] adv con aria di rimprovero

re·pro·duce [riːprə'djuːs] **1** v/t riprodurre **2** v/i riprodursi

re·pro·duc·tion [riːprə'dʌkʃn] riproduzione f

re·pro·duc·tive [riprə'dʌktɪv] adj riproduttivo

rep·tile ['reptaɪl] rettile m

re·pub·lic [rɪ'pʌblɪk] repubblica f

re·pub·li·can [rɪ'pʌblɪkn] **1** n repubblicano m, -a **2** adj repubblicano

re·pu·di·ate [rɪ'pjuːdɪeɪt] v/t (deny) respingere

re·pul·sive [rɪ'pʌlsɪv] adj ripugnante

rep·u·ta·ble ['repjʊtəbl] adj rispettabile

rep·u·ta·tion [repjʊ'teɪʃn] reputazione f; **have a good/bad ~** avere una buona/cattiva reputazione

re·put·ed [rep'jʊtəd] adj: **be ~ to be** avere la fama di essere

re·put·ed·ly [rep'jʊtədlɪ] adv a quanto si dice

re·quest [rɪ'kwest] **1** n richiesta f; **on ~** su richiesta **2** v/t richiedere

re·qui·em ['rekwɪəm] MUS requiem m inv

re·quire [rɪ'kwaɪə(r)] v/t (need) aver bisogno di; **it ~s great care** richiede molta cura; **as ~d by law** come prescritto dalla legge; **guests are ~d to …** i signori clienti sono pregati di …

re·quired [rɪ'kwaɪəd] adj (necessary) necessario

re·quire·ment [rɪ'kwaɪəmənt] (need) esigenza f; (condition) requisito m

req·ui·si·tion [rekwɪ'zɪʃn] v/t requisire

re·route [riː'ruːt] v/t aeroplane etc deviare

re·run ['riːrʌn] **1** n of programme replica f **2** v/t (pret **-ran**, pp **-run**) programme replicare

re·sched·ule [riː'ʃedjuːl] v/t stabilire di nuovo

res·cue ['reskjuː] **1** n salvataggio m; **come to s.o.'s ~** andare in aiuto a qu **2** v/t salvare

'res·cue par·ty squadra f di soccorso

re·search [rɪ'sɜːtʃ] n ricerca f

♦ **research into** v/t fare ricerca su

re·search and de·vel·op·ment ricerca f e sviluppo m

re·search as·sist·ant assistente ricercatore m, -trice f

re·search·er [rɪ'sɜːtʃə(r)] ricercatore m, -trice f

re'search proj·ect ricerca f

re·sem·blance [rɪ'zembləns] somiglianza f

re·sem·ble [rɪ'zembl] v/t (as)somigliare a

re·sent [rɪ'zent] v/t risentirsi per

re·sent·ful [rɪ'zentfʊl] adj pieno di risentimento

re·sent·ful·ly [rɪ'zentfʊlɪ] adv con risentimento

re·sent·ment [rɪ'zentmənt] risentimento m

res·er·va·tion [rezə'veɪʃn] of room, table prenotazione f; mental, special area riserva f; **I have a ~ in hotel, restaurant** ho prenotato

re·serve [rɪ'zɜːv] **1** n (store) riserva f; (aloofness) riserbo m; SP riserva f; **~s** FIN riserve fpl; **keep sth in ~** tenere qc di riserva **2** v/t seat, table prenotare; judgment riservarsi

re·served [rɪ'zɜːvd] adj person, manner riservato; table, seat prenotato

res·er·voir ['rezəvwɑː(r)] for water bacino m idrico

re·shuf·fle ['riːʃʌfl] **1** n POL rimpasto m **2** v/t POL rimpastare

re·side [rɪ'zaɪd] v/i fml risiedere

res·i·dence ['rezɪdəns] fml: house etc residenza f; (stay) permanenza f

'res·i·dence per·mit permesso m di residenza

'res·i·dent ['rezɪdənt] **1** n residente m/f **2** adj living in a building residente sul posto

res·i·den·tial [rezɪ'denʃl] adj district residenziale

res·i·due ['rezɪdjuː] residuo *m*

re·sign [rɪ'zaɪn] **1** *v/t position* dimettersi da; **~ o.s. to** rassegnarsi a **2** *v/i from job* dimettersi

res·ig·na·tion [rezɪg'neɪʃn] *from job* dimissioni *fpl*; *mental* rassegnazione *f*

re·signed [re'zaɪnd] *adj* rassegnato; **we have become ~ to the fact that …** ci siamo rassegnati al fatto che …

re·sil·i·ent [rɪ'zɪlɪənt] *adj personality* che ha molte risorse; *material* resistente

res·in ['rezɪn] resina *f*

re·sist [rɪ'zɪst] **1** *v/t* resistere a **2** *v/i* resistere

re·sist·ance [rɪ'zɪstəns] resistenza *f*

re·sis·tant [rɪ'zɪstənt] *adj material* resistente; **~ to heat / rust** resistente al calore / alla ruggine

re·sit ['riːsɪt] *v/t exam* ridare

res·o·lute ['rezəluːt] *adj* risoluto

res·o·lu·tion [rezə'luːʃn] *(decision)* risoluzione *f*; *made at New Year etc* proposito *m*; *(determination)* fermezza *f*; *of problem* soluzione *f*; *of image* risoluzione *f*

re·solve [rɪ'zɒlv] *v/t problem, mystery* risolvere; **~ to do sth** decidere di fare qc

re·sort [rɪ'zɔːt] *n place* località *f inv*; *holiday ~* luogo *m* di villeggiatura; *ski ~* stazione *f* sciistica; *as a last ~* come ultima risorsa

♦ **re·sort to** *v/t violence, threats* far ricorso a

♦ **re·sound with** [rɪ'zaʊnd] *v/t* risuonare di

re·sound·ing [rɪ'zaʊndɪŋ] *adj success, victory* clamoroso

re·source [rɪ'sɔːs] risorsa *f*; *financial ~s* mezzi *mpl* economici; *leave s.o. to his own ~s* lasciare qu in balia di se stesso

re·source·ful [rɪ'sɔːsfʊl] *adj* pieno di risorse

re·spect [rɪ'spekt] **1** *n* rispetto *m*; *show ~ to* avere rispetto per; *with ~ to* riguardo a; *in this / that ~* quanto a questo; *in many ~s* sotto molti aspetti; *pay one's last ~s to s.o.* rendere omaggio a qu **2** *v/t* rispettare

re·spect·a·bil·i·ty [rɪspektə'bɪlətɪ] rispettabilità *f inv*

re·spec·ta·ble [rɪ'spektəbl] *adj* rispettabile

re·spec·ta·bly [rɪ'spektəblɪ] *adv* rispettabilmente

re·spect·ful [rɪ'spektfʊl] *adj* rispettoso

re·spect·ful·ly [rɪ'spektflɪ] *adv* con rispetto

re·spec·tive [rɪ'spektɪv] *adj* rispettivo

re·spec·tive·ly [rɪ'spektɪvlɪ] *adv* rispettivamente

res·pi·ra·tion [respɪ'reɪʃn] respirazione *f*

res·pi·ra·tor [respɪ'reɪtə(r)] MED respiratore *m*

re·spite ['respaɪt] tregua *f*; *without ~* senza tregua

re·spond [rɪ'spɒnd] *v/i* rispondere

re·sponse [rɪ'spɒns] risposta *f*

re·spon·si·bil·i·ty [rɪspɒnsɪ'bɪlətɪ] responsabilità *f inv*; *accept ~ for* assumersi la responsabilità di; *a job with more ~* un lavoro con più responsabilità

re·spon·si·ble [rɪ'spɒnsəbl] *adj* responsabile (*for* di); *job, position* di responsabilità

re·spon·sive [rɪ'spɒnsɪv] *adj audience* caloroso; *be ~ of brakes* rispondere bene

rest[1] [rest] **1** *n* riposo *m*; *set s.o.'s mind at ~* tranquillizzare qu **2** *v/i* riposare; **~ on …** *(be based on)* basarsi su …; *(lean against)* poggiare su …; *it all ~s with him* dipende tutto da lui **3** *v/t (lean, balance)* appoggiare

rest[2] [rest] *n*: *the ~* il resto *m*

res·tau·rant ['restrɒnt] ristorante *m*

'res·tau·rant car RAIL vagone *m* ristorante

'rest cure cura *f* del riposo

rest·ful ['restfʊl] *adj* riposante

'rest home casa *f* di riposo

rest·less ['restlɪs] *adj* irrequieto;

545 **return**

have a ~ **night** passare una notte agitata

rest·less·ly ['restlɪslɪ] *adv* nervosamente

res·to·ra·tion [restə'reɪʃn] restauro *m*

re·store [rɪ'stɔː(r)] *v/t building etc* restaurare; (*bring back*) restituire

re·strain [rɪ'streɪn] *v/t dog, troops* frenare; *emotions* reprimere; ~ **o.s.** trattenersi

re·straint [rɪ'streɪnt] (*self-control*) autocontrollo *m*

re·strict [rɪ'strɪkt] *v/t* limitare; **I'll ~ myself to ...** mi limiterò a ...

re·strict·ed [rɪ'strɪktɪd] *adj view* limitato

re·strict·ed 'ar·e·a MIL zona *f* militare

re·stric·tion [rɪ'strɪkʃn] restrizione *f*

'**rest room** *Am* gabinetto *m*

re·sult [rɪ'zʌlt] *n* risultato *m*; *as a ~ of this* in conseguenza a ciò

♦ **result from** *v/t* risultare da, derivare da

♦ **result in** *v/t* dare luogo a; *this resulted in him feeling even worse* questo ha fatto sì che stesse ancora peggio

re·sume [rɪ'zjuːm] *v/t & v/i* riprendere

ré·su·mé ['rezumeɪ] *Am* curriculum vitae *m inv*

re·sump·tion [rɪ'zʌmpʃn] ripresa *f*

re·sur·face [riː'sɜːfɪs] **1** *v/t roads* asfaltare **2** *v/i* (*reappear*) riaffiorare

Res·ur·rec·tion [rezə'rekʃn] REL resurrezione *f*

re·sus·ci·tate [rɪ'sʌsɪteɪt] *v/t* rianimare

re·sus·ci·ta·tion [rɪsʌsɪ'teɪʃn] rianimazione *f*

re·tail ['riːteɪl] **1** *adv* al dettaglio **2** *v/i*: ~ **at ...** essere in vendita a ...

re·tail·er ['riːteɪlə(r)] dettagliante *m/f*

'**re·tail out·let** punto *m* (di) vendita

'**re·tail price** prezzo *m* al dettaglio

re·tain [rɪ'teɪn] *v/t* conservare

re·tain·er [rɪ'teɪnə(r)] FIN onorario *m*

re·tal·i·ate [rɪ'tælɪeɪt] *v/i* vendicarsi

re·tal·i·a·tion [rɪtælɪ'eɪʃn] rappresaglia *f*; *in ~ for* per rappresaglia contro

re·tard·ed [rɪ'tɑːdɪd] *adj mentally* ritardato

rethink [riː'θɪŋk] *v/t* (*pret & pp* -**thought**) riconsiderare

re·ti·cence ['retɪsns] riservatezza *f*

re·ti·cent ['retɪsnt] *adj* riservato

re·tire [rɪ'taɪə(r)] *v/i from work* andare in pensione

re·tired [rɪ'taɪəd] *adj* in pensione

re·tire·ment [rɪ'taɪəmənt] pensione *f*, *act* pensionamento *m*

re'tire·ment age età *f inv* pensionabile

re·tir·ing [rɪ'taɪərɪŋ] *adj* riservato

re·tort [rɪ'tɔːt] **1** *n* replica *f* **2** *v/t* replicare

re·trace [rɪ'treɪs] *v/t*: ~ **one's footsteps** ritornare sui propri passi

re·tract [rɪ'trækt] *v/t claws* ritrarre; *undercarriage* far rientrare; *statement* ritrattare

re·train [riː'treɪn] *v/i* riqualificarsi

re·treat [rɪ'triːt] **1** *v/i* ritirarsi **2** *n* MIL ritirata *f*; *place* rifugio *m*

re·trieve [rɪ'triːv] *v/t* recuperare

re·triev·er [rɪ'triːvə(r)] *dog* cane *m* da riporto

ret·ro·ac·tive [retrəʊ'æktɪv] *adj law etc* retroattivo

ret·ro·ac·tive·ly [retrəʊ'æktɪvlɪ] *adv* retroattivamente

ret·ro·grade ['retrəgreɪd] *adj move, decision* retrogrado

ret·ro·spect ['retrəspekt] *in ~* ripensandoci

ret·ro·spec·tive [retrə'spekt ɪv] *n* retrospettiva *f*

re·turn [rɪ'tɜːn] **1** *n* ritorno *m*; (*giving back*) restituzione *f*; COMPUT (*tasto m*) invio *m*; *in tennis* risposta *f* al servizio; *tax ~* dichiarazione *f* dei redditi; *by ~ (of post)* a stretto giro di posta; *~s (profit)* rendimento *m*; *many happy ~s (of the day)* cento di questi giorni!; *in ~ for* in cambio di **2** *v/t* (*give back*) restituire; (*put back*) rimettere; *favour, invitation* ricambiare 3 *v/i* (*go back, come back*) ritornare; *of symptoms, doubts etc* ricomparire

re·turn 'flight volo *m* di ritorno; **re·turn 'jour·ney** viaggio *m* di ritorno; **re·turn 'match** partita *f* (del girone) di ritorno; **re·turn 'tick·et** biglietto *m* (di) andata e ritorno

re·u·ni·fi·ca·tion [ri:ju:nɪfɪˈkeɪʃn] riunificazione *f*

re·u·nion [riːˈjuːnɪən] riunione *f*

re·u·nite [riːjuːˈnaɪt] *v/t* riunire

re·us·a·ble [riːˈjuːzəbl] *adj* riutilizzabile

re·use [riːˈjuːz] *v/t* riutilizzare

rev [rev] *n*: **~s per minute** giri al minuto

♦ **rev up** *v/t* (*pret & pp* **-ved**) *engine* far andare su di giri

re·val·u·a·tion [riːvæljuˈeɪʃn] rivalutazione *f*

re·veal [rɪˈviːl] *v/t* (*make visible*) mostrare; (*make known*) rivelare

re·veal·ing [rɪˈviːlɪŋ] *adj remark* rivelatore; *dress* scollato

♦ **revel in** [ˈrevl] *v/t* (*pret & pp* **-led**, *Am* **-ed**) godere di

rev·e·la·tion [revəˈleɪʃn] rivelazione *f*

re·venge [rɪˈvendʒ] *n* vendetta *f*; **take one's ~** vendicarsi; **in ~ for** per vendicarsi di

rev·e·nue [ˈrevənjuː] reddito *m*

re·ver·be·rate [rɪˈvɜːbəreɪt] *v/i of sound* rimbombare

re·vere [rɪˈvɪə(r)] *v/t* riverire

rev·e·rence [ˈrevərəns] rispetto *m*

Rev·e·rend [ˈrevərənd] REL reverendo *m*

rev·e·rent [ˈrevərənt] *adj* riverente

re·verse [rɪˈvɜːs] **1** *adj sequence* opposto; **in ~ order** in ordine inverso **2** *n* (*opposite*) contrario *m*; (*back*) rovescio *m*; MOT retromarcia *f* **3** *v/t sequence* invertire; **~ the car** fare marcia indietro; **~ the charges** TELEC telefonare a carico del destinatario **4** *v/i* MOT fare marcia indietro

revert [rɪˈvɜːt] *v/i*: **~ to** ritornare a

re·view [rɪˈvjuː] **1** *n of book, film*

censione *f*; *of troops* rivista *f*; *of situation etc* revisione *f* **2** *v/t book, film* recensire; *troops* passare in rivista; *situation etc* riesaminare

re·view·er [rɪˈvjuːə(r)] *of book, film* critico *m*, -a *f*

re·vise [rɪˈvaɪz] **1** *v/t opinion, text* rivedere; EDU ripassare **2** *v/i* EDU ripassare

re·vi·sion [rɪˈvɪʒn] *of opinion, text* revisione *f*; *for exam* ripasso *m*

re·viv·al [rɪˈvaɪvl] *of custom, old style etc* revival *m inv*; *of patient* ripresa *f*

re·vive [rɪˈvaɪv] **1** *v/t custom, old style etc* riportare alla moda; *patient* rianimare **2** *v/i of business etc* riprendersi

re·voke [rɪˈvəʊk] *v/t licence* revocare

re·volt [rɪˈvəʊlt] **1** *n* rivolta *f* **2** *v/i* ribellarsi

re·volt·ing [rɪˈvəʊltɪŋ] *adj* (*disgusting*) schifoso

rev·o·lu·tion [revəˈluːʃn] rivoluzione *f*

rev·o·lu·tion·a·ry [revəˈluːʃn ərɪ] **1** *n* POL rivoluzionario *m*, -a *f* **2** *adj* rivoluzionario

rev·o·lu·tion·ize [revəˈluːʃnaɪz] *v/t* rivoluzionare

re·volve [rɪˈvɒlv] *v/i* ruotare

re·volv·er [rɪˈvɒlvə(r)] revolver *m inv*

re·volv·ing 'door [rɪˈvɒlvɪŋ] porta *f* girevole

re·vue [rɪˈvjuː] THEA rivista *f*

re·vul·sion [rɪˈvʌlʃn] ribrezzo *m*

re·ward [rɪˈwɔːd] **1** *n financial* ricompensa *f*; *benefit derived* vantaggio *m* **2** *v/t financially* ricompensare

re·ward·ing [rɪˈwɔːdɪŋ] *adj experience* gratificante

re·wind [riːˈwaɪnd] *v/t* (*pret & pp* **-wound**) *film, tape* riavvolgere

re·write [riːˈraɪt] *v/t* (*pret* **-wrote**, *pp* **-written**) riscrivere

rhe·to·ric [ˈretərɪk] retorica *f*

rhe·to·ri·cal 'ques·tion [rɪˈtɒrɪkl] domanda *f* retorica

rheu·ma·tism [ˈruːmətɪzm] reumatismo *m*

rhi·no·ce·ros [raɪ'nɒsərəs] rinoceronte *m*

rhu·barb ['ruːbɑːb] rabarbaro *m*

rhyme [raɪm] **1** *n* rima *f* **2** *v/i* rimare; ~ **with** fare rima con

rhythm ['rɪðm] ritmo *m*

rib [rɪb] ANAT costola *f*

rib·bon ['rɪbən] nastro *m*

rice [raɪs] riso *m*

rice 'pud·ding budino *m* di riso

rich [rɪtʃ] **1** *adj* (*wealthy*) ricco; *food* pesante **2** *n*: **the** ~ i ricchi *mpl*

rich·ly ['rɪtʃlɪ] *adv deserved* pienamente

rick·et·y ['rɪkətɪ] *adj* traballante

ric·o·chet ['rɪkəʃeɪ] *v/i* rimbalzare

rid [rɪd]: **get** ~ **of** sbarazzarsi di

rid·dance ['rɪdns] *n* F: **good** ~! che liberazione!

rid·den ['rɪdn] *pp* → **ride**

rid·dle ['rɪdl] **1** *n* indovinello *m* **2** *v/t*: **be** ~**d with** essere crivellato di

ride [raɪd] **1** *n on horse* cavalcata *f*; *in vehicle* giro *m*; (*journey*) viaggio *m*; **do you want a** ~ **into town?** *Am* vuoi uno strappo in città? **2** *v/t* (*pret* **rode**, *pp* **ridden**): ~ **a horse** andare a cavallo; ~ **a bike** andare in bicicletta **3** *v/i* (*pret* **rode**, *pp* **ridden**) *on horse* andare a cavallo; *on bike* andare in bicicletta; *in vehicle* viaggiare; **he rode home** è andato a casa in bicicletta

rid·er ['raɪdə(r)] *on horse* cavallerizzo *m*, **-a** *f*; *on bike* ciclista *m/f*

ridge [rɪdʒ] *raised strip* sporgenza *f*; *of mountain* cresta *f*; *of roof* punta *f*

rid·i·cule ['rɪdɪkjuːl] **1** *n* ridicolo *m* **2** *v/t* ridicolizzare

ri·dic·u·lous [rɪ'dɪkjʊləs] *adj* ridicolo

ri·dic·u·lous·ly [rɪ'dɪkjʊləslɪ] *adv* incredibilmente

rid·ing ['raɪdɪŋ] *on horseback* equitazione *f*

ri·fle ['raɪfl] *n* fucile *m*

rift [rɪft] *in earth* crepa *f*; *in party etc* spaccatura *f*

rig [rɪg] **1** *n* (*oil* ~) piattaforma *f* petrolifera **2** *v/t* (*pret & pp* **-ged**) *elections* manipolare

right [raɪt] **1** *adj* (*correct*) esatto, giusto; (*suitable*) adat-

to; *not left* destro; **be** ~ *of answer* essere esatto; *of person* avere ragione; *of clock* essere giusto; **put things** ~ sistemare le cose; → **alright 2** *adv* (*directly*) proprio; (*correctly*) bene; (*completely*) completamente; *not left* a destra; ~ **now** (*immediately*) subito; (*at the moment*) adesso **3** *n civil, legal etc* diritto *m*; *not left* destra *f*; **the** ~ POL la destra; **on the** ~ a destra; **turn to the** ~, **take a** ~ girare a destra; **be in the** ~ avere ragione; **know** ~ **from wrong** saper distinguere il bene dal male

right-'an·gle angolo *m* retto; **at** ~**s to** ... ad angolo retto con ...

right·ful ['raɪtfʊl] *adj heir, owner etc* legittimo

'right·hand *adj* destro; **on the** ~ **side** a destra; **right·hand 'drive** MOT guida *f* a destra; *car* auto *f inv* con guida a destra; **right·hand·ed** [raɪt'hændɪd] *adj*: **be** ~ usare la (mano) destra; **right·hand 'man** braccio *m* destro; **right of 'way** *in traffic* (diritto *m* di) precedenza *f*; *across land* diritto *m* di accesso; **right 'wing** *n* POL destra *f*; SP esterno *m* destro; **right·'wing** *adj* POL di destra; **right 'wing·er** POL persona *f* di destra; **right-wing ex'trem·ism** POL estremismo *m* di destra

rig·id ['rɪdʒɪd] *adj material, principles* rigido; *attitude* inflessibile

rig·or *Am* → **rigour**

rig·or·ous ['rɪgərəs] *adj* rigoroso

rig·or·ous·ly ['rɪgərəslɪ] *adv check, examine* rigorosamente

rig·our ['rɪgə(r)] *of discipline* rigore *m*; **the** ~**s of the winter** i rigori dell'inverno

rile [raɪl] *v/t* F irritare

rim [rɪm] *of wheel* cerchione *m*; *of cup* orlo *m*; *of spectacles* montatura *f*

ring[1] [rɪŋ] (*circle*) cerchio *m*; *on finger* anello *m*; *in boxing* ring *m inv*, quadrato *m*; *at circus* pista *f*

ring[2] [rɪŋ] **1** *n of bell* trillo *m*; *of voice* suono *m*; **give s.o. a** ~ TELEC dare un colpo di telefono a qu **2** *v/t* (*pret* **rang**, *pp* **rung**) *bell* suonare; TELEC

chiamare **3** *v/i* (*pret* **rang**, *pp* **rung**)
of bell suonare; TELEC chiamare;
please ~ for attention suonare il
campanello

'ring·lead·er capobanda *m inv*;
'ring-pull linguetta *f*; 'ring road circonvallazione *f*

rink [rɪŋk] pista *f* di pattinaggio su
ghiaccio

rinse [rɪns] **1** *n for hair colour* cachet
m inv **2** *v/t* sciacquare

ri·ot ['raɪət] **1** *n* sommossa *f* **2** *v/i* causare disordini

ri·ot·er ['raɪətə(r)] dimostrante *m/f*

'riot police reparti *mpl* (di polizia)
antisommossa

rip [rɪp] **1** *n in cloth etc* strappo *m* **2** *v/t*
(*pret & pp* **-ped**) *cloth etc* strappare;
~ sth open aprire qc strappandolo

♦ rip off *v/t F customers* fregare F

♦ rip up *v/t letter, sheet* strappare

ripe [raɪp] *adj fruit* maturo

rip·en ['raɪpn] *v/i of fruit* maturare

ripe·ness ['raɪpnɪs] *of fruit* maturazione *f*

'rip-off *n* F fregatura *f* F

rip·ple ['rɪpl] *on water* increspatura *f*

rise [raɪz] **1** *v/i* (*pret* **rose**, *pp* **risen**)
from chair etc alzarsi; *of sun* sorgere;
of price, temperature aumentare; *of
water level* salire **2** *n* aumento *m*; *~
to power* salita *f* al potere; *give ~ to*
dare origine a

ris·en ['rɪzn] *pp → rise*

ris·er ['raɪzə(r)]: *be an early / a
late ~* essere mattiniero / alzarsi
sempre tardi

risk [rɪsk] **1** *n* rischio *m*; *take a ~* correre un rischio **2** *v/t* rischiare; *let's ~
it* proviamo

risk·y ['rɪskɪ] *adj* rischioso

ri·sot·to [rɪ'sɒtəʊ] risotto *m*

ris·qué [rɪ'skeɪ] *adj* osé

rit·u·al ['rɪtjʊəl] **1** *n* rituale *m* **2** *adj*
rituale

ri·val ['raɪvl] **1** *n in sport, love* rivale
m/f; *in business* concorrente *m/f* **2** *v/t*
competere con; *I can't ~ that* non
posso competere con quello

ri·val·ry ['raɪvlrɪ] rivalità *f inv*

riv·er ['rɪvə(r)] fiume *m*

'riv·er·bank sponda *f* del fiume;
'riv·er·bed letto *m* del fiume;
'riv·er·side **1** *adj* sul fiume **2** *n* riva *f*
del fiume

riv·et ['rɪvɪt] **1** *n* ribattino *m* **2** *v/t*
rivettare

riv·et·ing ['rɪvɪtɪŋ] *adj* avvincente

Riv·i·e·ra [rɪvɪ'eərə] *n*: *the Italian ~*
la riviera (ligure)

road [rəʊd] strada *f*; *it's just down
the ~* è qui vicino

'road·block posto *m* di blocco; 'road
hog pirata *m* della strada; 'road
hold·ing *of vehicle* tenuta *f* di strada; 'road map carta *f* automobilistica; road 'safe·ty sicurezza *f* sulle
strade; 'road·side: *at the ~* sul ciglio della strada; 'road-sign cartello *m* stradale; 'road·way carreggiata *f*, 'road works *npl* lavori *mpl*
stradali; 'road·wor·thy *adj* in buono stato di marcia

roam [rəʊm] *v/i* vagabondare

roar [rɔː(r)] **1** *n of engine* rombo *m*; *of
lion* ruggito *m*; *of traffic* fragore *m*
2 *v/i of engine* rombare; *of lion* ruggire; *of person* gridare; *~ with
laughter* ridere fragorosamente

roast [rəʊst] **1** *n beef etc* arrosto *m*
2 *v/t chicken, potatoes* arrostire;
coffee beans, peanuts tostare **3** *v/i of
food* arrostire; *in hot room, climate*
scoppiare di caldo

roast 'beef arrosto *m* di manzo

'roast·ing tin [rəʊstɪŋ] teglia *f* per
arrosti

roast 'pork arrosto *m* di maiale

rob [rɒb] *v/t* (*pret & pp* **-bed**) *person,
bank* rapinare; *I've been ~bed* mi
hanno rapinato

rob·ber ['rɒbə(r)] rapinatore *m*,
-trice *f*

rob·ber·y ['rɒbərɪ] rapina *f*

robe [rəʊb] *of judge* toga *f*; *of priest*
tonaca *f*; Am (*dressing gown*) vestaglia *f*

rob·in ['rɒbɪn] pettirosso *m*

ro·bot ['rəʊbɒt] robot *m inv*

ro·bust [rəʊ'bʌst] *adj* robusto

rock [rɒk] **1** *n* roccia *f*; MUS rock *m
inv*; *on the ~s drink* con ghiaccio;

marriage in crisi **2** v/t *baby* cullare; *cradle* far dondolare; (*surprise*) sconvolgere **3** v/i *on chair* dondolarsi; *of boat* dondolare

'**rock band** gruppo m rock; **rock** '**bot·tom**: *reach* ~ toccare il fondo; '**rock-bot·tom** adj *prices* bassissimi; '**rock climb·er** rocciatore m, -trice f; '**rock climb·ing** roccia f

rock·et ['rɒkɪt] **1** n razzo m **2** v/i *of prices etc* salire alle stelle

rock·ing chair ['rɒkɪŋ] sedia f a dondolo

'**rock·ing horse** cavallo m a dondolo

rock 'n' roll [rɒkn'rəʊl] rock and roll m inv

'**rock star** rockstar f inv

rock·y ['rɒkɪ] adj *shore* roccioso; (*shaky*) instabile

rod [rɒd] sbarra f; *for fishing* canna f

rode [rəʊd] pret → **ride**

ro·dent ['rəʊdnt] roditore m

rogue [rəʊg] briccone m, -a f

role [rəʊl] ruolo m

'**role mod·el** modello m di comportamento

roll [rəʊl] **1** n *of bread* panino m; *of film* rullino m; *of thunder* rombo m; (*list, register*) lista f **2** v/i *of ball etc* rotolare; *of boat* dondolare **3** v/t: ~ *sth into a ball* appallottolare qc; ~ *sth along the ground* far rotolare qc

♦ **roll over 1** v/i rigirarsi **2** v/t *person, object* girare; *loan, agreement* rinnovare

♦ **roll up 1** v/t *sleeves* arrotolare **2** v/i F (*arrive*) arrivare

'**roll call** appello m

roll·er ['rəʊlə(r)] *for hair* bigodino m

'**roll·er blade**® n roller blade m inv; '**roll·er blind** tenda f a rullo; **roll·er coast·er** ['rəʊləkəʊstə(r)] montagne fpl russe; '**roll·er skate** n pattino m a rotelle

roll·ing pin ['rəʊlɪŋ] matterello m

ROM [rɒm] abbr COMPUT (= *read only memory*) ROM f inv

Ro·man ['rəʊmən] **1** adj romano **2** n Romano m, -a f

Ro·man 'Cath·o·lic 1 REL cattoli-

co m, -a f **2** adj cattolico

ro·mance [rə'mæns] (*affair*) storia f d'amore; *novel* romanzo m rosa; *film* film m inv d'amore

ro·man·tic [rəʊ'mæntɪk] adj romantico

ro·man·tic·al·ly [rəʊ'mæntɪklɪ] adv romanticamente; ~ *involved with s.o.* legato sentimentalmente a qu

Rome [rəʊm] Roma f

roof [ruːf] tetto m; *have a* ~ *over one's head* avere un tetto sulla testa

'**roof rack** MOT portabagagli m inv

room [ruːm] stanza f; (*bedroom*) camera f (da letto); (*space*) posto m; *there's no* ~ *for ...* non c'è posto per ...

'**room mate** compagno m, -a f di stanza; '**room ser·vice** servizio m in camera; **room 'tem·per·a·ture** temperatura f ambiente

room·y ['ruːmɪ] adj *house, car etc* spazioso; *clothes* ampio

root [ruːt] n radice f; ~**s** *of person* radici fpl

♦ **root for** v/t F fare il tifo per

♦ **root out** v/t (*get rid of*) eradicare; (*find*) scovare

rope [rəʊp] corda f, fune f; *show s.o. the* ~**s** F insegnare il mestiere a qu

♦ **rope off** v/t transennare

ro·sa·ry ['rəʊzərɪ] REL rosario m

rose[1] [rəʊz] BOT rosa f

rose[2] [rəʊz] pret → **rise**

rose·ma·ry ['rəʊzmərɪ] rosmarino m

ros·trum ['rɒstrəm] podio m

ros·y ['rəʊzɪ] adj roseo

rot [rɒt] **1** n marciume m **2** v/i (*pret & pp* -**ted**) marcire

ro·ta ['rəʊtə] turni mpl; *actual document* tabella f dei turni; *on a* ~ *basis* a turno

ro·tate [rəʊ'teɪt] **1** v/i *of blades, earth* ruotare **2** v/t girare; *crops* avvicendare

ro·ta·tion [rəʊ'teɪʃn] *around the sun etc* rotazione f; *in* ~ a turno

rot·ten ['rɒtn] adj *food, wood etc* marcio; F (*very bad*) schifoso F; *what* ~ *luck!* che scalogna!; *what a* ~ *thing*

R

to do! che carognata!

rough [rʌf] **1** adj hands, skin, surface ruvido; ground accidentato; (coarse) rozzo; (violent) violento; crossing movimentato; seas grosso; (approximate) approssimativo; ~ **draft** abbozzo m **2** adv: **sleep ~** dormire all'addiaccio **3** v/t: ~ **it** F vivere senza confort **4** n in golf erba f alta

♦ **rough up** v/t F malmenare

rough·age ['rʌfɪdʒ] in food fibre fpl

rough·ly ['rʌflɪ] adv (approximately) circa; (harshly) bruscamente; ~ **speaking** grosso modo

rou·lette [ruːˈlet] roulette f inv

round [raʊnd] **1** adj rotondo; **in ~ figures** in cifra tonda **2** n of postman, doctor giro m; of toast fetta f; of drinks giro m; of competition girone m; in boxing match round m inv **3** v/t the corner girare **4** adv & prep → around

♦ **round off** v/t edges smussare; meeting, night out chiudere

♦ **round up** v/t figure arrotondare; suspects, criminals radunare

round·a·bout ['raʊndəbaʊt] **1** adj route, way of saying sth indiretto **2** n on road rotatoria f; '**round-the-world** adj intorno al mondo; **round trip** '**tick·et** Am biglietto m (di) andata e ritorno; '**round-up** of cattle raduno m; of suspects, criminals retata f; of news riepilogo m

rouse [raʊz] v/t from sleep svegliare; interest, emotions risvegliare

rous·ing ['raʊzɪŋ] adj speech, finale entusiasmante

route [ruːt] of car itinerario m; of plane, ship rotta f; of bus percorso m

rou·tine [ruːˈtiːn] **1** adj abituale **2** n routine f; **as a matter of ~** d'abitudine

row[1] [raʊ] n (line) fila f; **5 days in a ~** 5 giorni di fila

row[2] [raʊ] v/t & v/i boat remare

row[3] [raʊ] n (quarrel) litigio m; (noise) baccano m

row·dy ['raʊdɪ] adj turbolento

row·ing boat ['raʊɪŋ] barca f a remi

roy·al ['rɔɪəl] adj reale

roy·al·ty ['rɔɪəltɪ] (royal persons) reali mpl; on book, recording royalty f inv

rub [rʌb] v/t (pret & pp -bed) sfregare, strofinare

♦ **rub down** v/t to clean levigare

♦ **rub in** v/t cream, ointment far penetrare; **don't rub it in!** fig non rivoltare il coltello nella piaga!

♦ **rub off 1** v/t dirt levare (strofinando) **2** v/i: **it rubs off on you** ti si comunica

♦ **rub out** v/t with eraser cancellare

rub·ber ['rʌbə(r)] **1** n gomma f **2** adj di gomma

rub·ber 'band elastico m

rub·ber 'gloves npl guanti mpl di gomma

rub·bish ['rʌbɪʃ] immondizia f; (poor quality) porcheria f; (nonsense) sciocchezza f; **don't talk ~!** non dire sciocchezze!

'**rub·bish bin** pattumiera f

rub·ble ['rʌbl] macerie fpl

ru·by ['ruːbɪ] jewel rubino m

ruck·sack ['rʌksæk] zaino m

rud·der ['rʌdə(r)] timone m

rud·dy ['rʌdɪ] adj complexion rubicondo

rude [ruːd] adj person, behaviour maleducato; language volgare; **a ~ word** una parolaccia; **it's ~ to ...** è cattiva educazione ...

rude·ly ['ruːdlɪ] adv (impolitely) scortesemente

rude·ness ['ruːdnɪs] maleducazione f

ru·di·men·ta·ry [ruːdɪˈmentərɪ] adj rudimentale

ru·di·ments ['ruːdɪmənts] npl rudimenti mpl

rue·ful ['ruːful] adj rassegnato

rue·ful·ly ['ruːfəlɪ] adv con aria rassegnata

ruf·fi·an ['rʌfɪən] delinquente m/f

ruf·fle ['rʌfl] **1** n (on dress) gala f **2** v/t hair scompigliare; person turbare; **get ~d** agitarsi

rug [rʌg] tappeto m; (blanket) coperta f (da viaggio)

rug·by ['rʌgbɪ] SP rugby m inv

rug·by 'league rugby *m inv* a tredici; 'rug·by match partita *f* di rugby; 'rug·by play·er giocatore *m* di rugby; rug·by 'un·ion rugby *m inv* a quindici

rug·ged ['rʌgɪd] *adj coastline* frastagliato; *face, features* marcato

ru·in ['ruːɪn] 1 *n* rovina *f*; ~s rovine; *in* ~s *city, building* in rovina; *plans, career* rovinato 2 *v/t* rovinare; *be* ~ed *financially* essere rovinato

rule [ruːl] 1 *n of club, game* regola *f*; *(authority)* dominio *m*; *for measuring* metro *m* (a stecche); *as a* ~ generalmente 2 *v/t country* governare; *the judge* ~d *that ...* il giudice ha stabilito che ... 3 *v/i of monarch* regnare

♦ rule out *v/t* escludere

rul·er ['ruːlə(r)] *for measuring* righello *m*; *of state* capo *m*

rul·ing ['ruːlɪŋ] 1 *n* decisione *f* 2 *adj party* di governo

rum [rʌm] *drink* rum *m inv*

rum·ble ['rʌmbl] *v/i of stomach* brontolare; *of thunder* rimbombare

♦ rum·mage around ['rʌmɪdʒ] *v/i* frugare

ru·mour ['ruːmə(r)] 1 *n* voce *f* 2 *v/t*: *it is ~ed that ...* corre voce che ...

rump [rʌmp] *of animal* groppa *f*

rum·ple ['rʌmpl] *v/t clothes, paper* spiegazzare

rump·'steak bistecca *f* di girello

run [rʌn] 1 *n on foot* corsa *f*; *distance* tragitto *m*; *in tights* sfilatura *f*; *go for a* ~ andare a correre; *go for a* ~ *in the car* andare a fare un giro in macchina; *make a* ~ *for it* scappare; *a criminal on the* ~ un evaso, un'evasa; *in the short* ~ / *in the long* ~ sulle prime / alla lunga; *a* ~ *on the dollar* una forte richiesta di dollari; *it's had a three year* ~ *of play* ha tenuto cartellone per tre anni 2 *v/i* (*pret ran, pp run*) *of person, animal* correre; *of river* scorrere; *of trains, buses* viaggiare; *of paint, makeup* sbavare; *of nose* colare; *of play* tenere il cartellone; *of software* girare; *of engine, machine*

funzionare; *don't leave the tap* ~*ning* non lasciare il rubinetto aperto; ~ *for President in election* candidarsi alla presidenza 3 *v/t* (*pret ran, pp run*) correre; (*take part in: race*) partecipare a; *business, hotel, project etc* gestire; *software* lanciare; *car* usare; *risk* correre; *can I* ~ *you to the station?* ti porto alla stazione?; *he ran his eye down the page* diede uno sguardo alla pagina

♦ run across *v/t* imbattersi in

♦ run away *v/i* scappare

♦ run down 1 *v/t* (*knock down*) investire; (*criticize*) parlare male di; *stocks* ridurre 2 *v/i of battery* scaricarsi

♦ run into *v/t* (*meet*) imbattersi in; *difficulties* trovare

♦ run off 1 *v/i* scappare 2 *v/t* (*print off*) stampare

♦ run out *v/i of contract, time* scadere; *of supplies* esaurirsi

♦ run out of *v/t patience* perdere; *supplies* rimanere senza; *I ran out of petrol* ho finito la benzina; *we are running out of time* il tempo sta per scadere

♦ run over 1 *v/t* (*knock down*) investire; *can we run over the details again?* possiamo rivedere i particolari? 2 *v/i of water etc* traboccare

♦ run through *v/t rehearse, go over* rivedere

♦ run up *v/t debts, large bill* accumulare; *clothes* mettere insieme

run·a·way ['rʌnəweɪ] *n* ragazzo *m*, -a *f* scappato di casa

run-'down *adj person* debilitato; *part of town, building* fatiscente

rung[1] [rʌŋ] *of ladder* piolo *m*

rung[2] [rʌŋ] *pp* → ring

run·ner ['rʌnə(r)] *athlete* velocista *m/f*

run·ner 'beans *npl* fagiolini *mpl*

run·ner-'up secondo *m*, -a *f* classificato (-a)

run·ning ['rʌnɪŋ] 1 *n* SP corsa *f*; *of business* gestione *f* 2 *adj*: *for two days* ~ per due giorni di seguito

run·ning 'wa·ter acqua f corrente

run·ny ['rʌnɪ] adj substance liquido; nose che cola

'run-up SP rincorsa f; *in the ~ to* nel periodo che precede ...

'run·way pista f

rup·ture ['rʌptʃə(r)] **1** n rottura f; MED lacerazione f; (hernia) ernia f **2** v/i of pipe etc scoppiare

ru·ral ['ruərəl] adj rurale

ruse [ruːz] stratagemma m

rush [rʌʃ] **1** n corsa f; *do sth in a ~* fare qc di corsa; *be in a ~* andare di fretta; *what's the big ~?* che fretta c'è? **2** v/t person mettere fretta o premura a; meal mangiare in fretta; *~ s.o. to hospital / the airport* portare qu di corsa all'ospedale / aeroporto **3** v/i affrettarsi

'rush hour ora f di punta

Rus·sia ['rʌʃə] Russia f

Rus·sian ['rʌʃən] **1** adj russo **2** n russo m, -a f; language russo m

rust [rʌst] **1** n ruggine f **2** v/i arrugginirsi

rus·tle ['rʌsl] **1** n of silk, leaves fruscio m **2** v/i of silk, leaves frusciare

'rust-proof adj a prova di ruggine

rust re·mov·er ['rʌstrɪmuːvə(r)] smacchiatore m per la ruggine

rust·y ['rʌstɪ] adj also fig arrugginito; *I'm a little ~* sono un po' arrugginito

rut [rʌt] in road solco m; *be in a ~* fig essersi fossilizzato

ruth·less ['ruːθlɪs] adj spietato

ruth·less·ly adv spietatamente

ruth·less·ness ['ruːθlɪsnɪs] spietatezza f

rye [raɪ] segale f

'rye bread pane m di segale

S

sab·bat·i·cal [sə'bætɪkl] n of academic anno m sabbatico

sab·o·tage ['sæbətɑːʒ] **1** n sabotaggio m **2** v/t sabotare

sab·o·teur [sæbə'tɜː(r)] sabotatore m, -trice f

sac·cha·rin ['sækərɪn] n saccarina f

sa·chet ['sæʃeɪ] of shampoo, cream etc bustina f

sack [sæk] **1** n bag sacco m; *get the ~* F essere licenziato **2** v/t F licenziare

sa·cred ['seɪkrɪd] adj sacro

sac·ri·fice ['sækrɪfaɪs] **1** n sacrificio m; *make ~s* fig fare sacrifici **2** v/t sacrificare

sac·ri·lege ['sækrɪlɪdʒ] sacrilegio m

sad [sæd] adj triste; state of affairs deplorevole

sad·dle ['sædl] **1** n sella f **2** v/t horse sellare; *~ s.o. with sth* fig affibbiare qc a qu

sa·dis·m ['seɪdɪzm] sadismo m

sa·dist ['seɪdɪst] sadista m/f

sa·dis·tic [sə'dɪstɪk] adj sadistico

sad·ly ['sædlɪ] adv tristemente; (regrettably) purtroppo

sad·ness ['sædnɪs] tristezza f

safe [seɪf] **1** adj not dangerous sicuro; not in danger al sicuro; driver prudente; *is it ~ to walk here?* non è pericoloso camminare qui? **2** n cassaforte f

'safe·guard 1 n protezione f, salvaguardia f; *as a ~ against* per proteggersi contro **2** v/t proteggere

safe·keep·ing: give sth to s.o. for ~ dare qc in custodia a qu

safe·ly ['seɪflɪ] adv arrive, complete first test etc senza problemi; drive prudentemente; assume tranquillamente

safe·ty ['seɪftɪ] sicurezza f

'safe·ty belt cintura f di sicurezza;

'safe·ty-con·scious adj attento ai

                                  sandstone

problemi di sicurezza; **safe·ty 'first** prudenza *f*; **'safe·ty pin** spilla *f* di sicurezza

sag [sæg] **1** *n in ceiling* incurvatura *f* **2** *v/i* (*pret & pp* **-ged**) *of ceiling* incurvarsi; *of rope* allentarsi

sa·ga ['sɑːgə] saga *f*

sage [seɪdʒ] *n herb* salvia *f*

Sa·git·tar·i·us [sædʒɪ'teərɪəs] ASTR Sagittario *m*

said [sed] *pret & pp* → **say**

sail [seɪl] **1** *n of boat* vela *f*; *trip* veleggiata *f*; **go for a ~** fare un giro in barca (a vela) **2** *v/t yacht* pilotare **3** *v/i* fare vela; (*depart*) salpare

'sail·board 1 *n* windsurf *m inv* **2** *v/i* fare windsurf

'sail·board·ing windsurf *m inv*

sail·ing ['seɪlɪŋ] SP vela *f*

'sail·ing boat barca *f* a vela

'sail·ing ship veliero *m*

sail·or ['seɪlə(r)] marinaio *m*; **be a bad/good ~** soffrire / non soffrire il mal di mare

saint [seɪnt] santo *m*, -a *f*

sake [seɪk] *n*: **for my/your ~** per il mio / il tuo bene; **for the ~ of** per; **for the ~ of peace** per amor di pace

sal·ad ['sæləd] insalata *f*

sal·ad 'dress·ing condimento *m* per l'insalata

sal·a·ry ['sælərɪ] stipendio *m*

'sal·a·ry scale scala *f* salariale

sale [seɪl] vendita *f*; *at reduced prices* svendita *f*, saldi *mpl*; **for ~ sign** in vendita; **be on ~** essere in vendita

sales [seɪlz] *npl department* reparto *m* vendite

'sales as·sist·ant, **'sales clerk** *Am in shop* commesso *m*, -a *f*; **'sales fig·ures** *npl* fatturato *m*; **'sales·man** venditore *m*; **sales 'man·ag·er** direttore *m*, -trice *f* delle vendite; **'sales meet·ing** riunione *f* marketing e vendite; **'sales wom·an** venditrice *f*

sa·li·ent ['seɪlɪənt] *adj* saliente

sa·li·va [sə'laɪvə] saliva *f*

salm·on ['sæmən] (*pl* **salmon**) salmone *m*

sa·loon [sə'luːn] MOT berlina *f*; *Am*: *bar* bar *m inv*

salt [sɒlt] **1** *n* sale *m* **2** *v/t food* salare

'salt·cel·lar saliera *f*; **salt 'wa·ter** acqua *f* salata; **'salt-wa·ter fish** pesce *m* di mare

salt·y ['sɒltɪ] *adj* salato

sal·u·tar·y ['sæljʊtərɪ] *adj experience* salutare

sa·lute [sə'luːt] **1** *n* MIL saluto *m*; **take the ~** ricevere i saluti **2** *v/t & v/i* salutare

sal·vage ['sælvɪdʒ] *v/t from wreck* recuperare

sal·va·tion [sæl'veɪʃn] salvezza *f*

Sal·va·tion 'Ar·my Esercito *m* della Salvezza

same [seɪm] **1** *adj* stesso **2** *pron* stesso; **the ~** lo stesso, la stessa; **Happy New Year – the ~ to you** Buon anno! – Grazie e altrettanto!; **he's not the ~ any more** non è più lo stesso; **all the ~** (*even so*) eppure; **men are all the ~** gli uomini sono tutti uguali; **it's all the ~ to me** per me è uguale **3** *adv*: **all the ~** allo stesso modo; **I still feel the ~ about that** la penso sempre allo stesso modo

sam·ple ['sɑːmpl] **1** *n* campione *m* **2** *v/t food, product* provare

san·a·to·ri·um [sænə'tɔːrɪəm] casa *f* di cura

sanc·ti·mo·ni·ous [sæŋktɪ'məʊnɪəs] *adj* moraleggiante

sanc·tion ['sæŋkʃn] **1** *n* (*approval*) approvazione *f*; (*penalty*) sanzione *f* **2** *v/t* (*approve*) sancire

sanc·ti·ty ['sæŋktətɪ] santità *f*

sanc·tu·a·ry ['sæŋktjʊərɪ] REL santuario *m*; *for wild animals* riserva *f*

sand [sænd] **1** *n* sabbia *f* **2** *v/t with sandpaper* smerigliare

san·dal ['sændl] sandalo *m*

'sand·bag sacchetto *m* di sabbia; **'sand·blast** *v/t* sabbiare; **'sand dune** duna *f*

sand·er ['sændə(r)] *tool* smerigliatrice *f*

'sand·pa·per 1 *n* carta *f* smerigliata **2** *v/t* smerigliare

'sand·stone arenaria *f*

S

sand·wich ['sænwɪdʒ] **1** *n* tramezzino *m* **2** *v/t*: **be ~ed between two ...** essere incastrato tra due ...

sand·y ['sændɪ] *adj beach* sabbioso; *full of sand* pieno di sabbia; *hair* rossiccio

sane [seɪn] *adj* sano di mente

sang [sæŋ] *pret* → **sing**

san·i·ta·ry ['sænɪtərɪ] *adj conditions* igienico; *installations* sanitario

'san·i·ta·ry tow·el assorbente *m* (igienico)

san·i·ta·tion [sænɪ'teɪʃn] (*sanitary installations*) impianti *mpl* igienici; (*removal of waste*) fognature *fpl*

san·i·ty ['sænətɪ] sanità *f inv* mentale

sank [sæŋk] *pret* → **sink**

San·ta Claus ['sæntəklɔːz] Babbo *m* Natale

sap [sæp] **1** *n in tree* linfa *f* **2** *v/t* (*pret & pp -ped*) *s.o.'s energy* indebolire

sap·phire ['sæfaɪə(r)] *n jewel* zaffiro *m*

sar·cas·m ['sɑːkæzm] sarcasmo *m*

sar·cas·tic [sɑː'kæstɪk] *adj* sarcastico

sar·cas·tic·al·ly [sɑː'kæstɪklɪ] *adv* sarcasticamente

sar·dine [sɑː'diːn] sardina *f*

Sar·din·i·a [sɑː'dɪnɪə] Sardegna *f*

Sar·din·i·an [sɑː'dɪnɪən] **1** *adj* sardo **2** *n* sardo *m*, -a *f*

sar·don·ic [sɑː'dɒnɪk] *adj* sardonico

sar·don·ic·al·ly [sɑː'dɒnɪklɪ] *adv* sardonicamente

sash [sæʃ] *on dress* fusciacca *f*; *on uniform* fascia *f*; *on window* vetro *m* scorrevole (di finestra a ghigliottina)

Sa·tan ['seɪtn] Satana *m*

satch·el ['sætʃl] *for schoolchild* cartella *f*

sat·el·lite ['sætəlaɪt] satellite *m*

'sat·el·lite dish antenna *f* parabolica

sat·el·lite T'V TV *f inv* satellitare

sat·in ['sætɪn] *adj* satin *m inv*

sat·ire ['sætaɪə(r)] satira *f*

sa·tir·i·cal [sə'tɪrɪkl] *adj* satirico

sat·i·rist ['sætərɪst] satirista *m*

sat·i·rize ['sætəraɪz] *v/t* satireggiare

sat·is·fac·tion [sætɪs'fækʃn] soddisfazione *f*; *is that to your ~?* è di suo gradimento?

sat·is·fac·to·ry [sætɪs'fæktərɪ] *adj* soddisfacente; *just good enough* sufficiente; *this is not ~* non è sufficiente

sat·is·fy ['sætɪsfaɪ] *v/t* (*pret & pp -ied*) *customers, needs, curiosity* soddisfare; *requirement* rispondere a; *~ s.o.'s hunger* sfamare qu; *I am satisfied had enough to eat* sono sazio; *I am satisfied that ...* (*convinced*) sono convinto che ...; *I hope you're satisfied!* sei contento?

Sat·ur·day ['sætədeɪ] sabato *m*

sauce [sɔːs] salsa *f*, sugo *m*

'sauce·pan pentola *f*

sau·cer ['sɔːsə(r)] piattino *m*

sauc·y ['sɔːsɪ] *adj person, dress* provocante

Sa·u·di A·ra·bi·a [saʊdɪə'reɪbɪə] Arabia *f* Saudita

Sa·u·di A·ra·bi·an [saʊdɪə'reɪbɪən] **1** *adj* saudita **2** *n person* saudita *m/f*

sau·na ['sɔːnə] sauna *f*

saun·ter ['sɔːntə(r)] *v/i* passeggiare; *he ~ed in at 10.30* è arrivato tranquillamente alle 10.30

saus·age ['sɒsɪdʒ] salsiccia *f*

sav·age ['sævɪdʒ] **1** *adj animal* selvaggio; *attack, criticism* feroce **2** *n* selvaggio *m*, -a *f*

sav·age·ry ['sævɪdʒrɪ] ferocia *f*

save [seɪv] **1** *v/t* (*rescue*) salvare; *money, time, effort* risparmiare; (*collect*) raccogliere; COMPUT salvare; *goal* parare; *you could ~ yourself a lot of effort* potresti risparmiarti parecchi sforzi **2** *v/i* (*put money aside*) risparmiare; SP parare **3** *n* SP parata *f*

♦ **save up for** *v/t* risparmiare per

sav·er ['seɪvə(r)] *person* risparmiatore *m*, -trice *f*

sav·i·ng ['seɪvɪŋ] risparmio *m*

sav·ings ['seɪvɪŋz] *npl* risparmi *mpl*

'sav·ings ac·count libretto *m* di risparmio; **'sav·ings and 'loan** *Am* → **building society**; **'sav·ings bank** cassa *f* di risparmio

sa·vior *Am*, **sa·viour** ['seɪvjə(r)] REL salvatore *m*

sa·vor *etc Am → savour etc*

sa·vour ['seɪvə(r)] **1** *n* sapore *m* **2** *v/t* assaporare

sa·vour·y ['seɪvərɪ] *adj not sweet* salato (*non dolce*)

saw¹ [sɔː] **1** *n tool* sega *f* **2** *v/t* segare

saw² [sɔː] *pret → see*

◆ **saw off** *v/t* segare via

'saw·dust segatura *f*

sax·o·phone ['sæksəfəʊn] sassofono *m*

say [seɪ] **1** *v/t* (*pret & pp* **said**) dire; **can I ~ something?** posso dire una cosa?; **that is to ~** sarebbe a dire; **what do you ~ to that?** cosa ne dici?; **what does the note ~?** cosa dice il biglietto? **2** *n*: **have one's ~** dire la propria; **have a ~ in sth** avere voce in capitolo in qc

say·ing ['seɪɪŋ] detto *m*

scab [skæb] *on skin* crosta *f*

scaf·fold·ing ['skæfəldɪŋ] *on building* impalcature *fpl*

scald [skɔːld] *v/t* scottare; **~ o.s.** scottarsi

scale¹ [skeɪl] *on fish* scaglia *f*

scale² [skeɪl] **1** *n of map,* MUS scala *f; on thermometer* scala *f* graduata; *of project* portata *f;* **on a large ~** su vasta scala; **on a small ~** su scala ridotta **2** *v/t cliffs etc* scalare

◆ **scale down** *v/t* ridurre

scale 'draw·ing disegno *m* in scala

scales [skeɪlz] *npl for weighing* bilancia *fsg*

scal·lop ['skɒləp] *n* capasanta *f*

scalp [skælp] *n* cuoio *m* capelluto

scal·pel ['skælpl] bisturi *m*

scam [skæm] F truffa *f*

scam·pi ['skæmpɪ] *gamberoni mpl in pastella fritti*

scan [skæn] **1** *v/t* (*pret & pp* **-ned**) *horizon* scrutare; *page* scorrere; *foetus* fare l'ecografia di; *brain* fare la TAC di; COMPUT scannerizzare **2** *n* (*brain ~*) TAC *f inv; of foetus* ecografia *f*

◆ **scan in** *v/t* COMPUT scannerizzare

scan·dal ['skændl] scandalo *m*

scan·dal·ize ['skændəlaɪz] *v/t* scandalizzare

scan·dal·ous ['skændələs] *adj* scandaloso

Scan·di·na·vi·a [skændɪ'neɪvɪə] Scandinavia *f*

scan·ner ['skænə(r)] scanner *m inv*

scant [skænt] *adj* scarso

scant·i·ly ['skæntɪlɪ] *adv*: **~ clad** succintamente vestito

scant·y ['skæntɪ] *adj clothes* succinto

scape·goat ['skeɪpgəʊt] capro *m* espiatorio

scar [skɑː(r)] **1** *n* cicatrice *f* **2** *v/t* (*pret & pp* **-red**) *face* lasciare cicatrici su; *fig* segnare

scarce [skeəs] *adj in short supply* scarso; **make o.s. ~** squagliarsela F

scarce·ly ['skeəslɪ] *adv* appena; **there was ~ anything left** non rimaneva quasi più niente

scar·ci·ty ['skeəsɪtɪ] scarsità *f inv*

scare [skeə(r)] **1** *v/t* spaventare; **be ~d of** avere paura di **2** *n* (*panic, alarm*) panico *m;* **give s.o. a ~** mettere paura a qc

◆ **scare away** *v/t* far scappare

'scare·crow spaventapasseri *m inv*

scare·mon·ger ['skeəmʌŋgə(r)] allarmista *m/f*

scarf [skɑːf] *around neck* sciarpa *f; over head* foulard *m inv*

scar·let ['skɑːlət] *adj* scarlatto

scar·let 'fe·ver scarlattina *f*

scar·y ['skeərɪ] *adj* che fa paura

scath·ing ['skeɪðɪŋ] *adj* caustico

scat·ter ['skætə(r)] **1** *v/t leaflets, seeds* spargere; *crowd* disperdere **2** *v/i of people* disperdersi

scat·ter·brained ['skætəbreɪnd] *adj* sventato

scat·tered ['skætəd] *adj family, villages* sparpagliato; **~ showers** precipitazioni sparse

scat·ty ['skætɪ] *adj* sventato

scav·enge ['skævɪndʒ] *v/i* frugare tra i rifiuti

scav·eng·er ['skævɪndʒə(r)] *animal* animale *m* necrofago; (*person*) persona *f* che fruga tra i rifiuti

sce·na·ri·o [sɪ'nɑːrɪəʊ] scenario *m*

S

scene [si:n] scena *f;* (*argument*) scenata *f;* **make a ~** fare una scenata; **~s** THEA scenografia *f; jazz / rock ~* il mondo del jazz / rock; **behind the ~s** dietro le quinte

sce·ne·ry ['si:nəri] paesaggio *m;* THEA scenario *m*

scent [sent] *n of roses* profumo *m; of animal* odore *m*

scep·tic ['skeptik] scettico *m,* -a *f*

scep·ti·cal ['skeptikl] *adj* scettico

scep·ti·cal·ly ['skeptikli] *adv* scetticamente

scep·ti·cism ['skeptisizm] scetticismo *m*

sched·ule ['ʃedju:l] **1** *n of events, work* programma *m; for trains* orario *m; be on ~ of work, of train etc* essere in orario; **be behind ~** *of work, of train etc* essere in ritardo **2** *v/t put on schedule* programmare; **it's ~d for completion next month** il completamento dei lavori è previsto per il mese prossimo

sched·uled 'flight ['ʃedju:ld] volo *m* di linea

scheme [ski:m] **1** *n* (*plan*) piano *m;* (*plot*) complotto *m* **2** *v/i* (*plot*) complottare, tramare

schem·ing ['ski:mɪŋ] *adj* intrigante

schiz·o·phre·ni·a [skɪtsə'fri:nɪə] schizofrenia *f*

schiz·o·phren·ic [skɪtsə'frenɪk] **1** *n* schizofrenico *m,* -a *f* **2** *adj* schizofrenico

schol·ar ['skɒlə(r)] studioso *m,* -a *f*

schol·ar·ly ['skɒlə(r)lɪ] *adj* dotto

schol·ar·ship ['skɒlə(r)ʃɪp] (*scholarly work*) erudizione *f;* (*financial award*) borsa *f* di studio

school [sku:l] scuola *f*

'school bag (*satchel*) cartella *f;* **'school·boy** scolaro *m;* **'school·children** scolari *mpl;* **'school days** *npl* tempi *mpl* della scuola; **'school·girl** scolara *f;* **'school·mas·ter** maestro *m;* **'school·mate** compagno *m,* -a *f* di scuola; **'school·mis·tress** maestra *f;* **'school·teach·er** insegnante *m/f*

sci·at·i·ca [saɪ'ætɪkə] sciatica *f*

sci·ence ['saɪəns] scienza *f*

sci·ence 'fic·tion fantascienza *f*

sci·en·tif·ic [saɪən'tɪfɪk] *adj* scientifico

sci·en·tist ['saɪəntɪst] scienziato *m,* -a *f*

scis·sors ['sɪzəz] *npl* forbici *fpl*

scoff[1] [skɒf] *v/t food* sbafare

scoff[2] [skɒf] *v/i* (*mock*) canzonare

◆ **scoff at** *v/t* deridere

scold [skəʊld] *v/t* sgridare

scone [skɒn] focaccina *f* o dolcetto *m* da mangiare con il tè

scoop [sku:p] **1** *n for grain, flour* paletta *f; for ice cream* cucchiaio *m* dosatore; *of ice cream* pallina *f;* (*story*) scoop *m inv* **2** *v/t* (*pick up*) raccogliere

◆ **scoop up** *v/t* sollevare tra le braccia

scoot·er ['sku:tə(r)] *with motor* scooter *m inv; child's* monopattino *m*

scope [skəʊp] portata *f;* (*opportunity*) possibilità *f inv*

scorch [skɔ:tʃ] *v/t* bruciare

scorch·ing hot ['skɔ:tʃɪŋ] *adj* torrido

score [skɔ:(r)] **1** *n* SP punteggio *m;* (*written music*) spartito *m; of film etc* colonna *f* sonora; **what's the ~?** SP a quanto sono / siamo?; **have a ~ to settle with s.o.** avere un conto in sospeso con qu; **keep** (**the**) **~** tenere il punteggio **2** *v/t goal, point* segnare; (*cut*) incidere **3** *v/i* segnare; (*keep the score*) tenere il punteggio

'score·board segnapunti *m inv*

scor·er ['skɔ:rə(r)] *of goal, point* marcatore *m,* -trice *f;* (*score-keeper*) segnapunti *m/f inv*

scorn [skɔ:n] **1** *n* disprezzo *m;* **pour ~ on sth** deridere qc **2** *v/t idea, suggestion* disprezzare

scorn·ful ['skɔ:nful] *adj* sprezzante

scorn·ful·ly ['skɔ:nfulɪ] *adv* sprezzantemente

Scor·pi·o ['skɔ:pɪəʊ] ASTR Scorpione *m*

Scot [skɒt] scozzese *m/f*

Scotch [skɒtʃ] (*whisky*) scotch *m inv*

Scotch 'tape® *Am* scotch® *m*

scot-'free *adv*: **get off ~** farla franca

Scot·land ['skɒtlənd] Scozia *f*

Scots·man ['skɒtsmən] scozzese *m*

Scots·wom·an ['skɒtswʊmən] scozzese *f*

Scot·tish ['skɒtɪʃ] *adj* scozzese

scoun·drel ['skaʊndrəl] birbante *m/f*

scour[1] ['skaʊə(r)] *v/t* (*search*) setacciare

scour[2] ['skaʊə(r)] *v/t* pans sfregare

scout [skaʊt] *n* (*boy ~*) boy-scout *m inv*

scowl [skaʊl] **1** *n* sguardo *m* torvo **2** *v/i* guardare storto

scram [skræm] *v/i* (*pret & pp -med*) F filare F

scram·ble ['skræmbl] **1** *n* (*rush*) corsa *f* **2** *v/t* message rendere indecifrabile **3** *v/i* climb inerpicarsi; **he ~d to his feet** si rialzò in fretta

scram·bled 'eggs ['skræmbld] *npl* uova *fpl* strapazzate

scrap [skræp] **1** *n* metal rottame *m*; (*fight*) zuffa *f*; (*little bit*) briciolo *m* **2** *v/t* (*pret & pp -ped*) plan, project abbandonare

'scrap·book album *m inv*

scrape [skreɪp] **1** *n* on paintwork graffio *m* **2** *v/t* paintwork, one's arm etc graffiare; vegetables raschiare; **~ a living** sbarcare il lunario

♦ **scrape through** *v/i* in exam passare per il rotto della cuffia

'scrap heap cumulo *m* di rottami; **good for the ~** da buttare via; **scrap 'met·al** rottami *mpl*; **scrap 'pa·per** carta *f* già usata

scrap·py ['skræpɪ] *adj* work, writing senza capo né coda

scratch [skrætʃ] **1** *n* mark graffio *m*; **have a ~** to stop itching grattarsi; **start from ~** ricominciare da zero; **not up to ~** non all'altezza **2** *v/t* (*mark*) graffiare; because of itch grattare **3** *v/i* of cat, nails graffiare

scrawl [skrɔːl] **1** *n* scarabocchio *m* **2** *v/t* scarabocchiare

scraw·ny ['skrɔːnɪ] *adj* scheletrico

scream [skriːm] **1** *n* urlo *m*; **~s of laughter** risate *fpl* fragorose **2** *v/i* urlare

screech [skriːtʃ] **1** *n* of tyres stridio *m*; (*scream*) strillo *m* **2** *v/i* of tyres stridere; (*scream*) strillare

screen [skriːn] **1** *n* in room, hospital paravento *m*; of smoke cortina *f*; cinema, COMPUT, of television schermo *m*; **on the ~** in film sullo schermo; **on (the) ~** COMPUT su schermo **2** *v/t* (*protect, hide*) riparare; film proiettare; for security reasons vagliare

'screen·play sceneggiatura *f*, **'screen sav·er** COMPUT salvaschermo *m inv*; **'screen test** for film provino *m*

screw [skruː] **1** *n* vite *f* (metallica); V (*sex*) scopata *f* V **2** *v/t* V scopare V; F (*cheat*) fregare F; **~ sth to sth** avvitare qc a qc

♦ **screw up 1** *v/t* eyes strizzare; piece of paper appallottolare; F (*make a mess of*) mandare all'aria **2** *v/i* F (*make a bad mistake*) fare un casino F

'screw·driv·er cacciavite *m*

screwed 'up [skruːd'ʌp] *adj* F psychologically complessato

'screw top on bottle tappo *m* a vite

screw·y ['skruːɪ] *adj* F svitato

scrib·ble ['skrɪbl] **1** *n* scarabocchio *m* **2** *v/t & v/i* (*write quickly*) scarabocchiare

scrimp [skrɪmp] *v/i*: **~ and scrape** risparmiare fino all'ultimo soldo

script [skrɪpt] for film, play copione *m*; (*form of writing*) scrittura *f*

scrip·ture ['skrɪptʃə(r)]: **the (Holy) Scriptures** le Sacre Scritture *fpl*

'script·writ·er sceneggiatore *m*, -trice *f*

scroll [skrəʊl] *n* rotolo *m* di pergamena

♦ **scroll down** *v/i* COMPUT far scorrere il testo in avanti

♦ **scroll up** *v/i* COMPUT far scorrere il testo indietro

scrounge [skraʊndʒ] *v/t* scroccare

scroung·er ['skraʊndʒə(r)] scroccone *m*, -a *f*

scrub [skrʌb] *v/t* (*pret & pp -bed*) floors, hands sfregare (con spazzola)

S

scrub·bing brush ['skrʌbɪŋ] *for floor* spazzolone *m*

scruff·y ['skrʌfɪ] *adj* trasandato

scrum [skrʌm] *in rugby* mischia *f*

♦ **scrunch up** [skrʌntʃ] *v/t plastic cup etc* accartocciare

scru·ples ['skru:plz] *npl* scrupoli *mpl*; **have no ~ about doing sth** non avere scrupoli a fare qc

scru·pu·lous ['skru:pjʊləs] *adj* scrupoloso

scru·pu·lous·ly ['skru:pjʊləslɪ] *adv* (*meticulously*) scrupolosamente

scru·ti·nize ['skru:tɪnaɪz] *v/t text* esaminare attentamente; *face* scrutare

scru·ti·ny ['skru:tɪnɪ] attento esame *m*; **come under ~** essere sottoposto ad attento esame

scu·ba div·ing ['sku:bə] immersione *f* subacquea

scuf·fle ['skʌfl] *n* tafferuglio *m*

sculp·tor ['skʌlptə(r)] scultore *m*, -trice *f*

sculp·ture ['skʌlptʃə(r)] scultura *f*

scum [skʌm] *on liquid* schiuma *f*; (*pej: people*) feccia *f*

sea [si:] mare *m*; **by the ~** al mare

'sea·bed fondale *m* marino; **'sea·bird** uccello *m* marino; **'sea·far·ing** ['si:feərɪŋ] *adj nation* marinaro; **'sea·food** frutti *mpl* di mare; **'sea·front** lungomare *m inv*; **'sea·go·ing** *adj vessel* d'alto mare; **'sea·gull** gabbiano *m*

seal¹ [si:l] *n animal* foca *f*

seal² [si:l] **1** *n on document* sigillo *m*; TECH chiusura *f* ermetica **2** *v/t container* chiudere ermeticamente

♦ **seal off** *v/t area* bloccare l'accesso a

'sea lev·el: above / below ~ sopra / sotto il livello del mare

seam [si:m] *n on garment* cucitura *f*; *of ore* filone *m*

'sea·man marinaio *m*

seam·stress ['si:mstrɪs] sarta *f*

'sea·port porto *m* marittimo

'sea pow·er *nation* potenza *f* marittima

search [sɜ:tʃ] **1** *n for s.o. / sth* ricerca *f*; *of person, building* perquisizione *f*; **in ~ of** alla ricerca di **2** *v/t person,*

building, baggage perquisire; *area* perlustrare

♦ **search for** *v/t* cercare

search·ing ['sɜ:tʃɪŋ] *adj look* penetrante

'search·light riflettore *m*; **'search par·ty** squadra *f* di ricerca; **'search war·rant** mandato *m* di perquisizione

'sea·shore riva *f* (del mare)

'sea·sick *adj* con il mal di mare; **be ~** avere il mal di mare; **get ~** soffrire il mal di mare; **'sea·side** *n: at the ~** al mare; **go to the ~** andare al mare; **~ resort** località *f* balneare

sea·son ['si:zn] *n* stagione *f*; **in / out of ~** in / fuori stagione

sea·son·al ['si:znl] *adj* stagionale

sea·soned ['si:znd] *adj wood* stagionato; *traveller, campaigner etc* esperto

sea·son·ing ['si:znɪŋ] condimento *m*

'sea·son tick·et abbonamento *m*

seat [si:t] **1** *n* posto *m*; *of trousers* fondo *m*; POL seggio *m*; **please take a ~** si accomodi **2** *v/t* (*have seating for*) avere posti a sedere per; **please remain ~ed** state seduti, per favore

'seat belt cintura *f* di sicurezza

'sea ur·chin riccio *m* di mare

'sea·weed alga *f*

se·clud·ed [sɪ'klu:dɪd] *adj* appartato

se·clu·sion [sɪ'klu:ʒn] isolamento *m*

sec·ond¹ ['sekənd] **1** *n of time* secondo *m*; **just a ~** un attimo **2** *adj* secondo **3** *adv come in* secondo **4** *v/t motion* appoggiare

se·cond² [sɪ'kɒnd] *v/t:* **be ~ed to** essere assegnato a

sec·ond·a·ry ['sekəndrɪ] *adj* secondario

sec·ond·a·ry ed·u·ca·tion istruzione *f* secondaria

se·cond 'best *adj* secondo (dopo il migliore); **sec·ond 'big·gest** *adj* secondo in ordine di grandezza; **sec·ond 'class** *adj ticket* di seconda classe; **sec·ond 'floor** secondo piano *m*; *Am* terzo piano; **sec·ond 'gear** MOT seconda *f* (marcia); **'sec·ond hand** *n on clock* lancetta *f* dei secondi; **'sec·ond-hand** adj & adv di seconda mano

sec·ond·ly ['sekəndlɪ] adv in secondo luogo

sec·ond·'rate adj di second'ordine

sec·ond 'thoughts: *I've had ~ thoughts* ci ho ripensato

se·cre·cy ['siːkrəsɪ] segretezza f

se·cret ['siːkrət] **1** n segreto m; *do sth in ~* fare qc in segreto **2** adj segreto

se·cret 'a·gent agente m segreto

sec·re·tar·i·al [sekrə'teərɪəl] adj tasks, job di segretaria

sec·re·tar·y ['sekrətərɪ] segretario m, -a f; POL ministro m

Sec·re·tar·y of 'State in USA Segretario m di Stato

se·crete [sɪ'kriːt] v/t (give off) secernere; (hide away) nascondere

se·cre·tion [sɪ'kriːʃn] secrezione f

se·cre·tive ['siːkrətɪv] adj riservato

se·cret·ly ['siːkrətlɪ] adv segretamente

se·cret po'lice polizia f segreta

se·cret 'ser·vice servizio m segreto

sect [sekt] setta f

sec·tion ['sekʃn] sezione f

sec·tor ['sektə(r)] settore m

sec·u·lar ['sekjʊlə(r)] adj laico

se·cure [sɪ'kjʊə(r)] **1** adj shelf etc saldo feeling sicuro; job stabile **2** v/t shelf etc assicurare; s.o.'s help, finances assicurare

se·cu·ri·ty [sɪ'kjʊərətɪ] in job sicurezza f; in relationship stabilità f inv; for investment garanzia f; at airport etc sicurezza f

se'cu·ri·ties mar·ket FIN mercato m dei titoli

se'cu·ri·ty a·lert stato m di allarme; **se'cu·ri·ty check** controllo m di sicurezza; **se'cu·ri·ty-con·scious** adj attento alla sicurezza; **se'cu·ri·ty forces** npl police forze fpl dell'ordine; **se'cu·ri·ty forces** npl forze fpl di sicurezza; **se'cu·ri·ty guard** guardia f giurata; **se'cu·ri·ty risk** minaccia f per la sicurezza

se·date [sɪ'deɪt] v/t somministrare sedativi a

se·da·tion [sɪ'deɪʃn]: *be under ~* essere sotto l'effetto di sedativi

sed·a·tive ['sedətɪv] n sedativo m

sed·en·ta·ry ['sedəntərɪ] adj job sedentario

sed·i·ment ['sedɪmənt] sedimento m

se·duce [sɪ'djuːs] v/t sedurre

se·duc·tion [sɪ'dʌkʃn] seduzione f

se·duc·tive [sɪ'dʌktɪv] adj smile, look seducente; offer allettante

see [siː] v/t (pret saw, pp seen) vedere; (understand) capire; romantically uscire con; *I ~* capisco; *can I ~ the manager?* vorrei vedere il direttore; *you should ~ a doctor* dovresti andare dal medico; *~ s.o. home* accompagnare a casa qu; *I'll ~ you to the door* t'accompagno alla porta; *~ you!* F ciao! F

♦ **see about** v/t (look into) provvedere a; *I'll see about it* ci penso io

♦ **see off** v/t at airport etc salutare; (chase away) scacciare

♦ **see out** v/t: *see s.o. out* accompagnare qu alla porta

♦ **see to** v/t: *see to sth* occuparsi di qc; *see to it that sth gets done* assicurarsi che qc venga fatto

seed [siːd] single seme m; collective semi mpl; in tennis testa f di serie; *go to ~* of person, district ridursi male

seed·ling ['siːdlɪŋ] semenzale m

seed·y ['siːdɪ] adj bar, district squallido

see·ing (that) ['siːɪŋ] conj visto che

seek [siːk] v/t & v/i (pret & pp sought) cercare

seem [siːm] v/i sembrare; *it seems that ...* sembra che ...

seem·ing·ly ['siːmɪŋlɪ] adv apparentemente

seen [siːn] pp → **see**

seep [siːp] v/i of liquid filtrare

♦ **seep out** v/i of liquid filtrare

see·saw ['siːsɔː] n altalena f (a bilico)

seethe [siːð] v/i fig fremere di rabbia

'see-through adj dress, material trasparente

seg·ment ['segmənt] segmento m; of orange spicchio m

seg·ment·ed [seg'məntɪd] *adj* frazionato

seg·re·gate ['segrɪgeɪt] *v/t* separare

seg·re·ga·tion [segrɪ'geɪʃn] segregazione *f*

seis·mol·o·gy [saɪz'mɒlədʒɪ] sismologia *f*

seize [si:z] *v/t s.o., s.o.'s arm* afferrare; *power* prendere; *opportunity* cogliere; *of Customs, police etc* sequestrare

♦ **seize up** *v/i of engine* grippare

sei·zure ['si:ʒə(r)] MED attacco *m*; *of drugs etc* sequestro *m*

sel·dom ['seldəm] *adv* raramente

se·lect [sɪ'lekt] **1** *v/t* selezionare **2** *adj* (*exclusive*) scelto

se·lec·tion [sɪ'lekʃn] scelta *f*; *that/ those chosen* selezione *f*

se·lec·tion pro·cess procedimento *m* di selezione

se·lec·tive [sɪ'lektɪv] *adj* selettivo

self [self] (*pl* **selves** [selvz]) io *m*

self-ad·dressed 'en·ve·lope [selfə-'drest] busta *f* col proprio nome e indirizzo; **self-as'sur·ance** sicurezza *f* di sé; **self-as·sured** [self-'ʃʊəd] sicuro di sé; **self-ca·ter·ing a'part·ment** appartamento *m* indipendente con cucina; **self-'cen·tered** *Am*, **self-'cen·tred** [self'sentəd] *adj* egocentrico; **self-'clean·ing** *adj oven* autopulente; **self-con'fessed** [selfkən'fest] *adj* dichiarato; **self-'con·fi·dence** fiducia *f* in se stessi; **self-'con·fi·dent** *adj* sicuro di sé; **self-'con·scious** *adj* insicuro; *smile* imbarazzato; *feel* **~** sentirsi a disagio; **self-'con·scious·ness** disagio *m*; **self-con'tained** [selfkən'teɪnd] *adj flat* indipendente; **self con'trol** autocontrollo *m*; **self-de'fence**, **self-de'fense** *Am personal* legittima difesa *f*; *of state* autodifesa *f*; **self-'dis·ci·pline** autodisciplina *f*; **self-'doubt** dubbi *mpl* personali; **self-em'ployed** [selfɪm'plɔɪd] *adj* autonomo; **self-e'steem** autostima *f*; **self-'ev·i·dent** *adj* evidente; **self-ex'pres·sion** espressione *f* di sé;

self-'gov·ern·ment autogoverno *m*; **self-'in·ter·est** interesse *m* personale

self·ish ['selfɪʃ] *adj* egoista

self·less ['selflɪs] *adj person* altruista; *attitude, dedication* altruistico

self-made 'man *Am* **self-made man** *m inv*; **self-'pit·y** autocommiserazione *f*; **self-'por·trait** autoritratto *m*; **self-pos'sessed** *adj* padrone di sé; **self-re'li·ant** *adj* indipendente; **self-re'spect** dignità *f inv*; **self-'right·eous** *adj pej* presuntuoso; **self-'sat·is·fied** *adj pej* soddisfatto di sé; **self-'ser·vice** *adj* self-service; **self-ser·vice 'res·tau·rant** self-service *m inv*; **self-'taught** [self'tɔ:t] *adj* autodidatta

sell [sel] (*pret & pp* **sold**) **1** *v/t* vendere; *you have to* **~** *yourself* devi saperti vendere **2** *v/i of products* vendere

♦ **sell out of** *v/t* esaurire; *we are sold out of candles* abbiamo esaurito le candele

♦ **sell up** *v/i* vendere

'sell-by date data *f* di scadenza; *be past its* **~** essere scaduto

sell·er ['selə(r)] venditore *m*, -trice *f*

sell·ing ['selɪŋ] *n* COM vendita *f*

'sell·ing point COM punto *m* forte (che fa vendere il prodotto)

Sel·lo·tape® ['seləteɪp] scotch® *m*

se·men ['si:mən] sperma *m*

se·mes·ter [sɪ'mestər] *Am* semestre *m*

sem·i ['semɪ] *n* → *semidetached 'house*

'sem·i·cir·cle semicerchio *m*

sem·i·cir·cu·lar *adj* semicircolare

semi-'co·lon punto e virgola *m*

sem·i·con'duc·tor ELEC semiconduttore *m*

sem·i·de·tached ('**house**) [semɪdɪ-'tatʃt] villa *f* bifamiliare

semi'fi·nal semifinale *f*

sem·i·nar ['semɪnɑ:(r)] seminario *m*

sem·i'skilled *adj* parzialmente qualificato

sen·ate ['senət] senato *m*

sen·a·tor ['senətə(r)] senatore *m*, -trice *f*

send [send] *v/t* (*pret & pp* **sent**) mandare; **~ sth to s.o.** mandare qc a qu; **~ s.o. to s.o.** mandare qu da qu; **~ her my best wishes** mandale i miei saluti

♦ **send back** *v/t* mandare indietro

♦ **send for** *v/t doctor, help* (mandare a) chiamare

♦ **send in** *v/t troops* inviare; *next interviewee* far entrare; *application form* spedire

♦ **send off** *v/t letter, fax etc* spedire; *footballer* espellere

♦ **send up** *v/t* (*mock*) prendere in giro

send·er ['sendə(r)] *of letter* mittente *m/f*

se·nile ['si:naɪl] *adj pej* rimbambito

se·nil·i·ty [sɪ'nɪlətɪ] *pej* rimbambimento *m*

se·ni·or ['si:nɪə(r)] *adj* (*older*) più anziano; *in rank* di grado superiore; **be ~ to s.o.** *in rank* essere di grado superiore rispetto a qu

se·ni·or 'cit·i·zen anziano *m*, -a *f*

se·ni·or·i·ty [si:nɪ'ɒrətɪ] *in job* anzianità *f inv*

sen·sa·tion [sen'seɪʃn] (*feeling*) sensazione *f*; (*surprise event*) scalpore *m*; **be a ~** essere sensazionale

sen·sa·tion·al [sen'seɪʃnl] *adj* sensazionale

sense [sens] **1** *n* (*meaning*) significato *m*; (*purpose, point*) senso *m*; (*common sense*) buonsenso *m*; (*sight, smell etc*) senso *m*; (*feeling*) sensazione; **in a ~** in un certo senso; **talk ~, man!** ragiona!; **come to one's ~s** tornare in sé; **it doesn't make ~** non ha senso; **there's no ~ in trying / waiting** non ha senso provare / aspettare **2** *v/t* sentire

sense·less ['senslɪs] *adj* (*pointless*) assurdo

sen·si·ble ['sensəbl] *adj person, decision* assennato; *advice* sensato; *clothes, shoes* pratico

sen·si·bly ['sensəblɪ] *adv* assennatamente

sen·si·tive ['sensɪtɪv] *adj* sensibile

sen·si·tiv·i·ty [sensə'tɪvətɪ] sensibilità *f inv*

sen·sor ['sensə(r)] sensore *m*

sen·su·al ['sensjʊəl] *adj* sensuale

sen·su·al·i·ty [sensjʊ'ælətɪ] sensualità *f inv*

sen·su·ous ['sensjʊəs] *adj* sensuale

sent [sent] *pret & pp* → **send**

sen·tence ['sentəns] **1** *n* GRAM frase *m*; LAW condanna *f* **2** *v/t* LAW condannare

sen·ti·ment ['sentɪmənt] (*sentimentality*) sentimentalismo *m*; (*opinion*) opinione *f*

sen·ti·men·tal [sentɪ'mentl] *adj* sentimentale

sen·ti·men·tal·i·ty [sentɪmen'tælətɪ] sentimentalismo *m*

sen·try ['sentrɪ] sentinella *f*

sep·a·rate ['sepərət] **1** *adj* separato **2** *v/t* ['sepəreɪt] separare; **~ sth from sth** separare qc da qc **3** *v/i of couple* separarsi

sep·a·rat·ed ['sepəreɪtɪd] *adj couple* separato

sep·a·rate·ly ['sepərətlɪ] *adv* separatamente

sep·a·ra·tion [sepə'reɪʃn] separazione *f*

Sep·tem·ber [sep'tembə(r)] settembre *m*

sep·tic ['septɪk] *adj* infetto; **go ~** *of wound* infettarsi

se·quel ['si:kwəl] seguito *m*

se·quence ['si:kwəns] sequenza *f*; **in ~** di seguito; **out of ~** fuori tempo; **the ~ of events** l'ordine dei fatti

se·rene [sɪ'ri:n] *adj* sereno

ser·geant ['sɑ:dʒənt] sergente *m*

se·ri·al ['sɪərɪəl] *n* serial *m inv*

se·ri·al·ize ['sɪərɪəlaɪz] *v/t novel on TV* trasmettere a puntate

'se·ri·al kill·er serial killer *m/f inv*; **'se·ri·al num·ber** *of product* numero *m* di serie; **'se·ri·al port** COMPUT porta *f* seriale

se·ries ['sɪəri:z] *nsg* serie *f inv*

se·ri·ous ['sɪərɪəs] *adj illness, situation, damage* grave; *person, company* serio; **I'm ~** dico sul serio; **listen,**

this is ~ ascolta, è una cosa seria; *we'd better take a ~ look at it* dovremo considerarlo seriamente

se·ri·ous·ly ['sɪərɪəslɪ] *adv injured* gravemente; *(extremely)* estremamente; *~ though, ...* scherzi a parte, ...; *~? davvero?; take s.o. ~* prendere sul serio qu

se·ri·ous·ness ['sɪərɪəsnɪs] *of person* serietà *f inv; of situation, illness etc* gravità *f inv*

ser·mon ['sɜːmən] predica *f*

ser·vant ['sɜːvənt] domestico *m*, -a *f*

serve [sɜːv] **1** *n in tennis* servizio *m* **2** *v/t food, customer, one's country,* servire; *it ~s you / him right* ti / gli sta bene **3** *v/i give out food, in tennis* servire; *as politician etc* prestare servizio

♦ **serve up** *v/t meal* servire

serv·er ['sɜːvə(r)] COMPUT server *m inv*

ser·vice ['sɜːvɪs] **1** *n to customers, community service* servizio *m; for vehicle, machine* manutenzione *f; for vehicle* revisione *f; in tennis* servizio *m; ~s* servizi; *the ~s* MIL le forze armate **2** *v/t vehicle* revisionare; *machine* fare la manutenzione di

'**ser·vice ar·e·a** area *f* di servizio; '**ser·vice charge** *in restaurant, club* servizio *m;* '**ser·vice in·dus·try** settore *m* terziario; '**ser·vice·man** MIL militare *m;* '**ser·vice pro·vid·er** COMPUT fornitore *m* di servizi; '**ser·vice sec·tor** settore *m* terziario; '**ser·vice sta·tion** stazione *f* di servizio

ser·vi·ette [sɜːvɪ'et] tovagliolino *m*

ser·vile ['sɜːvaɪl] *adj pej* servile

ses·sion ['seʃn] *of parliament* sessione *f; with psychiatrist, consultant etc* seduta *f*

set [set] **1** *n of tools* set *m inv; of dishes, knives* servizio *m; of books* raccolta *f; group of people* cerchia *f;* MATH insieme *m;* (THEA: *scenery)* scenografia *f; where a film is made* set *m inv; in tennis* set *m inv; television ~* televisore *m* **2** *v/t (pret*

& pp set) *(place)* mettere; *film, novel etc* ambientare; *date, time, limit* fissare; *mechanism* regolare; *alarm clock* mettere; *broken limb* ingessare; *jewel* montare; *(typeset)* comporre; *~ the table* apparecchiare (la tavola); *~ a task for s.o.* assegnare un compito a qu **3** *v/i (pret & pp set) of sun* tramontare; *of glue* indurirsi **4** *adj views, ideas* rigido; *(ready)* pronto; *be dead ~ on (doing) sth* essere deciso a fare qc; *be very ~ in one's ways* essere abitudinario; *~ book / reading in course* libro / lettura in programma; *~ meal* menù *m inv* fisso

♦ **set apart** *v/t: set sth apart from sth* distinguere qc da qc

♦ **set aside** *v/t for future use* mettere da parte

♦ **set back** *v/t in plans etc* ritardare; *it set me back £400* F mi è costato 400 sterline

♦ **set off 1** *v/i on journey* partire **2** *v/t explosion* causare; *chain reaction, alarm* far scattare

♦ **set out 1** *v/i on journey* partire **2** *v/t ideas, proposal, goods* esporre; *set out to do sth (intend)* proporsi di fare qc

♦ **set to** *v/i start on a task* mettersi all'opera

♦ **set up 1** *v/t new company* fondare; *system* mettere in opera; *equipment, machine* piazzare; F *(frame)* incastrare F **2** *v/i in business* mettersi in affari

'**set·back** contrattempo *m*

set·tee [se'tiː] *(couch, sofa)* divano *m*

set·ting ['setɪŋ] *n of novel etc* ambientazione *f; of house* posizione *f*

set·tle ['setl] **1** *v/i of bird, dust, beer* posarsi; *of building* assestarsi; *to live* stabilirsi **2** *v/t dispute* comporre; *issue, uncertainty* risolvere; *s.o.'s debts, the bill* saldare; *nerves, stomach* calmare; *that ~s it!* è deciso!

♦ **settle down** *v/i (stop being noisy)* calmarsi; *(stop wild living)* mettere la testa a posto; *in an area* stabilirsi

♦ **set·tle for** v/t (*take, accept*) accontentarsi di

♦ **set·tle up** v/i (*pay*) regolare i conti; *in hotel etc* pagare il conto

set·tled ['setld] adj weather stabile

set·tle·ment ['setlmənt] of dispute composizione f; (*payment*) pagamento m

set·tler ['setlə(r)] in new country colonizzatore m, -trice f

'set-up n (*structure*) organizzazione f; (*relationship*) relazione f; F (*frameup*) montatura f

sev·en ['sevn] sette

sev·en·teen [sevn'ti:n] diciassette

sev·en·teenth [sevn'ti:nθ] diciassettesimo, -a

sev·enth ['sevnθ] n & adj settimo, -a

sev·en·ti·eth ['sevntɪɪθ] n & adj settantesimo, -a

sev·en·ty ['sevntɪ] settanta

sev·er ['sevə(r)] v/t arm, cable etc recidere; relations troncare

sev·e·ral ['sevrl] **1** adj parecchi **2** pron parecchi m, -ie f

se·vere [sɪ'vɪə(r)] adj illness grave; penalty, teacher, face severo; winter, weather rigido

se·vere·ly [sɪ'vɪəlɪ] adv punish severamente; speak, stare duramente; injured, disrupted gravemente

se·ver·i·ty [sɪ'verətɪ] of illness gravità f inv; of look etc durezza f; of penalty severità f inv; of winter rigidità f inv

sew [səʊ] v/t & v/i (pret -ed, pp sewn) cucire

♦ **sew on** v/t button attaccare

sew·age ['su:ɪdʒ] acque fpl di scolo

'sew·age plant impianto m per il riciclaggio delle acque di scolo

sew·er ['su:ə(r)] fogna f

sew·ing ['səʊɪŋ] n cucito m

'sew·ing ma·chine macchina f da cucire

sex [seks] sesso m; **have ~ with** avere rapporti sessuali con

sex·ist ['seksɪst] **1** adj sessista **2** n sessista m/f

sex·u·al ['seksjʊəl] adj sessuale

sex·u·al as'sault violenza f sessuale

sex·u·al ha'rass·ment molestie fpl sessuali; **sex·u·al 'in·ter·course** rapporti mpl sessuali

sex·u·al·i·ty [seksjʊ'ælətɪ] sessualità f inv

sex·u·al·ly ['seksjʊlɪ] adv sessualmente

sex·u·al·ly trans·mit·ted dis'ease [seksjʊlɪtrænz'mɪtɪd] malattia f venerea

sex·y ['seksɪ] adj sexy inv

shab·bi·ly ['ʃæbɪlɪ] adv dressed in modo trasandato; treat in modo meschino

shab·bi·ness ['ʃæbɪnɪs] of coat etc trasandatezza f

shab·by ['ʃæbɪ] adj coat etc trasandato; treatment meschino

shack [ʃæk] baracca f

shade [ʃeɪd] **1** n for lamp paralume m; of colour tonalità f inv; **in the ~** all'ombra **2** v/t from sun, light riparare

shad·ow ['ʃædəʊ] n ombra f

shad·y ['ʃeɪdɪ] adj spot all'ombra; character, dealings losco

shaft [ʃɑ:ft] of axle albero m; of mine pozzo m

shag·gy ['ʃægɪ] adj hair arruffato; dog dal pelo arruffato

shake [ʃeɪk] **1** n: **give sth a good ~** dare una scrollata a qc **2** v/t (pret **shook**, pp **shaken**) scuotere; emotionally sconvolgere; **~ hands** stringersi la mano; **~ hands with s.o.** stringere la mano a qu **3** v/i of hands, voice, building tremare

shak·en ['ʃeɪkən] **1** adj emotionally scosso **2** pp → **shake**

'shake-up rimpasto m

shak·y ['ʃeɪkɪ] adj table etc traballante; after illness, shock debole; grasp of sth, grammar etc incerto; voice, hand tremante

shall [ʃæl] v/aux ◊ future: **I ~ do my best** farò del mio meglio; **I shan't see them** non li vedrò ◊ suggesting: **~ we go now?** andiamo?

shal·low ['ʃæləʊ] adj water poco profondo; person superficiale

sham·bles ['ʃæmblz] nsg casino m F

shame [ʃeɪm] **1** n vergogna f; **bring ~ on ...** disonorare ...; **what a ~!** che peccato!; **~ on you!** vergognati! **2** v/t: **~ s.o. into doing sth** indurre qu a fare qc per vergogna

shame·ful ['ʃeɪmfʊl] adj vergognoso

shame·ful·ly ['ʃeɪmfʊlɪ] adv vergognosamente

shame·less ['ʃeɪmlɪs] adj svergognato

sham·poo [ʃæm'pu:] **1** n shampoo m inv; **a ~ and set** shampoo e messa in piega **2** v/t fare lo shampoo a

shape [ʃeɪp] **1** n forma f **2** v/t clay dar forma a; person's life, character forgiare; the future determinare

shape·less ['ʃeɪplɪs] adj dress etc informe

shape·ly ['ʃeɪplɪ] adv figure ben fatto

share [ʃeə(r)] **1** n parte f; FIN azione f; **do one's ~ of the work** fare la propria parte del lavoro **2** v/t dividere; s.o.'s feelings, opinions condividere **3** v/i dividere; **do you mind sharing with Patrick?** ti dispiace dividere con Patrick?

♦ **share out** v/t spartire

'share·hold·er azionista m/f

shark [ʃɑ:k] fish squalo m

sharp [ʃɑ:p] **1** adj knife affilato; mind, pain acuto; taste aspro **2** adv MUS in diesis; **at 3 o'clock ~** alle 3 precise

sharp·en ['ʃɑ:pn] v/t knife affilare; skills raffinare

sharp 'prac·tice pratiche fpl poco oneste

shat [ʃæt] pret & pp ▷ **shit**

shat·ter ['ʃætə(r)] **1** v/t glass frantumare; illusions distruggere **2** v/i of glass frantumarsi

shat·tered ['ʃætəd] adj F (exhausted) esausto; (very upset) sconvolto

shat·ter·ing ['ʃætərɪŋ] adj news, experience sconvolgente; effect tremendo

shave [ʃeɪv] **1** v/t radere **2** v/i farsi la barba **3** n: **have a ~** farsi la barba; **that was a close ~** ce l'abbiamo fatta per un pelo

♦ **shave off** v/t beard tagliarsi; from piece of wood piallare

shav·en ['ʃeɪvn] adj head rasato

shav·er ['ʃeɪvə(r)] electric rasoio m

'shav·ing brush ['ʃeɪvɪŋ] pennello m da barba

'shav·ing soap sapone m da barba

shawl [ʃɔ:l] scialle m

she [ʃi:] pron lei; **~ has three children** ha tre figli; **you're funny, ~'s not** tu sei spiritoso, lei no; **there ~ is** eccola

shears [ʃɪəz] npl for gardening cesoie fpl; for sewing forbici fpl

sheath [ʃi:θ] n for knife guaina f; contraceptive preservativo m

shed¹ [ʃed] v/t (pret & pp shed) blood spargere; tears versare; leaves perdere; **~ light on** fig fare luce su

shed² [ʃed] n baracca f

sheep [ʃi:p] (pl sheep) pecora f

'sheep·dog cane m pastore

sheep·ish ['ʃi:pɪʃ] adj imbarazzato

'sheep·skin adj lining di montone

sheer [ʃɪə(r)] adj madness, luxury puro; drop, cliffs ripido

sheet [ʃi:t] for bed lenzuolo m; of paper foglio m; of metal, glass lastra f

shelf [ʃelf] (pl shelves [ʃelvz]) mensola f; **shelves** scaffale msg, ripiani mpl

'shelf·life of product durata f di conservazione

shell [ʃel] **1** n of mussel etc conchiglia f; of egg guscio m; of tortoise corazza f; MIL granata f; **come out of one's ~** fig uscire dal guscio **2** v/t peas sbucciare; MIL bombardare

'shell·fire bombardamento m; **come under ~** essere bombardato

'shell·fish crostacei mpl

shel·ter ['ʃeltə(r)] **1** n (refuge) riparo m; construction rifugio m **2** v/i from rain, bombing etc ripararsi **3** v/t (protect) proteggere

shel·tered ['ʃeltəd] adj place riparato; **lead a ~ life** vivere nella bambagia

shelve [ʃelv] v/t fig accantonare

shep·herd ['ʃepəd] n pastore m

sher·ry ['ʃerɪ] sherry m inv

shield [ʃi:ld] **1** n scudo m; sports trophy scudetto m; TECH schermo m di protezione f **2** v/t (*protect*) proteggere

shift [ʃɪft] **1** n (*change*) cambiamento m; *period of work* turno m **2** v/t (*move*) spostare; *stains etc* togliere **3** v/i (*move*) spostarsi; *of wind* cambiare direzione; *that's ~ing!* F è un bolide!

'**shift key** COMPUT tasto m shift; '**shift work** turni mpl; '**shift worker** turnista m/f

'**shift·y** ['ʃɪftɪ] adj pej losco

'**shift·y-look·ing** adj pej dall'aria losca

shilly-shally ['ʃɪlɪʃælɪ] v/i (*pret & pp -ied*) F tentennare

shim·mer ['ʃɪmə(r)] v/i luccicare

shin [ʃɪn] n stinco m

shine [ʃaɪn] **1** v/i (*pret & pp shone*) *of sun, shoes, metal* splendere; *fig: of student etc* brillare **2** v/t (*pret & pp shone*) *torch etc* puntare **3** n *of shoes etc* lucentezza f

shin·gle ['ʃɪŋgl] *on beach* ciottoli mpl

shin·gles ['ʃɪŋglz] nsg MED fuoco m di Sant'Antonio

shin·y ['ʃaɪnɪ] adj surface lucido

ship [ʃɪp] **1** n nave f **2** v/t (*pret & pp -ped*) (*send*) spedire; (*send by sea*) spedire via mare

ship·ment ['ʃɪpmənt] (*consignment*) carico m

'**ship·own·er** armatore m

'**ship·ping** ['ʃɪpɪŋ] n (*sea traffic*) navigazione f; (*sending*) trasporto m (via mare)

'**ship·ping com·pa·ny** compagnia f di navigazione

'**shipshape** adj in perfetto ordine; '**ship·wreck 1** n naufragio m **2** v/t: *be ~ed* naufragare; '**ship·yard** cantiere m navale

shirk [ʃɜːk] v/t scansare

shirk·er ['ʃɜːkə(r)] scansafatiche m/f inv

shirt [ʃɜːt] camicia f; *in his ~ sleeves* in maniche di camicia

shit [ʃɪt] **1** n P merda f P; *bad quality goods, work* stronzata f P **2** v/i (*pret & pp shat*) cagare P **3** int merda P

shit·ty ['ʃɪtɪ] adj F di merda P

shiv·er ['ʃɪvə(r)] **1** v/i rabbrividire **2** n brivido m

shock [ʃɒk] **1** n shock m inv; ELEC scossa f; *be in ~* MED essere in stato di shock **2** v/t scioccare; *be ~ed by* essere scioccato da

'**shock ab·sorb·er** MOT ammortizzatore m

shock·ing ['ʃɒkɪŋ] adj behaviour, poverty scandaloso; F very bad allucinante F

shock·ing·ly ['ʃɒkɪŋlɪ] adv behave scandalosamente; bad, late, expensive terribilmente

shod·dy ['ʃɒdɪ] adj goods scadente; behaviour meschino

shoe [ʃuː] scarpa f

'**shoe·horn** calzascarpe m inv; '**shoe·lace** laccio m di scarpa; '**shoe·mak·er, shoe mender** calzolaio m; '**shoe-shop** negozio m di scarpe; '**shoe·string** n: *do sth on a ~* fare qc con pochi soldi

shone [ʃɒn] pret & pp → **shine**

♦**shoo away** [ʃuː] v/t children, chicken scacciare

shook [ʃʊk] pret → **shake**

shoot [ʃuːt] **1** n BOT germoglio m **2** v/t v/t (*pret & pp shot*) sparare; film girare; ~ s.o. colpire qu alla gamba; ~ s.o. for desertion fucilare qu per diserzione

♦**shoot down** v/t aeroplane abbattere

♦**shoot off** v/i (*rush off*) precipitarsi

♦**shoot up** v/i of prices salire alle stelle; of children crescere molto; of new suburbs, buildings etc spuntare; F of drug addict farsi F

shoot·ing star ['ʃuːtɪŋ] stella f cadente

shop [ʃɒp] **1** n negozio m; *talk ~* parlare di lavoro **2** v/i (*pret & pp -ped*) fare acquisti; *go ~ping* andare a fare spese

'**shop as·sis·tant** commesso m, -a f; '**shop·keep·er** negoziante m/f; **shop·lift·er** ['ʃɒplɪftə(r)] taccheggiatore m, -trice f; **shop·lift·ing** ['ʃɒplɪftɪŋ] n taccheggio m

shop·per ['ʃɒpə(r)] *person* acquirente *m/f*

shop·ping ['ʃɒpɪŋ] *activity* fare spese; *items* spesa *f*; *do one's ~* fare la spesa

'**shop·ping bag** borsa *f* per la spesa; '**shop·ping cen·ter** *Am*, '**shop·ping cen·tre** centro *m* commerciale; '**shop·ping list** lista *f* della spesa; '**shop·ping mall** centro *m* commerciale

shop 'stew·ard rappresentante *m/f* sindacale

shop 'win·dow vetrina *f*

shore [ʃɔː(r)] riva *f*; *on ~ not at sea* a terra

short [ʃɔːt] **1** *adj in length, distance* corto; *in height* basso; *in time* breve; *be ~ of* essere a corto di **2** *adv*: *cut a vacation / meeting ~* interrompere una vacanza / riunione; *stop a person ~* interrompere una persona; *go ~ of* fare a meno di; *in ~* in breve

short·age ['ʃɔːtɪdʒ] mancanza *f*

short 'cir·cuit *n* corto *m* circuito; **short-com·ing** ['ʃɔːtkʌmɪŋ] difetto *m*; '**short cut** scorciatoia *f*

short·en ['ʃɔːtn] **1** *v/t* accorciare **2** *v/i* accorciarsi

'**short·fall** deficit *m inv*; *in hours etc* mancanza *f*; '**short·hand** *n* stenografia *f*; **short-'hand·ed** *adj*: *be ~* essere a corto di personale; '**short·list** *n of candidates* rosa *f* dei candidati

short-lived ['ʃɔːtlɪvd] *adj* di breve durata

'**short·ly** ['ʃɔːtlɪ] *adv* (*soon*) tra breve; *~ before / after* poco prima / dopo

short·ness ['ʃɔːtnɪs] *of visit* brevità *f inv*; *in height* bassa statura *f*

shorts [ʃɔːts] *npl* calzoncini *mpl*

short·sight·ed [ʃɔːt'saɪtɪd] *adj also fig* miope; **short-sleeved** ['ʃɔːtsliːvd] *adj* a maniche corte; **short-staffed** [ʃɔːt'stɑːft] *adj* a corto di personale; **short 'sto·ry** racconto *m*; **short-tem·pered** [ʃɔːt'tempəd] *adj* irascibile; '**short-term** *adj* a breve termine; '**short time** *n*: *be on ~ of workers* lavorare a orario ridotto; '**short wave** RAD onde *fpl* corte

shot [ʃɒt] **1** *n from gun* sparo *m*; (*photograph*) foto *f*; (*injection*) puntura *f*; *be a good / poor ~* essere un buon / pessimo tiratore; *like a ~ accept, run off* come un razzo **2** *pret & pp → shoot*

'**shot·gun** fucile *m* da caccia

should [ʃʊd] *v/aux*: *what ~ I do?* cosa devo fare?; *you ~n't do that* non dovresti farlo; *that ~ be long enough* dovrebbe essere lungo abbastanza; *you ~ have heard him!* avresti dovuto sentirlo!

shoul·der ['ʃəʊldə(r)] *n* ANAT spalla *f*

'**shoul·der bag** borsa *f* a tracolla; '**shoul·der blade** scapola *f*; '**shoulder strap** spallina *f*

shout [ʃaʊt] **1** *n* grido *m*, urlo *m* **2** *v/t & v/i* gridare, urlare

♦**shout at** *v/t* urlare a

shout·ing ['ʃaʊtɪŋ] *n* urla *fpl*

shove [ʃʌv] **1** *n* spinta *f* **2** *v/t & v/i* spingere

♦**shove in** *v/i* passare davanti; *he shoved in in front of me* mi è passato davanti

♦**shove off** *v/i* F (*go away*) levarsi di torno

shov·el ['ʃʌvl] **1** *n* pala *f* **2** *v/t* spalare

show [ʃəʊ] **1** *n* THEA, TV spettacolo *m*; (*display*) manifestazione *f*; *on ~ at exhibition* esposto; *it's all done for ~ pej* è tutta una scena **2** *v/t* (*pret -ed*, *pp shown*) *passport, ticket* mostrare; *interest, emotion* dimostrare; *at exhibition* esporre; *film* proiettare; *~ s.o. sth*, *~ sth to s.o.* mostrare qc a qu **3** *v/i* (*pret -ed*, *pp shown*) (*be visible*) vedersi; *does it ~?* si vede?; *what's ~ing at the cinema?* cosa danno al cinema?

♦**show around** *v/t* far visitare

♦**show in** *v/t* far entrare

♦**show off 1** *v/t skills* mettere in risalto **2** *v/i pej* mettersi in mostra

♦**show up 1** *v/t s.o.'s shortcomings etc* far risaltare; *don't show me up in public* non farmi fare brutta figura

2 v/i F (*arrive, turn up*) farsi vedere F; (*be visible*) notarsi

'show busi·ness il mondo dello spettacolo

'show·case n vetrinetta f; fig vetrina f

'show·down regolamento m di conti

show·er ['ʃauə(r)] **1** n of rain acquazzone m; to wash doccia f; **take a** ~ fare una doccia **2** v/i fare la doccia **3** v/t: ~ **s.o. with praise** coprire qu di lodi

'show·er cap cuffia f da doccia; 'show·er cur·tain tenda f della doccia; 'show·er·proof adj impermeabile

show·jump·er ['ʃəudʒʌmpə(r)] cavaliere m, cavallerizza f di concorso ippico

'show·jump·ing concorso m ippico

'show-off pej esibizionista m/f

'show·room show-room m inv; **in** ~ **condition** mai usato

show·y ['ʃəui] adj appariscente

shrank [ʃræŋk] pret → **shrink**

shred [ʃred] **1** n of paper strisciolina f; of cloth brandello m; of evidence, etc briciolo m **2** v/t (pret & pp **-ded**) paper stracciare; in cooking sminuzzare

shred·der ['ʃredə(r)] for documents distruttore m di documenti

shrewd [ʃru:d] adj person, businessman scaltro; investment oculato

shrewd·ly ['ʃru:dli] adv oculatamente

shrewd·ness ['ʃru:dnɪs] oculatezza f

shriek [ʃri:k] **1** n strillo m **2** v/i strillare

shrill [ʃrɪl] adj stridulo

shrimp [ʃrɪmp] gamberetto m

shrine [ʃraɪn] santuario m

shrink[1] [ʃrɪŋk] v/i (pret shrank, pp shrunk) of material restringersi; level of support etc diminuire

shrink[2] [ʃrɪŋk] n F (psychiatrist) strizzacervelli m/f inv

'shrink-wrap v/t cellofanare

'shrink-wrap·ping process cellofanatura f; material cellophane® m inv

shriv·el ['ʃrɪvl] v/i avvizzire

Shrove 'Tues·day [ʃrəuv] martedì m grasso

shrub [ʃrʌb] arbusto m

shrub·be·ry ['ʃrʌbərɪ] arboreto m

shrug [ʃrʌg] **1** n alzata f di spalle **2** v/i (pret & pp **-ged**) alzare le spalle **3** v/t (pret & pp **-ged**): ~ **one's shoulders** alzare le spalle

shrunk [ʃrʌŋk] pp → **shrink**

shud·der ['ʃʌdə(r)] **1** n of fear, disgust brivido m; of earth etc tremore m **2** v/i with fear, disgust rabbrividire; of earth, building tremare; **I** ~ **to think** non oso immaginare

shuf·fle ['ʃʌfl] **1** v/t cards mescolare **2** v/i in walking strascicare i piedi; **he** ~**d into the bathroom** è andato in bagno strascicando i piedi

shun [ʃʌn] v/t (pret & pp **-ned**) evitare

shut [ʃʌt] (pret & pp **shut**) **1** v/t chiudere **2** v/i of door, box chiudersi; of shop, bank chiudere; **they were** ~ era chiuso

◆ shut down **1** v/t business chiudere; computer spegnere **2** v/i of business chiudere i battenti; of computer spegnersi

◆ shut off v/t chiudere

◆ shut up v/i F (be quiet) star zitto; **shut up!** zitto!

shut·ter ['ʃʌtə(r)] on window battente m; PHOT otturatore m

'shut·ter speed PHOT tempo m di apertura

shut·tle ['ʃʌtl] v/i fare la spola

'shut·tle·bus at airport bus m inv navetta; 'shut·tle·cock SP volano m; 'shut·tle ser·vice servizio m navetta

shy [ʃaɪ] adj timido

shy·ness ['ʃaɪnɪs] timidezza f

Si·a·mese 'twins [saɪə'mi:z] npl fratelli mpl/sorelle fpl siamesi

Si·cil·i·an [sɪ'sɪlɪən] **1** adj siciliano **2** n siciliano m, -a f

Sic·i·ly ['sɪsɪlɪ] Sicilia f

sick [sɪk] adj malato; sense of humour crudele; **I feel** ~ about to vomit ho la nausea; **I'm going to be** ~ vomit ho voglia di vomitare; **be** ~ **of** (fed up with) essere stufo di

sick·en ['sɪkn] **1** *v/t* (*disgust*) disgustare **2** *v/i*: **be ~ing for sth** covare qc

sick·en·ing ['sɪknɪŋ] *adj* disgustoso

'**sick leave** *n*: **be on ~** essere in (congedo per) malattia

sick·ly ['sɪklɪ] *adj person* delicato; *smell* stomachevole

sick·ness ['sɪknɪs] malattia *f*, (*vomiting*) nausea *f*

'**sick·ness ben·e·fit** *Br* indennità *f inv* di malattia

side [saɪd] *n of box, house* lato *m*; *of person, mountain* fianco *m*; *of page, record* facciata *f*; SP squadra *f*; *take ~s* (*favour one side*) prendere posizione; *take ~s with* parteggiare per; *I'm on your ~* sono dalla tua (parte); *~ by ~* fianco a fianco; *at the ~ of the road* sul ciglio della strada; *on the big / small ~* piuttosto grande / piccolo

♦ **side with** *v/t* prendere le parti di

'**side·board** credenza *f*; '**sideburns** *npl* basette *fpl*; '**side dish** contorno *m*; '**side ef·fect** effetto *m* collaterale; '**side·light** MOT luce *f* di posizione; '**side·line** **1** *n* attività *f inv* collaterale **2** *v/t*: *feel ~d* sentirsi sminuito; '**side·step** *v/t* (*pret & pp -ped*) scansare; *fig* schivare; '**side street** via *f* laterale; '**side·track** *v/t* distrarre; *get ~ed by* essere distratto da; '**side·walk** *Am* marciapiede *m*; '**side·ways** ['saɪdweɪz] *adv* di lato

siege [siːdʒ] *n* assedio *m*; *lay ~ to* assediare

sieve [sɪv] *n* setaccio *m*

sift [sɪft] *v/t* setacciare

♦ **sift through** *v/t details, data* passare al vaglio

sigh [saɪ] **1** *n* sospiro *m*; *heave a ~ of relief* tirare un respiro di sollievo **2** *v/i* sospirare

sight [saɪt] *n* vista *f*; *~s of city* luoghi *mpl* da visitare; *catch ~ of* intravedere; *know by ~* conoscere di vista; *be within ~* essere visibile da; *out of ~* non visibile; *out of ~ of* fuori dalla vista di; *what a ~ you are!*

come sei conciato!; *lose ~ of main objective etc* perdere di vista

sight·see·ing ['saɪtsiːɪŋ] *n* visita *f* turistica; *I enjoy ~* mi piace visitare i posti; *go ~* fare un giro turistico

'**sight·see·ing tour** giro *m* turistico

sight·seer ['saɪtsiːə(r)] turista *m/f*

sign [saɪn] **1** *n* (*indication*) segno *m*; (*road ~*) segnale *m*; *outside shop* insegna *f*; *it's a ~ of the times* è tipico dei nostri giorni **2** *v/t & v/i document* firmare

♦ **sign in** *v/i* firmare il registro (all'arrivo)

♦ **sign up** *v/i* (*join the army*) arruolarsi

sig·nal ['sɪgnl] **1** *n* segnale *m*; *be sending out the right / wrong ~s fig* lanciare il messaggio giusto / sbagliato **2** *v/i of driver* segnalare

sig·na·to·ry ['sɪgnətrɪ] *n* firmatario *m*, -a *f*

sig·na·ture ['sɪgnətʃə(r)] firma *f*

sig·na·ture 'tune sigla *f* musicale

sig·net ring ['sɪgnɪtrɪŋ] anello *m* con sigillo

sig·nif·i·cance [sɪg'nɪfɪkəns] importanza *f*, (*meaning*) significato *m*

sig·nif·i·cant [sɪg'nɪfɪkənt] *adj event etc* significativo; (*quite large*) notevole

sig·nif·i·cant·ly [sɪg'nɪfɪkəntlɪ] *adv larger, more expensive* notevolmente

sig·ni·fy ['sɪgnɪfaɪ] *v/t* (*pret & pp -ied*) significare

'**sign lan·guage** linguaggio *m* dei segni

'**sign·post** cartello *m* stradale

si·lence ['saɪləns] **1** *n* silenzio *m*; *in ~ work, march* in silenzio; *~!* silenzio! **2** *v/t* mettere a tacere

si·lenc·er ['saɪlənsə(r)] *on gun* silenziatore *m*; *on car* marmitta *f*

si·lent ['saɪlənt] *adj* silenzioso; *film* muto; *stay ~ not comment* tacere

sil·hou·ette [sɪluˈet] *n* sagoma *f*

sil·i·con ['sɪlɪkən] silicio *m*

sil·i·con 'chip *chip m inv* al silicio

sil·i·cone ['sɪlɪkəun] silicone *m*

silk [sɪlk] **1** *n* seta *f* **2** *adj shirt etc* di seta

silk·y ['sɪlkɪ] *adj hair, texture* setoso

sil·li·ness ['sɪlɪnɪs] stupidità *f inv*

sil·ly ['sɪlɪ] *adj* stupido

si·lo ['saɪləʊ] silo *m*

sil·ver ['sɪlvə(r)] **1** *n metal* argento *m*; *~ objects* argenteria *f* **2** *adj ring* d'argento; *colour* argentato

sil·ver-plat·ed [sɪlvə'pleɪtɪd] *adj* placcato d'argento; **'sil·ver·ware** argenteria *f*; **sil·ver 'wed·ding** nozze *fpl* d'argento

sim·i·lar ['sɪmɪlə(r)] *adj* simile

sim·i·lar·i·ty [sɪmɪ'lærətɪ] rassomiglianza *f*

sim·i·lar·ly ['sɪmɪləlɪ] *adv* allo stesso modo

sim·mer ['sɪmə(r)] *v/i in cooking* sobbollire; *with rage* ribollire

♦ **simmer down** *v/i* calmarsi

sim·ple ['sɪmpl] *adj method, life, dress* semplice; *(distinguish)* distinguere

sim·ple-mind·ed [sɪmpl'maɪndɪd] *adj pej* sempliciotto

sim·plic·i·ty [sɪm'plɪsətɪ] semplicità *f inv*

sim·pli·fy ['sɪmplɪfaɪ] *v/t (pret & pp -ied)* semplificare

sim·plis·tic [sɪm'plɪstɪk] *adj* semplicistico

sim·ply ['sɪmplɪ] *adv (absolutely)* assolutamente; *in a simple way* semplicemente; *it is ~ the best* è assolutamente il migliore

sim·u·late ['sɪmjuleɪt] *v/t* simulare

sim·ul·ta·ne·ous [sɪml'teɪnɪəs] *adj* simultaneo

sim·ul·ta·ne·ous·ly [sɪml'teɪnɪəslɪ] *adv* simultaneamente

sin [sɪn] **1** *n* peccato *m* **2** *v/i (pret & pp -ned)* peccare

since [sɪns] **1** *prep* da; *~ last week* dalla scorsa settimana **2** *adv* da allora; *I haven't seen him ~* non lo vedo da allora **3** *conj in expressions of time* da quando; *(seeing that)* visto che; *~ you left* da quando sei andato via; *ever ~ I have known her* da quando la conosco; *~ you don't like it* visto che non ti piace

sin·cere [sɪn'sɪə(r)] *adj* sincero

sin·cere·ly [sɪn'sɪəlɪ] *adv* con sinceri-

tà; *hope* sinceramente; *Yours ~* Distinti saluti

sin·cer·i·ty [sɪn'serətɪ] sincerità *f inv*

sin·ful ['sɪnful] *adj* peccaminoso

sing [sɪŋ] *v/t & v/i (pret sang, pp sung)* cantare

singe [sɪndʒ] *v/t* bruciacchiare

sing·er ['sɪŋə(r)] cantante *m/f*

sin·gle ['sɪŋgl] **1** *adj (sole)* solo; *(not double)* singolo; *bed, sheet* a una piazza; *(not married)* single; *with reference to Europe* unico; *there wasn't a ~ ...* non c'era nemmeno un ...; *in ~ file* in fila indiana **2** *n* MUS singolo *m*; *(~ room) (camera f)* singola *f*; *ticket* biglietto *m* di sola andata; *person* single *m/f inv*; *~s* in tennis singolo

♦ **single out** *v/t (choose)* prescegliere; *(distinguish)* distinguere

sin·gle-breast·ed [sɪŋgl'brestɪd] *adj* a un petto; **sin·gle-'hand·ed** [sɪŋgl-'hændɪd] *adj & adv* da solo; **sin·gle-mind·ed** [sɪŋgl'maɪndɪd] *adj* determinato; **Sin·gle 'Mar·ket** mercato *m* unico; **sin·gle 'moth·er** ragazza *f* madre; **sin·gle 'pa·rent** genitore *m* single; **sin·gle pa·rent 'fam·i·ly** famiglia *f* monoparentale; **sin·gle 'room** *(camera f)* singola *f*

sin·gu·lar ['sɪŋgjulə(r)] **1** *adj* GRAM singolare **2** *n* GRAM singolare *m*; *in the ~* al singolare

sin·is·ter ['sɪnɪstə(r)] *adj* sinistro

sink [sɪŋk] **1** *n* lavandino *m* **2** *v/i (pret sank, pp sunk)* of ship affondare; *of object* andare a fondo; *of sun* calare; *of interest rates, pressure etc* scendere; *he sank onto the bed* crollò sul letto **3** *v/t (pret sank, pp sunk) ship* affondare; *funds* investire

♦ **sink in** *v/i of liquid* penetrare; *it still hasn't really sunk in* of realization ancora non mi rendo conto

sin·ner ['sɪnə(r)] peccatore *m*, -trice *f*

si·nus ['saɪnəs] seno *m* paranasale; *my ~es are blocked* ho il naso bloccato

si·nus·i·tis [saɪnə'saɪtɪs] MED sinusite *f*

S

sip

sip [sɪp] **1** *n* sorso *m* **2** *v/t* (*pret & pp* **-ped**) sorseggiare

sir [sɜ:(r)] signore *m*; **Sir Charles** Sir Charles

si·ren ['saɪrən] sirena *f*

sir·loin ['sɜ:lɔɪn] controfiletto *m*

sis·ter ['sɪstə(r)] sorella *f*; *in hospital* (infermiera *f*) caposala *f*

'sis·ter-in-law (*pl* **sisters-in-law**) cognata *f*

sit [sɪt] (*pret & pp* **sat**) **1** *v/i* sedere; (*sit down*) sedersi; *for a portrait* posare; *of objects* stare; *of committee, assembly etc* riunirsi **2** *v/t exam* dare
♦ **sit down** *v/i* sedersi
♦ **sit up** *v/i in bed* mettersi a sedere; *straighten back* star seduto bene; *wait up at night* rimanere alzato

sit·com ['sɪtkɒm] sitcom *f inv*

site [saɪt] **1** *n* luogo *m* **2** *v/t new offices etc* situare

sit·ting ['sɪtɪŋ] *n of committee, court* sessione *f*; *for artist* seduta *f*; *for meals* turno *m*

'sit·ting room salotto *m*

sit·u·at·ed ['sɪtjʊeɪtɪd] *adj* situato; **be ~** trovarsi

sit·u·a·tion [sɪtjʊ'eɪʃn] situazione *f*; *of building etc* posizione *f*

six [sɪks] sei

six·teen [sɪks'ti:n] sedici

six·teenth [sɪks'ti:nθ] *n & adj* sedicesimo, -a

sixth [sɪksθ] *adj* sesto

six·ti·eth ['sɪkstɪɪθ] *n & adj* sessantesimo, -a

six·ty ['sɪkstɪ] sessanta

size [saɪz] dimensioni *fpl*; *of clothes* taglia *f*, misura *f*; *of shoes* numero *m*
♦ **size up** *v/t* valutare

size·a·ble ['saɪzəbl] *adj* considerevole

siz·zle ['sɪzl] *v/i* sfrigolare

skate [skeɪt] **1** *n* pattino *m* **2** *v/i* pattinare

skate·board ['skeɪtbɔ:d] *n* skateboard *m inv*

skate·board·er ['skeɪtbɔ:də(r)] skateboarder *m/f inv*

skate·board·ing ['skeɪtbɔ:dɪŋ] skateboard *m inv*

skat·er ['skeɪtə(r)] pattinatore *m*, -trice *f*

skat·ing ['skeɪtɪŋ] *n* pattinaggio *m*

'skat·ing rink pista *f* di pattinaggio

skel·e·ton ['skelɪtn] scheletro *m*

'skel·e·ton key passe-partout *m inv*

'skep·tic *etc Am* → **sceptic** *etc*

sketch [sketʃ] **1** *n* abbozzo *m*; THEA sketch *m inv* **2** *v/t* abbozzare

'sketch·book album *m* da disegno

sketch·y ['sketʃɪ] *adj knowledge etc* lacunoso

skew·er ['skjʊə(r)] *n* spiedino *m*

ski [ski:] **1** *n* sci *m inv* **2** *v/i* sciare

'ski boots *npl* scarponi *mpl* da sci

skid [skɪd] **1** *n* sbandata *f* **2** *v/i* (*pret & pp* **-ded**) sbandare

ski·er ['ski:ə(r)] sciatore *m*, -trice *f*

ski·ing ['ski:ɪŋ] sci *m inv*; **go ~** andare a sciare

'ski in·struc·tor maestro *m*, -a *f* di sci

skil·ful ['skɪlfʊl] *adj* abile

skil·ful·ly ['skɪlflɪ] *adv* abilmente

'ski lift impianto *m* di risalita

skill [skɪl] (*ability*) abilità *f inv*; **what ~s do you have?** quali capacità possiede?

skilled [skɪld] *adj* abile

skilled 'work·er operaio *m*, -a *f* specializzato, -a

skill·ful *etc Am* → **skilful** *etc*

skim [skɪm] *v/t* (*pret & pp* **-med**) *surface* sfiorare; *milk* scremare
♦ **skim off** *v/t the best* selezionare
♦ **skim through** *v/t text* scorrere

skimmed 'milk [skɪmd] latte *m* scremato

skimp·y ['skɪmpɪ] *adj account etc* scarso; *dress* succinto

skin [skɪn] **1** *n of person, animal* pelle *f*; *of fruit* buccia *f* **2** *v/t* (*pret & pp* **-ned**) scoiare

'skin div·ing immersioni *fpl* subacquee

skin·flint ['skɪnflɪnt] F spilorcio *m* F

'skin graft innesto *m* epidermico

skin·ny ['skɪnɪ] *adj* magro

'skin-tight *adj* aderente

skip [skɪp] **1** *n little jump* salto *m* **2** *v/i* (*pret & pp* **-ped**) saltellare; *with skipping rope* saltare **3** *v/t* (*pret & pp*

-ped) (*omit*) saltare

'**ski pole** racchetta *f* da sci

skip·per ['skɪpə(r)] NAUT skipper *m inv*; *of team* capitano *m*

'**skip·ping rope** ['skɪpɪŋ] corda *f* (per saltare)

'**ski re·sort** stazione *f* sciistica

skirt [skɜːt] *n* gonna *f*

'**ski run** pista *f* da sci

'**ski tow** sciovia *f*

skit·tle ['skɪtl] birillo *m*

skit·tles ['skɪtlz] *nsg* (*game*) birilli *mpl*

skive [skaɪv] *v/i* F fare lo scansafatiche F

skull [skʌl] cranio *m*

sky [skaɪ] cielo *m*

'**sky·light** lucernario *m*; '**sky·line** profilo *m* (contro il cielo); '**sky·scrap·er** ['skaɪskreɪpə(r)] grattacielo *m*

slab [slæb] *of stone* lastra *f*; *of cake etc* fetta *f*

slack [slæk] *adj rope* allentato; *person, work* negligente; *period* lento

slack·en ['slækn] *v/t rope* allentare; *pace* rallentare

◆ **slacken off** *v/i* rallentare

slacks [slæks] *npl* pantaloni *mpl* casual

◆ **slag off** [slæg] *v/t* P parlare male di

slain [sleɪn] *pp* → **slay**

slam [slæm] *v/t & v/i* (*pret & pp -med*) *door* sbattere

◆ **slam down** *v/t* sbattere

slan·der ['slɑːndə(r)] **1** *n* diffamazione *f* **2** *v/t* diffamare

slan·der·ous ['slɑːndərəs] *adj* diffamatorio

slang [slæŋ] slang *m inv*; *of a specific group* gergo *m*

slant [slɑːnt] **1** *v/i* pendere **2** *n* pendenza *f*; *given to a story* angolazione *f*

slant·ing ['slɑːntɪŋ] *adj roof* spiovente

slap [slæp] **1** *n blow* schiaffo *m* **2** *v/t* (*pret & pp -ped*) schiaffeggiare

'**slap·dash** *adj work* frettoloso; *person* pressapochista

slap-up '**meal** F pranzo *m* coi fiocchi

slash [slæʃ] **1** *n cut* taglio *m*; *in punctuation* barra *f* **2** *v/t skin, painting* squarciare; *prices, costs* abbattere; ~ *one's wrists* tagliarsi le vene

slate [sleɪt] *n* ardesia *f*

slaugh·ter ['slɔːtə(r)] **1** *n of animals* macellazione *f*; *of people, troops* massacro *m* **2** *v/t animals* macellare; *people, troops* massacrare

'**slaugh·ter·house** *for animals* macello *m*

Slav [slɑːv] *adj* slavo

slave [sleɪv] *n* schiavo *m*, -a *f*

'**slave-driv·er** F negriero, -a *f* F

sla·ve·ry schiavitù *f inv*

slay [sleɪ] *v/t* (*pret* **slew**, *pp* **slain**) ammazzare

sleaze [sliːz] POL corruzione *f*

slea·zy ['sliːzɪ] *adj bar, characters* sordido

sled(ge) [sled, sledʒ] *n* slitta *f*

'**sledge ham·mer** mazza *f*

sleep [sliːp] **1** *n* sonno *m*; *go to* ~ addormentarsi; *I need a good* ~ ho bisogno di una bella dormita; *I couldn't get to* ~ non sono riuscito a dormire **2** *v/i* (*pret & pp* **slept**) dormire

◆ **sleep in** *v/i* (*have a long lie*) dormire fino a tardi

◆ **sleep on** *v/t proposal, decision* dormire su; *sleep on it* dormirci su

◆ **sleep with** *v/t* (*have sex with*) andare a letto con

sleep·er ['sliːpə(r)] RAIL: *on track* traversina *f*; (*sleeping car*) vagone *m* letto; *train* treno *m* notturno; *be a light / heavy* ~ avere il sonno leggero / pesante

sleep·i·ly ['sliːpɪlɪ] *adv* con aria assonnata

'**sleep·ing bag** ['sliːpɪŋ] sacco *m* a pelo; '**sleep·ing car** RAIL vagone *m* letto; '**sleep·ing part·ner** *Br* COM socio *m* inattivo; '**sleep·ing pill** sonnifero *m*

sleep·less ['sliːplɪs] *adj night* in bianco

'**sleep walk·er** sonnambulo *m*, -a *f*

S

'sleep walk·ing sonnambulismo *m*

sleep·y ['sli:pɪ] *adj child* assonnato; *town* addormentato; *I'm ~* ho sonno

sleet [sli:t] *n* nevischio *m*

sleeve [sli:v] *of jacket etc* manica *f*

sleeve·less ['sli:vlɪs] *adj* senza maniche

sleigh [sleɪ] *n* slitta *f*

sleight of 'hand [slaɪt] gioco *m* di prestigio

slen·der ['slendə(r)] *adj figure, arms* snello; *chance, income, margin* piccolo

slept [slept] *pret & pp* → **sleep**

slew [slu:] *pret* → **slay**

slice [slaɪs] **1** *n also fig* fetta *f* **2** *v/t loaf etc* affettare

sliced 'bread [slaɪst] pane *m* a cassetta; *the greatest thing since ~* F il non plus ultra

slick [slɪk] **1** *adj performance* brillante; (*pej: cunning*) scaltro **2** *n of oil* chiazza *f* di petrolio

slid [slɪd] *pret & pp* → **slide**

slide [slaɪd] **1** *n for kids* scivolo *m*; PHOT diapositiva *f*; *in hair* fermacapelli *m inv* **2** *v/i* (*pret & pp* **slid**) scivolare; *of exchange rate etc* calare **3** *v/t* (*pret & pp* **slid**) far scivolare

slid·ing door [slaɪdɪŋ'dɔ:(r)] porta *f* scorrevole

slight [slaɪt] **1** *adj person, figure* gracile; (*small*) leggero; *no, not in the ~est* no, per nulla **2** *n* (*insult*) offesa *f*

slight·ly ['slaɪtlɪ] *adv* leggermente

slim [slɪm] **1** *adj* slanciato; *chance* scarso **2** *v/i* (*pret & pp* -**med**) dimagrire; *I'm ~ming* sono a dieta

slime [slaɪm] melma *f*

slim·y ['slaɪmɪ] *adj liquid* melmoso; *person* viscido

sling [slɪŋ] **1** *n for arm* fascia *f* a tracolla **2** *v/t* (*pret & pp* **slung**) (*throw*) lanciare

slip [slɪp] **1** *n on ice etc* scivolata *f*; (*mistake*) errore *m*; *a ~ of paper* un foglietto; *a ~ of the tongue* un lapsus; *give s.o. the ~* seminare qu **2** *v/i* (*pret & pp* -**ped**) *on ice etc* sci-

volare; *of quality etc* peggiorare; *he ~ped out of the room* è sgattaiolato fuori dalla stanza **3** *v/t* (*pret & pp* -**ped**) (*put*) far scivolare; *he ~ped it into his briefcase* l'ha fatto scivolare nella valigetta; *it ~ped my mind* mi è passato di mente

♦ slip away *v/i of time* passare; *of opportunity* andare sprecato; (*die quietly*) spirare

♦ slip off *v/t jacket etc* togliersi

♦ slip on *v/t jacket etc* infilarsi

♦ slip out *v/i* (*go out*) sgattaiolare

♦ slip up *v/i* (*make mistake*) sbagliarsi

slipped 'disc [slɪpt] ernia *f* del disco

slip·per ['slɪpə(r)] pantofola *f*

slip·per·y ['slɪpərɪ] *adj* scivoloso

'slip road rampa *f* di accesso

slip·shod ['slɪpʃɒd] *adj* trascurato

'slip-up (*mistake*) errore *m*

slit [slɪt] **1** *n* (*tear*) strappo *m*; (*hole*) fessura *f*; *in skirt* spacco *m* **2** *v/t* (*pret & pp* **slit**) *envelope, packet* aprire (*tagliando*); *throat* tagliare

slith·er ['slɪðə(r)] *v/i* strisciare

sliv·er ['slɪvə(r)] scheggia *f*

slob [slɒb] *pej* sudicione *m*, -a *f*

slob·ber ['slɒbə(r)] *v/i* sbavare

slog [slɒg] *n* faticata *f*

slo·gan ['sləʊgən] slogan *m inv*

slop [slɒp] *v/t* (*pret & pp* -**ped**) rovesciare, versare

slope [sləʊp] **1** *n* pendenza *f*; *of mountain* pendio *m*; *built on a ~* costruito in pendio **2** *v/i* essere inclinato; *the road ~s down to the sea* la strada scende fino al mare

slop·py ['slɒpɪ] *adj work, editing* trascurato; *in dressing* sciatto; (*too sentimental*) sdolcinato

sloshed [slɒʃt] *adj* F (*drunk*) sbronzo F

slot [slɒt] **1** *n* fessura *f*; *in schedule* spazio *m*

♦ slot in (*pret & pp* -**ted**) **1** *v/t* infilare **2** *v/i* infilarsi

'slot ma·chine *for vending* distributore *m* automatico; *for gambling* slot-machine *f inv*

slouch [slaʊtʃ] *v/i*: *don't ~!* su con la schiena!

slov·en·ly ['slʌvnlɪ] *adj* sciatto

slow [sləʊ] *adj* lento; *be ~ of clock* essere indietro

♦ **slow down** *v/t & v/i* rallentare

slow·coach *Br* F lumaca *f* F

slow·down *in production* rallentamento *m*

slow·ly ['sləʊlɪ] *adv* lentamente

slow 'mo·tion *n*: *in ~* al rallentatore

slow·ness ['sləʊnɪs] lentezza *f*

slow·poke *Am* F lumaca *f* F

slug [slʌg] *n animal* lumaca *f*

slug·gish ['slʌgɪʃ] *adj* lento

slum [slʌm] *n slum m inv*

slump [slʌmp] **1** *n in trade* crollo *m* **2** *v/i economically* crollare; *(collapse: of person)* accasciarsi

slur [slɜː(r)] **1** *n* calunnia *f* **2** *v/t (pret & pp -red) words* biascicare

slurp [slɜːp] *v/t* bere rumorosamente

slurred [slɜːd] *adj speech* impappinato

slush [slʌʃ] fanghiglia *f*; *(pej: sentimental stuff)* smancerie *fpl*

slush fund fondi *mpl* neri

slush·y ['slʌʃɪ] *adj snow* ridotto in fanghiglia; *film, novel* sdolcinato

slut [slʌt] *pej* sgualdrina *f*

sly [slaɪ] *adj* scaltro; *on the ~* di nascosto

smack [smæk] **1** *n on the bottom* sculacciata *f*; *in the face* schiaffo *m* **2** *v/t child* picchiare; *bottom* sculacciare

small [smɔːl] **1** *adj* piccolo **2** *n*: *the ~ of the back* le reni

small 'change spiccioli *mpl*; **small hours** *npl*: *the ~* le ore *fpl* piccole; **small·pox** ['smɔːlpɒks] vaiolo *m*; **'small print** parte *f* scritta in caratteri minuti; **'small talk** conversazione *f* di circostanza

smarm·y ['smɑːmɪ] *adj* F untuoso

smart [smɑːt] **1** *adj (elegant)* elegante; *(intelligent)* intelligente; *pace* svelto; *get ~ with* F fare il furbo con F **2** *v/i (hurt)* bruciare

smart al·ec(k) ['smɑːtælɪk] F sapientone *m* F; **'smart ass** P sapientone *m*; **'smart card** smart card *f inv*

♦ **smarten up** ['smɑːtn] *v/t* sistemare; *smarten o.s. up* mettersi in ghingheri

smart·ly ['smɑːtlɪ] *adv dressed* elegantemente

smash [smæʃ] **1** *n noise* fracasso *m*; *(car crash)* scontro *m*; *in tennis* schiacciata *f* **2** *v/t break* spaccare; *hit hard* sbattere; *~ sth to pieces* mandare in frantumi qc **3** *v/i break* frantumarsi; *the driver ~ed into ...* l'automobilista si è schiantato contro ...

♦ **smash up** *v/t place* distruggere

smash 'hit F successone *m*

smash·ing ['smæʃɪŋ] *adj* F fantastico

smat·ter·ing ['smætərɪŋ] *of a language* infarinatura *f*

smear [smɪə(r)] **1** *n of ink etc* macchia *f*; MED striscio *m*; *on character* calunnia *f* **2** *v/t*; *character* calunniare; *~ mud over the wall* imbrattare il muro di fango

'smear cam·paign campagna *f* diffamatoria

smell [smel] **1** *n* odore *m*; *it has no ~* non ha odore; *sense of ~* olfatto *m*, odorato *m* **2** *v/t* sentire odore di; *test by smelling* sentire **3** *v/i unpleasantly* puzzare; *(sniff)* odorare; *what does it ~ of?* che odore ha?; *you ~ of beer* puzzi di birra; *it ~s good* ha un buon profumo

smell·y ['smelɪ] *adj* puzzolente; *it's so ~ in here* qui dentro c'è puzza

smile [smaɪl] **1** *n* sorriso *m* **2** *v/i* sorridere

♦ **smile at** *v/t* sorridere a

smirk [smɜːk] **1** *n* sorriso *m* compiaciuto **2** *v/i* sorridere con compiacimento

smog [smɒg] smog *m inv*

smoke [sməʊk] **1** *n* fumo *m*; *have a ~* fumare **2** *v/t cigarettes etc* fumare; *bacon* affumicare **3** *v/i* fumare; *I don't ~* non fumo

smok·er ['sməʊkə(r)] *person* fumatore *m*, -trice *f*

smok·ing ['sməʊkɪŋ] fumo *m*; *no ~* vietato fumare

'smok·ing com·part·ment RAIL

S

carrozza *m* fumatori

smok·y ['sməʊkɪ] *adj room, air* pieno di fumo

smol·der *Am* → **smoulder**

smooth [smu:ð] **1** *adj surface, skin, sea* liscio; *sea* calmo; *transition* senza problemi; *pej: person* mellifluo **2** *v/t hair* lisciare

♦ **smooth down** *v/t with sandpaper etc* levigare

♦ **smooth out** *v/t paper, cloth* lisciare

♦ **smooth over** *v/t:* **smooth things over** appianare le cose

smooth·ly ['smu:ðlɪ] *adv without any problems* senza problemi

smoth·er ['smʌðə(r)] *v/t flames, person* soffocare; **~ s.o. with kisses** coprire qu di baci

smoul·der ['sməʊldə(r)] *v/i of fire* covare sotto la cenere; *fig: with anger, desire* consumarsi (**with** di)

smudge [smʌdʒ] **1** *n* sbavatura *f* **2** *v/t* sbavare

smug [smʌg] *adj* compiaciuto

smug·gle ['smʌgl] *v/t* contrabbandare

smug·gler ['smʌglə(r)] contrabbandiere *m*, -a *f*

smug·gling ['smʌglɪŋ] contrabbando *m*

smug·ly ['smʌglɪ] *adv* con compiacimento

smut·ty ['smʌtɪ] *adj joke, sense of humour* sconcio

snack [snæk] *n* spuntino *m*

'snack bar snack bar *m inv*

snag [snæg] *n (problem)* problema *m*

snail [sneɪl] chiocciola *f*, *in cooking* lumaca *f*

snake [sneɪk] *n* serpente *m*

snap [snæp] **1** *n* sound botto *m*; PHOT foto *f* **2** *v/t (pret & pp -ped) break* spezzare; *(say sharply)* dire bruscamente **3** *v/i (pret & pp -ped) break* spezzarsi **4** *adj decision, judgement* immediato

♦ **snap up** *v/t bargains* accaparrarsi

snap·py ['snæpɪ] *adj person, mood* irritabile; F *(quick)* rapido; *(elegant)* elegante

'snap·shot istantanea *f*

snarl [snɑ:l] **1** *n of dog* ringhio *m* **2** *v/t* ringhiare

snatch [snætʃ] **1** *v/t* afferrare; *(steal)* scippare; *(kidnap)* rapire **2** *v/i* strappare di mano

snaz·zy ['snæzɪ] *adj* F chic

sneak [sni:k] **1** *n (telltale)* spione *m*, -a *f* **2** *v/t (remove, steal)* rubare; **~ a glance at** dare una sbirciatina a **3** *v/i (tell tales)* fare la spia; **~ out of …** sgattaiolare fuori da …

sneak·ing ['sni:kɪŋ] *adj:* **have a ~ suspicion that …** avere il vago sospetto che …

sneak·y ['sni:kɪ] *adj* F *(crafty)* scaltro

sneer [snɪə(r)] **1** *n* sogghigno *m* **2** *v/i* sogghignare

sneeze [sni:z] **1** *n* starnuto *m* **2** *v/i* starnutire

sniff [snɪf] **1** *v/i to clear nose* tirare su col naso; *of dog* fiutare **2** *v/t smell* annusare

snig·ger ['snɪgə(r)] **1** *n* risolino *m* **2** *v/i* ridacchiare

snip [snɪp] *n* F *(bargain)* affare *m*

snip·er ['snaɪpə(r)] cecchino *m*

sniv·el ['snɪvl] *v/i pej* frignare

snob [snɒb] snob *m/f inv*

snob·ber·y ['snɒbərɪ] snobismo *m*

snob·bish ['snɒbɪʃ] *adj* snob *inv*

snook·er ['snu:kə(r)] biliardo *m*

snoop [snu:p] *n* ficcanaso *m/f inv*

♦ **snoop around** *v/i* ficcanasare

snoot·y ['snu:tɪ] *adj* snob *inv*

snooze [snu:z] **1** *n* sonnellino *m*; **have a ~** fare un sonnellino **2** *v/i* sonnecchiare

snore [snɔ:(r)] *v/i* russare

snor·ing ['snɔ:rɪŋ] *n* russare *m*

snor·kel ['snɔ:kl] *n* boccaglio *m*

snort [snɔ:t] *v/i* sbuffare

snout [snaʊt] *of pig* grugno *m*; *of dog* muso *m*

snow [snəʊ] **1** *n* neve *f* **2** *v/i* nevicare

♦ **snow under** *v/t:* **be snowed under with …** essere sommerso di …

'snow·ball palla *f* di neve; **'snow·bound** *adj* isolato dalla neve; **'snow chains** *npl* MOT catene *fpl* da neve; **'snow·drift** cumulo *m* di

neve; '**snow‧drop** bucaneve *m inv*;
'**snow‧flake** fiocco *m* di neve;
'**snow‧man** pupazzo *m* di neve;
'**snow‧storm** tormenta *f*

snow‧y ['snəʊɪ] *adj weather* nevoso;
roofs, hills innevato

snub [snʌb] **1** *n* affronto *m* **2** *v/t* (*pret*
& *pp* **-bed**) snobbare

snub-nosed ['snʌbnəʊzd] *adj* col
naso all'insù

snug [snʌg] *adj* al calduccio; (*tight-fitting*) attillato

♦ **snuggle down** ['snʌgl] *v/i* accoccolarsi

♦ **snuggle up to** *v/t* rannicchiarsi accanto a

so [səʊ] **1** *adv* così; ~ *hot / cold* così
caldo / freddo; *not ~ much* non così
tanto; ~ *much better / easier* molto
meglio / più facile; *you shouldn't*
eat / drink ~ much non dovresti
mangiare / bere così tanto; *I miss*
you ~ mi manchi tanto; ~ *am / do I*
anch'io; ~ *is she / does she* anche
lei; *and ~ on* e così via **2** *pron*: *I*
hope / think ~ spero / penso di sì; *I*
don't think ~ non credo, credo di
no; *you didn't tell me – I did ~* non
me l'hai detto – e invece sì; *50 or ~*
circa 50 **3** *conj* (*for that reason*) così;
(*in order that*) così che; *and ~ I*
missed the train e così ho perso il
treno; ~ *(that) I could come too*
così che potessi venire anch'io; ~
what? e allora?

soak [səʊk] *v/t* (*steep*) mettere a bagno; *of water, rain* inzuppare

♦ **soak up** *v/t liquid* assorbire; *soak*
up the sun crogiolarsi al sole

soaked [səʊkt] *adj* fradicio; *be ~ to*
the skin essere bagnato fradicio

soak‧ing (wet) ['səʊkɪŋ] *adj* bagnato fradicio

so-and-so ['səʊənsəʊ] F *unknown*
person tal dei tali *m/f inv*; (*euph:*
annoying person) impiastro *m*

soap [səʊp] *n for washing* sapone *m*

'**soap 'op‧e‧ra** soap (opera) *f inv*,
telenovela *f*

soap‧y ['səʊpɪ] *adj water* saponato

soar [sɔː(r)] *v/i of rocket etc* innalzar-

si; *of prices* aumentare vertiginosamente

sob [sɒb] **1** *n* singhiozzo *m* **2** *v/i* (*pret*
& *pp* **-bed**) singhiozzare

so‧ber ['səʊbə(r)] *adj* (*not drunk*) sobrio; (*serious*) serio

♦ **sober up** *v/i* smaltire la sbornia

so-'called *adj* cosiddetto

soc‧cer ['sɒkə(r)] calcio *m*

'**soc‧cer hoo‧li‧gan** hooligan *m/f inv*

so‧cia‧ble ['səʊʃəbl] *adj* socievole

so‧cial ['səʊʃl] *adj* sociale

so‧cial 'dem‧o‧crat socialdemocra-
tico *m*, -a *f*

so‧cial‧is‧m ['səʊʃəlɪzm] socialismo
m

so‧cial‧ist ['səʊʃəlɪst] **1** *adj* socialista
2 *n* socialista *m/f*

so‧cial‧ize ['səʊʃəlaɪz] *v/i* socializzare

'**soc‧ial life** vita *f* sociale; **so‧cial**
'**sci‧ence** scienza *f* sociale; **so‧cial**
se‧cu‧ri‧ty *Br* sussidio *m* della previdenza sociale; **so‧cial 'serv‧ic‧es**
Br npl servizi *mpl* sociali; '**so‧cial**
work assistenza *f* sociale; '**so‧cial**
work‧er assistente *m/f* sociale

so‧ci‧e‧ty [sə'saɪətɪ] società *f inv*;
(*organization*) associazione *f*

so‧ci‧ol‧o‧gist [səʊsɪ'ɒlədʒɪst]
sociologo *m*, -a *f*

so‧ci‧ol‧o‧gy [səʊsɪ'ɒlədʒɪ] sociologia *f*

sock[1] [sɒk] calzino *m*

sock[2] [sɒk] **1** *n* F (*punch*) pugno *m*
2 *v/t* F (*punch*) dare un pugno a

sock‧et ['sɒkɪt] *for light bulb* porta-
lampada *m inv*; *in wall* presa *f* (di
corrente); *of eye* orbita *f*

so‧da ['səʊdə] (~ *water*) seltz *m inv*

sod‧den ['sɒdn] *adj* zuppo

so‧fa ['səʊfə] divano *m*

'**so‧fa-bed** divano *m* letto

soft [sɒft] *adj pillow* soffice; *chair,*
skin morbido; *light, colour* tenue;
music soft; *voice* sommesso; (*lenient*)
indulgente; *have a ~ spot for* avere
un debole per

soft 'drink bibita *f* analcolica

'**soft drug** droga *f* leggera

soft‧en ['sɒfn] **1** *v/t butter etc* ammor-

S

bidire; *position* attenuare; *impact, blow* attutire **2** *v/i of butter, ice-cream* ammorbidirsi

soft·ly ['softlɪ] *adv speak* sommessamente

soft 'toy giocattolo *m* di pezza

soft·ware ['softweə(r)] software *m inv*

sog·gy ['sɒgɪ] *adj* molle e pesante

soil [sɔɪl] **1** *n* (*earth*) terra *f* **2** *v/t* sporcare

so·lar 'en·er·gy ['səʊlə(r)] energia *f* solare; **'so·lar pan·el** pannello *m* solare; **'solar system** sistema *m* solare

sold [səʊld] *pret & pp* → **sell**

sol·dier ['səʊldʒə(r)] soldato *m*

♦ **soldier on** *v/i* perseverare

sole[1] [səʊl] *n of foot* pianta *f* (del piede); *of shoe* suola *f*

sole[2] [səʊl] *adj* unico; (*exclusive*) esclusivo

sole[3] [səʊl] (*fish*) sogliola *f*

sole·ly ['səʊlɪ] *adv* solamente; *be ~ responsible* essere il solo / la sola responsabile

sol·emn ['sɒləm] *adj* solenne

so·lem·ni·ty [sə'lemnɪtɪ] solennità *f inv*

sol·emn·ly ['sɒləmlɪ] *adv* solennemente

so·li·cit [sə'lɪsɪt] *v/i of prostitute* adescare

so·lic·i·tor [sə'lɪsɪtə(r)] avvocato *m*

sol·id ['sɒlɪd] *adj* (*hard*) solido; (*without holes*) compatto; *gold, silver* massiccio; (*sturdy*) robusto; *evidence* concreto; *support* forte; *a ~ hour* un'ora intera

sol·i·dar·i·ty [sɒlɪ'dærətɪ] solidarietà *f inv*

sol·id·i·fy [sə'lɪdɪfaɪ] *v/i* (*pret & pp -ied*) solidificarsi

sol·id·ly ['sɒlɪdlɪ] *adv* built solidamente; *in favour of sth* all'unanimità

so·lil·o·quy [sə'lɪləkwɪ] *on stage* monologo *m*

sol·i·taire ['sɒlɪteər] *Am: card game* solitario *m*

sol·i·ta·ry ['sɒlɪtərɪ] *adj life, activity* solitario; (*single*) solo

sol·i·ta·ry con'fine·ment isolamento *m*

sol·i·tude ['sɒlɪtjuːd] solitudine *f*

so·lo ['səʊləʊ] **1** *n* MUS assolo *m* **2** *adj performance* solista; *flight* in solitario

so·lo·ist ['səʊləʊɪst] solista *m/f*

sol·u·ble ['sɒljʊbl] *adj substance* solubile; *problem* risolvibile

so·lu·tion [sə'luːʃn] soluzione *f*

solve [sɒlv] *v/t* risolvere

sol·vent ['sɒlvənt] **1** *adj financially* solvibile **2** *n* solvente *m*

som·ber *Am*, **som·bre** ['sɒmbə(r)] *adj* (*dark*) scuro; (*serious*) tetro

some [sʌm] **1** *adj* (*unspecified amount*) un po' di, del; (*unspecified number*) qualche; *del m*, *della f*, *dei m*; **would you like ~ water?** vuoi un po' d'acqua *o* dell'acqua?; **would you like ~ biscuits?** vuoi dei biscotti *o* qualche biscotto?; **~ people say that ...** alcuni dicono che ... **2** *pron* (*unspecified amount*) un po'; (*unspecified number*) alcuni *m*, -e *f*; **would you like ~?** ne vuoi un po'?; **give me ~** dammene un po'; **~ of the students** alcuni studenti

some·bod·y ['sʌmbədɪ] *pron* qualcuno; **'some·day** *adv* un giorno; **'some·how** *adv* (*by one means or another*) in qualche modo; (*for some unknown reason*) per qualche motivo; **'some·one** *pron* → **some·bod·y**

som·er·sault ['sʌməsɔːlt] **1** *n* capriola *f* **2** *v/i* fare una capriola

'some·thing *pron* qualcosa; **would you like ~ to drink / eat?** vuoi (qualcosa) da mangiare / bere?; **is ~ wrong?** c'è qualcosa che non va?; **'some·time** *adv* (*one of these days*) uno di questi giorni; **~ last year** l'anno scorso; **'some·times** ['sʌmtaɪmz] *adv* a volte; **'some·what** *adv* piuttosto; **'some·where 1** *adv* da qualche parte **2** *pron* un posto; **let's go ~ quiet** andiamo in un posto tranquillo

son [sʌn] figlio *m*

so·na·ta [sə'nɑːtə] MUS sonata *f*

song [sɒŋ] canzone *f*; *of birds* canto *m*

'**song·bird** uccello *m* canoro

'**song·writ·er** compositore *m*, -trice *f*

'**son-in-law** (*pl* **sons-in-law**) genero *m*

son·net ['sɒnɪt] sonetto *m*

soon [su:n] *adv* presto; **as ~ as** non appena; **as ~ as possible** prima possibile; **~er or later** presto o tardi; **the ~er the better** prima è, meglio è; **how ~ can you be ready?** fra quanto sei pronto?

soot [sʊt] fuliggine *f*

soothe [su:ð] *v/t* calmare

so·phis·ti·cat·ed [sə'fɪstɪkeɪtɪd] *adj* sofisticato

so·phis·ti·ca·tion [səfɪstɪˈkeɪʃn] *of person* raffinatezza *f*; *of machine* complessità *f inv*

sop·py ['sɒpɪ] *adj* F sdolcinato

so·pra·no [sə'prɑːnəʊ] *n* soprano *m/f*

sor·did ['sɔːdɪd] *adj affair, business* sordido

sore [sɔː(r)] **1** *adj* (*painful*) dolorante; *is it ~?* fa male? **2** *n* piaga *f*

sore 'throat mal *m* di gola

sor·row ['sɒrəʊ] *n* dispiacere *m*, dolore *m*

sor·ry ['sɒrɪ] *adj day, sight* triste; (*I'm*) **~!** *apologizing* scusa!; *polite form* scusi!; *(I'm) ~ regretting* mi dispiace; **I won't be ~ to leave here** non vedo l'ora di andarmene da qui; **I feel ~ for her** mi dispiace per lei

sort [sɔːt] **1** *n* tipo *m*; **~ of ...** F un po' ...; *is it finished? – ~ of* F è terminato? – quasi **2** *v/t* separare; COMPUT ordinare

♦ **sort out** *v/t papers* mettere in ordine; *problem* risolvere; **sort things out** sistemare le cose

SOS [esəʊ'es] SOS *m inv*

so-'so *adv* F così così

sought [sɔːt] *pret & pp* → **seek**

soul [səʊl] anima *f*; **the poor ~** il poverino, la poverina

sound[^1] [saʊnd] **1** *adj* (*sensible*) valido; (*healthy*) sano; *sleep* profondo; *structure, walls* solido **2** *adv*: **be ~ asleep** dormire profondamente

sound[^2] [saʊnd] **1** *n* suono *m*; (*noise*) rumore *m* **2** *v/t* (*pronounce*) pronunciare; MED auscultare; **~ one's horn** suonare il clacson **3** *v/i*: *that ~s interesting* sembra interessante; *that ~s like a good idea* mi sembra un'ottima idea; *she ~ed unhappy* dalla voce sembrava infelice

♦ **sound out** *v/t* sondare l'opinione di

'**sound bar·ri·er** muro *m* del suono

'**sound·bite** slogan *m inv*

'**sound ef·fects** *npl* effetti *mpl* sonori

sound·ly ['saʊndlɪ] *adv sleep* profondamente; *beaten* duramente

'**sound·proof** *adj* insonorizzato

'**sound·track** colonna *f* sonora

soup [su:p] minestra *f*

'**soup bowl** scodella *f*

souped-up [su:pt'ʌp] *adj* F truccato F

'**soup plate** piatto *m* fondo

'**soup spoon** cucchiaio *m* da minestra

sour ['saʊə(r)] *adj apple, orange* aspro; *milk, expression, comment* acido

source [sɔːs] *n* fonte *f*; *of river* sorgente *f*

sour 'cream panna *f* acida

south [saʊθ] **1** *adj* meridionale, del sud **2** *n* sud *m*; **to the ~ of** a sud di **3** *adv* verso sud

South 'Af·ri·ca Repubblica *f* Sudafricana

South 'Af·ri·can 1 *adj* sudafricano **2** *n* sudafricano *m*, -a *f*

South A'mer·i·ca Sudamerica *m*

South A'mer·i·can 1 *adj* sudamericano **2** *n* sudamericano *m*, -a *f*

south'east 1 *n* sud-est *m* **2** *adj* sud-orientale **3** *adv* verso sud-est; **it's ~ of ...** è a sud-est di ...

south'east·ern *adj* sud-orientale

south·er·ly ['sʌðəlɪ] *adj* meridionale

south·ern ['sʌðən] *adj* del sud

south·ern·er ['sʌðənə(r)] abitante *m/f* del sud

south·ern·most ['sʌðənməʊst] *adj* più a sud

S

South 'Pole polo *m* sud

south·wards ['saυθwədz] *adv* verso sud

south·'west 1 *n* sud-ovest *m* **2** *adj* sud-occidentale **3** *adv* verso sud-ovest; *it's ~ of ...* è a sud-ovest di ...

south'west·ern *adj* sud-occidentale

sou·ve·nir [su:və'nɪə(r)] souvenir *m inv*

sove·reign ['sɒvrɪn] *adj state* sovrano

sove·reign·ty ['sɒvrɪntɪ] *of state* sovranità *f inv*

So·vi·et ['səυvɪət] *adj* sovietico

So·vi·et 'U·nion Unione *f* Sovietica

sow¹ [saυ] *n* (*female pig*) scrofa *f*

sow² [səυ] *v/t seeds* seminare

sown [səυn] *pp* → **sow²**

soy·a bean ['sɔɪə] seme *m* di soia

soy(a) 'sauce salsa *f* di soia

spa [spɑː] località *f inv* termale

space [speɪs] *n* spazio *m*; *in car park* posto *m*

♦ **space out** *v/t* distanziare

'space-bar COMPUT barra *f* spaziatrice; **'space·craft** veicolo *m* spaziale; **'space·ship** astronave *f*; **'space shut·tle** shuttle *m inv*; **'space sta·tion** stazione *f* spaziale; **'space·suit** tuta *f* spaziale

spa·cious ['speɪʃəs] *adj* spazioso

spade [speɪd] *for digging* vanga *f*; *~s in card game* picche

'spade·work *fig* preparativi *mpl*

spa·ghet·ti [spə'getɪ] *nsg* spaghetti *mpl*

Spain [speɪn] Spagna *f*

span [spæn] *v/t* (*pret & pp* **-ned**) coprire; *of bridge* attraversare

Span·iard ['spænjəd] spagnolo *m*, -a *f*

Span·ish ['spænɪʃ] **1** *adj* spagnolo **2** *n language* spagnolo *m*

spank [spæŋk] *v/t* sculacciare

spank·ing ['spæŋkɪŋ] sculaccione *m*

span·ner ['spænə(r)] *Br* chiave *f* inglese

spare [speə(r)] **1** *v/t* (*do without*) fare a meno di; *can you ~ £50?* mi puoi prestare 50 sterline?; *can you ~ the time?* hai tempo?; *have money/*

time to ~ avere soldi/tempo d'avanzo; *there were 5 to ~* (*left over, in excess*) ce n'erano 5 d'avanzo **2** *adj* in più **3** *n* ricambio *m*

spare 'part pezzo *m* di ricambio; **spare 'ribs** *npl* costine *fpl* di maiale; **spare 'room** stanza *f* degli ospiti; **spare 'time** tempo *m* libero; **spare 'tire** *Am*, **spare 'tyre** MOT ruota *f* di scorta

spar·ing ['speə(r)ɪŋ] *adj*: *be ~ with* andarci piano con F

spar·ing·ly ['speə(r)ɪŋlɪ] *adv* con moderazione

spark [spɑːk] *n* scintilla *f*

spark·ing plug ['spɑːkɪŋ] candela *f*

spar·kle ['spɑːkl] *v/i* brillare

spark·ling 'wine ['spɑːklɪŋ] vino *m* frizzante

'spark plug candela *f*

spar·row ['spærəυ] passero *m*

sparse [spɑːs] *adj vegetation* rado

sparse·ly ['spɑːslɪ] *adv*: *~ populated* scarsamente popolato

spar·tan ['spɑːtn] *adj* spartano

spas·mod·ic [spæz'mɒdɪk] *adj* irregolare

spat [spæt] *pret & pp* → **spit**

spate [speɪt] *fig* ondata *f*

spa·tial ['speɪʃl] *adj* spaziale

spat·ter ['spætə(r)] *v/t mud, paint* schizzare

speak [spiːk] (*pret* **spoke**, *pp* **spoken**) **1** *v/i* parlare; *we're not ~ing* (*to each other*) (*we've quarrelled*) non ci rivolgiamo la parola; *~ing* TELEC sono io **2** *v/t foreign language* parlare; *the truth* dire; *~ one's mind* dire quello che si pensa

♦ **speak for** *v/t* parlare a nome di

♦ **speak out** *v/i* prendere posizione; *say what you think* farsi sentire

♦ **speak up** *v/i* (*speak louder*) parlare ad alta voce

speak·er ['spiːkə(r)] oratore *m*, -trice *f*; *of sound system* cassa *f*

spear [spɪə(r)] lancia *f*

spear·mint ['spɪəmɪnt] menta *f*

spe·cial ['speʃl] *adj* speciale; (*particular*) particolare

S

spe·cial ef·fects *npl* effetti *mpl* speciali

spe·cial·ist ['speʃlɪst] specialista *m/f*

spe·cial·i·ty [speʃɪ'ælətɪ] specialità *f inv*

spe·cial·ize ['speʃəlaɪz] *v/i* specializzarsi; **~ in ...** specializzarsi in; **we ~ in ...** siamo specializzati in …

spe·cial·ly ['speʃlɪ] *adv* → **especially**

spe·cial·ty ['speʃəltɪ] *Am* specialità *f inv*

spe·cies ['spiːʃiːz] *nsg* specie *f inv*

spe·cif·ic [spə'sɪfɪk] *adj* specifico

spe·cif·i·cal·ly [spə'sɪfɪklɪ] *adv* specificamente

spec·i·fi·ca·tions [spesɪfɪ'keɪʃnz] *npl of machine etc* caratteristiche *fpl* tecniche, specifiche *fpl*

spe·ci·fy ['spesɪfaɪ] *v/t* (*pret & pp -ied*) specificare

spe·ci·men ['spesɪmən] campione *m*

speck [spek] *of dust, soot* granello *m*

specs [speks] *npl* F (*spectacles*) occhiali *mpl*

spec·ta·cle ['spektəkl] (*impressive sight*) spettacolo *m*; (**a pair of**) **~s** (un paio di) occhiali *mpl*

spec·tac·u·lar [spek'tækjʊlə(r)] *adj* spettacolare

spec·ta·tor [spek'teɪtə(r)] spettatore *m*, -trice *f*

spec·ta·tor sport sport *m inv* spettacolo

spec·trum ['spektrəm] *fig* gamma *f*

spec·u·late ['spekjʊleɪt] *v/i* fare congetture (**on** su); FIN speculare

spec·u·la·tion [spekjʊ'leɪʃn] congetture *fpl*; FIN speculazione *f*

spec·u·la·tor ['spekjʊleɪtə(r)] FIN speculatore *m*, -trice *f*

sped [sped] *pret & pp* → **speed**

speech [spiːtʃ] (*address*) discorso *m*; *in play* monologo *m*; (*ability to speak*) parola *f*; (*way of speaking*) linguaggio *m*; **faculty / power of ~** facoltà / uso della parola; **her ~ was slurred** biascicava le parole

'speech de·fect difetto *m* del linguaggio

speech·less ['spiːtʃlɪs] *adj with*

shock, surprise senza parole

'speech ther·a·pist logopedista *m/f*;
speech 'ther·a·py logopedia *f*;
'speech writ·er ghost writer *m inv*

speed [spiːd] **1** *n* velocità *f inv*; (*quickness*) rapidità *f inv*; **at a ~ of 150 mph** a una velocità di 150 miglia orarie; **reduce your ~** rallentare **2** *v/i* (*pret & pp* **sped**) (*go quickly*) andare a tutta velocità; (*drive too quickly*) superare il limite di velocità

♦ **speed by** *v/i* sfrecciare; *of days* volare

♦ **speed up 1** *v/i* andare più veloce **2** *v/t* accelerare

'speed·boat motoscafo *m*

'speed bump dosso *m* di rallentamento

speed·i·ly ['spiːdɪlɪ] *adv* rapidamente

speed·ing ['spiːdɪŋ] *n when driving* eccesso *m* di velocità

'speed·ing fine multa *f* per eccesso di velocità

'speed lim·it *on roads* limite *m* di velocità

speed·om·e·ter [spiː'dɒmɪtə(r)] tachimetro *m*

'speed trap sistema *m* con cui la polizia individua chi supera il limite di velocità

speed·y ['spiːdɪ] *adj* rapido

spell[1] [spel] **1** *v/t*: **how do you ~ ...?** come si scrive ...?; **could you ~ that please?** me lo può dettare lettera per lettera? **2** *v/i* sapere come si scrivono le parole

spell[2] [spel] *n* (*period of time*) periodo *m*; (*turn*) turno *m*

'spell·bound *adj* incantato; **'spell-check** COMPUT controllo *m* ortografico; **do a ~ on ...** fare il controllo ortografico di ...; **'spell-check·er** COMPUT correttore *m* ortografico

spell·ing ['spelɪŋ] ortografia *f*

spend [spend] *v/t* (*pret & pp* **spent**) *money* spendere; *time* passare

'spend·thrift *n pej* spendaccione *m*, -a *f*

spent [spent] *pret* & *pp* → spend

sperm [spɜːm] spermatozoo *m*; (*semen*) sperma *m*

'sperm bank banca *f* dello sperma

'sperm count numero *m* degli spermatozoi

sphere [sfɪə(r)] *also fig* sfera *f*; ~ of influence sfera d'influenza

spice [spaɪs] *n* (*seasoning*) spezia *f*

spic·y ['spaɪsɪ] *adj food* piccante

spi·der ['spaɪdə(r)] ragno *m*

'spi·der's web ragnatela *f*

spike [spaɪk] *n on railings* spunzone *m*; *on plant* spina *f*; *on animal* aculeo *m*; *on running shoes* chiodo *m*

spill [spɪl] 1 *v/t* versare 2 *v/i* versarsi 3 *n of oil etc* fuoriuscita *f*

spin¹ [spɪn] 1 *n* giro *m*; *on ball* effetto *m* 2 *v/t* (*pret* & *pp* spun) far girare; *ball* imprimere l'effetto a 3 *v/i* (*pret* & *pp* spun) *of wheel* girare; my head is ~ning mi gira la testa

spin² [spɪn] *v/t* (*pret* & *pp* spun) *wool, cotton* filare; *web* tessere

♦ spin around *v/i of person, car* girarsi

♦ spin out *v/t* F far durare

spin·ach ['spɪnɪdʒ] spinaci *mpl*

spin·al ['spaɪnl] *adj* spinale

spin·al 'col·umn colonna *f* vertebrale, spina *f* dorsale

spin·al 'cord midollo *m* spinale

'spin doc·tor F persona *f* incaricata di far apparire un personaggio politico nella luce migliore; 'spin-dry *v/t* centrifugare; 'spin-dry·er centrifuga *f*

spine [spaɪn] *of person, animal* spina *f* dorsale; *of book* dorso *m*; *on plant, hedgehog* spina *f*

spine·less ['spaɪnlɪs] *adj* (*cowardly*) smidollato

'spin-off applicazione *f* secondaria

spin·ster ['spɪnstə(r)] zitella *f*

spin·y ['spaɪnɪ] *adj* spinoso

spi·ral ['spaɪrəl] 1 *n* spirale *f* 2 *v/i* (*rise quickly*) salire vertiginosamente

spi·ral 'stair·case scala *f* a chiocciola

spire ['spaɪə(r)] spira *f*, guglia *f*

spir·it ['spɪrɪt] *n* spirito *m*; we did it in

a ~ of cooperation abbiamo agito per spirito di collaborazione

spir·it·ed ['spɪrɪtɪd] *adj debate* animato; *defence* energico; *performance* brioso

'spir·it lev·el livella *f* a bolla d'aria

spir·its¹ ['spɪrɪts] *npl* (*alcohol*) superalcolici *mpl*

spir·its² ['spɪrɪts] *npl* (*morale*) morale *msg*; be in good / poor ~ essere su / giù di morale

spir·i·tu·al ['spɪrɪtjʊəl] *adj* spirituale

spir·i·tu·al·ism ['spɪrɪtjʊəlɪzm] spiritismo *m*

spir·i·tu·al·ist ['spɪrɪtjʊəlɪst] *n* spiritista *m/f*

spit [spɪt] *v/i* (*pret* & *pp* spat) *of person* sputare; it's ~ting with rain pioviggina

♦ spit out *v/t food, liquid* sputare

spite [spaɪt] *n* dispetto *m*; in ~ of malgrado

spite·ful ['spaɪtful] *adj* dispettoso

spite·ful·ly ['spaɪtfəlɪ] *adv* dispettosamente

spit·ting 'im·age ['spɪtɪŋ]: be the ~ of s.o. essere il ritratto sputato di qu

splash [splæʃ] 1 *n* (*noise*) tonfo *m*; (*small amount of liquid*) schizzo *m*; *of colour* macchia *f* 2 *v/t person* schizzare; *water, mud* spruzzare 3 *v/i* schizzare; *of waves* infrangersi

♦ splash down *v/i of spacecraft* ammarare

♦ splash out *v/i in spending* spendere un sacco di soldi (on per)

'splash·down ammaraggio *m*

splen·did ['splendɪd] *adj* magnifico

splen·dor *Am*, splen·dour ['splendə(r)] magnificenza *f*

splint [splɪnt] *n* MED stecca *f*

splin·ter ['splɪntə(r)] 1 *n* scheggia *f* 2 *v/i* scheggiarsi

'splin·ter group gruppo *m* scissionista

split [splɪt] 1 *n in leather* strappo *m*; *in wood* crepa *f*; (*disagreement*) spaccatura *f*; (*division, share*) divisione *f* 2 *v/t* (*pret* & *pp* split) *leather* strappare; *wood, logs* spaccare; (*cause disagreement in*) spaccare; (*divide*)

dividere **3** *v/i* (*pret* & *pp* **split**) *of
leather* strapparsi; *of wood* spaccarsi;
(*disagree*) spaccarsi
♦ **split up** *v/i of couple* separarsi
split per·son·al·i·ty PSYCH sdoppia-
mento *m* della personalità
split·ting ['splɪtɪŋ] *adj*: **~ headache**
feroce mal *m inv* di testa
spoil [spɔɪl] *v/t child* viziare; *surprise,
party* rovinare
♦ **spoil·sport** F guastafeste *m/f*
spoilt [spɔɪlt] *adj child* viziato; **be ~
for choice** avere (solo) l'imbarazzo
della scelta
spoke¹ [spəʊk] *of wheel* raggio *m*
spoke² [spəʊk] *pret* → **speak**
spo·ken ['spəʊkən] *pp* → **speak**
spokes·man ['spəʊksmən] portavoce *m*
spokes·per·son   ['spəʊkspɜːsən]
portavoce *m/f*
spokes·wom·an ['spəʊkswʊmən]
portavoce *f*
sponge [spʌndʒ] *n* spugna *f*
♦ **sponge off/on** *v/t* F vivere alle
spalle di
'**sponge cake** pan *m inv* di Spagna
spong·er ['spʌndʒə(r)] F scroccone
m, -a *f*
spon·sor ['spɒnsə(r)] **1** *n for immigration* garante *m/f inv*; *for membership* socio *m*, -a *f* garante; *of TV
programme, sports event, for
fundraising* sponsor *m inv* **2** *v/t for
immigration, membership* garantire
per; *TV programme, sports event*
sponsorizzare
spon·sor·ship ['spɒnsəʃɪp] spon-
sorizzazione *f*
spon·ta·ne·ous [spɒn'teɪnɪəs] *adj*
spontaneo
spon·ta·ne·ous·ly [spɒn'teɪnɪəslɪ]
adv spontaneamente
spook·y ['spuːkɪ] *adj* F sinistro
spool [spuːl] *n* bobina *f*
spoon [spuːn] *n* cucchiaio *m*
'**spoon·feed** *v/t* (*pret* & *pp* **-fed**) *fig*
scodellare la pappa a
spoon·ful ['spuːnfʊl] cucchiaio *f*
spo·rad·ic [spə'rædɪk] *adj* sporadico

sport [spɔːt] *n* sport *m inv*
sport·ing ['spɔːtɪŋ] *adj* sportivo; **a ~
gesture** un gesto sportivo
'**sports car** [spɔːts] Auto *f inv* sportiva; '**sports cen·ter** Am, '**sports
cen·tre** *indoor* palazzetto *m* dello
sport; '**sports jack·et** giacca *f* sportiva; '**sports·man** sportivo *m*;
'**sports med·i·cine** medicina *f* dello sport; '**sports news** *nsg* notizie
fpl sportive; '**sports page** pagina *f*
dello sport; '**sports·wear** abbigliamento   *m*   sportivo;   '**sports-
wom·an** sportiva *f*
sport·y ['spɔːtɪ] *adj* sportivo
spot¹ [spɒt] (*pimple*) brufolo *m*;
caused by measles etc foruncolo *m*;
part of pattern pois *m inv*; **a ~ of ...** (*a
little*) un po' di ...
spot² [spɒt] (*place*) posticino *m*; **on
the ~** (*in the place in question*) sul
posto; (*immediately*) immediatamente; **put s.o. on the ~** mettere in
difficoltà qu
spot³ [spɒt] *v/t* (*pret* & *pp* **-ted**)
(*notice*) notare; (*identify*) trovare
spot 'check *n* controllo *m* casuale
spot·less ['spɒtlɪs] *adj* pulitissimo
'**spot·light** *n* faretto *m*
spot·ted ['spɒtɪd] *adj fabric* a pois
spot·ty ['spɒtɪ] *adj with pimples*
brufoloso
spouse [spaʊs] *fml* coniuge *m/f*
spout [spaʊt] **1** *n* beccuccio *m*; *of
liquid* sgorgare **3** *v/t* F: **~ nonsense**
ciarlare
sprain [spreɪn] **1** *n* slogatura *f* **2** *v/t*
slogarsi
sprang [spræŋ] *pret* → **spring**
sprawl [sprɔːl] *v/i* stravaccarsi; *of city*
estendersi; **send s.o. ~ing** *of punch*
mandare qu a gambe all'aria
sprawl·ing ['sprɔːlɪŋ] *adj city, suburbs*
tentacolare
spray [spreɪ] **1** *n of sea water, from
fountain* spruzzi *mpl*; *for hair* lacca *f*;
(*container*) spray *m inv* **2** *v/t* spruzzare; **~ s.o. / sth with sth** spruzzare
qu / qc di qc
'**spray·gun** pistola *f* a spruzzo
spread [spred] **1** *n of disease, religion*

etc diffusione *f*; F *big meal* banchetto *m*; **2** *v/t* (*pret & pp* **spread**) (*lay*) stendere; *butter, jam* spalmare; *news, rumour, disease* diffondere; *arms, legs* allargare **3** *v/i* (*pret & pp* **spread**) diffondersi; *of butter* spalmarsi

'**spread·sheet** COMPUT spreadsheet *m inv*

spree [spri:] F: *go (out) on a ~ having fun* andare a far baldoria; *go on a shopping ~* andare a fare spese folli

sprig [sprɪg] rametto *m*

spright·ly ['spraɪtlɪ] *adj* arzillo

spring[1] [sprɪŋ] *n season* primavera *f*

spring[2] [sprɪŋ] *n device* molla *f*

spring[3] [sprɪŋ] **1** *n* (*jump*) balzo *m*; (*stream*) sorgente *f* **2** *v/i* (*pret* **sprang**, *pp* **sprung**) scattare; ~ *from* derivare da

'**spring·board** trampolino *m*; **spring 'chick·en** *hum*: *she's no* ~ non è più una ragazzina; **spring-'clean·ing** pulizie *fpl* di primavera; **spring 'on·ion** cipollotto *m*; '**spring·time** primavera *f*

spring·y ['sprɪŋɪ] *adj mattress, walk* molleggiato; *ground* morbido; *material* elastico

sprin·kle ['sprɪŋkl] *v/t* spruzzare; ~ *sth with* cospargere qc di

sprin·kler ['sprɪŋklə(r)] *for garden* irrigatore *m*; *in ceiling* sprinkler *m inv*

sprint [sprɪnt] **1** *n*: scatto *m*; *the 100 metres* ~ i cento metri piani **2** *v/i* fare uno scatto

sprint·er ['sprɪntə(r)] SP velocista *m/f*

sprout [spraʊt] **1** *v/i of seed* spuntare **2** *n* germoglio *m*; (**Brussels**) ~**s** cavolini *mpl* di Bruxelles

spruce [spru:s] *adj* curato

sprung [sprʌŋ] *pp* → **spring**

spun [spʌn] *pret & pp* → **spin**

spry [spraɪ] *adj* arzillo

spud [spʌd] F patata *f*

spur [spɜ:(r)] *n* sperone *m*; *fig* sprone *m*; *on the ~ of the moment* su due piedi

♦ **spur on** *v/t* (*pret & pp* **-red**) (*encourage*) spronare

spurt [spɜ:t] **1** *n*: *put on a* ~ *in race* fare uno scatto; *in work* accelerare il ritmo **2** *v/i of liquid* sprizzare

sput·ter ['spʌtə(r)] *v/i of engine* scoppiettare

spy [spaɪ] **1** *n* spia *f* **2** *v/i* (*pret & pp* **-ied**) fare la spia **3** *v/t* (*pret & pp* **-ied**) F scorgere

♦ **spy on** *v/t* spiare

squab·ble ['skwɒbl] **1** *n* bisticcio *m* **2** *v/i* bisticciare

squal·id ['skwɒlɪd] *adj* squallido

squal·or ['skwɒlə(r)] squallore *m*

squan·der ['skwɒndə(r)] *v/t money* dilapidare

square [skweə(r)] **1** *adj in shape* quadrato; ~ *mile* miglio quadrato **2** *n shape* quadrato *m*; *in town* piazza *f*; *in board game* casella *f*; MATH quadrato *m*; *we're back to* ~ *one* siamo punto e a capo

♦ **square up** *v/i* (*settle up*) fare i conti

square 'root radice *f* quadrata

squash[1] [skwɒʃ] *n vegetable* zucca *f*

squash[2] [skwɒʃ] *n game* squash *m inv*

squash[3] [skwɒʃ] **1** *v/t* (*crush*) schiacciare **2** *n*: *orange* / *lemon* ~ sciroppo *m* d'arancia / limone

squat [skwɒt] **1** *adj in shape* tozzo **2** *v/i* (*pret & pp* **-ted**) (*sit*) accovacciarsi; *illegally* occupare abusivamente

squat·ter ['skwɒtə(r)] squatter *m inv*, occupante *m/f* abusivo, -a

squeak [skwi:k] **1** *n of mouse* squittio *m*; *of hinge* cigolio *m* **2** *v/i of mouse* squittire; *of hinge* cigolare; *of shoes* scricchiolare

squeak·y ['skwi:kɪ] *adj hinge* cigolante; *shoes* scricchiolante; *voice* stridulo

squeak·y clean *adj* F pulito

squeal [skwi:l] **1** *n of pain, laughter* strillo *m*; *of brakes* stridore *m* **2** *v/i* strillare; *of brakes* stridere

squeam·ish ['skwi:mɪʃ] *adj*: *be* ~ avere lo stomaco delicato

squeeze [skwi:z] **1** *n of hand*,

shoulder stretta *f; **a ~ of lemon*** una spruzzata di limone **2** *v/t hand* stringere; *orange, lemon* spremere; *sponge* strizzare

♦ **squeeze in 1** *v/i to a car etc* infilarsi **2** *v/t* infilare

♦ **squeeze up** *v/i to make space* stringersi

squid [skwɪd] calamaro *m*

squint [skwɪnt] *n* strabismo *m*

squirm [skwɜːm] *v/i (wriggle)* contorcersi; **~ (with embarrassment)** morire di vergogna

squir·rel ['skwɪrəl] scoiattolo *m*

squirt [skwɜːt] **1** *v/t* spruzzare **2** *n* F *pej* microbo *m* F

St *abbr* (= *saint*) S. (= santo *m*, santa *f*); (= *street*) v. (= via *f*)

stab [stæb] **1** *n* F: **have a ~ at doing sth** provare a fare qc **2** *v/t* (*pret & pp* **-bed**) *person* accoltellare

sta·bil·i·ty [stə'bɪlətɪ] stabilità *f inv*

sta·bil·ize ['steɪbɪlaɪz] **1** *v/t prices, boat* stabilizzare **2** *v/i of prices etc* stabilizzarsi

sta·ble¹ ['steɪbl] *n building* stalla *f; establishment* scuderia *f*

sta·ble² ['steɪbl] *adj* stabile

stack [stæk] **1** *n (pile)* pila *f; (smokestack)* ciminiera *f;* **~s of** F un sacco di F **2** *v/t* mettere in pila

sta·di·um ['steɪdɪəm] stadio *m*

staff [stɑːf] *npl (employees)* personale *msg; (teachers)* corpo *m* insegnante

'staff·room *in school* sala *f* professori

stag [stæg] cervo *m*

stage¹ [steɪdʒ] *in life, project etc* fase *f; of journey* tappa *f*

stage² [steɪdʒ] **1** *n* THEA palcoscenico *m;* **go on the ~** *become actor* fare teatro **2** *v/t play* mettere in scena; *demonstration* organizzare

stage 'door ingresso *m* degli artisti; **'stage fright** attacco *m* di panico; **'stage hand** macchinista *m/f*

stag·ger ['stægə(r)] **1** *v/i* barcollare **2** *v/t (amaze)* sbalordire; *holidays, breaks etc* scaglionare

stag·ger·ing ['stægərɪŋ] *adj* sbalorditivo

stag·nant ['stægnənt] *adj also fig* stagnante

stag·nate [stæg'neɪt] *v/i of person, mind* vegetare

stag·na·tion [stæg'neɪʃn] ristagno *m*

'stag par·ty (festa *f* di) addio *m* al celibato

stain [steɪn] **1** *n (dirty mark)* macchia *f; for wood* mordente *m* **2** *v/t (dirty)* macchiare; *wood* dare il mordente a **3** *v/i of wine etc* macchiare; *of fabric* macchiarsi

stained-glass 'win·dow [steɪnd] vetrata *f* colorata

stain·less 'steel ['steɪnlɪs] **1** *n* acciaio *m* inossidabile **2** *adj* d'acciaio inossidabile

'stain re·mov·er smacchiatore *m*

stair [steə(r)] *n* scalino *m;* **the ~s** le scale

'stair·case scala *f*

stake [steɪk] **1** *n of wood* paletto *m; when gambling* puntata *f; (investment)* partecipazione *f;* **be at ~** essere in gioco **2** *v/t tree* puntellare; *money* puntare

stale [steɪl] *adj bread* raffermo; *air* viziato; *fig: news* vecchio

'stale·mate *in chess* stallo *m; fig* punto *m* morto

stalk¹ [stɔːk] *n of fruit* picciolo *m; of plant* gambo *m*

stalk² [stɔːk] *v/t animal* seguire; *person* perseguitare (con telefonate, lettere ecc)

stalk·er ['stɔːkə(r)] *persona f che perseguita qualcun altro con telefonate, lettere ecc*

stall¹ [stɔːl] *n at market* bancarella *f; for cow, horse* box *m inv*

stall² [stɔːl] **1** *v/i of engine* spegnersi; *of vehicle* fermarsi; *(play for time)* temporeggiare **2** *v/t engine* far spegnere; *people* trattenere

stal·li·on ['stæljən] stallone *m*

stalls [stɔːlz] *npl* platea *f*

stal·wart ['stɔːlwət] *adj support, supporter* fedele

stam·i·na ['stæmɪnə] resistenza *f*

stam·mer ['stæmə(r)] **1** *n* balbuzie *f* **2** *v/i* balbettare

stamp

stamp¹ [stæmp] **1** *n for letter* franco-bollo *m*; (*date* ~ *etc*) timbro *m* **2** *v/t letter* affrancare; *document, passport* timbrare; **~ed addressed enve-lope** busta *f* affrancata per la risposta

stamp² [stæmp] *v/t*: **~ one's feet** pe-stare i piedi

'**stamp col·lec·ting** filatelia *f*; '**stamp col·lec·tion** collezione *f* di francobolli; '**stamp col·lec·tor** col-lezionista *m/f* di francobolli

♦ **stamp out** *v/t* (*eradicate*) eliminare

stam·pede [stæm'piːd] **1** *n of cattle etc* fuga *f* precipitosa; *of people* fuggi-fuggi *m inv* **2** *v/i of cattle etc* fuggire precipitosamente; *of people* precipitarsi

stance [stɑːns] (*position*) presa *f* di posizione

stand [stænd] **1** *n at exhibition* stand *m inv*; (*witness* ~) banco *m* dei testi-moni; (*support, base*) base *f*; **take the ~** LAW testimoniare **2** *v/i* (*pret & pp* **stood**) (*be situated: of person*) stare; *of object, building* trovarsi; *as opposed to sit* stare in piedi; (*rise*) alzarsi in piedi; **~ still** stare fermo; **where do you ~ on the issue?** qual è la tua posizione sulla questione? **3** *v/t* (*pret & pp* **stood**) (*tolerate*) sopportare; (*put*) mettere; **you don't ~ a chance** non hai alcuna probabilità; **~ s.o. a drink** offrire da bere a qu; **~ one's ground** non mol-lare, tenere duro

♦ **stand back** *v/i* farsi indietro
♦ **stand by 1** *v/i* (*not take action*) sta-re a guardare; (*be ready*) tenersi pronto **2** *v/t person* stare al fianco di; *decision* mantenere
♦ **stand down** *v/i* (*withdraw*) ritirarsi
♦ **stand for** *v/t* (*tolerate*) tollerare; (*mean*) significare; *freedom etc* rap-presentare
♦ **stand in for** *v/t* sostituire
♦ **stand out** *v/i* spiccare; *of person, building* distinguersi
♦ **stand up 1** *v/i* alzarsi in piedi **2** *v/t* F **on date** dare buca a F
♦ **stand up for** *v/t* difendere

♦ **stand up to** *v/t* far fronte a

stan·dard ['stændəd] **1** *adj* (*usual*) comune; *model, size* standard *inv* **2** *n* (*level*) livello *m*; (*expectation*) aspet-tativa *f*; TECH standard *m inv*; **moral ~s** principi *mpl*; **be / not be up to ~** essere / non essere di buona qualità

stan·dard·ize ['stændədaɪz] *v/t* stan-dardizzare

'**stan·dard lamp** *Br* lampada *f* a ste-lo

stan·dard of 'li·ving tenore *m* di vita

'**stand·by 1** *n* ticket biglietto *m* stand-by; **on ~** at airport in lista d'at-tesa; **on ~** of troops etc pronto

'**stand·by pas·sen·ger** passeggero *m*, -a *f* in lista d'attesa

stand·ing ['stændɪŋ] *n in society etc* posizione *f*; (*repute*) reputazione *f*; **a musician of some ~** un musicista di una certa importanza; **a friendship of long ~** un'amicizia di lunga dura-ta

stand·ing 'or·der FIN ordine *m* per-manente

'**stand·ing room** posto *m* in piedi

stand·off·ish [stænd'ɒfɪʃ] *adj* sco-stante; '**stand·point** punto *m* di vi-sta; '**stand·still**; **be at a ~** essere fer-mo; **bring to a ~** fermare

stank [stæŋk] *pret* → **stink**

stan·za ['stænzə] *of poem* stanza *f*

sta·ple¹ ['steɪpl] *n* (*foodstuff*) ali-mento *m* base

sta·ple² ['steɪpl] **1** *n* (*fastener*) graffa *f* **2** *v/t* pinzare

sta·ple 'di·et alimentazione *f* base

'**sta·ple gun** pistola *f* sparachiodi

sta·pler ['steɪplə(r)] pinzatrice *f*

star [stɑː(r)] **1** *n in sky* stella *f*; *fig* star *f inv* **2** *v/t* (*pret & pp* **-red**): *a film* **~ring Julia Roberts** un film inter-pretato da Julia Roberts **3** *v/i* (*pret & pp* **-red**): *he* **~red in Psycho** è il protagonista di Psycho

'**star·board** *adj* a tribordo

starch [stɑːtʃ] *in foodstuff* amido *m*

stare [steə(r)] **1** *n* sguardo *m* fisso **2** *v/i* fissare; **~ at** fissare

'**star·fish** stella *f* di mare

stark [stɑːk] **1** *adj landscape* desola-

star·ling ['stɑːlɪŋ] storno *m*

star·ry ['stɑːrɪ] *adj night* stellato

star·ry-eyed [stɑːrɪ'aɪd]] *adj person* idealista

start [stɑːt] **1** *n (beginning)* inizio *m*; **make a ~ on sth** iniziare qc; **get off to a good / bad ~** *in marriage, career* cominciare bene / male; **from the ~** dall'inizio; **well, it's a ~!** è pur sempre un inizio! **2** *v/i* iniziare, cominciare; *of engine, car* partire; **~ing from tomorrow** a partire da domani **3** *v/t* cominciare; *engine, car* mettere in moto; *business* mettere su; **~ to do sth, ~ doing sth** cominciare a fare qc

start·er ['stɑːtə(r)] *part of meal* antipasto *m*; *of car* motorino *m* d'avviamento; *in race* starter *m inv*

'starting point punto *m* di partenza

'starting sal·a·ry stipendio *m* iniziale

star·tle ['stɑːtl] *v/t* far trasalire

star·tling ['stɑːtlɪŋ] *adj* sorprendente

starv·a·tion [stɑː'veɪʃn] fame *f*

starve [stɑːv] *v/i* soffrire la fame; **~ to death** morire di fame; **I'm starving** F sto morendo di fame

state¹ [steɪt] **1** *n* of car, house etc stato *m*, condizione *f*; *(country)* stato *m*; **the States** gli Stati Uniti; **be in a ~** essere agitato **2** *adj* di stato; *school* statale; *banquet etc* ufficiale

state² [steɪt] *v/t* dichiarare

'State De·part·ment *in USA* Ministero *m* degli Esteri

state·ment ['steɪtmənt] *to police* deposizione *f*; *(announcement)* dichiarazione *f*; *(bank ~)* estratto *m* conto

state of e'mer·gen·cy stato *m* d'emergenza

state-of-the-'art *adj* allo stato dell'arte

states·man ['steɪtsmən] statista *m*

state 'vis·it visita *f* ufficiale

stat·ic (e·lec·tric·i·ty) ['stætɪk] elettricità *f inv* statica

sta·tion ['steɪʃn] **1** *n* stazione *f* **2** *v/t* *guard etc* disporre; **be ~ed at** *of soldier* essere di stanza in / a

sta·tion·a·ry ['steɪʃənərɪ] *adj* fermo

sta·tion·er's ['steɪʃənərz] cartoleria *f*

sta·tion·er·y ['steɪʃənərɪ] articoli *mpl* di cancelleria

sta·tion 'man·ag·er dirigente *m* della stazione ferroviaria

'sta·tion wag·on *Am* giardiniera *f*

sta·tis·ti·cal [stə'tɪstɪkl] *adj* statistico

sta·tis·ti·cal·ly [stə'tɪstɪklɪ] *adv* statisticamente

sta·tis·ti·cian [stætɪs'tɪʃn] esperto *m*, -a *f* di statistica

sta·tis·tics [stə'tɪstɪks] *nsg science* statistica *f*; *npl figures* statistiche *fpl*

stat·ue ['stætjuː] statua *f*

sta·tus ['steɪtəs] posizione *f*

'sta·tus bar COMPUT barra *f* di stato

'sta·tus sym·bol status symbol *m inv*

stat·ute ['stætjuːt] statuto *m*

staunch [stɔːntʃ] *adj* leale

stay [steɪ] **1** *n* soggiorno *m* **2** *v/i in a place* stare; *in a condition* restare; **~ in a hotel** stare in albergo; **~ right there!** non ti muovere!; **~ put** non muoversi

♦ **stay away** *v/i* stare alla larga

♦ **stay away from** *v/t* stare alla larga da

♦ **stay behind** *v/i* rimanere

♦ **stay up** *v/i (not go to bed)* rimanere alzato

stead·i·ly ['stedɪlɪ] *adv improve etc* costantemente; *look* fisso

stead·y ['stedɪ] **1** *adj voice, hands* fermo; *job, boyfriend* fisso; *beat* regolare; *improvement, decline, progress* costante **2** *adv*: **be going ~** fare coppia fissa; **~ on!** calma! **3** *v/t (pret & pp -ied)* bookcase etc rendere saldo; **~ o.s.** ritrovare l'equilibrio

steak [steɪk] bistecca *f*, carne *f* (di manzo)

steal [stiːl] *(pret stole, pp stolen)* **1** *v/t money etc* rubare **2** *v/i (be a thief)* rubare; **~ in / out** *(move quietly)* entrare / uscire furtivamente

S

stealth·y ['stelθɪ] *adj* furtivo

steam [stiːm] **1** *n* vapore *m* **2** *v/t food* cuocere al vapore

♦**steam up 1** *v/i of window* appannarsi **2** *v/t*: **be steamed up** F *angry* essere furibondo

steam·er ['stiːmə(r)] *for cooking* vaporiera *f*

'**steam i·ron** ferro *m* a vapore

steel [stiːl] **1** *n* acciaio *m* **2** *adj* d'acciaio

'**steel·work·er** operaio *m* di acciaieria

'**steel·works** acciaieria *f*

steep[1] [stiːp] *adj hill etc* ripido; F *prices* alto; **that's a bit ~ expensive** è un po' caro

steep[2] [stiːp] *v/t* (*soak*) lasciare a bagno

stee·ple ['stiːpl] campanile *m*

'**stee·ple·chase** *in athletics* corsa *f* ad ostacoli

steep·ly ['stiːplɪ] *adv*: **climb ~** *of path* salire ripidamente; *of prices* salire vertiginosamente

steer[1] [stɪə(r)] *n animal* manzo *m*

steer[2] [stɪə(r)] *v/t car, boat* manovrare; *person* guidare; *conversation* spostare

steer·ing ['stɪərɪŋ] *of motor vehicle* sterzo *m*

'**steer·ing wheel** volante *m*

stem[1] [stem] *n of plant, glass* stelo *m*; *of word* radice *f*

♦**stem from** *v/t* derivare da

stem[2] [stem] *v/t* (*pret & pp* **-med**) (*block*) arginare

stench [stentʃ] puzzo *m*

sten·cil ['stensɪl] **1** *n* stencil *m inv* **2** *v/t* (*pret & pp* **-led**, *Am* **-ed**) *pattern* disegnare con lo stencil

step [step] **1** *n* (*pace*) passo *m*; (*stair*) gradino *m*; (*measure*) provvedimento *m*; **~ by** ~ poco a poco **2** *v/i* (*pret & pp* **-ped**) mettere il piede; **~ into / out of** salire in / scendere da

♦**step down** *v/i from post etc* dimettersi

♦**step forward** *v/i also fig* farsi avanti

♦**step up** *v/t* F (*increase*) aumentare

'**step·broth·er** fratellastro *m*; '**step-daugh·ter** figliastra *f*; '**step-fa·ther** patrigno *m*; '**step·lad·der** scala *f* a libretto; '**step·moth·er** matrigna *f*

'**step·ping stone** ['stepɪŋ] pietra *f* di un guado; *fig* trampolino *m* di lancio

'**step·sis·ter** sorellastra *f*

'**step·son** figliastro *m*

ster·e·o ['sterɪəʊ] *n* (*sound system*) stereo *m inv*

ster·e·o·type ['sterɪəʊtaɪp] *n* stereotipo *m*

ster·ile ['steraɪl] *adj* sterile

ster·il·ize ['sterəlaɪz] *v/t* sterilizzare

ster·ling ['stɜːlɪŋ] *n* FIN sterlina *f*

stern[1] [stɜːn] *adj* severo

stern[2] [stɜːn] *n* NAUT poppa *f*

stern·ly ['stɜːnlɪ] *adv* severamente

ster·oids ['sterɔɪdz] *npl* anabolizzanti *mpl*

steth·o·scope ['steθəskəʊp] fonendoscopio *m*

stew [stjuː] *n* spezzatino *m*

stew·ard ['stjuːəd] *n on plane, ship* steward *m inv*; *at demonstration, meeting* membro *m* del servizio d'ordine

stew·ard·ess [stjuːə'des] *on plane, ship* hostess *f inv*

stewed [stjuːd] *adj apples, plums* cotto

stick[1] [stɪk] *n wood* rametto *m*; (*walking ~*) bastone *m*; **out in the ~s** F a casa del diavolo F

stick[2] [stɪk] (*pret & pp* **stuck**) **1** *v/t with adhesive* attaccare; *needle, knife* conficcare; F (*put*) mettere **2** *v/i* (*jam*) bloccarsi; (*adhere*) attaccarsi

♦**stick around** *v/i* F restare

♦**stick by** *v/t* F: **stick by s.o.** rimanere al fianco di qu

♦**stick out** *v/i* (*protrude*) sporgere; (*be noticeable*) spiccare

♦**stick to** *v/t* F (*keep to*) attenersi a; F (*follow*) seguire

♦**stick together** *v/i* F restare uniti

♦**stick up** *v/t poster, leaflet* affiggere

♦**stick up for** *v/t* F difendere

stick·er ['stɪkə(r)] adesivo *m*

'**stick·ing plas·ter** cerotto *m*

'stick-in-the-mud F abitudinario *m*, -a *f*

stick·y ['stɪkɪ] *adj* hands, surface appiccicoso; *label* adesivo

stiff [stɪf] **1** *adj* brush, cardboard, leather rigido; *muscle, body* anchilosato; *mixture, paste* sodo; *in manner* freddo; *drink, competition* forte; *fine* salato **2** *adv*: **be scared ~** F essere spaventato a morte F; **be bored ~** F essere annoiato a morte F

stiff·en ['stɪfn] *v/i* irrigidirsi

♦ **stiffen up** *v/i of muscle* anchilosarsi

stiff·ly ['stɪflɪ] *adv* rigidamente; *fig* freddamente

stiff·ness ['stɪfnəs] *of muscles* indolenzimento *m*; *of material* rigidità *f*; *fig: of manner* freddezza *f*

sti·fle ['staɪfl] *v/t also fig* soffocare

sti·fling ['staɪflɪŋ] *adj* soffocante

stig·ma ['stɪgmə] vergogna *f*

sti·let·tos [stɪ'letəʊz] *npl* (*shoes*) scarpe *fpl* con tacco a spillo

still¹ [stɪl] **1** *adj* (*motionless*) immobile; *without wind* senza vento; *drink* non gas(s)ato; *it was very ~ outside* tutto era calmo fuori **2** *adv*: *keep / stand ~!* stai fermo!

still² [stɪl] *adv* (*yet*) ancora; (*nevertheless*) comunque; *she ~ hasn't finished* non ha ancora finito; *they are ~ my parents* sono pur sempre i miei genitori; *~ more* (*even more*) ancora più

'still·born *adj* nato morto

still 'life natura *f* morta

stilt·ed ['stɪltɪd] *adj* poco naturale

stilts [stɪlts] *npl* trampoli *mpl*

stim·u·lant ['stɪmjʊlənt] stimolante *m*

stim·u·late ['stɪmjʊleɪt] *v/t* stimolare

stim·u·lat·ing ['stɪmjʊleɪtɪŋ] *adj* stimolante

stim·u·la·tion [stɪmjʊ'leɪʃn] stimolazione *f*

stim·u·lus ['stɪmjʊləs] (*incentive*) stimolo *m*

sting [stɪŋ] **1** *n from bee* puntura *f*; *actual organ* pungiglione *m*; *from jellyfish* pizzico *m* **2** *v/t* (*pret & pp stung*) *of bee* pungere; *of jellyfish*

pizzicare **3** *v/i* (*pret & pp stung*) *of eyes, scratch* bruciare

sting·ing ['stɪŋɪŋ] *adj* remark, criticism pungente

sting·y ['stɪndʒɪ] *adj* F tirchio

stink [stɪŋk] **1** *n* (*bad smell*) puzza *f*; F (*fuss*) putiferio *m* F; *kick up a ~* F fare un casino F **2** *v/i* (*pret stank, pp stunk*) (*smell bad*) puzzare; F (*be very bad*) fare schifo F

stint [stɪnt] *n* periodo *m*; *do a ~ in the army* arruolarsi nell'esercito per un periodo; *do you want to do a ~ now?* vuoi darmi il cambio?

♦ **stint on** *v/t* F lesinare su

stip·u·late ['stɪpjʊleɪt] *v/t & v/i* stabilire

stip·u·la·tion [stɪpjʊ'leɪʃn] condizione *f*

stir [stɜ:(r)] **1** *n*: *give the soup a ~* mescolare la minestra; *cause a ~* fare scalpore **2** *v/t* (*pret & pp -red*) mescolare **3** *v/i* (*pret & pp -red*) *of sleeping person* muoversi

♦ **stir up** *v/t* fomentare

'stir-fry *v/t* (*pret & pp -ied*) saltare (in padella)

stir·ring ['stɜ:rɪŋ] *adj* music, speech commovente

stitch [stɪtʃ] **1** *n in sewing* punto *m*; *in knitting* maglia *f*; *~es* MED punti *mpl* (di sutura); *be in ~es laughing* ridere a crepapelle; *have a ~* avere una fitta al fianco **2** *v/t sew* cucire

♦ **stitch up** *v/t wound* suturare

stitch·ing ['stɪtʃɪŋ] (*stitches*) cucitura *f*

stock [stɒk] **1** *n* (*reserves*) provvista *f*; COM: *of store* stock *m inv*; *animals* bestiame *m*; FIN titoli *mpl*; *for soup etc* brodo *m*; *in ~ / out of ~* disponibile / esaurito; *take ~* fare il punto **2** *v/t* COM vendere

♦ **stock up on** *v/t* fare provvista di

'stock·brok·er agente *m/f* di cambio; **'stock cube** dado *m* (da brodo); **'stock ex·change** borsa *f* valori

stock·ing ['stɒkɪŋ] calza *f* (da donna)

stock·ist ['stɒkɪst] rivenditore *m*

S

'stock mar·ket mercato *m* azionario; **stock·mar·ket** 'crash crollo *m* del mercato azionario; 'stock·pile **1** *n of food, weapons* scorta *f* **2** *v/t* fare scorta di; 'stock·room magazzino *m*; stock-'still *adv*: **stand ~** stare immobile; 'stock·tak·ing inventario *m*

'stock·y ['stɒkɪ] *adj* tarchiato

stodg·y ['stɒdʒɪ] *adj food* pesante

sto·i·cal ['stəʊɪkl] *adj* stoico

sto·i·cism ['stəʊɪsɪzm] stoicismo *m*

stole [stəʊl] *pret* → **steal**

stol·en ['stəʊlən] *pp* → **steal**

stom·ach ['stʌmək] **1** *n* stomaco *m*; (*abdomen*) pancia *f* **2** *v/t* (*tolerate*) sopportare

'stom·ach·ache mal *m* di stomaco

stone [stəʊn] *n material* pietra *f*; (*pebble*) sasso *m*; (*precious ~*) pietra *f* preziosa; *in fruit* nocciolo *m*

stoned [stəʊnd] *adj* F *on drugs* fatto F

stone-'deaf *adj* sordo (come una campana)

'stone·wall *v/i* F menare il can per l'aia

ston·y ['stəʊnɪ] *adj ground, path* sassoso

stood [stʊd] *pret & pp* → **stand**

stool [stuːl] *seat* sgabello *m*

stoop [stuːp] **1** *n*: **walk with a ~** camminare con la schiena curva **2** *v/i* (*bend down*) chinarsi; (*have bent back*) essere curvo

stop [stɒp] **1** *n for train, bus* fermata *f*; **come to a ~** fermarsi; **put a ~ to** mettere fine a **2** *v/t* (*pret & pp* **-ped**) (*put an end to*) mettere fine a; (*prevent*) fermare; (*cease*) smettere; *person, car, bus* fermare; **it has ~ped raining** ha smesso di piovere; **I ~ped her from leaving** le ho impedito di andar via; **~ a cheque** bloccare un assegno **3** *v/i* (*pret & pp* **-ped**) (*come to a halt*) fermarsi; *of rain, noise* smettere

♦ stop by *v/i* (*visit*) passare

♦ stop off *v/i* fermarsi, fare sosta; *at post office* passare a

♦ stop over *v/i* fare sosta

♦ stop up *v/t sink* intasare

'stop·gap *person* tappabuchi *m/f inv*; *thing* soluzione *f* temporanea

'stop·o·ver *n* sosta *f*; *in air travel* scalo *m* intermedio

stop·per ['stɒpə(r)] tappo *m*

'stop sign (segnale *m* di) stop *m inv*

'stop·watch cronometro *m*

stor·age ['stɔːrɪdʒ]: *put sth in* ~ mettere qc in magazzino; *not much space for* ~ poco spazio per riporre la roba

'stor·age ca·pac·i·ty COMPUT capacità *f* di memoria

'stor·age space spazio *m* per riporre la roba

store [stɔː(r)] **1** *n large shop* negozio *m*; (*stock*) riserva *f*; (*storehouse*) deposito *m* **2** *v/t* tenere; COMPUT memorizzare

'store·room magazzino *m*

sto·rey ['stɔːrɪ] piano *m*

stork [stɔːk] cicogna *f*

storm [stɔːm] *n* tempesta *f*

'storm warn·ing avviso *m* di tempesta

storm·y ['stɔːmɪ] *adj also fig* tempestoso

sto·ry[1] ['stɔːrɪ] (*tale*) racconto *m*; (*account*) storia *f*; (*newspaper article*) articolo *m*; F (*lie*) bugia *f*

sto·ry[2] ['stɔːrɪ] *Am* → **storey**

stout [staʊt] *adj person* robusto; *defender* tenace

stove [stəʊv] *for cooking* cucina *f*; *for heating* stufa *f*

stow [stəʊ] *v/t* riporre

♦ stow away *v/i* imbarcarsi clandestinamente

'stow·a·way *n* passeggero *m*, -a *f* clandestino, -a

strag·gler ['stræglə(r)] persona *f* che rimane indietro

straight [streɪt] **1** *adj line* retto; *hair, whisky* liscio; *back, knees* dritto; (*honest, direct*) onesto; (*tidy*) in ordine; (*conservative*) convenzionale; (*not homosexual*) etero; **keep a ~ face** non ridere **2** *adv* (*in a straight line*) dritto; (*directly, immediately*) dritto, direttamente; (*clearly: think*) con chiarezza; ***stand up ~!*** stai dritto!; ***look s.o. ~ in the eye*** guardare qu dritto negli occhi; ***go ~*** F *of criminal* rigare dritto; ***give it to me ~*** F dimmi francamente; *~ ahead* avanti dritto; ***carry ~ on*** proseguire dritto; *~away, ~ off* immediatamente; *~ out* say sth chiaro e tondo

straight·en ['streɪtn] v/t raddrizzare

♦ **straighten out 1** v/t *situation* sistemare; F *person* mettere in riga F **2** v/i *of road* tornare diritto

♦ **straighten up** v/i raddrizzarsi

straight·for·ward adj (*honest, direct*) franco; (*simple*) semplice

strain¹ [streɪn] **1** n *physical* sforzo m; *mental* tensione f **2** v/t (*injure*) affaticare; *fig: finances, budget* gravare su

strain² [streɪn] v/t *vegetables* scolare; *oil, fat etc* filtrare

strain³ [streɪn] n *of virus* ceppo m

strained [streɪnd] adj teso

strain·er ['streɪnə(r)] *for vegetables etc* colino m

strait [streɪt] GEOG stretto m

strait-laced [streɪt'leɪst] adj puritano

strand¹ [strænd] n *of wool, thread* filo m; *of hair* ciocca f

strand² [strænd] v/t piantare in asso F; ***be ~ed*** essere bloccato

strange [streɪndʒ] adj (*odd, curious*) strano; (*unknown, foreign*) sconosciuto

strange·ly ['streɪndʒlɪ] adv (*oddly*) stranamente; *~ enough* strano ma vero

strang·er ['streɪndʒə(r)] *person you don't know* sconosciuto m, -a f; ***I'm a ~ here myself*** non sono di queste parti

stran·gle ['stræŋgl] v/t *person* strangolare

strap [stræp] n *of bag* tracolla f; *of bra, dress* bretellina f, spallina f; *of watch* cinturino m; *of shoe* listino m

♦ **strap in** v/t (*pret & pp -ped*) *with seatbelt* allacciare la cintura di sicurezza a

♦ **strap on** v/t allacciare

strap·less ['stræplɪs] adj senza spalline

stra·te·gic [strə'tiːdʒɪk] adj strategico

strat·e·gy ['strætədʒɪ] strategia f

straw¹ [strɔː] paglia f; ***that's the last ~!*** questa è la goccia che fa traboccare il vaso!

straw² [strɔː] *for drink* cannuccia f

straw·ber·ry ['strɔːbərɪ] fragola f

stray [streɪ] **1** adj *animal* randagio; *bullet* vagante **2** n *dog, cat* randagio m **3** v/i *of animal* smarrirsi; *of child* allontanarsi; *fig: of eyes, thoughts* vagare

streak [striːk] n *of dirt, paint* stria f; *fig: of nastiness etc* vena f **2** v/i *move quickly* sfrecciare **3** v/t: ***be ~ed with*** essere striato di

streak·y ['striːkɪ] adj striato

stream [striːm] **1** n ruscello m; *fig: of people, complaints* fiume m; ***come on ~*** *of plant* entrare in attività; *of oil* arrivare **2** v/i riversarsi

stream·er ['striːmə(r)] stella f filante

'stream·line v/t *fig* snellire

'stream·lined adj *car, plane* aerodinamico; *fig: organization* snellito

street [striːt] strada f; *in address* via f

'street·car *Am* tram m inv; **'street·light** lampione m; **'street·light·ing** illuminazione f stradale; **'street value** *of drugs* valore m di mercato; **'street·walk·er** F passeggiatrice f; **'street·wise** adj scafato F

strength [streŋθ] *of person, wind, emotion, currency* forza f; (*strong point*) punto m forte

strength·en ['streŋθn] **1** v/t rinforzare **2** v/i consolidarsi

stren·u·ous ['strenjʊəs] adj faticoso

stren·u·ous·ly ['strenjʊəslɪ] adv *deny* recisamente

stress [stres] **1** n (*emphasis*) accento m; (*tension*) stress m inv; ***be under ~*** essere sotto pressione **2** v/t *syllable* accentare; *importance etc* sottolineare

stressed 'out [strest] adj stressato

stress·ful ['stresful] adj stressante

S

stretch [stretʃ] **1** *n of land, water* tratto *m*; **at a ~** (*non-stop*) di fila **2** *adj fabric* elasticizzato **3** *v/t material* tendere; *small income* far bastare; **~ the rules** F fare uno strappo (alla regola); **he ~ed out his hand** allungò la mano; **a job that ~es me** un lavoro che mi impegna **4** *v/i to relax muscles* stirarsi; *to reach sth* allungarsi; (*spread*) estendersi; *of fabric*: *give* cedere; *of fabric*: *sag* allargarsi; **~ from X to Y** (*extend*) estendersi da X a Y

stretch·er ['stretʃə(r)] barella *f*

strict [strɪkt] *adj person* severo; *instructions, rules* tassativo

strict·ly ['strɪktlɪ] *adv*: **be brought up ~** ricevere un'educazione rigida; **it is ~ forbidden** è severamente proibito

strict·ness ['strɪktnəs] severità *f inv*

strid·den ['strɪdn] *pp* → **stride**

stride [straɪd] **1** *n* falcata *f*; **take sth in one's ~** affrontare qc senza drammi; **make great ~s** *fig* far passi da gigante **2** *v/i* (*pret* **strode**, *pp* **stridden**) procedere a grandi passi; **he strode up to me** avanzò verso di me

stri·dent ['straɪdnt] *adj* stridulo; *fig*: *demands* veemente

strike [straɪk] **1** *n of workers* sciopero *m*; *of oil* scoperta *f*; **be on ~** essere in sciopero; **go on ~** entrare in sciopero **2** *v/i* (*pret & pp* **struck**) *of workers* scioperare; (*attack*) aggredire; *of disaster* colpire; *of clock* suonare **3** *v/t* (*pret & pp* **struck**) (*hit*) colpire; *match* accendere (sfregando); *of idea, thought* venire in mente a; *oil* trovare; **~ one's head against sth** battere la testa contro qc; **she struck me as being ...** mi ha dato l'impressione di essere ...

♦ **strike out** *v/t* depennare

'strike·break·er crumiro *m*, -a *f*

strik·er ['straɪkə(r)] *person on strike* scioperante *m/f*; *in football* bomber *m inv*, cannoniere *m*, punta *f*

strik·ing ['straɪkɪŋ] *adj* (*marked*) marcato; (*eye-catching*) impressio-

nante; (*attractive*) attraente; *colour* forte

string [strɪŋ] *n* (*cord*) spago *m*; *of violin, tennis racket* corda *f*; **the ~s** MUS gli archi; **pull ~s** esercitare la propria influenza; **a ~ of** (*series*) una serie di

♦ **string along 1** *v/i* (*pret & pp* **strung**) F: **do you mind if I string along?** posso venire anch'io? **2** *v/t* (*pret & pp* **strung**) F: **string s.o. along** menare qu per il naso

♦ **string up** *v/t* F impiccare

stringed 'in·stru·ment [strɪŋd] strumento *m* ad arco

strin·gent ['strɪndʒnt] *adj* rigoroso

'string play·er suonatore *m*, -trice *f* di strumento ad arco

strip [strɪp] **1** *n* striscia *f*; (*comic ~*) fumetto *m*; *of soccer player* divisa *f* **2** *v/t* (*pret & pp* **-ped**) (*remove*) staccare; *bed* disfare; (*undress*) spogliare; **~ s.o. of sth** spogliare qu di qc **3** *v/i* (*pret & pp* **-ped**) (*undress*) spogliarsi; *of stripper* fare lo spogliarello

'strip club locale *m* di spogliarelli

stripe [straɪp] striscia *f*; *indicating rank* gallone *m*

striped [straɪpt] *adj* a strisce

'strip joint F → **strip club**

strip·per ['strɪpə(r)] spogliarellista *f*; **male ~** spogliarellista *m*

'strip show spogliarello *m*

strip'tease spogliarello *m*

strive [straɪv] *v/i* (*pret* **strove**, *pp* **striven**): **~ to do sth** sforzarsi di fare qc; **~ for sth** lottare per (ottenere) qc

striv·en ['strɪvn] *pp* → **strive**

strobe (**light**) [strəʊb] luce *f* stroboscopica

strode [strəʊd] *pret* → **stride**

stroke [strəʊk] **1** *n* MED ictus *m inv*; *when painting* pennellata *f*; *in swimming* bracciata *f*; *style of swimming* stile *m* di nuoto; **~ of luck** colpo di fortuna; **she never does a ~** (**of work**) non fa mai un bel niente **2** *v/t* accarezzare

stroll [strəʊl] **1** *n* passeggiata *f*; **go for**

a ~ fare una passeggiata **2** *v/i* fare due passi; **she ~ed back to the office** tornò in ufficio in tutta calma

strong [strɒŋ] *adj person, wind, drink, currency* forte; *structure* resistente; *candidate* valido; *taste, smell* intenso; *views, beliefs* fermo; *arguments* convincente; *objections* energico; **~ support** largo consenso

'**strong·hold** *fig* roccaforte *f*

strong·ly ['strɒŋlɪ] *adv believe, object* fermamente; *built* solidamente; **feel ~ about sth** avere molto a cuore qc

strong-mind·ed [strɒŋ'maɪndɪd] *adj* risoluto; '**strong point** (punto *m*) forte *m*; '**strong·room** camera *f* blindata; **strong-'willed** [strɒŋ-'wɪld] *adj* deciso

strove [strəʊv] *pret* → **strive**

struck [strʌk] *pret & pp* → **strike**

struc·tur·al ['strʌktʃərl] *adj* strutturale

struc·ture ['strʌktʃə(r)] **1** *n something built* costruzione *f*; *of novel, society etc* struttura *f* **2** *v/t* strutturare

strug·gle ['strʌgl] **1** *n (fight)* colluttazione *f*; *fig* lotta *f*; *(hard time)* fatica *f* **2** *v/i with a person* lottare; *(have a hard time)* faticare; **~ to do sth** faticare a fare qc

strum [strʌm] *v/t (pret & pp -med)* strimpellare

strung [strʌŋ] *pret & pp* → **string**

strut [strʌt] *v/i (pret & pp -ted)* camminare impettito

stub [stʌb] **1** *n of cigarette* mozzicone *m*; *of cheque, ticket* matrice *f* **2** *v/t (pret & pp -bed)*: **~ one's toe** urtare il dito del piede

◆ **stub out** *v/t* spegnere

stub·ble ['stʌbl] *on man's face* barba *f* ispida

stub·born ['stʌbən] *adj person* testardo; *defence, refusal, denial* ostinato

stub·by ['stʌbɪ] *adj* tozzo

stuck [stʌk] **1** *pret & pp* → **stick** **2** *adj* F: **be ~ on s.o.** essere cotto di qu F

stuck-'up *adj* F presuntuoso

stu·dent ['stjuːdnt] studente *m*, -essa *f*

stu·dent 'nurse infermiere *m*, -a *f* tirocinante

stu·dent 'teach·er insegnante *m/f* tirocinante

stu·di·o ['stjuːdɪəʊ] studio *m*; *(recording ~)* sala *f* di registrazione

stu·di·ous ['stjuːdɪəs] *adj* studioso

stud·y ['stʌdɪ] **1** *n* studio *m* **2** *v/t & v/i (pret & pp -ied)* studiare

stuff [stʌf] **1** *n* roba *f* **2** *v/t turkey* farcire; **~ sth into sth** ficcare qc in qc

stuff·ing ['stʌfɪŋ] *for turkey* farcia *f*; *in chair, teddy bear* imbottitura *f*

stuff·y ['stʌfɪ] *adj room* mal ventilato; *person* inquadrato

stum·ble ['stʌmbl] *v/i* inciampare

◆ **stumble across** *v/t* trovare per caso

◆ **stumble over** *v/t* inciampare in; *words* incespicare in

stum·bling-block ['stʌmblɪŋ] *fig* scoglio *m*

stump [stʌmp] **1** *n of tree* ceppo *m* **2** *v/t of question, questioner* sconcertare

◆ **stump up** *v/t* F sganciare F

stun [stʌn] *v/t (pret & pp -ned)* *of blow* stordire; *of news* sbalordire

stung [stʌŋ] *pret & pp* → **sting**

stunk [stʌŋk] *pp* → **stink**

stun·ning ['stʌnɪŋ] *adj (amazing)* sbalorditivo; *(very beautiful)* splendido

stunt [stʌnt] *n for publicity* trovata *f* pubblicitaria; *in film* acrobazia *f*

'**stunt·man** *in film* cascatore *m*

stu·pe·fy ['stjuːpɪfaɪ] *v/t (pret & pp -ied)* sbalordire

stu·pen·dous [stjuː'pendəs] *adj (marvellous)* fantastico; *mistake* enorme

stu·pid ['stjuːpɪd] *adj* stupido

stu·pid·i·ty [stjuː'pɪdətɪ] stupidità *f inv*

stu·por ['stjuːpə(r)] stordimento *m*; **in a drunken ~** stordito dall'alcool

stur·dy ['stɜːdɪ] *adj* robusto

stut·ter ['stʌtə(r)] *v/i* balbettare

sty [staɪ] *for pig* porcile *m*

style [stail] n stile m; (fashion) moda f; (fashionable elegance) classe f; (hair~) pettinatura f; **go out of ~** passare di moda

styl·ish ['stailiʃ] adj elegante

styl·ist ['stailist] (hair ~) parrucchiere m, -a f

sub·com·mit·tee ['sʌbkəmiti] sottocommissione f

sub·con·scious [sʌb'kɒnʃəs] adj subconscio; **the ~ (mind)** il subconscio

sub·con·scious·ly [sʌb'kɒnʃəsli] adv inconsciamente

sub·con·tract [sʌbkən'trakt] v/t subappaltare

sub·con·trac·tor [sʌbkən'traktə(r)] subappaltatore m, -trice f

sub·di·vide [sʌbdi'vaid] v/t suddividere

sub·due [səb'dju:] v/t sottomettere

sub·dued [səb'dju:d] adj person, voice pacato; light, colour soffuso

sub·head·ing ['sʌbhedɪŋ] sottotitolo m

sub·hu·man [sʌb'hju:mən] adj subumano

sub·ject ['sʌbdʒikt] **1** n of monarch suddito m, -a f; (topic) argomento m; EDU materia f; GRAM soggetto m; **change the ~** cambiare argomento **2** adj: **be ~ to** essere soggetto a; **~ to availability** nei limiti della disponibilità **3** v/t [səb'dʒekt] sottoporre; **be ~ed to criticism** essere criticato

sub·jec·tive [səb'dʒektɪv] adj soggettivo

sub·junc·tive [səb'dʒʌŋktɪv] GRAM congiuntivo m

sub·let ['sʌblet] v/t (pret & pp **-let**) subaffittare

sub·ma'chine gun mitra m

sub·ma'rine ['sʌbməri:n] sottomarino m, sommergibile m

sub·merge [səb'mɜ:dʒ] **1** v/t sommergere **2** v/i of submarine immergersi

sub·mis·sion [səb'mɪʃn] (surrender) sottomissione f; request to committee etc richiesta f

sub·mis·sive [səb'mɪsɪv] adj sottomesso

sub·mit [səb'mɪt] (pret & pp **-ted**) **1** v/t plan, proposal presentare **2** v/i sottomettersi

sub·or·di·nate [sə'bɔ:dɪnət] **1** adj employee, position subalterno **2** n subalterno m, -a f

sub·poe·na [sə'pi:nə] **1** n citazione f **2** v/t person citare in giudizio

♦ **subscribe to** [səb'skraɪb] v/t magazine etc abbonarsi a; theory condividere

sub·scrib·er [səb'skraɪbə(r)] to magazine abbonato m, -a f

sub·scrip·tion [səb'skrɪpʃn] abbonamento m

sub·se·quent ['sʌbsɪkwənt] adj successivo

sub·se·quent·ly ['sʌbsɪkwəntlɪ] adv successivamente

sub·side [səb'saɪd] v/i of waters, winds calare; of building sprofondare; of fears, panic calmarsi

sub·sid·i·a·ry [səb'sɪdɪərɪ] n filiale f

sub·si·dize ['sʌbsɪdaɪz] v/t sovvenzionare

sub·si·dy ['sʌbsɪdɪ] sovvenzione f

♦ **subsist on** v/t vivere di

sub·sis·tence farm·ing [səb'sɪstəns] agricoltura f di sussistenza

sub·sis·tence lev·el livello m minimo di vita

sub·stance ['sʌbstəns] (matter) sostanza f

sub·stan·dard [sʌb'stændəd] adj scadente

sub·stan·tial [səb'stænʃl] adj considerevole; meal sostanzioso

sub·stan·tial·ly [səb'stænʃlɪ] adv (considerably) considerevolmente; (in essence) sostanzialmente

sub·stan·ti·ate [səb'stænʃɪeɪt] v/t comprovare

sub·stan·tive [səb'stæntɪv] adj sostanziale

sub·sti·tute ['sʌbstɪtju:t] **1** n for person sostituto m, -a f; for commodity alternativa f; SP riserva f **2** v/t: **~ X for Y** sostituire Y con X **3** v/i: **~ s.o.** sostituire qu

sub·sti·tu·tion [sʌbstɪˈtjuːʃn] *(act)* sostituzione *f*; **make a ~** SP fare una sostituzione

sub·ti·tle [ˈsʌbtaɪtl] *n* sottotitolo *m*

sub·tle [ˈsʌtl] *adj* hint, difference sottile; *flavour* delicato

sub·tract [səbˈtrækt] *v/t* number sottrarre

sub·urb [ˈsʌbɜːb] sobborgo *m*; **the ~s** la periferia

sub·ur·ban [səˈbɜːbən] *adj* di periferia

sub·ur·bi·a [səˈbɜːbɪə] periferia *f*

sub·ver·sive [səbˈvɜːsɪv] **1** *adj* sovversivo **2** *n* sovversivo *m*, -a *f*

sub·way [ˈsʌbweɪ] *Br* (*passageway*) sottopassaggio *m*; *Am* metropolitana *f*

sub·ze·ro *adj*: **~ temperatures** temperature sottozero

suc·ceed [səkˈsiːd] **1** *v/i* (*be successful*) avere successo; **to throne** succedere; **~ in doing sth** riuscire a fare qc **2** *v/t* (*come after*) succedere a

suc·ceed·ing [səkˈsiːdɪŋ] *adj* successivo

suc·cess [səkˈses] successo *m*; **be a ~** avere successo

suc·cess·ful [səkˈsesfʊl] *adj* person affermato; *marriage*, *party* riuscito; **be ~** riuscire; **he's very ~** è arrivato

suc·cess·ful·ly [səkˈsesflɪ] *adv* con successo; **we ~ completed ...** siamo riusciti a portare a termine ...

suc·ces·sion [səkˈseʃn] (*sequence*) sfilza *f*; *to the throne* successione *f*; **in ~** di seguito

suc·ces·sive [səkˈsesɪv] *adj* successivo; **three ~ days** tre giorni di seguito

suc·ces·sor [səkˈsesə(r)] successore *m*

suc·cinct [səkˈsɪŋkt] *adj* succinto

suc·cu·lent [ˈsʌkjʊlənt] succulento

suc·cumb [səˈkʌm] *v/i* (*give in*) cedere; **~ to temptation** cedere alla tentazione

such [sʌtʃ] **1** *adj* (*of that kind*) del genere; **~ a** (*so much of a*) un / una tale; **~ as** come; **~ people** gente del ge-

nere; **he made ~ a fuss** ha fatto una tale scenata; **there is no ~ word as ...** la parola ... non esiste **2** *adv* così; **~ nice people** gente così simpatica; **as ~** (*in that capacity*) in quanto tale; **as ~** (*in itself*) di per sé

suck [sʌk] **1** *v/t lollipop etc* succhiare; **~ one's thumb** succhiarsi il dito **2** *v/i*: **it ~s** P (*is awful*) fa schifo P
 ♦ **suck up** *v/t* assorbire; *dust* aspirare
 ♦ **suck up to** *v/t* F leccare i piedi a F

suck·er [ˈsʌkə(r)] F *person* pollo F

suc·tion [ˈsʌkʃn] aspirazione *f*

sud·den [ˈsʌdn] *adj* improvviso; **all of a ~** all'improvviso

sud·den·ly [ˈsʌdnlɪ] *adv* improvvisamente

suds [sʌdz] *npl* (*soap ~*) schiuma *fsg*

sue [suː] **1** *v/t* fare causa a **2** *v/i* fare causa

suede [sweɪd] *n* pelle *f* scamosciata

suf·fer [ˈsʌfə(r)] **1** *v/i* (*be in great pain*) soffrire; (*deteriorate*) risentirne; **be ~ing from** soffrire di **2** *v/t loss*, *setback* subire

suf·fer·ing [ˈsʌfərɪŋ] *n* sofferenza *f*

suf·fi·cient [səˈfɪʃnt] *adj* sufficiente

suf·fi·cient·ly [səˈfɪʃntlɪ] *adv* abbastanza

suf·fo·cate [ˈsʌfəkeɪt] *v/t & v/i* soffocare

suf·fo·ca·tion [sʌfəˈkeɪʃn] soffocamento *m*

sug·ar [ˈʃʊgə(r)] **1** *n* zucchero *m* **2** *v/t* zuccherare

'sug·ar bowl zuccheriera *f*

sug·gest [səˈdʒest] *v/t* proporre, suggerire; **I ~ that we stop now** propongo di fermarci ora

sug·ges·tion [səˈdʒestʃən] *n* proposta *f*, suggerimento *m*

su·i·cide [ˈsuːɪsaɪd] *n* suicidio *m*; **commit ~** suicidarsi

'su·i·cide pact *n* patto *m* suicida

suit [suːt] **1** *n for man* vestito *m*, completo *m*; *for woman* tailleur *m inv*; *in cards* seme *m* **2** *v/t of clothes*, *colour* stare bene a; **~ yourself!** F fai come ti pare!; **be ~ed for sth** essere fatto per qc

sui·ta·ble [ˈsuːtəbl] *adj* adatto

sui·ta·bly ['su:təblɪ] adv adeguatamente

'**suit·case** valigia f

suite [swi:t] of rooms suite f inv; of furniture divano m e poltrone fpl coordinati; MUS suite f inv

sul·fur etc Am → **sulphur** etc

sulk [sʌlk] v/i fare il broncio

sulk·y ['sʌlkɪ] adj imbronciato

sul·len ['sʌlən] adj crucciato

sul·phur ['sʌlfə(r)] zolfo m

sul·phur·ic acid [sʌl'fjuːrɪk] acido m solforico

sul·try ['sʌltrɪ] adj climate afoso; sexually sensuale

sum [sʌm] somma f; in arithmetic addizione f; **a large ~ of money** una forte somma di denaro; **that's the ~ total of his efforts** quello è tutto quello che ha fatto

♦ **sum up** (pret & pp **-med**) **1** v/t (summarize) riassumere; (assess) valutare **2** v/i LAW riepilogare

sum·ma·rize ['sʌməraɪz] v/t riassumere

sum·ma·ry ['sʌmərɪ] n riassunto m

sum·mer ['sʌmə(r)] estate f

sum·mit ['sʌmɪt] of mountain vetta f; POL summit m inv

'**sum·mit meet·ing** → **summit**

sum·mon ['sʌmən] v/t convocare

♦ **summon up** v/t strength raccogliere

sum·mons ['sʌmənz] nsg LAW citazione f

sump [sʌmp] for oil coppa f dell'olio

sun [sʌn] sole m; **in the ~** al sole; **out of the ~** all'ombra; **he has had too much ~** ha preso troppo sole

'**sun·bathe** v/i prendere il sole; '**sun·bed** lettino m solare; '**sun·block** protezione f solare totale; '**sun·burn** scottatura f; '**sun·burnt** adj scottato

Sun·day ['sʌndeɪ] domenica f

'**sun·dial** meridiana f

sun·dries ['sʌndrɪz] npl varie fpl

sung [sʌŋ] pp → **sing**

'**sun·glass·es** npl occhiali mpl da sole

sunk [sʌŋk] pp → **sink**

sunk·en ['sʌŋkn] adj cheeks incavato

sun·ny ['sʌnɪ] adj day di sole; spot soleggiato; disposition allegro; **it's ~** c'è il sole

'**sun·rise** alba f; '**sun·set** tramonto m; '**sun·shade** ombrellone m; '**sun·shine** (luce f del) sole m; '**sun·stroke** colpo m di sole; '**sun·tan** abbronzatura f; **get a ~** abbronzarsi

su·per ['su:pə(r)] adj F fantastico

su·perb [suˈpɜːb] adj magnifico

su·per·fi·cial [suːpəˈfɪʃl] adj superficiale

su·per·flu·ous [suˈpɜːfluəs] adj superfluo

su·per·hu·man adj efforts sovrumano

su·per·in·tend·ent [suːpərɪnˈtendənt] of police commissario m

su·pe·ri·or [suːˈpɪərɪə(r)] **1** adj (better) superiore **2** n in organization, society superiore m

su·per·la·tive [suːˈpɜːlətɪv] **1** adj (superb) eccellente **2** n GRAM superlativo m

'**su·per·mar·ket** supermarket m inv, supermercato m

su·per·nat·u·ral 1 adj powers soprannaturale **2** n: **the ~** il soprannaturale

'**su·per·pow·er** POL superpotenza f

su·per·son·ic [suːpəˈsɒnɪk] adj flight, aircraft supersonico

su·per·sti·tion [suːpəˈstɪʃn] n superstizione f

su·per·sti·tious [suːpəˈstɪʃəs] adj person superstizioso

su·per·vise ['suːpəvaɪz] v/t supervisionare

su·per·vi·sor ['suːpəvaɪzə(r)] at work supervisore m

sup·per ['sʌpə(r)] cena f

sup·ple ['sʌpl] adj person, limbs snodato; material flessibile

sup·ple·ment ['sʌplɪmənt] supplemento m

sup·pli·er [səˈplaɪə(r)] n COM fornitore m

sup·ply [səˈplaɪ] **1** n fornitura f; **~ and demand** domanda e offerta; **supplies** rifornimenti **2** v/t (pret &

pp **-ied**) *goods* fornire; ~ **s.o. with sth** fornire qc a qu; **be supplied with** *fitted with etc* essere dotato di

sup·port [sə'pɔːt] **1** *n for structure* supporto *m*; (*backing*) sostegno *m* **2** *v/t building, structure* sostenere; *financially* mantenere; (*back*) sostenere; *football team* fare il tifo per

sup·port·er [sə'pɔːtə(r)] sostenitore *m*, -trice *f*; *of football team etc* tifoso *m*, -a *f*

sup·port·ive [sə'pɔːtɪv] *adj:* **be ~ towards s.o.** dare il proprio appoggio a qu

sup·pose [sə'pəʊz] *v/t* (*imagine*) supporre; *I* ~ *so* suppongo di sì; *it is ~d to ...* (*is meant to*) dovrebbe ...; (*is said to*) dicono che ...; *you are not ~d to ...* (*not allowed to*) non dovresti ...

sup·pos·ed·ly [sə'pəʊzɪdlɪ] *adv* presumibilmente

sup·pos·i·to·ry [sə'pɒzɪtrɪ] MED supposta *f*

sup·press [sə'pres] *v/t rebellion etc* reprimere

sup·pres·sion [sə'preʃn] repressione *f*

su·prem·a·cy [su:'preməsɪ] supremazia *f*

su·preme [su:'priːm] *adj* supremo

sur·charge ['sɜːtʃɑːdʒ] *for travel* sovrapprezzo *m*; *for mail* soprattassa *f*

sure [ʃʊə(r)] **1** *adj* sicuro; *I'm* ~ sono sicuro; *be* ~ *about sth* essere sicuro di qc; *make* ~ *that ...* assicurarsi che ... **2** *adv* certamente; ~ *enough* infatti; ~! F certo!

sure·ly ['ʃʊəlɪ] *adv* certamente; (*gladly*) volentieri; ~ *that's not right!* non può essere!; *oh,* ~ *you've heard of him* non puoi non conoscerlo

sure·ty ['ʃʊərətɪ] *for loan* cauzione *f*

surf [sɜːf] **1** *n on sea* spuma *f* **2** *v/t the Net* navigare

sur·face ['sɜːfɪs] **1** *n of table, object, water* superficie *f*; *on the* ~ *fig* superficialmente, in apparenza **2** *v/i of swimmer, submarine* risalire in su-

perficie, riemergere; (*appear*) farsi vivo

'sur·face mail posta *f* ordinaria

'surf·board tavola *f* da surf

surf·er ['sɜːfə(r)] *on sea* surfista *m/f*

surf·ing ['sɜːfɪŋ] surf *m inv*; *go* ~ fare surf

surge [sɜːdʒ] *n in electric current* sovratensione *f* transitoria; *in demand* impennata *f*; *of interest, financial growth etc* aumento *m*

♦ **surge forward** *v/i of crowd* buttarsi avanti

sur·geon ['sɜːdʒən] chirurgo *m*

sur·ge·ry ['sɜːdʒərɪ] intervento *m* chirurgico; *Br: place of work* ambulatorio *m*; *undergo* ~ sottoporsi a un intervento chirurgico; ~ *hours* orario *m* d'ambulatorio

sur·gi·cal ['sɜːdʒɪkl] *adj* chirurgico

sur·gi·cal·ly ['sɜːdʒɪklɪ] *adv* chirurgicamente

sur·ly ['sɜːlɪ] *adj* scontroso

sur·mount [sə'maunt] *v/t difficulties* sormontare

sur·name ['sɜːneɪm] cognome *m*

sur·pass [sə'pɑːs] *v/t* superare

sur·plus ['sɜːpləs] **1** *n* surplus *m inv* **2** *adj* eccedente

sur·prise [sə'praɪz] **1** *n* sorpresa *f*; *it'll come as no* ~ *to hear that ...* non ti sorprenderà sapere che ... **2** *v/t* sorprendere; *be ~d* essere sorpreso; *look ~d* avere l'aria sorpresa

sur·pris·ing [sə'praɪzɪŋ] *adj* sorprendente

sur·pris·ing·ly [sə'praɪzɪŋlɪ] *adv* sorprendentemente

sur·ren·der [sə'rendə(r)] **1** *v/i of army* arrendersi **2** *v/t weapons etc* consegnare **3** *n* resa *f*

sur·ro·gate 'moth·er [sʌrəgət] madre *f* biologica

sur·round [sə'raund] **1** *v/t* circondare; *be ~ed by ...* essere circondato da ... **2** *n of picture etc* bordo *m*

sur·round·ing [sə'raundɪŋ] *adj* circostante

sur·round·ings [sə'raundɪŋz] *npl of village etc* dintorni *mpl*; *fig* ambiente *m*

sur·vey ['sɜːveɪ] **1** *n of modern literature etc* quadro *m* generale; *of building* perizia *f*; *poll* indagine *f* **2** *v/t* [sə'veɪ] *(look at)* osservare; *building* periziare

sur·vey·or [sə'veɪə(r)] perito *m*

sur·viv·al [sə'vaɪvl] sopravvivenza *f*

sur·vive [sə'vaɪv] **1** *v/i* sopravvivere; *how are you? – I'm surviving* come stai? – si tira avanti; **his two surviving daughters** le due figlie ancora in vita **2** *v/t* sopravvivere a

sur·vi·vor [sə'vaɪvə(r)] superstite *m/f*; **he's a ~** *fig* se la cava sempre

sus·cep·ti·ble [sə'septəbl] *adj emotionally* impressionabile; **be ~ to the cold / heat** soffrire il freddo / caldo

sus·pect ['sʌspekt] **1** *n* indiziato *m*, -a *f* **2** *v/t* [sə'spekt] *person* sospettare; *(suppose)* supporre

sus·pect·ed [sə'spektɪd] *adj murderer* presunto; *cause, heart attack etc* sospetto

sus·pend [sə'spend] *v/t (hang)* sospendere; *from office, duties* sospendere

sus·pend·ers [sə'spendəz] *npl* giarrettiere *fpl*; *Am (braces)* bretelle *fpl*

sus·pense [sə'spens] suspense *f inv*

sus·pen·sion [sə'spenʃn] sospensione *f*

sus'pen·sion bridge ponte *m* sospeso

sus·pi·cion [sə'spɪʃn] sospetto *m*

sus·pi·cious [sə'spɪʃəs] *adj causing suspicion* sospetto; *feeling suspicion* sospettoso; **be ~ of** sospettare di

sus·tain [sə'steɪn] *v/t* sostenere

sus·tain·able [sə'steɪnəbl] *adj* sostenibile

swab [swɒb] tampone *m*

swag·ger ['swægə(r)] *n* andatura *f* spavalda

swal·low[1] ['swɒləʊ] **1** *v/t liquid, food* inghiottire **2** *v/i* inghiottire

swal·low[2] ['swɒləʊ] *n bird* rondine *f*

swam [swæm] *pret → swim*

swamp [swɒmp] **1** *n* palude *f* **2** *v/t:* **be ~ped with** essere sommerso da

swamp·y ['swɒmpɪ] *adj ground* paludoso

swan [swɒn] cigno *m*

swap [swɒp] *(pret & pp **-ped**)* **1** *v/t:* **~ sth for sth** scambiare qc con qc **2** *v/i* fare scambio

swarm [swɔːm] **1** *n of bees* sciame *m* **2** *v/i:* **the town was ~ing with …** la città brulicava di …

swar·thy ['swɔːðɪ] *adj face, complexion* scuro

swat [swɒt] *v/t (pret & pp **-ted**) insect, fly* schiacciare

sway [sweɪ] **1** *n (influence, power)* influenza *f* **2** *v/i* barcollare

swear [sweə(r)] *(pret swore, pp sworn)* **1** *v/i (use swearword)* imprecare; **~ at s.o.** dire parolacce a qu **2** *v/t (promise)* giurare; LAW, *on oath* giurare

♦ **swear in** *v/t:* **the witness was sworn in** il testimone ha prestato giuramento

'swear·word parolaccia *f*

sweat [swet] **1** *n* sudore *m*; **covered in ~** tutto sudato **2** *v/i* sudare

'sweat band fascia *f* asciugasudore

sweat·er ['swetə(r)] maglione *m*

'sweat·shirt felpa *f*

sweat·y ['swetɪ] *adj hands* sudato; *smell* di sudore

Swede [swiːd] svedese *m/f*

Swe·den ['swiːdn] Svezia *f*

Swe·dish ['swiːdɪʃ] **1** *adj* svedese **2** *n* svedese *m*

sweep [swiːp] **1** *v/t (pret & pp swept) floor, leaves* spazzare **2** *n (long curve)* curva *f*

♦ **sweep up** *v/t mess* spazzare via

sweep·ing ['swiːpɪŋ] *adj changes* radicale; **a ~ statement** una generalizzazione

sweet [swiːt] **1** *adj taste, tea* dolce; F *(kind)* gentile; F *(cute)* carino **2** *n* caramella *f*; *(dessert)* dolce *m*

sweet and 'sour *adj* agrodolce

'sweet·corn mais *m inv*

sweet·en ['swiːtn] *v/t drink, food* zuccherare

sweet·en·er ['swiːtnə(r)] *for drink* dolcificante *m*

'sweet·heart innamorato *m*, -a *f*

swell [swel] **1** *v/i of wound, limb* gonfiarsi **2** *n of the sea* mare *m* lungo

swell·ing ['swelɪŋ] *n* MED gonfiore *m*

swel·ter·ing ['sweltərɪŋ] *adj heat, day* afoso, soffocante

swept [swept] *pret & pp* → **sweep**

swerve [swɜːv] *v/i of driver, car* sterzare (bruscamente)

swift [swɪft] *adj* rapido

swim [swɪm] **1** *v/i* (*pret* **swam**, *pp* **swum**) nuotare; *go ~ming* andare a nuotare; *my head is ~ming* mi gira la testa **2** *n* nuotata *f*; *go for a ~* andare a nuotare

swim·mer ['swɪmə(r)] nuotatore *m*, -trice *f*

swim·ming ['swɪmɪŋ] nuoto *m*

'swim·ming baths *npl* piscina *f* pubblica; 'swim·ming cos·tume costume *m* da bagno; 'swim·ming pool piscina *f*

swin·dle ['swɪndl] **1** *n* truffa *f* **2** *v/t* truffare; *~ s.o. out of sth* estorcere qc a qu (con l'inganno)

swine [swaɪn] F *person* mascalzone *m*

swing [swɪŋ] **1** *n of pendulum etc* oscillazione *f*; *for child* altalena *f*; *a ~ to the left* una svolta verso la sinistra **2** *v/t* (*pret & pp* **swung**) far dondolare; *~ one's hips* ancheggiare **3** *v/i* (*pret & pp* **swung**) dondolare; (*turn*) girare; *of public opinion etc* indirizzarsi

swing-'door porta *f* a vento

Swiss [swɪs] **1** *adj* svizzero **2** *n person* svizzero *m*, -a *f*; *the ~* gli svizzeri

switch [swɪtʃ] **1** *n for light* interruttore *m*; (*change*) cambiamento *m* **2** *v/t* (*change*) cambiare **3** *v/i* (*change*) cambiare; *~ to* passare a

♦ switch off *v/t* spegnere

♦ switch on *v/t* accendere

'switch·board centralino *m*

'switch·o·ver *to new system* passaggio *m*

Swit·zer·land ['swɪtsələnd] Svizzera *f*

swiv·el ['swɪvl] *v/i* (*pret & pp* **-led**,

Am **-ed**) *of chair, monitor* girarsi

swol·len ['swəʊlən] *adj* gonfio

swoop [swuːp] *v/i of bird* scendere in picchiata

♦ swoop down on *v/t prey* scendere in picchiata su

♦ swoop on *v/t of police etc* piombare su

sword [sɔːd] spada *f*

swore [swɔː(r)] *pret* → **swear**

sworn [swɔːn] *pp* → **swear**

swum [swʌm] *pp* → **swim**

swung [swʌŋ] *pret & pp* → **swing**

syc·a·more ['sɪkəmɔː] sicomoro *m*

syl·la·ble ['sɪləbl] sillaba *f*

syl·la·bus ['sɪləbəs] programma *m*

sym·bol ['sɪmbəl] simbolo *m*

sym·bol·ic [sɪm'bɒlɪk] *adj* simbolico

sym·bol·ism ['sɪmbəlɪzm] simbolismo *m*

sym·bol·ist ['sɪmbəlɪst] simbolista *m/f*

sym·bol·ize ['sɪmbəlaɪz] *v/t* simboleggiare

sym·met·ri·c(al) [sɪ'metrɪkl] *adj* simmetrico

sym·me·try ['sɪmətrɪ] simmetria *f*

sym·pa·thet·ic [sɪmpə'θetɪk] *adj* (*showing pity*) compassionevole; (*understanding*) comprensivo; *be ~ towards an idea* simpatizzare per un'idea

♦ sympathize with ['sɪmpəθaɪz] *v/t person, views* capire

sym·pa·thiz·er ['sɪmpəθaɪzə(r)] *n* POL simpatizzante *m/f*

sym·pa·thy ['sɪmpəθɪ] *n* (*pity*) compassione *f*; (*understanding*) comprensione *f*; *don't expect any ~ from me!* non venire a lamentarti da me!

sym·pho·ny ['sɪmfənɪ] sinfonia *f*

'sym·pho·ny or·ches·tra orchestra *f* sinfonica

symp·tom ['sɪmptəm] *also fig* sintomo *m*

symp·to·mat·ic [sɪmptə'mætɪk] *adj*: *be ~ of fig* essere sintomatico di

syn·chro·nize ['sɪŋkrənaɪz] *v/t* sincronizzare

syn·o·nym ['sɪnənɪm] sinonimo *m*

S

sy·non·y·mous [sɪ'nɒnɪməs] *adj* sinonimo; *be ~ with* *fig* essere sinonimo di

syn·tax ['sɪntæks] sintassi *f inv*

syn·the·siz·er ['sɪnθəsaɪzə(r)] MUS sintetizzatore *m*

syn·thet·ic [sɪn'θetɪk] *adj* sintetico

syph·i·lis ['sɪfɪlɪs] sifilide *f*

Syr·i·a ['sɪrɪə] Siria *f*

Syr·i·an ['sɪrɪən] **1** *adj* siriano **2** *n* siriano *m*, -a *f*

sy·ringe [sɪ'rɪndʒ] *n* siringa *f*

syr·up ['sɪrəp] sciroppo *m*

sys·tem ['sɪstəm] (*method*) metodo *m*, sistema *m*; (*orderliness*) ordine *m*; (*computer*) sistema *m*; *the braking ~* il sistema di frenata; *the digestive ~* l'apparato digerente

sys·te·mat·ic [sɪstə'mætɪk] *adj* approach, *person* sistematico

sys·tem·at·i·cal·ly [sɪstə'mætɪklɪ] *adv* sistematicamente

sys·tems **'an·a·lyst** ['sɪstəmz] COMPUT analista *m/f* di sistemi

T

tab [tæb] *n for pulling* linguetta *f*; *in text* tabulazione *f*

ta·ble ['teɪbl] *n* tavolo *m*; *of figures* tabella *f*, tavola *f*; *sit at the ~* sedersi a tavola

'ta·ble·cloth tovaglia *f*; **'ta·ble lamp** lampada *f* da tavolo; **ta·ble of 'con·tents** indice *m*; **'ta·ble·spoon** cucchiaio *m* da tavola

ta·blet ['tæblɪt] MED compressa *f*

'ta·ble ten·nis ping pong *m*

tab·loid ['tæblɔɪd] *n newspaper* quotidiano *m* formato tabloid; *pej* quotidiano *m* scandalistico

ta·boo [tə'buː] *adj* tabù *m inv*

ta·cit ['tæsɪt] *adj* tacito

ta·ci·turn ['tæsɪtɜːn] *adj* taciturno

tack [tæk] **1** *n* (*nail*) chiodino *m* **2** *v/t* (*sew*) imbastire **3** *v/i of yacht* virare di bordo

tack·le ['tækl] **1** *n* (*equipment*) attrezzatura *f*; SP: *in rugby* placcaggio *m*; *in football, hockey* contrasto *m* **2** *v/t in rugby* placcare; *in football, hockey* contrastare; *problem, intruder* affrontare

tack·y ['tækɪ] *adj paint* fresco; *glue* appiccicoso; F (*cheap, poor quality*) di cattivo gusto

tact [tækt] tatto *m*

tact·ful ['tæktfʊl] *adj* pieno di tatto

tact·ful·ly ['tæktflɪ] *adv* con grande tatto

tac·tic·al ['tæktɪkl] *adj* tattico

tac·tics ['tæktɪks] *npl* tattica *f*

tact·less ['tæktlɪs] *adj* privo di tatto

tad·pole ['tædpəʊl] girino *m*

tag [tæg] (*label*) etichetta *f*

♦tag along *v/i* (*pret & pp* **-ged**) accodarsi

tail [teɪl] *n* coda *f*

'tail·back coda *f*; **'tail coat** frac *m inv*; **'tail light** luce *f* posteriore

tai·lor ['teɪlə(r)] sarto *m*, -a *f*

tai·lor-made [teɪlə'meɪd] *adj suit, solution* (fatto) su misura

'tail·wind vento *m* in coda

taint·ed ['teɪntɪd] *adj* contaminato

Tai·wan [taɪ'wɑːn] Taiwan *f*

Tai·wan·ese [taɪwə'niːz] **1** *adj* taiwanese **2** *n* taiwanese *m/f*; *dialect* taiwanese

take [teɪk] *v/t* (*pret* **took**, *pp* **taken**) prendere; (*transport*) portare; (*accompany*) accompagnare; (*accept: money, gift*) accettare; *maths, French, photograph, exam, shower, stroll* fare; (*endure*) sopportare; (*require*) richiedere; *how long does it ~?*

quanto ci vuole?; *I'll ~ it when shopping* lo prendo

♦ **take after** *v/t* aver preso da

♦ **take apart** *v/t* (*dismantle*) smontare; F (*criticize, beat*) fare a pezzi F

♦ **take away** *v/t pain* far sparire; (*remove: object*) togliere; MATH sottrarre; *take sth away from s.o.* togliere qc a qu; *to take away food* da asporto

♦ **take back** *v/t* (*return: object*) riportare; (*receive back*) riprendere; *person* riaccompagnare; (*accept back: husband etc*) rimettersi insieme a; *I take back what I said* ritiro quello che ho detto; *that takes me back* of music, thought etc mi riporta al passato

♦ **take down** *v/t from shelf* tirare giù; *scaffolding* smontare; *trousers* allungare; (*write down*) annotare

♦ **take in** *v/t* (*take indoors*) portare dentro; (*give accommodation*) ospitare; (*make narrower*) stringere; (*deceive*) imbrogliare; (*include*) includere

♦ **take off 1** *v/t clothes, 10%* togliere; (*mimic*) imitare; *can you take a bit off here?* to barber può spuntare un po' qui?; *take a day/week off* prendere un giorno/una settimana di ferie **2** *v/i of aeroplane* decollare; (*become popular*) far presa

♦ **take on** *v/t job* intraprendere; *staff* assumere

♦ **take out** *v/t from bag, pocket* tirare fuori; *stain, appendix, tooth, word* togliere; *money from bank* prelevare; *to dinner etc* portar fuori; *insurance policy* stipulare, fare; *take it out on s.o.* prendersela con qu

♦ **take over 1** *v/t company etc* assumere il controllo di; *tourists take over the town* i turisti invadono la città **2** *v/i of new management etc* assumere il controllo; (*do sth in s.o.'s place*) dare il cambio

♦ **take to** *v/t* (*like*) prendere in simpatia; (*form habit of*) prendere l'abitudine di; *take to drink* darsi all'alcol; *he immediately took to*

the idea la nuova idea gli è piaciuta subito

♦ **take up** *v/t carpet etc* togliere; (*carry up*) portare sopra; (*shorten*) accorciare; *judo, Spanish, new job* incominciare; *offer* accettare; *space, time* occupare; *I'll take you up on your offer* accetto la tua offerta

'**take·away** *meal* piatto *m* da asporto; (*restaurant*) ristorante *m* che prepara piatti da asporto

'**take-home pay** stipendio *m* in busta

tak·en ['teɪkən] *pp* → **take**

'**take·off** decollo *m*; (*impersonation*) imitazione *f*; '**take·o·ver** COM rilevamento *m*; '**take·o·ver bid** offerta *f* pubblica di acquisto, OPA *f*

ta·kings ['teɪkɪŋz] *npl* incassi *mpl*

tal·cum pow·der ['tælkəmpaʊdə(r)] talco *m*

tale [teɪl] storia *f*

tal·ent ['tælənt] talento *m*

tal·ent·ed ['tæləntɪd] *adj* pieno di talento; *he's not very ~* non ha molto talento

'**tal·ent scout** talent scout *m/f inv*

talk [tɔːk] **1** *v/i* parlare; *can I talk to …?* posso parlare con …?; *I'll ~ to him about it* gliene parlo **2** *v/t English etc* parlare; *business, politics* parlare di; *~ s.o. into doing sth* convincere qu a fare qc; *~ s.o. out of doing sth* dissuadere qu dal fare qc **3** *n* (*conversation*) conversazione *f*; (*lecture*) conferenza *f*; *~s* (*negotiations*) trattative *fpl*, negoziati *mpl*; *he's all ~ pej* è tutto chiacchiere

♦ **talk back** *v/i* ribattere

♦ **talk down to** *v/t* trattare dall'alto in basso

♦ **talk over** *v/t* discutere di

talk·a·tive ['tɔːkətɪv] *adj* loquace

talk·ing-to ['tɔːkɪŋtuː] sgridata *f*

'**talk show** talk show *m inv*

tall [tɔːl] *adj* alto

tall or·der bella impresa *f*

tall sto·ry baggianata *f*

tal·ly ['tælɪ] **1** *n* conto *m* **2** *v/i* (*pret & pp -ied*) quadrare

♦ **tally with** *v/t* quadrare con

tame [teɪm] *adj animal* addomesticato; *joke etc* blando

♦**tamper with** ['tæmpə(r)] *v/t* manomettere

tam·pon ['tæmpɒn] tampone *m*

tan [tæn] **1** *n from sun* abbronzatura *f*; *colour* marrone *m* rossiccio **2** *v/i* (*pret & pp* -**ned**) *in sun* abbronzarsi **3** *v/t* (*pret & pp* -**ned**) *leather* conciare

tan·dem ['tændəm] *bike* tandem *m inv*

tan·gent ['tændʒənt] MATH tangente *f*

tan·ge·rine [tændʒə'riːn] tangerino *m*

tan·gi·ble ['tændʒɪbl] *adj* tangibile

tan·gle ['tæŋgl] *n* nodo *m*

♦**tangle up**: *get tangled up of string etc* aggrovigliarsi

tan·go ['tæŋgəʊ] *n* tango *m*

tank [tæŋk] recipiente *m*; MOT serbatoio *m*; MIL carro *m* armato; *for skin diver* bombola *f* (d'ossigeno)

tank·er ['tæŋkə(r)] *ship* nave *f* cisterna; *truck* autocisterna *f*

tanned [tænd] *adj* abbronzato

Tan·noy® ['tænɔɪ] altoparlante *m*

tan·ta·liz·ing ['tæntəlaɪzɪŋ] *adj* allettante; *smell* stuzzicante

tan·ta·mount ['tæntəmaʊnt] *adj*: *be ~ to* essere equivalente a

tan·trum ['tæntrəm] capricci *mpl*; *throw a ~* fare (i) capricci

tap [tæp] **1** *n* rubinetto *m* **2** *v/t* (*pret & pp* -**ped**) (*hit*) dare un colpetto a; *phone* mettere sotto controllo; *he was ~ping his fingers on the table* tamburellava con le dita sul tavolo

♦**tap into** *v/t resources* attingere a

'**tap dance** *n* tip tap *m*

tape [teɪp] **1** *n magnetic* nastro *m* magnetico; *recorded* cassetta *f*; (*sticky*) nastro *m* adesivo; *on ~* registrato **2** *v/t conversation etc* registrare; *~ sth to sth* attaccare qc a qc col nastro adesivo

'**tape deck** registratore *m*; '**tape drive** COMPUT unità *f inv* di backup a nastro; '**tape meas·ure** metro *m* a nastro

tap·er ['teɪpə(r)] *v/i* assottigliarsi

♦**taper off** *v/i of production* calare gradualmente; *of figures* decrescere

'**tape re·cor·der** registratore *m* a cassette

'**tape re·cor·ding** registrazione *f* su cassetta

ta·pes·try ['tæpɪstrɪ] arazzo *m*

'**tape·worm** ['teɪpwɜːm] verme *m* solitario

tar [tɑː(r)] *n* catrame *m*

tar·get ['tɑːgɪt] **1** *n in shooting* bersaglio *m*; *for sales, production* obiettivo *m* **2** *v/t market* rivolgersi a

'**tar·get 'au·di·ence** target *m inv* di pubblico; '**tar·get date** data *f* fissata; '**tar·get 'fig·ure** target *m inv*; '**tar·get group** COM gruppo *m* target; '**tar·get language** lingua *f* d'arrivo; '**tar·get mar·ket** mercato *m* target

tar·iff ['tærɪf] (*price*) tariffa *f*; (*tax*) tassa *f*

tar·mac ['tɑːmæk] *at airport* pista *f*

tar·nish ['tɑːnɪʃ] *v/t metal* ossidare; *reputation* macchiare

tar·pau·lin [tɑː'pɔːlɪn] tela *f* cerata

tart[1] [tɑːt] *n* torta *f*

tart[2] [tɑːt] *n* F (*prostitute*) sgualdrina *f*; *pej: woman* stronza *f*

tar·tan ['tɑːtn] tartan *m*

task [tɑːsk] compito *m*

'**task force** task force *f inv*

tas·sel ['tæsl] nappa *f*

taste [teɪst] **1** *n* gusto *m*; *he has no ~* non ha nessun gusto **2** *v/t food* assaggiare; (*experience: freedom etc*) provare; *I can't ~ anything* non sento nessun sapore **3** *v/i*: *it ~s like …* ha sapore di …; *it ~s very nice* è molto buono

'**taste buds** *npl* papille *fpl* gustative

taste·ful ['teɪstfʊl] *adj* di gusto

taste·ful·ly ['teɪstfəlɪ] *adv* con gusto

taste·less ['teɪstlɪs] *adj food* insapore; *remark, person* privo di gusto

tast·ing ['teɪstɪŋ] *of wine* degustazione *f*

tast·y ['teɪstɪ] *adj* gustoso

tat·tered ['tætəd] *adj clothes, book* malridotto

tat·ters ['tætəz]: *in ~ of clothes* a brandelli; *of reputation, career* a pezzi

tat·too [tə'tuː] *n* tatuaggio *m*

tat·ty ['tætɪ] *adj* F malandato

taught [tɔːt] *pret & pp* → **teach**

taunt [tɔːnt] **1** *n* scherno *m* **2** *v/t* schernire

Taur·us ['tɔːrəs] ASTR Toro *m*

taut [tɔːt] *adj* teso

taw·dry ['tɔːdrɪ] *adj* pacchiano

tax [tæks] **1** *n* tassa *f*; *before / after ~* al lordo / al netto di imposte **2** *v/t* tassare

tax·a·ble 'in·come reddito *m* imponibile

ta·x·a·tion [tæk'seɪʃn] tassazione *f*

'**tax avoid·ance** elusione *f* fiscale; '**tax brack·et** fascia *f* di reddito; '**tax code** codice *m* fiscale; '**tax-de·duct·i·ble** *adj* deducibile dalle imposte; '**tax disc** *for car* bollo *m* (di circolazione); '**tax eva·sion** evasione *f* fiscale; '**tax-free** *adj* esentasse *inv*

tax·i ['tæksɪ] taxi *m inv*

'**tax·i dri·ver** tassista *m/f*

tax·ing ['tæksɪŋ] *adj* estenuante

'**tax in·spect·or** ispettore *m*, -trice *f* fiscale

'**tax·i rank**, **tax·i stand** stazione *f* dei taxi

'**tax·man** fisco *m*; '**tax ·pay·er** contribuente *m/f*; '**tax re·turn** *form* dichiarazione *f* dei redditi; '**tax year** anno *m* fiscale

TB [tiː'biː] *abbr* (= **tuberculosis**) tbc *f* (= tubercolosi *f*)

tea [tiː] *drink* tè *m inv*; *meal* cena *f*

'**tea·bag** ['tiːbæg] bustina *f* di tè

teach [tiːtʃ] (*pret & pp* **taught**) **1** *v/t subject* insegnare; *person* insegnare a; *~ s.o. to do sth* insegnare a qu a fare qc **2** *v/i* insegnare

tea·cher ['tiːtʃə(r)] insegnante *m/f*

tea·cher 'train·ing tirocinio *m* per insegnanti

tea·ching ['tiːtʃɪŋ] *profession* insegnamento *m*

'**tea·ching aid** sussidio *m* didattico

'**tea cloth** strofinaccio *m* da cucina;

'**tea·cup** tazza *f* da tè; '**tea drink·er** bevitore *m*, -trice *f* di tè

teak [tiːk] tek *m*

'**tea leaf** foglia *f* di tè

team [tiːm] *in sport* squadra *f*; *at work* équipe *f inv*

'**team mate** compagno *m*, -a *f* di squadra; **team 'spirit** spirito *m* d'équipe; '**team·work** lavoro *m* d'équipe

tea·pot ['tiːpɒt] teiera *f*

tear¹ [teə(r)] **1** *n in cloth etc* strappo *m* **2** *v/t* (*pret* **tore**, *pp* **torn**) *paper, cloth* strappare; *be torn between two alternatives* essere combattuto tra due alternative **3** *v/i* (*pret* **tore**, *pp* **torn**) (*run fast, drive fast*) sfrecciare

♦ **tear down** *v/t poster* strappare; *building* buttar giù

♦ **tear out** *v/t* strappare

♦ **tear up** *v/t paper* distruggere; *agreement* rompere

tear² [tɪə(r)] *n in eye* lacrima *f*; *burst into ~s* scoppiare a piangere; *be in ~s* essere in lacrime

tear·drop ['tɪədrɒp] lacrima *f*

tear·ful ['tɪəful] *adj person* in lacrime; *look, voice* piangente

'**tear gas** gas *m inv* lacrimogeno

'**tea·room** sala *f* da tè

tease [tiːz] *v/t person* prendere in giro; *animal* stuzzicare

'**tea serv·ice**, '**tea set** servizio *m* da tè; '**tea·spoon** cucchiaino *m* da caffè; '**tea strain·er** colino *m* da tè

teat [tiːt] capezzolo *m*; *made of rubber* tettarella *f*

'**tea to·wel** strofinaccio *m* da cucina

tech·ni·cal ['teknɪkl] *adj* tecnico

tech·ni·cal·i·ty [teknɪ'kælətɪ] (*technical nature*) tecnicismo *m*; LAW vizio *m* di procedura; *that's just a ~* è solo un dettaglio

tech·ni·cal·ly ['teknɪklɪ] *adv* tecnicamente

tech·ni·cian [tek'nɪʃn] tecnico *m*

tech·nique [tek'niːk] tecnica *f*

tech·no·log·i·cal [teknə'lɒdʒɪkl] *adj* tecnologico

T

tech·no·lo·gy [tek'nɒlədʒɪ] tecnologia f

tech·no·phob·i·a [teknə'fəʊbɪə] tecnofobia f

ted·dy bear ['tedɪbeə(r)] orsacchiotto m

te·di·ous ['tiːdɪəs] adj noioso

tee [tiː] n in golf tee m inv

teem [tiːm] v/i pullulare; **be ~ing with rain** piovere a dirotto; **be ~ing with tourists/ants** pullulare di turisti/formiche

teen·age ['tiːneɪdʒ] adj **problems** degli adolescenti; **gangs** di ragazzi; **~boy/girl** ragazzo m/ragazza f adolescente; **~ fashions** moda giovane

teen·ag·er ['tiːneɪdʒə(r)] adolescente m/f

teens [tiːnz] npl adolescenza f; **be in one's ~** essere adolescente; **reach one's ~** entrare nell'adolescenza

tee·ny ['tiːnɪ] adj F piccolissimo

teeth [tiːθ] pl → **tooth**

teethe [tiːð] v/i mettere i denti

'teething problems npl difficoltà fpl iniziali

tee·to·tal [tiː'təʊtl] adj **person** astemio; **party** senza alcolici

tee·to·tal·ler [tiː'təʊtlə(r)] astemio m, -a f

tel·e·com·mu·ni·ca·tions [telɪkəmjuːnɪ'keɪʃnz] telecomunicazioni fpl

tel·e·gram ['telɪɡræm] telegramma m

tel·e·graph pole ['telɪɡrɑːfpəʊl] palo m del telegrafo

tel·e·path·ic [telɪ'pæθɪk] adj telepatico; **you must be ~!** devi avere poteri telepatici!

te·lep·a·thy [tɪ'lepəθɪ] telepatia f

tel·e·phone ['telɪfəʊn] **1** n telefono m; **be on the ~** be speaking essere al telefono; possess a phone avere il telefono **2** v/t person telefonare a **3** v/i telefonare

'tel·e·phone bill bolletta f del telefono; **'tel·e·phone book** guida f telefonica; **'tel·e·phone booth** cabina f telefonica; **'tel·e·phone box** cabina f telefonica; **'tel·e·phone call** telefonata f; **'tel·e·phone con·ver·**

sa·tion conversazione f telefonica; **'tel·e·phone di·rec·to·ry** elenco m telefonico; **'tel·e·phone exchange** centralino m telefonico; **'tel·e·phone mes·sage** messaggio m telefonico; **'tel·e·phone num·ber** numero m telefonico

tel·e·pho·to lens [telɪfəʊtəʊ'lenz] teleobiettivo m

tel·e·sales ['telɪseɪlz] vendita f telefonica

tel·e·scope ['telɪskəʊp] telescopio m

tel·e·scop·ic lens [telɪskɒpɪk'lenz] lente f telescopica

tel·e·thon ['telɪθɒn] telethon m inv

tel·e·vise ['telɪvaɪz] v/t trasmettere in televisione

tel·e·vi·sion ['telɪvɪʒn] televisione f; **set** televisione f, televisore m; **on ~** alla televisione; **watch ~** guardare la televisione

'tel·e·vi·sion au·di·ence pubblico m televisivo; **'tel·e·vi·sion li·cence** canone m (televisivo); **'tel·e·vision pro·gramme** programma m televisivo; **'tel·e·vi·sion set** televisore m; **'tel·e·vi·sion stu·di·o** studio m televisivo

tell [tel] (pret & pp **told**) **1** v/t dire; story raccontare; **~ s.o. sth** dire qc a qu; **don't ~ Mum** non dirlo alla mamma; **~ s.o. to do sth** dire a qu di fare qc; **I've been told that ...** mi hanno detto che ...; **it's hard to ~** è difficile a dirsi; **you never can ~** non si può mai dire; **~ X from Y** distinguere X da Y; **I can't ~ the difference between ...** non vedo nessuna differenza tra ...; **you're ~ing me!** F a chi lo dici! **2** v/i (have effect) farsi sentire; **the heat is ~ing on him** il caldo si fa sentire su di lui; **time will ~** il tempo lo dirà

♦ **tell off** v/t rimproverare

tell·er ['telə(r)] in bank cassiere m, -a f

tell·ing ['telɪŋ] adj argument efficace; **a ~ sign** un segnale chiaro

tell·ing 'off rimprovero m; **give s.o. a ~** rimproverare qu

tell·tale ['telteɪl] **1** *adj* signs rivelatore **2** *n* spione *m*, spiona *f*

tel·ly ['telɪ] F tele *f*

temp [temp] **1** *n* employee impiegato *m*, -a interinale **2** *v/i* fare lavori interinali

tem·per ['tempə(r)] (*bad ~*): *have a **terrible** ~* essere irascibile; *be in a* ~ essere arrabbiato; *keep one's* ~ mantenere la calma; *lose one's* ~ perdere le staffe

tem·pe·ra·ment ['temprəmənt] temperamento *m*

tem·pe·ra·men·tal [temprə'mentl] *adj* (*moody*) lunatico; *machine* imprevedibile

tem·pe·rate ['tempərət] *adj* temperato

tem·pe·ra·ture ['temprətʃə(r)] temperatura *f*; (*fever*) febbre *f*; *have a* ~ avere la febbre; *take s.o.'s* ~ prendere la temperatura a qu

tem·ple¹ ['templ] REL tempio *m*

tem·ple² ['templ] ANAT tempia *f*

tem·po ['tempəʊ] ritmo *m*; MUS tempo *m*

tem·po·rar·i·ly [tempə'reərɪlɪ] *adv* temporaneamente

tem·po·ra·ry ['tempərərɪ] *adj* temporaneo, provvisorio

tempt [tempt] *v/t* tentare

temp·ta·tion [temp'teɪʃn] tentazione *f*

tempt·ing ['temptɪŋ] *adj* allettante; *meal* appetitoso

ten [ten] dieci

te·na·cious [tɪ'neɪʃəs] *adj* tenace

te·nac·i·ty [tɪ'næsɪtɪ] tenacità *f*

ten·ant ['tenənt] inquilino *m*, -a *f*, locatario *m*, -a *f fml*; *in office* affittuario *m*, -a *f*

tend¹ [tend] *v/t* (*look after*) prendersi cura di

tend² [tend]: ~ *to do sth* tendere a fare qc, avere la tendenza a fare qc; ~ *towards sth* avere una tendenza verso qc

ten·den·cy ['tendənsɪ] tendenza *f*

ten·der¹ ['tendə(r)] *adj* (*sore*) sensibile; (*affectionate*) tenero; *steak* tenero

ten·der² ['tendə(r)] *n* COM offerta *f* ufficiale

ten·der·ness ['tendənɪs] (*soreness*) sensibilità *f*; *of kiss, steak* tenerezza *f*

ten·don ['tendən] tendine *m*

ten·nis ['tenɪs] tennis *m*

'ten·nis ball palla *f* da tennis; **'tennis court** campo *m* da tennis; **'tennis pla·yer** tennista *m/f*; **'ten·nis rack·et** racchetta *f* da tennis

ten·or ['tenə(r)] MUS tenore *m*

tense¹ [tens] *n* GRAM tempo *m*

tense² [tens] *adj* voice, person teso; moment, atmosphere carico di tensione

♦ **tense up** *v/i of muscles* contrarre; *of person* irrigidirsi

ten·sion ['tenʃn] tensione *f*

tent [tent] tenda *f*

ten·ta·cle ['tentəkl] tentacolo *m*

ten·ta·tive ['tentətɪv] *adj* esitante

ten·ter·hooks ['tentəhʊks]: *be on* ~ essere sulle spine

tenth [tenθ] *n & adj* decimo, -a

tep·id ['tepɪd] *adj* water, reaction tiepido

term [tɜːm] periodo *m*; *of office* durata *f* in carica; EDU: *of three months* trimestre *m*; *of two months* bimestre *m*; (*condition, word*) termine *m*; *be on good/bad ~s with s.o.* essere in buoni/cattivi rapporti con qu; *in the long/short* ~ a lungo/breve termine; *come to ~s with sth* venire a patti con qc

ter·mi·nal ['tɜːmɪnl] **1** *n at airport, for containers*, COMPUT terminale *m*; *for buses* capolinea *m inv*; ELEC morsetto *m* **2** *adj illness* in fase terminale

ter·mi·nal·ly ['tɜːmɪnəlɪ] *adv*: ~ *ill* malato (in fase) terminale

ter·mi·nate ['tɜːmɪneɪt] **1** *v/t* contract, pregnancy interrompere **2** *v/i* terminare

ter·mi·na·tion [tɜːmɪ'neɪʃn] *of contract, pregnancy* interruzione *f*

ter·mi·nol·o·gy [tɜːmɪ'nɒlədʒɪ] terminologia *f*

ter·mi·nus ['tɜːmɪnəs] *for buses* capolinea *m inv; for trains* stazione *f* di testa

ter·race ['terəs] *of houses* fila *f* di case a schiera; *on hillside, at hotel* terrazza *f*

ter·raced house [terəst'haʊs] casa *f* a schiera

ter·ra cot·ta [terə'kɒtə] *adj* di terracotta

ter·rain [tə'reɪn] terreno *m*

ter·res·tri·al [tə'restrɪəl] **1** *n* terrestre *m/f* **2** *adj television* di terra

ter·ri·ble ['terəbl] *adj* terribile

ter·ri·bly ['terəblɪ] *adv play* malissimo; (*very*) molto

ter·rif·ic [tə'rɪfɪk] *adj* eccezionale; **~!** bene!

ter·rif·i·cal·ly [tə'rɪfɪklɪ] *adv* (*very*) eccezionalmente

ter·ri·fy ['terɪfaɪ] *v/t* (*pret & pp* **-ied**) terrificare; **be terrified** essere terrificato

ter·ri·fy·ing ['terɪfaɪɪŋ] *adj* terrificante

ter·ri·to·ri·al [terɪ'tɔːrɪəl] *adj* territoriale

ter·ri·to·ri·al 'wa·ters *npl* acque *fpl* territoriali

ter·ri·to·ry ['terɪtərɪ] *also fig* territorio *m*

ter·ror ['terə(r)] terrore *m*

ter·ror·is·m ['terərɪzm] terrorismo *m*

ter·ror·ist ['terərɪst] terrorista *m/f*

'ter·ror·ist at·tack attentato *m* terroristico

'ter·ror·ist or·gan·i·za·tion organizzazione *f* terroristica

ter·ror·ize ['terəraɪz] *v/t* terrorizzare

terse [tɜːs] *adj* brusco

test [test] **1** *n* prova *f*, test *m inv; for driving, medical* esame *m;* **blood ~** analisi *f inv* del sangue **2** *v/t soup, bathwater* provare; *machine, theory* testare; *person, friendship* mettere alla prova; **~ the water** *fig* tastare il terreno

tes·ta·ment ['testəmənt] testimonianza *f* (**to** di); **Old / New Testament** REL Vecchio / Nuovo Testamento

'test-drive: go for a ~ fare un giro di prova

tes·ti·cle ['testɪkl] testicolo *m*

tes·ti·fy ['testɪfaɪ] *v/i* (*pret & pp* **-ied**) LAW testimoniare

tes·ti·mo·ni·al [testɪ'məʊnɪəl] referenze *fpl* scritte

tes·ti·mo·ny ['testɪmənɪ] LAW testimonianza *f*

'test tube provetta *f*

'test tube ba·by bambino *m*, -a *f* (concepito, -a) in provetta

tes·ty ['testɪ] *adj* suscettibile

te·ta·nus ['tetənəs] tetano *m*

teth·er ['teðə(r)] **1** *v/t horse* legare **2** *n:* **be at the end of one's ~** essere allo stremo

text [tekst] testo *m*

'text·book libro *m* di testo

tex·tile ['tekstaɪl] tessuto *m*

tex·ture ['tekstʃə(r)] consistenza *f*

Thai [taɪ] **1** *adj* tailandese **2** *n person* tailandese *m/f; language* tailandese *m*

Thai·land ['taɪlænd] Tailandia *f*

than [ðæn] *adv:* **older / faster ~ me** più vecchio / veloce di me; **she's more French ~ Italian** è più francese che italiana

thank [θæŋk] *v/t* ringraziare; **~ you** grazie; **no ~ you** no, grazie

thank·ful ['θæŋkfʊl] *adj* riconoscente

thank·ful·ly ['θæŋkfʊlɪ] *adv* con riconoscenza; (*luckily*) fortunatamente

thank·less ['θæŋklɪs] *adj* ingrato

thanks [θæŋks] *npl* ringraziamenti *mpl;* **~!** grazie!; **~ to** grazie a

that [ðæt] **1** *adj* quel; *with masculine nouns before s+consonant, gn, ps and z* quello; **~ one** quello **2** *pron* quello *m*, -a *f;* **what is ~?** cos'è?; **who is ~?** chi è?; **~'s mine** è mio; **~'s tea** quello è tè; **~'s very kind** è molto gentile **3** *relative pron* che; **the person / car ~ you saw** la persona / macchina che hai visto; **the day ~ he was born** il giorno in cui è nato **4** *adv* (*so*) così; **~ big / expensive** così grande / caro **5** *conj* che; **I think ~ ...** credo che ...

thaw [θɔː] *v/i of snow* sciogliersi; *of*

frozen food scongelare

the [ðə] il *m*, la *f*; i *mpl*, le *fpl*; *with masculine nouns before s+consonant, gn, ps and z* lo *m*, gli *mpl*; *before vowel* l' *m/f*, gli *mpl*; **~ to ~ bathroom** al bagno; **~ sooner ~ better** prima è, meglio è

the·a·ter *Am* → theatre

the·a·tre ['θɪətə(r)] teatro *m*

'the·a·tre crit·ic critico *m* teatrale

the·a·tre·go·er ['θɪətəgəʊə(r)] frequentatore *m*, -trice *f* di teatro

the·at·ri·cal [θɪ'ætrɪkl] *also fig* teatrale

theft [θeft] furto *m*

their [ðeə(r)] *adj* il loro *m*, la loro *f*; i loro *mpl*, le loro *fpl*; *(his or her)* il suo *m*, la sua *f*, i suoi *mpl*, le sue *fpl*; **~ daughter / son** la loro figlia / il loro figlio

theirs [ðeəz] *pron* il loro *m*, la loro *f*; i loro *mpl*, le loro *fpl*; **it was an idea of ~** è stata una loro idea

them [ðem] *pron direct object* li *m*, le *f*; *referring to things* essi *m*, esse *f*; *indirect object* loro, gli; *after preposition* loro; *referring to things* essi *m*, esse *f*; *(him or her)* lo *m*, la *f*; **I know ~** li / le conosco; **I sold it to ~** gliel'ho venduto, l'ho venduto a loro

theme [θi:m] tema *m*

'theme park parco *m* a tema

'theme song canzone *f* principale

them·selves [ðem'selvz] *pron reflexive* si; *emphatic* loro stessi *mpl*, loro stesse *fpl*; *after prep* se stessi / se stesse; **they ~** loro stessi / stesse; **they enjoyed ~** si sono divertiti; **they only think about ~** pensano solo a se stessi / stesse; **by ~** *(alone)* da soli *mpl*, da sole *fpl*

then [ðen] *adv* *(at that time)* allora; *(after that)* poi; *(deducing)* allora; **by ~** allora

the·o·lo·gian [θɪə'ləʊdʒɪən] teologo *m*, -a *f*

the·ol·o·gy [θɪ'ɒlədʒɪ] teologia *f*

the·o·ret·i·cal [θɪə'retɪkl] *adj* teorico

the·o·ret·i·cal·ly [θɪə'retɪklɪ] *adv* teoricamente

the·o·ry ['θɪərɪ] teoria *f*; **in ~** in teoria

ther·a·peu·tic [θerə'pju:tɪk] *adj* terapeutico

ther·a·pist ['θerəpɪst] terapista *m/f*, terapeuta *m/f*

ther·a·py ['θerəpɪ] terapia *f*

there [ðeə(r)] *adv* lì, là; **over ~** là; **down ~** laggiù; **~ is ...** c'è ...; **~ are ...** ci sono; **is ~ ...?** c'è ...?; **are ~ ...?** ci sono ...?; **isn't ~?** non c'è ...?; **aren't ~?** non ci sono ...?; **~ you are** *giving sth* ecco qui; *finding sth* ecco; *completing sth* ecco fatto; **~ and back** andata e ritorno; **~ he is!** eccolo!; **~, ~!** *comforting* su, dai!

there·a·bouts [ðeərə'baʊts] *adv* giù di lì

there·fore [ðeəfɔː(r)] *adv* quindi, pertanto

ther·mom·e·ter [θə'mɒmɪtə(r)] termometro *m*

ther·mos flask ['θɜːməsflɑːsk] termos *m inv*

ther·mo·stat ['θɜːməstæt] termostato *m*

these [ðiːz] **1** *adj* questi **2** *pron* questi *m*, -e *f*

the·sis ['θiːsɪs] *(pl theses* ['θiːsiːz]*)* tesi *f inv*

they [ðeɪ] *pron* ◊ loro; **~'re going to the theatre** vanno a teatro; **~'re going to the theatre, we're not** loro vanno a teatro, noi no; **there ~ are** eccoli *mpl*, eccole *fpl* ◊ **if anyone looks at this, ~ will see that ...** se qualcuno ti guarda, vedrà che ...; **~ say that ...** si dice che ...; **~ are going to change the law** cambieranno la legge

thick [θɪk] *adj* spesso; *hair* folto; *fog, forest* fitto; *liquid* denso; F *(stupid)* ottuso

thick·en ['θɪkən] *v/t sauce* ispessire

thick·set ['θɪkset] *adj* tarchiato

thick·skinned ['θɪkskɪnd] *adj fig* insensibile

thief [θiːf] *(pl thieves* [θiːvz]*)* ladro *m*, -a *f*

thigh [θaɪ] coscia *f*

thim·ble ['θɪmbl] ditale *m*

thin [θɪn] *adj* sottile; *person* magro;

thing

hair rado; *liquid* fluido

thing [θɪŋ] cosa *f*; **~s** (*belongings*) cose *fpl*; **how are ~s?** come vanno le cose?; **it's a good ~ you told me** è un bene che tu me l'abbia detto; **what a ~ to do/say!** che razza di cosa da fare/dire!

thing·um·a·jig [ˈθɪŋʌmədʒɪg] F coso *m*, cosa *f* F

think [θɪŋk] *v/i* (*pret & pp* **thought**) pensare; **I ~ so** penso *o* credo di sì; **I don't ~ so** non credo; **I ~ so too** lo penso anch'io; **what do you ~?** cosa ne pensi?; **what do you ~ of it?** cosa ne pensi?; **I can't ~ of anything more** non mi viene in mente niente'altro; **~ hard!** pensaci bene!; **I'm ~ing about emigrating** sto pensando di emigrare

♦ **think over** *v/t* riflettere su

♦ **think through** *v/t* analizzare a fondo

♦ **think up** *v/t plan* escogitare

'think tank comitato *m* di esperti

thin-skinned [θɪnˈskɪnd] *adj fig* sensibile

third [θɜːd] *n & adj* terzo, -a

third·ly [ˈθɜːdlɪ] *adv* in terzo luogo

'third-par·ty terzi *mpl*; **third-par·ty in'sur·ance** assicurazione *f* sulla responsabilità civile; **third 'per·son** GRAM terza persona *f*; **'third-rate** *adj* scadente; **Third 'World** Terzo Mondo *m*

thirst [θɜːst] sete *f*

thirsty [ˈθɜːstɪ] *adj* assetato; **be ~** avere sete

thir·teen [θɜːˈtiːn] tredici

thir·teenth [θɜːˈtiːnθ] *n & adj* tredicesimo, -a

thir·ti·eth [ˈθɜːtɪɪθ] *n & adj* trentesimo, -a

thir·ty [ˈθɜːtɪ] trenta

this [ðɪs] **1** *adj* questo; **~ one** questo (qui) **2** *pron* questo *m*, -a *f*; **~ is easy** è facile; **~ is ...** *introducing s.o.* questo/questa è ...; TELEC sono ...; **3** *adv*: **~ big/high** grande/alto così

thorn [θɔːn] spina *f*

thorn·y [ˈθɔːnɪ] *adj also fig* spinoso

thor·ough [ˈθʌrə] *adj search, knowledge* approfondito; *person* scrupoloso

thor·ough·bred [ˈθʌrəbred] *horse* purosangue *inv*

thor·ough·ly [ˈθʌrəlɪ] *adv clean, search for* accuratamente; *know, understand* perfettamente; *agree, spoil* completamente; **~ stupid** stupidissimo

those [ðəʊz] **1** *adj* quelli; *with masculine nouns before s+consonant, gn, ps and z* quegli **2** *pron* quelli *m*, -e *f*; *with masculine nouns before s+consonant, gn, ps and z* quegli

though [ðəʊ] **1** *conj* (*although*) benché; **~ it might fail** benché possa non riuscire; **say it as ~ you meant it** dillo come se lo sentissi davvero; **it looks as ~ ...** sembra che ... **2** *adv* però; **it's not finished ~** non è finito, però

thought [θɔːt] **1** *n* pensiero *m* **2** *pret & pp* → **think**

thought·ful [ˈθɔːtful] *adj* pensieroso; *reply* meditato; (*considerate*) gentile

thought·ful·ly [ˈθɔːtflɪ] *adv* (*pensively*) con aria pensierosa; (*considerately*) gentilmente

thought·less [ˈθɔːtlɪs] *adj* sconsiderato

thought·less·ly [ˈθɔːtlɪslɪ] *adv* in modo sconsiderato

thou·sand [ˈθaʊznd] mille; **a ~ pounds** mille sterline; **~s of** migliaia di

thou·sandth [ˈθaʊzndθ] *n & adj* millesimo, -a

thrash [θræʃ] *v/t* picchiare; SP battere

♦ **thrash about** *v/i with arms etc* sferrare colpi in aria

♦ **thrash out** *v/t solution* mettere a punto

thrash·ing [ˈθræʃɪŋ] botte *fpl*; SP batosta *f*

thread [θred] **1** *n* filo *m*; *of screw* filettatura *f* **2** *v/t needle* infilare il filo in; *beads* infilare

thread·bare [ˈθredbeə(r)] *adj* liso

threat [θret] minaccia *f*

threat·en [ˈθretn] *v/t* minacciare

threat·en·ing [ˈθretnɪŋ] *adj* minaccioso; **~ letter** lettera *f* minatoria

three [θriː] tre

three 'quart·ers tre quarti *mpl*

thresh [θreʃ] *v/t corn* trebbiare

thresh·old ['θreʃhəʊld] *of house, new era* soglia *f;* **on the ~ of** sulla soglia di

threw [θruː] *pret →* **throw**

thrift [θrɪft] parsimonia *f*

thrift·y ['θrɪftɪ] *adj* parsimonioso

thrill [θrɪl] **1** *n* emozione *f; physical feeling* brivido *m* **2** *v/t:* **be ~ed** essere emozionato

thrill·er ['θrɪlə(r)] giallo *m*

thrill·ing ['θrɪlɪŋ] *adj* emozionante

thrive [θraɪv] *v/i of plant* crescere rigoglioso; *of business, economy* prosperare

throat [θrəʊt] gola *f;* **have a sore ~** avere mal di gola

throat loz·enge pastiglia *f* per la gola

throb [θrɒb] *v/i* (*pret & pp* **-bed**) pulsare; *of heart* battere; *of music* rimbombare

throb·bing ['θrɒbɪŋ] pulsazione *f; of heart* battito *m; of music* rimbombo *m*

throne [θrəʊn] trono *m*

throng [θrɒŋ] *n* calca *f*

throt·tle ['θrɒtl] **1** *n on motorbike* manetta *f* di accelerazione; *on boat* leva *f* di accelerazione **2** *v/t* (*strangle*) strozzare

♦ **throttle back** *v/i* decelerare

through [θruː] **1** *prep* (*across*) attraverso; (*during*) durante; (*by means of*) tramite; **go ~ the city** attraversare la città; **~ the winter / summer** per tutto l'inverno / tutta l'estate; **arranged ~ him** organizzato tramite lui **2** *adv:* **wet ~** completamente bagnato; **watch a film ~** guardare un film fino alla fine **3** *adj:* **be ~** *of couple* essersi lasciati; *have arrived: of news etc* essere arrivato; **you're ~** TELEC è in linea; **I'm ~ with ...** (*finished with*) ho finito con ...; **I'm ~ with him** ho chiuso con lui

'through flight volo *m* diretto

through·out [θruːˈaʊt] **1** *prep:* **~ the**

night per tutta la notte **2** *adv* (*in all parts*) completamente

'through train treno *m* diretto

throw [θrəʊ] **1** *v/t* (*pret* **threw**, *pp* **thrown**) lanciare; *into bin etc* gettare; *of horse* disarcionare; (*disconcert*) sconcertare; *party* dare **2** *n* lancio *m*

♦ **throw away** *v/t* buttare via, gettare

♦ **throw off** *v/t jacket etc* togliersi in fretta; *cold etc* liberarsi di

♦ **throw on** *v/t clothes* mettersi in fretta

♦ **throw out** *v/t old things* buttare via; *from bar, house etc* buttare fuori; *plan* scartare

♦ **throw up 1** *v/t ball* lanciare; **throw up one's hands** alzare le mani al cielo **2** *v/i* (*vomit*) vomitare

'throw-a·way *adj remark* buttato lì; (*disposable*) usa e getta *inv*

'throw-in SP rimessa *f*

thrown [θrəʊn] *pp →* **throw**

thrush [θrʌʃ] *bird* tordo *m*

thrust [θrʌst] *v/t* (*pret & pp* **thrust**) (*push hard*) spingere; *knife* conficcare; **~ sth into s.o.'s hands** ficcare qc in mano a qu; **~ one's way through the crowd** farsi largo tra la folla

thud [θʌd] *n* tonfo *m*

thug [θʌɡ] *hooligan* teppista *m; tough guy* bullo *m*

thumb [θʌm] **1** *n* pollice *m* **2** *v/t:* **~ a lift** fare l'autostop

thump [θʌmp] **1** *n blow* pugno *m; noise* colpo *m* **2** *v/t person* dare un pugno a; **~ one's fist on the table** dare un pugno sul tavolo **3** *v/i of heart* palpitare; **~ on the door** battere alla porta

thun·der ['θʌndə(r)] *n* tuono *m*

thun·der·ous ['θʌndərəs] *adj applause* fragoroso

thun·der·storm ['θʌndəstɔːm] temporale *m*

'thun·der·struck *adj* allibito

thun·der·y ['θʌndərɪ] *adj weather* temporalesco

Thurs·day ['θɜːzdeɪ] giovedì *m inv*

thus

608

thus [ðʌs] *adv* (*in this way*) così

thwart [θwɔːt] *v/t person, plans* ostacolare

thyme [taɪm] timo *m*

thy·roid gland ['θaɪrɔɪdglænd] tiroide *f*

Ti·ber ['taɪbə(r)] Tevere *m*

tick [tɪk] **1** *n of clock* ticchettio *m; in text* segno *m* **2** *v/i of clock* ticchettare **3** *v/t with a ~* segnare
♦ **tick off** *v/t* rimproverare; *item in a list* segnare

tick·et ['tɪkɪt] biglietto *m; in cloakroom* scontrino *m*

'ti·cket col·lec·tor bigliettaio *m*, -a *f*;
'ti·cket in·spec·tor controllore *m*;
'ti·cket ma·chine distributore *m* di biglietti; **'ti·cket of·fice** biglietteria *f*

tick·ing ['tɪkɪŋ] *noise* ticchettio *m*

tick·le ['tɪkl] **1** *v/t person* fare il solletico a **2** *v/t of material* dare prurito; *of person* fare il solletico

tickl·ish ['tɪklɪʃ] *adj*: **be ~** soffrire il solletico

ti·dal wave ['taɪdlweɪv] onda *f* di marea

tide [taɪd] marea *f*; **high ~** alta marea; **low ~** bassa marea; **the ~ is in/out** c'è l'alta/la bassa marea
♦ **tide over** *v/t* togliere d'impiccio

ti·di·ness ['taɪdɪnɪs] ordine *m*

ti·dy ['taɪdɪ] *adj* ordinato
♦ **tidy away** *v/t* (*pret & pp* **-ied**) mettere a posto
♦ **tidy up 1** *v/t room, shelves* mettere in ordine; **tidy o.s. up** darsi una sistemata **2** *v/i* mettere in ordine

tie [taɪ] **1** *n* (*necktie*) cravatta *f*; (SP: *even result*) pareggio *m*; **he doesn't have any ~s** non ha legami **2** *v/t knot, hands* legare; **~ a knot** fare un nodo; **~ two ropes together** annodare due corde **3** *v/i* SP pareggiare
♦ **tie down** *v/t with rope* legare; (*restrict*) vincolare
♦ **tie up** *v/t person, laces, hair* legare; *boat* ormeggiare; **I'm tied up tomorrow** sono impegnato domani

tier [tɪə(r)] *of hierarchy* livello *m; in stadium* anello *m*

ti·ger ['taɪgə(r)] tigre *f*

tight [taɪt] **1** *adj clothes* stretto; *security* rigido; *rope* teso; *hard to move* bloccato; *not leaving much time* giusto; *schedule* serrato; F (*drunk*) sbronzo F **2** *adv*: **hold s.o./sth ~** tenere qu/qc stretto; **shut sth ~** chiudere bene qc

tight·en ['taɪtn] *v/t screw* serrare; *belt* stringere; *rope* tendere; *control, security* intensificare
♦ **tighten up** *v/i in discipline, security* intensificare il controllo

tight-fist·ed [taɪt'fɪstɪd] *adj* taccagno

tight·ly ['taɪtlɪ] *adv* → **tight** *adv*

tight·rope ['taɪtrəʊp] fune *f* (per funamboli)

tights [taɪts] *npl* collant *mpl*

tile [taɪl] *on floor* mattonella *f; on wall* piastrella *f; on roof* tegola *f*

till[1] [tɪl] *prep & conj* → **until**

till[2] [tɪl] *n* (*cash register*) cassa *f*

till[3] [tɪl] *v/t soil* arare

tilt [tɪlt] **1** *v/t* inclinare **2** *v/i* inclinarsi

tim·ber ['tɪmbə(r)] legname *m*

time [taɪm] tempo *m;* (*occasion*) volta *f*; **~ is up** il tempo è scaduto; **for the ~ being** al momento; **have a good ~** divertirsi; **have a good ~!** divertiti!; **what's the ~?, what ~ is it?** che ora è?, che ore sono?; **by the ~ you finish** quando avrai finito; **the first ~** la prima volta; **four ~s** quattro volte; **and again** ripetutamente; **all the ~** per tutto il tempo; **I've been here for some ~** sono qui da un po'; **take your ~** fai con calma; **for a ~** per un po' (di tempo); **at any ~** in qualsiasi momento; (**and** about **~!** era ora!; **two/three at a ~** due/tre alla volta; **at the same ~** *speak, reply etc* contemporaneamente; (*however*) nel contempo; **in ~** in tempo; (*eventually*) col tempo; **on ~** in orario; **in no ~** in un attimo

'time bomb bomba *f* a orologeria; **'time clock** *in factory* bollatrice *f;*

toadstool

'time-con·sum·ing *adj* lungo; 'time dif·fer·ence fuso *m* orario; 'time-lag scarto *m* di tempo; 'time lim·it limite *m* temporale

time·ly ['taɪmlɪ] *adj* tempestivo

tim·er ['taɪmə(r)] cronometro *m*; *person* cronometrista *m/f*; *on oven* timer *m inv*

'time-sav·ing *n* risparmio *m* di tempo; 'time-scale *of project* cronologia *f*; 'time share *Br* (*house, apartment*) multiproprietà *f inv*; 'time switch interruttore *m* a tempo; 'time·ta·ble orario *m*; 'time-warp trasposizione *f* temporale; 'time zone zona *f* di fuso orario

tim·id ['tɪmɪd] *adj* timido

tim·id·ly ['tɪmɪdlɪ] *adv* timidamente

tim·ing ['taɪmɪŋ] (*choosing a time*) tempismo *m*; *that's good ~!* che tempismo!

tin [tɪn] *metal* stagno *m*; *container* barattolo *m*

tin·foil ['tɪnfɔɪl] carta *f* stagnola

tinge [tɪndʒ] *n of colour, sadness* sfumatura *f*

tin·gle ['tɪŋgl] *v/i* pizzicare
♦ tinker with ['tɪŋkə(r)] *v/t* armeggiare con

tin·kle ['tɪŋkl] *n of bell* tintinnio *m*

tinned [tɪnd] *adj* in scatola

'tin o·pen·er apriscatole *m inv*

tin·sel ['tɪnsl] fili *mpl* d'argento

tint [tɪnt] **1** *n of colour* sfumatura *f*; *in hair* riflessante *m* **2** *v/t hair* fare dei riflessi

tint·ed ['tɪntɪd] *glasses* fumé *inv*

ti·ny ['taɪnɪ] *adj* piccolissimo

tip¹ [tɪp] *n of stick, finger* punta *f*; *of cigarette* filtro *m*

tip² [tɪp] **1** *n* (*piece of advice*) consiglio *m*; *money* mancia *f* **2** *v/t* (*pret & pp* -ped) *waiter etc* dare la mancia a
♦ tip off *v/t* fare una soffiata
♦ tip over *v/t jug, liquid* rovesciare; *he tipped water all over me* mi ha rovesciato dell'acqua addosso

'tip-off soffiata *f*

tipped [tɪpt] *adj cigarettes* col filtro

Tipp-Ex® *n* bianchetto *m*

tip·sy ['tɪpsɪ] *adj* alticcio

tip·toe ['tɪptəʊ]: *on ~* sulla punta dei piedi

tire¹ ['taɪə(r)] **1** *v/t* stancare **2** *v/i* stancarsi; *he never ~s of it* non se ne stanca mai

tire² ['taɪə(r)] *Am n* → *tyre*

tired ['taɪəd] *adj* stanco; *be ~ of s.o. / sth* essere stanco di qu / qc

tired·ness ['taɪədnɪs] stanchezza *f*

tire·less ['taɪəlɪs] *adj* instancabile

tire·some ['taɪəsəm] *adj* (*annoying*) fastidioso

tir·ing ['taɪərɪŋ] *adj* stancante

Ti·rol → *Tyrol*

tis·sue ['tɪʃuː] ANAT tessuto *m*; (*handkerchief*) fazzolettino *m* (di carta)

'tis·sue pa·per carta *f* velina

tit¹ [tɪt] *bird* cincia *f*

tit² [tɪt]: *~ for tat* pan per focaccia

tit³ [tɪt] V (*breast*) tetta *f* V

ti·tle ['taɪtl] titolo *m*; LAW diritto *m*

'ti·tle-hold·er SP detentore *m*, -trice *f* del titolo

'ti·tle role *in play, film* ruolo *m* principale

tit·ter ['tɪtə(r)] *v/i* ridacchiare

to [tuː], unstressed [tə] **1** *prep* a; *~ Italy* in Italia; *~ Rome* a Roma; *let's go ~ my place* andiamo a casa mia; *walk ~ the station* andare a piedi alla stazione; *~ the north / south of ...* a nord / sud di ...; *give sth ~ s.o.* dare qc a qu; *from Monday ~ Wednesday* da lunedì a mercoledì; *from 10 - 15 people* tra 10 e 15 persone; *count ~ 20* contare fino a venti; *it's 5 ~ 11* sono le undici meno cinque **2** *with verbs*: *~ speak, ~ see* parlare, vedere; *learn ~ drive* imparare a guidare; *nice ~ eat* buono da mangiare; *too heavy ~ carry* troppo pesante da trasportare; *~ be honest ...* per essere franco ...; *~ learn Italian in order to* per imparare l'italiano **3** *adv*: *~ and fro* avanti e indietro

toad [təʊd] rospo *m*

toad·stool ['təʊdstuːl] fungo *m* velenoso

toast [təʊst] **1** *n* pane *m* tostato; (*drinking*) brindisi *m inv*; **propose a ~ to s.o.** fare un brindisi in onore di qu **2** *v/t* **bread** tostare; *drinking* fare un brindisi a

to·bac·co [təˈbækəʊ] tabacco *m*

to·bac·co·nist [təˈbækənɪst] tabaccaio *m*

to·bog·gan [təˈbɒgən] *n* toboga *m inv*

to·day [təˈdeɪ] oggi

tod·dle [ˈtɒdl] *v/i* of child gattonare

tod·dler [ˈtɒdlə(r)] bambino *m*, -a *f* ai primi passi

to-do [təˈduː] F casino *m* F

toe [təʊ] **1** *n* dito *m* del piede; of shoes, socks punta *f*; **big ~** alluce *m* **2** *v/t*: **~ the line** attenersi alle direttive

toe·nail [ˈtəʊneɪl] unghia *f* del piede

tof·fee [ˈtɒfɪ] caramella *f* al mou

to·geth·er [təˈgeðə(r)] *adv* insieme

toil [tɔɪl] *n* duro lavoro *m*

toi·let [ˈtɔɪlɪt] gabinetto *m*; place bagno *m*, gabinetto *m*; **go to the ~** andare in bagno

'toil·et pa·per carta *f* igienica

toi·let·ries [ˈtɔɪlɪtrɪz] *npl* prodotti *mpl* da toilette

'toi·let roll rotolo *m* di carta igienica

to·ken [ˈtəʊkən] (sign) pegno *m*; for gambling gettone *m*; (gift ~) buono *m*

told [təʊld] *pret & pp* → **tell**

tol·er·a·ble [ˈtɒlərəbl] *adj* pain etc tollerabile; (quite good) accettabile

tol·er·ance [ˈtɒlərəns] tolleranza *f*

tol·er·ant [ˈtɒlərənt] *adj* tollerante

tol·er·ate [ˈtɒləreɪt] *v/t* noise, person tollerare; **I won't ~ it!** non intendo tollerarlo!

toll[1] [təʊl] *v/i* of bell suonare

toll[2] [təʊl] *n* (deaths) bilancio *m* delle vittime

toll[3] [təʊl] *n* for bridge, road pedaggio *m*

'toll booth casello *m*

'toll road strada *f* a pedaggio

to·ma·to [təˈmɑːtəʊ] pomodoro *m*

to·ma·to ˈketch·up ketchup *m inv*

to·ma·to ˈsauce for pasta etc salsa *f* o sugo *m* di pomodoro; (ketchup) ketchup *m inv*

tomb [tuːm] tomba *f*

tom·boy [ˈtɒmbɔɪ] maschiaccio *m*

tomb·stone [ˈtuːmstəʊn] lapide *f*

tom·cat [ˈtɒmkæt] gatto *m* (maschio)

to·mor·row [təˈmɒrəʊ] domani; **the day after ~** dopodomani; **~ morning** domattina, domani mattina

ton [tʌn] tonnellata *f*

tone [təʊn] of colour, musical instrument tonalità *f inv*; of conversation etc tono *m*; of neighbourhood livello *m* sociale; **~ of voice** tono di voce

♦**tone down** *v/t* demands, criticism moderare il tono di

ton·er [ˈtəʊnə(r)] toner *m inv*

tongs [tɒŋz] *npl* pinze *fpl*; for hair ferro *m* arricciacapelli

tongue [tʌŋ] *n* lingua *f*

ton·ic [ˈtɒnɪk] MED ricostituente *m*

'ton·ic (wa·ter) acqua *f* tonica

to·night [təˈnaɪt] stanotte; (this evening) stasera

ton·sil [ˈtɒnsl] tonsilla *f*

ton·sil·li·tis [tɒnsəˈlaɪtɪs] tonsillite *f*

too [tuː] *adv* (also) anche; (excessively) troppo; **me ~** anch'io; **~ big / hot** troppo grande / caldo; **~ much rice** troppo riso; **~ many mistakes** troppi errori; **eat ~ much** mangiare troppo

took [tuːk] *pret* → **take**

tool [tuːl] attrezzo *m*; fig strumento *m*

toot [tuːt] *v/t* F suonare

tooth [tuːθ] (pl **teeth** [tiːθ]) dente *m*

'tooth·ache mal *m* di denti

'tooth·brush spazzolino *m* da denti

tooth·less [ˈtuːθlɪs] sdentato

'tooth·paste dentifricio *m*

'tooth·pick stuzzicadenti *m inv*

top [tɒp] **1** *n* of mountain, tree cima *f*; of wall, screen parte *f* alta; of page, list, street inizio *m*; (lid: of bottle etc, pen) tappo *m*; of the class, league testa *f*; (clothing) maglia *f*; (MOT: gear) marcia *f* più alta; **on ~ of** in cima a; **at the ~ of** list, tree, mountain in cima a; league in testa a; page, street all'inizio di; **get to the ~ of** company etc arrivare in cima; **get to the ~ of mountain** arrivare alla vetta; **be over the ~** (*exaggerated*) essere esagerato **2** *adj branches* più alto; *floor* ultimo; *management* di alto livello; *official* di alto rango; *player* migliore; *speed, note* massimo **3** *v/t* (*pret & pp* **-ped**): **~ped with cream** ricoperto di crema

♦**top up** *v/t glass* riempire; **top up the tank** fare il pieno

top 'hat tuba *f*

top·ic ['tɒpɪk] argomento *m*

top·ic·al ['tɒpɪkl] *adj* attuale

top·less ['tɒplɪs] *adj* topless *inv*

top·most ['tɒpməʊst] *adj branches, floor* più alto

top·ping ['tɒpɪŋ] *on pizza* guarnizione *f*

top·ple ['tɒpl] **1** *v/i* crollare **2** *v/t government* far cadere

top 'se·cret *adj* top secret *inv*

top·sy-tur·vy [tɒpsɪ'tɜːvɪ] *adj* sottosopra *inv*

torch [tɔːtʃ] *Br* pila *f*; *with flame* torcia *f*

tore [tɔː(r)] *pret* → **tear**

tor·ment ['tɔːment] **1** *n* tormento *m* **2** *v/t* [tɔː'ment] *person, animal* tormentare; **~ed by doubt** tormentato dal dubbio

torn [tɔːn] *pp* → **tear**

tor·na·do [tɔː'neɪdəʊ] tornado *m*

tor·pe·do [tɔː'piːdəʊ] **1** *n* siluro *m* **2** *v/t* silurare; *fig* far saltare

tor·rent ['tɒrənt] torrente *m*; *of lava* fiume *m*; *of abuse, words* valanga *f*

tor·ren·tial [tə'renʃl] *adj rain* torrenziale

tor·toise ['tɔːtəs] tartaruga *f*

tor·ture ['tɔːtʃə(r)] **1** *n* tortura *f* **2** *v/t* torturare

toss [tɒs] **1** *v/t ball* lanciare; *rider* disarcionare; *salad* mescolare; **~ a coin** fare testa o croce **2** *v/i*: **~ and turn** rigirarsi

to·tal ['təʊtl] **1** *n* totale *m* **2** *adj amount, disaster* totale; *stranger* perfetto

to·tal·i·tar·i·an [təʊtælɪ'teərɪən] *adj* totalitario

to·tal·ly ['təʊtəlɪ] *adv* totalmente, completamente

tot·ter ['tɒtə(r)] *v/i of person* barcollare

touch [tʌtʃ] **1** *n* tocco *m*; *sense* tatto *m*; *small detail* tocco *m*; *in rugby* touche *f*; **he felt a ~ on his shoulder** si è sentito toccare sulla spalla; **lose one's ~** perdere la mano; **kick the ball into ~** calciare la palla fuoricampo; **lose ~ with s.o.** perdere i contatti con qu; **keep in ~ with s.o.** rimanere in contatto con qu; **we kept in ~** siamo rimasti in contatto; **be out of ~** non essere al corrente; *with news* non essere al corrente; *with people* non avere contatti; **a ~ of** *little bit* un po' di ... **2** *v/t* toccare; *emotionally* commuovere **3** *v/i* toccare; *of two lines etc* toccarsi

♦**touch down** *v/i of aeroplane* atterrare; *SP* fare meta

♦**touch on** *v/t* (*mention*) accennare a

♦**touch up** *v/t photo* ritoccare; *sexually* palpeggiare

touch-and-'go: *it was* ~ la situazione era critica

touch·down ['tʌtʃdaʊn] *of aeroplane* atterraggio *m*

touch·ing ['tʌtʃɪŋ] *adj* commovente

touch·line ['tʌtʃlaɪn] *SP* linea *f* laterale

'**touch screen** schermo *m* tattile

touch·y ['tʌtʃɪ] *adj person* suscettibile

tough [tʌf] *adj person* forte; *question, exam, meat, punishment* duro; *material* resistente

♦**toughen up** ['tʌfn] *v/t person* rendere più forte

'**tough guy** F duro *m* F

tour [tʊə(r)] **1** *n* visita *f* **2** *v/t area* fare il giro di

'**tour guide** guida *f* turistica

tour·i·sm ['tʊərɪzm] turismo *m*

tour·i·st ['tʊərɪst] turista *m/f*

'**tour·ist at·trac·tion** attrazione *f* turistica; '**tour·ist in·dus·try** industria *f* del turismo; '**tour·i·st** (**in·for·'ma·tion**) **of·fice** azienda *f* (autonoma) di soggiorno; '**tour·ist sea·son** stagione *f* turistica

T

tour·na·ment ['tʊənəmənt] torneo *m*

'tour op·er·a·tor operatore *m* turistico

tous·led ['taʊzld] *adj* hair scompigliato

tout [taʊt] *n* bagarino *m*

tow [təʊ] **1** *v/t* car, boat rimorchiare **2** *n*: **give s.o. a ~** rimorchiare qu

♦tow away *v/t* car portare via col carro attrezzi

to·wards [tə'wɔːdz] *prep* verso; **rude ~** maleducato nei confronti di; **work ~ (achieving) sth** lavorare per (raggiungere) qc

tow·el ['taʊəl] asciugamano *m*

tow·er ['taʊə(r)] torre *f*

♦tower over *v/t* sovrastare

'tow·er block condominio *m* a torre

town [taʊn] città *f inv*; opposed to city cittadina *f*

town 'cen·tre centro *m*; town 'coun·cil consiglio *m* comunale; town 'coun·cil·lor consigliere *m*, -a *f* comunale; town 'hall municipio *m*

'tow·rope cavo *m* da rimorchio

tox·ic ['tɒksɪk] *adj* tossico

tox·ic 'waste scorie *fpl* tossiche

tox·in ['tɒksɪn] BIO tossina *f*

toy [tɔɪ] giocattolo *m*

♦toy with *v/t* object giocherellare con; idea accarezzare

'toy shop negozio *m* di giocattoli

trace [treɪs] **1** *n* of substance traccia *f* **2** *v/t* (find) rintracciare; (follow: footsteps) seguire; (draw) tracciare

track [træk] *n* (path) sentiero *m*; of race course pista *f*; (race course) circuito *m*; RAIL binario *m*; on record, CD brano *m*; **keep ~ of sth** tenersi al passo con qc; **keep record of sth** registrare

♦track down *v/t* rintracciare

'track·suit tuta *f* (da ginnastica)

trac·tor ['træktə(r)] trattore *m*

trade [treɪd] **1** *n* (commerce) commercio *m*; (profession, craft) mestiere *m* **2** *v/i* (do business) essere in attività; **~ in sth** commerciare in qc **3** *v/t* (exchange) scambiare; **~ sth for sth** scambiare qc con qc

♦trade in *v/t* when buying dare in permuta

'trade fair fiera *f* campionaria

'trade·mark marchio *m* registrato

trad·er ['treɪdə(r)] commerciante *m/f*

trade 'se·cret segreto *m* industriale

trades·man ['treɪdzmən] plumber etc operaio *m*; milkman etc fornitore *m*

trade(s) 'u·nion sindacato *m*

tra·di·tion [trə'dɪʃn] tradizione *f*

tra·di·tion·al [trə'dɪʃnl] *adj* tradizionale

tra·di·tion·al·ly [trə'dɪʃnlɪ] *adv* tradizionalmente

traf·fic ['træfɪk] *n* on roads, in drugs traffico *m*; at airport traffico *m* aereo

♦traffic in *v/t* (pret & pp **-ked**) drugs trafficare

'traf·fic cop F vigile *m* (urbano); 'traf·fic is·land isola *f* salvagente; 'traf·fic jam ingorgo *m*; 'traf·fic lights *npl* semaforo *m*; 'traf·fic po·lice polizia *f* stradale; 'traf·fic sign segnale *m* stradale; 'traf·fic war·den ausiliario *m* (del traffico)

tra·ge·dy ['trædʒədɪ] tragedia *f*

tra·gic ['trædʒɪk] *adj* tragico

trail [treɪl] **1** *n* (path) sentiero *m*; of person, animal tracce *fpl*; of blood scia *f* **2** *v/t* (follow) seguire; (drag) trascinare; caravan etc trainare **3** *v/i* (lag behind) trascinarsi; **they're ~ing 3-1** stanno perdendo 3 a 1

trail·er ['treɪlə(r)] pulled by vehicle rimorchio *m*; of film trailer *m inv*; Am (caravan) roulotte *f inv*

train[1] [treɪn] *n* treno *m*; **go by ~** andare in treno

train[2] [treɪn] **1** *v/t* team, athlete allenare; employee formare; dog addestrare **2** *v/i* of team, athlete allenarsi; of teacher etc fare il tirocinio

train·ee [treɪ'niː] apprendista *m/f*

train·er ['treɪnə(r)] SP allenatore *m*, -trice *f*; of dog addestratore *m*, -trice *f*

train·ers ['treɪnəz] *npl* shoes scarpe *fpl* da ginnastica

train·ing ['treɪnɪŋ] of new staff

formazione f; SP allenamento m; **be in ~** SP allenarsi; **be out of ~** SP essere fuori allenamento

'**train·ing course** corso m di formazione

'**train·ing scheme** programma m di formazione

'**train sta·tion** stazione f ferroviaria

trait [treɪt] tratto m

trai·tor ['treɪtə(r)] traditore m, -trice f

tram [træm] tram m inv

tramp [træmp] **1** n (vagabond) barbone m, -a f **2** v/i camminare con passo pesante

tram·ple ['træmpl] v/t: **be ~d to death** morire travolto; **be ~d underfoot** essere calpestato

♦ **trample on** v/t person, object calpestare

tram·po·line ['træmpəliːn] trampolino m

trance [trɑːns] trance f inv; **go into a ~** cadere in trance

tran·quil ['træŋkwɪl] adj tranquillo

tran·quil·li·ty [træŋ'kwɪlətɪ] tranquillità f

tran·quil·liz·er ['træŋkwɪlaɪzə(r)] tranquillante m

trans·act [træn'zækt] v/t deal, business trattare

trans·ac·tion [træn'zækʃn] transazione f

trans·at·lan·tic [trænzət'læntɪk] adj transatlantico

tran·scen·den·tal [trænsen'dentl] adj trascendentale

tran·script ['trænskrɪpt] trascrizione f

trans·fer [træns'fɜː(r)] **1** v/t (pret & pp **-red**) trasferire; LAW cedere **2** v/i (pret & pp **-red**) cambiare **3** n ['trænsfɜː(r)] trasferimento m; LAW cessione f; of money bonifico m bancario

trans·fer·a·ble [træns'fɜːrəbl] adj ticket trasferibile

'**trans·fer fee** for football player prezzo m d'acquisto

trans·form [træns'fɔːm] v/t trasformare

trans·for·ma·tion [trænsfə'meɪʃn] trasformazione f

trans·form·er [træns'fɔːmə(r)] ELEC trasformatore m

trans·fu·sion [træns'fjuːʒn] trasfusione f

tran·sis·tor [træn'zɪstə(r)] transistor m inv; radio radiolina f

tran·sit ['trænzɪt]: **in ~** of goods, passengers in transito

tran·si·tion [træn'sɪʒn] transizione f

tran·si·tion·al [træn'sɪʒnl] adj di transizione

'**tran·sit lounge** at airport sala f passeggeri in transito

'**trans·it pas·sen·ger** passeggero m, -a f in transito

trans·late [træns'leɪt] v/t tradurre

trans·la·tion [træns'leɪʃn] traduzione f

trans·la·tor [træns'leɪtə(r)] traduttore m, -trice f

trans·mis·sion [trænz'mɪʃn] trasmissione f

trans·mit [trænz'mɪt] v/t (pret & pp **-ted**) news, programme, disease trasmettere

trans·mit·ter [trænz'mɪtə(r)] for radio, TV trasmettitore m

trans·par·en·cy [træns'pærənsɪ] PHOT diapositiva f

trans·par·ent [træns'pærənt] adj trasparente

trans·plant [træns'plɑːnt] **1** v/t MED trapiantare **2** n ['trænsplɑːnt] MED trapianto m

trans·port [træn'spɔːt] **1** v/t goods, people trasportare **2** n ['trænspɔːt] of goods, people trasporto m; means of transport mezzo m di trasporto; **public ~** i trasporti pubblici

trans·por·ta·tion [trænspɔː'teɪʃn] of goods, people trasporto m; **means of ~** mezzo m di trasporto

trans·ves·tite [træns'vestaɪt] travestito m

trap [træp] **1** n trappola f; question tranello m; **set a ~ for s.o.** tendere una trappola a qu **2** v/t (pret & pp **-ped**) animal intrappolare; person incastrare; **be ~ped by enemy,**

flames, landslide etc essere intrappolato

trap·door ['træpdɔː(r)] botola *f*

tra·peze [trə'piːz] trapezio *m*

trap·pings ['træpɪŋz] *npl of power* segni *mpl* esteriori

trash [træʃ] (*garbage*) spazzatura *f*; *poor product* robaccia *f*; *despicable person* fetente *mlf*

trash·y ['træʃɪ] *adj goods, novel* scadente

trau·mat·ic [trɔː'mætɪk] *adj* traumatico

trau·ma·tize ['trɔːmətaɪz] *v/t* traumatizzare

trav·el ['trævl] **1** *n* viaggiare *m*; **~s** viaggi *mpl* **2** *v/i* (*pret & pp* **-led**, *Am* **-ed**) viaggiare; *I ~ to work by train* vado a lavorare in treno **3** *v/t* (*pret & pp* **-led**, *Am* **-ed**) *miles* percorrere

'**trav·el a·gen·cy** agenzia *f* di viaggio; '**trav·el a·gent** agente *mlf* di viaggio; '**trav·el bag** borsa *f* da viaggio; '**trav·el ex·pens·es** *npl* spese *fpl* di viaggio; '**trav·el in·sur·ance** assicurazione *f* di viaggio

trav·el·er *Am*, **trav·el·ler** ['trævələ(r)] viaggiatore *m*, -trice *f*

'**trav·el·er's check** *Am*, '**trav·el·ler's cheque** traveller's cheque *m inv*

'**trav·el pro·gram** *Am*, '**trav·el pro·gramme** *on TV etc* programma *m* di viaggi

trawl·er ['trɔːlə(r)] peschereccio *m*

tray [treɪ] *for food, photocopier* vassoio *m*; *to go in oven* teglia *f*

treach·er·ous ['tretʃərəs] *adj* traditore, infido

treach·er·y ['tretʃərɪ] tradimento *m*

tread [tred] **1** *n* passo *m*; *of staircase* gradino *m*; *of tyre* battistrada *m inv* **2** *v/i* (*pret* **trod**, *pp* **trodden**) camminare

♦ **tread on** *v/t s.o.'s foot* pestare

trea·son ['triːzn] tradimento *m*

trea·sure ['treʒə(r)] **1** *n also person* tesoro *m* **2** *v/t gift etc* custodire gelosamente

trea·sur·er ['treʒərə(r)] tesoriere *m*, -a *f*

treat [triːt] **1** *n* trattamento *m* speciale; *it was a real ~* è stato magnifico; *I have a ~ for you* ho una sorpresa per te; *it's my ~* (*I'm paying*) offro io **2** *v/t* trattare; *illness* curare; *~ s.o. to sth* offrire qc a qu

treat·ment ['triːtmənt] trattamento *m*; *of illness* cura *f*

treat·y ['triːtɪ] trattato *m*

tre·ble¹ ['trebl] *n* MUS: *boy's voice* voce *f* bianca; *register* alti *mpl*

tre·ble² [trebl] **1** *adv*: *~ the price* il triplo del prezzo **2** *v/i* triplicarsi

tree [triː] albero *m*

trem·ble ['trembl] *v/i* tremare

tre·men·dous [trɪ'mendəs] *adj* (*very good*) fantastico; (*enormous*) enorme

tre·men·dous·ly [trɪ'mendəslɪ] *adv* (*very*) incredibilmente; (*a lot*) moltissimo

trem·or ['tremə(r)] *of earth* scossa *f*

trench [trentʃ] trincea *f*

trend [trend] tendenza *f*

trend·y ['trendɪ] *adj* alla moda

tres·pass ['trespəs] *v/i* invadere una proprietà privata; *no ~ing* divieto d'accesso

♦ **trespass on** *v/t s.o.'s land, privacy* invadere; *s.o.'s rights, time* abusare di

tres·pass·er ['trespəsə(r)] intruso *m*, -a *f*

tri·al ['traɪəl] LAW processo *m*; *of equipment* prova *f*; *on ~* LAW sotto processo; *stand ~ for sth* essere processato per qc; *have sth on ~ equipment* avere qc in prova

tri·al pe·ri·od periodo *m* di prova

tri·an·gle ['traɪæŋgl] triangolo *m*

tri·an·gu·lar [traɪ'æŋgjulə(r)] *adj* triangolare

tribe [traɪb] tribù *f inv*

tri·bu·nal [traɪ'bjuːnl] tribunale *m*

tri·bu·ta·ry ['trɪbjutərɪ] *of river* affluente *m*

trick [trɪk] **1** *n to deceive* stratagemma *m*; (*knack*) trucco *m*; *a ~ of the light* un effetto di luce; *play a ~ on s.o.* fare uno scherzo a qu **2** *v/t* ingannare; **~ s.o. into doing sth** convincere qu con l'inganno a fare qc

trick·e·ry ['trɪkərɪ] truffa *f*

trick·le ['trɪkl] **1** *n* filo *m*; **a ~ of replies** poche risposte sporadiche **2** *v/i* gocciolare

trick·ster ['trɪkstə(r)] truffatore *m*, -trice *f*

trick·y ['trɪkɪ] *adj* (*difficult*) complicato

tri·cy·cle ['traɪsɪkl] triciclo *m*

tri·fle ['traɪfl] *n* (*triviality*) inezia *f*; *pudding* zuppa *f* inglese

tri·fling ['traɪflɪŋ] *adj* insignificante

trig·ger ['trɪɡə(r)] *n on gun* grilletto *m*; *on camcorder* pulsante *m* (di accensione)

♦ **trigger off** *v/t* scatenare

trim [trɪm] **1** *adj* (*neat*) ordinato; *figure* snello **2** *v/t* (*pret & pp* **-med**) *hair, hedge* spuntare; *budget, costs* tagliare; (*decorate*) *dress* ornare **3** *n* (*light cut*) spuntata *f*; **in good ~** in buone condizioni

trim·ming ['trɪmɪŋ] *on clothes* ornamento *m*; **with all the ~s** con tutti gli annessi e connessi

trin·ket ['trɪŋkɪt] ninnolo *m*

tri·o ['triːəʊ] MUS trio *m*

trip [trɪp] **1** *n* (*journey*) viaggio *m*, gita *f* **2** *v/i* (*pret & pp* **-ped**) (*stumble*) inciampare (**over** in) **3** *v/t* (*pret & pp* **-ped**) (*make fall*) fare inciampare

♦ **trip up 1** *v/t* (*make fall*) fare inciampare; *cause to make a mistake* confondere **2** *v/i* (*stumble*) inciampare; (*make a mistake*) sbagliarsi

tripe [traɪp] trippa *f*

tri·ple ['trɪpl] → **treble²**

trip·lets ['trɪplɪts] *npl* tre gemelli *mpl*

tri·pod ['traɪpɒd] PHOT treppiedi *m inv*

trite [traɪt] *adj* trito

tri·umph ['traɪʌmf] *n* trionfo *m*

triv·i·al ['trɪvɪəl] *adj* banale

triv·i·al·i·ty [trɪvɪ'ælətɪ] banalità *f inv*

trod [trɒd] *pret* → **tread**

trod·den ['trɒdn] *pp* → **tread**

trol·ley ['trɒlɪ] *in supermarket, at*

airport carrello *m*

trom·bone [trɒm'bəʊn] trombone *m*

troops [truːps] *npl* truppe *fpl*

tro·phy ['trəʊfɪ] trofeo *m*

trop·ic ['trɒpɪk] tropico *m*

trop·i·cal ['trɒpɪkl] *adj* tropicale

trop·ics ['trɒpɪks] *npl* tropici *mpl*

trot [trɒt] *v/i* (*pret & pp* **-ted**) trottare

trou·ble ['trʌbl] **1** *n* (*difficulties*) problemi *mpl*; (*inconvenience*) fastidio *m*; (*disturbance*) disordini *mpl*; **go to a lot of ~ to do sth** darsi molto da fare per fare qc; **no ~!** nessun problema!; **the ~ with you is …** il tuo problema è …; **get into ~** mettersi nei guai **2** *v/t* (*worry*) preoccupare; (*bother, disturb*) disturbare; *of back, liver etc* dare dei fastidi a

'trou·ble-free senza problemi

'trou·ble-mak·er attaccabrighe *m/f inv*

'trou·ble-shoot·er (*mediator*) mediatore *m*, -trice *f*

'trou·ble-shoot·ing mediazione *f*; *in software manual* ricerca *f* problemi e soluzioni

trou·ble·some ['trʌblsəm] *adj* fastidioso

trou·sers ['traʊzəz] *npl* pantaloni *mpl*; **a pair of ~** un paio di pantaloni

'trou·ser suit tailleur *m inv* pantaloni

trout [traʊt] (*pl* **trout**) trota *f*

tru·ant ['truːənt]: **play ~** marinare la scuola

truce [truːs] tregua *f*

truck [trʌk] (*lorry*) camion *m inv*

trudge [trʌdʒ] **1** *v/i* arrancare; **~ around the shops** trascinarsi per i negozi **2** *n* camminata *f* stancante

true [truː] *adj* vero; **come ~** *of hopes, dream* realizzarsi

tru·ly ['truːlɪ] *adv* davvero; **Yours ~** distinti saluti

trum·pet ['trʌmpɪt] tromba *f*

trum·pet·er ['trʌmpɪtə(r)] trombettiere *f*

trun·cheon ['trʌnʃn] manganello *m*

trunk [trʌŋk] *of tree, body* tronco *m*; *of elephant* proboscide *f*; (*large case*)

T

baule *m*; *Am* MOT bagagliaio *m inv*

trunks [trʌŋks] *npl for swimming* calzoncini *mpl* da bagno

trust [trʌst] **1** *n* fiducia *f*; FIN fondo *m* fiduciario; COM trust *m inv* **2** *v/t* fidarsi di; *I ~ you* mi fido di te

trusted ['trʌstɪd] *adj* fidato

trust·ee [trʌs'tiː] amministratore *m*, -trice *f* fiduciario, -a

trust·ful, trust·ing ['trʌstfʊl, 'trʌstɪŋ] *adj* fiducioso

trust·wor·thy ['trʌstwɜːðɪ] *adj* affidabile

truth [truːθ] verità *f inv*

truth·ful ['truːθfʊl] *adj* account veritiero; *person* sincero

try [traɪ] **1** *v/t* (*pret & pp -ied*) provare; LAW processare; *~ to do sth* provare a fare qc, cercare di fare qc **2** *v/i* (*pret & pp -ied*) provare, tentare; *you must ~ harder* devi provare con più impegno **3** *n* tentativo *m*; *in rugby* meta *f*; *can I have a ~?* of food posso assaggiare?; *at doing sth* posso fare un tentativo?

♦ **try on** *v/t clothes* provare

♦ **try out** *v/t new machine, method* provare

try·ing ['traɪɪŋ] *adj* (*annoying*) difficile

T-shirt ['tiːʃɜːt] maglietta *f*

tub [tʌb] (*bath*) vasca *f* da bagno; *of liquid* tinozza *f*; *for yoghurt, icecream* barattolo *m*

tub·by ['tʌbɪ] *adj* tozzo

tube [tjuːb] (*pipe*) tubo *m*; (*underground railway*) metropolitana *f*; *of toothpaste, ointment* tubetto *m*

tube·less ['tjuːblɪs] *adj tyre* senza camera d'aria

tu·ber·cu·lo·sis [tjuːbɜːkjʊ'ləʊsɪs] tubercolosi *f*

tuck [tʌk] **1** *n in dress* pince *f inv* **2** *v/t*: *~ sth into sth* infilare qc in qc

♦ **tuck away** *v/t* (*put away*) mettere via; (*eat quickly*) sbafare; *be tucked away* of house, village essere nascosto

♦ **tuck in 1** *v/t children* rimboccare le coperte a; *sheets* rimboccare **2** *v/i* (*eat*) mangiare; (*start eating*) incominciare a mangiare

♦ **tuck up** *v/t sleeves etc* rimboccarsi; *tuck s.o. up in bed* rimboccare le coperte a qu

Tues·day ['tjuːzdeɪ] martedì *m inv*

tuft [tʌft] ciuffo *m*

tug [tʌg] **1** *n* (*pull*) tirata *f*; NAUT rimorchiatore *m*; *I felt a ~ at my sleeve* mi sono sentito tirare la manica **2** *v/t* (*pret & pp -ged*) (*pull*) tirare

tu·i·tion [tjuː'ɪʃn] lezioni *fpl*

tu·lip ['tjuːlɪp] tulipano *m*

tum·ble ['tʌmbl] *v/i* ruzzolare; *of wall, prices* crollare

tum·ble·down ['tʌmbldaʊn] *adj* in rovina, fatiscente

tum·ble-dry·er ['tʌmbldraɪə(r)] asciugatrice *f*

tum·bler ['tʌmblə(r)] *for drinker* bicchiere *m* (*senza stelo*); *in circus* acrobata *m/f*

tum·my ['tʌmɪ] F pancia *f*

'tum·my ache mal di pancia

tu·mour ['tjuːmə(r)] tumore *m*

tu·mult ['tjuːmʌlt] tumulto *m*

tu·mul·tu·ous [tjuː'mʌltjʊəs] *adj* tumultuoso

tu·na ['tjuːnə] tonno *m*; *~ salad* insalata *f* di tonno

tune [tjuːn] **1** *n* motivo *m*; *in ~ instrument* accordato; *person* intonato; *out of ~ instrument* scordato; *person* stonato **2** *v/t instrument* accordare; *engine* mettere a punto

♦ **tune in** *v/i of radio, TV* sintonizzarsi

♦ **tune in to** *v/t radio, TV* sintonizzarsi su

♦ **tune up 1** *v/i of orchestra, players* accordare gli strumenti **2** *v/t engine* mettere a punto

tune·ful ['tjuːnfʊl] *adj* melodioso

tun·er ['tjuːnə(r)] (*hi-fi*) sintonizzatore *m*, tuner *m inv*

tune-up ['tjuːnʌp] *of engine* messa *f* a punto

tu·nic ['tjuːnɪk] tunica *f*; *protective* grembiule *m*; *of uniform* giacca *f*

tun·nel ['tʌnl] *n* galleria *f*, tunnel *m inv*

tur·bine ['tɜːbaɪn] turbina *f*

tur·bu·lence ['tɜːbjʊləns] *in air travel* turbolenza *f*

tur·bu·lent ['tɜːbjʊlənt] *adj* turbolento

turf [tɜːf] tappeto *m* erboso; (*piece*) zolla *f*

Tu·rin [tjʊ'rɪn] Torino *f*

Turk [tɜːk] turco *m*, -a *f*

Tur·key ['tɜːkɪ] Turchia *f*

tur·key ['tɜːkɪ] tacchino *m*

Turk·ish ['tɜːkɪʃ] **1** *adj* turco **2** *n language* turco *m*

tur·moil ['tɜːmɔɪl] agitazione *f*

turn [tɜːn] **1** *n* (*rotation*) giro *m*; *in road* curva *f*; *in variety show* numero *m*; **take ~s in doing sth** fare a turno a fare qc; **it's my ~** è il mio turno, tocca a me; **it's not your ~ yet** non è ancora il tuo turno; **take a ~ at the wheel** prendere il volante per un po'; **do s.o. a good ~** fare un favore a qu **2** *v/t wheel, corner* girare; **~ one's back on s.o.** girare le spalle a qu **3** *v/i of driver, car, wheel* girare; (*become*) diventare; **~ right/left here** gira a destra/sinistra qui; **it has ~ed sour/cold** è diventato acido/freddo; **he has ~ed 40** ha compiuto 40 anni

♦ **turn around 1** *v/t object* girare; *company* dare una svolta positiva a; (COM: *deal with*) eseguire; *order* evadere **2** *v/i of person* girarsi; *of driver* girare

♦ **turn away 1** *v/t* (*send away*) mandare via **2** *v/i* (*walk away*) andare via; (*look away*) girarsi dall'altra parte

♦ **turn back 1** *v/t edges, sheets* ripiegare **2** *v/i of walkers etc* tornare indietro; *in course of action* tirarsi indietro

♦ **turn down** *v/t offer, invitation* rifiutare; *volume, TV, heating* abbassare; *edge, collar* ripiegare

♦ **turn in 1** *v/i* (*go to bed*) andare a letto **2** *v/t to police* denunciare

♦ **turn off 1** *v/t TV, engine* spegnere; *tap* chiudere; F (*sexually*) far passare la voglia a **2** *v/i of driver* svoltare

♦ **turn on 1** *v/t TV, engine* accendere;

tap aprire; F (*sexually*) eccitare **2** *v/i of machine* accendersi

♦ **turn out 1** *v/t lights* spegnere **2** *v/i*: **as it turned out** come è emerso; **it turned out well** è andata bene

♦ **turn over 1** *v/i in bed* girarsi; *of vehicle* capottare **2** *v/t object, page* girare; FIN fatturare

♦ **turn up 1** *v/t collar, volume, heating* alzare **2** *v/i* (*arrive*) arrivare

turn·ing ['tɜːnɪŋ] svolta *f*

'turn·ing point svolta *f* decisiva

tur·nip ['tɜːnɪp] rapa *f*

'turn·out *of people* affluenza *f*; **'turn·o·ver** FIN fatturato *m*; *of staff* ricambio *m*; **'turn·stile** cancelletto *m* girevole; **'turn·ta·ble** piatto *m*; **'turn·up** *on trousers* risvolto *m*

tur·quoise ['tɜːkwɔɪz] *adj* turchese

tur·ret ['tʌrɪt] *of castle, tank* torretta *f*

tur·tle ['tɜːtl] tartaruga *f* marina

tur·tle·neck 'sweater maglia *f* a lupetto

Tus·ca·ny ['tʌskənɪ] Toscana *f*

tusk [tʌsk] zanna *f*

tu·tor ['tjuːtə(r)] EDU *insegnante universitario che segue un piccolo gruppo di studenti*; (*private*) ~ insegnante *m/f* privato, -a

tu·to·ri·al [tjuː'tɔːrɪəl] *n at university* incontro *m* con il tutor

tu·xe·do [tʌk'siːdəʊ] *Am* smoking *m inv*

TV [tiː'viː] tv *f inv*; **on ~** alla tv

T'V din·ner piatto *m* pronto; **T'V gui·de** guida *f* dei programmi tv; **T'V pro·gramme** programma *m* televisivo

twang [twæŋ] **1** *n in voice* suono *m* nasale **2** *v/t guitar string* vibrare

tweez·ers ['twiːzəz] *npl* pinzette *fpl*

twelfth [twelfθ] *n & adj* dodicesimo, -a

twelve [twelv] dodici

twen·ti·eth ['twentɪθ] *n & adj* ventesimo, -a

twen·ty ['twentɪ] venti

twice [twaɪs] *adv* due volte; **~ as much** il doppio; **~ as fast** veloce due volte tanto

twid·dle ['twɪdl] *v/t* girare; **~ one's**

thumbs girarsi i pollici
twig [twɪg] *n* ramoscello *m*
twi·light ['twaɪlaɪt] crepuscolo *m*
twin [twɪn] *n* gemello *m*
'**twin beds** *npl* due lettini *mpl*
twinge [twɪndʒ] *of pain* fitta *f*
twin·kle ['twɪŋkl] *v/i of stars, eyes* scintillare
twin 'room camera *f* a due letti
'**twin town** città *f inv* gemellata
twirl [twɜːl] **1** *v/t* fare roteare **2** *n of cream etc* ricciolo *m*
twist [twɪst] **1** *v/t* attorcigliare; **~ one's ankle** prendere una storta **2** *v/i of road* snodarsi; *of river* serpeggiare **3** *n in rope* attorcigliata *f*; *in road* curva *f*; *in plot, story* svolta *f*
twist·y ['twɪstɪ] *adj road* contorto
twit [twɪt] F scemo *m*, -a *f*
twitch [twɪtʃ] **1** *n nervous* spasmo *m* **2** *v/i (jerk)* contrarsi
twit·ter ['twɪtə(r)] *v/i* cinguettare
two [tuː] due; **the ~ of them** loro due
'**two-faced** *adj* falso; '**two-piece** (*woman's suit*) tailleur *m inv*; '**two-stroke** *adj engine* a due tempi; **two-way 'traf·fic** traffico *m* nei

due sensi di marcia
ty·coon [taɪ'kuːn] magnate *m*
type [taɪp] **1** *n (sort)* tipo *m*; **what ~ of ...?** che tipo di ...? **2** *v/t & v/i (use a keyboard)* battere (a macchina)
type·writ·er ['taɪpraɪtə(r)] macchina *f* da scrivere
ty·phoid ['taɪfɔɪd] febbre *f* tifoide
ty·phoon [taɪ'fuːn] tifone *m*
ty·phus ['taɪfəs] tifo *m*
typ·i·cal ['tɪpɪkl] *adj* tipico; **that's ~ of you / him!** tipico!
typ·i·cal·ly ['tɪpɪklɪ] *adv*: **~ American** tipicamente americano; **he would ~ arrive late** arriva sempre tardi
typ·ist ['taɪpɪst] dattilografo *m*, -a *f*
ty·ran·ni·cal [tɪ'rænɪkl] *adj* tirannico
ty·ran·nize [tɪ'rənaɪz] *v/t* tiranneggiare
ty·ran·ny ['tɪrənɪ] *n* tirannia *f*
ty·rant ['taɪrənt] tiranno *m*, -a *f*
tyre ['taɪə(r)] gomma *f*, pneumatico *m*
Ty·rol [tɪ'rɒl] Tirolo *m*
Ty·ro·le·an [tɪrə'liːən] *adj* tirolese
Tyr·rhe·ni·an Sea [taɪ'riːnɪən] mar *m* Tirreno

U

ug·ly ['ʌglɪ] *adj* brutto
UK [juː'keɪ] *abbr* (= **United Kingdom**) Regno *m* Unito
ul·cer ['ʌlsə(r)] ulcera *f*
ul·ti·mate ['ʌltɪmət] *adj* (*best, definitive*) definitivo; (*final*) ultimo; (*basic*) fondamentale
ul·ti·mate·ly ['ʌltɪmətlɪ] *adv* (*in the end*) in definitiva
ul·ti·ma·tum [ʌltɪ'meɪtəm] ultimatum *m inv*
ul·tra·sound ['ʌltrəsaʊnd] MED ecografia *f*
ul·tra·vi·o·let [ʌltrə'vaɪələt] *adj* ultravioletto

um·bil·i·cal cord [ʌm'bɪlɪkl] cordone *m* ombelicale
um·brel·la [ʌm'brelə] ombrello *m*
um·pire ['ʌmpaɪə(r)] *n* arbitro *m*
ump·teen [ʌmp'tiːn] *adj* F ennesimo
UN [juː'en] *abbr* (= **United Nations**) ONU *f inv* (= Organizzazione *f* delle Nazioni Unite)
un·a·ble [ʌn'eɪbl] *adj*: **be ~ to do sth** *not know how to* non saper fare qc; *not be in a position to* non poter fare qc
un·ac·cept·a·ble [ʌnək'septəbl] *adj* inaccettabile; **it is ~ that ...** è inac-

cettabile che ...

un·ac·count·a·ble [ʌnəˈkaʊntəbl] *adj* inspiegabile

un·ac·cus·tomed [ʌnəˈkʌstəmd] *adj*: **be ~ to sth** non essere abituato a qc

un·a·dul·ter·at·ed [ʌnəˈdʌltəreɪtɪd] *adj* (*fig: absolute*) puro; *activities* anti-americano

u·nan·i·mous [juːˈnænɪməs] *adj verdict* unanime; **be ~ on** essere unanimi su

u·nan·i·mous·ly [juːˈnænɪməslɪ] *adv vote, decide* all'unanimità

un·ap·proach·a·ble [ʌnəˈprəʊtʃəbl] *adj person* inavvicinabile

un·armed [ʌnˈɑːmd] *adj person* disarmato; **~ combat** combattimento senz'armi

un·as·sum·ing [ʌnəˈsjuːmɪŋ] *adj* senza pretese

un·at·tached [ʌnəˈtætʃt] *adj without a partner* libero

un·at·tend·ed [ʌnəˈtendɪd] *adj* incustodito; **leave sth ~** lasciare qc incustodito

un·au·thor·ized [ʌnˈɔːθəraɪzd] *adj* non autorizzato

un·a·void·a·ble [ʌnəˈvɔɪdəbl] *adj* inevitabile

un·a·void·a·bly [ʌnəˈvɔɪdəblɪ] *adv* inevitabilmente; **be ~ detained** essere trattenuto per cause di forza maggiore

un·a·ware [ʌnəˈweə(r)] *adj*: **be ~ of** non rendersi conto di

un·a·wares [ʌnəˈweəz] *adv*: **catch s.o. ~** prendere qu alla sprovvista

un·bal·anced [ʌnˈbælənst] *adj* non equilibrato; PSYCH squilibrato

un·bear·a·ble [ʌnˈbeərəbl] *adj* insopportabile

un·beat·a·ble [ʌnˈbiːtəbl] *adj team, quality* imbattibile

un·beat·en [ʌnˈbiːtn] *adj team* imbattuto

un·be·lie·va·ble [ʌnbɪˈliːvəbl] *adj* incredibile

un·bi·as(s)ed [ʌnˈbaɪəst] *adj* imparziale

un·block [ʌnˈblɒk] *v/t pipe* sbloccare

un·born [ʌnˈbɔːn] *adj* non ancora nato

un·break·a·ble [ʌnˈbreɪkəbl] *adj plates* infrangibile; *world record* imbattibile

un·but·ton [ʌnˈbʌtn] *v/t* sbottonare

un·called-for [ʌnˈkɔːldfɔː(r)] *adj* ingiustificato

un·can·ny [ʌnˈkænɪ] *adj resemblance, skill* sorprendente; (*worrying: feeling*) inquietante

un·ceas·ing [ʌnˈsiːsɪŋ] *adj* incessante

un·cer·tain [ʌnˈsɜːtn] *adj future, weather* incerto; *origins* dubbio; **what will happen? – it's ~** cosa succederà? – non si sa; **be ~ about sth** non essere certo su qc

un·cer·tain·ty [ʌnˈsɜːtntɪ] *of the future* incertezza *f*; **there is still ~ about ...** ci sono ancora dubbi su ...

un·checked [ʌnˈtʃekt] *adj*: **let sth go ~** non controllare qc

un·cle [ˈʌŋkl] zio *m*

un·com·for·ta·ble [ʌnˈkʌmftəbl] *adj* scomodo; **feel ~ about sth** sentirsi a disagio per qc; **I feel ~ with him** mi sento a disagio con lui

un·com·mon [ʌnˈkɒmən] *adj* raro; **it's not ~** non è raro

un·com·pro·mis·ing [ʌnˈkɒmprəmaɪzɪŋ] *adj* fermo; *in a negative way* intransigente

un·con·cerned [ʌnkənˈsɜːnd] *adj* indifferente; **be ~ about s.o. / sth** non darsi pensiero di qu / qc

un·con·di·tion·al [ʌnkənˈdɪʃnl] *adj* incondizionato

un·con·scious [ʌnˈkɒnʃəs] *adj* MED svenuto; PSYCH inconscio; **knock s.o. ~** stordire qu con un colpo; **be ~ of sth** (*not aware*) non rendersi conto di qc

un·con·trol·la·ble [ʌnkənˈtrəʊləbl] *adj anger, desire, children* incontrollabile

un·con·ven·tion·al [ʌnkənˈvenʃnl] *adj* poco convenzionale

un·co·op·er·a·tive [ʌnkəʊˈɒprətɪv] *adj* poco cooperativo

un·cork [ʌnˈkɔːk] *v/t bottle* stappare

U

un·cov·er [ʌnˈkʌvə(r)] *v/t* scoprire

un·dam·aged [ʌnˈdæmɪdʒd] *adj* intatto

un·daunt·ed [ʌnˈdɔːntɪd] *adj: carry on ~* continuare imperterrito

un·de·cid·ed [ʌndɪˈsaɪdɪd] *adj question* irrisolto; *be ~ about sth* essere indeciso su qc

un·de·ni·a·ble [ʌndɪˈnaɪəbl] *adj* innegabile

un·de·ni·a·bly [ʌndɪˈnaɪəblɪ] *adv* innegabilmente

un·der [ˈʌndə(r)] **1** *prep* (*beneath*) sotto; (*less than*) meno di; *it is ~ review / investigation* viene rivisto / indagato; *it is ~ construction* è in costruzione **2** *adv* (*anaesthetized*) sotto anestesia

un·der·age *adj: ~ drinking* alcolismo *m* minorile

'un·der·arm *adv throw* sottinsù

'un·der·car·riage carrello *m* d'atterraggio

'un·der·cov·er *adj agent* segreto

un·der'cut *v/t* (*pret & pp -cut*) COM vendere a minor prezzo di

'un·der·dog: they were the ~s dovevano perdere

un·der'done *adj meat* al sangue; *not cooked enough* non cotto abbastanza

un·der·es·ti·mate *v/t person, skills, task* sottovalutare

un·der·ex'posed *adj* PHOT sottoesposto

un·der'fed *adj* malnutrito

un·der'go *v/t* (*pret -went*, *pp -gone*) *surgery, treatment* sottoporsi a; *experiences* vivere; *~ refurbishment* venire ristrutturato

un·der·grad·u·ate studente *m*, -essa *f* universitario, -a

'un·der·ground 1 *adj passages etc* sotterraneo; POL: *resistance, newspaper etc* clandestino **2** *adv work* sottoterra; *go ~* POL entrare in clandestinità **3** *n* RAIL metropolitana *f*

'un·der·growth sottobosco *m*

un·der'hand *adj* (*devious*) subdolo

un·der'lie *v/t* (*pret -lay*, *pp -lain*) (*form basis of*) essere alla base di

un·der'line *v/t text* sottolineare

un·der'ly·ing *adj causes, problems* di fondo

un·der'mine *v/t s.o.'s position* minare

un·der·neath [ʌndəˈniːθ] *prep adv* sotto **2** *adv* sotto

'un·der·pants *npl* mutande *fpl* da uomo

'un·der·pass *for pedestrians* sottopassaggio *m*

un·der·priv·i·leged [ʌndəˈprɪvɪlɪdʒd] *adj* svantaggiato

un·der'rate *v/t* sottovalutare

'un·der·shirt *Am* canottiera *f*

un·der·sized [ʌndəˈsaɪzd] *adj* troppo piccolo

'un·der·skirt sottogonna *f*

un·der·staffed [ʌndəˈstɑːft] *adj* a corto di personale

un·der·stand [ʌndəˈstænd] (*pret & pp -stood*) **1** *v/t* capire; *I ~ that you ...* mi risulta che tu ...; *they are understood to be in Canada* pare che siano in Canada **2** *v/i* capire

un·der·stand·able [ʌndəˈstændəbl] *adj* comprensibile

un·der·stand·a·bly [ʌndəˈstændəblɪ] *adv* comprensibilmente

un·der·stand·ing [ʌndəˈstændɪŋ] **1** *adj person* comprensivo **2** *n of problem, situation* comprensione *f*; (*agreement*) intesa *f*; *on the ~ that we agree a price* a patto che ci troviamo d'accordo sul prezzo

'un·der·state·ment understatement *m inv*

un·der·take *v/t* (*pret -took*, *pp -taken*) *task* intraprendere; *~ to do sth* impegnarsi a fare qc

'un·der·tak·er impresario *m* di pompe funebri

'un·der·tak·ing (*enterprise*) impresa *f*; (*promise*) promessa *f*

un·der'val·ue *v/t* sottovalutare

'un·der·wear biancheria *f* intima

un·der'weight *adj* sottopeso

'un·der·world *criminal* malavita *f inv*; *in mythology* inferi *mpl*

un·der·write *v/t* (*pret -wrote*, *pp -written*) FIN sottoscrivere

un·de·served [ʌndɪ'zɜːvd] *adj* immeritato

un·de·sir·a·ble [ʌndɪ'zaɪərəbl] *adj features, changes* indesiderato; *person* poco raccomandabile; **~ element** *person* persona indesiderabile

un·dis·put·ed [ʌndɪ'spjuːtɪd] *adj champion, leader* indiscusso

un·do [ʌn'duː] *v/t* (*pret* **-did**, *pp* **-done**) *parcel, wrapping* disfare; *shirt* sbottonare; *shoes, shoelaces* slacciare; *s.o. else's work* annullare, sciupare

un·doubt·ed·ly [ʌn'dautɪdlɪ] *adv* indubbiamente

un·dreamt-of [ʌn'dremtɒv] *adj riches* impensato

un·dress [ʌn'dres] **1** *v/t* spogliare; **get ~ed** spogliarsi **2** *v/i* spogliarsi

un·due [ʌn'djuː] *adj* (*excessive*) eccessivo

un·du·ly [ʌn'djuːlɪ] *adv punished, blamed* ingiustamente; (*excessively*) eccessivamente

un·earth [ʌn'ɜːθ] *v/t ancient remains* portare alla luce; (*fig: find*) scovare

un·earth·ly [ʌn'ɜːθlɪ] *adv*: **at this ~ hour** a quest'ora (impossibile)

un·eas·y [ʌn'iːzɪ] *adj relationship, peace* precario; **feel ~ about** non sentirsela di

un·eat·a·ble [ʌn'iːtəbl] *adj* immangiabile

un·e·co·nom·ic [ʌniːkə'nɒmɪk] *adj* poco redditizio

un·ed·u·cat·ed [ʌn'edjʊkeɪtɪd] *adj* senza istruzione

un·em·ployed [ʌnɪm'plɔɪd] *adj* disoccupato; **the ~** i disoccupati

un·em·ploy·ment [ʌnɪm'plɔɪmənt] disoccupazione *f*; **~ benefit** sussidio *m* di disoccupazione

un·end·ing [ʌn'endɪŋ] *adj* interminabile

un·e·qual [ʌn'iːkwəl] *adj* disuguale; **be ~ to the task** non essere all'altezza del compito

un·er·ring [ʌn'erɪŋ] *adj judgement, instinct* infallibile

un·e·ven [ʌn'iːvn] *adj quality* irregolare; *ground* accidentato

un·e·ven·ly [ʌn'iːvnlɪ] *adv distributed, applied* in modo irregolare; **~ matched** *of two contestants* mal assortiti

un·e·vent·ful [ʌnɪ'ventful] *adj day, journey* tranquillo

un·ex·pec·ted [ʌnɪk'spektɪd] *adj* inatteso

un·ex·pec·ted·ly [ʌnɪk'spektɪdlɪ] *adv* inaspettatamente

un·fair [ʌn'feə(r)] *adj* ingiusto

un·faith·ful [ʌn'feɪθful] *adj husband, wife* infedele; **be ~ to s.o.** essere infedele a qu

un·fa·mil·i·ar [ʌnfə'mɪljə(r)] *adj* sconosciuto; **be ~ with sth** non conoscere qc

un·fas·ten [ʌn'fɑːsn] *v/t belt* slacciare

un·fa·vo·ra·ble *Am*, **un·fa·vou·ra·ble** [ʌn'feɪvərəbl] *adj report, review* negativo; *weather conditions* sfavorevole

un·feel·ing [ʌn'fiːlɪŋ] *adj person* insensibile

un·fin·ished [ʌn'fɪnɪʃt] *adj job, letter, building* non terminato; *business* in sospeso; **leave sth ~** non terminare qc

un·fit [ʌn'fɪt] *adj physically* fuori forma; **be ~ to ...** *morally* non essere degno di ...; **~ to eat / drink** non commestibile / non potabile

un·flap·pa·ble [ʌn'flæpəbl] *adj* F calmo, imperturbabile

un·fold [ʌn'fəʊld] **1** *v/t sheets, letter* spiegare; *one's arms* aprire **2** *v/i of story etc* svolgersi; *of view* spiegarsi

un·fore·seen [ʌnfɔː'siːn] *adj* imprevisto

un·for·get·ta·ble [ʌnfə'getəbl] *adj* indimenticabile

un·for·giv·a·ble [ʌnfə'gɪvəbl] *adj* imperdonabile; **that was ~ (of you)** è una mancanza imperdonabile

un·for·tu·nate [ʌn'fɔːtʃənət] *adj people* sfortunato; *event, choice of words* infelice; **that's ~ for you** è spiacevole per lei

un·for·tu·nate·ly [ʌn'fɔːtʃənətlɪ] *adv* sfortunatamente

un·found·ed [ʌnˈfaʊndɪd] adj infondato

un·friend·ly [ʌnˈfrendlɪ] adj poco amichevole; software di non facile uso

un·fur·nished [ʌnˈfɜːnɪʃt] adj non ammobiliato

un·god·ly [ʌnˈɡɒdlɪ] adj: **at this ~ hour** ad un'ora impossibile

un·grate·ful [ʌnˈɡreɪtfʊl] adj ingrato

un·hap·pi·ness [ʌnˈhæpɪnɪs] infelicità f inv

un·hap·py [ʌnˈhæpɪ] adj infelice; customers etc non soddisfatto; **be ~ with the service / an explanation** non essere soddisfatto del servizio / della giustificazione

un·harmed [ʌnˈhɑːmd] adj illeso

un·health·y [ʌnˈhelθɪ] adj person malaticcio; conditions malsano; food, atmosphere poco sano; economy traballante; balance sheet in passivo

un·heard-of [ʌnˈhɜːdɒv] adj inaudito

un·hoped-for adj insperato

un·hurt [ʌnˈhɜːt] adj illeso

un·hy·gi·en·ic [ʌnhaɪˈdʒiːnɪk] adj non igienico

u·ni·fi·ca·tion [juːnɪfɪˈkeɪʃn] unificazione f

u·ni·form [ˈjuːnɪfɔːm] **1** n of school pupil, air hostess divisa f; of soldier divisa f, uniforme f **2** adj uniforme

u·ni·fy [ˈjuːnɪfaɪ] v/t (pret & pp -ied) unificare

u·ni·lat·e·ral [juːnɪˈlætrəl] adj unilaterale

un·i·ma·gi·na·ble [ʌnɪˈmædʒɪnəbl] adj inimmaginabile

un·i·ma·gi·na·tive [ʌnɪˈmædʒɪnətɪv] adj senza fantasia

un·im·por·tant [ʌnɪmˈpɔːtənt] adj senza importanza

un·in·hab·i·ta·ble [ʌnɪnˈhæbɪtəbl] adj inabitabile

un·in·hab·it·ed [ʌnɪnˈhæbɪtɪd] adj building disabitato; region deserto

un·in·jured [ʌnˈɪndʒəd] adj incolume

un·in·tel·li·gi·ble [ʌnɪnˈtelɪdʒəbl] adj incomprensibile

un·in·ten·tion·al [ʌnɪnˈtenʃnl] adj involontario

un·in·ten·tion·al·ly [ʌnɪnˈtenʃnlɪ] adv involontariamente

un·in·te·rest·ing [ʌnˈɪntrəstɪŋ] adj poco interessante

un·in·ter·rupt·ed [ʌnɪntəˈrʌptɪd] adj sleep, work ininterrotto

u·nion [ˈjuːnɪən] POL unione f; (trade ~) sindacato m

u·nique [juːˈniːk] adj (also very good) unico; **with his own ~ humour / style** con quel senso dell'umorismo / quello stile tutto suo

u·nit [ˈjuːnɪt] of measurement unità f inv; (section: of machine, structure) elemento m; (part with separate function) unità f inv; (department) reparto m; MIL unità f inv; **we must work together as a ~** dobbiamo lavorare insieme come squadra

u·nit 'cost COM costo m unitario

u·nite [juːˈnaɪt] **1** v/t unire **2** v/i unirsi

u·nit·ed [juːˈnaɪtɪd] adj unito

U·nit·ed 'King·dom Regno m Unito

U·nit·ed 'Na·tions Nazioni fpl Unite

U·nit·ed 'States (of 'A·mer·i·ca) Stati mpl Uniti (d'America)

u·ni·ty [ˈjuːnətɪ] unità f inv

u·ni·ver·sal [juːnɪˈvɜːsl] adj universale

u·ni·ver·sal·ly [juːnɪˈvɜːsəlɪ] adv universalmente

u·ni·verse [ˈjuːnɪvɜːs] universo m

u·ni·ver·si·ty [juːnɪˈvɜːsətɪ] **1** n università f inv; **he is at ~** fa l'università **2** adj universitario

un·just [ʌnˈdʒʌst] adj ingiusto

un·kempt [ʌnˈkempt] adj hair scarmigliato; appearance trasandato

un·kind [ʌnˈkaɪnd] adj cattivo

un·known [ʌnˈnəʊn] **1** adj sconosciuto **2** n: **a journey into the ~** un viaggio nell'ignoto

un·lead·ed [ʌnˈledɪd] adj senza piombo

un·less [ənˈles] conj a meno che; **~ he pays us tomorrow** a meno che non ci paghi domani; **~ I am mistaken** se non mi sbaglio un·like [ʌn'laɪk] *prep* diverso da; *it's ~ him to drink so much* non è da lui bere così tanto; *the photograph was completely ~ her* la foto non le somigliava per niente; *~ Tom, I ...* a differenza di Tom, io ...

un·like·ly [ʌn'laɪklɪ] *adj* improbabile; *he is ~ to win* è improbabile che vinca; *it is ~ that ...* è improbabile che ...

un·lim·it·ed [ʌn'lɪmɪtɪd] *adj* illimitato

un·load [ʌn'ləʊd] *v/t* lorry, goods scaricare

un·lock [ʌn'lɒk] *v/t* aprire (con la chiave)

un·luck·i·ly [ʌn'lʌkɪlɪ] *adv* sfortunatamente

un·luck·y [ʌn'lʌkɪ] *adj* day, choice, person sfortunato; *that was so ~ for you!* che sfortuna hai avuto!

un·made-up [ʌnmeɪd'ʌp] *adj* face acqua e sapone

un·manned [ʌn'mænd] *adj* spacecraft senza equipaggio

un·mar·ried [ʌn'mærɪd] *adj* non sposato

un·mis·ta·ka·ble [ʌnmɪ'steɪkəbl] *adj* inconfondibile

un·moved [ʌn'muːvd] *adj*: *be ~ emotionally* non essere commosso

un·mu·si·cal [ʌn'mjuːzɪkl] *adj* person non portato per la musica; sounds disarmonico

un·nat·u·ral [ʌn'nætʃərl] *adj* non normale; *it's not ~ to be annoyed* è naturale essere seccati

un·ne·ces·sa·ry [ʌn'nesəsrɪ] *adj* non necessario; comment, violence gratuito

un·nerv·ing [ʌn'nɜːvɪŋ] *adj* inquietante

un·no·ticed [ʌn'nəʊtɪst] *adj* inosservato; *it went ~* passare inosservato

un·ob·tain·a·ble [ʌnəb'teɪnəbl] *adj* goods introvabile; TELEC non ottenibile

un·ob·tru·sive [ʌnəb'truːsɪv] *adj* discreto

un·oc·cu·pied [ʌn'ɒkjʊpaɪd] *adj* building, house vuoto; post vacante; *room* libero; *he doesn't like being ~ person* non gli piace stare senza far niente

un·of·fi·cial [ʌnə'fɪʃl] *adj* world record, leader non ufficiale; announcement ufficioso

un·of·fi·cial·ly [ʌnə'fɪʃlɪ] *adv* non ufficialmente

un·pack [ʌn'pæk] **1** *v/t* disfare **2** *v/i* disfare le valige

un·paid [ʌn'peɪd] *adj* work non retribuito

un·pleas·ant [ʌn'pleznt] *adj* person, thing to say antipatico; smell, taste sgradevole; *he was very ~ to her* si è comportato malissimo con lei

un·plug [ʌn'plʌg] *v/t* (*pret & pp -ged*) TV, computer staccare (la spina di)

un·pop·u·lar [ʌn'pɒpjʊlə(r)] *adj* person mal visto; decision impopolare; *an ~ teacher with the students* un insegnante che non ha la simpatia degli studenti

un·pre·ce·dent·ed [ʌn'presɪdentɪd] *adj* senza precedenti; *it was ~ for a woman to be ...* è senza precedenti che una donna sia ...

un·pre·dict·a·ble [ʌnprɪ'dɪktəbl] *adj* person, weather imprevedibile

un·pre·ten·tious [ʌnprɪ'tenʃəs] *adj* person, style, hotel senza pretese

un·prin·ci·pled [ʌn'prɪnsɪpld] *adj* senza scrupoli

un·pro·duc·tive [ʌnprə'dʌktɪv] *adj* meeting, discussion sterile; soil improduttivo

un·pro·fes·sion·al [ʌnprə'feʃnl] *adj* person, workmanship poco professionale; *it is ~ not to ...* è mancanza di professionalità non ...; *~ behaviour of doctor etc* scorrettezza *f* professionale

un·prof·it·a·ble [ʌn'prɒfɪtəbl] *adj* non redditizio

un·pro·nounce·a·ble [ʌnprə'naʊnsəbl] *adj* impronunciabile

un·pro·tect·ed [ʌnprə'tektɪd] *adj* borders indifeso; machine non riparato; *~ sex* sesso non protetto

U

un·pro·voked [ʌnprəˈvəʊkt] *adj* *attack* non provocato

un·qual·i·fied [ʌnˈkwɒlɪfaɪd] *adj* *worker, instructor* non qualificato; *doctor, teacher* non abilitato

un·ques·tio·na·bly [ʌnˈkwestʃnəblɪ] *adv* (*without doubt*) indiscutibilmente

un·ques·tion·ing [ʌnˈkwestʃnɪŋ] *adj* *attitude, loyalty* assoluto

un·rav·el [ʌnˈrævl] *v/t* (*pret & pp* **-led,** *Am* **-ed**) *string* dipanare; *knitting* disfare; *mystery, complexities* risolvere

un·rea·da·ble [ʌnˈriːdəbl] *adj* *book* illeggibile

un·re·al [ʌnˈrɪəl] *adj* *creature* irreale; *impression* inverosimile; **this is ~!** F incredibile!

un·rea·lis·tic [ʌnrɪəˈlɪstɪk] *adj* *person* poco realista; *expectations* poco realistico

un·rea·so·na·ble [ʌnˈriːznəbl] *adj* *person* irragionevole; *demand, expectation* eccessivo

un·re·lat·ed [ʌnrɪˈleɪtɪd] *adj* *issues* senza (alcuna) attinenza; *people* non imparentato

un·re·lent·ing [ʌnrɪˈlentɪŋ] *adj* incessante

un·re·li·a·ble [ʌnrɪˈlaɪəbl] *adj* poco affidabile

un·rest [ʌnˈrest] agitazione *f*

un·re·strained [ʌnrɪˈstreɪnd] *adj* *emotions* incontrollato, sfrenato

un·road·wor·thy [ʌnˈrəʊdwɜːðɪ] *adj* non sicuro

un·roll [ʌnˈrəʊl] *v/t* *carpet, scroll* srotolare

un·ru·ly [ʌnˈruːlɪ] *adj* indisciplinato

un·safe [ʌnˈseɪf] *adj* *bridge, vehicle, wiring, district* pericoloso; **~ to drink / eat** non potabile / non commestibile; **it is ~ to ...** è rischioso ...

un·san·i·tar·y [ʌnˈsænɪtrɪ] *adj* *conditions, drains* antigienico

un·sat·is·fac·to·ry [ʌnsætɪsˈfæktrɪ] *adj* poco soddisfacente

un·sa·vou·ry [ʌnˈseɪvrɪ] *adj* *person, reputation,* poco raccomandabile; *district* brutto

un·scathed [ʌnˈskeɪðd] *adj* (*not injured*) incolume; (*not damaged*) intatto

un·screw [ʌnˈskruː] *v/t* svitare

un·scru·pu·lous [ʌnˈskruːpjələs] *adj* senza scrupoli

un·self·ish [ʌnˈselfɪʃ] *adj* *person* altruista; *act, gesture, behaviour* altruistico

un·set·tled [ʌnˈsetld] *adj* *issue* irrisolto; *weather, stock market* instabile; *lifestyle* irrequieto; *bills* non pagato

un·shav·en [ʌnˈʃeɪvn] *adj* non rasato

un·sight·ly [ʌnˈsaɪtlɪ] *adj* brutto

un·skilled [ʌnˈskɪld] *adj* non specializzato

un·so·cia·ble [ʌnˈsəʊʃəbl] *adj* poco socievole

un·so·phis·ti·cat·ed [ʌnsəˈfɪstɪkeɪtɪd] *adj* *person, beliefs* semplice; *equipment* rudimentale

un·sta·ble [ʌnˈsteɪbl] *adj* *person* squilibrato; *structure, area, economy* instabile

un·stead·y [ʌnˈstedɪ] *adj* *ladder* malsicuro; **be ~ on one's feet** non reggersi bene sulle gambe

un·stint·ing [ʌnˈstɪntɪŋ] *adj* *support* incondizionato; *generosity* illimitato; *praise* senza riserve; **be ~ in one's efforts** prodigarsi negli sforzi

un·stuck [ʌnˈstʌk] *adj*: **come ~** *of notice etc* staccarsi; F *of plan etc* fallire

un·suc·cess·ful [ʌnsəkˈsesfʊl] *adj* *writer etc* di scarso successo; *candidate, party* sconfitto; *attempt* fallito; **he tried but was ~** ha provato ma non ha avuto fortuna

un·suc·cess·ful·ly [ʌnsəkˈsesflɪ] *adv* *try, apply* senza successo

un·suit·a·ble [ʌnˈsuːtəbl] *adj* *partner, clothing* inadatto; *thing to say, language* inappropriato; **be ~ for** non essere adatto per; **they're ~ for each other** non sono fatti l'uno per l'altra

un·sus·pect·ing [ʌnsəˈspektɪŋ] *adj* ignaro

un·swerv·ing [ʌnˈswɜːvɪŋ] *adj* loyalty, devotion incrollabile

un·think·a·ble [ʌnˈθɪŋkəbl] *adj* impensabile

un·ti·dy [ʌnˈtaɪdɪ] *adj* room, desk, hair in disordine

un·tie [ʌnˈtaɪ] *v/t* knot disfare; laces slacciare; prisoner slegare

un·til [ʌnˈtɪl] **1** *prep* fino a; *I can wait ~ tomorrow* posso aspettare fino a domani; *from Monday ~ Friday* da lunedì a venerdì; *not ~ Friday* non prima di venerdì; *it won't be finished ~ July* non sarà finito prima di luglio **2** *conj* finché (non); *can you wait ~ I'm ready?* puoi aspettare che sia pronta?; *they won't do anything ~ you say so* non faranno niente finché non glielo dici tu

un·time·ly [ʌnˈtaɪmlɪ] *adj* death prematuro

un·tir·ing [ʌnˈtaɪrɪŋ] *adj* efforts instancabile

un·told [ʌnˈtəʊld] *adj* riches incalcolabile; suffering indescrivibile; story inedito

un·trans·lat·a·ble [ʌntrænsˈleɪtəbl] *adj* intraducibile

un·true [ʌnˈtruː] *adj* falso

un·used[1] [ʌnˈjuːzd] *adj* goods mai usato

un·used[2] [ʌnˈjuːst] *adj*: be ~ to sth non essere abituato a qc; be ~ to doing sth non essere abituato a fare qc

un·u·su·al [ʌnˈjuːʒʊəl] *adj* insolito; it's ~ for them not to write non è da loro non scrivere

un·u·su·al·ly [ʌnˈjuːʒʊəlɪ] *adv* insolitamente

un·veil [ʌnˈveɪl] *v/t* memorial, statue etc scoprire

un·well [ʌnˈwel] *adj*: be / feel ~ stare / sentirsi male

un·will·ing [ʌnˈwɪlɪŋ] *adj*: be ~ to do sth non essere disposto a fare qc

un·will·ing·ly [ʌnˈwɪlɪŋlɪ] *adv* malvolentieri

un·wind [ʌnˈwaɪnd] (pret & pp -wound) **1** *v/t* tape svolgere **2** *v/i* of

tape svolgersi; of story dipanarsi; F (relax) rilassarsi

un·wise [ʌnˈwaɪz] *adj* avventato, imprudente

un·wrap [ʌnˈræp] *v/t* (pret & pp -ped) gift aprire, scartare

un·writ·ten [ʌnˈrɪtn] *adj* law, rule tacito

un·zip [ʌnˈzɪp] *v/t* (pret & pp -ped) dress etc aprire (la chiusura lampo di); COMPUT espandere

up [ʌp] **1** *adv*: ~ in the sky / ~ on the roof in alto nel cielo / sul tetto; ~ here / there quassù / lassù; be ~ (out of bed) essere in piedi; of sun essere sorto; (be built) essere costruito; of shelves essere montato; of prices, temperature essere aumentato; (have expired) essere scaduto; the road is ~ ci sono lavori in corso; what's ~? F che c'è?; ~ to the year 1989 fino al 1989; he came ~ to me mi si è avvicinato; what are you ~ to these days? cosa fai di bello?; what are those kids ~ to? cosa stanno combinando i bambini?; be ~ to something (bad) stare architettando qualcosa; I don't feel ~ to it non me la sento; it's ~ to you dipende da te; it is ~ to them to solve it their duty sta a loro risolverlo; be ~ and about after illness essersi ristabilito **2** *prep*: further ~ the mountain più in alto sulla montagna; he climbed ~ the tree si è arrampicato sull'albero; they ran ~ the street corsero per strada; the water goes ~ this pipe l'acqua sale su per questo tubo; we travelled ~ to Milan siamo arrivati fino a Milano **3** *n*: ~s and downs alti e bassi mpl

'up·bring·ing educazione f

'up·com·ing *adj* (forthcoming) prossimo

up'date 1 *v/t* file, records aggiornare; ~ s.o. on sth mettere qu al corrente di qc **2** *n* ('update) of files, records aggiornamento m; software version upgrade m inv; can you give me an ~ on the situation? può darmi gli

U

ultimi aggiornamenti sulla situazione?

up·grade *v/t computers, equipment etc* aggiornare; *memory* potenziare, aumentare; *(replace with new versions)* passenger promuovere a una classe superiore; *product* migliorare; *I ~d the monitor* ho comprato un monitor migliore; *we could ~ you to a bigger room* possiamo offrirle una camera più grande

up·heav·al [ʌp'hiːvl] *emotional* sconvolgimento *m*; *physical* scombussolamento *m*; *political, social* sconvolgimento *m*

up·hill [ʌp'hɪl] **1** *adv:* **go / walk ~** salire **2** *adj* ['ʌphɪl] *climb* in salita; *struggle* arduo

up·hold *v/t (pret & pp -held)* *traditions, rights* sostenere; *(vindicate)* confermare

up·hol·ster·y [ʌp'həʊlstərɪ] *coverings of chairs* tappezzeria *f*; *padding of chairs* imbottitura *f*

'up·keep *of old buildings, parks etc* manutenzione *f*

'up·load *v/t* COMPUT caricare

up·mar·ket *adj restaurant, hotel* elegante; *product* di qualità

upon [ə'pɒn] *prep* → **on**

up·per ['ʌpə(r)] *adj part of sth* superiore; *deck, rooms* di sopra; *the earth's ~ atmosphere* la parte più alta dell'atmosfera terrestre; *the ~ Thames* l'alto Tamigi

up·per 'class *adj accent* aristocratico; *family* dell'alta borghesia

up·per 'clas·ses *npl* alta borghesia *f*

'up·right 1 *adj citizen* onesto **2** *adv sit* (ben) dritto

'up·right (pi·an·o) pianoforte *m* verticale

'up·ris·ing insurrezione *f*

'up·roar *loud noise* trambusto *m*; *(protest)* protesta *f*

up·set 1 *v/t (pret & pp -set)* *drink, glass* rovesciare; *(make sad)* fare stare male; *(distress)* sconvolgere; *(annoy)* seccare **2** *adj (sad)* triste; *(distressed)* sconvolto; *(annoyed)* seccato; *be / get ~* prendersela

(about per*); get ~ about sth* prendersela per qc; *have an ~ stomach* avere l'intestino in disordine

up·set·ting *adj: it's so ~ (for me)* mi fa stare male, mi turba

'up·shot *(result, outcome)* risultato *m*

'up·side vantaggio *m*

up·side 'down *adv* capovolto; *turn sth ~* capovolgere qc

up·stairs 1 *adv* di sopra **2** *adj room* al piano di sopra

'up·start novellino *m* che si comporta in modo arrogante

up·stream *adv* a monte; *follow the river ~* risalire la corrente

'up·take: be quick on the ~ capire le cose al volo; *be slow on the ~* essere lento nel capire

up·tight *adj* F *(nervous)* nervoso; *(inhibited)* inibito

up-to-'date *adj information* aggiornato; *fashions* più attuale

'up·turn *in economy* ripresa *f*

up·wards ['ʌpwədz] *adv fly, move in* su; *~ of 10,000* oltre 10.000

u·ra·ni·um [jʊ'reɪnɪəm] uranio *m*

ur·ban ['ɜːbən] *adj areas, population* urbano; *redevelopment* urbanistico

ur·ban·i·za·tion [ɜːbənaɪ'zeɪʃn] urbanizzazione *f*

ur·chin ['ɜːtʃɪn] monello *m*, -a *f*

urge [ɜːdʒ] **1** *n* (forte) desiderio *m* **2** *v/t:* **~ s.o. to do sth** raccomandare (caldamente) a qu di fare qc

♦ **urge on** *v/t (encourage)* incitare

ur·gen·cy ['ɜːdʒənsɪ] urgenza *f*; *the ~ of the situation* la gravità della situazione

ur·gent ['ɜːdʒənt] *adj job, letter* urgente; *be in ~ need of sth* avere bisogno urgente di qc; *is it ~?* è urgente?

u·ri·nate ['jʊərɪneɪt] *v/i* orinare

u·rine ['jʊərɪn] urina *f*

urn [ɜːn] urna *f*

us [ʌs] *pron direct & indirect object* ci; *when two pronouns are used* ce; *after prep* noi; *they know ~* ci conoscono; *don't leave ~* non ci lasciare, non lasciarci; *she gave ~ the keys* ci ha dato le chiavi; *she gave them to ~*

ce le ha date; *that's for ~* quello è per noi; *who's that? – it's ~* chi è? – siamo noi

US [juːˈes] *abbr* (= *United States*) USA *mpl*

USA [juːesˈeɪ] *abbr* (= *United States of America*) USA *mpl*

us·a·ble [ˈjuːzəbl] *adj* utilizzabile

us·age [ˈjuːzɪdʒ] *linguistic* uso *m*

use [juːz] **1** *v/t* tool, skills, knowledge usare, utilizzare; word, s.o.'s car usare; a lot of petrol consumare; *pej*: person usare; *I could ~ a drink* F berrei volentieri qualcosa **2** *n* [juːs] uso *m*; *be of great ~ to s.o.* essere di grande aiuto a qu; *be of no ~ to s.o.* non essere d'aiuto a qu; *is that of any ~?* ti è d'aiuto?; *it's no ~* non c'è verso; *it's no ~ trying / waiting* non serve a niente provare / aspettare

♦ **use up** *v/t* finire

used¹ [juːzd] *adj* car etc usato

used² [juːst] *adj*: *be ~ to s.o. / sth* essere abituato a qu / qc; *get ~ to s.o. / sth* abituarsi a qu / qc; *be ~ to doing sth* essere abituato a fare qc; *get ~ to doing sth* abituarsi a fare qc

used³ [juːst]: *I ~ to know him* lo conoscevo; *I ~ to like him* un tempo mi piaceva; *I don't work there now, but I ~ to* ora non più, ma una volta lavoravo lì

use·ful [ˈjuːsfʊl] *adj* information, gadget utile; person di grande aiuto

use·ful·ness [ˈjuːsfʊlnɪs] utilità *f inv*

use·less [ˈjuːslɪs] *adj* information, advice inutile; F person incapace; machine, computer inservibile; *feel ~* sentirsi inutile; *it's ~ trying* there isn't any point non serve a niente provare

us·er [ˈjuːzə(r)] of product utente *m/f*

us·er'friend·ly *adj* software, device di facile uso

ush·er [ˈʌʃə(r)] *n* (at wedding) persona *f* che accompagna gli invitati ai loro posti; in a cinema maschera *f*

♦ **usher in** *v/t* new era inaugurare

ush·er·ette [ʌʃəˈret] maschera *f*

u·su·al [ˈjuːʒʊəl] *adj* solito; *it's not ~ for this to happen* non succede quasi mai; *as ~* come al solito; *the ~, please* il solito, per favore

u·su·al·ly [ˈjuːʒʊəlɪ] *adv* di solito

u·ten·sil [juːˈtensl] utensile *m*

u·te·rus [ˈjuːtərəs] utero *m*

u·til·i·ty [juːˈtɪlətɪ] (usefulness) utilità *f inv*; *public utilities* servizi pubblici

u·til·ize [ˈjuːtɪlaɪz] *v/t* utilizzare

ut·most [ˈʌtməʊst] **1** *adj* massimo **2** *n*: *do one's ~* fare (tutto) il possibile

ut·ter [ˈʌtə(r)] **1** *adj* totale **2** *v/t* sound emettere; word proferire

ut·ter·ly [ˈʌtəlɪ] *adv* totalmente

U-turn [ˈjuːtɜːn] inversione *f* a U; *fig*: in policy dietro-front *m inv*

V

va·can·cy [ˈveɪkənsɪ] at work posto *m* vacante; in hotel camera *f* libera; *~ for a driver* as advert autista cercasi; *do you have any vacancies?* avete bisogno di personale?; *"no vacancies"* "completo"

va·cant [ˈveɪkənt] *adj* building vuoto;

room libero; position vacante; look, expression assente

va·cant·ly [ˈveɪkəntlɪ] *adv* con sguardo assente

va·cate [veɪˈkeɪt] *v/t* room lasciar libero

va·ca·tion [veɪˈkeɪʃn] *Am* vacanza *f*;

be on ~ essere in vacanza

vac·cin·ate ['væksɪneɪt] v/t vaccinare; **be ~d against ...** essere vaccinato contro ...

vac·cin·a·tion [væksɪ'neɪʃn] vaccinazione f

vac·cine ['væksiːn] vaccino m

vac·uum ['vækjʊəm] **1** n also fig vuoto m **2** v/t floors passare l'aspirapolvere su

'**vac·u·um clean·er** aspirapolvere m inv; '**vac·u·um flask** termos m inv; **vac·u·um-'packed** adj sottovuoto

vag·a·bond ['vægəbɒnd] n vagabondo m, -a f

va·gi·na [və'dʒaɪnə] vagina f

va·gi·nal ['vædʒɪnl] adj vaginale

va·grant ['veɪgrənt] n vagabondo m, -a f

vague [veɪg] adj vago; **I'm still ~ about it** non ho ancora le idee chiare al riguardo

vague·ly ['veɪglɪ] adv vagamente

vain [veɪn] **1** adj person vanitoso; hope vano **2** n: **in ~** invano; **their efforts were in ~** i loro sforzi sono stati inutili

val·en·tine ['væləntaɪn] (card) biglietto m per San Valentino; **Valentine's Day** San Valentino

val·et ['væleɪ] **1** n person cameriere m personale **2** v/t ['vælət]: **have one's car ~ed** far lavare la macchina dentro e fuori

'**val·et ser·vice** for clothes servizio m di lavanderia; for cars servizio m completo di lavaggio

val·iant ['væliənt] adj valoroso

val·iant·ly ['væliəntli] adv valorosamente

val·id ['vælɪd] adj valido

val·i·date ['vælɪdeɪt] v/t with official stamp convalidare; s.o.'s alibi confermare

va·lid·i·ty [və'lɪdətɪ] of reason, argument validità f inv

val·ley ['vælɪ] valle f

val·u·a·ble ['væljʊəbl] **1** adj prezioso **2** n: ~**s** oggetti mpl di valore

val·u·a·tion [vælju'eɪʃn] valutazione

f; **at his ~** secondo la sua valutazione

val·ue ['væljuː] **1** n valore m; **be good ~** essere conveniente; **get ~ for money** fare un affare; **rise / fall in ~** aumentare / perdere di valore **2** v/t s.o.'s friendship, one's freedom tenere a; **I ~ your advice** ci tengo alla tua opinione; **have an object ~d** far valutare un oggetto

'val·ue-ad·ded tax imposta f sul valore aggiunto

valve [vælv] valvola f

van [væn] furgone m

van·dal ['vændl] vandalo m

van·dal·is·m ['vændəlɪzm] vandalismo m

van·dal·ize ['vændəlaɪz] v/t vandalizzare

van·guard ['vænguːd] n avanguardia f; **be in the ~ of** essere all'avanguardia di

va·nil·la [və'nɪlə] **1** n vaniglia f **2** adj ice cream alla vaniglia; flavour di vaniglia

van·ish ['vænɪʃ] v/i sparire

van·i·ty ['vænətɪ] of person vanità f inv

'**van·i·ty case** beauty-case m inv

van·tage point ['vɑːntɪdʒ] on hill etc punto m d'osservazione

va·por Am → **vapour**

va·por·ize ['veɪpəraɪz] v/t vaporizzare

va·pour ['veɪpə(r)] vapore m

'**va·pour trail** of aeroplane scia f

var·i·a·ble ['veərɪəbl] **1** adj variabile **2** n MATH, COMPUT variabile f

var·i·ant ['veərɪənt] n variante f

var·i·a·tion [veərɪ'eɪʃn] variazione f

var·i·cose '**vein** ['værɪkəʊs] vena f varicosa

var·ied ['veərɪd] adj range, diet vario; life movimentato

va·ri·e·ty [və'raɪətɪ] varietà f inv; (type) tipo m; THEA varietà f inv; **a ~ of things to do** varie cose da fare

var·i·ous ['veərɪəs] adj (several) vario; (different) diverso

var·nish ['vɑːnɪʃ] **1** n for wood vernice f; (nail ~) smalto m **2** v/t wood

ver·ni·ciare; *nails* smaltare

var·y ['veərɪ] *v/t* & *v/i* (*pret* & *pp* **-ied**) variare **2** *v/t* variare

vase [vɑːz] *vaso m*

vas·ec·to·my [və'sektəmɪ] vasectomia *f*

vast [vɑːst] *adj desert, knowledge* vasto; *improvement* immenso

vast·ly ['vɑːstlɪ] *adv* immensamente

VAT [viːeɪ'tiː, væt] *abbr* (= **value added tax**) IVA *f* (= imposta *f* sul valore aggiunto)

Vat·i·can ['vætɪkən]: **the ~** il Vaticano

vau·de·ville ['vɔːdvɪl] *Am* varietà *f inv*

vault[1] [vɔlt] *n in roof* volta *f; cellar* cantina *f*; **~s of bank** caveau *m inv*

vault[2] [vɔlt] **1** *n* SP volteggio *m* **2** *v/t* saltare

VCR [viːsiːɑː(r)] *abbr* (= **video cassette recorder**) videoregistratore *m*

veal [viːl] (carne *f* di) vitello *m*

veer [vɪə(r)] *v/i of car* sterzare; *of wind, party* cambiare direzione

veg [vedʒ] F verdure *fpl*

ve·gan ['viːgn] **1** *n* vegaliano *m*, -a *f* **2** *adj* vegaliano

vege·ta·ble ['vedʒtəbl] verdura *f*

ve·ge·tar·i·an [vedʒɪ'teərɪən] **1** *n* vegetariano *m*, -a *f* **2** *adj* vegetariano

ve·ge·tar·i·an·ism [vedʒɪ'teərɪən-ɪzm] vegetarianismo *m*

veg·e·ta·tion [vedʒɪ'teɪʃn] vegetazione *f*

ve·he·mence ['viːəməns] veemenza *f*

ve·he·ment ['viːəmənt] *adj* veemente

ve·he·ment·ly ['viːəməntlɪ] *adv* veementemente

ve·hi·cle ['viːɪkl] veicolo *m; for information etc* mezzo *m*

veil [veɪl] **1** *n* velo *m* **2** *v/t* velare

vein [veɪn] ANAT vena *f*; **in this ~** *fig* su questo tono

Vel·cro® ['velkrəʊ] velcro *m*

ve·loc·i·ty [vɪ'lɒsətɪ] velocità *f inv*

vel·vet ['velvɪt] *n* velluto *m*

vel·vet·y ['velvɪtɪ] *adj* vellutato

ven·det·ta [ven'detə] vendetta *f*

vend·ing ma·chine ['vendɪŋ] distributore *m* automatico

vend·or ['vendə(r)] LAW venditore *m*, -trice *f*

ve·neer [və'nɪə(r)] *on wood* impiallacciatura *f*; *of politeness etc* parvenza *f*

ven·e·ra·ble ['venərəbl] *adj* venerabile

ven·e·rate ['venəreɪt] *v/t* venerare

ven·e·ra·tion [venə'reɪʃn] venerazione *f*

ve·ne·re·al dis·ease [vɪ'nɪərɪəl] malattia *f* venerea

Ve·ne·tian [və'niːʃn] **1** *adj* veneziano **2** *n* veneziano *m*, -a *f*

ve·ne·tian 'blind veneziana *f*

ven·geance ['vendʒəns] vendetta *f*; **with a ~** a più non posso

Ven·ice ['venɪs] Venezia *f*

ven·i·son ['venɪsn] (carne *f* di) cervo *m*

ven·om ['venəm] *also fig* veleno *m*

ven·om·ous ['venəməs] *also fig* velenoso

vent [vent] *n for air* presa *f* d'aria; **give ~ to** *feelings, emotions* dare sfogo a

ven·ti·late ['ventɪleɪt] *v/t room, building* ventilare

ven·ti·la·tion [ventɪ'leɪʃn] ventilazione *f*

ven·ti·la·tion shaft condotto *m* di aerazione

ven·ti·la·tor ['ventɪleɪtə(r)] ventilatore *m*; MED respiratore *m*

ven·tril·o·quist [ven'trɪləkwɪst] ventriloquo *m*, -a *f*

ven·ture ['ventʃə(r)] **1** *n* impresa *f* **2** *v/i* avventurarsi

ven·ue ['venjuː] *for meeting, concert etc* luogo *m*

ve·ran·da [və'rændə] veranda *f*

verb [vɜːb] verbo *m*

verb·al ['vɜːbl] verbale

verb·al·ly ['vɜːbəlɪ] verbalmente

ver·ba·tim [vɜː'beɪtɪm] *adv* parola per parola

ver·dict ['vɜːdɪkt] LAW verdetto *m*; (*opinion, judgment*) giudizio *m*; **a ~**

V

of guilty / *not guilty* un verdetto di colpevolezza / non colpevolezza

verge [vɜːdʒ] *n of road* bordo *m*; **be on the ~ of ...** *ruin, collapse* essere sull'orlo di ...; **on the ~ of tears** sul punto di piangere

♦ **verge on** *v/t* rasentare

ver·i·fi·ca·tion [verɪfɪˈkeɪʃn] verifica *f*

ver·i·fy [ˈverɪfaɪ] *v/t* (*pret & pp* **-ied**) verificare

ver·mi·cel·li [vɜːmɪˈtʃeli] *nsg* vermicelli *mpl*

ver·min [ˈvɜːmɪn] *npl* animali *mpl* nocivi

ver·mouth [ˈvɜːməθ] vermut *m inv*

ver·nac·u·lar [vəˈnækjʊlə(r)] *n* vernacolo *m*

ver·sa·tile [ˈvɜːsətaɪl] *adj* versatile

ver·sa·til·i·ty [vɜːsəˈtɪlətɪ] versatilità *f inv*

verse [vɜːs] *poetry* poesia *f*; *part of poem, song* strofa *f*

versed [vɜːst] *adj*: **be well ~ in a subject** essere versato in una materia

ver·sion [ˈvɜːʃn] versione *f*

ver·sus [ˈvɜːsəs] *prep* SP, LAW contro

ver·te·bra [ˈvɜːtɪbrə] vertebra *f*

ver·te·brate [ˈvɜːtɪbreɪt] *n* vertebrato *m*

ver·ti·cal [ˈvɜːtɪkl] *adj* verticale

ver·ti·go [ˈvɜːtɪgəʊ] vertigini *fpl*

ver·y [ˈverɪ] **1** *adv* molto; **was it cold? – not ~** faceva freddo? – non molto; **~ fast** / **easy** molto veloce / semplice; velocissimo / semplicissimo; **the ~ best** il meglio **2** *adj*: **at that ~ moment** in quel preciso momento; **that's the ~ thing I need** è proprio quello che mi serve; **the ~ thought** il solo pensiero; **right at the ~ top** / **bottom** proprio in cima / in fondo

ves·sel [ˈvesl] NAUT natante *m*

vest [vest] canottiera *f*; *Am* (*waistcoat*) gilè *m inv*

ves·tige [ˈvestɪdʒ] vestigio *m* (*pl* vestigia *f*); **not a ~ of truth** neanche un'ombra di verità

vet¹ [vet] *n* (*veterinary surgeon*) veterinario *m*, -a *f*

vet² [vet] *v/t* (*pret & pp* **-ted**) *applicants etc* passare al vaglio

vet·e·ran [ˈvetərən] **1** *n* veterano *m*, -a *f*; MIL reduce *m/f* **2** *adj* veterano

vet·e·ri·na·ry 'sur·geon [ˈvetərɪnəri] veterinario *m*, -a *f*

ve·to [ˈviːtəʊ] **1** *n* veto *m* **2** *v/t* mettere il veto a

vex [veks] *v/t* (*concern, worry*) preoccupare

vexed [vekst] *adj* (*worried*) preoccupato; **the ~ question of ...** la questione controversa di ...

vi·a [ˈvaɪə] *prep* attraverso

vi·a·ble [ˈvaɪəbl] *adj life form, company* in grado di sopravvivere; *alternative, plan* fattibile

vi·brate [vaɪˈbreɪt] *v/i* vibrare

vi·bra·tion [vaɪˈbreɪʃn] vibrazione *f*

vic·ar [ˈvɪkə(r)] parroco *m* anglicano

vic·ar·age [ˈvɪkərɪdʒ] casa *f* del parroco

vice¹ [vaɪs] *for holding* morsa *f*

vice² [vaɪs] vizio *m*

vice 'pres·i·dent vice-presidente *m*

'vice squad buoncostume *f*

vi·ce ver·sa [vaɪsˈvɜːsə] *adv* viceversa

vi·cin·i·ty [vɪˈsɪnətɪ] *n*: **in the ~ of ...** *the church etc* nelle vicinanze di ...; **£500 etc** approssimativamente ...

vi·cious [ˈvɪʃəs] *adj dog* feroce; *attack, criticism* brutale

vi·cious 'cir·cle circolo *m* vizioso

vi·cious·ly [ˈvɪʃəslɪ] *adv* brutalmente

vic·tim [ˈvɪktɪm] vittima *f*

vic·tim·ize [ˈvɪktɪmaɪz] *v/t* perseguitare

vic·tor [ˈvɪktə(r)] vincitore *m*, -trice *f*

vic·to·ri·ous [vɪkˈtɔːrɪəs] *adj army* vittorioso; *team* vincente

vic·to·ry [ˈvɪktərɪ] vittoria *f*; **win a ~ over ...** riportare una vittoria su ...

vid·e·o [ˈvɪdɪəʊ] **1** *n* video *m inv*; *tape* videocassetta *f*; (*VCR*) videoregistratore *m* **2** *v/t* registrare

'vid·e·o cam·e·ra videocamera *f*;

'vid·e·o cas·sette videocassetta *f*;

'vid·e·o con·fer·ence TELEC

videoconferenza f; **'vid·e·o game** videogame m inv; **'vid·e·o phone** videotelefono m; **'vid·e·o re·cord·er** videoregistratore m; **'vid·e·o re·cord·ing** videoregistrazione f; **'vid·e·o·tape** videocassetta f; **'vid·e·o·tape li·bra·ry** videoteca f

vie [vaɪ] v/i competere

Vi·et·nam [vɪet'næm] Vietnam m

Vi·et·nam·ese [vɪetnə'miːz] **1** adj vietnamita m/f **2** n vietnamita m/f; language vietnamita m

view [vjuː] **1** n veduta f; of situation parere m; **in ~ of** considerato; **be on ~ of paintings** essere esposto; **with a ~ to** con l'intenzione di **2** v/t events, situation vedere; TV programme guardare; house for sale vedere **3** v/i (watch TV) guardare la TV

view·er ['vjuːə(r)] TV telespettatore m, -trice f

'view·find·er PHOT mirino m

'view·point punto m di vista

vig·or Am → **vigour**

vig·or·ous ['vɪɡərəs] adj vigoroso

vig·or·ous·ly ['vɪɡərəslɪ] adv vigorosamente

vig·our ['vɪɡə(r)] vigore m

vile [vaɪl] adj disgustoso

vil·la ['vɪlə] villa f

vil·lage ['vɪlɪdʒ] paese m

vil·lag·er ['vɪlɪdʒə(r)] abitante m/f (del paese)

vil·lain ['vɪlən] cattivo m, -a f; F criminal delinquente m/f

vin·di·cate ['vɪndɪkeɪt] v/t show to be correct confermare; show to be innocent scagionare; **I feel ~d by the report** il resoconto mi dà ragione

vin·dic·tive [vɪn'dɪktɪv] adj vendicativo

vin·dic·tive·ly [vɪn'dɪktɪvlɪ] adv vendicativamente

vine [vaɪn] (grape~) vite f; climber rampicante m

vin·e·gar ['vɪnɪɡə(r)] aceto m

'vine·yard ['vɪnjɑːd] vigneto m

vin·tage ['vɪntɪdʒ] **1** n of wine annata f **2** adj (classic) d'annata

vi·o·la [vɪ'əʊlə] MUS viola f

vi·o·late ['vaɪəleɪt] v/t violare

vi·o·la·tion [vaɪə'leɪʃn] violazione f

vi·o·lence ['vaɪələns] violenza f; **outbreaks of ~** episodi di violenza

vi·o·lent ['vaɪələnt] adj violento; **have a ~ temper** avere un carattere violento

vi·o·lent·ly ['vaɪələntlɪ] adv violentemente; **fall ~ in love** innamorarsi follemente

vi·o·let ['vaɪələt] n colour viola m; plant viola f

vi·o·lin [vaɪə'lɪn] violino m

vi·o·lin·ist [vaɪə'lɪnɪst] violinista m/f

VIP [viːaɪ'piː] abbr (= **very important person**) VIP m/f

vi·per ['vaɪpə(r)] snake vipera f

vi·ral ['vaɪrəl] adj infection virale

vir·gin ['vɜːdʒɪn] vergine m/f

vir·gin·i·ty [vɜː'dʒɪnətɪ] verginità f inv; **lose one's ~** perdere la verginità

Vir·go ['vɜːɡəʊ] ASTR Vergine f

vir·ile ['vɪraɪl] adj virile

vi·ril·i·ty [vɪ'rɪlətɪ] virilità f inv

vir·tu·al ['vɜːtjʊəl] adj effettivo; COMPUT virtuale

vir·tu·al·ly ['vɜːtjʊəlɪ] adv (almost) praticamente

vir·tu·al re·al·i·ty realtà f virtuale

vir·tue ['vɜːtjuː] virtù f inv; **in ~ of** in virtù di

vir·tu·o·so [vɜːtʊ'əʊzəʊ] MUS virtuoso m, -a f

vir·tu·ous ['vɜːtjʊəs] adj virtuoso

vir·u·lent ['vɪrʊlənt] adj disease virulento; fig: attack, hatred feroce

vi·rus ['vaɪərəs] MED, COMPUT virus m inv

vi·sa ['viːzə] visto m

vise [vaɪz] Am → **vice**[1]

vis·i·bil·i·ty [vɪzə'bɪlətɪ] visibilità f inv

vis·i·ble ['vɪzəbl] adj object, difference visibile; anger evidente; **not ~ to the naked eye** invisibile ad occhio nudo

vis·i·bly ['vɪzəblɪ] adv different visibilmente; **he was ~ moved** era visibilmente emozionato

vi·sion ['vɪʒn] (eyesight) vista f; REL etc visione f

vis·it ['vɪzɪt] **1** n visita f; **pay a ~ to**

the doctor / dentist andare dal medico / dentista; *pay s.o. a ~* fare una visita a qu **2** *v/t person* andare a trovare; *place, country, city* visitare; *doctor, dentist* andare da

vis•it•ing card ['vɪzɪtɪŋ] biglietto *m* da visita

'vis•it•ing hours *npl at hospital* orario *m* delle visite

vis•it•or ['vɪzɪtə(r)] *(guest)* ospite *m*; *to museum etc* visitatore *m*, -trice *f*; *(tourist)* turista *m/f*

vi•sor ['vaɪzə(r)] visiera *f*

vis•u•al ['vɪzjʊəl] *adj organs, memory* visivo; *arts* figurativo

vis•u•al 'aid sussidio *m* visivo

vis•u•al dis•play u•nit videoterminale *m*

vis•u•al•ize ['vɪzjʊəlaɪz] *v/t* immaginare; *(foresee)* prevedere

vis•u•al•ly im•paired ['vɪzjʊəlɪ] *adj* videoleso

vi•tal ['vaɪtl] *adj (essential)* essenziale; *it is ~ that …* è essenziale che …

vi•tal•i•ty [vaɪ'tælətɪ] *of person, city etc* vitalità *f inv*

vi•tal•ly ['vaɪtəlɪ] *adv: ~ important* di vitale importanza

vi•tal 'or•gans *npl* organi *mpl* vitali

vi•tal sta•tis•tics *npl of woman* misure *fpl*

vit•a•min ['vɪtəmɪn] vitamina *f*

'vit•a•min pill (confetto *m* di) vitamina *f*

vit•ri•ol•ic [vɪtrɪ'ɒlɪk] *adj* caustico

vi•va•cious [vɪ'veɪʃəs] *adj* vivace

vi•vac•i•ty [vɪ'væsətɪ] vivacità *f inv*

viv•id ['vɪvɪd] *adj* vivido

viv•id•ly ['vɪvɪdlɪ] in modo vivido

V-neck ['viːnek] maglione *m* con scollo a V

vo•cab•u•la•ry [və'kæbjʊlərɪ] vocabolario *m*; *list of words* glossario *m*

vo•cal ['vəʊkl] *adj to do with the voice* vocale; *expressing opinions* eloquente; *become ~* cominciare a farsi sentire

'vo•cal cords *npl* corde *fpl* vocali

'vo•cal group MUS gruppo *m* vocale

vo•cal•ist ['vəʊkəlɪst] MUS cantante *m/f*

vo•ca•tion [və'keɪʃn] *(calling)* vocazione *f* (**for** a); *(profession)* professione *f*

vo•ca•tion•al [və'keɪʃnl] *adj guidance* professionale

vod•ka ['vɒdkə] vodka *f inv*

vogue [vəʊg] *n* moda *f*; *be in ~* essere in voga

voice [vɔɪs] **1** *n* voce *f* **2** *v/t opinions* esprimere

'voice mail segreteria *f* telefonica

void [vɔɪd] **1** *n* vuoto *m* **2** *adj*: *~ of* privo di

vol•a•tile ['vɒlətaɪl] *adj personality, moods* volubile

vol•ca•no [vɒl'keɪnəʊ] vulcano *m*

vol•ley ['vɒlɪ] *n of shots* raffica *f*; *in tennis* volée *f inv*

'vol•ley•ball pallavolo *f*

volt [vəʊlt] volt *m inv*

volt•age ['vəʊltɪdʒ] voltaggio *m*; *high ~* alta tensione *f*

vol•ume ['vɒljuːm] volume *m*

vol•ume con'trol volume *m*

vol•un•tar•i•ly [vɒlən'teərɪlɪ] *adv* spontaneamente

vol•un•ta•ry ['vɒləntərɪ] *adj helper* volontario; *work* volontariato

vol•un•teer [vɒlən'tɪə(r)] **1** *n* volontario *m*, -a *f* **2** *v/i* offrirsi volontario

vo•lup•tu•ous [və'lʌptjʊəs] *adj woman, figure* giunonico

vom•it ['vɒmɪt] **1** *n* vomito *m* **2** *v/i* vomitare

♦ vomit up *v/t* vomitare

vo•ra•cious [və'reɪʃəs] *adj appetite* vorace

vo•ra•cious•ly [və'reɪʃəslɪ] *eat* voracemente; *fig: read* avidamente

vote [vəʊt] **1** *n* voto *m*; *right to vote* diritto *m* di voto **2** *v/i* POL votare; *~ for / against s.o. / sth* votare a favore di / contro qu / qc **3** *v/t*: *they ~d him President* l'hanno eletto presidente; *I ~ we stay behind* propongo di rimanere

♦ vote in *v/t new member* eleggere

♦ vote on *v/t issue* mettere ai voti

♦ vote out *v/t of office* respingere

vot•er ['vəʊtə(r)] POL elettore *m*, -trice *f*

vot·ing ['vəʊtɪŋ] POL votazione f
'vot·ing booth cabina f elettorale
♦ **vouch for** [vaʊtʃ] v/t truth of sth garantire; person garantire per
vouch·er ['vaʊtʃə(r)] buono m
vow [vaʊ] **1** n voto m **2** v/t: ~ **to do sth** giurare di fare qc
vow·el [vaʊl] vocale f
voy·age ['vɔɪɪdʒ] n by sea, in space viaggio m
V-sign ['viːsaɪn] for victory segno m di vittoria; **give s.o. the ~** mandare qu a quel paese
vul·gar ['vʌlgə(r)] adj person, language volgare
vul·ne·ra·ble ['vʌlnərəbl] adj vulnerabile
vul·ture ['vʌltʃə(r)] avvoltoio m

W

wad [wɒd] n of cotton wool batuffolo m; of paper fascio m; of banknotes mazzetta f
wad·dle ['wɒdl] v/i camminare ondeggiando
wade [weɪd] v/i guadare
♦ **wade through** v/t: **I've still got this lot to wade through** devo ancora leggermi tutto questo
wa·fer ['weɪfə(r)] biscuit cialda f; REL ostia f
'wa·fer-thin adj sottilissimo
waf·fle¹ ['wɒfl] n (to eat) tipo m di cialda
waf·fle² ['wɒfl] v/i parlare a vuoto
wag [wæg] (pret & pp **-ged**) **1** v/t finger scuotere; **the dog ~ged its tail** il cane scodinzolò **2** v/i: **the dog's tail was ~ging** il cane scodinzolava
wage¹ [weɪdʒ] v/t: ~ **war against** also fig fare la guerra a
wage² [weɪdʒ] n paga f; ~**s** paga f
'wage earn·er salariato m, -a f;
'wage freeze blocco m dei salari;
'wage ne·go·ti·a·tions npl rivendicazioni fpl salariali; **'wage pack·et** fig busta f paga
wag·gle ['wægl] v/t ears, loose screw, tooth etc far muovere; ~ **one's hips** ancheggiare
wag·gon Am, **wag·on** ['wægən] RAIL carro m merci; **be on the ~** F non bere alcolici

wail [weɪl] **1** n of person gemito m; of baby vagito m; of siren ululato m **2** v/i of person gemere; of baby vagire; of siren ululare
waist [weɪst] vita f
'waist·coat gilè m inv
'waist·line vita f
wait [weɪt] **1** n attesa f **2** v/i aspettare; **we'll ~ until he's ready** aspetteremo che sia pronto; **I can't ~ to …** non vedo l'ora di … **2** v/t meal ritardare
♦ **wait for** v/t aspettare; **wait for me!** aspettami!
♦ **wait on** v/t (serve) servire
♦ **wait up** v/i restare alzato ad aspettare
wait·er ['weɪtə(r)] cameriere m; ~**!** cameriere!
wait·ing ['weɪtɪŋ] n attesa f; **no ~ sign** divieto m di sosta
'wait·ing list lista f d'attesa
'wait·ing room sala f d'attesa
wait·ress ['weɪtrɪs] cameriera f
waive [weɪv] v/t (renounce) rinunciare a; (dispense with) fare al meno di, lasciar perdere
wake¹ [weɪk] (pret **woke**, pp **woken**) **1** v/i: ~ **(up)** svegliarsi **2** v/t svegliare
wake² [weɪk] n of ship scia f; **in the ~ of** fig a seguito di; **follow in the ~ of** seguire le tracce di
'wake-up call sveglia f (telefonica)

Wales [weɪlz] Galles *m*

walk [wɔːk] **1** *n* camminata *f*; *it's a long ~ to the office* è una bella camminata fino all'ufficio; *it's a short ~ to the office* l'ufficio è a due passi; *go for a ~* fare due passi **2** *v/i* camminare; *as opposed to taking the car, bus etc* andare a piedi; *(hike)* passeggiare; *learn to ~* imparare a camminare; *we ~ed for hours* abbiamo camminato per ore; *she ~ed over to the window* andò alla finestra **3** *v/t dog* portare fuori; *I'll ~ you home* ti accompagno a casa; *~ the streets (walk around)* girare in lungo e in largo

♦ **walk out** *v/i of husband etc, from theatre* andarsene; *(go on strike)* scendere in sciopero

♦ **walk out on** *v/t spouse, family* abbandonare

'walk·a·bout bagno *m* di folla; *go ~* F *of monarch, politician* fare un bagno di folla

walk·er ['wɔːkə(r)] *(hiker)* escursionista *m/f*; *for baby* girello *m*; *for old person* deambulatore *m*; *be a slow / fast ~* avere il passo lento / spedito

walk·ie-'talk·ie [wɔːkɪ'tɔːkɪ] walkie-talkie *m inv*

walk·ing ['wɔːkɪŋ] *n as opposed to driving* camminare *m*; *(hiking)* escursionismo *m*; *it's within ~ distance* ci si arriva a piedi

'walk·ing stick bastone *m* da passeggio

'walk·ing tour escursionismo *m*

'Walk·man® walkman *m inv*; **'walk·out** *strike* sciopero *m* selvaggio; **'walk·over** *(easy win)* vittoria *f* facile

wall [wɔːl] *external* muro *m*; *internal* parete *f*; *fig: of silence etc* muro *m*; *go to the ~ of company* andare in rovina; *~s of a city* mura *fpl*; *drive s.o. up the ~* F far diventare matto qu

wal·let ['wɒlɪt] portafoglio *m*

wal·lop ['wɒləp] **1** *n* F *blow* colpo *m* **2** *v/t* F colpire; *opponent* stracciare F

'wall·pa·per 1 *n* tappezzeria *f*, carta *f* da parati **2** *v/t* tappezzare

wall-to-'wall *adj*: *~ carpet* moquette *f*

wal·nut ['wɔːlnʌt] noce *f*

waltz [wɔːlts] *n* valzer *m inv*

wan [wɒn] *adj face* pallido

wan·der ['wɒndə(r)] *v/i (roam)* gironzolare; *(stray)* allontanarsi; *my attention began to ~* mi sono distratto

♦ **wander around** *v/i* girare

wane [weɪn] *v/i of interest, enthusiasm* calare

wan·gle ['wæŋgl] *v/t* F rimediare F

want [wɒnt] **1** *n*: *for ~ of* per mancanza di **2** *v/t* volere; *(need)* avere bisogno di; *~ to do sth* volere fare qc; *I ~ to stay here* voglio stare qui; *do you ~ to come too? – no, I don't ~ to* vuoi venire anche tu? – no, grazie; *you can have whatever you ~* puoi avere tutto ciò che vuoi; *it's not what I ~ed* non è quello che volevo; *she ~s you to go back* vuole che torni indietro; *he ~s a haircut* dovrebbe tagliarsi i capelli **3** *v/i*: *~ for nothing* non mancare di niente

'want ad annuncio *m* economico

want·ed ['wɒntɪd] *adj by police* ricercato

want·ing ['wɒntɪŋ] *adj*: *be ~ in* mancare di

wan·ton ['wɒntən] *adj cruelty, neglect* gratuito

war [wɔː(r)] *n* guerra *f*; *fig* lotta *f*; *be at ~* essere in guerra

war·ble ['wɔːbl] *v/i of bird* gorgheggiare

ward [wɔːd] *n in hospital* corsia *f*; *child minore m* sotto tutela

♦ **ward off** *v/t blow* parare; *attacker* respingere; *cold* combattere

war·den ['wɔːdn] *(traffic ~)* vigile *m* urbano; *of hostel* direttore *m*, *-trice f*; *of nature reserve* guardiano *m*, *-a f*; *Am: of prison* agente *m/f* di custodia

ward·er ['wɔːdə(r)] agente *m/f* di custodia

'ward·robe *for clothes* armadio *m*; *clothes* guardaroba *m*

ware·house ['weəhaʊs] magazzino *m*

'war·fare guerra *f*

'war·head testata *f*

war·i·ly ['weərılı] *adv* con aria guardinga

warm [wɔːm] **1** *adj* caldo; *welcome, smile* caloroso; **it's ~ of weather** fa caldo; **it's ~ in here** qui c'è caldo; **are you ~ enough?** ti fa freddo? **2** *v/t*: → **warm up**

♦**warm up 1** *v/t* scaldare **2** *v/i* scaldarsi; *of athlete etc* fare riscaldamento

warm·heart·ed ['wɔːmhɑːtıd] *adj* cordiale

warm·ly ['wɔːmlı] *adv dressed* con abiti pesanti; *welcome, smile* calorosamente

warmth [wɔːmθ] calore *m*; *of welcome, smile* calorosità *f inv*

'warm-up SP riscaldamento *m*

warn [wɔːn] *v/t* avvertire

warn·ing ['wɔːnıŋ] *n* avvertimento *m*; **without ~** senza preavviso

warp [wɔːp] **1** *v/t wood* deformare; *character* segnare **2** *v/i of wood* deformarsi

warped [wɔːpt] *adj fig* contorto

'war·plane aereo *m* militare

war·rant ['wɒrənt] **1** *n* mandato *m* **2** *v/t* (*deserve, call for*) giustificare

war·ran·ty ['wɒrəntı] (*guarantee*) garanzia *f*; **be under ~** essere in garanzia

war·ri·or ['wɒrıə(r)] guerriero *m*, -a *f*

'war·ship nave *f* da guerra

wart [wɔːt] verruca *f*

'war·time tempo *m* di guerra

war·y ['weərı] *adj* guardingo; **be ~ of** diffidare di

was [wɒz] *pret* → **be**

wash [wɒʃ] **1** *n*: **have a ~** darsi una lavata; **that skirt needs a ~** quella gonna va lavata **2** *v/t* lavare; **~ one's hands / hair** lavarsi le mani / i capelli **3** *v/i* lavarsi

♦**wash up** *v/i Br* (*wash the dishes*) lavare i piatti

wash·a·ble ['wɒʃəbl] *adj* lavabile

'wash·ba·sin, 'wash·bowl lavandino *m*

washed out [wɒʃt'aʊt] *adj* sfinito

wash·er ['wɒʃə(r)] *for tap etc* guarnizione *f*; → **washing machine**

wash·ing ['wɒʃıŋ] *washed clothes* bucato *m*; *clothes to be washed* biancheria *f* da lavare; **do the ~** fare il bucato

'wash·ing ma·chine lavatrice *f*

'wash·ing pow·der detersivo *m* per bucato

wash·ing-'up: **do the ~** lavare i piatti

wash·ing-'up liq·uid detersivo *m* per i piatti

wasp [wɒsp] vespa *f*

waste [weıst] **1** *n* spreco *m*; *from industrial process* rifiuti *mpl*; **it's a ~ of time / money** è tempo sprecato / sono soldi sprecati **2** *adj material* di scarto **3** *v/t* sprecare

♦**waste away** *v/i* deperire

'waste dis·pos·al (unit) tritarifiuti *m inv*

waste·ful ['weıstful] *adj person* sprecone; *methods, processes* dispendioso

'waste·land distesa *f* desolata; **waste·'pa·per** cartaccia *f*; **waste-pa·per 'bas·ket** cestino *m* della cartaccia; **'waste prod·uct** scorie *fpl* industriali

watch [wɒtʃ] **1** *n timepiece* orologio *m*; MIL guardia *f*; **keep ~** stare all'erta **2** *v/t film, TV* guardare; (*spy on*) sorvegliare; (*look after*) tenere d'occhio **3** *v/i* guardare

♦**watch for** *v/t* aspettare

♦**watch out** *v/i* fare attenzione; **watch out!** attento!

♦**watch out for** *v/t* fare attenzione a

'watch·dog *fig* comitato *m* di controllo

watch·ful ['wɒtʃful] *adj* vigile

'watch·mak·er orologiaio *m*, -a *f*

wa·ter ['wɔːtə(r)] **1** *n* acqua *f*; **~s** NAUT acque (territoriali) **2** *v/t plant* annaffiare **3** *v/i of eyes* lacrimare; **my mouth is ~ing** ho l'acquolina in bocca

W

♦ **water down** *v/t drink* diluire

'**wa·ter can·non** idrante *m*; '**wa·ter·col·or** *Am*, '**wa·ter·col·our** *n* acquerello *m*; '**wa·ter·cress** crescione *m*

wa·tered '**down** ['wɔːtəd] *adj fig* edulcorato

'**wa·ter·fall** cascata *f*

wa·ter·ing can ['wɔːtərɪŋ] annaffiatoio *m*

'**wa·ter·ing hole** hum bar *m inv*

'**wa·ter lev·el** livello *m* delle acque; '**wa·ter lil·y** ninfea *f*, **wa·ter·logged** ['wɔːtəlɒgd] *adj* allagato; '**wa·ter main** conduttura *f* dell'acqua; '**wa·ter mark** filigrana *f*; '**wa·ter mel·on** anguria *f*, cocomero *m*; '**wa·ter pol·lu·tion** inquinamento *m* dell'acqua; '**wa·ter·proof** *adj* impermeabile

'**wa·ter·shed** *fig* svolta *f*; TV *ora f dopo la quale sono ammessi programmi per un pubblico adulto*; '**wa·ter·side** *n*: **at the ~** sulla riva; '**wa·ter·ski·ing** *n* sci *m inv* nautico; '**wa·ter·tight** *adj compartment* stagno; *fig* inattaccabile; '**wa·ter·way** corso *m* d'acqua navigabile; '**wa·ter·wings** *npl* braccioli *mpl*; '**wa·ter·works**: **turn on the ~** F piangere

wa·ter·y ['wɔːtərɪ] *adj* acquoso

watt [wɒt] watt *m inv*

wave[1] [weɪv] *n in sea* onda *f*

wave[2] [weɪv] **1** *n of hand* saluto *m* (con la mano) **2** *v/i with hand* salutare (con la mano); **~ to s.o.** salutare qu (con la mano) **3** *v/t flag etc* sventolare

'**wave·length** RAD lunghezza *f* d'onda; **be on the same ~** *fig* essere sulla stessa lunghezza d'onda

wa·ver ['weɪvə(r)] *v/i* vacillare

wav·y ['weɪvɪ] *adj hair, line* ondulato

wax [wæks] *n for floor, furniture* cera *f*; *in ear* cerume *m*

way [weɪ] **1** *n* (*method, manner*) modo *m*; (*manner*) maniera *f*; (*route*) strada *f*; **this ~** (*like this*); (*in this direction*) da questa parte; **by the ~** (*incidentally*) a proposito; **by ~ of** (*via*) passando per; (*in the form*

of) come; **in a ~** (*in certain respects*) in un certo senso; **be under ~** essere in corso; **give ~** MOT dare la precedenza; (*collapse*) crollare; **X has given ~ to Y** (*been replaced by*) Y ha preso il posto di X; **have one's** (**own**) **~** averla vinta; **OK, we'll do it your ~** OK, faremo come dici tu; **lead the ~** *also fig* fare strada; **lose one's ~** smarrirsi; **be in the ~** (*be an obstruction*) essere d'intralcio; **it's on the ~ to the station** è sulla strada della stazione; **I was on my ~ to the station** stavo andando alla stazione; **no ~!** neanche per sogno!; **there's no ~ he can do it** è impossibile che ce la faccia **2** *adv* F (*much*); **it's ~ too soon to decide** è veramente troppo presto per decidere; **they are ~ behind with their work** sono molto indietro con il lavoro

way 'in entrata *f*; **way of 'life** stile *m* di vita; **way 'out** *n* uscita *f*; *fig: from situation* via *f* d'uscita

we [wiː] *pron* noi; **~'re the best** siamo i migliori; **they're going, but ~'re not** loro vanno, noi no

weak [wiːk] *adj physically, morally* debole; *tea, coffee* leggero

weak·en ['wiːkn] **1** *v/t* indebolire **2** *v/i* indebolirsi

weak·ling ['wiːklɪŋ] *morally* smidollato *m*, -a *f*; *physically* mingherlino *m*, -a *f*

weak·ness ['wiːknɪs] debolezza *f*; **have a ~ for sth** (*liking*) avere un debole per qc

wealth [welθ] ricchezza *f*; **a ~ of** una grande abbondanza di

wealth·y ['welθɪ] *adj* ricco

weap·on ['wepən] arma *f*

wear [weə(r)] **1** *n*: **~** (**and tear**) usura *f*; **clothes for everyday ~** vestiti per tutti i giorni; **clothes for evening ~** abiti da sera **2** *v/t* (*pret* **wore**, *pp* **worn**) (*have on*) indossare; (*damage*) logorare **3** *v/i* (*pret* **wore**, *pp* **worn**) (*wear out*) logorarsi; (*last*) durare

♦ **wear away 1** *v/i* consumarsi **2** *v/t* consumare

♦ **wear down** v/t resistance fiaccare

♦ **wear off** v/i of effect, feeling svanire

♦ **wear out 1** v/t (tire) estenuare; shoes consumare **2** v/i of shoes, carpet consumarsi

wea·ri·ly ['wɪərɪlɪ] adv stancamente

wear·ing ['weərɪŋ] adj (tiring) stancante

wear·y ['wɪərɪ] adj stanco

weath·er ['weðə(r)] **1** n tempo m; **be feeling under the ~** sentirsi poco bene **2** v/t crisis superare

'**weath·er-beat·en** adj segnato; '**weath·er fore·cast** previsioni fpl del tempo; '**weath·er·man** meteorologo m

weave [wiːv] **1** v/t (pret **wove**, pp **woven**) cloth tessere; basket intrecciare **2** v/i (move) zigzagare

web [web] of spider ragnatela f; **the Web** COMPUT il web m inv, la Rete f inv

webbed 'feet piedi mpl palmati

'**web page** pagina f web

'**web site** sito m web

wed·ding ['wedɪŋ] matrimonio m

'**wed·ding an·ni·ver·sa·ry** anniversario m di matrimonio; '**wed·ding cake** torta f nuziale; '**wed·ding day** giorno m del matrimonio; '**wed·ding dress** abito m or vestito m da sposa; '**wed·ding ring** fede f

wedge [wedʒ] **1** n to hold sth in place zeppa f; of cheese etc fetta f **2** v/t: ~ **open** tenere aperto

Wed·nes·day ['wenzdeɪ] mercoledì m inv

wee [wiː] adj F piccolo; **a ~ bit** un pochino

weed [wiːd] **1** n erbaccia f **2** v/t diserbare

♦ **weed out** v/t (remove) eliminare

'**weed-kill·er** diserbante m

weed·y ['wiːdɪ] adj F mingherlino

week [wiːk] settimana f; **a ~ tomorrow** una settimana a domani

'**week·day** giorno m feriale

week'end fine m settimana, weekend m inv; **at or Am on the ~** durante il fine settimana

week·ly ['wiːklɪ] **1** adj settimanale

2 n magazine settimanale m **3** adv settimanalmente

weep [wiːp] v/i (pret & pp **wept**) piangere

weep·y ['wiːpɪ] adj: **be ~** essere piagnucoloso

wee-wee ['wiː] **1** n F pipì f inv F; **do a ~** fare la pipì **2** v/i F fare la pipì

weigh [weɪ] v/t & v/i pesare

♦ **weigh down** v/t: **be weighed down** with with bags curvarsi sotto il peso di; with worries essere oppresso da

♦ **weigh on** v/t preoccupare

♦ **weigh up** v/t (assess) valutare

weight [weɪt] of person, object peso m; **put on / lose ~** ingrassare / dimagrire

♦ **weight down** v/t fermare con pesi

weight·less·ness ['weɪtləsnəs] assenza f di peso

'**weight·lift·er** pesista m/f

'**weight·lift·ing** sollevamento m pesi

weight·y ['weɪtɪ] adj fig: important importante

weir [wɪə(r)] chiusa f

weird [wɪəd] adj strano

weird·ly ['wɪədlɪ] adv stranamente

weird·o ['wɪədəʊ] n F pazzoide m/f

wel·come ['welkəm] **1** adj benvenuto; **make s.o. ~** accogliere bene qu; **it makes a ~ change** è un gradito cambiamento; **you're ~!** prego!; **you're ~ to try some** serviti pure **2** n also fig accoglienza f; fig: to news, proposal accoglienza f **3** v/t guests etc accogliere; fig: decision etc rallegrarsi di; fig: **she ~s a challenge** apprezza le sfide

weld [weld] v/t saldare

weld·er ['weldə(r)] saldatore m, -trice f

wel·fare ['welfeə(r)] bene m inv

wel·fare 'state stato m sociale; '**wel·fare work** assistenza f sociale; '**wel·fare work·er** assistente m/f sociale

well¹ [wel] n for water, oil pozzo m

well² [wel] **1** adv bene; **~ done!** bravo!; **as ~** (too) anche; **as ~ as** in addition to oltre a; **it's just as ~ you**

told me hai fatto bene a dirmelo; **very** *~ acknowledging an order* benissimo; *when you don't agree with sth but are doing it anyway* va bene; **~, ~! surprise** bene, bene!; **~ …** *uncertainty, thinking* beh … **2** *adj:* **be ~ while; feel ~** sentirsi bene; **get ~ soon!** guarisci presto!

well-'bal·anced *adj person, meal* equilibrato; *meal, diet* equilibrato; **well-be'haved** *adj* educato; **well-'be·ing** benessere *m*; **well-'built** *adj* ben fatto; *euph (fat)* robusto; **well-'done** *adj meat* ben cotto; **well-'dressed** *adj* ben vestito; **well-'earned** *adj* meritato; **well-'heeled** *adj* F danaroso

wel·lies ['welɪz] *npl* F → **wellingtons**

well-in'formed *adj* ben informato

wel·ling·tons ['welɪŋtənz] *npl* stivali *mpl* di gomma

well-'known *adj* famoso; **well-'made** *adj* ben fatto; **well-'mannered** *adj* ben educato; **well-'mean·ing** *adj* spinto da buone intenzioni; **well-'off** *adj* benestante; **well-'paid** *adj* ben pagato; **well-'read** *adj* colto; **well-'timed** *adj* tempestivo; **well-to-'do** *adj* abbiente; **well-'worn** *adj* liso

Welsh [welʃ] **1** *adj* gallese **2** *n language* gallese *m*; **the ~** i gallesi

went [went] *pret* → **go**

wept [wept] *pret & pp* → **weep**

were [wɜ:(r)] *pret pl* → **be**

west [west] **1** *n* ovest *m*, occidente *m*; **the West** POL l'Occidente *m*; *western part of a country* parte *f* occidentale del paese **2** *adj* occidentale **3** *adv* verso ovest; **~ of** a ovest di

west·er·ly ['westəlɪ] *adj* occidentale; **in a ~ direction** verso ovest

west·ern ['westən] **1** *adj* occidentale; **Western** occidentale **2** *n (film)* western *m inv*

West·ern·er ['westənə(r)] occidentale *m/f*

west·ern·ized ['westənaɪzd] *adj* occidentalizzato

west·ward ['westwəd] *adv* verso ovest

wet [wet] *adj* bagnato; *(rainy)* piovoso; **~ paint** *as sign* vernice fresca; **be ~ through** essere fradicio

wet 'blan·ket F guastafeste *m/f inv*

'wet suit *for diving* muta f

whack [wæk] **1** *n* F *(blow)* colpo *m*; F *(share)* parte *f* **2** *v/t* F colpire

whacked [wækt] *adj* F stanco morto

whack·ing ['wækɪŋ] *adj* F enorme

whale [weɪl] balena *f*

whal·ing ['weɪlɪŋ] *caccia* *f* alla balena

wharf [wɔ:f] *n* banchina *f*

what [wɒt] **1** *pron* (che) cosa; **~ is that?** (che) cos'è?; **~ is it?** *(what do you want)* (che) cosa c'è?; **~?** cosa?; *astonishment* (che) cosa?; **it's not ~ I meant** non è ciò che volevo dire; **~ about some dinner?** e se mangiassimo qualcosa?; **~ about heading home?** e se ce ne andassimo a casa?; **~ is the date today?** quanti ne abbiamo oggi?; **~ for?** *(why)* perché?; **so ~?** e allora? **2** *adj* che *inv*, quale; **~ colour is the car?** di che colore è la macchina?; **~ university are you at?** in quale università studi? **3** *adv:* **~ a brilliant idea!** che bella idea!

what·ev·er [wɒt'evə(r)] **1** *pron:* **I'll do ~ you want** farò (tutto) quello che vuoi; **~ I do, it'll be a probem** qualsiasi cosa faccia, ci saranno problemi; **~ the season** *regardless of* in qualunque stagione; **~ people say** qualunque cosa dica la gente; **~ gave you that idea?** cosa mai te lo ha fatto pensare? **2** *adj* qualunque; **you have no reason ~ to worry** non hai nessun motivo di preoccuparti

wheat [wi:t] grano *m*, frumento *m*

whee·dle ['wi:dl] *v/t* F: **~ sth out of s.o.** ottenere qc da qu con lusinghe

wheel [wi:l] **1** *n* ruota *f*, *(steering ~)* volante *m* **2** *v/t bicycle* spingere **3** *v/i of birds* roteare

♦ **wheel around** *v/i* voltarsi

'wheel·bar·row carriola *f*; **'wheel·chair** sedia *f* a rotelle; **'wheel**

clamp ceppo *m* bloccaruote

wheeze [wi:z] *v/i* ansimare

when [wen] *adv conj* quando **2** *conj* quando; ~ **I was a child** quand'ero bambino

when·ev·er [wen'evə(r)] *adv* (*each time*) ogni volta che; *regardless of when* in qualunque momento

where [weə(r)] **1** *adv* dove **2** *conj* dove; *this is ~ I used to live* io abitavo qui

where·a·bouts [weərə'baʊts] **1** *adv* dove **2** *npl*: *know s.o.'s ~* sapere dove si trova qu

where·as [weər'æz] mentre

wher·ev·er [weər'evə(r)] **1** *conj* dovunque; ~ *you go* dovunque tu vada **2** *adv* dove; ~ *can he be?* dove sarà mai?

whet [wet] *v/t v/t* (*pret & pp* **-ted**) appetite stuzzicare

wheth·er ['weðə(r)] *pron* se

which [wɪtʃ] **1** *adj* quale; ~ *one is yours?* qual è il tuo? **2** *pron interrogative* quale; *relative* che; *on / in* ~ su / in cui; *take one, it doesn't matter* ~ prendine uno, non importa quale

which·ev·er [wɪtʃ'evə(r)] **1** *adj* qualunque **2** *pron* quello che *m*, quella che *f*; ~ *of the methods* qualunque metodo

whiff [wɪf] *unpleasant* zaffata *f*; *catch a ~ of* sentire

while [waɪl] **1** *conj* mentre; (*although*) benché **2** *n*: *a long ~ ago* molto tempo fa; *wait a long ~* aspettare molto *o* lungo; *for a ~* per un po'; *in a ~* fra poco; *I'll wait a ~ longer* aspetto un altro po'

◆ **while away** *v/t* passare

whim [wɪm] capriccio *m*

whim·per ['wɪmpə(r)] **1** *n of person, baby* gemito *m*; *of animal* mugolio *m* **2** *v/i of person, baby* gemere; *of animal* mugolare

whine [waɪn] *v/i of dog* guaire; F (*complain*) piagnucolare

whip [wɪp] **1** *n* frusta *f* **2** *v/t* (*pret & pp* **-ped**) (*beat*) sbattere; *cream* montare; F (*defeat*) stracciare F

◆ **whip out** *v/t* F tirar fuori (fulmineamente)

◆ **whip up** *v/t* (*arouse*) sobillare; F *meal* improvvisare

whipped cream [wɪpt] panna *f* montata

whip·ping ['wɪpɪŋ] (*beating*) bastonata *f*; F (*defeat*) batosta *f*

'whip·ping cream panna *f* da montare

'whip·round F colletta *f*; *have a ~* fare una colletta

whirl [wɜ:l] **1** *n*: *my mind is in a ~* mi gira la testa **2** *v/i of blades etc* roteare; *of leaves* volteggiare; *of person* girarsi

'whirl·pool *in river* mulinello *m*; *for relaxation* vasca *f* per idromassaggio

whirr [wɜ:(r)] *v/i* ronzare

whisk [wɪsk] **1** *n* frusta *f*; *mechanical* frullino *m* **2** *v/t eggs* frullare

◆ **whisk away** *v/t* togliere in fretta

whis·kers ['wɪskəz] *npl of man* basette *fpl*; *of animal* baffi *mpl*

whis·ky of whisky *m inv*

whis·per ['wɪspə(r)] **1** *n* bisbiglio *m*; (*rumour*) voce *f* **2** *v/t & v/i* bisbigliare

whis·tle ['wɪsl] **1** *n sound* fischio *m*; *device* fischietto *m* **2** *v/i* fischiare **3** *v/t* fischiettare

whis·tle-blow·er ['wɪslbləʊə(r)] F *persona f che denuncia irregolarità all'interno della propria azienda*

white [waɪt] **1** *n in colour* bianco *m*; *of egg* albume *m*, bianco *m* F; *person* bianco *m*, -a *f* **2** *adj* bianco; *person* bianco; *go ~* sbiancare (in viso)

white 'Christ·mas natale *m* con la neve; **white 'cof·fee** *Br* caffè *m inv* con latte *o* panna; **white-col·lar 'work·er** impiegato *m*, -a *f*; **'White House** Casa *f* Bianca; **white 'lie** bugia *f* innocente; **white 'meat** carne *f* bianca; **'white·wash 1** *n* calce *f*, *fig* copertura *f* **2** *v/t* imbiancare (con calce); **white 'wine** vino *m* bianco

Whit·sun ['wɪtsn] Pentecoste *f*

whit·tle ['wɪtl] *v/t wood* intagliare

◆ **whittle down** *v/t* ridurre

whiz(z) [wɪz] *n*: *be a ~ at* F essere un genio in
♦ **whizz by**, **whizz past** *v/i of time*, *car* sfrecciare

'whizz-kid F mago *m*, -a f F

who [huː] *pron interrogative* chi; *relative* che; *the man ~ I was talking to* l'uomo con cui parlavo; *I don't know ~ to believe* non so a chi credere

who·dun(n)·it [huː'dʌnɪt] giallo *m*

who·ev·er [huː'evə(r)] *pron* chiunque; *(interrogative)* chi mai; *~ can that be?* chi sarà mai?

whole [həʊl] **1** *adj*: *the ~ town* tutta la città; *two ~ hours / days* ben due ore / giorni; *a ~ chicken* un pollo intero; *he drank / ate the ~ lot* ha bevuto / mangiato tutto; *it's a ~ lot easier / better* è molto più facile / meglio **2** *n* tutto *m*; *the ~ of the United States* tutti gli Stati Uniti; *on the ~* nel complesso

whole-heart·ed [həʊl'hɑːtɪd] *adj* senza riserve; **whole-heart·ed·ly** [həʊl'hɑːtɪdlɪ] *adv* senza riserve; **whole·meal 'bread** pane *m* integrale; **'whole·sale 1** *adj* all'ingrosso; *fig* in massa **2** *adv* all'ingrosso; **whole·sal·er** ['həʊlseɪlə(r)] grossista *m/f*; **whole·some** ['həʊlsəm] *adj* sano

whol·ly ['həʊlɪ] *adv* completamente

whol·ly owned 'sub·sid·i·ar·y consociata *f* interamente controllata

whom [huːm] *pron fml* chi; *to / for a ~* cui

whoop·ing cough ['huːpɪŋ] pertosse *f*

whop·ping ['wɒpɪŋ] *adj* F enorme

whore [hɔː(r)] *n* puttana *f*

whose [huːz] **1** *pron interrogative* di chi; *relative* il / la cui; *~ is this?* di chi è questo?; *a man ~ wife ...* un uomo la cui moglie ...; *a country ~ economy is booming* un paese dall'economia fiorente **2** *adj* di chi; *~ bike is that?* di chi è quella bici?; *~ car are we taking?* che macchina prendiamo?

why [waɪ] *adv* perché; *that's ~* ecco perché; *~ not?* perché no?; *the reason ~ he left* il motivo per cui se ne è andato

wick·ed ['wɪkɪd] *adj (evil)* malvagio; *(mischievous)* malizioso

wick·er ['wɪkə(r)] *adj* di vimini

wick·er 'chair poltrona *f* di vimini

wick·et ['wɪkɪt] porta *f*

wide [waɪd] *adj* largo; *experience* vasto; *range* ampio; *be 12 metres ~* essere largo 12 metri

wide-a·wake *adj* sveglio

wide·ly ['waɪdlɪ] *adv used*, *known* largamente; *it is ~ believed that ...* è una credenza diffusa che ...

wid·en ['waɪdn] **1** *v/t* allargare **2** *v/i* allargarsi

wide-'o·pen *adj* spalancato; **wide-'rang·ing** *adj* di largo respiro; **'wide·spread** *adj* diffuso

wid·ow ['wɪdəʊ] *n* vedova *f*

wid·ow·er ['wɪdəʊə(r)] vedovo *m*

width [wɪdθ] larghezza *f*; *of fabric* altezza *f*

wield [wiːld] *v/t weapon* brandire; *power* esercitare

wife [waɪf] (*pl* **wives** [waɪvz]) moglie *f*

wig [wɪg] parrucca *f*

wig·gle ['wɪgl] *v/t*: *~ one's hips* ancheggiare; *loose screw etc* muovere

wild [waɪld] **1** *adj animal*, *flowers* selvatico; *teenager*, *party* scatenato; *(crazy: scheme)* folle; *applause* fragoroso; *be ~ about ... (keen on)* andare pazzo per ...; *go ~* impazzire; *(become angry)* andare su tutte le furie; *run ~ of children* scatenarsi; *of plants* crescere senza controllo **2** *n*: *the ~s* le zone sperdute

wil·der·ness ['wɪldənɪs] *empty place* deserto *m*; *fig: garden etc* giungla *f*

'wild·fire: *spread like ~* allargarsi a macchia d'olio; **wild'goose chase** ricerca *f* inutile; **'wild·life** fauna *f*; *~ programme* programma *m* sulla natura

wild·ly ['waɪldlɪ] *adv* F terribilmente

wil·ful ['wɪlfʊl] *adj person* ostinato; *action* intenzionale; *action*

will¹ [wɪl] *n* LAW testamento *m*

will² [wɪl] *n* (*willpower*) volontà *f inv*

will³ [wɪl] *v/aux*: **I ~ let you know tomorrow** ti farò sapere entro domani; **~ you be there?** ci sarai?; **I won't be back** non tornerò; **you ~ call me, won't you?** mi chiamerai, vero?; **I'll pay for this – no you won't** questo lo pago io – no, lascia stare; **the car won't start** la macchina non parte; **~ you tell her that ...?** dille che ...; **~ you have some more tea?** vuoi dell'altro tè?; **~ you stop that!** smettila!

will·ful *Am* → **wilful**

will·ing ['wɪlɪŋ] *adj* disponibile; **are you ~ to pay more?** sei disposto a pagare di più?; **he was not ~ to accept** no ha voluto accettare

will·ing·ly ['wɪlɪŋlɪ] *adv* volentieri

will·ing·ness ['wɪlɪŋnɪs] disponibilità *f inv*

wil·low ['wɪləʊ] *n* salice *m*

'will·pow·er forza *f* di volontà

wil·ly-nil·ly [wɪlɪ'nɪlɪ] *adv* (*at random*) a casaccio

wilt [wɪlt] *v/i* of plant appassire

wi·ly ['waɪlɪ] *adj* astuto

wimp [wɪmp] F pappamolle *m/f*

win [wɪn] **1** *n* vittoria *f* **2** *v/t & v/i* (*pret & pp* **won**) vincere

◆ **win back** *v/t* riconquistare

wince [wɪns] *v/i* fare una smorfia

wind¹ [wɪnd] **1** *n* vento *m*; (*flatulence*) aria *f*; **get ~ of ...** venire a sapere ... **2** *v/t* **~ s.o.** togliere il fiato a qu

wind² [waɪnd] (*pret & pp* **wound**) **1** *v/i* of path, stream snodarsi; of plant avvolgersi **2** *v/t* avvolgere

◆ **wind down 1** *v/i*: **the party began to wind down** la gente cominciò ad andar via dalla festa **2** *v/t* car window abbassare; business chiudere gradualmente

◆ **wind up 1** *v/t* clock caricare; car window tirar su; speech, presentation concludere; business, affairs, company chiudere **2** *v/i*: **wind up in hospital** finire in ospedale

'wind·bag F trombone *m*

'wind·fall *fig* colpo *m* di fortuna

wind·ing ['waɪndɪŋ] *adj* tortuoso

'wind in·stru·ment strumento *m* a fiato

'wind·mill mulino *m*

win·dow ['wɪndəʊ] of house finestra *f*, of shop vetrina *f*; of car, train finestrino *m*; COMPUT finestra *f*; **in the ~** of shop in vetrina

'win·dow box fioriera *f*; **'win·dow clean·er** lavavetri *m/f inv*; **'win·dow·pane** vetro *m* (della finestra); **'win·dow seat** on plane, train posto *m* di finestrino; **'window-shop** *v/i* (*pret & pp* **-ped**): **go ~ping** guardare le vetrine; **window·sill** ['wɪndəʊsɪl] davanzale *m*

'wind·screen parabrezza *m inv*; **'wind·screen wip·er** tergicristallo *m*; **'wind·shield** *Am* parabrezza *m inv* **'wind·surf·er** person windsurfista *m/f*; board windsurf *m inv*; **'wind·surf·ing** windsurf *m inv*

wind·y ['wɪndɪ] *adj* weather, day ventoso; **it's getting ~** si sta alzando il vento

wine [waɪn] vino *m*

'wine bar enoteca *f*, bar *m inv*; **'wine cel·lar** cantina *f*; **'wine glass** bicchiere *m* da vino; **'wine list** lista *f* dei vini; **'wine mak·er** viticoltore *m*, -trice *f*; **'wine mer·chant** company azienda *f* vinicola; individual vinaio *m*, -a *f*

wing [wɪŋ] *n also* SP ala *f*

'wing·span apertura *f* alare

wink [wɪŋk] **1** *n* occhiolino *m*; **I didn't sleep a ~** F non ho chiuso occhio **2** *v/i* of person strizzare gli occhi; **~ at s.o.** fare l'occhiolino a qu

win·ner ['wɪnə(r)] vincitore *m*, -trice *f*

win·ning ['wɪnɪŋ] *adj* vincente

'win·ning post traguardo *m*

win·nings ['wɪnɪŋz] *npl* vincita *fsg*

win·ter ['wɪntə(r)] *n* inverno *m*

win·ter 'sports *npl* sport *m inv* invernali

win·try ['wɪntrɪ] *adj* invernale

wipe [waɪp] *v/t* (*dry*) asciugare; (*clean*) pulire; tape cancellare

W

♦ **wipe out** v/t (*kill*, *destroy*) distruggere; *debt* estinguere

wip·er ['waɪpə(r)] → **windscreen wiper**

wire ['waɪə(r)] **1** adj metallico **2** n fil m di ferro; ELEC filo m elettrico

wire·less ['waɪələs] radio f inv

wire 'net·ting rete f metallica

wir·ing ['waɪərɪŋ] n ELEC impianto m elettrico

wir·y ['waɪərɪ] adj person dal fisico asciutto

wis·dom ['wɪzdəm] saggezza f

'wis·dom tooth dente m del giudizio

wise [waɪz] adj saggio

'wise·crack n F spiritosaggine f

'wise guy pej spiritoso m

wise·ly ['waɪzlɪ] adv act saggiamente

wish [wɪʃ] **1** n desiderio m; **make a ~** esprimere un desiderio; **against his family's ~es** contro il volere della famiglia; **best ~es for birthday etc** tanti auguri; **as greetings** cordiali saluti **2** v/t volere; **I ~ that he'd stop** vorrei che la smettesse; **~ s.o. well** fare tanti auguri a qu; **I ~ed him good luck** gli ho augurato buona fortuna **3** v/i: **wish for** desiderare

'wish·bone forcella f (di pollo)

wish·ful 'think·ing ['wɪʃful] illusione f

wish·y-wash·y ['wɪʃɪwɒʃɪ] adj person insulso; colour slavato

wisp [wɪsp] of hair ciocca f; of smoke filo m

wist·ful ['wɪstful] adj malinconico

wist·ful·ly ['wɪstfəlɪ] adv malinconicamente

wit [wɪt] (*humour*) spirito m; person persona f di spirito; **be at one's ~s' end** non sapere più che fare; **keep one's ~s about one** non perdere la testa; **be scared out of one's ~s** essere spaventato a morte

witch [wɪtʃ] strega f

'witch·hunt fig caccia f alle streghe

with [wɪð] prep con; (*proximity*) con; (*agency*) con; (*cause*) di; (*possession*) con; **shiver ~ fear** tremare di paura; **a girl ~ blue eyes** una ragazza dagli o con gli occhi azzurri; **~ a**
smile / a wave con un sorriso / un gesto della mano; **are you ~ me?** (*do you understand*) mi segui?; **~ no money** senza soldi

withdraw [wɪð'drɔː] (*pret* **-drew**, *pp* **-drawn**) **1** v/t complaint, application, troops ritirare; money from bank prelevare; troops ritirare **2** v/i ritirarsi; ritirarsi

with·draw·al [wɪð'drɔːəl] of complaint, application, troops ritiro m; of money prelievo m; of troops ritiro m; from drugs crisi f inv di astinenza

with'draw·al symp·toms npl sindrome f da astinenza

with·drawn [wɪð'drɔːn] adj person chiuso

with·er ['wɪðə(r)] v/i seccare

with·hold v/t (*pret & pp* **-held**) information nascondere; consent rifiutare; payment trattenere

with·in prep (*inside*) dentro; in expressions of time nel giro di, entro; in expressions of distance a meno di; **is it ~ walking distance?** ci si arriva a piedi?; **we kept ~ the budget** abbiamo rispettato il budget; **it is not ~ my power** non rientra nelle mie competenze; **~ reach** a portata di mano

with'out prep senza; **~ you / him** senza (di) te/lui; **~ looking / asking** senza guardare / chiedere; **~ his seeing** senza che lo vedesse

with'stand v/t (*pret & pp* **-stood**) resistere a

wit·ness ['wɪtnɪs] **1** n testimone m/f; testimone m/f **2** v/t accident, crime essere testimone di; signature attestare l'autenticità di

'wit·ness box banco m dei testimoni

wit·ti·cis·m ['wɪtɪsɪzm] arguzia f

wit·ty ['wɪtɪ] adj arguto

wob·ble ['wɒbl] v/i of person vacillare; of object traballare

wob·bly ['wɒblɪ] adj person vacillante; object traballante; voice, hand tremante

wok [wɒk] wok m inv

woke [wəuk] pret → **wake**

wok·en ['wəʊkn] *pp* → **wake**

wolf [wʊlf] **1** *n* (*pl* **wolves** [wʊlvz]) *animal* lupo *m*; (*fig: womanizer*) donnaiolo *m* **2** *v/t*: ~ (**down**) divorare

'wolf whis·tle *n* fischio *m*

'wolf-whis·tle *v/i*: ~ **at s.o.** fischiare dietro a qu

wom·an ['wʊmən] (*pl* **women** ['wɪmɪn]) donna *f*

wom·an 'doc·tor dottoressa *f*

wom·an 'driv·er autista *f*

wom·an·iz·er ['wʊmənaɪzə(r)] donnaiolo *m*

wom·an 'priest donna *f* sacerdote

womb [wuːm] utero *m*

wom·en ['wɪmɪn] *pl* → **woman**

women's lib [wɪmɪnz'lɪb] movimento *m* di liberazione della donna

women's lib·ber [wɪmɪnz'lɪbə(r)] femminista *f*

won [wʌn] *pret & pp* → **win**

won·der ['wʌndə(r)] **1** *n* (*amazement*) stupore *m*, meraviglia *f*; *of science etc* meraviglia *f*; *no ~!* non mi stupisce!; *it's a ~ that …* è incredibile che … **2** *v/i* pensare **3** *v/t* domandarsi; *I ~ if you could help* mi chiedevo se potessi aiutarmi

won·der·ful ['wʌndəfʊl] *adj* stupendo

won·der·ful·ly ['wʌndəflɪ] *adv* (*extremely*) estremamente

won't [wəʊnt] → **will not**

wood [wʊd] legno *m*; *for fire* legna *f*; (*forest*) bosco *m*

wood·ed ['wʊdɪd] *adj* boscoso

wood·en ['wʊdn] *adj made of wood* di legno

wood·peck·er ['wʊdpekə(r)] picchio *m*; **'wood·wind** MUS fiati *mpl*; **'wood·work** *parts made of wood* strutture *fpl* in legno; *activity* lavorazione *f* del legno

wool [wʊl] lana *f*

wool·en *Am*, **wool·len** ['wʊlən] **1** *adj* di lana **2** *n* indumento *m* di lana

word [wɜːd] **1** *n* parola *f*; (*news*) notizie *fpl*; (*promise*) parola *f*; *is there any ~ from …?* ci sono notizie da …?; *you have my ~* hai la mia

parola; *have ~s* (*argue*) litigare; *have a ~ with s.o.* parlare con qu **2** *v/t article, letter* formulare

word·ing ['wɜːdɪŋ] formulazione *f*

word 'pro·cess·ing trattamento *m* testi

word 'pro·ces·sor *software* word processor *m inv*

wore [wɔː(r)] *pret* → **wear**

work [wɜːk] **1** *n* lavoro *m*; *out of ~* disoccupato; *be at ~* essere al lavoro; *I go to ~ by bus* vado a lavorare in autobus **2** *v/i of person* lavorare; *study* studiare; *of machine, (succeed)* funzionare; (*succeed*) funzionare; *I used to ~ with him* lavoravamo insieme; *how does it ~? of device* come funziona? **3** *v/t employee* far lavorare; *machine* far funzionare

♦ **work off** *v/t bad mood, anger* sfogare; *flab* smaltire

♦ **work out 1** *v/t problem* capire; *solution* trovare **2** *v/i at gym* fare ginnastica; *of relationship etc* funzionare

♦ **work out to** *v/t* (*add up to*) ammontare a

♦ **work up** *v/t*: **work up enthusiasm** entusiasmarsi; *I worked up an appetite* mi è venuto appetito; *get worked up* (*get angry*) infuriarsi; (*get nervous*) agitarsi

work·a·ble ['wɜːkəbl] *adj solution* realizzabile

work·a·hol·ic [wɜːkə'hɒlɪk] *n* F stacanovista *m/f*

'work·day *hours of work* giornata *f* lavorativa; *not a holiday* giorno *m* feriale

work·er ['wɜːkə(r)] lavoratore *m*, -trice *f*; *she's a good ~* lavora bene

'work·force forza *f* lavoro

work·ing ['wɜːkɪŋ] *adj day, week* lavorativo; *clothes* da lavoro; *lunch* di lavoro; *in ~ order* funzionante; **'work·ing class** classe *f* operaia; **'work·ing-class** *adj* operaio; **'work·ing con·di·tions** *npl* condizioni *fpl* di lavoro; **work·ing 'day** → **workday**; **'work·ing hours** *npl* orario *m* di lavoro; **work·ing**

W

'**knowledge** conoscenza f di base; **work·ing 'moth·er** madre f che lavora

'**work·load** carico m di lavoro; '**work·man** operaio m; '**work·man·like** adj professionale; '**work·man·ship** fattura f; **work of 'art** opera f d'arte; '**work·out** allenamento m; **work per·mit** permesso m di lavoro; '**work·shop** laboratorio m; *for mechanic* officina f; (*seminar*) workshop m inv; '**work sta·tion** work station f inv; '**work·top** piano m di lavoro; **work-to-'rule** sciopero m bianco

world [wɜːld] mondo m; **the ~ of computers / the theatre** il mondo dei computer / del teatro; **out of this ~** F fantastico

World 'Cup mondiali mpl (di calcio)

world-'class adj di livello internazionale

world-'fa·mous adj di fama mondiale

world·ly ['wɜːldlɪ] adj goods materiale; *not spiritual* terreno; *power* temporale; *person* mondano

world 'pow·er potenza f mondiale; **world 're·cord** record m inv mondiale; **world 'war** guerra f mondiale; '**world·wide 1** adj mondiale **2** adv a livello mondiale

worm [wɜːm] n verme m

worn [wɔːn] pp → **wear**

worn-'out adj shoes, carpet, part logoro; *person* esausto, sfinito

wor·ried ['wʌrɪd] adj preoccupato

wor·ried·ly ['wʌrɪdlɪ] adv con aria preoccupata

wor·ry ['wʌrɪ] **1** n preoccupazione f **2** v/t (pret & pp -ied) preoccupare; (upset) turbare **3** v/i (pret & pp -ied) proccuparsi; **it will be alright, don't ~!** andrà tutto bene, non preoccuparti!

wor·ry·ing ['wʌrɪɪŋ] adj preoccupante

worse [wɜːs] **1** adj peggiore; **things will get ~** le cose peggioreranno **2** adv peggio

wors·en ['wɜːsn] v/i peggiorare

wor·ship ['wɜːʃɪp] **1** n culto m **2** v/t (pret & pp -ped) venerare; fig adorare

worst [wɜːst] **1** adj peggiore **2** adv peggio **3** n: **the ~** il peggio; **if the ~ comes to the ~** nel peggiore dei casi

worst-case scen·'a·ri·o: the ~ la peggiore delle ipotesi

worth [wɜːθ] **1** adj: **be ~** valere; **it's ~ reading / seeing** vale la pena leggerlo / vederlo; **be ~** of (*deserve*) meritare **2** n valore m; **£20 ~ of petrol** 20 sterline di benzina

worth·less ['wɜːθlɪs] adj object senza valore; *person* inetto

worth·'while adj cause lodevole; **be ~** (beneficial, useful) essere utile; (worth the effort, worth doing) valere la pena

worth·y ['wɜːðɪ] adj degno; cause lodevole; **be ~ of** (deserve) meritare

would [wʊd] v/aux: **I ~ help if I could** ti aiuterei se potessi; **I said that I ~ go** ho detto che sarei andato; **I told him I ~ not leave unless ...** gli ho detto che non me ne sarei andato se non ...; **~ you like to go to the cinema?** vuoi andare al cinema?; **~ you mind if I smoked?** la disturba se fumo?; **~ you tell her that ...?** le dica che ...; **~ you close the door?** le dispiace chiudere la porta?; **I ~ have told you but ...** te l'avrei detto ma ...; **I ~ not have been so angry if ...** non mi sarei arrabbiato tanto se ...

wound¹ [wuːnd] **1** n ferita f **2** v/t also with remark ferire; with remark ferire

wound² [waʊnd] pret & pp → **wind²**

wove [wəʊv] pret → **weave**

wov·en ['wəʊvn] pp → **weave**

wow [waʊ] int wow

wrap [ræp] v/t (pret & pp -ped) parcel, gift incartare; (wind, cover) avvolgere

♦ **wrap up** v/i against the cold coprirsi bene

wrap·per ['ræpə(r)] incarto m

wrap·ping ['ræpɪŋ] involucro m

'**wrap·ping pa·per** carta f da regalo

wreath [riːθ] corona f; *for funeral* corona f funebre

wreck [rek] **1** n *of ship* relitto m; *of car* carcassa f; **be a nervous ~** sentirsi un rottame **2** v/t *ship* far naufragare; *car* demolire; *plans, career, marriage* distruggere

wreck·age ['rekɪdʒ] *of car, plane* rottami mpl; *of marriage, career* brandelli mpl

wrench [rentʃ] **1** n *tool* chiave f inglese; *injury* slogatura f **2** v/t *injure* slogarsi; *(pull)* strappare

wres·tle ['resl] v/i fare la lotta

♦ **wrestle with** v/t *problems* lottare con

wres·tler ['reslə(r)] lottatore m, -trice f

wres·tling ['reslɪŋ] lotta f libera

'**wres·tling match** incontro m di lotta libera

wrig·gle ['rɪgl] v/i *(squirm)* dimenarsi; *along the ground* strisciare

♦ **wriggle out of** v/t sottrarsi a

♦ **wring out** v/t *(pret & pp* **wrung***) cloth* strizzare

wrin·kle ['rɪŋkl] **1** n *in skin* ruga f; *in clothes* grinza f **2** v/t *clothes* stropicciare **3** v/i *of clothes* stropicciarsi

wrist [rɪst] polso m

'**wrist·watch** orologio m da polso

write [raɪt] *(pret* **wrote**, *pp* **written***)* **1** v/t scrivere; *cheque* fare **2** v/i scrivere; *of author* scrivere; *(send a letter)* scrivere

♦ **write down** v/t annotare, scrivere

♦ **write off** v/t *debt* cancellare; *car* distruggere

writ·er ['raɪtə(r)] autore m, -trice f; *professional* scrittore m, -trice f

'**write-up** F recensione f

writhe [raɪð] v/i contorcersi

writ·ing ['raɪtɪŋ] *as career* scrivere m; *(hand-writing)* scrittura f; *(words)* scritta f; *(script)* scritto m; **in ~** per iscritto

'**writ·ing pa·per** carta f da lettere

writ·ten ['rɪtn] pp → **write**

wrong [rɒŋ] **1** adj sbagliato; **be ~ of person** sbagliare; *of answer* essere errato; *morally* essere ingiusto; **it's ~ to steal** non si deve rubare; **what's ~?** cosa c'è?; **there is something ~ with the car** la macchina ha qualcosa che non va **2** adv in modo sbagliato; **go ~** *of person* sbagliare; *of marriage, plan etc* andar male **3** n *immoral action* torto m; *immorality* male m; **be in the ~** avere torto

wrong·ful ['rɒŋfʊl] adj illegale

wrong·ly ['rɒŋlɪ] adv erroneamente

wrong 'num·ber numero m sbagliato

wrote [rəʊt] pret → **write**

wrought 'i·ron [rɔːt] ferro m battuto

wrung [rʌŋ] pret & pp → **wring**

wry [raɪ] adj beffardo

X

xen·o·pho·bi·a [zenəʊ'fəʊbɪə] xenofobia f

X-ray ['eksreɪ] **1** n raggio m X; *picture* radiografia f; **have an ~** farsi fare una radiografia **2** v/t radiografare

xy·lo·phone [zaɪlə'fəʊn] xilofono m

Y

yacht [jɒt] *for pleasure* yacht *m inv*; *for racing* imbarcazione *f* da diporto

yacht·ing ['jɒtɪŋ] navigazione *f* da diporto

yachts·man ['jɒtsmən] diportista *m*

Yank [jæŋk] *n* F yankee *m inv*

yank [jæŋk] *v/t* dare uno strattone a

yap [jæp] *v/i* (*pret & pp* **-ped**) *of small dog* abbaiare; F *talk a lot* chiacchierare

yard¹ [jɑːd] *of prison, institution etc* cortile *m*; *for storage* deposito *m* all'aperto

yard² [jɑːd] *measurement* iarda *f*

yard·stick *fig* metro *m*

yarn [jɑːn] *n* (*thread*) filato *m*; F *story* racconto *m*

yawn [jɔːn] **1** *n* sbadiglio *m* **2** *v/i* sbadigliare

year [jɪə(r)] anno *m*; *I've known here for* ~s la conosco da (tanti) anni; *it will last for* ~s durerà anni; *we were in the same* ~ *at school* frequentavamo lo stesso anno; *be six* ~s *old* avere sei anni

year·ly ['jɪəlɪ] **1** *adj* annuale **2** *adv* annualmente; *twice* ~ due volte (al)l'anno

yearn [jɜːn] *v/i*: ~ *to do sth* struggersi dal desiderio di fare qc
♦ **yearn for** *v/t* desiderare ardentemente

yearn·ing ['jɜːnɪŋ] *n* desiderio *m* struggente

yeast [jiːst] lievito *m*

yell [jel] **1** *n* urlo *m* **2** *v/t & v/i* urlare

yel·low ['jeləʊ] **1** *n* giallo *m* **2** *adj* giallo

yel·low 'pag·es® *npl* pagine *fpl* gialle

yelp [jelp] **1** *n* guaito *m* **2** *v/i* guaire

yen [jen] FIN yen *m inv*

yes [jes] *int* sì; *say* ~ dire di sì

'yes·man *pej* yes man *m inv*

yes·ter·day ['jestədeɪ] **1** *adv* ieri; *the day before* ~ l'altro ieri **2** *n* ieri *m inv*

yet [jet] **1** *adv* finora; *the fastest* ~ il più veloce finora; *as* ~ up to now per ora; *it is as* ~ *undecided* rimane ancora da decidere; *have you finished* ~? (non) hai (ancora) finito?; *he hasn't arrived* ~ non è ancora arrivato; *is he here* ~? – *not* ~ è arrivato? – non ancora; ~ *bigger/ longer* ancora più grande/lungo **2** *conj* eppure; ~ *I'm not sure* eppure non sono sicuro

yield [jiːld] **1** *n from fields etc* raccolto *m*; *from investment* rendita *f* **2** *v/t fruit, harvest* dare, produrre; *interest* fruttare **3** *v/i* (*give way*) cedere

yob [jɒb] P teppista *m/f*

yo·ga ['jəʊɡə] yoga *m*

yog·hurt ['jɒɡət] yogurt *m inv*

yolk [jəʊk] tuorlo *m*

you [juː] *pron* ◊ *subject: familiar singular* tu; *familiar plural* voi; *polite singular* lei; *do* ~ *know him?* lo conosci/conosce/conoscete?; ~ *go, I'll stay* tu vai/lei vada/voi andate, io resto ◊ *direct object: familiar singular* ti; *familiar polite plural* vi; *polite singular* lei; *he knows* ~ ti/vi/ la conosce ◊ *indirect object: familiar singular* ti; *when two pronouns are used* te; *familiar polite plural* vi; *when two pronouns are used* ve; *polite singular* le; *did he talk to* ~? ti/vi/le ha parlato?; *I need to talk to* ~ devo parlarti/parlarvi/parlarle; *I told* ~ te/ve l'ho detto, glielo ho detto ◊ *after prep familiar singular* te; *familiar polite plural* voi; *polite singular* lei; *this is for* ~ questo è per te/voi/lei ◊ *impersonal*; ~ *never know* non si sa mai; ~ *have to pay* si

zombie

deve pagare; *fruit is good for ~* la frutta fa bene

young [jʌŋ] *adj* giovane

young·ster [ˈjʌŋstə(r)] ragazzo *m*, -a *f*

your [jɔː(r)] *adj familiar singular* il tuo *m*, la tua *f*, i tuoi *mpl*, le tue *fpl*; *polite singular* il suo *m*, la sua *f*, i suoi *mpl*, le sue *fpl*; *familiar & polite plural* il vostro *m*, la vostra *f*, i vostri *mpl*, le vostre *fpl*; *~ brother* tuo / suo / vostro fratello

yours [jɔːz] *pron familiar singular* il tuo *m*, la tua *f*, i tuoi *mpl*, le tue *fpl*; *polite singular* il suo *m*, la sua *f*, i suoi *mpl*, le sue *fpl*; *familiar & polite plural* il vostro *m*, la vostra *f*, i vostri *mpl*, le vostre *fpl*; *a friend of ~* un tuo / suo / vostro amico; *~ ... at end of letter* saluti ...; *~ sincerely* distinti saluti

your·self *pron reflexive* ti; *reflexive polite* si; *emphatic* tu stesso *m*, tu stessa *f*; *emphatic polite* lei stesso *m*,

lei stessa *f*; *did you hurt ~?* ti sei / si è fatto male?; *you said so ~* l'hai detto tu stesso / l'ha detto lei stesso; *keep it for ~* tienilo per te / lo tenga per sé; *by ~* da solo

your·selves *pron reflexive* vi; *emphatic* voi stessi *mpl*, voi stesse *fpl*; *did you hurt ~?* vi siete fatti male?; *can you do it ~?* potete farlo da voi?; *by ~* da soli *mpl*, da sole *fpl*

youth [juːθ] *n age* gioventù *f*; (*young man*) ragazzo *m*; (*young people*) giovani *mpl*

'youth club circolo *m* giovanile

youth·ful [ˈjuːθful] *adj* giovanile; *ideas* giovane; *idealism* di gioventù

'youth hos·tel ostello *m* della gioventù

Yu·go·sla·vi·a [juːgəˈslɑːvɪə] Jugoslavia *f*

Yu·go·sla·vi·an [juːgəˈslɑːvɪən] **1** *adj* jugoslavo **2** *n* jugoslavo *m*, -a *f*

yup·pie [ˈjʌpɪ] F yuppie *m/f inv*

Z

zap [zæp] *v/t* (*pret & pp* **-ped**) F COMPUT (*delete*) cancellare; (*kill*) annientare; (*hit*) colpire; (*send*) mandare
♦ **zap along** *v/i* F *move fast* sfrecciare

zapped [zæpt] *adj* F (*exhausted*) stanchissimo

zap·per [ˈzæpə(r)] *for changing TV channels* telecomando *m*

zap·py [ˈzæpɪ] *adj* F *car, pace* veloce; (*lively, energetic*) brioso

zeal [ziːl] zelo *m*

ze·bra [ˈzebrə] zebra *f*

ze·bra 'cross·ing *Br* strisce *fpl* pedonali

ze·ro [ˈzɪərəʊ] zero *m*; *10 below ~* 10 (gradi) sotto zero
♦ **zero in on** *v/t* (*identify*) identificare

ze·ro 'growth crescita *f* zero

zest [zest] (*enthusiasm*) gusto *m*; (*peel*) scorza *f*

zig·zag [ˈzɪgzæg] **1** *n* zigzag *m inv* **2** *v/i* (*pret & pp* **-ged**) zigzagare

zilch [zɪltʃ] F un bel niente

zinc [zɪŋk] zinco *m*

zip [zɪp] (*cerniera f*) lampo *f*
♦ **zip up** *v/t* (*pret & pp* **-ped**) *dress, jacket* allacciare; COMPUT zippare, comprimere

'zip code *Am* codice *m* di avviamento postale

zo·di·ac [ˈzəʊdɪæk] ASTR zodiaco *m*; *signs of the ~* segni *mpl* zodiacali

zom·bie [ˈzɒmbɪ] F (*idiot*) cretino *m*, -a *f*; *feel like a ~ exhausted*

sentirsi uno zombie
zone [zəʊn] zona f
zonked [zɒŋkt] *adj* P (*exhausted*) stanco morto
zoo [zu:] zoo *m inv*
zo·o·log·i·cal [zu:ə'lɒdʒɪkl] *adj* zoologico

zo·ol·o·gist [zu:'ɒlədʒɪst] zoologo *m*, -a f
zo·ol·o·gy [zu:'ɒlədʒɪ] zoologia f
zoom [zu:m] *v/i* F *move fast* sfrecciare
♦**zoom in on** *v/t* PHOT zumare su
zoom 'lens zoom *m inv*
zuc·chi·ni [zu:'ki:nɪ] *Am* zucchino *m*

Italian Verb Conjugations

You can find the conjugation pattern of an Italian verb by looking up the infinitive form in the dictionary. The numbers and letters given there after the infinitive refer to the conjugation patterns listed below.

The tables (**1a**, **2a**, **3a**, **4a**) show the full conjugations. The verb stem is given in ordinary type and the endings in *italics*. Compound tenses are given at **1a**. The three main conjugations (-are, -ere, -ire) are divided into four sets so as to illustrate the two different stress patterns of the second conjugation. Variations in form, stress pattern and vowel length are then shown for each of these four sets.

An underscore shows the stressed vowel in each conjugated form.

First Conjugation

1a mandare. The stem remains the same with regard to both spelling and pronunciation.

I. Simple Tenses

	indicativo			condizionale
pr	*imperf*	*p.r.*	*fut*	
mand*o*	mand*avo*	mand*ai*	mander*ò*	mander*ei*
mand*i*	mand*avi*	mand*asti*	mander*ai*	mander*esti*
mand*a*	mand*ava*	mand*ò*	mander*à*	mander*ebbe*
mand*iamo*	mand*avamo*	mand*ammo*	mander*emo*	mander*emmo*
mand*ate*	mand*avate*	mand*aste*	mander*ete*	mander*este*
mand*ano*	mand*avano*	mand*arono*	mander*anno*	mander*ebbero*

	congiuntivo		imperativo
pr	*imperf*		
mand*i*	mand*assi*		—
mand*i*	mand*assi*		mand*a*
mand*i*	mand*asse*		mand*i*
mand*iamo*	mand*assimo*		mand*iamo*
mand*iate*	mand*aste*		mand*ate*
mand*ino*	mand*assero*		mand*ino*

Participio presente: mand*ante*   *Participio passato*: mand*ato*
Gerundio presente: mand*ando*

II. Compound Tenses

1. Active voice
(Formed by placing *avere* before the verb form *participio passato*)

Infinito
passato: aver mand*ato*

Gerundio
passato: avendo mand*ato*

Indicativo
passato pross: ho mand*ato*
trapassato prossimo: av*e*vo mand*ato*

futuro anteriore: avr*ò* mand*ato*

Condizionale
passato: avr*e*i mand*ato*

Congiuntivo
passato: *a*bbia mand*ato*
trapassato: av*e*ssi mand*ato*

2. Passive voice
(formed by placing *essere* before the verb form *participio passato*)

Infinito
presente: *e*ssere mand*ato*, -a, -i, -e
passato: *e*ssere st*a*to (st*a*ta, st*a*ti, st*a*te) mand*ato*, -a, -i, -e

Gerundio
presente: essendo mand*ato*, -a, -i, -e
passato: essendo st*a*to (st*a*ta, st*a*ti, st*a*te) mand*ato*, -a, -i, -e

Indicativo
presente: s*o*no mand*ato*, -a
imperf: *e*ro mand*ato*, -a
passato remoto: fu*i* mand*ato*, -a
passato prossimo: s*o*no st*a*to (st*a*ta) mand*ato*, -a
trap. prossimo: *e*ro st*a*to (st*a*ta)

mand*ato*, -a
fut semplice: sar*ò* mand*ato*, -a
fut anteriore: sar*ò* st*a*to (st*a*ta) mand*ato*, -a

Condizionale
presente: sar*e*i mand*ato*, -a
passato: sar*e*i st*a*to (st*a*ta) mand*ato*, -a

Congiuntivo
presente: s*i*a mand*ato*, -a
imperf: f*o*ssi mand*ato*, -a
passato: sia st*a*to (st*a*ta) mand*ato*, -a
trapassato: f*o*ssi st*a*to (st*a*ta) mand*ato*, -a

Imperativo
si*i* mand*ato*, -a

This pattern applies to the compound tenses of all verbs

pr ind	p.r.	fut	pr congiunt	imper

1b cel*a*re. The stressed, closed *-e* in the stem becomes an open *e*.

pr ind	p.r.	fut	pr congiunt	imper
c*e*lo	cel*a*i	celer*ò*	c*e*li	—
celi*a*mo	cel*a*mmo	celer*e*mo	celi*a*mo	celi*a*mo
c*e*lano	cel*a*rono	celer*a*nno	c*e*lino	c*e*lino
		pp: cel*a*to		

1c lod*a*re. The stressed, closed *-o* in the stem becomes an open *o*.

pr ind	p.r.	fut	pr congiunt	imper
l*o*do	lod*a*i	loder*ò*	l*o*di	—
lodi*a*mo	lod*a*mmo	loder*e*mo	lodi*a*mo	lodi*a*mo
l*o*dano	lod*a*rono	loder*a*nno	l*o*dino	l*o*dino
		pp: lod*a*to		

1d cerc*a*re. The final consonant in the verb stem, *-c*, becomes *ch* before *i* and *e*.

pr ind	p.r.	fut	pr congiunt	imper
c*e*rco	cerc*a*i	cercher*ò*	c*e*rchi	—
cerchi*a*mo	cerc*a*mmo	cercher*e*mo	cerchi*a*mo	cerchi*a*mo
c*e*rcano	cerc*a*rono	cercher*a*nno	c*e*rchino	c*e*rchino
		pp: cerc*a*to		

pr ind	p.r.	fut	pr congiunt	imper

1e pagare. The final consonant in the verb stem, -g, becomes *gh* before *i* and *e*.

pago	pagai	pagherò	paghi	—
paghiamo	pagammo	pagheremo	paghiamo	paghiamo
pagano	pagarono	pagheranno	paghino	paghino

pp: pagato

1f baciare. The *i* is dropped if it is followed immediately by a second *i* or an *e*.

bacio	baciai	bacerò	baci	—
baciamo	baciammo	baceremo	baciamo	baciamo
baciano	baciarono	baceranno	bacino	bacino

pp: baciato

1g pigliare. The *i* is dropped if it is followed immediately by a second *i*.

piglio	pigliai	piglierò	pigli	—
pigliamo	piagliammo	piglieremo	pigliamo	pigliamo
pigliano	pigliarono	piglieranno	piglino	piglino

pp: pigliato

1h inviare. Verb forms in which the *i* is stressed retain the *i* even if it is followed by another *i*.

invio	inviai	invierò	invii	—
inviamo	inviammo	invieremo	inviamo	inviamo
inviano	inviarono	invieranno	inviino	inviino

pp: inviato

1i annoiare. Verbs ending in –*iare* with an unstressed *i* and a preceding vowel, drop the *i* which would be added.

annoio	annoiai	annoierò	annoi	—
annoiamo	annoiammo	annoieremo	annoiamo	annoiamo
annoiano	annoiarono	annoieranno	annoino	annoino

pp: annoiato

1k studiare. Verbs ending in –*iare* with an unstressed *i* and a preceding consonant, usually drop the *i* which would be added, even when the *i* in the verb stem is stressed: i.e. *tu studi*. Verbs ending in –*liare* always have -*lii*, eg *esiliare, esilii*.

studio	studiai	studierò	studi	—
studiamo	studiammo	studieremo	studiamo	studiamo
studiano	studiarono	studieranno	studino	studino

pp: studiato

1l abitare. In the verb forms in which the stem is stressed, the stress comes on the first syllable.

abito	abitai	abiterò	abiti	—
abitiamo	abitammo	abiteremo	abitiamo	abitiamo
abitano	abitarono	abiteranno	abitino	abitino

pp: abitato

pr ind	p.r.	fut	pr congiunt	imper

1m collaborare. In the verb forms in which the stem is stressed, the stress comes on the second syllable.

collaboro	collaborai	collaborerò	collabori	—
collaboriamo	collaborammo	collaboreremo	collaboriamo	collaboriamo
collaborano	collaborarono	collaboreranno	collaborino	collaborino
		pp: collaborato		

1n aggomitolare. In the verb forms in which the stem is stressed, the stress comes on the third or fourth syllable.

aggomitolo	~mitolai	~mitolerò	~mitoli	—
~mitoliamo	~mitolammo	~mitoleremo	~mitoliamo	~mitoliamo
~mitolano	~mitolarono	~mitoleranno	~mitolino	~mitolino
		pp: aggomitolato		

1o giocare. The stressed –o in the stem can be extended to –uo, but this is rarer.

gi(u)oco	giocai	giocherò	gi(u)ochi	—
giochiamo	giocammo	giocheremo	giochiamo	giochiamo
gi(u)ocano	giocarono	giocheranno	gi(u)ochino	gi(u)ochino
		pp: giocato		

1p andare. Two stems: and- and vad-. In fut and cond the e at the start of the ending is dropped.

vado	andai	andrò	vada	—
vai	andasti	andrai	vada	va, va', vai,
va	andò	andrà	vada	vada
andiamo	andammo	andremo	andiamo	andiamo
andate	andaste	andrete	andiate	andate
vanno	andarono	andranno	vadano	vadano
		pp: andato		

1q stare. Verb stem sta; p.r. (stetti etc); imperf del congiunt (stessi etc) as in the 2ⁿᵈ Conjugation; in fut and cond e becomes a.

sto	stetti	starò	stia	—
stai	stesti	starai	stia	sta', stai
sta	stette	starà	stia	stia
stiamo	stemmo	staremo	stiamo	stiamo
state	steste	starete	stiate	state
stanno	stettero	staranno	stiano	stiano
		pp: stato		

1r dare. Verb stem da; imperf del congiunt dessi etc; in the p.r. alternative forms detti, dette, dettero.

do	diedi, detti	darò	dia	—
dai	desti	darai	dia	da', dai
dà	diede, dette	darà	dia	dia
diamo	demmo	daremo	diamo	diamo
date	deste	darete	diate	date
danno	diedero, dettero	daranno	diano	diano
		pp: dato		

Second Conjugation – First Pattern

2a temere. The stem remains the same with regard to both spelling and pronunciation.

I. Simple Tenses

indicativo   condizionale

pr	imperf	p.r.	fut	
temo	temevo	temei, temetti	temerò	temerei
temo	temevo	temei, temetti	temerò	temerei
temi	temevi	temesti	temerai	temeresti
teme	temeva	temette	temerà	temerebbe
temiamo	temevamo	tememmo	temeremo	temeremmo
temete	temevate	temeste	temerete	temereste
temono	temevano	temettero, temerono	temeranno	temerebbero

congiuntivo   imperativo

pr	imperf	
tema	temessi	—
tema	temessi	temi
tema	temesse	tema
temiamo	temessimo	temiamo
temiate	temeste	temete
temano	temessero	temano

Participio presente: tem**e**nte   *Participio passato:* temuto
Gerundio presente: temendo

II. Compound Tenses

Auxiliary verb *essere* or *avere*, followed by *participio passato* (see 1a).

pr ind	p.r.	fut	pr congiunt	imper

2b avere. In *fut* and *cond* the final *e* in the ending is omitted.

ho	ebbi	avrò	abbia	—
hai	avesti	avrai	abbia	abbi
ha	ebbe	avrà	abbia	abbia
abbiamo	avemmo	avremo	abbiamo	abbiamo
avete	aveste	avrete	abbiate	abbiate
hanno	ebbero	avranno	abbiano	abbiano
		pp: avuto		

2c cadere. In *fut* and *cond* the final *e* in the ending is omitted.

cado	caddi	cadrò	cada	—
cadiamo	caddemmo	cadremo	cadiamo	cadiamo
cadono	caddero	cadranno	cadano	cadano
		pp: caduto		

2d calere. Used almost exclusively in 3rd person singular; now obsolete.

cale	calse	—	caglia	—
		pp: caluto		

pr ind	p.r.	fut	pr congiunt	imper

2e dolere. In *pr*, *g* is added between the verb stem and the ending *o* or *a*. In *fut* and *cond* *l* becomes *r* and the final *e* of the ending is dropped.

pr ind	p.r.	fut	pr congiunt	imper
dolgo	dolsi	dorrò	dolga	—
duole	dolse	dorrà	dolga	dolga
dogliamo	dolemmo	dorremo	dogliamo	dogliamo
dolgono	dolsero	dorranno	dolgano	dolgano
		pp: doluto		

2f dovere. In the forms with the emphasis on the stem vowel, *o* becomes *e*. Omission of *e* in *fut* and *cond*.

pr ind	p.r.	fut	pr congiunt	imper
devo	dovetti	dovrò	debba, deva	—
devi	dovesti	dovrai	debba, deva	devi
deve	dovette	dovrà	debba, deva	debba, deva
dobbiamo	dovemmo	dovremo	dobbiamo	dobbiamo
dovete	doveste	dovrete	dobbiate	dovete
devono	dovettero	dovranno	debbano, devano	debbano, devano
		pp: dovuto		

2g lucere. Used only in 3rd person singular and plural of *pr dell'ind* (luce, lucono), *imperf* (luceva, lucevano), *fut* (lucerà, luceranno), *pr del congiunt* (luca, lucano), and *imperf del congiunt* (lucesse, lucessero). Also *p pr* lucente, *ger* lucendo.

2h parere. In *fut* and *cond* the final *e* in the ending is omitted.

pr ind	p.r.	fut	pr congiunt	imper
paio	parvi	parrò	paia	—
pa(r)iamo	paremmo	parremo	pa(r)iamo	—
paiono	parvero	parranno	paiano	—
		pp: parso		

2i persuadere.

pr ind	p.r.	fut	pr congiunt	imper
persuado	persuasi	persuaderò	persuada	—
persuadiamo	persuademmo	persuaderemo	persuadiamo	persuadiamo
persuadono	persuasero	persuaderanno	persuadano	persuadano
		pp: persuaso		

2k piacere.

pr ind	p.r.	fut	pr congiunt	imper
piaccio	piacqui	piacerò	piaccia	—
piacciamo	piacemmo	piaceremo	piacciamo	piacciamo
piacciono	piacquero	piaceranno	piacciano	piacciano
		pp: piaciuto		

2l potere. In *fut* and *cond* the final *e* in the ending is omitted.

pr ind	p.r.	fut	pr congiunt	imper
posso	potei	potrò	possa	—
puoi	potesti	potrai	possa	—
può	poté	potrà	possa	—
possiamo	potemmo	potremo	possiamo	—
potete	poteste	potrete	possiate	—
possono	poterono	potranno	possano	—
		pp: potuto		

pr ind	p.r.	fut	pr congiunt	imper

2m rimanere. In *pr* g is added between stem and ending o or a; *p.r.* ending in –si and *pp* ending in –sto drop the –n from the stem; in *fut* and *cond* n becomes r.

rimango	rimasi	rimarrò	rimanga	—
rimani	rimanemmo	rimarremo	rimaniamo	rimaniamo
rimangono	rimasero	rimarranno	rimangano	rimangano
		pp: rimasto		

2n sapere. In *fut* and *cond* the e is dropped; 2nd person plural of *imperf* formed from *congiunt*.

so	seppi	saprò	sappia	—
sai	sapesti	saprai	sappia	sappi
sa	seppe	saprà	sappia	sappia
sappiamo	sapemmo	sapremo	sappiamo	sappiamo
sapete	sapeste	saprete	sappiate	sappiate
sanno	seppero	sapranno	sappiano	sappiano
	p pr: sapiente	*pp:* saputo		

2o sedere. The e in the stem becomes ie in forms with the emphasis on the stem vowel; in *pr* alternative forms with segg...

siedo, seggo	sedei	sederò	sieda, segga	—
sediamo	sedemmo	sederemo	sediamo	sediamo
siedono, seggono	sederono	sederanno	siedano, seggano	siedano, seggano
		pp: seduto		

2p solere. Only used in *pr*, *p.r.*, *ger* and *pp*. In *pr dell'ind* (except 2nd person singular: suoli) and *congiunt* it follows the pattern of *volere*.

soglio	solei	—	soglia	—
sogliamo	—	—	sogliamo	—
sogliono	—	—	sogliano	—
	ger: solendo		*pp:* solito	

2q tenere. Addition of g between stem and ending o or a. In *fut* and *cond* n becomes r.

tengo	tenni	terrò	tenga	—
tieni	tenesti	terrai	tenga	tieni
teniamo	tenemmo	terremo	teniamo	teniamo
tengono	tennero	terranno	tengano	tengano
		pp: tenuto		

2r valere. Addition of g between stem and ending o or a. In *fut* and *cond* n becomes r.

valgo	valsi	varrò	valga	—
valiamo	valemmo	varremo	valiamo	valiamo
valgono	valsero	varranno	valgano	valgano
		pp: valso		

pr ind	p.r.	fut	pr congiunt	imper

2s vedere. In *fut* and *cond* the final *e* in the ending is omitted.

vedo	vidi	vedrò	veda	—
vediamo	vedemmo	vedremo	vediamo	vediamo
vedono	videro	vedranno	vedano	vedano
	pp: visto			

2t volere. In *fut* and *cond l* becomes *r* and the final *e* of the ending is omitted; 2nd person plural of *imper* from the *congiunt*.

voglio	volli	vorrò	voglia	—
vuoi	volesti	vorrai	voglia	vogli
vuole	volle	vorrà	voglia	voglia
vogliamo	volemmo	vorremo	vogliamo	vogliamo
volete	voleste	vorrete	vogliate	vogliate
vogliono	vollero	vorranno	vogliano	vogliano
	pp: voluto			

Second Conjugation – Second Pattern

3a vendere. The stem remains the same with regard to both spelling and pronunciation.

I. Simple Tenses

	indicativo			condizionale
pr	imperf	p.r.	fut	
vendo	vendevo	vendetti, vendei	venderò	venderei
vendi	vendevi	vendesti	venderai	venderesti
vende	vendeva	vendette	venderà	venderebbe
vendiamo	vendevamo	vendemmo	venderemo	venderemmo
vendete	vendevate	vendeste	venderete	vendereste
vendono	vendevano	vendettero, venderono	venderanno	venderebbero

congiuntivo		imperativo
pr	imperf	
venda	vendessi	—
venda	vendessi	vendi
venda	vendesse	venda
vendiamo	vendessimo	vendiamo
vendiate	vendeste	vendete
vendano	vendessero	vendano

Participio presente: vendente   *Participio passato*: venduto*
          Gerundio presente: vendendo

*Participio passato of spandere is spanto.

II. Compound Tenses

Auxiliary verb *essere* or *avere*, followed by *participio passato* (see 1a).

pr ind	p.r.	fut	pr congiunt	imper

3b chiudere.

chiudo	chiusi	chiuderò	chiuda	—
chiudiamo	chiudemmo	chiuderemo	chiudiamo	chiudiamo
chiudono	chiusero	chiuderanno	chiudano	chiudano
		pp: chiuso		

3c prendere.

prendo	presi	prenderò	prenda	—
prendiamo	prendemmo	prenderemo	prendiamo	prendiamo
prendono	presero	prenderanno	prendano	prendano
		pp: preso		

3d fingere. The *pp* of *stringere* is *stretto*.

fingo	finsi	fingerò	finga	
fingiamo	fingemmo	fingeremo	fingiamo	fingiamo
fingono	finsero	fingeranno	fingano	fingano
		pp: finto		

3e addurre. Shorter form of *adducere*.

adduco	addussi	addurrò	adduca	—
adduci	adducesti	addurrai	adduca	adduci
adduce	addusse	addurrà	adduca	adduca
adduciamo	adducemmo	addurremo	adduciamo	adduciamo
adducete	adduceste	addurrete	adduciate	adduciate
adducono	addussero	addurranno	adducano	adducano
		pp: addotto		

3f assistere. In *p.r.* alternative forms end in –*etti*.

assisto	assistei	assisterò	assista	—
assistiamo	assistemmo	assisteremo	assistiamo	assistiamo
assistono	assisterono	assisteranno	assistano	assistano
		pp: assistito		

3g assolvere.

assolvo	assolsi, ~vetti	assolverò	assolva	
assolviamo	assolvemmo	assolveremo	assolviamo	assolviamo
assolvono	assolsero,	assolveranno	assolvano	assolvano
	assolvettero			
		pp: assolto		

3h assumere.

assumo	assunsi	assumerò	assuma	—
assumiamo	assumemmo	assumeremo	assumiamo	assumiamo
assumono	assunsero	assumeranno	assumano	assumano
		pp: assunto		

pr ind	p.r.	fut	pr congiunt	imper

3i bere. Conjugated according to the pattern of *bevere*. In *fut* and *cond* v becomes *r* and the *e* of the ending is dropped.

bevo	bevvi, bevetti	berrò	beva	—
bevi	bevesti	berrai	beva	bevi
beve	bevve, bevette	berrà	beva	beva
beviamo	bevemmo	berremo	beviamo	beviamo
bevete	beveste	berrete	beviate	bevete
bevono	bevvero, bevettero	berranno	bevano	bevano

pp: bevuto

3k chiedere.

chiedo	chiesi	chiederò	chieda	—
chiediamo	chiedemmo	chiederemo	chiediamo	chiediamo
chiedono	chiesero	chiederanno	chiedano	chiedano

pp: chiesto

3l concedere.

concedo	concessi, concedetti	concederò	conceda	—
concediamo	concedemmo	concederemo	concediamo	concediamo
concedono	concessero, concedettero	concederanno	concedano	concedano

pp: concesso

3m connettere.

connetto	connessi, connettei	connetterò	connetta	—
connettiamo	connettemmo	connetteremo	connettiamo	connettiamo
connettono	connessero, connetterono	connetteranno	connettano	connettano

pp: connesso

3n conoscere.

conosco	conobbi	conoscerò	conosca	—
conosciamo	conoscemmo	conosceremo	conosciamo	conosciamo
conoscono	conobbero	conosceranno	conoscano	conoscano

pp: conosciuto

3o correre.

corro	corsi	correrò	corra	—
corriamo	corremmo	correremo	corriamo	corriamo
corrono	corsero	correranno	corrano	corrano

pp: corso

pr ind	p.r.	fut	pr congiunt	imper

3p cuocere. In unstressed syllables *uo* becomes *o*. Imperf cocevo or cocessi.

cuocio	cossi	cuocerò	cuocia	—
cociamo	cocemmo	cuoceremo	cociamo	cociamo
cuociono	cossero	cuoceranno	cuociano	cuociano
	pp: cotto			

3q decidere.

decido	decisi	deciderò	decida	—
decidiamo	decidemmo	decideremo	decidiamo	decidiamo
decidono	decisero	decideranno	decidano	decidano
	pp: deciso			

3r deprimere.

deprimo	depressi	deprimerò	deprima	—
deprimiamo	deprimemmo	deprimeremo	deprimiamo	deprimiamo
deprimono	depressero	deprimeranno	deprimano	deprimano
	pp: depresso			

3s devolvere.

devolvo	devolvei, devolvetti	devolverò	devolva	—
devolviamo	devolvemmo	devolveremo	devolviamo	devolviamo
devolvono	devolverono, devolvettero	devolveranno	devolvano	devolvano
	pp: devoluto, devolto			

3t dire.

dico	dissi	dirò	dica	—
dici	dicesti	dirai	dica	
dice	disse	dirà	dica	
diciamo	dicemmo	diremo	diciamo	diciamo
dite	diceste	direte	diciate	dite
dicono	dissero	diranno	dicano	dicano
	pp: detto			

3u dirigere.

dirigo	diressi	dirigerò	diriga	—
dirigiamo	dirigemmo	dirigeremo	dirigiamo	dirigiamo
dirigono	diressero	dirigeranno	dirigano	dirigano
	pp: diretto			

3v discutere.

discuto	discussi	discuterò	discuta	—
discutiamo	discutemmo	discuteremo	discutiamo	discutiamo
discutono	discussero	discuteranno	discutano	discutano
	pp: discusso			

pr ind	p.r.	fut	pr congiunt	imper

3w esigere.

esigo	esigei, esigetti	esigerò	esiga	—
esigiamo	esigemmo	esigeremo	esigiamo	esigiamo
esigono	esigerono, esigettero	esigeranno	esigano	esigano

pp: esatto

3x esimere. Has no *pp*, and the *p.r. esimei* is rarely used. Instead the corresponding forms of *esentare* are used. Otherwise regular, following the pattern of *vendere* 3a.

3y espellere.

espello	espulsi	espellerò	espella	—
espelliamo	espellemmo	espelleremo	espelliamo	espelliamo
espellono	espulsero	espelleranno	espellano	espellano

pp: espulso

3z essere. Completely irregular. *Imperf dell'ind*: ero, eri, era, eravamo, eravate, erano; *imperf del congiunt*: fossi, fossi, fosse, fossimo, foste, fossero.

sono	fui	sarò	sia	—
sei	fosti	sarai	sia	sii
è	fu	sarà	sia	sia
siamo	fummo	saremo	siamo	siamo
siete	foste	sarete	siate	siate
sono	furono	saranno	siano	siano

pp: stato

3aa fare. Shorter form of *facere*. *Imperf* regular, following the pattern of *facere*: facevo etc.

faccio	feci	farò	faccia	—
fai	facesti	farai	faccia	fa', fai
fa	fece	farà	faccia	faccia
facciamo	facemmo	faremo	facciamo	facciamo
fate	faceste	farete	facciate	fate
fanno	fecero	faranno	facciano	facciano

pp: fatto

3bb fondere.

fondo	fusi	fonderò	fonda	—
fondiamo	fondemmo	fonderemo	fondiamo	fondiamo
fondono	fusero	fonderanno	fondano	fondano

pp: fuso

3cc leggere.

leggo	lessi	leggerò	legga	—
leggiamo	leggemmo	leggeremo	leggiamo	leggiamo
leggono	lessero	leggeranno	leggano	leggano

pp: letto

pr ind	*p.r.*	*fut*	*pr congiunt*	*imper*

3dd mescere.

mesco	mescei	mescerò	mesca	—
mesciamo	mescemmo	mesceremo	mesciamo	mesciamo
mescono	mescerono	mesceranno	mescano	mescano
		pp: mesciuto		

3ee mettere.

metto	misi	metterò	metta	—
mettiamo	mettemmo	metteremo	mettiamo	mettiamo
mettono	misero	metteranno	mettano	mettano
		pp: messo		

3ff muovere. In unstressed syllables *uo* becomes *o*.

muovo	mossi	muoverò	muova	—
muoviamo	movemmo	muoveremo	muoviamo	muoviamo
muovono	mossero	muoveranno	muovano	muovano
		pp: mosso		

3gg nascere.

nasco	nacqui	nascerò	nasca	—
nasciamo	nascemmo	nasceremo	nasciamo	nasciamo
nascono	nacquero	nasceranno	nascano	nascano
		pp: nato		

3hh nascondere.

nascondo	nascosi	nasconderò	nasca	—
nascondiamo	nascondemmo	nasconderemo	nascondiamo	nascondiamo
nascondono	nascosero	nasconderanno	nascondano	nascondano
		pp: nascosto		

3ii nuocere. In unstressed syllables *uo* becomes *o*.

nuoccio	nocqui	nuocerò	nuoccia	—
nociamo	nocemmo	nuoceremo	nociamo	nuociamo
nuocciono	nocquero	nuoceranno	nuocciano	nuocciano
		pp: nociuto		

3kk piovere. Used only in the 3rd person singular and plural, in the two participial forms and in the *ger*; *pr ind* piove, piovono; *p.r.* piovve, piovvero; *fut* pioverà, pioveranno; *pr congiunt* piova, piovano; *pp* piovuto.

3ll porre. When followed by an *r* in *fut* and *cond n* becomes *r*.

pongo	posi	porrò	ponga	—
poni	ponesti	porrai	ponga	poni
pone	pose	porrà	ponga	ponga
poniamo	ponemmo	porremo	poniamo	poniamo
ponete	poneste	porrete	poniate	ponete
pongono	posero	porranno	pongano	pongano
		pp: posto		

pr ind	p.r.	fut	pr congiunt	imper

3mm prefiggere.

prefiggo	prefissi	prefiggerò	prefigga	—
prefiggiamo	prefiggemmo	prefiggeremo	prefiggiamo	prefiggiamo
prefiggono	prefissero	prefiggeranno	prefiggano	prefiggano
		pp: prefisso		

3nn recere. Addition of *i* between stem and endings *o, a, u*.

recio	recetti	recerò	recia	—
reciamo	recemmo	receremo	reciamo	reciamo
reciono	recettero	receranno	reciano	reciano
		pp: reciuto		

3oo redigere.

redigo	redassi	redigerò	rediga	—
redigiamo	redigemmo	redigeremo	redigiamo	redigiamo
redigono	redassero	redigeranno	redigano	redigano
		pp: redatto		

3pp redimere.

redimo	redensi	redimerò	redima	—
redimiamo	redimemmo	redimeremo	redimiamo	redimiamo
redimono	redensero	redimeranno	redimano	redimano
		pp: redento		

3qq riflettere. In *p.r.* and in *pp* in the sense of "think about" forms usually end in *–ei* and *–uto*; in the sense of "reflect back" usually *–ssi, -sso*.

rifletto	riflettei, riflessi	rifletterò	rifletta	—
riflettiamo	riflettemmo	rifletteremo	riflettiamo	riflettiamo
riflettono	rifletterono, riflessero	rifletteranno	riflettano	riflettano
		pp: riflettuto, riflesso		

3rr rompere.

rompo	ruppi	romperò	rompa	—
rompiamo	rompemmo	romperemo	rompiamo	rompiamo
rompono	ruppero	romperanno	rompano	rompano
		pp: rotto		

3ss scegliere. The stem ending *gli* becomes *lg* before endings *o* and *a*.

scelgo	scelsi	sceglierò	scelga	—
scegli	scegliesti	sceglierai	scelga	scegli
sceglie	scelse	sceglierà	scelga	scelga
scegliamo	scegliemmo	sceglieremo	scegliamo	scegliamo
scegliete	sceglieste	sceglierete	scegliate	scegliete
scelgono	scelsero	sceglieranno	scelgano	scelgano
		pp: scelto		

pr ind	p.r.	fut	pr congiunt	imper

3tt scrivere.

scrivo	scrissi	scriverò	scriva	—
scriviamo	scrivemmo	scriveremo	scriviamo	scriviamo
scrivono	scrissero	scriveranno	scrivano	scrivano
		pp: scritto		

3uu spargere.

spargo	sparsi	spargerò	sparga	—
spargiamo	spargemmo	spargeremo	spargiamo	spargiamo
spargono	sparsero	spargeranno	spargano	spargano
		pp: sparso		

3vv spegnere. The stem sound *gn* becomes *ng* before the endings *o* and *a*.

spengo	spensi	spegnerò	spenga	—
spegni	spegnesti	spegnerai	spenga	spegni
spegne	spense	spegnerà	spenga	spenga
spegniamo	spegnemmo	spegneremo	spegniamo	spegniamo
spegnete	spegneste	spegnerete	spegniate	spegnete
spengono	spensero	spegneranno	spengano	spengano
		pp: spento		

3ww svellere.

svello	svelsi	svellerò	svella	—
svelliamo	svellemmo	svelleremo	svelliamo	svelliamo
svellono	svelsero	svelleranno	svellano	svellano
		pp: svelto		

3xx trarre.

traggo	trassi	trarrò	tragga	—
trai	traesti	trarrai	tragga	trai
trae	trasse	trarrà	tragga	tragga
traiamo	traemmo	trarremo	traiamo	traiamo
traete	traeste	trarrete	traiate	traete
traggono	trassero	trarranno	traggano	traggano
		pp: tratto		

3yy vigere. Common only in the following forms: 3rd person singular and

plural of *ind pr*, *imperf* and *fut*; *cond*; *congiunt imperf* and *p pr*
Ind pr: vige, vigono; *imperf*: vigeva, vigevano; *fut*: vigerà, vigeranno.
Congiunt imperf: vigesse, vigessero. *Cond*: vigerebbe, vigerebbero.
P pr: vigente.

3zz vivere.

vivo	vissi	vivrò	viva	—
viviamo	vivemmo	vivremo	viviamo	viviamo
vivono	vissero	vivranno	vivano	vivano
		pp: vissuto		

Third Conjugation

4a partire. The stem remains the same with regard to both spelling and pronunciation.

I. Simple Tenses

indicativo				condizionale

pr	imperf	p.r.	fut	
part*o**	part*i*vo	part*ii*	part*i*rò	part*i*rei
part*i*	part*i*vi	part*i*sti	part*i*rai	part*i*resti
part*e*	part*i*va	part*ì*	part*i*rà	part*i*rebbe
part*i*amo	part*i*vamo	part*i*mmo	part*i*remo	part*i*remmo
part*i*te	part*i*vate	part*i*ste	part*i*rete	part*i*reste
part*o*no*	part*i*vano	part*i*rono	part*i*ranno	part*i*rebbero

	congiuntivo		imperativo

pr	imperf		
part*a**	part*i*ssi		—
part*a**	part*i*ssi		part*i*
part*a**	part*i*sse		part*a**
part*i*amo	part*i*ssimo		part*i*amo
part*i*ate	part*i*ste		part*i*te
part*a*no*	part*i*ssero		part*a*no*

Participio presente: part*e*nte   *Participio passato*: part*i*to
Gerundio presente: part*e*ndo

* In *cucire* and *sdrucire* an *i* is added before *a* and *o*: *cucio, sdruciono* etc.

II. Compound Tenses

Auxiliary verb *essere* or *avere*, followed by *participio passato* (see 1a).

pr ind	p.r.	fut	pr congiunt	imper

4b sentire. The stressed, closed *-e* of stem ending becomes an open *-e*.

s*e*nto	sent*i*i	sent*i*rò	s*e*nta	—
sent*i*amo	sent*i*mmo	sent*i*remo	sent*i*amo	sent*i*amo
s*e*ntono	sent*i*rono	sent*i*ranno	s*e*ntano	s*e*ntano
	pp: sent*i*to			

4c dormire. The stressed, closed *-o* of stem ending becomes an open *-o*.

d*o*rmo	dorm*i*i	dorm*i*rò	d*o*rma	—
dorm*i*amo	dorm*i*mmo	dorm*i*remo	dorm*i*amo	dorm*i*amo
d*o*rmono	dorm*i*rono	dorm*i*ranno	d*o*rmano	d*o*rmano
	pp: dorm*i*to			

pr ind	p.r.	fut	pr congiunt	imper

4d finire. In the 1st, 2nd and 3rd person singular and 3rd person plural of *pr* (*ind* and *congiunt*) and *imper*, *isc* is added between stem and ending.

pr ind	p.r.	fut	pr congiunt	imper
finisco	finii	finirò	finisca	—
finisci	finisti	finirai	finisca	finisci
finisce	finì	finirà	finisca	finisca
finiamo	finimmo	finiremo	finiamo	finiamo
finite	finiste	finirete	finiate	finite
finiscono	finirono	finiranno	finiscano	finiscano
		pp: finito		

4e apparire.

pr ind	p.r.	fut	pr congiunt	imper
appaio, apparisco	apparvi, apparsi, apparii	apparirò	appaia apparisca	—
appariamo	apparimmo	appariremo	appariamo	appariamo
appaiono, appariscono	apparvero, apparsero, apparirono	appariranno	appaiano, appariscano	appaiano, appariscano
		pp: apparso		

4f aprire.

pr ind	p.r.	fut	pr congiunt	imper
apro	apersi, aprii	aprirò	apra	—
apriamo	aprimmo	apriremo	apriamo	apriamo
aprono	apersero, aprirono	apriranno	aprano	aprano
		pp: aperto		

4g compire. In most forms of the *pr ind*, *pr congiunt* and *imperf*, *compire* is conjugated according to the pattern of *compiere*. An *i* is therefore added between the stem and the ending except in forms whose ending begins with an *i*.

pr ind	p.r.	fut	pr congiunt	imper
compio	compii	compirò	compia	—
compiamo	compimmo	compiremo	compiamo	compiamo
compiono	compirono	compiranno	compiano	compiano
		pp: compito, compiuto; *p pr*: compiente; *ger*: compiendo		

4h gire. Defective verb. Apart from the forms listed below, is used only in the *imperf* (*ind* and *congiunt*) and in the *cond*. This verb is now obsolete.

pr ind	p.r.	fut	pr congiunt	imper
—	—	girò	—	—
—	gisti	girai	—	—
—	gì	girà	—	—
—	gimmo	giremo	—	—
gite	giste	girete	—	gite
—	girono	giranno	—	—
		pp: gito		

pr ind	p.r.	fut	pr congiunt	imper

4i ire. Defective verb. This verb is now obsolete. It was used only in *imperf dell'ind* (*ivo* etc) and in the following forms and persons:

—	2nd pers sg isti	—	—	—
—	—	1st pers pl iremo	—	—
2nd pers pl ite	—	2nd pers pl irete	—	2nd pers pl ite
—	3rd pers sg irono	3rd pers pl iranno	—	—
		pp: ito		

4k morire.

muoio	morii	mor(i)rò	muoia	—
moriamo	morimmo	mor(i)remo	moriamo	moriamo
muoiono	morirono	mor(i)ranno	muoiano	muoiano
		pp: morto		

4l olire. Defective verb. Used only in *imperf dell'ind* 3rd person singular (*oliva*) and 3rd person plural (*olivano*) and in *p pr* (*olente*). This verb is now obsolete.

4m salire. *Pr* as 4a, adding a *g* before *o* and *a*.

salgo	salii	salirò	salga	—
saliamo	salimmo	saliremo	saliamo	saliamo
salgono	salirono	saliranno	salgano	salgano
		pp: salito		

4n udire. *Pr* as 4a, with *u* becoming *o* in the forms in which the stem is stressed.

odo	udii	ud(i)rò	oda	—
udiamo	udimmo	ud(i)remo	udiamo	udiamo
odono	udirono	ud(i)ranno	odano	odano
		pp: udito		

4o uscire.

esco	uscii	uscirò	esca	—
esci	uscisti	uscirai	esca	esci
esce	uscì	uscirà	esca	esca
usciamo	uscimmo	usciremo	usciamo	usciamo
uscite	usciste	uscirete	usciate	uscite
escono	uscirono	usciranno	escano	escano
		pp: uscito		

4p venire.

vengo	venni	verrò	venga	—
vieni	venisti	verrai	venga	vieni
viene	venne	verrà	venga	venga
veniamo	venimmo	verremo	veniamo	veniamo
venite	veniste	verrete	veniate	venite
vengono	vennero	verranno	vengano	vengano
		pp: venuto		

Note sul verbo inglese

a) Coniugazione

Modo indicativo

1. Il tempo presente mantiene la stessa forma dell'infinito in tutte le persone, ad eccezione della 3ª singolare, a cui si aggiunge una -s all'infinito; ad es. *he brings*. Se l'infinito termina con una sibilante (ch, sh, ss, zz) si aggiunge -es, ad esempio *he passes*. Questa s ha due diverse pronunce: dopo una consonante sorda, si pronuncia sorda, ad es. *he paints* [peɪnts]; dopo una consonante sonora, si pronuncia sonora, ad es. *he sends* [sendz]; la pronuncia di -es è sonora, inoltre, quando la *e* fa parte della desinenza oppure della lettera finale dell'infinito, ad es. *he washes* ['wɒʃɪz], *he urges* ['ɜːdʒɪz]. Nei verbi che terminano per -y, la terza persona si forma sostituendo alla *y* -ies, ad es. *he worries, he tries*; sono tuttavia regolari i verbi che all'infinito hanno una vocale davanti alla -y, ad es. *he plays*. Il verbo *to be* è irregolare in tutte le persone: *I am, you are, he is, we are, you are, they are*. Altri tre verbi fanno eccezione alla terza persona singolare: *do - he does, go - he goes, have - he has*.

   Negli altri tempi, tutte le persone restano invariate. Il **passato** ed il **participio passato** si formano aggiungendo -ed all'infinito, ad es. *I passed, passed*, oppure aggiungendo soltanto -d nei verbi che all'infinito terminano in -e, ad es. *I faced, faced*. (Sono molti i verbi irregolari; cfr. sotto). Questa desinenza -(e)d si pronuncia generalmente [t]: *passed* [pɑːst], *faced* [feɪst]; tuttavia, quando compare negli infiniti che terminano con una consonante sonora, con un suono consonantico sonoro o con una *r*, si pronuncia [d]: *warmed* [wɔːmd], *moved* [muːvd], *feared* [fɪəd]. Quando l'infinito termina con -d o -t, la desinenza -ed si pronuncia [ɪd]. Quando l'infinito termina in -y, quest'ultima si trasforma in -ie, e quindi si aggiunge la -d: *try - tried* [traɪd], *pity - pitied* ['pɪtiːd]. I **tempi passati composti** si formano con l'ausiliare *to have* ed il participio passato: **passato prossimo** *I have faced*, **trapassato prossimo** *I had faced*. Con l'ausiliare *will* (*shall*) e l'infinito si forma il **futuro**, ad es. *I shall face;* con l'ausiliare *would* (*should*) si forma il **condizionale**, ad es. *I should face*.

   Per ciascun tempo esiste inoltre la forma continuata, che si costruisce con il verbo *to be* (= essere) e il participio presente (cfr. sotto): *I am going, I was writing, I had been staying, I shall be waiting*, ecc.

2. In inglese, il **congiuntivo** non esiste quasi più, ad eccezione di alcuni casi particolari (*if I were you, so be it, it is proposed that a vote be taken*, ecc.). Al presente, mantiene la stessa forma dell'infinito per tutte le persone, *that I go, that he go*, ecc.

3. In inglese, il **participio presente** ed il **gerundio** hanno la stessa forma e si costruiscono aggiungendo all'infinito la desinenza -ing: *painting, sending*. Tuttavia: 1) nei verbi che all'infinito terminano in -e muta, la desinenza fa cadere questa vocale, ad es. *love - loving, write - writing* (fanno eccezione *dye - dyeing, singe - singeing*, che conservano la -e:); 2) il participio presente dei verbi *die, lie, vie*, ecc. si scrive *dying, lying, vying*, ecc.

4. Esiste una classe di verbi in parte irregolari, che terminano con una sola consonante preceduta da vocale semplice accentata. In questi verbi, prima di aggiungere la desinenza -ing o -ed si raddoppia la consonante:

lob	lob*bed*	lob*bing*	compel	compel*led*	compel*ling*
wed	wed*ded*	wed*ding*	control	control*led*	control*ling*
beg	beg*ged*	beg*ging*	bar	bar*red*	bar*ring*
step	step*ped*	step*ping*	stir	stir*red*	stir*ring*

I verbi che terminano per -l, quando preceduta da vocale atona, raddoppiano la consonante dei due participi nell'ortografia inglese della Gran Bretagna, ma non in quella americana:

travel   travel*led, Am* traveled   travel*ling, Am* traveling

Nei verbi che terminano in -c, si sostituisce -ck alla c, prima di aggiungere le desinenze -ed e -ing:

traffic   traffic*ked*   traffic*king*

5. La **forma passiva** si forma esattamente come in italiano, con il verbo *to be* ed il participio passato: *I am obliged, he was fined, they will be moved,* ecc.

b) Verbi irregolari inglesi

Si riportano le tre forme principali di ciascun verbo: infinito, passato, participio passato.

alight	alighted, alit	alighted, alit	**cling**	clung	clung
arise	arose	arisen	**come**	came	come
awake	awoke	awoken, awaked	**cost**	cost	cost
be (am, is, are)	was (were)	been	**creep**	crept	crept
bear	bore	borne	**crow**	crowed, crew	crowed
beat	beat	beaten	**cut**	cut	cut
become	became	become	**deal**	dealt	dealt
begin	began	begun	**dig**	dug	dug
behold	beheld	beheld	**do**	did	done
bend	bent	bent	**draw**	drew	drawn
beseech	besought, beseeched	besought, beseeched	**dream**	dreamt, dreamed	dreamt, dreamed
bet	bet, betted	bet, betted	**drink**	drank	drunk
bid	bade, bid	bidden, bid	**drive**	drove	driven
bind	bound	bound	**dwell**	dwelt, dwelled	dwelt, dwelled
bite	bit	bitten			
bleed	bled	bled	**eat**	ate	eaten
blow	blew	blown	**fall**	fell	fallen
break	broke	broken	**feed**	fed	fed
breed	bred	bred	**feel**	felt	felt
bring	brought	brought	**fight**	fought	fought
broadcast	broadcast	broadcast	**find**	found	found
build	built	built	**flee**	fled	fled
burn	burnt, burned	burnt, burned	**fling**	flung	flung
burst	burst	burst	**fly**	flew	flown
bust	bust(ed)	bust(ed)	**forbear**	forbore	forborne
buy	bought	bought	**forbid**	forbad(e)	forbidden
cast	cast	cast	**forecast**	forecast(ed)	forecast(ed)
catch	caught	caught	**forget**	forgot	forgotten
choose	chose	chosen	**forgive**	forgave	forgiven
cleave (*cut*)	clove, cleft	cloven, cleft	**forsake**	forsook	forsaken

freeze	froze	frozen	**shrink**	shrank	shrunk
get	got	got, *Am* gotten	**shut**	shut	shut
give	gave	given	**sing**	sang	sung
go	went	gone	**sink**	sank	sunk
grind	ground	ground	**sit**	sat	sat
grow	grew	grown	**slay**	slew	slain
hang	hung,	hung,	**sleep**	slept	slept
	(*v/t*) hanged	(*v/t*) hanged	**slide**	slid	slid
have	had	had	**sling**	slung	slung
hear	heard	heard	**slink**	slunk	slunk
heave	heaved,	heaved,	**slit**	slit	slit
	NAUT hove	NAUT hove	**smell**	smelt, smelled	smelt, smelled
hew	hewed	hewed, hewn	**smite**	smote	smitten
hide	hid	hidden	**sow**	sowed	sown, sowed
hit	hit	hit	**speak**	spoke	spoken
hold	held	held	**speed**	sped, speeded	sped, speeded
hurt	hurt	hurt	**spell**	spelt, spelled	spelt, spelled
keep	kept	kept	**spend**	spent	spent
kneel	knelt, kneeled	knelt, kneeled	**spill**	spilt, spilled	spilt, spilled
know	knew	known	**spin**	spun, span	spun
lay	laid	laid	**spit**	spat	spat
lead	led	led	**split**	split	split
lean	leaned, leant	leaned, leant	**spoil**	spoiled, spoilt	spoiled, spoilt
leap	leaped, leapt	leaped, leapt	**spread**	spread	spread
learn	learned, learnt	learned, learnt	**spring**	sprang,	sprung
leave	left	left		*Am* sprung	
lend	lent	lent	**stand**	stood	stood
let	let	let	**stave**	staved, stove	staved, stove
lie	lay	lain	**steal**	stole	stolen
light	lighted, lit	lighted, lit	**stick**	stuck	stuck
lose	lost	lost	**sting**	stung	stung
make	made	made	**stink**	stunk, stank	stunk
mean	meant	meant	**strew**	strewed	strewed, strewn
meet	met	met	**stride**	strode	stridden
mow	mowed	mowed, mown	**strike**	struck	struck
pay	paid	paid	**string**	strung	strung
plead	pleaded, pled	pleaded, pled	**strive**	strove	striven
prove	proved	proved, proven	**swear**	swore	sworn
put	put	put	**sweep**	swept	swept
quit	quit(ted)	quit(ted)	**swell**	swelled	swollen
read [ri:d]	read [red]	read [red]	**swim**	swam	swum
rend	rent	rent	**swing**	swung	swung
rid	rid	rid	**take**	took	taken
ride	rode	ridden	**teach**	taught	taught
ring	rang	rung	**tear**	tore	torn
rise	rose	risen	**tell**	told	told
run	ran	run	**think**	thought	thought
saw	sawed	sawn, sawed	**thrive**	throve	thriven
say	said	said	**throw**	threw	thrown
see	saw	seen	**thrust**	thrust	thrust
seek	sought	sought	**tread**	trod	trodden
sell	sold	sold	**understand**	understood	understood
send	sent	sent	**wake**	woke, waked	woken, waked
set	set	set	**wear**	wore	worn
sew	sewed	sewed, sewn	**weave**	wove	woven
shake	shook	shaken	**wed**	wed(ded)	wed(ded)
shear	sheared	sheared, shorn	**weep**	wept	wept
shed	shed	shed	**wet**	wet(ted)	wet(ted)
shine	shone	shone	**win**	won	won
shit	shit(ted), shat	shit(ted), shat	**wind**	wound	wound
shoe	shod	shod	**wring**	wrung	wrung
shoot	shot	shot	**write**	wrote	written
show	showed	shown			

Numbers – Numerali

Cardinal numbers – I numeri cardinali

0	*zero* zero	80	*eighty* ottanta
1	*óne* uno	90	*ninety* novanta
2	*two* due	100	*one/a hundred* cento
3	*three* tre	101	*one/a hundred* centouno
4	*four* quattro		*and one*
5	*five* cinque	102	*one/a hundred* centodue
6	*six* sei		*and two*
7	*seven* sette	200	*two hundred* duecento
8	*eight* otto	201	*two hundred*
9	*nine* nove		*and one* duecento uno
10	*ten* dieci	300	*three hundred* trecento
11	*eleven* undici	400	*four hundred* quattrocento
12	*twelve* dodici	500	*five hundred* cinquecento
13	*thirteen* tredici	600	*six hundred* seicento
14	*fourteen* quattordici	700	*seven hundred* settecento
15	*fifteen* quindici	800	*eight hundred* ottocento
16	*sixteen* sedici	900	*nine hundred* novecento
17	*seventeen* diciassette	1,000	*one/a thousand* mille
18	*eighteen* diciotto	1,001	*one/a thousand* milleuno/
19	*nineteen* diciannove		*and one* mille e uno
20	*twenty* venti	2,000	*two thousand* duemila
21	*twenty-one* ventuno	3,000	*three thousand* tremila
22	*twenty-two* ventidue	4,000	*four thousand* quattromila
23	*twenty-three* ventitrè	5,000	*five thousand* cinquemila
28	*twenty-eight* ventotto		
29	*twenty-nine* ventinove	10,000	*ten thousand* diecimila
30	*thirty* trenta	100,000	*one/a hundred* centomila
40	*forty* quaranta		*thousand*
50	*fifty* cinquanta	1,000,000	*one/a million* un milione
60	*sixty* sessanta	2,000,000	*two million* due milioni
70	*seventy* settanta	1,000,000,000	*one/a billion* un miliardo

Notes:

i) In Italian numbers a comma is used for decimals:

    1,25 **one point two five** uno virgola venticinque

ii) A full stop is used where, in English, we would use a comma:

    1.000.000 = 1,000,000

Italian can also write numbers like this using a space instead of a comma:

    1 000 000 = 1,000,000

Ordinal numbers – I numeri ordinali

1st	*first*	1°	il primo, la prima
2nd	*second*	2°	secondo
3rd	*third*	3°	terzo
4th	*fourth*	4°	quarto
5th	*fifth*	5°	quinto
6th	*sixth*	6°	sesto
7th	*seventh*	7°	settimo
8th	*eighth*	8°	ottavo
9th	*ninth*	9°	nono
10th	*tenth*	10°	decimo
11th	*eleventh*	11°	undicesimo
12th	*twelfth*	12°	dodicesimo
13th	*thirteenth*	13°	tredicesimo
14th	*fourteenth*	14°	quattordicesimo
15th	*fifteenth*	15°	quindicesimo
16th	*sixteenth*	16°	sedicesimo
17th	*seventeenth*	17°	diciassettesimo
18th	*eighteenth*	18°	diciottesimo
19th	*nineteenth*	19°	diciannovesimo
20th	*twentieth*	20°	ventesimo
21st	*twenty-first*	21°	ventunesimo
22nd	*twenty-second*	22°	ventiduesimo
30th	*thirtieth*	30°	trentesimo
40th	*fortieth*	40°	quarantesimo
50th	*fiftieth*	50°	cinquantesimo
60th	*sixtieth*	60°	sessantesimo
70th	*seventieth*	70°	settantesimo
80th	*eightieth*	80°	ottantesimo
90th	*ninetieth*	90°	novantesimo
100th	*hundredth*	100°	centesimo
101st	*hundred and first*	101°	centunesimo
103rd	*hundred and third*	103°	centotreesimo
200th	*two hundredth*	200°	duecentesimo
1000th	*thousandth*	1000°	millesimo
1001st	*thousand and first*	1001°	millesimo primo
2000th	*two thousandth*	2000°	duemillesimo
1000000th	*millionth*	1000000°	milionesimo

Note:

Italian ordinal numbers are ordinary adjectives and consequently must agree:

her 13th granddaughter   la sua tredicesima nipote

Fractions – Frazioni

½	*one half, a half*	un mezzo
⅓	*one third, a third*	un terzo
⅔	*two thirds*	due terzi
¼	*one quarter, a quarter*	un quarto
¾	*three quarters*	tre quarti
⅕	*one fifth, a fifth*	un quinto
⅒	*one tenth, a tenth*	un decimo
1½	*one and a half*	uno e mezzo
2¾	*two and three quarters*	due e tre quarti
¹⁄₁₀₀	*one hundredth, a hundredth*	un centesimo
¹⁄₁₀₀₀	*one thousandth, a thousandth*	un millesimo

Approximate numbers – Valori approssimativi

a couple	un paio
about ten	una decina
about twenty	una ventina
about eighty	un'ottantina
about a hundred	un centinaio
hundreds (of people)	centinaia (di persone)
about a thousand	un migliaio
thousands	migliaia

Headword in **bold** Lemma in **grassetto**	**im•pact** ['ɪmpækt] *n of meteorite, vehicle* urto *m*; *of new manager etc* impatto *m*; (*effect*) effetto *m*
International Phonetic Alphabet Trascrizione fonetica internazionale	**in•sult** ['ɪnsʌlt] **1** *n* insulto *m* **2** *v/t* [ɪn'sʌlt] insultare
Translation in normal characters with gender shown in *italics* Traduzione in carattere normale, genere dei sostantivi in *corsivo*	**cou•ri•er** ['kʊrɪə(r)] (*messenger*) corriere *m*; *with tourist party* accompagnatore *m* turistico, accompagnatrice *f* turistica
Hyphenation points Dei punti dividono il lemma in sillabe	**con•sum•er 'con•fi•dence** fiducia *f* dei consumatori; **con'sum•er goods** *npl* beni *mpl* di consumo
Stress shown in headwords ' indica la sillaba accentata	**mouth•wa•ter•ing** *adj* che fa venire l'acquolina
Examples and phrases in **bold italics** Esempi e locuzioni in **grassetto corsivo**	**i•deal•ly** [aɪ'dɪəlɪ] *adv*: ***the hotel is ~ situated*** l'albergo si trova in una posizione ideale; ***~, we would do it like this*** l'ideale sarebbe farlo così
Indicating words in *italics* Discriminazioni di significato in *corsivo*	**montaggio** *m* (*pl* -ggi) TECH assembly; *di film* editing **definire** <4d> define; (*risolvere*) settle **imbalsamare** <1a> embalm; *animale* stuff **land•ing** ['lændɪŋ] *n of aeroplane* atterraggio *m*; *top of staircase* pianerottolo *m*